Contemporary Family Law

Taking a fresh and modern approach, *Contemporary Family Law: Principles and Practice* gives students all the information they need to develop a clear understanding of this fascinating area of the law. Covering the very latest developments in family law, each chapter uses contemporary cases as a window to introducing core legal concepts, principles and developments, emphasising the dynamism and evolving nature of family law, in which practitioners, campaigners, law reformers and students all play their part.

Key features include:

- Developments in family law are considered not only from a vantage point of judicial decision making but also from the perspective of the contribution made by solicitors, barristers and experts. This encourages students to develop a sense of their own potential agency when, as future practitioners, they represent their clients and engage in law reform;

- In considering legal argument and case determination, the book places equality front and centre, including access to justice;

- Each chapter provides further reading with online links and URLs and a set of self-test questions, including problem scenarios and discursive essay questions. Each form of assessment reflects the levels of educational attainment and mirrors testing techniques relevant to academic examination and legal professional and vocational practice courses.

This uniquely contemporary textbook will be essential reading for all students of family law.

Susan S. M. Edwards is Professor of Law at Northumbria University, Barrister, Door tenant at Red Lion Chambers London, expert witness, Emerita Professor of Law University of Buckingham, and has taught and published extensively in the area of family law, homicide, partner and child abuse and gender and human rights.

Judith Bray is a Barrister and Emerita Professor of Law at University of Buckingham. With many years' experience of teaching family law at degree level and for professional examinations, Judith has published extensively on property law and equity and trusts, particularly rights in the family home.

Contemporary Family Law
Principles and Practice

Susan S. M. Edwards and Judith Bray

Routledge
Taylor & Francis Group

LONDON AND NEW YORK

Designed cover image: standret/Getty Images ®

First published 2025
by Routledge
4 Park Square, Milton Park, Abingdon, Oxon OX14 4RN

and by Routledge
605 Third Avenue, New York, NY 10158

Routledge is an imprint of the Taylor & Francis Group, an informa business

British Library Cataloguing-in-Publication Data
A catalogue record for this book is available from the British Library

Library of Congress Cataloging-in-Publication Data
Names: Edwards, Susan S. M., author. |
    Bray, Judith, author.
Title: Contemporary family law : principles and practice / Susan S. M.
    Edwards and Judith Bray.
Description: Abingdon, Oxon [UK] ; New York, NY : Routledge, 2025. |
    Includes bibliographical references and index.
Identifiers: LCCN 2024032623 | ISBN 9781032563428 (hardback) |
    ISBN 9781032563404 (paperback) | ISBN 9781003435020 (ebook)
Subjects: LCSH: Domestic relations. | Adoption—Law and legislation. |
    Child support—Law and legislation.
Classification: LCC K670 .E325 2025 | DDC 346.01/5—dc23/eng/20240716
LC record available at https://lccn.loc.gov/2024032623

ISBN: 978-1-032-56342-8 (hbk)
ISBN: 978-1-032-56340-4 (pbk)
ISBN: 978-1-003-43502-0 (ebk)

DOI: 10.4324/9781003435020

Typeset in Bembo
by Apex CoVantage, LLC

Access the Support Material: www.routledge.com/9781032563404

For all our students wherever they are

Contents

Preface   *xxiii*
Susan S. M. Edwards
Abbreviations   *xxv*
Table of cases   *xxvii*
Table of statutes   *liii*
Table of statutory instruments   *lxiii*

1   Introduction to family law   1
     What is family law?   1
     Rights and obligations   3
     Evolving definitions of the family   4
     Excluded relationships   5
     Challenges to family law   6
         Divorce   6
         Financial matters   7
         Domestic abuse   7
         Children   7
         Child protection   8
     The international family   8
     Human rights   9
     International conventions   9
     Challenges to the operation of family justice   10
     Judging judges and justice   10
     Accountability   12
     The Future and the new Labour government   12
     Organisation of the text   13

2   State intervention in personal relationships   14
     Form v function   15

Which relationships should be recognised?   15
  A dual approach   15
    Civil partnerships and same-sex marriage   15
    Engagement to marry or enter into a civil partnership   17
  Relationships exempt from legal intervention   17
Definitions and formation of relationships   19
  Engagement   19
  Agreements to enter into a civil partnership   20
  Marriage   20
    History and background to marriage   20
    The right to marry   22
    Capacity to marry   23
    Age   24
    Prohibited degrees of relationship   25
  Already married or in a registered civil partnership   26
    Mental capacity   27
  Formalities of marriage   29
  Civil ceremonies   29
    Preliminary requirements   29
    The marriage ceremony   30
    Religious ceremonies   31
      Marriage in the Anglican Church   31
      The marriage ceremony   31
    Quaker and Jewish marriages   32
    Other religious marriages   32
  Marriages of the sick, the housebound or prisoners   32
  Informal marriage   33
    The concept of common law marriage has no validity   33
    Presumption of marriage by cohabitation and repute   33
    Non-qualifying marriages (also referred to as non-marriages) and void marriages 37
  Civil partners   38
    Capacity to register a civil partnership (CPA 2004, ss 3, 4)   38
    Age   40
    Already a civil partner or married   41
  Mental capacity   41
  Formalities of civil partnership   41
  Cohabitation   42
Self-test questions   45

3   Nullity and its consequences   48
Nullity: an important concept   48
Void or voidable relationships   49
  Void relationships   50
    Overseas marriages   54
    Marriage by cohabitation and repute   56
    Forced marriages   60
    Mistake   63

Sham marriages 63
Unsound mind 65
Or otherwise 66
Bars to relief where a marriage is voidable 68
Knowledge of the petitioner and injustice to the respondent 68
Delay 68
Grounds on which a civil partnership will be voidable 69
Bars to relief where a civil partnership is voidable knowledge of the
applicant and injustice to the respondent 70
Delay 70
Consequences of nullity for married couples and civil partners 70
Relationship status 70
Revocation of wills 71
Financial orders 71
Religious decrees of nullity 72
Self-test questions 72

4   Acquisition and protection of rights in the family home 75
The family home: an overview 75
Problems of home ownership 77
The Law Commission proposals – home sharing 78
Cohabitants and the family home 78
Sharing the family home 78
Background 78
Buying a house: legal ownership 79
Buying a house: the equitable title 80
Joint tenancy 80
Tenants in common 81
Informal trusts 82
There are two types of informal trust also referred to as implied
trusts: the constructive trust and the resulting trust 82
Resulting trusts 82
The presumption of advancement 83
Gifts or loans or monies attributable to some other motive 83
Constructive trusts 83
Agreements to share the property where the property is in the
sole name of one of the partners or family member 84
A more familial approach to agreements 86
Detrimental reliance 87
Financial detriment 87
Non-financial detriment 88
Quantification of the beneficial interest 89
The move to pragmatism 89
Property purchased in joint names – the high point of pragmatism in the
quantification of beneficial interests – Stack v Dowden (2007); Jones v
Kernott (2011) 91
Proprietary estoppel 96

Nature of the representation	*97*
Explicit representations	*97*
Implied representations	*98*
Detriment	*98*
Reliance	*99*
Wide range of remedies	*100*
Fee simple	*100*
An estoppel licence	*101*
Compensation	*101*
A problematic remedy	*102*
Matrimonial Proceedings and Property Act 1970, s 37	*102*
Civil Partnership Act 2004, s 65	*102*
The Law Reform (Miscellaneous Provisions) Act 1970,	
ss 2, 3; Civil Partnership Act 2004, s 74(5)	*102*
Family Law Act 1996, Part IV	*103*
Statutory right of occupation for spouses and civil partners	*103*
The family home	*103*
Effect of the statutory right on third parties	*104*
Potential for manipulation	*104*
Trusts of Land and the Appointment of Trustees Act 1996;	
rights of beneficiaries, creditors and the effect of bankruptcy	*104*
Beneficiaries	*104*
Creditors and bankruptcy	*104*
Exceptional circumstances	*105*
Self-test questions	*106*
5 Protecting adults from domestic abuse – the civil remedies	109
Contemporary definitions and very public cases	*110*
Domestic abuse may also include sexual abuse	*113*
Domestic abuse is also a pattern of abuse	*114*
History: challenging the common law	*115*
Legal landmarks	*116*
1970s reform measures	*117*
Explanations of domestic abuse	*117*
Post 1970s – feminist jurisprudential challenges	*119*
Domestic abuse incidence and the criminal law	*119*
Assault and coercive control	*121*
Protection from Harassment Act 1997	*123*
Civil remedies for domestic violence and abuse	*123*
Family Law Act 1996, Part IV ss 33–41, 43–49: occupation rights	*124*
Entitled persons	*124*
Types of occupation orders for entitled persons	*125*
Exercise of the court's discretion for entitled persons – the harm test	*126*
Duration of occupation orders for entitled persons	*128*
Non-entitled persons	*128*
Exercise of the court's discretion for former spouses or civil partners	*129*
Exercise of the court's discretion for cohabitants and former cohabitants	*130*

Circumstances where neither of the spouses, civil partners,
   former spouses, former civil partners or cohabitants have
   rights to occupy the property   130
Enforcement of occupation orders for both entitled and
   non-entitled persons   130
Number of occupation and non-molestation order applications
   and orders granted   130
Family Law Act 1996, Part IV: ss 42–42A, 43–49: non-molestation orders   131
   What constitutes non-molestation?   131
   Who may apply?   132
   The court's discretion   133
   Enforcement   133
      Undertakings   134
   Ex parte orders (without notice) occupation and non-molestation s 45(1)   134
      Return hearings   135
Other forms of abuse and legal protections   136
   Forced marriage   136
   The Forced Marriage (Civil Protection) Act 2007   138
   Dowry abuse   140
   Female genital mutilation protection orders   140
   Domestic violence/abuse protection orders and domestic
      violence/abuse protection notices   141
More protection needed: closing remarks   141
Self-test questions   145

6   Ending relationships   152
Divorce   152
   Statistical evidence of divorce   153
      Reasons for divorce and its consequences   154
   Background to divorce   154
   Matrimonial Causes Act 1973   155
   The five facts under the MCA 1973, s 1(2)   155
   The five facts   156
      Adultery and intolerability (MCA 1973, s 1(2)(a))   156
      Definition of adultery   156
      Intolerability   156
      Behaviour (MCA 1973, s 1(2)(b))   156
      Continuing cohabitation   158
      Desertion (MCA 1973, s 1(2)(c))   158
   Resumption of cohabitation   159
      Two years living apart and consent to the decree (MCA 1973, s 1(2)(d)) 159
      Resumption of cohabitation   160
      Five years living apart (MCA 1973, s 1(2)(e))   160
   The defence of grave hardship (MCA 1973, s 5)   160
      No divorce proceedings within a year of marriage   160
      A two-part process   160
The new procedure   161

Divorce under the Divorce, Dissolution and Separation Act 2020 161
Divorce based on irretrievable breakdown of marriage 161
   Proof of irretrievable breakdown 161
  Procedure for divorce 162
  Critique of the law leading to the Divorce, Dissolution and
    Separation Act 2020 163
  The road to reform 163
   Family Law Act 1996 163
   Family Justice Review 2011 164
  The Government's response 164
   Problems with the law of the MCA 1973 165
  Alternative divorce models 165
  Judicial separation 167
  Grounds for the decree 167
   Effect of a judicial separation order 168
Civil partnerships 168
  Dissolution (CPA 2004) 168
  Divorce in the religious courts 168
  Consequences of divorce 169
Self-test questions 170

7   Financial consequences of relationships 172
Part I ownership of personal property and rights to maintenance
during a relationship 173
  Personal property 173
  Trusts 174
   Express trusts 175
   Informal trusts 176
  Rights to maintenance during the relationship 176
   The abolition of a wife's right to be maintained at
    common law 176
   Contracts for maintenance 176
  Statutory rights to maintenance 176
   Matrimonial Causes Act 1973, s 27, Civil Partnership Act 2004,
    Sch 5, Part 9 176
   Domestic Proceedings and Magistrates' Courts Act 1978 177
   The court's discretion 177
   Conduct 178
Part II financial consequences of ending the relationship 178
  A general overview 178
  Reaching a financial settlement under the Matrimonial
    Causes Act 1973 (as amended by later legislation) 180
   Step one 180
   Step two 180
   Step three 181
   Step four 181
  Orders available to the court 181

Financial awards   181
Variation of periodical payments   183
Transfer of property   184
    Mesher orders   184
Martin orders   185
Leave to appeal   185
Looking afresh   186
A lack of overall guiding objective   189
Judicial intervention   189
Guidance from case law   189
A return to the statutory guidelines   193
    Attempts to marry the guidelines with the principle of fairness   196
'Non-relationship assets'   198
Post-separation assets   200
    Increase in earning capacity   201
Reform of the guidelines   207
Potential reform for the award of financial remedies   207
Relationship or pre-nuptial agreements   208
    Problematic nature of agreements   208
    The Law Commission – Matrimonial Property, Needs and
        Agreements Project   209
Judicial approaches to agreements   209
    Agreements made on relationship breakdown   209
    Pre-nuptial or pre-civil partnership agreements   211
    The dissent in Radmacher   214
    The aftermath of Radmacher   215
    Cohabitants   218
        The current debate   218
        Contract   220
        Indirect maintenance   221
    Fiancées and prospective civil partners   222
Self-test questions   223

8   The elderly, their rights in family life and death and its consequences   227
    Mental capacity amongst older people   227
    The four different ways under the Mental Capacity Act 2005
        that a substitute decision can be made on another's behalf   228
        a) Advance decisions or 'living wills'   229
        b) Lasting powers of attorney   229
        c) Deputies   230
        d) The court   230
Social care of the elderly   231
On whom should the burden of care fall?   231
    Adult children   231
Abuse of the elderly   232
    Addressing elder abuse   233
        The impact of death on family life   233

Presumption of death	234
Common law	234
The Presumption of Death Act 2013	234
Funeral arrangements	235
Rights and duties to deal with the deceased's body	235
Testate succession	237
Intestate succession: Administration of Estates Act 1925, s 46	238
Bona vacantia	240
The Inheritance (Provision for Family and Dependants) Act 1975 – applications for financial maintenance	240
Time bar	241
Applicants	241
Living together in the same household as if a spouse or civil partner	242
Proof of maintenance (s 1(3))	243
Assumption of responsibility (s 3(3)(4))	244
Reasonable financial provision	245
Applications by adult children	248
Family life after death	250
Re the Cremated Remains of AA [2018] ECC 7	251
Self-test questions	252
9 Family life – parents and carers: from parental rights to responsibilities	255
Parenting histories – the exclusive father	257
The biological father's rights are 'sacred'	258
Demise of paternal authority and rise of parental responsibility	259
Iterating the meaning of 'in the custody of the parent' – Hewer	260
Deciding in favour of non-biological over natural parents – J v C	261
Mothers over fathers – Re K	261
Kidnapping and child abduction – R v D	262
Today – who is a parent in fact?	263
The unfit parent	263
Genetic – biological parents and the natural parent presumption	265
Biological heterosexual family	265
Statutory exceptions to the natural parent presumption	267
Gestational – parentage	268
Reproductive technology and the legal parent	268
Transgender parentage and IVF	271
Three parents	273
Reproductive technology reform	273
Surrogacy	274
Surrogacy – international arrangements	276
Social and psychological parentage – the importance of attachment	277
Sexual orientation and parentage, gender reassignment and parentage	278
The limits of language	279
The transgender father	280
Legal parents and parental responsibility	281

'Parental responsibility' and its responsibilities   282
   Responsibility to care for the child   282
   Responsibility to ensure the child's education   282
   Responsibility for the child's religion – now of little relevance   283
   Responsibility to protect the child and not to inflict punishment or physical
      discipline   283
   Responsibility to consent to medical treatment of the child   284
   Responsibility to withhold consent or consent to marriage
      overridden by statute   284
   Responsibility involves administering the child's property
      and to enter into certain contracts with the child   284
   Responsibility to act for the child in legal proceedings   284
Parental responsibility: who is entitled?   285
   Mothers   285
   Fathers   285
   Unmarried fathers   285
Court orders parental responsibility   286
   Parental responsibility order   286
   Putting biological parentage to proof for the purpose of parental responsibility 287
   Mothers refusing consent to blood tests   287
      The local authority and proof of parentage   289
   Right of child to know   289
      Declaration of parentage and identity   289
      Putative fathers' right to know   290
      Birth fathers following adoption   290
   De facto fathers' right to truth   291
   Court denial of parental responsibility applications   291
   Terminating parental responsibility – circumstances   291
   Jade Ward 'Jade's Law' – suspending parental responsibility   293
      Termination – miscellaneous circumstances   293
   Parental responsibility when not the parent   294
Other parents – stepmothers' and stepfathers' parental responsibility   294
   Adoptive parents   294
   Foster parents   295
   Special guardians/guardians   295
Concluding remarks – family rights – article 8 'family life'   295
Self-test questions   296

10   Adoption – only permissible if nothing else will do   301
   History of UK adoption   303
   The legislation   304
   Who can be adopted? And who can adopt   304
      Who can adopt?   305
      Adoption by stepparents   306
      Adoption by relatives/foster parents   307
   The current legal framework   307
      Suitability and matching   307

From s 1(5) of the ACA 2002 to s 3 of the CFA 2014   309
Repealed – so what?   309
    Section 1(5) racial and cultural origin   310
Section 1(5) religious preferences   311
Post 2014   312
Court orders   313
    Overarching principles, judicial decision making and consent   313
    Dispensing with consent   315
        The chameleon concept of unreasonableness   315
    Challenges to dispensing with consent s 47(5)   318
    Waiting time   318
The placement order   319
    Appealing/revoking a placement order   320
    Upholding the placement order   321
Adoption order – when nothing else will do   321
    Adoption and the child's presence   322
Adoption or special guardianship order   322
    Appealing a special guardianship order   324
    Discharging a special guardianship order   325
    Dismissing appeals   326
    Appealing an adoption order and refusal   326
    Opposing the making of an adoption order   326
    Setting aside an adoption order   327
Other orders   329
    Residence orders rather than adoption   329
    Contact with parents   329
    Siblings   330
    Grandparents   331
International adoption   331
    The Hague Convention   332
    Conflicting principles: welfare v best interests   332
Closing remarks: 'nothing else will do'   334
    When adoption is cheap   334
    Post adoption contact   335
    Blood tie – Who do you think you are? and contact   336
Self-test questions   337

11   Adolescent autonomy – the right to decide and to participate in court
     proceedings   342
Rights of the child and adolescent: general principles and sources of law   343
    The voice of the child   345
    Three ages and stages of child rights   346
        Rights of the unborn   346
        Rights of infants and young children   347
        Rights of adolescents and 16–17-year-olds   349
Under 16-year-olds and the Gillick competence precept   350
    Sexual intercourse and the dissenters   352

Applying Gillick – how can an adolescent acquire competence?   353
   'Gillick competence' chronological age?   354
   Maturity to understand   354
'Gillick competence': only a right to refuse consent?   355
   The reaction of the academic community   358
   Analysis: 'Gillick competence' from consequences to competence   358
Refusing saying no no no to blood, organs, sedation   359
   Refusing organ transplant   361
   Refusing medication/sedation/sustenance   362
Wardship – trump card   363
   'Gillick competent': enough rope but not to hang themselves   364
   The competent/incompetent putative transgender adolescent   365
Adolescent participation in legal proceedings   367
   Test of competency   367
   Not old enough or not of sufficient understanding   368
   Simply inappropriate   370
   Changing attitudes?   371
   Competent – in family proceedings   372
   The more recent case law   373
Judicial activism or judicial paternalism   373
End game – a matter for Parliament!   376
Self-test questions   377

12   Putting child welfare first in child 'custody' and
    private disputes   381
Child custody throughout history   383
When parents fall out today   385
   Impact on children   386
Partnership – conciliation and mediation   387
The legal framework   388
Guiding principles of the Children Act   389
   Section 1 – child welfare paramount   389
     Who can apply for an order?   389
     Barring vexatious litigation – s 91(14)   390
The welfare checklist: six factors   391
   Failure to consider the statutory checklist   391
   Section 1(3)(a) 'The ascertainable wishes and feelings of the child
     concerned considered in the light of his age and understanding'   392
   Section 1(3)(b) 'physical, educational, and emotional needs'   393
   Section 1 (3)(c) 'The likely effect on the child of change in
     circumstances': status quo   394
   Section 1(3)(d) 'His age, sex, background and any other
     characteristic of his which the court considers relevant'   394
     Faith, culture intersecting with welfare   395
     Religious practices circumcision   397
   Giving quietus to media orchestrated orientalism – The Child AB   398
   Section 1(3)(e) 'any harm which he has suffered or is at risk of suffering'   399

Section 1(3)(f) 'How capable each of his parents, and any other person
in relation to whom the court considers the question to be relevant, is
of meeting his needs'   400
Section 8 – the orders   400
'No order' principle CA 1989, s 1(5)   400
Child arrangement order (CAO) for residence   401
Shared residence   402
Child arrangement order (CAO) for contact   403
Contact – who's right?   403
Contact with non-resident parent   403
Children voting with their feet – 'I don't care if I don't . . .'   404
Indirect letter contact   405
Abusive partners and contact strategies   406
'Pro contact' even where domestic violence   406
'Implacable hostility'   407
'Parental alienation'   407
Contemporary erratic landscape and domestic abuse   409
Contact with others – grandparents   409
Enforcing contact   410
Specific issue order   410
Disagreements, education, name change, health care   411
Prohibited steps order   412
Regional variations in orders   413
International relocation and abduction   414
Prohibited steps and different domiciles   414
Relocation residence and contact   414
Wardship and specific issue orders   415
International law   416
The Hague Convention   416
Removal and return, deciding the case, habitual residence   418
Non-Convention country abduction and recognising bilateral agreements   419
The child's voice in international relocation   420
Child's objections a paradigm case   421
No presumption in favour of applicant parent   422
Beyond objection – child at risk   422
Risk domestic abuse   424
A legitimacy crisis in private law   425
Self-test questions   427

13   The limitless jurisdiction of wardship   433
Contemporary high profile wardship cases   434
From the ancient to the modern jurisdiction of wardship   434
The inherent jurisdiction   436
Forced marriage   437
The confluence of the inherent jurisdiction and wardship   438
The legal framework of wardship   438
Practice direction   438
The official solicitor   439

Procedure and principles | 439
Test to be applied in wardship | 440
Strictly wardship | 440
Can anyone make an application in wardship? | 441
Applications without notice | 442
Restricting wardship: the Children Act 1989 | 442
Minors and the inherent jurisdiction | 443
Restricting wardship suborned to secretary of state power | 443
Restricting wardship – no wardship before birth | 444
Anticipatory declarations under the inherent jurisdiction after birth | 444
The limitless jurisdiction | 445
Practice direction 12d [1.2](a) – orders to restrain publicity | 445
Publicity privacy and children's rights | 445
Children of children who have killed | 445
Media intrusion 'Love child' | 446
Media interest – victims of child abuse | 446
Media interest – child victims of disasters | 447
Practice direction 12d [1.2](b) – orders to prevent undesirable association | 448
Child sexual exploitation | 448
Radicalisation | 449
Seek and find orders | 450
Practice direction 12d [1.2](c) – orders relating to medical treatment | 450
Reproduction, termination, sterilisation, life ending decisions | 450
Termination and sterilisation | 450
Surrogacy | 451
Life ending decisions – easing pain and suffering | 451
Ease suffering, or to prolong life? | 453
'Let die' | 453
'Treat to ease pain and suffering' | 453
From the child's perspective – intolerable life | 454
Resuscitation – more invasive | 454
Transplant decisions – invasive – sustaining life | 455
Recent disagreements | 457
No conflict, all parties agree | 458
Practice direction 12j (pd) wardship, abduction and habitual residence | 459
Not habitually resident | 460
Contact and wardship | 461
Wardship and unaccompanied asylum-seeking children | 462
Resisting deportation | 463
Reform of wardship | 463
Self-test questions | 463

14 Child protection: local authority, the court and public
law procedure | 467
High profile cases | 468
Child abuse – an historical denial | 468
Changing perceptions of abuse | 469
Slow death in full view of the protective agencies | 470

Abuse – from discrete incidents to totality context   472
   Totality context approach   473
     Physical abuse (non-accidental injury)   473
     Sexual abuse   474
     Emotional abuse   475
     Neglect   478
  Child abuse – an epidemic   478
  The legal and procedural framework of safeguarding   479
   The Children Act 1989 and partnership principle   480
   Children Act – significant harm – three thresholds   481
   The local authority – the investigative process   481
   Reporting suspicions: the referral process   482
     Turning the other way   482
     Moral panics and referrals   482
   Court ordered investigation: s 37 directions   484
     Child Protection Register   485
     Child protection plan   485
     Child protection conference   487
     Care plans   487
     Local authority – duty to investigate s 47   488
     Local authority failings   489
   Child protection and public authority liability and human rights   489
  Orders during the preliminary stage   490
   Emergency orders   490
     Emergency protection order   490
     Ex parte orders and human rights challenges   492
     Contact with the child and emergency protection order   493
   Exclusion order provision   494
     Police removal s 46   495
     Child assessment order s 43   496
  Court interim orders   497
   Division of functions   497
   Interim care orders   497
     The interim threshold   497
   Interim supervision order   498
  Child protection requires truth – fact finding expert
   opinion and the truthful parent   498
   What is truth? The medical expert   498
     Be vigilant   500
     Undoing earlier decisions and fresh medical evidence   502
    Protecting parents – the right not to self-incriminate   502
  Concluding remarks – how well is the local authority doing in child protection?   504
  Self-test questions   505

15 'Significant harm': judicial interpretations and state politics   510
  Social policy and the threshold   512
  The legal framework   513
   Section 31 – threshold finding of 'significant harm'   513

Split hearings   514
Evidence – burden and standard   515
What conduct falls under 'significant harm' s 31(10)?   516
  Judicial interpretation   517
    What degree of harm is recognised as significant?   517
    Objective and subjective tests   518
    How is the objective test of 'significant harm' measured?   519
    Similar children: similar to whom and to what?   519
  Debate – different but normal?   520
  Ethnic minority children in care   521
  Poverty, deprivation and s 17   522
  Providing a reasonable standard of parental care   523
    Observing the child or the standard of parental care: s 38(6) residential
      assessments   523
    Is there a right to a residential assessment?   524
Present significant harm: a temporal question   524
  'Is suffering'   524
    Is suffering – physical abuse – the factual basis   525
    Is suffering – sexual abuse – the factual basis   525
General principles pre-emptive strike   526
  Retrospectivism and prospectivism   526
  Evaluating the future risk of harm – facts not suspicion   527
  Finding significant harm – but for which harm?   527
  No finding of sexual abuse   527
The much contested case – Re H and R (1995) 'likely to suffer'   528
  Sexual abuse and probability theory   529
Care proceedings applications of sexual abuse in the shadow of Re H and R   530
  Setting the record nearly straight – Standard of proof – Re B (2008)   531
  Matters of proof and general allegations   533
Truth – uncertain perpetrators and physical injury   534
  The expansion of emotional harms   537
    Emotional abuse   538
    The radicalisation cases   538
  'No order' presumption (CA 1989, s 1(5))   540
  Parental cooperation   541
  Voluntary agreement (CA 1989, s 20)   543
Supervision orders   543
  Supervision v care   545
    Care orders at home   545
    Regional disparities – care supervision North and West and
      South and East divide   546
Finale – how better can we protect children?   547
  Proportionality question and the Human Rights Act (HRA)   547
Self-test questions   549

16 Financial provision for children   554
  Background to child support   555
    Child poverty   555

Child support: theoretical background to the financial support of children   555
Theoretical basis of child support   556
Child support: history   557
The background to the Child Support Act 1991   558
Recovery of maintenance prior to the Child Support Act 1991   559
The purpose of the Child Support Act 1991   560
Duty to maintain a qualifying child: Child Support Act 1991   560
A qualifying child   561
Age of qualifying child   561
Maintaining other children   561
What of children of the civil partnership union?   561
Resident parent   562
Person with care   562
The Child Support Agency – Child Support Act 1991 and maintenance
assessment   563
Failings of the CSA enforcement mechanism and subsequent reforms   563
Reform and the Child Maintenance and Other Payments Act 2008   565
Who pays – Whose child is it anyway? Paternity   566
Presumption of paternity   567
Whose child is it? – non-paternity issues   567
Parental responsibility – financial responsibility and contact issues   568
How much is a child worth? The maintenance formula   568
Maintenance calculations   569
Calculating the formula for payment   570
The basic rate   570
Adjustments to the formula   571
Enforcement   571
Domestic abuse cases   572
Evaluation of the Child Maintenance Service   572
Residual role of the courts   572
The private arena of child support   573
Financial provision for spouse carers   574
Clean break and children   574
The Children Act 1989, schedule 1, paragraph 1 and paragraph 2 – who
can make the application?   574
Financial orders under the Children Act 1989   575
Human rights and child support under the 1991 Act: legal challenges   577
Financial support for children: the future   578
Self-test questions   579

Index   582

Preface

We are delighted to have written the first edition of *Contemporary Family Law*. Family law has undergone change across nearly every aspect of the subject in recent years. One area of law which is still unchanged is the protection of rights of cohabitants. Property rights of a cohabitant still have no protection in law. Until legislation is introduced this area of law will continue to be governed by the complex rules of property law such as the law of trusts and proprietary estoppel. There are many new cases relying on these rules which have been dealt with in detail in Chapter 4. The law relating to death and inheritance has become increasingly important. The ever-growing number of decisions in this field demonstrates that no family law course can afford to ignore the fact that the death of a family member can involve as many difficulties and disputes as occur on divorce.

Human rights issues weave their way through most topics of family law, and we have attempted to illustrate, throughout the chapters, the way in which the European Court of Human Rights has been called upon to rule on disputes between individuals and the State.

The Domestic Abuse Act 2021 has introduced new ways of thinking about domestic violence with the terminology of 'domestic abuse' and an understanding of abuse as a pattern of behaviour involving coercive control. In the field of child law, the cases on relocation of children to an overseas jurisdiction after the breakdown of their parents' relationship continue to proliferate and no satisfactory solutions appear to have been found. Other important changes to the law include: parental status after infertility treatment, and surrogacy; the rights of grandparents; adoption and the fixity of language which does not always reflect family relationships and gender identities. Financial support for children is now dealt with under a new agency – the Child Maintenance Service – and we consider to what extent the problems of the Child Support Agency and its subsequent body have been addressed.

We have attempted to make the complexities of family law easier to understand not only for law students but also for all those who are interested in how family relationships are regulated by law. We have also introduced our readers to cases with which they will be familiar from media and more popular accounts to ease them into the doctrinal and procedural study of family law. We have tried to bring to life the individual stories and the role that solicitors and advocates play in shaping family law for without them judges would have little to do.

The book is a joint venture. Judith Bray is responsible for Chapters 2, 3, 4, 6, 7, 8 and 16 and Susan S. M. Edwards for Chapters 5, 9, 10, 11, 12, 13, 14 and 15. We have both written the introductory chapter, Chapter 1.

We would like especially to thank Mary Welstead, who co-authored with Susan S. M. Edwards editions 1 to 4 of the textbook *Family Law* (Oxford University Press, 2013), upon which this book is based, and whose insights have helped shape some aspects of this first edition of *Contemporary Family Law*. Mary is a regular contributor to *Family Law* which has allowed us to draw on her expertise in some of the chapters. We would like to thank Russell George, who originally approached us and with whom our journey of *Contemporary Family Law* began. The editorial team at Routledge, led by Emily Kindleysides and assisted by Chloe Herbert, and production team have supported us throughout and to them we also owe our thanks.

Susan S. M. Edwards

Judith Bray

Abbreviations

ACA	Adoption and Children Act
CA	Children Act
CAFCASS	Children and Family Court Advisory and Support Service
CAO	Child Assessment Order
CPA	Civil Partnership Act
CSA	Child Support Act
CSPSSA	Child Support, Pensions and Social Security Act
CYPA	Children and Young Persons Act
DPMCA	Domestic Proceedings and Magistrates' Court Act
ECHR	European Convention for the Protection of Human Rights and Fundamental Freedoms 1950
ECt HR	European Court of Human Rights
EPO	Emergency Protection Order
FLA	Family Law Act
FLRA	Family Law Reform Act
GRA	Gender Recognition Act
HFEA	Human Fertilisation and Embryology Act
IRM	Independent Review Mechanism
MCA	Matrimonial Causes Act
MFPA	Matrimonial and Family Proceedings Act
MPPA	Matrimonial Proceedings and Property Act
UNCRC	United Nations Convention on the Rights of the Child 1989

Table of cases

Canada
Duranceau, Re [1952] 3 DLR 714; 1952 Can LII 102 (ON CA) 246

EU
YC v United Kingdom (App. No 4547/10) (ECtHR 2012) 321

New Zealand
C v C [1942] NZLR 356 63
Harrild v Director of Proceedings [2003] 3 NZLR 289 347
Kempson v R [2020] NZCA 656 122
R v Lavallee [1990] 1 SCR 852; (1990) 108 NR 321 (SCC); (1988)
    52 Man.R.(2d) 274 (CA) 151

South Africa
Minister of Home Affairs and Another v Fourie and Another Lesbian and Gay
    Equality Project and Others v Minister of Home Affairs and Others [2006]
    1 LRC 677 (SA) 255

United Kingdom
A v A (Financial Provision for Child) [1995] 1 FCR 309 575
A v A (Financial Provision) [1998] 2 FLR 180 201
A v B (Appeal: Domestic Abuse) [2023] EWHC 1499 (Fam) 114, 119
A v B and C (Lesbian Co-Parents: Role of Father) [2012] EWCA Civ 285 280
A v Croatia [2010] (application no. 55164/08) 142
A v D (Serious domestic violence: mother's applications to terminate father's
    parental responsibility and to change child's name) [2013] EWHC 2963
    (Fam) 286, 292
A v East Sussex County Council [2010] EWHC 2771 (Admin) 491
A v East Sussex County Council and Chief Constable of Sussex Police [2010]
    EWCA Civ 743 496
A v G [2009] EWHC 736 (Fam) 386
A v General Medical Council and another [2004] EWHC 880 (Admin) 488
A v J [1989] 1 FLR 110 59
A v P (Surrogacy: Parental Order: Death of Applicant) [2011] EWHC 1738 (Fam) 277

A v Secretary of State for the Home Department [2016] CSHI 38 144
A v SM and HB (Forced Marriage Protection Orders) [2012] EWHC 435(Fam)............ 138
A v United Kingdom [1998] 27 EHRR 611.. 470
A (A Child: Female genital mutilation: asylum), Re [2019] EWHC 2475 (Fam).............. 124
A (A Child: Inherent jurisdiction: parens patriae, FMPO and passport orders),
    Re [2020] EWHC 451 (Fam) 138
A (A Child: Joint residence: parental responsibility), Re [2008] EWCA Civ 867 402
A (A Child: Mental Health of Mother), Re [2001] EWCA Civ 162.................................. 492
A (A Child: Wardship: Fact finding: Domestic Violence), Re [2015] EWHC
    1598 (Fam)... 520
A (A Child: Wardship: Habitual Residence), Re [2007] EWHC 3338 (Fam) 441
A (A Minor: Custody), Re [1991] 2 FLR 394 394
A (A Minor: Paternity: refusal of blood test), Re [1994] 2 FLR 463 287
A (Application for Care and Placement Orders: Local Authority Failings),
    Re [2015] EWFC 11, [2016] 1 FLR 1... 540
A (Children: Fact-Finding Hearing: Care Order), Re [2010] EWCA Civ 344 335
A (Children: Fact-Finding: Appeal), Re [2019] EWCA Civ 74....................................... 140
A (Children: Pool of Perpetrators), Re [2022] EWCA Civ 1348..................................... 537
A (Children), Re [2023] 1 WLR 1743 548
A (Conjoined Twins: Medical Treatment) (No 2), Re [2001] 1 FLR 267 451
A (Contact Order), Re [2010] EWCA Civ 208 369
A (Father: Knowledge of Child's Birth) (2011), sub nom M v F and others,
    Re [2011] EWCA Civ 273... 314
A (In the matter of Children) (AP) [2013] EWCA Civ 232; [2013] UKSC 60;
    [2012] EWCA Civ 1396 (CA)...419, 461
A (Male Sterilisation), Re (2000) 1 FLR 549 440
A (Supervised contact: Assessment of Impact of Domestic Violence), Re [2015]
    EWCA Civ 486 [2016] 1 FLR 689... 407
A and Another v B and Others [2022] EWHC 3089 (Fam); [2023] 1 WLR 677 123
A and B (Children: Restrictions on Parental Responsibility: Radicalisation and
    Extremism), Re [2016] EWFC 40; [2016] 2 FLR 977 293
A and B (Contact) (No 4), Re [2016] 2 FLR 429, FD 405
A and D (Children: Care Proceedings: Religious Upbringing), Re [2010] 2 FLR 151..... 396
A and D (Non-Accidental Injury: Subdural Haematomas), Re [2002] 1 FLR 337 500
A and Others (Adoption: notification of fathers and relatives), Re [2020] EWCA
    Civ 41...302, 315
A-M v A-M [2001] 2 FLR 6.. 34, 35
A, Re (Ward of Court) [2017] EWHC 1022 (Fam) 439, 444
A, Re [2023] EWCA 689... 291
AA v NA (Appeal: Fact-Finding) [2010] EWHC 1282 (Fam) 515
AAZ v BBZ [2016] EWHC 3234 (Fam)... 202
AB (A Child: Care Proceedings: Disclosure of Medical Evidence to Police),
    Re [2002] 1 FLR 579... 503
AB (Adoption: Joint Residence), Re [1996] 1 FLR 27 305
AB (In the family court at East London), Re [2017] Case No: ZE17C00153 398
AB v CD and Others [2021] EWHC 741 (Fam) 367
ABC (Fact finding gonorrhoea), Re (2022); [2023] EWCA Civ 437.............................. 537
ABC and Others v Derbyshire County Council and another [2023] EWHC 986 (KB).... 476
Addou v Bennabi [2022] EWHC 3465 (Fam) (An Algeria Case) 461
Agar-Ellis, Re (1883) 24 Ch D 317 (CA)..258–60, 283, 311, 383
Airedale NHS Trust v Bland [1994] 1 FRC 485; [1993] AC 789; [1993]
    2 WLR 316; [1993] 1 All ER 821 ....452, 459

Al M (Child Arrangements), Re [2021] EWHC 1577 (Fam)..434
Al M (Fact-finding), Re [2019] EWHC 3415 (Fam); [2020] 2 FLR 409 434
Al M (Fact-finding), Re [2021] EWHC 1162 (Fam) [2022] 2 FLR 136 434
Al M (Non-molestation Application), Re [2020] EWHC 3305 (Fam)...........................132
Al-Saedy v Musawawi (Presumption of Marriage) [2010] 2 FLR 287................................35
Allington v Allington [1985] FLR 586...394
An NHS Trust v Mother and others [2024] EWHC 2207 (Fam)....................................363
AR (A Child: Relocation), Re [2010] 2 FLR 1577 ....393, 422
ARB v IVF Hammersmith, sub nom R (the mother) and ARB (the appellant
    father) [2018] EWCA Civ 2803..274
Article 39 v Secretary of State for the Home Department and Others [2023]
    EWHC 1398 (Fam)...462
AS v CPW (Inward Return Order) [2020] 2 FLR 1000...415
Aspden v Elvy [2012] EWHC 1387 (Ch)..91
AT v SS [2015] EWHC 2703 (Fam) 422, 424
Attorney-General v Akhter and Khan [2020] EWCA Civ 122 ....36, 37, 46, 53, 55
Attorney-General's Reference (No. 45 of 2006), R v Stephenson [2006]
    EWCA Crim 1890 118
Axon v Secretary of State for Health and the Family Planning Association [2006]
    2 WLR 1130...374, 375
Aysha King (A Child) [2014] EWHC 2964 (Fam)...457
NP v BR [2019] EWHC 3854 (Fam) 461

B v B [1999] 1 FLR 715...127
B v B [2008] 2 FLR 1627..54, 113
B v B [2014] EWHC 1804...417
B v B (Consent Order: Variation) [1995] 1 FLR 9...210
B v B (Mesher Order) [2003] 2 FLR 285..184
B v B (Residence: Condition Limiting Geographic Area [2004] 2 FLR 979..................414
B v C [2023] EWHC 2524 (Fam)..294
B v El–B (Abduction: Sharia Law: Welfare of Child) [2003] 1 FLR 811 419
B v H (Habitual Residence: Wardship) [2002] 1 FLR 388 461
B v I (Forced marriage) [2010] 1 FLR 1721 ....62, 68
B v W (Wardship: Appeal) [1979] 3 All ER 83 441
B (A Child: Abduction: Article 13(b), Re [2021] 1 FLR 721; [2020] EWCA
    Civ 1057 ....422, 423
B (A Child: Abduction: Habitual Residence [2020] EWCA 1187 419
B (A Child: Care order: proportionality: criterion for review), Re [2013]
    3 All ER 929 548
B (A Child: Care proceedings: jurisdiction), Re [2013] EWCA Civ 1434 496
B (A Child: Immunization), Re [2003] EWCA Civ 1148 411
B (A Child: Placement order: findings of fabricated illness), Re [2015] EWCA
    Civ 1053 475
B (A Child: Post-adoption contact), Re [2019] EWCA Civ 29; [2019]
    Fam 389 ....302, 304, 330, 336
B (A Child: Residence Order), Re [2009] UKSC 5 ....267, 277, 394
B (A Child) [2012] EWCA Civ 1475 538
B (A Minor: Adoption: Parental Agreement), Re [1990] 2 FLR 383.............................317
B (A Minor: Care Order: Criteria), Re [1993] 1 FLR 815 526
B (A Minor: Wardship: Guardian Ad Litem), Re [1989] 1 FLR 268 439
B (A Minor: Wardship: Medical Treatment), Re [1981] 1 WLR 1421 453
B (A Minor: Wardship: Sterilisation), Re [1988] AC 199..450

B (A Minor), Re [1983] 4 FLR 683 394
B (Adoption: Father's Objections), Re [1999] 2 FLR 215 306
B (Adoption: Setting Aside), Re [1985] 1 FLR 1, [1985] Fam 239 327
B (Care or Supervision Order), Re [1996] 2 FLR 693 544
B (Care Proceedings: Expert Witness), Re [2007] EWCA Civ 556 524
B (Children: Care Proceedings: Standard of Proof) (CAFCASS intervening),
    Re [2008] 3 WLR 1; [2007] EWHC 2688 (Fam) 531, 532
B (Children: Non-accidental Injury), sub nom Re O and another (Children)
    (Non-accidental Injury), Re [2002] EWCA Civ 902; [2003] UKHL 18 514
B (Children: Sexual Abuse: Standard of Proof), Re [2008] UKHL 35 511
B (Children: Uncertain perpetrator), Re [2019] EWCA Civ 575 537
B (Children), Re [2000] 27 July 2000 (CA) 399, 400
B (Children), Re [2006] EWCA 1186 (Fam) 544
B (Contact: Child Support), Re [2006] EWCA Civ 1574 .... 568, 581
B (Deceased), Re (2000) 244
B (Leave to Remove), Re [2008] EWCA Civ 1034 415
B (Minors: Access), Re [1992] 1 FLR 140 404
B (Prohibited Steps Order), Re [2008] EWCA Civ 1055 412
B (Split Hearing: Jurisdiction), Re [2000] 1 FLR 334 514
B & L v UK [2006], 36536/02 26
B and G (Children: care proceedings), Re [2015] EWFC 3 516
B and K (Children: Section 91(14) Orders), Re [2024] EWFC 167 390
B and W (threshold criteria), Re [1999] All ER (D) 880 536
B–S (adoption application of s 47(5), Re [2013] EWCA 1146 322
B, O & N (Minors), Re [2003] UKHL 18; [2003] 1 FLR 1169; (2003)
    The Times, 4 April 536
B, RB v FB and MA (Forced Marriage: Wardship Jurisdiction), Re [2008]
    EWHC 1436 (Fam) 137, 440
B, Re [2008] UKHL 35 .... 516, 525
B, Re [2013] 3 All ER 929; [2013] 1 WLR 1911 .... 322, 514, 533
Bank of Ireland Home Mortgages Ltd v Bell [2001] All ER (Comm) 920 104
Barca v Mears [2004] EWHC 2170 (Ch) 105
Barder v Barder [1988] 1 AC 20 185–7
Barnes v Tyrrell [1982] 3 FLR 240 414
Barnsley Metropolitan Borough Council v JK and others [2024] EWHC 305 (Fam 289
Basham (Deceased), Re [1987] 1 WLR 1498 98
Baxter v Baxter [1948] AC 274 57
Baynes v Hedger [2009] EWCA Civ 374 244
Beale v Beale [1983] Lexis Citation 1243 386
Begum v Secretary of State for the Home Department [2024] EWCA Civ 152 540
Bell and another v Tavistock and Portman NHS Foundation Trust (University
    College London Hospitals NHS Foundation Trust and others intervening)
    [2021] EWCA Civ 1363; [2020] EWHC 3274 (Admin) 365, 366
Bell v Metropolitan Police Commissioner [2024] EWHC 379 (KB) 381
Bellinger v Bellinger [2003] UKHL 21; [2001] 2 FLR 1048 .... 22–4, 45, 281
Ben Hashem v Al Shayif [2008] EWHC 2380 (Fam) 51
Bibi v Chief Adjudication Officer [1998] 1 FLR 375 56
Bingham, Re [2015] EWHC 226 (Ch) 235
Bird v Secretary of State for Work and Pensions [2008] EWHC 3159 578
Birmingham City Council v AG and others [2009] EWHC 3720 (Fam) 525
Blackwell v Bull (1836) 1 Keen 176; 48 ER 274 4
Blagdon Cemetery, Re [2002] Fam 299 250

Blunkett v Quinn [2005] 1 FLR 648 .... 286, 287, 290, 404
Bokor-Ingram v Boker-Ingram [2009] EWCA Civ 412.. 186
Bolam v Friern Hospital Management Committee [1957] 2 All ER 118;
    [1957] 1 WLR 582.. 459
Borrows v HM Coroner for Preston [2008] EWHC 1387 (QB) 236, 237
Boudewijn v Johnson and Another [2022] EWFC 142 291
Bradley v Wife (1663) Keble's Reports 1685 Vol 1 637 115
BT v CU [2021] EWFC 87... 187
Buchanan v Milton [1999] 2 FLR 844.. 236
Buckland v Buckland [1968] P 296.. 60, 61
Burden v United Kingdom [2007] 1 FCR 69; (2006) 21 BHRC 640 ...... 6, 9, 16, 18, 19, 45
Burns v Burns [1984] Ch 317 86
Burris v Azadani [1996] 1 WLR 1372... 144
Burton v Islington Health Authority [1993] QB 204 (CA) 347
Button v Button [1968] 1 WLR 457 78

C v C (A Minor: Custody: Appeal) [1991] 1 FLR 223.. 391
C v C (Children: Investigation of Circumstances) [2005] EWHC 2935 (Fam)................ 484
C v C (Financial Relief: Short Marriage) [1997] 2 FLR 25 203
C v C [2001] EWCA Civ 1625... 132
C v C [2003] EWHC 3164 (Fam) 394
C (A Child: Ability to Instruct Solicitor), Re [2023] EWCA Civ 889 ....371, 376
C (A Child: Child's religious choice), Re [2012] Lexis citation 66 (Romford
    County Court) 397
C (A Child: Special Guardianship Order), Re [2019] EWCA Civ 2281 324
C (A Child) [2009] EWCA Civ 72... 390
C (A Child), Re [2007] EWCA Civ 1442 410
C (A Minor: Care: Child's Wishes), Re (1993) 1 FLR 832 ....370, 519
C (A Minor: Leave to Seek Section 8 Orders), Re [1994] 1 FLR 26............................. 370
C (A Minor: Wardship: Medical Treatment), Re [1989] 3 WLR 240 453
C (A Minor), Re [1995] 20 September CA, [1995] Lexis Citation 1364......................... 523
C (Abduction: Residence and Contact), Re [2006] 2 FLR 277...................................... 419
C (Adoption: Religious Observance), Re [2002] 1 FLR 1119 312
C (Adult: Refusal of treatment), Re [1994] 1 All ER 819 564
C (Child: Ability to instruct a solicitor), Re [2023] EWCA Civ 889 ....376, 390
C (Child's Wishes), Re [1993] 1 FLR 832; 1 FCR 810 523
C (Children: Care: Change of forename), Re [2016] EWCA Civ 374 ....411, 476
C (Detention: Medical Treatment), Re [1997] 2 FLR 180... 364
C (Interim Care Order: Residential Assessment), Re [1997] 1 FLR 1 524
C (Parental alienation: instruction of expert), Re [2023] EWHC 342 (Fam).................. 409
C (parental alienation'; instruction of an expert), Re [2023] EWHC 345 (Fam) 408
C (Permission to withdraw: Medical evidence: Interim Threshold not crossed),
    Re [2018] EWFC B37 498
C (Prohibition on Further Applications), Re [2002] EWCA Civ 292.............................. 390
C (Residence: Child's Application for Leave), Re [1996] FCR 461; [1995]
    1 FLR 927 ....373, 390
C (Responsible Authority), Re [2005] EWHC 2939 (Fam) 483
C (Welfare of Child: Immunisation), Re [2003] EWHC 1376 (Fam)......................411, 421
C & A (Children: acquisition and discharge of parental responsibility by an
    unmarried father), Re [2023] EWHC 516 (Fam) 294
C and V (Contact and Parental Responsibilit), Re [1998] 1 FLR 393 291
C-B (A Child: Care Proceedings: Human Rights Claim, Re [2004] 1 WLR 889............ 335

C, D and E (Children: Radicalisation: Fact-Finding), Re [2016] EWHC 3087 (Fam) 539
C, Re [1988] 1 All ER 705 330
CA v DR [2021] EWFC 21 577
Capehorn v Harris [2015] EWCA Civ 955 .... 88, 91
Catholic Care (Diocese of Leeds) v The Charity Commission for England
    and Wales [2010] EWHC 520 (Ch) 307
CDM v CM and others [2003] EWHC 1024 (Fam)... 348
CF v KM (Financial Provision for a Child: Costs of Legal Proceedings) [2011]
    1 FLR 208 575
CH (Care or Interim Care Order), Re [1998] 1 FLR 402... 541
Chalmers v Johns [1999] 1 FLR 392... 127
Chamberlain v De La Mare [1983] 4 FLR 434.. 414
Charman v Charman (No 4) [2007] FLR 1246...193–6, 226
Chief Constable and AA v YK and Others [2010] EWHC 2438 (Fam) 138
Child Maintenance and Enforcement Commission v Beesley and Whyman [2010]
    EWCA 1344 (Civ) 578
Churchill v Roach [2004] FLR 720.. 242
Clark [2003] EWCA Crim 1020... 501
CMX v EJX (French Marriage Contract) [2022] EWFC 136 217
Collins (An Infant), Re [1950] Ch 498 311
Coombes v Smith [1986] 1 WLR 808 99
Corbett v Corbett (otherwise known as Ashley) [1971] P 83... 58
Corbett v Corbett 2004.. 24
Cornick v Cornick [1994] 2 FLR 530 187
Cossey v United Kingdom (1990) 13 EHRR 622.. 281
County Council, A v DP, RS, BS (By the Children's Guardian) [2005] EWHC
    1953 (Fam)...498, 514
County Council, A v K, D and L [2005] EWHC 144 (Fam) 501
Coventry City Council v X, Y and Z (Care Proceedings: Costs: Identification
    of Local Authority) [2010] 1 FLR 977) 542
Covezzi and Morselli v Italy (2003) 38 EHRR 28 492
Cowan v Cowan [2001] EWCA Civ 679 ....189, 194, 207
Cox v Jones [2004] EWHC 1006; [2004] 3 CR 693..89, 103, 223
Cremated Remains of AA, Re [2018] ECC 7.. 251
Crossley v Crossley [2007] EWCA Civ 1491 211
CS v SBH and Others (Appeal FPR 2010, Rule 16.6: Sufficiency of Child's
    Understanding), Re [2019] EWHC 634 (Fam); [2019] 2 FLR 580....................367, 373
Cunliffe v Fielden [2006] Ch 361 248
CW v SG (parental responsibility: consequential orders) [2013] EWHC 854 (Fam) 292
G v G [1985] 1 WLR 647 391

D v Bury Metropolitan Borough Council; H v Bury Metropolitan Council [2006]
    1 WLR 917.. 486
D v D (Shared Residence Order) [2001] 1 FLR 495.. 402
D v D [1979] Fam 70 68
D v E (Termination of Parental Responsibility) [2021] EWFC 37................................... 292
D v East Berkshire Community Health NHS Trust and Others MAK and Another v
    Dewsbury Healthcare NHS Trust and another RK and Another v Oldham
    NHS Trust and Another [2005] UKHL 23; [2005] AC 373 490
D v Registrar General [1996] 1 FLR 707... 336
D (A Child: Abduction: Rights of Custody), Re [2007] 1 AC 619; [2006]
    UKHL 51.. 348, 377, 419, 423

D (A Child) & Another (2016) [2016] EWCA Civ 12 375
D (A Child), Re [2006] UKHL 51 420
D (A Child), Re [2014] EWCA Civ 1057 404
D (A Minor: Justices' Decision: Review), Re [1977] Fam 158 440
D (A Minor: Wardship: Sterilisation), Re [1976] Fam 185 .... 441, 451
D (Adoption Reports: Confidentiality), Re [1996] AC 593 329
D (An Infant: Adoption: Parent's Consent), Re [1977] AC 602 .... 278, 316, 389
D (Care: Natural Parent Presumption), Re [1999] 2 FLR 1023 266
D (Contact and Parental Responsibility: Lesbian Mothers and Known Father),
    Re (2006) EWHC 2 (Fam).. 267, 279, 282
D (Contact: Reasons for Refusal), Re [1997] 2 FLR 48.. 407
D (Leave to Remove: Appeal), Re [2010] EWCA Civ 50 415
D (Paternity), Re [2006] EWHC 3545 (Fam) 296
D (Unborn Baby: Emergency Protection Order: Future Harm), Re, sub nom
    30 Bury MBC v D (2009) EWHC 446 (Fam)... 444
D McG v Neath Port Talbot County Borough Council [2010] EWCA Civ 821............. 320
D-E v A-G [1845] 163 ER 1039 57
D, Re [1984] 1 AC 778...352, 460
Davies v Davies [2016] EWCA Civ 463 99
Davies v Taylor [1974] AC 207 527
Davis v Johnson [1979] AC 264; [1978] 2 WLR 553.. 2, 124
de Reneville v de Reneville [1948] P 100... 50
Depp II v News Group Newspapers Ltd and another [2020] EWHC 2911 (QB) 111
Devon County Council v EB and others, sub nom Re EY (Fact-Finding
    Hearing) [2013] EWHC 968 (Fam) 501, 502
Dibble v Pfluger [2010] EWCA 1005 (Civ) 223
Dodsworth v Dodsworth [1973] 228 EG 115 101
Dolan v Corby [2011] EWCA Civ 1664 128
Dorney-Kingdom v Dorney-Kingdom [2000] 2 FLR 85 184
Down Lisburn Health and Social Services Trust v H and another [2006] UKHL 36 317
Drake v Whipp [1996] 1 FLR 826; (1996) 28 HLR 53 (CA); [1995] EWCA Civ 25 95
DS v AC [2023] EWFC 46 ....132, 135
DW v Secretary for State for Work and Pensions and Another (2023) UKUT
    19 (AAC) 563, 571
DY (Capacity) Re [2024] EWCOP 4 436

E v D [2022] EWHC 1216 (Fam)... 424
E v L [2021] EWFC 60 200
E (A Child: Adoption by One Person) Re [2021] EWFC 45 306
E (A Child: Fact-finding hearing: assessment of biological parents), Re [2011]
    EWHC 3453 (Fam).. 538
E (A Minor: Wardship: Medical Treatment), Re [1993] 1 FLR 386; [1993]
    2 FCR 219E 359, 377
E (An Alleged Patient): Sheffield City Council v E and S, Re [2005] EWHC
    2808 (CH)... 28
E (By Her Litigation Friend EW) v London Borough of X [2006] 1 FLR 730 462
E (By Her Litigation Friend the Official Solicitor) v Channel Four; News
    International Ltd and St Helens Borough Council [2005] 2 FLR 913........................ 436
E (Care Proceedings: Social Work Practice), Re [2000] B 2 FLR 254............................ 477
E (Children: female genital mutilation protection orders) Re [2015]
    EWHC 2275 (Fam)... 140
E (Children: international abduction), Re [2011] UKSC 27... 417

E (SA) (A Minor: Wardship), Re [1984] 1 WLR 156 440
E and others v United Kingdom [2003] 36 EHRR 31 489
E-R (Child Arrangement order), Re [2016] EWHC 805 (Fam) 394
EA v NA [2018] EWHC 583 (Fam) 235
EC (Disclosure of Material), Re [1996] CA, sub nom Re C 2 FLR 725 (CA) 503, 504
Edwards v Lloyds Bank TSB [2004] EWHC 1745 105
EF, Re [2016] EWFC 69 411
El Gamal v Al Maktoum [2012] 2 FLR 387 36
Elkndo v Elsyed [2024] EWHC 2230 (Fam) 418, 462
Emma and Harry (children); A local authority v Mrs X (a mother) and others,
    Re [2023] EWFC 69 491
Enfield London Borough Council v A Mother and others [2024] EWHC 133 (Fam) 443
ES v AJ [2010] EWHC 1113 (Fam) 460
Espinosa v Bourke [1999] 1 FLR 74 246
Essex County Council v TLR and KBR (Minors) [1978] Fam Law 15 526
Estate of Singh (Deceased), Re [2023] All ER (D) 55 246
Evans and Another v Alder Hey Children's NHS Foundation Trust [2018]
    EWCA Civ 805 457
Evans v United Kingdom [2006] ECHR 10 270
Eves v Eves [1975] 1 WLR 1338 ....86, 88, 89
EY (Fact-Finding Hearing), Re [2023] EWCA Civ 1241 515

F v F (Ancillary Relief: Substantial Assets) [1995] 2 FLR 45 ....202, 211
F v M [2021] EWFC 4 ....110, 131, 409
F v M and Others [2023] EWFC 172 132
F v M, A and Secretary of State for the Home Department [2017] EWHC 949 (Fam) 444
F (A Child: Indirect Contact Through Third Party), Re [2006] EWCA
    Civ 1426, [2006] 3 FCR 553 ....399, 406
F (A Child: International Relocation Cases), Re [2015] EWCA Civ 882 422
F (A Child), Re [2009] EWCA Civ 313 391
F (A Child), Re [2011] EWCA Civ 258 536
F (A Minor: Adoption Parental Consent), Re [1982] 1 WLR 102 316
F (Adoption: Welfare of Child: Financial Considerations), Re [2004] 2 FLR 440 334
F (Children), Re [2016] EWCA Civ 546 371
F (Family Proceedings: Section 37 Investigations), Re [2006] 1 FLR 1122 484
F (In Utero: Wardship), Re [1988] 2 FLR 30 445
F (Orse A: A Minor: Publication of Information), Re [1977] Fam 58 448
F (Relocation), Re [2013] 1 FLR 645 422
F (Shared Residence Order), Re [2003] EWCA Civ 592 402
F and Another (Children: Discharge of special guardianship order), N v K and
    Others, Re [2021] EWCA Civ 622 326
F-H (Dispensing with Fact-Finding Hearing), Re [2008] EWCA Civ 1249 514
F, Re (In Utero) [1988] Fam 112 444
F, Re [1995] 1 FLR 956 403
Father Hudson's Society v Charity Commission [2009] PTSR 1125 307
Father v CD [2023] EWFC 192 409
Father v Maternal Aunt [2023] EWFC 20 485
Father, A (F) v A mother (M) and another [2023] EWHC 1955 (Fam) 485
Father, A v A Mother and Others [2024] EWHC 991 (Fam) 424
Father, A v Lancashire County Council [2010] 1 FLR 387, sub nom Re A and
    D [2010] 390
Father, The v The Mother [2023] EWFC 176 288

Father and another, A v [Zayn] (through his children's guardian, LC) and
    another [2024] EWFC 267 (B) 386
Ferguson and Others v UK (2012) (App. No.8254/11) 46
FF v KF [2017] EWHC 1093 (Fam) 202
First National Bank v Achampong (2004) 1 FCR 18; [2003] EWCA Civ 487 104
Fitzpatrick v Sterling Housing Association [2001] 1 AC 27 (HL) 5
Fleming v Fleming [2003] 1 EWCA 1841 (Civ) 183
Ford v Ford (1987) Fam Law 232 59
Fornah v Secretary of State for the Home Department, House of Lords [2006]
    UKHL 46, [2006] 3 FCR 381, [2007] 1 All ER 671 140
FRB v DRC (No. 3) [2020] EWHC 3696 (Fam) 187
Fred Perry Holdings v Genis [2015] 1 P & CR DG5 104
FZ v SZ and others (Ancillary Relief: Conduct) [2010] All ER (D) 189 206

G v G (Parental Order: Revocation) [2012] EWHC 1979 (Fam); [2013] 1 FLR 286 276
G (A Child: Care Order: Threshold Criteria), Re [2001] 1 FLR 872; UKHL 18 514
G (A Child: Parental Responsibility), Re [2006] EWCA Civ 745 277
G (A Child: Post-mortem report: delays), Re [2023] 1 FLR 218 481
G (A Child: Special Guardianship Order: Leave to Discharge), Re [2010]
    EWCA Civ 300 325
G (A Child) [2008] EWCA Civ 105 401
G (A Child) [2023] EWFC 168 393
G (A Minor: Interim Care Order: Residential Assessment), Re [2005]
    3 WLR 1166 524
G (Abduction: Children's Objections), Re [2010] EWCA Civ 1232 421
G (Adoption: Ordinary Residence), Re [2002] EWHC 2447 (Fam) 277
G (Adult Patient: Publicity), Re [1995] 2 FLR 528 438
G (Children: Abduction: Children's Objections), Re [2010] EWCA Civ 1232 381
G (Children: Contact), Re [2002] EWCA Civ 1012 277
G (Children: Education: Religious upbringing), Re [2012] EWCA
    Civ 1233 .... 361, 377, 396
G (Children: Fair hearing) [2019] EWCA Civ 126 498
G (Children: Residence Order: No Order Principle), Re [2006] 1 FLR 771 541
G (Children: Residence: Same-Sex Partner), Re (2006) UKHL 43; [2006] 1
    WLR 2305 .... 264, 267, 268, 277, 278, 394
G (Emotional Harm), Re [1999] Fam Law 852(2) 477
G (Interim Care Order: Residential Assessment), Re [2005] UKHL 68 524
G (Leave to Remove), Re [2007] EWCA Civ 1497; [2008] 1 FLR 1587 416
G (Parental Responsibility Order), Re [2006] EWCA Civ 745 264
G (Residence: Same-Sex Partner), Re [2005] 2 FLR 957 392
G and H (Leave To Revoke Placement Order), Re [2023] EWCA Civ 768 320
G and R, Re [1995] 2 FLR 867 .... 478, 527
G, Re [2006] 2 FLR 1092 567
Gallarotti v Sebastianelli [2012] EWCA Civ 865 91
Gammans v Ekins [1950] 2 KB 328 CA 4
Gandhi v Patel [2002] All ER (D) 436 53
Garland v Morris [2007] EWHC 2 (Ch) 249
George v George [1986] 2 FLR 347 132
Gereis v Yacoub [1977] 1 FLR 854 52
Ghaidan v Godin-Mendoza [2004] UKHL 30; [2004] 2 FCR 481 .... 5, 279
Gillick v West Norfolk and Wisbech Area Health Authority [1986] AC 112;
    [1986] Crim LR 113; [1985] UKHL 7; [1985] 3 All ER 403; [1984]

1 All ER 365; [1984] QB 581 .... 284, 342, 343, 349–60, 362–4, 366–8, 373–5, 377–80, 389, 392, 421, 433, 439, 496

Gissing v Gissing [1971] AC 886 85

Goodwin v UK (28957/95) [2002] IRLR 664; [2002] 2 FCR 577; [2002] 2 FLR 487 .... 24, 281

Görgülü v Germany [2004] 1 FLR 894 337

Gow (FC: Appellant) v Grant (Respondent) (Scotland) [2012] UKSC 29 219

GR (Care Order), Re [2010] EWCA Civ 871 497

Graham-York v York & Others [2016] 1 FLR 407; [2015] EWCA Civ 72; [2015] Fam Law 528 93

Grant v Baker [2016] EWHC 1782 (Ch) 106

Grant v Edwards [1986] Ch 638 .... 86, 97

Greasley v Cooke [1980] 1 WLR 1306 99

Gregory (Indi) v Nottingham University Hospitals NHS Foundation Trust and others [2023] EWCA Civ 1262 458

Grey v Grey (No 3) [2010] Fam Law 440 182

Grubb v Grubb [2009] EWCA Civ 976 127

GT v LT [2024] EWHC 2190 (Fam) 419

GT v RJ [2018] EWFC 26 422

Gudanaviciene & Others v Director of Legal Aid casework and the Lord Chancellor [2014] EWCA Civ 1622 382

Guest v Guest [2022] UKSC 27 .... 96, 100, 106, 108

Gully v Dix [2004] 1 FCR 453 243

GW v RW [2003] EWHC 611 (Fam) 204

H v A [2024] EWHC 476 (Fam) 417

H v D and others [2007] EWHC 802 (Fam) 461

H v H [2015] EWHC B24 (Fam) 177

H v H (Jurisdiction to Grant Wardship) [2011] EWCA Civ 796 460

H v R and Another (Attorney General for England and Wales intervening) [2021] EWHC 1943 (Fam) 290

H (A Child: Analysis of Realistic Options and SGOs), sub nom CH v London Borough of Hammersmith & Fulham and Others, Re [2015] EWCA Civ 406 326

H (A Child: Parental responsibility: vaccination), Re [2020] EWCA Civ 664 411

H (A Child: Residence), Re [2002] 3 FCR 277 277

H (A Minor: Care Proceedings: Child's Wishes), Re [1993] 3 WLR 1109; 1 FLR 440 .... 368, 372

H (A Minor: Section 37 Direction), Re [1993] 2 FLR 541 527

H (Abduction: Non-Convention Application: a Dominica Case), Re [2006] EWCA 199 (Fam) 461

H (Blood tests: Paternity), Re [1997] Fam 89 296

H (Children: Contact Order) No, Re 2 [2002] 1 FLR 22 404

H (Contact Order), Re [2010] EWCA Civ 448 391

H (Contact: Domestic Violence) [2006] 1 FLR 943 406

H (Contact: Domestic Violence), Re [1998] 2 FLR 42 406

H (Infants: Adoption: Parental Consent), Re [1977] 1 WLR 471 .... 316, 338

H (Minors: Local Authority: Parental Rights (No 3), Re [1991] Fam 151 286

H (Minors: Sexual abuse: standard of proof), Re [1996] AC 563 528

H (Minors: Wardship: Cultural Background), Re [1987] 2 FLR 12 283

H (Minors: Wardship: Cultural Background), Re [1987] 2 FLR 12 520

H (Minors), Re (unreported) 6 August 1992 368

H (Residence Order: Child's Application for Leave), Re (2000) 1 FLR 780 370

H and A (Children), Re [2002] EWCA 383 288
H and R (Child Sexual Abuse: Standard of Proof), Re [1996] 1 FLR 80;
    [1996] AC 563 (HL); [1996] 1 All ER 1; [1996] 1 FCR 509; [1995]
    1 FLR 643 (CA)... 474, 511, 514, 528–32, 545
H-B (child: contact), Re [2015] EWCA Civ 389.. 403
H-D (Children) [2001] EWCA Civ 402 411
H-N and Others (Children: Domestic Abuse: Finding of Fact Hearings),
    Re [2021] EWCA Civ 448; [2021] 2 FLR 1116 .... 109, 110, 113, 114, 409, 511, 515
H-W (Children) (No 2), Re [2022] UKSC 17.. 548
H, Re W (Adoption Parental Agreement), Re [1982] 4 FLR 614................................... 316
H, Re, Re G [2001] 1 FLR 646 315
Haase v Germany (2004) 2 FLR 39 492
Hadjuova v Slovakia [2003] App No 2660/03 142
Hale v Tanner [2000] 1 WLR 2377... 133
Hammond v Mitchell [1992] 1 WLR 1127 86
Hanlon v Law Society [1981] AC 124 (HL).. 179
Haringey London Borough Council v C (E Intervening) [2004] EWHC 2580 (Fam)...... 400
Haringey London Borough Council v C (E, E, F and High Commissioner of
    Republic of Kenya Intervening) [2007] 1 FLR 1035; [2006] EWHC
    1620 (Fam) 333, 395
Haringey London Borough Council v C, E, and Another [2005] 2 FLR 47 333
Harrow London Borough Council v Qazi [2004] 1 AC 98, [2003] UKHL 43 76
Hart v Hart [2018] Fam 93 198
Harthan v Harthan [1949] P 115... 57
Hartshorne v Gardner [2008] 2 FLR 1681 237
Hawksworth v Hawksworth (1861–73) 6 LR Ch App 539; [1861–73]
    All ER Rep 314 ....258, 259
Herefordshire Council v AB [2018] EWFC 10 543
Hewer v Bryant (1970) 1 QB 357 ....257, 259, 260, 343, 374
Hirani v Hirani [1983] 4 FLR 232... 60
His Highness Sheikh Mohammed Bin Rashid Al Maktoum v Her Royal
    Highness Princess Haya Bint Al Hussein And Others [2021] EWHC
    3480 (Fam)... 434
Hofstetter v Hofstetter [2009] EWHC 3282 (Admin) 312
Holtam v Arnold (1986) 2 BMLR 123 237
Horner v Horner [1982] Fam 90 132
Hosking v Michaelides [2004] All ER (D) 147.. 105
Hudson v Hathway [2022] EWCA Civ 1648.. 95
Hudson v Leigh (Status of Non-Marriage) [2009] EWHC 1306; [2009]
    2 FLR 1129.. 36, 37, 45, 54, 55
Humberside County Council v B [1993] 1 FLR 257 517
Huxley v Child Support Officer [2000] 1 FLR 898... 560
HW v WW [2021] EWFC B20.. 187
Hyde v Hyde (1866) LR1 P & D 130... 21, 22
HZ v GA [2024] EWHC 489 (Fam).. 423

I v I [2008] 1 FLR 201 183
Ibuna and another v Arroyo and another [2012] EWHC 428 (Ch)............................... 236
IJ overseas surrogacy: parental order) Re [2011] EWHC 921 (Fam) 276
Ilott v Blue Cross [2017] UKSC 17 ....249, 250
In the Matter of J (Children) [2009] EWCA Civ 365... 375
Ipecki v Mc Connell [2019] EWFC 19... 217

Islam Appellant and Secretary of State for The Home Department Respondent
      Regina v Immigration Appeal Tribunal and Another, Ex Parte Shah
      [Consolidated Appeals] [On Appeal from Reg v Immigration Appeal Tribunal
      and Another, Ex Parte Shah] [1999] 2 AC 629... 144

J v B (Ultra-Orthodox Judaism: Transgender) [2017] EWFC 4.. 397
J v C [1970] AC 668 .... 259, 261, 308, 311, 352, 523, 547
J v C (Child Financial Provision) [1999] 1 FLR 152 576
J v C (Void Marriage: status of children) J v C and another [2006] EWCA Civ 551 271
J v C [2007] Fam 1.. 70
J v J (Financial Orders: Wife's Long-Term Needs) [2011] EWHC 1010 (Fam)................ 202
J v S (Leave to Remove) [2010] EWHC 2098 (Fam) 415
J v S-T (formerly J: Transsexual: Ancillary Relief) [1997] 1 FLR 402............................. 206
J (A Child: Child arrangements order: recommendations of the guardian),
      Re: The father v The mother and another (2023) EWFC 35 484
J (A Child: Custody Rights: Jurisdiction: a Saudi Arabia Case), Re [2006] 1 AC 80 461
J (A Child), Re [2005] UKHL 40... 400
J (A Minor: Child in Care: Medical Treatment), Re [1993] Fam 15.............................. 454
J (A Minor: Contact), Re [1994] 1 FLR 729 407
J (A Minor: Wardship: Medical Treatment), Re [1990] 3 All ER 930 453
J (Adoption: Consent of Foreign Public Authority), Re [2002] EWHC 766 (Fam) 334
J (Adoption: Contacting Father), Re [2003] EWHC 199 (Fam) 314
J (Child Returned Abroad: Convention Rights), Re [2005] 2 FLR 802..................419, 420
J (Child's Religious Upbringing and Circumcision), Re [2000] 1 FLR 571..................... 396
J (Children: Non-accidental injury: past possible perpetrator in new family),
      Re [2012] 2 FCR 1.. 534
J (Jurisdiction: Abduction), Re [2015] UKSC 70 421
J (Leave to Issue Application for a Residence Order), Re [2002] EWCA Civ 1342 390
J (Special Guardianship), Re [2007] EWCA Civ 55 324
J & K (Abduction: Objections of Child), Re [2005] 1 FLR 273...................................... 422
J and others (Children: Interim Removal) [2023] EWCA Civ 1266 391
J, Re (Children: Non-accidental injury: past possible perpetrator in new family)
      [2012] 2 FCR 1... 536
JA, Re [1998] 1 FLR 231.. 420
Jagger v Hall (unreported, 1999)... 54
James v Thomas [2007] EWCA Civ 1007... 86, 88
Janos v Janos [1988] (25 August 1998, unreported) 386
JD and Another v B [2020] EWFC 16.. 386
Jelley v Iliffe [1981] Fam 128..243, 244
Jennings, Re [1994] Ch 256 248
JH v MF [2020] EWHC 86 (Fam).. 114
JL (A Child) (Leave to Apply to Revoke Placement Order) Re B v A Local
      Authority [2020] EWCA Civ 1253..302, 320
JL v SL [2015] EWHC 360 (Fam)... 193
Johnson v Walton [1990] 1 FLR 350... 132
Jones v Kernott [2011] UKSC 53; [2010] EWCA Civ 578; [2010] 1 All ER 947;
      [2009] EWHC 1713 (Ch)..84, 89, 91, 93, 95, 96, 108
JP v LP and Others (Surrogacy Arrangement: Wardship) [2014]
      EWHC 595 (Fam)... 451
Juffali v Juffali [2016] EWHC 1684 (Fam) 1 FLR 1508.. 202
JW (Children at Home Under Care order), Re [2023] EWCA
      Civ 944...498, 511, 545–7, 550

K v K (Minors: Property Transfer) [1992] 2 FLR 220 575
K v K (Relocation: Shared Care Arrangement) [2011] EWCA Civ 793 ....415, 563
K v L [2012] WTLR 153 226
K (A Child: deceased), Re [2017] EWHC 1083 (Fam) 236
K (A Child: Secure Accommodation Order: Right to Liberty), Re [2001]
    2 WLR 1141.. 282
K (A Minor) Re [2006] EWHC 1007; [2006] 2 FLR 883.....................................458, 459
K (Care Order), Re [2007] EWCA Civ 697 524
K (Care Proceedings), Re [2010] EWHC 3342 (Fam) 535
K (Care: Threshold Criteria), Re [2005] EWCA Civ 1226, [2006] 2 FLR 868 ....515, 535
K (Children: Adoption: Freeing Order), Re [2004] EWCA Civ 1181............................ 328
K (Children), Re [2016] EWHC 1606 (Fam) 539
K (Forced marriage passport order), Re [2020] EWCA Civ 190...............................138, 139
K (Infants), Re [1965] AC 201 440
K (Minors: Children: Care and Control), Re [1977] Fam 179.................................259, 261
K (Supervision Orders), Re [1999] 2 FLR 303 544
K, W and H (Minors), Re (1993) 4 Med LR 200 (Fam) 263
KA v MA (Pre-nuptial Agreement: Needs) [2018] EWHC 499 (Fam) 216
Kaha v Lahmer [2024] EWHC 2439 (Fam)...418, 462
Kaur v Gill [1988] Fam 110.. 104
Kaur v Singh [1972] 1 WLR 105.. 59
KD (A Minor) (Ward: Termination of Access), Re [1988] AC 806; [1988]
    1 All ER 577 .... 265, 266, 519
Kelley v Corston [1998] QB 686 209
Kelly v BBC [2001] 1 FLR 197.. 450
Kelly v Director of Public Prosecutions [2002] EWHC 1428 (Admin) 123
Kent County Council v C [1993] 1 FLR 308 541
Kettering General Hospital Trust NHS Foundation Trust v C and North
    Northamptonshire Council [2023] EWFC 12.. 445
Kiam v Crown Prosecution Service [2014] EWHC 1606 (Admin)................................ 496
King's College Hospital NHS Foundation Trust v Mrs R Mr R Nr (By his
    Children's Guardian) [2024] EWHC 910 (Fam)... 458
Kirklees Metropolitan District Council v S (Contact to Newborn Babies) [2006]
    1 FLR 333 493
Kokosinski v Kokosinski [1980] Fam 72 207
KR (Abduction: Forcible Removal by Parents), Re [1999] Fam Law 545 136
Kremen v Agrest [2012] 2 FLR 214 EWHC 45 (Fam).. 217
KY v DD (Injunctions) [2011] EWHC 1277 (Fam) 442

L (A Child: Care proceedings: responsibility for child's injury) [2006] EWCA
    Civ 49.. 517
L (A Child: Internal Relocation: Shared Residence Order), Re [2009] EWCA
    Civ 1008; [2009] EWCA Civ 20 ....386, 515
L (A Child) [2023] EWHC 3194 (Fam) 459
L v P (Paternity Test: Child's Objection) [2010] EWCA Civ 1145 566
L (A Minor: Police Investigation: Privilege), Re [1996], 1 FLR 731 (HL) 503
L (A Minor: Wardship: freedom of publication), Re [1988] 1 All ER 418..................... 447
L (Care: Assessment: Fair Trial), Re [2002] FLR 730... 345
L (Children), Re [2006] EWCA Civ 1282... 518
L (Children), Re [2012] EWCA Civ 721... 128
L (Medical Treatment: Benefit), Re [2004] EWHC 2713 (Fam) 456
L (Medical Treatment: Gillick competency), Re [1998] 2 FLR 810.............................. 360

L (Minors: Sexual Abuse: Disclosure), Re, V (Minors) (Sexual Abuse: Disclosure),
     Re [1999] 1 WLR 299 412
L (Section 37 Direction), Re [1999] 1 FLR 984 484
L and B (Children: Specific Issues: Temporary Leave to Remove from the
     Jurisdiction: Circumcision), Re [2016] EWHC 849 (Fam) 398
L and H (Residential Assessment), Re {2007] EWCA Civ 213 524
L-W (Enforcement and Committal: Contact; CPL v CHW and Others),
     Re [2010] EWCA Civ 1253 410
L, V, M, H (Contact: Domestic Violence), Re [2001] Fam 260; [2000]
     4 All ER 609 .... 295, 406
LA v PQ [2023] EWHC 1971 (Fam) 315
Lambert v Lambert [2003] Fam 103 .... 189, 205
Lancashire County Council v A [2000] 2 AC 147 534
Lancashire County Council v M and Others [2023] EWFC 30; [2023]
     EWHC 3097 (Fam) 515, 518, 533
Langdon v Horton [1951] 1 KB 666 CA 4
Langley v Liverpool City Council [2005] EWCA Civ 1173 496
Lawrence v Gallagher [2012] EWCA Civ 394 .... 188, 189, 195
LC (International Abduction: Child's Objections to Return), Re [2013]
     EWCA Civ 1058, [2014 1 FLR 1458 373
LC (Reunite: International Child Abduction Centre Intervening), Re [2014]
     UKSC 1 348
Leeds Teaching Hospitals NHS Trust v Mr and Mrs A and Others [2003]
     EWHC 259 (QB) 269
Leicester City Council v T [2016] EWFC 20 540
Lewisham London Borough Council v D & Others [2010] EWHC 1239 (Fam),
     Criteria for Territorial Jurisdiction in Public Law Proceedings (2008)
     2 FLR 1449 459
Liden v Burton [2016] EWCA Civ 275 .... 99, 107
Lilleyman v Lilleyman [2012] EWHC 821 (Ch) 245
Lindop v Agus; Bass and Hedley [2010] 1 FLR 631 243
Livesey v Jenkins [1985] 1 AC 424 186
Livingstone-Stallard v Livingstone-Stallard [1974] 2 All ER 766 157
Lloyds Bank plc v Rosset [1991] 1 AC 107 .... 84–9, 95
Local Authority, A v A Mother and others [2020] EWHC 3496 (Fam) 540
Local Authority, A v C (E and Another intervening) [2004] EWHC 2580 (Fam) 538
Local Authority, A v DG and Others, X and Y (Children: Disclosure of
     Judgment to Police) Y v Z (Publicity: Sch 1 Proceedings) [2014]
     EWHC 650.734 (Fam) 504
Local Authority, A v DL [2012] EWCA Civ 253 233
Local Authority, A v EBY and others [2023] EWHC 2494 (Fam) 491
Local Authority, A v HB and Others [2017] EWHC 1437 (Fam) 540
Local Authority, A v M [2016] EWHC 1599 (Fam) 539, 540
Local Authority, A v SB and Others [2022] EWFC 111 294
Local Authority, A v The Mother and Others [2024] EWFC 19 (B) 288
Local Authority, A v W and Others, sub nom Salford CC v W and Others
     (Religion and Declaration of Looked After Status) [2021] 4 WLR 21;
     [2021] EWHC 61 (Fam) 412, 413
Local Authority, A v X and others (M intervening) [2023] EWFC 121 288
Local Authority, A v Y, Z, and Others [2006] 2 FLR 41; [2006] Lexis
     Citation 579 .... 322, 323, 403
Lomas v Parle [2004] 1 FLR 812 123

London Borough Council, A v K and Others [2009] EWHC 850 (Fam)........................ 533
London Borough of Barnet v AL [2017] EWHC 125 (Fam) 411
London Borough of Enfield v E (Unconscionable Delay) [2024] EWFC 183 487
London Borough of Richmond v Mother and others [2023] EWFC 146 319
London Borough of Southwark v B [1993] 2 FLR 559.. 542
London Borough of Tower Hamlets v B [2015] EWHC 2491 (Fam)............................. 539
London Borough of Tower Hamlets v M & Others [2015] EWHC 869 (Fam) 449
Luckwell v Limata [2014] EWHC 502 (Fam) 217, 218

M v A [2023] CSOH 80...393, 410
M v D [2021] EWHC 1351 (Fam) 133
M v F [2024] EWFC 237 391
M v H (Educational Welfare) [2008] EWHC 324 (Fam).. 393
M v H (Private Law: Vaccination) [2020] EWFC 93 411
M v Netherlands [1993] 74 D & R 120 270
M v S [2024] EWFC 80 (B) 145
M (A Child: Refusal of Medical Treatment), Re [1999] 2 FLR 1097 .... 360, 361, 439, 442
M (A Child: Residence Order), Re [2003] EWCA Civ 1455 393
M (A Child) [2009] EWCA Civ 311 412
M (A Child), Re [2010] UKSC 12 371
M (A Minor: Application No. 2), Re [1994] 1 FLR 59.. 541
M (A Minor: Care Order: Threshold Conditions), Re [1994] 2 AC 424....................524–6
M (A Minor: Contact: Conditions), Re [1994] 1 FLR 272 399
M (A Minor: Wardship: Sterilization), Re [1988] 2 FLR 497.. 451
M (Abduction: Child's Objections: Appeal), Re [2014] EWCA Civ 1519..................... 421
M (Abduction: Child's Objections), Re [2007] EWCA Civ 260 348
M (Care Proceedings: Judicial Review), Re [2003] EWHC 850 (Admin) 491, 492
M (Child's Upbringing), Re (1996) 2 FLR 441 ....265, 266, 277, 333, 354
M (Children: Abduction: Rights of Custody), Re [2007] UKHL 55 422
M (Children: Jurisdiction Wardship) [2016] EWCA Civ 937 ....437, 443
M (Children: Ultra-Orthodox Judaism: Transgender) (Stonewall Equality Ltd
    and Another intervening), Re [2017] EWCA Civ 2164 397
M (Children), Re [2017] EWCA Civ 891 462
M (Children), Re [2019] EWCA 1364.. 540
M (Minors: Adoption Parental Agreement), Re [1985] 1 FLR 921 316
M (Minors: Adoption), Re [1991] 1 FLR 458 328
M (Minors: Children) (Repatriated Orphans), Re [2002] EWHC 852 (Fam) 516
M (Minors: Contact: Violent Parent), Re [1999] 2 FCR 56... 406
M (Placement Order), Re [2010] EWCA Civ 1257.. 321
M (Republic of Ireland: Child's Objections: Joinder of Children as Parties
    to Appeal), Re [2015] 2 FLR 1074; [2015] EWCA Civ 26 ....373, 422
M (Special Guardianship Order: leave to apply to discharge), Re [2021]
    EWCA Civ 442 326
M (Sperm Donor Father), Re [2003] Fam 94 402
M (Threshold criteria: Parental concessions), Re [1999] 2 FLR 728). In Re D
    (Children: Contact Order) (2005) EWCA Civ 825 475
M (Wardship Jurisdiction and Powers), Re [2015] EWHC 1433 (Fam)......................... 449
M and A (Disclosure of Information), Re [1999] 1 FLR 443... 412
M and R (Minors: Sexual Abuse: Expert Evidence), Re [1996] 4 All ER 25 530
M O C v Yusuf [2023] EWHC 2792 (Fam) 459
M-H (A Child) (Care Order), Re [2007] 2 FLR 1715 394
M-J (Special Guardianship Order), Re [2007] EWCA Civ 56....................................... 324

MA v JA and Her Majesty's Attorney General Respondent Intervener [2012]
    EWHC 2219 (Fam) 52
Mabon v Mabon [2005] EWCA Civ 634; [2005] 2 FLR 1011 .... 345, 349, 375, 376
MacLeod v MacLeod [2008] UKPC 64 210
Mairs v Secretary of State for Education and Skills [2005] EWHC 996 (Admin) 489
Manchester City Council v Maryan Yusef & Ors [2023] EWHC 2792 (Fam)
    return order 462
Manjra v Shaikh [2021] 1 FLR 106 135
Mansfield v Mansfield [2011] EWCA Civ 1086 198
Martin v Martin [1978] Fam 12 185
Martin v Myers [2004] EWHC 1543 35
Matharu v Matharu [1994] 2 FLR 597 101
McGrath v Wallis [1995] 2 FLR 114 83
Mensah v Islington Council and Another [2000] EWCA Civ 405 312
Mesher v Mesher [1980] 1 All ER 126 184–6
Messina (Formerly Smith Orse Vervaeke) v Smith (Messina intervening) [1971]
    P 322 63
Metropolitan Borough Council, A v DB [1997] 1 FLR 767 363
Michael and others v Chief Constable of South Wales Police and another
    (Refuge and others intervening) [2015] AC 1732 142
Midland Bank plc v Cooke [1995] 4 All ER 562 .... 89, 96
Miller v Miller/McFarlane v McFarlane [2006] UKHL 24; [2006]
    1 FLR 1186 .... 179, 190, 192–4, 196, 198, 202, 226
Mills v McCartney [2008] EWHC 401 (Fam) 204
Minton v Minton [1979] AC 593 196
Mizzi v Malta [2006] 1 FLR 1048 291
MLIA and Another v Chief Constable of Hampshire Police [2017]
    EWHC 292 (QB) 143
Moore v Holdsworth & Others [2010] EWHC 683 (Ch) 245
Mortgage Corporation v Silkin; Same and Shaire [2001] Ch 151; [2001] Ch 743 105
Mother, A v A Father [2024] EWFC 53 (B) 516, 541
Mr and Mrs C v D and others [2023] EWFC 10 .... 304, 317
Ms L, Re; Ms M (Declaration of parentage), Re [2022] EWFC 38 289
MS v AR [2019] IESC 10 348
Mundell v Name 1 [2019] EWCOP 50 65
Myerson v Myerson No. 2 (No 2) [2009] 2 FLR 147 .... 185, 186

N (A Child: International Abduction: Exercise of Inherent Jurisdiction),
    Re [2012] EWCA Civ 1086 460
N (A Minor: Adoption), Re [1990] 1 FLR 58 310
N (Children: Revocation of Placement Orders), Re [2023] EWCA Civ 1352 321
N (Contact: Minor Seeking Leave to Defend and Removal of Guardian),
    Re [2003] 1 FLR 652 369
N (In the Matter of: A Child) [2009] EWHC 1807 (Fam) 386
N (Leave to remove: Holiday), Re [2006] EWCA Civ 357 412
N (Leave to Withdraw: Care Proceedings), Re [2000)] 1 FLR 134 542
N (Recognition of Foreign Adoption), Re [2016] EWHC 3085 (Fam) 332
N v F (Financial Orders: Pre-Acquired Wealth) [2011] EWHC 586 (Fam) 199
N v K [2024] EWFC 245 (B) 286
N v N [2010] EWHC 717 (Fam) 199
N-B and others (Children: Residence: Expert Evidence), Re [2002]
    EWCA Civ 1052 394

NA v MA [2006] EWHC 2900 (Fam) 210
NB v MI (Capacity to Contract Marriage) [2021] EWHC 224 (Fam) 65
ND v GD [2021] EWFC 53 .... 202, 205
Negus v Bahouse [2008] 1 FCR 768 246
Newham London Borough Council v Attorney General [1993] 1 FLR 28 .... 516, 527
NHS Trust v X [2020] BMLR 7 393
NHS Trust, A v D [2000] 55 BMLR 19 .... 456, 458
NHS Trust, A v MB (A Child Represented by CAFCASS as Guardian ad
    Litem) [2006] EWHC 507 (Fam) 453, 455
NK v RK (By the Official Solicitor) X County Council AK [2023] EWCOP 37 436
Norfolk County Council v C [2007] EWHC 1556 (Fam) 502
Northampton AHA v Official Solicitor and the Governors of St Andrews
    Hospital (1994), Northampton Health Authority v The Official Solicitor and
    The Governors of St Andrews Hospital [1994] 1 FLR 162 (first reported as
    Re K, W and H (Minors) (Medical Treatment) [1993] 1 FLR 854 362
Northamptonshire County Council v S and Others [1993] Fam 136 541
Nottinghamshire County Council v Mother and others [2024] EWHC 666 (Fam) 514
NS v MI [2006] EWHC 1646 (Fam) 61, 137
NY (A Child: Reunite International and Others Intervening) sub nom Re NY
    (A Child), Re [2019] UKSC 49, [2019] 3 WLR 962, [2019] 2 FLR 124 .... 416, 439

O, Re; J, Re (Children) (Blood Tests: Constraint) [2000] Fam 139 .... 287, 288
O (A Minor: Care Proceedings: Education), Re [1992] 4 All ER 905 283
O and J (Paternity: Blood Tests), Re [2000] 1 FLR 418 295
O (Children: Privilege against self-incrimination), Re [2023] EWFC 14 504
O (Contact: Withdrawal of Application), Re [2004] 1 FLR 1258 386
O (Supervision Order), Re [2001] EWCA Civ 16; [2001] 1 FLR 923 547
O'Donoghue and Others v UK (2011) 23
O'Dwyer v O'Dwyer [2019] EWHC 1838 (Fam) 201
OG v AG (Financial Remedies: Conduct) [2020] EWFC 52 206
Opuz v Turkey [2009] Application no. 33401/02 142
Osman v United Kingdom [1999] 1 FLR 193 .... 489, 490
Owens v Owens [2018] UKSC 41; [2017]
    EWCA Civ 182 .... 2, 152, 156, 157, 160, 161, 163, 165, 166, 170
Oxley v Hiscock [2004] EWCA Civ 546 .... 90, 97

P (A Child: 2010] EWCA Civ 672 533
P (A Child: Abduction: Custody Rights), Re [2005] Fam 293 419
P (A Child: Adoption Order: Leave to Oppose Making of Adoption Order),
    Re [2007] EWCA Civ 616 318
P (A Child: Financial Provision), Re [2003] EWCA Civ 837 .... 221, 222, 576
P (A Child: Supervision: child in care); M v F and others, Re [2021]
    EWHC 1616 (Fam) 398
P (A Minor: Education), Re [1992] 1 FLR 316 392
P (A Minor: Residence Order: Child's Welfare), Re [2000] Fam 15
    (CA Civ Div); [1999] 3 All ER 734 .... 267, 277, 311, 396
P (A Minor), Re [1986] 1 FLR 272 450
P (A Minor), Re [1994] Lexis Citation 1679, 2633 .... 392, 393
P (An Infant: Adoption: Parental Consent), Re [1977] Fam 25 316
P (Children: Disclosure), Re [2022] EWCA Civ 495 504
P (Forced Marriage), Re [2010] EWHC 3467 (Fam) 138
P (Medical Treatment: Best Interests), Re [2004] 2 FLR 1117 .... 360, 374

P (Surrogacy: Residence), Re [2008] 1 FLR 177 274
P and L (Contact), Re [2011] EWHC 3431 (Fam); [2012] 1 FLR 1068 280
P v F [2023] EWHC 2730 (Fam) 390
P v Q [2023] EWHC 195 (Fam) 138
P v R (Forced Marriage: Annulment: Procedure) [2003] 1 FLR 661 61
P, C and S v United Kingdom (2002) 35 EHRR 31; (2002) 2 FLR 631 492
P, Re [2000] Fam 15 261
Padolecchia v Padolecchia (otherwise Leis) [1968] 2 WLR 173 50
Parlour v Parlour [2004] EWCA Civ 872 182
Pascoe v Turner [1979] 1 WLR 431 ....97, 98, 100
Paton v British Pregnancy Advisory Service Trustees [1979] QB 276 347
Paul v Constance [1977] 1 WLR 527 175
Paulik v Slovakia [2006] 46 EHHR 10 291
Payne v Payne [2001] EWCA Civ 166 415
Pazpena De Vire v Pazpena De Vire [2001] 1 FLR 460 34
Peter v Beblow (1993) 150 N.R. 1 (SCC); 1993 Can LII 126 (SCC);
    [1993] 1 S.C.R. 980 220
Pettitt v Pettitt [1968] 1 WLR 443 78
PF v CF [2016] EWHC 3117 (Fam) 132
PF v QF [2024] EWFC 10 (B) 72, 124
Pickard v Constable [2017] EWHC 2475 (Ch) 106
Poel v Poel [1970] 1 WLR 1469 414
Portsmouth NHS Trust v Wyatt (2004) EWHC 2247 (Fam) (2005)
    1 FLR 21; 84 BMLR 206 440
Potter v Potter [1975] 5 Fam Law 161 58
Practice Direction 12B–Child Arrangements Programme 382, 388, 432
Practice Direction 12D–Inherent Jurisdiction (Including Wardship)
    Proceedings [1, 2](a)–(c) 342, 438, 445, 446, 448, 450, 464
Practice Direction 12J– Family Proceedings Rules 2010 Child
    Arrangement & Contact Orders: Domestic Abuse, Violence and
    Harm 2008 ....381, 382, 390, 407, 409, 425, 426, 429, 431, 432, 459, 467, 473, 508
Practice Direction 12k: Children Act 1989: Exclusion Requirement 495, 509
Practice Direction 12Q Orders Under Section 91(14) of the Children Act 1989 431
Practice Direction 16A, Part 4, President's Direction (Representation of Children
    in Family Proceedings Pursuant to Family Proceedings Rules 1991
    Rule 9.5) [2004] 1 FLR 1188 ....371, 379
Practice Direction 27C, April 2023, of Family Proceedings Rules on the
    attendance of IDVA's and ISVA's at hearings in the Family Court 426
Practice Direction: Children Act 1989: Applications by Children (1993),
    r. 9.2A of the Family Proceedings Rules 1991 ....389–90, 431
Practice Direction: Custody and Access (1982) amended in 1992, 2004 and
    2015 PD 12B Child Arrangements Programme 387
Practice Direction (Public Law Proceedings: Guide to Case Management)
    April 2010 487
Practice Direction: Residence & Contact Orders: Domestic Violence and
    Harm (2009) 114
Practice Direction (Residence & Contact Orders: Domestic Violence (No 2) (2009) 410
Practice Direction, Split Hearings [2010] 2 FCR 271 515
Practice Direction (Ward of Court: Chancery Division) [1961] 1 WLR 580 435
Practice Guidance: Family Court – Duration of Ex Parte (Without Notice)
    Orders (18 January 2017) [5.114] 135
Public Guardian v RI & Ors [2022] EWCOP 22 229

Pugh v Pugh [1951] P 482..51
PW (Adoption), Re [2011] 1 FLR 96...327

Q v Q [2008] 1 FLR 935 97
Q (Implacable Contact Dispute), Re [2015] EWCA Civ 991................................404
Quincy Bell v MBA v The Tavistock and Portman NHS [2020]
    EWHC 3274 (Admin)..342

R v Adesanya (1974) *The Times*, July 16 and 17 520
R v Ali [2023] NI 415..472
R v Arthur (1981) 12 BMLR 1; [1981] *The Times*, 5 November.................452, 453
R v Besant [1879] NLR 11 Ch D 508..384
R v Birmingham Juvenile Court, ex parte G and others (Minors), sub nom
    R v Birmingham Juvenile Court, ex parte R (A Minor) [1990] 2 QB 573 542
R v Brooks (Tony Russel) [2023] EWCA Crim 554, [2023] 2 Cr App R (S) 40............120
R v Cannings [2004] EWCA Crim 1; [2004] 1 WLR 2607.................................501
R v Carmarthenshire County Council, ex parte White [2000] ELR 172..........282, 283
R v Carrigan [2021] EWCA Crim 1553..122
R v Central Independent Television plc [1994] Fam 192.....................................447
R v Challen [2019] Crim 916...120
R v Charles Bradlaugh and Annie Besant [1877] 2 QBD 569.............................384
R v Cheshire (Richard George) [2010] EWCA Crim 2148 118
R v Cordle (John William) [2016] EWCA Crim 1793...123
R v D [1984] AC 778 ....259, 262
R v de Mannerville [1804] 102 ER 1054...257
R v Dewhurst [2021] EWCA Crim 663..122
R v Dhaliwal [2006] All ER (D) 236 (CA) 120
R v E and F [2010] EWHC 4187 (Fam) 402
R v Ex parte Blood [1997] EWCA Civ 4003...271
R v Greenhill [1836] 4 Ad & El 624...257, 383
R v Halifax Justices ex parte Woolverton [1981] 2 FLR 369................................568
R v Halliday [1853] 17 JUR 56..257
R v Hopley [1860] 2 F & F 202 ....283, 343, 469, 470
R v Inhabitants of Darlington [1792] 4 TR 798; 100 ER 1308 4
R v Ireland and Burstow [1998] AC 147 121
R v Kent County Council, ex parte B [1996] Lexis Citation 1187 485
R v Kingswell [2022] EWCA Crim 814..122
R v Kirklees Metropolitan Borough Council Ex Parte C [1993] 2 FLR 187 363
R v Maw and another [1980] 1 CLR 841..406
R v P [2004] All ER (D) 191 123
R v R (Family Court: Procedural Fairness) Practice Note [2015] 1 WLR 2743 135
R v R [1992] 1 AC 599 116
R v R [2014] EWFC 48 135
R v Rausing (2012)..236
R v Registrar General, ex parte Smith [1991] 2 QB 393 336
R v Vinagre (1979) 69 Cr App R 104; C v Dixon [2009] EWHC 708 (QB) 118
R v Ward [1993] 2 All ER 577 501
R (A Child: IVF: Paternity of Child), Re [2003] EWCA Civ 182 ....269, 270
R (A Child: Possible Perpetrator), Re [2019] EWCA Civ 895.............................537
R (A Child: Wrongful retention: child's objections: discretionary return),
    Re [2023] EWHC 560 (Fam) 424
R (A Minor: Contact Biological Father), Re [1993] 2 FLR 762............................290

R (A Minor: Contempt), Re [1994] 2 FLR 185 449
R (A Minor: Wardship: Medical Treatment), Re [1992] 1 FLR 1014; [1991]
  4 All ER 177 .... 343, 353, 355, 356–8, 361, 362
R (Adoption: Contact), Re [2006] 1 FLR 373 330
R (IVF: Paternity of Child) (also Known as Re D) [2005] Fam 129 269
R (Mrs) v The Mother and another [2024] EWHC 263 (Fam) 461–2
R (No. 1) (Inter-Country Adoption), Re [1999] 1 FLR 104 520
R (No. 1), (Inter-Country Adoption), Re [1999] 1 FLR 1014, 1042 ....333, 348
R (on the application of A Child: Special Guardianship Order), Re [2007] Fam 41 324
R (on the application of Ahmadi) v Secretary of State for the Home
  Department [2002] EWHC 1897 (Admin) 463
R (on the application of Anton) v Secretary of State for the Home Department:
  Re Anton [2005] EWHC 2739 (Admin) 444
R (on the application of Baiai and others) v Secretary of State for the Home
  Department (2008) 2 FLR 1462 22
R (on the application of Burke) v GMC [2004] 3 FCR 579 459
R (on the application of EL) v Essex County Council [2017] EWHC 1041
  (Admin), [2017] Fam Law 818 312
R (on the application of FA(Sudan)) v Secretary of State for the Home
  Department [2021] EWCA Civ 59 144
R (on the application of Goodred) v Portsmouth City Council (Secretary of
  State for Education intervening) [2021] EWHC 3057 (Admin) 283
R (on the application of Green) v Secretary of State for the Department for
  Work and Pensions [2010] EWHC 1278 (Admin) 578
R (on the application of Howard League for Penal Reform) v Secretary of
  State for the Home Department and Department of Health [2002]
  EWHC 2497 (Admin), [2003] 1 FLR 484 344
R (on the application of JK) v Registrar General for England and Wales [2015]
  EWHC 990 (Admin) 268
R (on the application of Kehoe) v Secretary of State for Work and Pensions
  [2005] UKHL 48 .... 565, 577, 579, 580
R (on the application of McConnell and YY) v Registrar-General for England
  and Wales [2020] EWCA Civ 559 ....268, 280
R (on the application of Miller) (Appellant) v The Prime Minister (Respondent):
  Cherry and others (Respondents) v Advocate General for Scotland
  (Appellant) (Scotland) [2019] UKSC 41 11
R (on the application of Pinochet Ugarte) v Bow St Metropolitan Stipendiary
  Magistrate [2000] 1 AC 61, 119, 147 11
R (on the application of Plymouth City Council) v HM Coroner for the
  County of Devon and Secretary of State for Education and Skills [2005]
  EWHC 1014 (Admin); [2005] 2 FLR 1279 490
R (on the application of Quintavalle) v Human Fertilisation and Embryology
  Authority (Secretary of State for Health intervening) [2003] 2 AC 687 273
R (on the application of R) v Leeds Magistrates and others [2005] EWHC 1479
  (Admin) 282
R (on the application of Redmond) and Others v Health Service Commissioner
  [2005] EWCA Civ 1578 487
R (on the application of Rights of Women) v Lord Chancellor and Secretary of
  State for Justice [2016] EWCA Civ 91 382
R (on the application of Rose and another) v Secretary of State for Health Human
  Fertilisation and Embryology Authority, Court of Appeal – Administrative Court,
  and another [2002] EWHC 1593 (Admin) 273

R (on the application of SC, CB and 8 children) v Secretary of State for Work
    and Pensions and others [2021] UKSC 26.. 12
R (on the application of Steinfield and Keidan) v Secretary of State for
    International Development (in substitution for the Home Secretary and
    the Education) [2018] UKSC 32.. 16, 39
R (on the application of SWP) v Secretary of State for the Home Department
    [2022] EWHC 2067 144
R (on the application of TT) v Registrar General for England and Wales
    (AIRE Centre intervening) [2019] 3 WLR 1195, sub nom R (on the
    application of McConnell and YY) v Registrar-General for England and
    Wales [2020] EWCA Civ 559 272
R (on the application of W) v Essex County Council; R (on the application of F)
    v same; R (on the application of G) v same [2004] 1 FLR 1014 349
R (on the application of Williamson and Others) v Secretary of State for
    Education and Employment and Others [2005] 2 AC 426.............................344, 470
R, Re (1992) 373
Radmacher v Granatino [2010] UKSC 42 ....15, 208, 211–16, 218
Rampal v Rampal (No 2) [2001] 2 FCR 552 72
Ramsden v Dyson [1866] LR 1 HL 129 98
Ravel (A Bankrupt), Re [1998] 2 FLR 718 106
Rees v Hughes [1946] KB 517 235
Rees v United Kingdom (1987) 9 EHRR 56 281
Regina (Skelton and another) v West Sussex Senior Coroner [2021] 2 WLR 413 143
RH (a minor) (parental responsibility), Re [1998] 2 FLR 89... 286
Richards v Richards [1984] AC 174 389
Roberts, Re [1978] 1 WLR 653.. 71
Robson v Robson [2011] 1 FLR 751 200
Roddy (A Child: Identification: Restriction on Publication), Re [2003]
    EWHC 2927 (Fam)..374, 376
Ross v Collins [1964] 1 WLR 425... 4
Rossi v Rossi [2006] EWHC 1482 (Fam) 200
Rotherham Metropolitan Borough Council v G (A child) [2016] EWHC
    2660 (Fam)... 448
Rowe v Prance [1999] 2 FLR 787... 175
Rozanski v Poland [2006] 2 FLR 1163... 291
RW v Royal Borough of Windsor and Maidenhead [2023] EWFC 19; [2023]
    EWHC 1449 (Admin).. 390

S v AG (Financial Remedy: Lottery Prize) [2011] EWHC 2637 (Fam) 198
S v C (Abduction: Art. 13 Defence: Procedure) [2012] Fam Law 261; [2011]
    EWCA Civ 1385 422
S v F (Occupation Order) [2000] 1 FLR 255... 129
S v S (Non-Matrimonial Property Conduct) [2006] EWHC 2793 (Fam) 205
S v S (Otherwise C) [1956] P 1 58
S v S [1986] Fam 189 574
S v S [2007] EWHC 1975 (Fam) 207
R S (AP) v The Secretary of State for the Home Department [2011] CSOH 6................ 140
S (A Boy, born on [a date]) M v F and others, Re [2022] EWHC 214 (Fam) 140
S (A Child: Abduction: Article 13(b): Mental Health), Re [2023] EWCA Civ 208 423
S (A Child: Adoption), Re [2021] EWCA Civ 605... 314
S (A Child: Adoption: consent of child parent), Re [2017] EWHC 2729 (Fam) 301, 313
S (A Child: Contact and Residence Order), Re [2012] EWCA Civ 1031 474

S (A Child: Identification: Restriction on Publication), Re [2004] 1 AC 593 445
S (A Child: Transfer of Residence, Re [2010] Fam Law 1182 408
S (A Child), Re [2002] EWCA Civ 1795 414
S (A Child), Re [2010] EWCA Civ 465 460
S (A Child), Re [2021] EWCA Civ 605 326–7
S (A Minor: Blood Transfusion: Adoption Order Condition), Re [1994]
    2 FLR 416 308
S (A Minor: Consent to Medical Treatment), Re [1994] 1 FCR 604 .... 360, 363
S (A Minor: Independent Representation), Re [1993] Fam 263, 276G; [1993]
    2 FLR 437, 445 376
S (A Minor: Medical treatment), Re (1993) 1 FLR 376 368
S (A Minor) (Custody), Re [1991] 2 FLR 388 393
S (Adoption Order or Special Guardianship Order), Re [2007] EWCA Civ 54 323
S (Adult Patient: Sterilisation), Re [2001] Fam 15; [2000] 2 FLR 389; [2000]
    3 WLR 1288, [2000] 2 FCR 452 .... 438, 459
S (Children: Abduction: Asylum Appeal), Re [2002] 1 WLR 2548 459
S (Contact: Application by sibling), Re [1998] 2 FLR 897 403
S (In the Matter of: A Child) [2012] UKSC 10, on appeal from [2012] EWCA
    Civ 1385 sub nom S v C (Abduction: Art.13 Defence: Procedure) 422
S (Inherent Jurisdiction) Transgender Surgery Abroad [2023] EWHC 347 (Fam) 443
S (Minors: Care Order: Implementation of Care Plan), Re W (Minors) (Care Order:
    Adequacy of Care Plan), Re [2002] UKHL 10 497
S (Parental Alienation) Re [2020] EWCA Civ 568; [2020] EWHC 1940 (Fam) 408
S (Sexual Abuse Allegations: Local Authority Response), Re [2001] 2 FLR 776 488
S (Specific Issue Order: Religion: Circumcision), Re [2004] EWHC 1282 (Fam) 397
S (Split Hearing), Re [2014] 1 FLR 1421 515
S and A (Children: Care Orders: Threshold Criteria), Re [2001] 3 FCR 589 478
S-B (Children: Non-Accidental Injury), Re [2009] UKSC 17 527
S-B (Children: Perpetrator: non-accidental injury), sub nom S-B (2009) (children)
    (care proceedings: standard of proof), Re [2010] 1 All ER 705 535–7
S-B, Re 548
S-H (A Child) Placement Order, Re [2008] EWCA Civ 493 320
S-T (formerly J) v J [1998] Fam 103 71
SA (Vulnerable Adult with Capacity: Marriage), Re [2006] EWHC 2942; [2006]
    1 FLR 867 .... 27, 65, 438
Sadovska & Anor v Secretary of State for the Home Department (Scotland) [2017]
    UKSC 54 64
SB v RB [2008] EWHC 938 (Fam) 138
SC (A Minor), Re [1993] 1 FLR 431 372
Scott v Scott [1959] P 103 59
Scott v Sebright (1886) LR 12 PD 21 60
Seaton v Seaton [1986] 2 FLR 398 204
Secretary of State for Work and Pensions v M [2006] UKHL 11 561
Seddon v Oldham Metropolitan Borough Council [2015] EWHC 2609 (Fam) 330
SH v MM and RM (Prohibited Steps Order: Abduction) [2011] EWHC 3314 (Fam) 413
Sharland v Sharland [2015] UKSC 60 180
Sharp v Sharp [2017] EWCA 408 (Civ) 200
Sheffield and Horsham v United Kingdom [1970] 2 WLR 1306 281
Sheffield City Council v E and S [2004] EWHC 2808 (Fam) 65
Sheffield City Council v M and Others [2022] 2 FLR 812 138
Shelley v Westbrooke [1817] 37 ER 850, Jac 266 435
Singh v Entry Clearance Officer New Delhi [2004] EWCA Civ 1075 .... 267, 309, 333

Singh v Kaur [1978] 60
Singh v Singh [1971] P 226 .... 58, 60
SK (An Adult) (Forced Marriage: Appropriate Relief), Re (2004) EWHC
    (Fam) 3202 .... 136, 436, 437
Slough Children First applicant and Mother (1) F (2) SK (The Child) (3),
    sub nom Slough Children First v Mother, Father, SK (The Child) (2024)
    EWFC 31 518
SO (A Child Wardship Extension of protective Injunction) [2015] EWHC
    935 (Fam) 437, 443
South Glamorgan v W and B [1993] 1 FLR 574 364
Southwark London Borough Council v B [1998] 2 FLR 1095 526
Southwell v Blackburn [2015] EWCA Civ 1347 .... 99, 107
Special guardianship order K v Sheffield City Council [2011] EWCA Civ 635 324
Spencer v Camacho [1983] 4 FLR 662 132
Springette v Defoe [1992] 2 FLR 388 83
Stack v Dowden [2007] UKHL 17; [2007] 1 FLR 1858 .... 77, 80, 82, 83, 87–9, 91,
    93, 96, 97, 108
Stallion v Albert Stallion Holdings (Great Britain) Ltd [2010] EWCA Civ 1443 98
Stringer v Stringer [2006] EWCA Civ 1617 390
Stübing v Germany (Application No 43547/08) [2012] ECHR 656 .... 9, 25
Suggitt v Suggitt & Another [2012] EWCA Civ 1140; [2012] WTLR 1607;
    [2011] EWHC 903 (Ch); [2011] 2 FLR 875; 250
Sullivan v Sullivan [1818] 161 ER 728 66
Sutton v Mishcon de Reya and Gawor & Co [2004] EWHC 3166 (Ch) 221, 225
SY v SY (otherwise W) (No 2) [1963] P 37 57
Szechter v Szechter [1971] P 286 .... 59–61, 63

T v B [2010] EWHC 1444 (Fam) 280, 567
T v K and Others (Egyptian Fostering: UK Adoption) [2017] 2 FLR 943 309
T v T [2010] EWHC 2392 (Fam) 402
T (A Child: DNA tests: paternity), Re [2001] 2 FLR 1190 289
T (A Child: Non-Molestation Order), Re [2017] EWCA Civ 1889 132
T (A Child: Refusal of Adoption Order), Re [2020] EWCA Civ 797 326
T (A Child: Surrogacy: Residence Order) [2011] otherwise CW v NT and
    another, Re [2011] EWHC 33 (Fam) 275
T (A Child: Suspension of contact) (Section 91(14) CA 1989, Re [2015]
    EWCA Civ 719 390
T (A Minor: Child representation), Re [1993] 3 WLR 602 368
T (A Minor: Wardship: Medical Treatment), Re [1997] 1 All ER 906 455
T (A Minor), Re [1997] 1 WLR 242 459
T (Abduction: Child's Objections to Return), Re [2000] 2 FLR 192 421
T (Abuse: Standard of Proof), Re [2004] EWCA Civ 558 .... 501, 531
T (Adoption), Re [2012] EWCA Civ 191 329
T (Children) [2012] UKSC 36 548
T (Wardship: Review of Police Protection Decision) (No 2), Re [2008]
    EWHC 196 (Fam) 459
T (Wardship), Re [1993] 2 FLR 278 372
T and another (Appeal: Fair Hearings: Delegation of Judicial Functions,
    Re [2024] EWHC 2236 (Fam) 426
T and another (Children: Abduction: Recognition of Foreign Judgment),
    Re [2006] EWHC 1472 (Fam) 420
T and another (Children:Specific Issue Order), Re [2024] All ER 73 (Jul) 411

T, Re... 113
Tavli v Turkey [2007] 1 FLR 1136 ....291, 295
Tchenguizv Imerman [2010] EWCA Civ 908 ....180, 198
Thorner v Major [2009] 1 WLR 776..98, 101
TJ v RC [2023] EWFC 189 409
TL v Hammersmith and Fulham London BC, sub nom, Re T (a child:
    Residential Parenting Assessment) [2011] EWCA Civ 812; [2011] 3 FCR 343;
    [2012] 2 FLR 308... 524
TS (A Child) (Application to Revoke Adoption Order: Procedure in Non-Urgency
    Adoption Placement), sub nom ZH v HS and others (application to revoke
    adoption order [2019] EWHC 2190 (Fam) 329
Tyrer v United Kingdom [1978–79] (application No. 5856/72), [1978] ECHR;
    [1979–80] 2 EHRR 1 283

U (A Child); Re B (A Child) (Serious Injury: Standard of Proof), Re [2004]
    EWCA Civ 567 .... 3, 500
U (Abduction: Nigeria), Re [2010] EWHC 1179 (Fam)................................... 420
UD v DN [2022] EWCA 1947 (Civ) 577
University Hospital Lewisham NHS v Hamuth [2006] EWHC 1609 (Ch)...... 236

V (A Child) (Recognition of Foreign Adoption), Re [2017] EWHC 1733 (Fam)........... 332
V (A Minor), Re [1987] 2 FLR 89 316
Valier v Valier [1925] 133 LJ 830.. 63
Vaughan v Vaughan [1973] 1 WLR 1159.. 132
Venema v The Netherlands (2003) 1 FLR 552 492
Versteegh v Versteegh [2018] EWCA Civ 1050 217
Vince v Wyatt [2015] UKSC 14... 197

W v Middlesbrough Borough Council (Exclusion Order Evidence)
    [2000] 2 FLR 666... 495
W v W (nullity) [2001] Fam 111 23
W (A Child: Abduction: Jurisdiction: a Pakistan Case), Re [2003]
    EWHC 1820 (Fam).. 461
W (A Child: Care Proceedings), Re [2007] EWCA Civ 102 ....518, 525
W (A Child: Care proceedings), Re [2023] All ER (D) 53................................. 326
W (A Child: Public law proceedings: child's separate representation),
    Re [2016] EWCA Civ 1051.. 371
W (A Child), Re [2010] EWCA Civ 1449 328
W (A Minor: Medical Treatment: Court's Jurisdiction),
    Re [1993] Fam 64 ....360, 376
W (A Minor: Medical treatment), Re [1993] Fam 64; (1992) 9 BMLR 22;
    [1992] 4 All ER 627..343, 346, 361, 364–5
W (A Minor: Wardship: Jurisdiction), Re [1985] AC 791................................. 443
W (A Minor: Wardship: Medical Treatment), Re (1992)
    4 All ER 627...355, 356, 358, 373, 377
W (Abduction: Acquiescence: Children's Objections), Re [2010]
    EWHC 332 (Fam)... 348
W (Adoption: Homosexual Adopter), Re [1997] 3 All ER 620 ....279, 305
W (An Infant), Re [1971] AC 682.. 316
W (Children: Abuse: Oral Evidence), Re [2010] EWCA Civ 57 371
W (Children: Child abduction: intolerable situation), Re [2018] EWCA Civ 664.......... 422
W (Children: Leave to remove), Re [2008] 2 FCR 420..................................... 415

W (Children: Threshold Criteria: Parental Concessions), Re [2001] 1 FCR 139 475
W (Contact: Application by Grandparent), Re [1997] 1 FLR 793 .... 409, 410
W (Minors: Sexual Abuse Standard of Proof), Re [1994] 1 FLR 419 523
W (Minors), Re [1992] 2 FLR 332, [1992] Lexis Citation 1854 .... 395, 404
W (Representation of Child), Re [2017] 2 FLR 199; [2016] EWCA Civ 1051 .... 372, 373
W (Residence: Leave to Appeal), Re [2010] EWCA Civ 1280 410
W and M (Children), Re (2009) EWHC 3172 (Fam) 277
W and W v H (Child Abduction: Surrogacy) (No 2) [2002] 2 FLR 252, FD 276
W, Re [2017] 1 WLR 889 335
WA v AT (Child Abduction; Best Interest of the Children) [2024] IEHC 142 423
Waggott v Waggott [2018] EWCA Civ 727 201
Walkden v Walkden [2009] 3 FCR 25 187
Ward v Byham [1956] 1 WLR 496 557
Ward v Secretary of State for Social Services [1990] 1 FLR 119 70
Warwickshire County Council v A Mother and A Father and X and Z [2023]
    EWHC 399 (Fam) 408, 515
Watson (deceased), Re [1999] 1 FLR 878 242
Watson v Lucas [1980] 1 WLR 1493 5
WB v VM [2024] EWHC 302 (Fam) return order 462
Webster and Another v Norfolk County Council [2009] EWCA Civ 59 .... 328, 499
Webster v Webster [2008] 1 FLR 1240 247
Wellesley v Duke of Beaufort (1824–34) 4 ER 1078; (1828) 2 Bli NS 124 435
Wellesley v Wellesley [1824–34] ER 612 (HL) 435
Wellesley v Wellesley [2019] EWHC 11 (Ch) 250
Westwater v Secretary of State for Justice [2010] EWHC 2403 (Admin) 405
Whiston v Whiston [1995] Fam 198 .... 71, 72
White v White [2001] 1 All ER 1; [2001] 1 AC 596; [2000] 2 FLR 981
    [2000] UKHL 54 .... 179, 189, 190, 192, 195, 205
Williams v London Borough of Hackney [2018] UKSC 37 543
Williamson Regina (Williamson and others) v Secretary of State for
    Education and Employment [2005] AC 246 283
Williamson v Williamson [1986] 2 FLR 146 392
Windsor and Maidenhead. See RW v Royal Borough of Windsor and Maidenhead—
Winscom, Re [1865] 71 ER 573 257
Wookey v Wookey; Re S (a child) (injunction) [1991] Fam 121 118
WX v HX (Treatment of Matrimonial and Non-Matrimonial Property)
    [2021] EWFC 14 199
Wyatt (A Child) (Medical Treatment: Parents' Consent), Portsmouth NHS
    Trust v Wyatt and Wyatt, Southampton NHS Trust Intervening,
    Re [2004] EWHC 2247 (Fam) 454
Wyatt v Vince [2015] UKSC 14 .... 193, 225
Wye Valley NHS Trust v B [2015] EWCOP 60 228

X v Latvia (Application no. 27853/09) [2013] ECtHR 432
X v United Kingdom (1981) 4 EHRR 188; (1979) No. 7992/77,
    ECommHR (Plenary), 12 July 1978 489
X v X (Y and Z intervening) [2002] 1 FLR 508 210
X v Y [2024] EWFC 42 (B) 289
X and Y (Revocation of adoption orders [2024] EWHC 1059 (Fam) 327
X (A Child by His Litigation Friend), Re [2011] 2 FLR 794 441
X (A Child: No. 2): An NHS Trust v X, Re [2021] EWHC 65 (Fam) 355, 361
X (A Child), Re [2020] EWHC 3003 (Fam) 364

X (A Woman Formerly Known as Mary Bell) and another v O'Brien and
   others [2003] EWHC 1101 (QB).. 446
X (Children: No 3), Re [2015] EWHC 3651 (Fam) 450, 539
X (Children) and Y (children) (emergency protection orders), Re [2015]
   EWHC 2265 (Fam).. 493
X (Minors) v Bedfordshire County Council [1995] 2 AC 633; [1995] 3 All ER 353 490
X (Parental Responsibility Agreement: Children in Care), Re [2000] Fam 156 286
X and Y (Parental Order: Retrospective Authorisation of Payments),
   Re [2011] EWHC 3147 (Fam) 276
X Council v B (Emergency Protection Orders) (2005) 1 FLR 341.........................491, 492
X County Council v A [1985] 1 All ER 53 446
X, Re [2014] EWHC 4813 (Fam) 397
X, Y and Z v UK [1997] 2 FLR 892; (1997) 24 EHRR 143 ....256, 280, 281
X,Y and Z (Wardship: Disclosure of Material), sub nom X (minors),
   Re [1992] 1 FLR 84.. 447
X: Emergency Protection Orders, Re [2006] EWHC 510 (Fam) 491

Y (A Minor: Wardship: Assistance on Transition to Adulthood) Practice Note,
   Re [2018] 1 WLR 66... 449
Y (Children: No 3), Re [2016] EWHC 503 (Fam) 449
Y (Children: Occupation Order), Re [2000] 2 FCR 470.................................... 127
Y (Risk of Young Person Travelling to Join IS) (No 2), Re [2015] EWHC 2099 449
Y and another (Children) Care Proceedings: Split Hearing), Re [2003] EWCA
   Civ 669.. 514
Y and K (Split Hearing: Evidence), Re [2003] EWCA Civ 669 503
Yates v Yates [2012] EWCA Civ 532 182
Yemshaw v London Borough of Hounslow [2011] UKSC 3 115

Z v Kent [2018] 10 WLUK... 320
Z v United Kingdom [2001] 34 EHRR 97 489
Z v V and Others [2024] EWHC 365 (Fam)... 461
Z v Z (Contact in Prison) [2021] EWFC 47 405
Z v Z (No 2) [2011] EWHC 2878 (Fam) 215
Z (A Minor: Freedom of Information), Re [1995] 4 All ER 961...........................438, 446
Z, Re [1995] 4 All ER 961. [1996] 2 FCR 164 374
ZH v HS and others (Application to revoke adoption order) [2019]. See TS
   (A Child) (Application to Revoke Adoption Order: Procedure in
   Non-Urgency Adoption Placement)—

USA
Depp v Heard [2021] (108 Va. Cir. 382, Aug. 17, 2021 111
In the matter of Anonymous, A Minor (2001) 808 So.2d 1024
   (Ala. Civ.App.2001 ....353, 354
People (The) & C. Respondent v Joel Steinberg, A/K/A Joel Barnet Steinberg,
   Appellant [1992] 79 N.Y.2d 673, 595 N.E.2d 845, 584 N.Y.S.2d 770 473

Table of statutes

European Union

Brussels II Revised Regulation
(EC) No 2201/2003.............. 10, 331
Art. 4 .... 345, 378
Art. 14 461
Brussels Rules IIa 10
Brussels Rules IIb 420
Council Directive 93/13/EEC (1993)
On Unfair Terms in Consumer
Contracts
European Convention on
Human Rights and
Fundamental Freedoms
(ECHR) 1950 .... 3, 9, 55, 76, 142,
291, 296, 302, 344, 374, 456, 457,
463, 480, 493
Art.2 .... 142, 143, 345, 382, 456,
480, 489
Art.3 .... 142, 345, 382, 456, 463,
480, 489
Art.5 .... 142, 345
Art.6 ....9, 135, 142, 344, 345,
382, 390, 489, 492, 505, 577
Art. 6(1) 291
Art.8 ....9, 24, 27, 29, 37, 39, 71,
76, 105, 142, 237, 256, 257, 265,
267, 272, 281, 291, 295, 302, 314,
324, 329, 331, 335, 339, 341, 345,
374, 375, 382, 444, 445, 489, 492,
505, 562
Art. 8(1) 271
Art. 9 ....345, 359
Art. 9(2) 283
Art. 10 .... 345, 374, 445

Art. 12 ...... 9, 22–4, 26, 27, 29, 37, 142
Art. 13 489
Art. 14 ....9, 18, 39, 142, 345, 562
Protocol 12 9
Art. 1 18

International

Convention Relating to the Status of
Refugees 1951.................................9
Convention on the Prevention and
Punishment of the Crime of
Genocide 1948 9
Declaration of the Rights of the Child
1924 (extended 1959—
Principle 9.......................................479
Dublin Convention 1990 463
Hague Convention............ 331, 332, 412
Hague Convention on Parental
Responsibility and the Protection of
Children 1996 9
Art. 16(3) 283
Art. 22 283
Hague Convention on the Civil
Aspects of International Child
Abduction 1980 .... 9, 276, 371,
416, 417, 419–21, 423–5, 428, 439,
461
Arts. 1–4 416
Art. 1 416
Art. 3 419
Art. 3(a) 418
Art. 12 .... 417, 419, 421
Art. 13 .... 421, 422
Art. 13(b) 343, 345, 371, 422–4, 462

Art. 13(1)(b) 422, 423, 425, 432
Hague Convention on the Protection
    of Children and Co-operation in
    respect of Intercountry Adoption
    1973..332
International Covenant on Civil and
    Political Rights (ICCPR) 1966.......8
Art.23 8
Istanbul Convention (Council of
    Europe) On Preventing and
    Combating Violence against
    Women and Domestic Violence
    2012............................... 9, 143, 148
Art. 1 143
Art. 2 143
Maintenance Regulation 10
Refugee Convention 1951
Art. 1A(2) 144
United Nations Convention on the
    Rights of the Child (UNCRC)
    1989.......... 283, 337, 344, 345, 378,
    389, 392, 417, 421, 479, 556
Art. 2(2) 283
Art. 3 344
Art. 3(2) 479
Art. 6(1), (2).................................479
Arts. 7–9 337
Art. 9 403
Art. 11 417
Art. 12 345
Art. 12(1) 344
Art. 12(2) 344
Art. 16(1) 344
Art. 27 556
Art. 27(4) 556
Universal Declaration of Human
    Rights 1948....................................9
Washington Declaration on
    International Family Relocation
    2010...418

South Africa
Constitution—
    s. 9(1), (3).....................................256
United Kingdom
Abortion Act 1967—
    s. 1(1)(a) 347
Access to Health Records Act
    1990...352
Administration of Estates Act
    1925...238
    s. 46 238

s. 46(1) 240
s. 46(1)(i)..238
s. 46(2A) 238
s. 55(1)(x)..238
Administration of Justice Act 1970
    s. 1(2)..435
Adoption Act (AA) 1926 .... 301, 303
Adoption Act (AA) 1958 327
    s. 5 316
Adoption Act (AA) 1976 .... 267, 303,
    329
    s. 1(5)...310
    s. 6 311
    s. 7 308
    s. 12(1)..304
Adoption and Children Act (ACA)
    2002........... 279, 286, 294, 295, 302,
    304, 306, 309, 310, 312, 314, 317,
    318, 320, 322, 329, 336, 338, 392
    Pt. 3..306
    s. 1(1), (2)..318
    s. 1(4)....................310, 318, 322, 335
    s. 1(4)(d)..309
    s. 1(4)(f) 318
    s. 1(5).....................304, 308–10, 12
    s. 1(6)...322
    s. 3 307
    s. 4(1)..307
    s. 5 .... 266, 307
    s. 16(2)..317
    s. 16(2)(b)...316
    s. 19 313
    s. 18(1)..319
    s. 19(1)..313
    s. 21 .... 313, 314, 319
    s. 21(2)(a)–(c) 319
    s. 24(1), (2)(a), (3)...........................320
    s. 29(7)..304
    s. 39 .... 267, 306
    s. 42(5), (6)......................................329
    s. 44(3), (4)......................................329
    s. 45 .... 308, 312
    s. 45(2)..308
    s. 46 321
    s. 46(1) 294, 304
    s. 46(2)(a) 327
    s. 47 327
    s. 47(1)..321
    s. 47(2)(c) 318
    s. 47(4)..321
    s. 47(4)(b)(i) 313
    s. 47(4)(ii)...321

s. 47(5) 318, 322
s. 47(7) 326
s. 50 .... 294, 305, 321
s. 51 .... 294, 321, 330
s. 51(2) 306
s. 52(1) 329
s. 52(1)(a) 314
s. 52(1)(b) 314, 317
s. 83 331
s. 84 334
s. 109 307
s. 111 314
s. 111(2)(a), (b), (c) 285
s. 112 306
s. 115(1) 324
s. 115(6) 322
s. 120 .... 399, 477, 516
s. 144(4) 305, 306
Adoption (Intercountry Aspects) Act
   (AIAA) 1999 .... 331, 332, 334
s. 11 333
s. 12 333
s. 14 333
Aggravated Assaults Act (AAA)
   1853 116
Anti-Social Behaviour, Crime and
   Policing Act 2014—
s. 121 .... 61, 143
Asylum and Immigration
   (Treatment of Claimants, etc)
   Act 2004—
s. 19(3)(a), (c) 22
s. 19(3)(b) 22, 23

Bastardy Act 1575 .... 303, 557
Bastardy Laws (Amendment) Act
   1871 557
Better Regulating of the Future
   Marriages of the Royal Family
   Act 1722 30
Borders, Citizenship and Immigration
   Act (BCIA) 2009—
s. 55 331
British Nationality Act (BNA) 1981—
s 1(5) 332

CA 1975 .... 285, 329
CA 1981, s 41 284
Care Act 2014 232
Child Abduction Act (CAA)
   1984 414
s. 1 263

Child Abduction and Custody Act
   (CACA) 1985 ...... 414, 416, 417, 425
Sch. 1 439
Child Care Act 1980 543
Child Maintenance and Other Payments
   Act (CMOP) 2008 .... 564–6, 568
Pt. 1 566
Pt. 2 566
s. 2(1) 565
s. 2(2)(a) 566
s. 6 565
s. 42 561
Child Support Act 1991 ..... 284, 558–66,
   568, 571, 573, 575, 577, 579
s. 1(1) 560, 561, 566
s. 1(2) 561
s. 2 554
s. 3(1) 561
s. 3(2) 562
s. 3(3) 562
s. 4(1) 563
s. 6(10) 563
s. 8(1), (3) 572
ss. 11, 26, 27 566
s. 55 561
Child Support (Enforcement)
   Act 2023 571
Child Support, Pensions and
   Social Security Act (CSPSSA)
   2000 .... 564, 569
ss. 15, 17, 39(a) 564
s. 83 567
s. 83(2) 287
Childcare Act 2006—
s. 49 483
s. 50 483
Children Act 1989 .... 5, 13, 236, 260,
   271, 283, 284, 291, 297, 309, 322,
   325, 329, 367, 389, 390, 400, 401,
   411, 431, 433, 435, 440, 442, 443,
   459, 462–4, 467, 470, 471, 481, 487,
   494–6, 502, 507, 509, 511, 516, 517,
   525, 526, 536, 541, 543, 544, 547,
   550, 551, 553, 554, 559, 575
Pt. III 543, 544
Pt. IV 391, 497, 502
Pt. V 502
Pt. VI 543
Pt. VII 543
Pt. VIII 489
s. 1 .... 263, 26, 295, 302, 315, 317,
   333, 345, 426, 530

s. 1(1)... 278, 389
s. 1(2)...481
s. 1(2A) 425, 426
s. 1(2B) 426
s. 1(3)................................ 310, 391, 399
s. 1(3)(a) 344, 345, 392, 481
s. 1(3)(b)......................................393
s. 1(3)(c)......................................394
s. 1(3)(d)............................... 278, 394
s. 1(3)(e)............................... 399, 531
s. 1(3)(f) 400
s. 1(4)................................... 391, 541
s. 1(5).......... 400, 514, 540–2, 544, 547
s. 1(6), (7).....................................426
s. 2.......................................257, 285
s. 2(4)...................................257, 285
s. 2(5)...................................282, 285
s. 3...281
s. 3(5)...284
s. 4.......................................285, 286
s. 4(a) 285
s. 4(1)...................................314, 385
s. 4(1)(a)–(c) 286
s. 4(2A) 291, 292, 298
s. 4ZA(5)......................................291
s. 4A(1) 294
s. 4A(3) 291
s. 6(7)(b)......................................372
s. 8 .... 236, 282, 284, 293, 362, 367,
      372, 373, 381, 385, 387, 388, 391,
      395, 400, 401, 410, 412, 413, 435,
      436, 442, 443, 459, 484, 514
s. 8(1), (2)....................................402
s. 8(3)...329
s. 9(1)...443
s. 9(3)(c)......................................389
s. 10...292
s. 10(1)...329
s. 10(1)(a)(ii)................................372
s. 10(2)(b), (8) 389
s. 10(4)...347
s. 10(4)(a) 271, 282, 389
s. 10(5)...294
s. 10(5)(c) 410
s. 10(5A), (5B)................................389
s. 10(8)................................ 367, 372, 389
s. 11 402
s. 11(7)...403
s. 11(7)(c) 282, 402
ss. 11I, 11J....................................410
ss. 12(2), 13(1)(a) 402
ss. 14A–14F....................................295

s. 14A(3)(a) 304
ss. 14A(6)(b), 14D 324
s. 15 555
s. 17 .... 302, 334, 471, 483, 513, 522,
      523, 548, 549
s. 17(1)(b)....................................480
s. 17(10) 522
s. 20 ....480, 523, 543, 552
s. 22(5)(c) 309, 310, 399
s. 31 .... 277, 282, 399, 400, 449, 475,
      477, 481, 488, 497, 500, 511–16,
      518, 519, 524, 525
s. 31(1)(b)....................................543
s. 31(2) 497, 525, 527, 530, 531, 548
s. 31(2)(a) 513, 526, 528
s. 31(2)(b)...................... 516, 526, 528
s. 31(2)(b)(i) 513, 525, 534
s. 31(2)(b)(ii) 514, 517
s. 31(9) 487
s. 31(9)(b)....................................481
s. 31(10) 516, 519
s. 32(1)(a) 481
s. 33 411
s. 33(3)...411
s. 33(6)................................ 257, 266
s. 33(6)(a) 396
s. 34 493
s. 34(6)(a) 336, 396
s. 37 .... 381, 399, 443, 484, 485
s. 37(1) 462
s. 37(1)(2).....................................484
s. 37(2)(a) 497
s. 37(2)(b).....................................480
s. 38 488
s. 38(1) 497
s. 38(2) 497
s. 38(6) 277, 364, 523, 524, 552
ss. 38A, 38B 494
s. 43 ....496, 528
s. 43(1) 490, 496
s. 43(4)(b), (8), (9) 496
s. 44 .... 467, 483, 488, 496, 528
s. 44(1) 490
s. 44(1)(a)(i), (ii) 490
s. 44(1)(b)....................................490
s. 44(6) 492, 493
s. 44(6)(a), (b)...............................492
s. 44(7) 496
s. 44(10), (11) 491
s. 44(13) 493
s. 44A................................. 490, 494
s. 44B...494

s. 46 .... 445, 476, 488, 490, 495, 496, 528

s. 46(1) 495

s. 47 .... 467, 471, 481–3, 487, 488, 490, 513, 525

s. 47(7) 490

s. 76 552

s. 91(14) 267, 286, 292, 311, 324, 385, 390, 431

s. 91(14)A 390

s. 91(14)(4)......................................385

s. 94 391

s. 98 ....468, 502, 503, 509

s. 98(2)..503

s. 100 .... 411, 477, 516

s. 100(2) 460

s. 100(2)(c) 442

s. 100(3) 442, 443, 455

s. 100(4)(a) 460

s. 100(4)(b) 358, 370, 433, 442, 460

s. 105(1) 399

Sch. 1.................................. 555, 567

Sch. 1, para. 1 574

Sch. 1, para. 1(2)(c) 575, 576

Sch. 1, para. 2 574

Sch. 1, para. 4 .... 575, 576

Sch. 3, paras. 2, 3 545

Children Act 2004............................470

s. 11 480

s. 58(1)..470

Children and Adoption Act (CAA) 2006................................. 302, 410

Children and Families Act (CFA) 2014........266, 302, 304, 309, 388, 549, 551

s. 3 .... 309, 310, 312

ss. 5, 6 307

s. 9(2b)...336

s. 107[2A](1) 344

s. 139(6) 401

Sch. 2..401

Children and Young Persons Act 1969—

s. 1(2)..526

Children (Contact) and Adoption Act 2005...334

Civil Evidence Act 1968....................491

s. 14 503

Civil Partnership Act 2004 (CPA) 2004.........5, 6, 9, 15, 18, 38, 41, 42, 70, 125, 172, 174, 178, 216, 223, 279, 294, 306, 338, 561, 574, 579

Pt. 4A 188

s. 1(1)..40

s. 2...181, 183

s. 2(1)–(3)...40

s. 3 ....38, 56

s. 4 38

ss.5–27 41

s. 7 184

s. 13 182

s. 17(2) 41

s. 20 196

s. 21 188

s. 21(2)(a) 198

s. 21(2)(b), (c)................................202

s. 21(2)(d)..203

s. 21(2)(e)...204

s. 21(2)(f)..205

s. 21(2)(g)...205

s. 21(2)(h)...207

s. 23 196

s. 31(2) 41

s. 37 49

s. 38 181

s. 44–48 168

s. 49–53 49

s. 49 56

s. 50(1)..69

s. 50(1)(a)–(e) 69

s. 50(6)..69

s. 51 183

s. 51(1)(a), (b), (2)(a), (3)–(5) 70

s. 52 183

ss. 56, 57 168

s. 60 209

s. 65 102

s. 66 174

ss. 68, 69 209

s. 71 241

s. 72 574

s. 72(1)..71

s. 73 125

s. 74 .... 103, 180, 223

s. 74(5) 102

s. 246(1) 294

Sch. 1, pt. 1..40

Sch. 1, pt. 1, para. 2(2) 40

Sch. 4, pt. 2, para. 15(1), (5) 241

Sch. 5........... 71, 181–4, 188, 196, 198, 202, 203, 205, 207, 209

Sch. 5, pt. 9......................................176

Sch. 6..178

Civil Partnerships, Marriage and Deaths (Registration etc) Act 2019...........39

Congenital Disabilities (Civil Liability)
    Act 1976 347
Constitutional Reform Act 2005 439
Coroners Act 1988—
    s. 13 143
Coroners and Justice Act 2009—
    s. 5(2)..143
    s. 10(1)(a) 143
Counter-Terrorism and Security Act
    2015 (CTSA) 2015—
    s. 26 538
Crime and Security Act
    (CSA) 2010—
    s. 22(1)..141
    ss. 24–33 .... 124, 141
Criminal Justice Act 1988—
    s. 36 122
Criminal Justice Act 1991...................559
Criminal Justice Act 2003—
    s. 58 120
    s. 119 503
Criminal Law Amendment Act (1885)—
    s. 7 468
Custody of Infants Act, (CIA)
    (1839) 257, 384

Divorce, Dissolution and Separation Act
    (DDSA) 2020 .... 7, 49, 152, 153,
    156–8, 160–3, 166–70
    s. 1(1)..161
    s. 2 167
    s. 2(1)..168
    s. 3 161
Divorce Reform Act 155
Domestic Abuse Act (DAA)
    2021....... 7, 114, 115, 143, 144, 150,
    233, 425, 467, 511
    Pt. 3.............................. 124, 139, 149
    s. 1 .... 109, 110, 131, 140
    s. 1(3)..110
    s. 17 472
    s. 1(4)..111
    ss. 22–56 109
    ss. 22–49 141
    ss. 22–48 124
    s. 36(1)..141
    ss. 65–67 382
    s. 67 390
    s. 70 .... 109, 122
    ss. 72–74 143
    Sch. 3...143
    Practice Direction 12J 110, 131

Domestic Proceedings and
    Magistrates' Courts Act
    (DPMCA) 1978 .... 177, 178, 555
    ss. 1–3 177
    s. 4(2)..177
    ss. 6, 7, 25 177
    s. 25(1)...177
Domestic Violence and Matrimonial
    Proceedings Act (DVMPA)
    1976.....................2, 117, 124, 133
    s. 1 2
    s. 1(c) 124
    s. 2 110
Domestic Violence, Crime and Victims
    Act (DVCVA) 2004 .... 151, 553
    s. 5 .... 534, 549
    s. 9 472
Domestic Violence, Crime and
    Victims (Amendment) Act
    (DVCVAA) 2012 549
Domicile and Matrimonial Proceedings
    Act 1973 10
    s. 5(2)..10

Education Act 1996—
    s. 437 282
    s. 444(1) 282
Education and Adoption Act
    2016...312
Education (No 2) Act 1986—
    s. 47 283
Equality Act 2010.............................307
    s. 198 176
    s. 199 83
    s. 200 41
    s. 202 174

Family Law Act 1986 (FLA) 1986......461
    Pt. III..567
    s. 55 51
    s. 55A............................... 269, 287
    s. 58(1)...291
Family Law Act (FLA) 1996 ....79, 103,
    110, 124, 125, 131, 135, 138, 163,
    164
    Pt. II 164
    Pt. IV 75, 82, 103, 105, 124, 139
    Pt. IVA 138
    s. 30 .... 103, 124
    s. 31 104
    ss. 33–49 123
    ss. 33–41 124

s. 33 .... 103, 105
s. 33(1) 124, 125
s. 33(1)(a)(i) 126
s. 33(3) 124, 125
s. 33(3)(e)–(g) 126
s. 33(6) 103, 127, 128
s. 33(6)(a)–(d) 126
s. 33(7) 103, 126, 127
s. 33(10) 128
s. 34(1)(a) 104
s. 35 128
s. 35(3), (4) 128
s. 35(6) 104, 129
s. 35(8), (10) 129
s. 36 128
s. 36(3), (4) 128
s. 36(6) 130
s. 37 130
s. 40(1)(a) 126
s. 42 .... 110, 131
s. 42(2)(a) 132
s. 42(5) 133
s. 42A.....................110, 131, 133, 134
ss. 43–49 .... 124, 131
s. 45(1) 134
s. 45(3) 135
s. 46(3A) 134
s. 47(2) 130
s. 52 494
s. 55 52
s. 62(3) 125, 132
s. 62(3)(d) 133
s. 62(3)(f), (g) 125
s. 62(7) 125
s. 63(2) 139
s. 63A...442
s. 63H.4 138
s. 63H.4(2) 139
Sch. 6, paras. 1, 3 494
Family Law Protocol March 2002
    (Fourth Iteration 2015)...............387
Family Law Reform Act (FLRA)
    1969................................ 287, 357
Pt. III..288
s. 8 ....343, 349, 357, 366
s. 8(1)..349
s. 9 166
s. 20 287
s. 20(1) 288, 296
s. 20(6) 349
s. 21(3) 287, 288
s. 21(4) 287

Family Law Reform Act (FLRA)
    1987...272
s. 1 ....70, 71
Family Law (Scotland) Act 2006..........43
Female Genital Mutilation Act
    (FGMA) 2003 .... 124, 140
s. 4 143
Forced Marriage (Civil Protection)
    Act (FMPA) 2007.......... 61, 62, 123,
    136, 138, 151, 442
Freedom of Information Act (FOIA)
    2000...136

Gender Recognition Act (GRA)
    2004........5, 9, 21, 24, 58, 67, 69–71,
    272, 281
ss.1–4 272
s.1 24
s. 9(1)...272
s. 12 272
Guardianship of Infants Act
    (GOI) 1925 385
s. 1 259
ss. 5(1), 6...385
Guardianship of Infants Act
    (GOI) 1973 385
s. 1(1)...385

Housing Act (HA)1996
s. 177(1) 115
Human Fertilisation and Embryology
    Act (HEFA) 1990.......... 270, 272–4,
    299, 560
s. 2(1)...273
s. 3(1)(b)..273
s. 27 .... 267, 269
s. 28 ....70, 267, 269, 272
s. 28(2) 269, 272
s. 28(3) 269, 270
s. 28(6)(a) 269
s. 30 562
s. 30(7) 276
s. 31–31ZE.......................................273
s. 33, 34 274
s. 49(3) 272
s. 54(6) 274
Sch. 2, para. 1(1) 273
Sch. 3..271
Human Fertilisation and Embryology
    Act (HFEA) 2008 ...... 267, 271, 273,
    274, 300
s. 33 562

s. 33(1) 269
s. 35 562
s. 35(1) 269
s. 37, 38 271
s. 38(2)–(4) 269
s. 41 286
s. 54(8) 276
Human Fertilisation and Embryology
    (Deceased Fathers) Act 2003 271
s. 5A 271
Human Rights Act 1998 (HRA)
    1998 .... 9, 288, 344, 375, 379, 480,
    547
ss.3(1), 4 9
s.7 ....496, 577
s.7(1) 9

Immigration Act (IA) 2014 ....29, 41
s. 19 331
Immigration and Asylum Act 1999—
s. 115 144
Inheritance Act 1975. See Inheritance
    (Provision for Family and
    Dependants) Act 1975—
Inheritance (Family Provision)
    Act 1938 240
Inheritance (Provision for Family and
    Dependants) Act 1975 .... 45, 197,
    237, 240, 241, 245–50, 254
s. 1(1) 241
s. 1(1)(e) 241, 243, 245
s. 1(1A), (1B) 241
s. 1(2) 245, 248
s. 1(3) 243
s. 3 249
s. 3(1), (2)–(5) 247
s. 3(2) 247, 248
s. 3(2)(a), (b) 245
s. 3(3) 244, 245
s. 3(4) 244, 245
s. 4 241
Insolvency Act 1986—
s. 335A 105
s. 336 105

Land Charges Act 1972—
s. 2(7) 104
Land Registration Act 2002—
s. 31(10) 104
Law of Property Act 1925 ....79, 100
s. 52 ....80, 221
s. 52(1) 79

s. 53 80
s. 53(1)(b) 79
s. 53(1)(c) 95
s. 53(2) 82
Law of Property (Miscellaneous
    Provisions) Act 1989—
s. 2 80
Law Reform (Miscellaneous
    Provisions) Act 1949
s. 9 435
Law Reform (Miscellaneous
    Provisions) Act 1970 .... 180, 223
s. 1 223
s. 2 .... 102, 223
s. 3 102
s. 3(2) 223
Law Reform (Succession) Act 1995—
s. 2(3) 241
s. 3(1) 237
Legal Aid Sentencing and
    Punishment of Offenders Act
    (LASPO) 2012 .... 136, 382, 387
Limitation Act 1939 260
Limitation Act 1954 260
Limitation Act 1963 260
Local Government Act 1988—
s. 28 263

Marriage Acts 21
Marriage Act 1949 ....21, 26, 30, 35–7,
    52, 53, 256
Parts II–VI 29
ss. 1–3 23
s. 1 25
s. 31(1) 29
ss. 4, 14 31
s. 49 52
Sch. 1 ....23, 25
Marriage Act (Lord Hardwicke's
    Act) 1753 ....20, 32
Marriage and Civil Partnership
    Act (Minimum Age) 2022 .....24, 40,
    51, 56, 284
Marriage (Same Sex Couples)
    Act 2013 .... 5, 16, 49, 56
Married Women's Property
    Act 1870 173
Married Women's Property
    Act 1882 ....75, 173, 174, 225
s. 17 174
Married Women's Property Act
    (MWPA) 1964 174

s. 1 174
Matrimonial and Family Proceedings
    Act (MFPA) 1984......................573
Pt. III 178
Pt. IVB 382
s. 1 160
ss. 31Q-31Z..................................382
Matrimonial Causes Act (MCA)
    1857......................................154
Matrimonial Causes Act (MCA)
    1878—
s. 4(1), (2)..117
Matrimonial Causes Act (MCA)
    1923......................................155
Matrimonial Causes Act (MCA)
    1937......................................155
Matrimonial Causes Act (MCA)
    1973..........23, 24, 35, 69, 153, 155,
    160–2, 165, 166, 172, 174, 178, 186,
    195, 207, 248, 554, 555, 573, 574,
    579
Pt. II 71
s. 1(2)......................................66, 155
s. 1(2)(a) 156
s. 1(2)(b)................................. 156–8
s. 1(2)(c) 158
s. 1(2)(d)......................................159
s. 1(2)(e)......................................160
s. 2(3)......................................158
s. 2(5)............................... 159, 160
s. 2(6)......................................159
s. 5 160
s. 10 162
s. 10A...169
s. 10A(6) 169
ss. 11–16 49
ss. 11, 12, 13 23
s. 11(a)(i)–(iv)..............................51
s. 11(a)(iii) 52
s. 11(b)......................................56
s. 11(c) 23, 56
s. 11(d) 26, 56
s. 12 ....55, 57
s. 12(a) 57
s. 12(b)......................................58
s. 12(c) 27, 59, 66
s. 12(d) 27, 66
s. 12(e) 66
s. 12(f), (g)......................................67
s. 12(h)......................................67, 68
s. 13 68
s. 13(1) 68

s. 13(2) 68
s. 13(2A) 69
s. 13(3), (4)......................................68
ss. 23–25 ....573, 579
s. 23 .... 181, 183, 574
s. 24 184
s. 24(b), (c), (d)......................................188
s. 25 ......188–90, 192–5, 208, 212, 213,
    215, 216, 247, 573
s. 25(1) 196
s. 25(2) 194, 204
s. 25(2)(a) 198
s. 25(2)(b), (c)......................................202
s. 25(2)(d)......................................203
s. 25(2)(e)......................................204
s. 25(2)(f)......................................205
s. 25(2)(g)............................. 190, 205
s. 25(2)(h)......................................207
s. 25(3) 573
s. 25A...196
s. 27 .... 176, 177
s. 28 182
ss. 31, 32(1) 183
ss. 34–36 210
s. 34 .... 181, 209
s. 35 209
s. 52 574
Matrimonial Causes Act (MCA) 1984—
s. 25 562
Matrimonial Homes Act 1984 389
Matrimonial Proceedings and
    Property Act (MPPA) 1970 176
s. 37 .... 102, 223
Mental Capacity Act (MCA)
    2005.......................... 228, 233, 436
s. 1 228
ss. 2(1), 3......................................228
s. 4 230
s. 4(4)......................................228
s. 9(4)(b)......................................230
s. 24 229
Mental Health Act 1983 ...... 66, 353, 436
s. 2 363
s. 3 363
s. 1(2)......................................68
s. 136 476

National Assistance Act 1948—
s. 42 557
Nationality, Immigration and Asylum
    Act (NIAA) 2002—
Pt. 5A 331

Obscene Publications Act 1857 384
Offences Against the Person Act
 (OAPA) 1829—
 s. 1 116
Offences Against the Person Act
 (OAPA) 1861.............................121
 s. 21 122
 s. 43 116
 s. 57 27
Online Safety Act 2023 123
 s. 12 511

Pensions Act 1995 188
Poor Law Amendment Act 1834 557
Powers of Attorney Act 2023 230
Presumption of Death Act
 2013.................................... 234, 235
Preventing and Combating Violence
 against Women and Domestic
 Violence (Ratification of
 Convention) Act 2017................143
Protection from Harassment Act
 (PFHA) 1997.............. 110, 123, 133
 s. 2, 2A, 4, 4A 123
 s. 5 .... 123, 147
Protection of Freedoms Act 2012—
 s. 111 123
 s. 114 ....31, 41
Protocol for Judicial Case
 Management in Public Law
 Children Act Cases, June 2003 ...487

Rent Act...4

Senior Courts act 1981—
 s. 41(2)...441
 s. 61 435
 s. 90 439
 s. 116 236
 Sch. 1..435

Serious Crime Act (SCA) 2015—
 ss. 70–72 140
 s. 75 473
 s. 75(4)(a) 122
 s. 75A...122
 s. 76 ....120, 121
 s. 76(1)(b)......................................121
Sexual Offences Act (SOA) 1956—
 s. 6 352
Sexual Offences Act (SOA) 1967.......263
Sexual Offences Act (SOA) 2003—
 ss. 5–19, 47–51..............................474
 s. 53a..474
 s. 64 25
Supreme Court Act 1981. See Senior
 Courts act 1981—
Surrogacy Arrangements Act 1985—
 s. 2 276

Terrorism Act 2000—
 s. 41 540
Theft Act 1968.....................................233
Trusts of Land and Appointment of
 Trustees Act (TOLATA) 1996—
 s. 12 82
 s. 14 .... 82, 104, 105
 s. 15 104

Victims and Prisoners Act
 2024.................................... 145, 293
 s. 18(3)................................... 292, 293

Welfare Reform and Pensions
 Act 1999 188
Welfare Reform and Work Act
 (2016) 12
Wills Act 1837—
 s. 18 ....71, 237
 s. 18A..237
 s. 18B..237

Table of statutory instruments

Adoption (Northern Ireland) Order
    1987 (SI 1987/2203 (NI 22) 322
  art. 17(1) 322
  art. 18(1) 322
Adoption Agencies Regulations
    2005 (SI 2005/389)
  reg. 9 308
Adoptions with a Foreign Element
    Regulations 2005 (revised in
    February 2011) (SI 2005/392).....331

Child Support (Maintenance
    Calculations and Special Cases)
    Regulations 2000 (SI 2001/155)—
  reg. 8 563
Child Support Maintenance
    Calculation Regulations 2012 (SI
    2012/2677) 563, 568, 571, 572
Child Support (Variations) Regulations
    2000 (SI 2001/156) 571
Children and Families Act 2014
    (Commencement No. 2) Order
    2014 (SI 2014/889)—
  art. 4(f) 401
Civil Partnership (Opposite-sex
    Couples) Regulations 2019 (SI
    20191458) 5, 16
Civil Partnership (Opposite-sex Couples)
    Regulations 201

Equality Act (Sexual Orientation) 2007
    (SI 2007/1263) 308

Family Procedure (Amendment No. 2)
    Rules 2023 (SI 2023/1324) 387
Family Proceedings (Amendment) Rules
    1992 (SI 1992/456—
  r. 9 367
  r. 9.2A 368, 496
  r. 9.2A(4) 363
  r. 9.2A(6) 363
Family Proceedings (Amendment
    No 4) Rules 2005
    (SI 2005/1976) 503
Family Proceedings Rules (FPR) 1991
    (SI 1991/1247—
  r. 5.1 438
  r. 9.2A 367, 390, 496
  r. 9.2A(6) 375
  r. 9.5 ....371, 386, 428, 431
  r. 12.73 503
Family Procedure Rules (FPR) 2010
    (SI 2010/2955) 131, 381, 429
  Pt. 16 371
  r. 1 515
  r. 1.1 10
  r. 1.2 10
  r. 4.6 135
  r. 9.42 353
  r. 14.14 503
  r. 16.4 373
  r. 16.6 373
  r. 16.6(5) 373
  r. 18.10(3) 135
  r. 18.11 135

r. 10.73(c) 431
PD. 12G 503
PD. 14E 503
PD. 16A 371

Human Fertilisation and Embryology
    Authority (Disclosure of Donor
    Information) Regulations 2004
    (SI 2005/1511 273

Immigration (Procedure for
    Marriage) Regulations 2005
    (SI 2005/15) 22

Marriage Act 1949 (Remedial) Order
    2007 (SI 2007/438) 26

Marriages (Approved Premises)
    Regulations 1995
    (SI 1995/510) 30
Marriages and Civil Partnerships
    (Approved Premises)
    (Amendment) Regulations 2021
    (SI 2021/775) 30, 41

Non-Contentious Probate Rules 1987
    (SI 1987/2024)—
    r. 22 236

Sentencing Code—
    s. 360 133
Special Guardianship Regulations
    2005 (SI 2005/1109 324

1

Introduction to family law

What is family law?

Family law is the most relevant of all areas of law because it is the only one in which students of family law, academics and practitioners, have been personally involved from the moment of birth. It includes every aspect of legal intervention into the private lives of those who are related by blood or affinity, or who have, or have had, emotional ties with each other or whose interconnectedness is otherwise authorised by for example adoption or reproductive technology. The majority of those who fall within its sphere of influence tend to occupy, or will have been part of at some time, the same family home.

We might ask the question as did Lord Justice Peter Jackson in The Nicholas Wall Memorial Lecture, delivered in 2023, 'Is Family Law Law?' He said:

> Family law as practised in this country is a relatively recent creation. From the Middle Ages onwards, the dominant idea was that marriage was a sacrament. The gateway in and out was supervised by the church, applying ecclesiastical law. After marriage, the law strongly supported the husband's right to control his wife, her property and their children. As time went on, the courts of equity presided over a system of marriage settlements to protect the wife's property from the husband, but this was only of concern to the wealthy. Likewise, the Crown could intervene through wardship to prevent the property of infants, lunatics and idiots from falling into the wrong hands. So, matters rested until the middle of the 19th century.

Indeed, there is no better starting point for anyone interested in family law than Jackson LJ's lecture.

Over the last 150 years, family law has evolved a discrete core of its own which at times reflects views of the powerful regarding what constitutes a family, and why, and how, families should be regulated and also drives change which at times may conflict with public opinion. Women's reformers of the nineteenth century were called harridans and wreckers of the hearth and in 1984 when Baroness Hale joined

DOI: 10.4324/9781003435020-1

the Law Commission to help reform on domestic violence and divorce one media critic referred to her as 'one of the legal commissars subverting family values'. During this time, however, those who participate in these familial relationships have been granted legal rights and, in return, the adult participants have had legal responsibilities towards their children imposed upon them. Both the State's view and society's view of what constitutes the family has changed over time and these two views and other contested views within these two camps have repeatedly come into conflict. Developments in family law have been the result of contested struggle of power waging against the patriarchy in every area and most recently over same-sex marriage, divorce reform, property rights on divorce and whether cohabitants should be given greater legal rights and also concerning children's right to determine aspects of their life. Over the years there has been increasing State intervention in child protection.

Of course, there have been major reforms in some of these areas such as divorce reform and same-sex marriage whilst progress on other issues such as the rights of cohabitants has been almost non-existent.

The developments in family law owe much to Parliament and to public pressure regarding statutory reforms but also to the tenacity of family law practitioners pressing for a purposive approach to statutory interpretation where there is moot point to be argued when representing their clients. Judges apply the law, some judges interpret the law, and, in that interpretation, some also develop the law. In that process of interpretation Lord Denning in *Davis v Johnson* [1979] AC 264, a case which turned on whether the Domestic Violence and Matrimonial Proceedings Act 1976 with its purpose to protect an abused party from violence in the family home empowered the courts to exclude the aggressor from a joint tenancy, said:

> *[276] Some may say – and indeed have said – that judges should not pay any attention to what is said in Parliament. They should grope about in the dark for the meaning of an Act without switching on the light. I do not accede to this view.*

The House of Lords by a majority of 4 to 1 held that s 1 of the Act gave a county court the jurisdiction to exclude both a spouse and a cohabitee (in this case) irrespective of any property vested in the person excluded whether he be the sole or joint owner or tenant (see Law Commission Domestic Violence and Occupation of the Family Home 1989: 2.12).

As Lord Reid said at the House of Lords Constitution Committee (6 April 2022) 'we do not go looking for cases; they come to us'. This is also true of family law solicitors who are approached by those with difficult and troubling issues seeking a remedy. In most cases they simply apply the law to the situation. In some cases, a law to remedy the situation may not immediately be clear to exist, and they tell the client nothing can be done. Others may say: 'let's see if there is a remedy' and with good advocacy and a creative judge and purposive interpretation the boundaries of the law are shifted. In some cases where there is no room for manoeuvre the judges hearing the case respond and say, 'it is a matter for Parliament.' The recent change in the divorce laws can largely be attributed to the result of the failed attempt by Mrs Owens to be granted a divorce (*Owens v Owen* [2018] UKSC 41). Years of attempted reform of the divorce laws had come to nothing, but the plight of a woman forced to remain in a failed marriage for five years demonstrated to the court and to the Government that the law was overdue for reform. The Supreme Court was powerless to act, but no doubt their comments brought pressure on the Government to move swiftly on the issue.

Twenty-first-century family lawyers require not only a knowledge of, and an expertise in, the core area of family law; they also need a knowledge of financial matters, property law (both real and personal), the law of contract and tort, criminal law, the law of wills and trusts, conflict of laws, medical law, immigration law, public law in the context of housing and education, the law of evidence, and international and human rights law. They must be familiar with the social and biological sciences, including for example psychology, and reproductive technology and all areas of expert evidence if they are to put their case well and effectively probe and contest opposing argument. Inadequate preparation and research of expert argument can lead to abuse of process and injustice. Dame Elizabeth Butler-Sloss, when President of the Family Division, in *Re U (A Child); Re B (A Child) (Serious Injury: Standard of Proof)* [2004] EWCA Civ 567 called for caution and careful analysis of findings in Sudden Infant Death Syndrome (SIDS) cases:

> *The cause of an injury or an episode that could not be explained scientifically remained equivocal; recurrence was not in itself probative; particular caution was necessary in any case where the medical experts disagreed; the court always had to be on guard against the over-dogmatic expert; and the judge in care proceedings should never forget that today's medical certainty might be discarded by the next generation of experts.*

(See Ward 2020)

Rights and obligations

During the latter half of the twentieth century, a growing and more general respect for individual rights to self-determination and privacy gained momentum and the freedom for adults to contract with each other, free from State control, about the terms of their relationship, and to realise the legal recognition of those contracts. Family law appears to vacillate between the enforcement of privately negotiated contracts and the imposition of legal rights and obligations laid down by common law or statute.

Significantly, legal rights for women and children were developing and the historic suborned position of women and children of the family under the common law progressively eroded as equality and human rights norms developed within domestic law and the European Convention of Human Rights (ECHR) superseded. Heterosexual marriage as the only marital relationship was challenged embracing a union between other genders. Together with women's rights the voice and autonomy of the child/adolescent in all matters emerged. However, in matters relating to children's care and upbringing State intervention has increased protection for the most vulnerable whilst at the same time there is a growing concern that removing children from the birth family into adoption may not be the best outcome.

Evolving definitions of the family

The term 'family' in family law is not a term of art; it has no independent generalised legal meaning; it has changed over time, to its position today. Historical family laws reflected and enshrined patriarchal power and subornation of all other members. In *R v Inhabitants of Darlington* [1792] 4 TR 798; 100 ER 1308 Lord Kenyon CJ stated: 'In common parlance the family consists of those who live under the same roof with the pater familias: those who form . . . his fireside.' Servants were included in this definition and often lived with a family for the whole of their lives.

In *Blackwell v Bull* (1836) 1 Keen 176; 48 ER 274 Lord Langdale said:

> It is evident that the word family is capable of so many applications that if any one construction were attributed to it in wills, the intention of the testators would be more frequently defeated than carried into effect. Under different circumstances it means a man's household, consisting of himself, his wife, children and servants; it may mean his wife and children, or his wife; in the absence of wife and children, it may mean his brother and sisters or his next of kin, or it may mean the genealogical stock from which he may have sprung.

By the twentieth century, legal intervention into family life had become more incursive and definitions of the family narrowed. Rent Act legislation provides illustrations of this trend especially relating to the classification of a person as a member of a deceased tenant's family which would give him or her the right to continue to live in their family home, are infused with perceptions of the legitimacy of certain kinds of familial relationships.

In *Langdon v Horton* [1951] 1 KB 666 CA the Court of Appeal refused Rent Act protection to two elderly ladies who had lived for 30 years with their cousin in a house, which she had held a statutory tenancy prior to her death. The court held that all three had lived together for the sake of personal convenience and not because they were part of the same family. In *Gammans v Ekins* [1950] 2 KB 328 CA the Court of Appeal rejected the claim of a male cohabitant to remain in the family home on the death of his partner. Asquith LJ took the view that either the relationship was platonic, or it was not. If the relationship was platonic, Asquith LJ believed that to recognise the cohabitants as members of the same family would also require the court to accord the same status to 'two old cronies of the same sex innocently sharing a flat'. If the relationship were not platonic, Asquith LJ considered it: 'anomalous that a person could acquire a Rent Act protected status by living or having lived in sin, even if the relationship had not been a mere casual encounter but protracted in time and conclusive in character'.

In *Ross v Collins* [1964] 1 WLR 425 a woman claimed the right to succeed to a statutory tenancy on the death of her partner. She had lived with the deceased for a substantial period of time. She was 40 years younger than him and had looked after him dutifully, regarding him as a sort of elder relative, partly father, partly brother. Russell LJ ruled that this platonic, familial relationship was not within the definition of family because there was no kinship between the couple. He maintained that:

> two strangers cannot ever establish artificially a familial nexus by acting as brothers or as sisters, even if they refer to each other as such and consider their relationship to be tantamount to that. Nor can an adult man and woman who establish a platonic relationship

establish a familial nexus by acting as a devoted brother and sister or father and daughter would act, even if they address each other as such and regard their association as tantamount to such. Nor would they indeed be recognised as familial links by the ordinary man.

By 1980, the courts had begun to recognise that those living in stable heterosexual cohabiting relationships could be classified as members of each other's families in the context of landlord and tenant disputes.

In *Watson v Lucas* [1980] 1 WLR 1493 it was held that a married man, who had left his wife to live with another woman in a stable and long-term relationship, was a member of her family.

However, definition of family life and adult unions had historically eschewed and excluded same-sex unions. By 2000 in *Fitzpatrick v Sterling Housing Association* [2001] 1 AC 27, HL it was accepted that those in same-sex relationships could be members of each other's families. Lord Slynn viewed the essential hallmarks of a familial relationship as a degree of mutual interdependence, the sharing of lives, the caring and love for each other, and the commitment and support for each other. In *Ghaidan v Godin-Mendoza* [2004] UKHL 30; [2004] 2 FCR 481 the House of Lords held that the term *as husband and wife*, in Rent Act legislation, could be read to mean *as if they were husband and wife*. It, therefore, included a same-sex partner who had lived with the deceased in a spouse-like manner.

In accordance with the Gender Recognition Act 2004 (GRA 2004) transgendered persons, who have obtained a gender recognition certificate, may marry a member of the opposite sex to that of their newly acquired gender. Prior to the Act, they were restricted to marrying members of the opposite sex to their previous biological gender. The Civil Partnership Act 2004 (CPA 2004) has also given a quasi-spousal, and familial, status to same-sex couples who register their partnerships (see Chapter 2), the Marriage (Same Sex Couples) Act 2013 extends marriage to same-sex couples, and the Civil Partnership (Opposite-sex Couples) Regulations 2019 extends civil partnerships agreements to opposite sex couples.

As Jo Delahunty KC in her Gresham College lecture on 31 January 2019 'The 30th Anniversary of the Children Act 1989: Is It Still Fit for Purpose?' noted: 'The concept of the nuclear "family" that was the norm in 1989 is now a diverse reality. We have surrogacy, same sex marriage, civil partnership, and sexuality is no longer binary.'

Excluded relationships

There remain two categories of relationships, which although functionally familial, have only been granted limited legal rights. The first category consists of heterosexual and same-sex cohabitants. Their relationships are often identical to those of married couples and civil partners but have simply not been formalised. The Government asked the Law Commission to undertake a review of the law relating to cohabitants. Its recommendations were published in 2007 (Law Comm Cohabitation 2007), but no action has been taken. In 2008, the Labour Government announced that it would wait until research was completed on the cost and effectiveness of the recently implemented Scottish legislation. In 2011, Jonathan Djanogly, the Justice Minister explained that:

> *The findings of the research into the Scottish legislation do not provide us with a sufficient basis for a change in the law. Furthermore, the family justice system is in a transitional period, with major reforms already on the horizon. We do not therefore intend to take forward the Law Commission's recommendations for reform of cohabitation law in this parliamentary term.*
>
> (Djanogly 2011)

Professor Elizabeth Cooke, the Law Commissioner in charge of the cohabitation project at the time, responded and expressed the hope that there would be reform in the early days of the next Parliament. There is still no progress on recognition of the status of a cohabitant although Emily Thornberry MP (Shadow Attorney General in 2024) at the Labour Party Conference in 2023 stated that the Labour party is committed to the principle of widening recognition of cohabitants rights (Thornberry 2023).

The second category of familial relationships has been largely ignored by the legislators, and there are no plans to consider bringing it within the fold of the legal family in the foreseeable future. It consists of those who live together in the same household as members of a family but who have never engaged in sexual relationships with each other. This is either because they are closely related to each other, and they do not wish to have an illegal incestuous relationship, or because they are very close friends who have personally assumed responsibility for each other, but a sexual relationship is not a desired aspect of their friendship. These relationships also perform a familial function; many of the parties are elderly and would be unable to remain in their own homes were it not for the relationship.

The second excluded relationship – since an intimate relationship or, at least, a potential for it, is often the triggering factor for the legal recognition of adult relationships as familial – leaves adult sibling, and parent and adult child relationships without legal protection.

The case of *Burden v United Kingdom* (2006) 21 BHRC 640 in which two elderly sisters were denied the possibility of the inheritance tax relief, which is given to married and civil partners, is an example of such a relationship. The majority in *Burden* remarked that:

> *the relationship between siblings is qualitatively of a different nature to that between married couples and homosexual civil partners under the United Kingdom's CPA 2004. The very essence of the connection between siblings is consanguinity, whereas one of the defining characteristics of a marriage or CPA 2004 union is that it is forbidden to close family members. . . . The fact that the applicants have chosen to live together all their adult lives, as do many married and CPA 2004 couples, does not alter this essential difference between the two types of relationship.*

Challenges to family law

Divorce

Given that almost one in two marriages end in divorce, it was surprising that no legislation had been proposed to reform the divorce laws for so long, laws which had changed remarkably little since the 1970s. This was in spite of repeated calls for reform by practitioners, the judiciary and academics. It was probably the plight of

Mrs Owens who sought a divorce from her husband but found that she was trapped in a failed relationship for five years because he defended the petition which finally triggered Parliament to act.

The Divorce, Dissolution and Separation Act 2020 has simplified the divorce process allowing divorce or dissolution of a civil partnership if the applicant states that the marriage has irretrievably broken down. They no longer need proof: the statement is sufficient. Some have said this makes divorce too easy, but there is no evidence that forcing couples to stay together will prevent the breakdown of their marriage.

Financial matters

Financial and property disputes characterise much of the disputes relating to adult relationships. Equal division of a couple's assets continues to compete with judicial discretion as a fair solution to the problem of financial awards after the legal end of a relationship.

In the absence of legislation relating to home sharing, the family home, which is the cornerstone of family life, continues to tax the creative ingenuity of family lawyers and the judiciary in establishing rights by way of informal trusts and proprietary estoppel.

The law on financial provision on divorce is still a minefield. Couples have no certainty as to how a case will be decided, and litigation is often expensive and slow. Reform is long overdue, and practitioners await the recommendations of the Law Commission consultation to examine 50-year-old laws on finances after divorce and the ending of a civil partnership. There continues to be uncertainty as to whether a pre-nuptial agreement will be binding, and issues such as ownership of premarital assets are still unclear.

Where cohabitation breaks down there is still no legislation governing the distribution of assets. There is no right at all to maintenance. A claimant must rely on the complex rules of property law in order to establish rights in the family home. These are complicated and usually require the assistance of a lawyer and may result in a claimant losing all rights even after a long relationship and where there are children.

Domestic abuse

Intimate partner relationships we now understand are or become abusive with alarming prevalence. The Domestic Abuse Act 2021 has extended understanding of the dynamics of abuse and extends the definition of abuse to include coercive and controlling conduct and also includes a new offence of strangulation and suffocation. Parties protected have also been extended to include those who are 'personally connected' are or have been married, civil partners or are have been in an intimate relationship.

Children

The increasing emphasis in family law today is centred on the needs, rights and welfare of children from their conception to adulthood. Parenthood is concerned with obligations towards children rather than rights over them. Parenthood has evolved to include new forms of biological and social parent/child relationships. Medically assisted reproduction presents new challenges as does multi-parentage.

A new approach is required to transgender parenting concerning transgender identity and birth registration of children of the transgender parent and the binding of the terms mother and father with biological birth which survives in so far as registration is concerned notwithstanding change in gender identity.

Child protection

This often necessitates the removal of a child from the birth or caring family. In the endeavour to formalise as soon as possible a new family for the child a time target has been set for the completion of child protection proceedings. This has in some cases resulted in a too hasty adoption of the child into a new family. Adoption is being contested by some as an abrogation of the rights of the child to a family life with its natural parents and coupled with the pleas for more local authority funding to support families at the early stage to avert such draconian measures.

The international family

The family no longer remains in one village, city, county or country. It is a mobile institution; partners marry and form unions across international boundaries. They experience problems when the relationship breaks down and one partner wishes to return to his or her country of origin with the child of the union. The courts are faced with the impossible task of determining in which country a child should live and, thereby, effectively depriving the child of a relationship with one of his, or her, parents. Families also move from their country of origin because of war, genocide, persecution, famine, terrorism, environmental disasters and poverty. UK society has become multicultural, and family law is faced with disputes in which family members have different cultural, ethnic and religious expectations of family life and child rearing which lead to conflict not only between the State and the family but also between parents of different faiths and backgrounds. In addition, some migrants to the UK and also those who have settled here may have a different concept of family and their rights as parents and as adults one to another which may come into conflict with family law and equality norms of the UK. The Human Rights (HR) Committee stated with respect to the ICCPR in its General Comment 19 in 1990 on the Family, said:

> The Committee notes that the concept of the family may differ in some respects from State to State, and even from region to region within a State, and that it is therefore not possible to give the concept a standard definition. However, the Committee emphasizes that, when a group of persons is regarded as a family under the legislation and practice of a State, *it must be given the protection referred to in article 23*.
>
> (UN Human Rights Committee 2003;
> see also Banda and Eekelaar 2017, emphasis it is in original)

We live in a vibrant multi-cultural society with a rich mix of faiths and religions which brings with it many challenges. The proposed changes to the marriage laws should allow more certainty as to which ceremonies can be regarded as valid marriages. Although polygamy is not recognised in England and Wales the law has had to adapt to allow some rights to wives from a polygamous marriage.

Human rights

The Human Rights Act 1998 (HRA 1998) has had a significant impact on the development of family law although Baroness Hale has asserted that human rights instruments have not been used as much as she would like.

Family law must comply with the ECHR. Section 3(1), HRA 1998 provides that: 'so far as is possible to do so, primary legislation and subordinate legislation must be read and given effect in a way which is compatible with the Convention Rights'.

If this is not possible, HRA 1998, s 4 allows the High Court, the Court of Appeal, the Supreme Court and the Judicial Committee of the Privy Council to make a declaration of incompatibility. If remedial action is not taken by the Government after such a declaration, the case has to be dealt with by the European Court of Human Rights (ECtHR). An individual who believes that his or her human rights have been breached may take action against a public authority which acts in a way which is incompatible with any of the Convention Rights (see HRA 1998, s 7(1)).

The most important Articles of the ECHR for family lawyers are Article 6, the right to a fair trial; Article 8, the right to respect for private and family life; Article 12, the right to marry; and Article 14, the right to enjoy the Convention rights without discrimination. Protocol 12 of the ECHR provides for a self-standing right to freedom from discrimination, but the UK Government has not yet ratified the Protocol. Article 8 is subject to the very significant proviso that:

> there shall be no interference by a public authority with the exercise of this right except such as is in accordance with the law and is necessary in a democratic society in the interests of national security, public safety or the economic well being of the country, for the prevention of disorder or crime, for the protection of morals, or for the protection of the rights and freedoms of others.

The proviso is an attempt to balance the rights of the individual and the rights of the larger community, but it also limits severely the impact of Art 8 (see *Stübing v Germany (Application No 43547/08)* [2012] ECHR 656; *Burden v United Kingdom* [2006] 21 BHRC 640). The challenges and fears of challenges under the ECHR are now a constant theme throughout family case law. They have brought about dramatic changes in legislation to ensure conformity with the ECHR. The enactment of the GRA 2004 and the CPA 2004 were both products of challenges, and a fear of further challenges, under the ECHR.

International conventions

Family lawyers must also engage, where relevant, with the 1980 Hague Convention on the Civil Aspects of International Child Abduction and the 1996 Hague Convention on Parental Responsibility and the Protection of Children, as well as other European regulations. Family law issues also engage international conventions including amongst others The Universal Declaration of Human Rights 1948, the Istanbul Convention 2011 (The Council of Europe Convention on preventing and combating violence against women and domestic violence) and in some cases the Convention Relating to the Status of Refugees 1951, and Convention on the Prevention and Punishment of the Crime of Genocide. This list is by no means exhaustive, and the relevance of human rights instruments is of increasing relevance to developing advocacy in some complex family law cases.

Brussels II regulation, which contained the rules around divorce and children and the Maintenance Regulation, from 1 January 2021 no longer applies to England and Wales following the UK's exit from the EU. Domestic private international law applies and Brussels IIa rules as to jurisdiction are replicated by new provisions inserted into s 5(2) of the Domicile and Matrimonial Proceedings Act 1973. The UK courts will only allow a case to be initiated in the UK courts if they view the parties as being domiciled in this country. The issue will be based on factors such as nationality, residence, domicile and also where the main assets of the couple are kept.

Challenges to the operation of family justice

Challenges to the operation of family law have also come from changes to the family justice system and its operation including the rise of the digital court and remote hearings, the demise of legal aid funding and the increasing number of self-represented litigants.

The Covid pandemic from March 2020–19 July 2021 hastened the expansion of digital court and remote hearings. The President of the Family Division on 27 March 2020 said:

> Can I stress, however, that we must not lose sight of our primary purpose as a Family Justice system, which is to enable courts to deal with cases justly, having regard to the welfare issues involved [FPR 2010, r 1.1 'the overriding objective'], part of which is to ensure that parties are 'on an equal footing' [FPR 2010, r 1.2]. In pushing forward to achieve Remote Hearings, this must not be at the expense of a fair and just process.
>
> (see The Remote Access Family Court)

Judging judges and justice

Decisions of family law that are binding are made by Court of Appeal and Supreme Court judges, but the thousands of day-to-day cases are dealt with by Family Panel lay magistrates or district judges (magistrates' court) or by a district or Circuit judge.

District judges deal with the majority of family cases including private cases and public law cases concerning children and cases concerning financial remedies following divorce, as well as other types of family cases.

High Court judges sitting in the family court and in the Family Division of the High Court deal with the most complex cases relating to children and families. High Court judges sitting in the Family Division also deal with appeals from certain decisions of Circuit judges sitting in the family court. The supreme importance of judgments made in the High Court and the Supreme Court cannot be overstated for some of these very decisions determine what the law is, and some develop the law. Whilst the function of any judge is to be objective, nevertheless their interpretive nuances of statute as applied in particular cases may be influenced by character, background and personal views however much they and we might like to think that the judicial process of divining the law is immune and hermetically sealed from interpretation and individual discretion. Who sits in these courts and the make-up of these courts then is of supreme significance.

For example, United States Supreme Court Justice Ruth Bader Ginsburg's dying wish in 2020 was not to have President Trump choose her replacement. 'My most fervent wish is that I will not be replaced until a new president is installed.' She had made a stupendous difference during all her legal life to equality, to human rights and to family life and family law, and she did not want those advances undermined. Unfortunately, her wish could not be granted her and she died several weeks before the presidential election in October 2020 allowing Trump through an accelerated process of nomination to instate Amy Coney Barrett, the conservative favourite with 48–52 votes. As Supreme Court judges have a lifetime tenure (Clarence Thomas, currently the longest serving justice, has served as a Supreme Court judge for nearly 33 years) the long game of legal development in one way or another can be secured. Public concerns at the time were that the nine-member composition of the court could be skewed in favour of Republicans (with their illiberal views of what family life is and what relationships are permissible) could be engineered well into the future (see Ginsburg 2018).

Baroness Hale, the former president of the UK's Supreme Court, and her judgments have made a progressive mark in every area of the law including family law, family life and relationships. Baroness Hale spoke out over the prorogation of Parliament when 11 justices on the Supreme Court panel unanimously declared PM Boris Johnson's prorogation of Parliament unlawful. (*R (on the application of Miller) (Appellant) v The Prime Minister (Respondent) Cherry and others (Respondents) v Advocate General for Scotland (Appellant) (Scotland)* [2019] UKSC 41). Baroness Hale said: 'Our job was to stand up for the rights of parliament' (Hale 2021).

That said, it is for the advocate to put cases up to the law and if necessary to develop the law and press for change; judges can only adjudicate between opposing arguments. Baroness Hale and Ruth Bader Ginsburg have been described as trailblazers and champions of women's and family rights. But in one sense they have been neither, as they have been simply judges seeing life from a different perspective and upholding equality and going against the grain of decades of male thinking and male privilege and/or a particular privileged view of the world.

Judges must remain independent in every way, not only politically. And so, following a decision in the Pinochet case, (*R (Pinochet Ugarte) v Bow St Metropolitan Stipendiary Magistrate* [2000] 1 AC 61, 119 and 147) Senator Pinochet brought a petition to set aside an order made on 25 November 1998 because Lord Hoffman, one of the judges who had made the original decision, had connections with Amnesty International which was seen by Pinochet to blemish that independence. The division of power and the three branches of governance, parliament, the executive and the judiciary are fundamental to the constitution. Judges keep silent, aloof and aspire to being unbiased. But there are times when they walk the line, and some members of the senior judiciary have certainly spoken out when their office is undermined especially with regard to operational matters generally and the operation of the courts and access to justice. Access to family law remedies has been affected by the recent funding and legal aid crisis, and judges have spoken out about the impact on the family law justice system.

We have also witnessed a legal profession striking because of cuts to legal aid and the impact on their clients. We have also seen members of the Bar being critical of fellow judges. Whilst there is a judicial mechanism for inappropriate remarks by the judiciary, it has not silenced some members of the profession.

Judges also make an impact on law through what Mallory and Tyrrell (2024) call 'the extra judicial voice'. Significantly, past and present presidents of the Family

Division have also championed areas of family law and justice including enhancing understanding of domestic abuse and coercive control in lectures and speeches they have given away from the bench, and some of this extra judicial voice is heard and incorporated into the chapters in this book of *Contemporary Family Law*.

Accountability

An accountable family justice system also depends on transparency. It also depends on the diversity of its members, who must be reflective of the society it serves. Of solicitors, 53 per cent are women, 19 per cent are ethnic minorities and 6 per cent are disabled. There has been an increase in lesbian, gay and bi lawyers and there are trans lawyers – for example Robin White (she/her) and Reagan Persaud (she/her) – but as the 2021 'Landmark investigation and report on race and the Bar' found there remains discrimination, and barristers from ethnic minority backgrounds, and especially black and Asian women, face systemic obstacles to building and progressing a sustainable career. This is exacerbated by the cuts to legal aid funding since 2013 which means there are severe financial challenges at the self-employed publicly funded bar.

As for judicial diversity Asian judges now stand at 5 per cent, 1 per cent of judges are black and 2 per cent are from mixed ethnic backgrounds.

The diversity of all practitioners and judges across genders, socio-economic backgrounds and ethnicities, faiths and no faith and political opinion is important to the fair and just practice of family law. Diversity of the practitioner solicitor and barrister and the adjudicator judge impacts on understanding those who come to the law, their histories, their problems, their needs and ensures honouring the overarching principle and aspiration of the development of an equitable family law representing all humankind. We hope to instill through the pages of *Contemporary Family Law* that overriding human obligation.

The Future and the new Labour government

It is unclear what changes and reforms the Labour Government, in office since July 2024, will bring to family law.

The statements made up to present have been general and lacking in any detail. Few specific recommendations or commitments came out of the Labour Conference or manifesto or from the Minister for Children, Families and Wellbeing Janet Daby, MP. However, the transparency pilot already in situ promises to strengthen public confidence in the system with transparency regarding financial remedies and with the aim of diverting cases from the court process. With regard to financial arrangements between adults the new Government has indicated that it intends to bring in legislation to ensure that all pre nuptial agreements will be binding in the future. The austerity measure of the two child benefit limit which the Labour government has pledged to retain will further increase child and family poverty, contribute to an increasing number of cases of child neglect and impact on local authority applications to the court for child protection. A legal challenge to this measure in the Welfare Reform and Work Act (2016) in the Supreme Court in *R (on the application of SC, CB and 8 children) v Secretary of State for Work and Pensions and others* [2021] UKSC 26 found that the measure was lawful not disproportionate nor inappropriate.' (See Graham 2024).

Organisation of the text

The text is divided into two parts: Part I (Chapters 2–8) concerns the law relating to adult relationships and Part II (Chapters 9–16) the law relating to children. Each part is self-contained and may be read in whichever order the reader chooses. Chapters are variable in length and some themes appear across several chapters as family law issues in practice are not hermetically sealed.

References

Banda, Fareeda and John Eekelaar, 'International Conceptions of the Family' [2017] *International and Comparative Law Quarterly* 833

Cohabitation, 'Labour's Common-Law Marriage Pledge to Give Millions of Cohabiting Couples Property Rights' *The Times* (11.10.2023) www.thetimes.co.uk/article/labours-common-law-marriage-pledge-to-give-millions-of-cohabiting-couples-property-rights-d7xnq99w6 (accessed 25.05.2024)

Delahunty, Jo, 'Gresham College Lecture on 32 January 2019, the 30th Anniversary of the Children Act 1989 Is It Still Fit for Purpose?' www.2019-01-31_JoDelahunty_30thAnnive rsaryOfTheChildrenAct89.pdf (gresham.ac.uk) (accessed 24.05.2024)

Ginsburg, Ruth Bader, *My Own Words* (Simon & Schuster 2018)

Graham, Lewis, 'Has the Supreme Court Become More Restrained in Public Law cases?' (2024) 87 (5) *Modern Law Review* 1073

Hale, Brenda, *Spider Woman: A Life* (Bodley Head 2021)

House of Lords Constitution Committee (06.04.2022) https://committees.parliament.uk/oralevidence/10084/pdf/ (accessed 20.05.2024)

Jackson, Peter, 'The Nicholas Wall Memorial Lecture 2023 "Is Family Law Law"' [2023] *Family Law* 796 www.judiciary.uk/the-nicholas-wall-memorial-lecture-given-by-lord-justice-peter-jackson-is-family-law-law/ (accessed 11.05.2024)

Jonathan, Djanogly, 'House of Commons Hansard Ministerial Statements for 06.09.2011 (pt 0001) (parliament.uk)' https://publications.parliament.uk/pa/cm201011/cmhansrd/cm110906/wmstext/110906m0001.htm#11090644000011 (accessed 25.05.2024)

Law Commission Cohabitation (2007) https://lawcom.gov.uk/project/cohabitation/ (accessed 24.05.2024)

Law Commission Consultation (Review to Examine 50-Year-Old Laws on Finances After Divorce and the Ending of a Civil Partnership) https://lawcom.gov.uk/review-to-examine-50-year-old-laws-on-finances-after-divorce-and-the-ending-of-a-civil-partnership/ (accessed 24.05.2024)

Mallory, Connell and Hélène Tyrrell, 'The Extra Judicial Voice' [2024] *Legal Studies* 1

The Remote Access Family Court www.judiciary.uk/wp-content/uploads/2020/06/The-Remote-Access-Family-Court-Version-5-Final-Version-26.06.2020.pdf (accessed 24.05.2024)

Thornberry, Emily, 'Making the Law Work for Women – My Labour Conference Speech 2023' (10.10.2023) https://www.emilythornberry.com/shadow-attorney-general/2023/10/10/making-the-law-work-for-women-my-labour-conference-speech-2023 (accessed 30.8.2024)

UN Human Rights Committee (HRC), 'CCPR General Comment No. 19: Article 23 (The Family) Protection of the Family, the Right to Marriage and Equality of the Spouses' (27.07.1990) UN Doc HRI/GEN/1/Rev.6 at 149 (2003) para 2 www.refworld.org/legal/general/hrc/1990/en/38884 (accessed 25.05.2024)

Ward, Tony, 'Explaining and Trusting Expert Evidence: What Is a "Sufficiently Reliable Scientific Basis"?' [2020] *International Journal of Evidence and Proof* 233

2

State intervention in personal relationships

SUMMARY

The State's function in its involvement in personal relationships is to promote those economic and social policies, which it believes to be beneficial for itself and for society. This involvement takes the form of giving benefits to, and imposing burdens on, those parties who enter into personal relationships which meet with State approval. Those who are unable, or unwilling, to play the familial game in accordance with State expectations remain, for the most part, exempt from specific legal responsibilities for each other, and they receive negligible legal or economic advantages. Cohabitation is not a recognised relationship in England and Wales, so few rights arise from that relationship. One cohabitant cannot claim property rights from the other if the relationship breaks down, so any rights over property will derive from the law of property rather than from the relationship itself.

If benefits are to be given, and responsibilities enforced, it is necessary for the State to know who has entered into one of the approved familial relationships. The law, therefore, must define what constitutes such a relationship and what determines its point of entry and exit.

In this chapter, we consider the law relating to the formation, and nature, of the legally approved relationships of marriage and civil partnerships as well as the rather nebulous status of those who are engaged to be married or who have agreed to enter into a civil partnership. We also examine the nature of those informal cohabiting relationships in which the State has decided to intervene, albeit to a more limited degree. We note the minimal nature of State intervention in familial relationships involving siblings, and parent adult-child relationships.

There is an inevitable overlap in this chapter with the topics discussed in Chapter 3, and readers may find it helpful to read these two chapters in conjunction with each other.

DOI: 10.4324/9781003435020-2

Form v function

Which relationships should be recognised?

In determining which familial relationships should receive the special attention of the law, the State may take a formalistic approach, often referred to as following the 'bright-line rule', and define with precision the nature of the relationship and its entry point and the departure point. The purpose of this approach is to produce predictable and consistent results and leave no room for discretionary interpretation. If the relationship does not comply with the formal requirements, the partners will not be granted the status which is available to those in approved familial relationships. Katherine O'Donovan observed in 1993: 'Law regulates entry into marriage, the ceremony, the consummation and validity. In that sense law constitutes the marriage' (O'Donovan 1993). The position seems largely the same today although anticipated reform to the rules on formalities could allow a greater degree of individual control to the parties.

It is equally possible for the State to take a functional approach towards the family and bring any relationship, which performs the essential functions of the family in line with the State's expectations, within both its protective and demanding legal sphere.

A dual approach

English law takes a dual approach to familial relationships. Marriage was long regarded as the ideal family model; those who married acquired a status and were granted rights appropriate to that view. It has a fixed entry point with strict rules relating to its formation and dissolution. Those who enter into it may not, for the most part, determine the nature of the matrimonial contract for themselves; it is defined by law and, as will be seen, there is very limited opportunity to depart from it. Marriage gives the parties status, but it can also be regarded as a contract. Unlike most contracts the parties do not have freedom to lay down their own terms. They are limited to those terms laid down by the State. The intentions of the parties are not necessarily reflected in the outcome. The question of the enforceability of pre-nuptial contracts raised the question of whether parties to a marriage could predetermine the outcome should the marriage break down.

Baroness Hale commented:

> the parties are not entirely free to determine all its legal consequences for themselves. They contract into the package which the law of the land lays down. . . . . Nowadays there is considerable freedom and flexibility within the marital package but there is an irreducible minimum. This includes a couple's mutual duty to support one another and their children . . . The question for us is how far individual couples should be free to rewrite that essential feature of the marital relationship as they choose.
>
> (Radmacher v Granatino [2010] UKSC 42 para 132)

Civil partnerships and same-sex marriage

Since 2005, when the Civil Partnership Act 2004 (CPA 2004) came into force, State intervention has been extended to same-sex partnerships. These relationships have been granted the status of a form of quasi-marriage if the couple register a civil partnership. The rules relating to the formation and dissolution of same-sex partnerships are very similar to those relating to marriage, and civil partners are given almost all the rights and duties of married partners.

Under the Marriage (Same Sex Couples) Act 2013 same-sex couples are now allowed to be married in either civil or religious ceremonies. The civil ceremonies must follow the same rules and formalities as marriage between opposite sex couples and civil partnerships, but the rules governing religious ceremonies for same-sex couples are slightly more complex. Whether or not a couple can marry in a particular church of a particular denomination will depend on their rules. In most cases it will depend on whether the church has opted in to conduct a same-sex religious ceremony. The Act makes it clear that no individual within an organisation can be compelled to conduct a same-sex marriage.

Some opposite sex couples sought the right to enter into civil partnerships arguing that marriage is an ancient institution which in spite of changes in rules and form still carries with it a sense of patriarchal dominance. This was the argument of Rebecca Steinfield and Charles Keidan who argued that they were suffering discrimination because they were at the time unable to enter into a civil partnership. This argument was successful in the Supreme Court where they brought a case for judicial review. The Supreme Court held that the position on civil partnerships was incompatible with human rights (*R (On the application of Steinfield and Keidan) v Secretary of State for International Development (in substitution for the Home Secretary and the Education)* [2018] UKSC 32). The Civil Partnership (Opposite-sex Couples) Regulations 2019 were introduced shortly afterwards which allowed opposite sex couples to enter into civil partnerships.

Some argue that rather than confer status on couples who cohabit the whole question of formalised relationships should be revisited. The philosopher Clare Chambers has argued that marriage violates both equality and liberty so should not be recognised by the State, nor have any legal status (*Against Marriage: An Egalitarian Defence of the Marriage-Free State* (2017 OUP)). Her ideas may appear radical, but the numbers entering into formalised relationships have been steadily dropping over the past ten years, probably accelerated by Covid. There were 246,897 marriages in 2022. An increase assumed as a response to Covid after a decrease of 20.8 per cent in the number of marriages over the previous 30 years. Rather than extend the legal rights currently available to those who enter into marriage or civil partnership, another way of reforming the law could be to focus on the relationship and allow couples to opt in and access those rights and responsibilities currently enjoyed by parties to the two formal relationships in England and Wales today. (See later in this chapter *Burden and Burden v United Kingdom* (2006).) As argued by Carol Smart in 1984:

> *The aim is not to extend the legal and social definition of marriage to cover cohabitees or even homosexual couples, it is to abandon the status of marriage altogether and to devise a system of rights, duties or obligations which are not dependent on any form of 'coupledom' or marriage.*

(Smart 1984)

Engagement to marry or enter into a civil partnership

Engagements to marry and agreements to enter into a civil partnership are viewed by the State as a preliminary to the formal relationship of marriage or civil partnership. Fiancés have always received some legal rights, although these rights have lessened significantly over time. Those who agree to enter into a civil partnership may also benefit from those rights given to engaged couples.

Today, in the absence of formal betrothal ceremonies, it is not easy to determine what constitutes an engagement sufficient to bring the relationship within the law's sphere. It is not uncommon for couples who have no firm plan to marry, and who may not be free to marry because they have not divorced their existing partner, to describe themselves as being engaged.

Both heterosexual and same-sex cohabiting relationships perform some of the functions of marriage or civil partnership, and, for this reason, the State has given both categories of cohabitants limited legal protection and imposed limited responsibilities on them. It has, however, shown considerable reluctance to accord to them a similar status to spouses or civil partners.

Relationships exempt from legal intervention

There is one important category of cohabiting relationship in which the State has chosen, largely, not to intervene, even though it fulfils many of the approved familial functions. It is the non-sexual relationship which exists between adults, whether siblings, parent/adult child, or friends, who choose to live together and care for each other. During the passage of the Civil Partnership Bill through Parliament in 2003, concern was expressed at the State's neglect of these relationships. Lord Tebbit, a Conservative Peer, pointed out that persons in these relationships might be able to claim that the lack of provision for them is discriminatory and a breach of their human rights. He maintained that:

> *The financial and tax impact of the death of a parent who has been cared for by a son or daughter at the sacrifice of his or her own career and financial well-being is no less than that of the surviving member of a homosexual couple who may have made a similar commitment one to the other, but for perhaps a far shorter period. Daughters are made just as homeless when inheritance tax demands force the sale of their family home as those who would be members of civil partnerships under the provisions of the Bill. . . . When there is a relationship between a parent and a child who is particularly vulnerable, what happens then? The vulnerable child is left with an inheritance tax bill which forces the sale of the home in which he or she has lived, and has been cared for by parents, throughout the whole of their natural life. Are these not matters which are of concern to us here and now?*

> (Hansard, House of Lords, 24 June 2003)

Many would assert that Lord Tebbit's concerns were more connected with an interest in derailing the civil partnership legislation. However, his comments, once again, drew attention to the feelings of those who are excluded from entering into a legally recognised familial relationship either because they are within the prohibited degrees of relationship, or because they are platonic friends, and would regard it as inappropriate to marry or enter into a civil partnership.

THE DECISION OF THE EUROPEAN COURT OF HUMAN RIGHTS IN *BURDEN AND BURDEN v UK* (2006)

In 2006, in *Burden and Burden v United Kingdom* [2007] 1 FCR 69, two elderly spinsters made an application to the European Court of Human Rights (ECtHR) and complained, under Art 14 (prohibition of discrimination), taken in conjunction with Art 1 of Protocol 1 (the protection of property), of the European Convention on Human Rights 1950 (ECHR), that UK law discriminated against them by preventing them from registering a civil partnership. The consequence of this was that when the first of the sisters died, the survivor would be required to pay 40 per cent inheritance tax on the deceased's share of their family home. She might have to sell the home to pay the tax. By contrast, the survivor of a married couple, or a homosexual relationship registered under the CPA 2004, would be exempt from paying such a tax.

The Court rejected the application by four votes to three. Its ruling centred on the wide margin of appreciation enjoyed by a State in deciding whether, and to what extent, differential treatment is justified. It maintained that States may well need to strike a balance between the need to raise revenue and the social objectives in doing so, and were generally in a better position to determine their social and economic policies than the Court. A State's decision relating to these policies will, therefore, normally be respected by the Court unless it is evident that they are without reasonable foundation and consequently unjustifiable.

In a joint dissenting judgment, Judges Bonello and Garlicki maintained that once the UK legislature decided to extend the inheritance tax exemption to civil partners as well as married couples, it had failed to establish that it had behaved reasonably, and in a non-arbitrary manner, by not granting siblings who live together a similar right. In their opinion:

> The situation of permanently cohabiting siblings is in many respects – emotional as well as economical – not entirely different from the situation of other unions, particularly as regards old or very old people. The bonds of mutual affection form the ethical basis for such unions and the bonds of mutual dependency form the social basis for them. It is very important to protect such unions, like any other union of two persons, from financial disaster resulting from the death of one of the partners. . . .
>   . . . unless some compelling reasons can be shown, the legislature cannot simply ignore that such unions also exist.

The judges also acknowledged that:

> The situation of permanently cohabiting siblings under the UK legislation has also been negatively affected by the fact that – being within the prohibited degrees of relationship – they cannot form a civil partnership. In other words, they have been deprived of the possibility of choice offered to other couples.

In a second dissenting judgment, Judge Pavlovschi stressed that he was particularly influenced by the nature of the sisters' property which would be subject to inheritance tax:

> The case concerns the applicants' family house, in which they have spent all their lives and which they built on land inherited from their late parents. This house is not simply

a piece of property – this house is something with which they have a special emotional bond, this house is their home.

    It strikes me as absolutely awful that, once one of the two sisters dies, the surviving sister's sufferings on account of her closest relative's death should be multiplied by the risk of losing her family home because she cannot afford to pay inheritance tax in respect of the deceased sister's share of it.

    I find such a situation fundamentally unfair and unjust. It is impossible for me to agree with the majority that, as a matter of principle, such treatment can be considered reasonable and objectively justified. I am firmly convinced that in modern society there is no 'pressing need' to cause people all this additional suffering.

Joyce Burden on learning of the Court's decision commented:

If we were lesbians we would have all the rights in the world. But we are sisters, and it seems we have no rights at all.

THE DECISION OF THE GRAND CHAMBER IN *BURDEN v UK* (2008)

The Burden sisters did not give up and, in 2007 at their request, the Panel of the Grand Chamber of the ECtHR decided to refer their case to the Grand Chamber which refused to accept that a relationship between siblings could be seen as analogous to that of a married couple or civil partners. There was, therefore, no discrimination against the Burden sisters.

    In functional terms, it is difficult to see how the relationship between Joyce and Sybil Burden could properly be regarded in any way other than analogous with that of a married couple or same-sex partners. They had chosen to live with each other in their family home in a loving, committed and stable relationship for many decades, foregoing the possibility of marriage or civil partnership with any other person, yet unable to legalise that relationship because of their consanguinity. (See Dempsey 2009.) The sisters, not surprisingly, found it difficult to understand why:

two single sisters in their old age, whose only crime was to choose to stay single and look after their parents and two aunts to the end, should find themselves in such a position in the UK in the 21st century. We certainly do not regret our decision to look after our family for a single moment; we were glad to repay them for the happy, good, Christian upbringing they gave us . . . we have been fighting for 32 years just to gain the same rights, as regards inheritance tax, as married couples and couples in civil partnerships.

Definitions and formation of relationships

Engagement

Fiancés are given limited legal rights both during and at the end of their relationship. One of the problems for modern day law is the difficulty in determining precisely what constitutes an engagement. The term fiancé appears to encompass a wide array of relationships. At one extreme, a couple may describe themselves as engaged where the man has formally proposed marriage to the woman (it is still the norm for men to do the proposing except in leap years when custom provides that the woman may propose to her loved one); has presented her with a ring; a formal announcement has been made; the wedding date has been set, and the wedding plans are well under way. At the other extreme, a couple who cohabit and have children may refer to themselves as fiancées, yet have no intention of marrying in the near future, if ever. They may not be even be free to marry each other.

Historically, the term fiancé was more circumscribed. An engagement, or betrothal, was formally announced and an engagement ring was given to seal the promise to marry. The custom of giving an engagement ring began in 1477 when Maximilian, the Archduke of Austria, presented his fiancée Mary, Duchess of Burgundy with a diamond ring. It was possible prior to 1970 for a woman to sue for breach of promise if an engagement was broken because not only had she risked the possibility of marrying someone else but she might also have suffered damage to her reputation. Any property including the engagement ring transferred between the parties can be retained on the basis of the ordinary rules of property law if the engagement is later broken off, unless it is proved that the transfer was conditional on the marriage proceeding.

Agreements to enter into a civil partnership

There appears to be no exact counterpart of an engagement for prospective civil partners although in the period immediately prior to their civil partnership, one would assume that they have agreed to enter into one and made the necessary arrangements to complete the formalities.

Marriage

History and background to marriage

The first marriages were governed by the church and were deemed not to be a matter to be governed by the State. Valid marriages were officiated by a priest, and any challenge to the validity of the marriage was heard before an ecclesiastical court. Formalities were gradually introduced including reading the banns of marriage prior to any ceremony, the obtaining of a marriage licence and also regulation of the times and places when a marriage could take place. For a short period whilst Oliver Cromwell was governing the country, church marriages were banned and marriages could only take place in front of a magistrate. Although short lived, church marriages were reinstated when Charles II came to the throne, and it was now accepted that marriage was no longer governed solely by the church. This was a significant development. In the early seventeenth century parties to marriages often failed to adhere to the rules of place, time and officiate at marriage. These were referred to as 'clandestine marriages' conducted in private often in debtors' prisons such as the Fleet by unfrocked priests. (See Outhwaite 1992.) In response to this a number of Marriage Acts were passed; the most important was the Act of 1753 often referred to as Lord Hardwicke's Marriage Act. Many of the formalities laid down in that Act still govern marriages today: marriages had to take place in church, the service had to be conducted by a priest, in front of two witnesses and banns (an announcement of the forthcoming marriage inviting anyone to object if they had grounds) to be announced on three successive Sundays before the marriage. The marriage then had to be recorded in a register of marriages. With the exception of Jewish marriages and more recently the Quakers, marriages conducted by other faiths were not recognised. Civil ceremonies were finally introduced in 1836. People were now allowed to marry in a register office once a licence had been obtained and notice had been given as in religious ceremonies.

The provisions from the various Marriage Acts were consolidated into the Marriage Act 1949. This Act continues to govern the law on marriage today and there have been few changes save for the introduction of civil partnerships and same-sex marriages. Recognising the complexity of the rules for marriages the Government asked the Law Commission in 2015 to conduct research into the current law and make recommendations for change. The Law Commission published its report: Celebrating Marriage: A New Weddings Law, Law Com 408 in July 2022. The main finding was that the law governing marriage had failed to keep pace with modern life. The rules governing where marriages could take place have remained very restrictive; couples must opt for a civil or religious ceremony and have no option to incorporate their beliefs into the ceremony. Marriages outside in the open air are not allowed except in the grounds of approved premises. A number of recommendations were made, in particular the provision of a new 'weddings law' that would give couples greater choice. The principles governing the review included the need for certainty, simplicity, fairness and equality. It recognised that the interests of the State needed protection as well as the individual's wishes and beliefs. The recommendations attempt to remove unnecessary regulation which should result in more choice and cheaper weddings. The emphasis would rest with the status of the officiant rather than the location of the wedding. These are recommendations and have not been acted on by the Government.

Many people, including family lawyers, when asked to define marriage, automatically refer to the definition in *Hyde v Hyde* (1866) LR1 P & D 130 that

> *marriage is the voluntary union for life of one man to one woman to the exclusion of all others.*

This brief statement is neither an adequate description nor an accurate reflection of what marriage is today. Marriage can hardly be said to be for life. Divorce is easily obtainable and its incidence in England and Wales is high (see Chapter 6). Since the enactment of the Gender Recognition Act 2004 (GRA 2004), marriage is no longer restricted to those who were born respectively male and female.

Bigamous marriages entered into in jurisdictions which permit them may, in certain circumstances, be recognised by English law. Such marriages also appear to be socially accepted; the Queen invited the Sultan of Brunei and both his wives, as her guests, to the wedding of her youngest child in 1999. By the time her grandson married in 2011, the Sultan arrived at the wedding ceremony with only one wife; he had divorced the other one.

The definition in *Hyde* (1866) gives minimal information about the nature of marriage and the legal consequences which flow from it. By virtue of the marriage ceremony, couples agree to accept the spousal status but most of them will have little advance knowledge of the matrimonial rights and duties which attach to that status. They only become aware of such matters after the marriage, and by negative means; they must look to the legislation on nullity, divorce, property, death and domestic violence to discover the opaque terms of the contract which governs their new status.

Thorpe LJ in *Bellinger v Bellinger* (2001) 2 FLR 1048 explained that:

> the world that engendered those classic definitions [of marriage] has long since gone. We live in a multi-racial, multi-faith society. The intervening 130 years have seen huge social and scientific changes. Adults live longer, infant mortality has been largely conquered, and effective contraception is available to men and women as is sterilisation for men and women within marriage. Illegitimacy with its stigma has been legislated away: gone is any social condemnation of cohabitation in advance of or in place of marriage. Then marriage was terminated by death: for the vast majority of the population divorce was not an option. . . . Now more marriages are terminated by divorce than death. Divorce could be said without undue cynicism to be available on demand. These last changes are all reflected in the statistics establishing the relative decline in marriage and consequentially in the number of children born within marriage. Marriage has become a state into which and from which people choose to enter and exit. Thus I would now redefine marriage as a contract for which the parties elect but which is regulated by the state, both in its formation and in its termination by divorce, because it affects status upon which depend a variety of entitlements, benefits and obligations.

The right to marry

The ECHR Art 12 states that

> Men and women of marriageable age have the right to marry and to found a family, according to the national laws governing the exercise of this right.

In *R (on the application of Baiai and others) v Secretary of State for the Home Department* (2008) 2 FLR 1462, the House of Lords considered the right to marry under the Asylum and Immigration (Treatment of Claimants, etc) Act 2004, s 19(3)(b). The section requires the written permission of the Secretary of State to marry if one, or both parties, to the marriage is subject to immigration control unless entry clearance had been granted specifically for the purpose of marriage in the UK (s 19(3)(a)), or the relevant party was settled in the UK within the meaning of the Immigration Rules (s 19(3)(c)). The applicants had to pay a fee of £295 (Immigration (Procedure for Marriage) Regulations 2005).

Their Lordships held that the right to marry protected by Art 12 was a strong right. However, a Convention State could impose reasonable conditions on the right of a third country national to marry in order to check whether the proposed marriage was a genuine one or one of convenience for immigration purposes, and if so, prevent it. In order to prevent a breach, Art 12, s 19(3)(b) of the Act should be read as referring to person who

> *has the written permission of the Secretary of State to marry in the UK, such permission not to be withheld in the case of a qualified applicant seeking to enter into a marriage which is not one of convenience, and the application for, and grant of such permission not to be subject to conditions which unreasonably inhibit exercise of the applicant's right under Art 12 of the European Convention.*

The House of Lords also held that the current fee payable under the 2005 Regulations was set at a level which could infringe the right to marry. (See also *O'Donoghue and Others v UK* (2011).)

Capacity to marry

The law relating to the capacity to marry is laid down in the Marriage Act 1949, ss 1–3 and Sch 1 and the Matrimonial Causes Act 1973 (MCA 1973), ss 11, 12, 13.

MALE AND FEMALE

parties who wish to marry must be respectively male and female.

Until 2005, transgendered persons were not permitted to marry a member of the opposite sex to that of their newly acquired gender. If a transgendered person attempted to marry, the marriage was deemed to be a same-sex marriage and, therefore, invalid under the (MCA 1973, s 11(c)). Since 2013 same-sex marriage has been recognised in law which has addressed the problem of invalidity under the MCA. Before 2013, a male to female transgendered person could only marry a female, and a female to male transgendered person could only marry a male. Such marriages were rare and, to the outsider, looked remarkably like same-sex marriages. Transgendered persons were deemed to remain trapped in their birth gender. Unless they were found to be inter-sexed, their birth certificate could not be altered to reflect their adult-determined gender (see *W v W (nullity)* [2001]) Fam 111.

THE COURT OF APPEAL DECISION IN BELLINGER v BELLINGER (2001)

In *Bellinger* (2001), Thorpe LJ in a dissenting judgment concluded that:

> *To make the chromosomal factor conclusive, or even dominant, seems to me particularly questionable in the context of marriage. For it is an invisible feature of an individual, incapable of perception or registration other than by scientific test. It makes no contribution to the physiological or psychological self. Indeed in the context of the institution of marriage as it is today it seems to me right as a matter of principle and*

logic to give predominance to psychological factors just as it seems right to carry out the essential assessment of gender at or shortly before the time of marriage rather than at the time of birth.

THE HOUSE OF LORDS DECISION IN BELLINGER v BELLINGER [2003] UKHL 21

Mrs Bellinger appealed and the House of Lords held that a person, whose sex had been correctly diagnosed at birth, could not later become, or come to be regarded as, a person of the opposite sex. Their Lordships maintained that it was for Parliament rather than the courts to change the law on such an important matter because there was considerable uncertainty about the circumstances in, and purposes for, which gender reassignment should be recognised. It should not be dealt with in a piecemeal fashion. However, the House of Lords formally recorded the fact that the failure of the MCA 1973 to recognise gender reassignment for the purposes of marriage was incompatible with Articles 8 and 12. At the time of the decision there was still a body of opinion that viewed the approach of the court still working within the biological and heterosexual limits of *Corbett v Corbett* (Cowan 2004).

At the time of the decision in *Bellinger* (2003), the Government was already in the process of examining the law in this area because of the ECtHR's decision in *Goodwin v UK (28957/95)* [2002] IRLR 664 that the UK was in breach of Articles 8 and 12 by not allowing a transgendered person to marry a person of the opposite sex to his or her birth gender. The outcome of its deliberations was the enactment of the Gender Recognition Act 2004. Section 1 of that Act permits transgendered persons to apply for a gender recognition certificate from the Gender Recognition Panel (see Gov.UK). The Panel was set up to determine the gender identity of both pre-operative and post-operative transgendered persons over the age of 18. The applicant for such a certificate need not have undergone gender reassignment surgery if it would be inappropriate for them to do so. The grant of a certificate allows them to acquire a new gender from that registered on their birth certificate. If the trans-gendered person is already married to a person who is the opposite sex to that of his or her birth gender, only an interim certificate will be issued. A full certificate will be issued after an application has been made for a decree of nullity and the decree has been granted (see Chapter 3).

Age

The parties to a marriage must be over the age of 18. Until recently it was possible for those over 16 and under 18 to marry with parental consent. However concern had been expressed about the number of underage girls from the UK being forced into illegal marriages both in the UK and abroad (see further discussion in Chapters 3 and 5) and as a result of this concern the minimum age to marry was raised.

Under the Marriage and Civil Partnership Act (Minimum Age) 2022 the minimum age to marry has been raised to 18. This is now without exception. The Act also makes it a criminal offence if anyone does something with intent to cause a child to marry.

Prohibited degrees of relationship

The Marriage Act 1949, s 1, provides that a marriage between persons related by blood or marriage within the prohibited degrees of consanguinity or affinity is void.

It is also a criminal offence under the Sexual Offences Act 2003 (SOA 2003), s 64 for a person to have a sexual relationship with anyone who is within the prohibited degrees of relationship to him or her. The prohibition is based on a mixture of religious beliefs, social repugnance, genetics and social policy. Marriage within certain prohibited degrees of relationship risks the birth of children with genetic defects.

However, not all cultures take the same approach towards this issue; some regard it as totally inappropriate to marry cousins whilst others regard it as preferable to marry a close relation. Societal rules may depend on economic factors; marrying outside the family may bring greater wealth to poorer families. For wealthier families, marriage within the kin group family may safeguard their wealth and strengthen familial bonds.

In 1839, the scientist Charles Darwin married his first cousin, Emma Wedgwood. Of their ten children one daughter died of tuberculosis, aged 10, one died at birth and one at the age of 2. Five of the remaining seven children had serious illnesses or suffered some disability. Darwin expressed his concern about whether these problems were a consequence of his marrying his cousin.

In 2007, Anne Cryer, the Labour MP for Keighley, commissioned a report on marriage between cousins and proposed a ban on such marriages. The report claimed that 30 per cent of all births in the British Pakistani community had recessive gene disorders, and stated that more than 55 per cent of British Pakistanis are married to first cousins. The likelihood of unrelated couples having the same variant genes which cause recessive disorders is estimated to be 100–1. Between first cousins, the odds increase to as much as one in eight. In Bradford, more than three quarters of all Pakistani marriages are believed to be between first cousins. The city's Royal Infirmary Hospital has identified more than 140 different recessive disorders among local children, compared with the usual 20–30 (BBC, 16 November 2005).

Relationships which offend the consanguinity rule do occur, and often in circumstances where the siblings were not brought up together and maybe did not even know of each other's existence. A German brother and sister were separated whilst young and met and fell in love later in life. They had four children. The man was jailed for incest and appealed unsuccessfully to the ECtHR *(Stübing v. Germany* – *European Court Of Human Rights* 13 April 2012 (Application No. 43547/08)).

The Marriage Act 1949, Sch 1 (as amended) lists those relatives who may not marry. The list includes both blood relationships and relationships of affinity:

- father/daughter;
- mother/son;
- niece/uncle;

- nephew/aunt;
- brother/sister;
- grandparent/grandchild;
- half-siblings;
- adopted child/adoptive parent.

In the light of concern about the risk of destabilising the family, it is surprising that a person may marry his or her adopted sibling. Marriage between a stepchild and stepparent is also permissible if both parties are over 21 years of age and if the child, prior to the age of 18, has never been a child of the family in relation to the stepparent.

Prior to the decision in *B & L v UK* [2006] 36536/02 marriages between parents-in-law and children-in-law were restricted, under the Marriage Act 1949, except in circumstances where both parties were over 21 years of age and their spouses were dead, or they had obtained a personal Act of Parliament allowing them to marry.

B and L were a father-in-law and a daughter-in-law who wished to marry each other; he was aged 60 and was divorced from his son's mother; she was aged 40 and was divorced from his son. The couple claimed that the UK law which denied them the right to marry was a breach of their rights under Art 12 (the right to marry and found a family) of the ECHR. The ECtHR found that although UK law pursued the legitimate aim of protecting the integrity of the family, it did not prevent relationships between parents-in-law and children-in-law from happening, or even marriages from taking place if the parties were able to meet the exceptional circumstances provisions.

As a consequence of the Court's ruling, the prohibition on such marriages was removed by the Marriage Act 1949 (Remedial) Order 2007.

Transgendered persons also benefitted from the change in the law; for example a woman who is a male-to-female transgendered person, and who has obtained a gender recognition certificate, could now marry her ex-wife's father.

Already married or in a registered civil partnership

A person who is already married, or who is in a registered civil partnership, may not enter into a valid marriage in England and Wales.

If the parties to a bigamous or even a polygamous marriage have the personal capacity to marry under the law of their domicile in a country in which such marriages are legally recognised, their marriage will be recognised as valid (see MCA 1973, s 11(d)).

It is a criminal offence to marry bigamously in England and Wales (see Offences Against the Person Act 1861, s 57). Bigamy was first declared to be a crime in 1604 when the first Parliament of James 1 took action to restrain the

> *divers evil disposed persons who were bigamously marrying 'to the greate dishonour of God and utter undoinge of divers honest men's children and others', by ensuring that anyone found guilty would receive a sentence of death.*
>
> (Samuel Chapman 2001)

In 2009, the *Guardian* newspaper reported a story of a woman who was spared a prison sentence when she admitted that she had committed bigamy. She had in fact married five times between 1999 and 2007. She had lied about her marital status at each successive marriage, and she had used a succession of different names (*The Guardian* 2009).

Mental capacity

In order to marry, a person must be capable of understanding the nature of the marriage contract (MCA 1973, s 12(c), (d)).

Given the absence of a document which defines with any precision the nature of marriage and its duties and responsibilities, it is difficult to know what level of mental capacity is required to enter into marriage. Judicial statements relating to mental capacity have not helped in any significant way. They tend to be a little opaque and, probably, for very good reason; there is a reluctance to limit the emotional life of mentally vulnerable persons.

In *Re SA (Vulnerable Adult with Capacity: Marriage)* [2006] EWHC (Fam) the court discussed the question of capacity to marry, and the right to self-determination under Articles 8 and 12 of the ECHR, in the context of a vulnerable adult at risk of a forced marriage.

Ms SA was an 18-year-old deaf and mute young woman who could only communicate in British Sign Language (BSL). She was partially sighted, and was assessed as having the intellectual capacity of an early teenager, and the reading age of a 7-year-old. The psychologist who evaluated her acknowledged the problems in determining mental capacity in this context. Psychological testing uses both verbal and non-verbal communication; the former tests are inappropriate for a deaf person who is only capable of understanding non-verbal communication. He concluded that Ms SA had

> *a rudimentary but nevertheless clear and accurate understanding of the concept of marriage and of what a marriage contract would entail; that she has an accurate and realistic understanding of what a sexual relationship is, its effect and implications, and*

> *what would be expected within the relationship, and that she understands that a marriage can be legally ended in divorce.*
>
> However, he drew attention to the fact that Ms SA was unable to comprehend the very real possibility that her parents might take her to Pakistan, organise her marriage, whilst she was there to a man who would not, or could not, because of immigration rules, return with her and live in the UK. If that were to happen, she would be unable to express her concerns to anyone in Pakistan or obtain help to return to the UK. She might be compelled to remain in a country where she would be unable to communicate with anyone in BSL, including the man she might have been forced to marry. Such a possibility would result in her leading an isolated existence and her mental health would suffer severely.

Munby J reiterated what he had said in *Re E (An Alleged Patient): Sheffield City Council v E and S* [2005] EWHC 2808 (Ch). He maintained that the general rule of English law relating to capacity is to

> *understand the nature and quality of the act.*

In the context of marriage, a person wishing to enter into a valid marriage must know that he or she is taking part in a marriage ceremony and understands the words of the ceremony; he or she must also be able to appreciate the responsibilities which stem from the contract of marriage agreed to in that ceremony. According to Munby J, the marriage contract confers on the man and woman the status of husband and wife. From this status flow consequences. The parties are expected, *inter alia*, to live together, love only each other as husband and wife, and be responsible for each other's care and comfort.

Given the nebulous nature of the State-determined English marriage contract, it might be argued that Munby J's test is a very high hurdle for anyone who is contemplating marriage to leap and, particularly, persons as intellectually challenged as Ms SA. After all, it is not easy to appreciate the full significance of the marriage contract, which is unwritten, and can only be compiled from a reading of case law and statutes primarily relating to marital breakdown. This is not the reading matter of most couples who are about to embark on marriage, and certainly not of an adult on the borderline of learning ability with a reading age of a 7-year-old.

However, Munby J did not share this view. He maintained that the contract of marriage is essentially a very simple one, and does not require a high degree of intelligence to comprehend it.

He was, quite understandably, anxious to avoid discriminating against those of limited mental ability, were the test of capacity to marry to be set too high. Marriage and civil partnership remain the only legal means of establishing a stable relationship; a mentally disabled person living in a protected environment may be incapable of understanding the nature of the marriage contract (as indeed may many mentally able persons in advance of marrying) but may be capable of sustaining, and benefiting from, an emotional and loving relationship. The major argument against marriage of mentally incapacitated persons is the risk to any children born of such a marriage. However, that risk exists whether or not the couple marry; it could be taken care of by adequate preventative measures which would be overseen by those responsible for the mentally incapacitated person or persons.

The question remains as to whether a vulnerable adult might be able to succeed in challenging the denial of a right to marry under the ECHR, Articles 8 and 12.

Formalities of marriage

The formalities of marriage are laid down in the Marriage Act 1949, Parts II–VI (as amended).

They limit the ways in which a couple may choose to marry and are indicative of the values placed by the State on the serious nature of marriage. Currently the limitations on these formalities are under scrutiny. Marriages are subject to rules set out in the mid-twentieth century when social norms and expectations were very different. At the heart of the debate is the question as to whether couples embarking on marriage should have a greater degree of autonomy over the ceremony but still adhere to some basic structure and controls.

Today the formalities involve several stages. Firstly, notice must be given of the intention of the parties to marry; these rules differ as to whether the marriage is to take place under the rites of the Church of England or as a civil or secular marriage. Religious ceremonies of Quakers and Jewish people are recognised, but the notification of the intent to marry and the marriage itself must be registered at the local Registry Office. The formalities of marriage will change if the recommendations proposed by the Law Commission in their recent report Celebrating Marriage: A New Weddings Law (Law Com 408 2022) are adopted. The main recommendations concern the easing of restrictions on location of marriages. The current law remains in place until these recommendations are adopted.

Civil ceremonies

Preliminary requirements

Both parties must notify the registrar of their intention to marry; both parties must have resided in the district where they intend to marry for seven days; the parties have to supply details of their names, marital status, occupations, addresses and nationality, and these details are recorded in the marriage notice book. The parties then have to wait 28 days before the marriage can take place. If no objections are made the superintendent registrar will issue a certificate which allows the marriage to proceed. The 28-day waiting period was increased from 15 days in 2015 (Marriage Act 1949, s 31(1) as amended by the Immigration Act 2014). This was to give more time for objections to be made, in particular any objection on the basis of immigration fraud.

The marriage ceremony

The ceremony must take place in a registry office or in an approved place which has been licensed by the local authority. Such a venue must be a permanent structure and not a marquee but as a result of amendments to the Marriage Act 1949 (the Marriage (Approved Premises) Regulations 1995 and the Marriage and Civil Partnerships (Approved Premises) (Amendment) Regulations 2021) it is possible for marriages to take place in a wider variety of locations and can take place in open air locations where the main venue has approval for weddings. Normally, it must be open to the public to permit them to witness any marriage and make objections prior to or during the ceremony. Celebrity figures who wish to marry away from the public gaze have, usually, been forced to marry outside the jurisdiction. Wayne and Coleen Rooney married in Italy in 2009, and Keira Knightley married her husband the musician James Righton in France in 2013.

There was considerable debate prior to Prince Charles' marriage about whether he could remarry validly in a registry office because of the combined effects of the Act for the Better Regulating of the Future Marriages of the Royal Family Act 1722 and the Marriage Act 1949. The Lord Chancellor, Lord Falconer, decided that such a marriage would be valid.

The building must be secular in nature and have no connection with any religion. It must also be regularly available to the public for marriage ceremonies. Prince Charles and the Duchess of Cornwall were forced to abandon their original plan to marry in Windsor Castle when it was realised that the venue would have to be made available to other couples who might like to marry there.

(For a fuller discussion of the legal and historical background see Lucinda Maer 2008.)

Marriages whilst sky diving, swimming underwater or in other bizarre circumstances which seem to attract the interest of those who find the more acceptable forms of marriage ceremonies just a little dull, are not currently permissible under English law but may become available in the future. The recommendations of the Law Commission take the emphasis away from approved locations allowing the parties to choose their location for their marriage. The emphasis moves to the officiant who can only be within certain specific categories of people. These include registrars or an independent person registered to take marriages and whose main duties will be to ensure that both the parties consent to the marriage and the ceremony is witnessed by two witnesses and the parties sign the marriage document. The content of the ceremony will be far less strictly restricted.

Under the current law a superintendent registrar is responsible for conducting the civil ceremony whether it takes place in a registry office or other licensed venue. The couple may devise their own ceremony, but law forbids any religious element in it. The ceremony must include the statutory declaration using the contracting words that follow, or an alternative but essentially similar version, followed by the contracting words:

> *I do solemnly declare that I know not of any lawful impediment why I, ____ may not be joined in matrimony to ____, I call upon these persons here present to witness that I ____ do take thee ____ to be my lawful wedded husband/wife.*

The couple must then sign the register of marriages witnessed by two people.

Since 1 October 2012, the restriction on the times during which marriages could take place has been lifted for civil marriages (the Protection of Freedoms Act 2012, s 114 repeals the Marriage Act 1949, s 4). Now marriage may take place at any time.

Religious ceremonies

Where the parties wish to marry in a religious ceremony, different rules apply to different religious denominations. Each religious denomination has the right to refuse permission to a couple to marry in its own particular place of worship.

Marriage in the Anglican Church
Preliminary requirements
Because there is no separation of the Anglican Church and the State, Anglican clergy may deal with all the preliminary matters relating to marriage. Under the Marriage Act 1949, s 14 the publication of the marriage is made by publishing the banns of marriage on three successive Sundays during the church service. This allows for any objections to be made. There are two alternatives to the reading of the banns of marriage, use of a common licence which is the equivalent of the superintendent registrar's certificate or in very rare cases marriage under special licence which is a power exercised by the Archbishop of Canterbury who has extensive powers to authorise a marriage in any place at any time even where that place is unconsecrated.

The marriage ceremony
An Anglican priest may conduct the ceremony and formally register it. A couple have always had the right to be married in the parish church of a parish where one or both of them are resident or entered on the electoral roll. However, since October 2008, it is possible for those who wish to marry in the parish church of a parish with which one or both of them can demonstrate a 'qualifying connection'. A person has a qualifying connection with a parish if for instance that person:

■ was baptised in the parish; or had his or her confirmation entered in a church register book of a church or chapel in the parish; or has had his or her usual place of residence in the parish for at least six months.

There are several other qualifying connections which open up a marriage in an Anglican Church to a wider number of people.

■ The church may refuse to conduct a marriage where either of the parties has been divorced. The words of the marriage vows in the Anglican Church give some indication to the parties of what is expected of those who enter into a Christian marriage. In addition to the essential contracting words required by law, the couple also promise each other:

to have and to hold

from this day forward;

for better, for worse,

for richer, for poorer,

in sickness and in health,

to love and to cherish,

till death us do part.

Quaker and Jewish marriages

Quaker and Jewish marriages are not required to follow the rules for other religious denominations. The parties must fulfil the notification requirements, although in the case of Quaker marriage, notification is given to the Quaker authorities. Quaker and Jewish couples may marry wherever, and at whatever time they wish with the approval of their religious authorities. Approval will not be given for Jewish marriages to take place on Saturdays, the Jewish Sabbath or on Holy Days. Jewish and Quaker marriages do not have to be accessible to the public. The parties, in these religions, are regarded as performing the ceremony themselves; the ceremony, therefore, does not need to be conducted by a religious official or other approved person although such a person must be in attendance to register the marriage. These freedoms to conduct their own ceremonies derive from Lord Hardwicke's Marriage Act 1753.

Members of the Jewish faith and Quakers have never believed that a religious building is necessary to enable them to worship. They also have had an excellent reputation for record keeping and ensuring that anyone wishing to marry has the legal capacity to do so. It would seem that these long-standing historical facts are the major reasons for members of these religions having the right to marry in accordance with their beliefs. Jewish and Quaker marriages must be subsequently registered in the same way as a civil marriage.

Other religious marriages

Members of other religious denominations may marry in their place of worship if it has been registered for marriage ceremonies. Places of worship may be registered if the religion involves devotion to some form of deity. Many Catholic and Non-Conformist Christian religious ministers have registered their churches. Few Sikh, Hindu or Muslim places of worship have been registered.

Notification must be given to the registrar in advance, and a superintendent registrar must be present to register the marriage unless the religious minister has been authorised to perform the marriage ceremony.

Where their place of worship has not been registered, members of a religious denomination who wish to marry religiously will have to undergo two separate ceremonies, one in a registry office or other approved place, and one in their unregistered place of worship.

Marriages of the sick, the housebound or prisoners

The sick, housebound and prisoners may be married in hospital, at home or in prison, at any hour of the day or night, by licence of the Registrar General. They do not need to fulfil the requirements of notice.

Informal marriage

The concept of common law marriage has no validity

The expression common law marriage is frequently used in everyday speech to describe a couple who are not legally married but who live together and believe that they will be treated in the same way as legally married partners (see Law Com No 307 (2007) *Cohabitation: The Financial Consequences of Relationship Breakdown*, discussed later). In English law, the term has had no validity since 1753. If two people live together as if husband and wife, the same legal consequences do not flow from their relationship as would flow from a legally valid marriage. A significant number of people seem to believe that there is common law marriage and that it will give rise to similar rights as if they were formally married. The British Social Attitudes Survey of 2001 found that 56 per cent of people believed that unmarried partners definitely or probably had some rights (Barlow et al. 2001). Such attitudes continue to prevail 20 years later where results from the British Social Attitudes Survey carried out by the National Centre for Social Research in 2019 showed that 46 per cent of cohabiting couples were under the impression that cohabiting couples form a common law marriage which suggest they believe that rights will accrue from this status. Rebecca Probert charts the rise of the expression 'common law marriage' in her book *The Changing Legal Regulation of Cohabitation*. She writes of an increasing acceptance of people cohabiting together in the 1970s. She notes a move from using terms such as 'mistresses' and 'living in sin' towards 'cohabitation'. The term 'common law marriage' was adopted as a way of describing the relationship although such a term at the time was strictly a term describing an actual marriage celebrated overseas in unusual circumstances. She writes that by the end of the 1970s both cohabitants and the wider population began to believe that there were no legal differences between cohabitation and marriage (Probert 2012).

The Government became so concerned about this erroneous belief that in 2005, it funded the legal advice group, Living Together, to help eliminate the phrase 'common law marriage' and publicise the fact that it has no legal meaning. The findings from the British Social Attitudes survey suggest that this has not changed attitudes. Although married couples or those in a civil partnership still form the most common family form according to the ONS statistics cohabiting couples have been growing over the past five years. Between 1996 and 2021 the numbers of cohabiting couples rose from 1.5 million to 3.6 million which represents an increase of 144 per cent (see ONS 2021).

Presumption of marriage by cohabitation and repute

Where a marriage does not comply with the relevant formalities laid down by law, it may be rescued by the common law doctrine known as presumption of marriage by cohabitation and repute. Rayden and Jackson (1997) have explained that:

> *Where a man and woman have cohabited for such a length of time and in such circumstances, as to have acquired the reputation of being man and wife, a lawful marriage between them will be presumed [to have taken place], though there be no positive evidence of any marriage having taken place, particularly where the relevant facts have occurred outside the jurisdiction and this presumption can be rebutted only by strong and weighty evidence.*

The doctrine is based on the idea that it is conceivable that the documents recording the marriage might have been lost or indeed, the marriage may not have been documented in the first place. It is of particular importance to those who have always assumed that they were validly married outside the jurisdiction, and who would risk losing legal benefits which are only available to married persons. Caroline Bridge (2001) has suggested that:

> It is clear that the interests of a culturally diverse population in the UK require that a long-standing marriage should not be lightly struck down for want of compliance with the formalities of local law relied on many years later.

The following two decisions illustrate her point.

In *Pazpena De Vire v Pazpena De Vire* [2001] 1 FLR 460, a woman of German origin sought a decree of divorce. She maintained that she had been married for 35 years to an Argentinean-born man. There was no direct evidence of a marriage having taken place. The petitioner claimed that she and the respondent had used a proxy to whom they had granted a special power of attorney to contract the marriage for them in Uruguay. She had obtained an Argentinian passport on the strength of being married and had given birth to the respondent's child. The respondent denied that there was a valid marriage; he maintained that he himself had procured a fraudulent marriage certificate and that there was no other record of the marriage. His claims were backed up by strong expert evidence that the certificate might be fraudulent.

However, the court held that there was insufficient evidence to rebut the strong presumption of marriage arising from a long period of cohabitation as husband and wife and public recognition of them as such. Even if the certificate were a forgery, that did not prove that there had been no later ceremony. The petitioner was, therefore, held to have been validly married and entitled to seek a petition of divorce.

The woman, in *A-M v A-M* [2001] 2 FLR 6, sought to divorce, or obtain a decree of nullity from, her husband. She alleged that they were validly married, although there was no evidence of such a marriage. The couple were Middle Eastern Muslims. They had undergone a ceremony of marriage in London in a private home, intending it to be a formal Islamic marriage. The wife subsequently learned that the marriage was not valid under English law. She was advised that she should seek to validate it by marrying in a country which permitted polygamy. The couple went to Sharjah but were unable to regularise their status there. They would have had to obtain an Islamic divorce first in order to marry and this would not have been permissible under Islamic law merely to enable them to marry each other again in order to satisfy the demands of an overseas jurisdiction. They returned to England, had children and regarded themselves, and were regarded by others, as married. The wife became a British citizen and acquired a British domicile prior to the breakdown of the relationship.

The court held that there was a presumption of a valid marriage on the basis of cohabitation and repute; only strong and weighty evidence to the contrary would take that presumption away. The presumption was stronger in circumstances such as here, because the marriage presumed to have taken place could have taken place with minimal formality. A valid polygamous marriage could have been contracted in an Islamic country without a public ceremony and in the absence of the wife if she had signed a power of attorney.

Although there was no firm evidence that she had done so, she did frequently sign documents for her husband and it was conceivable that one of these had been a power of attorney.

The decision in *A-M v A-M* (2001) 2 FLR 6 was a most liberal interpretation of the doctrine of presumption of marriage by cohabitation and repute.

Today the doctrine seems to be applied more restrictively by the courts. The most recent decisions depend more on the extent to which the formalities of marriage have been ignored than on the contentions of the parties

In *Martin v Myers* [2004] EWHC 1543, the inheritance rights of the daughters of a deceased couple depended on their parents' having unmarried status. The inheritance rights of the remaining members of the family depended on the parents' having married status. The parents had cohabited for some 50 years and had seven children. The mother was always vague about her marital status, but all the family had always assumed that their parents were married until after their death when the inheritance issue arose, although on one occasion, when she was in her late 70s and ill in hospital, the mother had briefly suggested to one of her daughters that she and the daughters' father had never been married because they had been unable to afford to do so.

The court held that there could be no presumption of marriage because there was no reasonable doubt that they were not married. The mother herself had cast doubt on the presumption; the register of marriages had been searched and it was unlikely that an error had been made in the register. The couple had always been poor and never travelled, and the possibility of a marriage out of the jurisdiction was remote. The court pointed out that most of the authorities on presumption of marriage either predate the system of registration of marriages or relate to parties who may have been married abroad. The absence of a certificate is strong evidence to refute the presumption, unless marriage abroad is a real possibility.

In *Al-Saedy v Musawawi (Presumption of Marriage)* [2010] 2 FLR 287, the couple, although born in Iraq, were UK citizens and practising Muslims. The woman maintained that they had married in Damascus, a fact denied by the man. She also claimed that the presumption of marriage should be applied. The court rejected both claims, the former on the basis that there had been no ceremony in Damascus and the latter on the basis that there was insufficient evidence that the couple had actually cohabited and had held themselves out to be husband and wife.

It is important to distinguish between those marriages that can be found to be void under the Marriage Act 1949 and the Matrimonial Causes Act 1973 because some rights may flow from the failed marriage. If the court finds that it is a 'non-marriage' or 'non-existent marriage' or as better described today a 'non-qualifying ceremony' then no rights will flow. It cannot be void because the non-compliance goes to the very heart of the marriage ceremony. There are countless scenes in theatrical productions where the parties purport to get married but these scenes could never be considered valid marriages but merely 'non-qualifying ceremonies'. As the consequences are so significant it has proved challenging in the courts to distinguish between the two.

In *Hudson v Leigh (Status of Non-Marriage)* [2009] EWHC 1306 (Fam), a couple married in South Africa in the husband's home. Miss Hudson was a devout Christian whereas Mr Leigh was in his own words an atheist Jew. They planned a civil ceremony on their return to the UK. The ceremony in South Africa included words of a marriage ceremony, but key parts were omitted such as 'your lawful wife' and 'your lawful husband' and perhaps most significantly of all 'have been lawfully married by this ceremony'. The relationship broke down before the civil ceremony could take place, and the wife claimed financial provision. She had no right to do so if the ceremony was found to be a non-qualifying ceremony. She argued that the ceremony had failed to comply with certain formalities and so was void under the Marriage Act 1949. Bodey J reviewed the law on non-qualifying ceremonies and laid down four factors to be considered by the court in these cases:

a.   whether the ceremony or event set out or purported to be a lawful marriage;
b.   whether it bore all or enough of the hallmarks of marriage;
c.   whether the three key participants (most especially the officiating official) believed, intended and understood the ceremony as giving rise to the status of lawful marriage; and
d.   the reasonable perceptions, understandings and beliefs of those in attendance.

The list was not intended to be a definition of what constitutes a non-qualifying ceremony but guidance for future cases. These were applied to an Islamic wedding ceremony held in a flat which the wife believed to be a valid marriage but had failed to comply with fundamental aspects of the Marriage Act 1949 (*El Gamal v Al Maktoum* [2012] 2 FLR 387). In applying his own principles from *Leigh* Bodey J held the marriage to be a non-qualifying ceremony.

Chris Bevan observed that there was an emergent hierarchy in the factors to be considered in non-marriage cases as laid down by Bodey J in *Hudson v Leigh* with the parties' intentions playing a less significant role (Bevan 2013).

The complexities of this area of law are highlighted in the recent decision of the Court of Appeal in *Attorney-General v Akhter and Khan* [2020] EWCA Civ 122. The parties underwent a Muslim marriage ceremony in a restaurant in 1998 in London. They were both fully aware that this ceremony would not be regarded as a valid marriage. They had been advised by the imam that a civil ceremony was needed in order for their marriage to be recognised. After being together for 18 years and having had four children the relationship broke down and the wife brought a nullity petition on the basis that the marriage was void due to non-compliance with the formalities. The husband argued that there had been no marriage. At first instance Williams J found in favour of the wife and held that the marriage was void. His reasoning was based partly on Articles 8 and 12 of the ECHR and also that the ceremony bore all the hallmarks of a marriage such as witnesses, taken by an imam and also making of promises and confirmation that the parties were free to marry. In finding these key features of a marriage ceremony applying the principles of Bodey J from *Hudson v Leigh* he thought it closer to a void marriage than a non-qualifying ceremony. Applying Articles 8 and 12 of the ECHR he held that family life and marriage should be protected and so the fact that they had a ceremony with some of the features of a marriage should not be disregarded. In making this decision he acknowledged that he was taking a flexible approach and he must have had some sympathy with the wife who after a relationship of 18 years would have no rights to claim financial provision unless it was declared a void marriage.

The Court of Appeal unanimously held that this was a non-qualifying ceremony (preferring to use this as opposed to the term 'non-marriage') and found against the petitioner. It found that the Islamic ceremony fell far short of the formalities necessary to comply with the Marriage Act 1949. The parties knew that the ceremony did not comply with the formalities and that the defects were numerous including the fact that the building was not registered as a venue for marriages, nor was the imam registered to take marriages, no notice had been given to the superintendent registrar, no authorised person was present. Both parties knew that they needed to have a civil ceremony. The human rights arguments were rejected. The right to marry had not be violated since the parties had not married and neither had the right to family life been violated by the failure to uphold the Islamic marriage.

Non-qualifying marriages (also referred to as non-marriages) and void marriages

The divergence of the various cases on void and non-qualifying marriages has attracted considerable criticism particularly in relation to the court's approach to Islamic marriages (Probert 2018; O'Sullivan and Jackson 2017; Fiona Read 2012). The decision in *Akhter* shows that the formalities with regard to marriage are long overdue for reform. The very fact that the parties entered into a ceremony suggests that they felt that some weight was accorded to this rather than simply entering into cohabitation. The research of Rajnaara Akhter into Muslim attitudes to marriage were such that couples may be aware that the ceremony held did not comply with the required formalities but had simply failed to arrange a civil ceremony, whilst others did not realise that a civil ceremony was needed (Akhter 2015). Zainab Naqvi suggests that a way forward would be to recognise all Muslim monogamous marriages unless couples took the decision to opt out (Akhter et al. 2020).

The Law Commission recommendations in *Getting Married: A Consultation on Wedding Law* 2020 would address many of the issues that have arisen in the cases on non-qualifying ceremonies. It recognises that under the present law different rules apply to different religious groups so that Anglican, Quaker and Jewish marriages are treated differently to Muslim marriages which can cause unnecessary confusion. According to the Law Commission the current system 'is complicated, inconsistent, inefficient, unfair and needlessly restrictive'. The recommendations are such that the emphasis will be taken from the location of the ceremony and placed on the officiant. In the future, a non-qualifying ceremony will only occur where either or both the parties do not comply with the online registration process and the parties are both aware that the officiant does not have the authority to conduct marriages or where the marriage is a religious same-sex wedding and the relevant authority has not opted in to conduct same-sex weddings. It will also be a non-qualifying ceremony if the parties do not consent to the marriage as part of the ceremony and they do not sign the marriage document. These reforms combined with the other proposals bringing much of the formalities of marriage online would simplify the current framework, and it is envisaged that far fewer ceremonies would give rise to doubt.

Civil partners

In 2004, the CPA 2004 was enacted to allow same-sex partners to formalise their relationships by means of a registration process.

Because of the cultural and religious connotations of marriage, the Government had sought to achieve a compromise between those who were opposed to same-sex marriage and those who believed that marriage should be extended to same-sex partners. Although the Labour Government, which enacted the civil partnership legislation, refuted strongly the idea that civil partnership is equivalent to same-sex marriage, it was unable to give any satisfactory explanation as to how it differs from marriage; the explanations given lack any credibility. For instance the Government's Women and Equality Unit (now called the Equalities Hub) explained that:

> *Civil Partnership is a completely new legal relationship, exclusively for same-sex couples, distinct from marriage.*
>
> *The Government has sought to give civil partners parity of treatment with spouses, as far as is possible, in the rights and responsibilities that flow from forming a civil partnership.*
>
> *There are a small number of differences between civil partnership and marriage, for example, a civil partnership is formed when the second civil partner signs the relevant document, a civil marriage is formed when the couple exchange spoken words. Opposite-sex couples can opt for a religious or civil marriage ceremony as they choose, whereas formation of a civil partnership will be an exclusively civil procedure.*
>
> (Women and Equality Unit, 2005)

In spite of these protestations, the provisions of the CPA 2004 are remarkably similar to the law relating to married partners. Civil partnership is regularly referred to by the media and the general public as gay marriage. When the singer Elton John and his partner, David Furnish, registered their civil partnership in December 2005 soon after the CPA 2004 came into force, the media referred to it as the couple's wedding.

Somewhat surprisingly, even in 2009, the Law Commission, in its Consultation Paper (No 191), *Intestacy and Family Provision Claims on Death*, also chose to use the term spouse with reference to both a married partner and a civil partner.

Capacity to register a civil partnership (CPA 2004, ss 3, 4)

Until 2019 the parties to a civil partnership had to be of the same sex. For some years the Government refused to extend the provisions to heterosexual cohabitants maintaining that marriage was open to this group and, therefore, civil partnership was unnecessary for them. During the passage of the Civil Partnership Bill through Parliament, attempts were made to amend the Bill to allow family members of whatever sexual persuasion, who live together in non-sexual caring relationships, to enjoy the benefits of civil partnership. These attempts were almost certainly based on a desire by those, opposed to the legislation, to prevent its enactment, and the Government successfully resisted them. It argued that the amendment would create particular difficulties relating to property and inheritance between family members, and that problems relating to ancillary relief would arise if a civil partner, who later decided to marry, had first to terminate the partnership with the family member.

Under the Civil Partnerships, Marriage and Deaths (Registration etc) Act 2019 opposite sex couples are now allowed to enter into civil partnerships. This was largely in response to the decision in the case of *R (on the application of Steinfeld and Keidan) v Secretary of State for International Development* [2018] UKSC 32. Rebecca Steinfeld and Charles Keidan were an unmarried couple who applied to enter into a civil partnership. Their application was refused by the registrars because the parties were not of the same sex. The couple had strong views about marriage, believing that it was outdated and patriarchal institution. The couple brought a case against the Government arguing that the fact that they could not enter a civil partnership was a breach of their Article 8 rights to respect for their private and family life, as well as a breach of Article 14 the right to freedom of discrimination. Their application was refused at first instance and in the Court of Appeal but was upheld by the Supreme Court. It accepted that restricting civil partnership to same-sex couples was incompatible with both Articles 8 and 14. The Government had argued that it had not been clear whether civil partnership would be used by couples and so the Government wanted to evaluate the position before opening it up to opposite sex couples. Lord Kerr gave the sole judgment. In commenting on the argument of the Government he said:

> this does not derogate from the central finding that taking time to evaluate whether to abolish or extend could never amount to a legitimate aim for the continuance of the discrimination. The legitimate aim must be connected to the justification for discrimination and, plainly, time for evaluation does not sound on that. It cannot be a legitimate aim for continuing to discriminate.

As a result of this decision and pressure from interested groups civil partnerships were opened up to opposite sex couples in 2019. Today there is a question as to whether civil partnerships remain relevant where marriage is now available to both same-sex and opposite sex couples. (See Hayward and Fenwick 2018.) There are valid arguments that civil partnerships depend on compliance with rigid formalities so civil partnerships do not present couples with a simple alternative to marriage. (See Miles and Probert 2019.) If the proposed reform of the formalities of marriage are adopted perhaps there will be a greater appetite for marriage amongst couples who wish to formalise their relationship.

Age

In line with the raising of the minimum age for marriage, civil partners must have attained the age of 18.

Under The Marriage and Civil Partnership (Minimum Age) Act 2022 which came into effect in February 2023, no one under the age of 18 may enter into a civil partnership.

PROHIBITED DEGREES OF RELATIONSHIP

It is forbidden for a person to register a civil partnership with anyone who is within the prohibited degrees of relationship to him or her. CPA 2004, Sch 1, Part 1 lists those relatives who may not register a civil partnership. It divides them into absolute prohibitions (s 1(1)) and qualified prohibitions (s 2(1), (2), (3)).

Absolute prohibitions

A person may not register a civil partnership with his or her:

- adoptive child;
- adoptive parent;
- child;
- former adoptive child;
- former adoptive parent;
- grandparent;
- grandchild;
- parent;
- parent's sibling;
- sibling or half-sibling;
- sibling's or half-sibling's child.

Qualified prohibitions

A person may not register a civil partnership with any of the following unless:

> both of them have reached 21 years of age at the time when they register as civil partners of each other, and
> the younger has not at any time before reaching the age of 18 been a child of the family in relation to the other. CPA 2004, Sch 1, Part 1, para 2(2) defines a child of the family as a person who (i) has lived in the same household as that other person, and (ii) has been treated by that other person as a child of his family):

- a child of a former civil partner;
- a child of a former spouse;

- a former civil partner of a grandparent;
- a former civil partner of a parent;
- a former spouse of a grandparent;
- a former spouse of a parent;
- a grandchild of a former civil partner;
- a grandchild of a former spouse.

The absolute prohibitions reflect the determination of the Government not to extend the status of civil partnerships to those who are members of each other's family of origin.

Already a civil partner or married

A person who is already a civil partner or who is married may not register a civil partnership without first legally ending the existing relationship (see Chapter 6).

Mental capacity

In order to register a civil partnership, a person must understand the nature of the relationship and its consequences. It is presumed that the decisions relating to mental capacity to marry will be equally applicable to civil partners.

Formalities of civil partnership

The formalities are laid down in CPA 2004, ss 5–27 and are not dissimilar to those relating to marriage. Notice must be given 29 days in advance except where either party is seriously ill and may not survive. This is in line with the longer period of notice necessary for marriage which was raised as a result of concern over the rise in the number of 'sham' marriages (CPA 2004 as amended by the Immigration Act 2014). The information relating to a proposed registration must be made public in order that anyone may object on the grounds that the couple are not eligible to register a civil partnership.

Registration must take place in offices provided by a local authority, or in premises licensed by it for the registration of civil partnerships. Since 1 October 2012, there are no longer any restrictions on the timing of the ceremony (see the Protection of Freedoms Act 2012, s 114 which amends the Civil Partnership Act 2004, s 17(2) and repeals s 31(2)). The original idea of registration was that it would merely involve the parties signing a document.

As a result of s 202 of the Equalities Act 2010 and the Marriage and Civil Partnerships (Approved Premises) (Amendment) Regulations 2011 civil partnerships are no longer restricted to secular settings but now can take place in religious premises.

Although it is the choice of religious organisations as to whether they choose to hold civil partnerships, the partnership is totally dependent on registration. No specific words are necessary for the ceremony such as the exchange of vows in marriage. It is possible that a civil partnership could be regarded as void or voidable as a result of defects such as being under age or within the prohibited degrees. There are some differences with marriage, but the two remain distinct. Civil partnerships cannot be declared void as a result of non-consummation or venereal disease. These omissions are strange and suggest that when passing the legislation the Government did not consider a civil partnership as a sexual relationship. It is as if sexual relations which do not result in the procreation of children is less significant (see Crompton 2013). However, there was no attempt to change these rules when civil partnerships were opened up to opposite sex couples.

Cohabitation

The final category of relationship to be considered in this chapter is heterosexual and same-sex cohabitation. It remains a very popular family unit, and yet over the centuries it has had little legal recognition. Very few rights arise even where the length of the relationship has been long lasting and there are children. Although society has moved from disapproval of the relationship to acceptance it falls short of recognition. No property rights arise, and this is particularly stark in relation to the family home. The law largely ignores cohabitants so a person may cohabit within the prohibited degrees of relationship subject, of course, to the criminal law relating to under-age sexual relationships and incest.

Cohabiting partnerships do not bring about relationships of affinity; thus, a child of one cohabitant may marry his or her parent's partner although such a relationship is almost certain to cause family jealousies. An example from another jurisdiction is provided by the marriage of Woody Allen, the New York film director and actor, to Soon-Yi Previn, the adopted daughter of his long-term partner, Mia Farrow, and her ex-husband, Andre Previn.

Societal views vary on whether cohabiting relationships should be brought within a similar legal framework to that applicable to married couples and civil partners. During the passage of the Civil Partnership Bill through Parliament, the issue of according legal rights to cohabitants was debated. The Government took the view that heterosexual cohabitants did not require the protection of the CPA 2004 because they already had the right to marry, and same-sex cohabitants would, as a result of the CPA 2004, be given similar rights.

This approach ignores the fact that cohabitants do not belong to a heterogeneous group. There are heterosexual cohabitants who are unable to marry because one of them is already married and unwilling or unable to divorce. A minority group of cohabitants involves couples who have married in informal Islamic ceremonies in the UK, or have married polygamously in countries where that is permissible but did not have the capacity to do so in accordance with English law. Their marriages are void, and the parties only have the status of cohabitants. They may not realise that that is so until legal issues relating to marital status arise. Some cohabitants do not wish to marry or enter into a civil partnership because of the social, cultural and political significance attached to those relationships and would resent any possibility of State interference into a status which they have deliberately chosen for themselves. Other cohabitants, both heterosexual and of the same sex, may be contemplating formalising their relationships but may not yet be ready to do so. There are also those cohabitants who simply suffer from inertia and fail to marry or register a civil partnership. All of these groups may be unaware of the problematic consequences of informal relationships until they find themselves in a situation where they are denied rights, which are solely the prerogative of married couples or civil partners. This tends to occur at the end of a relationship.

It is difficult to produce accurate figures relating to cohabitation. According to The Office for National Statistics, the proportion of people living together and not married or in a civil partnership (both same-sex and opposite couples) had increased significantly from 20.6 per cent in 2011 to 24.3 per cent in 2021 (ONS 2020).

Such information, whilst helpful, does not give a complete picture. At what point in a relationship is a couple prepared to admit to cohabitation and convey that information on a census form? Couples vary in their perceptions of what constitutes cohabitation and when it begins. Some couples regard themselves as cohabitating although each retains a home of their own and they visit regularly. For other couples, cohabitation dates from the time one moves into the home of the other or when they acquire a new joint residence. For a further group cohabitation is determined when they have children. There are couples who claim to be married because they are indeed married but not to the person with whom they are cohabiting. Other couples do not admit to cohabiting because they wish to keep their status private, and some describe themselves as married because they actually believe that after a long period of cohabitation they have acquired the status of common law spouses; they are unaware that such a status no longer exists. It is likely therefore that the figure from the Office for National Statistics is an underestimate. It means that nearly a quarter of all people are living in a relationship that has no legal status and those in the relationship have very few rights. The granting of rights to cohabitants has been a contentious issue over many years.

In 2007, the Law Commission proposed a complex scheme of financial relief for cohabitants (*Cohabitation: The Financial Consequences of Relationship Breakdown*, Law Com No 307). It maintained on the basis of the statistical information available at that time that:

> *Cohabitation is therefore already a significant social practice. It is growing, and continued growth is forecast. This is, of course, not in itself a reason for law reform. But if it is accepted that the current law is inadequate and gives rise to unwelcome consequences, the fact that these consequences potentially affect a significant and increasing proportion of the population is highly relevant. The issues considered in this paper are therefore not issues that will go away. We urge Government to take the necessary steps to provide this increasingly significant section of society with legal remedies capable of dealing fairly with the financial consequences should they separate.*

In response to the Law Commission recommendations the Justice Minister, Jonathan Djanogly, in a written statement in September 2011, said that the Government had considered the Law Commission's report and the research which had been undertaken into the operation of the Family Law (Scotland) Act 2006, and had not found a 'sufficient basis' to enact new legislation. The Law Commissioner responsible for the proposals for reform, Elizabeth Cooke, immediately expressed the hope that reform would take place in the early days of the next Parliament

> *in view of the hardship and injustice caused by the current law. The prevalence of cohabitation, and of the birth of children to couples who live together, means that the need for reform of the law can only become more pressing over time.*

It was the second time in five years that the Law Commission had considered the vexed issue of cohabitation. In 2002, it also argued that:

> *the current law is inadequate and gives rise to unwelcome consequences, the fact that these consequences potentially affect a significant and increasing proportion of the population is highly relevant. The issues considered in this paper are therefore not issues that will go away. We urge Government to take the necessary steps to provide this increasingly significant section of society with legal remedies capable of dealing fairly with the financial consequences should they separate . . . We believe that further consideration should be given to the adoption, necessarily by legislation, of new legal approaches to personal relationships outside marriage, following the lead given by other jurisdictions (such as France, Australia and New Zealand).*
>
> *These approaches may include such mechanisms as the formal registration of civil partnerships, or less formally, a power for the court to adjust the legal rights and obligations of individuals who are or have been living together for a defined period or in defined circumstances.*
>
> (*Sharing Homes: A Discussion Paper* (2002)
> Law Com No 278)

Reform of the current law still seems unlikely. Since the lack of action on the Law Commission recommendations there have been a number of attempts at reform. Several Private Members' Bills have been introduced, the most recent Lord Marks' Cohabitation Rights Bill in 2020 which had a first reading but was affected by the Covid pandemic.

In 2022, a report was published by the Women and Equalities Committee on the question of the rights of cohabiting partners. In their report they noted the amendment virtual doubling of the numbers of couples cohabiting between 1996 and 2021, observing that cohabitants receive inferior protections to married couples and civil partners. The report added:

> *Notwithstanding the legal reality, many people believe in the so-called 'common law marriage myth', which is the erroneous belief that after a certain amount of time of living together, the law treats cohabitants as if they were married. On family breakdown, cohabitants must rely on complex property law and trusts principles. . . . The lack of legal protection on family breakdown means that women, including women from an ethnic minority background and those who have had a religious-only wedding, can suffer relationship-generated disadvantage. It is time the law adapted to the social reality of modern relationships while still recognising the social and religious status of marriage.*
>
> (Women and Equalities Commission)

The committee called on Parliament to revisit the Law Commission recommendations of 2007 and update where necessary and implement them.

The range of rights that need addressing include financial rights and rights in the family home as well as rights on intestacy and succession. On intestacy a spouse will automatically inherit rights in the estate, whereas a cohabitant can only claim rights under the Inheritance (Provision for Family and Dependants) Act 1975 which will involve expensive court proceedings and no guarantee of rights. It remains to be seen whether any future Government will add cohabitants rights to its programme of legislation, but reform is clearly long overdue.

Self-test questions

1. In view of the dwindling numbers of couples who choose to marry, has marriage outlived its usefulness as a legal relationship? If so, should it be replaced and if so what do you consider to be a suitable alternative?

2. Revisit the case of What in your view makes a marriage ceremony a 'non-qualifying ceremony'?

3. Why should relationships involving siblings, adult children and their parents, or other types of blood relationships, be excluded from the law relating to civil partnerships?

4. Would you wish to attempt to change the Government's view that it should not legislate to give cohabitants greater legal rights? Explain the reasons for your decision.

References

Akhtar, Rainaara C, 'Unregistered Muslim Marriages: An Emerging Culture of Celebratory Rites and Conceding Rites' in Joanna Miles, Perveez Mody and Rebecca Probert (eds) *Marriage Rites and Rights* (Bloomsbury 2015)

Bevan, Chris, 'The Role of Intention in Non-Marriage Cases Post *Hudson v Leigh*' (2013) 25 *Child and Family Law Quarterly* 80

Bridge, Caroline, 'Case Comment on *Pazpena de Vire*' [2001] *Family Law* 96

Chambers, Clare, *Against Marriage: An Egalitarian Defence of the Marriage Free State* (Oxford University Press 2017)

Chapman Samuel, [1991] 'Polygamy, Bigamy, Human Rights Law' *XLibris Corporation*

Cowan, Sharon, 'That Woman Is a Woman! The Case of Bellinger v Bellinger and the Mysterious Disappearance of Sex' [2004] *Feminist Legal Studies* 79

Dempsey, Brian, '*Burden v UK*: "Dissin" Lesbians or Decentring Marriage' [2009] *Family Law* 35

Gov.UK 'Judiciary.uk/Gender Recognition Panel'. www.gov.uk/apply-gender-recognition-certificate/how-to apply accessed 9 September 2024

The Guardian, 'Serial Bigamist With Five "Husbands" Spared Jail' (27.07.2009) www.theguardian.com/uk/2009/jul/27/serial-bigamist-emily-horne

Hayward, Andy and Helen Fenwick, 'From Same-Sex Marriage to Equal Civil Partnerships: On a Path Towards "Perfecting" Equality?' [2018] *Child and Family Law Quarterly* 30

Law Commission Getting Married: A Consultation Paper on Weddings Law (Law Com No 247, 2020)

Maer, Lucinda, 'Royal Marriages-Constitutional Issues SN/PC/034172' (2008) www.parliament. uk/documents/commons/lib/research/briefings/snpc-03417.pdf

Miles, Joanna and Rebecca Probert, 'Civil Partnership: Ties That (Also) Bind?' (2019) 31 *Child and Family Law Quarterly* 303

Naqvi, Zainab, 'At the Margins: Nikah Ceremonies in the UK – a Tool for Empowerment?' in Rajnaara Akhtar, Patrick Nash and Rebecca Probert (eds) *Cohabitation and Religious Marriage: Status, Similarities and Solutions* (Bristol University Press 2020)

O'Donovan, Katherine, 'Marriage: A Sacred or Profane Love Machine?' (1993) 1(1) *Feminist Legal Studies* 75

ONS, 'People's Living Arrangements in England and Wales: Census 2021' (2020) www.ons.gov. uk/peoplepopulationandcommunity/householdcharacteristics/homeinternet andsocialmediausage/articles/livingarrangementsofpeopleinenglandandwales/census2021

ONS, 'Marriages in England and Wales: 2021 and 2022' (2021) www.ons.gov.uk/ peoplepopulationandcommunity/birthsdeathsandmarriages/marriagecohabitationandcivil partnerships/bulletins/marriagesinenglandandwalesprovisional/2021and2022

O'Sullivan, Kathryn and Leyla Jackson, 'Muslim Marriage (Non) Recognition: Implications and Possible Solutions' (2017) 39(1) *Journal of Social Welfare and Family Law* 22

Outhwaite, RB (Brian), *Clandestine Marriage in England 1500–1850* (Hambledon Press 1992)

Probert, Rebecca, 'Common-Law Wives': The Creation of the Myth, 1973–1979' in *The Changing Legal Regulation of Cohabitation: From Fornicators to Family 1600–2010* (Cambridge University Press 2012)

Probert, Rebecca, 'The Presumptions of Marriage' (2018) 77 *Cambridge Law Journal* 77

Rayden, William and Joseph Jackson, *Law and Practice in Divorce and Family Matters* (Butterworths, 1997)

Read, Fiona, 'Non – Recognition of Islamic Marriages in England and Wales' [2012] *International Family Law* 452

Smart, Carol, *The Ties that Bind: Law and the Reproduction of Patriarchial Relations* (Routledge 1984)

Women and Equalities Commission https://commons/committees.parliament.uk/publications/ 23321/170094

Women and Equalities Unit www.womenandequalityunit.gov.uk/lgbt/faq.htm 2005

Further reading

Barker, Nicola, 'Civil Partnership: An Alternative to Marriage? *Ferguson and Others v UK*' (2012) *Family Law* 548 http://equallove.org.uk/the-legal-case/

Barlow, Anne, Carole Burgoyne, Elizabeth Clery and Janet Smithson, 'Cohabitation and the Law: Myths, Money and the Media' [2008] *British Social Attitudes* 29

Barlow, Anne and Grace James, 'Regulating Marriage and Cohabitation in 21st Century Britain' [2004] *Child and Family Law Quarterly* 2

Bull, Linzi, 'Cohabitation Outcomes After the Law Commission Report' [2008] *Family Law* 56

Celebrating Marriage: A New Weddings Law (Law Com 408 2022)

Crompton, Lucy, 'Civil Partnerships Bill 2004: The Illusion of Equality' [2004] *Family Law* 88

Cummings, Tristan, 'Equality as a Central Principle? The Law Commission's Solution to the Religious-Only Marriage Problem' [2021] *Child and Family Law Quarterly* 63

Cummings, Tristan, 'Gendered Dimensions and Missed Opportunities in *Akhter v Khan (Attorney-General and Others Intervening)*' (2020) 32 *Child and Family Law Quarterly* 239

Curry-Sumner, Ian, 'European Recognition of Same-sex Relationships: We Need Action Now' [2008] *International Family Law* 102

Family Justice Council, 'Cohabitation Concerns' [2009] *Family Law* 567

Gay, Oonagh and Lucinda Maer, 'Royal Marriages-Constitutional Issues SN/PC/034172' (December 2008) www.parliament.uk/documents/commons/lib/research/briefings/snpc-03417.pdf

Hale, B (Baroness Hale of Richmond), 'Unmarried Couples in Family Law' [2004] *Family Law* 419

Hansard HL Deb 24 June 2003 Vol 662 Cols 1368–1369

Hess, Edward, 'The Rights of Cohabitants and How Will the Law be Reformed' [2009] *Family Law* 405

Home Office Consultation on Same-Sex Couples and Civil Marriage (March 2012) www. homeoffice.gov.uk

Law Commission, 'Cohabitation: The Financial Consequences of Relationship Breakdown' (Law Com No 307)

Law Commission, 'Intestacy and Family Provision Claims on Death' (Consultation Paper No 191)

Law Commission, 'Sharing Homes, a Discussion Paper' (Law Com No 278, 2002) www.ons.gov. uk/peoplepopulationandcommunity/birthsdeathsandmarriages/families/bulletins/familie sandhouseholds/2020 www.publications.parliament.uk/pa/cm5803/cmselect/cmwomeq/ 92/summary.html

Probert, Rebecca, 'The Evolution of the Common Law Marriage Myth' [2011] *Family* Law 283

Probert, Rebecca, 'Lord Hardwicke's Marriage Act: Vital Change 250 Years on' 34 (2004) *Family Law* 583–589

Probert, Rebecca, Marriage, Law *and* Practice in the Long Eighteenth Century (Cambridge University Press 2009)

Probert, Rebecca, 'Why Couples Still Believe in Common-Law Marriage' [2011] *Family Law* 403

Probert, Rebecca and S Saleem, 'The Legal Treatment of Islamic Marriage Ceremonies' (2018) 7 *Oxford Journal of Law and Religion* 376

Ruth Deech Gresham Lectures (2010) www.gresham.ac.uk

Ruth, Gaffney-Rhys, 'Siblings and Civil Partnerships' [2007] *International Family Law Journal* 84

Scotland Cohabitation Research http:/www.crfr.ac.uk/researchproject/rp_cohabitation.html

Sham Marriages, *Family Migration: A Consultation* (UK Home Office 2011)

Welstead, Mary, 'Invitation to a Marriage: A Canadian Perspective' [2004] *Journal of Social Welfare and Family Law* 161

Welstead, Mary, 'Vulnerable Adults: The Inherent Jurisdiction and the Right to Marry: Re SA (Vulnerable Adult with Capacity: Marriage)' [2007] *Denning Law Journal* 259

3

Nullity and its consequences

SUMMARY

A couple may participate in a ceremony of marriage, or register a civil partnership, yet not acquire the status of spouse or civil partner because they failed to meet one or more of the requirements. Although their relationship may be judged to be a nullity, it may still have legal consequences. The law lays down quite strict rules as to what is considered to be a valid marriage ceremony. Recently such rules have been relaxed, allowing ceremonies in various settings to be regarded as marriage ceremonies but for many the rules are still fairly rigid and as a consequence their ceremony may fail to reach the standard required. The Law Commission recently recommended quite drastic reforms which would revolutionise the rules on what constitutes a valid marriage ceremony. At the time of writing these rules have not been adopted.

In this chapter we consider the law relating to nullity and its consequences. The law divides null relationships into two categories: those which are void and those which are voidable. We examine the differences between these two categories of relationships; we also draw attention to the nebulous concept of 'non-marriage' or 'non-qualifying ceremonies' which falls totally outside the ambit of the law of nullity and has no legal consequences. Inevitably, there will be an overlap with Chapter 2 and reference should be made to that chapter particularly with reference to the formalities of marriage.

This chapter is primarily concerned with marital relationships rather than civil partnerships because nullity in the case of the latter relationships has been a rare phenomenon to date.

Nullity: an important concept

For the majority of couples, the law relating to nullity of relationships is far less important today. Divorce has become more socially acceptable and, for the most part, decrees of divorce or orders for the dissolution of civil partnerships are easily

DOI: 10.4324/9781003435020-3

obtainable. It is likely to be even less important with the introduction of the Divorce, Separation and Dissolution Act 2020.

There are many, including family lawyers, who regard the concept of nullity as unnecessary, and have recommended its abolition.

The doctrine of nullity, however, cannot be discarded quite so readily. The most important reason for its retention for both spouses and civil partners is because of the contractual nature of their relationships. All contracts must satisfy certain legal requirements if they are to be valid. If the parties to a relationship are contracting with each other to enter into the new status of spouse or civil partner with legal responsibilities and legal rewards, a failure to comply with the essential contractual requirements would deny them that status.

Whilst many partners may not care whether a purported contract is declared to be at an end by either a decree of divorce, an order for the dissolution of a civil partnership, or a decree or order of nullity, others do. There are, for instance, those who for religious, cultural or social reasons would be unable to enter into a new relationship unless they were able to end their current relationship by way of a decree or order of nullity (it is unlikely that members of these groups are civil partners). Some of these partners will, of course, seek to have their relationships annulled by their religious authorities, but such declarations of nullity have no legal force if the couple were married under English law. They must also seek a decree of nullity from the civil courts if they wish to remarry in the jurisdiction of England and Wales.

More recently, the importance of nullity has proven to be a very useful remedy for those who have been forced into marriage (see later in this chapter and Chapter 5).

The Law Commission reviewed the law in 1970 (*Nullity of Marriage*, Law Com No 33) and has no further plans to reconsider the topic.

Its recommendations were incorporated into the Matrimonial Causes Act 1973 (MCA 1973) ss 11–16 which governs the law relating to nullity for opposite sex couples and since the introduction of Marriage (Same Sex Couples) Act in 2013 nullity for same-sex couples although the grounds differ slightly. The Civil Partnership Act 2004 ss 37, 49–53 makes similar provision for same-sex couples and now includes opposite sex also.

The separate categories of void and voidable relationships remain and, for the most part, no satisfactory explanations exist, other than historic ones, for this distinction.

Void or voidable relationships

Historically, marriage was under the jurisdiction of the ecclesiastical courts and so it was the church that could award a decree of nullity. Marriage was not the concern of the State. The judges in the ecclesiastical courts were concerned to administer law in a manner which would guard the sexual morals of the nation and ensure a satisfactory after-life for the souls of the parties who came before them. The validity of any given marriage was dependent on whether the couple had conformed with the religious views about sexual relationships. There were also other reasons why it was important to establish whether a marriage was valid or not e.g. inheritance purposes.

If a couple were living together and were found not to be validly married because of some serious obstacle to the marriage, such as a pre-existing marriage; marriage to a relation within the prohibited degrees of kindred; lack of consent, or an inability to sexually consummate the marriage, it was essential that the parties be separated by a decree of nullity (there was no divorce at this time). The decree declared that the marriage had never existed; it was said to be void *ab initio* (from the start). Marriages could be declared void at the request of a party other than one of the spouses and even after the death of the spouses. If a marriage was declared void *ab initio*, any children born during the relationship became illegitimate and risked disinheritance.

If the couple were found to be validly married, the court would order the parties to perform their marital obligations.

Eventually, the ecclesiastical courts were forced by the common law courts to distinguish between the more serious defects which would make a marriage void *ab initio* and those defects which were regarded as less fundamental. These latter defects were held to make the marriage merely voidable from the date of the court's decree. Non-consummation, for example, became a ground for making a marriage voidable rather than void. Voidable marriages could not be challenged by third parties, but only by a petition from either of the spouses themselves (see the scholarly judgment of Simon P in *Padolecchia v Padolecchia (otherwise Leis)* [1968] 2 WLR 173). Neither spouse could challenge the voidability of the marriage after a partner's death.

In *de Reneville v de Reneville* [1948] P 100 Lord Greene MR explained rather unsatisfactorily that

> So far as English law is concerned, there is a clear distinction between void and voidable marriages. . . . In what, for present purposes, does the distinction consist? It is argued that there is no real distinction by reason of the fact that in each case the form of the decree is the same and pronounces the marriage 'to have been and to be absolutely null and void to all intents and purposes in the law whatsoever'. It is, perhaps, unfortunate that a form of decree which was appropriate when a marriage was regarded as indissoluble and could only be got rid of by decreeing that it had never taken place is still used indiscriminately in the cases of both void and voidable marriages. . . . The substance, in my view, may be thus expressed. A void marriage is one that will be regarded by every court in any case in which the existence of the marriage is in issue as never having taken place and can be so treated by both parties to it without the necessity of any decree annulling it; a voidable marriage is one that will be regarded by every court as a valid subsisting marriage until a decree annulling it has been pronounced by a court of competent jurisdiction.

Void relationships

Those who enter into a purported marriage or civil partnership do not need to go to court to obtain a decree of nullity. Their relationship never came into existence; it was void *ab initio* and their status did not change. They never became spouses or civil partners. Such persons may enter into a new legal relationship. However, given that the void marriage or civil partnership will almost certainly be public knowledge, they may wish to avoid any misunderstanding about their status. The law permits either partner, in these circumstances, to petition for a decree of nullity. This can be done at any time; there is no requirement to wait for a year as required for divorce. This may be particularly relevant if either party wishes to marry, or enter into a civil partnership, with a new partner and does not wish to risk a public challenge to his or her capacity to do so. Although the Family Law Act 1986 (FLA 1986), s 55 allows a court to make a declaration of the validity of a person's marital status, it does not make provision for a declaration that a purported marriage was void *ab initio*.

A decree of nullity has the additional advantage that the parties may ask the court, at the time of the petition, to reallocate their assets between them in the same way as they may do so for those who obtain a decree of divorce or an order for the dissolution of a civil partnership (see *Ben Hashem v Al Shayif* [2008] EWHC 2380 (Fam) where assets were reallocated after a bigamous, and therefore, void marriage).

Logically, because the decree operates retrospectively, it may be obtained not only by the parties themselves, but also by any other interested party, and even after the death of either of them. For example, a third party, who stands to benefit from the deceased's estate were it not for the marriage or civil partnership of one of the other beneficiaries, might wish to challenge the validity of that beneficiary's relationship status.

grounds on which a marriage will be void – MCA 1973, s 11(a) (i) (ii) (iii) (iv)

The provisions of s 11(a)(i) were also considered in Chapter 2.
In *Pugh v Pugh* [1951] P 482, Pearce J explained the rationale behind s 11(a)(ii):

> *According to modern thought, it is socially and morally wrong that persons of an age at which we now believe them to be immature and provide for their education should have the stresses, responsibilities and sexual freedom of marriage and the physical strain of childbirth. Child marriages, by common consent, are believed to be bad for the participants and bad for the institution of marriage. Acts making carnal knowledge of young girls an offence are an indication of modern views on this subject.*

At the time Pearce J made these comments it was possible for those under 18 and over 16 to marry with parental consent.

That is no longer permitted and the minimum age for marriage is now 18 (Marriage and Civil Partnership (Minimum Age) Act 2022).

The main reason for this legislation was to address the growth in numbers of forced marriages particularly where one or both of the parties were under the age of 18. (For further discussion see also Chapter 5.) There remain countries where under-age marriage is still permitted; however, a person domiciled in England cannot evade the rule by marrying in such a country.

Under the MCA 1973, s. 11(a)(iii) it is laid down that marriage may be rendered void if the parties knowingly and wilfully do not comply with certain formalities delete the words 'relates to s.49 of the Marriage Act.

They have been amended over the past few years and will need to be completely reviewed if the recommendations of the Law Commission mentioned earlier are adopted by a future Government. There has always been a challenge as to what constitutes the irreducible core of a marriage ceremony and at what stage is it a non-qualifying ceremony as opposed to a void ceremony.

A number of cases have come before the courts in recent years under s 11(a)(iii), primarily involving overseas marriages or immigrant marriages which have been celebrated in England raising the question as to whether they reach a minimum in relation to the formalities set down by law sufficient for there to be a valid marriage recognised by the law in England and Wales. The decisions have not been readily reconcilable. Some marriage ceremonies have not complied with the formalities and have been accepted as giving rise to a valid marriage whilst others have been held to be void marriages. In a third category of cases, the ceremony has been held to be so far removed from the accepted idea of a marriage ceremony that it could only be viewed as a non-marriage or non-qualifying ceremony with no legal consequences.

Many of the recent cases appear to conflict, and it is arguable that some of the decisions in this area have been based on other principles of public policy. These relate primarily to the prevention of the circumvention of immigration rules via the spousal visa route, claims for welfare benefits based on spousal status, and the evasion of spousal support obligations.

The decision in *MA v JA and Her Majesty's Attorney General Respondent Intervener* [2012] EWHC 2219 (Fam) provided an interesting overview of the law relating to valid marriages, void marriages or non-marriages. Whether it makes it any easier to place a specific purported marriage ceremony into one of the three categories is debateable; the cases seem to be very fact dependent.

In *MA v JA*, the couple had lived together following a purported marriage ceremony in a mosque in Middlesbrough in 2002. They sought a declaration, under section 55 of the Family Law Act 1996, that they were validly married. The mosque was registered for marriage, and the Chairman of the Mosque, who was authorised to conduct marriages there, had witnessed the marriage. However, the imam, who conducted the ceremony, was not authorised to conduct marriages and had actually said that he believed he was only conducting a religious ceremony. The marriage was not registered as required by law. The couple were given a document stated to be a Contract of Marriage in accordance with Sharia law which was signed by the imam. Moylan J examined the history of the law and maintained that a sympathetic approach to a couple was permitted if they had not knowingly and wilfully breached certain requirements of the 1949 Act. He concluded that there had indeed been a marriage ceremony in the mosque and the parties had acted in good faith; they were therefore validly married.

By contrast, the parties in *Gereis v Yacoub* [1977] 1 FLR 854 went through a purported ceremony of marriage, at a Coptic Orthodox Church in London, knowing that it was not licensed for marriages under the Marriage Act 1949 and that the priest who conducted the ceremony was not licensed to conduct marriages. They were also aware that notice of the marriage had not been given to the superintendent registrar. The priest had advised the couple that a civil marriage ceremony should take place, but no such ceremony was carried out. The court held that the marriage was void rather than a non-marriage. It emphasised the importance that the ceremony had all

> the hallmarks of a Christian marriage; that it would be a monogamous marriage and a marriage for life.

In *Gandhi v Patel* [2002] All ER (D) 436, Jawaher Gandhi, a wealthy Indian astrologer and according to Park J, a ladies' man with several mistresses, went through a Hindu ceremony of marriage with Hasmita Gandhi, after she had consulted him astrologically. She claimed to have married in good faith and, therefore, to have become his wife. The ceremony took place in an Indian restaurant in London in considerable style, and it had complied fully with the requirements and traditions of a Hindu marriage. The Brahmin priest who conducted the ceremony maintained that he was only concerned with the rituals and requirements of his own faith, and not with the requirements of English law.

Park J held, rather obtusely, that the Hindu ceremony

> created something which was not a marriage of any kind at all, not even a marriage which was void. It might be described as a non-marriage rather than a void marriage. To draw a distinction between a non-marriage and a void marriage may seem artificial and elusive to the uninitiated – a class which until very recently included myself – but I am now convinced that the distinction exists, and that the relationship between Jawahar and Hasmita brought about by the Hindu ceremony fell into the category of non-marriages rather than void marriages . . . if a ceremony which takes place in England is to create a relationship which English law will recognise as a marriage, it must comply with the formal requirements of English law.

The distinction between a void marriage and a non-qualifying ceremony is often very fine. Valentine Le Grice commented on how hard it is to reconcile the reasoning in some cases ('A Critique of Non-Marriage' [2013] Fam Law 1278). One of the problems lies in trying to reconcile the various religious ceremonies with the rules set down for Christian ceremonies. Rebecca Probert comments on the flaws in this approach which render so many non-Christian ceremonies as non-qualifying. It is not comparing like with like (Probert 2002).

The decision in *Attorney-General v Akhter* [2020] EWCA Civ 122 has clarified some of the law on what constitutes a 'non-qualifying ceremony', but there remains some uncertainty. It is still not possible to point to particular characteristics which if left out would always render a ceremony to be 'non-qualifying'. There is also some confusion amongst parties wishing to get married as to what are the legal requirements for a valid marriage. The relaxation of the rules on where a marriage could take place as recommended by the Law Commission in 2022 would go some way towards addressing this issue by concentrating on the registration of the officiant rather than looking to the location of the ceremony. This would allow all religious ceremonies to be treated equally. This would also take away any question of bias against non-Christian ceremonies as there would be just one set of required formalities for all parties but scope for everyone to include in their ceremony religious content according to their faith.

There have been other more radical solutions such as the 'truly radical' solution suggested by John Eekelaar in 2013 that the law should allow a legal marriage to take place anywhere within England and Wales and in any form. The only requirements being that it is attested by two witnesses and prior to the ceremony rigorous formalities should be complied with such that it was clear the parties were eligible to marry (Eekelaar 2013). He accepted at the time of writing that his suggestion was radical, but the Law Commission recent recommendations make his solution appear far less radical and one that now requires serious discussion.

Overseas marriages

Marriages which take place abroad are dependent for their validity on the capacity of the couple to marry in a particular country and whether they have conformed with the relevant law relating to marriage in that location.

In *Jagger v Hall* (unreported, 1999), Mick Jagger, the wealthy rock star, and Jerry Hall, the well-known model, had married in a Hindu ceremony in Bali but had failed to register the marriage in accordance with Indonesian law. When the relationship broke down nine years later, the High Court found that although the ceremony did not conform with the required formalities of Indonesian law it did not give rise to a non-qualifying ceremony. This allowed Jerry Hall to petition for a decree of nullity on the grounds that the marriage was void *ab initio*, and obtain substantial financial relief in an out of court agreement.

In *B v B* [2008] 2 FLR 1627, a couple began a relationship in 1999. The woman maintained that after giving birth to two children, the man agreed with her that they would marry in California and have a blessing in a church in England at a later date. In 2003, they married in California in a hot air balloon. They returned to England and the church blessing took place. When the relationship broke down, the wife accepted that the marriage was not valid under Californian law, but maintained that she had acted in good faith at the time of the ceremony, and petitioned for a decree of nullity. The husband maintained that they had not obtained a licence in California and that the marriage was not void but a non-marriage. The court granted the wife's petition and said that was in the interests of public policy and justice to find the marriage to be void.

In *Hudson v Leigh (Status of non-marriage)* [2009] 2 FLR 1129, (see Chapter 2) an English couple who had lived together for 12 years and had had a daughter together decided to marry. The woman mainly lived in the man's second home in South Africa. She was a devout Christian and wanted to have a religious marriage ceremony. The man claimed to be a Jewish atheist and wanted a civil marriage. They agreed to have a religious ceremony in South Africa, even though it would not be legally binding and so it was further agreed that it would be followed soon after by a civil marriage in England. The South African ceremony took the form of a wedding; the woman wore a wedding dress, and their daughter was a bridesmaid. A wedding dinner was held at which the guests referred to the couple as having married that day. The couple returned to England and made arrangements for the civil ceremony. They took an oath stating that they were not already married but did explain to the registrar about the South African ceremony. The civil ceremony never took place, and the relationship broke down. The woman applied, *inter alia*, for a decree of nullity on the basis that the South African ceremony was void because it failed to comply with the formal requirements of South African law. The court rejected the woman's petition and declared that the ceremony gave rise to a non-marriage or as described today 'a non-qualifying ceremony'. It maintained that it was in the public interest to do so and, thereby, create certainty. The court explained that in deciding the effect of a ceremony, the particular facts of the case should be taken into account, including whether the ceremony purported to be a lawful marriage; whether it had all or enough of the hallmarks of marriage; whether the minister, or other officiating person, and the couple believed, and intended, that the ceremony gave rise to the status of a lawful marriage; and what were the reasonable perceptions and beliefs of those who attended the ceremony.

The criteria set out by Bodey J in *Hudson v Leigh* were then revisited in the Court of Appeal in *Attorney-General v Akhter* in 2020. Although the judgment attempts to clarify the law it also highlights how difficult it is to pick out the hallmarks of a marriage ceremony sufficient to allow it to be considered a ceremony failing for lack of formalities and therefore void. It is fair to comment that one problem in this case was that the judge at first instance tried to be as flexible as possible in his attempt to assist the wife in her very unfortunate position. For over 18 years she had believed she was married to her husband and in this belief she had cared and raised four children, but however unfortunate her position might be it was not possible to find this to be a marriage. As the Court of Appeal pointed out it was important to be certain when a ceremony qualified as a marriage not only to the parties concerned but to the State.

Sir Terence Etherton MR:

> *We also see no scope, as referred . . ., for the nature and effect of a ceremony to change over time, other than in the case of a voidable marriage as expressly provided for by s. 12 of the 1973 Act. Whether a ceremony created a valid marriage or a void marriage or was of no legal effect at all must be determined at the date of the ceremony. It would make no sense for its legal effect to fluctuate depending, . . ., on future events such as whether the parties did or did not have children. There is no support for this approach to the determination of the legal effect of a ceremony either in our domestic legislation or in the ECHR. . . . Further, to adopt this approach would also fundamentally undermine the need for the parties and the state to know, as from the date of the ceremony, whether the parties are or are not validly married.*

For a detailed discussion of the issues raised by this case see Akhtar et al. (2020).

Marriage by cohabitation and repute

In several decisions involving couples who have come to live in England from overseas, the courts have rescued them from the adverse consequences of non-marriages. The courts have found that they were validly married under the common law principle of presumption of marriage by cohabitation and repute. The principle was discussed in Chapter 2.

> **MCA 1973, s.11(b) that at the time of the marriage, either party was already lawfully married or in a civil partnership**

Marriage in England is a monogamous relationship. Anyone who attempts to marry whilst already married may also have committed the offence of bigamy, unless they reasonably believe that the first marriage was invalid or that the other party to it is dead. The marriage remains bigamous even where the first spouse dies after the second 'marriage' has taken place.

> **MCA 1973 s.11(c) a marriage was void where the parties were not respectively male and female but as a result of the Marriage (Same Sex Couples) Act 2013 this provision no longer applies.**

> **MCA 1973, s.11(d) In the case of a polygamous marriage entered into outside England and Wales, that either party was, at the time of the marriage, domiciled in England and Wales**

Polygamous marriages which have been celebrated abroad have become a more common occurrence in England. Immigrants return to their countries of origin, where polygamous marriages are legal, and marry. However, if either party to the marriage is domiciled in England the marriage will be void (see e.g. *Bibi v Chief Adjudication Officer* [1998] 1 FLR 375 where a woman from a polygamous marriage to a man domiciled in England was prevented from claiming a widow's allowance because her marriage could not be recognised in England).

> ### GROUNDS ON WHICH A CIVIL PARTNERSHIP WILL BE VOID
>
> The Civil Partnership Act 2004 (CPA 2004), ss 3 and 49 provide the grounds, which are very similar to those relating to void marriages, on which a civil partnership will be void. These provisions have been amended in line with the provisions on nullity of marriage
>
> - either of them is already a civil partner or lawfully married; or
> - either of them is under the age of 18 (as amended by the Marriage and Civil Partnership (Minimum Age) Act 2022); or
> - they are within the prohibited degrees of relationship; or
> - they both knew that key formality requirements had not been complied with.

Voidable relationships

A voidable relationship, unlike a void relationship, remains valid until either party has obtained a decree of nullity from the court. The decree has no retrospective effect. The parties are the only ones who may apply for the decree; no third party may do so.

> **Grounds on which a marriage will be voidable – MCA 1973, s 12**
> **s 12(a) that the marriage has not been consummated owing to the incapacity of either party to consummate it.**

This subsection retains as its basis the now rather outmoded views that the sole purpose of marriage is for procreation and the control of sexual behaviour in society. It provides that a marriage will be voidable if either party is unable to have sexual intercourse with the other. This is defined as penetrative sexual intercourse and this ground is not available to same-sex couples. It is questionable now whether such a provision should remain on the statute books. (Crompton 2013). The impotent party may rely on his or her own impotence to apply for a decree of nullity (see e.g. *Harthan v Harthan* [1949] P 115. Impotence requires a detailed and potentially embarrassing examination of the parties' sexuality or, rather, lack of it. The provision is also sexist in that males are, more obviously, and easily, able to prove an inability to consummate than females.

The incapacity must normally exist at the time of the marriage, but this requirement has been liberally and sensitively interpreted. If either of the spouses was capable at the time of the marriage but became impotent after the marriage, he or she may apply for a decree of nullity. Thus, where a spouse is injured after the marriage but prior to consummation of it, the marriage may be voidable even if the couple had had a sexual relationship prior to marriage. Given that intercourse need only take place once for a marriage to be consummated, it will be unfortunate for those spouses who consummate their marriage immediately after the wedding if one of them subsequently suffers an injury which prevents any further sexual relationship. Nullity will not be available; a divorce will be the only solution if either of them feels unable to live in a marriage without sex (see Chapter 6).

According to Dr Lushington, in *D-E v A-G* [1845] 163 ER 1039 for a plea of incapacity to succeed, there must be an inability to have ordinary and complete intercourse.

The incapacity need not be a generalised sexual impotence towards the world at large; it may relate only to a specific spouse.

In *Baxter v Baxter* [1948] AC 274 it was held that incapacity does not extend to an inability to have children nor is sexual intercourse incomplete when contraceptives have been used.

The reason for the incapacity may be physical or psychological and must be permanent and irremediable. The incapacity will be accepted as irremediable if it cannot be readily cured or would require dangerous medical intervention. Any refusal to have straightforward remedial treatment for any incapacity will be deemed to be a wilful refusal to consummate the marriage.

In *SY v SY (otherwise W) (No 2)* [1963] P 37 the court held there was no incapacity on the part of the wife because her vaginal defect could be remedied by simple surgery.

Psychological impotence may also be permanent and irremediable but is likely to be more difficult to prove than impotence resulting from a physical condition.

In *Singh v Singh* [1971] P 226 the parents of a Sikh girl, aged 17, arranged a marriage for her with a 21-year-old Sikh male. She met her husband for the first time at the registry office ceremony. She did not like him. She thought that he was neither as handsome nor as educated as she had been led to believe by her parents. After the civil ceremony, she returned home with her parents and refused to go ahead with the Sikh religious ceremony and have a sexual relationship with her husband. Subsequently, the wife petitioned for a decree of nullity on the grounds, *inter alia*, of her own incapacity because of an invincible repugnance, on her part, towards her husband.

The court rejected her allegation of incapacity and held she had not shown an invincible repugnance to having intercourse with the husband, because of some psychiatric or sexual aversion on her part. She merely did not wish to have a sexual relationship with him because she did not like what she had seen of him at the registry office ceremony.

The expectation of the court that a young girl can be expected to have a sexual relationship with a man whom she does not like, and whom she has never met before an arranged marriage ceremony, seems to be unnecessarily restrictive of the definition of invincible repugnance.

In *Corbett v Corbett* (otherwise known as Ashley) [1971] P 83, a transgendered person had had male-to-female gender reassignment surgery but was held to be incapable of having a sexual relationship because she had no vagina but merely a newly constructed cavity, which served as an artificial vagina.

In the light of the Gender Recognition Act 2004 it remains uncertain whether this decision remains good law.

s 12(b) that the marriage has not been consummated owing to the wilful refusal of the respondent to consummate it

Case law illustrates the fine line between an inability to consummate and a wilful refusal to consummate a marriage. Again this ground for nullity is only available to opposite sex couples. However, a spouse who wilfully refuses to consummate the marriage, unlike one who is incapable of doing so, may not rely on his or her own wilful refusal.

Wilful refusal, in *S v S (otherwise C)* [1956] P 1 was held to mean a settled and definite decision, without sufficient reason, not to have a sexual relationship with one's spouse. The husband left his wife and petitioned for nullity because his wife was indecisive about undergoing the necessary surgery to correct a physical defect which prevented consummation. The court held that indecisiveness did not constitute a wilful refusal.

In *Potter v Potter* [1975] 5 Fam Law 161, a wife successfully underwent treatment for her physical inability to have intercourse. In spite of this, her husband refused to have a sexual relationship with her. The wife petitioned for a decree of nullity on the grounds of the husband's wilful refusal to consummate. The court accepted that the husband was not wilful in his refusal but had merely lost his ardour whilst waiting for his wife's condition to be cured.

In *Ford v Ford* (1987) Fam Law 232, the husband was convicted of armed robbery and sentenced to five years' imprisonment prior to consummating his marriage. During his incarceration, there were opportunities to engage in sexual relations and it was common, although against prison rules, for prisoners to do so; we are not told how this was achieved. The husband refused to have a sexual relationship with his wife in prison and told her that he did not wish to live with her on his release. He also demanded to be taken to see a former girlfriend during parole visits rather than to his wife. The court held that the husband's behaviour showed a determination not to consummate the marriage and granted the wife a decree of nullity.

Failure to consummate a marriage until a religious ceremony has taken place, following a civil ceremony, will not constitute wilful refusal to consummate. However, failure to organise, or go through with, the religious ceremony may be interpreted as wilful refusal to consummate.

In *Kaur v Singh* [1972] 1 WLR 105, the parties, who were both Sikhs, married in a registry office on the understanding that they would not cohabit until a religious ceremony had been held in a Sikh temple. The husband refused to arrange the ceremony and was held to have wilfully refused to have a sexual relationship with his wife.

In *A v J* [1989] 1 FLR 110, the husband was prepared to arrange the religious ceremony following a civil ceremony of marriage, but the wife demanded that it be postponed indefinitely. The court granted the husband a decree of nullity on the grounds of the wife's wilful refusal to consummate.

It was held in *Scott v Scott* [1959] P 103 that the husband could not petition for a decree of nullity based on wilful refusal to consummate because he and his wife were not young and had agreed to a non-sexual, companionate marriage. It is possible for a couple to have a non-consummated valid marriage since it will remain valid until one of the parties takes action to declare it void.

s 12(c) that either party did not validly consent to it whether in consequence of duress, mistake, unsoundness of mind or otherwise

Duress

Consent lies at the heart of a marriage, and there cannot be a valid marriage in the absence of consent. Consent may be invalid because it was given under duress or alternatively it may be invalid because of a mistake on one or other of the parties.

A spouse who enters a marriage because of threats, force or duress has not freely consented to it. The threat need not emanate from the respondent spouse but may come from another source.

In *Szechter v Szechter* [1971] P 286, a woman was sentenced to three years' imprisonment in Poland for anti-Government activities. She knew that her health would suffer if she were to go to prison and that she would have no future in Poland at the end of her sentence. The man married her, having divorced his wife in order to do so, and thereby helped her to leave Poland and come to England. The woman claimed that she had married the man under duress and successfully applied for a decree of nullity in order to enable him to remarry his first wife. The court held that a spouse pleading duress must prove that their will was overborne by genuine and reasonably held fear caused by threat of immediate danger (for which the party is not himself responsible) to life, limb or liberty, so that the constraint destroys the reality of consent to ordinary wedlock.

Sir Jocelyn Simon P explained that a yielding of the lips but not of the mind could have no legal effect.

As a postscript to this decision, the man later divorced his first wife once more and remarried his second one.

In *Buckland v Buckland* [1968] P 296 the petitioner was falsely charged with a sexual offence against a young girl. In spite of his claim that he was innocent, he was told that he would be sent to jail for two years unless he married her. He was afraid of going to jail and did marry the girl. He proceeded to petition for a decree of nullity and was successful. Scarman LJ maintained that the fear or duress had to be objectively judged. The court also suggested that had he been justly accused of the offence, he himself would have been responsible for the threats and would have prevented him from petitioning for nullity.

The strict test in *Szechter* (1971) and *Buckland* (1968) was followed in two cases involving young immigrant girls who had been forced into marriage by their parents. In *Singh v Singh* (1971) and *Singh v Kaur* (1978), both girls were held not to have fulfilled the requirements of the arduous objective test. Their age and cultural background, which demanded parental obedience, was not taken into account.

In *Hirani v Hirani* [1983] 4 FLR 232, however, Ormrod LJ preferred the simple subjective test in *Scott v Sebright* (1866) in which Butt J explained that:

> the woman had been reduced by mental and bodily suffering to a state in which she was incapable of offering resistance to coercion and threats which in her normal condition she would have treated with the contempt she must have felt for the man who made use of them; and that, therefore, there never was any such consent on her part as the law requires for the making of a contract of marriage. Such being the case, I know of no consideration consistent with justice or with common sense which should induce me to hold this marriage binding.

He maintained that the question to be asked is:

> whether the pressure . . . is such as to destroy the reality of consent and overbear the will of the individual?

Forced marriages

Many of the duress cases are brought by young women who have entered into a 'forced marriage' arranged for them by family members where the parties have not been given a choice about the prospective marriage. It is common in a number of cultures for parents to select a spouse for their son or daughter, but usually it will only proceed where the parties agree to the choice.

Ormrod LJ's return to the 1866 test in *Hirani* (1983) was an important step forward. The test has re-emerged in recent years to play a significant role in the rescue of young adults who have been forced into marriage by their parents. Such marriages have become increasingly problematic for young second generation immigrants, both male and female – the phenomenon is not gender specific – who have been forced to marry, often by being taken to their parents' countries of origin to be married there. The Government has attempted to control such practices via the joint endeavours of the Foreign Office and the Home Office (see www.fco.gov. uk/), the Forced Marriage (Civil Protection) Act 2007, and, by enacting criminal legislation against the practice, s 121 of the Anti-Social Behaviour, Crime and Policing Act 2014, which criminalises attempts to force someone to enter into a marriage. This is a difficult provision to enforce as Gaffney-Rhys has shown; there is a fine line to be drawn between consent given freely to marriage and consent given under duress (Gaffney-Rhys 2015). Nevertheless nullity remains an essential remedy for young immigrants who marry because of cultural and familial pressure. In many cases, the treatment of some of these young spouses by their families would satisfy even the stricter test laid down in *Szechter* (1971) and *Buckland* (1968).

In *P v R (Forced Marriage: Annulment: Procedure)* [2003] 1 FLR 661, the petitioner was a 17-year-old British citizen of Pakistani origin whose parents persuaded her to attend a family funeral in Pakistan. They wished to remove her from England because she was involved in a relationship of which they disapproved. Whilst there, arrangements were made, against her will, for her to be married to a Pakistani cousin. She was terrified by her brother's threats of physical violence and also believed that if she refused to go through with the ceremony she would not be permitted to return to England. Her parents told her that her refusal to marry would bring shame on the family and that it would merit severe long-term punishment. The girl escaped to England and was granted a decree of nullity.

The judgment of Munby J, in *NS v MI* [2006] EWHC 1646 (Fam), gives a most helpful account of the doctrine of nullity in the context of forced marriage.

The petitioner in *NS v MI*, a young British girl aged 17, was taken to Pakistan by her parents, ostensibly for a holiday. Her passport was taken from her by her mother and she became, in effect, a prisoner trapped in Pakistan and was then forced to marry her 17-year-old cousin. He admitted that he only wanted to marry her in order to gain admission to the UK.

The marriage was not consummated, and the girl was allowed to return to the UK with her mother. She had nothing further to do with her husband and sought a decree of nullity on the grounds of duress. She maintained that her family had morally blackmailed her and threatened to commit suicide if she disobeyed their wishes *vis a vis* the marriage.

Munby J was most concerned to draw a distinction between arranged and forced marriages:

> *Arranged marriages are to be supported as a conventional concept in many societies. And for that very reason they are, I emphasise, not merely to be supported but to be respected. . . . We must guard against the risk of stereotyping. We must be careful to ensure that our understandable concern to protect vulnerable children (or, indeed, vulnerable young adults) does not lead us to interfere inappropriately – and if inappropriately then unjustly – with families merely because they cleave, as this family does, to mores, to cultural beliefs, more or less different from what is familiar to those who view life from a purely Euro-centric perspective*

Forced marriages, by contrast, he described as an appalling practice, a gross abuse of human rights and a form of domestic violence that dehumanises people by denying them their right to choose how to conduct their lives. He compared them to the barbarous practices of female genital mutilation and so-called honour killings.

Munby J explained that there could be no consent to marriage where the person marrying is able to say

> my tongue has sworn but my mind [that is, the mind as the seat of the mental faculties, perception, thought] is unsworn.

Pressure put to bear by a parent or close member of the family on a young vulnerable person, according to Munby J, is extremely powerful and, particularly so, when the threats are insidious and involve subtle arguments relating to matters of personal affection, duty, religious beliefs, and social and cultural conventions. He accepted that it might be necessary in certain circumstances to allow a vulnerable petitioner to give evidence from behind a screen or via a video link in order to protect him or her from intimidation by family members.

In *B v I (Forced marriage)* [2010] 1 FLR 1721 the court rescued a 16-year-old girl from the effects of a ceremony in Bangladesh by declaring it to be a non-marriage. The girl had been taken to Bangladesh by her parents and the day before she was due to return to England, an imam was brought to her bedroom and performed a ceremony in Bengali. The girl was instructed by her father to say 'I accept' at certain points during the ceremony. She thought that it was an engagement ceremony rather than an attempt to marry her to her absent cousin. The next day the cousin came to the girl's hotel and had sexual intercourse with her against her will. When she complained to her family, they explained that she was now married and must accept this. The girl returned to England with her family but without her cousin. It took her three years to gather together her courage to leave the family. This meant that she was time barred from pleading that the relationship was voidable for lack of consent (see later in this chapter). The court was very sympathetic to her plight and granted a declaration, under the inherent jurisdiction, that the ceremony she had undergone in Bangladesh was a non-marriage.

In 2005, the Forced Marriage Unit was established to lead on the Government's forced marriage policy giving advice and support. In 2022, it dealt with 302 cases of which 235 were female and 69 involved male parties. It operates both inside and outside the UK (www.gov.uk/government/statistics/forced-marriage-unit-statistics-2022/forced-marriage-unit-statistics-2022). The figure represents a considerable fall since 2019 when it advised on 1,355 cases. Indeed prior to 2020 the figures had been steadily rising. It is likely that the figures since 2020 have been impacted by Covid.

Forced marriage protection orders were introduced under the Forced Marriage (Civil Protection) Act 2007. The orders are civil orders in the form of injunctions which if breached will give rise to a criminal offence punishable by up to five years' imprisonment. Applications can be made by the applicant or by a third party, often the local authority. Once made the orders can contain prohibitions, restrictions and requirements as the courts consider to be appropriate to prevent a victim from being forced into a marriage. The fact that such orders are made under civil law is important where applicants are concerned not to criminalise family members.

A study in 2021 examining the use of Forced Marriage Protection Orders found that there is little known about how these orders function. The study found that the orders were breached in a substantial number of cases and also that victims with disabilities faced significant barriers to justice (Koack-Lundberg et al. 2022).

The issue of forced marriage is considered in more detail in Chapter 5.

Mistake

Voidable marriages based on mistake are rare. Mistake in this context has tended to be restricted to those relating to the identity of a spouse or to the nature of the ceremony.

In the New Zealand case of *C v C* [1942] NZLR 356, the wife claimed that she had married her husband in the erroneous belief that he was a famous boxer. The court held that this was not a mistake which invalidated the marriage. She had intended marrying her husband but thought that he had qualities which he did not have.

In *Valier v Valier* [1925] 133 LJ 830, the petitioner was an Italian who did not speak English. He was taken to a registry office and went through a ceremony of marriage without any realisation of what was happening. He had thought it was just a preliminary to a ceremony. It was held that he had not given a valid consent to the marriage.

Sham marriages

Sham marriages, also known as marriages of convenience, are normally undertaken to allow one party to gain a right of entry into England and British citizenship. Although the parties to such a marriage do not plan to live together but, rather, divorce at the earliest opportunity, the marriage is nonetheless valid.

In *Messina (formerly Smith Orse Vervaeke) v Smith (Messina intervening)* [1971] P 322, the woman, who was a prostitute, wished to escape arrest in Belgium for her criminal activities. She married a British citizen to obtain citizenship. The court was held that the marriage was valid even though the woman claimed to be mistaken as to the consequences of a sham marriage. She subsequently obtained a decree of nullity in Belgium which the English court also refused to recognise.

The decision is interesting in the light of *Szechter* (1971), which equally involved a sham marriage. In *Szechter*, public policy clearly favoured the spouse, who had engaged in activities against an unfriendly foreign Government during the Cold War, but not the one in *Messina* who had indulged in criminal behaviour in a country regarded as an ally. In 2011, the Government brought out a consultation paper with proposals, *inter alia*, to reform entry to the UK and prevent sham marriages which it believed were on the increase.

The Government consultation paper stated that:

> *Family migration must be based on a genuine and continuing relationship, not a sham or marriage of convenience, and not a forced marriage. We want to find an objective way of identifying whether a relationship is genuine and continuing or not. We therefore propose to define more clearly what constitutes a genuine and continuing relationship, marriage or partnership for the purposes of the Immigration Rules, and we invite views on how that definition should be framed.*

One of the suggestions in the paper was to consider making sham marriage a lawful impediment to marriage. It was not clear whether this would make such a marriage void or voidable. The responses to the paper showed the problems involved in defining what constitutes a genuine marriage in a manner which embraces the multiplicity of cultural views in the country.

In 2012, the immigration rules were tightened to prevent sham marriages. Minimum income requirements were imposed on any person seeking to bring a spouse or potential spouse into the UK from a non-EU country. Anyone seeking settlement in the UK from a non-EU country under the spousal rules must have been married for five years before making an application for settlement. The foreign spouse risks being deported and both spouses risk imprisonment. Photographs of such spouses in their wedding finery, handcuffed to a police officer on the day of the marriage, are now a common occurrence in the English press and, in 2012, a Church of England vicar was sent to jail for four years for conducting 250 sham marriages (*Daily Telegraph* 2009, 1 April 2012). In *Sadovska & Anor v Secretary of State for the Home Department (Scotland)* [2017] UKSC 54, the Supreme Court considered the issue of who bears the burden of proof in relation to an alleged marriage of convenience. Ms Sadovska, a Lithuanian citizen, had acquired the right of permanent residence. She began a relationship with Mr Malik, a Pakistani national. He had overstayed his student visa when it expired. They gave notice of their intention to marry but were then interviewed by immigration officers and detained. Removal decisions were made for both Mr Malik and Ms Sadovska. The decision with regard to Ms Sadovska was based on the attempt to enter into a marriage of convenience. The First-tier Tribunal dismissed their appeal, having placed the burden of proof on the Appellants to establish that their marriage was not one of convenience, on the balance of probabilities. However, the Supreme Court later found that Ms Sadovska had established rights which meant that the onus was on the respondent to prove that the grounds for her removal were made out. Therefore, the burden of proof was on the respondent to establish a marriage of convenience. The First-tier Tribunal had also failed to consider whether removing Ms Sadovska would be proportionate. Although Mr Malik did not have established rights, if he could produce evidence of a durable relationship the respondent would be obliged to facilitate his entry/residence or justify any refusal to do so. The Court therefore remitted the case to the First-tier Tribunal for a rehearing.

Baroness Hale considered the approach to marriages of convenience finding that earlier definitions had been moderated by the Commission's 2014 Handbook, such that the predominant, rather than sole, purpose of the marriage should be to gain rights of entry/residence. Incidental immigration and other benefits (e.g. tax advantages) that a marriage may bring are not relevant if it could be shown that this is not the predominant purpose of at least one party to the marriage. An issue arising in this case which remains problematic is the way that the court conflated the terms 'sham marriage' and 'marriage of convenience'. These terms are not always seen as interchangeable and indeed different jurisdictions tend to use them in different ways. The Home Office is now using an algorithm to determine whether a marriage should be investigated as a sham. The algorithm identifies couples that are suspected of getting married just to get around immigration controls and then refers them for investigation by officials. This has been heavily criticised by various public law bodies.

The Home Office faced a legal challenge in 2023 from the Public Law Project as to whether it is a valid way to identify 'sham' marriages and also accused the Home Office of using it in such a way that it was discriminatory. (For a more general discussion on this see Wray (2016); Davis et al. (2018).)

Unsound mind

> A marriage will be voidable if one of the parties shows that they did not understand the nature of the contract.

In marriage the parties must understand the general nature of marriage. The extent of understanding is explained by Mostyn J in *NB v MI (Capacity to Contract Marriage)* [2021] EWHC 224 (Fam) as follows: 'a putative spouse must have the capacity to understand in broad terms that marriage confers on the couple the status of a recognized union which gives rise to an expectation to share each other's society, comfort and assistance'.

(See also the cases on mental incapacity discussed in Chapter 2.)

If a mentally incapacitated adult does enter into a voidable marriage, they may require the help of the inherent jurisdiction to escape from it. The inherent jurisdiction is so wide that it almost certainly gives the courts the power to help in such circumstances (see *Re SA (Vulnerable Adult with Capacity: Marriage)* [2006] 1 FLR 867). If a voidable marriage can be shown to be damaging to the best interests of such a person, it would be unacceptable to leave him or her trapped in that marriage. Without the aid of the court, vulnerable adults would find it impossible to apply for a decree of nullity against their spouse's will.

In *Sheffield City Council v E and S* [2004] EWHC 2808 (Fam), a local authority brought proceedings in which the court had to decide whether a mentally disabled woman had the mental capacity to marry. The local authority brought the proceedings because they knew that the man had a history of violence. Munby P considered the test for capacity observing that

> *he or she must understand the nature of the marriage contract. This means that he or she must be mentally capable of understanding the duties and responsibilities that normally attach to marriage. That said, the contract of marriage is in essence a simple one, which does not require a high degree of intelligence to comprehend. The contract of marriage can be readily understood by anyone of normal intelligence.*

The judge made it clear that the court is engaged in deciding whether the parties have the capacity to marry not the merits of a particular marriage. He commented that marriage can immensely enrich the lives of many people of limited or borderline capacity. In *Mundell v Name 1* [2019] EWCOP 50, Mostyn J considered the extent of understanding of the full implications of marriage that was needed in order to have capacity. A deputy was acting for a party who had been awarded a substantial sum in compensation after a road accident and wanted to marry a woman living in his house with her children. He had learning difficulties and one of the main concerns of the deputy acting on his behalf was that if the marriage broke down and the partner made a claim for financial provision, the petitioner would be unable to provide for himself financially.

The court ruled that the petitioner did have capacity to marry. Mostyn J stated that: 'it would be inappropriate and, indeed, arguably dangerous to introduce into the test for capacity to marry a requirement that there should be anything more than a knowledge that divorce may bring about a financial claim', adding that even if the marriage did break down '[t]here are numerous authorities in the books which have effectively emphasised the near-immunity of personal injury awards from a financial claim'.

Or otherwise

The courts have rarely discussed the meaning of the words 'or otherwise', which are included in the MCA 1973, s 12(c).

Perhaps, more use could be made of them where one party is totally unaware of some significant fact relating to the spouse at the time of the marriage and might not have consented had they known about it. Such facts might include the existence of a mistress or a former cohabitant particularly one with children, or a woman who is pregnant by the man at the time of the marriage. A spouse who has not revealed that he or she is suffering from a serious communicable disease which does not come within the category of venereal disease might also mean that a valid consent could be questioned. Where a spouse marries under the influence of drink or drugs, and given the nature of the celebrations surrounding marriage, many do, it may be possible to maintain that a valid consent cannot have been given. In *Sullivan v Sullivan* [1818] 161 ER 728, a marriage was held to be voidable where the groom was so drunk he was unable to understand the nature of the ceremony. Such circumstances could be encompassed by the general umbrella of the words 'or otherwise'.

s 12(d) that at the time of the marriage either party, though capable of giving valid consent, was suffering (whether continuously or intermittently) from mental disorder within the meaning of the Mental Health Act 1983 of such a kind or to such extent as to be unfitted for marriage.

The MCA 1973, s 1(2) defines mental disorder somewhat liberally as 'mental illness, arrested or incomplete development of mind, psychopathic disorder and any other disorder or disability of mind'. The petitioner may rely on his or her own mental disorder.

s 12(e) that at the time of the marriage the respondent was suffering from venereal disease in a communicable form

It is unfortunate that s 12(e) is so limiting. HIV or AIDS do not come within the category of venereal disease nor do several other diseases which are also transmitted by means of intimate contact and have the potential to have serious consequences for the other spouses. This section applies to same-sex marriage but not to civil partnership. It seems an outdated and outmoded section and if retained should at least replace venereal disease with 'sexually transmitted disease'.

s 12(f) that at the time of the marriage, the respondent was pregnant by some other person than the petitioner.

A man is presumed, in the absence of evidence to the contrary, to be the father of any child born during marriage. This subsection is based on the view that it is unjust to expect a man to bring up another man's biological child when he may have married only because he believed the child to be his.

A wife may not petition on the basis that another woman is pregnant by her husband at the time of the marriage despite the fact that this event could have a profound effect on their future together.

This section has been retained for civil partnerships although in same-sex relationships it could only apply to women. If one party to a same-sex relationship of two women found that her wife was already pregnant in circumstances unknown to her wife then conceivably this section could apply in both a same-sex marriage and a civil partnership.

s 12(g) that an interim gender recognition certificate under the GRA 2004 has after the time of the marriage been issued to either party to the marriage

This provision is clearly based on policy, and perhaps compassion for the parties in a marriage where one or, less likely, both of the spouses have sought recognition in a new gender. Section 12(g) allows either spouse to marry a new partner without having to undergo divorce. It is, however, difficult to see how a change of gender, possibly undertaken many years after the marriage took place, nullifies what was a valid contract at the time of the marriage. This has been less of an issue since the introduction of same-sex marriage. This ground is controversial since categorisation of people into gender of male or female is regarded as outdated. There is no legal requirement to disclose other personal details on a marriage so it seems to stigmatise transgender people. (See Alex Sharpe (2012) where she argues that the requirement to disclose one's gender history is discriminatory and encroaches on privacy and even if it could be argued that there exists a right to know it ought to be trumped by considerations of justice, legal consistency and public policy.)

s 12(h) that the respondent is a person whose gender at the time of the marriage had become the acquired gender under the GRA 2004

This provision protects a person who marries and is unaware at the time of the ceremony that his or her spouse has acquired a gender recognition certificate under the GRA 2004. The provision appears to defeat the aims of the GRA 2004. It suggests that, although a gender recognition certificate has been issued, there remains some question over the true gender of the certificate holder. It was noted earlier that nullity based on mistake is rigidly interpreted; the provision under s 12(h) appears to statutorily extend the interpretation of nullity based on mistake.

Bars to relief where a marriage is voidable

An application for a decree of nullity in the case of a voidable marriage may be barred under the MCA 1973, s 13 in order to prevent injustice to a spouse who would suffer serious disadvantages if the decree were to be granted. There are no bars to an application for a decree of nullity in the case of a void marriage.

Knowledge of the petitioner and injustice to the respondent

> The MCA 1973, s 13(1) provides that a petition will not be granted if the petitioner, with the knowledge that the marriage was voidable, had led the respondent to believe that he or she would not do so, and it would be unjust to the respondent to grant the decree.

There are clearly two limbs to the section, and both must be satisfied.

In *D v D* [1979] Fam 70, the parties adopted two children at a time when the husband knew that he could have the marriage annulled because of his wife's wilful refusal to consummate the marriage. He was held to have conducted himself in a way that led the wife to believe that he would not seek an annulment. It could have been deemed unjust to annul the marriage as it would have left the wife on her own to care for the two adopted children but in this case the court considered that it would not be unjust to the respondent wife as she did not object.

Where the petitioner wishes to rely on venereal disease, pregnancy by another, or that he or she has married a transgendered person in possession of a gender recognition certificate, the MCA 1973, s 13(3) provides that the petitioner must be ignorant of those facts at the time of the marriage.

Delay

The MCA 1973, s 13(2) provides that any proceedings for nullity, where the petitioner is relying on grounds other than non-consummation, or the issue of an interim gender recognition certificate, must be brought within three years of the date of the marriage unless the court grants leave under the MCA 1973, s 13(4). The court will only grant leave to apply out of time where the petitioner has suffered from a mental disorder, and the court considers that it would be just to grant leave to apply out of time. The Mental Health Act 1983, s 1(2) defines mental disorder as 'mental illness, arrested or incomplete development of mind, psychopathic disorder and any other disorder or disability of mind'.

The case of *B v I (Forced Marriage)* discussed earlier in the chapter illustrates the difficulties that the time bar may present for a petitioner. In that case the court declared the marriage to be a 'non-marriage'. It would not have been able to waive the three-year time bar under the circumstances of the case.

The GRA 2004 inserts into the MCA 1973 a new s 13(2A), which provides that where the parties are married, any application for a decree of nullity must be made within six months of the issue of an interim gender recognition certificate.

Grounds on which a civil partnership will be voidable

CPA 2004, s 50(1) provides the grounds on which a civil partnership will be voidable:

- either of the parties did not validly consent to its formation (whether as a result of duress, mistake, unsoundness of mind or otherwise) (s 50(1)(a));
- at the time of its formation either of them, though capable of giving a valid consent, was suffering (whether continuously or intermittently) from mental disorder of such a kind or to such an extent as to be unfitted for civil partnership (s 50(1)(b));
- at the time of its formation, the respondent was pregnant by some person other than the applicant (this will only be relevant in a case involving a gender change under the Gender Recognition Bill and is subject to s 50(6) which provides that the court may not make a nullity order if the applicant knew of the pregnancy at the time of the formation of the civil partnership) (s 50(1)(c));
- an interim gender recognition certificate under the GRA 2004 has, after the time of the formation of the civil partnership, been issued to either civil partner (s 50(1)(d));
- the respondent is a person whose gender at the time of the formation of the civil partnership had become the acquired gender under the GRA 2004 (s 50(1)(e)).

It is presumed that the relevant decisions relating to voidable marriages will be followed.

There is a notable absence of any provisions relating to sexual consummation of the relationship or of the presence of venereal disease at the time the civil partnership is registered. It would seem that the legislators were unable to come to terms with the nature of sexual relations in same-sex relationships and were determined to avoid the issue completely. In November 2004, in the debate in the House of Lords on the Civil Partnership Bill, Baroness Scotland attempted to explain, with little success, that one of the major differences between marriage and civil partnership is that of consummation:

> in relation to marriage, for a marriage to be valid it has to be consummated by one man and one woman and there is a great deal of jurisprudence which tells you exactly what consummation amounts to, partial, impartial, penetration, no penetration. . . . There is no provision for consummation in the Civil Partnerships Bill. We do not look at the nature of the sexual relationship, it is totally different in nature.
>
> (House of Lords, Hansard 17 November 2004, col 1479)

It may be that an application could be made for a decree of nullity under the provisions for lack of valid consent in consequence of 'otherwise' (CPA 2004, s 50(1)(a)), where the respondent failed to reveal an intention not to have a sexual relationship or failed to reveal the existence of a communicable sexual disease.

Bars to relief where a civil partnership is voidable knowledge of the applicant and injustice to the respondent

The applicant may not obtain a decree of nullity if the respondent satisfies the court that, according to the provisions of the CPA 2004:

■   the applicant, with knowledge that it was open to him to obtain a nullity order, conducted himself in relation to the respondent in such a way as to lead the respondent reasonably to believe that he would not seek to do so (s 51(1)(a)); and

■   and that it would be unjust to the respondent to make the order (s 51(1)(b)).

There can be no grant of a decree where the applicant was aware, at the time of the registration of the partnership, that the respondent was pregnant, or was a person whose gender had become an acquired gender under the GRA 2004.

Delay

Except where a gender recognition certificate has been issued, CPA 2004, s 51(2)(a) provides that all applications must be made within three years of the registration of the civil partnership. In the case of a gender recognition certificate, the application must be made within six months of its issue (CPA 2004, s 51(5)).

Leave to apply after the three-year period has elapsed may be granted if the applicant has at some time during the three-year period suffered from mental disorder, and in all the circumstances of the case it would be just to grant leave for the institution of proceedings (CPA 2004, s 51(3)(4)).

Consequences of nullity for married couples and civil partners

Relationship status

In the case of a void relationship, either party may enter into a new marriage or civil partnership and treat the void relationship as having never existed whether or not they have sought a decree of nullity. In the case of a voidable relationship, the parties must obtain a decree of nullity from the court before they may claim that their relationship has ceased to exist.

In the case of a void relationship, because it is deemed to have never existed, the provision, or denial, of any benefit will be based on the status of the parties prior to the purported marriage or civil partnership. For example, any State benefits, or dispositions in a will, dependent on marital or civil partnership status will be forfeited.

Where a person enters into a voidable relationship, they lose their former status. On the grant of a decree of nullity, they are deemed not to revert to that status.

In *Ward v Secretary of State for Social Services* [1990] 1 FLR 119, a widow's pension was terminated when she remarried. The marriage was declared to be voidable; on the grant of the decree of nullity she was held not to revert to her status of widowhood. The decision meant that she could not reclaim her pension rights.

The decree of nullity does not normally affect the status of parenthood. However, in *J v C* [2007] Fam 1, the Court of Appeal held that as a consequence of the Human Fertilisation and Embryology Act 1990, s 28 and the Family Law Reform Act 1987, s 1, a transgendered female to male could not be held to be the father of children, conceived after donor insemination in a licensed clinic in 1986 and 1991, because at the time of conception his marriage was void. The GRA 2004 could not come to his aid because it does not provide for the retrospective recognition of a marriage which was entered into prior to the issue of the gender recognition certificate which the man had later obtained. Both the man and his children have lost their legal and social relationship with each other.

The man might have been able to bring a claim under Art 8 of the ECHR.

Revocation of wills

All wills are revoked on marriage or registration of a civil partnership (Wills Act 1837, s 18).

In *Re Roberts* [1978] 1 WLR 653, it was held that this includes a marriage, which is voidable. In the case of a void marriage, the will, of course, will not be revoked.

Financial orders

Under the provisions of the MCA 1973, Part II or the CPA 2004, s 72(1) and Sch 5 (see Chapter 7), in the case of both void and voidable relationships, either party may apply to the court for a financial order at the time they make an application for the decree or order of nullity.

It may seem strange that a party to a void relationship may be made responsible for the financial support of a partner even though that person never acquired the status of spouse or civil partner. The policy behind the law is to ensure that those who purport to enter into a new status, in the case of void relationships or who actually enter into a new status, in the case of voidable relationships, should not necessarily be allowed to escape from the obligations attached to such relationships on the grant of a decree or order of nullity.

In determining whether to make an order, and if so, its quantification, the courts have the same task as they have on divorce, judicial separation or dissolution of a civil partnership (see Chapter 7). The conduct of the parties has been regarded as a relevant factor in the decisions.

In *Whiston v Whiston* [1995] Fam 198, a man, who had lived with a woman for 15 years after they purported to marry, discovered that she already had a husband at the time of the marriage. He applied to the court for a decree of nullity and maintained that the woman should not be given financial relief because of her appalling conduct. The Court of Appeal refused the woman's claim for financial relief because to do so would allow her to assert rights directly arising from the commission of the crime of bigamy.

In *S-T (formerly J) v J* [1998] Fam 103, it was held that a female-to-male transgendered person should not receive any financial provision after his 'wife' was granted a decree of nullity. He had lied about his gender to the registrar by describing himself as a bachelor. Furthermore, he was found to have misled his 'wife' as to the nature of his birth gender. In the light of the fact that the 'marriage' had endured almost 20 years; that he had kept a penile prosthesis in a drawer in the bedroom; that he always backed out of the shower; and that the couple had two children by means of reproductive technology carried out in an infertility clinic, it is surprising that the court viewed his 'wife's' lack of knowledge as entirely blameless.

It was held in the later case of *Rampal v Rampal (No 2)* [2001] 2 FCR 552 that *Whiston v Whiston* had not set an automatic bar to applications for financial remedies consequent on a bigamist marriage. In *PF v QF* [2024] EWFC 10 (B), the court was asked to decide whether a wife who had entered a bigamous marriage could apply for financial relief. There were a number of features which were considered by the judge: the husband had initiated the marriage; both parties were aware that the wife's first marriage had not been annulled at the time of the second marriage; neither party had been misled; and the 'marriage' had been a long relationship of over 18 years. On the basis of this it was not appropriate to strike out the wife's claim. If the wife's claim to have her claim for financial relief heard was refused there would be a chance of real injustice.

Religious decrees of nullity

Roman Catholic Tribunals in England make provision for applications decrees of nullity for members of the Roman Catholic Church. The conditions for obtaining such a decree are not identical to those of the civil law. A person who has obtained a Catholic decree of nullity must first obtain a decree of divorce before marrying again within the jurisdiction. Gillian Douglas et al. carried out an extensive survey of the role of religious courts and their interaction with English law. Their research included an in-depth study of three religious courts: the Catholic National Tribunal for Wales in Cardiff; the Jewish London Beth Din, Family Division; and the Shariah Council of the Birmingham Central Mosque. They concluded from their research that none of the tribunals sought greater recognition by the State but recognised the role and interaction that they had with the civil courts, and all clearly recognised the boundaries between what they do and the sphere of the civil courts. In the case of all three religious courts studied each emphasised that they would not proceed until a civil divorce had been obtained by the parties but the religious courts had no power to compel a party to obtain a civil divorce. (See Douglas et al. (2011).)

Self-test questions

1. Do we need to categorise relationships which are capable of annulment into those which are void and those which are voidable?

2. Has the law on nullity outlived its usefulness? Discuss with reference to recent changes in the law on divorce.

3. Jeffrey married Kate ten years ago but was unable to consummate the marriage because he claimed that he found that he was not sexually attracted to her. At the date of the marriage, he suspected that he preferred men to women and had had several sexual relationships with men.

He has now met Karl with whom he wishes to have a permanent relationship. He would like to register a civil partnership with him. Karl registered a civil partnership four years ago with Liam but has since discovered that Liam was married to Miranda at the time of the registration.

Advise all parties on their current statuses and what, if any, action they need to take in order to enter into a new legal relationship.

4. Jonathan is a male-to-female transgendered person. He has not had gender reassignment surgery because the surgery could well require the need for blood transfusion and he belongs to a humanist organisation which is opposed to blood transfusion on health grounds. He has not yet obtained a gender recognition certificate. Three years ago, when Jonathan was aged 22, his father persuaded him that it was vital for the family business, in which Jonathan worked, to marry Helena, a daughter of a well-known criminal. Jonathan was also told that if he refused he would certainly lose his job, and that he could also 'expect a rough visit from Helena's dad and friends'. The marriage took place on Jonathan's 23rd birthday. He did not reveal to Helena that he was a transgendered person until after the marriage. Jonathan suggested to Helena that to please her father they should foster a baby boy with a view to adopting him, and Helena agreed. Last year, a 3-month-old baby came to live with them; they were told that they would be able to adopt the child this year. Helena gave up work to care for the baby and was supported by Jonathan's earnings. Immediately prior to the adoption date, Jonathan was offered the opportunity to work abroad. He decided to obtain a gender recognition certificate because he regrets his marriage to Helena and wishes to live life as a female.

Advise Jonathan whether he will be able to obtain a decree of nullity.

References

Akhtar, Rainaara, and Nash Rebecca Probert (eds), Cohabitation and Religious Marriage: Status, *Similarities and Solutions* (Bristol University Press 2020)

Crompton, Lucy, 'Where's the Sex in Same-Sex Marriage?' (2013) 43 *Family Law* 564

Daily Telegraph (2009) https://www.dailytelegraph.co.uk/news/religion/9042186/Clergyman-jailed-for-sham-marriage-scam.html (accessed 09.09.2024)

Davis, Nira Yuval, Georgie Wemyss and Kathryn Cassidy, 'Every Day Bordering, Belonging and the Re-Orientation of British Immigration Legislation' [2018] *Sociology* 228

Douglas, Gillian, Norman Doe, Sophie Gilliat-Ray, Russell Sandberg and Asma Khan, 'Marriage and Divorce in Religious Courts: A Case Study' [2011] *Family Law* 956

Eekelaar, John, 'Marriage: A Modest Proposal' [2013] *Family Law* 83

Forced Marriage www.homeoffice.gov.uk/media-centre/news/forced-marriage-new-law

Gaffney-Rhys, Ruth, 'The Criminalisation of Forced Marriage in England and Wales: One Year on' [2015] *Family Law* 1382

Le Grice, Valentine, 'A Critique of Non-Marriage' [2013] *Family Law* 1278

'Nullity of Marriage' (Law Com No 33)

Probert, Rebecca, 'When Are We Married? Void, Non-Existent and Presumed Marriages' (2002) 22 *Legal Studies* 398

Sharpe, Alex, 'Transgender Marriage and the Legal Obligation to Disclose Gender' (2012) 75 *Modern Law Review* 33

Wray, Helena, *Regulating Marriage Migration into the UK: A Stranger in the Home* (Routledge 2016)

Further reading

Barker, Nicola, *Not the Marrying Kind: A Feminist Critique of Same-Sex Marriage* (Palgrave Macmillan 2012)

Douglas, Gillian, 'Marriage – Nullity – *Akhter v Khan and the Attorney-General*' [2018] *Family Law* 1388

Gaffney-Rhys, Ruth, 'The Legal Response to Polygamous Marriages in England and Wales' [2011] *International Family Law* 319

House of Commons Library Standard Note, 'Immigration: Reforms to Family Migration Routes' www.parliament.uk/briefing-papers/SN06216

Hutchinson, Anne-Marie, Harriet Hayward and Teertha Gupta, 'Forced Marriage Nullity Procedure in England and Wales' [2006] *International Family Law* 20

Law Commission, 'Nullity of Marriage' (Law Com No 33, 1970)

Probert, Rebecca, 'How Would Corbett v Corbett Be Decided Today?' [2005] *Family Law* 382

UK Border Agency, 'Changes to Immigration Rules' www.ukba.homeoffice.gov.uk/sitecontent/newsarticles/2012/july/15-family-mig

UK Border Agency, 'Family Migration: Consultation' (July 2011) https://assets.publishing.service.gov.uk/media/5a7c95cc40f0b6629523a781/family-consultation.pdf

UK Home Office Response to Consultation on Family Migration (2012) www.ukba.homeoffice.gov.uk/sitecontent/. . ./news/cons-fam-mig.pdf

Welstead, Mary, 'A Constitutional Solution to Royal Marital Breakdown' [1994] *New Law Journal* 144

Welstead, Mary, 'The Virtue of Virginity' [2009] *New Law Journal* 95

4

Acquisition and protection of rights in the family home

SUMMARY

The family home is important both as a secure living space and as a potentially valuable but vulnerable asset. The loss of the home has profound effects on the welfare of the family, and on the State which has to support those who become homeless.

In this chapter, we consider what constitutes the family home and we consider a variety of different ways in which rights may arise in the family home. These include the doctrine of informal trusts, the doctrine of proprietary estoppel, the law of contract and the provisions of the FLA 1996, Part IV. Where the parties to a relationship are married or in a civil partnership rights in the family home arise automatically by virtue of the status of marriage but where the parties cohabit rights arise solely under property law.

By contrast cohabitants have no automatic property rights and must rely on property law principles in order to gain any rights in the family home. Contributions in kind and oral agreements may be relevant but only where they satisfy certain legal requirements which makes this area of law complex and unreliable. The status of a cohabitant has very limited recognition and none in relation to rights in the family home without proof of an intention that both should have rights. This is a difficult and controversial area of law, and we will examine efforts to extend some automatic rights in property to cohabitants. There is no current legislation that protects rights of cohabitants. This lack of rights for cohabitants causes many complications in family law, and we return to this as a theme a number of times in this book.

The family home: an overview

Historically, even married women were unable to claim rights in the family home, and this was so even if the property had been owned by the wife's family. The first recognition of a married woman's right in the family home can be found in the Married Women's Property Act 1882 which enabled a woman to hold property separately from her husband. Today, marriage and civil partnership will give rise to automatic rights in the family home and will not be solely dependent on financial

DOI: 10.4324/9781003435020-4

contributions. It means that there are two separate ways of resolving disputes of the family home when a relationship breaks down, dependent on whether or not the parties are married or in a civil partnership.

Unlike many European countries there is no recognition of family or communal property in England and Wales. The family home is just one asset within a family. As stated earlier on the breakdown of a relationship, resolution of ownership will depend on the status of the relationship. Where the parties cohabit the rules of property will apply. These rules have serious shortcomings when applied in a relationship as issues beyond the formalities of purchase e.g. length of the relationship, whether the couple have children, individual financial needs are not relevant. During the latter part of the twentieth century and the first years of the twenty-first century, the family home became the most valuable financial asset (often in close competition with a personal pension) for many families. Without a home in which to live, and without the knowledge that they are secure from eviction, no family can thrive satisfactorily; after food and clothing, shelter is the most basic of all human needs. Although a right to a family home is not recognised under the ECHR there is some recognition of property rights under Article 8.

It has been accepted that Art 8 (the right to respect for privacy and family life) of the European Convention 1950 (ECHR) includes respect for a person's home.

Lord Millett in *Harrow London Borough Council v Qazi* (2003) recognised that the home is a place where a person and his family:

> *are entitled to be left in peace from interference by the state or agents of the state. It is an important aspect of his dignity as a human being, and it is protected as such and not as an item of property.*

Between 1920 and 2021, a significant social change relating to home ownership occurred. In 1920, only 10 per cent of property in the UK was owner-occupied; by 2021, this figure had risen to 32.6 per cent owner occupation in England and 38.00 per cent in Wales (ONS 2021). This figure had risen to one-third (33 per cent) of households owned the accommodation they lived in outright (Miles 2003). During the 1980s, Margaret Thatcher's Government popularised the idea of a property-owning democracy which would have a stake in the economic system. Later Governments, regardless of political persuasion, took a similar approach even to the extent of providing help with mortgage interest payments when family members become unemployed.

For most families, this increase in home ownership has been achieved by means of heavy borrowings, normally secured by way of mortgage of their home. Many families were persuaded to take this risk because house price inflation gave them the opportunity to acquire capital. In 2007, average house prices rose by 10.9 per cent and the price of the average family home was £205,286. By March 2024, this had risen to £264,500 (Zoopla 2024). The home was seen as a source of wealth which could be passed on by inheritance from parent to child. It was regularly used as security for further borrowings to help finance, *inter alia*, such ventures as family businesses, university education, holidays, or to help adult offspring purchase their own family homes.

The cost of living crisis, the rise in house prices compared to income and uncertainty about future inflation has led to a reduction in owner occupation.

As more families have not only found it difficult to raise money to make a down payment on a home but have also had to face the risk of unemployment, they appear to have made the decision to rely on the increase in the supply of private sector rented property. This supply has been drastically reduced in recent years mainly due to the passage of legislation which has made it far less advantageous financially to let property as a landlord. Although many families are beginning to see the advantages of the freedom to move easily from one rented property to another, possibly to a new area, and without the risks and expensive maintenance involved in home ownership, the lack of affordable properties has made this option far less inviting or not even a possibility. This change may begin to have a significant effect on many aspects of family law such as financial provision on divorce and inheritance (see Chapters 6, 7).

Problems of home ownership

Where personal borrowings to fund the family home are exceptionally high, and when unemployment is a serious possibility, financial difficulties become commonplace. Families risk having to sell their property. After a period of exceptionally low interest rates, 2023 saw a rapid rise in interest rates. In some cases, where borrowers have been unable to make repayments on loans secured against the family home, lenders may attempt to repossess it, and bankruptcy may follow.

In these difficult circumstances, disputes can arise over ownership of the home, the rights of occupation in it, and the division of the proceeds of sale. Many couples do not lead the organised lives expected of them by the complexities of land law. The legal title to the property may have been conveyed into one, or even both, of their names but they may have failed to give any thought to the precise share of their beneficial interest in the property or may have failed to record it in writing. Where parties are not in a formal relationship and property rules apply, formalities such as recording an agreement in writing are often needed in order to gain rights.

In determining beneficial ownership where a couple has failed to clarify the matter, the law is supposedly bound by strict principles of property law. These principles have long been criticised as inappropriate in the family context. They do not reflect the informality with which many couples conduct their financial affairs. They have been particularly problematic for cohabitants who, unlike married couples or civil partners, do not have the benefit of the court's jurisdiction to redistribute their property as it thinks fit at the end of a relationship (see Chapter 7).

Various solutions have been proposed by the Law Commission on at least two occasions, but legislation has not followed.

Lady Hale in the House of Lords decision in *Stack v Dowden* [2007] UKHL 17 (see later in this chapter) commented that the lack of legislation in this area means that:

> *the evolution of the law of property to take account of changing social and economic circumstances will have to come from the courts rather than Parliament.*

The Law Commission proposals – home sharing

In 2002, the Law Commission produced *Sharing Homes: a Discussion Paper* (Law Com No 278). It examined the problems experienced by all those who share homes and emphasised the importance of persuading them to formalise their arrangements and declare the nature of their respective shares in the beneficial interest. The Law Commission proposed that any changes in the law should be by way of a default system which would apply only if home sharers had failed to specify the share of the beneficial interest. The report was inconclusive but took an approach which, very broadly, would take into account the home sharers' contributions to the property in determining their share. There has been no legislation resulting from the Commission's report.

Cohabitants and the family home

In 2007, the Law Commission's report, *Cohabitation: The Financial Consequences of Relationship Breakdown* (Law Com No 307) considered the problem of how to resolve disputes relating to family homes shared by the ever-growing number of cohabitants. It pointed out the difficulties of using strict property law to resolve these disputes. Its recommendations are considered in more detail in Chapter 7. As was seen in Chapter 2, the Government has made clear that it does not propose to legislate in the near future and give cohabitants greater rights than they now have. In 2022, the Women and Equalities Committee, a cross party group of MPs, made firm recommendations on the urgent need for reform of the law and greater education for the public on this issue. Those recommendations were not accepted by the Government. It leaves a cohabitant in a difficult position often having to rely on the expense of lawyers in order to establish rights in property (House of Commons Women and Equalities Committee).

Sharing the family home

Background

In England and Wales as there is no concept of family property or community of property, ownership of the family home in England and Wales is dependent on proof of ownership at law and in equity. There are wider issues involved in the problems associated with ownership of the family home. Writing in 'Unfair Shares for Women: The Rhetoric of Equality and the Reality of Inequality', Rosemary Auchmuty stated, in Lim and Bottomley (2007):

> As well as being the couple's greatest (or only) asset of worth, the home was the primary site of men's exercise of power. Symbolically as well as practically, it represented the last bastion of an outmoded patriarchal rule that lasted well beyond the implementation of sex equality legislation.

She continues by looking at cases where courts have taken a nuanced view of what constitutes a 'contribution' sufficient to give rise to rights in the family home citing cases such as *Button v Button* [1968] 1 WLR 457 and *Pettitt v Pettitt* [1968] 1 WLR 443. Her criticism is focussed on the way the court has always given excess weight to a direct financial contribution which has not always been available to women in relationships. She states: 'By constantly returning to rules requiring *direct financial contributions*, the courts have wilfully and deliberately discriminated against women, whose restricted access to money of their own has been well documented.'

The system of land ownership in England and Wales puts weight on ownership at law. It gives owners rights to deal in the land, e.g. sell the property or lease it to others, and therefore ownership at law is crucial in relation to control of the property. Ownership is recorded at the Land Registry and it is that record that is proof of title. The system also recognises that other rights might arise behind the title. These rights are called rights in equity; they do not allow the claimant to deal in the land, but they can be very valuable as ownership in equity relates to the share that each party can claim in the capital value.

Ownership at law is dependent on proof of registration, but proof of ownership in equity particularly where a party does not own the legal title is often complicated. Various rights can arise which although are not ownership of the title may give rise to rights of occupation. Rights of occupation are dealt with separately under the Family Law Act 1996, which gives spouses and civil partners automatic rights of occupation of the family home irrespective of property rights. It is also possible for a cohabitant to make an application to occupy the family home, but this can be more problematic where a cohabitant does not have property rights.

Buying a house: legal ownership

Where a couple purchase land jointly at law, both names will be recorded at the Land Registry. Purchase of the land requires a formal document called a deed under s 52(1) of the Law of Property Act 1925 and both parties must sign. Oral agreements cannot transfer rights at law. The purchase in joint names will automatically give rise to a trust of the family home. Ideally on purchase the parties declare their rights by way of express trust which must adhere to the formalities of the Law of Property Act 1925. Express trusts must be declared or evidenced in writing under s 53(1)(b), and it must be clear that the parties are creating an express trust of land. Trusts form a separate subject for study in law, but there are features which are important to understand in relation to the family home. These features are particularly important in relation to cohabitants. A key feature of a trust is the separation of ownership and enjoyment of property is separated from decision making and management in a trust.

So in a trust the person or persons owning at law (referred to as trustees) must make decision on behalf of everyone with rights in the property irrespective of whether or not he/she owns at law.

Example

Asma and Ben have lived together in rented property for five years. They have saved enough to purchase a house. If they buy jointly at law then all decisions about the house will have to be made jointly and all paperwork must be signed by both parties. So they take management decisions jointly.

If the property is purchased in the sole name of one party e.g. Asma, she will be sole owner at law and she will sign any documentation. She can take the decision to sell the property, but any decision taken by Asma in relation to the property must be taken on behalf of Ben as well as Asma.

Nevertheless, even if Ben does not own at law he may still have rights in the property and if the relationship breaks down Ben may be able to claim a share of the value but first he must show that he has rights in equity in the property.

In a perfect world all those who agree to share property together as their family home would decide how that property should be owned. If it is to be a genuine joint enterprise, and they propose sharing the profits and losses equally, they would decide to register the legal title in both their names, so in our example Ben and Asma would agree to both register as owners at law.

Buying a house: the equitable title

Most couples will not understand the complexities of property law without legal advice. Few will understand the difference between the legal and equitable estate, and so harsh legal reality hits when their relationship breaks down, or their partner dies, or a lender, with a secured interest in the property, takes action because loan payments have not been kept up to date. There are a number of different ways in which a partner can claim a share in property where he/she has not been registered as owner. According to Carnworth LJ, in the Court of Appeal decision in *Stack v Dowden* (2005), the various interpretations of these doctrines are confusing:

> To the detached observer, the result may seem like a witches' brew into which various esoteric ingredients have been stirred over the years, and in which different ideas bubble to the surface at different times. They include the implied trust, constructive trust, resulting trust, presumption of advancement, proprietary estoppel, unjust enrichment and so on. These ideas are likely to mean nothing to a layman and often little more to the lawyers who use them.

We will consider each of these in turn, but firstly where rights are established in equity there is another question to consider: do the parties own as joint tenants or tenants in common?

Assuming Asma and Ben purchase their house together and both have established rights then the next question is whether they own as joint tenants or tenants in common. This would be declared at purchase and in an ideal world will be done by express declaration.

Joint tenancy

Purchasers can indicate on the registration application form making clear that the beneficial interest is also to be shared equally.

This would comply with the formal requirements for property transactions to be in writing (Law of Property Act 1925, ss 52, 53, Law of Property (Miscellaneous Provisions) Act 1989, s 2), and it would be difficult for any person to challenge their decision at a later date.

If the parties choose a **joint tenancy** then if the relationship breaks down the value of the property is shared equally irrespective of their contributions but if one party dies then the survivor takes everything. Very broadly, if they decide to be **joint tenants**, each person owns all of the property. When one of them dies, his or her interest disappears. The survivor will now own all the property alone, and no share remains to be inherited under the deceased's will or on an intestacy (see Chapter 8). If the property is sold, the joint tenancy ends, and each person will be entitled to receive an equal share of the proceeds of sale (see generally Pawlowski (2016; 2013)).

Tenants in common

Alternatively they can choose to own their beneficial interests as **tenants in common** in which case they will own separate shares in specific proportions expressly. The share will pass on each party's death under a valid will or if no will has been made on intestacy.

Example

Assume Asma and Ben purchase property as joint tenants and this is expressly declared at the purchase. Two years after the purchase Asma is killed in a car accident and Ben becomes sole owner at law and in equity.

By contrast if at purchase they are declared to be tenants in common and Asma has left her share in the property to her brother Caleb, then Ben will own the property at law but Caleb will now have a half share.

If the parties have chosen to be tenants in common, each of them will own an agreed specific share of the beneficial interest in the property so it may not necessarily be a half share. If the property is sold while the parties are both alive each will receive the proportion of the proceeds of sale in accordance with their agreement.

The judiciary has regularly emphasised that disputes about family homes would disappear entirely if everyone expressly declared how they held the property in equity.

Unfortunately, the judicial cry has been ignored by so many, and the decisions discussed in this chapter illustrate this. One of the problems is that family lawyers and property lawyers approach the ownership of the family home in a completely different way. Property lawyers consider property rights as based on principles of property law ignoring wider issues of family life. Joanna Miles summed up the approach of family lawyers and family law as follows: 'Family law, by contrast, is often discretion based and concerned about familial status, and the consequences of relationship breakdown' (Miles 2003). Resolution of the family home by property lawyers is so often based on principles that seem far divorced from the realities of family life. In the following chapter the concept of common intention will be explored, but for many in their day to day family life common intention with regard to rights of ownership of the family home is rarely explicitly or implicitly discussed. The reliance on a concept that is so far divorced from family life has been criticised by many. See Nicola Glover and Paul Todd who wrote critically of what they referred to as the 'myth' of common intention (Glover and Todd 1996; see also Eekelaar 1987 and Maniscalco 2020).

One of the first questions to ask in relation to the title of the family home is whether or not the parties purchased the property at law in sole or joint names. If the parties have purchased property in the sole name of one party and have no express agreement about shares in the property then as discussed earlier in Lord Carnworth's judgment there are various ways in which a cohabitant can establish rights in property and also quantify the size of share each person holds. Each will be considered in turn.

Informal trusts

Most people arrange their financial affairs informally based on informal conversations. These can be accepted in law as proof of the intentions of the parties, but the law is rather confused on what constitutes proof. One of the advantages of informal trusts which include the family home as opposed to formal trusts of property is that they are not required to be in writing (Law of Property Act 1925, s 53(2)).

> If a person is able to establish the existence of such a trust, he or she acquires a beneficial interest in the property and, along with it a right to occupy the family home (Trusts of Land and Appointment of Trustees Act 1996, s 12; Family Law Act 1996, Part IV); a right to ask the court for sale or delay of sale of the home (Trusts of Land and Appointment of Trustees Act 1996, s 14), and an entitlement to a share in the proceeds of sale.

All these rights have the potential to prevail over the rights of third parties who acquire the property at a later date.

Rights in the family home acquired by way of proprietary estoppel give rise to not entirely dissimilar benefits.

There are two types of informal trust also referred to as implied trusts: the constructive trust and the resulting trust

The resulting trust is rarely used today to consider shares in the family home so the constructive trust will be considered in far more detail. Indeed, in *Stack v Dowden* a majority of the House of Lords criticised the use of the resulting trust in relation to the family home and so the doctrine in this context has been largely disregarded.

Resulting trusts

In the context of a family home, a resulting trust was said to come into existence in two types of situations. First where property was purchased in the sole name of one partner, and the other partner (or other family member) had made a financial contribution to the purchase price (the contribution could take the form of payments towards the overall cost of the property; the initial deposit; mortgage payments; legal fees; or the transfer of a discount, which had been granted to the claimant by the seller), there was a rebuttable presumption that the parties expected to share the beneficial interest in the property in proportion to their financial contributions. This presumption was based on the rather materialistic view that no one would make a financial contribution to another person's property without expecting something in return.

In the second situation, where property was purchased in the names of both persons without any explicit declaration of their respective beneficial interests, a rebuttable presumption arose that the beneficial interest would follow the legal interest, and it would be held in equal shares regardless of their respective financial contributions (see *Springette v Defoe* [1992] 2 FLR 388).

The presumption of advancement

It is material to note that the presumption of a resulting trust could be rebutted if the presumption of advancement applied. This rather archaic and paternalistic principle provided that where a husband, father or fiancé made a contribution towards the purchase price of a property, which was registered in his wife's, child's or fiancée's name, he was presumed to have made a gift of the property. There would be no resulting trust in his favour, meaning that he could not later claim a share even though he had provided the purchase monies. The principle did not apply to wives or fiancées who provide money towards the purchase price of their husbands' or fiancés' properties, nor does it apply to civil partners. The presumption of advancement could be rebutted by evidence to the contrary.

In *McGrath v Wallis* [1995] 2 FLR 114, Nourse LJ stated that:

> in its application to houses acquired for joint occupation, the equitable presumption of advancement has been reclassified as a judicial instrument of last resort. . . . For myself, I have been unable to recollect any subsequent case of this kind in which the presumption has proved to be decisive, even where one of the parties had since died.

In response to criticism the Equality Act 2010, s 199 abolished the presumption of advancement in future cases. However, the section has not yet been brought into force and it seems unlikely today that it will ever be brought into force which means this archaic principle could still apply, but the presumption is very weak and can easily be rebutted.

Gifts or loans or monies attributable to some other motive

No resulting trust could arise where there was evidence that the financial contribution was a gift or a loan or could be attributable to another motive.

(See generally for a discussion about the role of resulting trusts George and Sloan (2017).)

Constructive trusts

The constructive trust is the second type of informal trust and usually applies to the family home where one party seeks to establish rights. The trust arises because the court can draw conclusions from certain types of behaviour. Only certain behaviour will give rise to a trust and there has been repeated criticism of the limitations of what the court regards as behaviour sufficient to give rise to rights.

> **Example**
>
> Returning to Asma and Ben, if we assume the property was purchased in Asma's name alone then in order for Ben to claim a share the court will only accept:
>
> 1.   contributions to the purchase of the property by Ben; or
>
> 2.   an agreement between Asma and Ben that Ben is to get a share of the property.

Agreements to share the property where the property is in the sole name of one of the partners or family member

The law on constructive trusts can be found in three key decisions decided in the House of Lords and Supreme Court: *Lloyds Bank plc v Rosset* [1991] 1 AC 107; *Stack v Dowden* (2007); and *Jones v Kernott* (2011).

For many years, the decision of the House of Lords in ***Lloyds Bank v Rosset*** (1991) was regarded as the gold standard for establishing constructive trusts of the family home. Mr Rosset had purchased a semi-derelict farmhouse in his sole name, using money provided by the trustees of a family trust. Before the family moved into the property, Mrs Rosset spent every day at the house for four months. She monitored the builders' work, and went to the builders' merchants and organised the delivery of all the necessary materials. She helped plan all the renovations of the house and carried out a substantial part of the preparations prior to the decoration of the interior. During this period, Mr Rosset was mainly abroad, and Mrs Rosset had total responsibility for the renovation. In addition, she cared for their children.

Without his wife's knowledge, Mr Rosset obtained a bank overdraft and mortgaged the family home to the bank but he subsequently became unable to make the repayments. The bank commenced proceedings to sell the property. Mrs Rosset claimed that she had a beneficial share in the property by way of a constructive trust, which was binding on the bank.

The House of Lords rejected her claim; Lord Bridge explained in some detail the principles of constructive trusts. In his view, there were two types of agreements which could give rise to a constructive trust. The first required the court to ask the question:

> *whether there has, at any time prior to acquisition, or exceptionally at some later date, been any agreement, arrangement or understanding reached between them that the property is to be shared beneficially. The finding of an agreement or arrangement to share in this sense can only, I think, be based on evidence of express discussions between the partners, however imperfectly remembered and however imprecise their terms may have been.*
>
> *Once this agreement has been found, the person claiming a trust must show that he or she has acted to his or her detriment in reliance on the agreement or intention. The detriment in these circumstances must relate to the property in some way but need not necessarily be a financial contribution.*

The second type of agreement, according to Lord Bridge, is:

> in sharp contrast with [the first] situation is the very different one where there is no
> evidence to support a finding of an agreement or arrangement to share, however
> reasonable it might have been for the parties to reach such an arrangement if they had
> applied their minds to the question, and where the court must rely entirely on the
> conduct of the parties both as the basis from which to infer a common intention to
> share the property beneficially and as the conduct relied on to give rise to a
> constructive trust.

He maintained that only direct financial contributions, made by the claimant, and referable to the purchase of the property, could provide the dual function of the inference of an agreement or intention and the relevant detrimental reliance on it. Nothing else would be sufficient (see *Gissing v Gissing* [1971] AC 886).

Lord Bridge acknowledged the difficulties involved in determining the intentions of the parties in familial disputes at a time when the relationship had broken down. He explained that:

> Spouses living in amity will not normally think it necessary to formulate or define their
> respective interests in property in any precise way. The expectation of parties to every
> happy marriage is that they will share the practical benefits of occupying the
> matrimonial home no matter who owns it. But this is something quite distinct from
> sharing the beneficial interest in the asset, which the matrimonial home represents.
> These considerations give rise to special difficulties for judges who are called on to
> resolve a dispute between spouses who have parted and are at arm's length as to what
> their common intention or understanding with respect to interests in property was at a
> time when they were still living as a united family and acquiring a matrimonial home in
> the expectation of living in it together indefinitely.

The House of Lords maintained that in spite of the agreed joint venture to create a family home, there was insufficient evidence of the first type of agreement to share the beneficial interest. Indeed, there could have been no agreement because Mr Rosset had purchased the house and paid for its renovations from trust funds. He knew that the trustees would not have released the funds to him had they known that he was planning to share the beneficial interest with Mrs Rosset. Furthermore, there was no conduct from which the second type of agreement could be inferred because Mrs Rosset had provided no financial input for the purchase of the farmhouse.

The decision in *Rosset* (1991) limited the possibility of claims of beneficial interests in the family home. Beneficial interests are not part of the everyday conversation of most couples. They often fail to understand their significance and do not always make clear their agreements with each other. Inferred agreements equally elude them; women without financial resources are more likely to make non-financial contributions, often in the form of housekeeping and childcare, which enable their partners to earn the money to pay for the family home. If women do earn money, they are more likely to use it to purchase consumable household goods. In the absence of evidence of a clear agreement, neither of these types of contributions, according to *Rosset* (1991), permits a claim to a share in the beneficial interest of the family home. This decision highlights so clearly the different approach that a property lawyer will take to discussion of rights in the family to the approach taken by a family lawyer. The property lawyer focusses on a certain prescribed formula without which the claimant such as Mrs Rosset loses out; broader issues are ignored (see also *Burns v Burns* [1984] Ch 317). Where there has been a discussion about rights in the property case law shows us that the law makes quite fine distinctions between the different words used and also the contributions made. Simone Wong assesses the way the court has evaluated in the past the various contributions made towards a share of the family home arguing that courts have always focussed on direct contributions taking a property law approach as opposed to a relationship approach (Wong 2007).

In *James v Thomas* [2007] EWCA Civ 1007, Ms James sought to establish rights in the family home based on a promise 'you will be well provided for' and 'this will benefit us both' made by Mr Thomas with regard to the purchase of the house. It was held that there was no evidence of an express common intention. The approach here was to concentrate on the particular words used; had they been nuanced in a slightly different way, then the result could have been different.

A more familial approach to agreements

Prior to *Rosset* (1991), the courts had begun to develop an approach which recognised that the analysis of familial relationships and the discovery of relevant agreements are not a scientific exercise. The judiciary was prepared, by a sleight of hand, to find evidence of agreements in circumstances where the person who was the legal owner of the property had made an excuse about his or her motivation for purchasing the family home in his or her own name. Such an excuse could well have given rise to a belief that the legal owner would have liked to share the beneficial interest in the property had the circumstances been slightly different. However as can be seen in the cases that follow there were no express words of transfer to the other party.

> An example of this approach can be found in *Eves v Eves* [1975] 1 WLR 1338 where a male cohabitant told his female partner that the only reason why the property was to be acquired in his name alone was because she was under 21 years of age; this was accepted as a relevant agreement in the context of a constructive trust.

The rules for the minimum age of property ownership had recently been lowered to 18 so such a statement could have carried some meaning in the 1970s.

> A similar approach was taken in *Grant v Edwards* [1986] Ch 638 where a man had told his partner that he could not put the house in joint names because it might affect her divorce settlement. This was held to be evidence of a common intention to share the beneficial interest. (See also *Hammond v Mitchell* [1992] 1 WLR 1127.)

> ## Example
>
> In the earlier example of Asma and Ben, consider what would happen if Asma bought a property in her name and Ben had no spare cash to contribute to the sale. If she says to him, 'You want you to have some security. I hold the house for both of us,' the courts might interpret this as an express declaration and Ben will have a share even though he had not made any contribution to the purchase price.

Following *Rosset* (1991), the courts continued to accept the preceding approach as a way to overcome Lord Bridge's seemingly rigid principles. This strict approach was subject to criticism. It embedded a very biased approach to home sharing and contributions. It was often a matter of chance whether a conversation takes place that constitutes a representation of rights and further whether the claimant can adequately recall what was said. Inferences cannot be drawn from circumstances and weight cannot be laid on contributions to the family and household in order to establish rights in the family home.

However, some years later in the House of Lords decision in *Stack v Dowden* [2007] 1 FLR 1858 (see later), Lord Walker questioned Lord Bridge's view that only financial contributions would lead to an inference of a common intention to share the beneficial interest:

> *Whether or not Lord Bridge's observation was justified in 1991, in my opinion the law has moved on, and your Lordships should move it a little more in the same direction.*

Baroness Hale agreed, and said that *Rosset* (1991) had set the hurdle too high for claimants seeking to show that there was an implied intention, or agreement, to share the beneficial interest.

It must be stressed, however, that in *Stack v Dowden* (2007), it was not in dispute that there was a *Rosset* compliant agreement to share the beneficial interest because the property was registered in both partners' names. The decision centred on whether the couple's intention, manifested by that joint registration, had changed over time and if so what effect had it had on the partner's respective shares. Despite the statements of Lord Walker and Baroness Hale, as yet, there is no clear decision which has lowered the hurdle imposed in *Rosset* for the finding of agreements when the property is in the sole name of one of the partners. It will surely happen although one might comment that with rapidly rising house prices it has become far more likely that property is purchased in the joint names of two parties as opposed to one which will at least overcome the primary hurdle of finding an express common intention.

Detrimental reliance

In addition to the relevant intention or agreement, the claimant must also show detrimental reliance.

Financial detriment

It has generally been accepted that where the claimant has made a significant financial contribution to the property, that will also serve as proof of both the relevant intention and the necessary detrimental reliance.

Non-financial detriment

Where the court accepts the existence of an agreement or common intention, any conduct referable to the property has been accepted as sufficient detriment if it is found to be in reliance on the agreement or common intention of the parties.

In *Rosset* (1991), Lord Bridge found that Mrs Rosset's conduct was insufficient to be regarded as detriment. He explained that even if the Court had been prepared to find the relevant agreement or common intention, the conduct claimed as detrimental reliance was not only *de minimis*, but was also explicable by her desire to get her family happily installed in their new home prior to Christmas.

These comments seem outdated today especially since much of the behaviour of Mrs Rosset was directly referable to improvements to the property. Simone Wong further commented in her discussion on the shared home: 'From a feminist perspective, it has been argued that the little significance given to indirect contributions is not only discriminatory but also forms an effective barrier to female claimants successfully establishing the existence of the requisite common intention' (Lim and Bottomley 2007). It seems though that the courts have been more prepared to accept some types of behaviour at least as evidence of detrimental reliance than others.

In *Eves v Eves* (1975), Mrs Eves claimed that in reliance on the agreement she had

> stripped the wallpaper in the hall; painted the woodwork in the lounge and kitchen, and the kitchen cabinets, and generally cleaned the whole house; she painted the brickwork in the front of the house; using a 14 pound sledgehammer she broke up a large area of concrete covering the whole of the front garden and carried the pieces to a skip which had been hired for the purpose; she then prepared the front garden for turfing; she did work in the back garden and helped the defendant to demolish a shed there and to put up a new one.

The Court of Appeal was most impressed by this behaviour and granted her a beneficial share in the property but where Ms Eves claimed that she had contributed to the running of the house this behaviour was ignored.

It remains uncertain what other conduct might be accepted by the courts as a relevant detriment particularly if it is not directly referable to the property in some way. Such an approach is very narrow and excludes any reference to other aspects of family life. It has been subject to criticism from lawyers, the judiciary and academics [e.g.]. In *Stack v Dowden* (2007) comments were made by Lord Walker about the reasoning of Lord Bridge in *Rosset* that 'the law has moved'. This has been interpreted to suggest that other issues than purely monetary contributions or evidence of an express intention to share would suffice. Indeed Professor Martin Dixon has commented that there is now a third way to base a claim to a share in a sole owned property namely by basing it on inferences drawn from the parties' entire relationship (Dixon 2023). In *Capehorn v Harris* [2015] EWCA Civ 955, the Court of Appeal accepted that it was possible for the court to infer intention from conduct but there must be some clear evidence of this which can be objectively deduced as proof of intention.

The problem here is that often behaviour can be interpreted in several ways. As seen in *James v Thomas* discussed earlier, assisting in one's partner's business is not necessarily referable to a share in the family home.

Quantification of the beneficial interest

For many years the constructive trust cases which came before the courts were primarily concerned with the issue of agreement or common intention. More recent case law has centred on the quantification of the beneficial interest in circumstances where there was evidence of a *Rosset* compliant agreement.

On a strict interpretation of the law, where the agreement was implied from financial contributions, the claimant's share was said to be in proportion to the amount of his or her financial contribution to the property. Where there was evidence of an explicit agreement or an intention that the property should be shared, the conservative view was that the claimant should receive the share agreed.

The move to pragmatism

The courts found this conventional view to quantification unsatisfactory in the family home context, and attempts were made to replace it with a more holistic and pragmatic approach. It is now possible to consider the issue in a subjective manner rather than purely objectively. This new approach has evolved from cases of joint ownership in particular *Jones v Kernott* [2011] UKSC 53, so strictly the judgments should be viewed as *obiter* and not binding where the title is in sole ownership, but nevertheless the courts have been prepared to embrace the principles in sole ownership cases. The following decisions illustrate this pragmatism which was already detected before *Stack* and *Jones*.

The decision in *Midland Bank plc v Cooke* [1995] 4 All ER 562 was perhaps the first time a holistic approach was taken to quantification, although some might argue that Lord Denning's approach in *Eves v Eves* (1975) was the real starting point when he awarded Mrs Eves a one-third share in the beneficial interest in the property without any explanation why he had done so.

In **Cooke**, Mrs Cooke and her husband had been given a wedding present of £1,000 in 1971. They had used the money as a deposit towards the purchase of their first home, which was conveyed into the sole name of the husband; he subsequently made all the mortgage payments. Waite LJ held that this initial contribution gave rise to a **Rosset** compliant agreement that the couple were to share the beneficial interest in some unspecified proportion between them. He stressed that the couple had not, and indeed could not have, at the time of purchase, formulated with any precision what their final shares would be. He was, therefore, perfectly happy to quantify their respective shares on the basis of their conduct during the relationship. During a long marriage, Mrs Cooke had contributed financially to the household income, and made a major contribution to every aspect of the relationship including working on the property. Waite LJ explained that to give Mrs Cooke other than an equal share in the beneficial would be inequitable.

The decision in *Cox v Jones* [2004] EWHC 1006 (Ch) also illustrates a measure of flexibility towards quantification. Both partners were barristers. Ms Cox, the claimant, began to cohabit with Mr Jones, the defendant, in his flat in Lincoln's Inn; Ms Cox had a large dog. Mr Jones found life in the small flat with Ms Cox and the dog rather constricting, and Ms Cox and Mr Jones sought a larger family home in the country. The house, known as The Mill, required extensive renovation and was purchased in Mr Jones' sole name. Ms Cox managed and coordinated the project, but Mr Jones paid for the cost of all the works.

Ms Cox also found a flat, which she wished to purchase as an investment. Mr Jones paid the greater part of the purchase price, because Ms Cox had insufficient financial resources to do so. The price of the flat was discounted; Ms Cox had astutely persuaded the vendor to allow her to buy it at a low price in order to avoid the expense of placing it on the open market. This property, like The Mill, was also registered in Mr Jones' sole name.

The relationship broke down, and Ms Cox claimed a beneficial interest in both the house and the flat.

Mr Jones denied that there was any agreement to share the beneficial interest in the house jointly, and also argued that Ms Cox had exaggerated her contribution to the management of the renovation. The court found that there was express evidence of an agreement, albeit one which did not provide for an exact quantification of the parties' shares.

The court awarded Ms Cox a 25 per cent beneficial share in the house, based on her management of the project.

However with respect to the flat, the court took a more generous approach. Mr Jones maintained that he had purchased the flat as an investment for himself and denied that Ms Cox had any beneficial share in it. The court found an express agreement, made prior to the purchase of the property, that Mr Jones would hold it, as nominee, absolutely, for Ms Cox. She had acted to her detriment in reliance on that agreement by allowing Mr Jones to benefit from the discounted price, which had been secured by her negotiation skills alone, and she had managed the rental of the property afterwards. She was, therefore, held to have acquired a 100 per cent beneficial interest in the flat.

In *Oxley v Hiscock* [2004] EWCA Civ 546, the Court of Appeal maintained that the right question for the Court to ask:

> was what would be a fair share for each party having regard to the whole course of dealing between them in relation to the property.

> (Chadwick LJ)

Ms Oxley had purchased her council house in her sole name, in 1987, at the discounted price of £25,200, using money provided by Mr Hiscock, with whom she subsequently began to cohabit. Mr Hiscock had worked in Kuwait, and during the invasion by Iraqi troops in 1990, he was captured, taken to Baghdad and held as hostage. On his release, he returned home and a new property was purchased for £127,200. The funds for this property came from the proceeds of sale of the first house which amounted to £61,500, (£25,200 belonged to Mr Hiscock on the basis of his contribution, and £36,300 to Ms Oxley on the basis of the discount) £35,500 from Mr Hiscock's own savings and a mortgage loan of £30,000. The property was conveyed into the sole name of Mr Hiscock. Ms Oxley ignored warnings from her solicitor that she should ensure that the property be conveyed into the couple's joint names, and she refused to do so. After the purchase, both parties contributed towards the maintenance and improvement of the property from their pooled resources in the belief that each had a beneficial interest. By 2001, the mortgage had been paid off. The relationship between the parties broke down, the property was sold, and separate houses were purchased. Ms Oxley claimed that she had a 50 per cent beneficial interest in the proceeds of sale of the property. Her claim was granted.

Mr Hiscock appealed. He accepted that there was an intention that the beneficial interest should be shared but argued that it should be quantified in proportion to their respective contributions. The Court of Appeal granted his appeal and maintained that a fair division would be 60 per cent to Mr Hiscock and 40 per cent to Ms Oxley (see also *Gallarotti v Sebastianelli* [2012] EWCA Civ 865; *Aspden v Elvy* [2012] EWHC 1387 (Ch)).

In *Capehorn v Harris*, the Court of Appeal when considering the shares of the parties accepted that although in finding a share the courts were restricted to objective evidence once it was proved that a claimant had a share the courts were able to impute the intention of the parties.

Example

If the property discussed earlier had been registered in Asma's name and Ben had successfully argued that he had a share through the route of an express agreement or a contribution then the court can assess his share by referring what would be fair if Asma and Ben had sat down and thought about the issue. At this stage issues such as non-financial contributions such as child care and improvements to the property and length of relationship may be relevant and the court will then award a share which will be seen as 'fair' in all the circumstances.

Property purchased in joint names – the high point of pragmatism in the quantification of beneficial interests – *Stack v Dowden* (2007); *Jones v Kernott* (2011)

Where the family home is purchased in both names then the law presumes both parties will have a share.

In our example we can assume that both Asma and Ben are registered as owners of their family home. If the relationship breaks down and again the key question will be to determine the size of each share.

There are a number of cases decided over the past 17 years which have sought to lay down rules to be used by the court in quantifying the shares, although useful guidance in this area is still an area of uncertainty.

According to the House of Lords in **Stack v Dowden**, the starting point for quantification where the legal title is in the names of both parties is that the beneficial interest follows the legal interest and the partners have equal shares regardless of their financial contributions. If one partner wishes to dispute this division, he or she must produce evidence of a contrary intention. In its determination of such an intention, the court must take a holistic view of the whole course of dealing between the parties.

Mr Stack and Ms Dowden were unmarried. They had lived together with their four children for over 20 years before their relationship broke down. In 1983, Ms Dowden purchased a house, in her sole name, for £30,000. It had belonged to a man, whom Ms Dowden called Uncle Sidney. He had expressed the wish, before his death, that she should be allowed to buy it at a discount. She obtained a loan of £22,000 in her sole name; the remainder came from her own savings. She made all the payments on the loan and all the utility bills.

The couple both spent time altering, repairing, redecorating and generally improving their new home, although Mr Stack did more work than Ms Dowden. In 1993, the property was sold for £90,000. A new property was purchased. This time the legal title was put into the couple's joint names, but they did not specify how the beneficial interest in the property should be shared. The purchase monies were provided partly by Ms Dowden and partly by way of a mortgage in favour of the bank and by two endowment policies, one in the couple's joint names and one in Ms Dowden's sole name. The mortgage interest and joint endowment policy premiums, which eventually amounted to £33,747, were paid for by Mr Stack, and the capital was repaid by a series of lump sum payments, to which Mr Stack contributed £27,000 and Ms Dowden £38,435. Ms Dowden paid the premiums on the life policy in her name, and all the utility bills which were in her name, although Mr Stack claimed to have paid some of them. Throughout their relationship, the couple had separate bank accounts and separate investments and savings.

In 2002, the relationship broke down, and Ms Dowden remained in the family home with the children. Mr Stack wished to have the house sold and claim a 50 per cent share in the beneficial interest of the property. Ms Dowden maintained that his claim was unfair because of her greater financial contributions to its purchase. The judge ruled in favour of Mr Stack, and Ms Dowden appealed.

The Court of Appeal allowed her appeal and awarded her a 65 per cent share of the property. Mr Stack appealed to the House of Lords, and his appeal was denied. Their Lordships stated firmly that any division of the beneficial interest must be based on trust principles, and Lord Neuberger categorically rejected any possibility that judges should impose their own idea of a fair division based on the parties' long-term familial relationship. However, it maintained that it was important to take into account the realities of such relationships in determining the couple's intentions.

Baroness Hale, who gave the leading judgment, maintained that:

> In law, 'context is everything' and the domestic context is very different from the commercial world. Each case will turn on its own facts. Many more factors than financial contributions may be relevant to divining the parties' true intentions. These include: any advice or discussions at the time of the transfer which cast light upon their intentions then; the reasons why the home was acquired in their joint names . . . the purpose for which the home was acquired; the nature of the parties' relationship; whether they had children for whom they both had responsibility to provide a home; how the purchase was financed, both initially and subsequently; how the parties arranged their finances, whether separately or together or a bit of both; how they discharged the outgoings on the property and their other household expenses. When a couple are joint owners of the home and jointly liable for the mortgage, the inferences to be drawn from who pays for what may be very different from the

inferences to be drawn when only one is owner of the home. The arithmetical calculation of how much was paid by each is also likely to be less important. It will be easier to draw the inference that they intended that each should contribute as much to the household as they reasonably could and that they would share the eventual benefit or burden equally. The parties' individual characters and personalities may also be a factor in deciding where their true intentions lay. In the cohabitation context, mercenary considerations may be more to the fore than they would be in marriage, but it should not be assumed that they always take pride of place over natural love and affection. At the end of the day, having taken all this into account, cases in which the joint legal owners are to be taken to have intended that their beneficial interests should be different from their legal interests will be very unusual.

In spite of this strong statement, and her warnings about taking an arithmetical approach, Baroness Hale found that Ms Dowden and Mr Stack fell into that rare category of a couple who had kept their financial dealings very separate, and that, in this context, their differential contributions were significant. The Court of Appeal's decision was upheld.

If we analyse this decision there is guidance to couples when a relationship has come to an end, but it is important to note that the law makes it clear that the court is not involved in the same type of decision as in the breakdown of a marriage.

See the words of Tomlinson LJ in *Graham-York v York*:

> *the court is not concerned with some form of retributive justice. Thus it is irrelevant that it may be thought a 'fair' outcome for a woman who has endured years of abusive conduct by her partner to be allocated a substantial interest in his property on his death.*

Thus we see again the way the property law principles operate in the context of a family home. The context of a relationship other than the financial arrangements plays little part in deciding how the shares should be quantified.

In *Jones v Kernott* (2011), the Supreme Court revisited and attempted to clarify the principles in *Stack v Dowden* (2007). Ms Jones and Mr Kernott were an unmarried couple with two children. In 1985, the couple bought a family home which was conveyed into their joint names for £30,000. There was no discussion about their respective beneficial shares in the property. Ms Jones provided £6,000 towards the purchase price, and the balance came from an interest-only mortgage loan supported by an endowment policy.

Mr Kernott gave Ms Jones £100 per week. From that and her own earnings she paid for housekeeping, mortgage payments and other outgoings on the property, and the premiums on the endowment policy. Mr Kernott built an extension on the property which increased its value by 50 per cent of the purchase price.

In 1993, the couple separated and Ms Jones assumed total responsibility for all the outgoings and for the maintenance of the children. In 1996, Mr Kernott purchased a home for himself using his share of a further insurance policy. In 2006, he claimed a 50 per cent share in the family home.

Ms Jones argued that the original intention to share the property jointly had been altered because of the couple's separation; Mr Kernott's purchase of a new home in his sole name, and her subsequent responsibility for the outgoings on the house and for the children's maintenance. The judge at first instance and the High Court accepted that the partners had contributed unequally to the property and that fairness demanded that their beneficial shares should be unequal and awarded 10 per cent to Mr Kernott and 90 per cent to Ms Jones.

Mr Kernott appealed to the Court of Appeal. The Court of Appeal granted the appeal and held that the original agreement to share the property equally had not been displaced by the couple's later conduct.

Wall LJ said:

I described this case as a cautionary tale. So, in my judgment, it is. The purchase of residential accommodation is perhaps the single most important financial transaction which any individual transacts in a lifetime. It is therefore of the utmost importance, as it seems to me, that those who engage in these transactions, and those who advise them, should take the greatest care over such transactions, and must – particularly if they are unmarried or if their clients are unmarried – address their minds to the size and fate of the respective beneficial interests on acquisition, separation and thereafter. It is simply impossible for a court to analyse personal transactions over years between cohabitants, and the costs of so doing are likely to be disproportionate in any event. Cohabiting partners must, it seems to me, contemplate and address the unthinkable, namely that their relationship will break down and that they will fall out over what they do and do not own.

If this appellant and this respondent had truly intended that the appellant's beneficial interest in the property should reduce post separation, or if the property was to belong to the respondent when the appellant acquired his own house, they should have so decided and acted accordingly by adjusting their beneficial interests in the property. I cannot spell such an intention out of their actions.

Ms Jones appealed; the Supreme Court granted the appeal and restored the original order in her favour. It held that where the property was in joint names and one of the partners maintained that the intention to share the property equally had changed after the original purchase of the property, a court would have to decide whether there was such an intention and, if so, what the new division of the beneficial interest should be. There would be no difficulty if the couple had expressly agreed to such a change, but that is a rare occurrence. More usually, a court would have to infer the couple's intention from their conduct and in an objective way – not an easy task. The Supreme Court acknowledged that if a court is unable to infer the intention, it might have to resort to imputing an intention to them. This, according to the Court, means deducing what the couple, as reasonable people, would have intended, had they put their mind to the question of their respective shares of the beneficial interest. In so doing, a court would have to take into account the whole course of dealing between the partners during the relationship. This, according to the Supreme Court, is not the same as making a decision based on fairness – the analogy comes to mind how many angels can dance on the head of a pin!

There remains some confusion about Lady Hale's emphatic statement that the decision in *Kernott* only applies where property is purchased in joint names. One can only assume that she was referring to the maxim that equal division of the beneficial interest, in the absence of any supervening events, will be the assumption in such cases. As was discussed earlier, and as Lady Hale herself noted as a '*curious feature*', where the property is in the sole name of one partner, there will be no assumption that the property should be shared equally. Once a *Rosset* compliant agreement has been established, the courts have been taking a holistic approach to quantification for some time.

In *Hudson v Hathway* [2022] EWCA Civ 1648, a property was registered in joint names without an express declaration of trust. Both parties contributed to the mortgage repayments. Thus, initially the presumption of equal shares was invoked. Two years later, the parties separated but exchanged emails concerning the division of the equitable interest in the house. This resulted in Mr Hudson retaining his pension rights and shares but he would discontinue making mortgage repayments. In return, Ms Hathway would acquire the sole equitable interest in the house. Four years later, Mr Hudson sought the sale of the house and claimed that the equitable interest in the house ought to be divided equally between them. Ms Hathway claimed sole equitable ownership of the house based on a common intention constructive trust. The court held that:

a. Mr Hudson had disposed of his equitable interest in the house in favour of Ms Hathway via the email exchange. This constituted 'writing' 'signed' by him in accordance with s 53(1)(c) of the Law of Property Act 1925.

b. Additionally, in order to rebut the presumption of equal shares in the property Ms Hathway was required to adduce evidence of detriment and the evidence demonstrated that she had acted to her detriment by refraining from making a claim against other assets of Mr Hudson.

Readers who feel, and quite justifiably so, that decisions in this area of law have been somewhat confusing may be consoled by the words of Peter Gibson LJ in *Drake v Whipp* (1996) when he said in the context of informal trusts of the family home:

> *it is not easy to reconcile every judicial utterance in this well-travelled area of law.*

SUMMARY: *Quantifying shares in a trust of the family home*

The most significant changes that have evolved in quantification of shares in a trust can be summed up as follows . . .

1. Where title is in the sole name of one party there are two stages. Firstly the claimant must show that rights have been acquired through an informal trust. The claimant must show common intention either expressly or impliedly. *Obiter* comments in *Stack* also suggest that a claimant can acquire rights through conduct from the parties' course of conduct throughout the course of their relationship. If common intention can be proved then it must be supported by evidence of detrimental reliance which can be a range of conduct from monetary payments as well as behaviour that is not directly related to the property. The second stage is the quantification of the share in the property. In

sole owner cases this is more complicated. In most cases the parties will not have thought about this so the court must take guidance from the conduct of the parties. In particular it will look at the financial arrangements between the parties and can infer what the parties would expect as a share in the home from this. So where parties shared all bills and outgoings as in *Midland Bank v Cooke* then it is likely that the court would share the rights in the family home equally. It is also possible since *Kernott v Jones* for the courts to impute intention which is for the court to impute an intention as to the size of their share.

2. Quantification in joint ownership cases is much easier. The courts follow the maxim 'equity follows the law' so as the legal title is held jointly then the equitable title will follow it. This is only a starting point and any evidence to suggest the contrary will allow the courts to come to a different result as in *Stack v Dowden* and *Jones v Kernott*.

Proprietary estoppel

Proprietary estoppel is an alternative way to establish informal rights in the family home where the claimant does not own the legal title. It is based on the principle that it is inequitable for the legal owner to deny a right to anyone, who has acted to his or her detriment, in reliance on the legal owner's implied or explicit representation relating to the grant of rights in or over the property. It is a cause of action given to a volunteer whenever a landowner stands by and allows a volunteer who has acted on an assurance for instance by improving his property and incurring expenditure on the assumption that the property will be transferred to him. It is of particular value in families where one party, often a child of a family, has worked in a family business or a farm for many years and an assumption has been made that rights will be transferred to him or her. It can also be used between couples within a relationship. The cause of action is based on a promise or assurance by the landowner X that the claimant Y has rights in the property and Y has relied on that promise to their detriment.

This claim has become more important as an informal way of claiming rights in land where the strict formalities of transfer have not been satisfied. As the significance of the claim has grown so has the discussion of the proper basis of the claim. There is much discussion as to whether it is based on compensation for loss to the claimant or alternatively it is based on satisfaction of an expectation of rights held by the claimant.

In the recent case of *Guest v Guest* [2022] UKSC 27, the Supreme Court reviewed the law on proprietary estoppel, but the court was divided on what basis a remedy would be awarded. The majority agreed that a remedy should be based on satisfying the claimant's expectation as opposed to compensating the detriment of the claimant. In many cases this will make little difference to the actual remedy granted, but in cases where the detriment suffered has been modest but the expectation was of valuable property rights the result may be very different.

Proprietary estoppel is a claim firmly based in equity and it is awarded by the court on a discretionary basis. For the majority in the Supreme Court in *Guest* this discretion should be aimed at compensating the claimant for the loss of expectation. This should be seen as the harm done to the claimant. The case involved a family-run farm owned by the parents of the claimant. The claimant had a brother and also a sister, but it was the claimant Andrew who had been promised a significant share of the farm on the death of his parents. A number of assurances had been made over the years to Andrew, and on that basis he had continued to work on the farm for over 30 years. He received very low wages although he had lived rent free in one of the farm cottages. Whilst the parents were still alive relations between the claimant and his parents broke down and as a result the parents disinherited the claimant from any rights over the property. The father rewrote his will removing any rights in favour of the claimant. No contract or trust had been drawn up concerning the claimant's rights, and so he had to rely on the informal claim of proprietary estoppel which does not require written confirmation of rights but other factors. The High Court, Court of Appeal and Supreme Court all found in the claimant's favour, but there was some disagreement as to the appropriate remedy. The majority in the Supreme Court agreed that an award in proprietary estoppel is there to remedy or make good the unconscionable conduct of the defendant.

one of the principal functions of equity is to put right injustice to which the law is otherwise blind, by restraining the rigid application of legal rules where their implementation would be unconscionable.

(Lord Briggs)

The doctrines of proprietary estoppel and constructive trusts overlap; the latter has its roots in the former, and the two doctrines are often pleaded in the alternative. In all cases of a successful claim of a constructive trust of a beneficial interest in property, a claim based on proprietary estoppel would also succeed (see *Q v Q* [2008] 1 FLR 935). The reverse is not so. Judicial statements have been made to the effect that the two doctrines overlap or are even identical (see e.g., *Oxley v Hiscock* (2004); *Grant v Edwards* (1986)). This is clearly incorrect, as Lord Walker emphasised in *Stack v Dowden* (2007). There is a risk that if the constant attempts to merge the doctrines are successful the current requirements to ground an estoppel will be replaced by those of the constructive trust, and even if the holistic approach in *Stack* (2007) continues to prevail, the greater flexibility of proprietary estoppel will be lost.

For a successful claim in estoppel proprietary, three elements must be proved: a representation, reliance on that representation and proof of detriment. There is also a fourth element which has arisen in recent years which is proof of unconscionable conduct.

Nature of the representation

Explicit representations

The decisions involving explicit representations are rare.

In *Pascoe v Turner* [1979] 1 WLR 431, Mrs Turner had been Mr Pascoe's housekeeper and subsequently cohabited with him. After ten years of living together, he eventually informed her that he was leaving her to move in with a new woman. Mrs Turner was very distressed, but became somewhat consoled when Mr Pascoe informed her clearly, in front of witnesses, that the house and everything in it was hers. The court found that the explicit representation, albeit made in emotional circumstances, gave rise to an estoppel based right.

Implied representations

Most representations will not be quite so clear; family relationships tend to involve more hazy and imprecise arrangements which the parties may find difficult to recall during the bitter arguments which tend to accompany estoppel claims. They may be able to persuade the court that a representation may be inferred from all the circumstances of the case, taking into account a range of factors including, *inter alia*, the extent of the claimant's detriment, the nature of the parties' relationship and their respective housing needs.

The law concerning implied trusts has for many years been very strict about the type of evidence needed for common intention to be shown. Implied evidence suggesting property is to be shared between the parties always failed to be acceptable. By comparison an implied representation has been sufficient to give rise to property rights under the doctrine of proprietary estoppel. Even early cases on estoppel allowed a claim to be based on silence in the face of encroachment on land (*Ramsden v Dyson* [1866] LR 1 HL 129). So in the context of a family relationship it may be possible to imply rights over land.

A good illustration of this arises in the case of *Thorner v Major* [2009] 1 WLR 776 where a cousin David Thorner was able to claim rights in a farm owned by his father's cousin Peter Thorner in spite of only oblique assurances being made during the owner's lifetime. The clearest comment was made when he handed over a life assurance policy saying 'this will be for my death duties'. The younger cousin had worked for little or no pay for over 29 years. Although the Court of Appeal rejected the claim the House of Lords had no hesitation in upholding David's rights. The court looked at the entirety of the claim and its context. The lack of an express assurance did not defeat his claim.

Detriment

The detriment in estoppel claims, whether financial or otherwise, need not be referable to the property but must be capable of financial quantification (see *Stallion v Albert Stallion Holdings (Great Britain) Ltd* [2010] EWCA Civ 1443). It may well be at a level which would be insufficient to satisfy the requirement in the context of a constructive trust. Mrs Turner in *Pascoe v Turner* (1979), for example, spent very little on her improvements to the property and Cumming Bruce LJ recognised that this expenditure could not have given rise to a constructive trust of the property but he was prepared to grant an estoppel right.

The courts have accepted a very wide range of activities as evidence of detriment in the estoppel context; these include work on the property, care of the representor, working without wages, expenses of relocating to another country, and a disadvantage suffered by a close partner of the claimant.

In *Re Basham (deceased)* [1987] 1 WLR 1498, the claimant was the stepdaughter of the deceased. She had worked for him over a 30-year period helping to run a number of public houses and a garage. She had received no payment for this work. The claimant, her husband and their children all had a very close relationship with the deceased. On several occasions when the claimant and her husband considered moving away from the area because the husband had been offered good employment elsewhere, the deceased had dissuaded them from doing so. After the death of the claimant's mother, the claimant had cared for the deceased in his retirement. He told her that she would receive his cottage on his death in return for all her help. The court accepted that the claimant had acted to her detriment.

Detriment is not to be judged simply at the time of the representation because often the claimant is actually receiving a benefit at that point. It is only at the moment when the representor reneges on the representation that the conduct, which took place when the representation was made, may be viewed as detrimental.

In *Davies v Davies* [2016] EWCA Civ 463, a daughter of a farmer had devoted her life to the farm working for long hours at low wages relying on assurances that the farm would be hers one day. She left the farm after an argument with her parents and claimed a share which she said had been offered to her. The court took into account the different forms of detriment suffered which were more than merely financial; for example, her expertise in animal reproduction was extensive and would have earned much higher wages in another farm.

Detriment alone will never give rise to rights in property unless there has been an assurance of rights. Statements made in the context of cohabitation may give rise to an assurance, but general statements made will never be enough. So in the case of *Coombes v Smith* [1986] 1 WLR 808, a woman in a relationship claimed the right to live in a property owned by her partner based on her care for the property and their child. There was no evidence of a promise she had rights, merely evidence of detriment. Where there is evidence of a promise then rights for a cohabitant may arise. So in *Liden v Burton* [2016] EWCA Civ 275 and *Southwell v Blackburn* [2015] EWCA Civ 1347, there were successful claims. In *Southwell*, a woman had given up a secure tenancy on the basis of a promise from her partner that she would have a home for life. In *Liden*, statements made to the claimant that payments made were 'towards the house' were sufficiently clear to be seen as assurances and could therefore be linked to the detriment suffered. (See Lower 2018; Hayward 2015.)

Reliance

In familial situations, it is often the case that detriment can be viewed as related to a family obligation rather than specifically in reliance on any representations made to the claimant. The courts have recognised the dual nature of family behaviour and have tended to be liberal in their interpretation of reliance. They have accepted that once a claimant has acted to his or her detriment, it will be assumed that it was in reliance on the representation, and it is for the legal owner to prove otherwise.

In *Greasley v Cooke* [1980] 1 WLR 1306, Miss Cooke was the cohabitant of Mr Greasley who ran a butcher's shop. She had looked after the household for some 40 years, having arrived there aged 16 years. She had cared for Mr Greasley's mentally ill sister, Clarice, and helped in the shop. She was never paid for her services. He and his brother assured her that she would always have a home in the family property. After Mr Greasley's death, the family attempted to evict her.

Lord Denning maintained that the representations made to her:

> *were calculated to influence her, so as to put her mind at rest, so that she should not worry about being turned out. No one can say what she would have done if Kenneth and Hedley had not made those statements. It is quite possible that she would have said to herself: 'I am not married to Kenneth. I am on my own. What will happen to me if anything happens to him? I had better look out for another job now rather than stay here where I have no security.' So, instead of looking for another job, she stayed on in the house looking after Kenneth and Clarice. There is a presumption that she did so relying on the assurances given to her by Kenneth and Hedley. The burden is not on her but on them to prove that she did not rely on their assurances.*

Wide range of remedies

One of the greatest advantages of a successful claim based on proprietary estoppel is the ability of the court to grant whatever remedy it thinks fit. It is a particularly appropriate approach in family situations. Although the courts look at the nature of the representation in deciding on a remedy, they have accepted that the only feasible, and appropriate remedy based on all the circumstances of the parties, may be to grant the claimant an alternative remedy from that which he or she had been led to expect. Where a claim is made on the basis of an implied trust the court can only award one remedy namely an equitable interest. Remedies in proprietary estoppel are far more flexible and can be adapted to the circumstances of the claim.

The recent case of *Guest v Guest* has given the courts some guidance on the basis of the remedy in estoppel. The court was divided on what basis a remedy would be awarded, but the majority agreed that a remedy should be based on satisfying the claimant's expectation as opposed to compensating the detriment of the claimant. In many cases this will make little difference to the actual remedy granted, but in cases where the detriment suffered has been modest but the expectation was of valuable property rights the result may be very different.

Fee simple

The grant of a fee simple is the most valuable of all the remedies available in the context of proprietary estoppel. It gives the claimant the legal title to land and therefore rights of control over the property. The courts have been reluctant to award this particularly as it is based on informal assurances rather than compliance with the formalities of the Law of Property Act 1925.

In *Pascoe v Turner* (1979), the court granted Mrs Turner the fee simple of the property when Mr Pascoe and his 'heavies' attempted to evict her. Cumming Bruce LJ took the view that:

> *the equity cannot here be satisfied without granting a remedy which assures to the defendant security of tenure, quiet enjoyment and freedom of action in respect of repairs and improvements without interference from the plaintiff. The history of the conduct of the plaintiff in relation to these proceedings leads to an irresistible inference that he is determined*

to pursue his purpose of evicting her from the house by any legal means at his disposal with a ruthless disregard of the obligations binding on conscience. The court must grant a remedy effective to protect her against the future manifestations of his ruthlessness. It was conceded that if she is granted a licence, such a licence cannot be registered as a land charge, so that she may find herself ousted by a purchaser for value without notice. If she has in the future to do further and more expensive repairs she may only be able to finance them by a loan, but as a licensee she cannot charge the house. The plaintiff as legal owner may well find excuse for entry in order to do what he may plausibly represent as necessary works and so contrive to derogate from her enjoyment of the licence in ways that make it difficult or impossible for the court to give her effective protection.

In spite of the lack of an express assurance of rights the court was prepared to award the fee simple to the claimant in *Thorner v Major* (2009).

An estoppel licence

Where the court believes it appropriate to grant a right limited to the lifetime of the estoppel claimant, it may grant a licence.

In *Matharu v Matharu* [1994] 2 FLR 597, Mrs Matharu believed that she and her late husband had acquired the fee simple of the property from her father-in-law. The court gave her a licence to occupy the property for the rest of her life. It was accepted that the prime obligation of the father-in-law had been to his son, implying that had the claim been his, he might have been granted the fee simple. Now he was dead, it was more appropriate to simply protect Mrs Matharu for her lifetime.

Compensation

Family relationships, which begin happily, often end miserably, and it may be unreasonable to expect the parties to continue to live together, even if that is what was envisaged by the original representation.

In *Dodsworth v Dodsworth* [1973] 228 EG 115, a sister persuaded her brother and his wife to live with her in her bungalow on their return from Australia. The couple spent money on improvements to the bungalow, encouraged by the sister to believe that they would be able to share it with her as their home for as long as they wished to do so. Eventually, the relationship between the parties broke down. The sister became anxious to sell the bungalow and buy a smaller and less expensive one for herself. She could not do this if her brother and his wife were entitled to stay in the bungalow rent-free. She would therefore have to continue sharing her home for the rest of her life with the couple, with whom she was at loggerheads. The couple maintained that even if their expenditure was reimbursed, it would be insufficient to allow them to purchase a new home because property prices had appreciated since they first went to live in the bungalow.

The Court of Appeal was reluctant to grant the couple a licence as a remedy, even though the sister had died by the time the case reached the court. To allow the couple to remain in the bungalow, alone, would give them more than they had been led to expect from the original representation. They were awarded monetary compensation to the extent of their expenditure on the property, including an amount for their time and labour.

A problematic remedy

Although the flexible nature of proprietary estoppel makes it eminently suitable in the resolution of disputes in the family home, there are some disadvantages to it. Because the purpose of proprietary estoppel is to compensate the claimant for the detriment suffered, the doctrine can only be pleaded once the representation has been withdrawn. This means that claimants have no certainty, prior to the withdrawal, what their rights, in or over the property, are. A claimant is dependent on either the goodwill of the legal owner to continue to honour the representation, or if it is withdrawn, on the court's generosity once the claim is brought before it. A claimant may be fortunate and enjoy the court's grant of a fee simple, but may be unlucky and be given minimal compensation. Where the remedy is a licence, it is personal to the claimant and is not transferable to a third party which limits the possibilities for a claimant to move elsewhere and make a new start.

The dust is settling after the Supreme Court judgment in *Guest v Guest* but some question whether this has indeed made it easier or clearer as to what remedy will be awarded by the court after successfully arguing that rights arise. It still seems to have an element of a lottery ticket as to what type of remedy the court will award. Although Lord Briggs clarified the basis of any award as being in satisfaction of an expectation the strongly worded dissenting judgment of Lord Leggatt cast doubt on some of the established reasoning of the basis of proprietary estoppel (see Sloan 2023; Smyth and Dunbar 2024; Eldridge 2023; Waghorn 2023).

Matrimonial Proceedings and Property Act 1970, s 37

This little used provision allows married or engaged couples, either of whom have a beneficial interest in property, to acquire an enhanced share in that property if they have contributed substantially in money or money's worth to the improvement of the property without having to prove an agreement or representation. The provision is subject to the existence of any agreement between the couple to the contrary. Proof is required that the improvements made substantially improve the property; mere maintenance is not included and any work on the house that fails to improve it because it was so poorly executed cannot be relied on.

Civil Partnership Act 2004, s 65

The Civil Partnership Act 2004 (CPA 2004), s 65 makes similar provisions for civil partners, as those available to married partners.

The Law Reform (Miscellaneous Provisions) Act 1970, ss 2, 3; Civil Partnership Act 2004, s 74(5)

The Law Reform (Miscellaneous Provisions) Act 1970, s 2 makes provision for a couple who are engaged to be married but terminate their engagement to resolve their property ownership in accordance with any of the statutory provisions available to married couples. Section 3 provides that gifts exchanged on condition that the couple marry must be returned to the donor. However, engagement rings are presumed to be non-returnable unless there is evidence to the contrary.

The question of engagement rings played a significant role in the parties' stormy relationship in *Cox v Jones* (2004). Mr Jones gave Ms Cox an engagement ring, worth at least £10,000 possibly more. Mr Jones maintained that when he gave Ms Cox the ring, he made clear that if the engagement came to an end, he would be entitled to its return. The ring was flung out of windows; locked in a glove compartment; supposedly borrowed by Ms Cox, for sentimental reasons, after the engagement was over, and, finally, was turned into a pendant by Ms Cox which disappeared mysteriously before the court hearing. The judge rejected Mr Jones' version of events:

> *I have little difficulty in rejecting Mr Jones's version of events. His case on this point contains inconsistencies and implausibilities. First, I find the initial discussion implausible. It is common ground that the trip at the end of 1997 was a romantic one which both parties enjoyed very much. They were talking about marriage. Having heard the evidence, I reject as implausible the unromantic express remark which Mr Jones says that he made. I find it hard to accept that it would have been said in the context in which it was said to have been uttered.*

The CPA 2004, s 74 makes similar provisions for civil partners with respect to property ownership but makes no mention of engagement rings.

Family Law Act 1996, Part IV

Statutory right of occupation for spouses and civil partners

Where a spouse or civil partner has a beneficial estate or interest in, or contract to occupy, their family home, the Family Law Act 1996 (FLA 1996), s 30 provides the other spouse or civil partner, who does not possess any of these rights, with a statutory 'home right'. This right which might be broadly termed a right of occupation includes a right not to be evicted from the home except by court order, and a right, with a court order, to re-enter the home if they have been excluded from it.

The right is personal to the spouse or civil partner and may not be transferred to a third party. It comes to an end on: divorce, dissolution of a civil partnership, annulment of a marriage or civil partnership, death of a spouse or civil partner, or where it is formally terminated by agreement between the partners, usually when the home is sold. The right cannot be translated into money which limits the potential for a spouse or civil partner to leave the family home and purchase an alternative residence.

Where a spouse or civil partner, who has a home right, applies for an order under FLA 1996, s 33, the court will exercise its discretion in accordance with the broad provisions of s 33(6), (7). These provisions are considered in detail in Chapter 5.

The family home

A family home, for the purposes of the FLA 1996, is a property, or properties in which the spouses or civil partners have lived together. They may have two or more family homes, and the definition of family home includes not only apartments and houses, but also caravans and boats, indeed any structure in which two people may live together as a family.

Effect of the statutory right on third parties

One of the most important attributes of the home right is that, once it has come into existence, it acts as a charge on a spouse or civil partner's estate or interest in the home, and it has the potential to bind third parties who acquire the property (FLA 1996, s 31). The charge must, however, be registered under the Land Registration Act 2002, s 31(10) (or, in unregistered land, under the Land Charges Act 1972, s 2(7), as a class F land charge), if it is to be enforceable against third parties. Only one right can be registered even if there is more than one family home. Once the right is registered it will normally be protected against a subsequent third party who obtains an estate or interest in it. However, the FLA 1996, s 34(1)(a) provides that such a third party is in the same position as the spouse or civil partner from whom he acquired the property. Thus, the court may exercise its discretion under the FLA 1996, s 35(6) and determine the competing rights of the spouse or civil partner who has registered the family home right, and the third party. Such decisions are rare (see e.g. *Kaur v Gill* [1988] Fam 110).

Potential for manipulation

Where the family home is to be sold, the spouse or civil partner who has registered a home right will normally agree to arrange to remove it from the register prior to completion of the sale, because a failure to do so will almost certainly prevent sale. Often another family home is to be purchased and a home right will be subsequently registered against it. Spouses have, however, attempted to register a right or refused to have a registration removed because they wished to use it as a bargaining tool.

Trusts of Land and the Appointment of Trustees Act 1996; rights of beneficiaries, creditors and the effect of bankruptcy

Beneficiaries

As discussed earlier once it can be shown that two or more people own the family home a trust comes into being with all the attendant rights of beneficiaries under a trust. This area of law is complex, and decisions are based on property law principles which are ill-suited to decisions on family law. If the property is sole owned by one party then the other party can seek to prevent a sale. Rights arise under Trusts of Land and Appointment of Trustees Act 1996 (TOLATA), s 14 and are decided according to principles laid down in TOLATA, s 15 which include the purposes for which the property subject to the trusts is held. Once a relationship has broken down then it is difficult to argue that this purpose still subsists.

Creditors and bankruptcy

The interests of any secured creditor is also a matter under TOLATA, s 15 to be considered by the court. Case law suggests that the rights of the creditors will always take precedence over the rights of the family even where there are young children (see *Bank of Ireland Home Mortgages Ltd v Bell* [2001] All ER (Comm) 920; *First National Bank v Achampong* (2003) and *Fred Perry Holdings v Genis* [2015] 1 P & CR DG5). There are exceptions where sale has been postponed in the face of an application by a secured creditor (see *Mortgage Corporation v Silkin; Same and Shaire* [2001] Ch 151; *Edwards v Lloyds Bank TSB* [2004] EWHC 1745).

As the family home is often used to secure loans, it means that the family's occupation is put at risk in the event of bankruptcy. Even where a bankrupt's partner has a beneficial interest in the property which is binding on the trustee in bankruptcy, the latter may apply for an order for sale of the bankrupt's property under the Trusts of Land and Appointment of Trustees Act 1996, s 14. The trustee in bankruptcy may only take the bankrupt's share of the property on sale, leaving the partner's share intact. However, that share will more often than not be insufficient to purchase another family home.

Where a spouse or a civil partner has a right of occupation under the FLA 1996, Part IV which is a charge on the bankrupt's property, the trustee in bankruptcy may make an application under the FLA 1996, s 33.

In applications for a sale of the family home under the Trusts of Land and Appointment of Trustees Act 1996, s 14 or under the FLA 1996, s 33 the Insolvency Act 1986, ss 335A and 336 apply respectively. Both sections provide that in determining whether to order sale or not, the court must take into account the interests of the creditors, the conduct of the non-bankrupt partner relating to the bankruptcy, the needs of this partner, the needs of any children and all the circumstances of the case other than the bankrupt's needs. In addition, if the application for sale is made after the end of one year after the bankrupt's property is in the hands of the trustee in bankruptcy, the court must assume that the creditors take precedent unless the circumstances are exceptional. The courts have been flexible in allowing at least a delay in the sale of property

Exceptional circumstances

In *Barca v Mears* [2004] EWHC 2170 (Ch), the court questioned whether the narrow approach to exceptional circumstances was consistent with Art 8 of the ECHR.

The court held that in the general run of cases, the creditors' interests would prevail. However, it must be left open to the court to define what was exceptional in any given circumstances. Exceptional circumstances would not be limited to those cases where the consequences were unusual in the sense of going beyond the usual consequences of bankruptcy.

In *Hosking v Michaelides* [2004] All ER (D) 147, it was argued that the meaning given to the concept of exceptional circumstances in the past had been too restrictive and was incompatible with Art 8 of the ECHR. The court rejected this view and held that to be exceptional the circumstances need not be unique, unprecedented or very rare, but they cannot be ones that are routinely or normally encountered.

The exceptional circumstances relied upon by Mrs Michaelides concerned her physical and mental health. She had overdosed on drugs, was an alcoholic, was emotionally unstable and had a tendency to act impulsively. Her psychiatrist gave evidence that Mrs Michaelides was unable to cope with any stress and trauma and that she reacted in a way which was dissimilar to that of an ordinary person faced with similar circumstances. The sale of her family home would exacerbate her emotional difficulties, which would be dangerous for both her and her children.

The court, somewhat hesitantly, found that these were exceptional circumstances and deferred sale, but only for six months. It regarded its decision as generous; the creditors' needs should prevail over those of Mrs Michaelides and her children.

There are many examples where the courts have been prepared to at the very least postpone sale for a period of time. In *Re Ravel (A Bankrupt)* [1998] 2 FLR 718, a wife had suffered for many years from paranoid schizophrenia and, although she was stable and living at home, her doctor advised that 'adverse life events' (for example, a move to a smaller property away from supportive friends and family) could cause a relapse of her condition. The court held that the wife's circumstances justified a postponement of the order for sale for one year to enable suitable alternative accommodation to be found for her by the local authority. It rejected the postponement of six months (ordered at first instance) and also a postponement of five years holding that it would be too long for the creditors to wait for their money. In a more recent decision, *Pickard v Constable* [2017] EWHC 2475 (Ch), the district judge was held to have erred in postponing a possession order until the death or earlier permanent vacation of the property by its disabled occupant. The applicant had not presented any evidence that the local authority, in line with its statutory duty, would not be able to find the occupant alternative accommodation. A new possession order was made to be postponed for 12 months. Similarly, in *Grant v Baker* [2016] EWHC 1782 (Ch) it was held that the trial judge was wrong to postpone a sale of property order for a bankrupt's house until the bankrupt's daughter, who had special needs, no longer resided at the property – although the circumstances were exceptional, it was held that the judge had failed to give appropriate weight to the point that an indefinite suspension of the sale was incompatible with the underlying purpose of bankruptcy legislation.

In summary, there may be a chance to postpone sale of the family home where the trustee in bankruptcy makes an application but this is rare and only where there are exceptional circumstances which have been interpreted by the courts as severe ill-health of the bankrupt or family member.

Self-test questions

1. What advice would you give to an unmarried couple who wish to purchase a family home for the first time?

2. Smyth and Dunbar described the law on proprietary estoppel after the decision in *Guest v Guest* as 'clear as mud'. To what extent do you think that this is true?

3. William and Xavier are a same-sex couple who are not registered civil partners. In 2015, they purchased a property and registered the legal title in both their names; they had no discussions as to how the beneficial interest should be shared. Xavier borrowed 75 per cent of the purchase price from his employer, and William used a legacy from his parents to fund the remainder of the purchase price. After they moved into the property, William gave up his job as an investment banker and took responsibility for planning, planting and maintaining the couple's large garden. Last year, Xavier left to work abroad and William did not want to go with him. The couple decided to live apart and sell the property and buy two separate properties, one for each of them.

    Advise them how the court is likely to divide the beneficial interest between them if they are unable to agree on their respective shares in the property. Would your answer be any different if William and Xavier had entered into a registered civil partnership?

4. James, a merchant banker, was the owner of a flat in London. Kate, a legal secretary and James' long-term girlfriend, lived in a flat leased to her on an annual basis. In 2015, in order to give Kate some security, James purchased her flat for her. They continued to live separately until early 2020 when James invited Kate to live with him in a farmhouse, also owned by him. She accordingly quit her job and moved to the farmhouse. Kate did not seek new employment, but as the country went into lockdown during the Covid pandemic she spent her time supervising the renovation work on the farmhouse, overseeing any building work that could be done, and carrying out the decorating herself. James was unable to do this himself owing to his commitments in London on weekdays. In 2022, Kate and James both sold their flats in London and pooled the proceeds to purchase a terraced house in London. The house was registered in Kate's name alone because James thought that she should have some security if he were to die before her, but Kate insisted that everything they own should be shared by both of them. James used the house whilst he was working in London, and Kate very rarely visited it; she considered the farmhouse to be her real home. In 2023, Kate and James had a baby. Shortly after the birth she discovered that Laura had moved into the house in London to live with James, and that James proposed selling the farmhouse. Kate would like to stay in the farmhouse with Angelica, their daughter.

    Advise Kate what rights, if any, she might have in respect of both the farmhouse and the terraced house in London.

References

Auchmuty, Rosemary, 'Unfair Shares for Women: The Rhetoric of Equality and the Reality of Inequality' in Hilary Lim and Anne Bottomley (eds) *Feminist Perspectives on Land Law* (Routledge 2007) 171–193

Dixon, Martin, *Modern Land Law* (Routledge 2023) 182–191

Eekelaar, John, 'A Woman's Place – a Conflict Between Law and Social Values' [1987] *The Conveyancer and Property Lawyer* 93

Eldridge, Lorren, 'Looking a Guest Horse in the Mouth' [2023] *The Conveyancer and Property Lawyer* 101

George, Martin and Brian Sloan, 'Presuming too Little About Resulting and Constructive Trusts?' [2017] *The Conveyancer and Property Lawyer* 303

Glover, Nicola and Paul Todd, 'The Myth of Common Intention' (1996) 16 *Legal Studies* 325

Hayward, Andy, 'Cohabitants, Detriment and the Potential of Proprietary Estoppel: *Southwell v Blackburn*' (2015) 27(3) *Child and Family Law Quarterly* 303

House of Commons Women and Equalities Committee, 'Rights of Cohabiting Partners' www.commonscommittees-parliment.uk/publications/23321/documents/170094/default

Lower, Michael, '*Liden v Burton*: Proprietary Estoppel and the Family Home' [2018] *Conveyancer and Property Lawyer* 84–91

Maniscalco, Lorenzo, 'Common Intentions and Constructive Trusts: Unorthodoxy in Trusts of Land' (2020) 2 *The Conveyancer and Property Lawyer* 124

Miles, Joanna, 'Property Law v Family Law: Resolving the Problems of Family Property' (2003) 23 *Legal Studies* 624 www.ons.gov.uk/peoplepopulationandcommunity/healthandsocialcare/healthandwellbeing

ONS, 'Housing in England and Wales: 2021 Compared With 2011' (2021) www.ons.gov.uk/peoplepopulationandcommunity/housing/articles/housinginenglandandwales/2021compar edwith2011 (accessed 09.09.2024)

Pawlowski, Mark, 'Joint Owners, Severance and the Family Home [2016] *Family Law* 1238

Pawlowski, Mark and James Brown, 'Joint Purchasers and the Presumption of Joint Beneficial Ownership – A Matter of Informed Choice' (2013) 27 *Trusts Law International* 3

Sloan, Brian, 'Proprietary Estoppel in the Supreme Court: Banquo's Ghost' [2023] *Cambridge Law Journal* 13

Smyth, Claire-Michelle and Rupert Dunbar, 'Clear as Mud: Proprietary Estoppel After *Guest v Guest*' [2024] *Trusts and Trustees* 30

Waghorn, Alexander, 'Promises in Equity and at Law: Proprietary Estoppel After *Guest v Guest*' [2023] *Modern Law Review* 1504

Wong, Simone, 'The Shared Home: A rational Solution Through Statutory Reform?' in Hilary Lim and Anne Bottomley (eds) *Feminist Perspectives on Land Law* (Routledge 2007) 195

Zoopla, 'House Price Index: August 2024' (2024) www.zoopla.co.uk/discover/property-news/house-price-index/ (accessed 09.09.2024)

Further reading

Barlow, Anne, et al., 'Just a Piece of Paper? Marriage and Cohabitation', in Alison Park et al. (eds) *British Social Attitudes: Public Policy, Social Ties, the 18th Report* (Sage 2001) 29–57

Bray, Judith, 'The Financial Rights of Cohabiting Couples' [2009] *Family Law* 1151

Cooke, Elizabeth, 'In the Wake of Stack v Dowden: The Tale of TR1' [2011] *Family Law* 1142

Douglas, Gillian, Julia Pearce and Hilary Woodward, 'Dealing with Property Issues on Cohabitation Breakdown' [2007] *Family Law* 36

Goldrein, Iain, 'Bankruptcy and the Matrimonial Home: To Sell, or Exceptionally, Not to Sell' [2011] *Family Law* 1227

Hayward, Andy, 'Cohabitants, Detriment and the Potential of Proprietary Estoppel' (2015) 27 *Child and Family Law Quarterly* 303

Hayward, Andy, 'Common Intention Constructive Trusts and the Role of Imputation in Theory and Practice' [2016] *The Conveyancer and Property Lawyer* 233

Hayward, Andy, ' "Family Property" and the Process of Familiarisation of Property Law' [2012] *Child and Family Law Quarterly* 284

Hess, Edward, 'The Rights of Cohabitants: When and How Will the Law Be Reformed?' [2009] *Family Law* 405

Law Commission, 'Cohabitation: The Financial Consequences of Relationship Breakdown' (Law Com No 307, 2007)

Law Commission, 'Sharing Homes: A Discussion Paper' (Law Com No 278, 2002)

Pawlowski, Mark, 'Orders for Sale: The Creditor and the Family Home: Parts 1, 2' [2012] *Family Law* 18

Pawlowski, Mark, 'Resulting Trusts, Joint Borrowers and Beneficial Shares' [2010] *Family Law* 654

Sloan, Brian, 'Keeping Up with the Jones Case; Establishing Constructive Trusts in "Sole Legal Owner" Scenarios' [2015] *Legal Studies* 226

Tattersall, Mark, 'Stack v Dowden: Imputing and Intention' [2008] *Family Law* 249

Welstead, Mary, 'The Deserted Bank and the Spousal Equity' [1999] *Denning Law Journal* 113

Welstead, Mary, 'Domestic Contribution and Constructive Trusts: The Canadian Perspective' [1987] *Denning Law Journal* 151

Welstead, Mary, 'Proprietary Estoppel: A Flexible Familial Equity' [1995] *Conveyancer and Property Lawyer* 61

5

Protecting adults from domestic abuse – the civil remedies

SUMMARY

This chapter considers the nature and incidence of physical, sexual and psychological violence and abuse between current and former intimate partners, including women and other sex and genders. (Violence, assault and abuse against children is dealt with in Chapters 14 and 15.) The Domestic Abuse Act (DAA) 2021, s 1 establishes a much-needed statutory definition of domestic abuse which includes physical and sexual abuse, and extends the understanding of abuse to include threatening, coercive and controlling conduct, psychological, economic and financial abuse. The new definition is significant in recognising domestic abuse as a pattern of conduct involving tactics of control and a strategy of suborning the victim, rather than being perceived as one episodic and isolated violent event. 'Controlling or coercive behaviour in an intimate or family relationship' was also introduced as a specific crime under the Serious Crime Act (SCA) 2015, s 76. In *Re H-N and others (children) (domestic abuse: finding of fact hearings)* [2021] 2 FLR 1116, the Court of Appeal gave general guidance on the importance of focusing on a pattern of behaviour as opposed to a specific incident.

This chapter focuses on the civil remedies providing protection in the civil and family courts including non-molestation and occupation orders, forced marriage protection orders, female genital mutilation protection orders and domestic violence protection notices (DVPNs) and orders (DVPOs) DAA, ss 22–56 proposed the introduction of domestic abuse protection notices and orders. Relevant too, is the crime of non-fatal strangulation (DAA, s 70) which is a recurring feature of domestic abuse in criminal and family cases. An analysis of the annual trends in orders demonstrates a rise in applications for all protective orders and especially during the Covid pandemic where lockdown heightened the danger of abuse when victims were particularly vulnerable because of entrapment and isolation and the inaccessibility of support services cutting off their route for escape. Covid also accelerated the digitising of the courts and remote hearings resulting in the increase in unrepresented parties since notwithstanding legal aid as a right in domestic abuse cases the means test excluded many who could not afford private representation.

This chapter is as much a story about the law as it is about those who come to law for protection and their lived experience. It is a story which demonstrates that the development

DOI: 10.4324/9781003435020-5

of law is not reliant only on judges' determination in the higher courts but relies on tenacious solicitors working on the ground and advocates in the courtroom who through advocacy put arguments forward for judicial consideration and without whose determination the law regulating domestic abuse would simply have stood still. It is impossible to address the problem of domestic abuse without some consideration of the criminal law as the marginalisation of domestic abuse in the family justice system and the myths and stereotypes about domestic abuse that are still pervasive notwithstanding Practice Direction 12J – *Child Arrangements & Contact Orders: Domestic Abuse and Harm*, very much mirror the posture of the treatment of domestic abuse in the criminal justice process.

Contemporary definitions and very public cases

Historically, 'domestic violence' has been the term used to capture a variety of forms of abuse committed by intimate partners, largely by men on women, and where legal remedies required evidence of physical assault. Non-physical abusive conduct was however recognised as 'cruelty' in divorce petitions, recognised as 'molestation' for the purpose of non-molestation injunctions (Family Law Act (FLA) 1996) and in harassment offences which require a 'course of conduct' and 'putting a person in fear' (Protection from Harassment Act (PFHA) 1997). Research has shown that judges rarely granted a non-molestation order under the FLA, s 42, 42A unless there was physical violence.

The recent wider understanding of domestic abuse (DAA, s 1) has impacted on judges' understanding and approach to family law applications where domestic abuse is a feature. In *F v M* [2021] EWFC 4 in the family court where a mother had been subjected to controlling and coercive behaviour by the father, the court held that the significance of individual acts might only be understood properly within the context of wider behaviour. Hayden J in his postscript said: 'An intense focus on particular and specified incidents may be a counterproductive exercise. It carries the risk of obscuring the serious nature of harm perpetrated in a pattern of behaviour.' Sir Andrew McFarlane P with reference to non-molestation injunctions in the Court of Appeal said in *Re H-N* (noted earlier) that the term and understanding of domestic violence: '[23] . . . is now wholly outdated and hard to comprehend an approach which required evidence of actual bodily harm to a victim before a power of arrest could be attached to an injunction (section 2 of the DVMPA 1976)' [and is] '[52] old fashioned and no longer accepted [and] [25] As the present appeals illustrate, there are many cases in which the allegations are not of violence, but of a pattern of behaviour which it is now understood as abusive. This has led to an increasing recognition of the need in many cases for the court to focus on a pattern of behaviour and this is reflected by PD 12J'.

Section 1 DAA 'domestic abuse' replaces the term 'domestic violence' and recognises a range of behaviours. Section 1 (3) DAA Behaviour is 'abusive' if it consists of any of the following –

a.   physical or sexual abuse;
b.   violent or threatening behaviour;

c.   controlling or coercive behaviour;

d.   economic abuse (see subsection (4));

e.   psychological, emotional or other abuse; and it does not matter whether the behaviour consists of a single incident or a course of conduct.

(4)   "Economic abuse" means any behaviour that has a substantial adverse effect on B's ability to –

a.   acquire, use or maintain money or other property, or

b.   obtain goods or services.

The term 'other' abuse is purposely included to allow a wide discretion to police, prosecutors and the courts.

Whilst domestic abuse is experienced by all genders including those in heterosexual, same-sex relationships and other gendered or non-gendered relationships it is largely experienced by women, where perpetrators are men. Domestic abuse related crime recorded by the police shows that in the year ending March 2023, the victim was female in 73.5 per cent of domestic abuse-related crimes (889,918) (see Domestic Abuse Office for National Statistics November 2023 Main Point 1). This figure does not include abusive conduct where victims seek redress in the family court, although in some cases both criminal and civil remedies may be sought.

Domestic abuse is prevalent across all cultures, ethnicities and socio-economic backgrounds. In May 2024 a video was published online of P Diddy the rap singer violently abusing his partner Cassie Ventura in a hotel hallway (Vardy 2024). Diddy aka Sean Combs is facing numerous sexual misconduct lawsuits involving countless allegations from many victims. The legendary US singer Tina Turner spoke of the violence from her first husband, Ike Turner, who like so many abusers did not recognise his conduct as abusive, only his entitlement to abuse. He said: 'Sure, I've slapped Tina. . . . There have been times when I punched her to the ground without thinking. But I have never beat her' (Turner 1999). In 2009, the singer Rihanna was beaten by her boyfriend Chris Brown. He was sentenced to five years' probation in the US. She said, reflecting on how women want to keep their victimisation secret:

> But, for me, and anyone who's been a victim of domestic abuse, nobody wants to even remember it. Nobody even wants to admit it. So, to talk about it and say it once, much less 200 times, is like . . . I have to be punished for it. It didn't sit well with me.
>
> (Leibovitz 2015)

In the widely publicised case of *Depp v Heard* [2021] (108 Va. Cir. 382, Aug. 17, 2021), Johnny Depp brought a defamation action against Amber Heard following an article in which she alleged he was abusive. During divorce proceedings, Heard claimed that Depp had abused her physically, which he denied. An action for libel followed in London (*Depp II v News Group Newspapers Ltd and another* [2020] EWHC 2911 (QB)) when Depp sued News Group Newspapers Ltd over an article published in *The Sun* newspaper in which it was stated that Depp had abused Heard. The judge found that 12 of the 14 alleged assaults had been proved to the civil standard. Whilst Depp denied abusing Heard he sent this text to her:

> *[53] Once again, I find myself in a place of shame and regret. Of course I am sorry. I really don't know why or what happened. But I will never do it again. I want to get better for you. And for me. I must. My illness somehow crept up and grabbed me. I can't do it again. I can't live like that again. And I know you can't either. I must get better. And I will. For us both. I love you. Again, I am so sorry. So sorry. I love you and [f]eel so bad for letting you down. Yours.*

Nicol J dismissed his claim: '[585] I have reached these conclusions having examined in detail the 14 incidents on which the Defendants rely as well as the overarching considerations which the Claimant submitted; I should take into account.'

A subsequent trial in the US in relation to an article in the *Washington Post* written by Heard alleging Depp's violence towards her was not proven and the court found in favour of Depp awarding him compensatory and punitive damages of 15 million dollars. The court also found that Depp had defamed Heard in alleging that Heard and her friends had damaged Depp's penthouse. The claims and counterclaims continued, and eventually they dropped their subsequent appeals reaching a settlement.

Harriet Wistrich, Director of the Centre for Women's Justice, writes:

> *The tactics used by Depp in his claim against Amber Heard, have been described as a classic example of DARVO, 'deny, attack, and reverse victim and offender', a manipulation strategy where the abuser denies the abuse ever took place, attacks the victim for attempting to hold the abuser accountable, and claims that they, the abuser, are actually the victim in the situation, thus reversing the reality of the victim and offender. Like the term 'gaslighting' which has become more widely understood in recent years, identifying what is going on and naming the problem is the first step to resistance and fightback. It is critical that the courts and statutory agencies become wise to being unwittingly used by abusers to extend their manipulation of victims.*
>
> (Centre for Women's Justice)

Politicians, in supporting measures to protect women from domestic abuse, have also spoken out about their own experiences. In 2019, during a House of Commons debate on the Domestic Abuse Bill, Rosie Duffield MP spoke of her partner's coercive control of her.

> *Domestic violence has many faces . . . sometimes there are no bruises . . . abuse is often all about control and power . . . they don't threaten . . . control . . . not yet. . . . not at the start when they think you are sweet, funny, gorgeous . . . not when they want to impress you . . . not when they turn up on your third date with chocolates and jewelry. Not when they meet your parents . . . not when they meet the leader of your political party . . . it's when the ring is on your finger and the promises seem like threats . . .*

and you can spend all day at work only to find that on the way home they refuse to speak a single or solitary word to you . . . eventually when you are at home they will find a way to tell you what sin you have apparently committed . . . your dress was too short . . . the top you wore in the chamber was too low cut . . . or you didn't respond to a message quickly enough. It starts with a few emotional knocks . . . alternated with emotional gushes of romantic and everlasting love so you are left reeling . . . always in a hyper alert state . . . then it changes. His face changes and you know you have to stay calm silent and very careful . . . you know to do exactly as you are told . . . and then in the months that follow those patterns continue . . . reward . . . punishment and promises of happily ever after . . . alternated with abject rage, menace, silent treatment and coercive control . . . (whilst he lives in my home without contributing a single penny) and then the slow disappearance of any kindness, respect or loving behavior. . . . You are afraid to go home so one night when you muster up the courage you take his keys to your house from his pocket. He is locked out . . . he rages . . . phones you . . . texts you, but you muster up the courage to end it . . . and six months later you have the courage to smile and be happy again.

(Rosie Duffield YouTube) (See also Horley 2017)

Domestic abuse may also include sexual abuse

Domestic abuse can also involve sexual abuse of many kinds including rape as the following cases demonstrate.

In *Re H-N* [2021] noted earlier, four appeals were considered. *Re H* was dismissed. *Re H-N* was allowed on the basis that Tolson J's approach to the evidence was seriously flawed in respect of comments he made with regard to consent when dealing with allegations of sexual abuse, including that the victim ought to have physically resisted and he dismissed the fact (as accepted by both parties) that she was upset afterwards on the basis that she had difficulties in enjoying sex. In *Re B-B*, the appeal was allowed where both parents issued proceedings. The father sought an order that B-B live with him, and the mother, having obtained an ex parte non-molestation injunction, opposed his application and alleged rape which she had reported to the police and where case management was very poor, papers not filed and the hearing adjourned. On appeal the court said:

> [84] It is common ground that the judge, no doubt when under pressure and at a moment of intense irritation, said a number of ill-judged things at the hearing. . . .
> [108] In our judgment, the judge's unguarded comments, made to the mother, not only to have her child taken from her but to have her adopted and, on two further occasions, to refer the case to social services, have to be regarded as having had long lasting repercussions for her.

In *Re T* the appeal was allowed where there had been allegations of anal rape of the mother and where the judge made three findings of physical violence against the father yet failed to appreciate the significance of the findings she made. The Court of Appeal said:

> [180] . . . we cannot see on what basis the judge could conclude that coming up behind the mother (who was on the floor holding their baby) and putting a plastic bag over her head before saying that 'this was the way she would die' could be regarded as a 'prank'. This was, in our judgment, the second of two intimidating and highly abusive incidents of a similar type carried out within a few weeks of each other.

In *A v B (Appeal: Domestic Abuse)* [2023] EWHC 1499 (Fam) the judge in the family court fell into legal error by justifying B's sexual control of his partner with rape myths and stereotypes and erred in his reasoning regarding his finding that the sexual abuse allegation had not been proved and erred when he failed to consider her vulnerability. The appeal court took the opportunity to give general guidance regarding the need to focus on a pattern of behaviour as opposed to specific incidents. (See also *Re H-N and others* (2021) earlier in this chapter; *JH v MF* [2020] EWHC 86 (Fam)). These cases have drawn much criticism both from within and outside the judiciary.

Domestic abuse is also a pattern of abuse

Domestic abuse as pattern of behaviour as opposed to a specific incident has been well understood for several decades by those working and supporting victims of domestic abuse although not understood or adopted universally until the statutory definition in 2021. In the 1980s Ellen Pence, working with abused women in Duluth, Minnesota, USA, discovered how coercion was used as a tactic by abusers to maintain control. Pence devised what was called the 'power and control' wheel to identify the core tactics abusers used. She recognised that whilst coercion could be used by both men and women on partners in heterosexual and homosexual relationships what marked out coercive control by men in heterosexual relationships was their ability to use violence which in turn created in the putative victim/survivor a fear for her physical and sexual safety (Ellen Pence YouTube). Her thinking informed the work of front-line organisations working with domestic abuse victims in the UK. In 1989, the Law Commission in its Working Paper *Domestic Violence and Occupation of the Family Home* recognised threats, intimidation and coercion as part of a pattern of conduct (para 2.2) and noted for example 'sitting in a parked car outside someone's home or workplace is not objectionable in itself unless and until it is perceived as part of a pattern of conduct with no purpose other than that of unsettling or intimidating the person concerned' (para 3.28).

There were of course judges in UK courts prior to the enactment of the DAA 2021 who were cognisant of the several forms of domestic abuse. Sir Mark Potter, President of the Family Division, in *Practice Direction: Residence and Contact Orders: Domestic Violence and Harm* (2009) said:

> [2] . . . 'domestic violence' includes physical violence, threatening or intimidating behaviour and any other form of abuse which, directly or indirectly, may have caused harm to the other party or to the child or which may give rise to the risk of harm.

In *Yemshaw v London Borough of Hounslow* [2011] UKSC 3 when the Supreme Court considered the meaning of 'violence' in s 177(1) of the Housing Act (HA) 1996, with regard to whether a woman and her children should have been re-housed Lady Hale put this question:

> *Was this, in reality, simply a case of marriage breakdown in which the appellant was not genuinely in fear of her husband; or was it a classic case of domestic abuse, in which one spouse puts the other in fear through the constant denial of freedom and of money for essentials, through the denigration of her personality, such that she genuinely fears that he may take her children away from her however unrealistic this may appear to an objective outsider? This is not to apply a subjective test. . . . The test is always the view of the objective outsider but applied to the particular facts, circumstances and personalities of the people involved.*

Prior to the DAA 2021, the Government in 2012 had also defined domestic violence as:

> *Any incident or pattern of incidents of controlling, coercive or threatening behaviour, violence, or abuse between those aged 16 or over who are or have been intimate partners or family members regardless of gender or sexuality. This can encompass, but is not limited to, the following types of abuse: psychological, physical, sexual, financial, emotional.*

The Statutory Guidance Framework (2015) defined controlling behaviour as:

> *[12] . . . any act designed to make a person subordinate and/or dependent by isolating them from sources of support, exploiting their resources and capacities for personal gain, depriving them of the means needed for independence, resistance and escape and regulating their everyday behaviour.*

The Home Office in their guidance on 'Violence Against Women and Girls' defined coercive behaviour as: 'an act or a pattern of acts of assault, threats, humiliation and intimidation or other abuse that is used to harm, punish, or frighten their victim' reiterated in the 2023 Statutory Guidance on coercive and controlling behaviour. In November 2023, the Ministry of Justice published its policy paper and Government response, *Domestic abuse and the Family Court: Achieving cultural change*, setting out a series of improvements to be made in the family courts for victims and survivors. These recommendations will be addressed throughout this chapter.

History: challenging the common law

Historically, society and the law condoned and excused male violence and abuse against women especially in the domestic sphere. Originally called 'spousal' or 'wife abuse', it was seldom recognised. In *Lawe's Resolutions of Women's Rights* (Doddridge 1632: vol III 128) Justice Brooke asserted the current position. 'A man may beat an outlaw, a traitor, a Pagan, his villein or his wife because by the Law Common, these persons can have no action.' In *Bradley v Wife* [1663] Keble's Reports 1685 Vol 1 637, where a husband beat his wife, the court refused to bind him over unless it could be proved that her life was in danger: 'because by law he had power of castigation'. Husbands could rape wives and the Chief Justice of the Court of King's Bench, Sir Matthew Hale, said that husbands had immunity from prosecution if they raped them. 'The husband of a woman cannot himself be guilty of an actual rape upon his wife, on account of the matrimonial consent which she has given, and which she cannot retract' (Hale 1736: 472–474, 629). This prerogative remained until the House of Lords ruled in *R v R* [1992] 1 AC 599. Sir William Blackstone (1765: 445) later observed: 'The law thought it reasonable to entrust him with this power of chastisement in the same moderation that a man is allowed to correct his apprentices or children.' By contrast, a woman who in defending herself from a brutal husband killed him, was convicted of petit treason and until 1790 could be burned at the stake. In 1829, the Offences Against the Person Act (OAPA), s 1 abolished petit treason as a separate category of murder. (See Gavigan 1989.)

By the nineteenth century feminists turned to reform of the substantive law in their efforts to protect women from male violence. Frances Power Cobbe (1869) and Matilda Blake (1892) were amongst many who challenged this masculinist edifice of the common law wherein the male point of view was taken as objective truth. In 'Wife-Torture in England' (1869), Cobbe attempted to reframe the understanding of domestic violence describing it as 'domestic lynching' (221), replacing the term 'wife beating' with 'wife torture'. Women, she said, were: 'brought down by fear' (228) male abusers were excited by the signs of pain they inflicted (229) and women were blamed for male violence in a society that was largely indifferent (221). John Stuart Mill in supporting this agitation for protection wrote:

> *The vilest malefactor has some wretched woman tied to him against whom he can commit any atrocity except killing her, and if tolerably cautious, can do that without much danger of legal penalty . . . worst of all, she could not refuse her master even the worst familiarity but must submit to 'the lowest degradation of a human being' that of being made the instrument of an animal function contrary to her inclinations.*
>
> (1867, 1978: 35, 37)

Legal landmarks

In 1853, the Aggravated Assaults Act (AAA) was introduced, intended to provide women who were abused by male partners with greater access to the courts. The Act did not provide the remedy that was hoped for and instead 'down crimed' very serious cases of violence which should have been heard in the higher courts and consigned them to the magistrate's jurisdiction with their lesser sentencing powers (consolidated in the OAPA 1861, s 43, see Hansard Debate Brutal Assault legislation). Further, in a *Report to the Secretary of State for the Home Department, on the State of Law Relating to Brutal Assaults* (1875) justices themselves expressed reservations that s 43 of the AAA 1853 was being used to 'down crime' serious assault. Consider the case of William Babbington who was charged with assaulting his wife, kicking her with mining boots in the face, body and ribs and where four women testified against him as witnesses to the assault and his repeated kicking of her even after she had fallen to the ground. It was reported: 'The Bench, as it is only an occasional court, could not inflict a heavy penalty, gave the heaviest sentence they could – viz, fourteen days' hard labour and ordered the payment of seventeen shillings costs' (Edwards 2005). (See also further Behlmer 2011). By 1878, the Matrimonial Causes Act, ss 4(1), 4(2) provided some limited redress for victims of domestic violence and abuse and allowed for a separation order to a wife provided she could prove her husband's cruelty with a criminal conviction of aggravated assault. The court or magistrate 'if satisfied that the future safety of the wife is in peril' could then make a non-cohabitation order, a maintenance order and an order giving custody of any children under 10 years of age to the wife. During the House of Commons debate on the Guardianship of Infants Bill 1924 it was reported that: 'Sir Ernley Blackwell of the Home Office, who told us that out of ninety-nine cases of wife murder during the years 1901 to 1922, eighteen were connected with the question of obtaining separation orders.'

1970s reform measures

A century later, feminist reformers continued to challenge male perpetrators and a justice system that failed to offer domestic abuse victims protection. Police were reluctant to proceed with charging husband/cohabitants with criminal assault, the criminal courts were reluctant to convict, sentences were derisory, and civil courts granted injunctions only where physical violence was proven. Mrs X, in oral evidence to the *Select Committee on Violence in Marriage* (1974–5 [25]), said:

> I have had ten stitches, three stitches, five stitches, seven stitches, where he has cut me. I have had a knife stuck through my stomach; I have had a poker put through my face; I have no teeth where he knocked them all out; I have been burnt with red hot pokers; I have had red hot coals slung all over me; I have been sprayed with petrol and stood there while he has flicked lighted matches at me. . . . I have been to the police . . . and they held him in over the weekend and he came out on Monday. He was bound over to keep the peace. . . . On Tuesday he gave me the hiding of my life.

Jo Richardson MP, when presenting the Domestic Violence Bill 1975–76 in the House of Commons, which was later to become the Domestic Violence and Matrimonial Proceedings Act 1976 (DVMPA) to provide non-molestation and exclusion orders (the precursor to the currently existing civil remedies), reported a case where a husband with two previous convictions for assaulting his wife evaded punishment for non-fatal strangulation.

> During one attack, he tied a flex so tightly round her throat that her larynx was damaged, and she had to be fed through a tube in hospital. The man was taken to court, fined £2 and told to behave himself.
>
> (Domestic Violence Bill vol 905, col 862)

Explanations of domestic abuse

Domestic abuse is now recognised as a high-risk factor for more serious abuse and death and an act of male power and control. Understandings of domestic violence and abuse at any given time have shaped and informed legislation and policy of the time. Until the late 1980s, domestic violence and abuse was thought to occur only in homes where there was extreme deprivation, poverty and social problems.

Theorisations and understandings of domestic violence and abuse reflected the perceptions held at the time and reinforced myths and stereotypes about male and female behaviour including drug and alcohol abuse, addiction and instability in relationships. Strategies of male control and coercion were normalised and condoned as a part of married life, violent and controlling conduct was legitimised as a symbol of male prerogative and authority, and female partners were blamed and their conduct considered responsible for male violence.

In the 1960s and 1970s, domestic abuse was considered to be a matter of individual pathology (Gayford 1975). Studies of men who abused concluded that the cause of violence was alcohol, unemployment, drug addiction, violent personalities and women's provocation. Such thinking impacted on diagnostic categories about male violence such that 'morbid jealousy' and the 'Othello syndrome' recorded in Diagnostic and Statistical Manual (DSM-IV) and the International Classification of Diseases (ICD–10) were identified as medical conditions and used in the courtroom to excuse male violence against women. Pathological jealousy was raised in *Wookey v Wookey; Re S (a child) (injunction)* [1991] Fam 121 and *A-G's Reference (No 45 of 2006), R v Stephenson* [2006] EWCA Crim 1890, whilst the Othello syndrome formed part of the defence submission in *R v Vinagre* (1979) 69 Cr App R 104; *C v Dixon* [2009] EWHC 708 (QB) and *R v Cheshire (Richard George)* [2010] EWCA Crim 2148. A feminist analysis would locate the causes of male violence less in somatology or psychoanalytical foundation and rather more in an analysis of masculinist proprietorialness. Jackson and Rushton (1982: 17) wrote:

> *The problem is individualized [and] diverts attention away from the power structure of the family to the subordination of women within it and the oppression they experience as wives and mothers. The problem is restructured in terms of the unusual social or psychological characteristics of those who suffer from or give way to the temptation of violence.*

At the same time there were some studies of women victims of abuse which focused on individual pathology and maintained that women had provoked male violence. Pizzey and Shapiro (1982) theorised that women who were abused by several partners sought out violent men because they had a chemical addiction to violence. This dangerously gave some impetus for a revival of Freudian psychoanalytic theories of the first half of the twentieth century which promulgated the notion that women wished to be beaten (Deutsch 1958: 276). Such theorisations were reflected in criminal policy and in approaches to prosecution, defence submissions and judicial sentencing and in the civil justice process in protection of women from male violence. John Dean Wigmore, the American jurist, in his textbook on evidence asserted that rape allegations were invariably false and brought by a woman's psychic complexes, imagination and 'unchaste mentality' (1940: 459–460). The British jurist Glanville Williams (1962: 662) argued for the need for corroboration in sexual cases due to the 'danger of deliberately false charges, resulting from sexual neurosis, phantasy, jealousy'. And in his *Textbook of Criminal Law* (1978: 196) wrote: 'Many complaints of rape are false.'

In 2024, the Crown Prosecution Service (CPS) study on 'Rape and serious sexual offences' found that myths and stereotypes about consent continue to be held and the study perhaps surprisingly found that this was all the more so in the 18–24 years age group.

Post 1970s – feminist jurisprudential challenges

Challenging these earlier conceptions was the work of Gelles (1979) and feminist campaigners and front-line workers working with abused women (Hanmer and Saunders 1984; Patel 1989) and legal advocates (Fiora-Gormally 1978; Schneider 1986; Kennedy 1992; Sheehy 1994) and expert witnesses (Walker 1979, 1989) working in the courts, who argued that male violence against women was rooted in male hegemony and a masculinist law and legal system. Their understandings explored the structural conditions of gender inequity which defined the parameters of forced dependency (see Dobash and Dobash 1980), the social structures founded on patriarchy, and the legal system that refuted male violence and marginalised women's protection. The case of *A v B (Appeal: Domestic Abuse)* [2023] EWHC 1499 (Fam), an appeal in the Family Division of the High Court, demonstrates that time has not dispelled such 'cultural' and gendered forms of control nor outdated and inappropriate thinking and stereotyping by judges, where some of the judge's comments were found on appeal to be of 'concern', 'particularly inapt' and 'were unfortunate' since amongst several other matters he applied a higher standard of proof to the mothers' allegations of rape and made assumptions about patterns of consent and coercion.

Crenshaw (1991) in the US, and Patel (1989) together with the organisation Southall Black Sisters (SBS) in the UK, raised awareness of the experience of domestic violence and abuse by women of colour and the discrimination that they faced from a justice system as women and as women from minority ethnic communities. Radhika Coomaraswamy, the UN former Special Rapporteur on violence against women, its causes and consequences, speaking globally on the issue recognised that violence against women is linked to gender and that honour resides in the bodies of women and that crimes against women relating to honour have escaped national and international scrutiny largely because they are frequently presented as 'traditional or cultural practices requiring toleration and respect' (see Welchman and Hossain 2005).

Domestic abuse incidence and the criminal law

The extent of domestic violence and abuse is impossible to determine with any accuracy, as victims underreport and police underrecord. Motives for silence are myriad and have little changed over the years (see Edwards 1989, 1986), including lack of confidence in the criminal justice system, in the police (exacerbated by domestic violence and sexual abuse within police ranks and the murder of Sarah Everard by a serving police officer, and the Super Complaint brought by the Centre for Women's Justice which raised concerns about the policing of domestic abuse, (see Police perpetrated domestic abuse super complaint), lack of confidence in the civil and criminal courts, and concern with the delay in court) proceedings, shame, fear of losing one's children, and homelessness. Many women do not recognise the violence and abuse as unlawful, thinking they will not be believed and fearing retaliation.

Data on the incidence of domestic abuse need to be treated with caution as datasets are not always comparable and recording practices and definitions change over time.

For England and Wales year ending March 2022, 1,500,369 'domestic abuse-related incidents and crimes' were recorded and 1,453,867 year ending March 2023 (see Domestic Abuse Prevalence and Trends, Main point 2). Concerning the incidence of 'controlling and coercive conduct' (SCA, s 76) for the year ending March 2022, 41,626 were recorded and March 2023 there were 43,774 offences (see Domestic Abuse Prevalence and Trends Main point 5). Approximately 20 per cent of all homicides has involved the killing of female partners for several decades. For the year ending March 2020, 46 per cent (81 cases) of all adult female homicide victims were killed by an intimate partner. Year ending March 2022, female victims were killed by a partner or ex-partner in 33 per cent of cases (Homicide in England and Wales Appendix Table 32 and Main point 4). In 2023, of the 249 female domestic homicide victims, the suspect was male in 241 cases. In the majority of female domestic homicides, the suspect was a male partner or ex-partner (74.7 per cent) whereas in the majority of male domestic homicides, the suspect was a male family member (66.1 per cent) (Domestic abuse victim characteristics Main point 11).

In *R v Brooks (Tony Russel)* [2023] EWCA Crim 554, [2023] 2 Cr App R (S) 40, the appellant murdered his wife. The deceased was found with two ligatures around her neck, and in her throat were two socks, and a lint roller in her mouth. B appealed against a minimum term of 24 years and nine months imposed following his guilty plea to murder. A background of coercive control was noted. The court upheld a 12-year increase to a starting point of 15 years for an offence of murder, holding that there is no limitation on the degree of adjustment that a court can make in consideration of aggravating and mitigating factors.

Women subjected to violence and control, in preserving their own life, have killed the violent and abusive partner. In *R v Challen* [2019] Crim 916, after serving ten years in prison for murder and an earlier appeal having failed, Sally Challen the appellant who had killed her husband in 2010 was released from prison. On appeal, the court took into account that she had been a victim of coercive and controlling conduct. Her original conviction for murder was quashed and manslaughter diminished responsibility substituted (see Wistrich 2024: 205).

Domestic induced suicide is not uncommon (see *R v Dhaliwal* [2006] *R v Dhaliwal (appeal under s 58 of the Criminal Justice Act 2003) (CA)* [2006] All ER (D) 236). The 'Domestic Homicides and Suspected Victim Suicides' project recorded 215 deaths resulting from 208 incidents between March 2020 and March 2021, where 49 per cent were current or former intimate partner homicides and 18 per cent suspected victim suicides. A meta-analysis of three case-controlled studies found that the number of deaths by suicide was increased by tenfold among victims of intimate partner violence. Kelly Sutton took her own life in 2017 after domestic abuse and was found unconscious at the home she shared with partner Steven Gane. An original inquest ruled that she died from suicide. A second inquest ruled that she was unlawfully killed. In March 2018, Gane was convicted of controlling and coercive behaviour and assault occasioning actual bodily harm. Sutton sent a text to Gane shortly before he found her dead saying: 'Hope you feel bad, for this is your fault, you told me to do everyone a favour, so that's what I shall do. . . . Hope your life's better without me' (see Kelly Sutton).

Hoeger and Bates (2023) in their research found of 242 domestic abuse-related deaths recorded between April 2022 and March 2023, 93 were suspected suicides (see also Keynejad et al. 2022).

Assault and coercive control

Concerning assaults, both physical and psychological violence fall within the OAPA.

R v Ireland and Burstow [1998] AC 147 is an important and what appeared to be groundbreaking case to extend the meaning of assault recognising that inflicting grievous bodily harm, OAPA 1861, s 20, included the making of harassing telephone calls, writing menacing letters, visiting the victim's house and distributing insulting cards.

> *My Lords, it is easy to understand the terrifying effect of a campaign of telephone calls at night by a silent caller to a woman living on her own. It would be natural for the victim to regard the calls as menacing. What may heighten her fear is that she will not know what the caller may do next. The spectre of the caller arriving at her doorstep bent on inflicting personal violence on her may come to dominate her thinking. After all, as a matter of common sense, what else would she be terrified about? The victim may suffer psychiatric illness such as anxiety neurosis or acute depression. Harassment of women by repeated silent telephone calls, accompanied on occasions by heavy breathing, is apparently a significant social problem. That the criminal law should be able to deal with this problem, and so far as is practicable, afford effective protection to victims is self-evident.*
>
> (per Lord Steyn)

Although no physical violence was involved, it was accepted that the victim had been psychiatrically injured as evidenced by expert evidence of her severe depression. However despite this ruling the antiquated and inflexible OAPA provisions rarely extended to this kind of injury, and the House of Lords ruling the subject of much criticism thereby leaving much conduct outside the reach of the law.

By 2015 other forms of abuse were now recognised and prohibited in statute.

Section 76 Serious Crime Act SCA created a stand-alone offence of 'coercive and controlling conduct' for those 'personally connected' (s 76(1)(b)). Section 76 defined 'coercive and controlling conduct' as: 'a continuing act or a pattern of acts of assault, threats, humiliation, and intimidation or other abuse that is used to harm, punish, or frighten their victim and acts to control isolating them from family and friends'. (See also Bishop and Bettinson 2018.)

In *R v Dewhurst* [2021] EWCA Crim 663, the appellant was convicted of four counts of assault, one count of common assault and one count of coercive behaviour which included keeping the victim hostage, telling her she was worthless, head-butting her, threatening her with a weapon and taking control of her phone and Facebook account. In *R v Kingswell* [2022] EWCA Crim 814, the Solicitor General sought leave under s 36 of the Criminal Justice Act 1988 to refer the sentence to the court as unduly lenient where:

> *the victim reported multiple instances of controlling and coercive conduct by the defendant, amongst others: defendant threat to commit suicide; repeatedly smashing the victim's phone and a replacement phone, demanding money which was never repaid; punching her on the nose; forced her to leave their joint home; threw food at her; grabbed her by the throat with both hands, threw the victims phone and laptop out of the window.*

The Court of Appeal imposed a sentence of 33 months' imprisonment.

In 2022 1,925 cases of controlling behaviour reached the magistrates' court, and in 2023 that number was 2,720 (Domestic Abuse and the Criminal Justice System Table 16).

Further legislative reform in s 70 of the DAA inserted s 75A into the SCA 2015 creating a new offence of 'strangulation or suffocation'. The antiquated OAPA, s 21 recognised choking, strangulation and suffocation as an offence, but only where it was for the purpose of committing an indictable offence and in any event was rarely used. Under the DAA the offence of strangulation is a stand-alone offence and committed where: 'A intentionally strangles another person ("B") or A does any other act to B that affects B's ability to breathe and constitutes battery of B.' A defence is open to A if sufficient evidence of B's consent is adduced to raise an issue (s 75(4)(a)) but not if B suffers serious harm and A intended or was reckless as to that harm.

A compelling case for this new offence gathered further momentum following the murder by strangulation of Grace Millane in New Zealand by Jesse Kempson (see *Kempson v R* [2020] NZCA 656). Section 70 has significantly raised the understanding and recognition of strangulation and suffocation as a tactic of male violence against women. In *R v Carrigan* [2021] EWCA Crim 1553, the offence: '[11] included a period of strangulation when her breathing was interrupted.' The judge observed that this must inevitably take the offence into the top category of seriousness for the purposes of applying the relevant guideline and indicated that the appropriate starting point for that offence was 18 months' imprisonment with a range of between one and three years' imprisonment. Carrigan's appeal against sentence was rejected and twenty-seven months' imprisonment in respect of Count 2 to run concurrently to the other count was upheld.

An allegation of strangulation is now considered a red flag incident for police and front line practitioners and recognised as carrying a significant risk of serious and further abuse and death. Its prevalence is reflected in cases involving domestic abuse and violence in the civil and family courts. (See *A and another v B and others* [2022] EWHC 3089 (Fam); [2023] 1 WLR 677.)

Protection from Harassment Act 1997

Whilst the PFHA 1997 was not specifically introduced to prevent domestic violence, it has been used for that purpose. Sections 2 and 4 of the Act create two criminal offences: first, harassment; and secondly, putting a person in fear of violence. Both offences carry the option of a custodial sentence. The Protection of Freedoms Act 2012, s 111 inserted a new s 2A into the PFHA which provides for the offence of stalking and carries a potential maximum six-month prison sentence. A new s 4A provides for the offence of stalking which causes fear of violence or serious distress and carries a maximum five-year prison sentence. To be convicted of an offence, the accused must have pursued a course of conduct and not merely committed one act of harassment and whether acts constitute a course of conduct does not depend upon a mathematical calculation but is fact specific (see Crown Prosecution Service, 'Restraining Orders').

In *Kelly v Director of Public Prosecutions* [2002] EWHC 1428 (Admin), the court accepted that three phone calls in five minutes, in the middle of the night, from a man to a woman with whom the man had a previous relationship could be viewed as a course of conduct. In *R v P* [2004] All ER (D) 191, the defendant was divorced from his wife, she had obtained a restraining order under s 5 of the PFHA 1997, which prevented the defendant from making any direct or indirect contact with her or their children except through solicitors. The defendant repeatedly sent text messages and made silent calls from his mobile phone to her and the children and was found guilty of breaching the order. (See also *Lomas v Parle* [2004] 1 FLR 812; Edwards 1996: 220.)

The widespread use of the Internet, mobile phones and digital technology has increased the potential for harassment including cyber flashing (see McGlynn 2021; Online Safety Act 2023; 'Cyberflashing Convict BBC'). Research conducted by the charity Refuge in 2021 found that 1 in 3 women in the UK have experienced online abuse (perpetrated on social media or other online platform) at some point in their lives. The use of mobile phones and digital technology is part of a wider pattern of domestic abuse and in *R v Cordle (John William)* [2016] EWCA Crim 1793 the defendant sent a series of threatening texts as part of a campaign of domestic abuse: '[9] I'd like to see Tanya's face after the acid is put on her face. . . . God help you and your family. . . . "Acid's coming"'.

The national risk assessment protocol, the Domestic Abuse, Stalking and Harassment tool (known as DASH) which contains 27 questions and 11 stalking related questions has become the national risk assessment tool to assist police in identifying risk when domestic abuse is reported to them (see Robinson et al. 2016).

Civil remedies for domestic violence and abuse

The main civil remedies for domestic violence and abuse include occupation and non-molestation orders (ss 33 to 49 of the FLA), restraining orders (PFHA, s 5), forced marriage protection orders under the Forced Marriage (Civil Protection) Act 2007 (see *PF v QF* [2024] EWFC 10), female genital mutilation protection orders under the Female Genital Mutilation Act 2003 (see *Re A (a child) (female genital mutilation: asylum)* [2019] EWHC 2475 (Fam)) and domestic violence protection notices (DVPNs) and orders (DVPOs) ss 24 to 33 (Crime and Security Act (CSA) 2010). Following the DAA (ss 22–48) it is proposed that DVPNs and DVPOs will be replaced with domestic abuse protection notices (DAPNs) and domestic abuse protection orders (DAPOs), following the pilot commenced in 2023 in selected areas Gwent, Greater Manchester and three London boroughs (Croydon, Bromley and Sutton) (see New Practice Direction 36zg – Part 3 of The Domestic Abuse Act 2021: Provision During Piloted Commencement. See also Domestic Abuse Protection Notices and Domestic Abuse Protection Orders Draft statutory guidance for the police).

These remedies will be considered in turn.

Family Law Act 1996, Part IV ss 33–41, 43–49: occupation rights

Stand-alone domestic violence injunctions to restrain or exclude a party, to protect the abused party, usually the wife or female partner, were first introduced in the DVMPA 1976. The House of Lords in *Davis v Johnson* [1978] 2 WLR 553 resolved once and for all that s 1(c) of the DVMPA provided that the proprietorial right of a husband/partner party to occupy the matrimonial home in the event of his physical abuse of a wife or partner could be suspended. Part IV (FLA) amended these earlier remedies introducing a 'balance of harm test' into the jurisprudence. The Act is underpinned by the erstwhile value judgement that the protection of property rights is of overriding importance.

The FLA provides for certain categories of family members to apply to the court for an order relating to the occupation of the family home which includes any type of property which can reasonably be occupied in a domestic manner. In order to secure the Act's passage through Parliament, it was deemed necessary to differentiate between those family members who have statutory home rights, proprietary rights, contractual rights or other statutory rights in the family home (entitled) and those family members who have none of these rights (non-entitled). The first category of family members is referred to as 'entitled' and the second category as 'non-entitled' who despite their designation, do have some rights under the FLA. A third category of family members has no rights of occupation but rights to apply for non-molestation orders (see later in this chapter).

Entitled persons

The FLA 1996, s 33(1) provides that spouses or civil partners, who have a statutory home right to occupy their family home under s 30 of the Act (beneficial estate or interest or contract or by virtue of any enactment), may apply for one of the orders outlined in s 33(3).

Prior to the Civil Partnership Act 2004 (CPA) these rights were referred to as matrimonial home rights. 'Associated persons', who have a proprietary interest or contractual or statutory right relating to their family home, may also apply for a s 33(1) order. If they have none of these pre-existing rights, they remain outside the ambit of the FLA for the purposes of occupation orders.

Section 62(3) of the Act provides a wide definition of associated persons:

(3) For the purposes of this Part, a person is associated with another person if –
   (a)   they are or have been married to each other;
      (aa) they are or have been civil partners of each other;
   (b)   they are cohabitants or former cohabitants;
   (c)   they live or have lived in the same household, otherwise than merely by reason of one of them being the other's employee, tenant, lodger or boarder;
   (d)   they are relatives;
   (e)   they have agreed to marry one another (whether or not that agreement has been terminated);
      (ea) they have or have had an intimate personal relationship with each other which is or was of significant duration;
      (eza) they have entered into a civil partnership agreement (as defined by section 73 of the Civil Partnership Act 2004) (whether or not that agreement has been terminated);
   (f)   in relation to any child, they are both persons falling within subsection (4); or
   (g)   they are parties to the same family proceedings (other than proceedings under this Part).
(4) A person falls within this subsection in relation to a child if –
   (a)   he is a parent of the child; or
   (b)   he has or has had parental responsibility for the child.
(5) If a child has been adopted or falls within subsection (7), two persons are also associated with each other for the purposes of this Part if –
   (a)   one is a natural parent of the child or a parent of such a natural parent; and
   (b)   the other is the child or any person –
      (i)   who has become a parent of the child by virtue of an adoption order or has applied for an adoption order, or
      (ii) with whom the child has at any time been placed for adoption.
(6) A body corporate and another person are not, by virtue of subsection (3)(f) or (g) to be regarded for the purposes of this Part as associated with each other.

Types of occupation orders for entitled persons

The court may make regulatory or declaratory orders under the FLA, s 33(3). Regulatory orders are wide ranging and permit the applicant to return to the home and remain in it or part of it; state when and at what times the parties may occupy the home; prohibit, suspend or restrict the right to occupy the home; demand that one party leaves the home or part of it; exclude one party from part of the home or the area in which the home is situated. Declaratory orders state that the applicant has a right to occupy the family home, which the court may enforce and exclude the other entitled person. The court may also make orders under section 40(1)(a) impose on either party obligations as to – (i) the repair and maintenance of the dwelling-house; or (ii) the discharge of rent, mortgage payments or other outgoings affecting the dwelling-house, such as rent, mortgage payments, and renovation costs.

Exercise of the court's discretion for entitled persons – the harm test

In deciding whether to grant an occupation order, (3) An order under this section may –

(a) enforce the applicant's entitlement to remain in occupation as against the other person ('the respondent');

(b) require the respondent to permit the applicant to enter and remain in the dwelling-house or part of the dwelling-house;

(c) regulate the occupation of the dwelling-house by either or both parties;

(d) if the respondent is entitled as mentioned in subsection (1)(a)(i), prohibit, suspend or restrict the exercise by him of his right to occupy the dwelling-house;

(e) if the respondent has [home rights] in relation to the dwelling-house and the applicant is the other spouse [or civil partner], restrict or terminate those rights;

(f) require the respondent to leave the dwelling-house or part of the dwelling-house; or

(g) exclude the respondent from a defined area in which the dwelling-house is included.

It is generally assumed that the court must first apply the significant harm test in the FLA 1996, s 33(7). This is a duty imposed on the court. This test requires the court to first consider whether the applicant or any relevant child would be likely to suffer significant harm, which must be attributable to the conduct of the respondent, if the occupation order were not made. In this case the applicant who is experiencing domestic abuse likely will be applying for an order under s 33(3)(e)–(g) requiring the respondent to be removed from the home and/or prevented from entering a defined area. If the 'balance of harm' test results in the court finding that the harm to the respondent or a relevant child if an order were made would be as great or greater than that to the applicant or a relevant child if an order were not made, or where there is no finding of significant harm to either applicant or respondent, the court must look at all the circumstances to decide whether or not an order should be made.

The court must then proceed to the second exercise and here the court has a discretion to grant an order based on a wide range of factors, set out in the FLA 1996, s 33(6)(a)–(d) which might affect the rights of either party. These factors include housing needs, financial resources, the likely effect of any order, or any decision by the court not to exercise its discretion on the wellbeing of the parties and any relevant child, and the conduct of either of the parties. The child need not be a child of either of the parties, but any child who might be affected by the decision. The conduct need not be conduct towards the other party but conduct towards another relevant person which might indicate to the court the potential for future violent behaviour of the applicant or the respondent. Housing needs posed a particular difficulty during Covid.

In *Grubb v Grubb* [2009] EWCA Civ 976, Wilson LJ refused the husband leave to appeal against the award of an occupation order to his wife. He maintained that where the application was by an entitled person under s 33(6) it was unnecessary to go through the hoops of s 33(7). The husband, a farmer, owned a substantial estate which included the matrimonial home and several other properties. The wife applied for an occupation order of the home pending the finalising of the divorce proceedings. Thorpe LJ granted the order on the basis that the husband had been verbally abusive and domineering towards the wife and had refused to make any effort to provide the wife with alternative housing which he had available for this purpose on his estate. The courts are reluctant to award occupation orders unless the circumstances are exceptional.

Where both parties have proprietary rights in the family home, the courts have viewed the grant of an order as a draconian remedy because it interferes with these rights which have generally been regarded as sacrosanct. The harm claimed to have been suffered must result from the respondent's conduct and be more than a mere inconvenience, as is demonstrated in the following decisions.

In *Chalmers v Johns* [1999] 1 FLR 392, a mother and father had lived together for 25 years, occupying the family home as joint tenants. The police were called regularly to investigate assaults by the mother on the father, and vice versa. The mother was a recovering alcoholic and eventually decided to leave home with the 7-year-old daughter and move into temporary council accommodation. It was farther away from the daughter's school than the family home. The court refused to grant the mother an occupation order; neither the mother nor the child was likely to suffer significant harm attributable to the conduct of the father if the order were not made. There was no real risk of violence or any other harm to the child but merely inconvenience because of the child's longer journey to school.

In *Re Y (Children) (Occupation Order)* [2000] 2 FCR 470, a very 'dysfunctional' family lived in separate parts of the family home. The wife lived with the pregnant 16-year-old daughter; the husband lived with the 13-year-old son. The husband, who was a diabetic, applied for an occupation order. The daughter was at war with the father, but there was no evidence of violence by the mother towards her husband but only of his violence towards her. Harm to the husband, if any, resulted from his illness and not from his wife's conduct towards him. The court proceeded to determine occupation of the home using the discretionary factors in s 33(6). The pregnant daughter needed to be securely housed, and the family home was held to be large enough to accommodate all the parties separately. In *B v B* [1999] 1 FLR 715, the husband and wife were tenants of the family home. They lived there with their baby daughter and a child, aged 6, from the husband's previous marriage. The wife left home with the baby because of her husband's violence towards her; the husband and his 6-year-old remained in the home. The council re-housed her in unsuitable temporary bed and breakfast accommodation, and she applied to the court for, *inter alia*, an occupation order. The Court of Appeal held, after weighing the potential harm to the respective parties, that the husband's child would suffer more harm if an occupation order were made than the wife and baby would, if it were not; the position of the parties would simply be reversed. The husband and his child would be placed in accommodation similar to the unsuitable temporary accommodation which the wife and baby were already occupying. The child would have to change schools or be taken into the care of social services. The mother, on the other hand, would soon be re-housed by the council in more suitable permanent accommodation; the mother had, therefore, failed to satisfy the significant harm test. In *Dolan v Corby* [2011] EWCA Civ 1664, a couple occupied property together under a secure tenancy; the female party was granted a right of occupation on the basis of the man's verbal abuse; there was no physical violence. The man appealed. The Court of Appeal declined his appeal and said that because the grant of an occupation order excluded the other person who had rights in the property, it was a draconian order and can only be justified in exceptional circumstances. This did not mean that there had to be physical violence; exceptional circumstances could include many other factors.

Significantly in *Re L (Children)* [2012] EWCA Civ 721 the Court of Appeal upheld an occupation order made against the husband where the judge had been correct to find that both parents' conduct had contributed to a situation where the children's welfare had suffered significant harm as a consequence of the parents remaining in the same house while their relationship broke down. There was nothing in s 33(6) of the Act that limited the discretion to make an occupation order to cases in which there had been physical violence.

Duration of occupation orders for entitled persons

Because the order may be granted for an unlimited period, s 33(10) courts are reluctant in granting them. Judges are also aware that once an order has been granted, that status quo may prevail in any later ancillary proceedings related to a spouse's divorce, judicial separation or annulment, or to the dissolution, or grant of a separation or nullity order for a civil partner.

Non-entitled persons

> Under the FLA 1996, s 35 applications may be made for orders relating to occupation of the family home by former spouses or former civil partners. Section 36 of the Act makes provision for applications by heterosexual or same-sex cohabitants or former cohabitants who are living in, or who have lived in, a relationship as if a spouse or civil partner.

All these persons are defined as non-entitled if they have no statutory home right, proprietary, contractual or other statutory rights to occupy their family or former family home. The orders for which non-entitled persons may apply are very similar to those applicable to entitled persons except that if the court decides to make an order it has the additional power to grant the applicant the right not to be evicted or the right to enter the property for the duration of the order (ss 35(3) (4), 36(3) (4)). The reason for this is self-evident in that the non-entitled person would be unable to benefit from an order without first being allowed to remain in, or enter, the property. Entitled persons already have this right by way of a family home right or by way of property law.

Exercise of the court's discretion for former spouses or civil partners

Those applicants whose marriage or civil partnership has ended receive more preferential treatment than cohabitants, but less preferential treatment than married applicants. Section 35(6) requires the court to consider, in addition to all the factors relating to entitled applicants, *inter alia*, the length of time the parties have been apart, the length of time since the marriage or civil partnership formally ended, and the existence of certain proceedings between the parties relating to children, finances or property.

In *S v F (Occupation Order)* [2000] 1 FLR 255, the parents were divorced and their two children, a boy and a girl, aged 17 and 15, stayed with their mother in the former matrimonial home in London. Both parents had remarried and acquired new families. The mother eventually announced that she was moving to the country. Both children, who were at a critical stage in their education, were opposed to the move, in particular the son who indicated that he would not agree to it. The father applied for an occupation order which would permit him to move back with his new family into the matrimonial home and provide a home for his son there. The court considered, *inter alia*, the housing needs and resources of the parties and all their children; the effect on the health and wellbeing of the parties if the order was made; the conduct of the parties; and the length of the parties' separation. The father's financial position was far weaker, at least in the short term, than the mother's. The grant of an occupation order might lead to some financial inconvenience for the mother, whereas it would provide essential security for the son and the rest of the family. Regarding the conduct of the parties, the mother's sudden change of plan for her children and her failure to consult the father made her partly responsible at least for the son's implacable refusal to move. Although the parties had been separated for a long time each of them had a continuing parental responsibility for the children. The court, after balancing all the factors, granted an occupation order to the father which would permit him to return to the property for six months or until the financial proceedings between the parties were resolved. He was also ordered to undertake to make the mortgage payments.

Section 35(8) provides that if the court decides to make an order and it appears that the applicant or a child might suffer significant harm, it must then proceed to balance the harm which might result to the parties before determining the precise nature of the order. This differs from the provisions for entitled persons where, if there is evidence of significant harm, the balance of harm test is carried out first. It is only when the court rejects the evidence of significant harm that it proceeds to consider other relevant factors. Section 35 (10) provides that an order may be granted for up to six months and may be renewed for further periods of six months.

Exercise of the court's discretion for cohabitants and former cohabitants

Both cohabitants and former cohabitants are treated slightly differently from former spouses or civil partners, and it is questionable why this is so. They are the family members who are more likely to be at risk and they have few other legal rights enforceable against a former partner, such as financial maintenance, to help them if they need to find alternative accommodation. Section 36 (6) provides a list of factors which the court must consider in determining any order. They include the nature of the parties' relationship and in particular the level of commitment involved, the length of time they were together, whether they have joint children or children for whom they have joint responsibility, and the length of time that has passed since they ceased to live together. The balance of harm test for cohabitants is part of the court's overall discretion. Cognisant of the general approach that this category should be treated less generously than entitled persons or non-entitled former spouses or civil partners, any occupation order is limited to six months in the first instance and may be renewed for a further six months but for no longer.

Circumstances where neither of the spouses, civil partners, former spouses, former civil partners or cohabitants have rights to occupy the property

It will be rare to find a situation where none of these persons have rights to occupy the property which they are or have been occupying as their family home, it is likely to be limited to those who are squatting or who have bare licences. Section 37 provides for such an eventuality and allows orders of very limited effect to be made in favour of such applicants.

Enforcement of occupation orders for both entitled and non-entitled persons

Section 47(2) makes the attachment of a power of arrest mandatory if there has been violence or threats of violence towards the victim, unless the court is satisfied that it is not necessary to do so, and the applicant or child would be adequately protected.

This reverses the situation where hitherto it was a matter entirely at the discretion of the court whether to attach a power of arrest. Occupation orders do not automatically have a power of arrest.

Number of occupation and non-molestation order applications and orders granted

Non-molestation and occupation applications and orders granted are recorded in a different data set according to calendar year, and orders granted in one year may be recorded as applications in a previous year and so there are several reasons why the numbers of orders are not directly comparable across data sets. However, the pattern and trend is consistent across all data sets.

TABLE 5.1 Non-molestation and occupation orders applied for with notice and without notice and orders made

Year applications	Non-molestation	Orders made	Occupation	Orders made
With notice				
2022	30,952	36,567	5,907	2,109
2021	29,852	36,573	5,471	2,226
2020	29,856	37,129	6,129	2,482
Without notice ex parte				
2022	27,423	11,963	4,551	171
2021	26,046	13,567	4,064	182
2020	26,058	16,816	4,412	292

Source: Family Court Statistics Quarterly July to September 2022 Annual Applications and Orders Made. Data taken from Accessible Family Court Tables

Table 15 Applications and Orders Made for Domestic Violence Remedies in England and Wales, annually 2003–2022. www.gov.uk/government/statistics/family-court-statistics-quarterly-july-to-september-2022 (accessed 30.04.2024)

Family Law Act 1996, Part IV: ss 42–42A, 43–49: non-molestation orders

What constitutes non-molestation?

Non-molestation is not defined in the FLA 1996, but it has been clarified through case law and now through s 1 of the DAA 2021. Non-molestation includes a wide variety of threatening conduct such as physical violence, serious pestering, and psychological harassment and coercive and controlling conduct.

The most comprehensive definition is found in Practice Direction PD 12J *Child Arrangements & Contact Orders: Domestic Abuse and Harm* Family Procedure Rules 2010, as:

> any incident or pattern of incidents of controlling, coercive or threatening behaviour, violence or abuse between those aged 16 or over who are or have been intimate partners or family members regardless of gender or sexuality. This can encompass, but is not limited to, psychological, physical, sexual, financial, or emotional abuse. Domestic abuse also includes culturally specific forms of abuse including, but not limited to, forced marriage, honour-based violence, dowry-related abuse and transnational marriage abandonment.

(See *F v M* [2021] earlier, where there was a finding of coercive and controlling conduct.)

Earlier case law had also captured such conduct although orders were rarely granted unless there had been acts of physical violence. In *Vaughan v Vaughan* [1973] 1 WLR 1159, the husband continually called at his wife's home and workplace after their relationship was over. In *George v George* [1986] 2 FLR 347, the husband, whose wife had left him for a lesbian relationship, wrote angry letters to her and screamed abuse in an obscene manner when she collected the children. In *Spencer v Camacho* [1983] 4 FLR 662, the searching of a partner's personal property was held to be a form of harassment. In *Johnson v Walton* [1990] 1 FLR 350, a man sent private photographs picturing his partner in semi-nude poses to a newspaper. Ormerod LJ in *Horner v Horner* [1982] Fam 90 was one of the earlier trailblazers who understood the purpose of the legislation and the harm of the conduct. He said: 'I have no doubt that the word "molesting" . . . does not imply necessarily either violence or threats of violence. It applies to any conduct which can properly be regarded as such a degree of harassment as to call for the intervention of the court'. He accepted that a husband had molested his wife when the husband telephoned the school, where his wife was a teacher, to make unpleasant accusations against her. The husband had also placed posters making crude comments about his wife outside the school to draw the attention of parents who were collecting their children. In *C v C* [2001] EWCA Civ 1625, the court considered whether there had been a breach of a non-molestation order where the husband had made allegations to third parties including his children about his wife's sexual activities. Hale LJ agreed that this was a matter that required the intervention of the court [23]. *PF v CF* [2016] EWHC 3117 (Fam) demonstrates the importance of identifying the specific conduct complained of since the original order forbade the husband to threaten or use violence, yet the conduct complained of was intimidation, harassing and pestering. This was substituted in an amended order. In *F v M and others* [2023] EWFC 172 the husband (F) having made various and repeated unfounded allegations about M and her care of the children to social workers, professionals and the police was then made the subject of a non-molestation order containing terms of an exclusion zone. The court found that F had done this in part to try and gain litigational advantage, and that he had subjected M to coercive and controlling abusive and emotionally harmful behaviours [39]. In *Re T (A Child) (Non-Molestation Order)* [2017] EWCA Civ 1889 [42], Sir Andrew McFarlane reiterates the principles in *Horner* when granting the order. In *DS v AC* [2023] EWFC 46, Lieven J held there was no basis for the order iterating that not all unwanted conduct may amount to molestation.

In *Re Al M (Non-molestation Application)* [2020] EWHC 3305 (Fam), involving Princess Haya Bint Al Hussain and Sheik Mohammed bin Rashid Al-Maktoum, the court found, *inter alia*, that the father had acted in a manner aimed at intimidating and frightening the mother and that he had encouraged others to do so on his behalf and granted the order. (See also Chapter 12.)

Who may apply?

In accord with s 42(2)(a) all associated persons may apply, which s 62(3) (noted earlier) includes a wide range of familial relationships. One group of persons omitted from the list are persons who have had a non-cohabiting relationship with each other which cannot be described as intimate because there was no sexual aspect to it. If such persons experience molestation, they will be forced to seek alternative remedies under the PFHA 1997.

In *M v D* [2021] EWHC 1351 (Fam), an important point of principle was raised where the respondent was the appellant's 'stepnephew', namely the stepson of her sister. On 17 December 2020, the appellant applied, ex parte without notice, for a non-molestation order against the respondent, alleging that the respondent had been verbally abusive and threatening to the appellant, which included abusive telephone calls, social media posts and in person abuse. It was alleged that there had been threats of rape, murder and acid attacks. The district judge dismissed the appellant's application for a non-molestation order, holding that he was not satisfied, on the balance of probability, that the respondent and appellant were 'associated persons' for the purposes of FLA, s 62(d). The appeal court upheld the original judge's interpretation.

The court's discretion

Section 42(5) gives the court discretion to take into account all the circumstances of the case, including the need to safeguard the health, safety and wellbeing of the applicant or relevant child, in determining whether to exercise its powers and if so, how. It is a prospective directed provision, which is aimed at protecting the applicant from violence, rather than a retrospective centred one which punishes the perpetrator for having already molested the victim. Past conduct is a risk indicator of future violence. Non-molestation orders may be made for a fixed or an indefinite period depending on the nature of the requirements which will prevent harm to the applicant.

Enforcement

Those who have experienced molestation need to know that non-molestation orders will protect them from further similar behaviour or worse. Since the enactment of the Domestic Violence, Crime and Victims Act (DVCVA) 2004, there is no longer the possibility or need of a court to attach a power of arrest to an order. The DVCVA amended the FLA 1996, s 42A and made it a criminal offence to breach civil non-molestation orders, with a maximum penalty of five years' imprisonment. Section 360 of the Sentencing Code sets the penalty at six months custody or five years depending on culpability, harm and aggravating and mitigating factors.

Hale LJ in *Hale v Tanner* [2000] 1 WLR 2377 maintained that a custodial sentence should not be automatic. She accepted that when relationships break down, non-molestation orders might be thoughtlessly disregarded in the emotionally charged situation which exists at such times. She held that courts should consider all the circumstances before resorting to a custodial sentence. The court reduced the six-month prison sentence to 28 days. The respondent in this case, a woman, in breach of an injunction, had continued to make threatening telephone calls to her ex-boyfriend and his new girlfriend.

TABLE 5.2 Breach of non-molestation orders year ending December 2020 and December 2022 (latest figures)

Outcomes	Males	Females	Males	Females
Year	2020		2022	
Proceedings	2,346	133	1,173	76
Convictions	2,471	134	1,090	71
Sentenced	2,432	134	1,228	75
Custodial	413	7	298	9
Suspended	367	13	261	17
Community sentence	805	51	353	26
Fine	632	36	241	12

Source: From Table 17: Criminal justice outcomes for breach of a non-molestation order, England and Wales, year ending December 2020. Table 18: 2022 data for the same period www.ons.gov.uk/peoplepopulationandcommunity/crimeandjustice/datasets/domesticabuseandthecriminaljusticesystemappendixtables (accessed 30.04.2024)

Undertakings

Undertakings from the perpetrator party not to molest the applicant can also be given. They were once widely used, some 5,073 in 1999 (Judicial Statistics 1999).

Section 46(3A) FLA 1996 provides that:

> *the court shall not accept an undertaking under subsection (1) instead of making a non-molestation order in any case where it appears to the court that (a) that the respondent has used or threatened violence against the applicant or a relevant child, and (b) for the protection of the applicant or child it is necessary to make a non-molestation order so that any breach may be punishable under s 42A threshold.*

(See Speed 2022 for current position.)

Ex parte orders (without notice) occupation and non-molestation s 45(1)

Both non-molestation and occupation orders are limited and unless made ex parte, victim/survivor safety is compromised by waiting for a court hearing. The Association of Chief Police Officers (ACPO) in 'Tackling Perpetrators of Violence Against Women and Girls' noted: 'there is no readily available, consistent, affordable and timely access to the civil orders at this risky time.'

In securing immediate protection for the applicant, the court has the power to grant injunctions ex parte in the absence of the other party (without notice) where there is a 'real immediate danger of serious injury or irreparable damage'. The court has been extremely reluctant to grant ex-parte orders in the absence of the other party and especially so where occupation is concerned.

The Council of Circuit Judges said: 'it is a fundamental principle of natural justice that a court should not grant an order which involves a person's civil liberties and rights without giving them the opportunity to be heard' (see Home Affairs Committee Domestic Violence Inquiry p xxxvii). Such orders are challenged on human rights grounds and argued to be an abrogation of Article 6 'right to fair trial' (ECHR).

The Practice Guidance: Family Court – Duration of Ex Parte (Without Notice) Orders (18 January 2017) [5.114] sets out matters to be stated on the face of such orders and the Practice Guidance on non-molestation orders under the FLA 1996, July 2023 states:

> [5] When deciding whether it is 'just and convenient' to make an order without notice, It might, for example, be appropriate to make an order where the initial evidence suggests a pattern of coercive or controlling behaviour, and the court considers it is likely that the applicant could be further coerced or controlled into withdrawing the application; or where the court considers that the abuse (if proven) is likely [to have had such an impact on the applicant that they are likely to be deterred from proceeding if the respondent is given notice of an application.

In *Manjra v Shaikh* [2021] 1 FLR 106, a non-molestation order and an occupation order were made to regulate the continued co-occupation of the matrimonial home (specifically, forbidding the husband from entering the 'master' bedroom). In this case a 12-month maximum order was imposed. These orders were made exceptionally ex parte. In *DS v AC* [2023] EWFC 46, Lieven J reiterated the guiding principles.

Return hearings

Ex parte orders for both orders are to be listed for a return hearing within 14 days of the application (s 45(3)) so as to allow the other party to make representations and give his/her version. (See Practice Guidance duration of ex parte orders.) The target of 28 days may be all that can be achieved. An order made without notice must contain a statement of the right to make an application to set aside or vary the order under rule 18.11 in accordance with FPR 18.10(3). If the respondent does apply to set aside or vary the order the court must list the application as a matter of urgency, within a matter of days at most. In *R v R* [2014] EWFC 48; *R v R (Family Court: Procedural Fairness)* Practice Note [2015] 1 WLR 2743, an appeal against a non-molestation and occupation order, ex parte, was allowed due to procedural irregularities where an ex parte order was granted which also excluded the husband from the home. Jackson J set out the following principles relating to ex parte non-molestation applications. First, the default position of a judge in response to an ex parte application should always be 'why'. Second, the court should use its powers under FLA 1996 with caution. Third, extra injunctive powers such as exclusion area and prohibiting direct communication should not be routinely included in non-molestation orders. Fourth, the power to penalise for non-compliance with case management should be used fairly and apply FPR 4.6. Fifth, the court should guard against unfairness of the Legal Aid Sentencing and Punishment of Offenders Act 2012 whereby the applicant is entitled to legal aid, but the respondent is not.

Munby LJ (2020) in 'The Crisis in Private Law' has made a plea for research to be conducted on family law matters. Certainly, research needs to be conducted on the management of return hearings. A Freedom of Information Act (FOIA) 2000 request 220401011 (2022) made by Susan Edwards found that the Ministry of Justice (MoJ) does not collate information on return hearings.

Other forms of abuse and legal protections

Forced marriage

Forced marriage is a specific form of domestic abuse where one, or both, of the parties enter into marriage under duress. The force used may be emotional or physical, or both. The majority of these marriages involve young people, primarily females, under the age of 18, whose parents are immigrants from countries which support the practice. (See 'Right to Choose: The Consequences of Forced Marriage' YouTube.) Forced marriages may take place in England or in the country of origin of the victims' parents. Victims may be tricked into travelling abroad, on the pretext that a holiday, or a family gathering, has been arranged. It is very difficult for a young person to rebel against a forced marriage when he or she is in a strange place without financial resources or a passport (often confiscated by the parents on arrival in the country). (See also Patel et al. 2016.) Forced marriage can be dealt with under nullity provisions, the inherent jurisdiction or wardship, the Forced Marriage (Civil Protection) Act 2007 (FMPA) and criminal remedies.

The protection of those subject to forced marriage owes to the continual experience and lobbying of Anne-Marie Hutchinson, a solicitor and pioneer for change in the law on forced marriage and abduction and her groundbreaking work on forced marriage remedies and protection and international child abduction (see Anne-Marie Hutchinson: 'Forced Marriage and Violence Against Women in the Name of Honor' YouTube).

The first case was *Re KR (Abduction: Forcible Removal by Parents)* [1999] Fam Law 545.

In *Re SK (An Adult) (Forced Marriage: Appropriate Relief)* [2004] EWHC (Fam) 3202, a young adult woman resident in England was reported to be in Bangladesh. She was thought to be there against her will and at risk of a possible forced marriage. An application was made on her behalf, and without her knowledge, by her litigation friend.

[3] The request to take action on her behalf has come to Miss Anne-Marie Hutchinson of Dawson Cornwell, a solicitor with expertise in cases involving child abduction and forced marriage, from the Community Liaison Unit at the Foreign and Commonwealth Office to the High Court which held that it was within the court's inherent jurisdiction to make an order requiring members of the woman's family to arrange for her to be seen by an appropriate official at the High Commission in Dhaka to ascertain what her true wishes were.

Singer J also stated that other members of the woman's family in this country might be encouraged to give information about the woman's whereabouts as a result of the orders. The woman was interviewed and asked for the order to be withdrawn because by then she was not in need of the court's protection. The judgment ended with a strong condemnation of forced marriage. Singer J maintained:

> Although therefore in this particular case it seems that the anxieties giving rise to the proceedings may have been ill-founded, their utility has been to clarify to this family (if clarification may have been needed) the importance these courts place on the right of the individual to exercise choice in this most intimate area of decision-making. There can be no doubt that a very significant number of young persons find themselves coerced into marriage each year, or subject to that threat. The count was 105 during the past year through the Islamabad High Commission alone, of whom about 20% of those seeking assistance were male teenagers or young men. It seems reasonable to suppose that these known cases may constitute a representative sample only.

In a later case Munby J in *NS v MI* [2006] EWHC 1646 (Fam) stated firmly that there is a distinct difference between arranged marriages, where parents seek spouses for their children from their cultural community and allow their children a right of veto and forced marriages. He maintained that the arranged marriage which is a conventional concept in many immigrant cultures can be advantageous and should be respected and supported.

Any British person under the age of 18, who is at risk of a forced marriage, may be made a ward of court even if he or she is outside of the jurisdiction.

A further case came before the court in *Re B, RB v FB and MA* [2008] EWHC 1436 (Fam) in which a British father returned to Pakistan to live there. He died in Pakistan, and his wife who lived in Pakistan tried to force their 15-year-old daughter who also lived in Pakistan into marriage. The girl had a half-brother in Scotland whom she sought for help and also the British High Commission in Islamabad. At the British High Commission, in essence, she said:

> [3] 'I do not wish to be married to this man. I don't know him. He's too old. I've heard he's an alcoholic and I want to be taken out of this situation and I want to go and live with my brother in Scotland.' . . . [4] The High Commission was very responsive to this request. They knew she was a British national holding a British passport and informed the Forced Marriage Unit in London that they would be prepared to bring this young lady to this country to rescue her from the situation but required legal backing and court orders before they could do so.

Hogg J made her a ward of court and said: '[7] The difficulty as to jurisdiction is that she had no connection, other than her father's nationality, with this country. I had to ask myself whether the inherent jurisdiction and the old parens patriae principles could be extended to protect her.' The girl went to Scotland to join her half-brother who lived there. (Also discussed in Chapter 13.)

The dividing line between forced and arranged marriage can be a rather fine one. Young people who have been brought up to respect and obey their parents' wishes may find it difficult to object to an arranged marriage even where there are no threats although covert emotional pressure, sense of duty, respect and obligation may underlie some arranged marriages.

The Forced Marriage (Civil Protection) Act 2007

In response to the growing recognition of forced marriage and the campaigning of SBS as a member of the Home Office Working Group on Forced Marriage (1999) and Anne-Marie Hutchinson, Director of the Forced Marriage Commission, the statutory and practice multi-agency forced marriage guidelines was developed to accompany the Act. The Act provides legal remedies for victims, or prospective victims of forced marriage, and amends the FLA 1996 inserting a new Part 4A. The Act provides for applications for a Forced Marriage Protection Order (FMPO) by victims of forced marriages and those at risk of a forced marriage, and by third parties who are concerned that a forced marriage has been planned. An FMPO may be made against the respondent who is forcing someone to marry and against anyone who is associated with the coercion. The orders may contain a power of arrest (s 63H.4). Orders may relate to conduct, which is about to take place, or has already taken place, in the UK or abroad. They are open-ended and dependent on the circumstances. The courts may, *inter alia*, seize the respondent's passport (see *Re K forced marriage passport order* [2020] EWCA Civ 190), require the respondent to reveal the whereabouts of the victim, order the respondent not to contact the victim, allow the victim to assume a new identity, order that a marriage may not take place, order the respondent not to take the victim out of the country, and grant the victim a personal protection order (see *A v SM and HB (Forced Marriage Protection Orders)* [2012] EWHC 435 (Fam); *Re P (Forced Marriage)* [2010] EWHC 3467 (Fam)). In 2011, there were 1,468 instances where the FMU gave advice or support to those at risk of a possible forced marriage. Seventy-eight per cent of those helped were female and 22 per cent male (see *SB v RB* [2008] EWHC 938 (Fam)). Between 2011 and 2017 the FMU provided support in an average of 1,338 cases per year (see Forced Marriage Unit Statistics 2018 April 2020). In *Re A (a child) (inherent jurisdiction: parens patriae, FMPO and passport orders)* [2020] EWHC 451 (Fam), the court held that the evidence did not justify any relevant findings in respect of the mother's application for a forced marriage protection order (see for further discussion Proudman 2012; Welstead 2024).

Jurisdictional issues were considered in *P v Q* [2023] EWHC 195 (Fam). On appeal the judge was concerned that it raised an important point of public policy as set out. It was extraterritorial in its application and followed *Chief Constable and AA v YK and others* [2010] EWHC 2438 (Fam) where Sir Nicholas Wall P commented: '[17] Two aspects of the Act are immediately striking. The first is that it is very widely drawn. It is extra-territorial in its application and orders may be both made and discharged ex parte.' The appeal court in *P v Q* granted a FMPO to prevent Q from contacting P, holding that the judge did have jurisdiction to make a FMPO to protect P in circumstances where Q was a British citizen and was habitually resident here. Knowles J referred to the global reach of social media and the possibility it provided perpetrators to continue their abuse online wherever their victim lives. In *Sheffield City Council v M and Others* [2022] 2 FLR 812, the Bangladeshi parents living in England had daughters, A and B, aged 16 and 13. In November 2020, the father had purchased one-way tickets for himself and A and B to Bangladesh, the mother already being there, telling their school it would be for a short period to visit their paternal grandfather. A and B had previously missed at least three years of school in England due to an extended trip in Bangladesh. The local authority applied without notice for FMPOs in respect of A and B. Those orders were granted, and the parents were given notice. The orders were later extended multiple times at subsequent hearings. In making its application for a final FMPO, the local authority had relied on evidence which had been provided to the court but not disclosed to the parents ('the closed material'). SBS have been instrumental in the case of *Re K (Forced Marriage: Passport Orders)* (2020) earlier, where a forced marriage protection order which retained the applicant's passport was in place five years later which the Court of Appeal conceded breached her human rights. (See Southall Black Sisters You Tube.)

Breach of a forced marriage protection order is also a criminal offence with a maximum sentence of five years' imprisonment. Subsection (2) inserts a reference to Part 3 of the DAA into s 63(2) of the FLA 1996, which amends the definition of 'family proceedings' for the purposes of Part 4 of the FLA 1996. This amendment enables a judge (sitting in the family court of the Family Division of the High Court) hearing an application to make or vary a Domestic Abuse Protection Order (DAPO) to make a forced marriage protection order.

TABLE 5.3 Forced marriage protection order applications

Year	Applications under 17 years of age	Applications over 17 years of age
2010	57	55
2011	65	50
2012	51	38
2013	112	57
2014	115	53
2015	165	76
2016	176	97
2017	189	84
2018	233	83
2019	262	89
2020	160	89
2021	141	61
2022	199	69

Source: Table 16: Applications and disposals of Forced Marriage Protection Orders made in the High Court and county courts, England and Wales, annually 2009–2022. www.ons.gov.uk/peoplepopulationandcommunity/crimeandjustice/datasets/domesticabuseandthecriminaljusticesystemappendixtables. See also Forced Marriage Unit statistics. https://view.officeapps.live.com/op/view.aspx?src=https%3A%2F%2Fassets.publishing.service.gov.uk%2Fmedia%2F62d96400d3bf7f285e787797%2Fforced-marriage-unit-statistics-2021-figures-and-tables.ods&wdOrigin=BROWSELINK. (accessed 30.04.2024)

Dowry abuse

Dowry abuse has been recognised as one of the forms of economic and financial abuse in DAA, s 1 2021 (see *R S (AP) v The Secretary of State for the Home Department* [2011] CSOH 6). Hanisha Patel and Jasvinder Sanghera (2009) draw attention to dowry abuse where a woman is deemed not to have brought sufficient dowry, such as money or goods, into the relationship, and her husband's family may use physical abuse in an attempt to extract what it deems to be appropriate from her family (see CPS *Policy on Prosecuting Cases of Domestic Violence*).

'Stranding' or 'Transnational Marriage Abandonment' is recognised in Practice Direction 12J which states:

> *[3]. For the purposes of this Practice Direction – Domestic abuse also includes culturally specific forms of abuse including, but not limited to, forced marriage, honour-based violence, dowry-related abuse and transnational marriage abandonment. 'Abandonment' refers to the practice whereby a husband, in England and Wales, deliberately abandons or 'strands' his foreign national wife abroad, usually without financial resources, in order to prevent her from asserting matrimonial and/or residence rights in England and Wales.*

(See *Re A (Children: Fact-Finding: Appeal)* [2019] EWCA Civ 74; *Re S (a boy, born on [a date]) M v F and others* [2022] EWHC 214 (Fam).)

Female genital mutilation protection orders

FGM came to UK attention in *Fornah v Secretary of State for the Home Department*, House of Lords [2006] UKHL 46, [2006] 3 FCR 381, [2007] 1 All ER 671 when Zainab Esther Fornah, 15 years old as an unaccompanied minor, arrived at Gatwick airport claiming asylum. She had fled Sierra Leone where she had been captured by rebels, who had killed her family and repeatedly raped her. She did not want to return to her uncle's village fearing that she would be forcibly genitally mutilated, as was customary practice. Whilst her father was alive, he was able to protect her from this practice. In 2003, the Female Genital Mutilation Act (FGMA) was passed. (See Cook 2016.) The Act created several offences of aiding, abetting, counselling, procuring and helping in the act of FGM. Sections 70 and 71 of the Serious Crime Act 2015 (SCA) provide anonymity for complainants who are victims of FGM, and s 72 creates the offences of 'failing to protect a girl from risk of genital mutilation'. (See Female Genital Mutilation Legal Guidance.)

There are an estimated 137,000 women and girls living with FGM in England and Wales. In *Re E (children) (female genital mutilation protection orders)* [2015] EWHC 2275 (Fam), an order under the FGMP Act 2003 (the order) to protect the mother's three daughters from the father who on the evidence had intentions to have his three daughters subjected to the same procedure was made. (See also Gerry 2020.)

TABLE 5.4 Female genital mutilation applications

Year	Applications under 17	Applications over 17
2016	71	3
2017	99	1
2018	92	5
2019	105	1
2020	51	2
2021	34	1

Source: Table 17: Applications and disposals of Female Genital Mutilation Protection Orders, England and Wales, annually 2016–2022 HMCTS One Performance Truth (OPT) system. www.ons.gov.uk/people populationandcommunity/crimeandjustice/datasets/domesticabuseandthecriminaljusticesystemappendix tables (accessed 30.04.2024)

Domestic violence/abuse protection orders and domestic violence/abuse protection notices

In response to the limitations and delay in granting non-molestation and occupation order applications and securing immediate protection for victims of domestic abuse, the domestic violence protection notice (DVPN) and domestic violence protection order (DVPO) was introduced by ss 24 to 33 of the Crime and Security Act 2010 (CSA). Where there is insufficient evidence to charge an alleged perpetrator, the perpetrator can be removed from the home for a short period and prohibited from molesting the applicant. For the year ending March 2020, 4,468 DVPNs were issued and 6,267 DVPOs granted. Year ending March 2021, 10,046 DVPNs were issued and 7,995 DVPOs granted. Year ending March 2023, 11,886 DVPNs issued and 11,418 DVPOs applied for (see Government publications). The DAA 2021 ss 22–49 repeals the DVPN and DVPO by introducing the domestic abuse protection notice (DAPN) and the domestic abuse protection order (DAPO). A DAPN can now be 'given' (this word replaces 'issued') by a senior police officer (s 22(1)) of at least the rank of inspector). Unlike the earlier DVPOs, section 36(1) DAA establishes new criteria for the court when making a DAPO:

> *(1) Requirements imposed on a person by a domestic abuse protection order – must, as far as practicable, be such as to avoid – (a) conflict with the person's religious beliefs; (b) interference with the person's work or with the person's attendance at an educational establishment; (c) conflict with the requirements of any other court order or injunction to which the person may be subject.*
>
> (See Draft Statutory Guidance.)

More protection needed: closing remarks

In concluding this review of domestic abuse remedies, the remaining questions are how effective have they been? and what else needs to be done? Some fearless advocates and creative judges have developed more robust responses to domestic abuse in both adult and child safeguarding. Domestic abuse impacts in all areas of law. As later chapters with regard to children will demonstrate, across family law there is an unevenness in judicial attitudes and responses where domestic abuse is a component.

This final section explores the human rights protections, the public authority liability, the shortcomings of the refugee convention and/or advocacy and the courts to extend its protection to victims of domestic abuse, and the lesser protection afforded to migrant women experiencing domestic abuse in the UK.

The challenges are also evident where domestic abuse is an element in asylum, immigration and public law. However, across all areas of law human rights considerations remain overarching. Notwithstanding Brexit, the international human rights legislative framework remains an important superintendent.

The ECHR and the Istanbul Convention are of particular relevance. ECHR Articles 2, 3, 6, 8, 12 and 14 are of special relevance in the context of domestic abuse protection. The ECHR protects the right not to be subjected to domestic violence/abuse under Article 2, 'the right to life'; Article 3, 'the right not to be subjected to torture, inhuman or degrading treatment'; Article 5, 'the right to liberty'; Article 8, 'the right to respect for private and family life'; and Article 14, 'the right to enjoy Convention rights without discrimination'. (See *Hadjuova v Slovakia* [2003] App No 2660/03, *A v Croatia* [2010] (application no. 55164/08).)

The leading case law is found in *Opuz v Turkey* [2009] Application no. 33401/02, where a domestic violence perpetrator went on to kill his wife's mother. The European Court of Human Rights (ECtHR) held that Article 2 'right to life', Article 3 'degrading and inhumane treatment, and Article 6 'right to a fair trial' were engaged and that this was an act of 'gender-based violence' because of the State's failure to protect.

> [9] On 10 April 1995 the applicant and her mother filed a complaint with the Diyarbakır Public Prosecutor's Office, alleging that H.O and A.O had been asking them for money, and had beaten them and threatened to kill them. They also alleged that H.O and his father wanted to bring other men home. . . . H.O threatened to kill the applicants Mother 'Wherever you go, I will find and kill you!'

There had been a history of the applicant filing indictments with the police authorities. H.O subsequently carried out his threat and killed the applicant's mother. The applicant had withdrawn her previous complaints against her husband.

The ruling recognises the failure of public authorities to prosecute domestic violence perpetrators and protect victims of domestic violence. The ambit of this positive obligation on public authorities in the UK was tested in a civil action brought by the daughter of Lorraine Whiting who was killed by her partner, against the Chief Constable of Kent but no findings were made against the force (see Bawdon 2001).

The obligation of public authorities to protect was also tested in *Michael and others v Chief Constable of South Wales Police and another (Refuge and others intervening)* [2015] AC 1732 where police were called but the victim was stabbed to death before police arrived. (See also *MLIA and another v Chief Constable of Hampshire Police* [2017] EWHC 292 (QB)) (no finding in support of claimants.) See also Domestic Homicide Reviews, and the Centre for Women's Justice Report on the murder of Emma Day by her partner.

Regina (Skelton and another) v West Sussex Senior Coroner [2021] 2 WLR 413 concerned an inquest into the death of the claimants' daughter Susan Nicholson who was murdered on 17 April 2011 by her then partner, the second interested party, Robert Trigg. The inquest recorded a verdict of accidental death. Six years later Trigg was convicted of her murder. The original inquest verdict was quashed, and a new inquest was ordered under Coroners Act 1988, s 13. The coroner indicated that she intended to list a short hearing in order accurately to record the cause of death as unlawful killing. That was opposed by the claimants, who sought a wider inquest into the circumstances of their daughter's death under s 5(2) and s 10(1)(a) of the Coroners and Justice Act 2009 and, in particular, an investigation into whether the circumstances involved breaches by the police of their substantive obligations under Article 2 of the Convention for the Protection of Human Rights and Fundamental Freedoms to take positive preventative measures to protect life. The coroner ruled that there had been no arguable breach of any Article 2 duty by the police and that, accordingly, she was not under a procedural obligation to carry out an Article 2 compliant inquest. The coroner also rejected a submission by Trigg that he should be permitted to adduce evidence at the inquest which had not been considered at his criminal trial, with a view to showing that the claimants' daughter had not been unlawfully killed. The claimants sought judicial review of the coroner's decision.

The Istanbul Convention is a Council of Europe Convention on preventing and combating violence against women and domestic violence. The UK Government signed this Convention in 2012 but has yet to ratify it in legislation despite the Preventing and Combating Violence against Women and Domestic Violence (Ratification of Convention) Act 2017. It is of particular relevance to domestic abuse and violence and whilst the Istanbul Convention has been part of legal argument in cases involving immigration status it has not been used in legal argument in criminal or family cases. Article 1 sets out the purpose of the Convention as follows:

> *[t]o protect women against all forms of violence, and prevent, prosecute and eliminate violence against women and domestic violence; design a comprehensive framework, policies and measures for the protection of and assistance to all victims of violence against women and domestic violence; provide support and assistance to organisations and law enforcement agencies to effectively co- operate in order to adopt an integrated approach to eliminating violence against women and domestic violence.*

Article 2 of the Convention asserts that it applies to all forms of violence against women, including domestic violence, which affects women disproportionately, but that the states parties are encouraged to apply it to all victims of domestic violence.

The courts in England and Wales already have extraterritorial jurisdiction for some of the offences covered by the Convention (for example, female genital mutilation (by virtue of s 4 of the FGMA 2003) and forced marriage (by virtue of s 121 of the Anti-social Behaviour, Crime and Policing Act 2014)). The DAA extends this jurisdiction. (See further ss 72–74 and Schedule 3 DAA.)

It is incumbent on all those involved in the protection of victims of domestic abuse to use the power of these conventions in litigation and in the delivery of services and to hold individuals, public authorities, police, prosecutors, and the courts and the UK Government and its laws to account. (See *A v Secretary of State for the Home Department* [2016] CSHI 38; *R (on the application of FA(Sudan) v Secretary of State for the Home Department* [2021] EWCA Civ 59; *R on the application of SWP) v Secretary of State for the Home Department* [2022] EWHC 2067). (See also Grans 2018; Richardson and Speed 2019.)

The interpretation of other conventions fails to adequately protect victims of abuse and violence. Those who fear persecution in their home countries for reasons, *inter alia*, of membership of a particular social group are permitted to seek asylum in the UK. Women suffering from domestic violence abroad have had serious difficulties in bringing this form of persecution within the Convention grounds for seeking asylum in the UK. In *Burris v Azadani* [1996] 1 WLR 1372, two Pakistani women who had been forced to leave their homes by their husbands and risked being falsely accused of adultery in Pakistan, sought asylum. They maintained that the State would not protect them and that they would face the risk of criminal proceedings for sexual immorality if they were forced to return to Pakistan. They claimed that they were refugees since they had a well-founded fear of persecution for reasons of 'membership of a particular social group' within the meaning of the Refugee Convention 1951, Article 1A (2). The House of Lords granted their appeal and allowed them asylum. It held that on its true construction, Article 1A (2) applied to whatever groups might be regarded as coming within the Convention's anti-discriminatory objectives, namely those groups whose members shared a common unchangeable characteristic and were discriminated against in matters of fundamental human rights. Women could claim to be members of such a group if they lived in a society, such as Pakistan, which discriminated against them on the grounds of sex, and it was irrelevant that certain women might be able to avoid the impact of persecution. Furthermore, the persecution they feared was caused by their membership of a social group since the Pakistani State denied them protection from violence which it would have given to men. (See also *Islam Appellant and Secretary of State for The Home Department Respondent Regina v Immigration Appeal Tribunal and Another, Ex Parte Shah [Consolidated Appeals] [On Appeal from Reg v Immigration Appeal Tribunal and Another, Ex Parte Shah]* [1999] 2 AC 629; see also 'Domestic Abuse: Responding to Reports of Domestic Abuse from Asylum Seekers'.)

The domestic violence provisions and access to them continue to defy the equality norms and migrant women have no recourse to public funds, and so women asylum seekers in the UK, students on international visas etc are particularly vulnerable. Despite the Government's objective of providing protection for all under the DAA, migrant women were left out of the Act (see Patel and Walker 2023). Under s 115 of the Immigration and Asylum Act 1999 access to assistance and public funds was denied to those subject to immigration control, which precluded any person including women's victims of domestic abuse from claiming benefits and housing assistance unless there were exceptional circumstances. Two circumstances fall under exceptional circumstances including where there are compelling reasons related to the welfare of the child and on account of low income and destitution – 'the destitute domestic violence concession'. Perpetrators often use children of the family and a woman's immigration status as a way of controlling her.

The Government has continued to declare its commitment to preventing domestic abuse against women and girls. Importantly, intermediaries and IDVAs and ISVAs can assist women in court who seek protection from male abuse and violence. New provisions are introduced in the Victims and Prisoners Act 2024.

And robust counsel are already ensuring that victims have access to the support of IDVA's (see *M v S* [2024] EWFC 80 (B)).

Significantly, the Government's response to the Domestic Abuse Commissioner's Report: 'A Patchwork of Provision: how to meet the needs of victims and survivors across England and Wales' (2023) highlights the need to collaborate when commissioning support services for victims of domestic abuse, and Recommendation 7 calls for funding for behaviour-change interventions for perpetrators of domestic abuse to be scaled up.

This chapter ends with a salutary lesson from Lord Patten in the House of Lords debate on 'UK: Violence Against Women and Girls' June 2023:

Domestic violence has a number of manifestations – including the vanishingly small number of attacks by women on men in the home and the much greater number of lethal attacks on children by women and men who are in partnership in the home – but, of all these, the worst manifestation is that which this debate concentrates on: violence against girls and women. Getting the message across starts early – it has to start early – but one also has to remember, as Mary Tuck, the Home Office civil servant, again taught me, that just when you think you have taught one generation, there is another generation waiting in the wings, coming along as teenagers who will grow up, to be dealt with next.

Self-test questions

1. To what extent will the new domestic abuse prevention notices (DAPN) and domestic abuse prevention orders (DAPO) prevent further domestic abuse and protect victims of abuse and violence, and what advantages do they have over the former orders?

2. How important is the understanding of coercive control to protecting victims of domestic abuse, and what problems of proof arise for police and the courts?

3. Tony (he, him) and Brigitte (she, her) are married. They live in a two-bedroom flat, title to which is registered in the name of Brigitte. They have a son, Chaz, aged 2. Brigitte is pregnant and expects to give birth in three months' time. Tony is an alcoholic and also has a drug abuse problem; whilst reasonable when he is not drunk or taking drugs, he resorts to extreme forms of abusive and sometimes physically violent behaviour when drunk and abusing drugs. Earlier this year, Tony returned home drunk with a new friends Fili (she, her) and her two young sons, aged 4 and 6. He told Brigitte that he had rescued Fili from her violent female partner, Thomsin (she, her), and that from now on Fili and her two sons would be living in the flat that Brigette and Tony shared and would be living in the spare bedroom. Fili had been living previously with Thomsin in a house registered in Thomsin's sole name. When Brigitte understandably protested about the moving in of Fili and her two sons, Tony screamed at her and waved an antique sword in her face and told her to get out

of the flat. Brigitte was afraid and left the flat. She took her son, Chaz, with her, and they spent two weeks in a friend's house whilst the friend was out of the country on holiday. On the friend's return, Brigitte had nowhere to live. She wanted to return home but only if Tony, Fili and Fili's two children moved out. Fili was prepared to leave on condition that Thomsin (her former partner) would allow her and her two sons to live in Thomsin's house. However, as Fili is afraid of Thomsin she wants her brother Mike to move in to protect her. Meanwhile, Brigitte, who is about to give birth, and Chaz have nowhere permanent to stay. Advise Brigitte and Fili.

4. In 1999, John (he, him) and Krystyna (she, her) married. John moved into Krystyna's house which was registered in her sole name. In 2003, their twins were born, and John was unable to cope with the change in lifestyle. He was an artist and needed space and time to paint. He became increasingly irritated with the chaos in the house and moved out into a studio owned by Marcia (she, her) who was married to John's good friend, Lennie. After living in the studio for several weeks, John decided that he would like to have a long-term relationship with Lennie (he, him). Marcia understandably evicted John from the studio and also told Lennie to leave the family home, which was also registered in her sole name. However, John had always looked after the twins of the marriage (between himself and Krystyna) and refused to leave the children with Krystyna. John returned to the marital home with Lennie, and on their arrival, Krystyna threw a bottle of wine at Lennie's head. Lennie was treated at the local hospital. John now does not believe that Krystyna is fit to care for the twins. He wants to return to the house and live there with Lennie and his children. Lennie has volunteered to take care of all four children.
    Advise John.

References

Association of Chief Police Officers (ACPO) Tackling Perpetrators of Violence Against Women and Girls – ACPO Review for the Home Secretary (ACPO 2009) 48 [6.1.3] https://www.npcc.police.uk/documents/crime/2009/200909C RIVA W01.pdf (accessed 30.04.2024)

Bawdon, Fiona, 'I'm Going: I've Got No Blood Left in Me' www.theguardian.com/world/2001/apr/10/law.theguardian (accessed 30.04.2024)

Bishop, Charlotte and Vanessa Bettinson, 'Evidencing Domestic Violence, Including Behaviour That Falls Under the New Offence of "Controlling or Coercive Behaviour"' [2018] *The International Journal of Evidence & Proof* 3

Blackstone, Sir William, Commentaries on the Laws of *England* (Oxford University Press 1765)

Blake, Matilda M, 'The Lady and the Law' [1892] *Westminster Review* 364

Centre for Women's Justice Report on Emma Day www.centreforwomensjustice.org.uk/news/2021/4/23/murder-of-emma-day-by-her-former-partner-inquest-concludes-as-coroner-notes-systemic-failures (accessed 30.04.2024)

Cobbe, Frances Power, 'Wife-Torture in England' (1869) in Sheila Jeffreys (ed) *The Sexuality Debates* (Routledge 1987)

Cook, Kate, 'Female Genital Mutilation in the UK Population: A Serious Crime' (2016) 80 *Journal of Criminal Law* 88

Crenshaw, Kimberley, 'Mapping the Margins: Intersectionality, Identity Politics, and Violence Against Women of Color' [1991] *Stanford Law Review* 1241

Crown Prosecution Service, 'Policy on Prosecuting Cases of Domestic Violence' www.cps.gov.uk/publications/prosecution/domviolencepol.html. (accessed 30.04.2024)

Crown Prosecution Service, 'Restraining Orders – Section 5, Protection from Harassment Act 1997' https://www.cps.gov.uk/legal-guidance/restraining-orders-section-5-protection-harassment-act-1997 (accessed 30.04.2024)

Crown Prosecution Service, 'Study CPS and Equally Ours: Research into the Public Understanding of Rape and Serious Sexual Offences (RASSO) and Consent' www.cps.gov.uk/publication/cps-and-equally-ours-research-public-understanding-rape-and-serious-sexual-offences (accessed 30.04.2024)

DASH https://safelives.org.uk/sites/default/files/resources/Dash%20risk%20checklist%20quick%20start%20guidance%20FINAL.pdf (accessed 30.04.2024)

Deutsch, Helene, *Psychology of Women* (Grune and Strutton 1958)

Diagnostic and Statistical Manual www.academia.edu/11886511/DSM_IV_TR_Diagnostic_and_statistical_manual_of_mental_disorders (accessed 30.04.2024)

Dobash, Rebecca and Russell Dobash, *Violence Against Wives* (Open Books 1980)

Doddridge, *Lawe's Resolutions of Women's Rights* (1632)

Domestic Abuse Commissioner's Report, 'The Family Court and Domestic Abuse: Achieving Cultural Change, Government Response' (November 2023) www.gov.uk/government/publications/government-response-domestic-abuse-and-the-family-court-achieving-cultural-change (accessed 30.04.2024)

Domestic Abuse and the Criminal Justice System www.ons.gov.uk/peoplepopulationand community/crimeandjustice/datasets/domesticabuseandthecriminaljusticesystemappendix tables November 2022 edition of this dataset (accessed 30.04.2024)

Domestic Abuse and the Criminal Justice System www.ons.gov.uk/peoplepopulationand community/crimeandjustice/datasets/domesticabuseandthecriminaljusticesystem appendixtables November 2023 edition of this dataset (accessed 30.04.2024)

Domestic Abuse in England and Wales Overview www.ons.gov.uk/peoplepopulation andcommunity/crimeandjustice/bulletins/domesticabuseinenglandandwalesoverview/november2023 November 2023 (accessed 30.04.2024)

Domestic Abuse and the Family Court: Achieving Cultural Change www.gov.uk/government/publications/the-family-court-and-domestic-abuse-achieving-cultural-change (accessed 30.04.2024)

Domestic Abuse Prevalence and Trends, England and Wales www.ons.gov.uk/peoplepopulation andcommunity/crimeandjustice/articles/domesticabuseprevalenceandtrendsengland andwales/yearendingmarch2022 (accessed 30.04.2024)

Domestic Abuse Protection Notice www.gov.uk/government/consultations/statutory-guidance-on-domestic-abuse-protection-notices-and-protection-orders (accessed 30.04.2024)

Domestic Abuse Protection Notices and Domestic Abuse Protection Orders Draft Statutory Guidance for the Police https://assets.publishing.service.gov.uk/media/65cdf3ca130549000 c867a7d/Domestic+Abuse+Protection+Notices+and+Orders+Police+Statutory+Guida nce.pdf (accessed 24.05.2024)

Domestic Abuse: Responding to Reports of Domestic Abuse from Asylum Seekers https://assets.publishing.service.gov.uk/government/uploads/system/uploads/attachment_data/file/104975/Asylum_support_domestic_abuse.pdf (30.04.2024)

Domestic Abuse Victim Characteristics, England and Wales: Year Ending (March 2023) www.ons.gov.uk/peoplepopulationandcommunity/crimeandjustice/articles/domesticabuse victimcharacteristicsenglandandwales/yearendingmarch2023 (accessed 30.04.2024)

Domestic Homicide Reviews https://homicide-review.homeoffice.gov.uk/ (accessed 30.04.2024)

Domestic Violence Bill 1976 vol 905, col 862 https://api.parliament.uk/historic-hansard/commons/1976/feb/13/domestic-violence-bill (accessed 30.04.2024)

Domestic Violence Protection Notices www.gov.uk/government/publications/domestic-violence-protection-orders/domestic-violence-protection-notices-dvpns-and-domestic-violence-protection-orders-dvpos-guidance-sections-24-33-crime-and-security-act-2010 (accessed 30.04.2024)

Duffield, Rosie, 'MPs Moved to Tears by Rosie Duffield's Domestic Abuse Story' YouTube www.youtube.com/watch?v=XWvYVHiXqSg&t=25s (accessed 30.04.2024)

Edwards, Susan, '"Kicked, Beaten, Jumped on Until They Are Crushed" All Under Man's Wing and Protection' The Victorian Dilemma with Domestic Violence' (2005) in Judith Rowbotham and Kim Stevenson (eds) *Criminal Conversations: Victorian Crimes, Social Panic, and Moral Outrage* (Ohio State University Press 2005) 247

Edwards, Susan, *Policing Domestic Violence: Women, Law and the State* (Sage 1989)

Edwards, Susan, *Sex and Gender in the Legal Process* (Oxford University Press 1986)

Female Genital Mutilation Legal Guidance www.cps.gov.uk/legal-guidance/female-genital-mutilation (accessed 30.04.2024)

Gavigan, Shelley AM, 'Petit Treason in Eighteenth Century England: Women's Inequality Before the Law' (1989) *Canadian Journal of Women and the Law* 335

Gayford, JJ, 'Wife Beating: A Preliminary Survey of 100 Cases' [1975] *British Medical Journal* 194

Gelles, Richard, *Family Violence* (Sage 1979)

Gerry, Felicity, 'Why It Is Time for an FGM Commissioner – Practical Responses to Feminised Issues' [2020] *Family Law* 1317

Government's Response to the Domestic Abuse Commissioner's Report, 'A Patchwork of Provision' https://domesticabusecommissioner.uk/national-mapping-of-domestic-abuse-services/; https://assets.publishing.service.gov.uk/media/640207b38fa8f527f6680283/FINAL_Annex_A_-_DAC_Mapping_Report_Government_Response__clean_.pdf (accessed 30.04.2024)

Grans, Lisa, 'The Istanbul Convention and the Positive Obligation to Prevent Violence' [2018] *Human Rights Law Review* 133

Guardianship of Infants Bill https://api.parliament.uk/historichansard/lords/1924/jul/09/guardianship-of-infants-bill-hl#S5LV0058P0_19240709_HOL_53) (col 359) (accessed 30.04.2024)

Hale, Sir Matthew, *The History of the Pleas of the Crown* (Savoy 1736)

Hansard Debate Hansard question Assaults Upon Women – Question Volume 146: Debated on Monday 22.06.1857 Brutal Assaults – Legislation Volume 223: Debated on Thursday 29.04.1875 col 1825; HC Deb 29.07.1875 vol 226 cc172–173) https://hansard.parliament.uk/Commons/1856-02-04/debates/6035145a-921c-4e34-8d13-ec181d04e58f/AssaultsOnWomenAndChildren (accessed 01.05.2024)

Hoeger, Katharine and Lis Bates, 'Executive Summary, Findings and Recommendations: Domestic Homicides and Suspected Victim Suicides Year 3 Report (2020–2023)' www.vkpp.org.uk/assets/Files/Domestic-Homicides-and-Suspected-Victim-Suicides-2021-2022/Executive-Summary-Y3-Report.pdf (accessed 30.04.2024)

Home Affairs Committee Domestic Violence Inquiry https://committees.parliament.uk/committee/83/home-affairs-committee/news/100554/domestic-violence-and-abuse-inquiry/ (accessed 30.04.2024)

Home Office Statutory Guidance on Coercive and Controlling Behaviour www.gov.uk/government/publications/controlling-or-coercive-behaviour-statutory-guidance-framework/controlling-or-coercive-behaviour-statutory-guidance-framework-accessible (accessed 30.04.2024)

Home Office Violence Against Women and Girls www.homeoffice.gov.uk/crime/violence-against-women-girls/domestic-violence/ (accessed 30.04.2024)

Home Office Working Group on Forced Marriage (1999) https://edm.parliament.uk/early-day-motion/17745/a-choice-by-right-the-report-by-the-working-group-on-forced-marriages (accessed 30. 04.2024)

Homicide in England and Wales – Office for National Statistics (ons.gov.uk) www.ons.gov.uk/peoplepopulationandcommunity/crimeandjustice/articles/homicideinenglandandwales/march2022#the-relationship-between-victims-and-suspects (accessed 30.04.2024)

Horley, Sandra, *Power and Control* (Vermilion 2017)

House of Lords Debate, 'UK: Violence Against Women and Girls' (June 2023) https://hansard. parliament.uk/Lords/2023-06-29/debates/7487DBB6-577B-4BDD-8ACF-1D5ED362B7DA/UKViolenceAgainstWomenAndGirls vol 831 col 822 (accessed 30.04.2024)

Hutchinson, Anne-Marie, 'Forced Marriage and Violence Against Women in the Name of Honor' YouTube www.youtube.com/watch?v=PczVa0XUvLg (accessed 30.04.2024)

Jackson, Stevi and Pete Rushton, 'Victims and Villains: Images of Women in Accounts of Family Violence' [1982] *Women's Studies International Forum* 37

Judicial Statistics (1999) https://discovery.nationalarchives.gov.uk/details/r/C11518760 (accessed 30.04.2024)

Keynejad, Roxanne C, Sharli Paphitis, Sarah Davidge, Suzanne Jacob and Louise M Howard, 'Domestic Abuse Is Important Risk Factor for Suicide' (December 2022) *British Medical Journal Editorial* 1

Leibovitz, Annie, 'Rihanna in Cuba: The Cover Story' *Vanity Fair* (November 2015)

McGlynn, Clare, 'Criminalising Cyberflashing: Options for Law Reform' [2021] *Journal of Criminal Law* 171

Mill, John Stuart, On Liberty (Hackett Publishing 1867, 1978)

Ministry of Justice, 'Domestic Abuse and the Family Court: Achieving Cultural Change' www.gov.uk/government/publications/the-family-court-and-domestic-abuse-achieving-cultural-change (accessed 30.04.2024)

Munby, Sir James, 'The Crisis in Private Law' (2020) *Family Law* 448 https://transparencyproject.org.uk/the-crisis-in-private-law-by-sir-james-munby/ (accessed 12.05.2024)

Patel, Hanisha and Jasvinder Sanghera, 'Dowry Abuse' (2009) *Family Law* 1092

Patel, Pragna, 'Southall Black Sisters Two Struggles: Challenging Male Violence and the Police' in Christina Dunhill (ed) *The Boys in Blue* (Virago 1989)

Patel, Pragna, Sundari Anitha, Sulema Jahangir and Radhika Handa, 'Emerging Issues for International Family Law: Part 3: Transnational Marriage Abandonment and the Dowry Question' (2016) *The Family in Law* 1443

Patel, Pragna and Janaya Walker, 'The Domestic Abuse Act 2021 and Migrant Women' in Susan Edwards, David Malone and KC Jones Gillian (eds) *Blackstone's Guide to the Domestic Abuse Act 2021* (Oxford University Press 2023) 225–238

Pence, Ellen, 'Battered Women's Movement Leader' YouTube www.youtube.com/watch?v=r9dZOgr78eE (accessed 30.04.2024)

Pizzey, Erin and Jeff Shapiro, *Prone to Violence* (Hamlyn 1982)

Police Perpetrated Domestic Abuse Report on the Centre for Women's Justice Super Complaint www.gov.uk/government/publications/police-super-complaints-force-response-to-police-perpetrated-domestic-abuse/police-perpetrated-domestic-abuse-report-on-the-centre-for-womens-justice-super-complaint (accessed 14.05.2024)

Potter, Sir Mark, 'Practice Directions: Residence and Contact Orders: Domestic Violence and Harm' https://www.judiciary.uk/wp-content/uploads/JCO/Documents/FJC/Publications/Revised_PD_Domestic_Violence140109.pdf (accessed 24.10.2024)

Practice Guidance Family Court: Duration of Ex Parte (Without Notice) Orders (18 January 2017) https://www.judiciary.uk/wp-content/uploads/2017/01/pfd-practice-guidance-ex-parte-orders.pdf (accessed 30.04.2024)

Practice Direction New Practice Direction 36zg – Part 3 of the Domestic Abuse Act 2021: Provision During Piloted Commencement www.justice.gov.uk/documents/7815.pdf (accessed 20.05.2024)

Practice Direction: PD 12J Child Arrangements & Contact Orders: Domestic Abuse and Harm www.justice.gov.uk/courts/procedure-rules/family/practice_directions/pd_part_12j (accessed 30.04.2024)

Practice Guidance Non-Molestation Injunctions www.judiciary.uk/wp-content/uploads/2023/07/Practice-Guidance-Non-Molestation-Injunctions.pdf (accessed 30.04.2024)

Proudman, Charlotte, 'The Criminalisation of Forced Marriage' (2012) *Family Law* 460

Refuge Research – Online and Digital Abuse www.womensaid.org.uk/information-support/what-is-domestic-abuse/online-safety/ (accessed 30.04.2024)

Report to the Secretary of State for the Home Department, on the State of Law Relating to Brutal Assaults (1874) Parliamentary Papers, 1875, 61 (Cmd. 1138): 9. 48 48 (accessed 30.04.2024)

Report from the Select Committee on Violence in Marriage, Together with the Proceedings of the Committee (1974/5 H.C. 553) (accessed 30.04.2024)

Richardson, Kayliegh and Ana Speed, 'Two Worlds Apart: A Comparative Analysis of the Effectiveness of Domestic Abuse Law and Policy in England and Wales and the Russian Federation' [2019] *Journal of Criminal Law* 320

Right to Choose: The Consequences of Forced Marriage' YouTube www.youtube.com/watch?v=pSPxOa9tCOI (accessed 30.04.2024)

Southall Black Sisters, YouTube www.youtube.com/watch?v=irnjMln_m20 (accessed 30.04.2024)

Speed, Ana, '"Should I Stay, or Should I Go Now? If I Go There Will Be Trouble and if I Stay It Will Be Double": An Examination into the Present and Future of Protective Orders Regulating the Family Home in England and Wales' (2022) *Journal of Criminal Law* 179

Statutory Guidance on Domestic Abuse and Controlling and Coercive Behaviour www.homeoffice.gov.uk/crime/violence-against-women-girls/domestic-violence/ (accessed 30.04.2024); www.gov.uk/government/publications/controlling-or-coercive-behaviour-statutory-guidance-framework/controlling-or-coercive-behaviour-statutory-guidance-framework-accessible (accessed 30.04.2024)

Statutory Guidance www.gov.uk/guidance/forced-marriage (accessed 30.04.2024)

Statutory Guidance on Domestic Abuse Protection Notices and Orders www.gov.uk/government/consultations/statutory-guidance-on-domestic-abuse-protection-notices-and-protection-orders) (accessed 30.04.2024)

Sutton, Kelly www.bbc.co.uk/news/uk-england-beds-bucks-herts-51934477; www.judiciary.uk/wp-content/uploads/2020/04/Kelly-Sutton-2020-0076-Redacted.pdf (accessed 30.04.2024)

Turner, Ike, *Takin' Back My Name* (Awesome Books 1999)

Welstead, Mary, 'Extra-Territorial Applications for Forced Marriage Protection Orders' (2024) *Family Law* 927

Wigmore, John Dean, *Textbook on Evidence* (3rd edn, Little Brown 1940)

Williams, Glanville, 'Corroboration – Sexual Cases' [1962] *Criminal Law Review* 662

Vardy, Emma, 'Diddy Assault Video Cements Fall of Hip-Hop Icon' *BBC News* www.bbc.co.uk/news/world-us-canada-69042769.amp (accessed 23.05.2024)

Williams, Glanville, Textbook of Criminal Law (Stevens 1978)

Further reading

Barran, Diana, 'Developments in Protecting Victims of Domestic Abuse' [2009] *Family Law* 416

Behlmer, George, 'Summary Justice and Working-Class Marriage in England, 1870–1940' [2011] *Law and History Review* 229

Bishop, Charlotte, 'Prevention and Protection: Will the Domestic Abuse Act Transform the Response to Domestic Abuse in England and Wales?' [2021] *Child and Family Law Quarterly* 163

Centre for Women's Justice Blog on Perpetrators (13.06.2022) www.centreforwomensjustice.org.uk/new-blog-1/2022/6/13/cwj-manifesto-10-how-perpetrators-use-the-legal-systems-to-control-women (accessed 05.05.2024)

Cyber Flashing Convict www.bbc.co.uk/news/uk-england-essex-68543605 (accessed 26.05.2024)

Domestic Violence, Forced Marriage and 'Honour' Based Violence (HC 263-1 (2008)) https://publications.parliament.uk/pa/cm200708/cmselect/cmhaff/263/263i.pdf (accessed 05.05.2024)

Edwards, Susan and Mary Welstead, 'Death Before Familial Dishonour' (1999) *National Law Journal* 149

Equal Treatment Bench Book – Courts and Tribunals Judiciary www.judiciary.uk/about-the-judiciary/diversity/equal-treatment-bench-book/ (accessed 26.05.2024)

Fiora-Gormally, Nancy, 'Battered Wives Who Kill' (1978) 2 *Law and Human Behaviour* 133

Gill, Aisha, 'Making the Case for Legal Aid Funding for Victims/Survivors of Domestic Violence' [2012] *Family Law* 1128

Hale, Baroness, 'Practising Family Law Outside the Box' [2011] *Family Law* 1341

Hanmer, Jalna and Sheila Saunders, *Well Founded Fear* (Hutchinson 1984)

House of Commons Forced Marriage (HC 880) [2011] *Family Law* 767

Kennedy, Helena, *Eve Was Framed: Women and British Justice* (Chatto and Windus 1992)

Metropolitan Police, 'Review of MPS implementation of Forced Marriage (Civil Protection) Act 2007' (2010) www.mpa.gov.uk; https://publications.parliament.uk/pa/cm201012/cmselect/cmhaff/880/88004.htm (accessed 14.05.2024)

Pearce, Nasreen and Aisha Gill, 'Criminalising Forced Marriage Through Stand – Alone Legislation: Will It Work?' [2012] *Family Law* 534

Pizzey, Erin and Alison Forbes, *Scream Quietly or the Neighbours Will Hear* (Penguin 1974)

Robinson, Amanda L., Andy Myhill, Julia Wire, Jo Roberts and Nick Tilley, *Risk-Led Policing of Domestic Abuse and the DASH Risk Model* (College of Policing 2016) https://library.college.police.uk/docs/college-of-policing/Risk-led-policing-2-2016.pdf (accessed 25.05.2024)

Safe Lives https://safelives.org.uk (accessed 23.05.2024)

Sanghera, Jasvinder, *Daughters of Shame* (Hodder 2009)

Schneider, Elizabeth, 'Describing and Changing: Women's Self Defence Work and the Problem of Expert Testimony on Battering' [1986] *Women's Rights Law Report* 195

Sheehy, Elizabeth, 'Battered Woman Syndrome: Developments in Canadian Law After *R v Lavallee*' in Julie Stubbs (ed) *Woman Violence and the Law*, Monograph Series (Institute of Criminology 1994)

Taylor-Browne, Julie (ed) *What Works in Reducing Domestic Violence?* (Whiting and Birch 2001)

Walker, Lenore, *The Battered Woman* (Harper Row 1979)

Walker, Lenore, *Terrifying Love* (Harper Row 1989)

Wall, Sir Nicholas, 'Keynote Address at National Resolution Domestic Abuse Conference' www.innertemplelibrary.com/2012/03/annual-resolution-conference-speech-by-sir-nicholas-wall/ (accessed 20.05.2024)

Welchman, Lynn and Sara Hossain, *Honour* (Zed 2005)

Whitehead, L, 'Non-Molestation Orders: The New Provisions of the DVCVA 2004' [2010] *Family Law* 1299

Wistrich, Harriet, *Sisters in Law* (Torva 2024)

6

Ending relationships

SUMMARY

One of the accepted values of modern society is that many relationships will not last the lifetime of the parties and that, if a relationship has become unworkable, it is better for the parties to end it with the minimal of bitterness and hostility. In this chapter we consider the ways in which the State controls the legal ending of the relationships of marriage and civil partnerships. We also discuss the problematic nature of divorce law and consider the changes that have been made by the introduction of the Divorce, Dissolution and Separation Act 2020. The reforms introduced by this legislation cannot be underestimated. For years there had been calls for change but there was considerable opposition from groups who maintained that the institution of marriage must be upheld at all costs. This failed to take into account the fact that once a marriage has failed complex divorce laws will not persuade the parties to stay together. There is no evidence that making the divorce laws more difficult leads to more couples staying together. Iram Ellman commented: 'while legal barriers can affect the rate of formal divorce, it is far less clear they can affect the rate of actual marital demise' (Ellman 1997). As discussed later in the chapter it took the publicity surrounding the case of *Owens v Owens* in 2017 to persuade the Government to instigate a fresh review into the divorce laws which eventually culminated in the passage of the 2020 Act.

Because cohabiting relationships come into existence without any formal legal process, there are no legal means by which they may be formally ended. We also consider how certain religious authorities in England and Wales view some relationships as valid religious marriages and, therefore, within their divorce jurisdiction.

Divorce

Spouses and civil partners may not end their marriage or civil partnerships on demand. Just as they must meet certain legal requirements to enter into a relationship, they must also meet certain legal requirements to exit from it.

DOI: 10.4324/9781003435020-6

Once divorced, either partner becomes free to enter into a new marriage or civil partnership, or even remarry a previous partner, if he or she so wishes. The actors Elizabeth Taylor and Richard Burton divorced each other after ten years of marriage and remarried one year later, only to divorce again nine months after that second marriage.

A decree of divorce releases the parties from all the rights and obligations of marriage. However, it also grants new post-marital rights and imposes new post-marital obligations on the divorced couple. These rights and obligations relate primarily to children, finances and property and may mean that many couples will remain locked into a relationship with each other for many years after they have divorced. These rights and duties are considered in Chapters 7 and 16.

For many couples, divorce is both emotionally and practically damaging. It is not what they had hoped for when they embarked, with romantic optimism, on marriage. It is one of the more stress-inducing experiences of life which may be exacerbated by the primarily fault-based nature of the divorce process. The law on divorce changed in 2020. This change was preceded by decades of criticism and discussion amongst practitioners, the judiciary and academics about the weaknesses of the divorce law and what should replace it (see Shepherd 2009; Munby 2014).

The Divorce, Dissolution and Separation Act 2020 took effect in April 2022. Since then any couple seeking a divorce will do so under the new rules. The most significant change is the introduction under the Act of 'no-fault' divorce.

The applicant need simply to state on the relevant application form that the marriage has irretrievably broken down without need for proof. It is a move towards what has been described as divorce 'on demand'.

During this chapter we will look at the historical background to the introduction of divorce, the old law and the reasons for the reforms introduced over the years culminating in the 2020 Act.

Statistical evidence of divorce

Until 2020 divorce in the United Kingdom was governed by the Matrimonial Causes Act 1973. The changes introduced in the 1973 Act resulted in a large increase in the rate of divorce. Provisions for divorce after a period of separation allowed a number of people to divorce who had been deterred by the provisions in the previous law which were based on fault such as adultery. Traditionally there has always been a rise in the divorce rate immediately following any reform of the law which is mirrored across different jurisdictions. The divorce rate levelled off and from 2000 and 2020 the divorce rate steadily fell. In 2020, there were 102,438 divorces amongst opposite sex couples, down from 113,949 in 2009. This fall in the divorce rate could also be accounted for by the fall in the number of marriages that took place. The latest information from the Office for National Statistics (ONS) reveals that there was a decrease in the number of divorces in England and Wales in 2022, down to 80,057 compared to 113,505 in 2021. These figures may be distorted because of the change in the divorce laws in 2022. There may have been a number of couples who chose to delay taking divorce proceedings because it was recognised that the divorce process under the new rules had been simplified. There appears to be a small increase in the number of divorce applications the year following the introduction of the new rules in 2022 (Gov.UK 2023).

Reasons for divorce and its consequences

In spite of the fall in the divorce rate, it is still high. There has been considerable speculation about the reasons for this and the consequences for the institution of marriage and the effects on society. Social explanations for divorce include increased life expectancy; social changes in the nature of family life; higher expectations about marriage; a decrease in the birth rate; financial independence of women; and the fact that many marriages are based, unrealistically, on a romantic and idealised concept of love. Given these factors, it would be surprising if a significant number of marriages did not break down. Ruth Deech argued in 1990 that it is the divorce legislation itself which affects the divorce rate. She maintains that divorce increases whenever new divorce legislation, which makes divorce easier, comes into force (Deech 2009). This has been a consistent argument against introducing reforms to the divorce laws and in particular no-fault divorce.

Divorce may be beneficial in the long term for the individuals involved, but the consequences for society can be serious. Children are regarded as the most likely victims, but the health and welfare of the couple at the time of the divorce are also likely to be at risk. For the State, divorce has major economic consequences; medical treatment for stress and depression experienced by the couple is not without cost, and the level of welfare benefits will inevitably rise because many families will not have sufficient financial resources to enable them to fund their new life.

Background to divorce

The earliest divorces were only possible through an Act of Parliament passed in both houses of Parliament.

The earliest is possibly a divorce granted to Lord Roos of Belvoir Castle Leicester (www.historyofparliamentonline.org/volume/1660-1690/member/manners-john-1638-1711). It was a complicated and long process which involved gaining a separation from the ecclesiastical courts and then a divorce through an Act of Parliament. It took several years and included a declaration that the children of his wife should be declared illegitimate.

The difficulty of passing such an Act meant divorce was very rare and very few were awarded to women. Indeed according to parliamentary records only four divorces were awarded to women in 193 years of parliamentary divorce compared to 186 to men. The only grounds of divorce was adultery so instances of cruelty however repeated were insufficient to found divorce (see generally Phillips 1988; Stone 1990).

In 1857, the first of a number of Matrimonial Causes Acts was passed giving the courts power to dissolve a marriage without recourse to Parliament. This was a significant step taking the ending of a marriage and the law on separation away from the jurisdiction of the church and into the courts. In spite of this move, men and women continued to be treated differently when seeking a divorce; a situation that lasted until 1923. A man could divorce based on his wife's adultery whereas women had to prove adultery combined with another aspect such as bigamy, rape, bestiality or cruelty. Within a year the petitions for divorce had risen to over 250 per year of which approximately one third were brought by women. Nevertheless the new process was both daunting and expensive for anyone undertaking it. A divorce hearing was in open court often in front of a jury with the requirement of proof of certain evidence which were referred to as matrimonial offences. These 'offences' persisted in the later law on divorce where the law required proof of certain 'facts' before a divorce could be awarded. Subsequent Matrimonial Causes Acts of 1923 and 1937 relaxed some of the rules but still required proof of certain behaviour. The 1937 Act extended the grounds for divorce to desertion for three years or more, cruelty or because the other party was incurably of unsound mind. Divorce continued to rely on 'evidence' of a certain situation.

The law did not reflect a couple who accepted that their marriage was at an end and wished to part.

Matrimonial Causes Act 1973

Although divorce had become slightly more accessible, it still needed proof of one of the grounds which was still expensive, time consuming and sometimes unsuccessful. Often the parties both wanted divorce but were unable to satisfy the court on one of the required grounds. Stephen Cretney cited a case where after a trial lasting three days a divorce was denied in spite of cross petitions based on cruelty and adultery (Cretney 2005), reflecting on whether the State should force a couple who were clearly unhappy to remain married to each other. (For some general background to the family and attitudes to divorce in the twentieth century see the research published by the British Academy in 2010, Happy families? History and family policy.)

A report commissioned by the Archbishop of Canterbury (1966) supported the idea that divorce should be based on one ground, 'irretrievable breakdown of the marriage', which would be based on facts presented to the court. The report rejected the idea that divorce could be obtained by mutual consent. It has taken nearly 60 years for that to have been accepted. A second report by the Law Commission, Reform of the Grounds of Divorce: the Field of Choice (1966), also made a number of recommendations. There were some major differences between the two reports and the eventual result, The Divorce Reform Act, was a compromise between the two. It was later consolidated into the Matrimonial Causes Act 1973. Divorce under the Act depended on proving that the marriage had broken down irretrievably. In order to show irretrievable breakdown the petitioner had to prove one of five facts. A huge body of law grew up surrounding the requisite proof of each of these facts, and divorces were often refused where proof fell short of the required standard. The five facts under the 1973 Act will be discussed very briefly in the following section.

The five facts under the MCA 1973, s 1(2)

Three of the five facts listed in the MCA 1973, s 1(2) were fault-based and perpetuated the idea that divorce involved an aggressor and a victim. The reality is that it is often difficult to determine which partner can be said to be at fault in the failure of a marriage.

The fact relied on by the petitioner did not need to be the cause of the irretrievable breakdown of the marriage.

Once the petitioner had provided a statement of any one of the five facts, the court had to grant a decree of divorce unless it remained unconvinced that the marriage had irretrievably broken down. The Divorce, Dissolution and Separation Act 2020 has removed the need to prove any of the five facts today. It is enough to state in the application that the marriage has broken down irretrievably. The following section will cover very limited discussion on the older case law surrounding the five facts needed to prove irretrievable breakdown of marriage save for *Owens v Owens* (1917) which accelerated the move towards reform of the divorce process and will be discussed in more detail.

The five facts

Adultery and intolerability (MCA 1973, s 1(2)(a))

About 16 per cent of all divorce petitions relied on this fact before 2020; it was a way of obtaining a divorce easily and rapidly. Allegations were made that s 1(2)(a) led spouses to collude with each other and may even have encouraged adultery.

It was not necessary for the petitioner to know the identity of the person with whom the respondent had committed adultery (the co-respondent) but if it was known, the petitioner could name him or her in the petition.

Unless the respondent denied the adultery, the petitioner's word was accepted by the court without further proof or investigation.

Definition of adultery

To petition for divorce using this fact, the respondent must have had voluntary penetrative sexual intercourse with a member of the opposite sex.

Intolerability

The wording of s 1(2)(a) required that a petitioner, in addition to maintaining that the respondent had committed adultery, must also be able to state that he or she found it intolerable to live with the respondent. It would seem logical that the betrayed spouse should be able to seek a divorce stating that he or she finds it intolerable, as a result of the adultery, to continue living with the respondent. However, the courts made it clear that there need be no connection whatsoever between the adultery and the petitioner's claim of intolerability. One of the criticisms of allowing adultery as a reason for divorce was that it was open to abuse.

Behaviour (MCA 1973, s 1(2)(b))

Behaviour was the fact which was most commonly relied on to prove irretrievable breakdown of the marriage, around 48 per cent of petitions were based on this fact. It is readily understandable why the behaviour fact was so frequently relied on in divorce petitions. The very nature of living in an intimate relationship could almost certainly give rise to irritating behaviour. It is arguable that the majority of spouses could point to examples of behaviour which they could not reasonably be expected to tolerate.

Although s 1 (2)(b) was commonly referred to as the 'unreasonable behaviour' fact, it was not the respondent's behaviour itself which had to be unreasonable. It was the expectation that the petitioner should continue to live with the respondent's behaviour which must be seen as an unreasonable one.

The case law reflects changing views on what the court considered 'unreasonable behaviour'. Perhaps it is best summed up by the words of Dunn J in *Livingstone-Stallard v Livingstone-Stallard* [1974] 2 All ER 766 who considered unreasonable behaviour to be behaviour that:

> *would any right-thinking person come to the conclusion that this husband has behaved in such a way that this wife cannot reasonably be expected to live with him, taking into account the whole of the circumstances and the characters and personalities of the parties.*

This judgment of Dunn J suggests that there is a subjective element to the behaviour.

The Supreme Court had one final chance in *Owens v Owens* [2018] UKSC 41 to review the law on behaviour just a matter of a couple of years before the 2020 Act was passed. One may conclude that the facts of this case added weight to those who had for many years sought reform of divorce law.

The case concerned a couple, Tini and Hugh Owens, who had been married for 37 years. The couple was very wealthy and had substantial business interests. The wife petitioned on the basis of the unreasonable behaviour of the husband. Over the years fewer and fewer petitions for divorce were defended and it had become practically unheard of for a case to be heard in the appeal courts. The judge at first instance found the complaints of the wife to be 'flimsy' and 'scraping the barrel'. She complained of a number of incidents where the husband had criticised her publicly in front of a crowd of people or alternatively had refused to speak to her in a public place such as a restaurant. She said she found this humiliating. She also argued that he suffered from mood swings which resulted in serious arguments between the parties. In dismissing the petition the judge held that the wife was overly sensitive and that the husband had behaved in an 'old school' way. Mrs Owens appealed to the Court of Appeal. The judgment was delivered by Munby P who somewhat reluctantly upheld the decision of the judge at first instance. This was the first divorce case to be heard by the Court of Appeal for over 20 years and it gave the court and the Supreme Court who later heard the case a chance to comment on the state of the general law on divorce in the United Kingdom, in particular what must be proved in order to found a divorce based on unreasonable behaviour. In the words of Munby P:

> *Parliament has decreed that it is not a ground for divorce that you find yourself in a wretchedly unhappy marriage, though some people may say it should be. Such is the law which it is our duty to apply.*

The reason that the behaviour cited by Mrs Owens failed to satisfy the court was that in the circumstances the cumulative effect of the behaviour cited was not sufficient to meet the test even when looked at subjectively i.e. as stated by Munby P looking at this particular behaviour and this husband and this wife in the light of all the circumstances as well as the cumulative effect of the conduct of the respondent. This was because the test was only partially subjective and must be behaviour which reached a certain threshold which the court can conclude that it would be unreasonable for the petitioner to be expected to continue to live with the respondent.

The case was then heard by the Supreme Court who also upheld the judge at first instance but also criticised the state of the law on divorce in the United Kingdom.

The court recognised that social norms had changed over the years. Lord Wilson illustrated this by describing the moment when the behaviour of a husband may make it unreasonable for a wife to continue to live with him. In his words:

for the wife that moment now arrives earlier than it did before; it now arrives at the same time for both sexes in equivalent situations.

Although it is clear that Mrs Owens had expected the court to treat the different incidents of behaviour cited in her petition as cumulative the court also found it failed to reach the standard required. In view of the significance of the arguments in this case the family lawyers' organisation 'Resolution' had intervened. It was an opportunity for the Supreme Court to review the test for behaviour and to have substituted a purely subjective test. In that way divorce would be said to amount to what many have criticised as 'divorce on demand' by citing unreasonable behaviour. Nevertheless in spite of the court's reluctance to restate the law it's vociferous criticism of the way the law left Mrs Owens and the way it deprived her of a divorce when it was quite clear that her marriage had irretrievably broken down did lead to an almost immediate call for the law on divorce to be reviewed which then led to the introduction of the 2020 Act and the passage into law of 'no-fault' divorce removing behaviour as a fact to be proved before divorce was granted. (For a more detailed discussion of this case see Morgan 2019; Burton 2020.)

Continuing cohabitation

A spouse could not rely on the MCA 1973, s 1(2)(b) if he or she had lived with the respondent for a period or periods exceeding six months after the final occurrence of the behaviour on which the petition for divorce was based (MCA 1973, s 2(3)). He or she would have been deemed to be able to cope with the respondent's conduct. However, the court may exercise its discretion in the petitioner's favour.

And where the behaviour was ongoing, s 1(2)(b) was clearly irrelevant.

Desertion (MCA 1973, s 1(2)(c))

Divorce petitions based on desertion were rare, only 0.4 per cent relied on this fact. The petitioner had to be able to prove that the respondent had not lived in the same household as him or her for two years, had no justifiable reason for living apart, and had the intention to remain permanently apart from him or her throughout that period.

The respondent could be found to have deserted the petitioner even if they continued to live under the same roof. They would have had to prove that they are living totally separate lives in completely independent households – not an easy task to achieve and most difficult to prove.

The respondent could not be held to be in desertion if the petitioner had behaved in a manner which justified the respondent's departure or if the respondent, because of mental illness, was deluded into believing that the petitioner had behaved in such a way.

Adultery or conduct on the part of the petitioner, which would come within the behaviour fact, or mental or physical illness, might have been sufficient justification for the respondent to leave the petitioner without being held to be in desertion. Indeed, in these circumstances, the petitioner could have been held to be in constructive desertion of the respondent.

The respondent was not to be held to be in desertion if the petitioner has agreed to the separation.

There must have been an intention to desert. Spouses may have been physically apart from each other without intending to be in desertion. Work, illness or imprisonment may all lead to separation. However, if one party changed his mind and decided not to return, desertion would have been held to have commenced from that moment even if circumstances, in any event, would have prevented him from returning. The intention to desert need not have been communicated. This makes desertion difficult to prove, and it will have to be inferred from the circumstances.

Resumption of cohabitation

The petitioner may have resumed living with the respondent for a period or periods not exceeding six months without losing his or her right to rely on the respondent's desertion. However, in any subsequent petition for divorce, this period of cohabitation would not have counted towards the requisite two-year period of being apart (MCA 1973, s 2(5)).

Two years living apart and consent to the decree (MCA 1973, s 1(2)(d))

Twenty-five per cent of all divorces were based on this fact. It was most commonly pleaded where both parties wished to divorce, and in a non-acrimonious and private manner; it involved no publicity about the private lives of the spouses and was not fault-based. All the royal divorce petitions of the last century relied on this fact.

As with desertion, the parties could have lived under the same roof during the two-year period provided that they conducted separate households (MCA 1973, s 2(6)). This was obviously easier to achieve in a royal residence than in the homes of most potential divorcees. The case law did not always take into account the realities of everyday life. During times of economic recession, and where the divorcing couple had children, it could be difficult to maintain two separate households, yet the spouses may well have been living separate lives in every other way.

Resumption of cohabitation

The petitioner could have resumed living with the respondent for a period or periods not exceeding six months without losing the right to rely on two years' living apart. However, in any subsequent petition for divorce, this period of cohabitation would not have counted towards the requisite two-year period (MCA 1973, s 2(5)).

Five years living apart (MCA 1973, s 1(2)(e))

According to the Government consultation on divorce held in 2018 about 11 per cent of divorces relied on this fact (Ministry of Justice 2018). The spouses must have lived apart for five years, and there was no requirement that the respondent must consent to the decree. For the petitioner who relied on this fact, it was usually a case of last resort; all other possibilities would normally have been exhausted. In spite of the comment that this fact provides a *Casanova's charter* for men wishing to divorce their innocent wives unilaterally (Deech 1990), the majority of petitioners who relied on this fact were women.

The defence of grave hardship (MCA 1973, s 5)

The MCA 1973, s 1(2)(e) was considered controversial because it permitted the so-called innocent spouse to be divorced against his or her will. For that reason, where a petitioner alleged five years' living apart, the MCA 1973, s 5 allowed the respondent to plead that the dissolution of the marriage would result in grave financial or other hardship to him or her, and that it would in all the circumstances be wrong to dissolve the marriage. This right to defend divorce proceedings has been removed under the Divorce, Dissolution and Separation Act 2020. This also proved to be controversial because it removed any residual right to defend a divorce petition. The defended divorce had been very rarely used in recent years.

Munby P noted in *Owens v Owens*:

> In the year to January 2017 there were 113,996 petitions for divorce. The details are not published, but I understand that, over the same period, notice of intention to defend was given in some 2,600 acknowledgements of service (some 2.28 % of all petitions) while actual answers filed were about 760 (some 0.67 % of all petitions).

[see para 98] He concludes by asking the question: 'Can it really be justified, where its application is confined to such a minutely small number of cases?'

No divorce proceedings within a year of marriage

Under the Matrimonial Causes Act 1973 as amended by the Matrimonial and Family Proceedings Act 1984, s 1 no divorce proceedings can be initiated within a year of a marriage. This requirement has been retained by the 2020 Act.

A two-part process

Under the 1973 Act, the divorce decree was divided into two parts. The first part, the decree nisi, was pronounced in open court, normally without the attendance of either party. The second part, the decree absolute, was granted after a period of six weeks had elapsed. If there were no objections, the petitioner, or the respondent with the consent of the court, could apply for the decree absolute and it was only when this final decree had been made that the parties were free to marry again or enter into a civil partnership. The decree absolute could not be granted until the court was satisfied unless the court was satisfied that the financial arrangements are satisfactory.

The new procedure

Divorce under the Divorce, Dissolution and Separation Act 2020

The new Act came into effect in April 2022. It only applies to a divorce petition started after that date, so the old law will continue to apply to some divorces for a number of years. The Act applies to both civil partnerships and divorces and has also changed the law on judicial separation.

The key feature that 'irretrievable breakdown' of the marriage will be the sole ground for divorce replicates the law in the Matrimonial Causes Act 1973, but the five facts no longer need to be proved. The mere statement in the application that the marriage has broken down irretrievably is sufficient for the application to proceed.

Divorce based on irretrievable breakdown of marriage

S 1 *Divorce on breakdown of marriage*

(1) Subject to section 3, either or both parties to a marriage may apply to the court for an order ('a divorce order') which dissolves the marriage on the ground that the marriage has broken down irretrievably.

(2) An application under subsection (1) must be accompanied by a statement by the applicant or applicants that the marriage has broken down irretrievably.

(3) The court dealing with an application under subsection (1) must –
    (a) Take the statement to be conclusive evidence that the marriage has broken down irretrievably, and
    (b) Make a divorce order.

It means that the courts no longer need to examine the details of the marriage and its breakdown and in the future there will no longer be problems of proof as encountered in *Owens v Owens* (2017).

Proof of irretrievable breakdown

The proof lies in the statement made by the applicant (previously the petitioner) that the marriage has broken down. The courts will treat the statement by the applicant as conclusive proof of the facts.

The defence of grave hardship has been abolished. The only grounds under the 2020 Act to defend a divorce will be on the grounds of fraud, lack of jurisdiction or another procedural irregularity.

Procedure for divorce

Changes have been made to the procedure for divorce. The terminology and time scale before a final order is made have been changed.

> (4)   A divorce order –
>   (a)   is, in the first instance, a conditional order, and
>   (b)   may not be made final before the end of the period of six weeks from the making of the conditional order.
> (5)   the court may not make a conditional order unless –
>   (a)   in the case of an application that is to proceed as an application by one party to the marriage only, that party has confirmed to the court that they wish the application to continue, or
>   (b)   in the case of an application that is to proceed as an application by both parties to the marriage, those parties have confirmed to the court that they wish the application to continue;
>   And a party may not give confirmation for the purposes of this subsection before the end of the period of 20 weeks from the start of proceedings.

So the new procedure sets down a period of 20 weeks before the court can make a conditional divorce order. Six weeks after the conditional order has been made the court can make a final order. The total period between the service of the application and the final order if there is no objection is six months. There is provision in the Act to shorten the time periods set out. This may be in cases of terminal illness to allow a party to remarry in a hurry.

> s 10 of the Matrimonial Causes Act 1973 (as amended by the 2020 Act) will still apply so that no final order will be granted by the court unless it is satisfied on issues with regard to financial provision.

For example, it must be satisfied that the applicant should not be required to make any financial provision for the respondent or that any financial provision made by the applicant for the respondent is reasonable and fair or the best that can be made in the circumstances.

An important aspect of the Act is the use of modern straightforward language in the legislation. 'Decree Nisi' and 'Decree Absolute' are replaced by 'conditional' and 'final' order and the 'petition' and the 'petitioner' are referred to as the application and the applicant.

Some might argue it constitutes 'divorce on demand', but for many others it represents a long overdue reform. The different arguments and history of the move towards reform of the 1973 Act will be discussed briefly in the following section.

Critique of the law leading to the Divorce, Dissolution and Separation Act 2020

For many years, there was considerable despair over, and criticism of, the law relating to divorce (see e.g. Report of the Matrimonial Causes Procedure Committee (1985); *The Ground for Divorce* (Law Com No 192); *Looking to the Future, Mediation and the Ground for Divorce: the Government's Proposals* (Cm 2799, 1995)). In *Ground for Divorce* (1990), the Law Commission had considered what are the key features that any divorce law should include. One feature was to support those marriages capable of being saved but for those that cannot be saved then to be dissolved with the minimum of avoidable distress, bitterness and hostility.

Critics suggested that the existing law with its single ground of irretrievable breakdown with proof through five separate 'facts' was confusing, misleading, outdated and excessively legalistic. It failed to save marriages and fell short of allowing the civilised burial of dead relationships where there was no clear reason or fault for their breakdown. Critics also expressed dissatisfaction that although a marriage has broken down, divorce is not available without further proof of one of the five facts and that it was not necessary to show that the fact pleaded caused the breakdown of the marriage. The rigid rule that the couple must have been married for one year before a divorce petition was possible was also regarded as unnecessarily harsh. Couples who wanted a rapid and easy route out of marriage were more likely to rely on the fault-based facts of adultery and behaviour, often with collusion, if not actual perjury, and with little thought given to the consequences. The case of *Owens* showed that petitions alleging behaviour could be difficult to prove if the other party chose to defend the petition. For many years parties relying on behaviour as a ground of divorce with advice from lawyers had chosen to use as few examples of unreasonable behaviour as possible. They chose to take this course because they preferred to keep the details of their failing marriage from public discussion. High profile divorces such as the recent divorce of Johnny Depp and Amber Heard and Paul McCartney and Heather Mills have allowed the public to hear the details of their unhappy marriages, details which the parties would have preferred to keep private. Allegations of fault will usually lead to bitterness and hostility which may then lead to difficulties for the children of the marriage. Finally, a spouse who wanted a divorce could be held to ransom by the other party, who may make unfair demands in return for agreeing to a divorce or insist on the long wait of five years. Research carried out by Liz Trinder et al for the Nuffield Foundation showed that less than 30 per cent of respondents thought the petition matched the reason for the divorce whereas 60 per cent of petitioners thought that their petition represented the reason for their separation. They also found that 62 per cent of petitioners and 78 per cent of respondents said using fault-based grounds for divorce led to a greater degree of bitterness throughout the process although only one fifth had found that the use of fault had made sorting arrangements for the children more difficult (Trinder et al. 2017).

The road to reform

Family Law Act 1996

In 1996, the Family Law Act (FLA) received the Royal Assent. It sought to reform divorce by dividing marriages into those that might be saved and those that were clearly at an end. Couples seeking a divorce had first to attend an information meeting which it was hoped would lead the parties who wished to proceed to use mediation rather than the court process to resolve any outstanding matters concerning finances, arrangements for children and property. However, five years later, in 2001, the Lord Chancellor announced that Part II of the Act which related to divorce reform would not be brought into force and that Parliament would be asked to repeal it. It was clear from the trials that the information meeting failed to divert couples from using solicitors towards mediation. Indeed Richard Collier showed that more people used solicitors as opposed to mediation as a result of the information meetings (Collier 1999). This defeated the main aim of the Act which was to take away the acrimony that surrounds divorce by steering people towards mediation. It was also aimed at saving money because mediation saves on two legal teams. There was also an underlying hope that marriages would be saved because people would think through their relationships and decide that they would not divorce. What was found was that most people had thought about their relationship long before attending the information meeting.

Family Justice Review 2011

In spite of the failure of the divorce provisions of the 1996 Family Law Act key practitioners, judges and academics continued to call for reform. It was generally acknowledged now that divorce law was in an unfortunate state of limbo. The Family Justice Review produced its Final Report in 2011. The Review made minimal recommendations with respect to the divorce process. It concluded that:

> There is scope to increase the use of administrators in the courts to reduce burdens on judges and create a more streamlined process in the 98% of cases where divorce is uncontested. The current process requires judges to spend time in effect to do no more than check that forms have been filled in correctly, with accurate names and dates. This is a waste. To change it would not make any difference to the ease or difficulty of obtaining a divorce. It would just make more judge time available for more important things.

The Government's response

In its response to the Family Justice Review, the Government said that there would be no change to the substantive law of divorce other than the removal of the requirement for the court to consider arrangements for children in uncontested divorce cases. It did not wish to make divorce easier but, rather, wished to make the lives of the courts easier and allow uncontested divorces to be handled administratively in the courts by appropriately qualified persons, rather than by judges. The process for initiating divorce would begin with the 'online hub' which would provide divorcing couples with information.

A further attempt at the reform of divorce was the introduction of a Private Members' Bill in 2015 by Richard Bacon MP. This Bill attempted reform but instead introduced a further fact to prove irretrievable breakdown of marriage, namely 'divorce on the basis of mutual consent without a waiting period'. This failed to get beyond the second reading. Critics argued that this sixth fact based on 'no fault' would lead to an increase in marriages breaking down pointing to Canada where divorce had increased sixfold on the introduction of no-fault divorce in 1986.

Undoubtedly, it was the combination of the dire facts of *Owens v Owens* and the publication of the results of a number of research projects, in particular the research project sponsored by the Nuffield Foundation (see earlier) *Finding Fault? Divorce Law and Practice in England and Wales* that forced the Government to revisit the law on divorce. The Supreme Court hearing of *Owens* brought considerable public interest in the law and it became, not surprisingly, 'a *cause celebre*'. The research project made a number of findings including the key point that there was no evidence that fault reduces divorce. It also found that fault embittered the divorce process for both sides. The Government announced a consultation on reform of the law: *Reducing Family Conflict: Reform of the Legal Requirements for Divorce September 2018*. This time the proposal in the consultation was to abolish all the divorce facts and the possibility of defending a divorce save on procedural matters. In spite of some continued opposition from certain groups in particular some religious groups the Divorce, Dissolution and Separation Bill was introduced into Parliament in June 2019 receiving Royal Assent in June 2020 and implemented in April 2022.

Problems with the law of the MCA 1973

One of the key problems with the 1973 Act was the continuance of fault-based divorce.

There had been several reports examining divorce law following the 1973 Act. All accepted that the system was far from perfect but at least the Act had introduced certain 'facts' e.g. separation for two or five years which were longer based on fault. Nevertheless three other 'facts' – adultery, behaviour and desertion – were founded on fault.

It was found in both the Law Commission Reports of 1966 and 1990 that fault had no useful part to play in divorce and contributed to poor outcomes for the parties, in particular children. The Law Commission found divorce to be misleading and confusing. The law expected the petitioner to cite one of the facts as proof of the irretrievable breakdown of the marriage, but it was unlikely to be the real reason why it had broken down. It was also shown in the Nuffield Report of 2017 that frequently in undefended divorce the reasons were not even examined by the court. In *Owens* the divorce was defended so the behaviour cited in the petition was examined in detail in court, but it would not have been scrutinised had the petition been undefended. The irony is that the petition would have gone through without challenge and Tini Owens would have been granted her divorce rather than suffering the stress of three very public court cases and the publicity attached which allowed her marriage to be scrutinised by the general public. One of the key features of a good divorce law as stated in the 1966 Law Commission Report *The Field of Choice* was to buttress rather than undermine the stability of marriages. Far from buttressing marriages it was clear that the law failed to save marriages.

Alternative divorce models

There are a number of different models for divorce adopted across the world. One key feature is whether divorce should be fault-based or a granted on a no-fault model. The first divorces allowed in the UK were fault-based, and it was not until the 1973 Act that the no-fault 'facts' of separation for two or five years were introduced. Today many jurisdictions allow a combination of both or have moved towards the no-fault model. In Scotland divorce continues to be based on facts which include separation (no-fault) and adultery and behaviour (fault based). By comparison divorce in Australia has been on a no-fault basis since 1975. This is proved by separation for a year and proof that there is no likelihood of a resumption of living together. In Spain divorce is based on stating that the marriage has broken down and no proof is required. The court will grant the order once satisfied that the arrangements for the children and family finances are satisfactory.

1. **Fault–based divorce:** this requires proof of a 'fact' that the law perceives as behaviour allowing the parties to divorce. The most obvious example is adultery.

2. **Proof of irretrievable breakdown by one party:** this requires one party to state that the marriage has broken down irretrievably without requiring proof by stating a particular fact. This allows for divorce even where one party is opposed.

3. **Proof of irretrievable breakdown by both parties:** the difference between this model and the previous model is that for this divorce to proceed both parties must be in agreement. It means that the divorce proceeds because both parties wish it which is perceived as limiting acrimony between the parties. It could never be the sole ground for divorce because one party could refuse to agree as in the case of *Owens* which is highly unsatisfactory.

4. **Divorce based on a state of affairs:** this is divorce granted on a no-fault basis but proved by a state of affairs, usually separation.

5. **Divorce 'on demand' where divorce is granted because the parties request divorce:** this ground has always been treated with a certain amount of sceptism and fear. It is assumed that it would lead to instability. Parties could seek to divorce without really thinking through the consequences.

Divorce under the Divorce, Dissolution and Separation Act 2020 is granted on the basis of irretrievable breakdown of the marriage as stated by either one or both parties. It has removed fault and the need to prove certain facts. The need to prove certain facts had been subject to criticism for many years. The Law Commission Report in 1990 (Family Law: The Ground for Divorce) observed that 'the facts' were often manipulated e.g. behaviour cited in such a way as to satisfy the requirements of the petition but not always true and often exaggerated. In *Owens* Munby P had commented:

> the law which the judges have to apply and the procedures which they have to follow are based on hypocrisy and lack intellectual honesty. . . . It is ironic that collusion, which until the doctrine was abolished by section 9 of the 1969 Act was a bar to a decree, is now the very foundation of countless petitions and decrees.

Likely effect of the reforms?
Much of the criticism aimed at the reform of the divorce law was centred around the fact that it would encourage the breakdown of marriage by making it easier for

parties to divorce. It was perceived that if it is difficult for parties to divorce then they are more likely to stay together. Criticism of introducing no-fault divorce has come from many strands of society, in particular the church. The Christian Institute writes extensively under its 'apologetic' of the perceived dangers of divorce on society opposing strongly the introduction of no-fault divorce (The Christian Institute Apologetic, n.d.). Evidence from those countries where divorce procedures has been simplified has shown that the relaxation of strict rules generally leads to an increase in divorce applications, for example Canada, but this usually accounts for a backlog in those wishing to divorce but have been hesitant because of a perception that the procedure is complicated. In the months since the Divorce, Dissolution and Separation Act 2020 became law there has been an increase in divorce applications. According to Lubna Shuja, the President of the Law Society, the latest data show that in the nine months from when the new law came into effect, there were 89,123 divorce applications, 78 per cent from sole applicants and 22 per cent from joint applicants, including those for the dissolution of civil partnerships. In comparison, there were 77,449 divorce applications between April 2021 to December 2021, prior to the 'no-fault' law being introduced (Law Society 2023).

The full effect of the UK finally embracing the principle of no-fault divorce will be clearer once the anticipated spike in applications has ceased. Writing as a practitioner with experience of the new divorce procedure, Jemimah Fleet commented in 2023 on some of the positive improvements that the new legislation have brought: modernisation of the process with applications being made online (via the HMCTS portal) and service of the proceedings by email; the saving of unnecessary costs and anguish at the start of proceedings in attempting to agree particulars of a petition and negotiate about costs; the removal of Latin terminology. The grounds for disputing or 'defending' a divorce application are now very limited (relating to jurisdiction or the validity/subsistence of the marriage) (Fleet 2023).

Judicial separation

In a limited number of cases, spouses whose relationships are in difficulties may not wish to divorce but nevertheless want formal legal recognition that they no longer have to fulfil the requirements of the marriage contract. They may have cultural or religious objection to divorce, or they may have not been married for the one-year period of marriage which is an essential requirement for a divorce petition, before divorce proceedings can be started, or they may not be ready emotionally to divorce.

Grounds for the decree

The Divorce, Dissolution and Separation Act 2020 has reformed the law on judicial separation. Just as in divorce it is no longer necessary to prove one of the five facts in order to obtain a decree

The law is laid down in s 2 of the 2020 Act.

It states as follows:

'(1) Either or both parties to a marriage may apply to the court for an order (a "judicial separation order") which provides for the separation of the parties to the marriage.

(1A) An application under subsection (1) must be accompanied by –
 (a) if the application is by one party to the marriage only, a statement by that person that they seek to be judicially separated from the other party to the marriage, or
 (b) if the application is by both parties to the marriage, a statement by them that they seek to be judicially separated from one another.
(1B) The court dealing with an application under subsection (1) must make a judicial separation order.'

Effect of a judicial separation order

As a result of the order the parties are relieved from the nebulous obligations of the marriage contract, but they may not remarry. They may use the evidence presented for the decree of judicial separation to obtain a decree of divorce at some time in the future should they wish to do so. One of the major advantages of seeking the decree is that the spouses may seek court orders to resolve their financial affairs and make arrangements for their children's future.

Civil partnerships

Dissolution (CPA 2004)

CPA 2004, ss 44–48 has been amended by the Divorce, Dissolution and Separation Act 2020 as follows:
 It allows for one or both parties to apply for dissolution of the partnership bringing it in line with the new rules on divorce. There is no longer a need to prove fault or facts. The party or parties must state that the partnership has irretrievably broken down. The court must take this statement as conclusive evidence and make the order.

Separation Orders (CPA 2004, ss 56, 57) (as amended by the DDSA 2020)
 A civil partner may apply for a separation order in the same way as a spouse may apply for a decree of judicial separation but again since the 2020 Act came into force there is no longer need to prove one of the five facts but instead merely request the court to make an order. Similar consequences result in that the separated civil partners may live apart free from the obligations and rights of civil partnership but not enter into a new civil partnership or marriage.

Divorce in the religious courts

There are two major types of religious courts in England, the Sharia courts and the Jewish Beth Din, which deal with matters relating to divorce for their members. The courts within the two faiths are not homogenous in their treatment of divorce. They reflect the divisions of faith within the communities and one court may be more liberal than another. The Catholic Tribunal does not deal with divorce but only with matters of nullity.

Although Muslim males may divorce by pronouncing a talaq (the words 'I divorce you') three times either consecutively or on three separate occasions, a Muslim woman may only divorce if she has her husband's consent. If he does not consent, the woman must apply to a Sharia court to obtain a divorce. There are three types of divorce process, depending on whether the parties agree on the divorce, whether the husband has broken or failed to fulfil the agreements made in the Nikah or if the wife is suffering oppression. These are: Khula, Faskh and Tafreeq.

Orthodox Jewish spouses will require a Jewish divorce, known as a *Get*, from the Beth Din if they wish to marry again within their faith and, thereby, ensure the Jewish legitimacy of the wife's future children, and their descendants, in any new marriage. A *Get* can be granted on mutual consent of the parties and fault does not have to be shown. The *Get* is only in the power of the husband, and he can refuse to grant it, putting considerable pressure on the wife if she wishes to remarry. Recently, Lucy Greenwood and Feriha Tayfur examined the challenges for a Jewish woman where she is married to a man who refuses to grant her a *Get* and the problem it presents to her if she wishes to marry again (Greenwood and Tayfur 2022).

English law does not recognise any decree granted by religious courts as a legal decree of divorce. The couple, if validly married under English law, would also have to obtain a civil divorce in order to remarry within the jurisdiction. However, these religious decrees may be important for members of the Muslim and Jewish faith who wish to marry again in accordance with their religious beliefs. They may also be important for Muslim women who are not validly married in accordance with English law and are, therefore, regarded only as cohabitants. These women would have no recourse to the English court for financial provision. They may be helped by the Sharia court which may persuade the husband to make provision for them in accordance with Islamic principles or an agreement made at the time of the religious marriage. The Sharia court cannot enforce financial provision but where there was an agreement between the spouses, a civil court will be able to enforce that agreement as a contract.

The MCA, s 10A provides that a court may delay granting the decree absolute until the spouses have obtained a religious divorce from the appropriate religious court. Only the Jewish religious court is included within s 10A, but other religions may make a request to be included within the provisions of the Act (s 10A(6)). This section has been retained by the 2020 Act.

Consequences of divorce

Once the decree absolute has been granted, the spouses are free to lead separate lives free from the legal responsibilities, and without the legal advantages, of marriage. They may marry a new partner or enter into a civil partnership should they so wish. However, for many divorced couples, their lives will remain intertwined both financially and with respect to their children.

When a divorce or a dissolution takes place there are many other additional matters which will need to be resolved, such as the future of the family home and financial arrangements between the spouses or partners and arrangements for any children of the relationship. These issues are considered in further detail in Chapter 7, Chapter 12 and Chapter 16.

Self-test questions

1. If marriage and civil partnerships are contracts, why should they not be able to be brought to an immediate end by mutual agreement?

2. Will the provisions of the Divorce, Dissolution and Separation Act 2020 bring to an end acrimony between a couple when they divorce? Discuss.

3. David and Edward entered into a civil partnership one year ago. David has decided that he is a bi-sexual and has been having a sexual relationship with Fenella for the last six months; they now wish to marry. Fenella has been married to George for four years. Edward wishes to enter into a new civil partnership with Harry. George wishes to marry Imogen who has never been married.

   Advise David, Edward, Fenella and George how they may legally enter into their desired new relationships.

4. Discuss the various alternative divorce models. Is the 'no-fault' version brought in by the Divorce, Dissolution and Separation Act 2020 in England and Wales the best solution for couples whose relationship has broken down?

References

Burton, Frances, 'Owens v Owens: A Most Curious Case' [2020] Denning Law Journal 5

The Christian Institute Apologetic (n.d.) www.christian.org.uk/theology/apologetics/marriage-and-family/divorce/

Collier, Richard, 'The Dashing of a Liberal Dream? The Information Meeting, the "New Family" and the Limits of the Law' [1999] Child and Family Law Quarterly 257

Cretney, Stephen, Family Law in the Twentieth Century (Oxford University Press 2005)

Deech, Ruth, 'Divorce a Disaster' [2009] Family Law 1049

Deech, Ruth, 'Divorce and Empirical Studies' [1990] Law Quarterly Review 229

Ellman, Iram, 'The Misguided Movement to Revive Fault Divorce and Why Reformers Should Look Instead to the American Law Institute' (1997) 11 International Journal of Law, Policy and the Family 216

Fleet, J. 'The First Year of "No-Fault" Divorce – What Is the Practical Impact of the New Law?' [2023] Family Law 183

Gov.UK, 'Family Court Statistics Quarterly: January to March 2023' (2023) www.gov.uk/governemt/statistics/family-court-statistics-quarterly-january-to-march-2023 (accessed 09.09.2024)

Greenwood, Lucy and Feriha Tayfur, 'The Importance of Obtaining a Recognised Jewish Get When Jewish Couples Divorce and What More Is Being Done to Protect "Chained" Wives' [2022] Family Law 108

www.historyofparliamentonline.org/volume/1660-1690/member/manners-john-1638-1711 (accessed 09.09.2024)

www.judiciary.uk/wp-content/uploads/2014/05/munby-press-conference-290420141.pdf (accessed 09.09.2024)

Law Commission, 'Reform of the Grounds of Divorce: Field of Choice' (Law Com 3123 1966) https://lawcom.gov.uk/project/reform-of-the-grounds-of-divorce-the-field-of-choice/

www.theguardian.com/lifeandstyle/2017/mar/24/tini-owens-trapped-loveless-marriage-judges-refuse-divorce

Law Society, 'No Fault Divorce One-Year On', 2023, www.lawsociety.org.uk/contact-or-visit-us/press-office/press-releases/no-fault-divorce-one-year-on

Morgan, Polly, 'The Public Tragedy of the Owen's Divorce (2019) 41(1) *Journal of Social Welfare and Family Law* 100 www.ons.gov.uk/peoplepopulationandcommunity/birthsdeathsand marriages/divorce

Phillips, Roderick, *Putting Asunder: A History of Divorce in Western Society* (Cambridge University Press 1988)

Ministry of Justice, Reform of the Legal Requirements for Divorce (September 2018) https://consult.justice.gov.uk/digital-communications/reform-of-the-legal-requirements-for-divorce/supporting_documents/reducingfamilyconflictconsultation.pdf

Shepherd, Nigel, 'Ending the Blame Game: Getting No Fault Divorce Back on the Agenda' [2009] *Family Law* 122

Stone, Lawrence, *Road to Divorce: England 1530–1987* (Oxford University Press 1990)

Trinder, Liz, Debbie Braybrook, Caroline Bryson, Lester Coleman, Catherine Houlston and Mark Sefton, *Finding Fault?* Divorce Law and Practice in England and Wales (Nuffield Foundation 2017)

Further reading

Bainham, Andrew, 'Men and Women Behaving Badly: Is Fault Dead in English Family Law?' (2001) 21(1) *Oxford Journal of Legal Studies* 219

Barton, Chris, 'So Farewell Then, Goodbye to the "Good" Bits' [2022] *Family Law* 620

Cretney, Stephen, 'Breaking the Shackles of Culture and Religion in the Field of Divorce' [2015] *International Family Law Journal* 19

Douglas, Gillian, Norman Doe Sophie Gilliat-Ray, Russell Sandberg, and Asma Khan, 'Marriage and Divorce in Religious Courts: A Case Study' [2011] *Family Law* 956

Family Justice Review www.justice.gov.uk/downloads/publications/policy/moj/ family-justice-review-final-report.pdf

Hale, B, 'The Family Law Act 1996: Dead Duck or Golden Goose' in S Cretney (ed), *Family Law: Essays for the New Millennium* (Blackwell Synergy 2000)

Haskey, John, 'A History of Divorce Law Reform in England and Wales: Evolution, Revolution or Repetition?' [2018] *Family Law* 1407

Law Commission, 'The Ground for Divorce' (Law Com No 192, 1990)

Law Commission, 'Looking to the Future, Mediation and the Ground for Divorce: The Government's Proposals' (Cm 2799, 1995)

Levy, Deborah, Joanna Uzoka and Caoinhe Sykes, 'A Brief Overview of the Issue Relating to the Recognition of Talaq and Get in the UK' [2019] *Family Law* 386

McFarlane, Andrew, '"Am I Bothered?" The Relevance of Religious Courts to a Civil Judge' [2011] *Family Law* 946

Munby, James, 'The Family Justice Reforms: Judicial Office' (Press Conference May 2014)

Rafia, Arshad, *Islamic Family Law* (Sweet & Maxwell 2010)

Thompson, Sharon, 'Against Divorce? Revisiting the Charge of the Casanova's Charter' [2021] *Child and Family Law Quarterly* 193

Welstead, Mary, 'Divorce in England and Wales – Time for Reform' [2012] *Denning Law Journal* 21

7

Financial consequences of relationships

SUMMARY

When a formal relationship such as marriage or a civil partnership breaks down and is ended by divorce or by dissolution a number of practical arrangements must be made in relation to the couple's finances. By contrast where an informal relationship breaks down, however long-standing, there is a marked difference in the approach of the law as the parties have little if any legal right to claim financial support from the other party. This chapter is divided into two interrelated sections. In Part I, we consider the law relating to the ownership of personal property and rights to maintenance during familial relationships, albeit ones which may be in the final stages of breakdown. In Part II, we consider the law relating to the redistribution of both real and personal property, and the rights to maintenance after a relationship has been brought to a legal end. In this chapter we will consider the legal rights that arise both during a legal relationship and those that arise once a relationship has been brought to a legal end. There is considerable dissatisfaction amongst practitioners, the judiciary and academics about the state of the law concerning financial arrangements on divorce and dissolution of relationships. Those who are involved criticise the system as for being slow, time consuming and costly. Currently the Law Commission is engaged in a project reviewing the law on financial remedies and is due to report its findings in November 2024. The current law is governed by the Matrimonial Causes Act 1973 and the Civil Partnership Act 2004 which largely reflects the 1973 Act. One of the questions being asked by the Law Commission is whether there is a need for a clear set of principles, enshrined in law, to give more certainty to divorcing couples. We will also consider the lack of remedies for those in an informal relationship. Financial matters relating to children are considered in Chapter 16.

When relationships end financial difficulties and property disputes tend to follow. Financial arrangements which were appropriate during a relationship normally have to be dismantled when the couple go their separate ways to begin their new lives.

The law relating to the reallocation of resources at the end of a relationship has been severely criticised by the judiciary, lawyers, academic commentators, as well as those who have been personally affected by it. However, the regular calls for reform have remained unheeded by the Government. As a consequence, the judiciary has felt forced to indulge in law making. The undesired and undesirable outcome of this is uncertainty and a proliferation of fact specific cases.

High profile settlements on divorce tend to dominate the news and media. Stories such as Brad Pitt and Angelina Jolie engaged in a legal battle for ownership of a property and vineyard in Provence 'Miraval' which cost 25m euros to buy but has taken eight years and legal costs well in excess of its actual value tend to distort the real picture of how most people settle their financial affairs on divorce. Nevertheless there are similarities in the way legal costs are incurred and the delays in agreeing the final settlement.

Part I ownership of personal property and rights to maintenance during a relationship

Personal property

Whether a couple is married, in a registered civil partnership, engaged to be married or planning to enter into a civil partnership or cohabiting, each partner retains the right to his or her own personal property during the currency of the relationship. English law has no concept of community of property, and strict property principles apply in any determination of ownership.

When a relationship is working, many partners are unconcerned about the precise legal ownership of property. Purchases are paid for in a haphazard way, often in accordance with the division of labour within the relationship, or the state of the bank balance of either partner. The person who is primarily responsible for the home and children tends to pay for food, clothes and general housekeeping items. Even in a post-feminist world, it is more likely to be the woman who takes care of such matters. More expensive capital items tend to be funded by the highest earner in the family whether or not they are for that person's individual use. Within a relationship ownership of property particularly property purchased during the relationship is rarely questioned. Couples tend to ask questions about who owns what only when problems arise in the relationship, or a third party wishes to dispute the rights of one of the couple over a specific item of property.

The law relating to the resolution of disputes about the ownership of personal property in the family context can only be described as a hotchpotch. It consists of outdated statutory provisions and the judiciary's liberal, or not so liberal, interpretation of equitable remedies or contracts. There are some limited statutory provisions which deal specifically with financial rights within a relationship.

Until 1857 with the recognition of divorce, property rights of married women on divorce had not arisen as a separate issue. There were also very few rights for women to own property in their own right. The passage of the 1870 and the 1882 Acts were turning points allowing married women to keep property in their own names. The Married Women's Property Act 1870 provided that wages and property which a wife earned through her own work or inherited would be regarded as her separate property, and the Married Women's Property Act 1882 extended this principle to all property, regardless of its source or the time of its acquisition (see generally Hayward 2018). Rights for financial provision have gradually been extended culminating in the Matrimonial Causes Act 1973 but as discussed earlier the current statutory provision is now in need of reform.

MARRIED WOMEN'S PROPERTY ACT 1882, S 17; CIVIL PARTNERSHIP ACT 2004, S 66

A spouse, former spouse, civil partner or former civil partner may apply to the court for determination of the ownership of disputed property. So may fiancés or those who have agreed to enter into a civil partnership, if they terminate their relationship.

The provisions of both Acts are merely procedural and provide for a rapid resolution of disputes but not for the redistribution of property between the couple. The provisions are rarely used.

Married Women's Property Act 1964, s 1

Where a husband gives his wife a housekeeping allowance, the Married Women's Property Act 1964 (MWPA 1964), s 1 provides that any items purchased out of that allowance, or any savings made from it, are to be treated as belonging equally to both spouses, unless they have agreed otherwise. Where one spouse purchases an item, which is obviously for his or her sole use, an agreement will normally be implied that it belongs to the person using the item.

The provision is gender-biased, paternalistic and out of date with the reality of twenty-first-century life. It does not apply where a wife gives her husband an allowance, nor does it apply to civil partners. Thus a husband or civil partner who receives an allowance from a partner and purchases a lottery ticket from that allowance will be able to retain the winnings, unless they have agreed otherwise. A wife in similar circumstances will only be allowed to retain 50 per cent of any winnings.

As long ago as 1985, the Law Commission recommended the abolition of the Act (*Matrimonial Property* (Law Com No 175, 1985)), but the recommendation was not followed. A Private Members' Bill was introduced in 2005 by Rob Marris MP; it would have extended the provision of the 1964 Act to husbands and civil partners. The Bill was withdrawn for lack of support in 2006. The provision was finally amended by s 200 of the Equality Act 2010 so it would apply to husbands and wives and civil partners in the same way.

Trusts

As discussed in relation to the family home (see Chapter 4) trusts can be a useful way in establishing rights over family property. Reliance on express trusts for rights over land can prove difficult because formalities must be adhered to, but for personal property a declaration can be informal so long as there is an express declaration of a trust. For a lay person the Law of Trusts can prove a minefield and recourse to its principles and rules seem a very heavy handed way of dealing with issues over ownership over personal property.

Express trusts

A partner who wishes to claim ownership of property by virtue of an express trust must show that the legal owner demonstrated a clear intention to share the property. Unlike express trusts of real property which are required to be in writing (see Chapter 4), words alone may be sufficient to ground an express trust of personal property.

In *Paul v Constance* [1977] 1 WLR 527, Mr Constance, who was separated from his wife, began to cohabit with Mrs Paul. He received £950 as damages for personal injuries, which he deposited in a bank account in his sole name. He told Mrs Paul on many occasions that the money was as much hers as his, and that she was free to draw on the account with his signed agreement. The couple deposited further monies, including their joint bingo winnings, into the account. Mr Constance died intestate, and his wife wished to claim the contents of the bank account.

The Court of Appeal held that to establish the existence of an express trust it had to be shown that there was clear evidence from what had been said or done of an intention to create a trust. Scarman LJ accepted that the words need not be in stilted lawyers' language; the couple were

> simple people, unaware of the subtleties of equity, but understanding very well indeed their own domestic situation.

The words used by Mr Constance on many occasions to indicate that the money in the deposit account was as much Mrs Paul's as his, were held to be sufficient to constitute an express declaration of trust.

In *Rowe v Prance* [1999] 2 FLR 787, the Court of Appeal also found an express trust of personal property based on informal words. Mr Prance was a married man who had had a relationship with Mrs Rowe for 14 years. They agreed that Mr Prance would buy a boat in his name, which they would share and realise their dreams that he would leave his wife and sail around the world together. Mrs Rowe sold her own home and stored her furniture. In frequent discussions, Mr Prance referred to the boat as 'ours' or 'our boat'. He reassured Mrs Rowe that the boat would provide financial security for her. However, as is so often the case, Mr Prance could not bring himself to leave his wife, and Mrs Rowe succeeded in her demand to have the boat sold and receive half the proceeds of sale.

Informal trusts

Where there is insufficient evidence for the court to find that there was an express trust of personal property, it may be prepared to accept that a resulting or constructive trust has come into existence. Similar principles apply to informal trusts of personal property as apply to informal trusts of real property.

It is unusual for couples to contract expressly with each other about the ownership of personal property. If they have a clear, shared intention to create a legally binding contract, and there is appropriate consideration, a court will give effect to it, provided it is not contrary to public policy. In recent years cohabitants have started to use cohabitation contracts or agreements which formalise their property matters.

Such contracts are subject to the usual requirements for valid contracts:

i.   an intention to create legal relations must be shown;

ii. the terms of the agreements must be certain;

iii. there is consideration unless the agreement is in the form of a deed.

There has been very little litigation concerning the enforceability of cohabitation agreements unlike claims for rights in the family home under the law of trusts or proprietary estoppel.

Rights to maintenance during the relationship

The abolition of a wife's right to be maintained at common law

At common law, a husband had a duty to maintain his wife by providing her with accommodation, food and other necessities. It is questionable whether this right was of any real value. She could not demand that her husband provide her with an allowance; she could merely attempt to pledge his credit to tradesmen and depend on their goodwill to provide her with her essential needs. This was known as the agency of necessity and was abolished by the Matrimonial Proceedings and Property Act 1970 (MPPA 1970). The common law right to maintenance was abolished by the Equality Act 2010, s 198.

Contracts for maintenance

The courts have been most reluctant to find contracts for maintenance during an ongoing relationship; they do not see the policing of personal relationships as part of their role. A very conservative approach has been taken, and there has been a tendency to find both a lack of an intention to create legal relations and an absence of consideration.

Statutory rights to maintenance

Matrimonial Causes Act 1973, s 27, Civil Partnership Act 2004, Sch 5, Part 9

A spouse may apply for an order for maintenance under the Matrimonial Causes Act 1973 (MCA 1973), s 27, and a civil partner under the Civil Partnership Act 2004 (CPA 2004), Sch 5, Part 9 on the ground that the respondent spouse or civil partner has failed to provide reasonable maintenance.

The court determines whether there has been a failure to maintain and after considering all the circumstances of the case, whether to make an award and, if so, its amount. Orders may be made for secured or unsecured periodical payments, or unlimited lump sums. Payments secured against a capital sum or against property may continue to be paid in the event of the death or bankruptcy of the payer. All orders terminate if the payee remarries or dies. Applications under the Act are rare; it is an expensive procedure, but an order was made under s 27 in *H v H* [2015] EWHC B24 (Fam) even though the marriage had been very short but where the financial disparity between the parties was very marked.

Domestic Proceedings and Magistrates' Courts Act 1978

Spouses who require maintenance are more likely to take advantage of the Domestic Proceedings and Magistrates' Courts Act 1978 (DPMCA 1978).

It is less costly to make an application under this Act than under the provisions of the MCA 1973, s 27, and the magistrates' courts are easily accessible to most couples throughout the country; there is such a court in all towns.

The grounds of application under the DPMCA 1978, s 1 are: failure to provide reasonable maintenance for the applicant or a child of the family, behaviour of such a nature that the applicant cannot reasonably be expected to live with the spouse, or desertion. It must be questioned why there is not simply one single ground – failure to provide reasonable maintenance. Behaviour and desertion are the obsolete, leftover remnants of the old fault-based legislation which allowed the magistrates to grant maintenance orders at the same time as granting separation orders for those partners who were not prepared to seek a divorce.

The DPMCA 1978 has been described as 'poor person's justice' because its provisions limit the magistrates' powers. They may only award unsecured periodical payments, or lump sums up to £1,000 (s 2) unless it is a consent order. The court may also ratify consent orders agreed by the parties, or make an order reflecting payments which have already been made on a voluntary basis (ss 6, 7). Unlike an order under the MCA 1973, s 27, any order made under the DPMCA 1978 will end if the parties continue to live together for longer than six months from the date of the order (s 25(1)). All orders end if the payee remarries or dies (s 4(2)). They will also end if the payer dies.

The court's discretion

In determining whether to make an order, and if so, the amount and type of order, the court must have regard to all the matters laid down in DPMCA 1978, s 3. The wide-ranging list is analogous to the statutory guidelines in the MCA 1973, s 25 (see later in this chapter). It includes the parties' financial resources and needs; their earning capacity; their standard of living; their ages; any disabilities which either of them may have; the contribution of either of them, in the past or the future, to the welfare of the family; and the conduct of the parties if the court thinks it would be inequitable to disregard it.

Conduct

The courts have tended to ignore negative conduct, unless it is very grave.

CIVIL PARTNERSHIP ACT 2004, SCH 6

Under the CPA 2004, Sch 6, civil partners have been given all the same rights to maintenance as those of spouses under the provisions of the DPMCA 1978.

Part II financial consequences of ending the relationship

A general overview

Whether a relationship ends by a decree or order of nullity, a decree of divorce or dissolution order, a decree of judicial separation or a separation order, the court has wide powers to redistribute the couple's property. This includes all personal and real property, any pre- or post-relationship settlements made for the benefit of the couple and their family, life insurance policies, trusts of personal and real property, and pensions.

There is a tension in the law relating to the re-ordering of the parties' financial affairs which has been dominated by **three recurring themes**:

- First, private negotiation versus judicial determination. Should parties have the freedom to decide their financial affairs without the intervention of the courts?
- Second, the imposition of a clean break which ends any financial relationship between the couple versus financial orders which ensure the continuation of the couple's financial relationship. To what extent should financial responsibilities remain after a relationship has broken down?
- Third, equal division of assets based on fairness versus unequal division based on needs. How does the law treat assets of the parties? Should they be divided equally or should there be unequal weighting towards the party who is financially less well off?

These three themes are played out as the courts attempt the difficult task of exercising the extensive discretion given to them to deal with the parties' resources, and reallocate them as it thinks fit under the provisions of the MCA 1973, the CPA 2004, and the Matrimonial and Family Proceedings Act 1984 Part III in the case of relationships which have been legally ended abroad.

These issues have been part of the general discourse surrounding the resolution of financial issues on divorce (Cretney 2003; Barlow 2015; Fisher and Low 2009; Eekelaar 2006).

This process of redistribution has three purposes:

- to compensate a partner for his or her past contribution to the relationship;
- to share any gains generated during the relationship;
- to provide maintenance, where necessary, for a partner's future needs.

This tripartite approach is not always made explicit in the case law; the strands often appear to be entangled and the decisions confusing.

To avoid the costly process of settling their affairs by court order, modern legal policy has tended to favour private negotiated settlements for spouses and civil partners. Couples are encouraged to consult mediators or lawyers to help them reach agreement. If they succeed in doing so, once the agreement has been reviewed by a judge, it may be incorporated into a court order known as a consent order.

Although the reported case law is dominated by accounts of wealthy couples battling it out in the courts, it must be stressed that, in practice, many couples will attempt to reach an agreement with each other. All too often their resources are so limited that they are barely sufficient to provide satisfactorily for the needs of both of the parties and concessions on both sides are inevitable. There are also those who have no resources about which they can dispute; one or both partners will be forced to rely on State benefits.

In spite of the emphasis on the importance of agreements to resolve financial disputes, there remains a reluctance on the part of the State, which is both paternalistic and self-serving, to allow spouses and civil partners to have complete freedom of bargaining. An uneasy compromise has been reached with respect to agreements negotiated in advance of relationship breakdown.

The legislation has been subjected to frequent criticism, primarily for its lack of an overall objective, its discretionary nature which leads to unpredictability and the general perception that it is unfair. It is for this reason that the Law Commission has decided to undertake a complete review of the law. The considerable discretion given to the courts and the lack of clear guidelines has resulted in uncertainty and costly court cases where a considerable amount of the assets of the parties are spent on the legal costs.

Once an application for a financial remedy has been made after the relationship has ended, spouses and civil partners risk the loss of that absolute control which they had over their individual finances and property during their relationship.

In *Hanlon v Law Society* (1981), Lord Denning described the court's task in language which is strongly reminiscent of a quasi-lucky dip; all the spousal property is placed in a large bag and mixed up together:

> *The court then takes out the pieces and hands them to the two parties – some to one party and some to the other – so that each can provide for the future with the pieces allotted to him or to her. The court hands them out without paying any too nice a regard to their legal or equitable rights but simply according to what is the fairest provision for the future, for mother, and father and the children.*

One might argue that the situation has not really improved since Lord Denning criticised the process. There have been a number of key decisions over the past 20 years such as the joint cases of *Miller v Miller/McFarlane v McFarlane* (2006) and the earlier case of *White v White* (2001) which have endeavoured to give guidance on the statutory provisions.

Cohabitants with no formal relationship have little choice other than to negotiate private agreements with each other; there are no statutory provisions to enable a court to make financial awards in their favour at the end of a relationship.

Engaged couples have recourse to the minimal statutory provision of the Law Reform (Miscellaneous Provisions) Act 1970 and prospective civil partners to the provision of the CPA 2004, s 74. For the most part, however, they too have no alternative other than to rely on privately negotiated agreements.

The court must be satisfied about the financial arrangements made by the parties on the ending of the marriage or civil partnership. The arrangements may be made between the parties without recourse to court but in many cases where the breakdown of their relationship is acrimonious then the only solution for the parties is to have recourse to the courts.

Reaching a financial settlement under the Matrimonial Causes Act 1973 (as amended by later legislation)

Step one

Before making an application to court the parties must first attend a mediation information and assessment meeting (MIAM). Such meetings have been introduced in order to divert as many cases away from the court process as possible. In his forward to the Family Justice Review in 2012 the Chair, David Norgrave wrote:

> In private law we recommend a series of changes aimed at helping more people to sort out their affairs for themselves while protecting the interests of their children. . . . Generally it seems better that parents resolve things for themselves if they can. They are more likely to come to an understanding that will allow arrangements to change as they and their children change.
>
> (Family Justice Review 2012)

The Review showed how few people were aware of alternatives to the court process. It recommended a greater use of mediation and alternative dispute resolution, and the MIAM meetings were introduced as a result. The meeting of up to two hours is paid for by the Legal Aid Agency. It will inform the couple about the availability of mediation and also provide funding for anyone who is eligible. There is no compulsion to proceed to mediation if one or both parties do not wish to proceed and the mediator may also declare that the case is not suitable for mediation. The mediator will then issue a form enabling the parties to proceed to court.

Step two

Before the parties can proceed to a hearing the court will issue a 'directions order' the purpose of this is to provide the other party with information about their financial position. Although there is a duty to provide this information there is a temptation to try to conceal information from the other party in attempt to project oneself as having a weaker financial profile. In *Sharland v Sharland* [2015] UKSC 60, the Supreme Court set aside a consent order when evidence was presented to the court by the wife that the husband had deliberately concealed the true value of his company. It should be noted that documents accessed illegally by either party cannot be used in a later financial provision hearing (*Tchenguiz v Imerman* [2010] EWCA Civ 908).

Step three

There is one further step to be taken which also tries to encourage settlement between the parties without recourse to the courts. This is the Financial Dispute Resolution Appointment. It is a hearing before the judge who listens to the arguments of the parties and gives advice about their respective positions and feasibility of their arguments. If the case proceeds to a full hearing then the judge hearing the FDR will not be the judge at the final hearing. Many cases will settle at this stage or even between this hearing and the final hearing. In research carried out by Emma Hitchings et al. (2014) it was found that a settlement is usually reached through the solicitors acting for each party who negotiate to find a settlement that both accept. The timing of such a settlement depends on a number of factors such as the complexity of the case but also the emotional readiness of each party to reach a settlement which often comes as time passes. Parties tend to be distrustful of each other in the early stages of negotiation.

Step four

If a settlement has not been reached, then the last stage is a final hearing before a judge. Evidence will be heard from both parties and representations will be made on behalf of both parties. The judge will make an order on the basis of what is 'fair'. According to Ministry of Justice statistics 111,369 matrimonial cases – divorces, annulments and separations and 43,190 financial remedy cases (formerly known as 'ancillary relief') – financial provisions after divorce or relationship breakdown were started between January and December 2023 (https://data.justice.gov.uk/courts/family-courts). Of the applications for financial remedy, only a fraction proceed to a final hearing.

Orders available to the court

The orders available to the court fall into three categories:

- financial awards;
- property adjustment orders;
- pension orders.

Financial awards

maintenance prior to the legal ending of the relationship (MCA, s 34; CPA Schedule 5, s 38)
    In any application to legally end the relationship, the spouse or civil partner may apply for an interim order for maintenance.

Divorce proceedings take time, and one party may be in immediate financial need whilst these take place.

secured or unsecured periodical payments (MCA 1973, s 23; CPA Schedule 5, s 2)

Provided that a former spouse has not re-married or a civil partner has not entered into a new civil partnership, an application may be made for periodical payments or spousal maintenance. A former spouse or civil partner who cohabits rather than entering into a new legal relationship is not excluded from making an application. However, the cohabitation may be one of the factors the court will take into account in deciding whether to grant the application (see e.g. *Grey v Grey (No 3)* [2010] Fam Law 440).

The payments are made at regular intervals or, more unusually, may be capitalised and paid as a lump sum (see e.g. *Yates v Yates* [2012] EWCA Civ 532). They are normally made for the payee's maintenance but where there is insufficient capital available at the time of the divorce, the payments may be made to compensate a partner for his or her past contribution to the relationship. The order for payments may be nominal where the payer has insufficient income. This leaves open the possibility for the payee to make an application for the payments to be varied if the payer's income increases or the payer acquires capital at a future date. The order for payments may be long term or limited to a specific period of time if there is an expectation that the payee will become self-sufficient at some time in the future. Over the past 25 years the case law in this area tends to be dominated by high profile high money cases. These cases then set the rules for more modest cases of low profile parties.

In *Parlour v Parlour* [2004] EWCA Civ 872, the Arsenal footballer Ray Parlour was ordered to pay his ex-wife substantial periodical payments of £444,000 a year for four years, after which they would be reviewed. The award represented one-third of his future earnings. Mr Parlour had been a heavy drinker during the marriage. Mrs Parlour had realised that this problem was almost certain to ruin his career chances, and she had endeavoured to help him to change his lifestyle. Mr Parlour publicly praised her for her care and encouragement to overcome the problem, and he subsequently played for England and received the ultimate footballer's accolade of an English cap on ten different occasions.

The court accepted that there was insufficient capital to compensate Mrs Parlour adequately at the time of the divorce. However, Mr Parlour's earnings were exceptionally high, and well in excess of what was required for the reasonable needs of both parties. It was only fair that Mrs Parlour should receive a significant share of them; her husband's earnings would decline fairly rapidly, as he grew older and became unable to continue to play competitive football. The high award was not only for Mrs Parlour's current maintenance but also to allow her to save and provide for her future and become financially independent as soon as possible.

All periodical payments are a high-risk solution for the recipients because they end automatically on their remarriage or death, or on the death of the payer (MCA 1973, s 28; CPA 2004 Schedule 5, s 13) unless they have been secured against the payer's assets. Today it is unusual for periodical payments to be secured against an asset of the payer. The legislation ignores the fact that the payments may have been awarded as compensation for a spouse or civil partner's contribution to the relationship. Periodical payments may be viewed as a serious disincentive for the payee to consider entering into a new legal relationship, particularly if the court does not place a time limit on the payments. Payees who die lose the possibility of leaving what they had rightfully gained for their contribution during a relationship to their children or other beneficiaries. In such circumstances, the payer, or his or her estate, gains an unfair benefit.

Variation of periodical payments

If the parties' circumstances change after an award of periodical payments, either partner may apply to the court for a variation, discharge, or suspension of the payments, or a replacement of them with a capital order (MCA 1973, s 31; CPA, Schedule 5, s 51). When considering the application, the court also has the discretion to remit any arrears of periodical payments (MCA 1973, 32(1); CPA 2004, Schedule 5, s 52).

In *I v I* [2008] 1 FLR 201, the spouses had agreed a consent order, which included periodical payments, at a time when the husband had a draft contract for new employment which would give him a higher income. He failed to tell his wife about this matter. When he later began the new employment, the wife applied for the consent order to be set aside. The court held that the husband had been in breach of his duty to make full and frank disclosure of his circumstances. However, in deciding whether to set aside the order, the court had to consider what it would have done at the time of the original consent order had it had the information which the husband had withheld. Because the new employment was only a possibility at the time the consent order was made, the court would not have acted differently. The wife's application was refused.

A payee who wishes to remarry or enter into a new civil partnership, and whose periodical payments were compensatory rather than needs related, may be well advised to apply for an order of variation and for the periodical payments to be replaced with a capital order if possible. The capital order may be paid in instalments which, unlike periodical payments, may continue if the payee remarries or enters into a new civil partnership.

The payee's cohabitation with a new partner does not necessarily end periodical payments. If a request for variation is made, the court may take into account any actual or implied contribution of the payee's new partner.

In *Fleming v Fleming* [2003] 1 EWCA 1841 (Civ), a consent order was made which gave the wife, who was cohabiting with a new partner at that time, payments of £1,000 per month for four years. There was no provision in the order to prevent an application to extend the payments beyond that time. Shortly before the expiry date, the wife returned to court and asked for a variation of the order. The court held that cohabitation could not be treated in the same way as marriage which would automatically bring to an end the periodical payments. Nevertheless, the court should have regard to the cohabitation, including its financial consequences and its duration. Quite reasonably, the husband had an expectation that the payments would end four years after the order was made, and only in exceptional circumstances should that expectation be frustrated. The wife and her cohabitant had sufficient resources between them for their needs. The wife's application was refused.

LUMP SUM ORDERS (MCA 1973, S 23; CPA 2004, SCHEDULE 5, S 2)

Where there is sufficient capital, most spouses or civil partners are likely to prefer an order which allows complete freedom of control over their future finances. A capital order, in the form of an outright transfer of a lump sum or shares or instalment payments, will permit that control. The court may order sale of a partner's property to allow a capital order to be made.

Unlike periodical payments, the instalments of a capital transfer order will survive the remarriage or new civil partnership of a payee, and may survive the death of a payer as a charge against his or her estate.

PROPERTY ADJUSTMENT ORDERS (MCA 1973, S 24; CPA 2004, SCHEDULE 5, S 7)

For most couples, the family home will be their most important asset. Where it is of sufficient value, the court may order sale of the house and divide the proceeds between the parties to enable them to purchase individual properties. However, in many cases, the family home will not yield sufficient capital to allow for this. Alternative orders, which will allow one party to remain in the family home without doing too great an injustice to the other, will be necessary.

Transfer of property

Where one partner has sufficient capital, the other may be awarded a lump sum in return for the transfer of the family home. If there is insufficient capital to pay for such a transfer, a partner may be given the family home in return for renouncing any claim for periodical payments or for agreeing to a reduction in periodical payments.

Mesher orders

The court may make what is known as a Mesher order (see *Mesher v Mesher* [1980] 1 All ER 126). These orders, which go in and out of favour with the court, tend to be used only where there is insufficient capital to provide homes for both parties. The order provides for sale of the property at a specified point in the future such as when the children reach the age of 18 or complete their education.

One of the major drawbacks to Mesher orders is that they leave those partners who remain in the family home with a false sense of security and delay them from facing the reality of the future rather than seeking gainful employment. When the house is sold, they will have to find a new home at a time when financial resources or career potential to enable them to do so may be at their lowest ebb.

In *Dorney-Kingdom v Dorney-Kingdom* [2000] 2 FLR 855, Thorpe LJ recognised that Mesher orders could produce

> *a harsh situation in which the primary carer having discharged her responsibility to the children is then left in a position when she is unable to re-house herself as an independent person probably at a relatively vulnerable stage of life.*

However, he decided to grant the order because the family home was of sufficient value that the woman could be re-housed and the man adequately compensated on sale of the property at a time when the children would no longer need to be housed.

In *B v B (Mesher Order)* [2003] 2 FLR 285 the court declined to grant a Mesher order. It held that it was not appropriate to do so because the woman would make a significant contribution in the future by bringing up the child who was very young at the time of the court hearing. Her own income and future career opportunities would be severely affected. The man would very rapidly be able to recoup the cost to him of an outright transfer of the property to his ex–wife.

Martin orders

Martin orders, named after the decision in *Martin v Martin* [1978] Fam 12, are not dissimilar to Mesher orders and were devised to overcome the problems of Mesher orders. A Martin order allows a partner to remain in the family home for as long as he or she wishes or until the occurrence of an event, such as remarriage, a new civil partnership, cohabitation or death, when the property will be sold and the proceeds distributed in accordance with the court order.

In *Martin*, the husband had already been rehoused in council accommodation. The court allowed the wife to remain in occupation of the family home. A deferred sale under a Mesher order would not have given her sufficient money to purchase a new home for herself. She too would have required to be re-housed by the local authority.

One of the problems with both Mesher and Martin orders is that they keep the parties trapped into a financial relationship with each other which appears to conflict with the 'clean break principle' discussed later.

Where a capital order or orders relating to the family home were made in divorce, dissolution or nullity proceedings, they must normally be regarded as final unless exceptional circumstances arise. If this were not so, couples might be left with the permanent yet uncertain hope that, in the event of a dramatic change of fortune in the affairs of one of the partners, an application could be made to vary the original order. The courts have shown themselves most reluctant to vary orders. Their concern has been, insofar as is possible, to allow couples that certainty which will enable them to reorganise their lives as individuals and move forward.

Where the capital payments are ordered to be made by instalments, an application for variation is possible whilst any of the instalments remain outstanding (see *Myerson v Myerson No 2* (2009) later in this chapter).

Leave to appeal

A partner who wishes to have a capital order varied must first obtain the leave of the court. Secondly, if leave to appeal is granted, the court must take into account all the new facts before it, in determining whether to vary the order and, if so, what the new order should be. The courts appear to exercise their discretion on a case by case basis. The decisions are not easy to reconcile; they appear to contain elements of a generalised, and often, unarticulated view of fairness.

In *Barder v Barder* [1988] AC 20, the House of Lords laid down four conditions for a successful application for leave to appeal:

- there must have been a change of circumstances which occurred after the grant of the order; and which invalidated the basis on which it was made;

- the event must have occurred soon after the making of the original order;
- the application for leave should be made promptly;
- third parties must not be prejudiced by the grant of leave to appeal an original order.

In *Barder*, a consent order had been made, under which the husband was to transfer his share in the family home to his wife in order to end all further obligations between them. Five weeks later, the wife killed their two children and committed suicide. She left a will naming her mother as the beneficiary. The House of Lords held that the consent order had been based on the basic assumption that the wife and children would require a home for a substantial period of time, and that that assumption had been totally negated by their deaths. The husband's application for leave to appeal the original order was allowed.

In *Livesey v Jenkins* [1985] 1 AC 424, by a consent order, the husband transferred his half-share in the matrimonial home to the wife on the basis that she would live there and provide a home for herself and the children. She would also take over responsibility for the mortgage payments. Immediately prior to the making of the order, the wife became engaged and actually married two days after the family home was transferred to her. On hearing the news of her marriage, the husband successfully applied for leave to appeal the consent order. The House of Lords held that the court could not properly exercise its discretion under the MCA 1973 without adequate information on all the matters which it was required to consider. Each spouse owed a duty to each other and to the court to disclose any relevant facts; an intention to marry was one of them (see also *Bokor-Ingram v Boker-Ingram* [2009] EWCA Civ 412 where the court was prepared to set aside a *Mesher* order on the grounds of non-disclosure of facts by the husband, in this case that he was about to get a much better paid job).

Looking afresh

Once leave to appeal has been granted, the courts have stressed that in determining whether to grant a variation or not, although the matter is looked at afresh, the basis on which leave to appeal was granted is of prime importance.

The economic downturn led the husband in *Myerson v Myerson (No 2)* [2009] 2 FLR 147 to ask for a variation of a consent order. He and his wife had agreed that she should receive £11 million (43 per cent of the total assets) to be paid partly in instalments and partly in property transfer, and he would retain £14.5 million (57 per cent of the total assets).

The assets to be retained by Mr Myerson were primarily shares in his company plus various properties. When the global economy collapsed, his company's share price collapsed with it. This meant that his share of the assets dropped to 14 per cent and his wife's to 86 per cent.

The Court of Appeal gave Mr Myerson leave to appeal but refused to grant the appeal. By the time the appeal was heard the share prices had deteriorated still further, and the consent order would have left the husband with almost nothing. He argued that the fall in share prices meant that the consent order was unfair and unworkable, and that the relevant events were sufficiently dramatic to constitute new events as in **Barder** (1988). The Court of Appeal held that the natural processes of price fluctuations, however dramatic, were insufficient to allow the husband's appeal. He had agreed an order leaving him in control of both profits and losses of his shares which was speculative, and there was no justification to relieve him of the consequences of his agreement. The husband continued to enjoy control of the opportunities that went with the speculation (see also *Walkden v Walkden* [2009] 3 FCR 25).

Several cases came before the court where a claimant argued that the effect of the Covid pandemic was a reason to reopen a financial settlement. In *FRB v DRC (No 3)* [2020] EWHC 3696 (Fam), a very wealthy husband sought to reopen the settlement made in March 2020 in favour of his wife. The proceedings had been running since 2017, and the final settlement included the transfer of the former matrimonial home and payment of the outstanding mortgage as well as a lump sum payable in two instalments with interest payable if repayment was late. In addition annual periodical payments of £720k were ordered. He failed to transfer the home or pay the lump sums as agreed. Cohen J looked at the impact of the pandemic on his finances but concluded that it was not such that the order should be reopened.

A similar conclusion was reached in *HW v WW* [2021] EWFC B20; although the judge accepted that the pandemic could be seen as an intervening event which could in some circumstances allow an order to be reopened, the facts of this case were not such that it applied. HHJ Kloss stated:

> *The Covid 19 pandemic is an extraordinary event, different in nature and scale, to any similar world event in the lifetime of the parties. This is not an issue of market volatility which is periodically experienced, neither is it a national issue with predictable localised causes. It is akin to a war, with tentacles spreading across the world. I therefore find that in principle, the Covid 19 pandemic can open the door to a successful Barder claim.*

The Covid pandemic was also raised in *BT v CU* [2021] EWFC 87 where a husband who ran a company supplying meals for schools was directly impacted by the Covid pandemic. The court dismissed his application which sought to argue that Covid and its effects were unforeseen and unforeseeable, thereby falling outside the natural processes of price fluctuation. A similar argument had been raised over 25 years earlier in the case of *Cornick v Cornick* [1994] 2 FLR 530. (For a more general discussion of the effects of the Covid pandemic as a *Barder* event see Foy (2021).) In this case the wife was originally awarded a capital order which was equivalent to 50 per cent of the value of her husband's assets (she also obtained an order for periodical payments). Soon after the divorce, the husband's shares rose substantially in value. The court refused the wife's application for leave to appeal to set aside the original order. There had been no mistake made in the calculation of the shares and their sudden ascent was a fortuitous event. This did not constitute a sufficient change to invalidate the basis of the original order. This illustrates that the courts are very reluctant to apply *Barder* save for in the most exceptional circumstances since there are often fluctuations both up and down in valuations of assets.

PENSION ORDERS (MCA 1973, S 24(B), (C), (D); CPA 2004, SCHEDULE 5, PART 4A)

After the family home, pensions are usually a partner's next most valuable asset. Prior to 1996, the court had no power to directly re-allocate pension benefits. It could merely attempt to compensate a partner who risked the loss of pension benefits at the end of the relationship if there were sufficient resources to do so. The award of a lump sum payment, property settlement or additional periodical payments could be used to offset the loss ('pension offsetting'). Since 1996, through a succession of Acts, the courts have the power to deal more directly with pension benefits, although offsetting, of course, continues to remain a possibility.

Attachment orders: The Pensions Act 1995 gave the courts power to make earmarking orders ('pension earmarking'), now known as 'attachment orders'. These orders set aside a portion of the pension for the benefit of an ex-spouse and, since 2005, for the benefit of a civil partner, when the pension eventually comes on stream on a partner's retirement. These orders have proven to be unpopular and problematic. A former partner has no control over a beneficiary of a pension scheme who decides to delay the commencement of his or her pension beyond the proposed retirement date. If the former partner enters into a new legal relationship, he or she will lose the right to the income part of the pension, and he or she may also lose the lump sum portion of the pension because the court has the power to vary it prior to the pension holder's retirement. If the beneficiary dies prior to retirement, the benefits to the former partner will be reduced.

Pension sharing orders: In an attempt to deal with these problems, the Welfare Reform and Pensions Act 1999 introduced 'pension-sharing orders' for spouses and, since 2005, for civil partners. At the time of the divorce, or dissolution of the civil partnership, the pension will be valued and a transfer of a proportion of it made to the former partner (see *Lawrence v Gallagher* [2012] EWCA Civ 394. He or she may then add to that portion and build up a pension fund in his or her own right and under his or her own control. The significance of this is that it represents a clean break between the parties. it is less flexible because it does not allow the recipient to draw his/her share early, but it does mean the pension continues in existence even if the former partner dies or the recipient remarries or enters into a civil partnership.

In research carried out by Hilary Woodward on financial settlements of 369 court files she found that a very small minority used pension sharing orders, as most couples preferred the 'clean break' provisions where the pension value was offset by a payment of capital. Her work concluded also that the lack of orders may in fact be masking potential long-term unfairness between husbands and wives through poor quality pension disclosure (Woodward 2015).

The Exercise of the Court's Discretion – the Demise of the Statutory Guidelines (MCA 1973, s 25; CPA 2004, Schedule 5, s 21)

A lack of overall guiding objective

In Part I of this chapter, it was noted that there is no concept of community of property during a marriage or civil partnership in England and Wales; each partner has total freedom to deal with his or her own financial resources. It is not, therefore, surprising that many partners resent the power given to the court to redistribute property, which has up to that point belonged solely to one of them, when their relationship ends. Furthermore, they have no means of knowing in advance what form that redistribution will take; the court has total discretion over this reallocation process.

A certain sympathy should also be expressed for the judiciary, who have to deal with applications for financial orders, because the statutory guidelines lack any overall guiding objective to help them determine ones which may be viewed as fair, principled and predictable.

The decisions on financial orders are mainly cases about married couples, but *Lawrence v Gallagher* (2012) is an exception involving civil partners and it should be remembered that the principles will be equally applicable to civil partners as Thorpe LJ pointed out in **Lawrence**.

Judicial intervention

The lack of clear guidance from the legislation has given the courts a free hand in trying to formulate guidelines when making financial awards. Over the years principles have been developed, but the final result is still often uncertain. Practitioners have no choice but to advise the parties that the final outcome has much to do with individual judges. In cases where the family home, pensions and family assets are at stake this is far from ideal.

In *Cowan v Cowan* [2001] EWCA Civ 679, Thorpe LJ acknowledged that couples seeking advice from solicitors were often told that the order would all depend on the judge on the day. If the law was in such a state, how could sensible couples plan their future and reach agreements? He defended the fact that, in the absence of reform by Parliament, the judiciary had been forced to develop various mechanisms, which had no statutory basis, to help them reach decisions. This was written in 2001 and nearly 25 years later practitioners still advise that a final settlement on divorce or dissolution if a civil partnership is difficult to predict.

Guidance from case law

Several guiding principles have emerged over the past few years which have been applied in subsequent cases. The uncertainty lies in the degree of weight to be given to each guiding principle.

In *White v White* [2001] 1 AC 596, the House of Lords, and in *Lambert v Lambert* [2003] Fam 103, the Court of Appeal, used the concept of fairness as the guiding principle in the reallocation of property on divorce but also emphasised that all the factors in MCA 1973, s 25 should be considered to ensure a fair outcome for the parties. They maintained that there should be no discrimination between the contributions made by a husband and wife in their respective roles. Any proposed award should be checked against the yardstick of equality, and where appropriate, this could lead to an equal division of the assets.

The decisions led to confusion and debate about the circumstances in which equal division of assets would be a fair outcome. Nevertheless *White* does represent a turning point in the way the courts dealt with cases on financial provision. The fact that the term 'yardstick of equality' was introduced opened the possibility of a change in the legal approach and discourse surrounding distribution of assets on divorce. Alison Diduck refers to *White* as 'an altering of the narrative' and 'moving the courts away from the traditional family values of provider/dependent' (Diduck 2011).

The decisions in Miller v Miller; McFarlane v McFarlane *(2006)*

In the absence of Parliament's willingness to reform the law, the House of Lords, in the conjoined decisions of *Miller v Miller; McFarlane v McFarlane* [2006] UKHL indulged in judicial law. Their Lordships put a gloss on s 25 of the MCA 1973 and introduced principles, which they claimed to be consistent, practical and fair and would serve as clear guidelines in any future determination of the reallocation of spousal assets. Baroness Hale stressed the importance of finding a way forward to ensure

> *that so far as possible like cases are treated alike but also to enable and encourage the parties to negotiate their own solutions as quickly and cheaply as possible.*

Mr and Mrs Miller, who were both in their 30s, divorced after a short childless marriage of three years. On marriage, Mrs Miller had modified her career plans and, thereby, reduced her income. At that time, her husband was a successful fund manager with an income in excess of £1 million per year. He also owned shares worth £20 million. After the marriage, Mr Miller joined a new company and acquired £200,000 of shares which at the time of the divorce, had increased in value to around £15 million.

Mrs Miller was awarded a lump sum of £5 million and Mr Miller appealed. The Court of Appeal upheld the award which represented around 16 per cent of Mr Miller's total worth. The Appeal Court justified this significant award, in the context of such a short marriage, partly on the ground that the husband was responsible for the breakdown of the marriage; he had had an affair with another woman whom he subsequently married and with whom he had a child. The Court of Appeal, rather confusingly, stated that this was not conduct which should be taken into account under the MCA 1973, s 25(2)(g).

Mr Miller appealed and the House of Lords, whilst accepting that the award to Mrs Miller was at the upper limit in the light of a short marriage, dismissed his appeal.

By contrast, Mr and Mrs McFarlane had three children and had been married for 16 years. Mrs McFarlane had practised as a solicitor with Freshfields, a high-ranking London law firm. She gave up her career to enable her to care for the family and to help her husband advance his career as an accountant. On divorce, the husband had an annual salary of

£750,000 and capital of £3 million which consisted primarily of three family homes. The couple agreed to divide the capital equally between them, but, in the context of the husband's high earnings and the wife's sacrifice of her own career, this was viewed as inadequate compensation. She applied for and was given periodical payments of £250,000 per annum. The Court of Appeal restricted these to a five-year period; Mrs McFarlane appealed against this restriction. The House of Lords granted her appeal.

Lord Nicholls and Baroness Hale gave the two leading judgments. Their Lordships clarified the confusion relating to the issue of conduct, and the purpose of periodical payments. They reiterated that negative conduct should not be taken into account in assessing the size of an award unless it is of an extreme nature which it thought was not the case in the Miller's marriage. Positive conduct, on the other hand, could be taken into account. They also acknowledged that periodical payments are not merely limited to maintenance.

Baroness Hale stated that the overall aim of the court should be to set the parties on the road to independent living, and, in agreement with Lord Nicholls, centred her judgment on the concept of fairness. Both maintained that it should be the overarching principle in the determination of any award. According to Lord Nicholls, the concept of fairness is elusive:

> *it is an instinctive response to a given set of facts. Ultimately it is grounded in social and moral values. These values, or attitudes, can be stated. But they cannot be justified, or refuted, by any objective process of logical reasoning. Moreover, they change from one generation to the next. It is not surprising therefore that in the present context there can be different views on the requirements of fairness in any particular case.*

Given this acceptance of the relativist nature of fairness, it is interesting to note that Lord Nicholls had little difficulty in expounding, with Baroness Hale's agreement, the three elements of fairness:

- first, fairness requires that the needs of the spouses and their children, generated by the relationship, should be satisfied and for most couples there are insufficient resources to do more than that;

- second, fairness requires compensation to redress any future economic imbalance between the spouses as a result of the way in which they conducted their marriage. For instance, a husband's income earning capacity may have been increased because of his wife's supportive role in caring for the family. On divorce, the wife's earning capacity will almost certainly be less than had she worked throughout the marriage. She also loses the possibility of sharing in her husband's increased income, a possibility which may have been envisaged if she gave up work to help him in his career ambitions;

- third, fairness requires an equal sharing of the assets acquired during the marriage unless there is good reason to do otherwise. This was a natural conclusion from the fact that marriage is an equal partnership. Special and exceptional contributions should not be taken into account unless it would be inequitable to ignore them.

All three elements, according to Lord Nicholls:

> *are linked to the parties' relationship, either causally or temporally, and not to extrinsic, unrelated factors, such as a disability arising after the marriage has ended.*

Lord Nicholls' view had changed dramatically since his judgment in *White v White* (2000) where he stated that:

> *s 25 of the 1973 Act makes no mention of an equal sharing of the parties' assets, even their marriage-related assets. A presumption of equal division would be an impermissible judicial gloss on the statutory provision. That would be so, even though the presumption would be rebuttable. Whether there should be such a presumption in England and Wales, and in respect of what assets, is a matter for Parliament.*

Perhaps the most important and complex part of the judgment was the approach of Lord Nicholls and Baroness Hale to the categorisation, and subsequent division, of a couple's assets into 'matrimonial' and 'non-matrimonial' assets. The fact that the concept of 'matrimonial assets' does not exist in English law did not deter them. Lord Nicholls defined 'matrimonial assets' as the family home, however and whenever it was obtained, even one owned prior to marriage. He also included all other assets, which had been acquired during the marriage, other than gifts or inherited property. Property acquired prior to the marriage was excluded from his definition.

Baroness Hale added to Lord Nicholls list of 'matrimonial assets' the spouses' earning capacity. She excluded business or investment assets which had been unilaterally, or mainly, acquired by the efforts of one of the spouses. She believed that it was difficult to prove that these latter assets had been created with the help of the spouse who stayed at home, even if that support was a valuable contribution to the welfare and happiness of the family. She viewed these assets as speculative and risky; the spouse to whom they did not belong may not have shared in that risk.

Lord Nicholls and Baroness Hale agreed that 'matrimonial assets', but not 'non-matrimonial assets', should normally be divided equally. 'Non-matrimonial assets' might also be subject to reallocation depending on all the circumstances of the case. A short marriage, for instance, might be a good reason not to redistribute them between the spouses. Lord Nicholls had

> *an instinctive feeling that parties will generally have less call upon each other on the breakdown of a short marriage.*

Baroness Hale believed that there was

> *a perception that the size of the non-business partner's share should be linked to the length of the marriage.*

The decision in *Miller and McFarlane* (2006) which had promised principles and clarification, left so much unresolved. In particular, it failed to resolve:

- how needs should be quantified; Lady Hale identified 'needs' as those generated by the marriage but of course this issue is far more complex as cases will differ according to facts such as whether there are children/dependent relatives or whether either party suffers from a disability. Tom Hynes considered the challenges presented to lawyers in trying to meet 'needs' where there are limited assets (Hynes 2020).

'Needs' may also vary if the application for a financial remedy is brought sometime after the divorce as discussed in *Wyatt v Vince* [2015] UKSC 14.

■ the nature of 'matrimonial property' and how it differs from 'non-matrimonial property'; the definition of what constitutes 'matrimonial property' still troubles the judiciary. Some property naturally falls into the category such as the matrimonial home. Even where property is considered to be a 'non-matrimonial' asset it may still be brought into the equation of what is necessary to satisfy 'needs'. Bethany Hardwick of St Johns Chambers has sought to identify the approach taken towards assets as 'scientific' or 'artistic'. The 'scientific' approach seeks to initially identify all assets as being of either group and then essentially 'ring fences' non-matrimonial assets which have not become mingled during the marriage whereas the 'artistic' approach is broader brushed allowing equal division of all assets but accepting certain assets should be treated separately. This prevents the problems that arise where in a long marriage assets become mingled through joint use and enjoyment (Hardwick 2016).

■ the circumstances in which 'matrimonial property should be unequally distributed and the circumstances in which non-matrimonial property might be subject to distribution, equal or otherwise. Decisions since *Miller and McFarlane* (2006) have rarely ordered equal distribution on non-matrimonial property as stated by Mostyn J: 'Given that a claim to *share* non-matrimonial property (as opposed to having a sum awarded from it to meet needs) would have no moral or principled foundation it is hard to envisage a case where such an award would be made. If you like, such a case would be rare as a white leopard' (see *JL v SL* [2015] EWHC 360 (Fam)).

■ the relationship between the principle of fairness and s 25 of the MCA 1973. 'Fairness' was identified as the guiding principle in *White*, but applying it in practice is difficult as often a 'fair' outcome for one party may not be 'fair' for the other. Writing in 2011 Alison Diduck observed that: 'the judicially created objective of fairness is said by many to be indeterminate and to lack principled foundation.' She reflects on the move towards a principle of equality by the courts as not necessarily resulting in 'fair' decisions (Diduck 2011).

A return to the statutory guidelines

In *Charman v Charman (No 4)* [2007] FLR 1246, the Court of Appeal attempted to clarify the issues raised in *Miller and McFarlane*, and, in doing so, emphasised the importance of the statutory guidelines.

Mr and Mrs Charman met and married when they were very young and had no assets. At first, the wife worked as a civil servant until she became pregnant with the first of the couple's two children. The husband started his career as a junior clerk at Lloyds, and enjoyed a dramatic rise in the insurance industry. After 28 years of marriage, the couple decided to divorce. By this time their assets were valued at £131 million. Mrs Charman accepted that her husband had made a special contribution to the creation of this wealth and asked for a 45 per cent share of the assets to reflect this. Her husband offered her £20 million (a little over 15 per cent of the assets). The judge awarded Mrs Charman £48 million (36.5 per cent of the assets) having acknowledged Mr Charman's special contribution, and the future risk he would face with respect to the assets which he retained.

Mr Charman appealed; he maintained that the judge had made insufficient allowance for his special contribution and that he should have first considered the factors in s 25 of the MCA 1973 before determining the percentage division. Furthermore, he should have not included for division the £68 million of assets held in an offshore discretionary trust.

The Court of Appeal dismissed the husband's appeal. It maintained that:

- the starting point when determining financial awards clearly has to be the financial position of the couple;
- the court must then apply the guidelines in s 25(2) of the MCA (1973) to the facts and not in any particular order;
- the court need not postpone its consideration of the principle of equal sharing until after its consideration of s 25(2); the two go hand in hand;
- any decision to depart from equal sharing is part of the principle of equal sharing;
- all of the couple's assets are subject to the principle of equal sharing but the nature of the assets – e.g. 'non-matrimonial property' – may make it more likely that they should be shared unequally. Lady Hale's view, in *Miller and McFarlane*, of 'unilateral assets' which should be excluded from division, would lead to an unfair outcome;
- where the application of the three principles of fairness – needs, compensation and sharing – would give rise to conflicting outcomes, fairness must rule. If the result suggested by the needs principle is an award higher than that suggested by the sharing principle, the needs principle should determine the outcome. If the needs principle suggests a lower award than that suggested by the sharing principle, the sharing principle should determine the outcome;
- the approach taken in *Cowan v Cowan* (2001) which determined the respective needs of the spouses and then shared the surplus equally is unfair. It leads to disputes between the couple over the value of the assets as well as the appropriate level of their needs.

With respect to the offshore trust assets, the Court of Appeal held that where it is likely that trustees would advance the trust assets to one of the spouses, those assets may be viewed as the property of that spouse and available for redistribution.

Finally, the Court of Appeal stressed, yet again, the need for a review of the law relating to financial awards. In its view, the extent of social change affecting the nature of marital relationship, the increasing impact of globalisation and London's role as the 'divorce capital of the world', and the drive towards harmonisation of the law within Europe, have all made this review long overdue.

Commentators rejoiced that the decision in *Charman* (2007) was in the form of a single judgment. However, the judgment has muddied the waters of this area of law still further by taking a different approach from that of the House of Lords in *Miller and McFarlane*. It has not led to the certainty and predictability hoped for.

Following the decision in *Charman* (2007), Thorpe LJ, in *Lawrence v Gallagher* (2012), made clear that the principles he had outlined in that decision applied equally to civil partners. Once again, he emphasised the importance of the guidelines in the exercise of the court's discretion in determining financial awards. He criticised the judicial efforts (including his own) which have attempted to sideline the s 25 criteria and replace them with alternative principles:

> *Since the decision of the House of Lords in* White v White *the specialist judges have developed new approaches often expressed in newly minted phrases. I have myself contributed to this process to a limited degree. All this erudition is designed to guide the search for the fair outcome or to safeguard against the unfair outcome. But we must never forget the legislated check list which is designed to achieve the same ends.*

Mr Justice Ryder took a similar approach:

> *There is a prevalent practice of coining ever more sophisticated phrases which are intended by practitioners to highlight particular aspects of the notion of 'fairness'. That practice has created an expectation that the judge will consider the same in judgment. That expectation is inappropriate not least because the linguistic devices employed are not terms of art: they are no more than tools to assist in the interpretation of fact which should not be elevated to the status of factors that have to be considered alongside the section 25 criteria.*

Mr Lawrence and Mr Gallagher were a same-sex couple who had lived together for ten years before entering into a civil partnership in 2007. They applied for a dissolution of the partnership two years later. The couple agreed that the relationship should be treated as having lasted almost 12 years and should not be treated as merely a two-year one. Mr Lawrence was a high earning city analyst. His salary was £200,000 per year; he had deferred share options and a pension valued at £500,000. He had purchased a flat in the city prior to the relationship which at the date of the hearing was worth £2.4 million. Mr Gallagher was an actor who was currently earning £100,000 per year and had a share, worth £230,000 in the country cottage which the couple had bought. The cottage was valued at £900,000. He also had other assets worth £40,000.

Mr Gallagher maintained that the couple's assets which totalled around £4.1 million should be shared equally with a 5 per cent reduction to allow for the fact that the city flat had been purchased prior to he and Mr Lawrence living together. Mr Lawrence argued that as they were a joint career couple, each with their own resources, Mr Gallagher's claim should be limited to his needs of £420,000 and a share of the pension fund of £183,000.

Parker J proceeded to award a 42 per cent share of the total assets to Mr Gallagher which consisted of the cottage, a £200,000 share of the pension, and a lump sum of £577,000. She also awarded him a 45 per cent share of the deferred shares when they came on stream. Parker J viewed the relationship as one where the couple had intermingled their resources to provide them jointly with a high standard of living. The city flat was a partnership asset because it had become the couple's family home.

Mr Lawrence appealed and Thorpe LJ giving the judgment in the Court of Appeal allowed the appeal and reiterated the need to apply the statutory guidelines. He could find no rationality for Parker J's award. Although he accepted that she had conscientiously applied the statutory guidelines, he criticised her approach as one based primarily on a very theoretical interpretation of the sharing principle; her sums with the relevant discounts were clearly laid out in her judgement.

Thorpe LJ paid scant attention to Mr Lawrence's argument that he and Mr Gallagher were a joint career couple who had kept their resources separate. He ordered that the couple should each keep one of their homes, Mr Lawrence, the city flat because it was close to his work place and, Mr Gallagher, the country cottage because it was his 'pride and joy' and could be used to generate income as a bed and breakfast business. Thorpe LJ accepted that Parker J's order of pension sharing was appropriate but that the lump sum of £577,000 was not and should be reduced to £350,000. He appeared to base this reduction on three factors but failed to distinguish between them – a balancing out of the difference in value between the two properties, the needs of the couple in their future lives apart, and the principle of fair sharing. He gave no rational explanation as to how he reached the figure of £350,000.

Thorpe LJ's judgment illustrates that in spite of stressing the MCA guidelines, the Court of Appeal's award seems no more based on clear principle than that of Parker J; judicial discretion prevailed. Thorpe LJ's heartfelt plea for reform of this area of law is shared by many.

Attempts to marry the guidelines with the principle of fairness

Many of the decisions that follow, in which the guidelines were discussed, pre-date *Miller and McFarlane* and *Charman No 4*. They should be read bearing in mind the current attempts to apply the concept of fairness with them.

MCA 1973, s 25 (1), CPA 2004, Schedule 5, s 20
The duty of the court when making any award is to take into account all the circumstances of the case but, in so doing, its primary task is to consider the welfare of any minor child of the family under the age of 18.

The 'clean break' principle
MCA 1973, s 25A – the 'clean break' principle, CPA 2004, Schedule 5, s 23

In *Minton v Minton* (1978), Lord Scarman explained the 'clean break' principle in applications for financial awards:

> *The law now encourages spouses to avoid bitterness after family breakdown and to settle their money and property problems. An object of the modern law is to encourage each to put the past behind them and to begin a new life which is not overshadowed by the relationship which has broken down.*

Although the principle had its origins in judicial policy, it is now in statutory form. The court is specifically directed to consider whether it is possible to end all obligations between the partners, either at the time of the hearing or at a specified date in the future. The 'clean break' principle is normally extended to exclude any future application for provision from a deceased former partner's estate under the Inheritance (Provision for Family and Dependants) Act 1975 (see Chapter 8).

The 'clean break' principle has its limitations. It only applies to the partners; it cannot extend to ending financial provision for any children of the family. The principle reflects the fact that the legal end of a marriage or civil partnership terminates the partners' status and allows them to enter a new relationship. However, in practice, relationships generate responsibilities which must continue to be met even after the relationship is over. Emma Hitchings and Joanna Miles concluded in their research in 2018 that parties wanted a clean break but for a wife with young children who was unable to work because of child care responsibilities the clean break was not always ideal and the wife may suffer financially. A typical case quoted in the research is the transfer of the house to a wife but no further financial provision leaving her in a weak position with regard to outgoings and pension provision. As suggested by Hutchings and Miles: 'the clean break norm may under-protect economically vulnerable wives' (Hutchings and Miles 2018). The issue of the continuance of maintenance provision depends very much on financial equality between the parties. Where young children are involved the cost of child care which is very high in England and Wales remains a major issue. Katherine O'Donovan argued powerfully in 1982 for the abolition of maintenance but only on certain conditions such as equality of labour during the marriage and equal participation in wage-earning. She also discusses the payment of wages as a payment to a family unit rather than an individual. Undoubtedly, there has been progress in the 20 years since O'Donovan published these ideas, but the disparities between the parties persists. (See generally Diduck (2011); Fisher and Low (2009); Ferguson (2008).)

Without a clean break order it is always possible for one of the parties to return to court and make a claim reopening a relationship which has long ceased.

In *Vince v Wyatt* [2015] UKSC 14 a wife made an application for a financial order over 20 years after her divorce. The husband and wife had married in 1981 and at first had few assets; they embraced a 'neither worked new age hippy lifestyle' relying on benefits. They split up in 1984 but did not divorce until 1992; no financial order was made largely because there were no assets to distribute. They had two children, a son of the relationship who lived with Mr Vince and a daughter born before the relationship began who Mr Vince had treated as a child of the family. After the divorce Mr Vince became very wealthy with assets in 2015 of over £57 million. His wealth did not accrue until 13 years after they had split up. Ms Wyatt still had few assets and lived on benefits and so she sought financial provision from Mr Vince. Her application was turned down by the Court of Appeal but upheld by the Supreme Court. It accepted that as no financial order had been made in her favour at the time of the divorce leaving open the possibility of her returning to court and although her claim for £1.9 million was turned down she was awarded £300,000 reflecting her contribution to the family and in particular care for the children.

(See Ferguson 2015.)

> **MCA 1973, s 25(2)(a), CPA 2004, Schedule 5, s 21(2)(2)(a)**
> The court must take into account the income, earning capacity, property and other financial resources which each of the parties has or is likely to have in the foreseeable future, including in the case of earning capacity any increase in that capacity which it would in the opinion of the court be reasonable to expect a party to the marriage to take steps to acquire.

The partners must be absolutely honest about their available resources. If they are not, limitations are placed on how information about those resources may be obtained. In *Tchenguiz and others v Imerman* [2010] EWCA Civ 908, the Court of Appeal condemned the manner in which information was illegally obtained from the husband's computer even though it might prove the existence of resources which he was hiding to defeat his wife's application for a financial award.

'Non-relationship assets'

Since the decision in *Miller and McFarlane*, considerable confusion prevails about the redistribution of 'non-relationship' assets, and this continues today. The decision in *Hart v Hart* [2018] Fam 93 examines the meaning of non-relationship or non-matrimonial property. Moylan LJ explained that the term 'non-matrimonial' has been described to mean

> property "*from a source wholly external to the marriage*" *and it can . . . be broadly defined in the negative, namely as being assets (or that part of the value of an asset) which are not the financial product of or generated by the endeavours during the marriage. Examples usually given are assets owned by one spouse before the marriage and assets which have been inherited or otherwise given to a spouse from, typically, a relative of theirs during the marriage.*

Moylan LJ also showed that assets can be a combination of the two i.e. partly matrimonial and partly non-matrimonial. Examples could be where the family live in property once owned by the parents of either party but both parties have invested time and money into making improvements to the property. He held that it was better to adopt a more broad brush approach allowing the court to review all the assets rather than trying to separate them all from the start of the proceedings. In this case the husband had not provided the court with detailed information about the assets he owned so it made it more difficult for the court to use a more formulaic approach.

Where assets, which existed prior to the relationship, or were gifts, or inheritance, or lottery or other wins during the relationship, have been used to purchase a family home, or include a house which was subsequently used as the family home, the courts have tended to accept that they should be shared (see *Mansfield v Mansfield* [2011] EWCA Civ 1086 where the court refused to ring fence damages awarded to a husband in a personal injury action and *S v AG (Financial Remedy: Lottery Prize)* [2011] EWHC 2637 (Fam). In this case Mostyn J held that a lottery of £500,000 won by a wife where she had entered with a friend as a lone venture without the knowledge of her husband could be treated as non-matrimonial property and she was entitled to keep at least 80 per cent of the value). Where the future needs of a partner cannot be met from 'relationship assets' the courts have also ordered that 'non-relationship assets' be shared.

More recently, the concept of the metamorphosis of 'non-relationship assets' into 'relationship assets' has been developed. Mrs Justice Roberts referred to the process of the matrimonialisation of assets in *WX v HX (Treatment of Matrimonial and Non-Matrimonial Property)* [2021] EWFC 14. This was a complex case where both parties had contributed to very substantial assets although it was the husband who had made significant amounts of money from his job as a banker. Much of the family assets were kept in off-shore trusts funds, and the court had to decide which if any assets remained non-matrimonial assets and which became part of the matrimonial assets to be part of any decision on an award. The fact that the parties had been married for over 30 years and had had four children influenced the outcome in the case. Both parties brought assets into the marriage, but the husband's assets had been incorporated into the matrimonial property while the wife's had been kept separate and even though the husband had managed these assets this had not then turned them into matrimonial assets.

Case law suggests that it is more likely that assets will be matrimonialised in a longer marriage as there is more scope for them to be shared between the parties.

In *N v F (Financial Orders: Pre-Acquired Wealth)* [2011] EWHC 586 (Fam), the husband had £2.1 million of assets when he married. He continued in a highly paid career until 2007 when he decided to become a teacher earning £36,000 a year. This change of career meant that the family had to use the husband's assets to fund their expensive lifestyle. At the time of the divorce, the husband's capital amounted to £9.7 million. The husband offered the wife 43 per cent of this sum which she declined. Mostyn J awarded the wife a little less than 45 per cent of the capital and maintained that although the treatment of pre-matrimonial property was fact specific, the court's discretion had to be exercised in a predictable manner. The longer the marriage, the more likely it was that pre-matrimonial assets would lose their identity because they would be shared by both partners and treated as 'matrimonial assets'. Mostyn J suggested that the correct approach was to identify the extent to which these pre-matrimonial assets had become intermingled with 'matrimonial assets' before deciding whether to include them in the sharing process. The court should then test the fairness of any award as well as ensure that the needs of the applicant would be met. These needs were to be assessed by the standard of living during the marriage, by the value of the assets, by the percentage of the assets which were acquired prior to the marriage, and by whether the couple had made any prior agreement about the use, or sharing, of the assets.

The decision in *N v F* has been applauded by lawyers for its purported principled approach. It remains a little doubtful whether non-lawyers will be quite so enthusiastic. The decision demonstrates that judicial discretion inevitably plays an important role in determining a spousal financial award. It should also be noted that the costs of £652,200 were almost equivalent to the increase in the wife's financial award.

In *N v N* [2010] EWHC 717 (Fam), the couple had been married for a long time and had four children. The husband had been given significant assets by his family which were used to maintain his wife and children. Charles J held that a departure from equal division would be fair because the assets had been in the husband's family since the end of the eighteenth century, and it was reasonable that they should be preserved to be handed on to the next generation. Furthermore, the wife had always understood that the standard of living she had enjoyed during the marriage could not have continued, had she remained married to him, after her husband's retirement. She was awarded £5.3 million which represented a 32 per cent share of the total assets.

In *Robson v Robson* [2011] 1 FLR 751, the value of the husband's assets, which were largely inherited, amounted to over £22 million. They included an estate in Oxfordshire, a Scottish estate, land for development and two pension funds. The wife's assets were £343,500. Charles J awarded the wife £8 million on the basis that the husband's assets had been used to fund their extravagant lifestyle. The husband appealed. He maintained that the judge was wrong in assessing the wife's needs by the standard of living she had enjoyed during the marriage when she had been equally responsible for breakdown of the marriage, and was complicit in their reckless spending. The Court of Appeal reduced the wife's award to £7 million with minimal explanation but refused to ring fence any more than half the property inherited from the husband's family.

Writing in the *Child and Family Law Quarterly* in 2013, Jens Scherpe examined the approach of various jurisdictions towards non-matrimonial assets observing that across Europe the separation was much more marked. He suggested that there would be a move to greater demarcation in England and Wales (see Scherpe 2013). Some of the more recent decisions do seem to reflect this view.

Sharp v Sharp [2017] EWCA 408 (Civ) shows that it is perfectly possible for either party to acquire non-matrimonial property during the marriage. This couple had been married for six years. Both were high earners when they met but after a few years the wife began to receive large bonuses from her job. The couple had kept their finances largely separate during their marriage. When their relationship broke down she argued that the bonuses should be kept separate from the matrimonial assets. The Court of Appeal accepted the wife's argument. It was commented in *Sharp* that the marriage had been short and childless, and this factor had been found to be relevant to the conclusion drawn on the status of the assets of the wife. In a later case *E v L* [2021] EWFC 60, Mostyn J criticised this approach as follows: when applying the sharing principle 'for the court to start asking why there are no children, and whether this denotes a lesser extent of commitment to the relationship, is to make windows into people's souls, and should be avoided at all costs'.

The Appeal Court recently overturned a decision of the High Court on the basis that part of the £45m settlement in favour of the wife of a banker Clive Standish concerned non-matrimonial assets – assets which the husband argued had been acquired prior to the marriage. The award was reduced by £20m which reflected the biggest reduction in a financial award in legal history. This case is likely to be appealed and the issues that it raises would then be reviewed in the Supreme Court (see *The Times* 23 May 2024).

Post-separation assets

In *Rossi v Rossi* [2006] EWHC 1482 (Fam), the court maintained that property acquired, or created, by the sole efforts of one of the spouses (and without the use of any matrimonial property) after separation unless it is a bonus or other earned income which relates to the period prior to separation, should only be subject to reallocation in limited circumstances such as:

if the parties' resources are so small that the court has little choice;
if the marriage was so long that it is difficult to disentangle the matrimonial property and non-matrimonial property;
if the applicant spouse did not delay in making a claim;
if the spouse who owns the non-matrimonial property has treated the applicant spouse badly;
if the spouse who owns the after acquired asset is capable of making more money in the future from which the applicant spouse will not benefit.

Subsequent cases have followed these principles: in *Waggott v Waggott* [2018] EWCA Civ 727, Lord Justice Moylan said, 'any extension of the sharing principle to post-separation earnings would fundamentally undermine the court's ability to affect a clean break'. Later in *O'Dwyer v O'Dwyer* [2019] EWHC 1838 (Fam), Mr Justice Francis gave guidance that

if a bonus is earned during the marriage but not paid out until after the marriage has ended then there is every reason to treat it as matrimonial property in the true sense. Sharing bonuses that were generated or earned after the marriage ended would usually be possible only by reference to the principles of needs and compensation.

Increase in earning capacity

In determining available resources, the court may take into account any potential increase in the earning capacity of either partner. The courts rarely do so and where they have, have tended to show a gender bias in favour of women. This is hardly surprising given the research on the grave disparity that persists between the earning capacity of women as opposed to men. (See generally Ferguson 2008; Fisher and Low 2008; Westaway and McKay 2007.)

In *A v A (Financial Provision)* (1998), the husband and wife had been married for 13 years and had one son, aged 8, whom the husband adored. The husband, aged 64, was very wealthy; he had assets of over £200 million and an annual income of £1 million. The wife, aged 40, had an engineering degree but had never worked. The court awarded her a lump sum of £4.4 million because she bore the major responsibility for childcare. The court took note of the fact that during the marriage the husband in spite of his wealth had lived a very frugal life; nevertheless the court looked at the standard of living that the wife would expect to enjoy married to a wealthy man rather than the life she had at times enjoyed with him during their marriage. Singer J also took into account that:

'her role as mother to the husband's most treasured success, the son, would survive the marriage, continuing until she was over 50 years old'. It would not be reasonable, therefore, to expect her to seek full-time employment and increase her income unless she chose to do so.

> MCA 1973, s 25(2)(b), CPA 2004, Schedule 5, s 21(2)(b), the financial needs, obligations and responsibilities which each partner has or is likely to have in the foreseeable future.

This provision is, of course, closely linked with the standard of living (see later in this chapter) enjoyed by the partners during the relationship. Although the majority of reported cases involve wealthy couples, the resources of most couples' will leave them worse off than they were during the relationship and often insufficient to meet their future needs. The issue of 'needs' is a difficult issue when looking at financial provision cases. It has to be applied along with the other key principles of 'compensation' and 'sharing'. The law has moved a long way from simply equating 'needs' with basic necessities for life. Mostyn J took the opportunity in *FF v KF* [2017] EWHC (Fam) to consider the interpretation of needs in a number of high money cases citing examples such as *Juffali v Juffali* [2016] EWHC 1684 (Fam) 1 FLR 1508 (Mrs Juffali was awarded £62 million to meet her needs) and *AAZ v BBZ* [2016] EWHC 3234 (Fam) (the applicant wife was awarded £224 million for her needs).

He commented: 'Like equity in the old days, the result seems to depend on the length of the judge's foot.'

In *Miller/MacFarlane*, Lady Hale commented that 'needs were those that were linked to the parties' relationship either causally or temporally and not extrinsic unrelated factors such as a disability arising after the marriage had ended'. Her approach has been largely followed, but the courts have been prepared to diverge from this in some cases. In *ND v GD* [2021] EWFC 53, the court was prepared to make a higher award to a wife who shortly after the couple had separated had been diagnosed with early onset Alzheimer's disease. Much of the award came from non-matrimonial assets namely a portfolio of property left to the husband by his mother. It would seem that the comments of Lady Hale in *Miller/MacFarlane* are not regarded as a principle which must be followed in all cases and where the facts are unusual then it is possible to look at post-separation events and make provision for them; in those cases the court will revert to the principle of 'fairness'.

> MCA 1973, s 25(2)(c), CPA 2004, Schedule 5, s 21 (2)(c): the standard of living enjoyed by the family before the breakdown of the relationship

This provision will, of course, only be applicable if there are sufficient resources to take it into account. Where resources are plentiful, division of them is more likely to be subsumed within the sharing principle (see the comments of Moylan J in *J v J (Financial Orders: Wife's Long-Term Needs)* [2011] EWHC 1010 (Fam)).

In *F v F (Ancillary Relief: Substantial Assets)* [1995] 2 FLR 45, Thorpe J held that in determining the reasonable needs of a wife after a marriage to a very wealthy husband, it was important as a matter of principle that the court should use the standard of living of the ultra-rich and not the scales that would seem generous to ordinary people. He concluded that:

it would be wrong in principle to determine the application on some broad conclusion that if the wife cannot manage at the rate of a quarter of a million a year, she ought to be able to. I think that it is necessary to establish a yardstick that more nearly reflects the standard of living which has been the norm for the wife ever since marriage and for the husband for considerably longer.

The wife was judged to need a home worth £1.9 million; £300,000 to purchase a London flat; a chalet in Switzerland in which the wife would have a life interest; £685,000 to furnish the properties. The husband had already ceded chattels worth approximately £100,000, and the wife had been given jewellery worth £300,000. She would also need a maintenance fund of £5 million. The total cost to the husband would therefore be in the region of £9 million.

Thorpe J criticised the claim of £4,000 for the needs of the wife's Labrador dog and said:

After all, from the dog's point of view, there is not a lot of difference in being owned by a very rich family or simply a comfortably off family and I find it hard to see how a dog can cost as much as £4,000 per year.

MCA 1973, s 25(2)(d), CPA 2004, Schedule 5, s 21(2)(d): the age of each party to the relationship and the duration of the relationship

As a general principle the court will not be prepared to award a substantial sum to a claimant after a short marriage, but this is only a general rule and there are a number of cases where the courts have diverged from this principle. In *C v C (Financial Relief: Short Marriage)* [1997] 2 FLR 25, the wife met her husband when she was working as a high class prostitute. Their marriage lasted nine months during which a child was born. The judge in the lower court had been overtly impressed by the wife and her efforts at dealing with the numerous adverse events of her life; these included a husband who harassed her, redundancy, dyslexia, low self-esteem, and a lack of self-confidence, a nervous breakdown, dental problems, a road accident and a very sick child. Her career success as a prostitute was her only redeeming endeavour. He had described her as

an attractive lady, to whom her appearance is of critical importance. As will be seen, she has a fragile personality, and is vulnerable to emotional reverses, resulting in depression and loss of confidence and self-respect . . . in my view it is essential to her sense of self-worth and indeed to her effective functioning that she should present herself as attractively as possible. It is important to her to be well dressed and groomed, and thus she buys designer clothes, and spends considerable sums on hairdressing, fitness, make-up etc. I have no doubt that during the early and happier part of the cohabitation, the husband was pleased to indulge this expenditure, but as the quality of the parties' relationship quickly deteriorated, he began to resent and cavil at the cost, and for that reason reduced the wife's allowance. Nevertheless, I am satisfied that the parties enjoyed a very comfortable life-style during their cohabitation.

The Judge awarded the wife a lump sum of £195,000, on condition that she left the matrimonial home and transferred her interest in it to the husband, secured periodical payments of £19,500 a year for her and periodical payments of £8,000 a year to the child; and that a house belonging to the husband should stand charge as security for the periodical payments.

The husband appealed and Ward LJ explained the interrelationship between all the various factors listed in s 25(2) when considering the level of award after a short marriage. He thought that the circumstances and needs of the wife, who was aged 40, were exceptional enough to justify the award.

Where the marriage has been short, a period of cohabitation can be relevant in the assessment of the award. In *GW v RW* [2003] EWHC 611 (Fam), Mostyn J drew no distinction between the period where the parties had cohabited and the period later when they were married stating: 'where a relationship moves seamlessly from cohabitation to marriage without any major alteration in the way the couple live, it is unreal and artificial to treat the periods differently'.

This section would not be complete without mentioning the high profile case of *Mills v McCartney* [2008] EWHC 401 (Fam) which involved an application for a financial remedy after a short marriage. Ms Mills was awarded £24.3 million based on her reasonable needs in accordance with the standard of living during the marriage, although the judge did suggest that the hiring of private jets for trans-Atlantic flights was not one of those needs. He rejected her claim for a higher share of her husband's £400 million fortune which had been primarily generated long before he met her. Ms Mills' response to the judgment was to empty a jug of cold water over her husband's lawyer.

MCA 1973, s 25(2)(e), CPA 2004, s 21(2)(e): any physical or mental disability, of either of the parties to the relationship

This provision is related to the idea that marriage was traditionally considered to be a long-term commitment 'for better, for worse', an idea which is surely negated by the very fact that marriage and civil partnerships are so easily and frequently terminated. Whether a partner should have the responsibility of supporting an ex-partner who is disabled, particularly if the disability arose after the relationship ended, or through the applicant's own fault, remains questionable.

In *Seaton v Seaton* [1986] 2 FLR 398, the husband, aged 42, and the wife, aged 36, had been married for 14 years. They had no children. The wife was a teacher whose resources were limited. The husband had lost his job following criminal proceedings, and had a propensity to drink excessively. His wife had financially supported him. After the divorce, the husband suffered a major stroke, which severely incapacitated him. He could do little other than watch television and go out with friends; his parents took care of him.

The court held that to make any order for the wife to contribute to the husband's care would not enhance his life. His basic needs were already reasonably satisfied. It dismissed the husband's application for periodical payments, and ordered a clean break settlement.

As seen earlier in *ND v GD* the court was prepared to make a higher award to a wife who shortly after the couple had separated had been diagnosed with early onset Alzheimer's disease.

MCA 1973, s 25(2)(f), CPA 2004, Schedule 5, s 21(2)(f): the contribution which either of the parties has made or is likely in the foreseeable future to make to the welfare of the family, including any contributions by looking after the home or caring for the family.

The decisions in *White v White* (2000) *and Lambert v Lambert* (2003) emphasised that contribution should be judged in a non-sexist manner although whether these pronouncements have been carried through into decision making is itself questionable.

In *White* (2000), Lord Nicholls stated:

> *There should be no bias in favour of the money-earner and against the homemaker and the child-carer.*

In *Lambert* (2003), Mr Lambert pleaded that he had made a stellar contribution to the acquisition of the assets and maintained that his wife's contribution had been merely ornamental.

According to Thorpe LJ

> *special contribution remains a legitimate possibility but only in exceptional circumstances. It would be both futile and dangerous to even attempt to speculate on the boundaries of the exceptional. In the course of argument I suggested that it might more readily be found in the generating force behind the fortune rather than in the mere product itself. A number of hypothetical examples were canvassed ranging from the creative artist via the superstar footballer to the inventive genius, who not only creates but also develops some universal aid or prescription. All that seems to me to be more safely left to future case by case exploration.*

White did reset the thinking about the significance of home making and childcare. It has forced the courts to re-evaluate the way they view the relationship. In the past the focus was more on the financial contributions made by each party rather than any future economic loss suffered by a caregiver. Lisa Glennon (2008) argues that the focus of the discussion should be on the length of time dedicated to caring for the family.

MCA, 1973, s 25(2)(g), CPA 2004, Schedule 5, s 21(2)(g): the conduct of each of the parties, if that conduct is such that it would in the opinion of the court be inequitable to disregard it.

It will be rare for any court to take into account negative conduct (see *S v S (Non-Matrimonial Property Conduct)* (2006)). The court has taken a fairly restrictive view as to what type of conduct will be such that it would be inequitable to disregard it. Burton J referred to the type of conduct which may be relevant as having the 'gasp' factor. Conduct played a significant role in the divorce proceedings between Johnny Depp and Amber Heard where each cited examples of abuse suffered at the hands of the other party (*The Independent* 2023).

The following decisions illustrate the type of negative conduct which has affected financial awards.

In *J v S-T (formerly J) (Transsexual: Ancillary Relief)* [1997] 1 FLR 402, a decision on financial relief following a decree of nullity, the court accepted the wife's view that her transsexual husband had deceived her as to his gender over a period of 14 years. He had used a sexual prosthesis, which he kept in his bedside table; had always backed out of the shower; and had agreed to his wife having donor insemination to conceive their two children. In spite of this evidence, the wife maintained she had no knowledge of his true sexual identity. The husband was denied any financial relief because of his supposed deception.

In *FZ v SZ and others (Ancillary Relief: Conduct)* [2010] All ER (D) 189, Mostyn J regarded the individual conduct of each of the spouses as equally heinous and held that it cancelled out any effect it might otherwise have had on his final order.

The wife had made a false report to the police about her husband with respect to a breach of ouster orders, and the husband had reported his wife's parents to the tax authorities in their country of origin. Although the wife had taken documents belonging to her husband which concealed evidence of his assets, Mostyn J did not regard this as relevant conduct. Had she decided to breach locks on her husband's property or to open his post then he would have been prepared to find her guilty of relevant conduct and would reduce the level of the award. In *OG v AG (Financial Remedies: Conduct)* [2020] EWFC 52, Mostyn J differentiated between the different types of conduct that may be relevant in a case: 'litigation conduct' and the drawing of adverse inferences from a party's conduct, from 'gross and obvious personal misconduct' and, separately, 'wanton and reckless dissipation of assets' which supports the 'add back jurisprudence'. The instant case concerned personal conduct which can extend, obviously, to economic misconduct such as is alleged in this case. If one party economically oppresses the other for selfish or malicious reasons then, provided the high standard of inequitable to disregard is met, it may be reflected in the substantive award. The couple concerned had been married for over 25 years. They had built a successful business and had used the substantial profits to build a portfolio of property in various countries including Dubai. Mostyn J observed that both parties' conduct was reprehensible, but the wife was more 'sinned against than sinning'. Although it was a case where there should have been equal division of the assets he reduced the husband's share to reflect his behaviour and also reduced the wife's claim for costs in order to reflect her behaviour. He observed that:

> conduct should be taken into account not only where it is inequitable to disregard but only where its impact is financially measurable. It is unprincipled for the court to stick a finger in the air and arbitrarily to fine a party for what it regards as immoral conduct.

Conduct can, however, also be positive. It may be taken into account but only if it is exceptional.

In *Kokosinski v Kokosinski* [1980] Fam 72, the wife had faithfully, and lovingly, helped her husband to build up a family business and care for the home. The marriage was comparatively short but had been preceded by a 20-year period of cohabitation, because the husband could not divorce his previous wife. The court centred its decision on the wife's positive conduct rather than on the brevity of the marriage in order to achieve a fair outcome. She was awarded £8,000.

> MCA 1973, s 25(2)(h), CPA 2004, Schedule 5, s 21(2)(h): in the case of proceedings for divorce or dissolution or nullity of the relationship, the value to each of the parties to the relationship of any benefit which, by reason of the legal ending of the relationship, that party will lose the chance of acquiring.

In *S v S* [2007] EWHC 1975 (Fam), the court refused to take into account a wife's potential inheritance from her parents on the basis that there was no certainty that she would receive it because a will may be revised at any time prior to the death of the testator.

Reform of the guidelines

The lack of clear guidance from the legislation has given the courts a free hand in trying to formulate guidelines when making financial awards. In *Cowan v Cowan* [2001] EWCA Civ 679, Thorpe LJ acknowledged that couples seeking advice from solicitors were often told that the order would all depend on the judge on the day. If the law was in such a state, how could sensible couples plan their future and reach agreements? He defended the fact that, in the absence of reform by Parliament, the judiciary had been forced to develop various mechanisms, which had no statutory basis, to help them reach decisions. This judicial observation was written in 2001, and nearly 25 years later there is still no reform to the statutory provisions for financial settlement on divorce or dissolution of civil partnerships.

Potential reform for the award of financial remedies

In 2024, the Law Commission initiated a review 'Financial Remedies on Divorce' to examine the current legislation and make recommendations which would make a financial settlement more predictable and less costly for the parties.

As part of its analysis of existing law, the Law Commission has considering whether there is potential for reform in specific areas such as:

i) The discretionary powers given to judges over the division of financial assets, and whether there is a need for a clear set of principles, enshrined in law, to give more certainty to divorcing couples. There has been so much uncertainty about the guidelines listed in the Matrimonial Causes Act and about which of the guidelines should carry precedence. For the law on financial remedies to be cleared the judicial discretion needs to be addressed.

ii) Whether there should be wider powers given to the courts to make orders for children over the age of 18. The courts' powers with regard to children over the age of 18 cease except with regard to those in further education but for many children they are not able to support themselves for many years after the age of 18.

iii) How maintenance payments for an ex-spouse or civil partner should work.

iv) What consideration the courts should give to the behaviour of separating parties when making financial remedy orders. The courts have avoided making value judgments on the behaviour or conduct of one party and have tried to make awards based on financial issues alone. Some might argue that the courts should revisit this and decide whether or not behaviour in some cases should affect the final award.

v) Orders relating to pensions and whether they are overlooked when dividing the divorcing parties' assets.

vi) The factors judges must consider when deciding which, if any, financial remedy orders to make. The current list of factors laid down in s 25 of the Matrimonial Causes Act needs to be revisited to bring it into line with current standards and expectations (see https://lawcom.gov.uk/project/financial-remedies-on-divorce).

Relationship or pre-nuptial agreements

Given that such a high percentage of marriages end in divorce (civil partnerships are still sufficiently new not to be able to judge their ability to endure), it is readily understandable that couples, particularly wealthy ones and/or those entering into a legal relationship for a second time, might wish first to make an agreement which would take effect should their relationship break down at a future date. By doing so, they hope that they might avoid the court's discretionary reallocation of their assets.

Problematic nature of agreements

Traditionally the courts took little cognisance of agreements entered into prior to the marriage.

Largely as a result of the decision of the Supreme Court in *Radmacher v Granatino* [2010] UKSC 42 such agreements do carry weight, but they will not be binding on the court if it can be shown that:

a.   the parties did not enter into it freely and fully; or

b.   it would not be fair to hold the parties to the agreement given the circumstances at the time of the court hearing. Indeed courts continue to disregard the terms of any agreement where the financial arrangements are considered to be unfair. This contrasts with the attitude of courts in other jurisdictions where such agreements if entered into freely are binding.

Those who oppose the enforceability of relationship agreements argue that they may have been unfairly extracted from the partner with the weaker bargaining power as the price to pay for entering into a legal relationship. They also maintain that agreements made at the beginning of a relationship may be totally inappropriate when the relationship ends. The couple may have children and acquired property, and one partner may have sacrificed a career to allow the other to be successful.

Those in favour of enforcing agreements have argued that to deny adults the right to reach agreements is patronising.

Agreements made after a relationship has broken down may fall foul of the MCA 1973, ss 34, 35, or Schedule 5, ss 68, 69 of the CPA 2004 in the case of civil partners. Both statutes provide that a couple may not agree to oust the jurisdiction of the court in matters relating to financial remedies.

The decisions illustrate how frequently one of the partners regrets having signed an agreement when the consequences of doing so become starkly clear at the end of the relationship. Accusations of unfairness abound.

The Law Commission – Matrimonial Property, Needs and Agreements Project

The Law Commission commenced a project in 2009 to examine matrimonial property agreements. It is somewhat unfortunate that the title of the project appears to exclude civil partners when the project itself does include them. In 2012, the Law Commission extended the scope of the project to consider the extent to which one spouse or civil partner should be required to meet the needs of the other spouse or civil partner, and to examine the concept of 'non-matrimonial property' and the sharing of such property, when relationships end.

One of the recommendations by the Law Commission was that legislation be enacted to introduce 'qualifying nuptial agreements'. These would be enforceable contracts, not subject to the scrutiny of the courts, which would enable couples to make contractual arrangements about the financial consequences of divorce or dissolution. In order for an agreement to be a 'qualifying' nuptial agreement, certain procedural safeguards would have to be met. Qualifying agreements could not, however, be used to contract out of 'financial needs'. This recommendation has not been acted on.

The Law Commission undertook a new project in 2024 revisiting the reform options for the law governing finances on divorce and the ending of a civil partnership and this is expected to also cover nuptial agreements when it reports in November 2024.

Judicial approaches to agreements

Agreements made on relationship breakdown

A couple whose relationship has broken down may negotiate with each other and make an agreement about their financial affairs. Their agreement will be regarded as a maintenance agreement under the MCA 1973, s 34 or Schedule 5, s 60 of the CPA 2004 in the case of civil partners. Any clause purporting to oust the jurisdiction of the court will be unenforceable, but the remainder of the agreement may be enforced. Such agreements will often be ratified by the court as a consent order.

In *Kelley v Corston* [1998] QB 686, Butler-Sloss LJ explained that prior to making a consent order, the court may examine the spouses' agreement and

> *check, within the limited information made available, whether there are other matters which require the court to make enquiries. The court has the power to refuse to make the order*

although the parties have agreed it. The fact of the agreement will, of course, be likely to be an important consideration but would not necessarily be determinative. The court is not a rubber stamp.

The court may set aside a maintenance agreement because of the circumstances in which it was obtained, it is then free to consider any application for a financial award in accordance with the statutory guidelines.

In *B v B (Consent Order: Variation)* [1995] 1 FLR 9, the wife was very depressed at the time she agreed to a consent order. The court agreed to discount the agreement and vary the order. It accepted that the wife had been ill, and that her legal advisers had given her bad advice at the time the agreement was drawn up.

By contrast, in *X v X (Y and Z intervening)* [2002] 1 FLR 508, the court held that a wife could not renege on an agreement. The husband and wife were both practising Jews. When their relationship broke down, an agreement was reached that, in return for £500,000 provided by the wife's brother, the husband would petition for divorce using the adultery fact but would allow his wife to petition in reliance on the behaviour fact. The husband also agreed to grant the wife a Get, which would allow her to remarry in accordance with Jewish law, and he would remain silent about the events surrounding the divorce.

The husband signed the Get, and the decree of divorce was granted, at which point, the wife refused to take any action to obtain the £500,000 from her brother and pay it to the husband.

The court upheld the agreement and stated that it would not lightly allow parties to depart from a formal agreement, properly and fairly arrived at, after serious legal advice, unless there were good grounds for concluding that an injustice would be done. The wife had failed to establish any unconscionability, unfairness, inequality of bargaining power or exploitation by the husband. In fact it was the husband who would suffer injustice if the wife succeeded in her claim that she should not be held to the agreement.

In *NA v MA* [2006] EWHC 2900 (Fam), the wife had an affair with her husband's best friend. She and her husband decided to try and salvage the relationship, but the husband was only prepared to do so if the wife signed an agreement, drawn up by him, which was to take effect if their efforts were unsuccessful. In the agreement, the wife was to receive £3.3 million plus £252,000 per year for their joint lives or until remarriage. The husband had assets of about £120,000 million. The wife, who was in a state of severe stress, agreed to sign the agreement against the advice of her lawyer. The court overturned the agreement and awarded the wife a little over £9 million on the grounds that she had been put under emotional pressure by a very powerful husband so that she could not be held to have signed the agreement willingly. (See Hatwood (2007) for a fuller discussion on the implications of this case.)

In *MacLeod v MacLeod* [2008] UKPC 64, the Privy Council distinguished between agreements made when a relationship has broken down and those made prior to entry into it. It maintained that the former may be enforceable. In determining the weight to be given to such an agreement if one partner reneges on it and applies for a financial award, the statutory provisions governing the variation of maintenance agreements under MCA 1973, ss 34–36 must be the starting point. The Privy Council then proceeded to widen the grounds for the court's departure from enforcing the terms of the agreement if there has been:

- a change in circumstances which would produce manifest injustice;
- a failure to make proper provision for children;
- an attempt to improperly make the family rely on State support;
- unfair pressure on a signatory of the agreement.

Pre-nuptial or pre-civil partnership agreements

Until the decision in *Radmacher v Granatino* [2010] UKSC 42, the history of the enforceability of agreements made prior to entry into a relationship was somewhat chequered.

Thorpe J (as he then was), in *F v F (Ancillary Relief: Substantial Assets)* [1996] 2 FLR 45, stated that although such agreements were commonplace in the society from which the couple came, he did not attach any significant weight to it when the wife applied for a financial remedy. He said:

> *The rights and responsibilities of those whose financial affairs are regulated by statute cannot be much influenced by contractual terms which were devised for the control and limitation of standards that are intended to be of universal application throughout our society.*

His comment is in sharp contrast with his description of a pre-nuptial agreement 12 years later in *Crossley v Crossley* [2007] EWCA Civ 1491 as:

> *a factor of magnetic importance.*

The decision in *Radmacher* (2010)

The decision in *Radmacher* received major media coverage in which exaggerated claims suggested that the Supreme Court had decided that pre-nuptial agreements are enforceable, and that signatories to them would no longer be able to apply to the court for a financial order. That view is certainly not supported by a more detailed reading of the court's judgment which provides a complete history of nuptial agreements, and a commentary on marriage and financial orders.

Katrin Radmacher and Nicolas Granatino met in November 1997 whilst they were both living in London where Nicolas was working for JP Morgan. Katrin came from a very rich German family and Nicolas from a wealthy French family. At the time of their marriage, in 1998, Nicolas was earning about £120,000 per annum. Prior to the marriage, Katrin suggested that they should enter into a pre-nuptial agreement because not only did she want proof that Nicolas loved her for herself and not her money, but also because of her father's insistence on it. Katrin's family arranged for the agreement to be drawn up in Germany by the family notary, Dr Magis. It was somewhat draconian and provided that Nicolas would not benefit from Katrin's wealth either directly, or indirectly through any of their future children, nor she from his were he to acquire assets. The agreement did not mention the value of the couple's respective assets because Katrin had told the notary that she and Nicolas preferred to give each other this information separately. The notary insisted that the document should be translated and that Nicolas should have sufficient time to take advice and fully understand the implications of what he was signing. When the time came to sign, the notary was angry when he learned that the document had not been translated. He considered that he might postpone the execution of the agreement but, when told that the parties were unlikely to be in Germany again prior to the marriage, he was persuaded to continue. Speaking in English because Nicolas' German was not adequate, the notary explained the terms of the agreement in detail but did not give a verbatim translation of the document. The couple signed the agreement, which was binding under both German and French law, and soon after they married in London.

In 2000, Nicolas' employer sent him to work in New York and the family relocated there. Katrin did not like it, and they returned to London one year later.

In 2003, after the birth of two children, Nicolas decided to change career and embarked on a doctoral degree in biotechnology at Oxford University. Three years later, the couple separated and began proceedings for divorce in London. At that time, Katrin had assets of £54 million and an income of £2 million per annum. Nicolas earned £30,000 per annum as an academic researcher and had debts of £800,000. In spite of having signed the pre-nuptial agreement, Nicolas made an application for a financial award.

Baron J held that the pre-nuptial agreement was not enforceable as a valid contract under English law. She considered all the circumstances of the case under the MCA 1973, s 25, and accepted that in assessing Nicolas' needs she would take into account as one of the relevant factors that he had signed the pre-nuptial agreement. She concluded that:

> he understood the underlying premise that he was not entitled to anything if the parties divorced. In essence, he accepted that he was expected to be self-sufficient. As a man of the world that was abundantly clear. His decision to enter into the agreement must therefore affect the award.

However, Baron J found that the agreement was, *prima facie*, unfair because it did not meet the Home Office safeguards. In particular, the couple had two children; the preparation of the agreement had been very one-sided, and no negotiations between the couple had taken place; it was obviously not neutral; it attempted to deprive Nicolas of any financial help even if he was in need, and neither he nor Katrin had disclosed the extent of their assets. As a consequence of these findings, Baron J awarded Nicolas £700,000 towards his debts of £800,000 ; £25,000 to buy a car; £2.5 million to buy a home of his own in London, and € 630,000 to buy a home in Germany. The children were living with Katrin in Germany, and Nicolas needed a place where he could have the children to stay with him for visits. This latter home would remain in Katrin's ownership. He was also awarded a £2.5 million capital fund which would give him an annual income for life of £100,000. His own earning capacity had been reduced to £30,000 as a consequence of his change of career. Further periodical payments of £35,000 were awarded to him for the care of each of his two daughters until they ended their full-time education.

Baron J failed to explain with any precision how she had taken into account the existence of the pre-nuptial agreement in her calculation of the award, and Katrin appealed.

The Court of Appeal granted the appeal on the grounds that Baron J had barely given any weight to the pre-nuptial agreement and certainly not the decisive weight it deserved in her calculation of the award. She had not explained what effect the agreement had had on the award. The court maintained that Nicolas should receive an award which would allow him to fulfil his role as the father of his and Katrin's children and not for his own long-term needs; the £2.5 million fund for housing should be held by him only for the period that his daughters were in his care, and the capital fund should be reduced to provide for his needs only until the younger daughter's 22nd birthday. Nicolas appealed to the Supreme Court.

The Supreme Court refused to differentiate between pre-nuptial and post-nuptial agreements and maintained with great clarity that the MCA 1973, s 25 governs all applications for financial remedies. It is for the courts to exercise their discretion and determine an appropriate award and not the couple's agreement. However, there should be a presumption, or a starting point, in that discretionary process, that an agreement should be accorded weight under certain circumstances. Thus, one more gloss was put on s 25, and Nicolas Granatino's appeal was denied.

The Supreme Court outlined the principles, which the courts should apply when considering the weight that should be attached to nuptial agreements along the lines of the 1998 Home Office proposals (see earlier). It maintained that:

- duress, fraud or misrepresentation, or undue pressure, present at the time of the agreement would reduce the importance of the agreement, and what would have happened had these circumstances been absent;
- the couple's personal circumstances at the time of the agreement would be relevant. These would include such matters as their age and maturity, whether either or both had been married or been in long-term relationships before;
- the enforceability of the agreement in the couple's own home countries if it was drawn up there might be relevant;
- fairness would be an important factor.

In spite of the court's acknowledgement of the problem inherent in the concept of fairness and that it is fact dependent, it stated that it might be unfair to give effect to the agreement where:

- there were children;
- one of the couple had real needs or required to be compensated for looking after the family to allow the other to acquire wealth
- the agreement addressed uncertain future circumstances which changed over time or could not be envisaged at the time of the agreement; the longer the marriage had lasted the more likely that might be the case.

The court accepted that it might be fair to attach greater weight to the agreement where:

- the couple had given a well thought out approach to their finances which addressed their existing circumstances and not merely the contingencies of an uncertain future;
- the couple wished to exclude non-matrimonial property such as property owned prior to the relationship or acquired by one of them from a third party during the relationship.

The Supreme Court summarised its view succinctly:

> *The court should give effect to a nuptial agreement that is freely entered into by each party with a full appreciation of its implications unless in the circumstances prevailing it would not be fair to hold the parties to their agreement.*

In Katrin and Nicolas' situation, the Supreme Court maintained that Nicolas' earning ability had not been incapacitated during the marriage. He was able and it was his decision to give up a lucrative career. There was no need to compensate him. His needs were satisfied, and he would benefit from the award made to support his daughters whilst they were living with him until they reached an age of independence.

It is arguable that to some extent the Supreme Court's decision is sexist in that it viewed Nicolas' decision to change careers and earn less money as entirely his decision and that the financial consequences should be borne by him. No credit was given to him for agreeing to relocate to London when Katrin felt unhappy about living in New York, a decision which might have affected his career prospects. It must also be remembered that he was married to a very wealthy woman who did not object to the career change at the time it was made. Would the Supreme Court have taken the same approach to a woman, married to a wealthy man, who gave up a lucrative career to follow her own personal dreams? Little attention seems to have been paid to the circumstances surrounding the signing of the agreement. Nicolas was considered to be a man of the world; would a woman have been treated in the same way had she signed an untranslated agreement drawn up at the behest of her husband's parents?

What effect will the decision have on Nicolas and Katrin's children when they realise that their mother would not share even 10 per cent of her considerable fortune with their father?

The dissent in *Radmacher*

In an interesting and detailed dissenting judgment, Lady Hale began by stressing the fact that marriage and civil partnerships involve both contract and status. The law determines, to a certain extent, the nature of the contract into which a couple enters; they are not entirely free to decide the legal consequences of the contract for themselves. One of the consequences of the contract is that it imposes on the couple a duty of support for each other, and for their children and allows them to have recourse to law if the relationship ends.

Lady Hale acknowledged that the law relating to financial remedies in general, and nuptial agreements in particular, is in urgent need of reform but felt that it should be left to the legislature to do so and not the judiciary:

> *There is some enthusiasm for reform within the judiciary and the profession, and in the media, and one can well understand why. But that does not mean that it is right. This is a complicated subject upon which there is a large literature and knowledgeable and thoughtful people may legitimately hold differing views. Some may regard freedom of contract as the*

prevailing principle in all circumstances; others may regard that as a 19th century concept which has since been severely modified, particularly in the case of continuing relationships typically (though not invariably) characterised by imbalance of bargaining power (such as landlord and tenant, employer and employee). Some may regard people who are about to marry as in all respects fully autonomous beings; others may wonder whether people who are typically (although not invariably) in love can be expected to make rational choices in the same way that businessmen can. Some may regard the recognition of these factual differences as patronising or paternalistic; others may regard them as sensible and realistic. Some may think that to accord a greater legal status to these agreements will produce greater certainty and lesser costs should the couple divorce; others may question whether this will in fact be achieved, save at the price of inflexibility and injustice. Some may believe that giving greater force to marital agreements will encourage more people to marry; others may wonder whether they will encourage more people to divorce. Perhaps above all, some may think it permissible to contract out of the guiding principles of equality and non-discrimination within marriage; others may think this a retrograde step likely only to benefit the strong at the expense of the weak.

Although Lady Hale accepted that courts must take into account nuptial agreements as part of the discretionary exercise required by the MCA 1973, s 25, she felt that the majority decision of the Supreme Court placed an impermissible gloss on the section by giving agreements precedence. She regarded the majority view as inconsistent with the importance attached to the status of marriage in English law because it failed to differentiate between those in legal relationships and those who chose to simply cohabit. Lady Hale summarised her position in a slightly different way from that of the majority:

> *Did each party freely enter into an agreement, intending it to have legal effect and with a full appreciation of its implications? If so, in the circumstances as they now are, would it be fair to hold them to their agreement?*

Lady Hale concluded that she would have varied Byron J's order so that Nicolas Granatino would be allowed to enjoy his English home, or any home bought to replace it, for life. She also suggested that Nicolas' decision to leave his career in banking and study at Oxford was not as completely selfish as some may have thought it to be with the implication that he deserved some capital provision. After all Katrin had agreed to the decision:

> *And why should she not? The couple were rich enough each to be able to pursue their own dreams. She had not been happy in New York and perhaps she understood why her husband was no longer happy in banking. If the decision was taken for the good of the family as a whole, this would have been for the benefit of the children as well as their parents. Happy parents make for happy children. Discontented parents make for discontented children.*

The aftermath of *Radmacher*

In *Z v Z (No 2)* [2011] EWHC 2878 (Fam), a French couple signed a pre-nuptial agreement before marrying in France. They subsequently moved with their three children to England. The agreement provided that they were to retain separate ownership of their property. In 2008, the relationship broke down and divorce proceedings began. At this time the couple's assets amounted to around £15 million. Moor J considered the agreement and accepted that it was enforceable in so far as it excluded any sharing of the couple's individual assets. However, the agreement did not exclude the possibility of maintenance for the wife and Moor J awarded the wife £6 million for her needs which amounted to 40 per cent of the total assets.

The decisions on the enforceability of relationship agreements are totally fact dependent, and although they have the potential to be of significance in any application for a financial award, it remains the case that the courts' general discretion under the MCA 1973, s 25, and the similar provisions of the CPA 2004 in the case of civil partners, will prevail in situations where they would have unfair consequences. Those couples who make agreements with each other will have to continue to live with uncertainty.

In cases following *Radmacher* the courts consider the pre-nuptial agreement in the light of the provisos set down by the Supreme Court decision.

a. Did the parties freely enter into the agreement? This aspect is treated in the same way as a contract and so it must be clear to the court that the agreement was intended to create legal relations;

b. Was there any pressure put on either party to sign which could amount to undue influence or duress? The court considers each party to the agreement such as their relative ages, maturity, as well as the emotional state that they were in at the time of signing. In *KA v MA (Pre-nuptial Agreement: Needs)* [2018] EWHC 499 (Fam), a couple divorced in their mid-50s. They had one child together, aged 13, although the husband had three adult children from an earlier marriage. They had lived together for four years before marrying. The husband was reluctant to marry having experienced a complicated divorce from his first wife. He made agreement to a pre-nuptial agreement a condition of marriage. Under the terms of the agreement the husband would pay the wife a lump sum of £600,000 and periodical payments of £2,000 per month as well as payments towards the child. When the relationship broke down the wife sought to depart from the terms as she argued the amount offered did not meet her needs. She had received legal advice when she signed the agreement, but she had been warned by her solicitors that the terms would leave her in a much worse position than if she had divorced without it in place. She argued that she had been pressured into signing, but the court held it was entered into freely as the wife had received legal advice. The court upheld the agreement but was prepared to depart from the terms granting the wife a larger lump sum of £1.35 million in order to meet the wife's 'needs'. The case suggests that pre-nuptial agreements are still not fully binding in this country although clearly persuasive when the court assesses the needs of the parties under s 25. it is also likely that the court is more likely to depart from the terms of an agreement where the marriage can be described as long since the terms of the original agreement may be by that time regarded as unfair.

c. Legal advice. In most cases independent legal advice is an important point, but lack of legal advice at the time of signing the agreement may not always be fatal.

Versteegh v Versteegh [2018] EWCA Civ 1050 concerns a Swedish couple (living in England) but who had signed a standard Swedish pre-marital agreement (committing themselves to a separation of property regime) in Sweden the day before the wedding in 1993. After over 20 years of marriage they separated and on divorce in 2017 the wife sought to argue (amongst other things) that the judge should not have applied the pre-marital agreement to the financial settlement, because she had not received independent legal advice before she signed it. The Court of Appeal dismissed her appeal. The court found that the wife had a full appreciation of the implications of the pre-marital agreement, and there was evidence that she had tried to mitigate its effect during the marriage. Similarly in *CMX v EJX (French Marriage Contract)* [2022] EWFC 136, Moor J made an award in W's favour to meet her reasonable needs after upholding the validity of French marriage contract. The wife sought to argue that she was not bound by the pre-nuptial agreement which had been signed in France because she had not obtained independent legal advice, but Moor J reflected on the fact that it was the wife who had wanted the agreement in the first place and was fully aware of the consequences of signing it. 'This Wife is extremely intelligent. She had been working for three years in responsible employment. I cannot accept that she would not have known that the whole point of such Contracts was to deal with the position on divorce or separation given that there is no real need for them otherwise.' Even where legal advice is given the agreement may still not apply if it was not independent. In *Ipecki v Mc Connell* [2019] EWFC 19, the judge disregarded a pre-nuptial agreement because the advice given to a husband, who was the weaker of the two parties, came from the solicitor who had previously advised the wife. This could not be considered to be independent advice. In *Kremen v Agrest* [2012] 2 FLR 214 EWHC 45 (Fam), it was held that 'W did not freely enter into the agreement with a full appreciation of its implications. It was the product of pressure from H and there was a material absence of independent legal advice and disclosure.' This was a highly complex case which made legal advice all the more important. Mostyn J commented 'that a spouse would have to have a high degree of sophistication to have a full appreciation of what legal rights they are signing away'.

d.   Is the agreement fair? If the agreement has been entered into freely and with independent legal advice the second question to ask is whether under the circumstances at the time of the divorce the agreement could be regarded as 'fair'. This will be seen in a different light to cases where there is no agreement in force. As discussed earlier, 'needs' can be interpreted fairly generously where the parties have led an affluent lifestyle, but where there is a pre-nuptial agreement in place the courts will interpret 'needs' less generously.

Luckwell v Limata [2014] EWHC 502 (Fam) illustrates how a court will approach 'needs' in terms of an existing pre-nuptial agreement. The case concerned Victoria Luckwell who was the daughter of the director of the media company who created 'Bob the Builder'. Just 12 days before Victoria married her husband Francesco Limata the couple entered into a pre-marital agreement. It was agreed by both parties that if there had been no agreement the marriage would not have gone ahead. Francesco's claims were not, however, found by the High Court to be restricted to that which he was due to receive under the terms of the agreement although he received far less that he would have done had there been no agreement at all. Mr Justice Holman in his judgment made it absolutely clear that the judgment and decision was 'based entirely upon the needs of the husband, considered in conjunction with his role as a father'. The court awarded the husband £1,240,000 including £900,000 to buy a three-bedroom house. He commented that any order would require the 'damaging upheavals of sale' and moving to a smaller house in a less fashionable and less central area of London. 'I have concluded that the need to provide an adequate home in which the children can visit and stay with their father is very important and, insofar as the balance of welfare considerations is concerned, does outweigh the upheaval.' *Luckwell v Limata* is particularly interesting for its emphasis on sexual equality. Holman J added:

> *The court must be scrupulous to avoid gender discrimination or gender bias . . . . there must be no discrimination or bias based on gender alone, nor on any stereotypical view that a wife may be dependent upon her husband but not vice versa.*

[132]

He also quoted from the decision in *Radmacher v Granatino*, in which Lord Phillips said a 'nuptial agreement cannot be allowed to prejudice the reasonable requirements of any children of the family'.

In 2014, the Law Commission set out what it considered should be the main ingredients of a qualifying nuptial agreement as follows: –

Agreements will be qualifying nuptial agreements if the following requirements are met:

a.   The agreement must be contractually valid (and able to withstand challenge on the basis of undue influence or misrepresentation, for example).

b.   The agreement must have been made by deed and must contain a statement signed by both parties that he or she understands that the agreement is a qualifying nuptial agreement that will partially remove the court's discretion to make financial orders.

c.   The agreement must not have been made within the 28 days immediately before the wedding or the celebration of civil partnership.

d.   Both parties to the agreement must have received, at the time of the making of the agreement, disclosure of material information about the other party's financial situation.

e.   Both parties must have received legal advice at the time that the agreement was formed.

Paragraph 6.124: We have recommended that it should not be possible for a party to waive their rights to disclosure and legal advice (Law Commission 2014).

Cohabitants

The current debate

The financial position of cohabitants when relationships break down has been a recurrent theme in many chapters. As discussed earlier, there is an ongoing debate between those who believe that cohabitants should be treated in a similar way to spouses or civil partners when their relationships end, and those who believe that cohabitants should be free to decide their own affairs without any State intervention at the end of their relationships.

Ruth Deech, in her 2009–2010 Gresham College Lectures has vociferously expressed the view that:

> *Cohabitation is gradually gaining more recognition in English law, without any debate until very recently about the rights and wrongs of it. I can only echo what I said in my second lecture on maintenance, that women do not need and ought not to require to be kept by men after their relationship has come to an end. My preference is for the rights of the individual, or human rights, in this instance autonomy, privacy, a sphere of thought and action that should be free from public and legal interference, namely the right to live together without having a legal structure imposed on one without consent or contract to that effect. It is better not to have legal interference in cohabitation and leave it to be dealt with by the ordinary law of the land, of agreements, wills, property and so on. . . . But I would argue that cohabitation law retards the emancipation of women, degrades the relationship, takes away choice, is too expensive and would extend an already unsatisfactory maintenance law for married couples to another large category. I rate most highly personal autonomy and the use of agreements to settle legal boundaries with others – the respect for individuals' expectations and contribution rather than stereotyping and fitting every couple into the traditional marriage mould.*

By contrast, Lady Hale in the UK Supreme Court judgment in *Gow (FC) (Appellant) v Grant (Respondent) (Scotland)* (2012), suggested that there are lessons to be learned from the Scottish legislation which permits a cohabitant to apply for a financial order at the end of a cohabiting relationship. She applauded the Law Commission's demands for a change in the existing law which she believed brought about injustice. The increase in cohabitation, and births of children in cohabiting relationships, and the general belief that the law offers protection to cohabitants requires law reform which would provide a remedy for them. Rather than treating them in the same way as married couples or civil partners, the law should concentrate on balancing out the gains and losses flowing from the cohabiting relationship (Law Commission 2007).

The Law Commission considered the financial problems facing heterosexual and same-sex cohabitants when their relationships end. It made recommendations based on two years of research and it remains uncertain whether the Government will act upon the recommendations.

The Commission found that many cohabitants suffered hardship at the end of a relationship which had serious consequences not just for them but also for their children, and they might be forced to rely on State benefits. The Commission found that a substantial majority of people believed that cohabitants should have the right to apply for financial relief from their partner at the end of a relationship; whilst a minority felt that cohabitants should be given information about the current law and decide on the basis of this whether to marry or enter into a civil partnership, and thereby receive protection.

According to the Commission neither of these options was acceptable because some cohabitants are in relationships which are not as committed as marriage and they have deliberately chosen that route. They would be reluctant to have legal responsibilities thrust upon them, and are prepared to accept that they have no rights. At the other extreme there are those cohabitants who are not free to legalise their relationships, or who live with partners who refuse to do so; it would be unfair to deny them rights.

The Commission, therefore, recommended that cohabitants should be given rights to financial relief at the end of a relationship in order to

> provide economically vulnerable members of society with the private means to rebuild their lives and to ensure a fairer division of assets on relationship breakdown and to ensure that the pluses and minuses of the relationship were fairly shared between the couple.

The Law Commission's proposed scheme would not apply to all cohabitants but only to those who could bring themselves within the following rules:

- the couple had not agreed to opt out of the scheme;
- the applicant had made contributions to the relationship, which gave rise to consequences which were ongoing at the end of the relationship, either in the form of a benefit to the respondent or an economic disadvantage to the applicant;
- the cohabitants must have had a child together or had lived together for a specified number of years. The Commission made no specific recommendation about time but suggested a period between two and five years might be regarded as appropriate;
- the decision and amount of any financial award would be at the court's discretion.

Certain aspects of the scheme resemble closely the concept of proprietary estoppel, or the Canadian concept of constructive trusts based on unjust enrichment (see e.g. *Peter v Beblow* (1993)).

In the absence of any remedy along the lines of Lady Hale's view, cohabitants whose relationships end have little choice other than to resort to the principles of resulting or constructive trusts, proprietary estoppel which were discussed in Chapter 4, or argue the existence of a contract or apply for indirect maintenance. It was found in research carried out in 2008 by Anne Barlow, Carole Burgoyne, Elizabeth Cleary and Janet Smithson that there remains a high degree of ignorance amongst cohabitants about their lack of rights. Having to resort to reliance on complex areas such as constructive trusts and proprietary estoppel in order to claim rights in property puts them at a grave disadvantage.

Contract

Cohabitants who draw up a legally binding cohabitation contract, by deed, or accompanied by consideration, are comparatively rare (Tennant et al. 2006).

Under contract law, cohabitation agreements may be enforceable on relationship breakdown if the couple are able to establish that:

- they intended to create a legally enforceable contractual relationship with each other;
- they had both put their minds to the terms of the agreement and agreed them without pressure from either of each other or a third party;

- the terms were expressed with precision and were not contrary to public policy;
- the consideration, if the contract was not made by deed, was not illegal.

In *Sutton v Mishcon de Reya and Gawor & Co* [2004] EWHC 3166 (Ch), the court considered a most unusual and rather bizarre contract between two male cohabitants, Sutton, an airline steward and a male prostitute, and Staal, a wealthy businessman. Staal was to become Sutton's sexual slave and give him all his financial assets. Not surprisingly, the relationship broke down. Sutton unsuccessfully sued two firms of solicitors for negligence. Both had warned that the agreement was likely to be unenforceable at law.

What is of interest to the family lawyer in Hart J's judgment, in this hardly typical situation, are his comments on the enforceability of cohabitation contracts. He maintained that a property contract between two people who were having a sexual relationship and cohabited with each other could be valid. There must be no undue influence in obtaining the consent of either party, and the sexual relationship must involve no criminal conduct. A contract for payment for sexual services would not be valid. With the endorsement of the principle from Hart J cohabitation contracts do play some part in protecting rights of cohabitants, but very few couples use them and even when they are used there are traps for the unwary. As Mark Pawlowski (2004) commented where the parties are in a close relationship there is a presumption against finding an intention to create legal relation.) The agreement must also be in the form of a deed rather than merely in writing. The legal requirements of s 52 of the Law of Property Act which deals with the transfer of land are often misunderstood. As in any contract there is a need for the terms to be clear. For a cohabitation contract to be binding most couples would need the assistance of a lawyer.

Indirect maintenance

Although a cohabitant may not claim maintenance from a partner at the end of a relationship, the courts have made awards for children and thereby indirectly contributed to the maintenance of the cohabitant who is caring for them.

In *Re P (A Child) (Financial Provision)* [2003] EWCA Civ 837, an unmarried mother separated from a very wealthy man and applied for maintenance for their child. Thorpe LJ explained that the mother had no personal entitlement but merely an allowance as the child's primary carer. He acknowledged that distinguishing between these two factors could be difficult, but her allowance should not be diminished by the absence of any direct claim in law. The court:

> *must recognise the responsibility, and often the sacrifice, of the unmarried parent (generally the mother) who is to be the primary carer for the child, perhaps the exclusive carer if the absent parent disassociates from the child. In order to discharge this responsibility the carer must have control of a budget that reflects her position and the position of the father, both social and financial.*

Thorpe LJ took a broad brush approach based on principles similar to those used on determining financial remedies on divorce. He awarded the mother £1 million to purchase a house which would revert to the father at the end of the child's education,

£10,000 for furnishings and periodical payments of £70,000 per annum. However, he explained that the mother should not be able to save from this allowance to provide a pension for her future but should spend it all on an annual basis, and account to the father for her expenditure.

In spite of the seemingly generous nature of the award in Re P (2003), it does not resolve the issue of what a mother, who has devoted her life and sacrificed her career to caring for a child, does when the child becomes independent. The decision draws attention to the difficulties for unmarried partners who are left without means of financial support when their child-rearing role ends. Where there are no children of the relationship, a former cohabitant in need of maintenance because she has no resources of her own and is unable to work will be forced to rely on State benefits.

The research into the misunderstandings amongst the general population about rights of cohabitants is very extensive (see Barlow et al. 2001; Douglas et al. 2009; Tennant et al. 2006). Douglas et al. having looked at over 50 cases either directly from cohabitants themselves or through legal advisors who saw trends in the outcomes. Long relationships left parties with nothing even where child care had prevented career progression. As discussed in Chapter 4 rights in the family home for a cohabitant are decided solely on principles of property law and often where the house was in sole ownership the other cohabitant often failed to establish any rights in equity. In their summary on their research, Douglas et al. refer to a suggestion made by Lady Hale over 40 years ago.

> As a society, we may still not be ready to adopt the proposal, originally made nearly 30 years ago, by Brenda Hoggett, as she was then known, to drop marriage as the key criterion for legal recognition and protection and to look instead at the substance of peoples relationships. But we are surely ready to address the substantial unfairness that the current law produces for those couples who separate after having lived together outside marriage. For the legal policy response to this challenge to prove effective, however, we have argued that it will be necessary both to recognise unjust enrichment as the key to understanding the problems that couples may face, and to promote more effective self-regulation to obviate such problems in the first place.

As the formalities of marriage become less tightly regulated this suggestion by Lady Hale may be more of a feasible solution to the question of establishing rights for cohabitants.

Fiancées and prospective civil partners

Historically, the term fiancé/fiancée was used to describe an unmarried man or woman who was formally engaged to be married. The man would offer a ring to the woman as a sign of their commitment to marry. The purpose of the engagement was to allow a period of time to prepare for the wedding and for any objections to be raised to the proposed marriage. If a man terminated the engagement, he could be sued for breach of promise because of the potential damage to a woman's reputation. This was based on the assumption that a woman may have agreed to have a sexual relationship with a man because he had agreed to marry her; she might also have risked giving birth to a child. A woman could not be sued for breaking the engagement. All actions for breach of promise ended in England with the enactment of the Law Reform (Miscellaneous Provisions) Act 1970 s 1.

There is no precise legal definition of the term fiancé/fiancée. More recently, the term has become a quasi-respectable title used in the tabloid press to describe partners who are cohabiting, and who may have little intention of marrying in the future, and may not even be free to do so.

If an engaged couple, or prospective civil partners, end a relationship, the Law Reform (Miscellaneous Provisions) Act 1970, or the CPA 2004, s 74 for civil partners, make limited provision for the resolution of property disputes when an engagements or prospective civil partnerships are terminated. The Acts do not permit the court to reallocate the property but merely determine who owns it. The policy behind the law is the recognition that a couple may acquire possessions in advance of the legal relationship, either as presents or because they have purchased them themselves for their future life together. (See e.g. *Dibble v Pfluger* [2010] EWCA 1005 (Civ) which concerned the purchase of a house by an engaged couple.) The Court of Appeal applied s 2 of the Law Reform (Miscellaneous Provisions) Act 1970 which provides that when a couple terminate their agreement to marry, property in which either or both had a beneficial interest during the engagement is subject to the same rules as determine the rights of husbands and wives in equivalent circumstances, including s 37 of the Matrimonial Proceedings and Property Act 1970 (MPPA 1970). Section 37 provides that where a spouse contributes in money or money's worth to the improvement of real or personal property in which either spouse has a beneficial interest, the contributing spouse (subject to any contrary agreement) acquires a share or an enlarged share in the property.

It remains uncertain who may bring themselves within the ambit of the provisions. For instance, could those who have cohabited for ten years with a person who is not free to marry or enter into a civil partnership be permitted to apply under the Act if they maintain that they plan to formalise their relationship in the future?

The symbol of any committed relationship is often a ring. Although an engagement ring is normally a gift given in contemplation of marriage, s 3(2) of the 1970 Act provides that it may only be recovered by the donor if it was made on the express or implied condition that it must be returned if the engagement is ended by either party. There is no equivalent provision relating to rings exchanged by prospective civil partners.

In *Cox v Jones* [2004] 3 CR 693 Mr Jones and Miss Cox became engaged in 1998. Mr Jones gave her a ring valued at around £10,000. He claimed that he told Miss Cox that, if their engagement came to an end, she must return the ring to him. After the engagement ended, Miss Cox requested a jeweller to set the stone from the ring into a new pendant which was valued at £18,000. The court had little difficulty in rejecting Mr Jones' version of events. It found it implausible that any fiancé could express such an unromantic remark; Miss Cox could retain the pendant.

Self-test questions

1. Consider the competing concepts of 'sharing, compensation and needs'. How do the courts currently apply the principles in cases on financial provision?

2. Explain how the courts approach the definition of matrimonial and non-matrimonial assets. Is it possible for an asset acquired prior to the marriage to become a matrimonial asset during a marriage? Discuss your conclusions with reference to recent case law.

3. Clara and Daphne have cohabited happily for the last ten years. They have been advised by friends that they should draw up a cohabitation contract, but they are worried that it would not be enforceable. Advise them on their current legal position and whether a cohabitation contract would be enforceable.

4. Marietta and Nathan married 15 years ago and have three children. When they married Nathan had shares in his parents' business worth £25 million. Nathan was a heart surgeon in both private and national health hospitals, and earned £300,000 per annum. Marietta was a lawyer earning £250,000 per annum with an international law firm. Nathan owned a house worth £1 million at the time of the marriage which became the family home.

   The couple signed a pre-nuptial agreement in which they agreed that Nathan's shares would remain his in the event of a divorce, and that Marietta would make no claim for any financial award. Seven years ago Marietta was tired with travelling around the world for work, and was concerned about leaving the children in the care of nannies. She agreed with Nathan that she would give up her position and go to art school to pursue her interest in painting. Since then, she has not worked.

   The couple have now decided that their relationship is over and wish to divorce. Marietta has no resources of her own and wants to apply for a financial award. Nathan has told her that she will not succeed because everyone knows that pre-nuptial agreements are now enforceable.

   Advise Marietta.

References

Barlow, Anne, ' Solidarity, Autonomy and Equality: Mixed Messages for the Family?' (2015) 27(3) *Child and Family Law Quarterly* 223

Barlow, Anne, Carole Burgoyne, Elizabeth Cleary and Janet Smithson, '*Cohabitation and the Law: Myths, Money and the Media*' in *British Social Attitudes: The 24th Report* (Sage 2008)

Barlow, Anne, Simon Duncan, Grace James and Alison Park, 'Just a Piece of Paper? Marriage and Cohabitation' in Alison Park National Centre for Social Research (ed) *British Social Attitudes: Public Policy, Social Ties: 18th Report* (Sage 2001)

Cretney, Stephen, *Family Law in the Twentieth Century: A History* (Oxford University Press 2003)

https://data.justice.gov.uk/courts/family-courts

Diduck, Alison, 'Ancillary Relief: Complicating the Search for Principle' (2011) 38 *Journal of Law and Society* 272

Diduck, Alison, 'What Is Family Law For?' (2011) 64 *Current Legal Problems* 287

Douglas, Gillian, Julia Pearce and Hilary Woodward, 'Cohabitants, Property and the Law: A Study of Injustice' (2009) 72(1) *Modern Law Review* 24

Eekelaar, John, 'Property and Financial Settlement on Divorce – Sharing and Compensating' [2006] *Family Law* 754

Family Justice Review 'Family Justice. Final Report' (2012) www.gov.uk/governmenr/publications/family-justice-final-report/2012

Ferguson, Lucinda, 'Family, Social Inequalities and the Persuasive Force of Interpersonal Obligation' [2008] *International Journal of Law, Policy and the Family* 61

Ferguson, Lucinda, '*Wyatt v Vince*: The Reality of Individualised Justice – Financial Orders, Forensic Delay, and Access to Justice' (2015) 27(2) *Child and Family Law Quarterly* 195

Fisher, Hayley and Hamish Low, 'Who Wins, Who Loses and Who Recovers from Divorce?' in Joanna Miles and Rebecca Probert (eds) *Sharing Lives, Dividing Assets: An Interdisciplinary Study* (Hart 2009)

Foy, Emily, '*Barder*: Where Are We Now?' [2021] *Family Law Journal online* 30 March.

Glennon, Lisa, 'Obligations Between Adult Partners: Moving from Form to Function' (2008) 22 *International Journal of Law, Policy and the Family* 22

Hardwick, Bethany, 'What's Mine Is (*Not) Yours – the Treatment of Non-Matrimonial Property: No Longer a Lawless Science?' [2016] *Family Law e-news* 18 November

Hatwood, Margaret, 'NA v MA: When Is an Agreement Not an Agreement?' [2007] *Family Law*

Hayward, Andy, 'The Married Women's Property Act 1882' in Erica Rackley and Rosemary Auchmuty (eds) *Women's Legal Landmarks: Celebrating the History of Women and Law in the United Kingdom and Ireland* (Hart Publishing 2018)

Hitchings, Emma, Joanna Miles and Hilary Woodward, 'Assembling the Jigsaw Puzzle: Understanding Financial Settlement on Divorce' [2014] *Family Law* 209

Hynes, Tom, 'Limited Assets: Meeting Reasonable Needs – Is There Enough to Go Around?' [2020] *Family Law* 618

The Independent, 'Johnny Depp v Amber Heard: A Timeline of Their Relationship, Allegations, and Court Battles' (2023) www.independent.co.uk/news/world/americas/johnny-depp-amber-heard-trial-b2343074

Law Commission, 'Matrimonial Property, Needs and Agreements Law Comm 343' (2014) www.lawcom.gov.uk/project/matrimonial-property-needs-and-agreements/

'Matrimonial Property' (Law Com No 175, 1985)

O'Donovan, Katherine, 'Should All Maintenance of Spouses Be Abolished?' [1982] *Modern Law Review* 424

Pawlowski, Mark, 'Cohabitation Contracts – The Sutton Case' [2004] *Family Law* 199

Scherpe, Jens, 'A Comparative Overview of the Treatment of Non-Matrimonial Assets, Indexation and Value Increases' [2013] *Child and Family Law Quarterly* 61

Tennant, Rosalind, Jean Taylor, and Jane Lewis *Separating from Cohabitation: Making Arrangements for Finances and Parenting* (Department for Constitutional Affairs Research Series 2006)

The Times, 'Judges Cut Banker's £45m Divorce Payment to £25m' hp03ktrvd (24.05.2024) www.thetimes.com/uk/law/article/judges-cut-bankers-£45m-divorce-payment-to-25m

Westaway, Jenny and Stephen McKay, *Women's Financial Assets and Debts* (Fawcett Society 2007)

Woodward, Hilary, 'Everyday Financial Remedy Orders: Do They Achieve Fair Pension Provision on Divorce?' [2015] *Child and Family Law Quarterly* 151

Further reading

Barlow, Anne, 'Solidarity, Autonomy and Equality: Mixed Messages for the Family' [2015] *Child and Family Law Quarterly* 223

Baroness Hale of Richmond, 'What's the Deal? Marital Property Agreements, Past, Present and Future' [2011] *International Family Law* 282

Bradley, Charlotte, 'Resolution International Committee: The English Pre-Nup: A Different Animal to the European Marriage Contract?' [2011] *International Family Law* 73

Bradley, Charlotte and Emily Moore, 'The Maintenance Conflict: Crystal Ball Gazing Versus a Meal Ticket for Life' [2011] *Family Law* 733

Bray, Judith, 'The Financial Rights of Cohabiting Couples' [2009] *Family Law* 1151

Chandler, Alexandra, 'The Law Is Now Reasonably Clear: The Court's Approach to Non-Matrimonial Assets' [2012] *Family Law* 163

Cooke, Elizabeth, 'The Law Commission's Consultation on Marital Property Agreements' [2011] *Family Law* 145

Cooke, Elizabeth, 'Miller/McFarlane: Law in Search of Discrimination' [2006] *Family Law* 753

Deech, Ruth, 'What's a Woman Worth' (Gresham College Lecture) [2009] *Family Law* 1140

Douglas, Gillian, Julia Pearce and Hilary Woodward, 'Dealing with Property Issues on Cohabitation Breakdown' [2007] *Family Law* 36

Douglas, Gillian, Julia Pearce and Hilary Woodward, 'The Law Commission's Cohabitation Proposals: Applying them in Practice' [2008] *Family Law* 351

Edwards, Susan, 'Division of Assets and Fairness: "Brick Lane" – Gender, Culture and Ancillary Relief on Divorce' [2004] *Family Law* 809

Eekelaar, John, 'Property and Financial Settlement on Divorce – Sharing and Compensating' [2007] *IFL Journal* 18

Harris, Peter, Robert George and Jonathan Herring, 'With This Ring I Thee Wed (Terms and Conditions Apply) [2011] *Family Law* 367

Hatwood, Margaret and Lehna Hewitt, 'Do Family Courts in England and Wales Discriminate Against Husbands?' [2012] *Family Law* 674

Hess, Edward, 'The Rights of Cohabitants: When and How Will the Law Be Reformed?' [2009] *Family Law* 405

Kingdom, Elizabeth, 'Cohabitation Contracts and the Democratisation of Personal Relations' (2000) 8(1) *Feminist Legal Studies* 5

Law Commission, 'Cohabitation: The Financial Consequences of Relationship Breakdown' (Law Com No 307, 2007)

Law Commission, 'First Report on Family Property – a New Approach' (Law Com No 52, 1973)

Law Commission, 'Matrimonial Property' (Law Com No 175, 1985)

Law Commission, 'Transfer of Money Between Spouses' (Law Com No 90, 1985)

Miles, Joanna, '*Charman v Charman (No 4)* – Making Sense of Need, Compensation and Equal Sharing After *Miller/McFarlane*' [2008] *Child and Family Law Quarterly* 378

Miles, Joanna and Rebecca Probert (Eds), *Sharing Lives,* Dividing Assets: An Inter-Disciplinary Study (Hart 2009)

Rains, Robert, 'A Prenup for Prince William and Kate? England Inches Towards Twentieth Century Law of Antenuptial Agreements: How Shall It Enter the Twenty-First?' [2011] *Florida Journal of International Law* 447

Scherpe, Jans, 'Marital Agreements and Matrimonial Property' [2012] *Family Law* 865

Thompson, Sharon, 'Levelling the Prenuptial Playing Field: Is Independent Legal Advice the Answer?' [2011] *International Family Law* 327

Welstead, Mary, 'Judicial Reform or an Increase in Discretion – the Decision in *Miller v Miller; McFarlane v McFarlane*', Chapter 3 in *International Survey of Family Law* (Jordans 2008)

Welstead, Mary, '*Miller v Miller; McFarlane v McFarlane* (2004) UKHL 24, Fairness Remains an Elusive Concept' [2006] *Denning Law Journal* 209

Welstead, Mary, 'The Sharing of Pre-matrimonial Property on Divorce: *K v L*' [2012] *Family Law* 185

8

The elderly, their rights in family life and death and its consequences

SUMMARY

When considering family life the focus tends to be on relationships and young people, but this ignores the elderly who make up a large section of the population. In this chapter we will consider the rights of older people in particular in relation to mental capacity, their care and also issues surrounding death, in particular what happens to their property after death, which of course is relevant to all ages. Many people die intestate without making a valid will and so their estate is distributed according to statute often in a way that is quite contrary to what they would have intended. We address this question and look at changes in the law. We will also explore the difficult topic of elder abuse which has only been recognised comparatively recently. Finally, we will consider how the court may intervene and order distribution of an estate of a deceased in favour of a family member where they have been left out of a will.

The Census 2021 results show that the population of England and Wales has continued to age since 2011. The number of people aged 65 years and over increased from 9.2 million in 2011 to over 11 million in 2021, and the proportion of people aged 65 years and over rose from 16.4 per cent to 18.6 per cent. In 2021, 3.3 million people aged 65 years and over were living alone in England and Wales 30.1 per cent of the older population (Census 2021). This raises a number of issues particularly as people tend to become more vulnerable as they age. The law has in place some protection for vulnerable older people, although currently the protection is piecemeal and is often derived from rights that cover all vulnerable adults.

Mental capacity amongst older people

As people age they become more susceptible to health conditions which impact on their mental capacity. According to Age UK policy paper published in March 2020 748,000 were living with dementia and this is expected to grow to 1.3 million by 2040 (Age UK 2023a). Not all people living with dementia will lack mental capacity, but many become too ill to manage their own affairs.

DOI: 10.4324/9781003435020-8

Currently the key legislation governing the law on capacity for all vulnerable adults is the 2005 Mental Capacity Act. The Act states in s 1 that it should be presumed that a patient has capacity unless there is evidence that they have not. It therefore places the burden of proof on any doctor or carer to prove that the person lacks capacity.

The Act defines mental capacity in s 2(1)

as a person lacks capacity in relation to a matter if at the material time he is unable to make a decision for himself in relation to the matter because of an impairment of, or a disturbance in the functioning of, the mind or brain

Under s 3 the Act considers those situations where a person is unable to make a decision as being unable to understand the information relevant to the decision and retain that information or use or weigh that information as part of a process of making a decision and finally to communicate his decision. The law leans in favour of the individual in the sense that the Act specifically mentions that all practical steps must be taken for a person to 'reach capacity' (s 4(4)). The law is concerned about protecting those persons who lack capacity because of a mental impairment or disturbance; it is this that is significant so that if a relative challenges a will then unless it can be shown that the testator lacked mental capacity or that person is entitled to make a claim based on dependency the provisions in the will must stand. Gifts in wills that appear to be foolish or eccentric cannot be challenged since the law in England and Wales upholds testamentary freedom although some would question the logic of this seeing that the law is prepared to intervene in so many other areas. (See Hedlund 2021.)

The Act also specifically mentions that decisions on capacity must be made without reference to a person's age, appearance or a condition of his, or an aspect of his behaviour which might lead others to make unjustified assumptions about his capacity. The Act is clearly envisaging decision being made about an older person who presents as unkempt and perhaps slightly eccentric which must be ignored when assessing capacity.

Once lack of capacity has been established then a substitute decision must be put in place, but this does not totally ignore the wishes of the patient. In *Wye Valley NHS Trust v B* [2015] EWCOP 60, a patient aged 73 lacked capacity to make decision which included his medical treatment. He had a severely infected foot which required amputation and without this treatment he was likely to die in a matter of days or weeks. He made it clear that he opposed this fully understanding that it would lead to his death and the court respected his views and feelings and did not order the amputation.

The four different ways under the Mental Capacity Act 2005 that a substitute decision can be made on another's behalf

They are as follows:

a) Advance decisions or 'living wills'

These are decisions specifically associated with future medical care and are in reality decisions made by an individual who has capacity and is over the age of 18 in anticipation of a time when he or she may lack capacity. It allows that individual to specify how he or she wishes to be treated in the future if at any time he or she loses capacity. Advance decisions are governed by s 24 of the Mental Capacity Act 2005.

They are limited in that they only relate to the refusal of treatment. An example would be someone who wished at a later stage in life to refuse life-saving antibiotic treatment for a serious infection at a stage when they lacked capacity to consent. Where the treatment is life-saving as in the aforementioned example then the decision must be in writing and signed by the individual and witnessed.

Any decision can be amended at a later stage whilst a person has the capacity to do so. So it is strictly limited to individuals preparing for a future stage when they are unable to give consent but pre-empting how they would have wanted to be treated.

b) Lasting powers of attorney

A lasting power of attorney (LPA) allows an individual to anticipate a time when he or she may not have capacity to appoint one or more other people to make decisions on his or her behalf.

Occasionally the court will inquire as to whether or not an individual had capacity to appoint anyone to act on his or her behalf. In *Public Guardian v RI & Ors* [2022] EWCOP 22, the donor had a learning disability and a diagnosis of chronic schizophrenia. He had purportedly executed a LPA in December 2009. It was found over ten years later that he had not had the mental capacity to do so. The court found that the certificate provider had made no mention of the individual's mental disability and there was no evidence that he had experience in dealing with disability.

There are two kinds of LPA.

A property and financial affairs LPA appoints someone to manage P's finances. This could be a friend, relative or someone with professional expertise such as a solicitor. More than one person can be appointed, and the LPA will set out whether they must agree or whether they can each act independently. This type of power of attorney can be used even where the individual continues to have mental capacity. It can be used as soon as it is registered if the individual gives permission. The LPA allows others to decide such matters as the management of a bank account or the payment of a bill and even the sale of one's home.

The second type of LPA is concerned with the health and welfare of an individual. LPA appoints someone to make decisions about P's health and well-being, including potentially where they live and whether life-sustaining treatment should be withdrawn. This type of LPA can only be exercised once an individual loses mental capacity. The decisions must always be based on what is in the best interests of the individual (see s 4 of the Mental Capacity Act 2005).

(The scope of the powers will be set out in the document and the donor can include restrictions on the powers granted: s 9(4)(b).) An LPA must be made by P while he or she still has capacity to do so, and both types of LPA must be filed with the Office of the Public Guardian. The LPA concerning Health and Welfare comes into effect once P loses the capacity to manage their own money and/or health, when it must also be registered with the Court of Protection. The Powers of Attorney Act 2023 introduces a digitised system for registering Powers of Attorney which aims to make the system quicker, easier to access and more secure. The paper system will be maintained. Some fear that there may be an increase in abuse of the system. Holly Chantler, Director of Solicitors for the Elderly, commented that the new system must be matched with 'proper checks and balances in the making and use of powers of attorney and the supervision and regulation of attorneys'. She also said that it was imperative that the Office of Public Guardian has the necessary powers and resources to supervise and investigate attorneys effectively. She was concerned that organisations such as banks, care homes and the police who should be acting as 'gatekeepers' to help prevent abuse do not sufficiently understand the capacity and vulnerability of individuals (*The Times* September 28, 2023).

c) Deputies

Once a person has been declared to have lost mental capacity then it is no longer possible to make an LPA. Instead, someone will need to apply to the Court of Protection to be appointed as a deputy on his or her behalf unless it is a single decision in which case the court can decide on the individual's behalf.

The deputy can be a member of the family, or it can be a professional person such as a solicitor. The deputy normally makes decisions about financial affairs which can include the decision to sell someone's house. The appointment of a deputy can take up to six months.

d) The court

The Court of Protection can make decisions on behalf of another concerning their health and welfare when an individual is found to lack capacity to do so on his or her behalf. all decisions must be made in the best interests of the person (s 4 of the Mental Capacity Act 2005).

Decisions of the court must consider the views of the patient under the court as well as the family views. It is then up to the court to consider how much weight to place on each of these views.

Social care of the elderly

According to figures released by Age UK in 2023 a 65-year-old man can expect to live another 18.5 years, and a 65-year-old woman 21. In 2023, there are 11 million people aged over 65 in England. When the NHS was founded and our adult social care system established 75 years ago, one in two people died before the age of 65. Now, fewer than one in seven people do so. This places a very high burden of care on society as the elderly are more likely to suffer from long-term health conditions and will be in need of some assistance and care. The population aged 85+, the age group most likely to need health and care services, is also projected to rise rapidly, increasing by 8.2 per cent in the next five years and by 62.7 per cent by 2043 (126,000 and 956,000 people, respectively). This level of growth is not new. Between 2010 and 2020, the population in England over 65 grew by over 22 per cent or 1.9 million people (Age UK 2023b).

The rise in numbers living beyond 65 poses a theoretical and practical question about their care:

i)   firstly, on whom does the burden of care fall? This is a question that has some similarity to the questions raised in Chapter 16 about the financial support of children living in single parent homes. Should the burden of care fall on adult children, or should this burden fall on the shoulders of the State?

ii)   secondly, a practical question arises as to how care is provided and what level of financial support should be given to the elderly and their carers. Further, should this be means tested so that those who can afford to do so carry the financial burden of their care leaving those who cannot afford to pay dependent on state funding?

On whom should the burden of care fall?

Adult children

With rising costs of care in the UK and an ageing population, discussion of who should shoulder the costs of care for the elderly has become very topical. Amy Mullin explored the question of whether adult children should be responsible for the care of elderly parents in her article 'Filial responsibilities of dependent children' (2010). She argued that it is entirely appropriate for that burden to be shouldered by adult children but the basis of such an argument appears to be based on a moral duty. Others have also argued in favour of some of the burden of care for elderly parents falling on the shoulders of adult children but struggle to find ways of managing this. Jane English suggests that any obligation placed on children to support elderly parents should be based on friendship, but she points out the problems of enforcement as the law rarely enforces rights based on friendship (English 1979).

If an obligation to support elderly parents was to be enforceable against adult children, then it is difficult to find a legal basis for such an obligation. The obligation placed on the shoulders of parents to support children arises after they have taken a conscious decision to have a child; adult children do not consciously make the same decision with regard to their parents.

In a study across Europe of a range of family obligations carried out by Jane Millar and Andrea Warman in 1996 it was found that there was a wide degree of variation between different European countries in the duties placed on adult children in relation to care for elderly parents. The findings revealed that where the legal obligations had been removed from adult children, then the State had largely stepped in to take on the burden. This was particularly true of Scandinavian countries. In the UK as there had never been a legal obligation placed on adult children to provide support then the system was far more piecemeal (Millar and Warman 1996; see also Oldham 2001 which describes the responsibilities under French law in detail).

Of course, this ignores the hours of often unpaid care that are provided by adult children for their parents and the fact that this releases the State from bearing the cost and responsibility (see Pickard 2015; Arber and Ginn 1992).

> The State does have a statutory duty under the Care Act 2014 to provide care which covers a range of services. This includes not only the person whose welfare is the concern, but also any carer that they have. The Act is not exclusively about the elderly. but it is significant because it places a legal duty on the State to provide care.

It is clear that the State struggles to meet this commitment especially with regard to the elderly. It is beyond the scope of this chapter to cover the rocky road to possible reform to the funding of the social care system but following recommendations made in July 2011, the independent Commission on Funding of Care and Support, chaired by Sir Andrew Dilnot, published its report, *Fairer Care Funding*. This set out proposals for reform of adult social care, including on the support individuals should be given to help pay for care and what they should contribute themselves. Plans for a social care levy were introduced which would go in part towards the care of the elderly. These recommendations were welcomed by many across the NHS, carers and those responsible for care of elderly people (see comments on the report made by The King's Fund (2013), an independent think tank which addresses health issues in the community), but the proposed plan has not yet been implemented and state funding of social care continues to be the subject of political debate. (See House of Lords Library 2023.)

Abuse of the elderly

The abuse of elderly people must have existed over history, but it is only comparatively recently that it has become recognised as a separate category of abuse. The term 'elder abuse' was not in general use until the 1980s. By the 1990s interest in the subject had increased and there have now been a number of surveys looking at the extent of elder abuse in society. In particular work carried out by Manthorpe et al. on *The U.K. National Study of Abuse and Neglect Among Older People* which looked at the extent of the problem. They found that 2.6 per cent of people over 66 reported suffering mistreatment and neglect from close family members or friends or care workers. This rose to 4 per cent once neighbours and acquaintances were included in the calculation (see Manthorpe et al. 2007). There have been further studies which suggest that the findings of Manthorpe et al. were fairly conservative. A study by Yon et al. – which considered data from 52 other studies across 28 countries – found that as many as 1 in 6 people aged 60 or over had experienced some form of abuse in a single year. The abuse was defined as 'a single, or repeated act, or lack of appropriate action, occurring within any relationship where there is an expectation of trust which causes harm or distress to an older person' (Yon et al. 2017). Psychological abuse was the most common in Yon et al's study closely followed by financial, neglect, physical and sexual abuse.

Addressing elder abuse

There is no specific criminal offence of elder abuse. Depending on the type of abuse it could fall within several different statutes e.g. the Theft Act where property is taken or The Domestic Abuse Act 2021 where the abuse is caused by someone personally connected with the elder person.

The Mental Capacity Act 2005 created a specific offence where a person lacking in mental capacity is ill-treated or neglected but such an offence relies on the elderly person lacking capacity. Where a person has mental capacity the inherent jurisdiction of the court is still available to deal with a situation where abuse is suspected.

In *A Local Authority v DL* [2012] EWCA Civ 253, a 50-year-old man lived with his parents who were both over 80. Although the mother was physically disabled neither were mentally disabled. The carer who visited daily to assist the mother was aware of the son's high level of control over the parents; he sought to limit visits from others, and he also abused them both mentally and physically. There could be no redress under the Mental Capacity Act 2005, but the Court was able to hear the case under its inherent jurisdiction. The facts of the case illustrate how complex cases of elderly abuse can be, as not only was it difficult to find grounds to bring a case against the son the elderly parents were both very reluctant to bring criminal charges against him in spite of the abuse they had suffered.

One possible way to address the issues which elderly abuse presents is to specifically grant rights to the elderly in the form of a charter rather than leave those who have suffered abuse to rely on other legislation which is often too wide and too vague and may not apply.

The impact of death on family life

Death is an inevitable and, in most cases, an involuntary event in family. Death happens to everyone and the legal, emotional, practical, social and financial consequences for the family are far reaching. No discussion of family law can ignore the subject of death. It will often alter the status of family members and allow surviving spouses or civil partners to enter into new legal relationships. A regrouping of the family may take place, and new associated familial relationships may come into existence.

It is regarded as an important part of family life, and in some cases a legal duty, to bury or cremate the remains of family members.

Presumption of death

Each year, significant numbers of people disappear without trace, leaving behind them great uncertainty about their fate, some as a result of personal stress and others because of natural disasters.

The tsunami in South East Asia in December 2004, in which 220,000 died, left many believing that their partners and other family members were dead. They were left without the satisfaction of the certainty that this was so. Where no body is found, it is not usually possible for a death certificate to be issued. The family of the deceased or the personal representatives may have to apply for a legal declaration of presumption of death to permit the deceased's estate to be distributed.

In 1974, Lord Lucan, a well-known English aristocrat, disappeared from his family home in London after the murder of the family nanny. He was legally presumed dead in 1992.

Common law

At common law, a declaration of presumption of death can be made after a person has been absent for seven years. There must have been no communication between the missing person and those with whom he or she would have been expected to make contact. The person applying for the declaration must have made enquiries about the missing person and there must be no evidence that he or she is still alive.

A declaration of presumption of death at common law did not terminate a marriage. Therefore, if a spouse remarried after a declaration of presumption of death, and the person who had been presumed dead re-appeared, the new marriage would be held to be void.

The seven-year rule and the risk of an invalid marriage caused great hardship to surviving spouses who were left in limbo. It led to a change in the law to enable spouses and civil partners to apply for a statutory presumption of death.

The Presumption of Death Act 2013

The Presumption of Death Act 2013 which came into force on 1 October 2014 changed the common law rules and allows a court to make a conclusive declaration that a missing person is presumed dead. This is effective for all purposes and against all persons. The property of the missing person can pass to others and any marriage or civil partnership will come to an end. Under the Act an application can be made to the High Court for a declaration that a missing person who is thought to have died or who has been missing for at least seven years. Anyone can apply to the court under the Act but if the applicant is not a spouse or civil partner, parent, child or sibling then the court must be satisfied that he/she has sufficient interest to do so. The court must be satisfied that the missing person was domiciled in England and Wales for the preceding year on the date when he or she was last known to be alive or the applicant is the spouse or civil partner of the missing person and is domiciled in England and Wales at the date the application is made or was habitually resident there for the preceding year.

There are provisions allowing an application to vary or revoke the order if the missing person returns. In *EA v NA* [2018] EWHC 583 (Fam), Mr Justice Keehan granted a declaration of presumed death under the Act following a claim made by the wife of an Iraqi national who she had assisted in making an application for a British passport. As soon as he obtained the passport he had deserted her. At no time had she met his family who were living in Nottingham. In 2010 five years after they had met she received a phone call from a relative telling her that he died in Iraq, but no details were given to her of the circumstances. Seven years after receiving this information she made an application seeking a declaration that he was presumed dead. Although the judge held that he could not be satisfied that her husband was dead, he was satisfied that the missing husband has not been known to be alive for a period of at least seven years.

Although Lord Lucan was legally presumed dead under the common law rules seven years after his disappearance, his son and heir Lord Bingham made an application to the court under the Act when it was passed for a declaration that Lord Lucan was presumed dead. This was important since under the Presumption of Death Act 2013 a finding of the court is conclusive as to the death of the missing individual. (See *Re Bingham* [2015] EWHC 226 (Ch), where the Court concluded that Lord Lucan had died on the seventh anniversary of his last being seen alive.)

Funeral arrangements

Rights and duties to deal with the deceased's body

When a person dies, there is a duty at common law to dispose of the body in a proper manner. According to Scott LJ in *Rees v Hughes* [1946] KB 517:

> *There is an obligation at common law, in the nature of a public duty, which rests on certain persons in whose possession a dead body may be – a husband being one – to bury it. . . . [W]here a man dies possessed of personal property, the duty of burying his body falls primarily on his personal representatives . . . and this duty entitles the personal representative to absolute priority of reimbursement out of the estate.*

Where children are involved and the parents have separated the court may have to rule as to who should have the authority to arrange the disposal, and thus, coincidentally, usually, where the body is to be buried and perhaps according to what rites. The question of whether the court has jurisdiction to order that a body be buried, due to a delay in making the arrangements by those who would normally be expected to do so, was decided in a recent case *Re K (A Child: deceased)* [2017] EWHC 1083 (Fam). It was held that no order in respect of a child's body or burial can be made under the Children Act 1989. By s 8 of the Children Act 1989 a specific issue order is 'an order giving directions for the purpose of determining a specific question which has arisen, or which may arise, in connection with any aspect of parental responsibility for a child'. The Act applies to the exercise of parental responsibility for a child, defined as a person under the age of 18. While parental responsibility extends, at least for a parent who has the means to do so, to providing for the burial of his or her deceased child, it does not extend to regulating events arising after the child's death. Christopher Sharp QC examined the relevant law in *Re K*. He pointed to a judgment by Lady Hale when she was sitting as a High Court judge in the case of *Buchanan v Milton* [1999] 2 FLR 844 at para [845]–[846] where she said: 'There is no right of ownership in a dead body. However, there is a duty at common law to arrange for its proper disposal. This duty falls primarily upon the personal representatives of the deceased.' He concluded that rather than rely on complex property law rules the issue should be decided under the court's inherent jurisdiction (see Sharp 2017).

In *R v Rausing* (2012), Hans Kristian Rausing, a multi-millionaire who inherited a fortune from Tetra Pak carton manufacture, was charged with the offence of preventing the lawful and decent burial of his wife's body. He had wrapped the body up under several layers of bin bags in a sealed room where it had remained for one or two months. The court accepted that he was distressed and too confused after her death to organise a funeral. He was given a suspended prison sentence (BBC News 2012).

Provided there is no dispute, the certificate will normally be given to the person who registers the death. In many cases, this will be a friend or relative of the deceased. However, from a strict legal standpoint, the deceased's representatives (if there is a will, the executors or, in the case of an intestacy, those appointed as the administrators of the deceased's estate are the only persons who have the right, and duty, to deal with the body). However, the deceased's wishes may also be taken into account (see *Ibuna and another v Arroyo and another* [2012] EWHC 428 (Ch)). This case concerned a dispute between an estranged wife and the deceased's life partner as to who should have the right to take possession of the body of the deceased. The daughter of the deceased had been appointed his executrix. The deceased had indicated that he wished his life partner to make the arrangements for his burial. Where there is a dispute about the validity of a will and therefore, the identity of the executors, the person in possession of the body may have the right to deal with the body (see *University Hospital Lewisham NHS v Hamuth* [2006] EWHC 1609 (Ch)).

In *Borrows v HM Coroner for Preston* [2008] EWHC 1387 (QB), a 15-year-old boy had committed suicide whilst in a Young Offenders Institution. He had lived with his uncle and his family for some time before his incarceration because of his mother's drug addiction. He had re-established contact with his mother just before he was sentenced. The uncle planned to cremate the body because that was the boy's wish, but his mother wanted to bury it.

The court held that the best person to be appointed as administrator of the boy's estate was set out in the order of priority in Rule 22 of the Non-Contentious Probate Rules (SI 1987/2024).

If there is a dispute over priority, s 116 of the Supreme Court Act 1981 applies and the court must consider whether there are any special circumstances to vary the order of priority, and exercise its discretion. Art 8 (the right to respect for private and family life) of the European Convention on Human Rights 1950 (ECHR) and the jurisprudence of the European Court of Human Rights (ECtHR) require the deceased's wishes to be taken into account. The mother in *Borrows* was found to be incapable of making the funeral arrangements. The uncle and his family were the deceased's psychological family, and the deceased had a strong connection with the area in which they lived. The uncle, therefore, was given the right to arrange his deceased nephew's cremation.

In *Hartshorne v Gardner* [2008] 2 FLR 1681, the deceased died intestate at the age of 44 in a car accident. His divorced parents both wished to arrange the funeral for their son. The mother wished to have him cremated, and the father wished to have him buried at some distance from the mother's home but close to where the son had lived. The mother maintained that it would be difficult for her to visit the grave because of its distance from her home. The coroner refused to release the body until the parents had reached agreement or the court had decided which of them should take precedence.

The court held that both parents had equal rights but chose to exercise its discretion in favour of the father because he had had a close relationship with the deceased compared with the mother. Furthermore, the deceased's fiancée and siblings all supported the father's wishes relating to the funeral arrangements.

In *Holtam v Arnold* (1986) 2 BMLR 123, the deceased had left his wife in order to cohabit with the plaintiff. The cohabitant made arrangements for the funeral but the court held that the deceased's wife, on the intestacy, was entitled to letters of administration of her husband's estate and, therefore, had the right to dispose of the body. Had the deceased left a will, his executors would have had the right to arrange the funeral.

Testate succession

Freedom of testation means that all sane adults have the right to make a will which will ensure that their property will be distributed after their death in whatever way they have specified. There is no obligation to make provision for a spouse, civil partner, cohabitant, other family member, or a friend who was maintained by the deceased during his or her lifetime.

If the deceased fails to provide for any of these persons, an application for limited provision from the deceased's estate may be made under the Inheritance (Provision for Family and Dependants) Act 1975 which is discussed later in this chapter.

The Wills Act 1837, ss 18, 18B provides that every will is revoked by a valid marriage or civil partnership. However, if the will was made by the testator with the assumption that marriage or civil partnership to a specific person was in his or her mind, and that the will should not be revoked by the marriage or civil partnership, it will be enforceable.

Under Section 18A of the Wills Act 1837 as amended by the Law Reform (Succession) Act 1995 s 3(1) if a person has made a will and then subsequently divorces or his/her civil partnership is dissolved their former spouse or civil partner is deemed for the purpose of the testator's will to have died on the date that the marriage or civil partnership ended (the date on which the decree absolute or decree of dissolution was issued). This has several consequences: firstly if the former spouse or civil partner was appointed executor under the will that appointment does not take effect; secondly any gift under the will will fail and any substitute provision will take effect. Thirdly if the former spouse was the only beneficiary and there were no substitute provisions then the estate would be distributed in accordance with the rules of intestacy. This can be problematic as the distribution under the rules of intestacy may not be in accordance with the deceased's wishes. The section only applies on divorce or dissolution and not separation.

Intestate succession: Administration of Estates Act 1925, s 46

Intestate succession will take place where the deceased leaves no will or where the will is invalid.

According to a survey carried out by Canada Life in 2023, one in three adults have not made a will. Many believe they do not have sufficient assets to warrant the making of a will, some believe the costs involved will be too high, whilst others believe that their property will automatically pass to their family. Where a couple cohabit then this is unlikely to be true as cohabitants do not automatically inherit on the death of a partner. The intestacy rules often work in a way that is contrary to the intentions of the deceased see Canada Life (2024).

If a spouse or civil partner dies intestate, the property will be distributed in accordance with the Administration of Estates Act 1925. Section 46(2A) of the Act provides that a spouse or civil partner must survive for 28 days after the death of a partner to come within the intestacy rules. If he or she dies within that period, the property of the person who dies first will be distributed as if there is no surviving spouse or civil partner.

If the parties are divorced or judicially separated, or the civil partnership has been dissolved, or a separation order has been granted, or if a decree or order of nullity has been granted, or the marriage or civil partnership was void *ab initio*, they will receive nothing on an intestacy.

Section 46(1)(i) of the Act provides that a surviving spouse or civil partner takes all the personal chattels unless they have to be sold to pay the intestate's debts.

Section 55(1)(x) defines personal chattels in a rather quaint manner:

Carriages, horses, stable furniture and effects (not used for business purposes), motor cars and accessories (not used for business purposes), garden effects, domestic animals, plate, plated articles, linen, china, glass, books, pictures, prints, furniture, jewellery, articles of household or personal use or ornament, musical and scientific instruments and apparatus, wines, liquors and consumable stores, but they do not include any chattels used at the death of the intestate for business purposes nor money or securities for money.

The distribution of the deceased's estate after the personal chattels have been taken by the surviving spouse or civil partner depends on whether there are other surviving relatives. The rules of intestacy changed in July 2023. The amount that a partner or spouse can inherit if there are surviving children was raised to £322,000 for deaths after July 2023.

Where there is a spouse or civil partner and children or other direct descendants, the surviving spouse or civil partner has a right to a statutory legacy of £322,000 (provided the deceased's estate is sufficient) and half the remainder.

Whatever remains is held on trust in equal shares for the deceased's children who are alive at the time of his or her death.

There is no formal statutory legacy if the deceased dies, leaving a surviving spouse or civil partner without issue, as the whole estate goes to the spouse or civil partner.

For cohabitants, the rules of intestacy can be very harsh. There is no automatic right to the property of the deceased with the possible exception of the family home.

This aspect of the intestacy laws has been heavily criticised. With the numbers of cohabitants rising annually and the numbers choosing to marry it seems sensible for the law to reflect the practicalities of family life. In 2011, the Law Commission considered the rights of cohabitants on the death of a partner and recommended that cohabitants should be able to inherit if they had cohabited for over five years. This was not acted on. As discussed in earlier chapters, the 'common law myth' survives and many people are unaware of the lack of rights of cohabitants compared to married couples and civil partners. Research has shown that most people think that it was right that cohabitants should automatically inherit if his/her partner died intestate. Reflecting on two large scale research projects in 2008 carried out by Sheffield and Cardiff Universities Williams, Potter and Douglas showed that a large majority of the general public would support some automatic provision being made for a surviving cohabitant, with a greater share being felt appropriate both the longer the relationship had lasted and if the partners had had children (Williams 2008).

There is one exception to the rule which is dependent on property law rules rather than intestacy: if the legal and equitable title to the family home is in joint names and held as a joint tenancy the law allows the survivor to take the property absolutely.

Where a person dies intestate leaving no spouse or civil partner or children then the law has drawn up a list of which relatives of the deceased should inherit. The list is very old-fashioned and can result in relatives who have had little or no contact with the deceased inheriting a share of the property when close friends and partners can claim nothing. The logic of this list has been subject to criticism, and some have reflected on the changes made recently to the rules which result in spouses and civil partners benefiting often at the expense of children (Cooke 2009; Burns 2013).

The deceased's estate is inherited in the following order of precedent:

- first, by the direct descendants;
- secondly, by the parents;
- thirdly, by the deceased's brothers or sisters or their direct descendants;
- fourthly, by the deceased's half brothers and sisters;
- fifthly, by the grandparents;
- sixthly, by the deceased's aunts and uncles.

If any of these have died before the deceased but have living children, the children will take their parent's share.

Bona vacantia

The Administration of Estates Act 1925, s 46(1) provides that if there are none of the relatives listed above who are surviving at the time of the deceased's death, the estate goes as *bona vacantia* to the Crown. It is believed that the Crown acquires several million pounds each year by way of *bona vacantia*.

The Treasury Solicitor may make an *ex gratia* payment to anyone who makes an application on the ground that the deceased could reasonably have been expected to make provision for them. The process is very informal; applications by email are possible. The Treasury Solicitor has complete discretion to make a decision (see www.bonavacantia.gov.uk). The factors which will be taken into account include:

a.   the size and nature of the deceased's estate;

b.   the length and nature of the relationship between the deceased and the applicant;

c.   any legal or moral obligations which the deceased had towards the applicant;

d.   the way in which the applicant behaved towards the deceased, including the contribution (if any) made by the applicant to the welfare of the deceased;

e.   any other matter which, in the particular circumstances, the Treasury Solicitor considers relevant.

No application will be considered if the person is eligible to make a claim under the Inheritance Act 1975. This rule excludes the possibility of many claims to the Treasury Solicitor because there will be few applicants eligible to claim an *ex gratia* payment who would not have a right to apply under the Inheritance Act 1975. Possible applicants might include immediate relatives or close friends, who were not being maintained by the deceased prior to death and do not, therefore, come within the ambit of the 1975 Act but to whom the deceased owed some form of moral obligation,

The Inheritance (Provision for Family and Dependants) Act 1975 – applications for financial maintenance

The principle of testamentary freedom has been jealously guarded in England and Wales for many years. This contrasts with many European countries where testamentary freedom is limited. It was accepted as early as 1938 that it would be right to allow certain classes of people to apply to the court where they felt they had been unfairly left out of a will.

The Inheritance (Family Provision) Act 1938 was fairly limited in its remit, but the Act that followed, the Inheritance (Family Provision) Act 1975, was more radical. It was considered to be a revolutionary development at the time of its enactment. The Act has the potential to provide financial maintenance for a wide range of family members, and other dependants including mistresses and cohabitants, who have received no reasonable financial provision from the deceased's estate either by will or because of the rules relating to intestacy.

During its passage through Parliament, it was referred to as the '*Mistresses' Charter*' (Hansard HC Deb 16 July 1975 vol 895). It has been said repeatedly that the Act does not allow the court to rewrite the deceased's will or modify the intestacy rules. However, in reality, any order made under the Act will have to be met out of the legacies intended by the testator, or where there is an intestacy, out of the statutory legacies.

Time bar

Because any award which the court makes will affect the rights of other beneficiaries, s 4 of the Act provides that any application must be made within six months of the valid grant of probate (in the case of testate succession), or from the date when letters of administration are first taken out (in the case of intestate succession). The period may be extended at the court's discretion.

Applicants

Section 1(1) of the Act defines the categories of those who may apply:

a. spouses or civil partners: included in this category are judicially separated spouses or civil partners, parties to a voidable marriage or civil partnership which has not been annulled prior to the deceased's death. Parties who have entered into a void marriage or civil partnership in good faith, and who have not applied for the relationship to be annulled, are also included provided they have not remarried or entered into a new civil partnership;

b. former spouses or civil partners who have not remarried or entered into a new civil partnership and have not been barred from applying under the terms of the divorce settlement or the civil partnership dissolution settlement;

c. children, including adopted children;

d. any person who is not a child of the deceased but who was treated as a child of the deceased in relation to a marriage to which the deceased was a party;

e. any other person who immediately before the death of the deceased was being maintained, either partly or wholly, by the deceased.

Section 1(1A), (1B) of the Act provides that any person living in the same household as the deceased, as if a spouse or civil partner of the deceased, during the two years immediately preceding the death of the deceased may also make an application. Prior to the insertion of these sections (see Law Reform (Succession) Act 1995, s 2(3), CPA 2004, s 71, Sch 4, Pt 2, para 15(1), (5)), heterosexual or same-sex cohabitants had to apply under s 1(1)(e) with all the attendant problems of proving dependency. The task of such couples has been made significantly easier by s 1(1A), (B).

Living together in the same household as if a spouse or civil partner

Courts continue to struggle with the meaning of 'living together in the same household as if a spouse or a civil partner'. House and household do not have the same meaning, although, it is implicit in several of the decisions that the courts have tended to confuse the two concepts. Whether a person is living in the same household as another depends on the particular facts of the case. Applicants have been more likely to succeed where they meet the judiciary's fairly conservative expectations that they were fulfilling one of the traditional roles associated with marriage and were living in the same house as the deceased, and had had a sexual relationship with the deceased.

In *Re Watson (deceased)* [1999] 1 FLR 878, the applicant and the deceased had had a relationship for 30 years. For the first 20 years, they did not live together because they both cared for their elderly parents. When they were eventually free to live together, the applicant kept her house but left it unoccupied. She declined to marry the deceased; she preferred her freedom, although she only took advantage of it to get together with her female friends. She cooked and cleaned for the deceased and contributed towards half the cost of the outgoings. The couple lived companionably together, having abandoned their sexual relationship prior to moving in together, until the deceased went into hospital where he died intestate. He left no surviving relatives. An application was made under the Inheritance Act. The deceased's estate consequently passed to the Crown as *bona vacantia*, and the Treasury Solicitor maintained that the applicant's relationship with the deceased was merely a house-sharing arrangement. This argument centred on the applicant's refusal to marry, her lack of sexual relations with the deceased once they began living together, her retention of her own home and her sharing of the outgoings on the deceased's house.

The court rejected this approach and maintained that the question to be asked was whether, in the opinion of a reasonable person with normal perceptions, could it be said that the two people in question were living together as husband and wife. In so doing, it acknowledged the multifarious nature of marital relationships. The court suggested that:

> it cannot be doubted that it is not unusual for a happily married husband and wife in their mid-fifties (which was the age of the parties when they started living together in the present case) not merely to have separate bedrooms, but to abstain from sexual relations. Mr Watson and Miss Griffiths lived alone together for over 10 years in a house where they shared the bathroom and the living rooms. He went out to work and earned the bulk of the household's income, while she did the housekeeping . . . the shopping, the washing, the cooking and the gardening. No doubt, they ate together every day and that they enjoyed the living rooms jointly.

The court concluded that the applicant had lived as if she were the wife of the deceased.

In *Churchill v Roach* [2004] FLR 720, a middle-aged couple, who were lovers for many years, finally purchased adjoining houses and subsequently combined them into one house in which they lived together. The man died before they had lived together in the house for the requisite two years. The court maintained that the relationship lacked the following features which it thought to be indicative of living together as if a husband or wife:

a.   elements of permanence;

b.   frequency and intimacy of contact;

c.   an element of mutual support;

d.   a degree of voluntary restraint upon personal freedom;

e.   an element of community of resources.

The court did however permit the woman to claim under s 1(1)(e) of the Act on the basis that the deceased had been maintaining her immediately before his death.

(See also *Lindop v Agus; Bass and Hedley* [2010] 1 FLR 631, where the court upheld a claim under the Act by a cohabitant who could not prove that she had lived with the deceased for two years immediately before the deceased died but could prove dependency.)

An application will not fail if there is a good reason why a couple, who had lived together for two years, were not actually doing so at the time of the death. One obvious good reason is where the deceased was hospitalised. In such circumstances, he or she was clearly still a member of the applicant's household.

In *Gully v Dix* [2004] 1 FCR 453, the applicant had left the deceased three months prior to his death because he had a drink problem. It was to be a trial separation, and the relationship had not ended. The court accepted that the parties had been living together in the same household immediately prior to death. In Ward LJ's words

> *so the steadfastness of a commitment to live together may wax and wane, but so long as it is not extinguished it survives.*

Proof of maintenance (s 1(3))

Section 1(3) of the Inheritance Act provides that applicants who make a claim under s 1(1)(e) will be treated as being maintained by the deceased, if the deceased, other than for full valuable consideration, was making a substantial contribution in money or money's worth towards their needs. The provision was intended, partly, to prevent employees who lived with the deceased from making a claim.

In *Jelley v Iliffe* [1981] Fam 128, Stephenson LJ explained his interpretation of s 1(3):

> *The court has to balance what [the deceased] was contributing against what [the applicant] was contributing, and if there is any doubt about the balance tipping in favour of [the deceased's] being the greater contribution, the matter must go to trial. If, however, the balance is bound to come down in favour of the [applicant's] being the greater contribution, or if the contributions are equal, there is no dependency.*

This approach to maintenance could mean an applicant who has made a significant contribution by caring for the deceased for very little reward would appear to lose out. The lazier an applicant has been, the more likely they could be considered to have received more than they have given and be rewarded under the Act.

However, Stephenson LJ suggested that a balance must be struck and

> the court must use common sense and remember that the object of Parliament in creating this extra class of person who may claim benefit from an estate was to provide relief for persons of whom it could be said that they were wholly or partially dependent on the deceased. It cannot be an exact exercise of evaluating services in pounds and pence.

Rather strangely, he did suggest that companionship could be evaluated as valuable consideration. What price one puts on such an imponderable remains a mystery.

In *Re B (deceased)* (2000), a mother and her severely disabled daughter lived in a property which was purchased using 25 per cent of the mother's money and 75 per cent of the damages which had been awarded to the daughter for severe mental and physical disabilities sustained at birth. Her father had left home when she was born and played no part in her life; her affairs were dealt with by the Court of Protection which had made regular payments to the mother for the daughter's maintenance but no specific allowance for herself.

When the daughter died intestate, the estate passed to the mother and father in equal shares. The mother successfully applied for reasonable provision from her daughter's estate. She argued that her daughter had maintained her. The Court of Appeal maintained that it would have been obvious to the Court of Protection that the payments to the daughter were also being used to meet her mother's financial and material needs to enable her to look after her daughter's needs. The Court of Protection could be seen as acting as the conscience of a patient and making provision for those to whom the patient would have felt a moral obligation if mentally capable of doing so.

Assumption of responsibility (s 3(3)(4))

Sections 3(3)(4) of the Act requires the court to take into account the extent to which, and the basis on which, the deceased assumed responsibility for an applicant's maintenance.

In *Jelley v Iliffe* (see earlier), Stephenson LJ took a fairly liberal approach to the assumption of responsibility and stated that where one person had made a substantial contribution to another person's needs, it raised an inference of an assumption of responsibility and dependency.

In *Baynes v Hedger* [2009] EWCA Civ 374, the deceased, a well-known wealthy sculptor, had had a very private lesbian relationship with the applicant's mother for 40 years. The deceased was also the applicant's godmother. She had been very involved with all of her partner's children and had made gifts during her lifetime to them but had been exceptionally generous towards her goddaughter. She had bought her a flat and had provided her with other forms of financial help. Not satisfied, the goddaughter had attempted to obtain further financial help by telling the deceased that she knew the nature of her relationship with her mother. In her will, the deceased had left her house, worth £2 million, to a charity, £2,500 to the applicant and the residuary estate of £400,000 to her partner for life and then to her partner's children, excluding the goddaughter.

The applicant's debts exceeded £400,000 and she asked the court for an award of £800,000, under the Inheritance Act, to help her avoid bankruptcy.

In the High Court in 2008, Lewison J accepted that the goddaughter was eligible to make a claim under s 1(1)(e) of the Act but refused to make an order in her favour. He considered s 3(4) of the Act and held that the deceased had wanted to pay off her goddaughter's debts to make her financially independent and had not assumed a responsibility or an obligation for her ongoing maintenance. The goddaughter appealed unsuccessfully. The Court of Appeal emphasised that the first question a court must address is whether an applicant, to whom s 3(3) or (4) applies is eligible to make a claim. Lewison J had failed to do so; he had accepted the goddaughter's eligibility to apply and then concluded that the deceased had not assumed responsibility for the maintenance of her goddaughter. Given this conclusion, he should have held that she was ineligible to apply for maintenance in the first place.

Reasonable financial provision

Applicants must be able to show that the effect of the deceased's will or the rules relating to intestacy means that they have not received reasonable financial provision from the deceased's estate.

> Reasonable financial provision is defined in s 1(2) of the Act. A different test for what constitutes reasonable financial provision is applied for spouses and civil partners to that of other applicants.

For the surviving spouse or civil partner, it means such financial provision as it would be reasonable in all the circumstances of the case for them to receive, whether or not it was required for their maintenance. In *Moore v Holdsworth* [2010] EWHC 683 (Ch), a wife was allowed to continue living in the family home after the death of her husband. Prior to his death he had severed the joint tenancy of the property and left his half share of the property to a nephew and niece. This would have meant that the property would have to be sold, but the order of the court allowed her to continue living there for the rest of her life and should she be unable to live there since she suffered from a long-term health condition, then an alternative property must be purchased for her.)

> S3 (2)(a)(b) provides that the court should take into account the age of the spouse or civil partner, the duration of the relationship, any contribution made to the welfare of the family and the potential size of any financial award which the applicant might have received had the relationship ended other than on death.

(See e.g. *Lilleyman v Lilleyman* [2012] EWHC 821 (Ch), where the court considered the type of award that might have been made had the parties divorced. The parties had only been married for two and a half years so the court drew analogies with financial provision in cases of short marriages.)

In *Re Estate of Singh (deceased)* [2023] All ER (D) 55, a husband had sought to disinherit his wife after 66 years of marriage. Under his will he left all his estate to his two sons and left nothing to his wife or four daughters. He claimed that he wished his property to pass down the male line of the family. At the time of his death the wife was living with one of her daughters; she was registered disabled and lived on a number of state benefits. The court reviewed the case as if it had ended in divorce and awarded her a half share of the estate.

This standard may be extended to a surviving spouse or civil partner whose legal separation took place not more than 12 months before the death of the deceased. It may also be extended to a former spouse or civil partner who has not entered into a new legal relationship and whose divorce, or dissolution of the civil partnership, was granted not more than 12 months prior to the deceased's death.

For all other applicants, reasonable financial provision means such financial provision as it would be reasonable in all the circumstances of the case for the applicant to receive for his or her maintenance.

In *Espinosa v Bourke* [1999] 1 FLR 747, the Court of Appeal declined to define the exact meaning of the term maintenance but suggested that:

> *it connotes only payments which, directly or indirectly, enable the applicant in the future to discharge the cost of his daily living at whatever standard of living is appropriate to him. The provision that is to be made is to meet recurring expenses, being expenses of living of an income nature. This does not mean that the provision need be by way of income payments. The provision can be by way of lump sum, for example, to buy a house in which the applicant can be housed, thereby relieving him pro tanto of income expenditure . . . there may be cases in which payment of existing debts may be as appropriate as a maintenance payment; for example, to pay the debts of an applicant in order to enable him to continue to carry on a profit-making business or profession.*

In *Negus v Bahouse* [2008] 1 FCR 768, the deceased, Mr Bahouse, had been divorced twice and had one son. He had asked Ms Negus to live with him and give up her work as a receptionist. He had treated her generously, paying for all her needs in addition to giving her a small allowance of £250 a month. They had enjoyed dining in expensive restaurants and having luxurious holidays. Mr Bahouse had purchased a home for them. Eventually, after the couple had lived together for over seven years, his health declined. He became very depressed and committed suicide while Ms Negus was away for a weekend visiting her mother. Mr Bahouse's estate was worth £2 million. He had left a will leaving most of his property to his son, and legacies of £75,000 each to his three siblings. Ms Negus made a successful application under the Inheritance Act because she was not mentioned in the will. She had already acquired a half share of Mr Bahouse's pension policy worth £459,000, and a half share of a property in Spain worth £200,000; the remaining half shares belonged to his son.

In assessing what would be an appropriate amount for maintenance for Ms Negus, Judge Kaye QC referred to the Canadian decision in *Re Duranceau* (1952) where

> *in somewhat poetic language, the court said that the question is: 'Is the provision sufficient to enable the dependant to live neither luxuriously nor miserably, but decently and comfortably according to his or her station in life?'*

What is proper maintenance must in all cases depend upon all the facts and circumstances of the particular case being considered at the time, but I think it is clear on the one hand that one must not put too limited a meaning on it; it does not mean just enough to enable a person to get by; on the other hand, it does not mean anything which may be regarded as reasonably desirable for his general benefit or welfare.

He took into account Ms Negus' age, the length of her relationship with Mr Bahouse, his generosity to her and their lifestyle during his lifetime, and his promises to her to ensure her long-term security. It would be unjust to assume that Ms Negus would find employment at the age of 50; she had no recent work experience. The court awarded her the English home free of mortgage plus £240,000 on the basis that this, together with her share of the pension fund and the Spanish property, would give her an adequate income to meet her estimated needs of around £39,000 a year.

(See also *Webster v Webster* [2008] 1 FLR 1240, where the court awarded a cohabitant the family home and also reasonable financial provision from the deceased's estate.)

It shows that it is possible for a cohabitant to use the 1975 Act as a way of claiming financial provision where the deceased has died intestate or alternatively where the will of the deceased makes little or no provision for the claimant.

FACTORS TO BE CONSIDERED BY THE COURT

Once an applicant has proven eligibility to apply for an award from the deceased's estate, the court must have regard to a number of factors laid down in s 3(1) of the Act. The section is remarkably similar to the discretionary factors to which the court must have regard under the MCA 1973, s 25 (see Chapter 7), in making ancillary awards on divorce. The factors are:

a. the applicant's financial needs and resources;
b. other applicants' financial needs and resources;
c. any beneficiaries' financial needs and resources;
d. any obligation or responsibility which the deceased had towards the applicant or any beneficiary;
e. the size and nature of the estate;
f. any physical or mental disability of the applicant or beneficiary;
g. any other matter, including the conduct of the applicant or any other person, which the court considers to be relevant.

Section 3(2)–(5) expands on these factors; s 3(2) is of particular interest. It provides, *inter alia*, that, in the case of married applicants, the court shall have regard to

the provision which the applicant might reasonably have expected to receive if on the day on which the deceased died the marriage, instead of being terminated by death had been terminated by a decree of divorce.

This provision was considered by the Court of Appeal in *Cunliffe v Fielden* [2006] Ch 361. Mrs Cunliffe was aged 48 when she married the deceased in 2001; her husband died one year later and left an estate of £1.3 million. Mrs Cunliffe was named in the will as a beneficiary under a discretionary trust. The trustees offered her a £200,000 lump sum. She rejected this and applied for provision under the Inheritance Act. The judge at first instance awarded her £800,000. The executors appealed. The Court of Appeal granted the appeal and in doing so, Wall LJ drew attention to the problematic nature of the Inheritance Act 1975, s 3(2). He explained that:

> there is self-evidently a profound difference between a marriage which ends through the death of one of the spouses, and a marriage which ends through divorce . . . . A marriage dissolved by divorce involves a conscious decision by one or both of the spouses to bring the marriage to an end. That process leaves two living former spouses, each of whom has resources, needs and responsibilities. In such a case the length of the marriage and the parties' respective contributions to it assume a particular importance when the court is striving to reach a fair financial outcome. However, where the marriage, as here, is dissolved by death, a widow is entitled to say that she entered into it on the basis that it would be of indefinite duration, and in the expectation that she would devote the remainder of the parties' joint lives to being his wife and caring for him. The fact that the marriage has been prematurely terminated by death after a short period may therefore render the length of the marriage a less critical factor than it would be in the case of a divorce.

Wall LJ acknowledged that Mrs Cunliffe had married on the basis that her husband was considerably older than she was and that she might well have expected to spend time caring for her husband in his old age. She was entitled to assume that she need not revert to her position as a single woman when her husband died and that she would be financially secure for the rest of her life.

In spite of these comments, Wall LJ thought that, in the light of a short marriage, it would be inappropriate for Mrs Cunliffe to expect to be maintained at the same level she had enjoyed during the marriage. He proceeded to look at what he perceived to be Mrs Cunliffe's reasonable needs, in spite of the fact that s 1(2) of the Act provides that in the case of a married applicant the court may make an award whether or not it is required for maintenance. He stated that she had a need for a home at a lesser value that the former matrimonial home, and income providing her with reasonable maintenance. He judged that to be £600,000.

This decision shows some similarity with the approach taken by the courts to financial provision on divorce and the court is expressly instructed under the legislation to consider the principles that would be applied on divorce. Some of the same principles are applied but it seems that the application of the Matrimonial Causes Act will leave the spouse with considerably more than the spouse making an application under the Inheritance Act.

Applications by adult children

Applications under the Inheritance Act by adult children have proved to be problematic; the courts have tended to take a very restrictive approach towards them.

For instance, in *Re Jennings* [1994] Ch 256, Nourse LJ maintained that, although the Act made provision for applications by adult children, such applications would only be successful where there were special circumstances. The applicant was aged

50; the deceased, his father, had never provided for him during his lifetime. The court took the approach that because the deceased had not taken on any obligations or responsibilities towards his son during his lifetime, in accordance with s (1)(d) of the Act, it should not make provision for him now.

A similar approach was taken by the court in *Garland v Morris* [2007] EWHC 2 (Ch). Here, the parents of two sisters separated and the mother subsequently committed suicide. Prior to her death, she had had regular contact with the younger daughter and had made a will in which she left her entire estate to her. As a consequence, the father decided to leave £300,000 to the older daughter and nothing to the younger one. When he died the younger daughter applied for provision from his estate under the Inheritance Act 1975. She had minimal career prospects and had a young child; she was in financial difficulties. All her inheritance from her mother had been spent on a house which had required extensive renovations. Prior to her father's death, she had had nothing to do with him. The older daughter had had a good relationship with her father who had helped her financially during his lifetime. He wanted that help to continue after his death. He did ask her not to let her younger sister starve after he had died, and on his death, she gave her sister £6,000.

The court refused to grant the applicant's claim. It held that there is no need for a child of a deceased parent to prove that there was a moral obligation to provide for him or her, but merely to show that taking into account all the facts, and the factors in s 3 of the Act, it was unreasonable for a parent to exclude him or her from the will. Here, the failure to provide was not unreasonable; the father and his younger daughter had not had a relationship for a long time, and she had already benefited substantially from her mother's will.

The attitude of the courts towards applications by adult children for financial provision has become slightly more generous in recent years as illustrated by the Supreme Court case *Ilott v Blue Cross* [2017] UKSC 17. In this case a mother and daughter had become estranged when the daughter left home aged 17. When the mother died they had been estranged for over 26 years. Under the will the mother left her estate to three animal charities and left the daughter nothing. She made a claim under the 1975 Act. The daughter had very little money; she rented her house and relied on state benefits. The judge at first instance made an award of £50,000 and the Court of Appeal increased this to £143,000 representing over a quarter of the estate. The Supreme Court reinstated the award by the High Court judge basing its decision on the words of the statute i.e. what constitutes 'reasonable financial provision'. It held that maintenance is assessed on the facts of each case but is payment to 'enable the applicant in future to discharge the cost of his daily living at whatever standard of living appropriate to him'. In this case the court took note of the current standard of living enjoyed by the daughter. The case revealed how little guidance the legislation gives as to what constitutes reasonable provision for an applicant, but it also suggests that in spite of the apparent flexibility that the Act gives the court it does not allow the court the freedom to rewrite wills in favour of disappointed children or family members. Lady Hale commented on the state of our law saying that:

> it has not, or not yet, recognised a public interest in expecting or obliging parents to support their adult children so as to save the public money.

(See Sloan 2019)

John Wilson and Rebecca Bailey-Harris have suggested in an article written before *Ilott* was decided that the courts' approach in successful claims by adult children is one of satisfying disappointed reasonable expectation in a manner analogous to that of proprietary estoppel. In *Suggitt v Suggitt* [2011] EWHC 903 (Ch), the adult son actually made an application under both the principles of proprietary estoppel and the Inheritance Act but deferred his claim under the Act until his estoppel claim had been heard. Several of the decisions relating to claims by adult children do appear to have an estoppel element to them (see Wilson and Bailey-Harris 2005).

Although *Re Ilott v Blue Cross* [2017] UKSC 17 appears to have suggested that the courts have shown a more generous attitude towards adult applications for provision under the 1975 Act this has not been consistent. Express reasons from the deceased as to why the deceased has made little or no provision for the applicant does appear to carry weight. Even where there is 'need' as in the case of *Ilott*, the court may still refuse to make an award. In *Wellesley v Wellesley* [2019] EWHC 11 (Ch), a claim was brought by Tara Wellesley against her father's estate worth £1.3m and Tara had been left £20,000. The rest of the estate was left to his fourth wife for life, to be divided on her death between his son and five step children. Tara made a claim using the Inheritance Provision for Family and Dependants Act (1975) for a substantial part of the estate, arguing that she needed such funds as would allow her to train and work as an artist. She had been estranged from the Earl for over 30 years mainly because the Earl disapproved of her lifestyle which was described as 'chaotic' and included heavy drinking and drugs. Early attempts by the Earl to help Tara failed and the relationship broke down and was never repaired. Tara had a child of her own at the time of the application who was aged 21 and lived in a residential home for adults with special needs. She had not worked for some years and lived on state benefits but had hopes of becoming an artist. Her father had left her £20,000 and the judge awarded Tara nothing from the estate over the £20,000 she had already been left. The main reason for this was the long estrangement, and the judge placed the blame for this on the daughter. He did however say that even without the estrangement her claim would have failed. This is due to Tara living within her means, having had no financial support from the Earl during her adult life; she was capable of working; and if she needed help to get back into work she could use her £20,000 legacy. The judge placed weight on testamentary freedom, and perhaps in this case the fact that the claimant had been left a sum of money was persuasive whereas in the case of *Ilott* the claimant had been left nothing.

Family life after death

The final burial place of a family member can cause issues within a family. Where one member wishes to exhume and rebury a body the issue must be decided by an ecclesiastical court.

In *Re Blagdon Cemetery* [2002] Fam 299, the appellants' son had died in an industrial accident in 1978 whilst living some distance from their home. They arranged for his body to be buried in consecrated ground in Somerset close to where they were living at the time of his death. They subsequently moved home several times and finally retired to Suffolk. They wished to exhume their son's body and have it reburied near to their new home in a family burial plot which they had purchased for the benefit of themselves and their son. They wished to honour the memory of their son and visit his grave in its intended new location and, eventually, join him there.

Requests for exhumation and reburial of bodies from consecrated ground are made by petition to the Consistory Court of the Anglican Church under ecclesiastical law. The court's Chancellor declined the parents' request.

The parents appealed to the Arches Court in Canterbury which allowed the appeal. It held that there was a presumption that Christian burial was permanent, that bodily remains should not be portable, and a faculty for exhumation would only be granted in rare circumstances. It cited a paper written by the Bishop of Stafford (2001) which explained that:

> The permanent burial of the physical body/the burial of cremated remains should be seen as a symbol of our entrusting the person to God for resurrection. We are commending the person to God, saying farewell to them (for their 'journey'), entrusting them in peace for their ultimate destination, with us, the heavenly Jerusalem. This commending, entrusting, resting in peace does not sit easily with 'portable remains', which suggests the opposite: reclaiming, possession, and restlessness; a holding onto the 'symbol' of a human life rather than a giving back to God.

The Arches Court held that it was for the parents to show their circumstances were special. Old age, poor health and a move to a new area were not sufficient reasons in themselves. However, the court accepted as exceptional circumstances the son had died suddenly at an age when it might be expected that he had no view about where he might be buried, and there was no link between him, or his parents, and the community in the place in which he was buried. It was simply the most convenient place at the time. The court granted the parents' request. In so doing, it made some interesting observations on family life, albeit family life post death:

> The concept of a family grave is, of course, of long standing. In a less mobile society in the past, when generations of a family continued to live in the same community, it was accepted practice for several members of a family to be buried in one grave. Headstones give a vivid picture of family relationships and there are frequent examples of one or more children predeceasing their parents due to childhood illnesses, which were incurable. Burials in double or treble depth graves continue to take place at the present time. They are to be encouraged. They express family unity and they are environmentally friendly in demonstrating an economical use of land for burials.

Exhumation and reinterment can also be ordered in cases where there are exceptional circumstances such as sexual abuse of a member of the family as illustrated in the case that follows.

Re the Cremated Remains of AA [2018] ECC 7

The judgment of HH Judge Eyre QC, the Lichfield Diocesan Chancellor, is summarised on the Ecclesiastical Law Association website:

> The petitioner proposed to be buried in the same grave as her late sister and parents. However, when her sister's husband died, his cremated remains were interred in the same

grave, notwithstanding that a granddaughter of the late sister had specifically asked the parish priest not to inter the husband's remains in the same grave, alleging that the husband had subjected her to repeated sexual abuse when she was young, and it would cause great distress to the family to have his remains in the same grave where the remains of some members of the family were already interred and where other members of the family wished their remains to be interred.

The Chancellor decided that the continuing family distress which would be caused by allowing the husband's remains to be left in the grave amounted to exceptional circumstances justifying exhumation. He therefore granted a faculty for the exhumation of the husband's cremated remains and for re-interment of the remains in another churchyard.

Self-test questions

1. What does the law relating to intestate succession in England and Wales reveal about the meaning of family?

2. The courts should have much wider powers to interfere with testamentary freedom. Discuss with reference to case law.

3. The law does not permit spouses or civil partners to avoid their financial responsibilities towards each other on the legal ending of their relationships but does so on death. How would you ensure that partners whose relationships end by death are not in a worse financial situation than they would be if they decided to legally terminate their relationships during their lifetime?

4. Henrietta lived with Inigo for the last ten years prior to his death last week. His widow, Jane, has lived in an institution because she has been mentally ill for the last 12 years. Inigo did not divorce her because he felt that to do so would make her condition worse. Inigo and Jane had three children who are all adults.

   Inigo's children disliked their father intensely because they believed that he was the cause of their mother's illness. They also hate Henrietta because they believe that their father might have eventually rescued their mother from the institution if he had not gone to live with Henrietta. They wish to oppose Henrietta's wishes about the organisation of Inigo's funeral, to show the strength of their feelings against her. They want the undertaker to arrange the cremation of their father and dispose of the ashes for them; they do not wish to attend the cremation and have ordered the undertaker not to arrange any funeral service. Henrietta would like to organise Inigo's burial in the churchyard of the small village in Oxfordshire in which they had lived together.

   Advise Henrietta.

References

Age UK, 'Living With Dementia' (2023a) www.ageuk.org.uk/globalassets/age-uk/documents/policy-positions/health-and-wellbeing/dementia-policy-position-mar-2020.pdf[0] (accessed 09.09.2024)

Age UK, 'The State of Health and Care of Older People' (2023b) www.ageuk.org.uk/globalassets/age-uk/documents/reports-and-publications/reports-and-briefings/-july-2023 (accessed 09.09.2024)

Arber, Sara and Jay Ginn, 'Class and Caring: A Forgotten Dimension' (1992) 26(4) *Sociology* 619

BBC News, 'Eva Rausing Death: Husband Charged With Burial Delay' (01.08.2012) https://www.bbc.co.uk-england-london-19078646 (accessed 10.09.2024)

Burns, Fiona, 'Surviving Spouses, Surviving Children and the Reform of Total Intestacy Law in England and Scotland: Past, Present and Future' [2013] *Legal Studies* 85

Canada Life, 'Half of UK Adults Don't Have a Will' (2024) https://www.canadalife.co.uk/news/over-half-of-uk-adults-do-not-have-a-will (accessed 10.09.2024)

Census, 'Profile of the Older Population Living in England and Wales in 2021 and Changes Since 2011' (2021) www.ons.gov.uk/peoplepopulationandcommunity/birthsdeathsandmarriages/ageing/articles/profileoftheolderpopulationlivinginenglandandwalesin2021andchangessince2011/2023-04-03 (accessed 09.10.2024)

Cooke, Elizabeth, 'Wives, Widows and Wicked Stepmothers: A Brief Examination of Spousal Entitlement on Intestacy' [2009] *Child and Family Law Quarterly* 423

English, Jane, 'What Do Grown Children Owe Their Parents?' in *Having Children: Philosophical and Legal Reflections on Parenthood* (Oxford University Press 1979)

www.ftadviser.com/your-industry/2023/04/05/half-of-uk-adults-do-not-have-a-will

Hedlund, Richard, 'The End to Testamentary Freedom' (2021) 41 *Legal Studies* 55

House of Lords Library, 'Reforming Adult Social Care: House of Lords Committee Report' (2023) https://lordslibrary.parliament.uk/reforming-adult-social-care-house-of-lords-committee-report (accessed 10.09.2024)

The Kings Fund, 'Paying for Social Care' (2013) www.kingsfund.org.uk/insight-and-analysis/reports/paying-social-care-dilnot (accessed 10.09.2024)

Manthorpe, Jill, Simon Biggs, Claudine McCreadie, Anthea Tinker, Amy Hills, Madeleine O'Keefe, Melanie Doyle, Rebecca Constantine, Shaun Scholes and Bob Erens, *The U.K. National Study of Abuse and Neglect Among Older People* (Department of Health 2007)

Millar, Jane and Andrea Warman, Family and Parenthood: Policy & Practice (Family Policy Studies Centre 1996)

Mullin, Amy, 'Filial Responsibilities of Dependent Children' (2010) 25 *Hypatia* (Special Issue: Current Work in Feminist Ethics and Social Theory) 157

Oldham, Mika, 'Financial Obligations Within the Family: Aspects of Intergenerational Maintenance and Succession in England and France' (2001) 60(1) *Cambridge Law Journal* 128

Pickard, Linda, 'A Growing Care Gap? The Supply of Unpaid Care for Older People by Their Adult Children in England to 2032' (2015) 35(1) *Ageing and Society* 96

Sharp, Christopher, 'The Family Court's Jurisdiction to Direct the Burial of a Child: Re K' [2017] *Family Law* 844

Sloan, Brian, 'Ilott v The Blue Cross (2017): Testing the Limits of Testamentary Freedom' in B Sloan (ed) *Landmark Cases in Succession Law* (Hart Publishing 2019)

The Times, 'Warnings Over Power of Attorney Digital Plan' (2023) www.thetimes.com/uk/healthcare/article/warnings-over-power-of-attorney-digital-plan (accessed 09.09.2024)

Williams, Catherine, Garfield Gary Potter and Gillian Douglas, 'Cohabitation and Intestacy: Public Opinion and Law Reform' [2008] *Child and Family Law Quarterly* 499

www.webarchive.nationalarchives.gov.uk/ukgwa/20130221121534/http://www.dilnotcommission.dh.gov.uk/our-report

Wilson, John and Rebecca Bailey-Harris, 'Family Provision: The Adult Child and Moral Obligation Family Law' (2005) 35 *Family Law* 555

Yon, Yongjie, Christopher Mikton, Zachary Gassoumis and Kathleen Wilber, 'Elder Abuse Prevalence in Community Settings: A Systematic Review and Meta-Analysis' (2017) 5(2) *The Lancet Global Health* e147

Further reading

Conway, Helen, 'Dead, but Not Buried: Bodies, Burial and Family Conflicts' [2004] *Legal Studies* 23

Douglas, Gillian, Hilary Woodward, Alun Humphrey, Gareth Morrell and Lisa Mills, 'Inheritance and the Family: Public Attitudes' [2010] *Family Law* 1308

Francis, Andrew, 'Family Provision: What Is the Trouble with Modern 1975 Act Disputes?' [2012] *Family Law* 1246

Hale, Brenda, 'The Quest for Equal Treatment' [2005] *Public Law* 571

Haskey, John, 'Intestacy and Surviving Kin: Law Commission Research' [2010] *Family Law* 964

Hill, Christopher, 'Theology of Burial' (September 2001) www.chichester.anglican.org/

Law Commission, 'Overview: Intestacy and Family Provision Claims on Death' (2011) www.lawcom.gov.uk

Ross, Sidney, *Inheritance Act Claims: Law and Practice* (4th edn, Sweet and Maxwell 2023)

Sloan, Brian, 'Testamentary Freedom and Caring Adult Offspring in England & Wales and Ireland' in Katherina Boele-Woelki, Joanna Miles and Jens Scherpe (eds) *The Future of Family Property in Europe: Proceedings of the 4th Conference of the Commission on European Family Law* (Intersentia 2010)

Welstead, Mary, 'Truly a Charter for Mistresses' [1990] *Denning Law Journal* 117

9

Family life – parents and carers

From parental rights to responsibilities

SUMMARY

In this chapter is considered firstly, what is a family, and who is a parent, and how modern family life has changed over the years to include a range of carers. Today, the current position is that a parent, father and mother, two fathers or two mothers, heterosexual, homosexual, transsexual now termed transgender, biological and acquired, and other parties, take on the parenting role. Today, these adults have 'responsibilities' for children in their care such that any notion of a paternal or proprietorial right over a child is extinguished. Secondly, the meaning of 'parental responsibility', who in law has this responsibility and how those who do not might acquire it, for example stepparents, adoptive parents, other family members and foster parents, is considered. Thirdly, an overarching theme and consideration here is the increasing alignment of family law with the lived experience of family life that shapes the law.

Family law of the nineteenth century reflected the bourgeois family and authorised a middle class and privileged model of family life which was heterosexual, gendered and male dominated, where families outside that orthodox model were faulted and condemned. Lawmakers desired the institution of the family and marriage to further certain objectives. The changing face of twenty-first-century family law is driven by the social realities of family life and the changing family law reflects the temporality of law. Whilst law once required life to adapt itself to its edicts, Sir James Munby in his 2018 lecture 'Changing Families' acknowledged: 'The law must adapt itself to these realities.' The common law with its entrenched prejudices has been challenged and to name but two areas of reform, same-sex parent relationship families and transgendered parent families now have full legal status. Justice Sachs, in *Minister of Home Affairs and Another v Fourie and Another Lesbian and Gay Equality Project and Others v Minister of Home Affairs and Others* [2006] 1 LRC 677 (2006) SA, said of the common law:

DOI: 10.4324/9781003435020-9

> *[114] I conclude that the failure of the common law and the Marriage Act to provide the means whereby same-sex couples can enjoy the same status, entitlements and responsibilities accorded to heterosexual couples through marriage, constitutes an unjustifiable violation of their right to equal protection of the law under s 9(1) and not to be discriminated against unfairly in terms of s 9(3) of the Constitution. Surrogacy arrangements and development in reproductive technology and IVF treatment has also changed possibilities of conception.*

The vastly changing demography and ethnography of contemporary Britain, the changing status of the position of women, the strive towards sex and gender equality, together with an increasingly diverse population requires understanding and accommodation of different cultural, social, ethnic, gendered and religious considerations when deciding family law matters. As Simone de Beauvoir (1974) recognised: 'humanity is not an animal species, it is a historical reality.' In 1801, the first census of England and Wales counted 8.9 million people, and by 2020, this number was just under 60 million. Ninety per cent (53.8 million) identified with at least one UK national identity (English, Welsh, Scottish, Northern Irish, British and Cornish); less than half of the population (46.2 per cent, 27.5 million people) described themselves as 'Christian'; 'No religion' was the second most common response (37.2 per cent, 22.2 million), followed by 'Muslim' (6.5 per cent, 3.9 million) and 'Hindu' (1.7 per cent, 1.0 million) (2021 Census figures).

These and other characteristics are matters the law is obliged to consider in construing its welfare obligation to the child. A family law reflective of the lived experience of family life and the rights of its members has also been furthered and championed by the European Convention on Human Rights (ECHR) especially Article 8 which protects 'the right to privacy and to family life', and also by forward thinking and creative advocates and judges courageous in developing the law championing equality and protecting human rights. Munby LJ (2018) in 'Changing families,' (earlier) on this point said:

> *in contemporary Britain the family takes an almost infinite variety of forms. Many marry according to the rites of non-Christian faiths. People live together as couples, married or not, and with partners who may not always be of the opposite sex. Children live in households where their parents may be married or unmarried. They may be brought up by a single parent, by two parents or even by three parents. Their parents may or may not be their natural parents. They may be children of parents with very different religious, ethnic or national backgrounds. They may be the children of polygamous marriages. Their siblings may be only half-siblings or step siblings. Some children are brought up by two parents of the same sex. Some children are conceived by artificial donor insemination. Some are the result of surrogacy arrangements. The fact is that many adults and children, whether through choice or circumstance, live in families more or less removed from what, until comparatively recently, would have been recognised as the typical nuclear family.*

(See Fletcher 1966; Young and Wilmott 1957 for a detailed study of earlier family life.) Some children may be raised by a cisgender mother and a trans man father (see *X, Y and Z v UK* [1997] 2 FLR 892 discussed later).

Parenting histories – the exclusive father

It is suggested for the purpose of this discussion that there have been three significant trajectories over the last 150 years with regard to the law's framing of families and legal parenting. Firstly, the common law for centuries reflected male privilege and accorded the father 'rights' over his children however cruel and violent his conduct to his wife or his child. His power was absolute. Secondly, during the last 50 years, this patriarchal and proprietorial right of the father over 'his' child was challenged; as Lord Denning said in *Hewer v Bryant* [1970] 1 QB 357 the parental right 'dwindled'. It is to be noted here that the notion and terminology of parental right was a fiction since in reality it was only ever a patriarchal right. Thirdly, the exclusivity of the male proprietorial right over children of the family was expressly removed by the Children Act (CA) 1989, s 2(4) and replaced by the legal requirement of 'parental responsibility' (CA, s 2) for children of the family extending to both fathers and mothers. Whilst any individual parental rights have been displaced, there is nonetheless the potential, under some circumstances, of the residuality of a form of a parental right accorded by Article 8, ECHR, 'right to family life'. Alongside and paralleling these three developments there have been shifts in understanding different gender identities, heterosexual and homosexual as well as other sexual and asexual identities. Most recently these gender identities have led to contested positions on and around the limitations of language, conceptualisation, thinking and understanding which have under certain circumstances tied the concept and identity of motherhood or fatherhood to biological sex (discussed later in this chapter). Judith Butler helps in an understanding of how language entraps within a binarism (Butler 1999, 2024; see also Butler YouTube). As Butler (2024: 14) writes: 'at the beginning of life when we are generally called a girl or a boy, ... we are suddenly placed in confrontation with a powerful interpellation from elsewhere', this as we shall see later has consequences for other descriptors and constructs like mother and father.

The common law eschewed the biological, psychological and social reality of the role of the biological mother in the parenting function excluding her from legal recognition, treating her as an underclass and instead, enshrining the biological father as the legal parent. 'His' rights over 'his' children were absolute. He had the right to custody and control despite absence of any attachment or bonding with his children, his physical absence from their lives, or his adultery or his cruelty towards the mother or children of the family. In *R v de Mannerville* [1804] 102 ER 1054, a father forcibly abducted without legal recrimination his 8-month-old baby who was still being breastfed by its mother. In *R v Greenhill* [1836] 4 Ad & El 624, the court ordered Mrs Greenhill to hand over to the father their three daughters (all under 6 years of age) notwithstanding the fact that he had been guilty of cruelty to both his wife and the children.

By 1839, Parliament passed the Custody of Infants Act 1839 (CIA), which in certain circumstances allowed the courts to override paternal hegemony by making an order granting custody to the mother of any child up to the age of 7 years, and to grant the mother access and visitation rights until the children reached the age of majority. Notwithstanding, judges, in interpreting the law, took a restrictive view of what Parliament had intended (see *R v Halliday* [1853] 17 JUR 56, and *Re Winscom* [1865] 71 ER 573) and held steadfastly to a chauvinistic view that a mother's position under the law should be suborned and that a father's right was inviolable. Pressure for reform continued and by the Custody of Infants Act 1873 (CIA) the mother's right to custody of her children from 7 years until they reached 16 years of age was endorsed. However, its practical impact was limited as few women had the means to take their case through the courts and when they did judges rarely acceded to their claims (see Maidment 1984, 1985, see also Abramowicz 1999).

Feminist legal scholars over the decades have theorised and analysed this male hegemony. Rosalind Coward (1983) debates the natural psychological drive of paternity to ensure the inheritance of property by genetic offspring citing Havelock Ellis (1885) who observed: 'it was undoubtedly on the rock of property that the status of women and the organisation on which it rested'. Within Marxist scholarship, Engels (1884) recognised that the family was instrumental in perpetuating private property. Firestone (1972) explored sex class and male culture across all institutions and the family as an ideological state apparatus of this hegemony suborning women whilst privileging men.

The biological father's rights are 'sacred'

That the father's absolute authority in the family was 'sacred' is demonstrated in the case of *Re Agar-Ellis* (1883) 24 Ch D 317.

Mr Agar-Ellis, a Protestant-Anglican, married a woman who was a Roman Catholic. He made a promise to her that the children of the marriage would be raised as Roman Catholics. Soon after the birth of their first child, he changed his mind. The wife however continued to take the children to Roman Catholic services and so he obtained an injunction restraining her from doing so and took their daughter, Harriet, along with their other children, away from the mother and arranged for them to be looked after by an Anglican clergymen and others. When Harriet was 16 years of age, she asked to be allowed to spend her holidays with her mother. An application was made by the mother to the court seeking such permission. The court refused the application on the ground that it had no jurisdiction to interfere with a father's legal right. Malins VC, in pronouncing judgment, said:

> *This is perhaps the strongest case that has ever occurred showing the misery that ensues from mixed marriages. . . . The authority of a father to guide and govern the education of his child is a very sacred thing, bestowed by the Almighty, and to be sustained to the uttermost by human law. It is not to be abrogated or abridged, without the most coercive reason.*

Sir Baliol Brett MR went further and asserted: 'The rights of a father are sacred rights because his duties are sacred duties.'

A father's authority also transcended beyond the grave; he had the power to appoint testamentary guardians, extending a father's reach even after his death. In *Hawksworth v Hawksworth* (1861–73) 6 LR Ch App 539, [1861–73] All ER Rep 314, a Roman Catholic man married a Protestant woman and died leaving a child by her of 6 months old who had been baptised as Roman Catholic. The child was brought up by the mother up to the age of eight and a half years in the principles of the Church of England. The court declared that when dealing with a child the strictest regard to the religion of the father was to be had and directed that the child be brought up in the dead father's faith. James LJ said:

> *having arrived at this age of eight and a half years, when it is important that the future religious belief of the child should be attended to – the question now is whether any other religion can be adopted as the religion of the child than that which was the religion of the father. I am of opinion that no other religion can be adopted than the religion of the father.*

Concurring, Mellish LJ asserted:

> *The rule, of law is that the religion of the father is to prevail over the religion of the mother, even in a case where the father has died and the mother survives, and that rule, of course, we cannot alter.*

Demise of paternal authority and rise of parental responsibility

By 1925, the patriarchal hegemony was slowly eroding.

The Guardianship of Infants Act, s 1 provided:

> Where in any proceeding before any court . . . the custody or upbringing of an infant . . . is in question, the court, in deciding that question, shall regard the welfare of the infant as the first and paramount consideration, and shall not take into consideration whether from any other point of view the claim of the father, or any right at common law possessed by the father, in respect of such custody [or] upbringing . . . [as]superior to that of the mother, or the claim of the mother is superior to that of the father.

It took nearly a century after *Agar-Ellis* and *Hawksworth* for the absolute authority of the father to be challenged and abrogated in the cases that follow. The House of Lords exerted its influence in four leading cases in different areas of law, reflecting the changing times. Interpreting firstly, the meaning of 'in the custody of the parent' (*Hewer* earlier); secondly, deciding whether the rights of natural parents could be overridden (*J v C* [1970] AC 668, later in this chapter); thirdly, deciding whether a mother's rights to custody might prevail over a father's (*Re K (Minors) (Children: Care and Control)* [1977] Fam 179) and fourthly, in *R v D* [1984] AC 778, (later in this chapter) deciding whether a father had an absolute right of custody over his child permitting him to forcibly abduct the child.

By CA 1989, 'rights' over children of the family had been superseded by responsibilities for children of the family. During the House of Lords debate on the Children Bill 1989, Lord Mackay of Clashfern said:

> *Your Lordships will have noted a change of terminology in the Bill. The fundamental concept in this area of law is no longer to be expressed variously in terms of rights, duties, authority or even powers of parents, but simply as 'parental responsibility'. The phrase, recommended by the Law Commission, is apt to my mind. It emphasises that the days when a child should be regarded as a possession of his parent – indeed when in the past they had a right to his services and to sue on their loss – are now buried forever. The overwhelming purpose of parenthood is the responsibility for caring for and raising the child to be a properly developed adult both physically and morally.*

(vol 502 col 487)

Iterating the meaning of 'in the custody of the parent' – *Hewer*

In *Hewer v Bryant* (1970), mentioned earlier, a boy who was an agricultural trainee was seriously injured in a motor accident at work allegedly caused by the negligent driving of a motor truck in which the plaintiff was a passenger. The farmer who employed the boy at the time of the accident went bankrupt. The parents thought their son had a good prospect of making a full recovery and made no claim in damages against the farmer. However, the boy had been mentally injured by the accident and did not make a full recovery and his memory was impaired. The parents applied for leave to bring an action for damages out of time under the Limitation Act 1963, which was refused. The question arose as to whether the boy was within the care and control of his parents or under the disability of infants. His lawyers argued that he was under the disability of infants and not within the care and control of his parents. If this argument succeeded it would allow the boy to bring a civil action in tort for damages for personal injury against his employers which was not time barred. The court held that the question of custody was a question of fact and not a state of law, and that a person is only in the custody of his parents if he is in their effective care and control at the time when the action actually accrued to him. Lord Denning in a landmark ruling said:

> *I would utterly reject the notion that an infant is, by law, in the custody of his father until he is 21. These words 'in the custody of the parent' were first used in a Statute of Limitations in the year 1939. During the next year youngsters fought the Battle of Britain. Was each of them at that time still in the custody of his father? The next use of the words was in the Statute of 1954, since which time pop-singers of 19 have made thousands of pounds a week, and revolutionaries of 18 have broken up universities. Is each of them in the custody of his father? Of course not, neither in law nor in fact . . . I would get rid of the rule in re Agar Ellis 24 Ch D 317 and of the suggested exceptions to it. That case was decided in the year 1883. It reflects the attitude of the Victorian parent towards his children. He expected unquestioning obedience to his commands. If a son disobeyed, his father would cut him off without a shilling. If his daughter had an illegitimate child, he would turn her out of the house. His power only ceased when the child became 21. I decline to accept a view so much out of date . . . the legal right of a parent to the*

custody of a child ends at the 18th birthday; and even up till then, it is a dwindling right which the courts will hesitate to enforce against the wishes of the child, and the more so the older he is. It starts with a right of control and ends with little more than advice.

Deciding in favour of non-biological over natural parents – *J v C*

In *J v C* [1970] AC 668, referred to as the 'blood tie baby case' by Ward LJ in *Re P* [2000] Fam 15 at 41, the House of Lords considered a case which turned upon the parental 'right' and the welfare of the child in the context of adoption. The child's biological parents had through no fault of their own demonstrated their inability to care adequately for him. The boy was taken into care at 4 days old in 1958, as his birth mother became ill with tuberculosis, and placed in the care of foster parents acting on behalf of the local authority. In 1960, his natural parents returned to Spain and took the child, by that time aged 2 years, with them, the mother having made a reasonable recovery. In 1961, when the boy was 3 he was returned to England into the care of his foster parents as his mother became once again unable to care for him. In 1963, his natural parents asked for his return to Spain. The child was made a ward of court in order that a determination of the future stability of the child's care could be made. The court in wardship ruled that the child should remain with the foster parents in England, subject to their raising him in the Roman Catholic faith and also ensuring that the child understood his cultural language of Spanish. Circumstances changed for the foster parents and in 1967 they returned to court over the issue of whether the child, now aged 9, could attend a Church of England choir school where he had won a scholarship place. The parents objected and issued a summons for care and control. The court of first instance, in considering the long-term interests of the child, held that the welfare of the child would be best served by remaining with the foster parents. The decision was upheld by the Court of Appeal, and the House of Lords. Lord Donovan said:

> *although the claim of natural parents to the custody and upbringing of their own children is obviously a most weighty factor to be taken into consideration in deciding what is in the best interests of the infant, yet the legislature recognised that this might not always be the determining factor, whether the parents were impeachable or not.*

Lord MacDermott concluded: 'the court should act cautiously, and in opposition to the parent only when judicially satisfied that the welfare of the child requires it.'

Mothers over fathers – *Re K*

A further inroad into paternal hegemony was made in the case of *Re K (Minors) (Children: Care and Control)* [1977] Fam 179, where the mother had engaged in an extra marital relationship. The parents were married in 1969, a boy was born in 1971 and a girl in 1974. The father was an Anglican clergyman. By March 1975, the wife had begun an extra marital relationship. The father refused to grant the mother a divorce, and the mother continued to live in the matrimonial home because she wanted to be with her children. She applied to the magistrates' court for custody whilst the father applied to have the children made wards of court and for custody. The judge in the wardship proceedings found that the mother was an excellent mother; he ordered that the children should remain wards of court until they reached the age of majority and concluded that, until further order, custody of the children should be given to the mother on the ground that she was the 'natural guardian and protector of very young children'. The father appealed and the court held that in considering the care and control of a minor, the welfare of the minor was the first and paramount consideration and the court should not balance the welfare of the minor against the wishes of an unimpeachable parent or against the justice of the case as between the parents.

Kidnapping and child abduction – *R v D*

The question of the proprietorial paternal right fell once again to be determined in a case in the criminal court which turned on all too familiar facts, of the abduction and kidnapping and taking away of children by fathers (see Edwards 2024).

In *R v D* [1984] AC 778, the defendant was convicted of kidnapping the 5-year-old daughter of the marriage. The child had been made a ward of court. On the night in question the father intent on abducting his daughter in defiance of a court order was determined to take the child, if necessary by force, away from her mother. He enlisted the assistance of two men, who with the father pushed their way into the flat where the mother and child were living.

> *The appellant had a rope in his hand. Hunter wore a stocking mask and plastic gloves and carried a knife. He unscrewed the doorbell. One of the men had a pair of scissors and a knife. Another wore a stocking mask and plastic gloves and carried a knife.*

The father took the child whilst one of the accomplices remained in the flat for five hours and showed the mother an object which he said was a gas bomb which could be exploded at any time should she try to escape. The imprisonment of the mother in the flat for several hours allowed the appellant to escape with the child and take her to New Zealand. The mother followed and was subsequently awarded custody and control of the daughter and upon her return to England with the child, the father once again abducted the daughter. The defendant appealed the conviction to the Court of Appeal. The Court of Appeal, Watkins LJ, Mustill and Skinner JJ, quashed the conviction and refused the Crown leave to appeal to the House of Lords, but certified that two points of law of general importance were involved in the decision: firstly, whether the common law offence of kidnapping exists in the case of a child victim under the age of 14 years, and secondly, whether in any circumstances a parent may be convicted of such an offence where the child victim is unmarried and under the age of majority.

These two points were considered by the judicial committee of the House of Lords. The House of Lords then reversed the decision of the Court of Appeal. Lord Brandon said:

> *Since the nineteenth century, however, the generally accepted social conventions relating to the paramountcy of a father's position in the family have been progressively*

whittled away, until now, in the second half of the twentieth century, they can be regarded as having disappeared altogether. Parents are treated as equals in at least most respects, and certainly in relation to their authority over their children. English law, both common law and statute law, has recognised this fundamental change in the position of a father in the family.

Nonetheless, Lord Brandon said that invoking the criminal law in such cases of kidnapping would require exceptional circumstances and was not desirable (AC 778,807). The Child Abduction Act 1984, s 1 soon followed and made such conduct a criminal offence. Paternal rights were no longer inviolable, and the welfare of the child was a weighty factor. By the CA 1989, s 1 the welfare of the child was not merely a weighty factor but the paramount consideration.

Today – who is a parent in fact?

In so far as the law was concerned by the legal template of the nineteenth century and first half of the twentieth century the parent was only ever heterosexual, monogamous and biological. Diduck and Kaganas (2012: 3) open their book *Family law, Gender and the State* with these words:

> *In the light of recent family law reforms, it may be provocative, if not downright peculiar, to suggest that the idea of the family in English law is dependent for its meaning on the monogamous sexual relationship (either actual or symbolically) between a man and a woman.*

But largely hidden from history were those parents, mothers and fathers, who did not identify with the binarism of male and female identity, who were bravely emerging openly declaring their sexual preference and in custody battles fighting for the right to custody of their children whilst the courts deemed them unfit to care for their children who were wrested from them.

The unfit parent

Any identity and sexual preference other than heterosexual was considered immoral and therefore relevant to conduct and parenting. With regard to male homosexuality, it was regarded as a criminal offence until 1967 Sexual Offences Act partially decriminalised it whilst discussion in places of education that condoned homosexuality was outlawed in s 28 of the Local Government Act 1988.

'(1) A local authority shall not –
   (a) intentionally promote homosexuality or publish material with the intention of promoting homosexuality;
   (b) promote the teaching in any maintained school of the acceptability of homosexuality as a pretended family relationship.'

The difficulties and obstacles that have beset the lesbian mother or gay father in securing custody of their children are replete throughout all jurisdictions. In Britain and North America and Australia, the courts have regarded homosexuality as detrimental to 'the best interests of the child' and instrumental in 'scarring children for life' whilst a heteronormative model of family life prevailed. Upon matrimonial dispute and breakdown, custody has been awarded to the heterosexual parent unless that parent is deemed 'unfit'. Lesbianism has been considered as axiomatically antipathetical to the interests of the child and incongruous with the construction of motherhood (See Edwards 1996 Chapter 2; see Hanscombe and Forster 1981). Campaigning groups such as 'Action for Lesbian parents' were set up to provide support for lesbian parents trying to secure access and custody of their children (*Sunday Times* 15 January 1978).

And so, in many respects Re G *(Children) (Residence: Same-Sex Partner)* [2006] UKHL 43 was a legal landmark.

A case which involved a dispute between the children's mother and her former female partner Ms C, in which all their Lordships concurred with Baroness Hale's judgment. The context is that of a lesbian couple CW, the natural mother, and CG, the partner, who both made the conscious decision to have children together, and together arranged for anonymous donor insemination at a clinic abroad and brought up the children together until their relationship broke down and where the natural mother CW raises the children and CG applied for shared residence [11]. The CA awarded residence to CG in part because of the conduct of the natural mother in deliberately disobeying the court's order [43]. The House of Lords reversed the decision. In this case Baroness Hale identified three types of parenting: (1) genetic, (2) gestational, and (3) social and psychological. This typology still remains a sound lens in 2024–5 through which to examine the lived reality of parenting. Baroness Hale said:

[33] There are at least three ways in which a person may be or become a natural parent of a child, each of which may be a very significant factor in the child's welfare, depending upon the circumstances of the particular case. The first is genetic parenthood: the provision of the gametes which produce the child. . . . [34] The second is gestational parenthood: the conceiving and bearing of the child. [35] The third is social and psychological parenthood: the relationship which develops through the child demanding and the parent providing for the child's needs, initially at the most basic level of feeding, nurturing, comforting and loving, and later at the more sophisticated level of guiding, socialising, educating and protecting.

(See further Callus 2012)

Whilst this question, who is the parent? had hitherto been defined from the biological parents' vantage point this question is now considered from a child's viewpoint and experience. In Re G *(Parental Responsibility Order)* [2006] EWCA Civ 745, an application to suspend a parental responsibility order, Hedley J said of the judge who had made the original order, 'What he did, in acknowledging the fact that the order he was proposing to make might appear rather unjust to the father, was try to look at the case through the eyes of the child.' Such approaches implement the spirit of the CA 1989, s 1, and the centrality of the child in family law and the requirement to apply the test of 'welfare of the child as paramount' in all matters relating to care and upbringing.

Genetic – biological parents and the natural parent presumption

Biological heterosexual family

The law has historically approached the question of parentage by considering the biological link between adult and child within a heterosexual arrangement and unless another arrangement better serves the welfare of the child, will rarely interfere. And that 'other arrangement' was cognised at that time as a heterosexual foster carer arrangement. And has been the norm, the language of mother and fathers, the role of motherhood and fatherhood has been tied to biological sex. This particular question of language and materialism and the way in which the social totality of the family and parenting take place in language will be addressed further later in this chapter.

Lord Templeman articulated the biological parent presumption in *Re KD (A Minor) (Ward: Termination of Access)* [1988] 1 All ER 577 when he said: 'The best person to bring up a child is the natural parent. It matters not whether the parent is wise or foolish, rich or poor, educated or illiterate, provided the child's moral and physical health are not endangered.' Whilst the presumption has been displaced it still remains a weighty 'consideration' in court decision making. However, it is to be noted that Article 8, ECHR, 'the right to family life' gives credence to this consideration, and in matters of placing a child for adoption, or in the making of special guardianship orders or connected foster carer orders, a placement within the natural family is preferred if at all possible.

The natural parent presumption held firm in this following case. In *Re M (Child's Upbringing)* [1996] 2 FLR 441 (see Chapters 10, 11) (P) and his mother were living with a white family in Transvaal, South Africa. Lord Justice Neil summarised the facts of the case:

> The appellant is a white South African of Afrikaner descent. She came to England in 1969 when she was about 23 years of age. In 1973 she married an Englishman and acquired British nationality. . . . The family (the husband having died) returned to the United Kingdom bringing the boy [P] with them with the consent of his natural/biological parents. The natural parents had worked as housekeeper and nanny to the appellant's children. . . . The appellant, who had become attached to P, offered to take responsibility for him in a way that would enable him to remain as a member of the household because of the increasing instability in South Africa. The appellant together with her daughters and P arrived in the United Kingdom on 16 March 1992. The appellant told the immigration authorities that she wished to adopt P and P was given leave to remain for three months. After some time, she issued an application for an adoption order and residence order. On 29 September 1994, P became a ward of court. P's natural parents objected to the applications and wanted him returned to them.

The original agreement between the natural parents and the prospective adoptive mother that P should be allowed to live in England subject to his visits to his parents and then his return when the political situation stabilised, broke down and the matter came before the court in an appeal by the appellant and a cross-appeal by the parents. The appeal court concluded that P should be returned to his natural parents even though P, who was 10 years of age at the time, had expressed the wish to remain with the appellant whom he regarded as the psychological parent and with whom a strong attachment had been formed. Thorpe J, in the court of first instance, based his decision to return the child to his parents in South Africa on Lord Templeman's reasoning in *Re KD* (above) and said:

> It begs the question: who is the natural parent, when the issue is to determine who should have the daily care of a child when one applicant is the biological parent and the other the psychological parent? I know of no statement of principle, in any decided case, that particularly guides the resolution of that competing claim. . . . It is the function of the judge to choose that solution which promotes welfare, or, more relevantly, is likely to prove the least damaging to the child in its intellectual, physical, emotional and psychological development . . . the child's development must be Zulu development and not Afrikaans or English development.

The Court of Appeal dismissed the appeal and allowed the cross-appeal. As for P he finally determined his own future by returning to the UK in December 1996 when he was 12 years old to be raised by his white foster mother following an agreement made between his parents and his foster mother (see *Daily Telegraph*, Australia, December 6, 1996).

The importance of racial origin, cultural and linguistic background, and religious persuasion cannot be underestimated, and they are mandatory factors to consider when placing children in care, and foster placements (CA 1989, s 33(6)) and also was the case when matching children with adoptive parents (Adoption and Children Act 2002 (ACA), s 5). However, whilst the children and Families Act has removed that strict duty when matching for adoption and replaced it with the duty to consider the rather less precise requirement of ethnicity it is unlikely that any judge would eschew the ACA, s 5 factors.

Judges are not immune from the social context in which they decide cases before them. Regarding *Re M*, the court drawing on the expert opinion evidence considered most thoroughly factors of race, culture and language. On this point, by the mid-1980s, Anglo-American-Australian jurisdictions were making strides to reconcile themselves with their colonial past. In Australia, during the twentieth century, aboriginal children had been forcibly removed from their natural parents and adopted into white families; such forcible removal had been Government policy for many years during the nineteenth and twentieth centuries. (See Grenville 2010.) In the UK, intra-racial adoption whilst encouraged in the 1970s as a positive move towards embracing multiculturalism, was considered by the 1990s to be a potentially harmful practice which denied children the full possibility of realising their own cultural identity and heritage.

Court decision making continued to maintain the agreed position that compelling factors would be needed to displace the natural biological heterosexual parent. In *Re D (Care: Natural Parent Presumption)* [1999] 2 FLR 1023, the court asserted that: 'only compelling factors could override the right of a child to be reared by a natural parent' making an order authorising the placement of the child in the father's care and not the grandmothers. (See also *Lord* Nicholls in *Re G (Children) (Residence: Same-Sex Partner)* (2006) earlier in this chapter.)

However, in *Re P (a minor) (residence order: child's welfare)* [2000] Fam 15, the court reiterated that there was no presumptive right to be raised by natural parents, in a case where a child of the Jewish faith (N) with medical needs could not be cared adequately by his natural parents and was fostered within a non-practising Roman Catholic family, who undertook to observe orthodox Jewish dietary and dress requirements since no suitable Jewish family was found. An application by N's parents to vary the residence order was refused by the judge on the ground that, since N did not have the ability to appreciate or understand her religious heritage, the benefit to her of a Jewish upbringing did not outweigh other considerations, namely the exceptionally strong attachment of N to her foster parents and the risk of harm inherent in such a move. Following the emotional harm of possible protracted litigation the court made an order under s 91(14) of the CA 1989 restricting further applications unless with leave of the court and with new conditions arising.

In *Singh v Entry Clearance Officer New Delhi* [2004] EWCA Civ 1075, where different considerations applied, in recognising family life and the role of adoptive parents for the purposes of Article 8 (in the context of an immigration appeal) Dyson LJ said:

> [21] *These close personal ties will be presumed to exist as between children and their natural parents, but exceptionally the presumption may be displaced. The notion of family life is not, however, confined to families based on marriage, and may encompass other relationships.*

This was reiterated in *Re B (A Child) (Residence Order)* [2009] UKSC 5 where the parents separated before the child was born and both parents agreed that it was best for the child to be reared by the grandmother. At a later stage the father changed his mind and objected to a residence order being made to her. The judge felt he was bound by the case of G (2006) (cited earlier) and made an order in favour of the father. An appeal was made to the Supreme Court. The court in allowing the appeal stated that: 'The child had lived virtually all of his life with his grandmother, he had naturally formed a strong bond with her and there was reason to apprehend that, if that bond was broken, his current stability would be threatened' ([19][20][38][41]).

Statutory exceptions to the natural parent presumption

There are two statutory exceptions to the natural parent consideration: firstly, where a child is adopted (Adoption Act 1976, s 39 Adoption and Children Act 2002 (ACA)) and secondly, where reproduction and childbirth follows from sperm or egg donation (Human Fertilisation and Embryology Act 1990, (HFEA) ss 27, 28, Human Fertilisation and Embryology Act 2008). Adoption terminates the legal responsibility (parental responsibility) of natural parents or legal parents (see Chapter 10). Where a person donates genetic material (eggs, sperm, embryos) that person relinquishes any rights to biological parentage in relation to any child that may be born as a result.

In *Re D (Contact and Parental Responsibility: Lesbian Mothers and Known Father)* [2006] EWHC 2 (Fam) (discussed later in this chapter) where a voluntary arrangement was made by a male and a lesbian woman by which she was impregnated and had a child, Black J concluded:

There is no doubt that Mr B is committed to D and that there is an attachment between them, even though from D's point of view, the degree of it is moderated by the relative infrequency of her contact with Mr B. Mr B has a real importance in her life, both in practical terms through her contact with him and because of the simple and incontrovertible but less tangible fact that he is her father. It is imperative that they continue to have contact and that a positive relationship should be fostered between them, allowing her to know that he loves her unquestioningly and wants what is best for her and to understand and appreciate his role originally in her conception and now in her life. D will also benefit from getting to see another world through him and his extended family.

Gestational – parentage

Baroness Hale in *Re G (Children) (Residence: Same-Sex Partner* (2006) (see earlier in this chapter) identified the gestational parent as the second parenting type which involves the conceiving and bearing of the child. The possibilities of conception and childbearing have been revolutionised by reproductive technologies and surrogacy arrangements whilst language and concepts are struggling to keep up with these developments. And the constructs and terminology of mother and father with regard to trans parenting have also been recently challenged and contested. (*See R (on the application of JK) v Registrar General for England and Wales* [2015] EWHC 990 (Admin); R *(McConnell and YY) v Registrar-General for England and Wales* [2020] EWCA Civ 559.)

Reproductive technology and the legal parent

For the last three decades IVF (in vitro fertilisation)/ICSI (intra-cytoplasmic sperm injection) treatment has enabled an embryo to be carried for women unable to conceive or carry a foetus to full term and to single women and lesbian women without the need for sexual intercourse with a person of the male sex. Significantly, since the NHS removal of the financial barriers to licensed treatment for female same-sex couples the numbers of same-sex couples entering IVF programmes has increased (See HFEA Fertility data).

Since 1991 when the HFEA started recording information there have been around 1.3 million (IVF) cycles and over 260,000 donor insemination (DI) cycles, resulting in around 390,000 babies born. The HFEA licenses fertility clinics, and it is an offence to operate without a licence. In 2024, the HFEA responding to a BBC programme said,

We are very concerned about the issues raised by the BBC Spotlight NI programme on the Logan Wellbeing Centre in Belfast. This is not a HFE Authority licensed clinic, and it is a criminal offence for treatments that fall under HFE Authority law to be carried out in a non-licenced clinic.

(See HFEA March 2024 Press release)

Where a person has donated sperm or eggs then that person relinquishes any rights over that 'genetic material'. The donor is no longer the legal parent. (See Pila 2019.)

The HFEA 1990, s 27 (2008 Act, s 33(1)) defines a 'mother' as: '(1) The woman who is carrying or has carried a child as a result of the placing in her of an embryo or of sperm and eggs'. Section 28 (2008 Act, s 35(1)) defines a 'father' thus:

(1) If – (a) at the time of the placing in her of the embryo or of the sperm and eggs or of her artificial insemination, W was a party to a marriage with a man or a civil partnership with a man, and (b) the creation of the embryo carried by her was not brought about with the sperm of the other party to the marriage or civil partnership, then, subject to section 38(2) to (4) the other party to the marriage or civil partnership is to be treated as the father of the child unless it is shown that he did not consent to the placing in her of the embryo or the sperm and eggs or to her artificial insemination (as the case may be).

The legal moment articulated by the phrase 'placing in her' mirrors the legal moment of 'conception' as being the specific point in time for legal responsibility. In *Re R (A Child) (IVF: Paternity of Child)* [2003] EWCA Civ 182 the mother, D, and her partner, B, were unmarried, and sought IVF treatment which required the fertilisation of D's eggs with sperm from a donor. In accordance with IVF procedure, B signed a form acknowledging and consenting to being the father of any child born in consequence. D and B separated when implantation in D had taken place, and about which B (the putative father) had no knowledge. On an application by B, the judge declared, under HFEA 1990, s 28(3) that B was the legal father of the child. The Court of Appeal allowed D's appeal. B appealed this decision to the House of Lords. The House of Lords in *R (IVF: Paternity of Child) (also Known as Re D)* [2005] UKHL 33 dismissed the ruling of the Court of Appeal, holding that s 28(3) should apply only to cases falling clearly within it and most importantly that the legal determination of who is the parent should not be based on a fiction, especially where deception was involved; that the embryo had to have been placed in the woman when treatment services were provided for her and the man together; and that, although they had originally been so provided for D and B, they had not been when implantation had taken place.

Consent of all parties is required, and problems have arisen where technology has failed and also where a party dies and embryos or genetic material is stored for later use.

A legal conundrum arose where a baby of mixed raced parentage had been born to a white couple following a mix up with the genetic material. In *Leeds Teaching Hospitals NHS Trust v Mr and Mrs A and others* [2003] EWHC 259 (QB) the court resolved the matter by constituting the family in accordance with the practical reality. In this case, a married (white) couple (Mr and Mrs A) were undergoing IVF treatment and gave birth to twins of 'mixed race' parentage. At the time Mr and Mrs A (a white couple) were undergoing IVF treatment, so too, were Mr and Mrs B (a married black couple). Mr B's sperm was mistakenly used to fertilise Mrs A's eggs and the embryos were then implanted into Mrs A. Mrs A gave birth to mixed-race twins. Who then was the legal father? Mr B, applied for a declaration of parentage (s 55A of the Family Law Act 1986) although s 28(6)(a) provides that the donor of sperm used in licensed fertility treatment will not be the father of any resulting child. Mr A, in attempting to exercise his right in bringing himself within the rules of s 28(2) of the HFEA 1990, needed to establish himself as being married at the time to the mother or else if not, then within s 28(3) which established the partner as the father provided, they are treated together. So, which claim prevailed? Dame Elizabeth Butler-Sloss, P ruled that the black sperm donor was to be the legal father, although the twins would actually live with their white mother and her white husband as a family. The genetic claim to fatherhood prevailed since:

> [27] *The insurmountable problem, in my view, to that approach, is the question – to what did he consent? . . . The 'course of treatment' to which he consented was that outlined in Mrs A's consent form. As I set out above, Mrs A consented to her eggs being used and mixed with her husband's sperm. She did not consent to her eggs being mixed with named or anonymous donated sperm. She consented to the placing of not more than two resulting embryos in her uterus. [and] This was clearly an embryo created without the consent of Mr and Mrs A. [And] [44] Mr B is the biological father of the twins in circumstances in which he has had no opportunity to forge any relationship with them. Although he was clearly not a consenting sperm provider other than in a treatment process with his wife, it is, on the facts of this sad case, only the use of his sperm that connects him with the twins. 'In M v Netherlands [1993] 74 D & R 120 the European Commission declared inadmissible a case on somewhat stronger facts than the present. In that case, the biological father agreed to be a sperm donor to a lesbian couple and after the birth of the child visited regularly and babysat on occasions. When he sought greater contact with the child and the couple broke off contact with him, his application to the courts was dismissed. On his application to the European Court, the commission rejected it out of hand and stated at para 1 of the judgment: "Family life . . . implies close personal ties in addition to parenthood. The Commission considers that the situation in which a person donates sperm only to enable a woman to become pregnant through artificial insemination does not of itself give the donor a right to respect for family life with the child".'*

This outcome, and one seemingly contrary to the ruling in *Re R* (earlier) perpetuated a fiction, albeit that the HFEAct rules had been correctly applied, since parental status could not be conferred on a husband whose wife had given birth after IVF treatment because he had neither consented to the placing in his wife of the embryo since it was actually placed in error, nor had the couple undergone 'treatment together' within the meaning of the HFEAct 1990. The solution proposed that Mr and Mrs A adopt the two children who are twins albeit that Mrs A was in any event the legal mother by virtue of the genetic tie and also that she carried and gave birth to the children (see Weathers 2009).

Further legal complexities arose governing the use and legality of the embryo on at a date to be determined in the future. In *Evans v United Kingdom* [2006] ECHR 10, the applicant and her then partner, J, were told in 2000 that the applicant had pre-cancerous tumours in both ovaries, and that her ovaries would have to be removed. Prior to the operation, a number of eggs were extracted for (IVF) treatment, and it was explained to the applicant and J that each of them would have to sign a form consenting to such treatment. In 2002, the relationship broke down, and J withdrew his consent to further use of the embryos. The applicant commenced proceedings seeking an injunction requiring J to restore his consent to the storage and use of the embryos. That claim was dismissed; and that decision upheld on appeal and by the European Court of Human Rights. Mrs Evans said: 'I am distraught at the court's decision. It's very hard for me to accept that the embryos will now be destroyed and that I will never become a mother.' (See further Maddox 2017.) The judges said they did not consider that Ms Evans's desire to have a genetically related child was entitled to greater respect than Mr Johnston's decision not to have a child with her. But the decision must have fallen on one side. Harris-Short (2010: 81) considers it falls on Mrs Evans side and writes:

> *Schedule 3 of the 1990 Act which requires the 'effective' consent of both gamete provides to the continued storage and future use of the disputed embryos, is incompatible with Natalie Evans' right to reproductive freedom as protected under Article 8 (1) of the European Convention on Human Rights.*

The 2008 Act introduces more rigid conditions called 'agreed fatherhood conditions' (HFEAct 2008, ss 37, 38) to address the procreative liability of each party.

The issue of posthumous parents and what use can be made of genetic material arises when one of the consenting parties dies was raised in *R v Ex p Blood* [1997] EWCA Civ 4003 and is provided for in the Human Fertilisation and Embryology (Deceased Fathers) Act 2003, which provides for certain deceased men to be registered as fathers if written consent was given and not withdrawn (5A). Sloan (2021) takes up this extraordinary case.

> *In 2015, The Independent newspaper reported the case of a man who had 'failed' a paternity test in the United States because (it eventually transpired) the genetic material in his saliva was shown to be different from that in his sperm. This was said to be the first reported instance of a paternity test being 'fooled' by what is known as a 'human chimera'. Such a chimera has extra genes, in this instance apparently absorbed from a twin lost in early pregnancy. The result was that, according to the tests, the 'true' genetic father of the child in question was the man's twin, who had never been born.*

As technology advances the courts will be required to adjudicate.

Transgender parentage and IVF

The fixity of thinking and language (see Butler 1999) and equality norms has posed barriers to transgender parents seeking access to services, legal recognition and also access to recognition of sexual identity.

> In *J v C (Void Marriage: status of children) J v C and another* [2006] EWCA Civ 551, the applicant had been born female but lived as a male. In 1977, he purported to marry the respondent, without informing her that he was 'transsexual' (the terminology used at that time). Two children were conceived by donor insemination. The marriage was subsequently declared void and the question for determination was whether the purported husband was a parent of the children. The court held:
>
> > *since the 1989 Act did not define the term 'parent' used in section 10(4)(a) it was necessary to look elsewhere for an applicable statutory definition; that, in the context*

> *of artificial insemination by donor, parenthood was defined by both the Family Law Reform Act 1987 and the Human Fertilisation and Embryology Act 1990 and it was necessary to determine which statute applied; that it was clear from sections 28(2) and 49(3) of the 1990 Act that the Act did not apply if the artificial insemination had taken place before section 28 had commenced, and it was immaterial that the embryo resulting from the insemination had been carried by the mother after its commencement; that, therefore, since the artificial insemination of the respondent which led to the birth of the younger child had taken place before the commencement of section 28 of the 1990 Act, that Act did not apply and the case was governed by the 1987 Act (post, paras 17–19, 21–22, 26).*

This meant that the applicant who wished to be recognised as the legal father was not the legal father and changes in the law recognising his reassignment could not change the legal position that pertained at the time of insemination.

In *R (TT) v Registrar General for England and Wales (AIRE Centre intervening)* [2019] 3 WLR 1195, sub nom *R (McConnell and YY) v Registrar-General for England and Wales* [2020] EWCA Civ 559), the claimant, who had been registered as female at birth, transitioned to live in the male gender including those who have had gender reassignment surgery and been granted a gender recognition certificate under the Gender Recognition Act 2004, s 1–4. The claimant then underwent IVF, became pregnant and gave birth to a child. Under s 9(1) of the 2004 Act, the legal effect of a gender recognition certificate was that a person 'becomes for all purposes the acquired gender' However, s 12 provided that, 'The fact that a person's gender has become the acquired gender under this Act does not affect the status of the person as the father or mother of the child'. The Registry Office informed the claimant that he would have to be registered as the child's 'mother' on the birth certificate, although the registration could be in his then (male) name. McConnell sought judicial review. His primary claim was to be regarded and registered, as the child's 'father', or otherwise 'parent' or 'gestational parent'. His secondary and alternative claim, on the basis that domestic law required his registration as 'mother', was for a declaration of incompatibility under s 4 of the HRA 1998 on the ground that the domestic regime was incompatible with his and/or the child's rights under art 8 (right to respect for private and family life) and art 14 (prohibition of discrimination). The judge dismissed the claim and granted a declaration that the claimant was the child's 'mother', holding that 'mother', in the context of a birth, applied to the person who carried a pregnancy and gave birth to a child, irrespective of their legal gender. The claimant appealed to the Court of Appeal which held that s 12 of the 2004 Act had both retrospective and prospective effect and the judge had been correct, applying the ordinary interpretation of s 12, to register the claimant as the mother of the child (see [29]–[35], [39]).

This conundrum will continue. As Coward and Ellis (1977: 1) note 'an understanding of mankind, social history and the laws of how society functions' are rooted in language and as the aforementioned case demonstrates, fixed in language. And the terms mother and father are performative (Austin 1962).

Three parents

Developments in reproductive technology have detached childbearing and birthing from heterosexual partnerships and from the experience of sexual intercourse. Assisted reproductive technology has made it is possible to screen genetic material by the introduction of healthy DNA from a third biological parent to achieve a child born without genetic disease (such a muscular dystrophy) thereby introducing a 'third parent'. The technological possibilities have prompted a deluge of moral arguments. The law nevertheless has to navigate through the complexities which the following case demonstrates.

In *R on the application of Quintavalle) v Human Fertilisation and Embryology Authority (Secretary of State for Health intervening)* [2003] 2 AC 687, the court considered whether the HFE Authority had the statutory authority to permit tissue typing in conjunction with pre-implantation genetic diagnosis (HFEA 1990, ss 2 (1), 3 (1)(b), Sch 2, para 1(1)) in considering the case of Zain Hashmi, aged 6, with a genetic disorder, beta thalassemia major which required daily drugs and regular blood transfusions to keep him alive, and who needed a tissue type transplant from a sibling. The court considered that the authority had that power.

Such developments raise ethical questions and also challenge existing notions of parentage (see Gallagher 2023). In this case, six of Sharon Bernardi's children died within days of birth. Her son Edward survived to the age of 21, although he was often ill, and she desperately wanted to bear and raise children with a prospect of survival. (See Sharon Bernardi YouTube.) (See also BBC One – Sunday Morning Live, 'Should we be allowed to design our babies?'.)

Reproductive technology reform

Baroness Ruth Deech (2018), former Chairperson of the HEFAuthority reflecting on the past 20 years of IVF and its impact on the family, is concerned that IVF treatment has not kept up with social realities. She raises important questions including the problems that may arise since donor anonymity was ended in 2005 and the consequences that might follow when the child born of the donation reaches the age of 18 and is able to discover the identity of the sperm donor (Human Fertilisation and Embryology Authority (Disclosure of Donor Information) Regulations 2004 (SI 2005/1511). In accord with the HFEAct 2008, the donor can now make inquiries but will not be told of the child's identity.

In *R (on application Rose and another) v Secretary of State for Health Human Fertilisation and Embryology Authority, Court of Appeal – Administrative Court, and another* [2002] EWHC 1593 (Admin), the applicant (child) said: 'genetic connections are important to me'. Scott Baker J said in this case:

> *Joanna Rose was born in Reading in 1972, long before the Human Fertilisation and Embryology Act 1990 (the 1990 Act) and indeed well before the Warnock Committee on Human Fertilisation and Embryology whose report in 1984 led to the 1990 Act. At the time of her conception more or less complete secrecy was the order of the day, but attitudes have changed a great deal during her lifetime.*

The HFEA 1990, s 31–31ZE establishes the donor register.

Baroness Deech also raises other concerns including that a sibling may accidentally meet and fall in love with another sibling, both from the same donor sperm, and where for example revelation of sperm donor can save life as in 'saviour sibling' (see Sample 2010) or where there is a known genetic disease in the family, so that PGD would be authorised. The courts have also had to rule on a case where an IVF baby was born and a claim for wrongful parenthood was made. (See *ARB v IVF Hammersmith* [2018] EWCA Civ 2803 sub nom *R (the mother) and ARB (the appellant father)*).

Widening NHS funding in cases involving same-sex applicants has also removed the potential barriers to licensed treatment for female same-sex couples.

Several recommendations were made in November 2023 to modernise fertility law to reflect changing times including broadening enforcement powers, inspections, financial penalties and patient protection and proposing that the Act be amended to enable the removal of donor anonymity from the birth of any child born from donation and clinics required by law to inform donors and recipients of the potential for donor identity to be discovered through, for example, DNA testing websites, social media or further means other than the HFEAct. Further proposals to register all donors and recipients to have implications counselling sessions before starting treatment and an overhaul of the consent regime in the Act. Finally, a proposal that the Act should explicitly give the HFE Authority greater discretion to support innovation in treatment and research and be 'future proofed' to accommodate future scientific developments and new technologies (Horsey and Jackson 2003).

Surrogacy

What is the legal position of the woman whose womb is hired for the purpose of the gestation and embryonic development and nurturing of a child? Surrogacy is where a woman hires out her womb and makes arrangements to carry the child until birth and then relinquishes the child upon birth to the surrogate parents. Many surrogate 'mothers' perform this service for a family relative unable to conceive and in some cases for financial gain. The law on surrogacy provides that the surrogate (and potentially her partner if she is married or in a civil partnership) is recognised as the legal parent under the HFEA 1990, s 33. And if the surrogate is not married or in a civil partnership the intended father will become the legal father, but only if he has a genetic link to the child. Intended parents must apply to the court for a parental order after the birth of the child to become legal parents (s 34 of the HFEA) which can be time consuming and protracted, and it is by no means straightforward as s 54(6) of the HFEA requires that both the surrogate and any other person who is the child's legal parent must give their free and informed consent to the making of a parental order. In 2021, only 436 parental orders were granted in England and Wales, but as Welstead (2023) points out the actual figures for surrogate births are likely to be higher as not all intended parents apply for a parental order.

Surrogacy case law shows how things go wrong where there is secrecy, deception and change of mind and parties then turn to the court for a remedy. In *Re P (Surrogacy: Residence)* [2008] 1 FLR 177 two children N and C, were born by way of surrogacy agreements. The mother had five children, each by a different father and the last two children were born as a result of surrogacy arrangements. The first of these children was conceived following artificial insemination. During the pregnancy the mother told the biological father of the child that she had miscarried the baby and raised the fourth child as her own. Some years later the mother re-registered with the surrogacy agency and signed another surrogacy agreement. She became pregnant through artificial insemination, and once again informed the biological father that she had miscarried. But before she gave birth, her eldest daughter informed the agency of the mother's deceptions. After the fifth child was born, the biological father commenced proceedings for a residence order and the biological father of the fourth child applied for contact.

Similarly, *Re T (a child) (surrogacy: residence order)* [2011] otherwise *CW v NT and another* [2011] involved a case where the surrogate did not honour her agreement to give up the child. Baker J summarises the case as follows:

> [8] *After Mr and Mrs W were married, they tried to have a baby themselves, but because Mrs W had lost part of her womb as a result of cancer . . ., their attempts resulted in a series of miscarriages. These failures led them to consider surrogacy, . . .' finding a surrogate through the internet,. . . [56] After a contested hearing, Coleridge J. made a residence order . . . in favour of the father. He applied the principle that the test when choosing between two competing residential parental regimes was in which home was the child most likely to mature into a happy and balanced adult and to achieve his fullest potential as a human. . . . He found that the mother and her husband had set out to deceive both the couples with whom they had reached a surrogacy agreement because of a desperate desire to parent more children by any means. He . . . granted residence to the father and his wife with regular contact to the mother.*

This was reversed on appeal where the judge found:

> [73] *On balance, I have reached the clear conclusion that T's welfare requires her to remain with her mother. In my judgment, there is a clear attachment between mother and daughter. To remove her from her mother's care would cause a measure of harm. It is the mother who, I find, is better able to meet T's needs, in particular her emotional needs. I am satisfied that the mother would foster contact and a close relationship between T and her father. I am less confident that Mr and Mrs W would respect the relationship between T and her mother were they to be granted residence. [74] I therefore order that T shall reside with her mother. [75] There will be interim visiting contact between T and her father until the hearing in February, to be arranged by the guardian. At that hearing, I will review progress and make whatever orders are necessary for T's long-term future, including future contact.*

(See Edwards 1989 202, for a case on who in 1989 was considered suitable for treatment.)

The law is confusing and complex. In March 2023, the Law Commission and the Scottish Law Commission published the full joint report with recommendations similar to the proposals set out in the consultation paper. (*Law Commission and Scottish Law Commission, 'Building families through surrogacy: a new law'*, Law Com No 411, Scot Law Com No 262 (2023)). The Commission offered some reassurance:

> *Our recommendations will ensure that surrogacy continues to operate on an altruistic, rather than a commercial basis. They seek to protect the best interests of the child by providing greater certainty to surrogates and to intended parents as regards legal parental status (a*

*term we use to describe legal parenthood). In line with the shared intentions of the surrogate
and the intended parents, our recommendations enable the intended parents to be recognised
as the legal parents from birth, as long as that remains the wish of the surrogate, while
protecting the surrogate's autonomy throughout pregnancy and childbirth.*

Welstead (2023) has charted the development of surrogacy law and surrogacy
cases for two decades and in a critique of the Law Commission recommendations
argues that the law: 'does not adequately reflect changes in societal attitudes towards
surrogacy' and that traditional surrogacy arrangements should not be included in the
new pathway on the basis that, as the surrogate is the biological mother, the
arrangement is closer to adoption. She also argues that surrogates should be
remunerated for the nine months of gestation, birth and recuperation; since creating
a baby is no mean feat, it could therefore potentially be exploitive not to pay the
surrogate for valuable work. (See Welstead 2019, 2023.) Under HFEA 1990, s 30(7)
(Surrogacy Arrangements Act 1985 s 2) no money or other benefit, other than for
expenses reasonably incurred, could be given or received in relation to surrogacy,
unless such payment had been authorised by the court. (See Brown 2021.) In *W and
W v H (Child Abduction: Surrogacy) (No 2)* (2002) an English surrogate mother entered
into a surrogacy agreement in California with a married couple, where such
agreements are legally binding. The surrogate mother was implanted with an egg
from an anonymous donor, fertilised by her husband. After implantation, the
surrogate mother found she was carrying twins. The surrogate mother issued civil
proceedings in California, resulting in an order declaring that the Californian couple
should have custody of both the children at birth. But when the surrogate mother
returned to England, she decided that she wanted to keep the twins. The Californian
couple brought proceedings under the Hague Convention on the Civil Aspects of
International Child Abduction 1980. The English court dismissed the application for
summary return to California. (See also Re *X and Y (Parental Order: Retrospective
Authorisation of Payments)* [2011], *G v G (Parental Order: Revocation)* [2012]; Gamble
and Ghevaert 2011).

The Law Commission on Surrogacy has made a series of recommendations
including that the surrogate would have a right to withdraw consent at any time
between the treatment which resulted in her pregnancy and the end of the 6th week
elapsing following the child's birth. Welstead says of this recommendation,
'permitting the surrogate to withdraw consent to the surrogacy is perhaps the most
negative aspect of the surrogacy report'.

Surrogacy – international arrangements

What is the position where a surrogacy agreement has been entered into abroad? Since
different laws pertain, couples may find themselves regarded as parents in countries
overseas but are not accorded such legal status in the UK. The position for example in
India, Ukraine and some US states including California and Illinois, is not congruent
with English law. For example, in *Re IJ Overseas Surrogacy: Parental Order)* [2011]
EWHC 921 (Fam), the child was conceived in the Ukraine as a result of fertilisation of
an egg from an anonymous donor. The sums of money involved made such an
arrangement illegal under UK law (s 54(8) of the HFEA 2008). The claimants were the
legal parents with regard to Ukraine law and wanted to bring their child into the UK.

However, under domestic law the legal parents of the child were the defendants who were a married couple. It was held that the legal parents were the Ukrainian couple, and a parental order was made pursuant to an overseas surrogacy arrangement.

In *A v P (Surrogacy: Parental Order: Death of Applicant)* [2011] EWHC 1738 (Fam), Mr and Mrs A entered into a surrogacy agreement in India. The child, B, was genetically related to Mr A. He was handed over to them and brought to this country. They commenced proceedings for a parental order, but Mr A died. The court made an order relating to both Mr and Mrs A. The complexity of international surrogacy has been addressed by Munby LJ in 'International surrogacy' (2019).

Social and psychological parentage – the importance of attachment

The third type of parenting identified by Baroness Hale in *Re G* (discussed earlier) is social and psychological. Good parenting (biological or acquired) depends on bonding, and forming an emotional relationship with the child (see *Re B* (2009) (discussed earlier). Attachment lies at the very heart of the parent/child relationship and the degree of attachment of parent/carer to child and child to parent/carer is considered an important indicator of the stability and strength of a relationship. Absence of attachment may indicate neglect or emotional harm (CA 1989, s 31) or that a local authority placement for a child with a foster carer is unsuitable. (See in Chapter 15 where the role of residential assessments (CA 1989, s 38(6)) as a mechanism by which attachment can be observed in a structured and supervised setting is considered (see *Re W and M (Children)* (2009)). The strength of the psychological relationship was taken into consideration in determining the question 'with whom should a child live?' In *Re M (Child's Upbringing)* (1996) (earlier) where Thorpe LJ recognised, 'this case is further complicated by the fact that this boy has two psychological parents, and they are both psychological mothers' (see Chapters 10 and 11). In *Re G (Children: Contact)* (2002), the court recognised: 'the adoptive parents are effectively the psychological parents and the only ones that C and T know'. And in *Re G (Adoption: Ordinary Residence)* [2002] EWHC 2447 (Fam), the court observed: 'LA and FD are undoubtedly the girls' psychological parents. They are, I believe, entirely devoted to the girls' welfare and will treat them as their daughters for the remainder of their lives.'

Under certain circumstances, the biological relationship may yield to the psychological relationship, when for example there are rival claims for residence which can better serve child welfare. In *Re H (A Child) (Residence)* [2002] 3 FCR 277 it was asserted:

> *in cases where the child had been for a long time in the settled care of a non-parent, that non-parent would effectively have become the child's psychological parent. When weighing the rival claims of the biological parent over the psychological parent, . . . such considerations had to be qualified by what was best for the welfare of the child.*

In *Re G (A Child) (Parental Responsibility)* [2006] EWCA Civ 745, where the child had been conceived as a result of a 'one night stand', the child had grown up with another person acting in the role of the father and for all intents and purposes he was the psychological father of the child. In *Re P (A Minor) (Residence Order: Child's Welfare)* (2000), the psychological tie was considered to outweigh the blood tie. The natural parents appealed and the Court of Appeal in dismissing the appeal of the parents held:

> that on an application to vary a residence order there was no presumption that a child's natural parents were to be preferred to his foster parents, and the court's primary consideration under section 1(1) of the Children Act 1989 was the child's welfare; that although, in assessing the child's welfare, the court was required under section 1(3)(d) of the Act of 1989 to have regard to the child's background, including his cultural and religious heritage, that was only one factor to be weighed in the balance and was not a paramount consideration; that, given N's exceptional attachment to her foster parents and the grave risk of long-term harm if she were moved from them, her need for an uninterrupted settled life outweighed the need for a religious life; and that, accordingly, N's welfare dictated that she should not be moved from her foster parents.

Echoing Baroness Hale in *Re G (Children) (Residence: Same-Sex Partner)* [2006] UKHL 43 (earlier) Dey and Wasoff (2006) write:

> Family law requires reform in many jurisdictions in response to change in family forms and relationships. . . . Many 'family practices' . . . no longer conform to the norms embodied in family law. The growth in lone parent families, the prevalence of divorce and remarriage, and alternative ways of managing intimate relationships (such as cohabitation and 'living apart together') have eroded the normative purchase of marriage and the nuclear family.

The family census data 2021 provides a picture of the reality of contemporary family life. There were 16.9 million families in England and Wales; 81.3 per cent of families were couples and 18.7 per cent were lone parents, 41.8 per cent of lone parents were aged 50 years and over, while 3.6 per cent were aged 24 years and under, 5.0 per cent (613,000) of children had a second parent or guardian's address that they stayed at for more than 30 days per year, and 1.7 per cent of all couple families were same sex. Of all same-sex families, 52.6 per cent were male and 47.4 per cent were female, and 23.9 per cent of female couples and 6.5 per cent of male couples had children (Children in Families in England and Wales: Census 2021).

Sexual orientation and parentage, gender reassignment and parentage

The issues raised here bring the same-sex family within Baroness Hale's first biological category regarding one partner and regarding the other within the social and psychological acquired parent category. The law's approach to same-sex couples has been discriminatory. Lord Wilberforce in *Re D (An Infant) (Adoption: Parent's Consent)* [1977] AC 602 said:

> new attitudes at the time should not entitle the courts to relax the vigilance and severity with which they should regard the risk of children, at critical ages, being exposed or introduced to ways of life which as this case illustrates, may lead to severance from normal society to psychological stresses and unhappiness . . . which may scar him for life.

And dispensed with a father's objection to the child being adopted by the former wife's new husband. Singer J led the way in challenging law's cruelty to homosexual parents in *Re W (Adoption: Homosexual Adopter)* [1997] 3 All ER 620 and held that in the context of adoption there was nothing in the Adoption Regulations to prevent a homosexual adopting a child and allowed a 49-year-old lesbian in a permanent relationship to adopt, overturning the former orthodoxy.

Baroness Hale further championed this development towards equality when she said in *Ghaidan v Godin-Mendoza* [2004] UKHL 30:

> *if (a) couple are bringing up children together, it is unlikely to matter whether or not they are the biological children of both parties. Both married and unmarried couples, both homosexual and heterosexual, may bring up children together. One or both may have children from another relationship: this is not at all uncommon in lesbian relationships and the court may grant then a shared residence order so that they may share parental responsibility.*

The limits of language

The fixity of language and its function in structuring social relations and the institution of the family and roles within it is recognised in *Re D (Contact and Parental Responsibility: Lesbian Mothers and Known Father)* [2006] EWHC 2 (Fam) where A and C, the first and second respondents, were a lesbian couple who advertised for a man to father a child. The applicant, B, responded to the advertisement and as a result D was born. Both A, as the biological mother, and C had parental responsibility because of a joint residence order. B, the biological father, sought parental responsibility to which A and C objected. The court granted parental responsibility to B with conditions that he did not contact any health professional or the school without the consent of A or C. A and C were perfectly happy for B to be recognised as D's father, but they opposed any order that would recognise him as the 'parent'.

Black J said:

> *This application falls to be decided at a time of considerable change in the law affecting same sex couples. It is now possible for a same sex couple to register their relationship as a civil partnership under the Civil Partnership Act 2004, the material provisions of which came into force on 5 December 2005. Civil partnerships are enduring relationships, which end only on death, dissolution or annulment. In many ways, the law applicable to civil partners is aligned with the law relating to married couples, for instance the provision for financial relief corresponds to the provision made for financial relief in connection with marriages. With the commencement of the Adoption and Children Act 2002, it will be possible for a same sex couple to adopt a child, provided they are living together as partners in an enduring family relationship.*

In addition, Black J praised the invaluable expert report which had interrogated and criticised the linguistic limitations placed on attempts to describe such newly emergent family relationships:

> *Dr Sturge (in her report) refers to the deficiencies of our language in the present context, pointing out that there is 'a range of difficulties that the present terminology does not cover', including whether two women can be 'parents', whether children's psychological thinking can accommodate three 'parents', and what the biological father should be called if not a*

'parent'. 'Mummy' and 'Daddy' and the variants on these names are readily recognisable but there is no recognised name for the woman or man in a same sex relationship who stands in the position of a parent but does not have a biological relationship to the child of the family (57).

In *T v B* [2010] EWHC 1444 (Fam) a lesbian couple had a child together via IVF. They had a joint application. They had separated and the child stayed with the birth mother and her new partner whilst the former partner applied for residence and contact; the couple was awarded joint residence. The birth mother then applied for financial support from her former partner, and the court held that the former partner was a parent in the social and psychological sense but not in a legal sense (see Chapter 16).

Heteronormativity is no longer privileged, but as Hedley J observed in *Re P and L (Contact)* [2011] EWHC 3431 (Fam), [2012] 1 FLR 1068 where two men (same sex) and two women (same sex) were involved and contact with the children was being considered: 'this is still new territory'. In *A v B and C (Lesbian Co-Parents: Role of Father)* [2012] EWCA Civ 285, where in addressing the fixity of language and concepts, Black LJ said: 'Despite the passage of time, the courts continue to struggle to evolve a principled approach to cases such as this one.' (See Diduck 2007.)

Since 2004 the transgendered parent has been recognised as a legal parent in his or her newly acquired gendered status. (See Welstead 2015.)

The transgender father

The lack of recognition of a female to male post operative 'transsexual' in the new sex/gender was the subject of *X, Y and Z v United Kingdom* (1997). The term at that time was 'transsexual' and was understood and constructed as the issue of a person wanting to change and become recognised in the opposite gender male or female, and many in that journey wished to be rid of secondary sex characteristics that visibly trapped them in their biological sex of male or female.

In this case X a female to male post–operative 'transsexual' living with a woman Y cis gender partner who conceived following IVF and gave birth to two children, wanted to be recognised as the father of the children. (See Edwards 1996.)

As can be seen in this case the problem of the fixity of 'mother' and 'father' encountered by Freddy McConnell (*R (McConnell and YY) v Registrar-General for England and Wales* [2020] EWCA Civ 559) had already presented itself nearly three decades earlier.

The application of *X, Y and Z v United Kingdom* (1997) 24 EHRR 143 to the European Court of Human Rights raised fundamental issues about children's rights to a named parent as 'father' and also the right of a transsexual parent to be called father and recognised as a father to his children since legal rules governing parenthood and gender identity is predicated on biological essentialist criteria. The position of the child Z was that the birth certificate had a nil entry for the father, and yet Z knows X to be its father. X had assumed the role of parental responsibility for the child de jure although acquiring legal rights of fatherhood were prohibited. The result was not only a denial of the official recognition of fatherhood and all its interpellations for X, but the child was also denied the benefits of a named father through the intransigence of the law to recognise and validate the social reality which broke the law's pact with biological essentialism in family relationships. The ECtHR said that the community has interest in maintaining a coherent system of family law prioritising the best interests of the child.

> When deciding whether a relationship can be said to amount to 'family life', a number of factors may be relevant, including whether the couple live together, the length of their relationship and whether they have demonstrated their commitment to each other by having children together or by any other means [36].

And that X was not prevented from acting as Z's father in social sense and could, with Y, apply for joint residence order in respect of her. The court concluded that there had been no violation of the right to family life Article 8 (14 votes to six).

(See also *Rees v United Kingdom* (1987) 9 EHRR 56; *Cossey v United Kingdom* (1990) 13 EHRR 622 and *Sheffield and Horsham v United Kingdom* [1970] 2 WLR 1306, together with the cases of *Goodwin v UK* [2002] 2 FCR 577, [2002] 2 FLR 487, and *Bellinger v Bellinger* [2003] UKHL 21.)

By 2004, the Gender Recognition Act (2004) deemed that provided a person had been granted a Gender Recognition certificate which did not require the person to have surgery to remove secondary sex characteristics or create artificial sex characteristics that person could be known for all intents and purposes including as a mother or father in that person's preferred gender. Following this statute the applicant in *X, Y, and Z* (mentioned earlier) finally succeeded in being recognised as the legal father to his children. (See Stephen Whittle YouTube, see also Welstead 2015).

Brown (2024) cites McCandless and Sheldon (2010: 202) who had already recognised what they described as 'the tensions inherent in continuing to map our legal determinations of parenthood to a family model that is unmoored from its traditional underpinnings' these tension surface in *McConnell* mentioned earlier.

Legal parents and parental responsibility

Turning now to parental responsibility those persons recognised as legal parents have 'parental responsibility' for a child in their care. Parental responsibility involves 'all the rights, duties, powers, responsibilities and authority which by law a parent of a child has in relation to the child and his property' (CA 1989, s 3). Legal parenthood carries the responsibility to register a child's name within six weeks of birth, acquire automatic responsibility if the mother, automatic responsibility for the father if married to the mother or if named on birth certificate as the father. Legal parenthood carries the 'right' to make an application for example for a residence or contact order, specific issue order (to change a child's name or to apply for a prohibited steps order to prevent a child being removed from the country (CA 1989, s 8).

Not all biological fathers have parental responsibility for their children (see *Re D* (2006) earlier) but a biological father with or without parental responsibility has the right to make a private law application without requiring the leave of the court (CA 1989, s 10(4)(a)). Other parties who may have some biological connection to the child, for example, grandparents, aunts or siblings, may acquire parental responsibility where a residence order or special guardianship order is made in their favour. In addition, the local authority may have parental responsibility for a child where a care order has been made (CA 1989, s 31). More than one person can have parental responsibility for a child (CA 1989, s 2(5)). Where other parties have parental responsibility for the child, this responsibility lasts for the duration of the order made in their favour (s 11(7)(c)); that is to say, where a relative or a foster parent is granted a contact order or in the case of residence and the child is living with them. When that residence order ceases, so too does their parental responsibility for the child.

'Parental responsibility' and its responsibilities

Some of the more salient aspects of parental responsibility are noted next, including caring and protecting the child from harm, ensuring the education of the child and providing medical treatment, administering property and acting for the child in legal proceedings. All of these aspects are considered in a context of how best to provide for a child's welfare.

Responsibility to care for the child

This means the responsibility and duty to determine the place and manner of the upbringing of the child. Conflict frequently arises over upbringing between parents who are unmarried, or who have been married or in civil partnerships and later separate or divorce (see Chapter 12 as to residence and contact and especially the insuperable difficulties of relocation, especially international relocation). Conflict may arise between parents and the State necessitating the involvement of the court in wardship or the local authority (see Chapters 13 and 14, 15 respectively). A failure or inability to adequately care will result in loss of residence or else an order for defined contact, or else where significant harm is found (s 31) a child will be removed and taken into care, and may be adopted.

Responsibility to ensure the child's education

Parents have a responsibility and duty to ensure that the child receives an education, whether by going to school or else by being educated at home. If the local education authority is not satisfied that the child is attending school and no provision is made elsewhere, they can make an application to the court for a school attendance order (section 437 of the Education Act 1996). A parent who disobeys a school attendance order is guilty of an offence section 444(1) (see *R (on the application of R) v Leeds Magistrates and others* [2005] EWHC 1479 (Admin); *Re K (A Child) (Secure Accommodation Order: Right to Liberty)* [2001] 2 WLR 1141, *R v Carmarthenshire*

County Council, ex parte White [2000] ELR 172). Where school attendance is so infrequent as to be capable of potentially harming the child, a care order under the CA 1989 may be made (see *Re O (A Minor) (Care Proceedings: Education)* [1992] 4 All ER 905). In *R (on the application of Goodred) v Portsmouth City Council (Secretary of State for Education intervening)* [2021] EWHC 3057 (Admin), a challenge by application of leave for judicial review of the local authority's requirement that the claimant mother prove that her children are receiving suitable education at home was made.

Responsibility for the child's religion – now of little relevance

In the past, raising a child within the Christian religion was considered a key function and requirement of a parent's role as emphasised in *Agar-Ellis* cited earlier. Today, religious upbringing in any faith whilst it is no longer a requirement of parental responsibility is nevertheless of varying importance in particular cultures and communities. For some communities and families, religious upbringing remains central to the parental role of guidance and everyday living, and in this regard it is important that the courts have an understanding of how faith intersects with the parental role and upbringing of a child.

Responsibility to protect the child and not to inflict punishment or physical discipline

Under the common law a father had the right to chastise a child, although it must not be for the 'gratification of passion' (see *R v Hopley* [1860] 2 F & F 202). There is no right today to chastise a child or to discipline for disobedience. Judicially ordered punishment has been held to be degrading (see *Tyrer v United Kingdom* [1978–79]), and corporal punishment is prohibited in State schools by the Education (No 2) Act 1986, s 47. In *Williamson Regina (Williamson and others) v Secretary of State for Education and Employment* [2005] AC 246, the claimants who were teachers and parents wished to exercise their right as Christians to hold and manifest their belief in mild corporal punishment of pupils. The court held that their right was not absolute and that the interference with their religious right, to hold and manifest their belief which included, they argued, a right to use mild corporal punishment, was justified under Art 9(2) and necessary in a democratic society for the protection of the rights and freedoms of others, namely, children (see Chapter 14). The United Nations Convention on the Rights of the Child (UNCRC) (1989) also imposes obligations on member states to protect children from domestic violence. Article 2(2) of the Convention provides protection from discrimination or punishment and claims of culture and educational tradition yield to this prohibition.

In *Re H (Minors) (Wardship: Cultural Background)* [1987] 2 FLR 12, the parents came from a different cultural background, but the court found that this was no defence to physical punishment. C, then 3 years old, had been put out in the snow, naked from the waist down, as a punishment. There were constant reports of the children being left unattended. In mitigation from the mother's point of view, she had a difficult pregnancy at that time and gave birth to a child two days later which died. Bruising was found on P when he was hit with a stick, and evidence of hitting of C across the face with a flip-flop, and L was found alone when she was only 2½ years old.

The court held:

> *Where the court in the discharge of its parental duties was dealing with children of foreign ethnic origins and culture it must consider the situation against the reasonable objective standards of that culture so long as they did not conflict with minimal acceptable standards of child care in England, and always provided that the one criterion on which its decision was based was the welfare and best interests of the children concerned.*

Responsibility to consent to medical treatment of the child

Parental responsibility includes ensuring that medical treatment is provided. Failure to do so may result in criminal liability. CA 1989, s 3(5) introduced a further possible proxy, a person who:

> *(a) does not have parental responsibility for a particular child; but (b) has care of the child may, subject to the provisions of the CA 1989, do what is reasonable in all the circumstances of the case for the purpose of safeguarding or promoting the child's welfare.*

Another proxy decision-maker would be the court itself in wardship (see CA 1989, s 8 and CA 1981, s 41 for the wardship jurisdiction and Chapter 13). The parents will give consent for their children unless the child is of the age where he or she may give consent (see 'Gillick competent' *Gillick v West Norfolk and Wisbech Area Health Authority* [1986] AC 112 discussed in Chapter 11 and later). Failure to provide medical care for a child may also result in a child being taken into care if significant harm to a child is found as a result of lack of adequate medical attention.

Responsibility to withhold consent or consent to marriage overridden by statute

Young children who wish to marry without parental consent may do so in Scotland where the age of marriage without parent consent is 16 years. The Marriage and Civil Partnership (Minimum Age) Act 2022, however, has prohibited marriage and civil partnerships until parties are 18 in England and Wales. The new law also applies to cultural or religious marriages that are not registered with the local council.

Responsibility involves administering the child's property and to enter into certain contracts with the child

Parents have the right to administer the child's property. See the Child Support Act 1991 in Chapter 16.

Responsibility to act for the child in legal proceedings

Rules of civil litigation insist that someone else acts on the child's behalf. This is important in care proceedings where the court will appoint a children's guardian, to represent the child. Where a child has sufficient understanding (see Chapter 11, Adolescent rights: autonomy and participation) he or she may apply for leave to apply for an order under CA 1989 in his or her own right.

Parental responsibility: who is entitled?

In accordance with CA 1989, s 2, more than one person may have parental responsibility for the same child at the same time (s 2(5)).

The following parties have parental responsibility:

- the mother (whether a child is born outside or within marriage);
- the married father;
- the unmarried father if ACA 2002, s 111(2)(a)(b)(c) applies; if mother and father jointly register birth;
- the unmarried father if he is granted a court order under CA 1989, s 4;
- same-sex partners if civil partnership at time of fertility treatment or donor insemination;
- the adoptive parents of an adopted child;
- if a child is a ward of court the court until further order;
- a guardian appointed by a parent, by deed or will, after the parent's death;
- a local authority in whose favour a care order has been made until further order;
- the CA 1975 created the institution of custodianship repealed in CA 1989, under which many parental rights are given to the foster parent, but some rights remain with the natural parent;
- stepparents under CA 1989, s 4(a); and
- special guardians.

Mothers

The law confers automatic parentage (parental rights and responsibilities) on the mother. This represents a complete volte-face when compared with the total lack of legal status of mothers in the nineteenth and first half of the twentieth century. The CA 1989, s 2(4) abolished the old patriarchal rule stating: 'The rule of law that a father is the natural guardian of his legitimate child is abolished.'

Fathers

The biological father (where the father is married to the mother) is automatically the legal parent. And, where the man is married to the mother there is a rebuttable presumption that he is the father. Where the parties are not married, but the father's name is registered on the certificate of birth, he becomes the legal parent and acquires parental responsibility. This follows the provision in the ACA (2002), s 111.

Unmarried fathers

Birth characteristics in England and Wales: 2021 records show that in 2021 there were 624,828 live births. Of this number, 320,713 were registered to women outside of marriage or civil partnership. This represents 51.3 per cent of the total. Prior to

2002 an unmarried father could only acquire parental responsibility if he had been granted a parental responsibility order under s 4 of the CA 1989. The 2002 Act was an attempt to introduce some equality between parents. Further, following changes to birth registration in 2009 it became compulsory to register the father on the birth certificate. The impetus behind this requirement was to establish paternity and enable accountability and ensure the financial support of the child by the unmarried father. The mother was therefore required to provide the birth registrar with details about the father. Certain exemptions provided in s 41 of the HFEA 2008 included where the father had died and where the mother is uncertain about who the father is, where the father lacks capacity (Mental Capacity Act 2005) and where the mother has reason to fear for her own safety or the safety of the child.

Court orders parental responsibility

The CA 1989, s 4(1)(b) introduced 'parental responsibility agreements' which provide a means by which parents, who no longer reside together, can have an amicable agreement that allows them to both participate in the raising of the children.

In *Re X (Parental Responsibility Agreement: Children in Care)* [2000] Fam 156, the mother entered into an agreement with the father that he should have parental responsibility, this was upheld by the court. (See also *A v D (serious domestic violence: mother's applications to terminate father's parental responsibility and to change child's name)* [2013] EWHC 2963 (Fam).)

Parental responsibility order

Where the conditions under CA 1989, s 4(1)(a) and (b) are not present, the unmarried father may apply to the court for parental responsibility in accordance with s 4(1)(c). The decision of the court is governed by the degree of commitment and attachment of the applicant to the child (see *Re H (Minors) (Local Authority: Parental Rights (No 3)* [1991] Fam 151 and the application of the welfare principle (*Re RH (a minor) (parental responsibility)* [1998] 2 FLR 89). Applications for parental responsibility may also be a strategy to exercise control on the other partner thereby weaponising parental responsibility. In *N v K* [2024] EWFC 245 (B) the court refused an order where the father who had previous convictions for domestic violence had not demonstrated genuine reasons, commitment or attachment, and made a barring order under s 91(14) CA to prevent further litigation. The appearance of the real father wishing to have contact may not always be in the best interest of the child.

In *Blunkett v Quinn* [2005] 1 FLR 648, the biological father wished to establish whether he was, in fact, the father, and if he was the father, then to establish his parental responsibility s (4)(1)(c) of the CA 1989, and to exercise his rights and responsibilities as the child's lawful parent. David Blunkett, the then Home Secretary, applied to the court for a contact order in respect of the son of Kimberly Quinn which was established that he was the father. This was not the wish of Kimberly Quinn. The two-year-old child lived with the respondent mother and her husband. David Blunkett sought a parental responsibility order and a contact order. The mother denied that the applicant was the child's father. A conciliation appointment was listed. Following paternity testing, and in a blaze of publicity it was discovered that David Blunkett was indeed the father of the child.

In 2008, the fathers of 14 per cent of children born outside marriage were not registered. Ed Miliband, the leader of the Labour party, was not named on the birth

TABLE 9.1 Parental responsibility orders applied for by year in private law

	2011	2013	2015	2017	2019	2020	2021	2022
Parental resp applics-3a	3,822	3,397	1,244	1,117	962	813	704	508
No of children involved in applics-3b	5,496	4,725	1,632	1,468	1,236	1,059	925	665
Parental responsibility orders granted-4a	3,479	3,007	2,186	2,000	1,456	1,072	1,132	1,059

Source: Family Court Statistics Quarterly July to September 2022 Annual Applications and Orders Made. Data taken from Accessible Family Court Tables www.gov.uk/government/statistics/family-court-statistics-quarterly-july-to-september-2022 (accessed 30.04.2024)

certificate of his 15-month–old son, Daniel, as per September 2010. As an unnamed and unmarried father, he had no legal parental responsibility for his son. In May 2011, he married the mother of his two children and then applied for parental responsibility for his two sons.

Putting biological parentage to proof for the purpose of parental responsibility

In cases where the identity of the biological father is unknown, uncertain or contested (*Blunkett v Quinn*) and the mother or father wishes to establish parentage for the child, or a party undertaking the role of the father wishes to dispute another's parentage, an order for a declaration of paternity (under the Family Law Act 1986, s 55A, as amended by the Child Support, Pensions and Social Security Act 2000, s 83(2)) may be made. The Family Law Reform Act 1969 (FLRA 1969), s 20 provides that applications are only permitted in the course of other applications and do not stand alone and confer a discretion on the court. The FLRA 1969 provides that a sample will only be taken with the consent of the person concerned, although the court will draw inferences from a refusal s 21(3) (see *Re A (a minor) (paternity: refusal of blood test)* [1994] 2 FLR 463).

A number of principles guide the exercise of discretion, including the child's right to know the truth of his or her genetic progenitor, and the right of a biological father to know his progeny. However, blood testing will only be ordered if it is considered to be in the child's best interests (see Wallbank 2004) which is the overriding consideration and this remains the position. Under FLRA 1969, s 21(3):

> A blood sample may be taken from a person under the age of sixteen years, not being such a person as is referred to in sub-section (4) of this section – (a) if the person who has the care and control of him consents; or (b) where that person does not consent, if the court considers that it would be in his best interests for the sample to be taken.

The court can override a parents refusal and if the child is 16 years or over then the child is competent to give or refuse consent. (See Chapter 11.)

Mothers refusing consent to blood tests

The court can overrule a mother's refusal if it is in the best interests of the child. Consider the two cases that follow. In *Re O; Re J (Children) (Blood Tests: Constraint)* [2000] Fam 139 two separate cases, were brought together before the court because they both turned on the same issue, where a male applicant had obtained an order under FLRA 1969, s 20(1) for obtaining blood tests in order to determine the paternity of a child who was the subject of the proceedings. In each case, the mother, whose consent is required under FLRA 1969, s 21(3), refused to consent to the child's blood being tested. The court held that as the law stood, the person with the care and control of a child had been given the absolute right to refuse to allow a sample of blood to be taken from the child making it a matter for the mother to grant or withhold consent. Wall J (per curiam) said:

> *Knowledge of a child's paternity is increasingly regarded not only as a matter of prime importance to a child, but as being both his right and in his interests. If a direction for blood tests cannot be enforced, the court and the child concerned are deprived of the means of acquiring that knowledge, and the court is thrown back on the unsatisfactory and blunt instrument of drawing an inference against the person with the care and control of the child. If Parliament does not implement reform, the law in this area will continue not to serve the best interests of children. In these circumstances, it is anticipated that reform may need to be achieved when the Human Rights Act 1998 comes into force, by the point being taken that Pt III of the 1969 Act is not human rights' compliant.*

[434]

In *Re H and A (Children)* [2002] EWCA 383, the applicant sought an order for testing the children's blood to determine paternity; the mother opposed the application. Mr and Mrs R had been married. Some 22 years later Mrs R gave birth to twin girls. Mrs R had been having a relationship with Mr B. Mrs R had told Mr B that he was the father whilst Mr R had no suspicion that the twins were anybody else's than his own. Mrs R and Mr B had an argument and as a result Mr B issued an application for contact and parental responsibility. Mr R appealed. (The decision of Wall J in *Re O; Re J*, mentioned earlier, where the court had ruled that a parent with care and control could refuse consent, was no longer good law.) The heartache and possibility of undermining family stability is evident in Mr R's evidence, and it is worth comparing the courts approach to this possibility with its approach to relocation where the stability of the mother is a central feature of the court's decision making.

Mr R said:

> *If there was any chance, if there was only a 1% chance that Mr B is the father of these children it would impair everybody's lives, including my own. I couldn't act − if it is true then that Mr B is the father of G and L then I don't − well, I'm almost certain that I couldn't cope with that at all and I would have to let the family unit go because I couldn't look after somebody else's children, if you like . . . I don't think I could cope.*

The Court of Appeal concluded that the appeal should be allowed, and the application remitted for retrial.

A direction can be sought from the court (see *A Local Authority v The Mother and Others* [2024] EWFC 19 (B) where '(d) The Court grants the father's applications for Declaration of Parentage and Parental Responsibility Orders for the youngest three children.'

(See earlier *The father v The mother* [2023] EWFC 176; *A local authority v X and others (M intervening)* [2023] EWFC 121.)

The local authority and proof of parentage

In *Barnsley Metropolitan Borough Council v JK and others* [2024] EWHC 305 (Fam) in public law D had been conceived through the insemination of his father and his grandfather's sperm to his mother. After D's parents had separated, D and his sibling (E) had lived with their mother but the authority had issued public law proceedings because of concerns about serious harm to the children attributable to their mother's actions and neglect. The court held, among other things, that the authority did not have a sufficient personal interest in the determination of its application for a declaration of D's parentage.

Right of child to know

This issue of a child's right to know has engaged domestic courts and the ECtHR in a succession of cases. Whilst the right to know has driven the development of the law and is now treated as axiomatic, Professor Fortin has argued that there also subsists a right not to know. Her argument is predicated on a concern that the child also has a right to family stability which may be blown asunder where disclosures of this kind are made. (See Fortin 2009; Herring and Foster 2012.) In *Re T (a child) (DNA tests: paternity)* [2001] 2 FLR 1190 concerned the right of the mother and her husband. Bodey J balanced the right to know with the right of the de facto family to stability and refused an application for paternity testing. (See Marshall 2018.)

In *X v Y* [2024] EWFC 42 (B) the parties involved: X the father; Y the mother (who had separated; the mother forming a new relationship with Z) and the child, A (a boy aged 6) represented through his r16.4 Guardian (CG). The first issue to be decided by the court is whether the child is told that the Father is his biological father. '14. At some point, and it is unclear precisely when, the Mother and Z decided that they would pretend to all that A was the son of Z. This has necessarily entailed lying to the child about his parentage, lying to both V and W (the children of their family) lying to the community, their friends, A's school and anyone else with whom they interact. They decided to change A's name as part of creating and maintaining this lie, and lied to various authorities such as the Local Authority, and the Court in an attempt to obtain paperwork that enabled them to successfully conceal A's parentage from him and from everyone else.' The mother's position was that even when A reaches 18 years old he should not know the truth it would be 'evil' to tell him [at 36]. The judge concluded

[98]. I am satisfied that when I ask myself the question, should this Court uphold A's right to know his parentage, or will that knowledge be contrary to his best interests? The answer, is that his right prevails and indeed it is in his best interests for to know. There are no cogent child-focused reasons for denying him that knowledge.

Declaration of parentage and identity

A progeny's knowledge of parentage may also be crucial to identity for a range of reasons. In *Re Ms L; Re Ms M (declaration of parentage)* [2022] EWFC 38 two separate unrelated progenies sought to 'correct the historical record on their original birth certificates', adding the 'name and identity of their birth father and thus formally complete their birth history'. In the first case an adoptive child, L, applied for a declaration of parentage on the basis that such a declaration was personally a very important step for her as it strongly related to her identity and that a practical benefit of a declaration of parentage for her would be her ability to acquire dual citizenship. In the case of M, M was born in 1964, and her birth mother was from an aristocratic family and was unmarried. No one in the birth mother's family knew at the time of the pregnancy, the birth of the baby, and/or the subsequent adoption. Within two months of her birth, M was placed with substitute parents. M had some later contact with her birth mother, but all other members of M's birth family rejected her. M applied for a declaration of parentage to take citizenship of the country of her father – BH's nationality, and was planning to relocate to live in the country of her birth father and his family. After the application had been issued, a bone from the body of BH was exhumed, and M was able to persuade the authorities in that country, with support from BH's family, to test her DNA against the bone of the deceased.

> [23] In most unusual, but extremely fortuitous, circumstances unconnected with this application (the details of which it is unnecessary to rehearse here) in late October 2021 (after this application had been issued) a bone from the body of BH (buried in his home country in Europe) was exhumed, and Ms M was able to persuade the authorities in that country, with support from BH's family, to test her DNA against the bone of the deceased. This DNA test confirmed to a very high degree of probability indeed that the deceased (BH) is her birth father. Ms M wishes to take citizenship of the country of BH's nationality, and has started to form plans to relocate to live in the country of her birth father and his family.

This DNA test confirmed to a very high degree of probability indeed that the deceased (BH) was her birth father.

Putative fathers' right to know

Putative fathers frequently bring applications with regard to paternity testing (*Blunkett v Quinn* earlier). In *Re R (A Minor) (Contact Biological Father)* [1993] 2 FLR 762 Butler Sloss LJ held that a putative father has the right to know the truth where the parents separated and sometime later the father sought contact with the daughter; however, the girl, of 5½, has been brought up in the belief that the mother's cohabitee is her natural father.

> I agree with the judge that the child and her father cannot meet at this moment. But I differ from the judge in leaving the long-term decision in limbo. I believe the child has not only the right to see her father; if this can eventually be realised without causing her damage, she also has a right in this case to know the truth.
>
> [768]

Birth fathers following adoption

In *H v R and another (Attorney General for England and Wales intervening)* [2021] EWHC 1943 (Fam) the court declined to make a declaration of parentage in favour of the applicant, Mr H, the birth parent of an adopted child. The court found that to do so would be manifestly contrary to public policy for the purposes of s 58(1) of the Family Law Act 1986. In *Boudewijn v Johnson and Another* [2022] EWFC 142, Mostyn J granted a declaration of parentage to an adult adoptee who was a half sibling which resulted in the name of the biological father (who had died) being registered on the registration of birth enabling Amy the daughter concerned to secure Jamaican citizenship by descent.

De facto fathers' right to truth

In *Mizzi v Malta* [2006] 1 FLR 1048 the husband sought to dispute the paternity of the child. Maltese law permitted this but within time limits. The husband was outside the time limit. The Maltese court found this was a breach of the husband's Article 8 right, which was overturned on appeal. The ECHR held there had been a breach of Articles 6(1) and 8 and held that whilst time limits could be in the interests of children, such limits should not altogether prohibit the use of the legal remedy. (See also *Rozanski v Poland* [2006] 2 FLR 1163, *Paulik v Slovakia* [2006] 46 EHHR 10, *Tavli v Turkey* [2007] 1 FLR 1136.)

Court denial of parental responsibility applications

The court in considering applications for parental responsibility will take into consideration the rights of all parties and the welfare of the child. In *Re C and V contact and parental responsibility* [1998] 1 FLR 393 the appellant was the father of the second of two children S and R. He applied for contact in respect of both children and for parental responsibility for R. The mother opposed all the applications. R had medical problems which the mother could attend to. The judge denied the applicant the orders in respect of R and the order in respect of S. On appeal, the court granted parental responsibility in connection with R and contact in respect of S.

All applications to the court for termination of parental responsibility are not successful. Importantly in *Re A* [2023] EWCA 689, whilst the Court of Appeal dismissed an appeal by the appellant mother it was also tasked to decide whether to grant a declaration of incompatibility. The Children Act 1989 (CA 1989) made a distinction between married and unmarried parents with respect to the court's power to revoke parental responsibility. Where parents were married, or were in a civil partnership, there was no power to revoke the parental responsibility of a father or second female parent whilst concerning unmarried fathers, unmarried second female parents or stepparents where, CA 1989, ss 4(2A), 4ZA(5) or 4A(3) the court had the power to bring their parental responsibility to an end. In this case however the application for a declaration of incompatibility failed.

Terminating parental responsibility – circumstances

Domestic violence by the father and sexual abuse of step children or otherwise a criminal record of sexual abuse of children has on some occasions outweighed any right to parental responsibility and been the subject of recent discussion (see Bassam 2024). In 2022, 25 terminations of parental responsibility were made. However, such orders are relatively infrequent averaging about 12 per year from 2013 onwards in private law and even fewer in public law proceedings (see Accessible Family Court Tables 2022 Table 4a). Following the changes introduced by the Victims and Prisoners Act (2024) s 18(3) amending the Children Act (CA 1989) s 10 (see below). A proposal to include child sex offenders tabled as an amendment to the Criminal Justice Bill on 10 May 2024 was later abandoned being lost by a mere ten votes. However, the Labour government, (elected July 2024) Ministry of Justice spokesperson, has said that they will bring forward legislation to restrict parental responsibility for any parent convicted of child sexual offences. Significantly in September 2024 a convicted rapist of the child's mother and a adult stranger resulted in parental responsibility being removed from the father for the child (Summers 2024).

In *Child arrangements – D v E (Termination of Parental Responsibility)* [2021] EWFC 37 where the father was a sex offender and the mother sought a child arrangements order that there be no contact, a specific issue order to change the child's surname, the termination of the father's parental responsibility pursuant to s 4(2A) and an order pursuant to s 91(14) of the 1989 Act. The probation service concluded that the father posed a risk to adolescents, particularly in the form of sexual grooming, and a serious risk to intimate partners.

> *There was no evidence demonstrating an attachment between the father and the child, nor had he demonstrated the level of commitment that would support the making of a parental responsibility order. The father had taken no steps to address his offending behaviour and had failed to engage with the legal process designed to reinstitute his relationship with the child. Were he to have parental responsibility there was a significant risk he would use it to seek to control the mother.*

MacDonald J said: 'the removal of parental responsibility was a serious step that had to be justified on the available evidence and be proportionate' [5].

In *CW v SG (parental responsibility: consequential orders)* [2013] EWHC 854 (Fam) the mother's application for an order terminating the father's parental responsibility in respect of their child, D, was granted in circumstances where the father had been convicted of sexually abusing the mother's two elder daughters.

A v D (serious domestic violence: mother's applications to terminate father's parental responsibility and to change child's name) [2013] EWHC 2963 (Fam). Here, the father had a criminal record of offending involving violence related offences, severe domestic violence against the mother which the child had witnessed, at the time of the hearing, serving a term of imprisonment for GBH against the mother. Wood J terminated parental responsibility of the father:

> *[27] To leave the father as a joint holder of parental responsibility would lead to the mother having perforce to have dealings with the father which would, on any objective view of the evidence, be intolerable to her, and which would more probably than not lead to a profound instability for her, with the inevitable consequences for the deterioration in the arrangements for the children as she sought to combat the seriously undermining effects upon her of such an intrusion. This finding rests significantly but not exclusively on the mother's evidence, which I accept, that this father is interested in controlling her above all*

else and, frankly, not in A at all. Even though he has evinced no real interest in A, his capacity to create mischief by deploying his parental responsibility if he retained it would remain. I cannot risk this comparatively new-found security being jeopardised.

Jade Ward 'Jade's Law' – suspending parental responsibility

Jade's Law, introduced through the Victims and Prisoners Act 2024, applies an automatic suspension of parental responsibility in cases where a perpetrator has killed a partner or ex-partner with whom they share children through s 18(3) by imposing a prohibited steps order under section 8 of the Children Act. This started its passage in 2022 with the proposal that parental responsibility should be removed from those who committed serious offences originally moved by Mark Tami MP.

> *On 26 August 2021 Jade was brutally murdered by her estranged husband, Russell Marsh, in a premeditated attack. On 12 April 2022, Marsh was given a life sentence with a minimum of 25 years in prison. After Jade ended their relationship a week before her murder, Marsh had reportedly told friends that if he could not have Jade, no one could. Marsh was a controlling figure throughout their relationship, who would tell Jade who she could see and speak to, and what she could wear and do. When Jade stood up to him, she was killed as punishment.*

(Hansard 2022, see also BBC News 12 April 2022.) Marsh was able to exert his control over their children as he had parental responsibility. Jade's children were later raised by her parents. They had to ask Marsh permission if they wanted to take the children on holiday etc.

> *I understand that Jade's parents have been told that if they want to take their grandsons on holiday abroad, they need permission from the father. A convicted parent must also be consulted on issues such as where the children go to school and the medical treatment they receive. Effectively, Marsh has the right to veto decisions made by Jade's parents and pursue a family court hearing.*

Her murderer was able to continue to take part in decisions relating to their four children inflicting further trauma on them and Jade's parents.

Termination – miscellaneous circumstances

In *Re A and B (Children: Restrictions on Parental Responsibility: Radicalisation and Extremism)* [2016] EWFC 40, [2016] 2 FLR 977 whilst granting an application to terminate a father's parental responsibility, Russell J warned that allegations must be supported by evidence where the findings sought in respect of radicalisation were vague, and generalised.

> *[119] . . . I emphasise this, extremism, or radicalisation, is a sensitive subject and there must be no suggestion that the courts would accept or tolerate any suggestion that adherents of the Islamic faith, or any other faith, are, ipso facto, supporters of extremism.*

In *B v C* [2023] EWHC 2524 (Fam) MacDonald J considered an application to terminate parental responsibility where it was conferred on a person by operation of Spanish law by fraud. Parental responsibility acquired under foreign law subsists in England and Wales by operation of Article 16(3) of the 1996 Hague Convention. MacDonald J held that it was manifestly contrary to public policy to accept the application of Spanish law in this case, meaning that the person did not hold parental responsibility in England and Wales (Article 22, 1996 Hague Convention).

Parental responsibility when not the parent

The court considered the status of the man acting as father when the discovery was made by declaration of non-paternity that he was not the biological father. (See Craddock 2023.) In *A Local Authority v SB and Others* [2022] EWFC 111 before HHJ Moradifar, the court reached a different conclusion less than a year later in *Re C & A (children) (acquisition and discharge of parental responsibility by an unmarried father)* [2023] EWHC 516 (Fam) (below).

Other parents – stepmothers' and stepfathers' parental responsibility

Where a parent remarries, the new spouse becomes the stepparent of any children of the previously married partner. Under the ACA 2002, amending CA 1989, s 4A(1):

Where a child's parent ('parent A') who has parental responsibility for the child is married to a person who is not the child's parent ('the step-parent') (a) parent A or, if the other parent of the child also has parental responsibility for the child, both parents may by agreement with the step-parent provide for the step-parent to have parental responsibility for the child; or (b) the court may, on the application of the step-parent, order that the step-parent shall have parental responsibility for the child.

The Civil Partnership Act 2004 (CPA) provides that civil partners are eligible to apply for parental responsibility on the same basis as stepparents under CPA 2004, s 246(1). The CA 1989, s 10(5) is amended so that any civil partner in a civil partnership (whether or not subsisting) may make an application for a residence order or contact order in respect of a child who is a child of the family. (See further Chapter 12.)

Adoptive parents

An order of the court placing a child for adoption establishes the adoptive parent as the legal parent. ACA 2002, s 46(1) states:

An adoption order is an order made by the court on an application under section 50 or 51 giving parental responsibility for a child to the adopters or adopter. (2)   The making of an adoption order operates to extinguish (a) the parental responsibility which any person other than the adopters or adopter has for the adopted child immediately before the making of the order.

In these circumstances, parental responsibility of other parties, including natural parents, is terrminated. (See further Chapter 10.)

Foster parents

When a child is being cared for by foster parents and a residence order is made in their favour parental responsibility is conferred upon them by virtue of the CA 1989, s 10. The foster carer(s) may be a single adult or an adult couple in a family arrangement. Foster parents also care for children when a care order has been made by the courts. In these circumstances the local authority has parental responsibility. (See further Chapter 10.)

Special guardians/guardians

Special guardianship orders (SGOs) were introduced following the ACA 2002 to support parental responsibility (see Special Guardianship Regulations 2005, Department of Education and Skills 2005) s 115 of the ACA 2002 which inserts sections 14A–F into the CA 1989. A court may make a special guardianship order in respect of the child on the application of any guardian of the child including anyone amongst others who has the consent of all those with parental responsibility for the child. When considering whether to make a special guardianship order, the welfare of the child is the court's paramount consideration and the welfare checklist in s 1 of the CA 1989 applies. Such orders do not terminate the parental responsibility of other parties. (See further Chapter 10, Chapter 14.)

Concluding remarks – family rights – article 8 'family life'

Whilst this chapter began with setting out the demise and gradual eradication of the proprietorial right of fathers over their children and the development of the notion of responsibility for the child the ECHR Article 8 protects the 'Right to Respect for Private and Family Life', where

1. Everyone has the right to respect for his private and family life, his home and his correspondence.
2. There shall be no interference by a public authority with the exercise of this right except such as is in accordance with the law and is necessary in a democratic society in the interests of national security, public safety or the economic well-being of the country, for the prevention of disorder or crime, for the protection of health or morals, or for the protection of the rights and freedoms of others.

However, Article 8 might not always be the panacea. In *Re L, V, M, H* [2001] *Fam* 260 Thorpe LJ warned of the 'wariness of the terminology of rights'.

Where there is a clash of convention rights the best interests of the child trumps other considerations. This clearly has been subject to shifting interpretation over time juxtaposed with the particular facts of the case. So in 2007 *Tavli* the court held that the right of the child to know his or her genetic origins is not to prevail over 'effective respect for family life'. In *Re O and J (Paternity: Blood Tests)* [2000] 1 FLR 418, for example where both mothers simply did not want to know the child's origins the judge said there was no jurisdiction to compel either of the mothers in the instant case to give their consent to samples being taken of their respective children's blood, and remitted the cases to the county court for further directions and/or adjudication on the merits of the respective applications. This case underscores that whilst the child's right not to know is a weighty consideration the need to preserve family stability may be weightier. (See Fortin 2009.)

But in *Re D (Paternity)* [2006] EWHC 3545 (Fam) where the child opposed paternity testing the court adopted a half-way house position. The child had been reared by a woman he assumed was the paternal grandmother and was settled with her. The applicant wanted to prove that he was the father and wanted contact with the boy. The court departed from the test in *Re H (Blood tests: Paternity)* [1997] Fam 89, and in applying s 20(1) of the Family Law Reform Act 1969 held that the child's welfare will outweigh any 'right to know' and ordered a sample to be taken to be used only in the future if the child wished to know. One wonders how this was communicated to the child and how this uncertainty and potential possible revelation would always be omnipresent. Right to know ones parentage as developed considerably from these cases depending on circumstances and the age of the child concerned. Issues of surrogacy have also introduced new situations. Significantly, Jade's Law discussed in Chapter 12 removes parental responsibility from those who have been convicted of killing their child's other parent. It is yet to be seen how women who in self-defence kill an abuser parent will come within the interpretation of this putative provision.

The interpretation of the best interest of the child in each particular case will depend on the arguments put by creative advocates in this area of wide discretion.

Self-test questions

1. Florence and Zebedee have raised two children, Tim (7 years) and Stevie (10 years). Jimmy, a former boyfriend of Florence, has returned from Ecuador. He is claiming to be Stevie's father. He intends to settle in England and wants to have contact with Stevie and to be part of his life. He has made several applications to the court (1) for DNA testing for proof of parentage, (2) an application for parental responsibility and (3) an application for joint/shared residence. Zebedee has been known as the father to Stevie from his birth, and Zebedee and Stevie have a very close relationship. Florence is opposing all three applications. The family is a very close and happy one, and the children know nothing about Jimmy.

    What principles should the court take into consideration when deciding whether to grant these applications? In your answer refer to relevant statute and case law.

2. The termination of parental responsibility is a draconian step; under what circumstances might it be terminated, and can such termination be justified when the right to family life under the European Convention on Human Rights (ECHR) is engaged for both the child and the person with parental responsibility?

3. Sukhi (she/her) and Madison (she/her) are a same-sex couple. They both entered into an agreement to undergo IVF treatment. After the embryo was implanted in Sukhi, Madison started a new relationship with Eva (she/her). Madison no longer wants a child with Sukhi but wants a child with Eva. Sukhi is due to give birth in two weeks' time.

    Meanwhile, Eva who wants to undergo IVF treatment with Madison has just separated from her husband Martin (he/him) who is serving a prison sentence for possession of indecent photographs of children. However, prior to this conviction he lived with Eva and helped raise a girl, Mary (6 years), and a boy, Peter (8 years), although he never married Eva. Now he is in prison, and he is anxious about his status as father to Mary and Peter and is considering applying to the court for parental responsibility. In respect of the two children, Eva needs some advice regarding these several complex issues including IVF treatment and also the protection of her children from Martin as he is due to come out of prison in 16 months' time.

    Advise Eva and Sukhi.

4. Diduck and Kaganas (2012: 3) open their book *Family Law, Gender and the State* with these words: 'In the light of recent family law reforms, it may be provocative, if not downright peculiar, to suggest that the idea of the family in English law is dependent for its meaning on the monogamous sexual relationship (either actual or symbolically) between a man and a woman'.

    Discuss this statement in charting the notion and understanding of parenthood over the decades.

References

Abramowicz, Sarah, 'English Child Custody Law, 1660–1839: The Origins of Judicial Intervention in Paternal Custody' [1999] *Columbia Law Review* 1391

Accessible Family Court Tables July–September 2022 Table 4a, 'Number of Orders in Public and Private law (Children Act) Made in Family Courts in England and Wales, by Type of Order, Annually 2011–2022 and Quarterly Q1 2011–Q3 2023 [note 1][note 2]' Family Court Statistics Quarterly: July to September 2022 – GOV.UK (www.gov.uk) (accessed 30.08.2024)

Bassam, Adiba, 'In What Circumstances Is Removal of Parental Responsibility Justified and Is Further Guidance Necessary?' [2024] *Family Law* 885

BBC News, 'Jade Marsh: Russell Marsh Jailed for Estranged Wife's Murder' (12.04.2022) www.bbc.co.uk/news/uk-wales-61077140 (accessed 22.04.2024)

BBC One – Sunday Morning Live, Series 6, Episode 15, 'Should We Be Allowed to Design Our Babies?' www.bbc.co.uk/programmes/p034fm3j (accessed 05.05.2024)

Bernardi, Sharon, 'I Lost 7 Children to Mitochondrial Disease' YouTube www.youtube.com/watch?v=Zb6NWmFLiDs) (accessed 11.05.2024)

Brown, Alan, 'Surrogacy Law Reform in the UK: The Ambiguous Position of Payments to the Surrogate' [2021] *Child and Family Law Quarterly* 95

Butler, Judith, 'Speaks on Gender' YouTube www.youtube.com/watch?v=wz9PZTU5V9M (accessed 05.05.2024)

Callus, Thérèse, 'A New Parenthood Paradigm for Twenty-First Century Family Law in England and Wales? [2012] *Legal Studies* 347

Census Figures, 'Census – Office for National Statistics' (2021) www.ons.gov.uk/census (accessed 11.05.2024)

Child Rapists to Automatically Have Parental Responsibility Stripped www.gov.uk/government/news/child-rapists-to-automatically-have-parental-responsibility-stripped (accessed 19.05.2024)

Children Bill Children Bill [H.L.] HL Deb (06.12.1988) vol 502 cc487–540 https://api.parliament.uk/historic-hansard/lords/1988/dec/06/children-bill-hl (accessed 05.05.2024)

Children in Families in England and Wales: Census 2021, 'Children in Families in England and Wales – Office for National Statistics' www.ons.gov.uk (accessed 05.05.2024)

Coward, Rosalind, *Patriarchal Precedents Sexuality and Social Relations* (Routledge 1983)

Craddock, Toby, 'Parental Responsibility and the Falsehood of Paternity: Interpreting s 4(2A) of the Children Act 1989' [2023] *Family Law* 1330

de Beauvoir, Simone, *The Second Sex* (Penguin 1974)

Deech, Ruth, 'Reflections on 40 Years of IVF and Its Impact on the Family' [2018] *Family Law* 1296

Dey, Ian and Fran Wasoff, 'Mixed Messages: Parental Responsibilities, Public Opinion and the Reforms of Family Law' [2006] *International Journal of Law, Policy and the Family* 20

Diduck, Alison and Felicity Kaganas, *Family law Gender and the State* (3rd edn, Hart 2012)

Edwards, Susan, 'Kidnapping' in *Elgar Encyclopedia of Crime and Criminal Justice* (2024) www.elgaronline.com/display/book/9781789902990/b-9781789902990.kidnapping.xml (accessed 05.05.2024)

Edwards, Susan, 'Protecting the Honour of Innocent Men' in Christina Dunhill (ed) *The Boys in Blue: Women's Challenge to the Police* (Virago 1989) 192

Ellis, Havelock, *Women and Marriage: or Evolution in Sex* (Kessinger Publishing 1888, 2010)

Engels, Frederich, *The Origin of the Family Private Property and the State* (Penguin 1884, 1986)

Firestone, Shulamith, *The Dialectic of Sex* (Paladin 1972)

Fletcher, Ronald, The Family *and* Marriage in Britain (Penguin 1966)

Fortin, Jane, 'Children's Right to Know Their Origins: Too Far, Too Fast?' (2009) 21 *Child and Family Law Quarterly* 336

Gallagher, James, 'Baby Born from Three People's DNA in UK First' *BBC* (9.05.2023) www.bbc.co.uk/news/science-environment-65538866 (accessed 05.05.2024)

Gamble, Natalie and Louisa Ghevaert, 'International Surrogacy: Payments, Public Policy and Media Hype' (2011) *Family Law* 504

Grenville, Kate, 'A True Apology to Aboriginal People Means Action as Well' *The Guardian* (14.02.2010)   www.theguardian.com/commentisfree/2010/feb/14/australia-aboriginals-apology-disadvantaged (accessed 05.05.2024)

Hansard, 'Parental Responsibility for People Convicted of Serious Offences' (Col 2WH) (2022) https://hansard.parliament.uk/Commons/2022-11-07/debates/E6A02687-8AE0-471D-97D9-9E6666811889/ParentalResponsibilityForPeopleConvictedOfSeriousOffences (accessed 20.05.2024)

Harris-Short, Sonia, 'Resisting the March Towards 50/50 Shared Residence: Rights, Welfare and Equality in Post-Separation Families' [2010] *Journal of Social Welfare and Family Law* 257

Herring, Jonathan and Charles Foster, ' "Please Don't Tell Me", the Right Not to Know' (2012) *Cambridge Quarterly of Healthcare Ethics* 26

HFEA Human Embryology and Fertilisation Authority 2024 Press Release www.hfea.gov.uk/about-us/news-and-press-releases/2022/hfea-responds-to-bbc-spotlight-ni-programme-the-babymaker-uncovered/ (accessed 05.05.2024)

HFEA Human Embryology and Fertilisation Authority Fertility Data (2019) www.hfea.gov.uk/about-us/publications/research-and-data/fertility-treatment-2019-trends-and-figures/ (accessed 05.05.2024)

HFEA Human Embryology and Fertilisation Authority Fertility Data (2021) www.hfea.gov.uk/about-us/publications/research-and-data/fertility-treatment-2021-preliminary-trends-and-figures/ (accessed 05.05.2024)

HFEA Human Embryology and Fertilisation Authority Modernising Fertility Law. www.hfea.gov.uk/about-us/modernising-the-regulation-of-fertility-treatment-and-research-involving-human-embryos/modernising-fertility-law (accessed 05.05.2024)

Horsey, Kirsty and Emily Jackson, 'The Human Fertilisation and Embryology Act 1990 and Non-Traditional Families' [2003] *Modern Law Review* 1472

Law Commission and Scottish Law Commission, 'Building Families Through Surrogacy: A New Law' (Law Com No 411, Scot Law Com No 262, 2023)

Maddox, Neil, 'Inheritance and the Posthumously Conceived Child' [2017] *Conveyancer and Property Lawyer* 408

Marshall, Jill, 'Secrecy in Births, Identity Rights, Care and Belonging' (2018) 30 *Child and Family Law Quarterly* 167

Munby, James, 'Changing Families: Family Law Yesterday, Today and Tomorrow – a View from South of the Border' University of Edinburgh (20 March 2018) www.judiciary.uk/wp-content/uploads/2018/03/speech-pfd-changing-families-edinburgh.pdf (accessed 05.05.2024)

Munby, James, 'International Surrogacy Forum: The Way Forward 2019' https://podbay.fm/p/cambridge-law-public-lectures-from-the-faculty-of-law/e/1562856577 (accessed 05.05.2024)

Pila, Justine, 'Property in Human Genetic Material: An Old Legal Question for a New Technological Age' in Tamara K Hervey and David Orentlicher (eds) *The Oxford Handbook of Comparative Health Law* (Oxford University Press 2019)

Sample, Ian, 'Girl, Nine, Benefits from UK's First IVF "Saviour Sibling" Therapy' *The Guardian* (21.12.2010) www.theguardian.com/society/2010/dec/21/girl-first-ivf-saviour-sibling (accessed 05.05.2024)

Sloan, Brian, 'The "Chimera" of Parenthood' (2021) 84(3) *Modern Law Review* 503

Special Guardianship Regulations 2005 Department of Education and Skills (2005) www.legislation.gov.uk/uksi/2005/1109/contents/made (accessed 05.05.2024)

Summers, Hannah, 'Father who is convicted rapist stripped of parental responsibility for daughter' The Observer' 14 September 2024

Wallbank, Julie, 'The Role of Rights and Utility in Instituting a Child's Right to Know Her Genetic History' [2004] *Social and Legal Studies* 245

Weathers, Helen, 'Why am I Dark Daddy the White Couple Mixed Race Children' Mail Online (13.06.2009) www.dailymail.co.uk/news/article-1192717/Why-I-dark-daddy-The-white-couple-mixed-race-children-IVF-blunder.html#ixzz13qcbaqpT (accessed 05.05.2024)

Welstead, Mary, 'The Law Commissions' Report on Surrogacy – a Missed Opportunity' [2023] *Family Law* 1074

Welstead, Mary, 'A New Pathway to Domestic Surrogacy (Building Families Through Surrogacy: A New Law: The Law Commission's Joint Consultation Paper' [2019] *Family Law* 1031

Welstead, Mary, 'Transgendered Persons: Children and Birth Registration' [2015] *Family Law* 1001

Whittle, Stephen, YouTube www.youtube.com/watch?v=nR-FR_sD_mo (accessed 05.05.2024)

Young, Michael and Peter Wilmott, *Family and Kinship in East London* (Penguin 1957)

Further reading

Austin, John L, 'Performative Utterances' in *How to Do Things with Words* (Oxford University Press 1962)

Barton, Chris, 'British Minority Ethnics, Religion and Family Law(yers)' [2008] *Family Law* 1217

Blackstone, William, *Blackstone's Commentaries on the Laws of England* (Clarendon Press 1765, 1857)

Butler, Judith, Gender Trouble (Routledge 1999)

Butler, Judith, Who's Afraid of Gender? (Allen Lane 2024)

Coward, Rosalind and John Ellis, *Language and Materialism* (Routledge 1977)

Davis, Liam, 'The Evolution of Birth Registration in England and Wales and Its Place in Contemporary Law and Society' [2024] *Modern Law Review* 317

Diduck, Alision, 'If Only We Can Find the Appropriate Terms to Use the Issue Will Be Solved: Identity and Parenthood' (2007) 19(4) *Child and Family Law Quarterly* 458

Edwards, Susan, *Sex and Gender in the Legal Process* (Blackstone Press 1996)

Engels, Frederich, The Origin of the Family, *Private Property, and the State* (Penguin 1884, 1986)

Hanscombe, Gillian and Jackie Forster, Rocking the Cradle: Lesbian Mothers, *A Challenge to Family Living* (Sheba 1981)

Maidment, Susan, *Child Custody and Divorce* (Croom Helm 1984)

Maidment, Susan, 'Women and Childcare: The Paradox of Divorce' in Susan Edwards (ed) *Gender,* Sex and the Law (Croom Helm 1985, 2024)

McCandless, Julie and Sally Sheldon, 'The Human Fertilization and Embryology Act 2008 and the Tenacity of the Sexual Family Form' [2010] Modern *Law Review* 175

Pote, Andrew and Sonja MacLeod, 'Is M for Mother? Applying Current Legislative Frameworks on the Implications of "Genetically" Parenting a Child to the Issue of mDNA Transfer' [2012] *Family Law* 23

Welstead, Mary, 'This Child Is My Child; This Child Is Your Child; This Child Was Made for You and Me; Surrogacy in the UK' in Bill Atkin (ed) *The International Survey of Family Law 2010* (Jordans 2010)

10

Adoption – only permissible if nothing else will do

SUMMARY

When a child is adopted all rights of birth parents are extinguished and unless the birth parent agrees, the child, when an adult, is denied any disclosure in their search for their natural parent. As Cobb J said in *Re S (a child) (adoption: consent of child parent)* [2017] EWHC 2729 (Fam): '[1] An adoption order, involving the permanent severance of all family ties of a child, is one of the most significant of all court orders available in the law of England and Wales.'

Adoption today claims, wherever possible, to favour adoption within the birth family, representing a shift from a time not so very long ago when adoption occurred behind closed doors, in secret, and where orders were only made to those outside the birth family. Since 2002, adopted children can register their names on the UK Birth Adoption Register, a publicly accessible site, and record their wish to contact and be connected by a birth parent. The digital age in any event has meant that it is much easier for children to search for birth parents and for parents to search for children. The success of the programme 'Long Lost Family' broadcast since 2011, relies on the emotional connection made with those who watch it as they witness the emotional and psychological importance for the many separated by adoption from birth parents and the importance to them of discovering genetic family ties. Declarations of parentage arising from adoption is considered in Chapter 9.

Most adoptions today involve babies and small children for whom local authority care orders in child protection proceedings have been made. This profile from the care system into adoption is a very different profile from the circumstances pertaining at the time of the 1926 Adoption Act, when those placed for adoption were infants of single mothers who because of cruel social mores and social stigma at that time their mothers were considered to bring shame upon their families and upon the children to whom they gave birth. As for the adoptive parents, the newly born child offered parenthood to married couples unable to conceive.

DOI: 10.4324/9781003435020-10

The statutory framework is provided in the Adoption and Children Act (ACA) (2002), the Children and Adoption Act (CAA) (2006) and the Children and Families Act (CFA) (2014). The 'welfare of the child as paramount' test lies at the heart of the Children Act (CA) (1989) s 1, and is the test applied when the court considers an application for adoption. This is also the test applied which allows the court to dispense with parental consent to adoption where the welfare of the child requires it, notwithstanding that it is open to an Article 8 'right to privacy and family life' European Convention of Human Rights (ECHR) challenge, especially as dispensing with parental consent, from the parents' vantage point, is an attack on their civil rights, and a draconian measure so very, very final. Contact with birth family and all its members is also claimed to be encouraged, however as Sir Andrew McFarlane said in *Re B (A Child) (Post-adoption contact)* [2019] EWCA Civ 29: '[61] notwithstanding that contact is encouraged both at the placement for adoption stage and at the adoption hearing the ultimate decision is for the adopters'.

However, there is a conflict in contemporary adoption practice between those who regard contact with the birth family as important and inevitable and those who favour the historical legal severance, discussed by Young and Neil (2009) Sloan (2014) amongst others.

The transracial adoption debate and countervailing practices which have waxed and waned over the years continue with protagonists on both sides of the debate.

The chapter considers both domestic and international adoption arrangements (see *Child adoption: Adopting a child from overseas*), the legal and procedural framework, and the overarching principles, and provides an evaluation of current tensions and debates within adoption practice which whilst favouring open adoption and continuing contact with family members, legal practice demonstrates this is actually rarely realised.

The chapter concludes with a reflection on McFarlane LJ's 2023 lecture, 'Adapting Adoption to the Modern World' and his seminal question – 'Is adoption really the best option in achieving a balance between child protection and the right to family life?' The court explores just this balance in *Re A and others (adoption: notification of fathers and relatives)* [2020] EWCA Civ 41. Here, the court considered the relevant statutory material including the ECHR, Article 8 'right to family life' and s 17 of the CA 1989 which imposes a duty on local authorities to promote the upbringing of children in need by their families so far as is consistent with their welfare. As Cobb J notes: 'the statutory material provides strong indicators of the importance of the engagement of the wider family in the adoption process'. Underhill LJ in *JL (A Child) (Leave to Apply to Revoke Placement Order) Re B v A Local Authority* [2020] EWCA Civ 1253 reiterated this principle: '[18] The law requires children where possible to be brought up in their natural families. Adoption is a measure of last resort.'

Whilst adoption arrangements are matters for the families concerned and are heard in the privacy of the family court, adoption is for some especially when public figures and celebrities are involved a very public matter when reported in the media. Clare Short, former Labour MP for Ladywood, Birmingham, and Government Minister (who resigned from her post following the UK invasion of Iraq in 2003) when a university student, gave up her son for adoption when he was 6 weeks old. She was very publicly reunited with him in 1996, some 31 years later (See White 1996).

Many high profile adoptions involve children from overseas and children from areas of war, deprivation and conflict. Such adoptions involve complex legal inter-country arrangements (discussed later).

History of UK adoption

Legal adoption was first introduced by the Adoption Act 1926. Children available for adoption at that time had been abandoned, orphaned or where a birth was forcibly relinquished by the mother. The film 'Philomena' based on the 2010 book, *The Lost Child of Philomena Lee*, by Martin Sixsmith poignantly details the real-life story of an elderly woman who had been searching for her son for 50 years and Sixsmith's efforts to help her find him. In 1951, Philomena became pregnant after having casual sex with a man she did not know at a county fair. She was sent by her father to Sean Ross Abbey, Roscrea, Ireland, a convent run by the Sisters of the Sacred Hearts of Jesus and Mary. After giving birth, she was forced to work in the convent laundry for four years, with little contact with her son. The nuns then gave her son up for adoption. She kept her lost son a secret from her family for nearly 50 years. The son and his natural mother had both been involved in a lifelong search for the other. However, the son dies only years before Philomena finds out the truth about what happened to him. Both the son and Philomena at different times return to the convent searching for answers. The nuns tell the son that his mother abandoned him and tell the mother that they cannot help her.

With the overwhelming stigma attached to pregnancy outside marriage, both for the pregnant mother and her born child, social mores as well as economic hardship forced women to give up their babies at birth. Gender discrimination against women and repressive attitudes to sex outside marriage, and not only in the church, created a climate of shame around such pregnancies and the children born in consequence. Women in despair concealed their pregnancies, attempted abortion and in some cases were driven to killing their newly born. Rose (1986) examines the context of women driven to kill their newborn in the nineteenth century. The derogatory term 'bastard' was once used to describe such children, and the Bastardy Act of 1575 provided the power to search for the fathers of illegitimate children. As Peter Jackson LJ in the 2023 Nicholas Wall Memorial Lecture: 'Is Family Law Law?' noted: 'A Treatise on the Law of Adulterine Bastardy by Sir Harris Nicholas KCMG, 1836, captures the spirit of the legal age. For an adulterous wife to produce an illegitimate child struck at the social order in a nightmare manner.' These attitudes persisted well into the 1970s when poverty, unmarried parenthood and social stigma continued to wrest newly born infants from mothers.

There are no data recording the number of adoptions prior to 1930. During the 1950s there were approximately 13,000 adoptions annually and by 1968 that figure had risen to 25,000. This was partly the result of the more relaxed attitudes to sexual intimacy and a resultant rise in pregnancies outside marriage. This led to directives being introduced following the Adoption Act 1976, requiring the courts to consider alternative legal solutions, such as custodianship or residence. In response to these alternate legal solutions, the wider availability of contraception and more mothers keeping their babies, by 1980 the number of adoption orders fell to 8,026. By 1996, the number of newly born babies placed for adoption had fallen to about 50 per year and newly borns were relinquished for adoption by mothers because of illness or inability of the parent to care for the child. Single or unmarried women were no longer coerced into surrendering their babies. Changing social attitudes to single mother parenthood, the development and availability of IVF treatment (accounting for the birth of 390,000 babies since 1991 (HFEA figures) were reflected in the changing pattern of adoption orders and their steady decline discussed by Theis and others (2021) 'Adoption in the 21st century,' and by Baroness Hale in her lecture with the same title 'Adoption in the 21st Century' (2021).

By 2003, 4,870 adoption orders were made, and there was a corresponding rise in the special guardianship order (SGO) which was implemented in 2005 (CA 1989, s 14A(3)(a)). In 2011, 4,734 adoption orders were made, and the decline continued. In 2022, 3,997 and in 2023, 2,960 orders were made. (Family Court Accessible Tables, Table 18; See Douglas 2003). In 2022, the Joint Committee on Human Rights published the written evidence received as part of its inquiry into the adoption of children of unmarried women between 1949 and 1976.

The legislation

The ACA 2002, s 46(1) re-enacts the Adoption Act 1976 (AA), s 12(1). Whilst adoption had been described as a 'legal transplant' because it severs the child's legal connection with the birth parents through transferring parental responsibility from the birth to the adoptive parents, the 2002 Act reflects a shift in recognising a new form of 'open' adoption where a contact order, if appropriate, may be made for the child and the birth family, although it is noted later despite the legislation and the research evidence the adoptive families are likely opposed to such a proposal (see for example *Re B (A Child)* [2019] Fam 389). The introduction of SGOs under s 29(7) of the ACA 2002 (implemented 2005), obviated the need for adoption where a child can be looked after by a family member and is explored in detail by Harwin et al. (2019) in the Special Guardianship BPG report. A snapshot of the second quarter of 2022/2023 indicates that 790 orders for placement, 680 adoption orders and 940 orders for SGOs were made. (See Coram statistics.)

The Children and Families Act 2014 repealed s 1(5) of the ACA replacing the several traits of culture and language etc to be considered with the term 'ethnicity' which is intended to be all encompassing without being unduly restrictive. Now adoption is about as it was before the welfare of the child but also about a duty to consider ethnicity. New nomenclature may have yielded to political pressure but has not supplanted the need to consider all the s 1(5) factors in the ACA.

Who can be adopted? And who can adopt

A person can only be adopted if he or she is under 19 years of age, although the application must be made before the person is 18 years old.

In the case of *Mr and Mrs C v D and others* [2023] EWFC 10 the applicants, who were married, returned to the UK with two boys of 12 and 10 years. The applicants said they had found them begging on the streets of Bangladesh. The boys were in fact the half-nephews of the male applicant. Upon discovery, the couple were charged with immigration offences and the authorities intended to deport the boys, but the departmental files were lost. Meanwhile, the couple applied for residence and an interim residence order was made. Later, they issued adoption proceedings with the consent of the boys' mothers (the fathers could not be found). The boys wanted to be adopted. The Home Office, at the end of the six-year legal process, opposed adoption and so did the children's guardian. At the time of the hearing the elder boy was nearly 18 years of age, his brother nearly 16 years. The Home Office said the boys could stay in the UK until they were 18 years old and then they would be deported. The court granted applications for adoption, taking the view that although the applicants had misled the authorities, which was conduct to be deprecated, they genuinely sought the psychological advantages for the boys of having a real family and, indeed, this was the only family the boys knew. Those psychological links could best be preserved by adoption, which, unlike residence, was for life.

During the year ending 31 March 2022, 88 (2.2 per cent) of 3,997 children adopted were under 1 year old. In 2022, 2,522 (63 per cent) of 3,997 children adopted were aged between 1 and 4 years. In 2022, 782 (19.5 per cent) of 3,997 were aged between 5 and 9 years old. In 2022, 346 (8.6 per cent) of 3,997 were aged between 10 and 15 years. (See Family Court Statistics Quarterly Accessible Tables, Table 19 and Figure 9, 2022.)

The older the child, the more difficult it is to secure a positive experience because of attachment and adjustment and where a child is 12 years or older, adoption may not be in the best interests of the child and the local authority will look to other alternatives. But with any child older than an infant severing a child from the natural family can be devastating.

Who can adopt?

The ACA 2002, s 50 rules, provide that a heterosexual (married or unmarried couple) or homosexual couple may adopt if there is sufficient permanency in their relationship and are 'living as partners in an enduring family relationship' (s 144(4)). Under the old law, the courts circumvented the statutory restrictions on couples living together by allowing one member of a heterosexual couple to proceed with an adoption application. In *Re AB (Adoption: Joint Residence)* [1996] 1 FLR 27 Cazalet J made an adoption order in favour of the foster father of a 5-year-old child together with a joint residence order in favour of both foster parents.

Case law also reflects the changing attitudes towards parenting and notions of 'fit' parents and suitability based on heteronormative preference and judges who spoke out against such privileging of heteronormative parenting. In *Re W (Adoption: Homosexual Adopter)* [1997] 3 All ER 620 Singer J held that there was nothing in the Adoption Regulations to prevent a homosexual, a married or unmarried couple, or a single person, adopting a child. In this case, a 49-year-old lesbian woman in a stable relationship was allowed to adopt a child (cited in Chapter 9). He said: '[58] Any other conclusion would be illogical, arbitrary and inappropriately discriminatory in a context where the court's duty was to give first consideration of the need to safeguard and promote the welfare of the child throughout its childhood.'

The ACA 2002 recognises that the contemporary family of the twenty-first century may include parents who may be married, unmarried, heterosexual or of different genders. As Bamforth (2007) writes:

> The CPA 2004 also allows for the same assessment criteria for adoption to apply to married, unmarried, partnered and un partnered couples. Courts tended until comparatively recently to be troubled by the presence of lesbians or gay men as would be adopters. However, the Adoption and Children Act 2002 allowed for adoption orders to be applied for on the same basis by same sex and opposite sex couples living together in 'enduring family relationships', and the CPA 2004 includes civil partners within that Act.

The lived experience and reality of the pansexuality of family life is reflected in the increasing number of adoption orders made to same-sex couples, 673 of 3,997 (17 per cent) in 2022 and sole carers 826 of 3,997 (21 per cent). In *E (A Child) (Adoption by One Person) Re* [2021] EWFC 45 where two people who had separated after being in a relationship, having never been married or civil partners, could nevertheless be a 'couple' for the purposes of the ACA 2002 Pt 3, s 144(4) so as to permit one to apply for an adoption order under s 51(2) in respect of a child born to the other while they were in a relationship.

Adoption by stepparents

The ACA 2002, s 39 provides for adoption by partners of the child's natural parent. The new stepparent may wish to achieve some certainty and stability for the child and to formalise his/her/their responsibility for the child. Adopting the child ensures parental responsibility for the stepparents but extinguishes the rights and responsibilities of the 'left behind' natural parent. About one-half of all 7,326 adoption orders made in 1994 resulted from applications made by stepparents. In 2005, following the introduction of the special guardianship order (SGO), this number fell to less than one fifth (866) of all adoption orders and by 2011 constituted 533 (11 per cent) of 4,705 orders, falling further by 2022 to 266 (7 per cent) of 3,997 orders granted.

The following case demonstrates the complex and difficult issues for the birth parent, posed by a stepparent wanting to adopt their child.

In *Re B (Adoption: Father's Objections)* [1999] 2 FLR 215 the natural father had abducted the child on three occasions and received a sentence of imprisonment. The mother remarried, and the stepfather wanted to adopt. The natural father objected. The judge concluded that the welfare of the child demanded an adoption order, and he then went on to dispense with the consent of the father on the basis that the refusal of the father to give his agreement was unreasonable. The father appealed. The court dismissed the appeal. The wide ambit given to courts in their determination of their limitless discretion in the application of unreasonableness is discussed later.

Stepparents may also acquire parental responsibility through a stepparent parental responsibility agreement (s 112 of the ACA) which may obviate the need for adoption and will certainly diminish any acrimony between birth parents since the non-resident spouse no longer loses their parental status or their legal relationship of parental responsibility with the child. George (2024) discusses stepparent adoption after the death of a parent.

Orders for special guardianship are discussed separately later in this chapter.

Adoption by relatives/foster parents

The adoptive parent and the local authority, despite the principle of openness in adoption, have considered any contact between the child to be adopted and the birth family as a risk to the stability of the relationship between the adoptive parent and the child. The *Review of Adoption Law* in 1993 similarly chimed and considered that there would be few situations where adoption by relatives or contact with the birth family would be desirable. However, many children when adults seek out birth parents and birth family members as they wish to complete what they consider is a missing part in their life.

The current legal framework

Under ACA 2002, s 3, adoption services may only be provided by the local authority or a registered adoption society.

Every local authority is under the duty to maintain a service within their area. Under the ACA 2002, s 4(1) 'adoption agencies', that is, the local authority or a registered service, have a responsibility for selecting and assessing the suitability of prospective adopters and placing children for adoption with suitable adopters. This includes the provision of support services (this is discussed in detail later and set out in the Children and Families Act (CFA) 2014, s 5 and 6). (See Adoption Support PACT). In accordance with ACA 2002, s 5, local authorities must prepare a clear adoption plan for the provision of services. Section 109 ACA 2002, requires the court to draw up a clear plan for the child with a view to ensuring that any delay in the provision of a placement order or adoption order is avoided.

Any person wishing to proceed with an adoption application must undergo a process of assessment. A home study is carried out by the adoption agency in which the suitability of the prospective adopters is assessed.

Adoption services are subject to the law. The Equality Act 2010 and the Equality Act (Sexual Orientation) Regulations (in force 2007) prohibit discrimination in the provision of goods, facilities and services based on sexual orientation. In *Father Hudson's Society v Charity Commission* [2009] PTSR 1125 a charity which did not provide adoption services to homosexuals for religious doctrinal reasons including defences of the heterosexual institution of marriage as a basis for raising children and a rejection of homosexuality could not continue to refuse to provide services to a person on grounds of sexual orientation. See also *Catholic Care (Diocese of Leeds) v The Charity Commission for England and Wales* [2010] EWHC 520 (Ch).

Suitability and matching

Placing a child for adoption depends upon the suitability of prospective adoptive parents, and the courts must be satisfied in this regard. This involves police checks, health checks and references. The safety and welfare of the child is paramount and under Adoption Agencies Regulation 2005 the agency must conduct Disclosure and Barring Service (DBS) checks on the prospective adopter and any adult members of their household.

> The ACA 2002, s 45, specifies two grounds in assessing the suitability (see the Adoption Agencies Regulations 2005, SI 2005/389, under s 9): firstly, stability and permanence of a relationship (s 45(2)) and secondly, religious persuasion, racial origin, and cultural and linguistic background (s 1(5)). Prior adoption law specified only religion (AA 1976, s 7) which stated: 'An adoption agency shall in placing a child for adoption have regard (so far as is practicable) to any wishes of a child's parents and guardians as to the religious upbringing of the child.'

At that time the provision held in its contemplation the Christian faith and conflicts between those of the Catholic and Protestant faith arose as was evident in *J v C* [1970] AC 668. Under the old law, adoption agencies both private and local authority developed their own views of relevant criteria and excluded certain types of persons. For example, some local authorities excluded those with children of their own, those who held certain religious views or those with no religious belief, those who were considered health risks, including smokers and those who were considered to be overweight. In *Re S (A Minor) (Blood Transfusion: Adoption Order Condition)* [1994] 2 FLR 416 the adoptive parents who were Jehovah's Witnesses had to give an undertaking that they would not impede blood transfusion if required by the child. Staughton LJ allowed their appeal, and the undertaking was rescinded.

Local authorities also put an age limit on prospective adoptive parents; it was set for women, at 35 years, and for men, at 40 years and could also stipulate conditions which seem absurdly proscriptive today. (See Adoption and Children Bill 2002.) In the House of Commons debate, 9 November 2011, David Simpson MP said this:

> *It is nonsense for social services to restrict the number of prospective parents just because someone is over 40, or 45. One of the prospective parents who had come to see me and who had been told that they could not adopt was told that one reason was they were over 45, so when the child reached their teenage years, the prospective father could not play football with them. That is absolute nonsense'.*
>
> (col 82wh)

By 2013, the Statutory guidance held:

> *Any practice that classifies couples/single people in a way that effectively rules out the adoption because of their status, age or because they and the child do not share the same racial or cultural background is not child-centered and is unacceptable.*
>
> (83[4.5])

And so these irrelevant criteria were finally consigned to history and the factors of relevance to ensuring child welfare given statutory precedence.

From s 1(5) of the ACA 2002 to s 3 of the CFA 2014

Section 1(5) ACA requires that in placing the child for adoption, the adoption agency must give: 'due consideration to the child's religious persuasion, racial origin and cultural and linguistic background'. This is also found in the CA 1989, s 22(5)(c) as factors to be considered by the local authority when 'looking after children'. The importance of these factors was enunciated by Munby J in *Singh v Entry Clearance Officer New Delhi* [2004] EWCA Civ 1075.

More recently the factors were considered in *T v K and Others (Egyptian Fostering: UK Adoption)* [2017] 2 FLR 943 where the child Z was found abandoned by a British worker T and her Egyptian husband K who has married in an Islamic ceremony in Egypt. The identity, background and religion of Z's parents is unknown; she was born on or around 29 October 2010 and found abandoned as a newborn baby on 30 October 2010 in a cardboard box in a street in Isna or Esna, a city south of Luxor, Egypt. T and K later separated. T brought her adopted daughter Z to England and Z was made a ward of court and care and control granted to T. At a later stage K opposed the proposed adoption when it was clear that T did not wish to return to Egypt. The court said:

> [75] It is a reality that part of the consequences of this child being adopted by T will inevitably mean there is no possibility of those larger factors in respect of Egyptian heritage and culture being fully restored. The court accepts that this is a significant loss and a matter that I must consider pursuant to s 1(4)(d) of the ACA 2002 and weigh in the balance. I can, and I do, that her background is Egyptian is not disputed; nor does any party, including T seek to ignore it or set it aside. In the wider sense Egypt is Z's home country, but, as far as this child is concerned her home is with T, and it is in England where she has spent most of her life.

Russell J refused the application by the Ministry to return Z to Egypt pursuant to the inherent jurisdiction 'it is in her best interests and her welfare throughout her life to remain in England and become the adopted child of the applicant'.

Repealed – so what?

The ACA, s 1(5) 'due consideration' factor was repealed in 2014 under the CFA, s 3 'Repeal of ethnicity requirement' which appears in the headline of the statutory provision itself. However, the term 'ethnicity' is found neither in the ACA 2002 nor in the CA 1989, whilst s 22(5)(c) of the CA remains unaffected and requires consideration of 'religion, race, cultural and linguistic background' when placing children in care or accommodating them.

Under the CFA 2014 as Edwards argues (2015a, 2015b) 'ethnicity' is the new term used under which these earlier ACA, s 1(5) considerations still sit and is now the standard bearer for cultural relativism and cultural pluralism.

The question and concern are whether the CFA configuration permits a relegation of some of these several considerations when considering the welfare of the child, or has it merely repositioned these factors. Certainly, critics were understandably concerned that this new emphasis would seriously displace the importance of race, religion and linguistic background when placing a child for adoption. The House of Lords select committee had advised that 'ethnicity' was to be placed on the welfare checklist (Adoption and Children Act, s 1(4) and Children Act 1989, s 1(3)) as one of the several factors to be considered. This, however, has not been accommodated. The committee concluded: 'to remove mention of religion, race, culture and language altogether will run the risk of these important factors of identity being neglected in matching decisions'.

This following section considers how the s 1(5) provision has been applied prior to 2014 and the continuing application of these principles post 2014 under the 'ethnicity' requirement.

Section 1(5) racial and cultural origin

This consideration has changed over time and depends on the needs of the child and the availability of a family that can match these characteristics. It is known that in 2024–5 there is a disproportionate number of children of 'mixed heritage' in care because of the lack of mixed heritage adopters and the rigidity of 'matching' each characteristic which as families became more diverse culturally, ethnically, faith, became impossible and the overall purpose of placing a child with a loving family became submerged. (See Edwards 2015a, 2015b.) It was this that led to the CFA, s 3 'ethnicity' repeal. The considerations under s 1(5) remain just as relevant today in 2024–5 if not even more so, as such the earlier case law is of continuing relevance. What follows is some detail of that contested journey.

The tension inherent in the interpretation of s 22(5)(c) of the CA (and later in s 1(5) AA) is reflected in the following case. In Re N (A Minor) (Adoption) [1990] 1 FLR 58 a child was born in 1984 of Nigerian parents. The mother placed the child with white foster parents and then went to the USA. The unmarried father also lived in the USA and sought to have contact with the child. In 1987, the foster parents agreed to adopt and to dispense with the mother's agreement. The father applied for care and control. Bush J clearly frustrated by the statutory requirement said:

'in my view the emphasis on colour rather than cultural upbringing can be mischievous and highly dangerous when you are dealing in practical terms with the welfare of children.' In February 2011, the Government, in response to the crisis for black children and minority ethnic children who were losing out on not being placed with loving families, published revised guidance 'Adoption Guidance Adoption and Children Act 2002', (First revision: February 2011 Department of Education 2013 guidance). 'If the prospective adopter can meet most of the child's needs, the social worker must not delay placing a child with the prospective adopter because they are single, older than other adopters or does not share the child's racial or cultural background'.

A concern at the centre of Government debate on Adoption, Jessica Lee MP said:

It is easy to be simplistic about this topic, but it is difficult to accept that it is better for a black and minority ethnic child to have to remain in care for all of their childhood instead of being placed in a loving home because there is not an ideal ethnic match.

(Col 79WH)

However, views on interracial adoption were then as now contested on both sides and continue to be a matter for vociferous debate, which is discoursed by Sargent (2015) and Hayes (2014) amongst others.

The Association of Black Social Workers in evidence to the House of Commons Select Committee said:

> *The most valuable resource of any ethnic group is its children. Nevertheless, black children are being taken from black families by the process of the law and being placed in white families. It is, in essence, 'internal colonialism' and a new form of the slave trade, but only black children are used.*
>
> (Cited in McRoy and Griffin 2012)

In another context and time Frantz Fanon's *Black Skin White Masks* (1967) explored the impact of colonialism on the black identity. He would no doubt argue that irreparable psychological harm would be done to a black child adopted into a non-black and especially a white family.

Section 1(5) religious preferences

Religion is also an important factor in assessing suitability of adoptive parent(s) and placement. The AA 1976, s 6, placed an emphasis on religion holding in its contemplation of the Christian faith only. This emphasis on religion reflected the central place Catholicism and Protestantism held for centuries in British society (remember *Agar-Ellis* [1883] 24 Ch D 317; *Re Collins (An Infant)* [1950] Ch 498, and *J v C* [1970] AC 668 which involved disputes between Catholics and Protestants, discussed in Chapter 9). Malins VC said of *Agar-Ellis* when referring to marriage between a Roman Catholic wife and a Protestant husband: 'This is perhaps the strongest case that has ever occurred shewing the misery that ensues from mixed marriages.'

So, in *Re P (A Child) (Residence Order: Child's Welfare)* [1999] 3 All ER 734 where a Down's syndrome child of orthodox Jewish parents was accommodated by the local authority, the parents having accepted that they could not adequately care for her, and since a suitable Jewish family could not be found the child was placed with Catholic foster parents, in a short-term placement. After three years, the court made a residence order in favour of the foster parents and the natural parents sought the child's return to them. After a further four years, the birth parents applied for a variation of the residence order and return of the child. The court made a further order restricting future application without leave of court under CA 1989, s 91(14). The parents appealed contending (i) that a child had a presumptive right to be brought up by its own parents and in its own religion and that the judge had failed to give sufficient weight to N's religious and cultural heritage; (ii) that the judge had erred in principle in his approach to contact; and (iii) that the judge should not have made an order under s 91(14). The court said:

> *The undoubted importance for an orthodox Jew of his religion which provides a way of life which permeates all activities, is a factor to be put in the balancing exercise, particularly in considering the welfare of the daughter of a rabbi. But N's religious and cultural heritage cannot be the overwhelming factor in this case for the reasons set out by the judge nor can it displace other weighty welfare factors.*

In *Re C (Adoption: Religious Observance)* [2002] 1 FLR 1119 a child of a mixed background with Jewish, Irish Roman Catholic and Turkish-Cypriot Muslim faithed elements was placed for adoption with a Jewish couple. The guardian for the child issued proceedings for judicial review of the local authority's decision to place the child with the Jewish couple, arguing that the couple were unsuitable, on the basis that they were 'too Jewish', and that C should be placed in an essentially secular home. The court held that where a child's heritage was very mixed, it would rarely be possible for it all to be reflected in the identity of the adoptive home. Wilson J explained:

> As society becomes increasingly complex with children often having diverse ethnicity and cultures in their background, it is even more important that social workers should avoid 'labelling' a child and ignoring some elements of his background. Children of mixed origin should be helped to understand and take pride in all elements in their racial heritage and feel comfortable about their origins but must not displace welfare. What that means however may straddle opposing positions and change over time.

Post 2014

Notwithstanding the repeal of s 1(5) race and religion continue to be important considerations and are considered under the umbrella of the new nomenclature of 'ethnicity' CFA s 3. However arguably the non-specific term provides room for inconsistency. 'Black Lives Matter' certainly has a perspective on this repeal and it has led to much concern.

There are no firm conclusions here, however personal testimonies about the negative side are powerful. In *Mensah v Islington Council and Another* [2000] EWCA Civ 405 Mensah brought an action for psychological damage against the respondents, Islington Council and East Sussex County Council. Mr Mensah also sought an apology from the local authority since, in 1966 as the child of a Nigerian mother and a Ghanaian father who was placed with elderly white foster parents, he suffered personality and identity problems.

The ACA 2002, s 45 provides for the regulation of agency decisions in respect of suitability (see the Education and Adoption Act (2016) and suitability of adopters). A system of review introduced by the ACA 2002 ensures that what are called 'qualifying determinations', which are decisions which conclude that a prospective applicant is unsuitable, are subject to an independent review. In addition, there is a formal complaints mechanism, and prospective adopters can make a complaint to the local authority. Research has shown that objections are grouped around three main subject areas; these related to the prospective adopter's health, their parenting capacity or because of information supplied by referees.

Judicial review of the decision of adoption agencies is available for prospective adopters who are considered unsuitable. However, judicial review is limited, and procedural unfairness is the relevant factor. (See *Hofstetter v Hofstetter* [2009] EWHC 3282 (Admin); *R (on the application of EL) v Essex County Council* [2017] EWHC 1041 (Admin), [2017] Fam Law 818.)

Court orders

The orders the court can make with regard to adoption include:

a placement order (s 19, s 21);

an adoption order;

a special guardianship order.

Overarching principles, judicial decision making and consent

The ACA 2002, s 19(1) requires the consent of the birth parents to the adoption before any placement or adoption order can be made (and a mother cannot give consent until six weeks after childbirth s 47(4)(b)(i). However, parents rarely willingly give their consent and so the notion of consent is a fiction. Assenting to relinquishing their child for adoption better expresses their position. Where parents refuse to consent, as they invariably do, the court will override their refusal in the pursuit of the welfare of the child principle. Cobb J in *Re S (a child) (adoption: consent of child parent)* [2017] EWHC 2729 (Fam) said:

> *[1] Some, albeit relatively few, adoption orders are made with the consent of the birth parents; in the majority of applications for adoption orders, the court will need to consider whether the welfare of the child requires that parental consent be dispensed with.*

It is intended that parental relinquishing of their child otherwise 'consent' will be witnessed by an officer of the Children and Family Court Advisory and Support Service (CAFCASS) to ensure that the parents fully understand the placement process and what adoption means.

Parents are required to sign Form A 104 in which this following declaration is made:

> *I understand that, once the application for the adoption order has been started in the court, my child may only be returned to me if the court so orders. When the adoption order is made, I understand that I will no longer legally be treated as the parent and that my child will from then on become part of the applicant(s)' family. I will have no right to have my child returned to me. I also understand that I will have no right to contact my child unless it is by arrangement with the applicant(s) or under a court order, when the court will decide on the contact arrangements it considers are most appropriate. Until the adoption order is made, I am entitled to apply to the court for an order for contact with my child at any time. Once the adoption order is made, I will*

*only be entitled to apply for a contact order if the court gives permission. I under-
stand that when the application for an adoption order is heard, this document may be
used as evidence of my consent to the making of the order, unless I inform the court
otherwise.*

Consent to adoption is required of all those with parental responsibility. So, for
example where the unmarried father or the absent father has parental responsibility
(see CA 1989, s 4(1); ACA 2002, s 111) then his consent is required, as is the consent
of the mother of the child.

Notwithstanding the legal requirement of securing consent, the refusal to consent
by any party with parental responsibility does not determine the issue and may be
dispensed with if the welfare of the child requires it. Section 52(1)(b) sets out the
grounds where consent may be dispensed with. Section 52(1)(a) provides for
dispensing with consent where the parent or guardian cannot be found or is incapable
of giving consent. (The ACA 2002 abolishes the former freeing order and introduces
a placement order (s 21) which authorises the local authority to place a child for
adoption with prospective adopters deemed suitable.)

Re S (A Child) (Adoption) [2021] EWCA Civ 605 [5–7] concerns consent of the child's parents and
sets out the line of authority on the nebulous concept of 'competence' to consent. Whilst consent of
those with parental responsibility must be sought, knowledge of the impending birth of a child or
child born for whom a plan has been made to place for adoption may under certain case specific
circumstances be withheld from those with parental responsibility who might otherwise oppose the
placement and adoption order and/or wish to put themselves forward to adopt the child. The
circumstances have to be exceptional and are fact specific.

In *Re J (Adoption: Contacting Father)* [2003] EWHC 199 (Fam) an unmarried
17-year-old became pregnant. She had never cohabited with the father. The father
left the area, and the mother did not tell him that she was pregnant. After the child's
birth, she put the child up for adoption. The child had cystic fibrosis, as did the
father's brother's child. The social worker pressured the mother to reveal the name
of the child's father. She assured the mother that the information would only be
revealed if and when the child required it as an adult; the father would not be told.
The mother reluctantly agreed to give the information. Immediately, the local
authority sought declarations under Article 8 that it was in the child's best interests
for the father to be informed of his existence, and that it was lawful for the LA to
inform the father. The court was concerned about protecting the mother from any
possible abusive conduct and held that Article 8 was not engaged because her
relationship with the child's father had been transitory and insubstantial.

However, in *Re A (Father: Knowledge of Child's Birth)* (2011) also known as *M v F
and others* [2011] EWCA Civ 273 the court held that the knowledge of adoption
could not be withheld from a father where the mother placed her baby for adoption

and sought a declaration authorising the local authority not to inform her husband who was the father. The family was from Afghanistan and had been granted asylum and the father was diagnosed with post-traumatic stress disorder following his treatment under the Taliban. He was volatile and violent to the mother. The court held in dismissing the mother's appeal that exceptional circumstances were required before the court would sanction the withholding of information about the existence of a child from a parent who was the father. '[37] The thrust of these cases is, therefore, that the court will not be persuaded to sanction the withholding of information about the existence of a child from that child's parent or to dispense with service on him of proceedings in relation to the child in anything other than exceptional circumstances where there are, as the President put it in *Re H, Re G*, "strong countervailing factors"'.

Re A and others (adoption: notification of fathers and relatives) [2020] EWHC Civ 41 involved three cases in which the mothers concerned were pregnant. The Court of Appeal set out the principles governing whether the putative father or relatives should be informed. In the case of Child A, the guardian appealed against a declaration order that the local authority was not obliged to notify the father of the plan for adoption. In this case the guardian's appeal would be allowed (see [98–99] of the judgment). 'The mother's account does not provide a strong objective basis for discounting him as a suitable carer . . . the appeal should be allowed'. In the case of Child B, the mother appealed against a judge's decision to refuse to grant an injunction against the local authority from contacting the maternal family group. The court dismissed the mother's appeal (see [105–106]). Child C was born as a result of rape. The LA appealed against the decision to refuse an order to permit the local authority to contact other relatives. C's appeal was be dismissed (see [112]).

> *The distressing circumstances of the conception and the impact of them on the mother, which the judge fully considered, had to be set alongside the fact that C's father has parental responsibility for her and is the father/stepfather of her siblings. To proceed without notifying him of the birth would be an extremely strong course to take and in my view the judge was right to resist the temptation to do so.*

A different decision was made in *LA v PQ* [2023] EWHC 1971 (Fam) where it was held that the local authority was not obliged to notify relatives, maternal and paternal, that the mother had placed the child for adoption or to assess their suitability as carers. A family placement was not realistic because the mother was an unmarried woman of the Muslim faith and risked the ostracism of her community if the existence of a child were to be discovered.

Dispensing with consent

The chameleon concept of unreasonableness

The dismissal of challenges by parents who refuse to consent is authorised only if the 'welfare of the child requires it' and is the effect of s 1 of the CA 1989 and the paramountcy of child welfare. Prior to this time dispensing with parental consent relied on a less weighty vision of welfare, the courts being required only to 'consider' welfare. In determining such cases the case law saw the development of a most nebulous quasi-legal test of 'unreasonableness' which permitted dispensing with consent on vague and esoteric grounds. The judicial thread discoursing this 'unreasonableness' concept where the parent refused to consent under s 16 (2)(b) was found in some form in Adoption Act 1958, s 5. The leading cases on unreasonableness reveal a litany of judgments where judges not surprisingly struggled with the opaque concept. (See: *Re W (An Infant)* [1971] AC 682; *Re P (An Infant) (Adoption: Parental Consent)* [1977] Fam 25; *Re H (Infants) (Adoption: Parental Consent)* [1977] 1 WLR 471; *Re M (Minors) (Adoption Parental Agreement)* [1985] 1 FLR 921; *Re H, Re W (Adoption Parental Agreement)* [1982] 4 FLR 614; *Re F (A Minor) (Adoption Parental Consent)* [1982] 1 WLR 102; and *Re V (A Minor)* [1987] 2 FLR 89.) Unreasonableness and the unreasonable parent in reality defined a parent who was unwilling to consent or agree to what the adoption agency and court considered best for the child or a parent. Judicial paternalism decided what was best for the child, and any dissent from that was deemed not simply a different view but an unreasonable one. An unreasonable parent was labelled as such because the court said the parent was not considering what was best for a child's welfare.

In *Re W* [1971] (discussed earlier) where the mother withheld her consent, her appeal to the Court of Appeal was upheld on the ground that her conduct had not been culpable or blameworthy. However, it was a decision later overturned by the House of Lords. Lord Hailsham delivering the judgment tries to explain the test:

> *Section 16(2)(b) lays down a test of reasonableness. It does not lay down a test of culpability or self-indulgent indifference or failure or probable failure of parental duty. It is not for the courts to embellish, alter, subtract from, or add to the words which, for once at least; . . . Parliament has employed without any ambiguity at all. . . . The test . . . is reasonableness not culpability. . . . From this it is clear that the test is reasonableness and not anything else. It is not culpability. It is not indifference. It is not failure to discharge parental duties. It is reasonableness and reasonableness in the context of the totality of the circumstances. But although welfare per se is not the test, the fact that a reasonable parent does pay regard to the welfare of his child must enter into the question of reasonableness as a relevant factor. It is relevant in all cases if and to the extent that a reasonable parent would take it into account. It is decisive in those cases where a reasonable parent must so regard it.*

In *Re D (an infant) (adoption: parent's consent)* [1977] AC 602 where a father who was homosexual refused to consent to his son's adoption by his former wife's partner/husband, Noakes J in the court of first instance dispensed with his consent. The Court of Appeal's unsung heroes, Stephenson LJ and Orr LJ upheld the father's appeal, but the House of Lords reinstated the finding of the judge of first instance. Wilberforce LJ said:

> *My Lords, I would add two observations in this difficult and painful case. First, as I have already said, there is nothing in the present decision which would warrant or support a general principle of dispensing with a parent's consent on the grounds of homosexual conduct alone. . . . This case has to be decided as it does, for reasons which are individual*

to it and to these parents. . . . Whatever new attitudes Parliament, or public tolerance, may have chosen to take as regards the behaviour of consenting adults over 21 inter se, these should not entitle the courts to relax, in any degree, the vigilance and severity with which they should regard the risk of children, at critical ages, being exposed or introduced to ways of life which, as this case illustrates, may lead to severance from normal society, to psychological stresses and unhappiness and possibly even to physical experiences which may scar them for life. . . . I think that the reasonable parent in the circumstances here shown would inevitably want to protect his boy from these dangers, that this parent, to his credit, recognised this, and that the trial judge so decided. . . . For these reasons I would restore the judge's decision and allow the appeal.

In *Re B (A Minor) (Adoption: Parental Agreement)* [1990] 2 FLR 383 in a case where a child aged 11 having lived with foster parents for seven years with no current access to the mother but contact by telephone and cards and where the foster parents encouraged contact the child wished to be adopted and the foster parents applied for adoption, but the mother refused to agree. Butler-Sloss LJ held:

the question then arises as to whether this court should substitute its own discretion upon the facts before us. . . . In our judgment, a reasonable parent in the position of the mother would recognise the overwhelming force of the negative points and the unreasonableness of refusing to agree to the freeing for adoption. We, therefore, hold that the mother has unreasonably withheld her agreement under s 16(2) s 52(1)(b) of the ACA 2002.

This chameleon like concept of unreasonableness falls away once welfare as paramount becomes the overriding principle following the CA 1989 s 1 and its assimilation in the ACA 2002.

Rather more cogent justifications are required to dispense with consent such that in *Down Lisburn Health and Social Services Trust v H and another* [2006] UKHL 36 the mother who was an alcoholic and unable to care adequately for her youngest child who was 4 and could not meet her welfare needs found her consent was properly dispensed with.

In *Mr and Mrs C v D and others* [2023] EWFC 10 an unusual case, where the application was made ten days before the person turned 18 years the court dispensed with the parents' consent.

[27] T was born in 2004. M and F separated when she was 4 or 5 years old, F played very little role in her upbringing and has a conviction for sexual assault on a minor and is a registered sex offender which has had a traumatising impact on the family, including T. T describes an unhappy childhood, characterised by an abusive relationship between her parents, and verbally and physically abusive behaviour by her parents towards her and domineering and bullying behavior of S. [28] Public law proceedings were brought by the LA in 2016, a care order was made in respect of S, and a 12-month supervision order in respect of T. [29] In 2018, T met the applicants upon being referred to them for educational services.

> *[31] Their personal relationship developed. Over time, she began to be treated as part of their family . . . T has become very close to them, refers to them as Mum and Dad, and has taken their surname by deed poll. The applicants in their written evidence describe T as a remarkable young woman and I am satisfied that they are devoted to her and want the very best that they can provide for her. T wants to be adopted.*

Challenges to dispensing with consent s 47(5)

Once the court has decided that the welfare of the child requires consent to be dispensed with under s 47(2)(c) the opportunity for challenge by a party with parental responsibility is limited and a change of circumstance is required before leave is given. The welfare of the child is paramount (ACA 2002, s 1(2)) and when considering whether to make an adoption order or dispense with consent the welfare checklist in the ACA 2002, s 1(4) applies (discussed also in Chapter 12). In *Re P (A Child) (Adoption Order: Leave to Oppose Making of Adoption Order)* [2007] EWCA Civ 616 the court reiterates this principle that a judicial decision upon a parent's application for leave to oppose an adoption order is:

> *a decision relating to the adoption of a child' for the purposes of s 1(1) of the 2002 Act with the result that: "[t]he paramount consideration of the court . . . must be the child's welfare, throughout his life' (s 1(2) of the 2002 Act). [19] The 2002 Act recognizes that for many, particularly older children, maintaining contact with birth relatives, parents and siblings is not simply to be desired by them but essential to their development and wellbeing"*
> (See the findings of Triseliotis 2010.)

With 'maintaining contact' in mind, s 1(4) (f) requires the court to consider:

> the relationship the child has with relatives, and [with any other person who is a prospective adopted with whom the child is placed] and any other person in relation to whom the court or agency considers the relationship to be relevant, including:

> (i)   the likelihood of any such relationship continuing and the value to the child of its doing so,

> (ii) the ability and willingness of any of the child's relatives, or of any such person, to provide the child with a secure environment in which the child can develop, and otherwise to meet the child's needs,

> (iii) the wishes and feelings of any of the child's relatives, or of any such person, regarding the child.

Waiting time

The delay in the adoption process has been a perennial problem and has come under increasing criticism as uncertainty for a child undermines the welfare principle. The

Family Justice Review (Sir David Norgrove, November 2011) expressed concern about the time it took for a child to be adopted (2.7 years from being placed in care) and proposed a time limit for courts in completing care and placement proceedings, of six months (26 weeks). In 2024, the proportion of children waiting 18 or more months since entering care and 18 or more months since the grant of placement order has increased, taking longer than the time frame of 26 weeks.

In 2016, in 62 per cent of cases the 26-week time frame was met and in 2021 this fell to 23 per cent (Family Court Statistics Quarterly Accessible Tables 2022: Table 8).

Efforts to avoid delay in meeting the time framework of 26 weeks to achieve stability and certainty for the child in adoption at the same time negates the possibility of making a special guardianship order (an order which would allow the child to live with a family member) since a SGO cannot be considered unless the child concerned has lived with the prospective special guardian for one year. Two negative possibilities potentially follow the objective of meeting the time frame: firstly the possibility of an erroneous decision being made or secondly, a SGO cannot be made because of the time frame thereby forcing adoption as the only option. Notwithstanding, the number of special guardianship orders has risen.

The placement order

A placement order (ACA 2002, s 21) is an order authorising a local authority to place a child for adoption. This can only be made where the child is subject to a local authority care order (ACA 2002, s 21(2) (a)) or where there is no parent or guardian (s 21(2)(c)) and either there is parental consent, or if there is no parental consent, then the court has already deemed that the circumstances are such that parental consent should be dispensed with, (s 21(3)(b)) or else the parents cannot be found. Without a placement order or the consent of the parents or the court dispensing with consent, children in the care system cannot be placed for adoption (ACA 2002, s 18(1)).

London Borough of Richmond v Mother and others [2023] EWFC 146 sets out the requirement for consideration of alternatives to adoption and the paramountcy of the welfare principle in decision making.

> *[105] In my assessment the combination of welfare and holistic analysis points firmly in favour of a care and placement order. I recognise this brings with it significant negatives, but it is the only option which at this time on the evidence available can provide [the Child] with the security and permanence of his welfare demands. Sadly, the other options placed before me will simply not meet [the Child]'s welfare needs and there is no other option that will do other than the making of a placement order with a plan for adoption.[106]. I appreciate the parents cannot actively consent to this outcome. I consider for the reasons given above that [the Child]'s welfare requires the making of these orders and I accordingly dispense with the parents' consent under s 52 of the 2002 Act.*

Appealing/revoking a placement order

There is a power to appeal and revoke a placement order (s 24(1)), but that power is used very sparingly and requires leave of the court. Under s 24(3) the court cannot give leave under subsection (2)(a) unless satisfied that there has been a change in circumstances since the order was made.

The unlikely prospect of revocation is reiterated in *Re JL* [2020] EWCA Civ 1253

> *[5] . . . for understandable reasons many birth parents whose children have been made subject to a placement order are devastated by the outcome and want to take any lawful step as is open to them to stop adoption going ahead. Sadly, many applications for leave to apply to revoke a placement order are made with no prospect of success whatsoever.*

A few cases are successful and are decided on a case-by-case basis. The following case demonstrates the importance of adhering to due process. In *D McG v Neath Port Talbot County Borough Council* [2010] EWCA Civ 821 the Court of Appeal allowed the appeal of the mother against a care and placement order. The basis of the care order was neglect and inadequate parenting, where the mother had learning difficulties. Since the guardian had recommended that two assessments be made and only one had been completed, the court took the view that all avenues towards rehabilitation had not been fully explored.

Allowing the appeal in *Re S-H (A Child) Placement Order* [2008] EWCA Civ 493 the court held, per Wilson LJ:

> *This unusual case demonstrates that it will occasionally be proper for the court to grant a parent leave to apply to revoke a placement order under s 24(2)(a) of the Adoption and Children Act 2002 ('the Act') notwithstanding the absence at present of any real prospect that a court would find it to be in the interests of the child to return to live with the parent.*

The kind of change in circumstances (s 24(3)) advantageous to the welfare of the child is demonstrated in the following cases. In *Re JL* [2020] EWCA Civ 1253 (noted above) where a grandmother, already a foster carer for two of her grandchildren, applied for leave to revoke a placement order in respect of a further grandchild because of her change in circumstances, in that she had moved from a two bedroomed flat to a three bedroomed house, a special guardianship order was made in her favour.

In *Re G and H (Leave To Revoke Placement Order)* [2023] EWCA Civ 768 a grandmother's application for leave to revoke was allowed where a change of mind by a family member about putting themselves forward as a potential carer for the children could have amounted to a change of circumstances within the meaning of s 24(3). In *Z v Kent* [2018] 10 WLUK where a care order and a placement order had been made there were procedural irregularities and material grounds for the revocation of the placement order as the maternal grandmother had not been informed of the birth. The court held that there were failings by the local authority not to inform, but nonetheless the court decided that the child should stay with the carers under a SGO and the placement order for adoption was revoked.

Upholding the placement order

Most applications are not successful. In *Re M (Placement Order)* [2010] EWCA Civ 1257 the mother appealed against an order for care and placement made without her consent. The mother had substance abuse problems and could not take care of her child and wanted the child to remain in care whilst she tried to rehabilitate herself with a longer-term ambition of being able to care for her child. The court took the view that the mother would not comply with any rules and requirements and that the delay of the care plan would be disadvantageous for the child. In *YC v United Kingdom (App No 4547/10)* (European Court of Human Rights 2012) where a mother appealed a placement order in respect of her child where there had been substance abuse and domestic abuse by the father. The mother alleged an abrogation of her Article 8 rights to privacy and family life, which the court held was not violated.

In *Re N (Children: Revocation of Placement Orders)* [2023] EWCA Civ 1352 the mother appealed against the making of a placement order. She had made significant changes to her life since the making of the order. She had distanced herself from the father who was abusive. At an earlier hearing:

[2] The deputy judge found that the father had repeatedly assaulted the mother but that she had lied about it or retracted complaints and had failed to separate from him or protect the children from being exposed to such incidents. Neither parent had engaged with the child protection plans and the work and support offered. In July 2020, the father had breached the exclusion requirement, and the mother subsequently retracted her report to the police.

The judge concluded in dismissing the appeal:

[36] I have great sympathy for this mother, who has courageously tried to repair the daunting problems in her life. The recorder rightly placed considerable weight on the changes she had made. However, he found that they had not brought her to the point where she can meet the children's needs.

In 2021, 3,899 applications were made for placement orders. It is not known how many of these were appealed and how many appeals were successful. (Family Court Accessible Tables, Table 18). Following the making of a placement order a final adoption order can be made, ACA 2002, s 46, s 47(1) and (4). Sections 50 and 51 give parental responsibility for the child to the adopter(s).

Adoption order – when nothing else will do

Conditions for making adoption orders are set out in s 47(4)(ii). An order cannot be made unless three conditions are met: firstly that the parents' consent or else the consent has been dispensed with; secondly, that the child has been placed for adoption with the consent of the parent and the mother having given her consent when the child was at least 6 weeks old and or the child is placed for adoption under a placement order; and thirdly, that the child (a) is the subject of a Scottish permanence order which includes provision granting authority for the child to be adopted, or (b) is free for adoption by virtue of an order made, under Article 17(1) or 18(1) of the Adoption (Northern Ireland) Order 1987 (SI 1987/2203 (NI 22)).

An adoption order can be made by the High Court, county court or magistrates' court. The application must be made at the court in the district where the child lives. *Re B – S (adoption application of s 47(5)* [2013] EWCA 1146 iterates that adoption is only granted when nothing else will do. '[74] The judge must keep at the forefront of his mind the teaching of in *Re B* [2013] 1 WLR 1911 in particular that adoption is the "last resort" and only permissible if "nothing else will do" '.

Adoption and the child's presence

Rule 14.15 Rule 32(6) President's Guidance: Listing Final Hearings in Adoption cases (Dated 3rd October 2008) provides that the court cannot make an adoption order unless the applicant and the child personally attend the final hearing. However, rule 32(6) is subject to rule 32(7) which gives the court discretion to direct that the applicant or the child need not attend the final hearing; this provision permits the court, where appropriate, to direct that the attendance of the applicant or the child or both of them at the final hearing is not required.

Each parent or guardian must be 'joined' as a party ('respondents') as well as the adoption agency, whether a local authority or voluntary organisation, which has care of the child. Adoption documents are confidential. If the adoption is refused, the child must be returned to the adoption agency within seven days of the order. The agency will then try to find another suitable placement. The court can also make a short-term order, which gives the applicants parental responsibility for a period of not more than two years.

Adoption or special guardianship order

The ACA 2002, like the CA 1989, requires the court to be satisfied that the order it makes is better than an alternative order or better than making no order at all (s 1(6)). The court must always consider all the options (s 1(4)) i.e. SGO, foster care arrangements and can attach conditions to the adoption order, such as allowing the birth parent to have contact with the child (see *A Local Authority v Y, Z, and others* [2006] 2 FLR 41) or attaching conditions.

A special guardianship order (SGO) may be made in any family proceeding under s 115(6).

TABLE 10.1 Annual trends in adoption and placement orders granted

Year	Adoption orders	Placement orders
2011	4,705	5,118
2012	5,260	6,477
2013	6,074	6,256
2014	6,750	4,300
2015	6,196	4,390
2016	5,825	4,571
2017	5,438	4,690
2018	4,926	4,412
2019	5,012	3,868
2020	3,832	3,174
2021	4,432	3,434
2022	3,997	3,150

Source: Table 18 and Table 19 Family Court Statistics Quarterly Accessible Tables 2023 www.gov.uk/government/statistics/family-court-statistics-quarterly-july-to-september-2023/family-court-statistics-quarterly-july-to-september-2023 (accessed 30.4.2024)

In adoption cases it is made largely to kinship carers, such that total severance from the birth family may not be required. As Mitchell (2008) observes: 'Special guardianship is less intrusive on the family life of the birth family than adoption.'

In *A Local Authority v Y, Z, and others* [2006] 2 FLR 41 SGOs were made in respect of three children. The Deputy High Court Judge explaining the provision said:

> *Special guardianship, therefore, operates as follows. It creates parental responsibility – the bundle of rights and duties a parent has in respect of a child – in the special guardian or guardians. The parental responsibility already vested in others – in this case the mother – is not extinguished.*

However, whereas parental responsibility is normally a matter for exercise in partnership between those holding it, under a special guardianship order it is exercised exclusively by the special guardian or guardians.

In *Re S (Adoption Order or Special Guardianship Order)* [2007] EWCA Civ 54 the authority's care plan was for S to be adopted. The foster mother applied to adopt the child. The child's mother applied to discharge the care order and pursue contact. The judge decided that the child should live with the foster mother, but declined to make an adoption order, making a special guardianship order under s 14A(6)(b) of the CA 1989 to the foster mother. Wall LJ reiterated the benefits of the provision:

> We would add, however, that, although the 'no order' principle as such is unlikely to be relevant, it is a material feature of the special guardianship regime that it is 'less intrusive' than adoption. In other words, it involves a less fundamental interference with existing legal relationships. The court will need to bear Article 8 of ECHR in mind, and to be satisfied that its order is a proportionate response to the problem, having regard to the interference with family life which is involved. In choosing between adoption and special guardianship, in most cases Article 8 is unlikely to add anything to the considerations contained in the respective welfare checklists. Under both statutes the welfare of the child is the court's paramount consideration, and the balancing exercise required by the statutes will be no different to that required by Article 8. However, in some cases, the fact that the welfare objective can be achieved with less disruption of existing family relationships can properly be regarded as helping to tip the balance.

In *Special guardianship order K v Sheffield City Council* [2011] EWCA Civ 635 the child concerned had been left with the maternal grandmother who lived with her lesbian partner. The local authority brought care proceedings. The court granted the maternal grandmother a SGO and made an order under s 91(14) restricting any further applications to the court for a period of two years and four months to introduce some calm and stability to the child's life since the child had been living harmoniously with the maternal grandmother. As for the parents, they had divorced, and the father had married another woman in Pakistan and the mother had made several attempts to abduct the child.

Appealing a special guardianship order

Birth parents or applicants can apply for a variation but only with leave of the court and where there are exceptional circumstances. (CA 1989, ss 14D inserted by ACA 2002, s 115(1) see also the consequential Special Guardianship Regulations 2005 (SI 2005/1109,)

(See *Re R (A Child) (Special Guardianship Order)* [2007] Fam 41; *Re J (Special Guardianship)* [2007] EWCA Civ 55; *Re M-J (Special Guardianship Order)* [2007] EWCA Civ 56.) In *Re C (A Child: Special Guardianship Order)* [2019] EWCA Civ 2281, the mother appealed from the SGO made in respect of her daughter ("C") aged 5. The order was made in favour of the paternal grandparents. The mother and father had mental health difficulties and were unable to care for the child. The local authority obtained an emergency protection order in 2019 and an interim care order which confirmed C's placement with the grandparents. The mother wished the child to be returned to her care under a supervision order.

[85] The judge had found that there was a "significant chance . . . that the mother's current progress in terms of her mental health will not be sustained". And [81] was "not satisfied" that the mother "would, at the moment [or] in the longer term, be able to meet those needs". Also, the judge was concerned that the mother [at 35] has difficulty accepting not just the validity of Western medicine but that such medicine is not in itself harmful. He also said that: "Perhaps at its most extreme the mother has suggested that both she and C ought to be capable of being 'breatharians', meaning that they should be able to survive without food and possibly water". The judge was concerned on the likely welfare consequences for C.

The appeal was dismissed.

Discharging a special guardianship order

Discharging a SGO may follow a change in circumstances or lack of due process. In *Re G (A Child) (Special Guardianship Order: Leave to Discharge)* [2010] EWCA Civ 300, an application made by the mother for leave to discharge a SGO in favour of the maternal grandmother was initially refused. It was later allowed following a

TABLE 10.2 Number of special guardianship orders applied for and made in public and private proceedings and number of children involved

SGO orders	2011	2015	2021
Applications			
Public law – 3a	159	121	183**
Children involved – 3b	278	222	307
Private law – 3a	1,212	1,496	1,114
Children involved – 3b	1,642	2,032	1,527
Orders Made			
Public law – 4a	1,977	3,621	3,984**
Children involved – 4b	2,973	5,514	6,124
Private law* – 4a	980	1,455	952
Children involved – 4b	1,313	1,949	1,293

Source: Taken from family court accessible tables July–September 2023 Table 3a, Number of orders applied for in Public and Private law (Children Act) applications made in the family courts in England and Wales, by type of order and Table 3b Number of children involved in Public and Private law (Children Act) applications made in the family courts in England and Wales, by type of order. * Excludes Combined Supervision Orders and Special Guardian Orders Table 4a and Table 4b www.gov.uk/government/statistics/family-court-statistics-quarterly-july-to-september-2022 ** (accessed 30.04.2024)

change in the mother's circumstances and behaviour. In *Re M (special guardianship order: leave to apply to discharge)* [2021] EWCA Civ 442, the appeal was allowed following a significant change and improvement in the mother's mental health. The court was not required to make findings of fact, but the application had to provide credible evidence to show that there had been the necessary change, and that leave should be granted (see paras 14, 17, 22–25, 28–31, 33–34 of judgment).

As to failures of due process in *Re H (A Child) (Analysis of Realistic Options and SGOs)* [2015] EWCA Civ 406, sub nom *CH v London Borough of Hammersmith & Fulham and others* the SGO was set aside because of a lack of due process where: '[7] procedurally and substantively there had been errors of law . . . without a thorough examination of the viability of a SGO to a non-relative, and apparently with little opportunity being given to the father to challenge the proposal'. In *Re F and another (children) (discharge of special guardianship order) N v K and others* [2021] EWCA Civ 622, the girls concerned were subject not only to a SGO but also to a care order. The issues arising from this appeal centred on whether as a matter of law the two orders can coexist and, if they can, whether in the circumstances of this case the judge was wrong to allow the SGO to continue. The court ruled the two orders incompatible.

Dismissing appeals

In *Re W (a child) (care proceedings)* [2023] All ER (D) 53, the Court of Appeal dismissed the mother's permission to appeal against a SGO made in respect of her son, W. At the conclusion of care proceedings brought by the local authority, a SGO was made in favour of W's maternal uncle, the mother's brother R and his partner C.

Appealing an adoption order and refusal

In *Re T (A Child) (Refusal of Adoption Order)* [2020] EWCA Civ 797, the child, now 3, had lived with his maternal grandmother and stepgrandfather under a special guardianship order since he was 2 days old, as his birth mother suffered from mental illness, had criminal convictions and posed a threat to the grandparents and the child. The grandparents appealed the judge's refusal to make an adoption order. Their appeal was allowed, the mother's consent was dispensed with as the welfare of the child was paramount, and an adoption order made.

The Court of Appeal again considered the relative merits of adoption orders and special guardianship orders and the circumstances in which a family placement may need to be secured by the making of an adoption order rather than a special guardianship order.

Opposing the making of an adoption order

Under s 47(7) the court cannot exercise its discretion to grant permission to oppose the making of an adoption order unless satisfied that there has been a sufficient change of circumstances since the making of the placement order. In *S (A Child) Re*

[2021] EWCA Civ 605 a mother (M), a litigant in person, appealed against the court's refusal of her application under the Adoption and Children Act 2002, s 47 for permission to oppose the making of an adoption order in respect of her son (Z).

The local authority had issued care proceedings in respect of Z and four of his siblings on the basis of neglect and emotional harm. The court made final care orders in February 2019, together with a placement order in respect of Z. Z was placed with prospective adopters, and an application by M to revoke the placement order was refused. M applied for permission to oppose the making of an adoption order in respect of Z on the basis that her circumstances had changed. Her application was refused, the judge holding that there had been insufficient change to enable him to exercise his discretion to grant permission to oppose. In reaching his conclusions, the judge did not have sight of the judgment of the court which made the placement order on due process grounds the appeal was allowed.

Setting aside an adoption order

Once an adoption order is made, adoption is final (ACA 2002, s 46(2)(a)). The court will not set aside an adoption order unless the procedure is flawed or there is an abuse of process. In *Re X and Y (Revocation of adoption orders)* [2024] EWHC 1059 (Fam) the court said it had no power to revoke. This finality and irreversibility is nowhere more starkly demonstrated than in the case of *Re B (Adoption: Setting Aside)* [1985] 1 FLR 1, [1985] Fam 239. The applicant B, who was adopted when a young child, made an application to set aside the adoption order after he discovered that his birth culture, religion and ethnicity were fundamentally different from the religion and ethnicity he had acquired from his adoptive parents and being so different, led him to be considered a spy when he applied to emigrate to Israel. B was born in 1959 to an English mother and a Kuwait father of the Muslim faith. The couple was not married. Three weeks after B was born, his mother put him up for adoption. The adoptive parents, who were of the Jewish faith, knew that the father of B was from the Gulf and assumed he also was a Jew. In 1968, the adoptive parents discovered that B's natural mother was not of the Jewish faith; nevertheless, the boy was received into the Jewish faith. When B was 27 years of age he intended to emigrate to Israel. On his arrival in Israel, the authorities suspected him of being an Arab spy, and refused him entry. B then made enquiries as to the background of his birth parents, discovering that his mother was English and his father a Kuwaiti. Consequently, he was rejected from Jewish culture. In an effort to resolve these issues of cultural identity and rejection, he made an application to have the original adoption order set aside. The judge said that as the order had been made in accordance with correct procedure, there was no jurisdiction to have the order set aside. His appeal was unsuccessful.

In *Re PW (Adoption)* [2011] 1 FLR 96 the applicant, aged 69, was the middle child of three girls born to married parents. Both her parents died when she was 17 and the parents of her closest friend offered her a home and adopted her (Adoption Act 1958). She lived with them until she was 23 and later married in her adoptive name and her children's birth certificates showed that name. The applicant stated that at the time of the adoption she was not asked about her wishes and feelings and applied to have the adoption order set aside or revoked. The court dismissed the application. The application was delayed by 51 years and there had been no serious procedural irregularity.

However, decisions made on incomplete information, or the result of procedural errors may exceptionally allow an adoption order being set aside. Consider the very different cases that follow.

In *Re M (Minors) (Adoption)* [1991] 1 FLR 458 the natural father agreed to the adoption by the stepfather of his two daughters, aged 11 and 12 years. The natural mother, unbeknown to the father, had terminal cancer and died within three months of the adoption order being made. The stepfather was subsequently unable to care for the girls who then went to reside with the paternal grandparents. The natural father, who had settled in America with a new wife, wanted the care and custody of the two children. All parties involved agreed that this was in the best interests of the girls. The father appealed on the grounds that the decision had been made in the absence of the knowledge of his wife's terminal illness. Glidewell LJ said, per curiam:

> *I should say, as a postscript, that this is, if not unique, at the very least a wholly exceptional case. I say that because I do not want the setting aside of this adoption order in these circumstances to be thought of as being some precedent for any related set of facts in some other cases.*

In *Re K (Children) (Adoption: Freeing Order)* [2004] EWCA Civ 1181, a freeing order (freeing the child for adoption, the order that preceded the introduction of the placement order) was set aside on the application of an Indian mother who argued that she had been coerced by her husband and his family into silence during the care and freeing proceedings relating to her elder child who had undoubtedly suffered non-accidental injuries.

Whether it is open to the court to set aside adoption orders where medical expert evidence is flawed was considered in *Webster and another v Norfolk County Council* [2009] EWCA Civ 59 where freeing orders for adoption were made dispensing with consent in respect of a child and two siblings. Following an appeal and fresh evidence which found the original evidence on which these decisions were made flawed the court considered whether it was appropriate to dispense with the adoption orders and concluded that it was not. However, Wall LJ said this:

> *The four children concerned, namely Brandon, his sister and his two brothers, have been denied the opportunity to argue that they should grow up together with their parents as a family. [3] For Mr and Mrs Webster, the parents of the children concerned, the case has been a disaster . . . they have been wrongly accused of physically abusing one of their children, and three of their children have been removed wrongly and permanently from their care. The only mitigation, from their point of view is the local authority's belated recognition that they are fit and able to care for Brandon.*

He nevertheless held that in the meantime the children had settled with their new families. This was a miscarriage of justice not just an error.

In *Re W (A Child)* [2010] EWCA Civ 1449, the mother had not been given notice of the adoption hearing. The child had been placed with adopters when he was 4 years of age and had no contact with his mother since he was 2½ years of age. The mother was at that time addicted to drugs, but she had been drug-free for two years. She applied to have the adoption order set aside on the basis that the original reason for adoption was no longer operative. The court held that the order was procedurally flawed and must be set aside. However, she had to persuade the court that there had been a change of circumstances and that it was in the child's best interests justifying the grant of leave. In *Re T (Adoption)* [2012] EWCA Civ 191, care proceedings were ongoing in relation to the parents' seven children; the parents had been imprisoned for offences against them. Separate proceedings were brought in relation to the youngest, now 2 years of age, who had been placed with prospective adopters. The parents sought permission to oppose the adoption application. The appeal was successful on the basis of procedure and due process. The mother's lack of representation could not be overcome, since she had neither seen nor read the guardian's report 'even though it contained no privileged information relating to a third party which might have substantiated the exercise of a judicial discretion not to disclose' (following the guidance in *Re D (Adoption Reports: Confidentiality)* [1996] AC 593).

In *TS (A Child) (Application to Revoke Adoption Order: Procedure in Non-Urgency Adoption Placement)* [2019] EWHC 2190 (Fam) also known as *ZH v HS and others (application to revoke adoption order)* [2019] EWHC 2190 (Fam)), on the birth mother's application, the order was revoked which had been made in favour of an aunt and uncle where there had been numerous substantive and procedural flaws. The birth mother, a Somali national, fled from Somalia with one of her children, leaving her husband and her other children behind in Somalia. Having become separated from her mother, the child entered the United Kingdom on her own and was placed in the care of the paternal aunt and her husband. The aunt and uncle wished to adopt the child, and the court issued a non-agency adoption application. On 12 October 2016 the court made an adoption order in respect of the child in the aunt's and uncle's favour, having failed to identify that the respective requirements of ss 42(5)(6), 44(3)(4) and 52(1) of the ACA 2002 had not been met.

Other orders

Residence orders rather than adoption

A significant number of original applications for adoption fail and a residence order under CA 1989, ss 8(3) 10(1) may otherwise be made. Failure is a matter of concern as it is destabilising for a child caught in such an uncertain process. The CA 1975 provided alternative orders including joint custody or custodianship, and courts were required to make these orders when they were better for the child than making an adoption order. Following the AA 1976, there was a decline in adoption orders which affected stepparents although the CA 1989 repealed the restriction. The ACA 2002 has reverted to provision of a variety of alternative orders. This is because the pendulum has swung towards retaining links with the natural family and maintaining links with other relatives. In addition, the question of Article 8, the right to privacy and family life, is more pressing from the perspective of all parties.

Contact with parents

In furthering the objective of contact with natural parents, whilst there is a provision for contact most adoptive parents oppose contact and in such cases the courts do not wish to undermine the adoptive placement by insisting upon it. In *Seddon v Oldham Metropolitan Borough Council* [2015] EWHC 2609 (Fam), where an adoption order had been made, although letterbox contact was to take place each year, a mother's application for contact was refused. In *Re B (A Child)* [2019] Fam 389, the birth parents applied for contact, but prospective adoptive parents opposed, and their appeal was dismissed. The court ruled that although s 51 of the ACA 2002 had introduced a bespoke statutory regime for the regulation of post-adoption contact, the law remained that it would only be in an extremely unusual case that a court would make an order stipulating contact arrangement to which the adopters of a child did not agree. While there might be justification in considering some form of direct contact, the ultimate decision as to what contact was to take place was for the adopters.

The court noted per curiam:

> Any change from previous practice because of new research by social work and adoption professionals, which may be moving towards the concept of greater openness in post-adoption contact arrangements between an adopted child and her natural parents and siblings, will be reflected in welfare decisions made by adopters, or by a court, on a case-by-case basis. These are matters of welfare and not of law.

([59] [64–65])

Siblings

The court reiterated the position that had pertained for siblings. In *Re C* [1988] 1 All ER 705, a foster parent made an application to adopt a girl of 13 in the care of the local authority. The girl was in care with her younger brother, and she was attached to him. The court took the view that it did not have the power to make a condition of contact with the brother on the adoption order. The House of Lords, however, said that an adoption order could be made with a condition of contact with the younger brother. Their Lordships re-affirmed that it was usual to have a permanent and final break. Lord Ackner added:

> The court will not, except in the most exceptional case, impose terms or conditions as to access to members of the child's natural family to which the adopting parents do not agree. To do so would be to create a potentially frictional situation which would be hardly likely to safeguard or promote the welfare of the child.

In *Re R (Adoption: Contact)* [2006] 1 FLR 373, the mother could not care for the child, and she had been cared for instead by her half-sister, who was 17 years. The child was placed for adoption, but her half-sister wanted contact. The adoption panel recommended direct contact of three times per year. The half-sister considered this insufficient. She was refused leave to apply for a contact order. Wall LJ said: 'So contact is more common, but nonetheless the jurisprudence I think is clear. The imposition on prospective adopters of orders for contact with which they are not in agreement is extremely, and remains extremely, unusual.'

The review of children's social care report examined the contact arrangements for those children recorded as having at least one sibling not placed with them for adoption. Of the 256 cases reviewed, contact was proposed between 70 per cent of the children and a sibling living elsewhere (n = 177). Proposed contact arrangements were most often letterbox, although just more than a fifth (n = 38, 21 per cent) were for face-to-face contact. (See Independent review of children's social care report).

Doughty (2019) reviews the potential psychological value of the sibling bond for human development, particularly during childhood (see Azmitia and Hesser 1993; Davies 2015) reflecting on Lowe (2000) who asked why adoption must automatically sever the legal relationship between a child and siblings and grandparents.

Grandparents

Contact with grandparents may be very important in the life of the child, but it is also contact that the adoptive parents consider undermines a child settling with them.

There are currently 14 million grandparents in the United Kingdom of whom 1% have grandchildren living with them. Many more grandparents play an important role in the lives of their grandchildren, one in three 'family carers' are themselves single-parent grandparents.

(See Grandparents rights).

International adoption

Turning now to international adoption arrangements, adoption is not common practice across the world. Each country has its own arrangements, and, in some countries, adoption is unacceptable, or not encouraged. (See Brulard et al.) This is the case where patriarchal progeny is rooted in family structures and tradition. Different social attitudes amongst particular groups in the UK have led to some communities not putting themselves forward as prospective adopters to the detriment of many children seeking a family. For example, in the UK 2 per cent of adoptions approved were to Muslim families, 0 per cent to Jewish families, 32 per cent to Christian families and 32 per cent to families with no religion (Coram Adopter characteristics 2020–2021).

In EU member states, few children are accommodated by the local authority and there are few adoptions.

Clear rules and procedures govern the adoption of children from outside the UK since Brexit Brussels 11 no longer applies. Pinder (2022a) sets out the complexities and formalities. They include the Adoption (Intercountry Aspects) Act AIA 1999, SI 2005/392, the Adoptions with a Foreign Element Regulations 2005 revised in February 2011 and the Hague Convention. The immigration rules that also impact on overseas adoptions are complex, including s 55 of the Borders, Citizenship and Immigration Act (BCIA) 2009, and the weight to be given to the public interest factor under Article 8 (see Part 5A of the Nationality, Immigration and Asylum Act (NIAA) 2002, inserted by s 19 of the Immigration Act (IA) 2014). So children coming to the UK as adopted children or for the purpose of adoption are expected to meet the requirements set out in the Immigration a Certificate of Eligibility as required under paragraph 309B of the Immigration Rules where an adoptive parent or parents habitually resident in the UK (a) intend to bring a child who is habitually resident outside the UK to the UK for the purpose of adoption, or (b) where the adoption has taken place less than 12 months before the date on which the child will be entering the UK (s 83 of the ACA).

If the adoption is to be finalised in the UK, then an application under para 316D of the Immigration Rules will need to be made. If the adoption has already been finalised in the child's state of origin, the child will become British if at least one parent is British and the parent(s) are habitually resident in the UK, under s 1(5) of the British Nationality Act 1981 ('the 1981 Act'). If neither parent is British, then usually an application under para 310 of the Immigration Rules for indefinite leave to enter ('ILE') must be made. There are also some countries which are subject to further adoption restrictions. The UK has restricted applications from Cambodia, Guatemala, Nepal, Haiti, Ethiopia and Nigeria because of factors including child trafficking, lack of records and corruption in these countries.

The rules are set out in Adopting a Child from Abroad to UK.

Intercountry adoption should only take place where it is in the best interests of the child and with respect for the child's fundamental rights. Any person wishing to adopt a child from outside the jurisdiction must be assessed for suitability and must apply for an 'eligibility certificate' from a casework team at the Department for Education.

Humanitarian reasons generally provide the motive for international adoption. As Douglas (2003) writes: 'Within the UK, more than 10,000 unaccompanied children are living with friends, relatives or strangers, having made their way here or having been sent here from abroad. Some will end up in de facto adoptions.'

The prolonged length of time taken to adopt a child from within the jurisdiction together with the restrictions on suitability has also led those seeking to find a family to make an application for a child from overseas.

The Hague Convention

The Hague Convention on the Protection of Children and Co-operation in respect of Intercountry Adoption 1973 governs such adoptions. At the heart resides the 'best interests' test. The Adoption (Intercountry Aspects) Act 1999, amends adoption legislation to include intercountry adoption, including the amendment of certain provisions for example, s 11 six months residence required for certain intercountry adoptions; s 12 registration of certain intercountry adoptions; and s 14 restriction on bringing children into the UK for adoption. The HC applies where both contracting states are signatories. The HC provides important safeguards including a period of assessment of potential adopters. If the adoption is determined in a non-Hague Convention country recognition of the adoption requires an application to the High Court. The relevant case is Re N (Recognition of Foreign Adoption) [2016] EWHC 3085 (Fam) which considered the issue of domicile and Re V (A Child) (Recognition of Foreign Adoption) [2017] EWHC 1733 (Fam).

Conflicting principles: welfare v best interests

There is no uniform international family law or child law standard of what is best for children in a multicultural, multifaith world. And making child welfare paramount displaces any competing rights. Since European human rights law has given considerable manoeuvre to member states as it is founded on a margin of appreciation then the 'best interests' rather than 'welfare as paramount' test allows for such flexibility. For example, intercountry 'humanitarian' adoption may, in its 'rescue mode', gloss over or ignore assumptions that prefer one culture over another. Already we have seen in *Re M* (Child's Upbringing) [1996] 2 FLR 441 (the South African case discussed in Chapter 9) how the Court did not wish to be seen as preferring one culture over another in arriving at its decision for advancing the child's welfare.

In *Re R (No 1) (Inter-Country Adoption)* [1999] 1 FLR 1042 the wife visited Romania in 1993, intending to adopt a child. In July 1994, R's natural parents, who had 13 children, agreed that R, who was 5 years old, suffered with a severe squint and was withdrawn, could go with the wife on a visit to the UK. Formal consent to a visit for medical treatment was given before a public notary, and the wife gave an undertaking to return R to Romania within three months. In September 1994, R was registered at a local school, and the husband and wife had begun to set in motion an application for adoption of R. In deciding the case, that R should be a ward of court with care and control to the husband and wife and contact with the natural family, Bracewell J applied the welfare test and the welfare checklist, applying CA 1989, s 1 and said:

> *When considering the placement of AM, the welfare test demands that her parents are only displaced if they are unable to provide an adequate quality and standard of parenting for her particular needs now and in the future. The case is not a contest between a middle-class lifestyle in Wales with all the comforts and advantages, and on the other hand poverty and deprivation in Bucharest. Natural parents are prima facie the best people to bring up their daughter, whatever their position in life, whether they are rich or poor, wise or foolish, intellectual or illiterate. In respect of placement, the welfare checklist, s 1 of the Children Act 1989, applies and I propose to consider the list.*

At the Parliamentary Assembly of the Council of Europe on 26 January (recommendation 1443 (2000)) the Assembly affirmed: 'The purpose of international adoption must be to provide children with a mother and father in a way that respects their rights, not to enable foreign parents to satisfy their wish for a child at any price' ([87] in *Singh v Entry Clearance Officer New Delhi* [2004] EWCA Civ 1075 referred to in Chapter 9).

In *Haringey London Borough Council v C (E, E, F and High Commissioner of Republic of Kenya Intervening)* [2007] 1 FLR 1035 following the decision in *Haringey London Borough Council v C, E, and another* [2005] 2 FLR 47, the child concerned was placed for adoption, the local authority plan was approved, and a freeing order made, dispensing with parental consent. The child was the victim of child trafficking. The woman acting in the capacity of the child's mother believed that she had given birth to the child in a miracle birth. At the time of the application, the woman believed she was experiencing another spiritual pregnancy. The child, however, was well cared for by the woman and her partner and there was a bond between them. But it was not in the interests of the child to remain in this environment where the adult carers both deluded themselves and continued to do so regarding the child's origins. Egede (2011) discusses this case and its context in considerable detail.

The Children (Contact) and Adoption Act 2005 concerns intercountry adoptions and provides that the Secretary of State can impose restrictions on intercountry adoptions from the country concerned because of practices in a particular country (such as the trafficking of children or the removal of children from their parents without consent) and extends the provision in the earlier Adoption (Intercountry Aspects) Act 1999. Section 84 of ACA 2002 does, however, facilitate the lawful removal of children from the UK for the purpose of adoption overseas, and provides for the making of an order granting parental responsibility to prospective adoptive parents and extinguishing it in every other person.

In *Re J (Adoption: Consent of Foreign Public Authority)* [2002] EWHC 766 (Fam), an abandoned child was brought to the UK by a UK couple for the purpose of adoption, and all the necessary procedures had been followed in Kordan. The consent of the natural parents was dispensed with on the grounds that they could not be found, and an adoption order was made. (See Colgan 2023, Pinder 2022a, 2022b.)

Closing remarks: 'nothing else will do'

Sir Andrew McFarlane has said that adoption should only be considered if nothing else will do and that adoption is a measure of last resort.

When adoption is cheap

Criticisms of adoption focusing on resources assert that instead of putting resources into rehabilitating and supporting families (s 17 of the CA) the option of a route into adoption through care proceedings with the lowered threshold (See Munby LJ 2015, 15th View) is attractive because it is cheaper. Cynics would say that cuts to Government funding for children's social care funding for natural parents who are struggling means that adoption may be the thrifty answer to the cuts to the children's social care budget. In *Re F (Adoption: Welfare of Child: Financial Considerations)* [2004] 2 FLR 440 where the local authority argued it could not pay for the fostering placement to continue at the current rate (nearly £131,000 per annum, of which the foster parents received £53,000) the court held that it was in the children's best interests to stay where they were, in a fostering placement. It is evident that care orders and placement orders are applied for in unison and care plans consider at the outset that adoption will be the end game. The experience of those in adoption confirm what we already know: that children already in care provide the main route into adoption and adoption performance indicators and time targets result in fast-tracking children from care to adoption. (See Adoption Barometer.) Certainly, a balance must be struck between the policy desire to settle a child permanently within a family and without delay and placing a child too late and doing damage, or not putting up a child for adoption at all and returning the child to an abusive or neglectful family or remaining in a care home or with a succession of foster carers, have we got the balance right? (See Doughty 2019.) Can we measure which option is best between stability and permanence for a child in a speedy placement and adoption whilst being removed from their natural family, versus instability in the interim but with the prospect of rehabilitation with the natural family even in the future?

The 'rights' of family members in this process and the right of the child to family life with the birth family may now have some renewed support given that Article 8 the right to family life also embraces the right of parents as well as children when after all adoption is so very final. There is a tension between considering parental rights and right to family life which requires giving parents time to rehabilitate themselves and improve their caring skills or their mental health and seek the necessary rehabilitative treatment.

What value if any at all is placed on the prospect of rehabilitation with the natural family? As Lewis (2004) writes: 'it is worth reflecting on the duty of a local authority to support families in partnership and in voluntary agreements' (discussed in Chapter 14 and 15). See *Re C-B (A Child) (Care Proceedings: Human Rights Claim)* [2004] 1 WLR 889. In *Re A (Children) (Fact-finding Hearing: Care Order)* [2010] EWCA Civ 344, a mother was in a relationship with an abusive partner who was father to the children. The mother agreed to separate from him but was seen with him at a later stage (there was, however, some dispute as to eyewitness identification).

A full care order was made on behalf of the authority and a placement order in respect of the two children. The mother appealed. The Court of Appeal criticised the judge in the court of first instance:

> The failure to mention Article 8 of the Convention was flawed. In a case where the care plan led to adoption the full expression of the terms of art 8 had to be explicit in judgment because, ultimately, there could be no greater interference with family life. The judge should have turned his mind to the established attachment to a loving mother who, with targeted assistance, might be able to provide some form of future mothering. Where the positive features of a parents' care had been highlighted, it was only proper that steps be taken to foster and support the positives so that rehabilitation was given a reasonable prospect of success.

(See [57–59], [62] and [64] of the judgment.)

Post adoption contact

What of the commitment to post adoption contact ACA 2002, s 1(4) (see *Re W* [2017] 1 WLR 889)? There are different forms of openness, e.g. involvement of the birth parents with the selection of adoptive parents, indirect contact with the child after adoption, contact with the child after adoption and provisions for the discovery of birth parents.

> The CARA review, we collated information on the planned contact arrangements between the child and members of their birth family of 369 children for whom we had information about post-adoption contact, 363 had a plan for contact with birth mothers (98.4 per cent). All but one arrangement was for letterbox contact. For one child, voluntarily relinquished at birth, face-to-face contact was requested by birth parents and proposed by the local authority, with the proviso that the adoptive parents agree. For just six children (1.6 per cent) no contact was anticipated. In these instances, either birth mothers had died or had explicitly asked for no contact.

In *Re B (A Child) (Post-adoption contact)* [2019] EWCA Civ 29 Sir Andrew McFarlane, P is clear that, although the legislation is now different, the court's approach is not. The CFA 2014, s 9 [51A] 2b) inserted additional clauses into s 34(6) (a) of the CA 1989 to strengthen the ability of a local authority to refuse contact on child welfare grounds.

> *(6) An authority may refuse to allow the contact that would otherwise be required by virtue of subsection (1) or an order under this section if – (a) they are satisfied that it is necessary to do so in order to safeguard or promote the child's welfare.*

Findings from a recent consultation found that contact has a significant impact on children's wellbeing and the current tradition of 'no contact' or only letterbox contact needed to change. This finding is important especially at a time when digitalisation and social media enables discovery of birth families and is increasingly a search upon which many wish to embark.

Blood tie – Who do you think you are? and contact

The Registrar General is required to keep records of natural parents, so it is possible for the adopted child to trace the original birth registration. Since 1975, 70,000 adults who were adopted in 'out of family' adoptions have received their original birth records. After 1976, adopted adults may have access to this information and those who want such information are provided with counselling, since mothers who were ensured confidentiality may not wish the babies they once placed for adoption, now adults, to come into their lives. Clare Short MP (discussed earlier) had indicated that if her son ever wished to contact her, she also desired such a reunion.

The ACA 2002 provides no absolute right to birth records on the part of the adopted child, however. If there are public policy reasons, the Registrar General can refuse such access, as in the case of the conviction of a son for murder, as in *R v Registrar General, ex parte Smith* [1991] 2 QB 393. Here, the applicant who was 31 was adopted as a baby. He had no knowledge of his parents. He was suffering from a psychotic illness. In 1977, he was convicted of murder and in 1979, killed a fellow prisoner whom he believed was his adoptive mother. In 1987, he instructed solicitors to apply for access to his birth records; his application was refused on public policy grounds. The Divisional Court dismissed his application for judicial review, and the Court of Appeal dismissed his appeal.

In *D v Registrar General* [1996] 1 FLR 707, the natural mother sought information about the wellbeing of her child who had been adopted and the local authority refused to supply that information. She applied to the Registrar General in order that such information should be provided to her. The test for authorising such disclosure was that it was of benefit to the adopted person rather than the birth family. The application was dismissed. The focus of the openness debate in recent years, however, has rested on the child's right to know his or her genetic identity, and it is this issue which has driven open adoption in current adoption law and practice.

It is interesting that, at a time when the family is multifaceted, and relationships rather than blood ties are important, genetic identity also looms large in public policy and law. The Houghton Report (1972) considered this to be important. Human rights legislation and the UNCRC 1989 reinforced the right of a child to know his or her history and biological origins:

> *Article 7: Each child should be registered immediately after birth, and has the right from birth to a name, to acquire a nationality, and as far as possible to know and be cared for by his or her parents.*
>
> *Article 8: Each child has the right to preserve his or her identity, including nationality, name and family relations as recognised by law, without unlawful interference.*
>
> *Article 9: Children shall not be separated from their parents against their will, unless competent authorities which are subject to judicial review determine through the applicable legislation and procedures that such separation is necessary for the best interests of the child. All parties to such procedures shall be given an opportunity to participate in the proceedings and to make their views known. A child separated from one or both parents has the right to maintain personal relations and direct contact with both parents on a regular basis, unless this is contrary to the child's best interests. Where separation results from state action such as detention, imprisonment, deportation or exile, the state shall provide essential information about the absent family member's whereabouts to the child or another member of the child's family on request, unless to do so would be detrimental to the child's wellbeing.*

Judges are presented with competing arguments from different perspectives but all advancing as they see it a human rights claim. In *Görgülü v Germany* [2004] 1 FLR 894, the European Court of Human Rights emphasised that the severance of family ties could be justified only in 'very exceptional circumstances'.

The 'Lived experience' evidence and conclusions of the adoption barometer findings make a number of cogent recommendations including the need to improve support for birth family contact, adopters to be offered specific training and support relating to their child's contact arrangements. All contact plans to be reviewed regularly with the family and experienced staff at their agency to ensure that all participants – including birth family – are well supported. The report concluded that contact with birth siblings was the most enduring (13). (See also Hansen 2019, Doughty 2019, Mitchell 2020.)

Self-test questions

1. At the centre of Government debate on adoption, in 2011 Jessica Lee MP said: 'It is easy to be simplistic about this topic, but it is difficult to accept that it is better for a black and minority ethnic child to have to remain in care for all of their childhood instead of being placed in a loving home because there is not an ideal ethnic match.'
    Countervailing views on interracial adoption were then, as now, contested on both sides and continue to be a matter for vociferous debate.
    Discuss with reference to social policy, statute and case law.

2. If adoption is a draconian measure of last resort how important are special guardianship orders in dealing with shortcomings of the birth family?

3. Explain the circumstances in which a parent's consent to adoption will be dispensed with. Is the test under the Adoption and Children Act 2002 sufficiently specific? remembering that '(It) ought to be recognised by all concerned with adoption cases that once formal consent has been given or perhaps once the child has been placed with adopters, time begins to run against the mother and, as time goes on, it gets progressively more and more difficult for her to show that withdrawal of her consent is reasonable' (per Ormrod LJ in *Re H (Infants)* (1977).
    To what extent is former case law still of relevance?

4. Monica (she/her) has been taking drugs for some time, and her partner Pete (he/him) has mental health problems, takes drugs and also has a criminal record. The local authority received reports from neighbours about the child being left alone in the evenings and during the weekend and also evidence of drug taking around the premises. Soosoo, their 18-month-old baby girl, has already been taken into interim foster care. The final hearing for a care order with a longer-term plan of adoption forms part of the local authorities' care plan. Monica and Peter, the parents of Soosoo, have refused to cooperate with the local authority and have obstructed the local authority throughout the investigation. The maternal grandmother, Mildred, has made an application for a special guardianship order in respect of Soosoo. A drug assessment of both parties, however, found no evidence of drug abuse prepared as part of the evidence for the final hearing.
    Advise the local authority, Monica, Pete and Mildred.

References

Adopting a Child from Abroad to UK www.theukrules.co.uk/rules/children/childcare/adoption/adopting-a-child-from-overseas/#:~:text=As%20a%20rule%2C%20you%20can%20adopt%20a%20child,and%20suitable%20to%20adopt%20a%20child%20from%20overseas (accessed 03.05.2024)

Adopting a Child from Overseas www.gov.uk/child-adoption/adopting-a-child-from-overseas (accessed 02.05.2024)

Adoption Barometer www.adoptionuk.org/the-adoption-barometer (accessed 03.05.2024)

Adoption and Children Bill Hansard, Lords Debates, vol 639, col 882 (16.10.2002) https://hansard.parliament.uk/Lords/2002-10-16/debates/653afbb8-64aa-4b0b-814a-4448924b574a/AdoptionAndChildrenBill (accessed 30.04.2024)

Adoption Guidance, Adoption and Children Act 2002 (First Revision: February 2011 Department of Education 2013 guidance) https://dera.ioe.ac.uk/id/eprint/1919/ (accessed 03.05.2024)

Adoption Law Review HC Deb vol 213 cc1045-76 (12.11.1992) https://api.parliament.uk/historic-hansard/commons/1992/nov/12/adoption-law-review (accessed 03.05.2024)

Adoption Support PACT UK www.pactcharity.org/adoption-support/(accessed 03.05.2024)

Azmitia, Margarita and Joanne Hesser, 'Why Siblings Are Important Agents of Cognitive Development: A Comparison of Siblings and Peers' (1993) 64 *Child Development* (2) 430–444

Bamforth, Nicolas, 'The Benefits of Marriage in All but Name? Same Sex Couples and the Civil Partnership Act 2004' [2007] *Child and Family Law Quarterly* 133

Coram Adopter Statistics: England | CoramBAAF.) See for earlier profile Adoption Leadership Board headline measures and business intelligence (publishing.service.gov.uk)

Coram Statistics Coram-i – ASG Data https://coram-i.org.uk/asglb/data/ (accessed 02.04.2024)

Davies, Katherine, 'Siblings, Stories and the Self: The Sociological Significance of Young People's Sibling Relationships' (2015) 49 *Sociology* (4) 679–695.Douglas, Gillian, Adoption: Changing Families, *Changing Times* (Routledge 2003) https://drive.google.com/file/d/1idBSUQkBULspjn0CBmad8fvBcnt6zzqx/view (accessed 11.05.2024)

Edwards, Susan, '"Ethnicity" Legally Constructed: Part 2" [2015b] *Family Law* 158

Edwards, Susan, '"Ethnicity" Matters in Adoption and Child Custody: Part 1: Some Conceptual Considerations' [2015a] *Family Law* 52

Egede, Hephzibah, 'Shrouded Gender and Reproductive Issues in Child Welfare and Protection Proceedings' [2011] *Denning Law Journal* 202

Family Court Statistics Quarterly Accessible Tables (July–September 2022) www.gov.uk/government/statistics/family-court-statistics-quarterly-july-to-september-2022 (accessed 02.04.2024)

Family Court Statistics Quarterly Tables Accessible Tables (July–September 2023) www.gov.uk/government/statistics/family-court-statistics-quarterly-july-to-september-2023 (accessed 02.04.2024)

Fanon, Franz, *Black Skins, White Masks* (Grove Press 1967)

George, Rob, 'Step-Parent Adoption After the Death of a Parent: Article 8 and Family Relationships' [2024] *Family Law* 711

Grandparents Rights www.manches.com/Content/Resources/files/Children%20-%20Grandparents'%20Rights%20or%20Responsibilities.pdf- (accessed 02.05.2024)

Hale, Baroness, 'Adoption in the 21st Century and the Bridget Lindley Memorial Lecture' (March 2021) www.judiciary.uk/guidance-and-resources/adoption-in-the-21st-century-and-the-bridget-lindley-memorial-lecture-march-2021/

Harwin, Judith, Bachar Alrouh, Lily Golding, Tricia McQuarrie, Karen Broadhurst and Linda Cusworth, 'The Contribution of Supervision Orders and Special Guardianship to Children's Lives and Family Justice' (March 2019) www.nuffieldfjo.org.uk/resource/special-guardianship-a-review-of-the-evidence. www.judiciary.uk/wp-content/uploads/2020/06/PLWG-SGO-Final-Report-1.pdf (accessed 11.05.2024)

Hayes, John, 'Adoption in England: The End of Placements Dictated by Race, Culture, Religion and Language' [2014] *Family Law* 1288

House of Commons Debate Adoption (09.11.2011) https://publications.parliament.uk/pa/cm201011/cmhansrd/cm111109/halltext/111109h0001.htm#11110978000468 Col 82WH (accessed 03.05.2024)

House of Commons Debate Adoption (09.11.2011) https://publications.parliament.uk/pa/cm201011/cmhansrd/cm111109/halltext/111109h0001.htm#11110978000461 Col 79WH (accessed 11.05.2024)

House of Lords Select Committee Adoption www.publications.parliament.uk/pa/ld201213/ldselect/ldadopt/94/9407.htm (accessed 30.04.2024)

Human Embryology and Fertilisation Authority Figures (HFEA) www.hfea.gov.uk/about-us/media-centre/key-facts-and-statistics/ (accessed 30.04.2024)

Independent Review of Children Social Care Report www.gov.uk/government/publications/independent-review-of-childrens-social-care-final-report (accessed 02.05.2024)

Jackson, Peter, 'The Nicholas Wall Memorial Lecture 2023 "Is Family Law Law"' [2023] *Family Law* 796 www.judiciary.uk/the-nicholas-wall-memorial-lecture-given-by-lord-justice-peter-jackson-is-family-law-law/ (accessed 11.05.2024)

Joint Committee on Human Rights the Violation of Family Life: Adoption of Children of Unmarried Women 1949–1976: Government Response to the Committee's Third Report Fifth Special Report of Session (2022) 2 https://committees.parliament.uk/work/1522/the-right-to-family-life-adoption-of-children-of-unmarried-women-19491976/ (accessed 02.04.2024)

Lewis, Jane, 'Adoption: The Nature of Policy Shifts in England and Wales' (2004) 18 *International Journal of Law, Policy and the Family* 235

Lowe, Nigel 'English Adoption Law; Past, Present and Future' in S. N. Katz, J. Eekelaar and M. Maclean (eds) *Cross Currents* (Oxford University Press 2000)

McFarlane, Andrew, 'Adapting Adoption to the Modern World' 2023 lecture www.judiciary.uk/speech-by-sir-andrew-mcfarlane-adapting-adoption-to-the-modern-world/ (accessed 02.05.2024)

McRoy, Ruth and Amy Griffin, 'Transracial Adoption Policies and Practices: The US Experience' [2012] *Adoption and Fostering* 38

Mitchell, Emily, 'Post Adoption Contact and Placement Orders – When Should We Argue for the Former and Challenge the Latter?' [2020] *Family Law* 1209

Munby, Sir James, '15th View from the President's Chambers: Care Cases: The Looming Crisis' 2015 www.judiciary.uk/wp-content/uploads/2014/08/pfd-view-15-care-cases-looming-crisis.pdf (accessed 02.05.2024)

Norgrove, David, 'Family Justice Review' Norgrove Report (2011) https://assets.publishing.service.gov.uk/government/uploads/system/uploads/attachment_data/file/217343/family-justice-review-final-report.pdf (accessed 02.05.2024)

Pinder, Sarah, 'The Ins and Outs of Applying for a Child to Enter the UK for Adoption Purposes' [2022a] *Family Law* 1489

Pinder, Sarah, 'Inter-Country Adoptions – a Nationality and Immigration Perspective' [2022b] *Family Law* 1290

Report of the Departmental Committee on the Adoption of Children 'The Houghton Report' (Home Office, Scottish Education Department) (Cmnd 5107 1972)

Rose, Lionel, Massacre of the Innocents: Infanticide *in Great Britain 1800–1939* (Routledge 1986)

Sargent, Sarah, 'Transracial Adoption in England: A Critical Race and Systems Theory Analysis' [2015] *International Journal of Law in Context* 412

Sixsmith, Martin, *The Lost Child of Philomena Lee* (Macmillan 2010)

Sloan, Brian, 'Post-Adoption Contact Reform: Compounding the State-Ordered Termination of Parenthood?' (2014) *Cambridge Law Journal* 378

Statutory Guidance on Adoption https://assets.publishing.service.gov.uk/media/5a7badc640f0b645ba3c5dff/adoption_statutory_guidance_2013.pdf (accessed 03.05.2024)

Theis, Lucy et al., 'Family Justice Council: Adoption in the 21st Century' [2021] *Family Law* 618

Triseliotis, John, 'Contact Between Looked After Children and Their Parents: A Level Playing Field?' [2010] *Adoption and Fostering* 59

UK Birth Adoption Register www.ukbirthadoptionregister.com/search.php?posted=1&searchin=1&searchfor=Land&day=na&month=na&year=na (accessed 02.05.2024)

White, Michael, 'Short and Son Reunited' www.guardian.co.uk/politics/1996/oct/17/labour.uk (accessed 02.05.2024)

Young, Julie and Elsbeth Neil, 'Contact After Adoption' in Gillian Schofield and John Simmonds (eds) *The Child Placement Handbook: Research, Policy and Practice* (BAAF 2009)

Further reading

Brulard, Yves and Létitia Dumont, 'Comparative Study Relating to Procedures for Adoption Among the Member States of the European Union, Practical Difficulties Encountered in This Field by European Citizens Within the Context of the European Pillar of Justice and Civil Matters and Means of Solving These Problems and of Protecting Children's Rights' Jls/2007/C4/017-30-Ce-0157325/00-64FinalReportwww.econbiz.de/Record/comparative-study-relating-procedures-adoption-among-member-states-european-union-practical-difficulties-encountered-this-field-european-citizens/10010527789 (accessed 14.05.2024)

Colgan, Shauna, 'Inter-Country Adoptions – a Nationality and Immigration Law Perspective' [2023] *Irish Journal of Family Law* 73

Doughty, Julie, 'Rights and Relationships of Children Who Are Adopted from Care' [2019] *International Journal of Law, Policy and the Family Journal* 1

Edwards, Olivia, 'Race and culture in family law' [2021] *Family Law* 1174

Gheera, Manjit and Rob Long, 'Inter-Racial Adoption' Standard Note: SN/SP/6351 29 October 2014 Section Social Policy Section (parliament.uk) https://researchbriefings.files.parliament. uk/documents/SN06351/SN06351.pdf (accessed 11.05.2024)

Hansen, Sarah, 'Birth Relationships After Adoption – Is There a Role for Article 8?' [2019] *Child and Family Law Quarterly Journal* 211

Mornington, Alicia-Dorothy and Alexandrine Guyard-Nedelec, 'Is Poverty Eroding Parental Rights in Britain? The Case of Child Protection in the Early Twenty-First Century' in Nicolás Brando and Gottfried Schweiger (eds) Philosophy *and Child Poverty Reflections on the Ethics and Politics of Poor Children and their Families* (Springer 2019)

The Violation of Family Life: Adoption of Children of Unmarried Women 1949–1976: Government Response to the Committee's Third Report, This Is a Government Response to a House of Lords and House of Commons Committee Joint Report Fifth Special Report of Session 2022–2 https://publications.parliament.uk/pa/jt5803/jtselect/jtrights/1180/report.html (accessed 03.05.2024)

11

Adolescent autonomy – the right to decide and to participate in court proceedings

SUMMARY

This chapter focuses on the adolescent's right to speak and be heard in matters affecting their care and upbringing, to determine their own medical treatment, and to participate in legal proceedings that directly affect them. The older the child, the weightier their right to be heard and their wishes to be respected. The case of *Gillick v West Norfolk and Wisbech Area Health Authority and Another* [1985] AC 112 established a legal landmark and victory for children's rights, and the principles established in that case remain the normative test for determining an adolescent right to self-determination.

The post-*Gillick* case law 40 years on demonstrates that the scope for adolescent self-determination and participation in decisions which affect those under 16 years, remains limited and that judges are reluctant to give effect to the principle of adolescent self-determination even where the adolescent is considered competent to exercise a choice. This is especially so where the consequence of adolescent autonomy is life threatening or else determinative as in for example regarding gender dysphoria treatment. It has been suggested that in cases regarding gender dysphoria treatment the courts in their decision making indicate a narrowing of the Gillick principle of self-determination and autonomy. (See *Quincy Bell v MBA v The Tavistock and Portman NHS* [2020] EWHC 3274 (Admin)) (discussed further later in this chapter, see also Eskenazi and Williams (2023) and Hirst (2021).)

Where judges have sought to limit the Gillick principle they have resolved cases before them by either finding the adolescent 'not competent' to make the desired decision, or if considered 'competent' then the adolescent's wishes are overruled by invoking the protective jurisdiction of wardship. (See Chapter 13 and Practice Direction 12D – *Inherent Jurisdiction (Including Wardship) Proceedings*.)

DOI: 10.4324/9781003435020-11

However, where the matter concerns international relocation of residence and one of the parents want the adolescent to move with them to another jurisdiction the wishes of the child/adolescent carry considerable weight and are specifically provided for in Article 13b of the Hague Convention on the Civil Aspects of International Child Abduction (1980) in force (1983).

Rights of the child and adolescent: general principles and sources of law

To the nineteenth-century legal and public imagination, children had no need for rights, since they were protected by parent fathers. Far from being protected they could be physically abused, beaten until half-dead by fathers and by those acting on behalf of fathers who had absolute authority. (See *R v Hopley* [1860] 2 F & F 202.) It was not until the latter half of the twentieth century that paternal rights over their offspring to do with their children as they wished dwindled (see *Hewer v Bryant* 1 QB 357 in Chapter 9). As paternal rights over the child diminished the child's right to self-determination became imagined and increasingly recognised in both domestic and international law and asserted itself as a relevant consideration in statute, case law and in international conventions.

There are several sources of legal authority to this effect. In this chapter it is suggested that there are at least six such sources of law (although this number is not cast in stone) which enshrine the ambition of the principle of the child and especially an adolescent's right to a voice in decision making in matters that affect them.

Firstly, the Family Law Reform Act 1969 (FLRA 1969), s 8, grants 16- to 17-year-olds the right to consent to their own medical treatment, for example treatment by a dentist or doctor and here there is a presumption of competence.

The consent of a minor who has attained the age of sixteen years to any surgical, medical or dental treatment which, in the absence of consent, would constitute a trespass to his person, shall be as effective as it would be if he were of full age; and where a minor has by virtue of this section given an effective consent to any treatment it shall not be necessary to obtain any consent for it from his parent or guardian.

Secondly, the momentous decision in *Gillick* [1986], introduced in Chapter 9 and discussed at length in this chapter, conceded that adolescents who have sufficient understanding and maturity to make their own decisions in certain matters should be allowed to do so, but where that decision conflicts with the parental view or view of those with authority in medical matters for example, the adolescent's wish should not carry a right of veto but be considered equally weighty. The case law discussed in this chapter reveals differences of judicial interpretation of this case. Some judges demonstrate resolve to limit the application of *Gillick* to its own facts or else otherwise try to narrow the ambit of its application to the matter of consent to treatment and rule that refusal to consent to treatment falls outside the principle in *Gillick* (see Lord Donaldson in *Re R (A Minor) (Wardship: Medical Treatment)* [1992] 1 FLR 1014 and *Re W (a minor) (medical treatment)* (1992) 9 BMLR 22) whilst other judges adopt a more creative and purposive approach.

Thirdly, in domestic law, the Children Act CA 1989, s 1(3)(a) places a duty upon the court, in exercising its jurisdiction over any matter relating to the care and upbringing of the child or in relation to the child's property, to consider: 'the ascertainable wishes and feelings of the child concerned considered in the light of his age and understanding'. (This is considered in Chapter 12.)

Fourthly, the international framework of child and adolescent autonomy and rights is found in the United Nations Convention on the Rights of the Child (UNCRC) (1989) which safeguards the right of participation in legal decisions and imposes obligations on member states to implement national laws which enforce those rights. As of 2024, 196 countries, including all member states of the European Union, had ratified the UNCRC. The UNCRC applies to persons under 18 years of age, and Article 12(1) asserts:

> *States parties shall assure to the child who is capable of forming his or her own views the right to express those views freely in all matters affecting the child, the views of the child being given due weight in accordance with the age and maturity of the child. (2) For this purpose, the child in particular be provided the opportunity to be heard in any judicial and administrative proceedings affecting the child.*

Article 12(2) is a conditional provision as the UNCRC is not directly enforceable by the courts. It establishes a framework for child matters internationally by providing a set of minimum standards, although it is not formally integrated into the European Convention on Human Rights (ECHR) or UK domestic law. Munby J in *R (Howard League for Penal Reform) v Secretary of State for the Home Department and Department of Health* [2002] EWHC 2497 (Admin), [2003] 1 FLR 484 said the UNCRC could and should be consulted by the courts in England and Wales, in so far as it proclaims, reaffirms or elucidates the contents of human rights, in particular the nature and scope of Convention rights under the Human Rights Act 1998. Baroness Hale of Richmond in *R (Williamson) v Secretary of State for Education and Employment* [2005] AC 246, asserted: 'Above all, the state is entitled to give children the protection they are given by an international instrument to which the UK is a party, the United Nations Convention on the Rights of a Child.' The Children's Commissioner under s 107[2A](1) of the Children and Families Act (CFA) 2014: 'must, in particular, have regard to the United Nations Convention on the Rights of the Child in considering for the purposes of the primary function what constitute the rights and interests of children (generally or so far as relating to a particular matter)'. Other articles of relevance include Article 16(1) which asserts: 'No child shall be subjected to arbitrary or unlawful interference with his or her privacy, family, home or correspondence, nor to unlawful attacks on his or her honour and reputation.' The right to participation must be read alongside Article 3, of the UNCRC, which stipulates that all organisations involved with children should work towards what is best for the child. Children's views and the views of adolescents should be considered in matters regarding issues within the family, at school, regarding children's health and in all aspects of their lives.

Fifthly, the ECHR (which is enforceable) (per Human Rights Act 1998) protects everyone including children and their right to self-determination and participation. Article 6, 'fair trial' rights guarantee adolescents and children the right to be heard in legal proceedings. Article 6 ECHR provides that: 'in the determination of his civil rights and obligations . . . everyone is entitled to a fair and public hearing within a reasonable time by an independent and impartial tribunal established by law.' The right to family life is contained in Article 8 ECHR. (See *Re L (Care: Assessment: Fair Trial* [2002] FLR 730, *Mabon v Mabon* [2005] EWCA Civ 634, [2005] 2 FLR 1011.) As MacDonald (2009) notes:

> *The provisions of s 1 of the 1989 Act and the United Nations Convention have a slightly different emphasis to Arts 6 and 8 of the European Convention. Section 1(3)(a) of the 1989 Act and Art 12 of the UNCRC emphasise participation of the child in the decision-making process through the articulation and expression of their wishes and feelings. Arts 6 and 8 emphasise the participation of the child in that decision making process in broader terms, through the adequate and independent representation of the child's interests within that process.*

Other rights that are protected and relevant here include the right to life (Article 2); the right to be free from inhuman and degrading treatment (Article 3); the right to liberty (Article 5); the right to family life and privacy (Article 8); the right to religious thought (Article 9); the right to freedom of expression (Article 10); and the right to freedom from discrimination (Article 14).

Sixthly, Article 13(b) of the Hague Convention on the Civil Aspects of International Child Abduction (91 signatories by 2024), whilst its purpose is to effect the return of a child to his or her 'habitual residence', permits the judicial authority to refuse to order the 'abducted' child to be returned if the child 'objects to being returned and has attained an age and degree of maturity at which it is appropriate to take account of its views'. (See Chapter 12.)

The voice of the child

Parkinson 2024 asserts:

> *Following the UN Convention 1989 on the Rights of the Child, the Brussels II Revised Regulation (Art 4) upheld the child's right to be heard in matters relating to parental responsibility for the child, in accordance with the child's age and maturity. The Council of Europe's Guidelines on Child-Friendly Justice 2010 iv [26] state that the child's right to be heard should be guaranteed both in court and out-of-court proceedings.*

The Family Justice Review (Norgrove 2011) advised that children: 'should as early as possible be supported to make their views known and older children should be offered a menu of options to lay out the ways in which they could – if they wish – do this [9]'.

Findings from the Nuffield Family Justice Observatory revealed that children and young people said they were not given information and not able to participate in decisions affecting them. They did not feel listened to, causing them significant distress. (See Symonds et al. 2022.) The Family Mediation Council ('FMC') Code of Practice states that children aged 10 years and above should be offered the opportunity to express their views if they wish. However actually specifying that the child should be aged 10 or above contravenes advice from the UN Committee on the Rights of the Child which asserts that State signatories to the 1989 Convention should not set age limits in law or in practice that would restrict the child's right to be heard. The 13th European Forum on the Rights of the Child 2020 ended with these words from children who participated:

> We need a strategy that is inclusive of all children and that supports children in vulnerable situations, and we need a strategy that supports and promotes our right to participate in decisions that affect us. Because nothing should be decided for children without children. It's time to normalise child participation.

So how has the family justice system responded to the voice of the child over the years?

Three ages and stages of child rights

Where the child/adolescent is of an age where they can express their views, then their competence is assessed based on an understanding of the issue in question in accordance with their age and development. Children's rights to self-determination are not absolute or fixed but incremental. Lord Donaldson in *Re W (a minor) (medical treatment)* [1992] recognised: 'Adolescence is a period of progressive transition from childhood to adulthood.' It is suggested here that the law has contrived at least three 'ages' or stages of childhood. Firstly, the rights of the unborn which include rights to protection when in utero; secondly, the rights of infants and young children which include rights to protection and to be listened to, but not the right of self-determination or participation; and thirdly, the right of adolescents which include rights to protection, to be listened to, have their views considered, and also the right to self-determination and participation. There is no exactitude as to where the law draws the bright line with regard to the chronological age or indeed stage of development regarding these three stages and their corresponding degrees of legal autonomy. Indeed, thresholds of consent to marry, and age of childhood have moved forward over the decades. Any attempt to draw and organise such boundaries is largely artificial and driven by social policy concerns. Mary Douglas captures this artificiality when she writes:

> It is no new thing for the law to be drawing the line between the biological and social events, choosing the moment when a foetus is enough of a person to require legal protection, deciding when a marriage has been physically consummated, deciding on the definitions of death, rape, cruelty, indecency, and a standard of living above starvation. At less public and weightier levels the same assessment and drawing of boundaries proceeds through the whole social process. Physical nature is masticated and driven through the cognitive meshes to satisfy social demands for clarity, which compete with logical demands for consistency.
>
> (Douglas 1973: 113)

Burin (2014) discusses the medical, philosophical, moral and pragmatic arguments for the bright line of birth and personhood.

Rights of the unborn

The rights of the unborn to protection has had an uncertain status. '[T]he rules according to legal rights at birth are in modern times one founded on convenience.

It does not rest on medical or moral principle.' (See *Harrild v Director of Proceedings* [2003] 3 NZLR 289.) Whilst the unborn does not have rights in its own name, the right to develop to full capacity is protected before birth (Infant Life Preservation Act 1929). And when born, and the infant becomes a person in law, the person can sue for any injury inflicted whilst in the womb before personhood is acquired. (See Congenital Disabilities (Civil Liability) Act 1976, the common law would have allowed recovery prior to the passage of the Act. See *Burton v Islington Health Authority* [1993] QB 204 (CA).) Sir George Baker in *Paton v British Pregnancy Advisory Service Trustees* [1979] QB 276 articulates what remains the legal position: 'The foetus cannot, in English law, in my view, have any rights of its own at least until it is born and has a separate existence from the mother. That permeates the whole of the civil law of this country.'

Brenda Hoggett (Baroness Hale) (1984) wrote:

> Once the unborn child is capable of being born alive it is an offence intentionally to cause the child's death before he has an existence independent of his mother except where this is done in good faith in order to save the mother's life. This indicates that the mother's life takes priority over the child's and also that doctors may take steps to protect the mother's health even at some risk to the baby provided that there is no intention that the baby should die. Where an unborn child is not capable of being born alive of course the pregnancy may be terminated if the risk to the mother's life or health would be greater in letting it continue Abortion Act 1967 s 1(1)(a). Neither a married nor unmarried father has the right to prevent a mother from having a lawful abortion: Paton v British Pregnancy Advisory Service Trustees *[1979]* above, otherwise, an unborn child is not a person with legal rights and status until he is born (or it now seems, on the point of birth).
>
> (Hoggett 1984: 11–12, see also Atkins and Hoggett 1984)

Rights of infants and young children

The question of the young child's right to be consulted, and to speak and be heard in legal decisions about their care and upbringing depends on the issue in question and is fact specific. The right to consideration exists in proportionate relationship to the age, understanding and development of the child. An infant is not able to express his or her wishes and feelings about, for example, which parent he wishes to live with, or whether to have a transplant operation. An infant's best interest will be advanced by the guardian acting for the child and the wishes of those who have parental responsibility for the child. A 4-year-old child can express some view on both these matters but is not capable of assessing what might be in their best interest. However, for the 10-year-old, whose parents have separated, their wishes and feelings concerning with whom they wish to live will have considerable weight but will not be determinative, but a child of such years may not be considered sufficiently competent to exercise an opinion about complex medical matter.

The child's wishes and feelings are voiced in all matters through the children's guardian who represents the child and is appointed by the court. In some cases, the older child and adolescent, if considered competent to do so, may appoint their own representative or solicitor who is not appointed by the court and has a duty directly to the child as client (s 10(4) of the Children's Act 1989).

The court will also consider whether the wishes and feelings expressed are truly those held by the child or whether the expressed wishes are those of one of the parents and whether those wishes expressed are in the child's best interests. For example: 'Parental alienation', considered later in this chapter (and in Chapter 12) may lead the court to take the view that the child's apparent wishes and feelings are not his own. In *CDM v CM and others* [2003] EWHC 1024 (Fam) where the resident parent had persuaded the children that the non-resident parent had physically and sexually abused them and also that the paternal grandparents were physical abusers, the court considered that the child's reluctance to see the father was the result of the resident parent's false and distorted belief system about the non-resident parent, which the children had imbibed.

Having ascertained those genuine wishes, the court will consider how far they should be taken into account in accordance with the issue in question. Cobb J in an article 'Seen but not heard' (2015) asserts:

> As Baroness Hale memorably said in Re D (Re D (Abduction: Rights of Custody) [2006] UKHL 51, [57]) '. . . as any parent who has ever asked a child what he wants for tea knows, there is a large difference between taking account of a child's views and doing what he wants'. It was acknowledged in that case that at 4½ years old, D was not of an age where a court would accept that he had 'attained an age and degree of maturity at which it is appropriate to take account of its views'. But the time of the appeal was when he was 8, it was a different story; so, the court listened more carefully. That said, there is no threshold below which a child cannot be sufficiently mature for the purposes of the child's objections defence, nor are there even any presumptions although, as a matter of common sense, one will be able to say, for example, that an infant will not be old enough and a normal 15-year-old is likely to be. (Re W (Abduction: Acquiescence: Children's Objections) [2010] EWHC 332 (Fam)). This year, the Supreme Court developed the point further (Re LC (Reunite: International Child Abduction Centre Intervening) [2014] UKSC 1 [87]). It's not just the articulated objections; in the more mature child, one is looking at the perception of her situation: The relevant reality is that of the child, not of the parents. This approach accords with our increasing recognition of children as people with a part to play in their own lives, rather than as passive recipients of their parents' decision'.

In *Re R (No 1) (Inter-Country Adoption)* [1999] 1 FLR 1014, a case which involved a 10-year-old child, Bracewell J observed:

> The wishes and feelings of AM are clear. I am abundantly satisfied that she wants to stay where she is and to be part of her present family where she has put down roots. She has, in effect, voted with her feet . . . I find that although she wants to keep in touch with her birth family, she would be devastated if she had to return. Her wishes cannot be decisive of outcome because a child of her age and understanding may know what she wants but not necessarily what she needs. However, wishes of this intensity must be given due consideration when balancing all the factors.

Where the child objects to a proposal the Supreme Court in *MS v AR* [2019] IESC 10 set out the three-stage approach identified by Potter P in *Re M (Abduction: Child's Objections)* [2007] EWCA Civ 260. This approach involves ascertaining if a child does in fact object and, if so, what weight should attach to the objection, given the maturity of the child.

Rights of adolescents and 16–17-year-olds

The approach of the court in more recent times is summarised boldly by Thorpe LJ in *Mabon v Mabon* [2005] earlier:

> *Although the tandem model has many strengths and virtues, at its heart lies the conflict between advancing the welfare of the child and upholding the child's freedom of expression and participation. Unless we in this jurisdiction are to fall out of step with similar societies as they safeguard article 12 rights, we must, in the case of articulate teenagers, accept that the right to freedom of expression and participation outweighs the paternalistic judgment of welfare.*

Fine words indeed; let us then explore how and under what conditions these sentiments are realised.

Firstly, as stated earlier under FLRA 1969, s 8, 16–17-years-olds are presumed in law to be competent. Section 8(1) asserts:

> *The consent of a minor who has attained the age of sixteen years to any surgical, medical or dental treatment which, in the absence of consent, would constitute a trespass to his person, shall be as effective as it would be if he were of full age; and where a minor has by virtue of this section given an effective consent to any treatment it shall not be necessary to obtain any consent for it from his parent or guardian.*

This is a rebuttable presumption. The adolescent can say 'yes' but it would seem, not 'no' to treatment. Is it a capacity to refuse? In *R (on the application of W) v Essex County Council; R (on the application of F) v same; R (on the application of G) v same* [2004] 1 FLR 1014, the court asserted:

> *Section 20(6) as we have seen, requires the local authority to ascertain and give due consideration to the child's wishes regarding the provision of accommodation. Plainly when dealing with 16-year-old children, who are likely to have minds of their own and may well be Gillick competent – see Gillick v West Norfolk and Wisbech Area Health Authority (1986) AC 112 a local authority has to have regard to the realities. In particular, a local authority has to have regard to the reality that young people faced with proffered support packages which are perceived as being unacceptable may well reject the support being offered and simply vote with their feet.*

Is this correct or does this undermine the competence principle?

In 2024 NHS guidance said that a competent 16–17-year-old cannot refuse treatment if it is considered in their best interests to receive it. This guidance is clearly batting the decision back to the court and back to the uncertainty of the nebulous concept of 'best interests' and privileging the residual power of the court's paternalism always in the shadows.

Under 16-year-olds and the Gillick competence precept

The case of *Gillick* has been referred to severally in this chapter but what was it about and what did it decide exactly?

In *Gillick v West Norfolk and Wisbech Area Health Authority* [1986] discussed earlier, the Department of Health and Social Security (now the Department of Health) issued a notice to all area health authorities detailing guidance on the treatment of young people under 16 years of age seeking contraceptive advice. It was anticipated that where such advice was being given to adolescents under 16 years their parents would attend such consultations and that it would be most unusual to provide contraceptive advice to a young person without parental consent/ knowledge. This is because in the case of a person under 16 parental responsibility requires parents to act on behalf of their minor offspring in all including medical matters. The guidance stated:

> There is widespread concern about counselling and treatment for children under 16. Special care is needed not to undermine parental responsibility and family stability. The Department would therefore hope that in any case where a doctor or other professional worker is approached by a person under the age of 16 for advice in these matters, the doctor, or other professional, will always seek to persuade the child to involve the parent or guardian (or other person in loco parentis) at the earliest stage of consultation, and will proceed from the assumption that it would be most unusual to provide advice about contraception without parental consent.

The plaintiff, Mrs Victoria Gillick, a mother of five girls and five boys, wrote to the local authority asking for an assurance that no contraceptive advice would be given to any of her daughters without her knowledge and consent:

> Concerning the new D.H.S.S. guidelines on the contraceptive and abortion treatment of children under both the legal and medical age of consent, without the knowledge or consent of the parents, can I please ask you for a written assurance that in no circumstances whatsoever will any of my daughters (Beatrice, Hannah, Jessie and Sarah) be given contraceptive or abortion treatment whilst they are under 16 in any of the family planning clinics under your control, without my prior knowledge, and irrefutable evidence of my consent? Also, should any of them seek advice in them, can I have your assurance that I would be automatically contacted in the interests of my children's safety and welfare? If you are in any doubt about giving me such assurances, can I please ask you to seek legal medical advice.

The local authority refused to give any such an assurance, since few if any young girls would discuss contraception with their parents and in consequence would not seek medical help resulting in unwanted pregnancies and unsafe terminations and putting them at risk. Mrs Gillick responded by initiating an action by writ for a declaration that the DHSS guidelines on the contraceptive and abortion treatment of children were unlawful, and adversely affecting parental responsibility.

Woolf J in the court of first instance, refused to grant the declarations sought by Mrs Gillick and dismissed the action. Woolf J's judgment is historic. Woolf J said this:

> The fact that a child is under the age of 16 does not mean automatically that she cannot give consent to any treatment. Whether or not a child is capable of giving the necessary consent will depend on the child's maturity and understanding, and the nature of the consent which is required. The child must be capable of making a reasonable assessment of the advantages and disadvantages of the treatment proposed, so the consent if given can be properly and fairly described as true consent . . . since the interests of parents, I consider, are more accurately described as responsibilities or duties.

Mrs Gillick appealed Woolf J's judgment to the Court of Appeal (*Gillick v West Norfolk and Wisbech Area Health Authority and another* (CA) [1985]), and Eveleigh, Fox and Parker LJJ's unanimously reversed Woolf J's decision in the court of first instance on the ground that a girl under 16 years of age was incapable of consenting to medical treatment or prohibiting a doctor from seeking the consent of her parents and, as such, the DHSS guidance was contrary to law. Eveleigh LJ concluded:

> I do not intend to lay down a rule that in every case, no matter what the question is, no matter who the child is, the parent must be consulted before any important decision can ever be arrived at in relation to the child.

The DHSS then appealed the Court of Appeals decision to the House of Lords who allowed the appeal (Lords Brandon and Templeman dissenting). For the majority, Lords Fraser, Scarman and Bridge held that the legislation indicated that Parliament regarded contraceptive advice and treatment as essentially medical matters and that a girl under 16 years had the legal capacity to consent to medical examination and treatment. They also noted that the parental right to control a child was a 'dwindling right'. Lord Fraser said:

> Once the rule of the parents' absolute authority over minor children is abandoned, the solution to the problem in this appeal can no longer be found by referring to rigid parental rights at any particular age. The solution depends upon a judgment of what is best for the welfare of the particular child. . . . There is a dwindling scale of parental rights from birth to the age of majority.

Lord Scarman echoed the demise of parental authority:

> Parental rights are derived from parental duty . . . the dwindling right . . . of a parent yields to the child's right to make his own decisions when he reaches a sufficient understanding and intelligence to be capable of making up his own mind on the matter

> *requiring decision . . . the underlying principle of the law was exposed by Blackstone*
> *and can be seen to have been acknowledged in the case law. It is that parental rights*
> *yield to the child's right to make his own decisions when he reaches a sufficient un-*
> *derstanding and intelligence to be capable of making up his own mind on the matter*
> *requiring decision.*

(One doubts however whether Sir William Blackstone ever intended such a consequence.)

Sexual intercourse and the dissenters

Lord Brandon, who, whilst he had championed the principle of the rights of the child in *Re D* [1984] 1 AC 778 (see Chapter 9), dissented in *Gillick*, which may have seemed a volte face not following principle, since Lord Brandon changed course because of the substance of the case which involved a teenage girl having sexual intercourse still frowned upon in 1985. Lord Brandon's dissent palpably demonstrated how adherence to principle is precarious and is so often driven by factual scenarios. He said: 'The only answer which the law should give . . . is "Wait till you are 16."' Lord Templeman said: '[199e] . . . an unmarried girl under the age of 16 does not in my opinion, possess the power in law to decide for herself to practice contraception. [201c]'. He went on to say rather glibly, 'There are many things which a girl under 16 needs to practise but sex is not one of them,' a remark which became sensationalised in media strap lines. He continued:

> *Parliament could declare this view to be out of date. But in my opinion the statutory*
> *provisions discussed in the speech of noble and learned friend Lord Fraser and the provisions*
> *of s 6 of the Sexual Offences Act 1956 indicate that as the law now stands an unmarried*
> *girl under 16 is not competent to decided to practise sex and contraception.*

Gillick establishes in law, for the first time, the adolescent's right to make decisions as a free-standing right and enshrines in law the importance of considering a minor/adolescent wishes in accord with intellect and understanding. This places the child in a new subject position in law, far beyond *J v C* [1970] AC 668 (Chapter 9), where the interests of the child were perceived through the lens of judicial paternalism. *Gillick* represents a watershed moment, a brightline in establishing for adolescents the right to autonomy before they have attained full age. It has implications for health care professionals, for patient confidentiality, for schooling and for the courts, not only in medical, but in all matters. The Access to Health Records Act 1990 further embellishes this autonomy picture in allowing a child under 16, deemed 'Gillick competent' by a doctor, to veto the parent's access to medical information held by that doctor where disclosure may result in the patient child suffering harm to wellbeing, even though the parent can consent to treatment which the child cannot veto (Radcliffe Hospital Confidentiality Guidelines). Doctors require properly informed consent before treating anyone, including adolescent patients. (See Clause 3.5 of the NMC Code of Professional Conduct:

standards for conduct, performance, and ethics.) The Health and Care Professionals Council assert:

> For children under 16, you may need to get consent from someone with parental responsibility. This could be the child's mother or father; the child's legally appointed guardian; a person with a residence order for the child; a local authority designated to care for the child; or a local authority or person with an emergency protection order for the child. Some children under 16 can give consent if they can fully understand the information given to them. This is known as 'Gillick competence'.
>
> (See Consent and confidentiality)

Applying *Gillick* – how can an adolescent acquire competence?

Acquiring competence (either for the purpose of determining medical or related treatment or else as competent under Family Proceedings Rules, r 9.42 for the purpose of participation in legal proceedings) is not a fixed or absolute quality. Competence to determine contraceptive treatment does not mean that the same individual would be considered competent to make a decision with regard to refusing a blood transfusion. Competence is situation specific and assessed in the light of particular circumstances.

This is what Woolf J had groundbreakingly determined in the High Court in *Gillick* when he said that it depended on the nature of the consent which is required. It is not a fixed trait or quality like hearing or sight, nor is it a constant quality.

Lord Donaldson in *Re R (A Minor) (Wardship: Medical Treatment)* [1992] 1 FLR 1014 highlighted the fluid nature of competence when considering an adolescent with psychological issues.

> But, even if she was capable on a good day of a sufficient degree of understanding to meet the Gillick criteria, her mental disability, to the cure or amelioration of which the proposed treatment was directed, was such that on other days she was not only 'Gillick incompetent', but actually sectionable. No adolescent in that situation can be regarded as 'Gillick competent' and the judge was wholly right in so finding in relation to R.

The case law demonstrates that the threshold required in 'comprehending the outcome and the procedures involved' is so often set at an unreachable level, far above that which might be expected of, or even attainable by, an adult.

The US case of *In the matter of Anonymous, a Minor* [2001] 808 So.2d 1024 (Ala. Civ.App.2001) similarly reflects the high threshold that is required. Here an 'unemancipated minor' petitioned the court to review the judgment of the Court of Civil Appeals affirming the trial court's denial of the minor's petition for a waiver of parental consent to an abortion. The adolescent was denied an abortion on the grounds that as she was not provided with the opportunity to be fully informed of the procedure and without the full facts, she could not be said to understand the procedure.

'Gillick competence' chronological age?

In considering whether a minor is Gillick competent the courts have taken into account the three characteristics of age, understanding and maturity. Age is the first hurdle which must be navigated before the question of competence can be considered.

In the case of *Re M (Child's Upbringing)* [1996] 2 FLR 441 (discussed in Chapter 9) where there was conflict between the natural parents and the foster parents with regard to the question of with whom the child should live which led to an application for adoption, the fact that the child was 10 years of age and not 12 years of age assumed considerable significance in the court's reasoning. Thorpe J (in the court of first instance) ruled that the boy concerned should be returned to South Africa to his biological parents notwithstanding that he had expressed more than a wish to remain in the United Kingdom with his prospective adoptive mother. Thorpe J accepted that if, in two years' time, the boy, who was 10 years of age at the hearing, still wished to remain with the foster parents in England, his wishes would 'have' to be taken into account.

Thorpe J clearly considered that the wishes of a 12-year-old boy would be harder to ignore. That '12 years of age' once the common brightline may have been lowered slightly in recent years.

Maturity to understand

Once the age threshold is met, whatever that might be with regard to a particular issue, an assessment of the adolescent's maturity and ability to understand what is involved is then required. Lord Scarman, in *Gillick*, said:

> *When applying these conclusions to contraceptive advice and treatment it has to be borne in mind that there is much that has to be understood by a girl under the age of 16 if she is to have legal capacity to consent to such treatment. It is not enough that she should understand the nature of the advice which is being given: she must also have sufficient maturity to understand what is involved.*

The meaning of 'to understand what is involved' is not fixed, it is really quite imprecise. How much, and how deep an understanding is required? In the case of *In the matter of Anonymous, a Minor* (2001) cited earlier, understanding 'what was involved' required an ability to understand the medical procedure of aborting a foetus including the two-stage process which involved the insertion of an extra amniotic catheter, and an intravenous infusion cannula, and the connection of infusions of the abortifacient drugs to the catheter and, if appropriate, to the cannula, and the regulation of those infusions. The matter of death and the matter of the moral and ethical issues involved, both questions of supreme philosophical importance, were also required. Post-*Gillick* case law lacks a clear protocol regarding consistent treatment as to age, threshold of maturity and the degree of understanding and vacillates in the wind depending on the facts and the opinions of judges. Judges simply cannot agree. The application of the legal principle of adolescent self-determination and autonomy seems to yield to the outcome and consequences of the desired wishes pleaded by the adolescent and judicial judgment and discretion.

'Gillick competence': only a right to refuse consent?

Since *Gillick* was decided, the courts have through cases before the courts debated its meaning and its potential application and whether 'Gillick competence' is confined to an adolescent's capacity to consent to medical treatment, or whether 'if young people have the right to consent to medical treatment, logically they should have the right to refuse treatment' (Cretney and Masson 2003: 504). There does seem to be agreement amongst family law scholars that logic should prevail, and the principle should apply to cases which raise the issue of consent and those where refusal of consent is in issue.

For some time the courts were tethered by two significant decisions of Lord Donaldson (Master of the Rolls at the time) who in interpreting Lord Scarman's ruling in *Gillick*, held Gillick competence to apply only to those cases where the issue in question related to an adolescent's capacity to consent to medical treatment limiting *Gillick* (see *Re R (A Minor) (Wardship: Medical Treatment)* [1992] 1 FLR 1014, and *Re W (A Minor) (Wardship: Medical Treatment)* [1992] 4 All ER 627). It is significant that in the case of *Re X (A Child) (No 2): An NHS Trust v X* [2021] EWHC 65 (Fam) (discussed later) the court referred to these two decisions and held that they remain the law rejecting the plaintiff's argument that these judgments were out of date and no longer applied.

In *Re R (A Minor) (Wardship: Medical Treatment)* [1992] 1 FLR 1014 the competence of an adolescent to refuse tranquilising sedation was in question. The adolescent girl, R, was 15 years and 10 months old. She was on the local authority's 'at-risk' register and was received into voluntary care after a fight with her father. The local authority obtained a place of safety order and an interim care order. She was admitted into an adolescent psychiatric unit where she was sedated from time to time because of her suicidal and volatile behaviour. Specialists in the unit wanted to sedate her in order to treat her because she had psychotic episodes. When she was in a lucid state she objected to the continuation of the medication and doctors feared that if the medication was withdrawn psychosis would return. R telephoned her social worker protesting against this continuation of treatment. The local authority who had parental responsibility decided that they could not give authorisation to such treatment under these circumstances and made an application to the court to have her made a ward of court. In wardship proceedings the court considered: (i) whether the judge had power to override the decision of a ward to refuse medication and treatment irrespective of whether the minor was competent to give her consent; and (ii) whether the ward had the requisite capacity to accept or refuse such medication or treatment. The Official Solicitor (James Munby QC as he then was) as guardian for the child appealed, contending that if a child had the right to give consent to medical treatment, then the parents', and a fortiori the wardship court's right to give or refuse consent terminated.

Lord Donaldson did not agree and said:

> Consent by itself creates no obligation to treat. It is merely a key, which unlocks a door. Furthermore, whilst in the case of an adult of full capacity there will usually only be one keyholder, namely the patient, in the ordinary family unit where a young child is the patient there will be two key holders, namely the parents, with a several as well as a joint right to turn the key and unlock the door. If the parents disagree, one consenting and the other refusing, the doctor will be presented with a professional and ethical, but not a legal, problem because, if he has the consent of one authorised person, treatment will not without more constitute a trespass or a criminal assault.

The court concluded that the Gillick competence test was of general importance, but not decisive as James Munby (her counsel at that time) had argued. So, an adolescent refusing treatment did not have the ultimate say in the matter or a right of veto, but their refusal was a factor. Lord Donaldson even goes so far as to rewrite what Lord Scarman says by stating what Lord Scarman's intentions were:

> I do not understand Lord Scarman to be saying that, if a child was 'Gillick competent', to adopt the convenient phrase used in argument, the parents ceased to have an independent right of consent, as contrasted with ceasing to have a right of determination, or veto. . . . If Lord Scarman intended to go further than this and to say that in the case of a 'Gillick competent' child, a parent has no right either to consent or to refuse consent, his remarks were obiter. . . . Furthermore, I consider that they would have been wrong. . . . One glance at the consequences suffices to show that Lord Scarman cannot have been intending to say that the parental right to consent terminates with the achievement by the child of 'Gillick competence'.

Farquharson LJ in his judgment and in a blanket stroke dismissed the possibility that an adolescent with mental health problems could ever achieve Gillick competence:

> 'Gillick competence' is not open to her . . . for my part I would find it difficult to import the criteria applied in Gillick to the facts of the present case. We are not here solely concerned with the developing maturity of a 15-year-old child, but with the impact of a mental illness upon her.

R failed the test of competence.

In *Re W (a Minor) (Wardship: Medical Treatment)* [1992] 4 All ER 627, the issue of consent or its refusal arose to be determined where the minor was deemed competent. It is to be noted that the legal situation is somewhat different since young people (aged 16 and 17) should be treated in the same way as adults and presumed that they have capacity unless there is significant evidence to suggest otherwise. Was there significant evidence to suggest otherwise?

W was 16 years of age and suffering from highly advanced anorexia. She was transferred against her wishes to a London specialist clinic for the treatment of eating disorders. She was so thin that her arms were encased in plaster to protect them, and she was fed via a nasogastric tube. The question arose whether, under s 8 of the FLRA 1969, such a minor had an exclusive right to consent to such treatment and therefore her right to refuse medical treatment was absolute. The risk of significant harm to her resulted in an application under the wardship jurisdiction which authorised treatment on the ground that within one week she would suffer irreversible harm. W's appeal failed.

W wanted to die. As Lord Donaldson in the Court of Appeal acceded:

Fate has dealt harshly with W. She is now aged 16, having been born on 31 March 1976. She has an older sister, now aged 18, and a younger brother, now aged 13. In November 1981, when she was 5, her father died of a brain tumour and in September 1984, when she was 8, her mother died of cancer.

Her fate was that her short life up until then had been an excoriating series of tragedies. In 1984, she was orphaned and taken into care. In 1989, her foster mother had breast cancer; in 1990, her grandfather died. W was considered Gillick competent. Thorpe J said she was competent, so did the judges in the Court of Appeal. Thorpe J asserted:

There is no doubt at all that [W] is a child of sufficient understanding to make an informed decision. I am quite satisfied of that. . . . I am convinced that she has a good intelligence and understands what is proposed as treatment. She is adamant that under no circumstances would she consent to further use of a nasogastric tube, whether or not she was drugged to such a degree that she felt little discomfort as it was pushed down into her stomach. I believe that her fear of losing control of her eating and thus developing into an adult woman, which makes her fight against her ever-present hunger, is understandable. She is by no means so severely undernourished that her thinking is physically impaired. (The starving people in Belsen, and Ethiopia recently, were noted to be clear in mental powers, which are preserved above all else.)

[641]

In accordance with the FLRA 1969, W could consent to treatment without interference although the question of refusal to medical treatment is not specifically covered by the provision. Indeed, Nolan LJ in the Court of Appeal commenting on the effect of this statute in this case made it clear that the 16- and 17-year-old was in possession of 'the same capacity as an adult to surgical, medical or dental treatment'.

Lord Donaldson in deciding the case embarked on a new concept, this time and in this case, it had to be more robust ego – the flak jacket! He said:

the purpose of seeking consent from a patient (whether adult or child) . . . has two purposes, the one clinical and the other legal. The clinical purpose stems from the fact that in many instances the co-operation of the patient . . . is a major factor contributing to the treatment's success. Failure to obtain such consent . . . will usually make it much more difficult to administer the treatment. I appreciate that this purpose may not be served if consent is given on behalf of, rather than by the patient. . . . On reflection I regret my use in Re R of the key holder analogy . . . because keys can lock as well as unlock. I now prefer the analogy of the legal 'flak jacket' which protects from claims by the litigious whether he acquires it from his patient who may be a minor over the age of 16, or a 'Gillick competent' child under that age or from another person having parental responsibilities which include a right to consent to treatment of the minor. Anyone who gives him a flak jacket (i.e. consent) may take it back, but the doctor only needs one and so long as he continues to have one, he has the legal right to proceed.

Lord Donaldson was also mindful to assert that even competent adolescents do not have an exclusive right of veto to determine their own treatment. Indeed, he had said earlier in *Re R* that Gillick competence was not decisive, and he showed it, once again, not to be so in *Re W*.

So what self-determination, or autonomy might come within a 'competent' adolescent's grasp? Lord Donaldson's demonstrated that in *Re W* competency was worth very little. W was competent, but the wardship court overrode her expressed wishes in their role of parens patriae protector in accordance with the CA 1989 s100 (4) (b) in applying the welfare test and in the prevention of significant harm. At common law the role of the court has always been to prevent death and preserve life at least until the minor reaches majority (otherwise a capacitous adult). This overriding obligation will be returned to later.

The case law suggests that self-determination is negated where the adolescent displays behavioural problems. Farquharson LJ had said in *Re R*, that an adolescent displaying certain behavioural difficulties was, in his view, incompetent by virtue of her psychological difficulties. Lord Donaldson arrived at the same outcome in *Re W*, although he accepted that W was competent, he went on to say in general terms that a feature of anorexia is that it can destroy the ability to make an informed decision.

The reaction of the academic community

In 1992, Gillian Douglas courteously described *Re R* and *Re W* as a 'retreat from Gillick'. Fortin robustly said: 'In a remarkable U-turn, the Court of Appeal in *Re R* and *Re W* radically undermined the liberal sentiments expressed only a few years earlier by the House of Lords' (Fortin 2003: 84).

Analysis: 'Gillick competence' from consequences to competence

Applying the law to the fact is the fulcrum of legal method. However, law and legal principles are derived from a set of facts which then may take the form of a rule for later cases. This deductive logic doesn't always work to do justice. The facts in Gillick were indeed case specific such that some judges presented with new scenarios attempted to confine the test of competence to the facts whilst others expanded its application, honouring the principle.

In many cases the courts faced with a question of a minor's refusal of consent to treatment or otherwise demands for treatment (see gender dysphoria later in this chapter) start from the other end of the periscope considering consequences first and principle second. This is because the welfare of the child is paramount and because the courts paternalism will continue to impose their view of what is best. Simon Lee (1989: 85) observed:

> There are two reasons for disagreements on such matters of law and morals. One is starting from different moral premises, intuitions, or priorities. The other concludes with different predictions as to the factual consequences which would follow from a decision. So, when the judges rely on public policy in the third, consequentialist sense, their disagreement might be due to a different estimation of the consequences, whether X or Y would actually happen, and/or due to a different moral evaluation of the desirability of those consequences, whether X or Y would be good or bad.

There are no hard and fast rules. However, we find that the anorexic and the adolescent with behavioural problems who refuse treatment and the gender dysphoric adolescent who demands treatment are unlikely candidates for legally recognised autonomy.

When an adolescent refuses to consent to life-saving or medically necessary treatment, the court has several options. The court may either deem the adolescent 'incompetent' and then with little problem proceed to order the medically prescribed treatment. The court may deem the adolescent 'competent' and must then decide whether to let the adolescent's wishes prevail or invoke its powers under the wardship jurisdiction on the grounds that the adolescent will suffer significant harm if permitted to realise the consequences. When a Gillick competent adolescent's wishes are overridden by invoking the inherent jurisdiction/wardship, this leads to the criticism that Gillick competence is just a mirage of autonomy since it makes no difference at all.

Refusing saying no no no to blood, organs, sedation

This history of adolescents' refusal has not been without considerable controversy.

An adolescent following an accident or due to an inherited medical condition may need blood transfusions or other blood products. A Jehovah's Witness (JW) in following the precepts of the faith is prohibited from submitting to life-saving blood products, nor can parents decide on their behalf. JW's regard blood as sacred. David Ziebart (2007) raises the issue of Article 9 of the ECHR in this context and challenges the courts in their overruling of children who follow this religious observance. Article 9 provides:

> 1. Everyone has the right to freedom of thought, conscience, and religion; this right in-cludes freedom to change his religion or belief and freedom, either alone or in commu-nity with others and in public or private, to manifest his religion or belief, in worship, teaching, practice and observance.
>
> 2. Freedom to manifest one's religion or beliefs shall be subject only to such limitations as are prescribed by law and are necessary in a democratic society . . . for the protec-tion of the rights and freedoms of others.

In *Re E (a Minor) (Wardship: Medical Treatment)* [1993] 1 FLR 386, [1993] 2 FCR 219E a Jehovah's Witness of 15 years and nine months refused to consent to a blood transfusion (a decision supported by his parents). E was deemed incompetent, yet Ward J was impressed by his intelligence and said:

> *I find that he has no realisation of the full implications, which lie before him as to the process of dying. He may have some concept of the fact that he will die but as to the manner of his death and to the extent of his and his family's suffering I find he has not the ability to turn neither his mind to it nor the will to do so. Who can blame him for that?*

In *Re S (a Minor) (Consent to Medical Treatment)* [1994] 1 FCR 604, a 15-year-old Jehovah's Witness with a rare blood disease refused a blood transfusion (a decision supported by the parents). Johnson J concluded that:

> *whilst as she gave evidence I was so very strongly impressed by her integrity and her commitment; I believe they were the integrity and commitment of a child and not of somebody who was competent to make a decision that she tells me she has made . . . an understanding that she will die is not enough. For her decision to carry weight she should have a greater understanding of the manner of the death and pain and the distress.*

What then is the integrity and commitment of a child and what then satisfies the threshold of a 'greater understanding of pain, of death and the distress'?

In *Re L (Medical treatment Gillick competency)* [1998] 2 FLR 810, a 14-year-old girl who was Jehovah's Witness required a blood transfusion, to which she would not consent. She had signed an Advanced Medical Directive prohibiting the use of blood. Sir Stephen Brown P acknowledged that her religious beliefs were strongly held, and, in her case, she was 'mature for her age' but she too was disqualified because she did not understand death, and so declared that she was 'not Gillick competent'; treatment was ordered.

By 2004, Johnson J articulates what is quickly causing difficulty for the courts as adolescent autonomy takes a firmer foothold. In *Re P (Medical Treatment: Best Interests)* [2004] 2 FLR 1117, in deciding for P (John), a 16-year and 10-month-old Jehovah's Witness with an inherited condition, hypermobility syndrome, which manifests in fragility of blood vessels and bleeding, John refused treatment. Given that he is in the 16–17-year-old age group Gillick competence does not strictly apply. Johnson J said:

> *[9] There may be cases as a child approaches the age of 18 when his refusal would be determinative. A court will have to consider whether to override the wishes of the child approaching the age of majority when the likelihood is that all that will have been achieved will have been the deferment of an inevitable death and for a matter of months. Here, however, I am reminded of the words of Nolan LJ., (as he then was) in* Re W (A Minor) (Medical Treatment: Court's Jurisdiction): *'In general terms the present state of the law is that an individual who has reached the age of 18 is free to do with his life what he wishes, but it is the duty of the court to ensure so far as it can that children survive to attain that age.'*

Johnson J clearly struggles with these moral and legal considerations. Whilst he made an order in the terms sought by the NHS Trust, he makes it clear that blood treatment must be the absolute last resort, adding the words 'unless no other form of treatment is available' and he did so, he said, 'reluctantly'. His reluctance arose because of John's age, since with regard to a 16–17-year-old there is a presumption of consent and John was so clearly able to articulate his wishes, as John said: 'I am my own person. I have a separate mind. It makes no difference what my parents think. I make my own decisions.'

We see a shift from earlier cases. Johnson J had dealt with S in 1994 (earlier in this chapter) and with 15-year-old M in 1999 (discussed later) and clearly finds it difficult to justify overruling P, a 16–17-year-old competent young person approaching majority, recognising too that his decision is merely 'deferring death'.

Fortin in her critique of these decisions has said: 'case law establishes far less stringent requirements when assessing an adult patient's competence to refuse treatment (than a child). These requirements are difficult to justify on logical grounds to the teenagers themselves' (2003: 133, see also Gilmore and Herring 2011).

By 2012, had the position changed? As Munby J said in *Re G (children) (Education: Religious upbringing)* [2012] EWCA Civ 1233: 'The tenets and faith of Jehovah's Witnesses will not prevent the court ordering a child to receive a blood transfusion, even though both the parents and the child vehemently object.' The current position is as it was, and *Re X (A Child) (No 2): An NHS Trust v X* [2021] EWHC 65 (Fam) provides a most thorough analysis of earlier decisions. In this case, X who was 15 years old and suffered who from sickle cell, was a Jehovah's Witness and deemed competent. She applied for declarations that she had the requisite decisional capacity to exclusively decide her own medical treatment, refusing consent to blood transfusions should the occasion arise. The NHS trust wanted a clear legal framework available for the resolution of the next crisis requiring immediate medical intervention and transfusion. The court refused to make a two-year 'rolling order' in favour of the NHS authorising blood transfusions to be performed on X if clinically indicated until she was 18 but rejected X's argument that since competent her wishes were determinative as if a capacitous adult when she became 16 years of age [27].

The judge accepted legal argument that heed needed to be paid to the standards of 2021 but said that it did not entitle the court to overturn the learning of the law and overthrow *Re R (a minor) (wardship: medical treatment)* [1991] 4 All ER 177, and *Re W (a minor) (medical treatment)* [1992] 4 All ER 627, merely because society's views had changed, even assuming that they had [161], concluding that the change, which was requested, was a matter for Parliament.

Bridge (1999), Coggon and Miola (2011), and Daniel (2009) consider the moral, ethical and autonomy issues that arise from these several decisions.

Refusing organ transplant

Where gravely ill adolescents who are in need of an organ transplant refuse to consent to transplant surgery, because the procedure is so invasive, it is more difficult to override their wishes (see Hall 2006).

In *Re M (Child: Refusal of Medical Treatment)* [1999] 2 FLR 1097 a 15½-year-old adolescent was close to death. The court ordered that doctors should be allowed to treat the adolescent with a heart transplant. The doctors applied to the High Court for authorisation to carry out the operation. They contacted the judge, Johnson J, at home in the evening, who immediately contacted the Official Solicitor at his home. As the Official Solicitor was in London, he was unable, in the time available, to see M himself and to ascertain from M her wishes and to hear representations on behalf of the child. The Official Solicitor appointed a local solicitor, Mr Winter, to act as his agent. Mr Winter interviewed M that same evening and his notes contained these reflections from M:

> if I don't have the operation I will die. I really don't want a transplant – I am not happy with it – I don't want to die. . . . If I had the transplant, I wouldn't be happy. If I were to die my family would be sad. . . . Death is final – I know I can't change my mind. I don't want to die, but I would rather die than have the transplant and have someone else's heart, I would rather die with 15 years of my own heart. If I had someone else's heart, I would be different from anybody else – being dead would not make me different from anyone else. I would feel different with someone else's heart.

Johnson J having considered M's wishes and the views of the Official Solicitor's representative concluded that M was overwhelmed by events and said:

> Whilst I am very conscious of the gravity of the decision, I was making in overriding M's wish, it seemed to me that seeking to achieve what was best for her required me on balance to give the authority that was asked.

M was considered incompetent although the court did not expressly say so, nor was this expression used by the court. However, the fact that M was considered to be 'overwhelmed by her circumstances' weighed heavily, and for all practical purposes she was considered incompetent. Her mother wanted her to undergo a transplant.

In 2008, Hannah Jones, 13 years of age, succeeded in the High Court in refusing a transplant. 'I am not a normal thirteen-year-old I am a very deep thinker. I have had to be with my illness. Its hard to know I am going to die but I know what's best for me' (see *Hannah's Choice* by Kirsty Jones and Hannah Jones, 2010). As it happened subsequent to this hearing Hannah consented to a transplant. In 2018, she reunited with her surgeon. (See Hannah Jones BBC News.)

Refusing medication/sedation/sustenance

Doctors require informed consent before treating adolescent patients with medication. This question has been partially addressed in respect of the child R (*Re R (a Minor) (Wardship: Medical Treatment)* (1992) (earlier) which involved administering sedation. In *Northampton AHA v Official Solicitor and the Governors of St Andrews Hospital* (1994) *Northampton Health Authority v The Official Solicitor and The Governors of St Andrews Hospital* [1994] 1 FLR 162 (first reported as *Re K, W and H (Minors) (Medical Treatment)* [1993] 1 FLR 854), the issue as to whether three adolescents who refused treatment were Gillick competent arose. A consultant psychiatrist of the hospital applied for CA, s 8 specific issues orders regarding the future administration of emergency medication for the patients, two were aged 15, and one 14 years old. When admitted they were required to consent to the hospitals administering oral or intramuscular tranquillising treatment should an emergency situation determine that such medication was necessary. Consent to such medication had been given by all families, but the adolescents refused consent. The first adolescent was diagnosed as suffering from 'unsocialized adolescent conduct disorder' and was said to have had an 'extremely disturbed and chaotic adolescence'. In her case no emergency medication had been administered, as it had not been considered necessary. The second adolescent was diagnosed with 'adolescent conduct disorder' and described as having had an extremely disturbed adolescence, and in her case the staff at St Andrew's hospital found it necessary to administer a tranquillising drug, Droperidol. The third adolescent was diagnosed with 'bipolar effective disorder' and on the day of her admission was considered to be mentally ill, and the professionals treating her were of the opinion that her admission could have been secured under the Mental Health Act. She had been prescribed Lithium. In her case, an application was made under the Family Proceedings Rules 1992, r 9.2A(4) to remove the guardian ad litem and an application made under r 9.2A(6): 'that the minor concerned has sufficient understanding to participate as a party in the proceedings concerned or proposed without guardian ad litem'. In determination of this issue the guardians were called and asked: 'Do you consider that J, do you consider that D, has sufficient understanding to participate in the proceedings concerned without a next friend or guardian ad litem?' Both guardians said: 'No.' Consequently, the Official Solicitor acted for all three adolescents. Thorpe J in *K, W and H* held that none of these three is Gillick competent. 'I am in no doubt at all that the treatment methods that St Andrews have developed to deal with these extremely difficult cases are not open to reasonable criticism or question, quite apart from a challenge to their legality.' (See also refusing to consent to compulsory detention *R v Kirklees Metropolitan Borough Council Ex Parte C* [1993] 2 FLR 187 and refusing to consent to Caesarean section *A Metropolitan Borough Council v DB* [1997] 1 FLR 767.)

In the medical cases, *Re S (a Minor) (Consent to Medical Treatment)* [1994] 1 FCR 604 discussed earlier, amongst others, the threshold of understanding required by the court might be said to be virtually unattainable even by a competent adult. There are further obstacles to overcome since the courts consider that those who are dying or are seriously ill are 'overwhelmed by circumstance' and dying or serious illness, or those with mental health issues are considered devoid of the ability to make an informed choice and so they are considered incompetent. It is to be noted that euthanasia is only permitted (in countries that permit euthanasia) where the person is fully and freely making the decision to end their life.

In *An NHS Trust v Mother and others* [2024] EWHC 2207 (Fam) the trust made an application to the court to permit forced feeding and restraint in order to so of a 12 year old girl with anorexia with which the parents were in agreement. However a potential conflict between the Code of Practice under the Mental Health Act 1983 and what was lawful where a patient was not compulsorily detained under s 2 or s 3 of the Act arose which may be the subject of a later challenge.

Wardship – trump card

Even if an adolescent is Gillick competent, there is no absolute right for a competent minor under 16 to refuse treatment, which also applies to an adolescent of 16 to 17 years. Gillick competent minors do not stand on the same ground as 'competent' adults, since a finding of competence is not determinative and welfarism supervenes. The court trumps the adolescent's wishes by invoking the inherent jurisdiction/ wardship jurisdiction. Judges have repeatedly said that, even where the adolescent is competent, he or she does not have the right of veto. Inspection of the case law demonstrates that the weight attached to the adolescent's wishes depends on the issue and the consequences that would flow should an adolescent's wishes be allowed to prevail. Especially in cases where the adolescent's decision may lead to their own death their right to autonomy is suspended as in *Re X (A Child)* [2020] EWHC 3003 (Fam).

'Gillick competent': enough rope but not to hang themselves

Wardship allows the court to act on behalf of the adolescent. It has been said of the wardship jurisdiction that it is a protective cloak (discussed in Chapter 13), but, looked at through the eyes of an adolescent, it may well be perceived as a fearsome obstacle which denies their autonomy.

Of wardship Lord Donaldson said in *Re W* [1992] 9 BMLR 22 [33], [1993] Fam 64 [81]):

> the inherent powers of the court under its parens patriae jurisdiction are theoretically limitless and that they certainly extend beyond the powers of a natural parent. . . . There can therefore be no doubt that it has power to override the refusal of a minor, whether over the age of 16 or under that age but 'Gillick competent'. It does not do so by ordering the doctors to treat, which, even if within the court's powers, would be an abuse of them, or by ordering the minor to accept treatment, but by authorising the doctors to treat the minor in accordance with their clinical judgment, subject to any restrictions which the court may impose.

In *South Glamorgan v W and B* [1993] 1 FLR 574, a 15-year-old adolescent who suffered from depression refused to undergo psychiatric assessment, which she was permitted to refuse under CA 1989, s 38(6). Douglas Brown J said: 'I am not prepared to find on that evidence that she is "*Gillick* incompetent",' and then went on to exercise the inherent jurisdiction to overrule her refusal.

In *Re C (Detention: Medical Treatment)* [1997] 2 FLR 180, a 16-year-old adolescent girl was suffering from anorexia. She refused recommended treatment and absconded from the clinic. The local authority applied for an order authorising her detention in the clinic. The court ruled that:

> *that power included the authorisation of her detention in the clinic for the purposes of treatment, and the power to authorise the use of reasonable force if necessary for that purpose. The precedent set in* Re W *(a minor) (Consent to Medical Treatment) was followed.*

The adolescent who achieves competence will little understand how, having won the first round of the fight in satisfying the competence threshold, they are then prevented from realising their wishes. And so, the dilemma for adolescents persists. On the one hand the courts have a duty to respect the child and the wishes of the adolescent and even more so the older the adolescent, however, where those wishes are considered to conflict with what the court considers is best for their welfare, then the inherent protective jurisdiction of wardship is invoked. The courts have repeatedly taken the stance that their duty is to keep adolescents alive to reach majority. Who can blame them for that! Lord Justice Nolan in *Re W* [1992] earlier, said it was the duty of the court to keep an adolescent alive until they attained 18 years. Lord Donaldson said: 'As I put it in the course of the argument, and as I sincerely believe, "good parenting involves giving minors as much rope as they can handle without an unacceptable risk that they will hang themselves".'

The competent/incompetent putative transgender adolescent

Here, the question arose as to whether children under 16 who experience gender dysphoria would be deemed by the court to be capacitious, that is to say to have the capacity to consent to treatment that inhibits and blocks puberty and even if deemed competent would a court allow them to access treatment? Gender dysphoria is a state of being where one's sex assigned at birth does not align with one's perceived gender. Some children experiencing psychological consequences of this dysphoria seek treatment to enable transition before adulthood. Puberty for such individuals is traumatic as it is a physical manifestation of the body and sex, which they have feared they would become. Recognised treatment with puberty blockers pauses the changes of breast development or facial hair; later treatments from 16 years of age may include cross sex hormones including estrogen for a person transitioning to the female gender and testosterone for a person transitioning to the male gender. In 2019/2020, 161 children under 16 were referred by GIDS to the trust for puberty blockers, of whom three were aged 10 or 11, thirteen were aged 12, ten were aged 13, twenty-four were aged 14, forty-five were aged 15, fifty-one were aged 16, and fifteen were aged 17 or 18. The number of referrals to GIDS has increased from 97 in 2009 to 2,519 in 2019 (reported in *Bell and another v Tavistock and Portman NHS Foundation Trust (University College London Hospitals NHS Foundation Trust and others intervening)* [2021] EWCA Civ 1363 [20]). Until 2011, PBs were only available at GIDS for those aged 16 or older. In 2011, PBs started to be prescribed for those aged 12–15 and in mid-puberty.

The Divisional Court in *Bell and another v Tavistock and Portman NHS Foundation Trust (University College London Hospitals NHS Foundation Trust and others intervening)* [2020] EWHC 3274 (Admin) before the President of the Queen's Bench Division, Lord Justice Lewis and Mrs Justice Lieven, in a claim for judicial review of the competence of children to consent to puberty blocker treatment for gender dysphoria ruled that children and young persons under 18 are not competent to give consent to the administration of puberty blocking drugs [90] nor are parents in executing parental responsibility on their own behalf.

The claimant Quincy (Keira) Bell, who transitioned from male to female and is now in the process of transitioning back to female, and Mrs A (the mother of a child who theoretically might be offered puberty blocker treatment) challenged: 'the continuing practice of [Tavistock] through its [GIDS], to prescribe puberty-suppressing hormone blockers to children under the age of 18 who experience gender dysphoria'. It was described as a "continuing activity or policy" [4] [2021] judgment]. The relief they sought was a declaration that Tavistock's *current practice of prescribing hormone blocking treatment to children which is anticipatory of, and inextricably linked to, cross-sex hormone treatment, absent an order from the Court in its welfare jurisdiction that the treatment is in the child's best interest, is unlawful.*

([4] of 2021 judgment)

The court considered whether [133] a young person under the age of 16 could achieve Gillick competence in respect of the decision to take PBs for GD, and in respect of a young person aged 16 or over, given that for those 16–17 years of age s 8 of the FLRA 1969 there is a presumption of capacity, would their consent be determinative [146]. The court concluded that:

[151] A child under 16 may only consent to the use of medication intended to suppress puberty where he or she is competent to understand the nature of the treatment. That includes an understanding of the immediate and long-term consequences of the treatment, the limited evidence available as to its efficacy or purpose, the fact that the vast majority of patients proceed to the use of cross-sex hormones, and its potential life changing consequences for a child. There will be enormous difficulties in a child under 16 understanding and weighing up this information and deciding whether to consent to the use of puberty blocking medication. It is highly unlikely that a child aged 13 or under would be competent to give consent to the administration of puberty blockers. It is doubtful that a child aged 14 or 15 could understand and weigh the long-term risks and consequences of the administration of puberty blockers. [152] Given the long-term consequences of the clinical interventions at issue in this case and given that the treatment is as yet innovative and experimental, we recognise that clinicians may well regard these as cases where the authorisation of the court should be sought prior to commencing the clinical treatment. [153]. We have granted a declaration to reflect the terms of this judgment.

On appeal to the Court of Appeal in *Bell and another v Tavistock and Portman NHS Foundation Trust (University College London Hospitals NHS Foundation Trust and others intervening)* [2021] EWCA Civ 1363, Lord Burnett of Maldon LCJ, Sir Geoffrey Vos, Master of the Rolls, and Lady Justice King, the Court of Appeal ruled:

[86] Moreover, the effect of the guidance was to require applications to the court in circumstances where the Divisional Court itself had recognised that there was no legal obligation to do so. It placed patients, parents, and clinicians in a very difficult position. In practice the guidance would have the effect of denying treatment in many circumstances for want of resources to make such an application coupled with inevitable delay through court involvement. Furthermore, the guidance that there should be an application to the court in circumstances where child, parents and clinicians all consider the treatment to be in the best interests of the child would be inconsistent with the conclusion of the Supreme Court in An NHS Trust. . . . And as such was wrong in law.

In *AB v CD and Ors* [2021] EWHC 741 (Fam), AB sought a declaration that a mother with parental responsibility was empowered to consent to the administration of Puberty Blockers on behalf of a 15-year-old daughter. Lieven J said: 'the very essence of Gillick is in my view, that a parent's right to consent or determine treatment cannot trump or overbear the decision of the child.'

Adolescent participation in legal proceedings

A child's voice and participation have a place in family proceedings cases. A child's voice may be heard in mediation appointments as well as up unto the more formal involvement of a child in participating in family proceedings. Such formal participation may involve being joined as a party to the proceedings or being a party to the proceedings in their own right. It may involve dispensing with a guardian and instructing a solicitor. Such adolescent participation is involved where applications are made for CA, s 8 child arrangement orders for residence, contact, prohibited steps and specific issues or for other applications including care, supervision or adoption. Section 10(8) of CA 1989 provides that leave to make an application may only be granted if the court is satisfied that the child has sufficient understanding to make the proposed application. As Williams J said in *CS v SBH and others* [2019] EWHC 634 (Fam):

> [51] *The decision of the House of Lords in* Gillick v West Norfolk and Wisbech AHA *[1985] UKHL 7 [1986] AC 112, remains the cornerstone of our current approach to questions relating to the capacity or competence of a child or young person to take decisions for themselves.*

Where the child wants to join the proceedings as a party, Rule 16 (2) provides that the court may make a child a party to proceedings if it is in their best interests. A child should only be joined as a party if the facts of the case demand it and with guidance offered as to what circumstances might justify this decision. (See Enhancing the Participation of Children and Young People in Family Proceedings: Starting the Debate [12].)

Being joined as a party means that the joined party can have access to the court documents submitted in evidence and have a bigger role in the proceedings (see Part 16 Representation of children and reports in proceedings involving children).

Test of competency

The child will need to satisfy the test of competency which is governed by the Family Proceedings Rules 1991 (SI 1991/1247 (L 20)), r 9.2A (as inserted by Family Proceedings (Amendment) Rules 1992 (SI 1992/456 (L 1)), r 9), detailed by Sir Thomas Bingham MR in *Re S (A Minor) (Independent Representation)* [1993] 2 FLR 437. The rules apply only to proceedings under the 1989 Act or the inherent jurisdiction of the High Court with regard to minors. Each decision made by the court is fact specific as the cases that follow demonstrate.

The rule distinguishes between those cases where a minor wishes to begin or continue with the proceedings without a next friend or to defend proceedings without a guardian having never had one, or where the minor has had a next friend or guardian but wishes to dispense with the guardian or next friend and continue the proceedings without them. In the first situation the minor must be considered to have sufficient understanding to participate; second, the minor must be capable of giving instructions. Sir Thomas Bingham in *Re S* (1993) in referring to the authorities' states: 'We accept that what has come to be known as "Gillick competence" is the appropriate test in relation to the sufficiency of a child's understanding under the Act and rules.' The earlier case law reflects a reluctance with which adolescent participation in legal proceedings was regarded.

Not old enough or not of sufficient understanding

Age has been considered by the courts to be an important starting point for assessments of competency for legal participation. Sir Thomas Bingham in *Re S* (1993) did not consider a 12-year-old boy old enough to fully participate. In the course of divorce proceedings, the son S, aged 12, asked for leave to make an application for a residence order. S wanted to live with his father. He was fearful that unless he was able to make representations to the court, the court would attach insufficient weight to his wishes.

> *The Official Solicitor's recommendation to the court, supported by the consultant psychiatrist, is that S should continue to live with his mother but should continue to have contact with his father, although less often than at present. The father challenges that recommendation and contends that S should live with him. In this he is supported by S. It is this divergence of view between S and the Official Solicitor as his guardian ad litem which gives rise to the present appeal.*

On appeal, Sir Thomas Bingham, said: 'The judge's conclusion that this boy lacks sufficient understanding to participate as a party in these emotionally complex and highly fraught proceedings is impregnable.'

The court referred to three other cases supporting its opinion: *In Re H (Minors)* (unreported) 6 August 1992; Transcript No. 769 of 1992, a case concerning children aged 10 and 7, Butler-Sloss LJ said: 'I would expect that rule 9.2A would be extremely valuable for the older teenager and is most unlikely to be used in regard to younger children.' In *Re T (A Minor) child representation* [1993] 3 WLR 602, Thorpe J in proceedings launched under rule 9.2A by a 13-year-old without a guardian said: 'with a child of only 13 years of age, I doubt whether, on an application for leave, I would have been persuaded that she had sufficient understanding to participate without the aid of a guardian'. In *Re H (A Minor) (Care Proceedings)* [1993] 3 WLR 1109, Thorpe J rejected a submission that almost any child of 15 years and eight months must be taken to have sufficient understanding to instruct a solicitor (p 340). In *H*, a ward of court and the defendant, in wardship proceedings, applied to continue the proceedings without the Official Solicitor acting as his guardian ad litem. The application was opposed by the Official Solicitor and the boy's parents. It was accepted by the boy that if the Official Solicitor was removed as guardian ad litem he should remain in the case as amicus curiae. Granting the application, that in the circumstances of the case, the court was satisfied that the child had a sufficient understanding to participate as a party in the proceedings without a guardian ad litem; that there was clearly a role for the Official Solicitor to play when removed from the post of guardian ad litem in order for a child to instruct his own solicitor; and that, accordingly, in such circumstances the role of amicus should be (at 1110) extended so that the Official Solicitor could act as an independent adviser to the court, but that it would not be appropriate for the Official Solicitor when invited to act as amicus to be joined as a party to the proceedings (1114B, H,–1115D).

In *Re N (Contact: Minor Seeking Leave to Defend and Removal of Guardian)* [2003] 1 FLR 652, a boy of 11 years and four months wished to remove the guardian ad litem (children's guardian). Coleridge J held:

> I have come to the conclusion that in this particular case and against the background of this particular long and stormy application, L does not have sufficient understanding to participate in the proceedings and give instructions that are fully considered, in the sense of fully considered as to their implications. His wishes and feelings are clear beyond any doubt. That the guardian has communicated those to the court on numerous occasions is also beyond any doubt. He feels that he has not been listened to. What that means in practice, however, of course to an adolescent is that the adults are not doing what he wants. That is very often the state of affairs in applications similar to this.

The court dismissed the applications by the adolescent for leave to defend the proceedings and for removal of the guardian.

In *Re A (Contact Order)* [2010] EWCA Civ 208, per Wall LJ at [43] [44] a 12-year-old who wished to be separately represented was refused separate representation. In care proceedings the local authority sought to terminate contact between R, a 12-year-old boy, and his mother. His parents sought to remove the guardian and replace his solicitor on the basis that the guardian, while supporting R's wish to continue to have contact was presenting the case as she saw it and not as R saw it. The trial judge refused the application on the basis that although the child was bright and articulate, he lacked the maturity to comprehend and weigh all the complex considerations involved and to reach a proportionate, balanced consideration. The appeal was dismissed. Lord Justice Thorpe was clear the trial judge's decision was the correct one.

> *There are cases involving children in post-pubertal adolescent rebellion for whom it is very difficult for a guardian to act. Their position, their wishes, their feelings, their opinions so conflict with an objective view of welfare that there has to be a parting of the ways, and our system generously provides for two distinct and equally constituted litigation teams thereafter. That is an extremely expensive solution, and in present days when the family justice system is obliged to seek economy wherever and whenever it can, orders granting separate representation under this rule should, in my opinion, be issued very sparingly. This was a perfectly standard situation in which the child's wishes were only an ingredient within the review of the guardian and only one element upon which the guardian had to report to the court [145].*

Simply inappropriate

Whilst competency is the test judges have also been influenced by the moral dimension and have made subjective judgements about whether such a child should be joined as a party or separately represented in cases that also involve their parents.

In *Re C (A Minor) (Care: Child's Wishes)* (1993) a single parent father of 64 years of age and in poor health was solely responsible for the upbringing of two children, a girl of 13 and a boy of 12 years. The girl was arrested for shoplifting. She and her friend had reported to the police incidents which involved their ill treatment and rape by male friends of her father. The local authority applied to remove her from her father and place her in their care. The court made a care order. The girl wanted to remain with her father, and the father appealed. His appeal to the Family Division of the High Court was dismissed. Waite J said that that the father was unable to meet the girl's needs:

> I agree with comments that were made by her guardian ad litem, both in the original report and in evidence on this appeal. Those are to the effect that C is too young to carry the burden of decisions about her own future, and too young to have to bear the weight of responsibility for a parent who lacks authority and plays on her feelings of protectiveness.

And later, Waite J said: 'She would be sad, of course, but she must learn and be helped to make the best of it.' Waite J also added that young children should be discouraged from attending High Court appeals since, even where children are competent to assess the situation, it was simply inappropriate. The adolescent's wishes were overridden because the court considered that the threshold of significant harm CA 1989, s 100(4)(b) had been met. 'C is too young to carry the burden of decisions about her future', and participation in court proceedings should be avoided because 'it undermines the stability and lightness of heart which could be called the natural birthright of every child'.

Judges have also expressed a concern that independent participation may embolden children in battles with parents (see Houghton-James 1994). *Re C (a Minor) (Leave to Seek Section 8 Orders)* [1994] 1 FLR 26 involved a 15-year-old girl's application for a specific issue order regarding a holiday and a residence order to confirm the lawfulness of her living with her friend's family instead of her own. The court said that if she were to be given leave, 'C might interpret being given leave as having achieved some advantage against her parents in a situation where she should be dealing directly with them.'

In *Re H (Residence Order: Child's Application for Leave)* [2000] 1 FLR 780, a 12-year-old sought leave to apply for a residence order to reside with the father. He felt that unless he was able to make representations to the court on his own behalf then little weight would be attached to his views. In this case, leave was refused by Johnson J who considered it disadvantageous in the family situation of a child seeing all the evidence in a case between the parents. He went on: 'there would be the spectre (a word I choose deliberately) of a mother being faced across courtroom by solicitor or counsel acting on behalf of the child she bore'.

However, where the matter of return following removal to another jurisdiction is concerned and the adolescent objects, international conventions take a more liberal view. The Hague Convention on the Civil Aspects of International Child Abduction special provision Art 13(b) more readily recognises autonomy no doubt because of the draconian consequences of a child not wishing to return to the other parent (discussed in Chapter 12). (See International parental child abduction.)

How far attitudes have developed regarding the participation of the child in the proceedings is still a matter of considerable disagreement. In *Re W (children) (Abuse: Oral Evidence)* [2010] EWCA Civ 57 when RW wished to give evidence and was heard in the Court of Appeal it was suggested that the whole issue of children giving evidence should be reviewed by the Family Justice Council. But in *Re M (A child)* [2010] UKSC 12, whilst the presumption was removed against children giving evidence unless exceptional circumstances Hughes LJ said:

> *Whatever Re W (children) may say about a necessary change in practice in relation to the starting point in relation to children of that age, I have no doubt at all that they would never have been and should not be even now.*

Changing attitudes?

Re W (a child) (public law proceedings: child's separate representation) [2016] EWCA Civ 1051 the Court of Appeal considered the issue as to separate representation of a child in public law proceedings. In this case there was conflict between the child and the guardian's instructions. The issue was whether the girl was able, having regard to her understanding, to give her own instructions. It was held that the issue of separate representation was to be considered alongside the developments in relation to children giving evidence as highlighted by *Re F (Children)* [2016] EWCA Civ 546. The court held in this case:

> *A judge should be very slow to reach a conclusion that the understanding of a child, who had previously instructed a solicitor and was now a year older, had diminished. The fact that a child's view coincided with that of her parents does not necessarily mean it was not her own view or that she did not have sufficient understanding to instruct a solicitor. Insufficient weight had been given to matters such as the child's age and her history of instructing her own solicitor. The child should have been permitted to instruct a solicitor.*

(See Practice Direction 16A Part 4, President's Direction (Representation of Children in Family Proceedings Pursuant to Family Proceedings Rules 1991 Rule 9.5) [2004] 1 FLR 1188.)

In a very complex case, *Re C (Child: Ability to Instruct Solicitor)* [2023] EWCA Civ 889, the Court of Appeal found the boy had been alienated by the father and where the boy was critical of the family justice system the Court of Appeal held that he had wrongly been allowed to instruct his own solicitor in care proceedings and said:

> *(1) The decision that the boy had the ability to instruct a solicitor directly was wrong in the distinctive circumstances of the case. Part 16 of the FPR 2010 and PD 16A and the*

authorities showed that the assessment of whether a child had the ability to instruct a solicitor was based on a broad consideration of all relevant factors and opinions from solicitors and experts: Re W (Representation of Child) *[2016] EWCA Civ 1051, [2017] 2 FLR 199. It was case specific and driven by a practical assessment of the child's understanding in the particular context of the case.*

Competent – in family proceedings

Where the minor is considered competent in respect of the matter before the court, it is likely that the wishes of the child concur with the decision the court would in any event have made. In *Re H (A Minor) (Care Proceedings: Child's Wishes)* [1993] 3 WLR 1109, 1 FLR 440, a 15½-year-old male adolescent had been made a ward of court on the application of his parents. His parents and sister went to live in France when H was 14. He stayed in England and lived with the R family. Mr R was later arrested for sexual offences against another boy and the local authority removed H, his parents taking him back to France. He ran away and returned to England and was in the care of another family, wishing to have nothing to do with his own family. He was receiving counselling and had made a suicide attempt. The Official Solicitor was acting as guardian ad litem. The adolescent applied to have him removed (under CA 1989, s 6(7)(b)) and to have his own solicitor, as he did not feel that the Official Solicitor was representing his views. His application was granted, and the court said the test was that the court must be satisfied that he had sufficient understanding to participate as a party in the proceedings without guardian ad litem (give evidence, be cross-examined, etc) and that the test for understanding is that the adolescent must understand what is happening now and what will happen in the future. Booth J stated: 'This is an exceptional case' (and perhaps took a unique view). But, in our view, what is exceptional in this case is the fact that judicial paternalism did not render the adolescent incompetent. What is best for the adolescent, the court said, was not correctly an issue for them:

> *[I]n those circumstances, I am satisfied that H has sufficient understanding to participate as a party in the proceedings and should be permitted to do so. It is not for the court in applying that test to take into account what the court may or may not consider to be in the best interests of the child . . . I will remove the Official Solicitor and will allow H to instruct his own solicitors, but I will invite the Official subject to his consent to do so, to act as amicus to the court.*

Similarly, in *Re SC (A Minor)* [1993] 1 FLR 431, an adolescent female aged 15 years who was living in a children's home wished to apply for a residence order to allow her to live in the home of a long-standing friend. An application under CA 1989, s 10(1)(a)(ii) was transferred to the High Court. The court was satisfied that the adolescent had sufficient understanding to make a s 8 application as required by CA 1989, s 10(8). She was granted leave.

In *Re T (Wardship)* [1993] 2 FLR 278, the court upheld the right of a 13-year-old girl to represent her case, where T had contended on her appeal that once she had satisfied her solicitor that she had the required degree of understanding to give him instructions, she was entitled to make her own judgement as to what those instructions might be.

In *Re C (Residence: Child's Application for Leave)* [1995] 1 FLR 927, the child's parents had separated and initially there was an order that she and her brother should live with their mother. In 1992, it was ordered that the child should live with the father. There were contact difficulties and at Christmas 1994 the child (aged 14 years) remained with the mother. The adolescent sought leave to make an application under the CA 1989, s 8, that she be permitted to live with the mother. The court granted the application.

The more recent case law

For the more recent jurisprudence see the following cases, *Re LC (International Abduction: Child's Objections to Return)* [2013] EWCA Civ 1058, [2014 1 FLR 1458, *Re M (Republic of Ireland) (Child's Objections) (Joinder of Children as Parties to Appeal)* [2015] 2 FLR 1074, and *Re W (representation of child)* [2017] 2 FLR 199.

In *Re CS (Appeal FPR 2010, Rule 16.6: Sufficiency of Child's Understanding)* [2019] EWHC 634 (Fam), [2019] 2 FLR 580 in the course of preliminary hearing a dispute arose as to who should act for the child in a matter as to with whom the child should live. [6] The child had been a party to the proceedings with a guardian appointed for her pursuant to FPR 16.4 and a solicitor appointed who was not the solicitor. The child's wish was to live with her mother. The child wrote several letters to the judge.

> The court remained the ultimate arbiter of whether a child had understanding or sufficient understanding to act without a children's guardian. The Queen's Bench Division ruled in determining preliminary issues which arose concerning the dismissal of a mother's application to vary an order that the child live with her father (the decision). The court held that an appeal against the decision was a continuation of the first instance proceedings and, accordingly, FPR 16.6(5) (concerning a child's application for the removal of the litigation friend or children's guardian) applied. It further held that, on the facts of the case, the child did not have sufficient understanding to conduct an appeal without a children's guardian, that the guardian who had been appointed in the earlier proceedings remained appointed, and that the solicitor appointed by that guardian was not obliged to conduct the proceedings in accordance with instructions received from the child but, rather, in accordance with instructions received from the guardian.

Judicial activism or judicial paternalism

The family court recognises that judicial paternalism, espoused by Lord Donaldson in *Re R* (1992) above and *Re W* (1992) above, must be balanced against adolescent participation both in 'consent to' and 'refusal of consent' to treatment and in participation in hearings that affect them and their right to autonomy. Munby LJ is determined that adolescent rights and autonomy is a principle not merely to be realised but to be defended. Thorpe LJ is of like mind, in defending the importance of legal principle over consequences in embracing adolescent rights. Johnson J recognises even if reluctantly, that the wishes of a 'Gillick competent' adolescent cannot simply be held back.

The post 2004 legal landmarks however are cases which do not involve life and death or serious welfare matters. In *Re P* (2004) discussed earlier, although Johnson J did not accede to the adolescent's wishes, nonetheless in his judgment and reasoning he demonstrated that judges no longer could justify making a decision contrary to an adolescent's wishes merely on the basis of outcomes. As Johnson J said:

> In the words of Balcombe LJ. in Re W (A Minor) (Medical Treatment: Court's Jurisdiction) [1993] As children approach the age of majority, they are increasingly able to take their own decisions concerning their medical treatment. . . . It will normally be in the best interests of a child of sufficient age and understanding to make an informed decision that the court should respect its integrity as a human being and not lightly override its decision on such a personal matter as medical treatment. All the more so if that treatment is invasive.

In *Re Roddy (A Child) (Identification: Restriction on Publication)* [2003] EWHC 2927 (Fam), the question arose as to whether Angela, who was 16 years old, was entitled to sell her story to the media. She had been in care, had given her child up for adoption and there was an injunction preventing publicity made. She wished to vary that injunction so she could tell her story. The lawyers acting for her couched her case in terms of Article 8 and 10 of the ECHR, on the basis that a child or an adolescent is equally entitled to protection by the ECHR rights. Munby J in true Denningesque style, so reminiscent of Lord Denning in *Hewer v Bryant* [1970] 1 QB 357 (see Chapter 9), said:

> We no longer treat our 17-year-old daughters as our Victorian ancestors did, and if we try to do so it is at our – and their – peril. . . . She is what Ward LJ described in Re Z [1996] 2 FCR 164 at 189, [1995] 4 All ER 961 at 984 as a 'competent teenager taking (her) story to the press'. She is, to use the language of Woolf J (as he then was) in Gillick's Case [1984] 1 All ER 365 at 373–374, [1984] QB 581 at 596: 'capable of making a reasonable assessment of the advantages and disadvantages' of what is proposed. In my judgment (and I wish to emphasise this) it is the responsibility – it is the duty – of the court not merely to recognise but, as Nolan LJ said, to defend what, if I may respectfully say so, he correctly described as the right of the child who has sufficient understanding to make an informed decision, to make his or her own choice. . . . For, as Balcombe LJ recognised, the court must recognise the child's integrity as a human being. And we do not recognise Angela's dignity and integrity as a human being – we do not respect her rights under arts 8 and 10 – unless we acknowledge that it is for her to make her own choice, and not for her parents or a judge or any other public authority to seek to make the choice on her behalf.

In *Axon v Secretary of State for Health and the Family Planning Association* [2006] 2 WLR 1130, the contest was between the parent and the local health authority, and the issue concerned whether the adolescent had the right to determine her contraceptive treatment unimpeded, or with no interference by parental wishes, and in the absence of their knowledge. The matter was the substance of *Gillick* and arguably had already been decided in 1986. However, in the case of *Axon* what was new was the advent of the HRA 1998; the emergence of the right to family life (Art 8) and how broadly that Article could be construed. Mrs Axon, through judicial review, challenged the lawfulness of the 2004 guidance. The new guidance had extended the remit of matters over which a doctor could treat an adolescent patient to include sexually transmitted diseases and abortion; in addition, the guidance stated that involving parents would be considered to be the exception. Silber J asserted at [86]:

> The speeches of Lord Fraser, Lord Scarman and Lord Bridge do not indicate or suggest that their conclusions depended in any way upon the nature of the treatment proposed because the approach in their speeches was and is of general application to all forms of medical advice and treatment.

The court concluded (per Silber J) that the parental right to respect for privacy of family life 'dwindles as their child gets older' [129]. He went on to assert that: 'the parent only retains such rights to family life and to be notified about medical treatment if but only if the young person so wishes', and declaring that Article 8 was not engaged, he said:

> A third reason why I do not consider that the 2004 Guidance interferes with any article 8 rights of a parent is that it is established that a child's article 8 rights overrides similar rights of a parent . . . where the rights under article 8 of the parents and those of the child are at stake, the child's rights must be the paramount consideration.

The case of *Mabon v Mabon and others* (2005), earlier, raised the issue of the adolescent's right to representation in a private law dispute. The applicants were three boys aged 17, 15 and 13, each of whom wanted their own solicitor and each to be separately represented in their parents' dispute, which involved residence and contact. The judge in the court of first instance found that they failed the test of competence under r 9.2A (6) Family Proceedings Rules 1991 (SI 1991/1247). His Honour Judge Dixon found that involvement in the proceedings in this way would result: 'in unquantifiable emotional damage from contact with the material in this case' (quoted by Thorpe LJ [18]). Thorpe LJ in the Court of Appeal said that it was simply unthinkable to exclude young men from knowledge of and participation in legal proceedings that affected them so fundamentally. They had been seen by an experienced family practitioner who had no doubts as to the sufficiency of their understanding: they were educated, articulate and reasonably mature for their respective ages. Thorpe LJ said:

> Unless we in this jurisdiction are to fall out of step with similar societies as they safeguard art 12 rights, we must, in the case of articulate teenagers, accept that the right to freedom of expression and participation outweighs the paternalistic judgment of welfare.
> (also cited in *D (A Child) & Anr (2016)* [2016] EWCA Civ 12 [47])

In *the Matter of J (Children)* [2009] EWCA Civ 365, the question of the weight to be given to Gillick competent children/adolescents, who have expressed a specific wish, arose. Two boys who were the subject of a care order: namely S, 16 years of age, and Adam, 14 years of age, applied for permission to appeal the order of His Honour Judge Newton, in which he dismissed their application to discharge a care order made by him in February 2008.

In *C (Child: Ability to instruct a solicitor)* [2023] EWCA Civ 889), a 14-year-old boy, A, was allowed to instruct his own solicitor in proceedings brought by his parents to discharge care orders in respect of him and his sister B, who was 13. The care orders were made to protect the children from parental conflict and from behaviour by their father that had severely alienated them from their mother. Prior to the decision the judge had met with A. The mother appealed. The Court of Appeal said: '[72] I have nevertheless concluded, with real reluctance, that the decision that A has the ability to instruct a solicitor directly was wrong in the distinctive circumstances of this case.'

It still remains as Sir Thomas Bingham MR in *Re S (A Minor) (Independent Representation)* [1993] Fam 263, 276G, [1993] 2 FLR 437, 445: expressed it:

> any solicitor accepting instructions from a child in this situation must exercise a scrupulous, conscientious and responsible judgment.
>
> (See Zakaria 2023)

End game – a matter for Parliament!

Of course, the cases of *Roddy* and *Mabon* rest on the right to publicity and private law, matters of residence and contact and legal representation. The decisions of the parties involved do not result in any serious or significant harm. Johnson J in *P* was dealing with a life and death issue and his judgment clearly reflects his own disquiet with the position he found himself in and his part in enforcing a decision on a recalcitrant adolescent on no other basis than that the decision the adolescent would otherwise wish to make was irreversible and in extremis.

Death is a terrible consequence, and others might argue that forcible sedation of minors is inhumane. The judge in the court of first instance in *Mabon* considered the process of litigation involving adolescents to have terrible consequences.

What should the law's primary focus be – the empowerment of young people? the protection of their right to autonomy? (See Fortin 2006). And what if in the exercise of that right they are positively harmed? Where does the court stand then, does it have a duty to protect them from such harm as Nolan LJ has asserted? The contemporary vexed moral question is this: on the one hand the courts have a contract with the welfare of the child as paramount principle, so as Nolan LJ in *Re W (A Minor) (Medical Treatment: Court's Jurisdiction)* [1993] Fam 64, said: 'it is the duty of the court to ensure so far as it can that children survive to attain that age (majority)'. On the other hand, the courts have a contract with the adolescent in international and domestic conventions to respect their wishes. Yet the courts will draw a line and suspend the adolescent's right to expression and self-determination if it considers that the adolescent requires protection from him or herself and will not, to use Lord Donaldson's expression, give the adolescent enough rope to hang himself, and will instead delay death, as it did in E, *Re E (A Minor) (Wardship: Medical Treatment)* [1993] 1 FLR 386, who when an adolescent, the court compelled to undergo a life-saving blood transfusion. Ward J said in his judgment that in later years, E would be likely to 'suffer some diminution in his convictions'. When E reached the age of 18 years, he demonstrated that his convictions were as strong as they had ever been, and he exercised his right as a competent adult to refuse treatment when he later needed it. As a result of his refusal, he died. (See *Re G* (2012)[81].)

What should the law do? Should it be bound by principle and embrace Gillick competence and thereby let the living die, or perhaps find something more workable and moral solution perhaps by excluding cases involving death as a consequence from the competence consideration. Or is this too much interference with individual liberty and we remain with the charade of deciding whether competent or not competence and with wardship trumping all. The right of self-determination for Jehovah's Witnesses and for those seeking gender dysphoria treatment has been passed up from the courts to Parliament.

We are reminded that perhaps we really have not come that far when we consider the skeleton argument of Mr Munby QC (as he then was) summarised as follows by Nolan LJ in *Re W* (1992) at 646:

> [1] A judge exercising the inherent jurisdiction in relation to a 16- or 17-year-old child should, as a matter of course, ascertain the wishes of the child. [2] In the case of all normal surgical, medical, or dental treatment the child's decision should determine the matter, whether or not the court thinks this is in the child's best interests. [3] There will, however, be cases which are 'extraordinary' or fall into a 'special category'. In such cases, but only in such cases, the child's decision should not be allowed to determine the matter. In such cases the court must give proper weight to the child's wishes, and be slow to reject them, but in the final analysis should be free to determine for itself what the child's best interests require. . . . (4) Included within the 'extraordinary' or 'special' category might be, for example, cases where the child is proposing to submit to a sterilisation, an abortion, the removal of an organ for donation, or some similar non-therapeutic procedure, or where the child is refusing to submit to some procedure necessary to prolong or save the child's life or to protect the child from really serious and irreparable harm.
>
> (Munby LJ's emphasis)

Self-test questions

1. Baroness Hale observed in *Re D (A Child)* (2007):

   'There is a growing understanding of the importance of listening to the children involved in children's cases. It is the child, more than anyone else, who will have to live with what the court decides. Those who do listen to children understand that they often have a point of view which is quite distinct from that of the person looking after them. They are quite capable of being moral actors in their own right. Just as the adults may have to do what the court decides whether they like it or not, so may the child. But that is no more reason for failing to hear what the child has to say than it is for refusing to hear the parents' views.'

In what way and to what extent have the courts embraced the wishes of children and adolescents?

2. 'The post-Gillick case law 40 years on demonstrates that the scope for adolescent self-determination and participation in decisions which affect those under 16 years, remains in practice limited and that judges are reluctant to give effect to the principle of adolescent self-determination even where the adolescent is considered competent to exercise a choice. This is especially so where the consequence of adolescent autonomy is life threatening or else determinative as in gender dysphoria treatment.'

Discuss.

3. A child's voice and participation has a place in family proceedings cases. A child's voice may be heard in mediation appointments as well as up unto the more formal involvement of a child participating in family proceedings. Such formal participation may involve being joined as a party to the proceedings or being a party to the proceedings in their own right.

Discuss the development of this recognition of child autonomy through consideration of the legal cases.

4. Parkinson (2024) asserts: 'Following the UN Convention 1989 on the Rights of the Child, the Brussels II Revised Regulation (Art 4) upheld the child's right to be heard in matters relating to parental responsibility for the child, in accordance with the child's age and maturity. The Council of Europe's Guidelines on Child-Friendly Justice 2010 iv [26] state that the child's right to be heard should be guaranteed both in court and out-of-court proceedings.' The Family Justice Review (Norgrove 2011) advised that children: 'should as early as possible be supported to make their views known and older children should be offered a menu of options to lay out the ways in which they could – if they wish – do this [9]'.

Discuss the importance of these developments and their impact on the domestic law and case determination.

References

Bridge, Caroline, 'Religious Beliefs and Teenage Refusal of Medical Treatment' [1999] *Modern Law Review* 585

Burin, Achas K, 'Beyond Pragmatism: Defending the "Bright Line" of Birth' [2014] *Medical Law Review* 494

Cobb, Neil, 'Seen but Not Heard?' [2015] *Family Law* 144

Coggon, John and José Miola, 'Autonomy, Liberty, and Medical Decision-Making' [2011] *Cambridge Law Journal* 523

Consent to Treatment – Children and Young People – NHS (2024) www.nhs.uk/conditions/consent-to-treatment/children/ (accessed 03.05.2024)

Daniel, Richard, 'Mature Minors and Consent to Treatment: Time for Change' [2009] *International Family Law Journal* 233

Douglas, Gillian, 'The Retreat from Gillick' [1992] *Modern Law Review* 569

Douglas, Mary, *Rules and Meanings* (Penguin 1973)

Enhancing the Participation of Children and Young People in Family Proceedings: Starting the Debate www.judiciary.uk/wp-content/uploads/JCO/Documents/FJC/voc/Participation_of_young_people.pdf [12]

Eskenazi, Delphine and Sarah Williams, 'Trans Gender Matters and Family Law – Comparative European Approaches' [2023] *International Family Law Journal* 149

European Forum on the Rights of the Child 2020 https://commission.europa.eu/ec-events/13th-european-forum-rights-child-towards-eu-strategy-rights-child-2020-09-29_en (accessed 03.05.2024)

Family Mediation Council ('FMC') Code of Practice www.familymediationcouncil.org.uk/us/code-practice/(accessed 03.05.2024)

Fortin, Jane, 'Accommodating Children's Rights in a Post HRA Era' [2006] *Modern Law Review* 299

Fortin, Jane, *Children's Rights and the Developing Law* (Butterworths 2003)

Gilmore, Stephen and Jonathan Herring, '"No" Is the Hardest Word: Consent and Children's Autonomy' [2011] *Child and Family Law Quarterly* 3

Hall, Ananda, 'Children's Rights, Parents' Wishes and the State: The Medical Treatment of Children' [2006] *Family Law* 317

Hirst, Hannah, 'The Legal Rights and Wrongs of Puberty Blocking in England' [2021] *Child and Family Law Quarterly* 115

Hoggett, Brenda, *Parents and Children* (Sweet and Maxwell 1984)

Houghton-James, Hazel, 'Children Divorcing Their Parents' [1994] *Journal of Family and Social Welfare* 185

International Parental Child Abduction www.gov.uk/guidance/international-parental-child-abduction (accessed 03.05.2024)

Jones, Hannah, 'Heart Transplant Patient Reunited with Her Surgeon' *BBC News* www.bbc.co.uk/news/av/uk-43110989 (accessed 03.05.2024)

Jones, Kirsty and Hannah Jones, *Hannah's Choice* (HarperCollins 2010)

Lee, Simon, *Judging Judges* (Faber and Faber 1989)

MacDonald, Alistair, 'The Child's Voice in Private Law: Loud Enough?' (2009) *Family Law* 40

Norgrove, Sir David, 'Family Justice Review, Executive Summary' (2011) para 9 www.gov.uk/government/publications/family-justice-review-final-report (accessed 03.05.2024)

Nuffield Family Justice Observatory www.nuffieldfjo.org.uk/ (accessed 03.05.2024)

Parkinson, Lisa, 'What About Me? It's My Life Too!' [2024] *Family Law* 439

Practice Direction 12D – Inherent Jurisdiction (Including Wardship) Proceedings www.justice.gov.uk/courts/procedurerules/family/practice_directions/pd_part_12d (accessed 03.05.2024)

Practice Direction 16A – Representation of Children www.justice.gov.uk/courts/procedurerules/family/practice_directions/pd_part_16a (accessed 03.05.2024)

Practice Direction Part 16 – Representation of Children and Reports in Proceedings Involving Children (justice.gov.uk) www.justice.gov.uk/courts/procedure-rules/family/parts/part_16 (accessed 03.05.2024)

Radcliffe Hospital Confidentiality Guidelines (Oxford Radcliffe Hospitals Confidentiality Guidelines), July 30, 2007, 2010 Oxford Radcliffe Hospitals NHS Trust www.ouh.nhs.uk/about/information-governance/ (accessed 03.05.2024)

Symonds, Jon, Esther Dermott, Emma Hitchings and Eleanor Staples, 'Separating Families: Experiences of Separation and Support' (2022) Nuffield Family Justice Observatory www.

nuffieldfjo.org.uk/resource/separating-families-experiences-of-separation-and-support (accessed 03.05.2024)

Zakaria, Mitali, 'Assessing Competence and Representing Children on Direct Instructions' [2023] *Family Law* 1138

Ziebart, Daniel, 'Jehovah's Witnesses – Medical Care, Minors and the Religious Rite/Right' [2007] *Denning Law Journal* 219

Further reading

Atkins, Susan and Brenda Hoggett, *Women and the Law* (Routledge 1984)

Bart, Avraham, Georgina Antonia Hall and Lynn Gillam, 'Gillick Competence: An Inadequate Guide to the Ethics of Involving Adolescents in Decision-Making' (2024) *Journal of Medical Ethics* 157

Birch, Jessica, 'Mature Minors and the Refusal of Medical Treatment: A Misuse of Gillick?' Durham theses, Durham University. Durham E-Theses Online (2017)

Clark, Beth A. and Alice Virani, ' "This Wasn't a Split-Second Decision": An Empirical Ethical Analysis of Transgender Youth Capacity, Rights, and Authority to Consent to Hormone Therapy' (2021) *Journal of Bioethical Inquiry* 151

Cretney, Stephen and Judith Masson, *Principles of Family Law* (Sweet and Maxwell 2003)

Diduck, Alison and Felicity Kaganas, Family Law, *Gender, and the State* (Hart 2012)

Douglas, Gillian, 'The Retreat from Gillick' (1992) *Modern Law Review* 569

Fortin, Jane, 'The Gillick Decision – Not Just a High-Water Mark' in Stephen Gilmore, Jonathan Herring and Rebecca Probert (eds) *Landmark Cases in Family Law* (Hart Publications 2011)

Huntington, Clare and Elizabeth S Scott, 'Conceptualizing Legal Childhood in the Twenty-First Century' (2020) *Michigan Law Review* 1371

Raitt, Fiona, 'Hearing Children in Family Law Proceedings: Can Judges Make a Difference?' (2007) *Child and Family Law Quarterly* 204

12

Putting child welfare first in child 'custody' and private disputes

SUMMARY

In this chapter the principle of the welfare of the child in court decision making in private disagreements between parents and those caring for a child who have a legal parental responsibility, takes central place. The welfare principle is the overarching consideration for the court when making a s 8 Children Act (CA) 1989, child arrangement order (CAO) when disputes arise, or when parents separate and live apart with regard to making living and caring arrangements for the child, and contact with other parties including grandparents, siblings, aunts, uncles and other family members. A wide range of matters may arise requiring the courts adjudication including contact between child and parent/carer, regulating any change a parent/carer may wish to make, changing a child's family name, place of residence, matters of schooling, medical treatment, oversees holidays, religious education or leisure pursuits. There are times when prohibiting a party from, for example, removing a child from the jurisdiction will require the courts intervention. Child abduction and relocation, where a parent without a court order takes a child out of the country to a different jurisdiction, is as Thorpe LJ said: 'two sides of the same coin' (Re *G (Children) (Abduction: Children's Objections)* [2010] EWCA Civ 1232). (See also *Bell v Metropolitan Police Commissioner* [2024] EWHC 379 (KB).)

Domestic abuse by a parent towards the other parent or by a parent towards a child may arise. Bellamy and Lord (2003) found that where domestic abuse was a feature, in many cases what commences as an application by the abused party for 'no contact' between the alleged perpetrator and the child may then lead to a public law investigation (s 37 of the CA). Bainham (2013) points to the confluence of private and public law in both directions. In 2016, the Cobb J 'Harm report' published findings from the family courts on the 'Review of Practice Direction 12J FPR 2010 *Child Arrangement and Contact Orders: Domestic Violence and Harm*'. The Practice Direction was first introduced in 2008 which obliged the family judiciary to approach issues of domestic violence by following the directions. By 2024–5 there is evidence and general concern that the directions are not being consistently applied and a 'pro contact' culture persists, and with regard to international child abduction children are being returned to situations where there is domestic abuse.

DOI: 10.4324/9781003435020-12

At the same time despite judicial training (see Judicial College Prospectus 2024) there is criticism of judges who still fail to appreciate the problem of domestic abuse where there is acrimony over separation and child contact notwithstanding guidance under Practice Direction (PD) 12B *Child Arrangements Programme* and Practice Direction (PD) 12J *Child Arrangements & Contact Orders: Domestic Abuse and Harm.*

Sir James Munby in his (2020) lecture 'The Crisis in Private Law' expresses concern over the withdrawal of legal aid from most private law disputes following the Legal Aid, Sentencing and Punishment of Offenders Act (LASPO) (2012) and the impact this has had on children resulting in unacceptable delays to court hearings because of funding. The eligibility requirements for legal aid introduced by LASPO have been challenged under Articles 2, 3, 6 and 8 of the European Convention on Human Rights (ECHR). (See Marshall et al. 2018.) With regard to the exceptional funding provision in *Gudanaviciene & Others v Director of Legal Aid casework and the Lord Chancellor* [2014] Collins J said the guidance issued by the Lord Chancellor is in 'certain respects unlawful', 'too restrictive' and 'not in accordance with the law'. LASPO reform has led to a rise in litigants in person (LIP) from 2014 onwards. By June 2023, the proportion of disposals where neither the applicant nor respondent had legal representation in private law cases had risen to 40 per cent. (See 'A Handbook for Litigants in Person' Figure 4: Proportion of private law disposals by type of legal representation of the parties, January to March 2012 to April to June 2023 and Table 10).

In *R (Rights of Women) v Lord Chancellor and Secretary of State for Justice* [2016] EWCA Civ 91 a challenge was made to LASPO and its impact on protecting women experiencing domestic abuse.

The increases in LIP led in many cases to the empowerment of the perpetrator in court proceedings over child arrangement orders whereby he would through cross examination of the abused party weaponise court hearings and also by making repeated applications following decisions of the court. The Domestic Abuse Act (DAA) 2021 ss 65–67 responded to this situation by inserting a new Part 4B (ss 31Q-31Z) into the Matrimonial and Family Proceedings (MFPA) 1984. This represents a long overdue reform introducing into family proceedings an automatic prohibition on perpetrators or alleged perpetrators of abuse from cross examining their victims.

Notwithstanding Munby LJ's concern with what he calls 'The Crisis in Private Law', a gradual and progressive march towards greater protection of children and provision for their care is demonstrated over the years. Its success depends on raising the public debate, the political obligation, and the quality and courage of advocacy and of judges in all levels of the family courts. This chapter charts the evolution and development of this area of family law and includes some consideration of international child custody cases.

Custody conflict over child arrangements in private law cases becomes very public where high profile parties are concerned. Kelly Clarkson and Brandon Blackstock were locked in conflict and over co-parenting due to the breakdown of trust between them. The court granted Clarkson primary physical custody of daughter and son and is reported to have said: 'The Court finds that under the circumstances present in this case, the interest in providing stability and continuity for the minor children weighs in favor of Petitioner having primary custody.' (See Trepany 2020.)

A conflict over international relocation resulted in the death of two of the parties involved in the following case. In 2023, Stephen Alderton shot dead Joshua Dunmore, his daughter's former partner and the father of the child, and his daughter's former partner's father in the battle for custody over his grandson. His daughter had remarried a US national, and she wanted to take her son (Alderton's grandson) to America. Joshua Dunmore (the child's father) had opposed the application for relocation. Alderton was convicted of manslaughter and a prison sentence of 27 years was handed down. Alderton said he did not know what came over him. (See Moore and Russell 2023.).

Child custody throughout history

The custody of children of marriage throughout history had never been a matter of what was in the interests of the child nor a matter that included any consideration of the mother's interests. Custody of children was a matter of property. At common law children were treated as chattel. (See Montgomery 1988.) As explored in Chapter 9, a father's rights were sacred (see *Re Agar-Ellis* [1883] 24 Ch D 317) and a child had no voice or say in any matter. Prior to this case the Custody of Infants Bill (1839) was debated in the House of Lords reflecting the pressure for reform. Lord Lyndhurst, speaking of the law's cruelty, detailed a case where the mother was completely cut out of any relationship with her child.

> *The father was a French emigrant, who married a woman possessed of some landed property, yielding 700l. a-year. A settlement was made on him on their marriage of the interest of 200l. in the event of his surviving his wife. They had one child, which was an infant at the breast at the time that he referred to. The husband was dissatisfied with the settlement and endeavoured to induce his wife to make a will in his favour. There were reasons which induced her to refuse him. What did he do? He immediately threatened to take possession of the child and take it to the continent by law. The child was not weaned, and the mother, in the greatest distress and agony, thought she had a right to it under the circumstances, and made her escape to her mother's. The father got hold of the child by stratagem, which made it necessary for the mother to make an application to the Lord Chancellor for relief. The case was heard by Lord Eldon; he said he was powerless, and the mother was obliged to see her child put in the care of a stranger. Here was a case of extreme cruelty and hardship, and all inflicted for the basest purposes.*
>   (See Custody of Infants Bill 1839 vol 49 cc485–94)

Lord Wynford considering the interests of children said:

> *That was a wise law, for the father was responsible for the rearing up of the child; but when unhappy differences separated the father and mother, to give the custody of the child to the father, and to allow access to it by the mother, was to injure the child for it was natural to expect that the mother would not instil into the child any respect for the husband whom she might hate or despise. The effects of such a system would be most mischievous to the child and would prevent its being properly brought up.*
>   (Custody of Infants col 492)

Lord Denman said judges found the state of the law 'odious' citing the case of *R v Greenhill* [1836] 4 Ad. & E. 624 before himself and the judges of the Court of

King's Bench, and said that he believed that there was not one judge who had not felt ashamed of the state of the law, and that: 'it was such as to render it odious in the eyes of the country' (Custody of Infants col 493).

Caroline Norton led a campaign to change the law (see Caroline Norton and Angela Burdett-Coutts (2021) YouTube). The Custody of Infants Act (CIA) (1839) permitted a mother to petition the court for custody of her children up to the age of 7, and for access in respect of older children. As Baroness Hale said in her 2023 lecture, 'Matrimony Patriarchy and the Welfare of Children': 'and thus began the long march of statutory intervention to cure the injustice of the common law, a march which only reached its destination in 1973 [at 10.36]'. (See also Abramowicz 1999.)

In that long march Annie Besant was denied the custody of her 8-year-old daughter who was removed from her care (*R v Besant* [1879] NLR 11 Ch D 508). Why? Annie Besant, known as heroine of the East End of London, was many things, including a birth control campaigner having seen the misery of poor families, poverty and deprivation exacerbated by the financial burden of looking after many children, women in poor health and with multiple pregnancies. Women who married in England at that time bore an average of more than six children, and there was a high rate of maternal and infant mortality. In her efforts to alleviate women's suffering Besant republished and updated a pamphlet with Charles Bradlaugh, written by Charles Knowlton entitled 'Fruits of Philosophy: An Essay on the Population Question' (1832) which addressed the issue of birth control, family deprivation and material mortality in childbirth.

In *R v Charles Bradlaugh and Annie Besant* [1877] 2 QBD 569, Bradlaugh and Besant were indicted under the Obscene Publications Act (1857) for conspiracy to corrupt public morals. The jury found that the book was calculated to deprave public morals but exonerated the defendants from any corrupt motives in publishing it. A verdict of guilty was entered. In the later 1879 custody case before James, Baggallay and Bramwell LJJ, the Court of Appeal ruled on two grounds, firstly, on Besant's declaration of being of no religious faith and secondly, her coauthorship of the revision and publication of the pamphlet. The CA concluded:

> *It is impossible for us not to feel that the conduct of the Appellant in writing and publishing such works is so repugnant, so abhorrent to the feelings of the great majority of decent Englishmen and Englishwomen, and would be regarded by them with such disgust, not as matters of opinion, but as violations of morality, decency, and womanly propriety, that the future of a girl brought up in association with such a propaganda would be incalculably prejudiced.*

[521]

It is interesting to note that Dr Henry Allbutt, who had also written a book on birth control, 'The Wife's Handbook,' (1888) opens up the first chapter with this statement: 'From the first marriage-night no woman under forty-five years of age can consider herself Safe,' and in his Preface to the 1888 seventh edition he wrote:

The truth is this – the heads of the medical profession in England are opposed to cheap medical knowledge for the people. They like to keep the poor hard-working man and woman in ignorance of certain important facts. They do not like a poor married woman to know the means by which she can keep from the workhouse by having only as many children as she can bring up in comfort.

Allbutt was never prosecuted in the criminal court, nor did he lose custody of his children, although the Royal Society of Medicine voted in secret to have his name removed from the medical register.

By the Guardianship of Infants Act (GOI) 1925 both parents, mother and father, were placed on an equal footing and the welfare of the child placed as 'the first and paramount consideration' (s 5(1)). Section 6 permitted party to come to court where there were disputes. Section I(1) of the Guardianship Act 1973 reasserted the spirit of the 1925 Act:

> *the court, in deciding that question, shall regard the welfare of the minor as the first and paramount consideration, shall not take into consideration whether from any other point of view the claim of the father . . . in respect of such legal custody, upbringing, administration or application is superior to that of the mother, or the claim of the mother is superior to that of the father.*

When parents fall out today

When parents live separately from one another there may be a dispute between them as to where, and with whom, their children will live. They may agree on a solution out of court (indeed most do) or resort to a court-based resolution of a child arrangement order for residence or contact (s 8 of the CA 1989). Differences of habit, taste, political opinion, interests, faith, culture and background, which seemed so very minor, between the parties, when they were in love, become major battlegrounds now they have fallen out. If the parties form new relationships and new families, a parent may wish to change the child's family name to the name of the new partner so that the child will feel part of the newly constituted family (a change of name is prohibited, unless a 'specific issue order' (s 8 of the CA) has decided the matter in the applicant's favour). A stepfather or stepmother who is now a central part of the child's life may want that parenting arrangement to be formalised through a 'parental responsibility order' (CA 1989, s 4(1)) or a 'special guardianship order' (SGO) or through adoption. Such conflicts relating to care and upbringing may persist throughout the child's minority and become so acrimonious with the parties making repeated court applications contesting orders that are not made in their favour, such that the court in bringing to a halt such aggravated proceedings impose a CA, s 91(14) order. Under s 91(14)(4) there must be a material change of circumstance before leave for any further applications to the court may be granted.

Fortunately, for many children, parents reach amicable agreements in determining what is best for the children of the family without recourse to the courts. Research conducted by Blackwell and Dawe (2003) found that only 10 per cent of parents come to court over contact. No research has been conducted since to determine whether this position has changed. It is likely that with legal aid cuts, austerity, and the move towards mediation and out of court resolution, this percentage has fallen markedly.

In *Re L (A Child) (Internal Relocation: Shared Residence Order)* [2009] EWCA Civ 20, the judge recognised the battle that so frequently ensues:

> *[69] L must therefore be able to appreciate that even though her parents are separated, they have respect for each other. Most disputes about children following parental separation have nothing to do with the children concerned: they are about the parents fighting all over again the battles of the past and seeking retribution for the supposed ills and injustices inflicted on them during the relationship.*

In *The Matter of N (A Child)* [2009] EWHC 1807 (Fam), the unhappiness of litigation is palpably apparent, as Munby J explained.

> *[2] The proceedings began on 17 October 2003, when N was only 2½ years old, and have continued ever since with unabated vigour. The President of the Family Division recently described the attitude of the parents until July 2008 as "acrimonious, confrontational and emotionally fraught in relation to N's residence and parental contact".*

(See also *A v G* [2009] EWHC 736 (Fam) [1].) dispute *A father and another v [Zayn] (through his children's guardian, LC) and another* [2024] EWFC 267 (B).

Impact on children

The impact on children of these 'custody battles' is great.

In *Beale v Beale* [1983] Lexis Citation 1243, the court welfare officer in her report said: 'Gary knows that both parents are fighting over him which, he says, is putting him under a long-term strain; he is trying to be loyal to both parents, but the situation is not doing him any good.' In *Janos v Janos* (25 August 1998, unreported), CA, the court welfare office reported: 'Timothy, reacting to the bonds formed in two opposing directions, is confused. This results in his behaving in a way that is only too familiar to the court.' The child at the centre of *Re O (Contact: Withdrawal of Application)* [2004] 1 FLR 1258 poignantly articulated the experience of the custody battlefield: 'It's like a war. You know they are fighting, and they are fighting over me.' The judge in *JD and Anor v B* [2020] EWFC 16 where there were allegations and cross allegations said: 'In the battle between the parents, both children risk being run over by the tanks.'

Research into the operation of the Family Proceedings Rules 1991, r 9.5 discovered: 'Many contested contact and residence disputes are emotionally abusive to the child, but the parents are so caught up in their petty squabbles they don't see that' (166).

Partnership – conciliation and mediation

The courtroom is a place of last resort; all effort is directed at encouraging parties to resolve matters outside court proceedings. Partnership is a guiding principle where conciliation and mediation in assisting parties towards agreement on parenting is aimed at avoiding court proceedings.

The Family Law Protocol March 2002, now in its fourth iteration 2015, is intended to (a) develop a conciliatory approach to the resolution of family disputes; (b) encourage the narrowing of the issues in dispute; (c) work towards the effective and timely resolution of disputes; (d) minimise any risks to the parties and/or the children; (e) treat safety as a primary concern; (f) have regard to the interests of the children and long-term family relationships; and (g) endeavour to ensure that costs are not unreasonably incurred. The Protocol endorses the Resolution Code of Practice, which is a commitment to resolve disputes in a non-confrontational and constructive way in order to encourage agreements. At a 'first directions hearing' or Conciliation Appointment, it is the duty of the advocate to investigate the issues, inquire into the possibility of a settlement and give directions to the client.

The Principal Registry of the Family Division operates a conciliation scheme (Practice Direction (PD): *Custody and Access* (1982) amended in 1992, 2004 and 2015 PD 12B *Child Arrangements Programme*). Under a district judge's direction (Children: Conciliation) (2004) all s 8 applications for a CAO for residence, contact, specific issue and prohibited steps are automatically placed in the conciliation list to allow both parents to see if an agreement can be reached and where the child is 8 years old or above the child is encouraged to attend. No order can be made at the conciliation appointment unless the parents/parties reach an agreement. If conciliation fails, the court will give directions for the future conduct of the application. (See The Family Procedure (Amendment No. 2) Rules 2023 in force on 8 April 2024.)

Whilst agreement between adult parties outside a court settlement is best, Mant and Wallbank (2017: 150) express the concern that: 'In the neoliberal context of LASPO, mediation has again been promoted as a means of diverting families away from public funding such as legal aid and encouraged them to take responsibility for what are seen as "private" disputes.' Conciliation appointments rose in 2004–2005 to 1,141 from 549 the previous year. Research conducted by Hunt and Roberts (2005) found that 50–95 per cent of mediating parents achieved settlement (cited in Stevenson 2006). Research is desperately needed to shed light on the contemporary situation. Sir Andrew McFarlane P in 'A View from the President's Chambers: July 2023' reported on the success of the two Pathfinder pilot projects in North Wales and Dorset, a project in which the court interacts with separated parents in conflict, with a view to resolving disputes for the benefit of their child. The project allows for information sharing and also giving children a greater say.

Whilst the Government removed legal aid from private family disputes in the LASPO reforms, the Family Mediation voucher scheme was introduced for divorcing and separating couples whether or not they have children and extended to family members, e.g. grandparents, to help settle arrangements for children. Cases eligible for a mediation voucher include a dispute/application regarding a child, a dispute/application regarding family financial matters where a dispute/application relating to a child is also involved. Parties are encouraged to seek legal advice from a solicitor, during and at the end of mediation, to ensure that the agreement reached is best for them. However, the parties in mediation may also need a solicitor to draw up a Court Order to make the agreement formal. The Ministry of Justice (MOJ) conducted research into the Family Mediation Voucher Scheme which was introduced during the pandemic (March 2020–September 2021). The MOJ research summarises the findings from the first 7,214 families using the scheme. Across all responses, 69 per cent of families were able to reach agreement on some or all issues and are classed as a successful diversion from court. The total number of children in the family justice system in ongoing child arrangement cases has increased from 42,009 in August 2018 to 85,706 in August 2022. The average length of time taken to resolve child arrangement cases from issue to final order has also almost doubled from 22 weeks in 2016 to 41 weeks in 2021 (see 4 [13] Family Voucher Scheme analysis). The recent Government consultation 'Supporting earlier resolution of private family law arrangements' (2023) proposes to increase funding for mediation. However, Munby LJ said in evidence to the 'Children and Families Act 2014 Committee Report' that 'one of the great disasters and one of the great mistakes by government in 2013 was identifying mediation as the non-court solution'. (Cited in 'A Failure of Implementation' (Children and Families Act 2014 Committee Report – Hansard – UK Parliament).

The legal framework

The orders for child arrangement which the court can make under the CA 1989 (s 8) include:

Residence – an order determining where and with whom a child is to live;
Contact – an order requiring the parent with residence to allow the person named in the order to have contact with the child;
Prohibited steps – an order to prohibit a party from making a particular arrangement, or doing something, which involves the child;
Specific issue – an order addressing a particular question regarding upbringing or care which needs the court to resolve.

Practice Direction (PD) 12B *Child Arrangements Programme* sets out a protocol to ensure that the court approaches such applications with consistency and within a clear framework. Private law cases are dealt with by magistrates, district judges or deputy district judges. The caseload of all private applications for 2022 including s 8 orders for child arrangements provides an indication of the volume of court work where 54,404 applications were made and 90,542 total orders were applied for (a single application can include several orders) involving 80,262 children (Table 2 Family Court accessible tables July–Sept 2023). Turning specifically to post separation support and dispute resolution, a total of 83,932 s 8 orders for residence, contact, specific issue and prohibited steps were applied for in 2022 (Table 3a Family Court accessible tables July–Sept 2023). As Munby LJ repeatedly acknowledges very few of these decisions are reported and research needs to be conducted to enable an understanding of what is happening on the ground (see Munby 2016, 2020). Walsh's 2023 research which concludes this chapter provides important insights.

Guiding principles of the Children Act

Section 1 – child welfare paramount

Prior to 1989 CA, when the court considered any matter relating to the child, the child's welfare was only one of a number of factors and the conduct of parties and other matters could trump the court's final decision. So, for example if a mother was a lesbian, up until 1970s, she would be regarded as an 'unfit' mother and sexual preference likely resulted in the custody of the children being awarded to the other heterosexual party of the marriage. The film 'Carol' (2015) starring Cate Blanchett explores just this. The courts also regarded the homosexual father as an unfit parent. (See *Re D (An Infant) (Adoption: Parent's Consent)* [1977] AC 602; see Chapter 9.)

Despite the statutory duty in the GOI 1973 to place the child's welfare as 'first and paramount', judges continued to take into account other factors in exercising their discretion. In *Richards v Richards* [1984] AC 174, a dispute between a married couple regarding the occupation of the matrimonial home, where there were children and where the applicant had made an application for an ouster injunction to remove the other party from the home because of continual arguments and 'an altercated atmosphere', the House of Lords, in interpretating the Matrimonial Homes Act (1984) refused to allow the child's welfare to be placed 'first and paramount' and said it was only one of four factors (discussed in Edwards and Halpern 1988).

The CA 1989 resolved any uncertainty when statute established s 1(1): 'When the court determines any question with respect to – the upbringing of a child; or the administration of a child's property or the application of any income arising from it, the child's welfare shall be the court's paramount consideration.' This mirrors international obligations when on 20 November 1989, the United Nations Convention on the Rights of the Child (UNCRC) 1989, Article 3, held that the best interests of the child shall be the primary consideration.

Who can apply for an order?

Section 10(4)(a) CA provides that a parent, guardian, special guardian, stepparent by marriage or civil partnership, who has parental responsibility and any person in whose favour a residence order has been made, may apply for any of the orders for child arrangement (CAO – residence, contact) and prohibited steps or specific issue order.

In the case of a CAO 'residence only' application, local authority foster parents may apply (s 10(5A) of the CA) and also a relative of the child including a grandparent, uncle, aunt, brother, sister, half-brother, half-sister, stepparent (s 10(5B) of the CA) but the child must have been living with the applicant for over a year prior to the application (s 9(3)(c) of the CA 1989).

The child may also make an application for leave to apply for an order under s 10(8) CA, which may be granted if the court is satisfied that the child has sufficient understanding and satisfies the test of competency which follows *Gillick v West Norfolk and Wisbech Area Health Authority* [1986] AC 112, and the guidance (see s 10(2)(b), 10(8) CA, Practice Direction PD: *Children Act 1989: Applications by*

Children (1993), r 9.2A of the Family Proceedings Rules 1991). See for case development, *Re C (Residence: Child's Application for Leave)* [1996] FCR 461, *Re J (Leave to Issue Application for a Residence Order)* [2002] EWCA Civ 1342, *Re C (Child: Ability to instruct a solicitor)* [2023] EWCA Civ 889. See further Chapter 11.)

Barring vexatious litigation – s 91(14)

Section 67 of the DAA (2021) inserts a new s 91(14)A into the CA 1989, which requires, in addition to change of circumstances, that leave to make an application be granted by the court. The insertion of this section follows recommendations made by Cobb J's 'Harm report' which is a review of the Practice Direction 12J *Child Arrangements and Contact Orders*. Such 'barring' orders are to protect parents and children when further proceedings would risk causing harm, in particular where proceedings themselves could be part of a strategy of continuing domestic abuse. Such an order can be made by the court of its own motion, or pursuant to an application by a person.

Article 6 'right to fair trial' arguments have been raised in this context since any further litigation is prohibited and estopped. The court has held that barring a party from repeated applications and needless prolongation of litigation where harm is occasioned to the other parties, especially the child, is not incompatible with an applicant's Article 6 rights. A s 91(14) order can be made ex parte, in exceptional circumstances, but not where the applicant is a litigant in person (see *Re C (Prohibition on Further Applications)* [2002] EWCA Civ 292, *C (A Child)* [2009] EWCA Civ 72).

In *Stringer v Stringer* [2006] EWCA Civ 1617 where a s 91(14) order had been imposed on the father, restricting any application by him for residence or contact to the children until they reached the age of 16 years was considered a step too far!

In *A Father v Lancashire County Council* [2010] 1 FLR 387 sub nom *Re A and D* [2010] a father was initially refused contact with his daughter until she was 16. The local authority, in addition to the orders for which it applied, applied for an order under s 91(14). The judge in declining to make such an order said in his concluding remarks:

> *[85] Any further unwarranted litigation would be very likely to leave the court on the next occasion to conclude that the last resort had arrived and, therefore, to take steps to prevent further applications by an order under section 91(14) or otherwise.*

The vexatious litigant may present more of a problem where legal aid is now restricted. In making a decision to impose a s 91(14) order the courts are also required to balance the rights of the parents. (See *Re T (A Child) (Suspension of contact) (Section 91(14) CA 1989*, [2015] EWCA Civ 719); *P v F* [2023] EWHC 2730 (Fam); *Windsor and Maidenhead* [2023] EWFC 19.) See also *M v F* [2024] EWFC 237 (B). Consider also *Re:B and K (Children: Section 91(14) Orders)* [2024] EWFC 167 where there was 10 years of litigation history and the court imposed a barring order to prevent any further vexatious litigation.

The welfare checklist: six factors

The court must apply the welfare checklist when considering a s 8 order. Section 1(4) asserts:

> Where (a) the court is considering whether to make, vary or discharge a s 8 order, and the making, variation or discharge of the order is opposed by any party to the proceedings; or (b) the court is considering whether to make, vary or discharge an order under Part IV (care/supervision) then, the checklist in s 1(3) applies.

In considering the welfare checklist under s 1(3) a court shall have regard in particular to the following factors:

> (a) the ascertainable wishes and feelings of the child concerned (considered in the light of his age and understanding); (b) his physical, emotional and educational needs; (c) the likely effect on him of any change in his circumstances; (d) his age, sex, background and any characteristics of his which the court considers relevant; (e) any harm which he has suffered or is at risk of suffering; (f) how capable each of his parents, and any other persons in relation to whom the court considers the question to be relevant, is of meeting his needs.

Failure to consider the statutory checklist

Should a judge fail to consider any of these factors the decision may be open to appeal (CA 1989, s 94). Overturning the decision of the lower court may apply but only when a judge has: 'exceeded the generous ambit within which a reasonable disagreement is possible' (per Lord Fraser in *G v G* [1985] 1 WLR 647). (See also *Re F (A Child)* [2009] EWCA Civ 313.) In *Re H (Contact Order)* [2010] EWCA Civ 448, a married couple separated shortly after the birth of their disabled child, Z. Mother became the sole carer. Father applied for contact. At the interim hearing the judge made a shared residence order, involving several periods of contact with the father prior to the final hearing. The mother appealed. The appeal was allowed on the basis that the judge had failed to take account of a number of checklist factors. In *J and others (Children: Interim Removal)* [2023] EWCA Civ 1266, where the judgment had contained no analysis of the risk of the children suffering emotional harm if removed from the father's care, the appeal was allowed.

Some of the principles that operated pre-1989 still remain 'good' law. However, 'mother is best' is now only a consideration for the court and presumptions about the unfitness of homosexual parent of either gender 'to parent' are totally repudiated (see Fenton-Glynn 2020). In *C v C (A Minor) (Custody: Appeal)* [1991] 1 FLR 223 the marriage broke down. The mother was in a lesbian relationship; the court of first instance awarded custody to the mother, and the father appealed. The Court of Appeal allowed the appeal and said:

> *The fact that the mother has a lesbian relationship with Ms A does not of itself render her unfit to have the care and control of her child. It is, however, an important factor to be*

taken into account in deciding which of the alternative homes, which the parents can offer the child is most likely to advance her welfare. The judge did not give proper consideration to this factor. That is why I would allow this appeal and order a rehearing.

Attitudes to a person's sexual partner preference and capacity for parenting have changed as have legal reforms in protecting equality rights reflected in the Civil Partnership Act (2004). (See the decision of the Court of Appeal in *Re G (Residence: Same-Sex Partner)* [2005] 2 FLR 957 and the Adoption and Children Act ACA 2002 permitting adoption by same-sex partners.)

Section 1(3)(a) 'The ascertainable wishes and feelings of the child concerned considered in the light of his age and understanding'

This principle derives from the case of *Gillick v West Norfolk and Wisbech Area Health Authority* [1986] AC 112 (considered in Chapters 9 and 11) and the obligations of state parties to implement the UNCRC. The child's wishes and the opportunity to express them must be balanced alongside age and understanding. It must also be considered whether the child's views are not unduly influenced by a parent who might attempt to alienate the child from the other parent (parental alienation). In *Williamson v Williamson* [1986] 2 FLR 146, where the children of 14 and 15 years of age said that they did not wish to live with their mother and 'voted with their feet' by arriving at the home of their father, this was a factor taken into account on appeal. In *Re P (a minor)* [1994] Lexis Citation 1679, two children wanted to remain with their father. The mother appealed against the decision submitting, among other reasons, that the judge was wrong to place such weight upon the wishes of a girl of 12 years who had from time to time vacillated and who had from time to time shown her divided loyalties to two parents, both of whom she deeply loved. The views of Lee James at the age of 8 years, it is submitted, should not weigh heavily in the scales and justify a removal from a mother who offered them a good home and was capable and willing to offer them the proven stability of her care. The Court of Appeal was included not to upset the judge in the court of first instance and only allowed the appeal on the basis that:

> *It would therefore be prudent to direct, and I would direct, that both parties file further evidence by Monday which we think is 19 September and I will be corrected if I am wrong about that. That should be a fortnight before the hearing and should give sufficient time for the children's views to have been made known to the parents and for them to have considered them.*

In *Re P (A Minor) (Education)* [1992] 1 FLR 316 where a 14-year-old boy did not want to attend Stowe School in Buckinghamshire as a boarder, but wanted instead to attend the local secondary school, the Perse school, in Cambridge, Butler-Sloss LJ in the Court of Appeal said:

> *The courts, over the last few years, have become increasingly aware of the importance of listening to the views of older children and taking into account what children say, . . . paying proper respect to older children who are of an age and the maturity to make their minds up as to what they think is best for them.*

(See also *G (A child)* [2023] EWFC 168, *M v A* [2023] CSOH 80), *NHS Trust v X* [2020] BMLR 7.)

In *Re P (a minor)* [1994] Lexis Citation 2633, the child said to the father, 'Go away. I don't want to see you.'

The Judge said:

> *[17] I have come to the conclusion that the child's wishes in this respect, although they do not blot out from sight all other considerations, are very important and he is right in saying he wants to be left alone. He not only wants to be left alone, he is entitled to be left alone. . . . Therefore, I have to say with greatest possible sympathy to this father he is wasting his time on appeal. What he must do is comply with the Judge's order and wait, painful though that must be, for the time when his son will, as I very sincerely hope he will, come round*

and dismissed the father's appeal.

Section 1(3)(b) 'physical, educational, and emotional needs'

The physical needs of a child include housing, food, other material provisions and, if disabled or with special needs, appropriate physical, emotional support, and environment. In *Re M (A Child) (Residence Order)* [2003] EWCA Civ 1455, a child, C, 2 years old, had been placed into the care of foster parents by the local authority. At an interim hearing, the judge heard evidence that C's natural father and his new partner, L, should not be ruled out as future long-term carers of C. The social worker contended that given the very special needs of C, and the demands that she would place on any parent, it would not be prudent to return her to the care of her father and L in their household which already contained six other children. At the hearing, the judge concluded that despite those parties' misgivings, the father and L demonstrably had the capacity to meet C's needs and ordered the transferral of C from foster care to the father's house under a residence order, supported by a supervision order. The guardian, supported by the local authority, appealed. The appeal was dismissed.

Educational needs include type of school, continuity in education, and proximity of school and education at home. (See Specific Issue Order in *M v H (Educational Welfare)* [2008] EWHC 324 (Fam).) In *Re AR (A Child: Relocation)* [2010] 2 FLR 1577, where the court held that A's physical and educational needs would be equally well met in London or Troyes (France), the court said that the child: 'has a strong emotional need to have a meaningful participation in his upbringing by F; this would be adversely affected were he to be relocated to France.'

Emotional needs raise issues of attachment and parenting. In *Re S (A Minor) (Custody)* [1991] 2 FLR 388, an appeal from an order where custody was ordered to the father and access to the mother, Butler-Sloss LJ in allowing the appeal and remitting the case to a new bench of justices for a fresh hearing, said:

> *The welfare of the child is the first and paramount consideration. . . . It used to be thought many years ago that young children should be with their mother, that girls approaching puberty should be with mother and that boys over a certain age should be with father. Such presumptions if they ever were such, do not in my view, exist today.*

A long line of cases echoes this sentiment (see *Re A (A Minor) (Custody)* [1991] 2 FLR 394). The 'mother best principle', argues McGlynn (2000), privileges the mother/child relationship in law and devalues fatherhood. Importantly, neither is fatherhood allowed to override the best interests of the child (see *Re E-R (Child Arrangement order)* [2016] EWHC 805 (Fam).)

The child's attachment to siblings is also of relevance. In *C v C* [2003] EWHC 3164 (Fam), Sumner J said: 'It is not usually advisable to separate siblings who are close in age and obviously allied with one another.' Half-sibling attachment was also considered in *Re N-B and others (Children) (Residence: Expert Evidence)* [2002] EWCA Civ 1052, and in *Re M-H (A Child) (Care Order)* [2007] 2 FLR 1715, where the court recognised the advantage of the child being brought up with his half-sibling. Notwithstanding, Isaac's (2022) research demonstrates that sibling attachment is not given the importance in court that it holds for the child. (See also Monk and Macvarish 2019, Gilmore et al. 2023.)

Section 1 (3)(c) 'The likely effect on the child of change in circumstances': status quo

A fundamental rule of good childcare is stability and continuity (see *Re B (A Minor)* [1983] 4 FLR 683, per Ormrod LJ). That precept remains constant. In *Allington v Allington* [1985] FLR 586, for the first 18 months of her life, a baby girl had lived with her parents. Although the mother then left the home and her baby and went to live with another man the court ruled in favour of the mother because the baby had in effect spent most of its life with its mother. In *Re B (A Child) (Residence Order)* [2009] UKSC 5, the status quo principle was raised, where being raised by a grandmother trumped a father's paternal rights. Lord Kerr of Tonaghmore JSC in the House of Lords judgment leads with this statement.

> *This appeal requires a revisiting of a vexed but highly important topic. The significance of parenthood in private law disputes about residence and contact has exercised many courts over many years but one might have thought that the final word on the subject had been uttered in the comprehensive and authoritative opinion of Baroness Hale of Richmond in In re G (Children) (Residence: Same-sex Partner)* [2006] 1 WLR 2305.

The court, in allowing the appeal ruled that: 'The judge had . . . erred in allowing the question of the child's so-called right to be raised by his biological parent to define the outcome of the residence debate' and said that the issue of rights had become a distraction over welfare.

Section 1(3)(d) 'His age, sex, background and any other characteristic of his which the court considers relevant'

Age and sex of a child are relevant factors, as is background and any other characteristic for example, class, culture, ethnicity, race, language, religion and gender. Patterns of migration (detailed in Chapter 9) create a diverse multi-faithed and multi-cultural society. Faith and culture, where a factor in family disputes, have presented the court with some challenges. Jivraj and Herman (2009) explored how

'Christian normativity' informed judicial understandings of 'secularity' and child welfare when dealing with Jewish, Muslim and Sikh faithed families. These faith/culture characteristics are important considerations in decision making in child welfare. However, there are also concerns that presumptions about culture and value judgements are made unwisely and, in some cases, discriminately (see Edwards 2023, Ahdash 2018, 2023).

Faith, culture intersecting with welfare

The diversity of culture understood in its broadest sense, concern with a predominantly white family law judiciary (see Introduction) and the diversity of cultural backgrounds of families coming to law necessitate a deep dive into how these factors are considered when welfare of the child is paramount. In some cases, judges continue to make assumptions about cultures and faiths that Jivraj and Herman had observed in 2009.

Religious faith may be given more or less weight depending on the particular facts of a case. However, the central question for the court is how faith intersects with the welfare of the child. This principle was articulated in *Haringey LBC v C and E and another intervening* [2006] EWHC 1620 (Fam) [2007] 1 FLR 1035. Ryder J opined:

> [76] *Religious, racial, and cultural factors are integral elements of welfare and may on the facts of a particular case provide both the positive and negative factors and context by and within which decisions have to be made. However, despite the respect that will be given to private and family life, and the right to freedom of thought, conscience and religion, and the freedom to manifest religion or belief . . . the safeguarding of the welfare of vulnerable children and adults ought not to be subordinated by the court to any particular religious belief.*

Ryder J again importantly said:

> I start with the proposition that the nature of a child's religious persuasion evolves as the child matures. In the case of a very young child, whose concept of faith is undeveloped, his religious persuasion is necessarily that of his parents. . . . Some children follow their parent's faith throughout their lives, others do not. . . . Once he is developmentally of an age to make a choice, the choice is his. In such circumstances, it would be absurd to impugn a local authority for failing to sustain the religious persuasion of a child who had decided for himself that he did not wish to follow his parent's faith.

The wishes of the parents/carers as to matters of faith take secondary importance where the child is not likely to be reared in an environment where the faith of the non-resident parent(s) is not practiced, as the following cases demonstrate. In *Re W (Minors)* [1992] 2 FLR 332, the mother and her family were of the Jewish faith. The father was not. The parents separated; the mother had residence and the father had contact with the children. The father sought a s 8 specific issue order relating to his daughter's proposed attendance at a Jewish school, to which he objected, and sought a prohibited steps order in respect of the preparation of his son for bar mitzvah. The matter was transferred to the High Court because of its complexity. The final determination is unreported but raises the difficulties in such cases.

In *Re P (A Child) (Residence Order: Child's Welfare)* [1999] 3 All ER 734, the child was born into an orthodox Jewish family. Her father was a rabbi. She was mentally handicapped. The judge made a residence order to the foster parents with reasonable contact to the natural parents. The parents appealed, arguing that a child had a presumptive right to be brought up by her own parents and in her own religion. The judge found that because of her disability the child was unlikely to have any perception of her religious and cultural heritage so that culture or faith could not be the overwhelming factor, nor could it displace other weighty welfare factors, including the exceptional attachment of the child to the foster parents (who were not of the Jewish faith) and of them to her, and the evidence of the harm to her which a move would cause. The appeal was dismissed.

In *Re J (Child's Religious Upbringing and Circumcision)* [2000] 1 FLR 571, the English mother, a non-practising Christian, met the father, a non-practising Muslim whilst on holiday in Turkey in 1992. They married in Turkey and returned to England. Their son, J, was born in March 1994. The parents separated when J was 2½ years old. The child was brought up by the mother. His only contact with Islam was through his father, and he himself did not have any Muslim friends or mix in Muslim circles. When J was 5 years old, the father applied for a specific issue order that J be circumcised. The judge held that it was not in J's best interests to be circumcised. The father appealed. The Court of Appeal decided that circumcision was not a matter that one parent could decide, it was a matter for both parents and any disagreement should be referred to the court for its determination, each case being decided on its own facts.

In *Re A and D (Children) (Care Proceedings: Religious Upbringing)* [2010] 2 FLR 151, the court considered an application by a father for contact. The father was Muslim and had two children by different mothers. Before the birth of his first child, he had been convicted of unlawful sexual intercourse with a 15-year-old girl. The court ordered 'no contact' with the older child. The younger child was taken into care due to the mother's addiction, and then placed with the maternal grandparents. The father was granted contact on four occasions each year. The maternal grandparents were not of the Islamic faith but were agreeable to raising the child in the Muslim faith. The father opposed the placement and made several applications to the court, arguing human rights breaches. The court conceded that the local authority was required under s 33(6)(a) of the CA to ensure that a child in care is brought up in the religion of its parents with a full appreciation and understanding of its heritage and also that if the religion of the parents' changes, the authority must take that into account, subject always to promoting the child's welfare. But the order remained and contact with the father was refused.

In *Re G (children) (Education: Religious upbringing)* [2012] EWCA Civ 1233, the mother and the father come from families of Chassidic (Hasidic) Charedi community of ultra-orthodox Jews. They entered into an arranged marriage in 2000 which was unhappy. In 2010, the father, at the mother's request, left the family home, and the marriage irretrievably broke down. The issue between the parties arose with regard to the schooling of the children. The Court of Appeal found no fault with Copley J's treatment of the issue of religious upbringing in considering the emotional impact on the children:

[85] If the children were to go to the schools of [father's] choosing, I think there is a high risk that their relationship with their mother would become problematic. . . . Conversely, if the children go to a school of [mother's] choosing, there will be considerable losses also . . . I also think that there is some merit in the observation that a more accepting community composed of children from a variety of backgrounds will make it easier for the children to adjust to being children of a separated family.

The father's appeal was dismissed. (See also for similar faithed factors, *Re C (A child) (Child's religious choice)* [2012] Lexis citation 66, Romford County court; *Re X* [2014] EWHC 4813 (Fam).)

In *J v B (Ultra-Orthodox Judaism: Transgender)* [2017] EWFC 4, Jackson J considered the competing claims in a contact contest between a mother and a transgendered male to female 'father' living in an ultra-orthodox Charedi community as 'a collision between two unconnecting worlds [185]'. How should the court decide the children's welfare where it interconnected with a legal and human rights duty to foster gender equality and tolerance and human rights claim to sensibilities of a religious life and where faith/community norms stood in diametric opposition to such gender expression? Jackson J concluded:

[187] So, weighing up the profound consequences for the children's welfare of ordering or not ordering direct contact with their father, I have reached the unwelcome conclusion that the likelihood of the children and their mother being marginalized or excluded by the ultra-Orthodox community is so real, and the consequences so great, that this one factor, despite its many disadvantages, must prevail over the many advantages of contact.

Notwithstanding Jackson J's refusal of the father's application for contact he did express his serious concerns that: 'the practices within the community and in particular its schools amounted to unlawful discrimination against, and victimisation of, the father and the children because of the father's transgendered status [178]'. (See Edwards 2018.) On appeal (*Re M (children) (Ultra-Orthodox Judaism: Transgender) (Stonewall Equality Ltd and another intervening)* [2017] EWCA Civ 2164, the Court of Appeal took a different view about the weight that should be attached to equality norms and held that in substance, the father had made good all three grounds of appeal. The father's appeal was allowed.

Religious practices circumcision

Applications to allow or prohibit the circumcision of male children has also arisen for the court's consideration particularly in Jewish and Muslim families for whom this is an important mark of their faith. The courts have decided these cases on the lived experience of the child now and in the future. In *Re S (Specific Issue Order: Religion: Circumcision)* [2004] EWHC1282 (Fam), the parties, a Muslim mother and Hindu father, brought up their children as Hindus 'with Islamic influences'. After the birth of the children, the mother asked the father to convert to Islam, which he was not prepared to do. Instead, with assistance from the mother's family, the father underwent a Muslim ceremony of marriage in which he held himself out, falsely, as a Muslim no doubt to satisfy other family members or to succumb to pressures. After the separation of the mother and father, the mother applied to the court for permission for both children to become Muslim, and for a specific issue order to allow her son to be circumcised. The father opposed the application for a specific issue order. The court refused the mother's application and held that children of mixed heritage should be allowed to decide for themselves which, if any, religion they wished to follow. Circumcision was not in the son's best interests at present, because it would limit his freedom of choice. Similarly, in *Re L and B (Children) (Specific Issues: Temporary Leave to Remove from the Jurisdiction: Circumcision)* [2016] EWHC 849 (Fam), the court continued a prohibited steps order preventing the children from being removed from England and Wales and refused the father's application for the children's circumcision opining that circumcision was a matter for the child at maturity to make for himself [146]. This was followed in *Re P (a child) (supervision: child in care); M v F and others* [2021] EWHC 1616 (Fam). P was subject to an interim care order in favour of the local authority. He had lived all his life with extended maternal family members (Mr and Mrs R) who were likely to become his permanent carers under a special guardianship order (SGO). P's parents were Muslim. Mr and Mrs R were not. P's mother sought the court's authorisation for P to be circumcised, in accordance with the custom of the Muslim faith. The court determined that on balance, the decision to circumcise P would be deferred until he was able to make his own choice.

Giving quietus to media orchestrated orientalism – The Child AB

This section cannot be left without a mention of the local authority and the media's inflaming of racist attitudes towards different cultures. No criticism can be made of the court in this particular case. The facts of the case of *Re AB in the family court at East London* [2017] Case No: ZE17C00153 were widely misreported in the media. (See Edwards 2018: 49–50.) Child AB, the media story said, was a "white" British child being "taken over" by an "alien" Muslim culture when child "AB," who was 5 years old, was removed from her mother's care in March 2017 and placed with foster parents. *The Times* newspaper printed on 28 August a bigoted and inaccurate headline: 'Christian child forced into Muslim foster care – Concern for girl who had cross removed and was encouraged to learn Arabic' embellished with a pixelated photograph (taken from behind the subject) of a young child with flowing blonde hair, her hand held by a woman dressed in a long black tunic (gelabaya) though not a picture of the child and foster mother in question (see Norfolk 2017).

When the case of AB came to court the presiding judge Sapnara J remarked on the media reports and the photograph. '[14.21] The court expresses its concern that photographs of the child and foster carer have been published in the press' (Albeit at that time, a day after the hearing, the judge was unaware that the photograph was a fake). The Independent Press Standards Organisation (IPSO) received 200 complaints in connection with the press report. The foster placement was in fact a short-term respite placement which, in any event, ended on 29 August 2017, the day following the media story. The maternal grandparents of labelled 'Christian child' AB were of the Muslim faith, and AB was of dual nationality. *The Times* 3 October 2017 changed course and published this headline: 'Muslim fosterers gave "warm care" to Christian girl in Tower Hamlets'. And on 2 November 2017, the London Borough of Tower Hamlets was given permission to publish an alternative version 'Tower hamlets rejects concern over Muslim family' rebutting the original inaccurate claims.

The case involved the following parties: the applicant – the London Borough of Tower Hamlets, the first respondent – the mother (CD), the second respondent – the child (AB) through her children's guardian (EF), the putative father (GH), the presumptive father (IJ) and the maternal grandparents – Mr KL and Mrs MN. AB was placed with foster carers under emergency arrangements following a police protection order, as at that time there was 'no culturally matched foster placement' [14.2]. (See local authority obligation noted earlier s 22(5)(c) of CA 1989.) The mother raised some concerns about the placement and on 27 June 2017 the court directed the local authority to produce a statement to address the cultural appropriateness of the foster care placement [14.8]. The allegations against the foster parents were disputed by the local authority [14.9] whilst the children's guardian had no concerns about the child's welfare or placement and reported that the child was settled [14.10]. The mother made an application on 27 June and 29 August 2017 for the child to be placed with the maternal grandmother [14.12]. By 29 August, an assessment of the grandmother had been made, she was deemed a suitable carer as a special guardian and stated she wished to return to her country of origin with the child [14.15].

An investigation by IPSO discovered inaccurate reporting and upheld the complaint by the local authority against *The Times* newspaper. Significantly, Sir Martin Narey, chairing the Government's review into fostering, said the AB case could result in 'professionals reverting to more cautious race and religious-based decisions when placing children' and would turn the clock back 15 years to when Department for Education guidance discouraged what were called 'trans-racial placements' (see *The Guardian* 2 September 2017) (see Edwards 2018, 2021).

Section 1(3)(e) 'any harm which he has suffered or is at risk of suffering'

Bainham (2013) demonstrates that private and public law are by no means hermetically sealed and explores the confluence between private and public law in cases where harm which is serious may amount to the significant harm threshold under s 31 of the CA and where in private law a s 37 investigation may be ordered. (See Chapter 14.)

Section 1(3) 'Any harm' means ill-treatment or the impairment of health or development (CA 1989, s 105(1)) in its very broadest sense. The threshold of 'any harm' is not the same as 'significant harm' (s 31), which is the threshold required in care proceedings when an order is made for a care or supervision order where the harm includes physical, sexual, mental harm or neglect or might include the child being exposed to the father's alleged violence to the mother (ACA 2002, s 120) as in *Re M (A Minor) (Contact: Conditions)* [1994] 1 FLR 272 or the harm from directly witnessing the violence of a father to a mother (*Re F (A Child) (Indirect Contact through Third Party)* [2006] 3 FCR 553). Already in 1989 the Law Commission in its Working paper on 'Domestic Violence and Occupation of the Family Home' recognised 'Abuse or violence directed at a spouse or cohabitant will also affect children living in the home, because of their intimate contact, may also be at risk of either emotional or physical harm' (2.17).

'Any' harm might also involve a parent administering: 'a wrong dose of medicine, possibly because of difficulties in appreciating what was written on the instructions' (*Re B (Children)* [2000] 27 July 2000 CA). Harm might include where a parent believes that a child has been born through miracle birth (see *Haringey London Borough*

Council v C (E intervening) [2004] EWHC 2580 (Fam) where, in this case, significant harm amounting to significant harm under s 31 of the CA was found. Harm to a child might also be because a mother is deluded and thinks that she is the reincarnation of Elizabeth 1st, or the posting on social media of abusive words or images intended to harass.

Another example of harm is provided in *Re J (A Child)* [2005] UKHL 40. Here, the father was from Saudi Arabia and the mother from Iraq. The mother came to the UK as a student with their son and filed for a divorce. The father filed an application for a specific issue order, s 8, requiring the child to be returned to Saudi Arabia. The court decided that the child should remain with the mother. The factor tipping the balance was that the father had raised allegations about the mother's association with another man, albeit subsequently withdrawn. The judge had heard expert evidence about, among other things, the effect of such allegations in Saudi Arabian society and was concerned that such an allegation might have dramatic effects in Saudi Arabia and on the child ([64]). The judge declined to order that the child be summarily returned to Saudi Arabia. The father appealed. The Court of Appeal reversed the decision. The mother appealed and the House of Lords allowed the appeal and restored the orders made by the trial judge.

Section 1(3)(f) 'How capable each of his parents, and any other person in relation to whom the court considers the question to be relevant, is of meeting his needs'

The court will also consider the standard of care, material circumstances, geographical location, the character of new partners and the child's relationship with all parties. With regard to material advantages, the courts have accepted that 'affluence and happiness are not necessarily synonymous'. In *Re B (Children)* [2000] 27 July 2000 CA, Hale LJ said: 'those needs then have to be considered in the light of the sixth factor, factor (f) which is how capable each of the parents (and any other person in relation to whom the court considers the question to be relevant) is of meeting those needs'.

Munby LJ in 'Parents with a Learning Disability' (2018) discusses cases involving parents with a learning difficulty or physical disability and explores the principles of fairness, the understanding and application of which that have changed radically in the last three decades. The decision to remove a child from its family's care must be based on failure to offer 'good enough' parenting.

Having considered all the factors on the welfare checklist the court must move to the second stage, to consider whether it is better to make an order or not to make an order at all.

Section 8 – the orders

'No order' principle CA 1989, s 1(5)

Under the CA 1989, there is a presumption against making a court order. Section 1(5) provides that a court will only make an order if doing so would be better for the child than making no order at all. The intention is to allow parents to make arrangements for themselves and to preserve joint and several parental responsibility.

This is based on the experience that, if at all possible, it is better to support parties towards agreement without interference from the court and aligns with the spirit of partnership, mediation and conciliation (discussed earlier). If parents cannot agree, an order may become inevitable. But disagreement is not the only basis for an order, as an order may be needed to confirm and give stability to existing arrangements, and with the future in mind to clarify the respective roles of parents, or just to reassure and support the parent with whom the child is living. The 'no order' principle places the burden on the person making the application to explain, and persuade, the court why an order is better than leaving things as they are. An order for 'no order' is not the same as a decision to order 'no contact' (discussed later). It is assumed that an order for 'no order' will diminish as mediation in the early stages may likely resolve issues at this point. There are no statistics available on orders for 'no order' available. However, figures were available in earlier years.

Child arrangement order (CAO) for residence

Section 8 orders for residence and contact were only recently renamed 'child arrangement orders'. Words in s 8 heading being substituted (22.4.2014) by Children and Families Act 2014 (c. 6), s 139(6), Sch. 2 para. 3; SI 2014/889, art. 4(f). Prior to 1989 the terms used were 'custody' and 'access'. The new language of 'child arrangement order' was thought to enable an improved relationship between the caring parties in the interests of the children of the family in their care.

Prior to 1989 the terms 'custody' and 'access' were used such that in *G (A Child)* [2008] EWCA Civ 105, Ward LJ stated:

> *The whole purpose of the Act in getting rid of the concept of custody and access, with concomitant thoughts that they each carry different rights and power and authority and regulation and control, all of that should have been swept away, so that you have an order which conveys no right but simply regulates a factual state of affairs,*
>
> [18]

TABLE 12.1 Order of 'no order'

	Residence	Contact	Prohibited steps	Specific issue
2000	941	2,067	185	118
2005	662	2,381	175	142
2011	354	662	146	70
2022	n/a	n/a	n/a	n/a

Source: Judicial statistics for 2000, https://discovery.nationalarchives.gov.uk/details/r/C11518761

Statistics for 2005, www.gov.uk/government/statistics/judicial-statistics-revised-england-and-wales-for-the-year-2005

Statistics for 2011–2022, www.gov.uk/government/statistics/judicial-and-court-statistics-annual (accessed 30.04.2024)

The terminology of 'child arrangement order' post 2014 is a further attempt to use language to reduce contest and acrimony between parents. Language is performative to use the term used by John Austin (1962). Whilst words describe a reality, they have the power to act on or act out a particular reality.

A child arrangement order may include a condition of residence which settles the arrangements to be made as to the person with whom a child is to live (CA 1989, s 8(1)). It can be ordered in favour of one party (resident parent) but also in favour of two persons who do not live together. Where a residence order is made no person may change the child's surname (s 13(1)(a)) or remove the child from the jurisdiction for longer than one month. If a residence order is made to a person who does not have parental responsibility, for example a grandparent, that person will acquire parental responsibility by virtue of the order (s 12(2)) (see *Re M (Sperm Donor Father)* [2003] Fam 94). Residence orders may be made for a fixed period (s 11(7)(c)) and anyone who is entitled to apply for an order can also apply for a variation or discharge of a residence order (s 8(2) CA).

Shared residence

The CA 1989, s 11 allows for a joint or shared residence order; such orders are important in striving towards a level playing field for partners. In *D v D (Shared Residence Order)* [2001] 1 FLR 495, the parties separated, and the children spent nearly half of the time with their father. The judge made a joint/shared residence order which was upheld on appeal, albeit the court said at that time: 'it will be unusual to make a shared residence order.' Wilson J in *Re F (Shared Residence Order)* [2003] EWCA Civ 592 summed up the aspiration of joint or shared residence and the importance of 'performative' language (see Austin 1962) in achieving a specific goal:

> *Speaking for myself, I make no bones about it: to make a shared residence order to reflect the arrangements here chosen by the judge is to choose one label rather than another. . . . But labels can be very important. Indeed, where there is proximity of homes and arrangements between the two parents can be easily facilitated such cases are better suited to joint residency.'*

Sir Mark Potter confirmed this sentiment and objective in *Re A (a child) (joint residence: parental responsibility)* [2008] EWCA Civ 867 when he said: 'The making of a shared residence order is no longer the unusual order it once was.'

In *R v E and F* [2010] EWHC 4187 (Fam), the child lived with her mother and her civil partner who had acquired parental responsibility. The father was in a same-sex relationship and had not acquired parental responsibility although he visited the child regularly. After a dispute and dissatisfaction with contact the father issued an application for staying contact and parental responsibility. The mother responded and issued an application for a joint residence order with her civil partner. At the child's request overnight contact was agreed with the father. The court made a joint residence order in favour of the mother and her civil partner, approved contact of 50 days per year with the father and dismissed the father's application for parental responsibility and shared residence.

In *T v T* [2010] EWHC 2392 (Fam), a shared residence order between the mother and the father was in place. In this case the mother was in a civil partnership and the father was in a long-standing same-sex relationship. The shared residence order was altered to include the mother's partner. This was done with the father's consent, and he was awarded 152 days contact time per year since there was a concern with regard to the situation should the mother die. The parties were eager to secure the child's long-term future. In this case the judge acknowledged that shared, and joint residence can also lead to disharmony.

> *What is profoundly disappointing is to see how, in practice, instead of bringing greater benefits for children, shared joint residence can simply serve as a battlefield for the adults in the children's lives, so that even when the practicalities of how child's time should be split are agreed or determined by the court they continue to fight over what label is to be put on the arrangement. This can never have been intended when shared/joint residence orders were commended by the courts as a useful tool.*

Child arrangement order (CAO) for contact

Contact – who's right?

Article 9 of the UNCRC asserts that contact is the right of the child as is iterated in *Re F* [1995] 1 FLR 956.

> The starting point always, is that every child has a right to be brought up in the knowledge of his non-custodial parent. This is a right which the courts are determined to preserve. It is not the right of a parent to contact the child. However, the approach of the courts is that fathers should only be denied contact in wholly exceptional cases. These exceptional circumstances include domestic violence, illness, criminality, and eccentricity.

Whilst the views of the child are all important, they are not always decisive.

Contact orders may also be applied for in respect of other relatives – siblings (*Re S (Contact: Application by sibling)* [1998] 2 FLR 897 although contact was refused; – grandparents (see *A Local Authority v Y, Z, and others* [2006] Lexis Citation 579 where contact was approved).

Contact with non-resident parent

It is the responsibility of a parent to ensure that the child sees the other parent with whom he does not live. (See *Re H-B (child) (contact)* [2015] EWCA Civ 389.) In many cases contact works well and will be defined as to when and where contact will take place.

Under CA 1989, s 11(7) the court can attach conditions to contact. Many parents have defined contact, where contact is confined to times, places and conditions, etc. Contact with a child may be direct, indirect, supervised or at a contact centre or by card or letter – 'letterbox' contact. Contact directions set out the conditions of contact and also orders for 'no contact'.

In *Re B (Minors: Access)* [1992] 1 FLR 140, where a father who was socially awkward and suffered from anxiety, and where his eccentric behaviour, e.g. walking along a street with a plastic bag on his head, distressed his children, an application for contact with them was refused. However, on appeal, the Court of Appeal said that: 'a father who was genuinely fond of his children, but who exhibited eccentric, bizarre behaviour, capable of baffling or distressing a child, should not be prevented from having defined access to his children'.

In *Re H (Children) (Contact Order) No 2* [2002] 1 FLR 22 the father, who had Huntington's chorea, and was also violent and abusive towards the mother, applied for contact. Direct contact had been withdrawn following his threats to kill himself and the children with petrol and sleeping pills and he telephoned the mother and members of his own family, but without revealing his whereabouts, to announce that he intended to kill the children and commit suicide. The children wanted direct contact with their father. The judge refused direct contact as there was evidence the mother might have a nervous breakdown if this were to be imposed. On appeal, the Court of Appeal was critical of the judge's failure to analyse the nature of the harm of which the father was capable and also of the judge's rejection of professional recommendations for supervised contact. It allowed the appeal to the limited extent of directing a review of the father's application for direct contact.

Some parents/carers will have supervised contact, where contact with the child is supervised by a child contact social worker (contact coordinator) and may take place in a contact centre. David Blunkett, a former Home Secretary, who was blind, was awarded two hours' supervised contact per month with his son who was aged 3. The visits were ordered to take place under the personal supervision of a friend of Ms Quinn (*Blunkett v Quinn* [2005] 1 FLR 648).

Children voting with their feet – 'I don't care if I don't . . .'

Some children do not want any contact with a parent and attempts by the courts to enforce such contact usually break down.

In *Re W (Minors)* [1992] Lexis Citation 1854 the child said: 'I don't care if I don't see him for the rest of my life.' A no contact order was made under the circumstances, although the court said that there is no reason why the children should not see or communicate with their father if and when they wish to do so.

In *Re D (a child)* [2014] EWCA Civ 1057, it was proportionate for the court to order 'no contact' between the child and his father because the child had such entrenched negative views and was maintaining his opposition to contact. This was not the view taken in *Re Q (Implacable Contact Dispute)* [2015] EWCA Civ 991 where numerous unsuccessful attempts at enforcing contact were made. The 8-year-old child had lived with his mother following the parents' separation in 2008. In 2014, the children's guardian reported that the child was emotionally traumatised by the thought of contact with the father. The judge found that the father had never done his son any deliberate harm but held that the child had been influenced by the mother's hostility towards the father. In *Re A and B (Contact) (No 4)* [2016] 2 FLR 429, FD although a daughter was opposed to any form of contact with her father, the court nevertheless made an order for indirect contact as it considered that would be in her best interests.

Indirect letter contact

Even where parents have committed grave criminal offences, in some cases the offending parents have been permitted indirect contact by letter. In *Westwater v Secretary of State for Justice* [2010] EWHC 2403 (Admin), a father who was in prison for committing sexual offences on young children sought judicial review against the decision not to allow him visiting contact with his children. He had been allowed 'level 2 contact' only (level 2 contact is by written correspondence only, level 1 involves no contact at all, level 3 provides for written correspondence and telephone calls, and level 4 also permits photographs and prison visits). The judicial review succeeded since the proper assessment framework had not been followed and an assumption had been made given the nature of the offender for level 2 contact only.

> *[51] With respect to the authors of the opinions recorded, there was no assessment material which analysed the risk. While it would be an entirely reasonable opinion to hold that a prisoner who maintained his innocence in respect of his sexual offences against children is still a risk to children generally, the risk to his own daughter is specific to her and will be a unique combination of factors including her own needs, wishes and feelings and the interruption in her relationship with her father. The risk will be in context, for example, it will be specific to the prison resources and facilities which have to be taken into account. All of that requires assessment. That is what a multi-agency approach relying on the Framework would provide. . . . [54] Accordingly, I shall quash the decision and direct that an assessment in accordance with the guidance and procedures issued by the Secretary of State be undertaken and a new decision made.*

In *Z v Z (Contact in Prison)* [2021] EWFC 47, the father had committed grave sexual offences including two counts of raping a female child under the age of 13, three counts of sexual assault on a female child under the age of 13, two counts of assault by penetration of a female child under the age of 13, one count of distributing an indecent photograph or pseudo photograph of a child and four counts of possessing an indecent photograph or pseudo photograph of a child including indecent images, of which 20,407 images ranged from Level 1 to Level 5 on the COPINE scale. The offences involved the sustained sexual abuse of a female child, aged 11 years, known to the father over a period of approximately 18 months. He was sentenced to 26 years in prison with a parole eligibility on 2 April 2025. The mother supported contact. The children of 16 and 14 who had not seen their father for ten years (he having been imprisoned in 2011) wanted contact. The court approved the consent order agreed by all parties that there be indirect supervised contact between the children and the father as provided for in that order and under the auspices of the written agreement signed by each of the parents.

Abusive partners and contact strategies

In some cases, abuse, coercion and control and physical and sexual violence become instruments and a tactic of hurting or controlling the other party and a bargaining tool where access to children becomes weaponised. Contact with a father who has been violent to the mother is both damaging and harmful to the child. In protecting the mother, children themselves may feel they have no other option but to resort to violence in defending a mother from the abuse of a violent father (see *R v Maw and another* [1980] 1 CLR 841). In some cases, children themselves are murdered during contact visits with fathers (see Chapter 5). The Women's Aid Federation of England reported on 'Twenty-Nine Child Homicides,' where 29 children from 13 different families had been murdered by their fathers during contact (Saunders 2004). In 2016, a Women's Aid report entitled 'Nineteen Child Homicides' continued to evidence the risk to children.

'Pro contact' even where domestic violence

However domestic violence and abuse to the mother has never been a bar to child contact with the violent party. Wall J said, in *Re H (Contact: Domestic Violence)* [1998] 2 FLR 42 where a recorder's order for contact was upheld: 'As a matter of principle, domestic violence of itself cannot constitute a bar to contact.' However, in *Re M (Minors) (Contact: Violent Parent)* [1999] 2 FCR 56 where the mother was subjected to domestic violence and the father had a drinking problem, the justices refused to order contact which was upheld on appeal. A significant watershed followed in *Re L, V, M, H (Contact: Domestic Violence)* [2000] 4 All ER 609 which involved four separate cases where the fathers' application for contact had been refused because of violence to the mother and the risk to children of physical or emotional harm. The fathers' appeals to the Court of Appeal were all dismissed. However, the court ruled that domestic violence would only be a factor in their consideration.

A denial of contact in a domestic abuse case was overturned on appeal (see *H (Contact: Domestic Violence)* [2006] 1 FLR 943) and in *Re F (A Child) (Indirect Contact Through Third Party)* [2006] EWCA Civ 1426 an order for indirect contact was made between the child and the father where the father had been violent to the mother and the mother and child had relocated and taken on new identities for their safety.

Post-*Re L* cases are inconsistent and allow for a wide ambit of discretion, (see Barnett 2014) such that criticism of the courts in their approach to domestic abuse and contact continues into 2024–5 and has been the subject of wide concern and debate (see Proudman 2021b, see also Bettinson and Burton 2022).

In *Re A (Supervised contact: Assessment of Impact of Domestic Violence)* [2015] EWCA Civ 486 [2016] 1 FLR 689, the parents separated, and the father had not seen the 3-year-old daughter for a year, there had been allegations of sexual abuse and what was described as 'low level violence'. The judge ordered direct contact. The mother appealed and said that insufficient consideration had been given to the father's conduct. The appeal was dismissed [59]. The appeal court held that the risk had been sufficiently considered. It was at this time that the Cobb J review of Practice Direction PD 12J *Child Arrangements and Contact Orders: Domestic Abuse and Harm* was being undertaken into its implementation by the courts. When published in 2016 the 'Harm Report' found that it was far from clear that the PD guidelines on domestic abuse and protection were being consistently implemented.

'Implacable hostility'

As part of the 'custody battles' and during the lifetime of the child a parent may display hostility to the other parent and may try to alienate the child from a relationship with the other parent. Over the last two decades the terms 'implacable hostility', and 'parental alienation' are to be found in reports and witness statements and also in court findings and judgments. What is also evident is that both of these terms are used in proceedings usually by the partner who has been alleged to have used violence against the other partner as a strategy to 'gaslight' the violence and abuse and to seek an advantage in custody disputes over children. (See further McKenzie Friend, Contest and Fact Finding).

It will be for the courts to tease out the truth in a fact-finding hearing. Of 'implacable hostility' Balcombe LJ in *Re J (A Minor) (Contact)* [1994] 1 FLR 729 remarked: 'I would like to say that judges should be very reluctant to allow the implacable hostility of one parent (usually the parent who has a residence order in his or her favour) to deter them from making a contact order where they believe the child's welfare requires it.' Hale J in the Court of Appeal, in *Re D (Contact: Reasons for Refusal)* [1997] 2 FLR 48 displayed some scepticism over the use of the term and said:

> It is important to bear in mind that the label 'implacable hostility' is sometimes imposed by the law reporters and can be misleading. In some cases, the judge or the court finds that the mother's fears, not only for herself but also for the child, are genuine and rationally held.

Where a party makes an application for 'no contact' regarding the other party it may not be a strategy to get back at the other parent nor an expression of hostility to the other parent but a genuine desire to protect the children of the family.

'Parental alienation'

Concerning 'parental alienation' this has been turned into a term of art which rather mistakenly has become viewed as a problem of the child rather than a factual scenario that genuinely exists in some cases, or else an allegation weaponised against the other parent to deflect attention away from real concerns. Disputed theorisations of parental alienation and discussion of who is a qualified expert was raised most recently in *Re C (parental alienation'; instruction of an expert)* [2023] EWHC 345 (Fam). Allegations of parental alienation are frequently made by a party who is abusive and controlling in an attempt to defeat the other party's application and has been the subject of much recent debate (see Beck 2024; Reed 2024).

Bellamy J in *Re S (A Child: Transfer of Residence* [2010] Fam Law 1182 noted:

> The concept of alienation as a feature of some high conflict parental disputes may today be regarded as mainstream. Here the courts are concerned that the child's wish for no contact with a parent should not be a posture instigated by the parent with residence. The courts have dealt with such situations by granting contact to the non-resident parent, or where appropriate by transferring residence altogether.

In this case, the father abandoned his attempts to enforce the residence order. By consent, it was ordered that there should be a residence order to the mother, a supervision order to the local authority, and indirect contact to the father by the provision of school reports and photographs. A University of Manchester research project studied 45 cases in which the mother alleged domestic abuse by the father. In 39 cases, the father made counter-allegations of parental alienation by the mother and in the other six cases, the father threatened allegations of parental alienation or claimed that the mother was mentally unstable (reported in Parkinson 2024).

Most recently in *Warwickshire County Council v A Mother and A Father and X and Z* [2023] EWHC 399 (Fam) Lieven J cites *Re S [Parental Alienation]* [2020] EWCA Civ 568, [2020] EWHC 1940 (Fam) as the authoritative guidance on dealing with such allegations, although offers some qualification in the context of X and Z's family. She adds:

> There are a number of cases concerning alleged 'parental alienation'. This is a highly fact specific scenario in which labels and generalisations are not in my view helpful. In a very large number of cases that appear before the Family Courts, particularly concerning private law, the parents have some degree of animosity towards each other and whether consciously or unconsciously may influence the views of the children about the other parent. It must however be remembered that children are autonomous human beings who have their own feelings and their own perceptions. That becomes particularly true as they become older and begin to wish to assert their own personalities separately from parental control . . . [23] [and] I fully accept Judge Watson's judgment and the facts that she found. I also accept that I have the immense benefit of hindsight. However, I do not think that the label of parental alienation is at all helpful, indeed in this case it has been thoroughly unhelpful, by embedding conflict and a sense that one parent is right and justified, and the other parent wrong and has acted inappropriately. This case is an example of how the adversarial process of litigation, particularly when combined with lengthy delays, serves to entrench positions, and produce poor outcomes for the children [67].

In *TJ v RC* [2023] EWFC 189 the judge rejected the allegation of parental alienation and refused to make any order to either party. Recent concerns with the credibility of psychology experts and the promulgation of an erroneous theoretical perspective that parental alienation is a psychological condition of the child prompted Sir Andrew McFarlane P in *Re C (parental alienation: instruction of expert)* [2023] EWHC 342 (Fam) to clarify the position: 'the identification of alienating behaviour should be the courts focus rather than any quest to determine whether the label "parental alienation" can be applied,' and ruled that it was a question of fact and not of diagnosis for a psychologist.

Contemporary erratic landscape and domestic abuse

Where domestic abuse is a feature and 'no contact' is part of an application the contemporary landscape is still far from certain. In *Father v CD* [2023] EWFC 192, the father applied for a child arrangement order (CAO) that would provide for the children to live with or alternatively, spend time with him. The father had perpetrated serious domestic abuse against the mother, including rape and physical abuse, to which the children were exposed. An order was made that refused contact. The father's refusal to accept the decision of the court resulted in him still persisting in some contact with the children and he made an application to have some role in the children's education whereupon he requested that the school should make available to him the children's school reports. The court quite rightly refused his application. His application was a demonstration of an abusive parent's determination to maintain some kind of presence and coercive control in the child's and in the mother's life. (See further Chapter 5.)

In *F v M* [2021] EWFC 4, Hayden J was one of the several voices that urged greater prominence to be given to coercive and controlling behaviour in child arrangement proceedings.

> *Among other things, F had been found to be profoundly dangerous to women, whom he had identified as vulnerable, and also dangerous to children. The risks that F presented to women had been identified as not only to their emotional and physical well-being but also to their sexual safety.*

An understanding of coercive and controlling conduct is found in *Re H-N and ors (Children) (Domestic Abuse: Finding of Fact Hearings)* [2021] EWCA Civ 448 where the Court of Appeal confirmed that there are many cases in which the allegations are not of violence, but of a pattern of behaviour which it is now understood as abusive. However, it remains unclear in the absence of court-based research the extent to which coercion and control is understood and to what extent the PD 12J is now applied, especially since there is still much recent criticism which is discussed in the closing remarks of this chapter.

Contact with others – grandparents

Certainly, the role of grandparents is extremely significant in the child's life and the courts have recognised that contact may be beneficial (see *Re W (Contact: Application by Grandparent)* [1997] 1 FLR 793). Research findings show that when parents separate 42 per cent of grandparents lose contact with their grandchildren. Griggs (2009) reported that 200,000 children were living with their grandparents as kinship carers, and that placement with grandparents was the preferred choice of 65 per cent of parents in the event that they were unable to care for their children. Grandparents require leave of the court to apply for a s 8 order with respect to a child, save where the criteria under s 10(5)(c) are made out, namely where they have a residence order, or the child has resided with them for a period of three years or, finally, that they have the consent of those with parental responsibility. (See Davey and Lindsey 2023.) In *Re W (Residence: Leave to Appeal)* [2010] EWCA Civ 1280, the mother refused to participate in the court process and permit the child to have contact with the father. The mother had failed to provide the child for 28 out of 34 contact sessions. The father was a drug addict. A residence order was made in favour of the paternal grandmother. The mother sought leave to appeal, and permission was refused (see Spitz 2012).

Enforcing contact

The CAA 2006 Act gives powers to the courts to enforce contact where it has been ordered by the court and case law has shown that where there is hostility to contact by the residential parent for no good reason then residence may be transferred to the parent with contact, as in *Re C (A Child)* [2007] EWCA Civ 1442. The 2006 Act makes provision for monitoring contact, including warning notices for failure to comply including (an 'enforcement order') imposing on the person an unpaid work requirement (inserting s 11 I and 11 J) into the CA 1989). In addition, the *Practice Direction (Residence and Contact Orders: Domestic Violence (No 2)* (2009) issues guidance setting out how such cases should be handled. In *Re L-W (Enforcement and Committal: Contact; CPL v CHW and Others)* [2010] EWCA Civ 1253, the mother applied for an enforcement order of contact where the father was supposed to make the child available for contact one Saturday a month. The father was found guilty of contempt and appealed against the committal order. Cafcass reported that the child did not want to see his mother. The court found that whether the father had 'allowed' the child to have contact was not an appropriate question with regard to assessment of whether there had been a breach said to justify committal. The appeal was allowed in part and most of the enforcement orders and the compensations orders and committal were set aside.

Specific issue order

A specific issue order empowers the court to give directions for the purpose of determining a specific question which has arisen with regard to parental responsibility, e.g. moving the child to another part of the country, a change of name, immunisation, circumcision, holiday or police interviewing of a child. The need for such orders arises where there is disagreement. (See a case from the Scottish jurisdiction *M v A* [2023] [CSOH] 80.)

Disagreements, education, name change, health care

In *H-D (Children)* [2001] EWCA Civ 402 where the parents had separated and the mother wanted to move with the children to another part of the country, the father had made an application for a prohibited steps order pending the final decision of residence and contact. The judge accepted undertakings from the mother. The judge made an order of residence to the mother and contact to the father and made a specific issue order so that the mother could control the choice of the children's schools (the children concerned were two boys – J who was 8½ years of age and K who was 5 years old) because, the judge considered that the mother would struggle to keep the boys at their present school, and provided that she should give two months' notice to the father if she wanted to change schools.

Changing the name of a child may help integrate a child into a new second family with the new partner usually the stepfather's family name but it is considered a draconian step by the natural father whose name up until recently children of the family have most likely taken albeit that recently children may take both parents' names as for example Smith-Jones. Changing a forename or preventing the use of a forename as the following case demonstrates may also be considered necessary to protect the child from ridicule or bullying (see the CA in *Re C (Children) (Care: Change of forename)* [2016] EWCA Civ 374, cited in Chapter 14).

Immunisation and use of medical versus homeopathic remedies is also another potential area of parental disagreement (see *Re H (a child) (parental responsibility: vaccination)* [2020] EWCA Civ 664; *M v H (Private Law: Vaccination)* [2020] EWFC 93).

In *Re C (Welfare of Child: Immunisation)* [2003] EWHC 1376 (Fam), the applications concerned two children (from two different families) aged 4 and 10 years, neither of whom had received any form of immunisation against infectious diseases. In each case, the child lived with the mother, who was opposed to immunisation, while the non-resident father approved of immunisation. Both fathers applied for a declaration requiring immunisation. Both mothers argued that immunisation involved risks and would cause undue distress. The court held that appropriate immunisation was in the best interests of the children (see also *Re B (A Child) (Immunization)* [2003] EWCA Civ 1148; *Re EF* [2016] EWFC 69; *London Borough of Barnet v AL* [2017] EWHC 125 (Fam) where the mothers refused to permit immunisation). In *Re H (a child parental responsibility) vaccination* [2020] EWCA Civ 664 the CA held that the judge had been correct to find that the vaccination of a healthy child in care was a matter which a local authority could properly consent to and arrange pursuant to its powers under s 33 of the Children Act 1989 as it was not an issue that had necessitated an application to the High Court for leave to invoke its inherent jurisdiction under s 100 of the Act. The Court of Appeal, dismissing the parents' appeal, held that the declaration made by the judge that the respondent authority had lawful authority, pursuant to s 33(3) to consent to and make arrangements for the vaccination of the child, notwithstanding the objection of the parents, would stand. A strict following of procedure and process is required for the success of any application. In *Re T and another (Children:Specific Issue Order)* [2024] All ER 73 (Jul) the Court of Appeal allowed an appeal where it found inter alia that the ground rules had not been spelled out, the order lacked clarity, evidential issues were not apparent and the order was unnecessary and disproportionate.

Prohibited steps order

This is a preventative order made by the court that no step which could be taken by the parents in meeting their parental responsibility should be taken without the consent of the court. Prohibited steps are modeled on the wardship jurisdiction where the court can require that no important step in the child's life is taken without the consent of the court. The steps must be identified in the order.

Arranging summer holidays for children can be something of a special problem where parties are separated and pose real worries and concerns where parents live in separate jurisdictions. Parents may fear that the parent wishing to take a child on holiday may use this opportunity to abduct the child and not return the child and therefore will often apply for a prohibited steps order. In *Re N (Leave to remove: Holiday)* [2006] EWCA Civ 357, the mother had been refused leave to send her two children on a holiday to relatives in Slovakia. The Court of Appeal granted consent but deferred the visit until the following year when the court considered the two children would be better equipped to deal with an unaccompanied flight, especially as it also involved a change of plane. In *M (A Child)* [2009] EWCA Civ 311, an appeal against an order made in September 2009 permitting a father to take a 7-year-old child on holiday to France and/or Cameroon was allowed. In this case the mother was concerned that the court should obtain expert evidence on the legal situation in Cameroon (a non-Hague Convention country) and how the child could be recovered in the event that the father retained him there before permission were given. In addition, the mother wanted the father to provide an undertaking to return the child and effect a notarised agreement in the High Commission of Cameroon in London. However, the notarised agreement anticipated by the judge was not possible, nor was the case adjourned for expert evidence. (See also *A Local Authority v W and others* [2021] 4 WLR 21.)

A prohibited steps order may be applied for simply to prevent a party removing the children. In *Re M and A (Disclosure of Information)* [1999] 1 FLR 443, the local authority social services department became involved with the family. The children were living with their grandparents. On 9 January 1998, the grandparents issued an application for residence and a prohibited steps order to prevent the mother from removing the children from their care. That application was ex parte. The judge granted the grandparents leave to apply for the s 8 order, committed the interim residence of both children to the grandparents, made a prohibited steps order, and provided for a further hearing to take place. In *Re L (minors) (Sexual Abuse: Disclosure) Re V (Minors) (Sexual Abuse: Disclosure)* [1999] 1 WLR 299, in two separate proceedings for care orders, findings of sexual abuse were made against the appellants. There was evidence of an unusual and unhealthy sexual relationship between the child, C, and W. The judge held that W posed a risk of significant harm both to D and C unless some protective measures were kept in place, including a prohibited steps order and retaining the boys' names on the Child Protection Register. In *Re B (Prohibited Steps Order)* [2008] EWCA Civ 1055, the English father applied for a prohibited steps order and a residence order, wanting to prevent the mother, who came from Northern Ireland, from taking the child to live in Northern Ireland. Judicial consent was not needed for such a removal, as Northern Ireland was within the UK. The judge prohibited the mother from transferring the child's residence to Northern Ireland, although she was permitted to take him there for holidays. No order was made in relation to residence on the basis that the mother would continue to be the primary carer. The mother appealed, and the Court of Appeal set the order aside because certain authorities had not been considered. (See also *SH v MM and RM (Prohibited Steps Order: Abduction)* [2011] EWHC 3314 (Fam).)

A prohibited steps order may be applied for with regard to differences in faithed upbringing. In *A local authority v W and others* [2021] sub nom *Salford CC v W and Ors (Religion and Declaration of Looked After Status)* [2021] EWHC 61 (Fam), MacDonald J dismissed the mother's application for a prohibited steps order concerning the children's religious upbringing where the maternal aunt and uncle under a SGO wished to have the children initiated baptised into the Roman Catholic faith as they had been attending Roman Catholic Masses. MacDonald J dismissed the mother's application for a s 8 order stating that the conclusion reached in this instance was 'not to pronounce judgment on the relative merits' of each denomination, but merely a matter of the children's welfare [85].

Regional variations in orders

It is a matter of concern expressed by successive Presidents of the Family Divisions that there are wide variations in private as well as public law orders for children.

TABLE 12.2 Private law applications made and orders granted for contact, residence, prohibited steps and specific issues

Year	CAO-contact	CAO-residence	CAO-prohibited steps	CAO-specific issue
2022-Applications	32,563	25,392	12,881	12,202
2022-Granted*	46,528	44,557	12,501	8,076
2021-Applications	34,623	25,631	12,745	11,918
2021-Granted*	51,119	46,997	12,152	7,333
2020-Applications	35,397	25,703	12,656	10,930
2020-Granted*	46,444	41,163	10,984	5,897
2015-Applications	24,288	15,781	8,779	6,345
2015-Granted*	49,959	34,020	9,653	4,690
2022-Applications	25,742	23,199	11,508	6,278
2022-Granted*	70,856	24,975	11,215	3,732

Source: Table 3a and Table 4a Post Separation Support and Dispute Resolution, Applications and Number of Orders Granted annually Accessible Family Court Tables July-Sept 23 https://www.gov.uk/government/statistics/family-court-statistics-quarterly-july-to-september-2022 (accessed 5.05.2024)

Note: The number of disposals shown in table 4 are not equal to the corresponding number of applications made during the year, because: disposals in one year may relate to applications made in earlier years; and an application for one type of order may result in another type of order.

Following a parliamentary question on 4 March 2004, variations in Child Custody orders were published (see Child Custody – Hansard – UK Parliament). More recently regional variations have been the subject of comment by Sir Andrew McFarlane (see Chapter 15).

International relocation and abduction

Prohibited steps and different domiciles

When parents are domiciled in different towns or in different countries, managing residence and contact is fraught. The court, in exceptional circumstances, has imposed conditions (see *Re S (A Child)* [2002] EWCA Civ 1795). In *B v B (Residence: Condition Limiting Geographic Area* [2004] 2 FLR 979 where a condition, which would not be enforceable today in 2024–5, requiring the mother to live within the M25 was imposed to facilitate contact between the non-resident parent and the child.

In contested residence/contact disputes one parent may abduct their own children in the absence, or in defiance, of a court order. Child abduction by a parent is a national and international problem.

The Child Abduction Act (CAA) (1984) prevents a person from removing a child from within and outside the UK. The Child Abduction and Custody Act (CACA) (1985) makes further provision and incorporates the Hague Convention and European Convention into domestic law.

The Law Commission's report on 'Child Custody' (1986) noted:

> *[2.59] Clearly, the grant of leave to take the child abroad for a long time can have a serious effect upon the links between the child and his other parent. Nevertheless, the courts have generally taken the view that this alone is not a sufficient reason to interfere with a reasonable way of life which the custodial parent has chosen to adopt.*

(See *Poel v Poel* [1970] 1 WLR 1469, *Barnes v Tyrrell* [1982] 3 FLR 240, *Chamberlain v De La Mare* [1983] 4 FLR 434.) There are four areas in which these disputes can arise. Firstly, where a child has been taken overseas without the other parent's consent. Secondly, where a child has been retained in a foreign country following an overseas trip. Thirdly, where there is a risk that a child will be abducted overseas. And fourthly, where one parent is trying to exercise rights of residence or access in a foreign country.

Relocation residence and contact

Where one party wishes to relocate to another jurisdiction, such separations dislocate the family and contact with the non-resident parent is likely to be infrequent. Herring and Taylor (2006) note that in such cases a significant number of non-resident parents fail to keep in contact with the child five years after separation. Some parents, however, are forced to relocate to the new place of residence to be near to their children.

Children in relocation disputes, at least until 2011, were likely but not in all cases to be relocated with their mother. That approach had been guided by the view that the welfare of the child is served best where the mother's mental wellbeing is secured. This is no longer the case. The leading case for a decade was *Payne v Payne* [2001] EWCA Civ 166 where a mother was granted leave to relocate to New Zealand. In *Re W (children) (leave to remove)* [2008] 2 FCR 420, the Swedish parents had three children, aged 11, 13 and 15, and moved to London so the father could develop his career. The mother wished to move back to Sweden. The court considered:

> *the oldest child was an autonomous person with clear rights, that all family members were Swedish nationals, and their habitual residence was the consequence of the attraction of the financial market in which the father traded was a matter to be stressed. Accordingly, the appeal would be allowed.*

In *Re B (Leave to Remove)* [2008] EWCA Civ 1034, the mother sought leave to take her children back to Germany. It was recognised that although refusal would exacerbate the mother's already depressive state nevertheless relocation was refused, since removal would have severed contact with the father.

In *J v S (Leave to Remove)* [2010] EWHC 2098 (Fam), a different decision was reached on similar facts. A Japanese mother was living in the UK with her children. She was divorced from the father and very unhappy. She wanted to return with the children to Japan. In this case the court granted permission because it was felt her health would suffer if permission was refused. The mother was required to arrange contact and be flexible with regard to the children maintaining contact with the father.

By 2010, Wall LJ in *Re D (Leave to Remove; Appeal)* [2010] EWCA Civ 50 asserted:

> *There has been considerable criticism of* Payne v Payne *in certain quarters, and there is a perfectly respectable argument for the proposition that it places too great an emphasis on the wishes and feelings of the relocating parent and ignores or relegates the harm done to children by a permanent breach of the relationship which children have with the parent left behind.*

So in *K v K (relocation: shared care arrangement)* [2011] EWCA Civ 793 where there was a shared residence agreement in place which made all the difference the Payne principle fell away. In *K* the Cafcass officer considered that the move would not be in the best interests of the children. The judge granted an order in favour of the mother. The father appealed, and the Court of Appeal found in his favour. In this impossible situation case law has demonstrated a very fact specific outcome.

Wardship and specific issue orders

In *AS v CPW (Inward Return Order)* [2020] 2 FLR 1000, an application in wardship for a summary inward return order was made and whether mother should be given retrospective permission to relocate child was considered. The father applied to the High Court in wardship for a summary inward return order in respect of B who was taken by the mother on 7 July 2019, to her country of Sierra Leone and left there with her family. The mother cross-applied on 20 February 2020 for an order permitting her retrospectively to relocate B to Sierra Leone until the summer of 2022 to enable her son to conclude his GCSEs at a school in Freetown.

> In *Re NY (A Child) (Reunite International and Others Intervening)* sub nom *Re NY (A Child)* [2019] UKSC 49, [2019] 3 WLR 962, [2019] 2 FLR 1247, the Supreme Court held that an application for a return order, whether outward or inward, should, save in exceptional circumstances, be formulated as an application for a specific issue order in the family court.

International law

Where children are taken abroad against the other party's wishes international law is engaged and in such cases the voice of the child and the child's objections to return carry a special weight where there are certain circumstances. In some cases when couples separate abduction and relocation without court authority may simply be a case of a parent wishing to secure an advantage and a future with a child in another jurisdiction, and in some cases it may also involve a parent escaping from domestic abuse.

As Thorpe LJ recognised in *Re G (Leave to Remove)* [2007] EWCA Civ 1497, [2008] 1 FLR 1587

> *[9] These cases are particularly traumatic for the parties, since each of them conceives so much as being at stake. They are very, very difficult cases for the trial judges. Often the balance is very fine between grant and refusal. The judge is only too aware of how heavily invested each of the parents is in the outcome for which they contend. The judges are very well aware of how profoundly the decision will affect the future lives of the children and how difficult it will be for the disappointed parent to adjust to the outcome.*

The Hague Convention

By 2024, 103 contracting states joined the Hague Convention on the Civil Aspects of International Child Abduction 1980 in force 1983. The Convention enforces the return of abducted children to the jurisdiction for the custody matters to be determined there. The Child Abduction and Custody Act (1985) implements the Hague Convention. (See International parental child abduction and also George and Netto (2023) for an overview of this area.) How does the Convention operate and has it drifted from its purpose?

> Articles 1–4 of the Hague Convention state:
>
> [Article 1] The objects of the present Convention are: (a) to secure the prompt return of children wrongfully removed to or retained in any Contracting State; and (b) to ensure

that rights of custody and of access under the law of one Contracting State are effectively respected in other Contracting States.

[Article 2] Contracting States shall take all appropriate measures to secure within their territories the implementation of the objects of the Convention. For this purpose, they shall use the most expeditious procedures available.

[Article 3] The removal or the retention of a child is to be considered wrongful where:

(a) it is in breach of rights of custody attributed to a person, an institution or any other body, either jointly or alone, under the law of the State in which the child was habitually resident immediately before the removal or retention; and

(b) at the time of removal or retention those rights were actually exercised, either jointly or alone, or would have been so exercised but for the removal or retention. The rights of custody mentioned in sub-paragraph (a) above, may arise in particular by operation of law or by reason of a judicial or administrative decision, or by reason of an agreement having legal effect under the law of that State.

[Article 4] The Convention shall apply to any child who was habitually resident in a Contracting State immediately before any breach of custody or access rights. The Convention shall cease to apply when the child attains the age of 16 years.

The Supreme Court held in *Re E (children) (international abduction)* [2011] UKSC 27:

(2) The whole of the Hague Convention was designed for the benefit of children, not of adults. The best interests, not only of children generally, but also of any individual child involved, were a primary concern in the Hague Convention process. In that connection, their best interests had two aspects: to be reunited with their parents as soon as possible, so that one did not gain an unfair advantage over the other through the passage of time; and to be brought up in a 'sound environment', in which they were not at risk of harm. The Hague Convention was designed to strike a fair balance between those two interests.

This primary purpose is echoed in *H v A* [2024] EWHC 476 (Fam) where Cusworth J said:

[48] as pointed out by Mostyn J in B v B [2014] EWHC 1804, the objective of the Convention is to ensure that a child who has been removed unilaterally from the country of his or her habitual residence in breach of rights of custody is returned forthwith in order that the courts in that country can decide his or her long term future.

In addition, the UNCRC 1989, is binding on UK courts. Article 11 requires states parties to take measures to prevent the transfer and abduction of children. The Convention also provides for bilateral and multi-lateral agreements. The Child Abduction and Custody Act 1985 under its schedules embeds international conventions into UK law.

Addressing these issues and in an effort to establish an international standard, in March 2010, the *Washington Declaration on International Family Relocation* was agreed but it is not binding on a UK court.

> The declaration establishes a series of principles:
>
> - the best interests of the child should be the paramount (primary);
> - the right of the child separated from one parent to maintain personal relations and direct contact with both parents on a regular basis in a manner consistent with the child's development, except if the contact is contrary to the child's best interest;
> - the views of the child having regard to the child's age and maturity;
> - the parties' proposals for the practical arrangements for relocation, including accommodation, schooling and employment;
> - here relevant to the determination of the outcome, the reasons for seeking or opposing the relocation;
> - any history of family violence or abuse, whether physical or psychological;
> - the history of the family and particularly the continuity and quality of past and current care and contact arrangements;
> - pre-existing custody and access determinations;
> - the impact of grant or refusal on the child, in the context of his or her extended family, education and social life, and on the parties;
> - the nature of the inter-parental relationship and the commitment of the applicant to support and facilitate the relationship between the child and the respondent after the relocation;
> - whether the parties' proposals for contact after relocation are realistic, having particular regard to the cost to the family and the burden to the child;
> - the enforceability of contact provisions ordered as a condition of relocation in the State of destination;
> - issues of mobility for family members; and
> - any other circumstances deemed to be relevant by the judge (See Washington Declaration).

Removal and return, deciding the case, habitual residence

A child is wrongfully removed where there is a breach of rights of custody (residence). (See *Kaha v Lahmer* [2024] EWHC 2439 (Fam); *Elkndo v Elsyed* [2024] EWHC 2230 (Fam).). Rights of custody Article 3 (a) HC are determined in accordance with the law of the country where the child is 'habitually resident'. Habitual residence applies where a child has been resident in a country for some time, and a child's habitual residence is largely a matter of fact. Children are therefore returned to the country of habitual residence for these cases to be decided in many of these instances.

In *Re P (A Child) (Abduction: Custody Rights)* [2005] Fam 293, the mother and father were US citizens and 'habitually resident' in New York. The mother was granted sole custody, with contact to the father. The mother took the child to England. The father claimed that he had not consented to the child's removal, that the removal was in breach of his rights of custody and therefore in breach of Article 3 of the Hague Convention. He invoked Article 12 of the Convention and applied for the child's return. The court allowed the father's appeal, *inter alia*, as the Hague Convention required the court to give the expression 'rights of custody' an autonomous interpretation; the reference in Article 3 to 'rights of custody' applied to a person under the law of the child's habitual residence and that, accordingly, the court had to order the immediate return of the child to New York under Article 12 of the Convention. (See *Re D (A Child) (Abduction: Rights of Custody)* [2006] UKHL 51: *Re C (Abduction: Residence and Contact)* [2006] 2 FLR 277.) (See for a recent decision *GT v LT* [2024] EWHC 2190 (Fam).)

In deciding matters of jurisdiction the Supreme Court on 9 September 2013 handed down judgment *in the matter of A (Children) (AP)* [2013] UKSC 60 [2012] EWCA Civ 1396 & [2013] EWCA Civ 232. This was a landmark decision in relation to issues of jurisdiction where the Supreme Court held that there was [54] no legal rule akin to that whereby a child automatically takes the domicile of his parents, and held that domicile is 'the place which reflects some degree of integration by the child in a social and family environment', the purposes and intentions of the parents being merely one of the relevant factors. (See also *B (A Child) (Abduction: Habitual Residence* [2020] EWCA 1187.)

Non-Convention country abduction and recognising bilateral agreements

The Convention's reach is limited and where countries are not signatories retrieving a child is beyond the scope of domestic courts. There are some bilateral agreements for example as between France, and Algeria and Morocco. The courts have adopted divergent rules with regard to non-Convention cases. In 2008, half of abduction cases were in non-Hague countries. In *Re J (Child Returned Abroad: Convention Rights)* [2005] 2 FLR 802, the court said that there was no warrant in statute or authority 'for the principles of the Hague convention to be extended to countries which are not parties to it' [22].

In *B v El-B (Abduction: Sharia Law: Welfare of Child)* [2003] 1 FLR 811, the key issue was whether the application of Sharia law to the custody of children was to be respected by English courts in international child abduction cases or to be considered as potentially in conflict where the fundamental principle that the child's welfare should be protected operated. A Lebanese mother brought the children to England in breach of an order of the Lebanese court. The case was brought under the wardship jurisdiction, as Lebanon was not a signatory to the Hague Convention. The welfare of the child had to be considered in relation to the circumstances. Here, both parents were devout Muslims, and this was also the religious and the cultural background of the children. Under Muslim law, the transfer of legal custody of children from mother to father takes place at the ages of 7 for boys and 9 for girls. The court found that there was no substance in the suggestion that Sharia law was not to be regarded as child centred.

The apparent suggestions in *Re JA* [1998] 1 FLR 231 that welfare was not the test in Sharia law needed to be taken in the context of a case where the family had lived in England for substantial periods and where there was expert evidence of harm to the mother and child if return to the United Arab Emirates was ordered. A careful review of the welfare issues might lead to a refusal to return an abducted child in certain cases, but it was not an outright rejection of Sharia law. See *Re J (Child Returned Abroad: Convention Rights)* [2005] 2 FLR 802.

In *Re T and another (Children) (Abduction: Recognition of Foreign Judgment)* [2006] EWHC 1472 (Fam), the Spanish judgment was recognised because, as the court explained, if the court did not make an order for the return of the children to Spain, it would be failing to give effect to its recognition of the Spanish judgment and thus failing to accord precedence to Brussels IIb [Brussels Convention II] over the Hague Convention in that respect. The primary rationale underlying the Hague Convention was to ensure that decisions as to the welfare of children, and questions where and with which parent they should reside, were taken in the country of the child's habitual residence. The mother had initiated proceedings in Spain, so by the time the matter came before the English court the matter would have already been heard before a Spanish court in possession of all the relevant facts as to welfare decisions, and as to the father's removal of the children. The Spanish court had specifically vested interim custody in the father on the basis that the children should continue to reside in England with the father as their main carer, and with appropriate and beneficial educational arrangements, pending a full and final hearing. By virtue of the relevant Spanish law, that interim custody order was not capable of appeal and would remain in place till the resolution of divorce and/or separation proceedings. In those circumstances, if the court was obliged to return the children, it would defeat rather than assist the overall purpose of the Hague Convention. However, by application of the provisions of Brussels II b, such a result was avoided.

In *Re U (Abduction: Nigeria)* [2010] EWHC 1179 (Fam), the mother abducted her children from their home in Nigeria and brought them to England. The mother alleged that she was a victim of domestic violence. Summary return of the children was ordered because it was held that the relevant State within Nigeria had enacted domestic violence legislation and that protection from domestic violence was available. In addition, the father was prepared to arrange and pay for separate accommodation and to pre-register a version of his undertakings with the Nigerian court and was also prepared to prepay money to lawyers to represent the mother in Nigerian proceedings. (For a review of case law see Welstead (2024) and Basi and Halliday (2023).)

The child's voice in international relocation

Where international relocation is concerned the Convention and the courts give more weight to the child's voice than anywhere else in family law disputes. Baroness Hale in *Re D (A Child)* [2006] UKHL 51 said:

> *There is a growing understanding of the importance of listening to the children involved in children's cases. It is the child, more than anyone else, who will have to live with what the*

court decides. Those who do listen to children understand that they often have a point of view which is quite distinct from that of the person looking after them. They are quite capable of being moral actors in their own right. Just as adults may have to do what the court decides whether they like it or not, so may the child. But that is no more reason for failing to hear what the child has to say than it is for refusing to hear the parents' views.

(See also *Re M (Abduction: Child's Objections: Appeal)* [2014] EWCA Civ 1519, *Re J (Jurisdiction: Abduction)* [2015] UKSC 70).)

The resolution of child abduction has been guided by the principle of the best interests of the child and the paramountcy of the child's welfare, and the best solution is generally considered to be to return the child to his or her country of residence. Whilst the original problem to be combated was the removal of the child from the status quo (habitual residence), this can only be one factor to be considered. The welfare of the child is not always protected by the habitual residence presumption (see *Re C* earlier). Where the country of origin does not resolve issues of domestic violence and custody in family proceedings by making child welfare paramount considering instead the rather more moveable feast of best interests, then it is not surprising that mothers will take a course of forcible abduction in an effort to resolve custody battles and in some cases to gain protection from domestic violence. In such cases, children need to be consulted and the older the child the weightier his or her views not only because the child may be approaching Gillick competence (see *Gillick v West Norfolk and Wisbech Area Health Authority* [1986] AC 112), but because of the length of time he or she has been reared in a particular jurisdiction and the importance of the other associations and relationships that have been formed during that time. Under the Hague Convention there is an effective presumption in favour of ascertaining the views of the child. Under Article 12 of the Convention, where wrongful removal or retention is established, the Courts are bound to order that child's immediate return to the country of his habitual residence.

Child's objections a paradigm case

Article 13 HC provides that a court is not bound to order the return of a child if: '[the Court] finds that the child objects to being returned and has attained an age and degree of maturity at which it is appropriate to take account of its views'. This is known as the 'Child's Objections Defence'. In *Re T (Abduction: Child's Objections to Return)* [2000] 2 FLR 192, Ward LJ said that where the child who has attained a degree of maturity objects to being returned this is a factor that must be taken into consideration.

In *Re G (Abduction: Children's Objections)* [2010] EWCA Civ 1232, the court said:

There is, in this branch of international family law, a growing perception that the judge at trial should hear the voice of the child: that is implicit from the Hague Convention itself but made explicit by the United Nations Convention on the Rights of the Child 1989. Of course, the manner in which the judge hears the child is a matter of local custom and tradition.

In this jurisdiction, judges in the High Court have not traditionally in modern times heard the voice of the child directly but through the officer of the court, the Cafcass officer. The tradition is now under scrutiny, debate, and revision. The subcommittee of the Family Justice Council that is concerned to ensure the safeguarding of the rights of children has forcefully expressed the view that judges in this jurisdiction should be meeting children and hearing their voice in carefully arranged conditions; given the fact that E was seeking to communicate her views to the decision-maker, it is perhaps with hindsight a pity that His Honour Judge Barnett did not have the opportunity of meeting her and hearing from her own lips.

The leading authority on the child's objections exception is *Re M (Republic of Ireland) (Child's Objections) (Joinder of Children as Parties to Appeal)* [2015] EWCA Civ 26 and as to discretion, the leading authority is *Re M (Children) (Abduction: Rights of Custody)* [2007] UKHL 55.

In *Re J & K (Abduction: Objections of Child)* [2005] 1 FLR 273, the court ordered return of the children to Malta in a case where notwithstanding that the older of two boys expressed a fear of return, it ordered that both children be returned to Malta. It held that the future of a child is usually best decided in the court of the State of his habitual residence.

In *GT v RJ* [2018] EWFC 26, an application by a mother to relocate to the Ukraine with her two children had been dismissed because of her contemptuous regard for the court's authority.

(See also *S v C (Abduction: Art 13 Defence: Procedure)* [2011] EWCA Civ 1385, [2012] Fam Law 261.)

No presumption in favour of applicant parent

The Court of Appeal reviewed the law on external relocation in the light of the international obligations in *Re AR (A Child: Relocation)* [2010] 2 FLR 1577, *Re F (Relocation)* [2013] 1 FLR 645, and *Re F (A Child) (International Relocation Cases)* [2015] EWCA Civ 882, and held that there was no presumption created by Article 13(1)(b) of the Hague Convention in favour of the applicant parent, although the reasonable proposals of the parent with a residence order wishing to live abroad carry great weight.

Beyond objection – child at risk

The second part of Article 13b allows a refusal for return if the child would be exposed to 'risk'. Risk has involved a range of considerations including intolerable situation (*Re W (children) (child abduction: intolerable situation)* [2018] EWCA Civ 664), deteriorating health of the mother (*Re B (2021)* later in this chapter), physical or psychological harm, domestic abuse (*AT v SS* [2015] EWHC 2703 (Fam)) and inadequate standard of care *Re B (a child) (abduction: Article 13(b))* [2020] EWCA Civ 1057.

How intolerable is to be determined by the court upon the evidence. Barnett argues that the courts tend to apply this defence to a high standard, resulting in numerous children and their mothers being compelled to return to the jurisdiction of their abusers. *In the Matter of S (a Child)* [2012] UKSC 10, on appeal from [2012] EWCA Civ 1385 sub nom *S v C (Abduction: Art.13 Defence: Procedure)* where the mother removed the child to England in early February 2011 without informing the father, the father applied for the child's return to Australia under the Convention. At first instance, Charles J had declined to order W's return to Australia. A return order was refused because it would expose the child to the grave risk referred to in Article 13(1) (b). The Court of Appeal ordered W's immediate return which was overturned by the Supreme Court. The Supreme Court considered the child's health at the epicentre of a decision to return a child to the jurisdiction and also the mothers mental health which would create a situation that was intolerable for the child.

In *Re S (A Child) (Abduction: Article 13(b): Mental Health)* [2023] EWCA Civ 208 on appeal, a father's application for summary return of the child was refused. The Court of Appeal said:

> *[115]. The fact that a risk within the scope of article 13(b) exists is not legally determinative because, under the 1980 Convention, it gives the court a discretion not to make a summary return order. However, it is well established that the discretion will almost inevitably be exercised by refusing to make a return order.*

As Baroness Hale said in *Re D (A Child) (Abduction: Custody Rights)* [2007] 1 AC 619,

> *[55] it is inconceivable that a court which reached the conclusion that there was a grave risk that the child's return would expose him to physical or psychological harm or otherwise place him in an intolerable situation would nevertheless return him to face that fate. There is no justification in this case for exercising the discretion other than by refusing to make a summary return order.*

In the Irish case of *WA v AT (Child Abduction; Best Interest of the Children)* [2024] IEHC 142 recognised, where the mother had removed the children from Ireland to Poland '[9.3] Notwithstanding any of these concerns, the best interests of the children now require that they remain in Poland, despite the significant damage done to the boys by the dismantling of their relationship with their father.'

In *Re B (A Child: Abduction: Article 13(b))* [2021] 1 FLR 721, [2020] EWCA Civ 1057, the mother of the now 3-year-old child was born in Bosnia in 2017 and came to the UK as an asylum seeker when she was 14. The family travelled backwards and forwards between England and Bosnia thereafter. The mother suffered from long-standing mental health difficulties and often left the child with the father in Bosnia while she travelled to England for treatment. On several occasions the mother alleged that the father had been violent towards her and had taken the child, refusing to return her to the mother. In 2019, the mother was granted a restraining order against the father by the Bosnian court and subsequently brought the child to England without informing the father. The father was granted custody, the mother appealed, and her appeal was allowed and the father's application under the Hague Convention 1980 dismissed.

However, in *HZ v GA* [2024] EWHC 489 (Fam), the mother went with the child to New Zealand. The mother is from the UK and father from New Zealand. The mother stayed in New Zealand because of the Covid pandemic. Later the mother and child left for England for a holiday but stayed in the UK and the mother made an application to relocate to the UK. A psychiatrist gave evidence for the mother and the impact on her health should she have to return to New Zealand. The court found that the mother had failed to satisfy an article 13b defence and ordered return of the child to New Zealand.

Risk domestic abuse

The risk that tips the balance is one determined by the court. In *A Father v A Mother and others* [2024] EWHC 991 (Fam), the court [50] cited MacDonald J who said in *E v D* [2022] EWHC 1216 (Fam) at [32]: 'There is a distinction to be drawn between the practical arrangements for the child's return and measures designed or relied on to protect the children from an Art 13(b) risk.' Clearly this was not a case of practical arrangements but involved domestic abuse by the father towards the mother and the children's objections to return.

In *AT v SS* [2015] earlier, where there was evidence of domestic abuse nonetheless the court ordered return of the child.

[68] Whilst the Convention provides for any return to take place forthwith, there will have to be a short delay in this case whilst the necessary arrangements are made for the reception of S in Holland. These arrangements will include the need to notify the CCPB of the decision of this court, the need for an interim foster care or kinship placement to be identified as detailed above and the need for arrangements to me for transporting S to the Netherlands in the event that the mother persists in her stated intention not to accompany her child to that jurisdiction. The timing of the return of S will need to account for the resolution of these practical issues.

In *A Father v A Mother and others* [2024] EWHC 991 (Fam) (see earlier), M alleges that F was abusive and controlling, there was a history of allegations of serious domestic abuse, and there was an injunction against F for protection against domestic violence by the Miami-Dade court amongst other conduct. The father had no in person contact with the children since their removal. The court heard M's allegations of domestic abuse as part of the overall picture and considered them of a very serious nature. *Re R (a child) (wrongful retention: child's objections: discretionary return)* [2023] EWHC 560 (Fam) was applied and the court said: 'It is likely if not obvious, beyond this summary application, this issue will need to be considered by the family court' whilst holding that the father had no rights of custody and also that the facts indicated that a no return order would be made.

There is a concern shared amongst some family practitioners that the Hague Convention is not honouring its purpose. Evidence suggests that 75 per cent of applicants are made by mothers and in 70 per cent of cases domestic abuse is a component, but nevertheless children are ordered to return despite a risk to them and or the mother. Adrienne Barnett in a Policy Briefing on the Hague Convention calls for changes to the Hague Convention including a defence against return in circumstances of domestic violence/abuse, explicit acknowledgment of the impact of domestic violence/abuse on children, provision for a stay on return orders in domestic abuse cases and enable welfare hearings to be held remotely to permit the taking parent to litigate in a safe location. Also: restrict the circumstances in which it is appropriate to rely on 'protective measures' and in any event ensure that courts cannot accept undertakings as a means of defeating the Article 13(1)(b) defence in domestic violence/abuse cases, and ensure that children's wishes and feelings are explored in all cases involving domestic violence/abuse.

Reem Alsalem, the UN Special Rapporteur on violence against women and girls, wants to make changes to the implementation of the Convention in the UK to ensure that the Child Abduction and Custody Act 1985 is compatible with the Domestic Abuse Act 2021. This particularly relates to the definition of domestic abuse, and the recognition that children living with domestic abuse are victims in their own right.

A legitimacy crisis in private law

This chapter concludes with reflections on the crisis in private law drawing on the concerns of the senior family law judiciary, practitioners and academics (see Monk et al. 2023).

Sir James Munby for several years has expressed grave concerns about private family law, in 2016 in 'Care Cases A Looming Crisis,' 15th View from the President's Chambers, and the 'The Crisis in Private Law' (2020). Some of these concerns are echoed by the current President Sir Andrew McFarlane in his 'View from the President's Chambers 2023' and his lecture on 'Domestic Abuse and the Family Court' (2020) Fam Law 19, and by Peter Jackson LJ in his lecture 'Is Family Law Law?' (2023). Munby LJ's (2020) findings on the current crisis in private law reflect his concerns and also records and compiles complaints made about the family justice system. Many of the complaints that have come to his attention are not only about the failures in the system but also the failings of judges including: judges do not comply with the President's Guidance of 2017 and are not applying section 1(2A) of the 1989 Act, and are failing to give effect to the statutory policy and are not sufficiently alert to an understanding of the problem of domestic abuse in all its forms and its effects on the parent and the children, especially when there is an allegation of coercive and controlling behaviour. Munby LJ notes that despite PD 12J, *Child Arrangements & Contact Orders: Domestic Abuse and Harm*, there is an increasing tendency to revert to a culture of 'contact at all costs'. Further, that while judges are unwilling to accept evidence from domestic abuse experts they are too accepting of some supposedly expert evidence in support of allegations of parental alienation, and that in some cases where there has been a fact-finding hearing the findings have been skewed by judicial attitudes which are uninformed, lacking in understanding, out-of-date or even misogynistic.

And on the other side of the water, complaints have been made that judges are not sufficiently alert to the behaviour of women who are alienating their children from their fathers and that judges are not sufficiently robust in ensuring that their orders are actually complied with by recalcitrant mothers.

What is generally agreed by senior judges, practitioners and academics is that family judges fail to understand the risk posed by violent and coercive partners. In *Re: T and another (Appeal: Fair Hearings: Delegation of Judicial Functions* [2024] EWHC 2236 (Fam) an earlier judge was criticised for failure to have regard to para 35 PD 12j in a case which involved a number of applications including for indirect contact with children of the family and where there was a non-molestation and occupation order in place in respect of the mother of the child. The main issue upon which there is broad concern relates to judges ordering contact where there are allegations of violence. This arises because of judicial failure to understand domestic abuse and its impacts, but also the CA, s 1(s 1(2A), (2B) (6) (7)) establishes that unless there is a 'risk of suffering harm' there is a presumption that contact will further the child's welfare.

Walsh (2023) in a view from the ground presents research findings of a case file review of CAO applications flagged as containing a risk of harm and concludes from these findings that PD 12J is insufficient in ensuring safety as a priority in contact determinations notwithstanding that paragraph 5 adds to the PD the duty of risk elimination. Walsh points out that paragraph 35 appears to clarify that whilst there is a duty of risk minimisation since the phrase 'unmanageable risk of harm' also appears this has the potential to undermine protection where there is a risk of harm if that risk is considered manageable. Walsh also raises the problem of cases which make no mention of domestic abuse in the order and asks what is the obligation then imposed by the PD? Of the 684 cases initially examined in the research the majority of applications were made by fathers and only a minority of applicants were legally represented with domestic abuse alleged in 72 per cent of cases. Walsh concluded that despite clear risks there were significant levels of unsupervised and overnight contact. Walsh says there is a legitimacy crisis (see also Hunter and Barnett 2013).

With regard to the system problem, the lack of funding has attracted litigation and criticism and with the highest volume of private cases and litigants in person requiring clear support and advice, more needs to be done despite the support through court initiatives in a number of the 52-district family judge court centres and the mediation scheme which has not attracted universal support. The withdrawal of legal aid funding to private cases save those in which an allegation of domestic violence has been made has had a dramatic effect. Academics and practitioners have been vocal with some practitioners breaking rank and talking rather more publicly to the media about the impact of the lack of funding and the failings of judges and the system (see Proudman 2021a). Many see mediation as a response to lack of funding.

Will or can the Government's consultation paper on 'Supporting earlier resolution of private family law arrangements' (2023) address any of these problems?

The Consultation outcomes repeated the failings of judges and of the system and pledged to inject more resources into mediation, speed up the process of case resolution, and provide training and support to those where there are allegations of abuse. There are some positive steps for example:

[15] A further positive step has been the issue, in April 2023, of FPR Practice Direction 27C on the attendance of IDVA's and ISVA's at hearings in the Family Court. An IDVA is an 'Independent Domestic Violence Adviser', and an ISVA is an 'Independent Sexual Violence Adviser'. PD27C firmly establishes the default setting, which is that an IDVA or ISVA, who is providing support for a party, should attend any hearing if that party wishes them to do so. The default position may only be departed if it is in the interests of justice to do so.

Self-test questions

1. Jack (he/him) and Helene (she/her) now live separately and have a joint/shared child arrangement order for residence in favour of their two children Irene (she/him) and Mark (he/him). Helene has met Charles (he/him) who has a property business in New York and Helene wants to move to America with her two children to live with him. She made an application to the court for relocation. Meanwhile Jack has friends and family in Albania and on one residence visit he removes the children without court authorisation and without telling Helene and takes them on a trip to Albania. He tells the children it is for a holiday. Jack remains in Albania with the two children and goes into hiding in a remote village. After nine months they are tracked down by the authorities. The children like Albania, have learnt the language, made friends and connected with their Albanian family. Advise Helene.

2. Mildred (she/her) left the matrimonial home and resided at several addresses with June her daughter. Mildred has had a series of partners and is living in temporary accommodation. June is well cared for and settled in the local school. The father, Steve continues to live in the matrimonial home, a large four bedroomed property. Steve is a caring and loving father. Steve's parents, June's paternal grandparents, live nearby. Both maternal and paternal grandparents have retired and are able to provide help and assistance with the daily care of the June. Mildred and Steve have both applied for sole residence of June. Advice both parties.

3. Mr and Mrs Khan divorced in April 2010. Mr Khan is a practicing Muslim; Mrs Khan does not have any religious beliefs. They have one son Ali, aged 3. Ali is living with his mother, Mrs Khan, who has now reverted to her name before marriage and calls herself Mrs Sheila Magnolia. She is now cohabiting with Bill Smith (he/him) who she met at a friend's party. Mr Khan (Ali's father) wants Ali to be circumcised as he believes that is central to Ali's identity. He also wants to take Ali to Afghanistan for the summer school holidays to stay with the paternal grandparents. Mr Khan is also concerned that Ali is going to be enrolled at a Roman Catholic nursery which is near to where Sheila lives. He is also concerned that Sheila might marry Bill Smith and that Ali might be adopted.

   You are acting for Mr Khan. What orders might you apply for on his behalf, and what principles will guide the court?

4. Mr and Mrs Rose have separated because of Mr Rose's violent behaviour. He was recently convicted of an assault on Mrs Rose in the magistrates' court. The children, Babs (she/her) (11 years) and Sid (he/him) (12 years), want to have contact with their father. Mrs Rose opposes contact with their father because of his violent temperament and his controlling and coercive conduct towards her and the children during their married life. The paternal grandparents have a very warm and loving relationship with their grandchildren and are anxious that any contact between them and the children might be opposed by Mrs Rose following the divorce. The children love their paternal grandparents who have been very involved with the children since they were small including picking

them up from school and taking them on holiday and on outings. Their mother feels she has no alternative but to oppose contact between the children and the grandparents because of the father's violence.

Sid doesn't want to be caught in the crossfire of his parents' litigation and wants to be separately represented so that he might have a more vocal say in the outcome of what in effect will be his future. He wants to live with his mother and to have contact with his paternal grandparents.

Advise all parties.

References

Abramowicz, Sarah, 'English Child Custody Law, 1660–1839: The Origins of Judicial Intervention in Paternal Custody' [1999] *Columbia Law Review* 1391

Allbutt, Henry, *The Wife's Handbook* (R Forder 1888)

Ahdash, Fatima, 'Countering Terrorism in the Family Courts: A Dangerous Development' [2023] *Modern Law Review* 1197

Ahdash, Fatima, 'The Interaction Between Family Law and Counter-Terrorism: A Critical Examination of the Radicalisation Cases in the Family Courts' [2018] *Child and Family Law Quarterly* 389

Austin, John L, 'Performative Utterances' in *How to Do Things with Words* (Oxford University Press 1962)

Bainham, Andrew, 'Private and Public Children Law; an Under Explored Relationship' [2013] *Child and Family Law Quarterly* 138

Barnett, Adrienne, 'Contact at All Costs? Domestic Violence and Children's Welfare' [2014] *Child and Family Law Quarterly* 439

Barnett, Adrienne, 'Policy Briefing on the Hague Convention' www.hague-mothers.org.uk/document-tag/adrienne-barnett/ (accessed 04.05.2024)

Basi, Mani Singh and Alex Halliday, 'Setting Aside 1980 Hague Convention Return Orders: Where Are We Now?' [2023] *Family Law* 1371

Beck, Jenny, '"PA": Reluctance, Resistance, and Refusal – Lets Lose the Pseudo-Science' [2024] *Family Law* 660

Bellamy, Christopher and G. Lord, 'Research into the Operation of Rule 9.5 of the Family Proceedings Rules 199: Final Report to the Department for Constitutional Affairs' (DCA, 2006, 2003) [2006] *Family Law* 298

Bettinson, Vanessa and Mandy Burton, 'Domestic Abuse and Child Arrangement Proceedings: Identifying and Assessing the Risk of Harm, Including Coercive and Controlling Behaviour' [2022] *Child and Family Quarterly* 3

Blackwell, Alison and Fiona Dawe, *Non-Resident Parent Contact* (Office for National Statistics 2003)

Child Custody – Hansard – UK Parliament https://hansard.parliament.uk/commons/2004-03-02/debates/13393f34-2a93-4403-8845-a1720b410372/ChildCustody (accessed 28.04.2024)

Children and Families Act 2014 Committee Report– Hansard – UK Parliament, 'A Failure of Implementation' (col 74GC) https://hansard.parliament.uk/lords/2023-09-06/debates/9A988CF8-B7BF-4133-8E98-1F7DD809CAD2/AFailureOfImplementation%28ChildrenAndFamiliesAct2014CommitteeReport%29 (accessed 28.04.2024)

Custody of Infants Bill, HL Deb 18.07.1839 vol 49 cc485-94 (1839) https://api.parliament.uk/historic-hansard/lords/1839/jul/18/custody-of-infants (col 488) (accessed 28.04.2024)

Davey, Samantha M and Jaime Lindsey (eds) *Grandparents and the Law, Rights and Relationships* (Bloomsbury 2023)

Edwards, Olivia, 'Race Culture and the Law' [2021] *Family Law* 1174

Edwards, Susan, 'Negotiating Faith, Culture and Gender in J v B and the Child AB' [2018] *Family Law* 56

Edwards, Susan, *The Political Appropriation of the Muslim Body Islamophobia Counter Terrorism Law and Gender* (Palgrave Macmillan 2021)

Edwards, Susan, 'Radicalisation: Antithetical Jurisdictions of Protection and Punishment' [2023] *Family Law* 684

Edwards, Susan and Ann Halpern, 'Conflicting Interests: Protecting Children or Protecting Title to Property' [1988] *Journal of Social Welfare and Family Law* 110

Family Court Statistics Quarterly Accessible Tables (July–September 2022) https://w.ww.gov.uk/government/statistics/family-court-statistics-quarterly-july-to-september-2022 (accessed 28.04.2024)

Family Mediation Voucher Scheme Analysis https://assets.publishing.service.gov.uk/media/6419 cd288fa8f547c7ffd692/family-mediation-voucher-scheme-analysis.pdf (accessed 28.04.2024)

Fenton-Glynn, Claire, 'Deconstructing Parenthood: What Makes a "Mother"?' [2020] *Cambridge Law Journal* 34

Friend, McKenzie, '"Contest and Fact Finding" How Do Family Courts Deal with Domestic Violence Allegations?' www.youtube.com/watch?v=GW2GelvyI1o (accessed 28.04.2024)

George, Rob and James Netto, 'Concurrent Convention and Non-Convention Cases: Child Abduction in England and Wales' [2023] *Laws* 70

Gilmore, Stephen, Daniel Monk, Ruth Lamont and Jonathan Herring, 'Reflections on Future Directions in Family Law' [2023] *Child and Family Law Quarterly* 99

Griggs, Julia, *Grandparents Plus* Prepared for Grandparents Plus and the Equality and Human Rights Commission (EHRC), Protect, Support, Provide: Examining the Role Played by Grandparents in families at risk of poverty 2010' (2009) https://issuu.com/equalityhuman rights/docs/protect_support_provide_full (accessed 28.04.2024)

Hale, Baroness, 'Matrimony, Patriarchy and the Welfare of Children' Selden Society and Four Inns of Court Annual Lecture (2023) recorded on 29 November 2023 at Gray's Inn, London, YouTube 2023 www.youtube.com/watch?v=8D1doc1LXaI&t=26s (accessed 28.04.2024)

Herring, Jonathan and Richard Taylor, 'Relocating Relocation' [2006] *Child and Family Law Quarterly* 517

Hunt, Joan and Ceridwen Roberts, *Family Policy Briefing 4: Intervening in Litigated Contact: Ideas from Other Jurisdictions* (Oxford University Press 2005) www.nuffieldfoundation.org/sites/default/files/files/fpb4-ref6.pdf (accessed 13.05.2024)

International Parental Child Abduction www.gov.uk/guidance/international-parental-child-abduction (accessed 28.04.2024)

Isaacs, Elizabeth, 'Sibling Contact: Messages from Research Re Mutuality of Parentage' [2022] *Family Law* 442

Jackson, Peter, 'The Nicholas Wall Memorial Lecture, Given by Lord Justice Peter Jackson "Is Family Law Law?"' (11.05.2023) www.judiciary.uk/the-nicholas-wall-memorial-lecture-given-by-lord-justice-peter-jackson-is-family-law-law/ (accessed 03.05.2024)

Jivraj, Suhraiya and Didi Herman, '"It Is Difficult for a White Judge to Understand": Orientalisation, Racialisation and Christianity in English Child Welfare Cases' [2009] *Child and Family Law Quarterly* 283

Judicial College Prospectus (2024) www.judiciary.uk/wp-content/uploads/2023/11/Judicial-College-Prospectus-2023-2024.pdf (accessed 28.04.2024)

Justice Neil Cobb Report, 'Harm Report' Review of Practice Direction 12J FPR 2010 Child Arrangement and Contact Orders: Domestic Violence and Harm (2016) www.judiciary.uk/wp-content/uploads/2017/01/PD12J-child-arrangement-domestic-violence-and-harm-report-and-revision.pdf (accessed 03.05.2024)

Knowlton, Charles, 'Fruits of Philosophy: An Essay on the Population Question' (1832) Fruits of Philosophy, by Charles Knowlton (gutenberg.org) www.gutenberg.org/files/38185/38185-h/38185-h.htm (accessed 25.05.2024)

Law Commission, 'Domestic Violence and Occupation of the Family Home' Working Paper No 113 (HMSO 1989)

Law Commission, 'Family Law Review of Child Law: Custody' Working Paper No 96 (1986) https://cloud-platform-e218f50a4812967ba1215eaecede923f.s3.amazonaws.com/uploads/sites/30/2016/08/No.096-Family-Law-Review-of-Child-Law-Custody.pdf (accessed 03.05.2024)

Litigants in Person: A Handbook for Litigants in Person, Figure 4: Proportion of Private Law Disposals by Type of Legal Representation of the Parties, January to March 2012 to April to June 2023 www.judiciary.gov.uk/publications/handbook-litigants-person-civil-221013/ (accessed 28.04.2024)

Mant, Jess and Julie Wallbank, 'The Post-LASPO Landscape: Challenges for Family Law' [2017] *Journal of Social Welfare and Family Law* 149

Marshall, Emma, Sue Harper and Hattie Stacey, 'The Public Law Project' (2018) Research Briefing Paper Family Law and Access to Legal Aid https://publiclawproject.org.uk/resources/family-law-and-access-to-legal-aid/ (accessed 03.05.2024)

McFarlane, Sir Andrew, 'Domestic Abuse and the Family Court' (2020) *Family Law* 19 www.judiciary.uk/wp-content/uploads/2019/11/PSU-domestic-abuse-FINAL-1.pdf (accessed 03.05.2024)

McFarlane, Sir Andrew, 'A View from the President's Chambers' (2023) www.judiciary.uk/guidance-and-resources/a-view-from-the-presidents-chambers-july-2023/) (accessed 28.04.2024)

McGlynn, Claire, 'Ideologies of Motherhood in European Community Sex Equality Law' [2000] *European Law Journal* 29

Monk, Daniel and Jan Macvarish, 'Siblings, Contact and the Law: An Overlooked Relationship?' [2019] *Family Law* 180

Montgomery, Jonathan, 'Children as Property?' [1988] *The Modern Law Review* 323

Moore, Orla and Sam Russell, 'Stepen Alderton Admits Gunsot Murders of Father and Son' *BBC News* (2023) www.bbc.co.uk/news/uk-england-cambridgeshire-66042969 (accessed 28.04.2024)

Munby, Sir James, 'The Crisis in Private Law in the English Family Court' [2020] *Family Law* 448 https://transparencyproject.org.uk/the-crisis-in-private-law-by-sir-james-munby/ (accessed 03.05.2024)

Munby, Sir James, 'President's Guidance Family Proceedings: Parents with a Learning Disability' [2018] *Family Law* 596

Munby, Sir James, '14th View from the President's Chambers: Care Cases: Settlement Conferences and the "Tandem" Model' (2016) *Family Law* 1102

Munby, Sir James, '15th View from the President's Chambers: Care Cases: The Looming Crisis' [2016] *Family Law* 1227 www.judiciary.uk/wp-content/uploads/2014/08/pfd-view-15-care-cases-looming-crisis.pdf (accessed 28.04.2024)

Norfolk, Andrew, 'Christian Child Forced Into Muslim Foster Care – Concern for Girl Who Had Cross Removed and Was Encouraged to Learn Arabic' *The Times* (28.06.2017) https://www.thetimes.com/uk/society/article/christian-child-forced-into-muslim-foster-care-by-tower-hamlets-council-3gcp6l8cs

Norton, Caroline and Angela Burdett-Coutts, 'The Continuing Victorian Narrative: Caroline Norton & Angela Burdett-Coutts (youtube.com)' (2021) www.youtube.com/watch?v=wQhPDu33sj8 (accessed 28.04.2024)

Parkinson, Lisa, 'What About Me? It's My Life Too!' [2024] *Family Law* 439

Practice Direction 12B 'Child Arrangements Programme' www.justice.gov.uk/courts/procedure-rules/family/practice_directions/pd_part_12b (accessed 28.04.2024)

Practice Direction 12J Child Arrangements & Contact Orders: Domestic Abuse and Harm www.justice.gov.uk/courts/procedure-rules/family/practice_directions/pd_part_12j#:~:text=Factors%20to%20be%20taken%20into%20account%20when%20determining,order%20for%20contact%20only%20if%20it%20is%20satisfied- (accessed 28.04.2024)

Practice Direction 12Q Orders Under Section 91(14) of the Children Act 1989 www.justice.gov. uk/courts/procedure-rules/family/practice_directions/practice-direction-12q-orders-under-section-9114-of-the-children-act-1989 (accessed 28.04.2024)

Practice Direction Children Act 1989: Applications by Children (1993) https://www.justice.gov. uk/courts/procedure-rules/family/practice_directions/pd_part_12k (accessed 28.04.2024)

Proudman, Charlotte, 'Analysis of the Historic Court of Appeal case on the Family Court' (2021a) *Violence Against Women* www.centreforwomensjustice.org.uk/analysis (accessed 28.04.2024)

Proudman, Charlotte, 'A Critical Examination of the Family Court's Approach to Domestic Abuse in Private Law Children Cases: Where Are We Now? Part I' [2021b] *Family Law* 803

Reed, Lucy, 'The Presumption of Parental Involvement 10 Years On' [2024] *Family Law* 947

Research into the Operation of Rule 9.5 of the Family Proceedings Rules 1991 www.dca.gov. uk/family/familyprocrules_research_3.pdf p 166 (accessed 28.04.2024)

Saunders, Hilary, 'Twenty-Nine Child Homicides: Lessons Still to Be Learnt on Domestic Violence and Child Protection' (2004) Women's Aid Federation, England www.judiciary. uk/wp-content/uploads/JCO/Documents/FJC/Publications/twenty_nine_child_ homicides.pdf (accessed 28.04.2024)

Spitz, Louise, 'Grandparents: Their Role in 21st Century Families' [2012] *Family Law* 1254

Stevenson, M, 'Compulsory Mediation – a Discussion' [2006] *Family Law* 986

Supporting Earlier Resolution of Private Family Law Arrangements (2023) Government Consultation Paper www.gov.uk/government/consultations/supporting-earlier-resolution-of-private-family-law-arrangements (accessed 28.04.2024)

Tower Hamlets Rejects Concern Over Muslim Family www.bbc.co.uk/news/uk-41833590 (accessed 30.04.2024)

Trepany, Charles, 'Kelly Clarkson Reveals She "Definitely Didn't See" Her Divorce Coming' (2020) USAtoday.*Com* https://eu.usatoday.com/story/entertainment/celebrities/2020/09/ 21/kelly-clarkson-reveals-she-definitely-didnt-see-her-divorce-coming/5860265002/ (accessed 28.04.2024)

Walsh, Kieron, 'The Gap Between Facts and Norms: Contact, Harm, and Futility' [2023] *Child and Family Law Quarterly* 27

Washington Declaration www.icmec.org/wp-content/uploads/2015/10/Washington_Declaration_ EN.pdf (accessed 28.04.2024)

Welstead, Mary, 'International Relationships and Child Abduction' [2024] *Family Law* 81

Women's Aid, 'Nineteen Child Homicides: What Must Change so Children Are Put First in Child Contact Arrangements and the Family Courts?' (2016) www.womensaid.org.uk/ wp-content/uploads/2016/01/Child-First-Nineteen-Child-Homicides-Report.pdf (accessed 28.04.2024)

Further reading

Andrews, Danielle M, 'Note, Non-Muslim Mothers v. Egyptian Muslim Fathers: The Conflict Between Religion and Law in International Child Custody Disputes and Abductions' [1999–2000] *Suffolk Transnational Law Review* 595

Bainham, Andrew, Bridget Lindley, Martin Richards and Liz Trinder (eds), *Children and Their Families* (Hart Publishing 2003)

Cross, Rebecca and Malvika Jaganmohan, A Practical Guide to Practice Direction *12J and Domestic Abuse in Private Law Children Proceedings* (Law Brief Publishing 2021)

Hunter, Rosemary and Adrienne Barnett, 'Fact-Finding Hearings and the Implementation of Practice Direction 12J' [2013] *Family Law* 431

George, Rob, The Relocation Research Project 2012 Under Dr Rob George Authorised by Sir Nicholas Wall P Under FPR Rule 10.73(c) *Fam Law Week* 1304/2012

Gilmore, Stephen, 'The Payne Saga: Precedent and Family Law Cases' [2011] *Family Law* 970

Handbook Litigants in Person www.judiciary.gov.uk/publications/handbook-litigants-person-civil-221013/

Henderson, ME, 'Note, U.S. State Court Review of Islamic Law Custody Decrees-When Are Islamic Custody Decrees in the Child's Best Interest?' (1988) 36 *Brandeis Journal of Family Law* 423, 426

Hermann, Didi, An Unfortunate Coincidence: Jews, *Jewishness, and English Law* (Oxford University Press 2011)

Holt, Kim, 'Territory Skirmishes with DIY Advocacy: A Dickensian Misadventure' [2013] *Family Law* 1150

Lamont, Ruth, 'Child Protection in International Family Law and the Determination of Where a Child "Belongs" for the Purpose of Jurisdiction' [2022] *Child and Family Law Quarterly* 401

Kaganas, Felicity and Shelley Day Sclater, 'Contact Disputes: Narrative Constructions of Good Parents' [2004] *Feminist Legal Studies* 1

Langdon-Down, Grania, 'Islamic Family Law; Culture Clash' *Law Society Gazette* (2006) 103(48) 14

www.lawsociety.org.uk/Support-services/Advice/Articles/Litigants-in-person-new-guidelines-for-lawyers-June-2015/ (accessed 11.05.2024)

Maclean, Mavis and John Eekelaar, 'Legal Representation in Family Matters and the Reform of Legal Aid: A Research Note on Current Practice' [2012] *Child and Family Law Quarterly* 2

McFarlane, Andrew, Madeleine Reardon and Alexander Laing, *Hershman and McFarlane, Children Law and Practice* (Bloomsbury 2024)

Momoh, Onyoja, 'The Interpretation and Application of Article 13(1) b) of the Hague Child Abduction Convention in Cases Involving Domestic Violence: Revisiting X v Latvia and the Principle of "Effective Examination"' [2019] *Journal of Private International Law* 626

Monk, Daniel, Ruth Lamont, Herring Jonathan and Gilmore Stephen, 'Reflections on Future Directions in Family Law' [2023] *Child and Family Law Quarterly* 99

Mums on the Run Failed by the Family Court' video www.bbc.co.uk/programmes/p0g7gsly (accessed 24.05.2024)

Practice Direction 12B: Child Arrangements Programme, the Revised and Up Dated

Practice Direction 12J: Child Arrangements and Contact Orders: Domestic Abuse and Harm and the revised President's Practice Guidance (18.01.2017): Family Court – Duration of Ex Parte (Without Notice) Orders

Reed, Lucy, *The Family Court Without a Lawyer: A Handbook for Litigants in Person: A Handbook for Litigants in Person* (Bath Publishing 2022)

van Rossum, Wibo, 'The Clash of Legal Cultures Over the "Best Interests of the Child"' (2010) *Utrecht Law Review* 33 www.utrechtlawreview.org/ (accessed 11.05.2024)

Williams, Kim, *Litigants in Person: A Literature Review* (Research Summary 2/11, Ministry of Justice 2011) https://assets.publishing.service.gov.uk/government/uploads/system/uploads/attachment_data/file/217374/litigants-in-person-literature-review.pdf (accessed 11.05.2024)

Young, James, 'The Constitutional Limits of Judicial Activism: Judicial Conduct of International Relations and Child Abduction' [2003] *Modern Law Review* 823

13

The limitless jurisdiction of wardship

SUMMARY

In this chapter the jurisdiction of wardship in protecting the interests of children is considered. Family lawyers may only occasionally encounter the need for such an application; nevertheless, the fact that the Official Solicitor steps in to act for the child, that the circumstances which involve such intervention are unusual and that the reach and use of wardship is limitless indicate this clearly much-needed jurisdiction deems a detailed consideration. There are some restrictions on the use of the jurisdiction, and the Children Act 1989 (CA) prohibits the local authority from using wardship to achieve its purpose unless there are exceptional circumstances and where there is or there would be significant harm to the child (s 100(4)(b)). The very sad deaths of babies and young children involves often an understandable conflict of opinion of what is in the child's best interests between parents and doctors which arose in the cases of Baby Gregory, Charlie Gard, Aysha King, and Alfie Evans, Isaiah Haastrup, and Zainab Abbasi (see Isaiah Haastrup news feature otherwise see under name) where the court in wardship made a decision with respect to the medical treatment of a terminally ill or gravely ill infant or young child. Wardship has also been invoked to prevent a 'Gillick competent' (*Gillick v West Norfolk and Wisbech Area Health Authority* [1986] AC 112) adolescent from refusing life-saving and other medical treatment. Recent applications by local authorities in care proceedings have invoked in some cases the warding of minors in families where it is alleged that they are at risk of being 'radicalised' (see Ahdash 2023, Edwards 2023). Such intervention has been argued to be social engineering whilst the term 'radicalisation' and its meaning is nebulous. The Law Commission (1987) said that wardship was a declining jurisdiction as other statutory powers superseded. It is not possible to determine whether wardship is declining as statistics on applications are not available. What is apparent is that the jurisdiction remains important, has expanded its reach and is limitless.

DOI: 10.4324/9781003435020-13

Contemporary high profile wardship cases

Wardship was invoked in a case involving the current ruler of Dubai, his wife and their two young children. The case of *His Highness Sheikh Mohammed Bin Rashid Al Maktoum v Her Royal Highness Princess Haya Bint Al Hussein And Others* [2021] EWHC 3480 (Fam) following child arrangements – *Re Al M (Child Arrangements)* [2021] EWHC 1577 (Fam) involved a final hearing to determine the welfare of two children, aged 14 and 10, both of whom were wards of court and lived with their mother as agreed between the parents, Her Royal Highness Haya bint Al Hussein and His Highness Sheikh Mohammed bin Rashid Al Maktoum. In the wardship proceedings, two fact-finding hearings made findings of forced abduction, restraint and house arrest of two of the father's older daughters (*Re Al M (Fact-finding)* [2019] EWHC 3415 (Fam), [2020] 2 FLR 409) and the deployment of highly sophisticated hacking software to infiltrate the mobile telephones of the mother, her security staff and solicitors (*Re Al M (Fact-finding)* [2021] EWHC 1162 (Fam) [2022] 2 FLR 136). The mother sought an order permitting her to make arrangements for, and give sole consent to, any assessment or treatment of the children in relation to their medical, dental, ophthalmic, orthodontic, psychological, therapeutic or educational needs. The court ordered the wardship to continue and granted the mother's application to be given sole responsibility to determine all issues relating to the children's medical care and education.

Paula Yates (a television presenter in the 1980s and 1990s) died in 2000 and left her 4-year-old daughter, Tiger Lily, orphaned. The child's natural father, Michael Hutchence, lead singer of INXS, had died in 1997. Tiger Lily's paternal grandparents lived in Australia and wanted custody whilst Bob Geldof (musician) and the former husband of Yates, who had custody of their three daughters, sought custody of Tiger Lily so that she could be raised in a family with her three half-sisters. Tiger Lily was made a ward of court and in 2007 Geldof, having fostered Tiger Lily, was granted an adoption order in his favour (see Graves and Martin 2000).

From the ancient to the modern jurisdiction of wardship

The jurisdiction of wardship is derived from the principle that all subjects owe an allegiance to the Crown who as *parens patriae*, protects its subjects, and, has a special obligation to care for those who cannot look after, or make decisions for themselves. Once a child is made a 'ward of court', the court then becomes in effect the judicious parent and no decision can be made about the infant or child without the court's permission.

Wardship originated in the Court of Chancery, which had a jurisdiction in equity to protect equity wardship and was described in the sixteenth century as protecting 'all infants, as well as idiots and lunatics'. Joseph Chitty, in his *Treatise on the Law of the Prerogatives of the Crown*, explains:

[t]he King is in legal contemplation the guardian of his people; and in that amiable capacity is entitled, (or rather it is his Majesty's duty, in return for the allegiance paid him,) to take care of such of his subjects, as are legally unable, on account of mental incapacity, whether it proceed from 1st nonage: 2. idiocy: or 3. lunacy: to take proper care of themselves and their property.

(155)

Until the 1800s, the equitable jurisdiction was largely limited to cases where the ward had property which needed protection.

In times gone, by, wardship was inextricably linked to property, and was most frequently used to prevent wealthy children from falling into the hands of fortune-hunters who might dissipate their inheritance or lead them into what their families might regard as an undesirable marriages. The link with property gradually came to be regarded as a formality and was finally severed by s 9 of the Law Reform (Miscellaneous Provisions) Act 1949, which enabled a child to become a ward of court whenever an application was made for that purpose.

(See [3.2] Law Commission 1987)

The concept of the child's welfare was then broadened in scope to include the child's 'moral, religious, and physical welfare'. In *Shelley v Westbrooke* [1817] 37 ER 850 Jac 266, the children were removed from a father's control where the court found that he was 'acting on irreligious and immoral principles' in deserting his family and living with another woman. In *Wellesley v Duke of Beaufort* (1824–34) 4 ER 1078; (1828) 2 Bli NS 124, the Court of Chancery had jurisdiction to appoint a guardian for infants, being wards of the court, where Wellesley was 'living in a state of adultery' and had encouraged his children in 'swearing and keeping low company'. Wellesley's appeal was dismissed by the House of Lords (*Wellesley v Wellesley HL* [1824–34] ER 612).

By 1971, the wardship jurisdiction was transferred from the Chancery Division Practice Direction PD (Ward of Court) [1961] 1 WLR 580 to the Family Division under the Administration of Justice Act 1970, s 1(2) (see now Supreme Court Act 1981, s 61, Sch 1). Under modern wardship once warded, the court has parental responsibility for the child, which continues until the order for wardship is discharged which can be of several months' or years' duration. Following the CA 1989, a s 8 prohibited steps order (see Chapter 12) affords, in certain circumstances, the protection which was formerly secured under wardship. In other respects, the CA curtails the wardship jurisdiction by prohibiting the power to commit a child into the care of the local authority.

In 1951, there were 71 wardship orders; in 1973, 622; in 1988, 3,704; in 1990, 6,227 wardship orders; and following the CA 1989 by 1991, they had fallen to 4,961 orders. (See also Law Commission [3.3] for early figures.) By 2002, statistics on wardship were no longer published. Rosie Winterton, MP, in a reply to Mr Vaz, MP, who tabled a Commons question asking for information on the extent of wardship, said this:

The Children Act 1989 came into force on 14 October 1991. Under the Act, the use of wardship by local authorities is severely limited. Leave to make an application for any exercise of the court's inherent jurisdiction must be granted by the High Court. Applications by private individuals are not restricted, but the same results can generally be achieved by obtaining a prohibited steps or specific issue order under s 8 of the Act. Statistics have not been collected since 1991 because the number of wardship orders made has been negligible.

(See 'Wardship orders, Hansard')

A FOI request made by Susan Edwards in 2023 was unable to furnish any up-to-date statistics. John Mitchell, District Judge at Bow County Court, in 1991 with the help of Alan Sealey of the Statistical Support Office of the Court Service identified the annual numbers of originating summonses.

Since 1991 Judicial Statistics has not recorded the number of wardship cases but collected data shows that after an uncertain 3 years the numbers remain steady at about 420–40 cases a year. In 1993 269 originating summonses were issued in the Principal Registry of the Family Division, in 1994 349 in the country as a whole, in 1995 277, in 1996 437, in 1997 437, in 1998 431 and in 1999 418.

(Mitchell 2001a)

The inherent jurisdiction

The inherent jurisdiction provides protection to any individual, regardless of age, who is incapacitated. (See *Re SK (An Adult) (Forced Marriage: Appropriate Relief)* (2004).) So, for example, in the case of *E (By Her Litigation Friend the Official Solicitor) v Channel Four; News International Ltd and St Helens Borough Council* [2005] 2 FLR 913, Pamela, a 32-year-old woman with a learning disability (mental impairment – within the meaning of the Mental Health Act 1983) and diagnosed with dissociative identity disorder (DID), needed protection. DID manifests as different 'personalities' and in Pamela's case, there were four personalities in addition to Pamela herself: 'Sandra', 'Andrew', 'Margaret' and 'Susan'. Channel Four television wished to complete and then broadcast a film on Pamela and her condition. An application was made to the court under the inherent jurisdiction because it was argued on her behalf by the Official Solicitor and the local authority that she was not able to give her consent. The Official Solicitor and local authority sought an interim injunction. The injunction failed on the basis that her lack of capacity had not been established, although the court recognised that there was a narrow margin and even if it had acceded the incapacity to consent, it held that the making of the film was not necessarily against her best interests.

There is also an overlap with the Court of Protection. In *NK v RK (By the Official Solicitor) X County Council AK* [2023] EWCOP 37, the court said:

[6]R's family seeks an order (either under the Mental Capacity Act or the inherent jurisdiction) that it is in R's best interests to implement a 'supportive framework' around R to encourage R to repair and maintain her relationship with her immediate and wider family and friends. I . . . refuse the Applicant's deemed application for an order under the court's inherent jurisdiction. I find that R is not under undue influence, nor is she being coerced, pressured, or otherwise constrained, in her decision making in relation to contact with her family.

(See also *Re DY (Capacity)* [2024] EWCOP 4.)

Forced marriage

By 2004, the problem of women being forced into marriage was becoming known as solicitors who in an attempt to find some remedy in existing law turned first to wardship. Who and what drives the law, is it parliamentary law making, or the Supreme Court judges and judges in the Court of Appeal? Certainly the teaching of law focuses on precedent decisions of the superior courts, and always with a judge made focus but without the litigant or person seeking a remedy and tenacious advocate prepared to put the question up even to ofttimes an unyielding law and take action on behalf of a person needing in this case protection and a remedy there would be little for the higher court to determine.

In *Re SK (An Adult) (Forced Marriage: Appropriate Relief)* (2004) earlier, the question arose as to whether wardship extended to adults who were, through being forced to enter into marriage against their will, deprived of the capacity to make their own decisions. Anne-Marie Hutchinson OBE (solicitor) of Dawson Cornwell drove the law and made such an application to the court as at the time no other protective powers seemed available to deal with this situation. Hutchinson feared that SK might be being kept by relatives and family in Bangladesh against her will and her return to the UK deliberately delayed as part of an attempt to marry her forcibly. Singer J in the High Court in a most sensitively aware and progressive judgment that helped change the course of forced marriage ruled:

> *An adult cannot be made a ward of court, but the inherent jurisdiction of the High Court can, in an appropriate case, be relied upon and utilised to provide a remedy. I believe that the inherent jurisdiction now, like wardship . . . is a sufficiently flexible remedy to evolve in accordance with social needs and social values.*

So, the general rule is that a person over the age of 18 years cannot be warded, however the inherent jurisdiction can be invoked to protect such a person and the importance of this jurisdiction was emphasised in *Re SK* (earlier).

Exceptionally in *SO (a child Wardship Extension of protective Injunction)* [2015] EWHC 935 (Fam) in the context of wardship proceedings, where the court had ruled that a young person was at risk of harm and had granted an injunction to protect her from that risk, the court ruled that it had the power, as part of the protective measures available in wardship and under the inherent jurisdiction generally, to extend that protection beyond the young person's 18th birthday. S, who was almost 18 at the date of the instant hearing, lived with M in Australia. Both M and S were British nationals. The wardship proceedings had commenced when S was aged 2, at which time she was unlawfully abducted from the UK by her father (F) and taken to Australia, before being recovered and returned to M's care. F had been convicted on two occasions of incitement to solicit M's murder and was still serving a prison sentence in Australia and due to be released in three years. (Compare this case with *M Children Jurisdiction Wardship* [2016] EWCA Civ 937 later.)

The confluence of the inherent jurisdiction and wardship

With regard to minors under 18 years of age, the inherent jurisdiction and wardship can both be used. In *Re Z (A Minor) (Freedom of Information)* [1995] 4 All ER 961, Ward LJ asserted: 'For all practical purposes the jurisdiction in wardship and the inherent jurisdiction over children is one and the same thing.' In *Re S (Adult Patient: Sterilisation)* [2001] Fam 15, [2000] 2 FLR 389, [29–30] and [403] respectively, Thorpe LJ described this as: 'a distinction without a difference', going on to say that the two jurisdictions are 'to be exercised upon the same basis, namely that relief would be granted if the welfare of the patient required it and equally refused if the welfare of the patient did not'. In *Re SA* [2006] 1 FLR, Munby J said this: '[39] In *Re G (Adult Patient: Publicity)* [1995] 2 FLR 528, at 530, Sir Stephen Brown P described the jurisdiction as "not strictly 'parens patriae'" but similar in all practical respects to it'.

The legal framework of wardship

Wardship is part of the wider protective inherent jurisdiction which protects adults and minors. The wardship jurisdiction whilst under the wing of the inherent jurisdiction applies only to those under 18 years. The High Court has the power to make orders in wardship. Applications must be made in accordance with the Family Proceedings Rules 1991 (SI 1991/1247 (L20)): '5.1 – (1) An application to make a minor a ward of court shall be made by originating summons and, unless the court otherwise directs, the plaintiff shall file an affidavit in support of the application when the originating summons is issued.'

Practice direction

The Practice Direction 12d – *Inherent Jurisdiction (Including Wardship) Proceedings* provides guidance on the ambit of this jurisdiction and procedure. '[1.2] The court may under its inherent jurisdiction, in addition to all of the orders which can be made in family proceedings, make a wide range of injunctions for the child's protection of which the following are the most common –

    (a)   orders to restrain publicity;

    (b)   orders to prevent an undesirable association;

    (c)   orders relating to medical treatment;

    (d)   orders to protect abducted children, or children where the case has another substantial foreign element; and

    (e)   orders for the return of children to and from another state'.

The Practice Direction was amended following Sir James Munby LJ's judgment in *Re A Ward of Court* [2017] EWHC 1022 (Fam) which involved a specific question of whether police officers who wished to interview a ward were required to make an application to the wardship court for permission. The court clarified that had never been the case.

The official solicitor

The Official Solicitor is normally appointed as litigation friend to represent the child's interests.

> *The Official Solicitor is an officer of the Supreme Court appointed by the Lord Chancellor under s 90 of the Senior Courts Act 1981 (formerly the Supreme Court Act 1981, renamed by the Constitutional Reform Act 2005) and performs duties pursuant to statute, rules of court, direction of the Lord Chancellor, at common law, or in accordance with established practice. The Official Solicitor's work is now largely acting as 'litigation friend' (or in family proceedings, 'guardian ad litem' or 'next friend') of last resort for those who lack litigation capacity.*
>
> (*Jowitt's Dictionary of English Law* 2019)

(See also the role of the Official Solicitor in wardship cases discussed in Chapter 11 which involve Gillick competent adolescents including *Re M (Child: Refusal of Medical Treatment)* [1999] 2 FLR 109, the girl who did not want a heart transplant.) The Official Solicitor represents minors but only when there is no other suitable person or agency available to take on this role. (See *Re B (A Minor) (Wardship: Guardian Ad Litem)* [1989] 1 FLR 268.) In some cases, a child/adolescent may wish for independent representation by appointing their own solicitor to directly and exclusively represent their interests. A child/adolescent may also be represented by a children's guardian appointed by the court.

Procedure and principles

The child becomes a ward of court immediately on the originating summons and the court may make, in addition to all of the orders which can be made in family proceedings, a wide range of injunctions for the child's protection. For a review of the relevant case law and the principles and correct law to be applied see *NY [a child]* [2019] UKSC 49. In this case a father applied under the Hague Convention on the Civil Aspects of International Child Abduction 1980 set out in Schedule 1 to the Child Abduction and Custody Act (CACA) 1985 for a summary order for the return of his daughter from England to Israel which was opposed by the mother. The application was granted, and the mother appealed. The Court of Appeal ruled that it had not been open to the judge to make an order under the Convention and setting aside the order invoked the inherent jurisdiction and made an order for the immediate return of the child to Israel, in substitution for his order under the Convention.

Test to be applied in wardship

In wardship proceedings, the test of 'best interests of the child' prevails. The 'best interests test' has been severally articulated as ensuring the welfare of the child and predates the 1989 welfare paramount test. As stated by Hedley J in *Portsmouth NHS Trust v Wyatt* (2004) EWHC 2247 (Fam) (2005) 1 FLR 21 [23], 84 BMLR 206:

> *Best interests must be given a generous interpretation. As Dame Elizabeth Butler-Sloss P said in Re A (Male Sterilisation) (2000) 1 FLR 549 at 555: . . . best interests encompass medical, emotional and all other welfare issues. . . . The infinite variety of the human condition never ceases to surprise, and it is that fact that defeats any attempt to be more precise in the definition of best interest.*

Wardship proceedings are governed by the child's welfare which is placed first and paramount (note this was the language and the order of the construct and principle pre-1989 Children Act). In *Re K (Infants)* [1965] AC 201, a case which concerned the disclosure of the guardian ad litem's report in wardship proceedings, Lord Devlin quoted with approval the dictum of Ungoed-Thomas J, the trial judge, who said that the jurisdiction: 'is not based on the rights of parents, and its primary concern is not to ensure their rights but to ensure the welfare of the children'. In *Re D (A Minor) (Justices' Decision: Review)* [1977] Fam 158, Dunn J expressed the principle in this way: 'the golden thread, which runs through the whole of this court's jurisdiction, the welfare of the child, which is considered in this court first, last and all the time'. Lord Scarman in *Re E (SA) (A Minor) (Wardship)* [1984] 1 WLR 156 said: 'In exercising wardship jurisdiction, the court is a true family court. Its paramount concern is the welfare of its ward'.

Strictly wardship

Who can be warded?

The jurisdiction of wardship applies to those who are:

- under 18 years;
- not necessarily British subjects (e.g. children seeking asylum);
- not necessarily residing in England and Wales (e.g. a child removed from the jurisdiction by child abduction, and *Re B, RB v FB and MA (Forced Marriage: Wardship Jurisdiction)* [2008] EWHC 1436 (Fam) later in this chapter.

Can anyone make an application in wardship?

Any individual may bring an application by originating summons to make a child a ward of court (Supreme Court Act 1981, s 41(2)) including, for example, a health care professional, a relative, neighbour, friend, an organisation, a charitable body or a solicitor.

The following cases consider the range of persons who can make an application. In *Re D (A Minor) (Wardship: Sterilisation)* [1976] Fam 185, an educational psychologist made an application in wardship. Here, the mother of an 11-year-old handicapped girl was concerned that her daughter, because she had no understanding of sexual matters and was therefore vulnerable, might become pregnant. The mother made arrangements for her daughter to be sterilised. This concerned the educational psychologist who made an application in wardship. The court ruled against the proposed sterilisation finding that it was not in the child's best interests.

In *B v W (Wardship: Appeal)* [1979] 3 All ER 83, an appeal before the House of Lords, the appellant and his wife were the grandparents of two wards of court, one a boy of 14 years of age and the other a girl of 7 who were the children of the appellant's daughter and her husband. At the beginning of his judgment Ormrod LJ in the CA recognised and acknowledged the insuperable inherent difficulties between the parties concerned:

> *Whenever grandparents find it necessary to make their grandchildren wards of court and to make their own son or daughter a defendant, the situation is one which could scarcely be more difficult or more disadvantageous for the children; litigation between parents and their children is a very unfavourable situation.*

Mrs Justice Lane had originally made an order committing the two wards of court into the care of the local authority and made detailed provisions as to access to the children's maternal grandparents. The grandfather (B) appealed against this order, seeking care and control himself. Lord Diplock delivered the decision of the HL and restored the order of Mrs Justice Lane.

In *Re A (A Child) (Wardship: Habitual Residence)* [2007] EWHC 3338 (Fam), the father sought political asylum and was granted indefinite leave to remain in the UK. His wife gave birth to a child in the UK. The father took the mother and the child to Kurdistan purportedly for a holiday, but the family remained there. The marriage deteriorated and a court in Kurdistan granted custody of the child, A, to the father. The father told the mother she could not see A. The mother left Kurdistan and issued wardship proceedings in respect of A in the UK. A jurisdictional issue arose over the question of 'habitual residence'. The court said that the jurisdiction of the court rested on the fact-based concept of 'habitual residence' and since the child's habitual residence was Kurdistan then the child should be returned to Kurdistan.

In *Re X (A Child by His Litigation Friend* [2011] 2 FLR 794, E lived in London with the mother. When he was about 17 years old, he contacted a solicitor and said that his mother was planning to take him to Nigeria and force him into a marriage.

[3] Acting by Ms Hutchinson, a partner in that firm, as his next friend, E obtained a forced marriage protection order under s 63A of the Family Law Act 1996, inserted into that Act by the Forced Marriage (Civil Protection) Act 2007. . . . On E's instructions the order was not served on the mother. No doubt the plan was to keep the order in abeyance until it was absolutely clear that adversary proceedings between E and his own mother were necessary in order to protect him from subjection to a marriage against his will. . . . [5] The non-return of E to England led to the issue by him as plaintiff, again acting by Ms Hutchinson as his next friend, of an originating summons in wardship. He remained a ward of court until his recent birthday. On the date of issue of the originating summons an order was made for E's return to England.

In *Re B, RB v FB and MA (Forced Marriage: Wardship Jurisdiction)* [2008] EWHC 1436 (Fam), a 15-year-old girl who was a British national said she wanted to move to Scotland to live with her half-brother as her mother in Pakistan had made arrangements for her to marry in Pakistan. As a child can be warded who is not necessarily residing in England and Wales the court said: 'in these very dire circumstances, the tentacles of this court should stretch towards Pakistan to rescue the child from the circumstances she found herself in.'

Applications without notice

Applications can be made ex parte without notice and the urgency of some situations may require it (see for example *Re M*, the heart transplant case cited in Chapter 11) but as Munby J points out in the following case ex parte applications must only be granted where strictly necessary.

In *KY v DD (Injunctions)* [2011] EWHC 1277 (Fam), the mother of a 5-year-old child made a without notice application, asking the court to: (i) make the child a ward of court; (ii) prohibit the father from removing the child from the mother's care and control; (iii) make a passport order in respect of the father; and (iv) order an inter partes hearing in two weeks' time. The child who had been warded then was dewarded and other ancillary orders including a passport order, and a prohibited steps (s 8 CA 1989) order preventing the child from being removed from the jurisdiction were made. In this case Munby J expressed concern about ex parte applications and reiterated the guiding principles.

Restricting wardship: the Children Act 1989

The CA 1989, s 100(3) ended the use of wardship by the local authority unless if, without the intervention of the court, the child would be likely to suffer 'significant harm' (s 100(4)(b)). Section 100(2)(c) provides:

No court shall exercise the High Court's inherent jurisdiction with respect to children – (c) so as to make a child who is the subject of a care order a ward of court;(3) No application for any exercise of the court's inherent jurisdiction with respect to chil-

dren may be made by a local authority unless the authority has obtained leave of the court. (4) The court may only grant leave if it is satisfied that – (a) the result which the authority wish to achieve could not be achieved through the making of any order of a kind to which subsection (5) applies; and (b) there is reasonable cause to believe that if the court's inherent jurisdiction is not exercised with respect to the child, he is likely to suffer significant harm.

The CA 1989 imposes two prohibitions with respect to a child who is in the care of the local authority subject to a care order. Firstly, no s 8 order other than a child arrangement order for residence can be made (see s 9(1)) and secondly, a child subject to a care order cannot be made a ward.

In *M Children Jurisdiction Wardship* [2016] EWCA Civ 937, the court could not exercise its jurisdiction to authorise the local authority to provide care for a 17-year-old adolescent. Further, there was no jurisdiction to extend T's wardship, or the terms of the order, beyond T's 18th birthday. (See the difference with the earlier case of *SO (a child Wardship Extension of protective Injunction)* [2015] EWHC 935.)

In *Enfield London Borough Council v A Mother and others* [2024] EWHC 133 (Fam), an application for leave was made by the London Borough of Enfield to seek an order from the court under its inherent jurisdiction in relation to a 17-year-old child, V, a ward of court, in circumstances where immediately before her 17th birthday in November 2023, she was the subject of an interim care order. The court held that it could not make an order.

Minors and the inherent jurisdiction

In *S (Inherent Jurisdiction) Transgender Surgery Abroad* [2023] EWHC 347 (Fam) following an application by the local authority for leave under s 100(3) of the CA, to determine one matter alone with regard to the child that of transgender surgery abroad, a judge invoked the inherent jurisdiction of the High Court and '[3] ordered that Sam was not to undergo any gender reassignment surgery without the permission of the court and he was not to leave, or be removed from, the jurisdiction for the purpose of undergoing any surgery until further order'. Five days before the final hearing was due to commence in January 2022, the local authority applied to withdraw its application to invoke the inherent jurisdiction on the basis that, on recent evidence put before the court, it could not prove its case. Sir Andrew McFarlane P was critical of the local authority application.

> *[13] Can I make it plain that, by criticising the legal approach described in the s 37 report, I do not seek to criticise its author, who was a newly qualified social worker. My criticism is of the corporation, rather than any individual.*

Restricting wardship suborned to secretary of state power

That the wardship court is suborned to the Secretary of State powers has been reiterated in a long line of authorities. In *Re W (A Minor) (Wardship: Jurisdiction)* [1985] AC 791, the Court of Appeal held that the High Court cannot exercise its powers so as to intervene in an area entrusted by Parliament to another public authority, in the instant case – the Secretary of State. In *R (Anton) v Secretary of State for the Home Department: Re Anton* [2005] EWHC 2739 (Admin), the court refused to grant an injunction which would prevent a child from being deported. Munby J said that the fact that a child was a ward could not limit or confine the powers of the Secretary of State. Although he also made it clear that it had not been fair of the immigration authorities to allow family proceedings due to be heard imminently to be adjourned without informing the parties that removal directions had already been set for before the adjourned date. It was unfair because it must have been obvious that with knowledge of the true facts the other side would never have allowed the hearing to be adjourned. He also granted similar relief in the judicial review proceedings and directed that the family proceedings proceed to a full hearing.

In *F v M, A and Secretary of State for the Home Department* [2017] EWHC 949 (Fam), in granting the declaration sought the court said:

> [1] The Secretary of State's grant of refugee status to a child was an absolute bar to any order by the Family Court seeking to affect the return of the child to alternative jurisdiction. The determination of refugee status itself, and therefore its consequences, was the Secretary of State's sole responsibility.

(See earlier *Re A Ward of Court* [2017] EWHC 1022 (Fam).)

Restricting wardship – no wardship before birth

Where pregnant mothers and/or their partners are alcohol/drug/substance users the safety of their unborn and newly born babies has resulted in the local authority making an application in wardship to protect the child of a pregnant mother to be even before its birth. In such cases the court has repeatedly held that it has no jurisdiction. In *Re F (In Utero)* [1988] Fam 112, the local authority applied ex parte for leave to issue a summons making in effect a foetus a ward of court where a mentally disturbed woman prone to drug abuse was pregnant and shortly due to give birth. The judge held that the court had no wardship jurisdiction over an unborn child.

Anticipatory declarations under the inherent jurisdiction after birth

Other questions have arisen relating to whether it is for the wardship jurisdiction to determine matters relating to concealing from a party a birth plan for an unborn child. In *Re D (Unborn Baby) (Emergency Protection Order: Future Harm)* (2009) sub nom *30 Bury MBC v D* [2009] EWHC 446 (Fam), Munby J said:

> [5] Putting the point in slightly different form, the question is whether, despite the requirements of Article 8 of the European Convention, it is lawful for the local authority not to involve the mother and her partner fully in the birth planning for her future child as would normally be required. [6] . . . I am therefore concerned, it seems to me, and Mr. Hayden is entirely content with this approach, with the inherent jurisdiction of the High Court to grant anticipatory declaratory relief, declaring in appropriate circumstances that some future course of conduct is either unlawful or, as Mr. Hayden would invite me to declare in the present case, lawful. The question therefore, and it seems to me a question

which arises wholly independently of the best interests of the mother, is whether it is lawful in the circumstances for the local authority not to share its thinking and its care plan with the mother and her partner prior to the point at which, immediately following the birth, the child is removed, as I would anticipate by the police in the exercise of their powers under Section 46 of the Act.

In *Kettering General Hospital Trust NHS Foundation Trust v C and North Northamptonshire Council* [2023] EWFC 12, the trust applied under the inherent jurisdiction for anticipatory declarations relating to an unborn child. The application was made without notice to C who was 37 weeks pregnant. C was HIV positive and had declined anti-retroviral treatment during her pregnancy. C was due to give birth by planned caesarean section on 24 January 2023. The Trust's application was intended to secure the administration of anti-retroviral medication to the baby, commencing immediately upon birth and to continue for 28 days. Whilst the court had no jurisdiction to make any order either under the Children Act 1989 or its wardship jurisdiction, see *Re F (In Utero) (Wardship)* [1988] 2 FLR 307. The court held that:

[3] The circumstances met the criteria of exceptionality. The fact that the baby might be able to live with HIV does not mean that he should: that would be wholly contrary to his best interests. The doctors and medical team were entirely right to identify the immediate medical treatment as an imperative which established a secure basis for what remained an exceptional declaration.

The limitless jurisdiction

Practice direction 12d [1.2](a) – orders to restrain publicity

Publicity privacy and children's rights

The media is always eager to report stories of 'interest to the public' especially where parents have committed grave criminal offences or where the child is the 'love child' of a public figure or celebrity. An order in wardship can restrain any individual from publishing any details which would enable the identity of the child concerned to become known. Whilst in the earlier cases the court in wardship imposed an outright ban on publishing details potentially harmful to the child, recent case law *Re S (A Child) (Identification: Restriction on Publication)* [2004] 1 AC 593 balances Article 10 of the ECHR (right to freedom of expression) with the protective purpose of wardship and Article 8 right to privacy.

Children of children who have killed

Mary Bell and Norma Bell (who were not related) were both accused of killing Martin Brown, 4 years of age, and Brian Howe, 3 years of age, in May and July 1968. Norma Bell was acquitted of the murder and manslaughter of both boys. Mary Bell was found guilty of manslaughter on the grounds of diminished responsibility. At the time of the killings, Mary Bell was 10 years of age. After serving 12 years in a juvenile detention centre, she was released. When she was 24 years old, she gave birth to a baby girl. The birth of Mary Bell's daughter was of interest to the public and attracted media attention and intrusion. An application was made and granted in wardship to ward the baby and an injunction granted to prohibit publication of her whereabouts (see Practice Direction 12d – *Inherent Jurisdiction (Including Wardship) Proceedings* [1.2 (a)].

In *X County Council v A* [1985] 1 All ER 53, a successful application by summons in the wardship proceedings for an order restraining the respondents, News Group Newspapers Ltd, by themselves, their servants or agents, from (i) publishing the name or identity of the ward or the parents of the ward or any information which would lead to their identification; (ii) publishing the address, locality, or area of the ward or the parents or any information which could lead to the identification of its location; (iii) publishing the identity, name or address, or any information by which the same could be established, of the ward's maternal grandmother, until the ward reached 18 years of age, was made.

A further injunction was granted in 1995 following renewed media interest in Bell and her daughter, who by that time was an adolescent. Exceptionally, in 2003, an injunction was granted *contra mundum* to protect the anonymity of both Mary Bell and her daughter (see *X (A Woman Formerly Known as Mary Bell) and another v O'Brien and others* [2003] EWHC 1101 (QB)).

Media intrusion 'Love child'

Cecil Parkinson, Secretary of State for Trade and Industry (under Margaret Thatcher a former British Prime Minister's Government) had an intimate relationship with Sara Keays, his secretary. Their daughter, Flora, was born in 1983, suffering from learning disabilities. Her mother, in pursuit of treatment for her daughter, attended the Peto Institute, a facility for treatment of learning disabilities. A documentary was made of the work of the Institute and Flora was one of the children filmed in the documentary. An injunction was sought to prevent the transmission of the documentary. In *Re Z (A Minor) (Freedom of Information)* [1995] 4 All ER 961, Flora (Z) was made a ward of court, and an injunction was granted restraining publication of her identity. On appeal, Ward LJ said that Cazalet J, the original judge who had refused a request by Miss Keays to lift the existing injunction, was correctly of the view that the welfare of the child would be harmed and not advanced by her being involved in the making and publication of the film.

Media interest – victims of child abuse

In the 1980s an unprecedented number of cases of child sexual abuse involving very young children were diagnosed in Middlesbrough, Cleveland (discussed in Chapter 14 and Chapter 15). Sixty-seven of the 125 children who were diagnosed as having been sexually abused between February and July of 1987 were made wards of court.

In *Re X, Y and Z (Wardship: Disclosure of Material)* [1992] sub nom X (minors) Re 1 FLR 84, a newspaper made an application for leave (1) to have access to wardship files relating to certain wards or ex-wards; and (2) to disclose documents for the purposes of a libel suit in which the newspaper was the defendant and in which two paediatricians were the plaintiffs. The two paediatricians sued for libel, following the publication in the newspaper of two articles accusing the doctors of incompetent and irresponsible promulgation of unsound techniques, in particular reflex and dilation, which were used as diagnostic indicators in the investigation of child sexual abuse, and which subsequently led to children being removed from their families. The newspaper pleaded justification, relying on a number of case histories including the *X*, *Y* and *Z* children. The court held, on the basis of the authorities, that the privilege of confidentiality in wardship proceedings was that of the court, not the child, and the court had a dispensing power to authorise publication in particular instances, having regard to the welfare of the child, and the public interest in the due administration of the wardship jurisdiction, in accordance with its parental functions. The application failed, and the originating summons was dismissed.

In *R v Central Independent Television plc* [1994] Fam 192, in a case where a mother was concerned that a television programme on sexual abuse would lead to the identification of her son as a victim, since it did not directly involve the care or upbringing of a child the injunction was not granted and Waite LJ in the Court of Appeal said:

> *No child, simply by virtue of being a child, is entitled to a right of privacy or confidentiality. That is as true of a ward of court (or child in respect of whom the inherent jurisdiction is otherwise invoked) as of any other child. Any element of confidentiality concerning a child in respect of whom the court's jurisdiction is invoked belongs not to the child but to the court. It is imposed to protect the proper functioning of the court's own jurisdiction and will not be imposed to any further extent than is necessary to afford that protection.*

Media interest – child victims of disasters

On 23 May 1987, the *Daily Mail* newspaper published an article, which referred to a ward of court. The ward, L, aged 12 years, had been a passenger on the Herald of Free Enterprise when the ferry sank off Zeebrugge. L lost her parents and grandmother when the ferry sank. The funeral of the child's parents and grandmother took place on 22 May. The article described the events at the funeral and referred to L by name and to the fact that she was a ward of court. The question arose as to whether, as a ward of court, the newspaper, in disclosing the name of the child, was in contempt. Booth J found that the newspaper had not committed a contempt of court, since the article complimented L on her courage, and it did not contain inaccurate information (*Re L (a minor) (wardship: freedom of publication)* [1988] 1 All ER 418).

Practice direction 12d [1.2](b) – orders to prevent undesirable association

In *Re F. (Orse. A.) (A Minor) (Publication of Information)* [1977] Fam 58, where the ward (F) was a minor just 16 years of age who had formed an association with a man (R) and to whom F's parents took the strongest objection on moral grounds. F left home and on 16 February 1976, her parents applied ex parte to Arnold J for her to be made a ward of court. Arnold J also granted an injunction against R, forbidding him to 'harbour or to communicate' with F. The Official Solicitor applied ex parte to Tudor Evans J for orders and injunctions until further order to restrain the Daily Telegraph Ltd. proprietors of *The Daily Telegraph* newspaper and its editor Mr William Deedes, and against the proprietors of the *Evening Mail*, Slough and its editor Mr Martin Edward Macklin Davies, from publishing any information whatsoever relating to the proceedings. The Court of Appeal held that: 'it is not a contempt to publish information about a ward of court which does not relate to wardship proceedings heard in private (post, pp. 86D, 99C-D).'

Nigel Lowe in his paper 'Inherently Disposed to Protect Children' (2012) considers how the inherent jurisdiction can be used. The Practice Direction PD 12D *Inherent Jurisdiction (Including Wardship) Proceedings* (updated 10 April 2014) gives specific examples of 'undesirable association' (para 3.1) which in addition to the preceding has recently been used in cases where local authorities are seeking to prevent extremist connections and child sexual exploitation. 'Seek and find' orders are also specifically mentioned in para 1.2.

Child sexual exploitation

The problem of human trafficking and child exploitation has been recognised for several years. Most recently the Telford Child Sexual Abuse Inquiry published in July 2022 exposed the extent of child sexual exploitation in the Telford area where wardship could have been used to protect these young girls if anyone had engaged with the idea that they were being exploited and were vulnerable instead of labelling them streetwise and that they had made a life style choice (vol 4 para 9.45 1121).

For example, in *Rotherham Metropolitan Borough Council v G (A child)* [2016] EWHC 2660 (Fam), Rotherham Council sought orders to protect a female Child G from what it believed to be child sexual exploitation by four males identified as HH, LL, MM and NN. The four males are described in this judgment as 'associated males' associated with Child G. An application was granted for a Reporting Restriction Order to protect the identity of Child G, her family members and the four associated males to include provision for lifelong anonymity.

Other cases have involved undesirable associations of underage girls with older men so in *Re R (A Minor) (Contempt)* [1994] 2 FLR 185 a married man in his 30s with six children formed a relationship with a 14-year-old girl. She was warded and injunctions were granted prohibiting contact between the two.

Radicalisation

Family lawyers are familiar with the interventive protection of the wardship and care proceedings jurisdiction in circumstances where children are at risk of being exposed to extreme political or religious views and behaviour, specifically 'radicalisation'. The approach of the family court has been broadly welfare centric through the wardship jurisdiction and s 31 of the Children's Act 1989 (CA) in the protection of minors and safeguarding (discussed in Chapter 12, 14). The wardship jurisdiction has been invoked in such cases because of its international reach. However, the use of wardship in these circumstances is contested (Ahdash 2023, Edwards 2015, 2023).

In *Re Y (Children) (No 3)* [2016] EWHC 503 (Fam) three adult parents who travelled to Syria with four children were stopped and detained at the Turkish/Syria border. The children were made wards of court and the parents detained in UK police custody. However, the local authority could not meet the standard of proof required in order for a care order to be granted, unable to provide evidence that the parents intended to travel to Syria to join ISIS. The interim care orders were discharged, and the children returned to their parents. In *Re M (Wardship Jurisdiction and Powers)* [2015] EWHC 1433 (Fam), Sir James Munby used wardship to obtain the return of four siblings aged between 20 months and 7 years whose parents had removed them from the jurisdiction to Turkey and then Moldova since it was thought the family's purpose might be to join ISIS.

Adolescents have also travelled unaccompanied to join ISIS, persuaded or groomed and trafficked by persons outside their immediate family. For adolescent males the concern has been the risk to them of physical harm in fighting, witnessing violence and death. In *Re Y (Risk of Young Person Travelling to Join IS) (No 2)* [2015] EWHC 2099, Hayden J made orders in wardship where Y, 16 years of age, had grown up within a family where there was a commitment to waging Jihad in Syria, two of Y's brothers had died and Y's uncle was unlawfully detained in Guantánamo Detention Centre and there was a concern that he needed much support. In *Re Y (A Minor) (Wardship: Assistance on Transition to Adulthood)* Practice Note [2018] 1 WLR 66 and reading the tragic circumstances and the risk of future harm to this teenager, no one can be in any doubt of the continuing vulnerability of this young man reaching majority whilst empathising with his feelings of aggrievement and injustice. Concerned for his welfare and the jurisdiction's inability to protect and safeguard and 'preserve Y's life' [6] when he reached 18 years of age, unusually a bespoke package was devised by the local council to continue until Y is 21, including an appointed social worker. In *London Borough of Tower Hamlets v M & Others* [2015] EWHC 869 (Fam) following the grant of wardship, Hayden J was asked to make orders to retrieve the passports of several adolescent girls to prevent any attempt to travel to ISIS territory. Such a measure necessitated careful consideration in the event the passports were surrendered through non-legal means and parental cooperation.

In *Re X (Children) (No 3)* [2015] EWHC 3651 (Fam) where children accompanied by their mother were intercepted prior to boarding a flight destined for Turkey, Sir James Munby, in discharging the care and wardship proceedings, said: 'The local authority, for its part, has not proved either that the materials found at her home have the significance which was suggested or, more generally, that she is a radical or extremist' [111].

Seek and find orders

Seek and find orders so called have been made in the following circumstances. Madeleine McCann, who was a child who had gone missing whilst holidaying with her parents in Praia da Luz, Lagos, Portugal, on the evening of 3 May 2007, following the parents application, became a ward of court, on 2 April 2008, as the result of proceedings which started on 17 May 2007. 'The purpose of the proceedings was to call upon the extensive powers of the High Court to require assistance to be given in the search for a missing child' (see Scott 2008). In *Kelly v BBC* [2001] 1 FLR 197, the boy concerned had run away from home in order, it was thought, to join a religious cult. A 'seek and find' order was made. Munby J later held that the media did not require permission to interview the ward or to publish or broadcast the interview.

Practice direction 12d [1.2](c) – orders relating to medical treatment

Reproduction, termination, sterilisation, life ending decisions

Where there is a concern that there may be a conflict between the several parties – parents, patient and doctors – the court in wardship is tasked with deciding such matters. Earlier cases raised issues of termination of pregnancy and sterilisation, whilst more recent case law concerns issues of surrogacy and transgender treatment.

Termination and sterilisation

In *Re P (A Minor)* [1986] 1 FLR 272, a 15-year-old girl wanted an abortion, and her mother was opposed to it. The local authority made an application in wardship. The girl had already given birth to a child when she was 13 years old. The court held that the girl could have an abortion and applied the welfare of the child as the paramount consideration in the court's decision. The parent's objection to the abortion and offer to care for the unborn child were factors taken into consideration, but the court held that such factors could not weigh above other factors in balancing the needs of the ward and the dangers to her mental health if such a termination were to be refused.

Sterilisation raises many moral and ethical questions, especially where the minor concerned is mentally vulnerable. The court in wardship has authorised sterilisation in several cases where the adolescent was unable to understand sexual relations and pregnancy and childbirth. Consider these following cases. In *Re B (A Minor) (Wardship: Sterilisation)* [1988] AC 199 the House of Lords ruled in favour of sterilisation in a case where a local authority had the care of the adolescent girl. B, a girl of 17 years, suffered from a moderate degree of mental handicap but had a very limited intellectual development. Her ability to understand speech was that of a 6-year-old and her ability to express herself that of a 2-year-old child. In *Re M (A Minor) (Wardship: Sterilization)* [1988] 2 FLR 497 the local authority made an application in wardship for leave to carry out a sterilisation operation on a 17-year-old girl who was physically normal but had a mental age of 5 or 6 years. The court authorised the surgery.

Such procedures on those with inhibited mental capacity have been much contested challenging as they do basic reproductive rights. Heilbron J in *Re D (A Minor) (Wardship)* [1976] Fam 185 did not authorise sterilisation as the child would be able at some point to make an informed decision. She described as: 'a basic human right . . . the right of a woman to reproduce'.

Surrogacy

JP v LP and Others (Surrogacy Arrangement: Wardship) [2014] EWHC 595 (Fam) involved a partial surrogacy arrangement, the surrogate mother providing the egg and the husband the sperm. The mother's friend carrying the child. Within months, the marriage had broken down. The spouses obtained a shared residence order and undertook to seek a parental order to regularise the child's status, and it was not until 2012 that the question of the child's status was finally transferred to the High Court after the mother had sought sole residence. The surrogate mother was added as a party to the proceedings. The court said: '[5] Given the wholly exceptional circumstances wardship was the most appropriate way to manage the overall use of parental responsibility as between the father, the legal mother and the psychological mother of the child (see [35]–[37])'. (See Horsey and Sheldon 2012). (See Chapter 9 for discussion of surrogacy).

Life ending decisions – easing pain and suffering

Wardship is used to protect adolescents from the consequences of taking life-ending decisions when refusing blood products or donated organs (See Chapter 11). Wardship is also invoked where babies and young children are not competent to make medical decisions for themselves and where parents, in exercising parental responsibility, do not agree with the medical plan of care proposed by medical professionals. Where babies and young children are terminally ill or are so sick that they are unlikely to live, for even a short while, decisions must be made with regard to their ongoing medical care, including decisions regarding how to numerously feed, medicate, provide pain relief, ventilate or resuscitate, or a decision may need to be taken with regard to authorising a heart, heart and lung, or liver transplant for a child. Or as in the following unique and exceptional case a decision regarding the life of one party which will bring about the death of the other. In *Re A (Conjoined Twins: Medical Treatment) (No 2)* [2001] 1 FLR 267, the twins who were joined at birth required separation which would result in the weaker of the two dying. Jodie and Mary were born in August 2000 and were ischiopagus (joined at part of the pelvis) tetrapus (with four legs). They each had their own brain, heart, lungs, liver and kidneys, although Mary's brain, heart and lungs were defective. One 'crucial anatomical fact' was that the arterial circulation ran from Jodie to Mary. Because of the defects in Mary's vital organs already identified, she was not capable of independent existence, but if there were an elective separation, the prognosis for Jodie would be for at least a reasonable quality of life. If the twins were not separated, Jodie's heart would fail within a matter of months through the strains imposed on it. It was accepted that separation entailed rapid death for Mary (see Burnet 2001).

The court in wardship held that it was necessary to operate in order to save the life of one child where the death of both was imminent, knowing that the separation would result in the death of the weaker child.

Loving parents may reach a decision to consent to resuscitating a child or consenting to an organ transplant in the desire of 'treating the child to live'. Loving parents may equally reach a decision that they do not wish their child to be resuscitated, or to receive a donated organ, since in their view it is kinder to 'treat' the child by allowing him or her to die with medication to alleviate pain and suffering. Doctors caring for very sick children always work with the 'sword of Damocles' over their heads, fearing criminal prosecution. The question is who ultimately decides: parents, doctors or judges? (See for further discussion Cantor 2006.)

Such was the predicament of Dr Leonard Arthur, who was described as 'letting' a very sick baby (John Pearson) die and faced a criminal prosecution for murder. In *R v Arthur* (1981) *The Times*, 5 November, Dr Leonard Arthur was indicted for the murder of John Pearson, a charge that was dropped and attempted murder substituted. John Pearson was born on 28 June 1981 and was suffering from Down's syndrome as well as other related disabilities and conditions. His parents did not want him to live. Dr Arthur prescribed 'nursing care only' and doses of dihydrocodeine to sedate the baby, who died three days later. The jury driven by the moral rather than legal claim found Dr Arthur 'not guilty'.

What is the moral basis for prolongation of life as against letting an individual die without further suffering? The ethics of such a decision are much contested. The language used and the contextual framing of the primary objective has over the years moved from 'letting a child die' to 'treatment to ease pain and suffering'. What is being done is justified or else condemned by and through the use of language and rhetoric which is 'performative' (see Searle 1969, Austin 1958). That is to say, when a word is spoken or written it becomes a relational entity. Words are very powerful in framing action and are used to justify and condone a behaviour or act, or otherwise condemn the decision or action that is being taken.

The language used in these cases has moved through a number of positions from (a) 'letting a child live' or 'letting a child die', which carries perhaps a negative connotation of omission, to (a) 'treatment to live' and (b) 'treatment to die' which inscribes the action as 'treatment' carrying a positive inflection rather than a negative expression of an act of failing. Most recently, the medical approach has centred on (c) easing pain and suffering as the primary objective (see Bertini 2024).

Over the years wardship judges in these extremely difficult cases demonstrate a shift in the use of language towards the primary objective of which is to ease suffering and not merely to prolong life. These ethical questions are considered in the following cases. Lord Goff of Chieveley said, in *Airedale NHS Trust v Bland* (1993):

I agree (with Professor Glanville Williams) that the doctor's conduct in discontinuing life support can properly be categorized as an omission. It is true it may be difficult to describe what the doctor actually does as an omission, for example where he takes some positive step to bring life support to an end. But discontinuation of life support is, for present purposes, no different from not initiating it in the first place. In each case the doctor is simply allowing his patient to die in the sense that he is desisting from taking a step which might, in certain circumstances, prevent his patient from dying as a result of his pre-existing condition.

Ease suffering, or to prolong life?

'Let die'

In *Re B (A Minor) (Wardship: Medical Treatment)* [1981] 1 WLR 1421, a baby was born with Down's syndrome, duodenal atresia and intestinal blockage. The parents thought it kinder to 'let her die'. Doctors, fearing criminal prosecution, given the *Arthur* case cited earlier, contacted the local authority, who made the baby a ward of court. The court of first instance refused to consent to the treatment to live. But on appeal and in the light of the *Arthur* case, the Court of Appeal authorised surgery since it said the baby should not be (in the performative utterance of the court) 'condemned to die'.

However, as the following cases demonstrate, each case turns on its own particular facts, since suffering, prognosis of duration of life and quality of life for the child differs from case to case. The court said in *An NHS Trust v MB (A Child Represented by CAFCASS as Guardian ad Litem)* [2006] EWHC 507 (Fam): 'For every case and every child is unique, and this case concerns M alone.'

'Treat to ease pain and suffering'

Re C (A Minor) (Wardship: Medical Treatment) [1989] 3 WLR 240 reflects the use of language, which embodies a moral position that allowing a child to die can indeed be a positive which involves treatment of the child. This shift from considering merely the consequences of life and death to weighing up the suffering of the child can be seen in the case of Baby C. C was made a ward of court shortly after her birth. The court considered the case from a perspective of the importance of giving treatment to ease pain and suffering rather than giving treatment to prolong life and accepted the opinion of medical staff that the aim of nursing care should be to ease the ward's suffering rather than achieve a short prolongation of life, and in such circumstances considered it inappropriate to include in the court's directions any specific instructions as to how the ward was to be treated. Lord Donaldson, Master of the Rolls, said: 'Baby C is dying. Nothing that the court can do, or the doctors, can alter that fact' and refuted Ward J's description in the lower court when he said in the course of his judgment, that leave would be given to 'treat the ward to die'. Lord Donaldson said: 'No one would uphold such a phrase,' and in the amended judgment said that Baby C who was born with severe hydrocephalus should be treated: 'in such a way that she may end her life and die peacefully with the greatest dignity and the least pain, suffering and distress'.

In *Re J (A Minor) (Wardship: Medical Treatment)* [1990] 3 All ER 930, the court made an order that a premature 27-week baby born as a result of an accident which resulted in brain damage, blindness, paralysis and epilepsy, should be treated with antibiotics if he developed a chest infection but not reventilated unless doctors deemed it appropriate. Lord Donaldson said:

Again I have to cavil at the use of such an expression as 'condemn to die' and 'the child must live' in Templeman LJ's judgment, which, be it noted, was not a reserved judgment. . . . The decision on life and death must and does remain in other hands. What doctors and the court have to decide is whether, in the best interests of the child patient, a particular decision as to medical treatment should be taken which as a side effect will render death more or less likely. This is not a matter of semantics.

Prolongation of life however was ruled as the objective by the court of first instance in *Re J (A Minor) (Child in Care: Medical Treatment)* [1993] Fam 15. As a result of serious head injuries sustained when he was 1 month old, J, who was born in January 1991, became profoundly mentally and physically handicapped, suffering from microcephaly, cerebral palsy, cortical blindness, severe epilepsy and requiring to be fed by a nasogastric tube. The local authority shared parental responsibility under a care order. The judge directed that if J were to suffer a life-threatening event while in the health authority's care and the required drugs and equipment were or could reasonably be made available, the health authority should cause such measures (including artificial ventilation) to be applied so long as they were capable of prolonging his life. The health authority appealed. The Court of Appeal, allowing the appeal, held that in the exercise of its inherent jurisdiction the court would not order a medical practitioner to treat his patient in a manner contrary to his clinical judgement. Accordingly, the order would be set aside.

From the child's perspective – intolerable life

Resuscitation – more invasive

In *Re Wyatt (A Child) (Medical Treatment: Parents' Consent)* [2004] *Portsmouth NHS Trust v Wyatt and Wyatt, Southampton NHS Trust Intervening* [2004] EWHC 2247 (Fam), the parents opposed medical opinion that the child should not be resuscitated in the event of a respiratory crisis. C was 11 months old and born at 26 weeks' gestation weighing 458g (approximately one pound). She suffered from, *inter alia*, poor kidney function and respiratory difficulties and required ventilation for most of her first three months of life. She had also suffered severe brain damage. Since resuscitation is considered more invasive than feeding and drug treatment, a higher level of justification for this procedure is required. The court approached its task by considering the course of action from the child's vantage point or subject position. Hedley J enumerated the medical evidence ([15–19]) which reported that she could feel pain and distress and that it was unlikely, although not impossible, that she experienced pleasure. To supply C with the necessary supplemental oxygen her head was covered with a transparent plastic box. When removed from the box she generally became distressed and turned blue. In July 2004, she contracted an infection, which had led to a deterioration of her condition. The realistic prognosis for her survival for a further 12 months was 5 per cent. The unanimous medical opinion was that it was not in C's best interests to artificially ventilate her in the future. The applicant NHS Trust sought a declaration, which would, in essence, permit them to discontinue invasive and aggressive treatment of C.

The parents believed it was their duty to maintain C's life, as they believed she was not yet ready to die. They also believed that they had experienced C's reacting to them ([12–14]). The court held that the test was not whether life would be tolerable to the decider but whether the child in question, if capable of exercising sound judgment, would consider the life intolerable. The medical evidence held that further aggressive and invasive treatment would be intolerable to C and such treatment would not be in her best interests. Accordingly, a declaration in similar terms to that contended for by the applicant NHS Trust was granted.

Ethical considerations and understanding shifted again in later cases which focused on a concept of whether life had become intolerable. In *A NHS Trust v MB* [2006] EWHC 507, the child of 18 months suffered from severe spinal muscular atrophy, which was incurable and degenerative. The trust caring for the child was concerned about whether the child's life had become intolerable. The parents opposed any discontinuation of ventilation. The medical witnesses were unanimous that it was in MB's best interests to withdraw treatment, but the judge decided that it was not in the child's best interests to discontinue ventilation and so granted ventilation. The judge however held that it was in the child's best interest to withhold procedures that went beyond ventilation including CPR (cardio-vascular resuscitation).

Transplant decisions – invasive – sustaining life

Where the treatment proposed involves an organ transplant, the courts have tended to give less weight to any presumption of treatment to live. As Butler-Sloss LJ recognised: 'But to prolong life . . . is not the sole objective of the court.' (See *Re T (A Minor) (Wardship: Medical Treatment)* [1997] 1 All ER 906). (See also du Bois-Pedain 2005.) In *Re T*, the child was born with a life-threatening liver defect and a transplant was required. His parents, who had taken him with them to live abroad, were both healthcare professionals with experience in the care of young, sick children. They did not wish T to undergo transplant surgery and refused their consent to an operation should a suitable liver become available. The doctors who had treated T in England were of the opinion that his parents were not acting in his best interests and referred the matter to the relevant local authority, which applied under CA 1989, s 100(3) for the court to exercise its inherent wardship jurisdiction. The judge held that the mother's refusal to accept the unanimous advice of the doctors and her refusal to consent to the operation was not the conduct of a reasonable parent and he ordered that T be returned to the jurisdiction within 21 days to be assessed for transplant surgery. On appeal by the mother, the court said that 'it was in his best interests to require his future treatment to be left in the hands of his parents'. Accordingly, the judge's order was set aside. Roch J said this:

> This brings me face to face with the problem of formulating the critical equation. In truth it cannot be done with mathematical or any precision. There is without doubt a very strong presumption in favour of a course of action which will prolong life, but, even excepting the 'cabbage' case to which special considerations may well apply, it is not irrebuttable. . . . The presumption in favour of the sustaining of life is not irrebuttable and perhaps has less weight where the issue is whether to prolong or not to prolong life by means of organ transplantation. I agree that this appeal should be allowed.
>
> (See Michalowski 1997)

In *A National Health Service Trust v D* [2000] 55 BMLR 19, a child was born prematurely with serious disabilities, including a chronic, irreversible and worsening lung disease, heart failure, hepatic and renal dysfunction, and severe developmental delay. In June 2000, the applicant applied for a declaration that, in the event of any future respiratory and/or cardiac failure or arrest, the child should not be resuscitated but should be given palliative care to ease pain and suffering and 'to permit his life to end peacefully and with dignity'. In this case, the parents opposed the application, contending that it was premature. The court held that, having regard to:

> the minimal quality of life, the short life span left, the irreversible and worsening lung condition, any possible very limited short-term extension that mechanical ventilation might give him had to be weighed, from his assumed standpoint, against the increasing pain and suffering caused by further mechanical ventilation.

The court referred to the 'palliative treatment' proposed as being in the best interests of the child, and answering counsel's submissions added that such a declaration did not disclose any breach of the ECHR, there could be no infringement of Article 2 because the treatment as advised was in the best interests of the child, and Article 3, which required that a person was not subjected to inhuman or degrading treatment included the right to die with dignity.

Similarly, in *Re L (Medical Treatment: Benefit)* [2004] EWHC 2713 (Fam), two National Health Service Trusts applied for a declaration about the future care of a 9-month-old baby, following disagreements between the trusts and the baby's mother over his future care. The baby was born with Edward's Syndrome, a genetic disorder that caused him to suffer multiple heart defects, chronic respiratory failure, gastroesophageal reflux, severe developmental delay, epilepsy and hypertonia. The baby's condition was incurable, and he was unlikely to survive beyond a year. Any treatment given would be palliative, not curative. The mother contended that the baby had not deteriorated to the extent set out in the medical reports and that the medical profession was giving up too soon. The trusts sought a declaration that it would be lawful not to provide further aggressive treatment, either by artificial ventilation or by cardiac massage. The court ruled:

> [26] In L.'s best interests, seen in the broadest possible way, taking into account his emotional need to continue his relationship with his mother and the sort of life he would lead permanently connected to a mechanical ventilator, I would exclude intubation and the use of mechanical ventilation as not being in his best interests. [27] The purpose of mechanical ventilation would be to enhance palliative care. It would not be to cure him. I am entirely satisfied that the risks outweigh the benefits, and of course in coming to that conclusion I do of course take into account that I am looking at an issue of palliative care. I will therefore in due course make the declaration sought by the two Trusts.[28] Very little has been said about cardiac massage. L. appears to have been successfully revived twice after cardiac arrests by this method, once in August and on the other occasion on 8 October. I understand the process to be that two fingers are used to massage the heart through the skin by repeated thrusts and push, about a hundred a minute over the chest to squash the heart in order to stimulate it. One appears to have to go three to four centimetres in through the chest in order to achieve the proper pressure. The process continues until a proper level of

cardiac output, that is to say, a response to a sufficient level. It may continue for a several minutes.[29] After discussion, the Trusts have agreed not to pursue this matter. The mother does not want it excluded as a possibility. In my view, the Trusts are right to come to that conclusion. I recognise that all the treating doctors and almost all the experts oppose the idea of cardiac massage, but as I have said, it has been used twice, and whatever part it may have played in resuscitation on 8 October, that part cannot have been negative. I consider it should remain as an option. It is in the best interests of L. that that it should remain an option.

Recent disagreements

In *Aysha King (a Child)* [2014] EWHC 2964 (Fam), Aysha who was 5 years old suffered from an inoperable and life limiting brain tumour (Medulla blastoma)[4] and was warded following the parents' disagreement with the hospital regarding his treatment 'in particular, the type of radiotherapy to be administered'. The parents wanted the hospital to offer proton therapy which the doctors said was neither recommended nor funded. The parents then found a centre in Prague offering proton therapy and removed Aysha from Southampton General hospital and took him to France. The local authority filed an application in the High Court seeking permission to invoke the inherent jurisdiction making Ashya a ward of court and 'directions as to necessary medical treatment'. In order to affect Aysha's return to ensure that he would not suffer, a European arrest warrant was also issued. He was later dewarded. Baker J said: '[36] I have been informed that Ashya has been formally admitted to hospital in Prague. It follows that he has now ceased to be a ward of court.' (In 2016, following the publication of a prospective Phase II trial the NHS decided it would pay for children with medulloblastoma to travel abroad to receive proton therapy. (Aysha King survived.)

In 2017, Charlie Gard was made a ward of court in order to resolve the conflict between parents and medical professionals caring for him. Charlie Gard suffered from a life limiting condition, mitochondrial DNA depletion syndrome. The parents wished to pursue experimental treatment in the US which US doctors originally willing to treat their son considered futile as it was treatment that required to be commenced immediately. The position of Great Ormond Street Hospital (GOSH) caring for Charlie was that palliative care should be provided. The parents unsuccessfully appealed the court's decision accepting the GOSH recommendations to the Court of Appeal and the Supreme Court and the ECHR. Charlie Gard died in 2017. (See Welstead 2023, Jonas 2021.)

In the case of Alfie Evans, *Evans and Another v Alder Hey Children's NHS Foundation Trust* [2018] EWCA Civ 805, the parents appealed an order made by Hayden J on 11 April 2018. By that order Hayden J declared that it would be lawful for artificial ventilation, being provided to Alfie, to be withdrawn at the date and time specified in the order. Alfie was terminally ill with a severe and progressive neurodegenerative condition and an MRI scan undertaken at the beginning of February 2018 revealed, to quote from the Court of Appeal's previous judgment, 'the almost total destruction of his brain' [13]. Hayden J concluded:

Alfie's need now is for good quality palliative care. By this I mean care which will keep him as comfortable as possible at the last stage of his life. He requires peace, quiet and privacy in order that he may conclude his life, as he has lived it, with dignity [62].

Hayden J determined that the parents' proposals were 'irreconcilable with Alfie's best interests'. This decision was upheld by the Court of Appeal which expressly stated that to transfer Alfie to another country could not possibly be in Alfie's best interests. The Supreme Court refused permission to appeal [67]. (See the case of Indi Gregory, *Gregory v Nottingham University Hospitals NHS Foundation Trust and others* [2023] EWCA Civ 1262. See also Bertini 2024.)

See also *King's College Hospital Nhs Foundation Trust v Mrs R Mr R Nr (By his Children's Guardian)* [2024] EWHC 910 (Fam).

Wardship will continue to impose itself as an important jurisdiction with the best interests of the child at its centre. The case of *A National Health Trust* (earlier) indicates that the modern subject position of the court in wardship is to place itself in the position of the child in determining where the best interests of the child lie. Hence in such cases, discussions of whether the child's life is painful or intolerable now become relevant. This suggests a departure from the earlier position in wardship where the court stood in the place of the judicious parent and in a default position that prolongation of life was always the correct course. It is established that the doctor will not be forced to treat against his judgement and conscience. Doctors now seem increasingly unwilling to accede to pressure.

No conflict, all parties agree

Where the medical professionals and both parents agree with the proposed course of action, the decision for the court is less problematic. In *K (A Minor) Re* [2006] EWHC 1007; [2006] 2 FLR 883, where a 5½-month-old child was suffering from congenital myotonica dystrophy and in care of the local authority, the NHS Trust made an application to the court to remove the feeding tube and move to a regime of palliative care to allow the child to die peacefully. The parents both approved of what the doctors proposed as did the child's guardian. Sir Mark Potter P granted the declaration to allow her to die peacefully, saying it would: 'not only be a mercy, but it is in her best interests'.

[42] This is a comparatively unusual case to come before the court in the sense that the declaration sought is non-contentious, all parties concerned being in agreement with the views of the medical professionals involved that life-prolonging treatment should cease. Indeed, I was told in the course of argument that, had the necessity for parental consent simply rested with the father and mother in this case, the matter would not have come to court, the medical professionals being satisfied that their ethical and legal obligations would not be breached by the action now proposed. However, the case is now before the court for

decision, and the court is not tied to or bound by the clinical assessment of what is in K's interests. The court must reach its own conclusion on the basis of a broad spectrum of considerations after careful consideration of the evidence before it. See Re T (A Minor) *[1997] 1 WLR 242 [250] per Butler-Sloss LJ;* Airedale National Health Service Trust v Bland *[1994] 1 FRC 485 [530];* R (Burke) v GMC *[2004] 3 FCR 579 per* Munby J *[93]–[95].*

In applying the 'best interests' test the court said:

Dame Elizabeth Butler-Sloss P made clear in Re S (Adult Patient: Sterilisation) *[2001] Fam 15 at 30E, [2000] 3 WLR 1288, [2000] 2 FCR 452: at p 28 that the principle of the 'best interests' of the patient as applied by the court extends beyond the considerations governing the propriety and advisability of medical treatment developed in the* Bolam Case *[1957] 2 All ER 118, [1957] 1 WLR 582 and 'The judicial decision will incorporate broader ethical, social, moral and welfare considerations'.*

Practice direction 12j (pd) wardship, abduction and habitual residence

In cases where the child is abducted by one of the parents and removed to another jurisdiction wardship proceedings are commenced for return of the child. These circumstances are also dealt with under s 8 prohibited steps orders CA 1989 (See Chapter 12 as there is some understandable overlap here and areas of law are not hermetically sealed). The prohibited steps order is more focused than the wardship jurisdiction. Wardship provides that no matter concerning a child can be executed without leave of the court.

Where the cases are complex wardship may be preferred over a s 8 order. Whilst s 8 prohibited steps orders are considered in Chapter 12 some of the more complex wardship cases are considered here. For example, see orders for return of the child *Lewisham London Borough Council v D (Criteria for Territorial Jurisdiction in Public Law Proceedings)* (2008) 2 FLR 1449, L (a child), Re [2023] EWHC 3194 (Fam) return order for a 4-year-old who had been removed to Algeria and *M O C v Yusuf* [2023] EWHC 2792 (Fam) where a return order was ordered for a child from Somalia. The question of habitual residence is determinative.

In *Re S (Children) (Abduction: Asylum Appeal)* [2002] 1 WLR 2548, the appellant and respondent were the parents of two sons, aged 5 and 3 years. The family was from India and resided in India until June 2001, when the appellant and her sons came to England for a holiday. They stayed with the respondent's family and the appellant then went to live with a family friend. The appellant said that the respondent had been violent towards her and decided not to return to India. The respondent denied the allegations. He issued an originating summons seeking the summary return of the children to India. The children were made wards of court.

In *Re T (Wardship: Review of Police Protection Decision) (No 2)* [2008] EWHC 196 (Fam), the child had been abducted at the age of 6 months by the father and taken to India for two years, and had been made a ward of court. When the father returned to England with the child, the child was removed from the paternal home and placed in the mother's care. The father was subsequently arrested and charged with the criminal offence of child abduction (see Chapter 9 and *Re D* (1984)).

In *Re S (A Child)* [2010] EWCA Civ 465, the local authority was concerned that a 7-year-old child was being neglected and applied for an emergency protection order. The order was refused. The mother took the child to Spain, where the father lived. Notwithstanding, the local authority continued with an application for care proceedings and the child was made a ward of court, with the requirement that she return to the jurisdiction. The issue was whether the child had lost habitual residence in England when she was removed to Spain. The court held that the judge was entitled to make the child a ward of court, and to conclude that the CA 1989, s 100(2)(4)(a) applied and that the child was likely to suffer significant harm s 100(4)(b) if the inherent jurisdiction was not exercised.

Not habitually resident

ES v AJ [2010] EWHC 1113 (Fam) turned on the question whether the children were 'habitually resident' in England. The court was satisfied that there was an agreement between the parents to send the twins to Cameroon. The twins were currently habitually resident in Cameroon and so the English court had no jurisdiction, and it was decided that the mother could pursue remedy there (see Chapter 12).

In *H v H (Jurisdiction to Grant Wardship)* [2011] EWCA Civ 796, the father was a British national of Afghanistan origin. He married in Afghanistan. The child was born in Afghanistan, and the mother came to England on a visa, leaving the child in Afghanistan in the care of an uncle. Several months later the mother left the father, because of domestic violence. The child was allegedly 'abducted' from the uncle's home; the court issued wardship proceedings. The child was warded, the father appealed, and wardship was discharged:

> there was no jurisdiction over a child who was not and never had been habitually resident or present in the country in circumstances in which jurisdiction had not been conceded, even implicitly. In this case jurisdiction had been challenged at the first opportunity and that challenge had been maintained thereafter at every hearing, (see paras [47], [50], [52]).

In *Re N (A Child) (International Abduction: Exercise of Inherent Jurisdiction)* [2012] EWCA Civ 1086 the mother and father had one child (T). The mother was a citizen of Thailand. The father was a national of Lebanon but had gained British citizenship as a result of a previous marriage. The family had spent time in various jurisdictions and settled in the United Kingdom in 2009. At that stage, T had become habitually resident in the UK, but she was not a UK citizen. The Court of Appeal, Civil Division, upheld a finding that it had not been appropriate for the court to exercise its inherent jurisdiction and order the return of a child to this jurisdiction where the child was no longer habitually resident in the UK. It was not until after that time that the mother made her application to the High Court on 18 August 2011 and the conclusion, therefore, of Wood J was that at that time, the time of the application when the court's jurisdiction was first invoked, that the child T was no longer habitually resident here.

In 2013, in *the matter of A (Children) (AP)* [2013] UKSC 60 on appeal from [2012] EWCA Civ 1396 and [2013] EWCA Civ 232 concerning habitual residence, abduction and wardship, the mother made a wardship application to the English court in 2011. Jackson J made all four children wards of court and ordered that they be brought to England and Wales by the father. The father challenged the jurisdiction of the English court. The proceedings came before Parker J who found that all four children were habitually resident in England. She relied on the judgment of Charles J in *B v H (Habitual Residence: Wardship)* [2002] 1 FLR 388, a case with almost identical facts.

The father appealed to the Court of Appeal, where it was unanimously held that it was 'quite hopeless' for him to argue that the three oldest children did not remain habitually resident in England. However, the majority (Rimer and Patten LJJ) held that it would be 'divorced from reality' to find that the youngest child, who had been born in Pakistan and had never set foot in this jurisdiction, was habitually resident here holding that physical presence in a country at some point was a pre-requisite for habitual residence in that country. Thorpe LJ dissented, also relying on *B v H* (discussed earlier). The mother appealed to the Supreme Court who laid down principles including that there is a single test for habitual residence, and it is a question of fact.

If a child is not habitually resident in England and Wales or any other member state, Article 14 of the Brussels II Revised Regulation permits the use of other bases of jurisdiction within national law. There remains in existence under the national law of England and Wales a 'nationality' based parens patriae jurisdiction that applies to British nationals within inherent jurisdiction/wardship proceedings, regardless of habitual residence or physical whereabouts. This jurisdiction can be exercised in exceptional cases, where Article 14 is engaged, unless that jurisdiction is excluded by the Family Law Act 1986. (See a complex case involving care proceedings and the inherent jurisdiction of wardship *Z v V and others* [2024] EWHC 365 (Fam). See also where countries are outside the Hague Convention (*Re J (A Child) (Custody Rights: Jurisdiction)* [2006] 1 AC 80 – a Saudi Arabia case; *Re W (A Child) (Abduction: Jurisdiction)* [2003] EWHC 1820 (Fam) – a Pakistan case; and *Re H (Abduction: Non-Convention Application)* [2006] EWCA 199 (Fam) – a Dominica case, *Addou v Bennabi* [2022] EWHC 3465 (Fam) – Algeria case.) (See further Turner et al. 2013).

Contact and wardship

In *H v D and others* [2007] EWHC 802 (Fam), a complex inter-jurisdictional residence and contact matter between the parties, the court made the children wards of court and Sumner J set out the ambit of wardship powers:

> *[57] It can be exercised irrespective of the proceedings in which the need to protect the children arose. It can be exercised where there are concurrent proceedings in another territorial jurisdiction. It can also be exercised if the child's presence is transient provided there is a good enough reason, such as damage or risk of damage to the child's well-being.*

(See also *NP v BR* [2019] EWHC 3854 (Fam) involving a transfer of living arrangements from mother to father and protracted litigation. See also *Mrs R v The*

Mother and another [2024] EWHC 263 (Fam).) In *Re M Children* [2017] EWCA Civ 891, involving custody and access issues of four children wardship was invoked where the return of the younger two children to Estonia was ordered by the Estonia court. In response, the mother relied upon Article 13(b) of the Convention, asserting that she had been the victim of domestic violence perpetrated by the father and that he had sexually assaulted her eldest daughter (the allegations including rape) and had frequently physically assaulted her second child. Roderic Wood J, who heard the Hague application in July 2014, decided that having regard to the protective measures available in Estonia and the undertakings offered by the father, grave risk/intolerability under Article 13(b) was not established. However, he found that the children objected to being returned and declined to order their return. The court held that the Estonia order could not be upheld. (See also *WB v VM* [2024] EWHC 302 (Fam) return order, *Manchester City Council v Maryan Yusef & Ors* [2023] EWHC 2792 (Fam) return order.) See also in complex abduction cases and breach of return orders the invocation of wardship *Kaha v Lahmer* [2024] EWHC 2439 (Fam); *Elkndo v Elsyed* [2024] EWHC 2230 (Fam).

Wardship and unaccompanied asylum-seeking children

An increasing number of children arrive in the UK as unaccompanied minors or as members of families seeking asylum. In *E (By Her Litigation Friend EW) v London Borough of X* [2006] 1 FLR 730, E obtained a visa and came to the UK with an older sister. The older sister said E was 17 years of age. She arrived in England and lived with a woman she believed to be her mother. By 2004, the relationship had broken down and she then lived with foster parents. The 'mother' wanted to return to Ghana with E, but E refused. She was made a ward of court, and the local authority was ordered to prepare a report under CA 1989, s 37(1). The court held that in the light of the uncertainty as to her present circumstances wardship would not be discharged until her 18th birthday. (See *The Care Matters* White Paper 2007: 116.)

In January 2023, 4,600 unaccompanied asylum-seeking children were accommodated in Home Office hostels. It transpired that a number of refugee children disappeared from hostels where they should be protected and safe. Article 39, a registered charity, made an application to the court in wardship. In *Inherent jurisdiction – Article 39 v Secretary of State for the Home Department and Others* [2023] EWHC 1398 (Fam):

> *[1] The Applicant, Article 39, a registered charity which promotes and protects the rights of children in England . . . seeks to trigger the Court's inherent jurisdiction to make wardship orders in relation to a number of unaccompanied asylum-seeking ('UAS') children who have gone missing from Home Office run accommodation in Brighton and Hove. [12] Article 39 wants the Court to ensure that it has the relevant information about the children and to consider whether it should make further orders in respect of them under its wardship jurisdiction.*

Following an extensive review of the authorities, the court said this is not an appropriate case in which the court should or could exercise its wardship jurisdiction. Sir Andrew McFarlane ruled that the children could not be protected as wards of court because they are already protected by the CA 1989 and local authorities have a duty to uphold their safeguarding for unaccompanied asylum-seeking children who are in their area.

Resisting deportation

In *R (on the application of Ahmadi) v Secretary of State for the Home Department* [2002] EWHC 1897 (Admin), the Ahmadi family, who were victims of torture, fled Kabul on the back of a lorry with their children. They claimed asylum in the UK having travelled via Germany. They had applied for asylum in Germany where their application was refused notwithstanding that under the Dublin Convention, the appropriate country in which to make an asylum application is the first country of arrival, which in this case was Germany. The claimants stated that conditions in Germany for asylum seekers were so poor that to return them to Germany would be in breach of Article 3 (inhuman and degrading treatment) of the ECHR. They sought refuge in a mosque in Stourbridge until they were arrested by police for deportation, during which time the family were kept in detention at Harmondsworth Detention Centre, London. The children, a daughter aged 5 and son aged 3, were made wards of court and an emergency application was made to Bennett J in the Family Division, for their release from detention. The family were finally deported to Germany in 2004.

The ambit and uses of wardship are wide and vital to child protection in complex and differing situations.

Reform of wardship

The Law Reform Commission for the UK considered the matter of the reform of wardship in 1987 considering that its usefulness had by and large been supplied by statutory reform. The Law Reform Commission of Ireland in 2005 recommended the abolition of the wardship jurisdiction and its replacement with a new Public Guardianship system. (See in particular, paras. 4.61, 6.41, 6.56, 6.58 and 6.62 of the 2003 Consultation Paper and para. 7.96 et seq. of the 2005 Consultation Paper, 'Vulnerable Adults and the Law: Capacity'.) Clearly statutory reform has not supplanted the usefulness of wardship.

Despite these proposals it is clear that wardship remains a very important protective jurisdiction which impacts on all areas of law relating to children where children cannot be adequately protected by other legislation. Regrettably, the number of wardship proceedings are no longer recorded. Collation of family proceedings data is a reflection of public interest and political will. Statistics compiled by the Department of Education (DOE) and the Ministry of Justice (MOJ) record the number of forced marriage protection orders and female genital mutilation protection orders where numbers are far less than wardship but reflect the importance of these two areas and the importance of accountability. Wardship, as this excursion has demonstrated, continues to be an important safeguard in the protection of minors as society becomes more complex especially with interjurisdictional matters.

Self-test questions

1. 'Contrary to fears which were expressed before the Children Act 1989 came into force, wardship remains vigorously alive . . . wardship remains an important last resort in a variety of situations where a child's welfare requires the intervention of the High Court' (Mitchell 2001b).

Discuss, with reference to case law and the range of circumstances and situations in which wardship since 2010 continues to provide important protection for children.

2. Ann is 18 months old and has a rare condition known as dilated cardiomyopathy. She will need a heart transplant before she is 3 years of age, otherwise she will die. Her parents, Saad and Marianna, do not want her to have the operation as her brother Julian also has the condition and had a heart transplant. Sadly, he had a stroke following surgery and is now severely mentally handicapped. The doctors treating Ann believe that a heart transplant is in her best interests.

Advise the doctors and the parents.

3. The *Practice Direction 12d – Inherent Jurisdiction (Including Wardship) Proceedings* states: '1.1 It is the duty of the court under its inherent jurisdiction to ensure that a child who is the subject of proceedings is protected and properly taken care of. The court may in exercising its inherent jurisdiction make any order or determine any issue in respect of a child unless limited by case law or statute. Case law establishes that such proceedings should only be commenced exceptionally where it is clear that the issues concerning the child should not be resolved under the Children Act 1989, for example, for reasons of urgency, of complexity or of the need for particular judicial expertise in the determination of a cross-border issue.'

Discuss the reach of wardship and cases where wardship should not have been brought and cases which were wrongly brought under the jurisdiction and where other statutory provisions might have otherwise been used to achieve the purpose for which the order was sought.

4. Olivia Fox has completed a term of imprisonment for child cruelty towards her young daughter Mary Ellen who was 4 years of age at the time. She is due to be released and plans to reside in the former matrimonial home in a small village in London Brooke. The Rosetta family adopted her daughter whilst Olivia was serving her term of imprisonment. The *London Brooke Herald* wants to publish Olivia Fox's release from prison as the lead story. Mary Ellen is 12 years of age.

What course of action, if any, is open to the Rosettas, Mary Ellen's adoptive parents?

References

Ahdash, Fatima, 'Countering Terrorism in the Family Courts: A Dangerous Development' [2023] *Modern Law Review* 1197

Bertini, Ilaria, 'Young Children's Best Interests and the Withdrawal of Life-Saving Treatments in the UK' [2024] *Child and Family Law Quarterly* 59

Burnet, David, 'Case Commentary: Conjoined Twins, Sanctity and Quality of Life, and Invention the Mother of Necessity' [2001] *Child and Family Law Quarterly* 91

Cantor, Neil, 'On Hastening Death Without Violating Legal and Moral Prohibitions' [2006] *Loyola University Chicago Law Journal* 101

du Bois-Pedain, Antje, 'Doctors, Patients and the Courts, Legitimising Restrictions on the Continued Provision of Lifespan Maximising Treatments for Severely Handicapped Non-Dying Babies' [2005] *Child and Family Law Quarterly* 535

Edwards, Susan, 'Radicalisation: Antithetical Jurisdictions of Protection and Punishment' [2023] *Family Law* 684

Evans, Alfie, 'Alfie Evans: Legal Battle Toddler Dies' *BBC News* www.bbc.co.uk/news/uk-43933056 (accessed 12.05.2024)

Gard, Charlie, www.bbc.co.uk/news/health-40554462 (accessed 28.04.2024)

Graves, David and Geoffrey Lee Martin, 'Geldof Wins Custody' (2000) www.telegraph.co.uk/news/uknews/1378636/Geldof-wins-custody-of-Paula-Yatess-daughter.html (accessed 28.04.2024)

Gregory, Baby, 'Indi Gregory: Critically Ill Baby Dies After Life Support Turned Off' *BBC News* www.bbc.co.uk/news/uk-england-derbyshire-67400915 (accessed 28.04.2024)

Haastrup, Isaiah www.independent.co.uk/topic/isaiah-haastrup (accessed 28.04.2024)

Horsey, Kirsty and Sally Sheldon, 'Still Hazy After All These Years: The Law Regulating Surrogacy' [2012] *Medical Law Review* 67

Independent Inquiry – Telford Child Sexual Exploitation the Crowther Report (July 2022) www.iitcse.com/ (accessed 12.05.2024)

Jonas, Monique, 'The Discourse of Dignity in the Charlie Gard, Alfie Evans and Isaiah Haastrup Cases' [2021] *Medical Law Review* 24

King, Aysha, www.theguardian.com/society/2014/sep/01/ashya-king-timeline (accessed 12.05.2024)

Law Commission Working Paper No 101, 'Family Law Review of Child Law: Wards of Court Law Commission Scottish Law Commission' (April 1987) https://cloud-platform-e218f50a4812967ba1215eaecede923f.s3.amazonaws.com/uploads/sites/30/2016/08/No.101-Family-Law-Review-of-Child-Law-Wards-of-Court.pdf (accessed 12.05.2024)

Law Reform Commission Consultation Paper, 'Vulnerable Adults and the Law: Capacity' LRC CP 37-2005 www.lawreform.ie/_fileupload/consultation%20papers/cp37.htm (accessed 12.05.2024)

Lowe, Nigel, 'Inherently Disposed to Protect Children' in Rebecca Probert and Chris Barton (eds) *Fifty Years in Family Law Essays for Professor Stephen Cretney* (Intersentia 2012) 161

Michalowski, Sabine, 'Case Commentary: Is It in the Best Interests of a Child to Have a Life-Saving Liver Transplantation?' [1997] *Child and Family Law Quarterly* 179

Mitchell, John, 'Whatever Happened to Wardship?' Part 1 [2001a] *Family Law* 130

Mitchell, John, 'Whatever Happened to Wardship?' Part 2 [2001b] *Family Law* 212

Scott, Tim, 'McCann, Madeleine, 'Madeleine: Ward of Court, LP Information' 2008 submission by Tim Scott QC High Court of Justice 2 July 2008 Open Court www.gerrymccannsblogs.co.uk/Nigel/id130.htm (accessed 12.05.2024)

Susan Edwards "Protecting schoolgirls from terrorism grooming", *International Journal of Family Law 2015*, 3. 236-248

'Telford Child Sex Abuse Went on for Generations, Inquiry Finds' *BBC News* www.bbc.co.uk/news/uk-england-shropshire-61983584 (accessed 12.05.2024)

Turner, James, Richard Harrison KC and Peter Newman, 'Jurisdiction and Meaning of Habitual Residence' *Law Society Gazette* (13.09.2013) www.lawgazette.co.uk/law/jurisdiction-and-meaning-of-habitual-residence/5037615.article (accessed 28.04.2024)

Wardship Orders (Hansard) HC Deb vol 385 cc836-7W (16.05.2002) https://api.parliament.uk/historic-hansard/written-answers/2002/may/16/wardship-orders (accessed 28.04.2024)

Welstead, Mary, 'In Search of a Chimera: The Best Interests' Test in Determining Life or Death for Baby A' (2023) *Family Law* 222

Further reading

Austin, John L, *Philosophical Papers* (Oxford University Press 1958)

Care Matters: Time for Change – GOV.UK (www.gov.uk) www.gov.uk/government/publications/care-matters-time-for-change (accessed 12.05.2024)

Chitty, Joseph, *Treatise on the Law of the Prerogatives of the Crown* (Butterworth 1838) https://archive.org/details/atreatiseonlawp00chitgoog (accessed 12.05.2024)

Illich, Ivan, *Medical Nemesis* (Boyars 1975)

Morris, Anne, 'Selective Treatment of Irreversibly Impaired Infants: Decision-Making at the Threshold' [2009] *Medical Law Review* 347

Searle, John, *Speech Acts: An Essay in the Philosophy of Language* (Cambridge University Press 1969, 1999)

Stringer, E and T Lumley, *A Long Way to Go* (New Philanthropy Capital 2007)

Taylor, Rachel, 'Case Commentary: Re S (A Child) (Identification: Restrictions on Publication) and a Local Authority v W: Children's Privacy and Press Freedom in Criminal Cases' [2006] *Child and Family Law Quarterly* 269

14

Child protection

Local authority, the court and public law procedure

SUMMARY

This chapter considers the sexual, physical and emotional abuse and neglect of children, and the new learnings and understandings which move from an incident approach to child protection to looking at the totality of abusive situations following Practice Direction (PD) 12J *Child Arrangements & Contact Orders: Domestic Abuse and Harm*, and the Domestic Abuse Act (DAA) 2021, with its understanding of coercive control. The focus in this chapter is concentrated on the role of the local authority and their statutory obligation to take steps to protect a child in their area (s 17 of the Children Act (CA)) designated as 'a child in need'. The local authority is under an obligation to provide supportive services and where there is a suspicion of 'significant harm' (CA, s 47) intervention is mandated by law. The local authority is under a duty to investigate s 47, and also has a range of powers including the emergency removal of a child from the home to secure their future protection (s 44). This chapter outlines the procedural stages which the local authority must take once a child has been referred to them and considers the several interim orders that can be made prior to a final order for care or supervision and other ancillary orders (discussed in Chapter 15).

The statutory framework is found in the CA 1989. The preliminary investigatory stages include convening a care conference, placing a child on the child 'at risk' register, and where necessary instigating emergency measures (ex parte) which authorise the immediate removal of a child from the home.

In addition, this chapter considers two features essential to the investigation which are also relevant to the determination of final orders (see Chapter 15): firstly, the importance of the medical expert in determining injury and how it was likely caused and secondly, the privilege against self-incrimination established to encourage parent/carers to disclose the cause of injuries to the child so the child can be protected. Concerning the medical expert, a mistake as to causation may result in a child being returned home to abusive parents/carers or else a child being removed from blameless parents/carers and placed into local authority care with the prospect of adoption. The second theme considered vital to a child protection investigation is the importance of encouraging parents to cooperate and disclose fully and

DOI: 10.4324/9781003435020-14

frankly the circumstances of the alleged harm so that appropriate child protection measures may be put in place for the child concerned and all the children of the family. The importance of discovering the truth is furthered by CA 1989, s 98, the privilege against self-incrimination, which prohibits disclosures from being admitted into evidence in any parallel criminal investigation. However, since the police make applications to the court for part disclosure, the prospect of police applications being successful threatens to undermine the parties' frankness about how a child came to suffer the injury thus thwarting and undermining steps made for the child's future protection.

This chapter concludes with examining some further obstacles, raised by senior judges, practitioners and academics, to an effective child protection process and attempts to mitigate them, including the Public Law Online project which addresses delay in these hearings and adherence to the 26 weeks target for public law matters (see Jackson 2023, Gilliatt 2023) and the transparency project which facilitates greater transparency in the family court and therefore greater accountability.

High profile cases

In recent years partly as a response to the 'MeToo' movement many public figures have talked about the abuse they experienced as children. Their experience and personal insights reinforce the reality that child abuse, physical, sexual and emotional, happens in all families. Their experiences are important to assist in understanding its prevalence and ubiquity.

Child abuse – an historical denial

Child abuse was thought not to exist and if it did it happened only in other people's families (see Miller 1984). Lord Justice McFarlane in his 2017 lecture 'Holding the Risk' considers some of this history where nineteenth-century patriarchal power authorised and extolled the physical chastisement of children and a father's power was rarely if ever impeached. Instances of both physical and sexual assault against children were documented throughout the nineteenth century, even if largely ignored. Edwards (1981: 138) for example reported on the Thomas Fellows evidence in 'The Edwin Chadwick Papers 1838–40' which described how girls were invariably 'seduced' (raped) by their employers and then when pregnant dismissed. On 11 January 1868, the *Illustrated Police News* carried a story of a mill manager who, it was alleged, had committed an 'outrage' (a euphemism of that time for rape) on a 12-year-old girl. In the debate on the Criminal Law Amendment Bill (1884) it was recognised that no offence was more frequent. Yet, when the Bill became law s 7 of the Criminal Law Amendment Act (1885) provided that a 'guardian' or 'master' was to be charged with misdemeanour or assault only, and that: 'it shall be a defense to any charge under this section to show that such a girl had been unchaste previously to the time of the offence charge'. Tardieu (Professor of Legal Medicine in Paris) meticulously documented the extent of child physical and sexual abuse in 'A Medico-legal Study of Assaults on Decency' (1857) citing figures for 1858–69 in France, of

9,125 accusations of rape or attempted rape on children (reported by Masson 1984: 199 nb.8). Dr Sandor Ferenczi (1932) observed:

> *Even children of respected, high-minded puritanical families fall victim to real violence or rape, much more often than one dared to suppose. Either the parents themselves seek substitution for their lack of [sexual] satisfaction in this pathological manner, or else trust persons such as relatives (uncles, aunts, grandparents) tutors servants, who misuse the ignorance and innocence of children. The immediate explanation – that these are only sexual fantasies of the child, a kind of hysterical lying – is unfortunately made invalid by the number of such confessions, of assaults upon children, committed by patients actually in analysis.*

Notwithstanding, in order to conceal and protect perpetrators' narratives of child victims as liars, evil, money extorters, seducers of men or later in psychoanalytical theory, as 'hysterics' were promulgated by powerful patriarchs. Many eminent medical and legal professionals said children made false allegations. In 1886, Dr Routh in an address to the British Gynecological Society said that women and young girls were: 'the most decided liars in creation. . . . As medical jurists we should never forget the mendacity of these women'. The 'eminent' gynaecologist Lawson Tait, police surgeon to Birmingham City Police, wrote: 'Two dirty little wretches of ten and twelve, who had been thrashed by their father for stealing, promptly turned round on him with a charge of having seduced them' (Edwards 1981: 126, 128).

Changing perceptions of abuse

Cretney and Masson (2003: 712) wrote, with reference to physical assault somewhat provocatively but appositely that, 'child maltreatment is a socially constructed phenomenon which reflects the values and opinions of a particular culture at a particular time'. In *R v Hopley* [1860] 2 F & F 202 Hopley, a schoolmaster at a school in Eastbourne wrote to the father of one of the boys at the school seeking the father's permission to chastise the boy and, as he stated in his letter to the father, he asked if he might 'continue it at intervals, even if he held out for hours'. The father replied stating: 'I do not wish to interfere with your plan.' The schoolmaster did just that, beating him for hours, until eventually the child died. The court had to decide whether the beating was excessive, since only moderate chastisement was permissible. The jury found Hopley guilty. He was sentenced to four years' imprisonment.

By 1961, a century later, health care professionals agreed that physical abuse of children occurred within the family. McFarlane LJ (2017) also referred to the work of Henry Kemp who coined the term 'battered child syndrome' after seeing children in accident and emergency departments with unexplained 'accidental' injuries. Baroness Hale, former President of the Supreme Court, in a lecture celebrating the 40th anniversary of the Family Rights Group in 2014, in an indictment of the child protection system, said:

> *Throughout the 1980s . . . were terrible scandals, such as those of Jasmine Beckford, Kimberley Carlile and Tyra Henry, where vulnerable children had been returned to or left at home to die at the hands of their parents or, more often, their parents' partners. Social workers were not doing enough to protect them.*
>
> (Hale 2014, cited in Delahunty 2019)

By 1989, the CA specifically recognised physical, sexual, emotional abuse and neglect as 'significant harm' and by 1998, following the decision in *A v United Kingdom* [1998] 27 EHRR 611 parents could no longer beat or cane their children, or as had occurred in *Hopley* (discussed earlier) authorise someone else to do so. In this case A was caned by his stepfather, S. The stepfather was prosecuted in criminal proceedings and acquitted of assault causing actual bodily harm. The European Court of Human Rights (ECtHR) held that failure to criminalise such behaviour violated A's right not to be subjected to inhuman or degrading punishment. The CA 2004 criminalised such conduct in s 58(1). 'In relation to any offence specified in subsection (2) battery of a child cannot be justified on the ground that it constituted reasonable punishment'. The provision was tested in *R (on the application of Williamson and others) v Secretary of State for Education and Employment and others* [2005] 2 AC 426. The claimants were teachers and parents of children at Christian independent schools who brought proceedings for judicial review to challenge the lawfulness of the ruling that teachers could not stand in the place of parents and administer physical punishment to children who misbehaved (see Chapter 12).

Slow death in full view of the protective agencies

Despite the momentous changes the CA 1989 introduced, abuse of children and child death continued of those already known to local authority social services departments. In 2001, Gillian Shepherd, MP, reported in the House of Commons the death of yet another abused child (See Shepherd 2001):

> *Lauren Wright my constituent, died from a blow to her abdomen, with extreme bruising all over her body, on 6 May 2000, two days before the date of the case conference that Norfolk social services had finally organised to discuss her plight. From her birth she had been known to Hertfordshire social services. She was known to Norfolk social services for the three years before her death. . . . Lauren's treatment at the hands of her stepmother, who was convicted of her manslaughter, took place in public, observed by the local community, and under the supervision of doctors, social workers, and teachers. Trial evidence revealed that the stepmother was seen hitting the child and screaming abuse at her, that she fed her pepper sandwiches, that she put bugs from the garden in her food, and that she turned off the taps so tightly that the child could not get a drink of water.*

Lauren's class teacher said at the trial:

> *often, she was covered with lots of small bruises and with major bruises about once a month. These included black eyes, bruising on her face and scratches across her back. . . . In the words of her head teacher, her physical deterioration had been 'apparent for at least five months before she died'.*

In 2000, Victoria Climbié, 8 years old, died of starvation, hypothermia, neglect and abuse at the hands of her great-aunt and her aunt's partner. Lord Laming opened the Victoria Climbié Inquiry (2003) with these words:

> *at the end Victoria spent the cold winter months, bound hand, and foot, in an unheated bathroom, lying in the cold bath in a plastic bag in her own urine and faeces and having to*

eat what food she could get by pressing her face onto the plate of whatever was put in the bath beside her . . . at the time of her last admission to hospital her body temperature was so low it did not register on a standard thermometer and her legs could not be straightened . . . this once lively, bright, and energetic child had been reduced to a bruised, deformed, and malnourished state in which her life ebbed away because of the total collapse of her body systems. As the very experienced pathologist Dr Carey told us: 'All non-accidental injuries to children are awful and difficult for everybody to deal with', but in terms of the nature and extent of the injury and the almost systematic nature of the inflicted injury, I certainly regard this as the worst I have ever dealt with, and just about the worst I have ever heard of.

The report made 18 recommendations including: (rec 13) the need to prescribe a clear step-by-step guide on how to manage a case through either a CA 1989, s 17 or a s 47 track, with built-in systems for case monitoring and review. Deaths of children continued. On 3 August 2007, Baby P died from multiple bruising, a broken back and ribs (injuries perpetrated by Tracey Connelly and her partner Steven Barker). 'Baby P was known to the social services for many months . . . he was said to have been visited on sixty occasions by health care and social work professionals and was also on the child at risk register' (Campbell et al. 2008).

And sadism and cruelty and child deaths continued. In 2021, the NSPCC recorded 223 child deaths involving abuse or neglect and conducted case reviews to see what can be learned. The 'Multi-agency safeguarding and domestic abuse paper' (2022) comprised of 50 rapid reviews, 13 serious case reviews (SCRs), seven local child safeguarding practice reviews (LCSPRs), one serious youth violence review, and one joint SCR and domestic homicide review totaling 72 domestic homicide reviews. One of the key findings emerging was the lack of a coordinated multi-agency response to domestic abuse. Nothing new, since in 2001 the internal local authority investigation into the death of Lauren Wright concluded that there was poor communication and a lack of urgency. The 'Safeguarding paper' found that in cases involving pre-birth and babies nearly all involved death or serious injury to the child through deliberate harm/physical abuse or accidental/negligent harm (for example, through co-sleeping). Infants suffered abusive head trauma, fractures consistent with non-accidental injury and neglect, substance misuse and domestic abuse. Pre-school children suffered similar injuries to those concerning babies, including non-fatal neglect. Children of primary school age included sexual abuse of the child by family members. Cases involving adolescents involved five taking their own life. Other issues included gang involvement, knife crime, criminal exploitation, sexual abuse and exploitation, teenage pregnancy, child/adolescent to parent violence, including one case of murder.

Most recently, Arthur Labinjo-Hughes (see ITV news YouTube) and Star Hobson (see Mistry 2021) died from gross and sadistic cruelty inflicted by parents and stepparents. Both deaths were the subject of a National Review.

Evidence from video footage and text messages seen at the criminal proceedings revealed a shocking scale of physical abuse and neglect suffered by Arthur. A total of 130 bruises were found on Arthur's body at the time of his death. Blood tests indicated very high levels of sodium, suggesting the possibility of salt poisoning, for which Emma Tustin was convicted. In the days leading up to his murder, CCTV footage showed that Arthur had been forced

> *to stand to attention alone in the hallway of the house for most of the day, without water.*
> *He was made to sleep downstairs on a hard floor without a mattress.*
>   (*National Review into the Murders of Arthur Labinjo-Hughes*
>   *and Star Hobson* para 1.20)

The *National Review into the Murders of Arthur Labinjo-Hughes and Star Hobson* recognised failures of the local authorities involved and also of agencies and others. The recommendations of the National Review are considered in the closing remarks in this chapter.

The DAA 2021, s 17 called for Domestic Homicide Reviews (DHRs) (which had already become law in April 2011, following s 9 of the Domestic Violence, Crime and Victims Act (DVCVA) 2004) to be reported to the Domestic Abuse Commissioner to ensure a nationwide coordination and learning. Community safety partnerships (CSPs) have the responsibility to commission DHRs. Agencies taking part include police, health trusts, GP practices, probation, adult social care, children's social care, housing providers and local domestic abuse specialist organisations.

Deaths of children continue. In *R v Ali* [2023] NI 415, the defendant was arrested on suspicion of the murder of Hunter McGlennon, the 11-month-old child of his partner. He alleged that the child had fallen onto the floor from a sofa. He took the child, who was blue, freezing and had bruises on his head, to his partner who was staying with her family. An ambulance was called. The child was pronounced dead at the hospital. In police interviews, he said the child's death was an accident. The medical evidence found a significant head injury, including extensive visible bruising, rib fractures and an injury to his penis, all of which were inconsistent with a fall from a sofa.

> *[16] The substantial medical evidence is directly in contradiction of the Respondent's account. It describes a child who was subjected to a forceful assault causing a range of significant injuries . . . head injury, characterised by subdural and subarachnoid haemorrhage associated with extensive retinal haemorrhages as well as widespread, multifocal bruises to the scalp. This severe head injury would be expected to have caused unconsciousness and would account for his clinical presentation and subsequent death. Neither a fall from a sofa and the attempts to rouse Hunter described by Mr Ali would be [not] expected to have caused such severe head injuries . . . his bruising was said to be caused by multiple blunt blows.*

Ali was convicted and sentenced to a prison. A sentence of 16 years was imposed by the Northern Ireland Court of Appeal following an Attorney General referral.

Abuse – from discrete incidents to totality context

The approach to child abuse in the family courts, until recently, has been incident focused reflecting the approach adopted within the criminal law offence framework, notwithstanding that the family courts have heard in position statements in local authority applications for some while evidence of a myriad of behaviours constituting abusive and harmful conduct. In addition, the construction of 'significant harm', and the collation and recording of official data on child abuse, has also reflected an incident-based approach. The prevalence of child abuse is recorded in one of four categories: physical, sexual, emotional and neglect, although they are by no means discrete. (See Barnett 2017.)

Totality context approach

The recognition of coercive and controlling control as a strategy of domestic abuse and as a crime (Serious Crime Act (SCA), s 75) recalibrates thinking on adult and child abuse. Coercive and controlling conduct once accepted and condoned as a patriarchal right which suborned women and children was normalised and regarded as appropriate male conduct which Shulamith Firestone in the *Dialectic of Sex* (1972) calls 'male culture'. However, Munby LJ (2020) makes the point that few judges even after Practice Direction (PD) 12J *Child Arrangements & Contact Orders: Domestic Abuse and Harm*, which expressly recognises controlling and coercive conduct, acknowledged the totality of domestic abuse albeit that coercive control also underpins much of child abuse.

In addition, mothers in particular whose children have been abused by intimate partners and stepparents have been frequently blamed for not protecting the child and intervening to prevent the other partners violence. Susan Brownmiller in *Waverley Place* (1990), a fictional account of wife-battering and child-killing based on the case of *People v Steinberg* (1989) (see below) where Joel Steinberg was indicted for second degree (depraved indifference) murder, first degree manslaughter, and seven charges that were severed or dismissed and he was acquitted of murder but convicted of manslaughter, and the Appellate court affirmed the conviction.

> There was no dispute at trial that Lisa's death was a homicide. Even the defense expert agreed that the child's death was caused by brain trauma as a result of abuse. The medical testimony, including Lisa's treating physicians and the post- mortem examination, confirmed beyond a reasonable doubt that Lisa's death was a consequence of an assault and a failure to obtain prompt medical attention.

Brownmiller in her book and in television interviews at the time criticised Hedda Nussbaum for apparently standing by as the 6-year-old adopted child of Nussbaum and Joel Steinberg (Lisa Steinberg) was killed by Steinberg. Yet when Nussbaum gave evidence for the prosecution against Steinberg the court was to hear evidence of Nussbaum's abuse at his hands which included extreme physical abuse and coercive and controlling conduct. She suffered a broken nose and underwent a splenectomy. Of his total control of her she said in evidence: 'I ate when Joel said I could . . . I slept when Joel said I could . . . I went to the bathroom when Joel said I could.' The Appellate court (per Kaye J) also noted: 'Moreover, there was evidence of Nussbaum's debilitated physical condition on November 1 from which a jury could infer that she did not deliver the fatal injury.' (*The People & C. Respondent, v. Joel Steinberg, A/K/A Joel Barnet Steinberg, Appellant* [1992] 79 N.Y.2d 673, 595 N.E.2d 845, 584 N.Y.S.2d 770.) For a discussion in the UK of attitudes to abused mothers' failure to protect children see Thompson (2020).

Physical abuse (non-accidental injury)

Signs of physical abuse of children include bruising, black eyes, grazing, burns, blindness, deafness, paralysis, fracture, subdural haematoma and retinal haemorrhaging.

An injured child may come to the attention of the police and/or local authority, both of whom have a statutory duty to protect. Anyone can refer a child to the local authority, but a doctor or teacher has a statutory duty to report any concerns. Perpetrators of abuse routinely deny responsibility for the injuries, claiming that such injuries are accidental (AI). The task of a child protection investigation involves careful piecing together of evidence of injury and other relevant medical and behavioural evidence which goes towards establishing causation in determination of how the child has been harmed.

In *Re S (A Child) (Contact and Residence Order)* [2012] EWCA Civ 1031, the trial judge recognised the impact of the father's coercive control of the mother on his parenting of the child. The father's conduct included following the mother in his car, sending her numerous bullying and derogatory text messages, insisting that the child be enrolled at a nursery of his choice, and restricting the mother from living and working where she chose. Although the mother had been physically violent to the father, the judge concluded that he was the abusive parent, recognising that his conduct formed a pattern of domineering and controlling behaviour, which was an inseparable aspect of his own parenting of the child.

Sexual abuse

Sexual abuse includes indecent touching, rape of a child, forcing a child to watch pornography or forcing a child into prostitution, sexual grooming and child sexual exploitation in all its forms. (See for offences Sexual Offences Act (SOA) 2003 ss 5–19, 47–51 53 a.) Sexual abuse of children like physical abuse, but even more so, until very recently, was thought simply not to exist or else the victim was responsible. These attitudes of disbelief and presumptions about the victim's responsibility and contributory negligence have also had an impact within the courtroom and have infected juries and judicial opinion and assessment. (Stereotypes of likely and unlikely perpetrators and victims have had an impact on judicial reasoning and judgments in criminal and family cases (See *Re H and R (Child Sexual Abuse: Standard of Proof)* [1996] 1 FLR 80 especially Lord Nicholls' judgment discussed in Chapter 15.)

The discovery of a number of sexual abuse cases in Middlesbrough, Cleveland, in 1987 raised awareness of the problem of sexual abuse and contested the myths about sexual abuse that had held family members beyond reproach, discovering that boys were at risk and that anal rape of young children, as well as vaginal rape of girls, formed part of this pattern of abuse. (See Edwards 1996 for detailed discussion.)

> In total 125 children were diagnosed as having been sexually abused between February and July 1987 in Middlesbrough General Hospital: 66 children became wards of court. In the wardship cases, 27 were dewarded and went home with the proceedings dismissed; 24 went home on conditions as to medical examination of the children, and two went home on interim care orders. Nine children who were wards of court remain in care of the County Council and away from families. Of those not made wards of court, 27 were the subject of place of safety orders. In all, 21 children remain in care. We understand that out of the 121 children 98 are at home.
>
> (Cleveland Inquiry 1988: 12)

In *Re W (Children) (Threshold Criteria: Parental Concessions)* [2001] 1 FCR 139, the local authority initiated care proceedings in relation to three boys aged 15, 12 and 11 years because of: (i) their poor physical presentation; (ii) non-intentional physical injuries; (iii) sexualised behaviour, including masturbation and simulated sex, in particular inappropriate sexualised behaviour by one of the boys towards his mother which took place during a supervised contact visit in full view of his father and social worker; and (iv) allegations of sexual abuse, in particular against their father. The parental concessions were inadequate because they had not accepted any responsibility (see also *Re M (threshold criteria: parental concessions)* [1999] 2 FLR 728). In *Re D (Children: Contact Order)* [2005] EWCA Civ 825, the local authority commenced care and adoption proceedings in relation to four children, S, aged 16; L, aged 11; L, aged 7; and T, aged 4, where:

> it was alleged by the authority that both parents had subjected S, L and L to repeated acts of sexual abuse including sexual intercourse, indecent touching, oral sex, exposure to pornography, exposure to an adult sex object, participation in a sex game involving family members removing all of their clothing, sexual activity between the adults in the children's presence and sexual abuse of one child in the presence of one or more of the other children; that S had sexually abused his sisters, L and L, and that the parents had failed to protect them from such abuse.

In both these two cases, the judge found that the threshold criteria in the CA 1989, s 31 was satisfied.

Emotional abuse

Emotional abuse arises in a context of cruelty and unkindness, ranging from belittlement and humiliation of a child to making a child feel hopeless, unworthy and unwanted, telling a child that he or she will never amount to anything, that s/he is useless, ridiculing the child, controlling the child in everything s/he does, blaming the child for every mishap, and isolating and cutting the child off from friends and family members.

Placing expectations which are too high for the child's developmental capabilities and diminishing a child's confidence and self-esteem, and unfairness in discipline and punishment and unequal treatment of siblings. For example, Tracey Wright (Lauren Wright's stepmother) 'openly discriminated against the child, teasing and bullying her while lavishing praise on her own children'. (See Batty 2001). Bullying and scapegoating, threats of violence, attempts to frighten the child with homelessness, making an adolescent eat cigarettes to stop him from smoking, are all part of emotional abuse.

Other forms of emotional abuse are demonstrated in the following cases. Allegations of fabricated illness and harm **(FII)** made by a parent about the child to draw attention to the parent can include the fabrication of signs and symptoms, falsification of medical records, samples and also correspondence and also deliberately inducing illness. In *Re B (a child) (placement order: findings of fabricated illness)* [2015] EWCA Civ 1053,

> There were . . . increasing concerns about fabricated illness in relation to EB whom the mother said was going blind, having seizures showing autistic traits. The mother's mental

health deteriorated to the extent that the police attended at her property, and she was detained under s 136 of the Mental Health Act 1983. She remained in hospital for a period as a voluntary patient. An emergency protection order was accordingly made in respect of EB, who was aged 19 months, and an interim care order was made.

Care and placement orders were made in respect of the child upheld on appeal.

In *ABC and others v Derbyshire County Council and another* [2023] EWHC 986 (KB) in a case where there was a concern about the possibility of fabricated illness (FII), four claimants brought an action against police who under s 46 of the CA 1989 had removed two children for their protection. The factual evidence found:

[15] Both children were regularly seen by medical professionals within the NHS and private sector for a series of issues. The concerns raised by ABC and DEF about GHI included suspected allergies/gastroenterological issues, benign joint hypermobility syndrome, energy levels, Mast Cell Activation Syndrome ('MCAS') Postural Tachycardia Syndrome ('PoTS') and Ehlers-Danlos Syndrome ('EDS'). There was a family history of similar gastrointestinal and connective tissue disorders. In respect of JKL, the concerns related to allergies, energy levels, his height (he was short for his age) backache and other matters. [16] In 2014 the children came under the care of Dr S, an NHS Consultant Paediatrician. On 3 March 2017, Dr S made a referral to D1's children's social care team, seeking an urgent assessment regarding FII in respect of GHI and JKL. By way of background, she explained in the letter that both children had had asthma and eczema in the past, with concerns about dietary intolerances and 'significant dietary manipulations'. She said that GHI had been discussed at a medical professionals' meeting in July 2015. There was a concern that ABC was seeking multiple medical opinions from practitioners throughout the country, mostly on a private basis, many of whom did not have paediatric expertise. A private psychology report had described GHI as binge eating, stealing food, feeling isolated from her peers and expressing suicidal ideation. She had missed extensive schooling due to medical appointments. The doctors were concerned that she was at risk of emotional harm, as a result of which GHI had been admitted to the local children's hospital for two weeks (referred to during the trial as the 'in-stay'). No food allergies or intolerances were proven and after the admission, ABC and DEF 'agreed not to seek further external reviews' of GHI.

The police decided that it was not appropriate to discuss the concerns with the parties ABC and DEF and work with them under child protection procedures, and officers removed the children GHI and JKL into police protection. Earlier in the day ABC and DEF had been arrested on suspicion of child cruelty offences. An interim care order (ICO) was granted and in an extremely complex case the court dismissed the human rights abuses claims brought by the defendants and ruled that police intervention had been entirely appropriate.

Another extraordinary and unusual example of emotional abuse is found in the case of *Re C (Children) (Care: Change of forename)* [2016] EWCA Civ 374 where exceptionally, the court countenanced a change of forenames where the mother of twins who were taken into care wanted to call them 'Cyanide' and 'Preacher'.

[4] The children were said to have been conceived as a result of rape and the midwife at the hospital where the mother had given birth to the children, contacted the local authority to

tell them of her concern that the mother was proposing to name the children respectively 'Preacher' (for the boy) and 'Cyanide' (for the girl). The local authority brought it to the court's attention at the interim care order hearing. The mother said that she had chosen the name 'Cyanide' because 'this is how Hitler killed himself'.

The mother remained determined that the children should be called 'Preacher' and 'Cyanide'.

The case was transferred to the High Court, and the local authority made an application to invoke the inherent jurisdiction of the court under wardship, s100 CA 1989. The judge said:

It does not need expert evidence or academic research to appreciate that a name which attracts ridicule, teasing, bullying or embarrassment will have a deleterious effect on a child's self-esteem and self-confidence with potentially long-term consequences for him or her,

and authorised a change of name.

Families may quite legitimately change a name for other reasons. In families children may take on a version of the parental name as for example in the case of Nigella Lawson named after her father Nigel Lawson. However, in a case where the father is called 'Norman' and the daughter called Norma after him and the marriage breaks down because of Norman's abuse to his wife and divorce follows, the mother may wish to rename the young daughter, such a move being considered appropriate for all concerned.

Since the Adoption and Children Act (ACA 2002, s 120) it is now recognised that a child who witnesses domestic violence/abuse between parents can suffer immeasurable emotional harm which may amount to the threshold standard of s 31 'significant harm' for a care order. Witnessing domestic violence or abuse and emotional abuse were the most commonly experienced types of child abuse in 2020. (See Figure 1 Main point 3 'Child Abuse in England and Wales'.)

The signs and symptoms of emotional abuse manifest in low self-esteem, a lack of confidence, fearfulness, self-deprecation, nervousness, speech disorders and other physical and mental disorders, and attempted suicide. In *Re G (Emotional Harm)* [1999] Fam Law 29 (851), the court dismissed the mother's appeal against the care order in respect of her two children since there was sufficient evidence of emotional harm to the children in the form of the children's disturbed behaviour, their emotional instability and inconsistent parenting within the home.

In *Re E (Care Proceedings: Social Work Practice)* [2000] 2 FLR 254, Bracewell J made care orders in respect of four children:

After a 12-day hearing I have found threshold criteria established under s 31 of the Children Act 1989 in respect of three children, E aged 16, P aged 15 and I aged 3. A substantial part of the history in evidence has concerned two older children, F who is now 24, and D, who died aged 16 in 1997. I have found that over a period of some 20 years the four oldest children in this family have been successively emotionally, physically and sexually abused. . . . The children have been in and out of care, have been placed on and removed from the child protection register, files have been opened and closed. The four children in turn have each exhibited remarkably similar characteristics of serious sexualised behaviour, emotional disturbance, anti-social conduct, difficulties in school, suicidal tendencies and serial rejection by the parents.

A similar pattern is found in *Re S and A (children) (Care Orders: Threshold Criteria)* [2001] 3 FCR 589. S and A, were taken into care. The judge found that they were suffering from emotional harm. The mother had been married four times. In 1995, she commenced a relationship with A's father. That relationship ended before the birth of A. The mother said that three of her relationships were characterised by violence. To escape the violence she had to leave the home and take refuge in local authority bed and breakfast accommodation. She suffered from depression and at one point had taken an overdose. The children experienced six moves into alternative care. An expert found S to be unhappy and disorientated. An expert of the mother considered that she would need a prolonged programme of therapy before she would be capable of caring for her children.

Neglect

This includes the failure of parent carers to provide adequate care for children, medical attention, food, shelter and to protect them from drug and alcohol use and abuse by parents. Signs of neglect include children who are inadequately or improperly clothed, unwashed, and are hungry and tired. It can include parents/ carers leaving children unsupervised at weekends and evenings and during school holidays. Such situations often occur where there is an introduction of a new partner. And whilst no one factor constitutes neglect, 'more than any single form of abuse, the detection and diagnosis of neglect is dependent on establishing the importance and collation of sometimes small, apparently undramatic single pieces of factual information which, when seen together are of considerable significance' (Judge Christina Lyon, Lyon et al. 2003: 87).

Where there is a finding of neglect, children are frequently made the subject of a care order (see e.g. *Re G and R* [1995] 2 FLR 867 Chapter 15). Local authority intervention is often too late, and children die. Paul Bridge was 15 months old when he died on 7 March 1993. The Bridge Child Care Consultancy Service reported that Paul was found dead in a pool of urine which caused burns and septicaemia (see *Paul: Death Through Neglect* Ward 1991).

Child abuse – an epidemic

Data on child abuse, the extent of local authority intervention and court outcome are found across a range of data sets which are difficult to navigate. Monitoring local authority intervention and court outcome is important in holding those protecting children, both the local authority and the courts, to account. Table 14.1 provides some indication of the prevalence of categories of abuse recorded by the local authority.

TABLE 14.1 Number of children who were the subject of a child protection plan on 31 March by category of abuse

Category of abuse	2019	2020	2021	2022	2023
Neglect	25,330	26,010	24,120	24,430	25,050
Physical abuse	4,170	3,820	3,650	3,780	3,630
Sexual abuse	2,230	1,970	1,930	1,930	1,890
Emotional abuse	18,460	18,380	18,840	19,480	19,000
Multiple	2,070	1,330	1,480	1,280	1,210
Total	52,260	51,510	50,010	50,920	50,780

Source: NSPCC statistics Child protection plan statistics: England 2019–2023
December 2023 https://learning.nspcc.org.uk/media/3neb415q/child-protection-plan-register-statistics-england-2019-2023.pdf (accessed 5.05.2024)

As of 31 March 2019, 52,260 children in England were the subject of a child protection plan (CPP) and 2,820 children in Wales were on the Child Protection Register (CPR) because of experience or risk of abuse or neglect. Neglect was the most common category of abuse recorded in England, and emotional abuse was the most common recorded category in Wales.

As of 31 March 2019, 49,570 children in England and 4,810 children in Wales were looked after by their local authority because of experience or risk of abuse or neglect (Main point 2 'Child abuse extent and nature'.). Annual trends over the last decade provide an important barometer of how child protection is being tackled amid growing criticism. The categorisation of types of abuse reflects the incident driven approach over the years.

The legal and procedural framework of safeguarding

International law and domestic law protect children from abuse. The United Nations Convention on the Rights of the Child (UNCRC 1989) states in Article 3(2):

> *States Parties undertake to ensure the child such protection and care as is necessary for his or her well-being, taking into account the rights and duties of his or her parents, legal guardians, or other individuals legally responsible for him or her.*

Article 6(1) and (2) provides, '(1) States Parties recognise that every child has an inherent right to life. (2) States Parties shall ensure to the maximum extent possible the survival and development of the child.'

Principle 9 of the Declaration of the Rights of the Child states, 'The child shall be protected against all forms of neglect, cruelty and exploitation.'

The Human Rights Act 1998, incorporating the European Convention on Human Rights (ECHR) provides protection for everyone, including children. Article 2 provides that 'everyone's right to life should be protected by law', and Article 3 provides 'no one shall be subjected to torture, or to inhuman or degrading treatment or punishment'. Section 11 of the CA 2004 also places a duty on certain people and bodies to make arrangements to ensure that their functions are discharged with regard to the need to safeguard and promote the welfare of children (see The Statutory Guidance 'Safeguarding and promoting the welfare of children' under s 11 of the CA 2004). These provisions set out the international and human rights framework along with domestic legislation.

The Children Act 1989 and partnership principle

At the heart of CA 1989, s 17(1)(b) is the ideology of partnership, where:

It shall be the general duty of every local authority . . . (a) to safeguard and promote the welfare of children within their area who are in need; and (b) so far as is consistent with that duty, to promote the upbringing of such children by their families.

Section 37(2)(b) provides that:

Where the court gives directions under this section the local authority concerned shall, when undertaking the investigation, consider whether they should provide assistance or services for the child or his family.

The partnership aspiration developed partially in response to the overwhelming public concern over the methods employed by local authorities following what happened in Cleveland, where children were removed by police and social workers in dawn raids from homes and where parents were not consulted prior to or at the point of removal, nor kept informed months and, in some cases, even years afterwards (see Butler-Sloss 1988). The idea of partnership developed out of the precept that cooperation between parents/carers and the local authority, and a principle of non-intervention, could protect children and advance their welfare best and so it was anticipated that arrangements for child protection might also be made with parents on a voluntary basis (CA 1989, s 20).

There is however a wealth of evidence demonstrating that there is little support given to families that need it which might if provided obviate child protection especially relating to neglect at a later stage. That may seem a bleak picture. Fortin (1998) argues that research suggests that children are not receiving the assistance they need within the home. Proudman (2012) suggests that by 2012 little had changed. Whereas partnership and support services might make a real difference to families they are expensive and there is no guarantee that there will be an outcome of real difference at the end. The preferred local authority route is not through support services but child protection, through the removal of the child and placement with foster carers and finally adoption. This reflexive route to child protection through adoption is a resonating concern in 2023 with some arguing that such removal of a child from the family is breaching family rights (see McFarlane LJ 2017).

Children Act – significant harm – three thresholds

The CA 1989 is concerned with three thresholds of harm. The first is found in s 1(3)(a) of the CA – 'any harm the child is at risk of suffering' (discussed earlier in Chapter 12) and is a factor on the welfare checklist which must be considered when any child arrangement order (CAO) is being made, varied or discharged. The second threshold is the suspicion of significant harm required to open a s 47 CA child protection investigation. The third threshold is proof of significant harm required to be satisfied to the civil standard before the court can make a care or supervision order under s 31 of the CA, and where the court must be satisfied that the child 'is suffering or likely to suffer significant harm'.

This term 'significant harm' has a specific legal meaning (statutory interpretation is discussed in Chapter 15). Whilst CA 1989 itself does not define 'child abuse', it defines 'harm'. Under s 31(9)(b): 'Harm' means ill-treatment or the impairment of health or development including, for example, impairment suffered from seeing or hearing the ill-treatment of another'. 'Development' means physical, intellectual, emotional, social or behavioural development. 'Health' means physical or mental, and 'ill treatment' includes sexual abuse and forms of ill treatment, which are not physical.

The local authority – the investigative process

It is the local authority who initiates the investigative process under their duty to safeguard. Obviating delay, providing a clear plan and timetable are overriding objectives. CA 1989, s 1(2) asserts: 'In any proceedings in which any question with respect to the upbringing of a child arises, the court shall have regard to the general principle that any delay in determining the question is likely to prejudice the welfare of the child.' Section 32(1)(a) asserts: 'A court shall . . . – (a) draw up a timetable with a view to disposing of the application – (i) without delay, and (ii) in any event within twenty-six weeks beginning with the day on which the application was issued.'

In *Re G (a child) (post-mortem report: delays)* [2023] 1 FLR 218, the court was highly critical of the delay following the death of a child and said (1) that the timescales that were now regularly encountered in care proceedings following the death of a child were wholly outside those required by Parliament and were plainly contrary to the welfare of any surviving sibling and that it was necessary to consider what alternative processes might be followed to meet the needs of the child protection proceedings without having to wait up to a year to receive results of a post-mortem exercise commissioned by the police or coroner. McFarlane LJ (2017) has expressed concern about the delay in concluding child protection proceedings.

Reporting suspicions: the referral process

Any individual can report their suspicions and concerns for the safety of a child to the local authority. Gibbons et al. (1995) found that 23 per cent of referrals came from educational professionals, 17 per cent from health professionals, 17 per cent from neighbours and family friends, 13 per cent from social services, 12 per cent from police, 6 per cent were anonymously reported, and 'others' reported in 12 per cent of cases. In 2003, there were 570,220 referrals of children to local authority social services child protection teams in England (DfES 2004) and 547,000 referrals year ending 31 March 2009 rising even further in 2022 to 650,270 (see Children in Need, Reporting Year 2022 statistics). In 2023 this number was 640,430 (see 'Children in Need, Reporting Year 2023 statistics').

Turning the other way

Following the death of Lauren Wright one local resident reported:

> *This whole village has got its head in the sand, nobody wants to talk about what went on here, but they must have been blind in Chestnut Avenue if they did not see what was happening to that child. She was wandering round like a rag doll, but they chose to say nothing.*
>
> (2001)

Moral panics and referrals

Whilst there is a rise in referrals Devine and Parker (2023) report that only 88 per cent of referrals result in a s 47 investigation. Research is much needed to understand

TABLE 14.2 Number of referrals by source in the year to 31 March 2019 to 2023

	2019	2020	2021	2022	2023
Police	189,910	184,760	195,270	191,840	184,530
Schools	117,190	117,010	81,180	129,090	128,650
Health services	95,070	96,300	95,670	96,170	92,350
LA services	86,810	90,810	87,260	87,300	90,070
Individual	51,950	52,290	50,940	53,160	53,020
Other legal agency	23,780	25,180	23,910	26,020	26,520
Education services	15,580	13,630	8,490	13,350	12,600
Anonymous	15,580	13,770	13,430	11,600	11,150
Housing	8,540	8,300	6,550	6,640	7,240
Other	35,780	31,630	29,180	27,840	27,560
Unknown	10,730	9,300	5,890	7,250	6,730

Source: Children in Need, Reporting year 2023 – Explore education statistics – https://explore-education-statistics.service.gov.uk/find-statistics/characteristics-of-children-in-need (accessed 12.05.2024)

the basis on which the several reporting agencies police, social services, education, housing etc. and the public, base their concerns especially as there are no grounds for so many of them. Undoubtedly, the impact of statutory responsibilities and possible litigation falls on schools, and childcare providers, who, if they fail face civil litigation for negligence. Regulatory bodies for example Ofsted inspections of safeguarding (sections 49 and 50 of the Childcare Act 2006 on the quality and standards of provision that is registered on the Early Years Register) may result in childcare providers referring unnecessarily rather than making a decision.

The local authority area where a child resides is responsible for the cost of a 'child in need' and care investigation and any subsequent care arrangements. In *Re C (Responsible Authority)* [2005] EWHC 2939 (Fam), where the children were placed on the Child at Risk Register (CAR) and then taken into foster care, the paternal grandparents later offered to care for the children. After an authority assessment of the grandparents the children moved in to live with them in a different local authority area. The mother later withdrew her consent and the issue which fell to be decided was which of the two local authorities was responsible for the children. The court held that the new authority was the responsible authority, as the children had resided in the new authority area for 11 months.

When a referral is made, children's services have 24 hours to determine what type of response is required. In arriving at a decision, the local authority must consider whether to take no action, or to take immediate action (an emergency protection order (EPO) s 44 discussed later) or, where no immediate action is required undertake an initial assessment, obtain reports and interview family members. An initial assessment should be completed within seven days of the date of the referral. At the conclusion, a determination of whether the child is a 'child in need' (s 17) or not is made. If the child is identified as a 'child in need' a plan will be devised which identifies the services the child requires. This is followed by a case conference to decide whether to initiate a s 47 CA 1989 inquiry and make a core assessment (see later).

TABLE 14.3 Children in need child protection referrals and completed assessments 2013 to 2023

	Children in need (as of 31 March)	Children in need per 10,000 children (as of 31 March)	Child protection plans (as of 31 March)	Child protection plans per 10,000 children (as of 31 March)	Referrals (year to 31 March)	Completed assessments (year to 31 March)
2013	378,030	330.9	43,190	37.8	593,470	x
2014	395,480	343.7	48,300	42.0	657,780	u
2015	390,130	336.6	49,690	42.9	635,620	550,810
2016	393,910	337.3	50,310	43.1	621,470	571,640
2017	389,040	330.1	51,080	43.3	646,120	606,910
2018	404,710	341.0	53,790	45.3	655,630	631,090
2019	399,510	334.2	52,260	43.7	650,930	644,730

Source: Characteristics of Children in Need https://explore-education-statistics.service.gov.uk/find-statistics/characteristics-of-children-in-need#releaseHeadlines-tables (accessed 5.05.2024)

Court ordered investigation: s 37 directions

In private law family proceedings where, for example, the parties are applying for a s 8 CA 1989 child arrangement order (CAO) for residence/contact, specific issue or prohibited steps orders (discussed in Chapter 12) the court may direct the local authority to investigate the child's circumstances if there are concerns regarding welfare or, for example, allegations of domestic abuse. Section 37(1)(2) provides:

> Where, in any family proceedings in which a question arises with respect to the welfare of the child, it appears to the court that it may be appropriate for a care or supervision order to be made with respect to him, the court may direct the appropriate authority to undertake an investigation of the child's circumstances (2) Where the court gives a direction under this section the local authority concerned shall, when undertaking the investigation, consider whether they should – (a) apply for a care order or for a supervision order with respect to a child; (b) provide services or assistance for the child or his family; or (c) take any other action with respect to the child.

In *Re L (Section 37 Direction)* [1999] 1 FLR 984, a girl, aged 6, was cared for from birth by her maternal grandmother. The judge had made a number of directions, one being a direction for a s 37 investigation which was the subject of the application for leave to appeal by the maternal grandmother. The court held that, in making the s 37 direction in reliance upon some evidence regarding the mother on the basis that it might eventually justify a care or supervision order, the judge had been wrong, since the evidence in the case was nowhere near the threshold at which public law powers could be invoked. It was plain that the court should not order the local authority to conduct a s 37 investigation unless it appeared that it might be appropriate to make a public law order. In *Re F (Family Proceedings: Section 37 Investigations)* [2006] 1 FLR 1122, where the children no longer wanted to see their mother, a position supported by the father, who was considered to be in complete subjugation to their views and their reaction and attitude to their mother (in which he was complicit). This all caused the boys emotional harm which was likely to be significant. Whilst the children were not to be removed from the father's care, a s 37 direction was required unless the father would give his consent to the children being seen by a psychiatrist as the court needed to know what the boys were thinking, how they were performing at school and whether they needed therapy. (See also *C v C (Children) (Investigation of Circumstances)* [2005] EWHC 2935 (Fam), in which a s 37 investigation was ordered where the child said the mother had smacked the children whilst the father said children do not love her, are afraid of her, that she is a liar, and that she should have nothing to do with them.)

In *Re J (a child) (child arrangements order: recommendations of the guardian)* (2023) *The father v The mother and another* [2023] EWFC 35, the residence of 'J' was transferred to his father following a s 37 report by Children's Services and a joint psychologist's assessment of all the parties.

In this case:

> It is also important to note that the mother has not had the benefit of legal representation throughout this matter . . . she has failed to engage properly throughout, showing scant regard for court orders . . . the mother has a history of failing to engage with the court

process, throughout the interview with the mother she presented the father as a violent and aggressive individual who had sexually harmed the child. There did not appear to be any clear evidence that what she had stated was accurate . . . the mother has a history of failing to engage with the court process.

In *Father v Maternal Aunt* [2023] EWFC 204, a case which involved several hearings but due to matters including allegations of domestic abuse, and also the child holding her father responsible for the suicide of her mother, a s 37 investigation was ordered.

[1] A is a girl aged 12 years. She is the eldest of three siblings. She has lived with her father and siblings since November 2019. She was placed in the care of her father by an order made in a family court in the Midlands pending the final determination of cross applications by both parents that the children should live with them.

There was no final hearing because in January 2020 the mother ended her life.

[2]. Since July 2023, A has been with her maternal aunt in the North. Her father does not agree that she should remain there. He is the only person with parental responsibility for her.

However, in *A father (F) v A mother (M) and another* [2023] EWHC 1955 (Fam), a s 37 report was ordered following the move to Germany and dispute between the parents as to residence and contact proceedings concerning with whom the child should live. The local authority concluded that: 'the current concerns do not warrant a care or supervision order at this stage.'

This confluence of private into public and public into private law is also considered in Chapter 12. (See Bainham 2013.)

Child Protection Register

When a child has been referred to the local authority, the first stage of the investigative process involves checking the Child at Risk Register to discover whether a child or member of the family is registered and, if registered, to consider the nature of the past concerns with regard to any particular child (see Table 14.1).

Child protection plan

Once a child is placed on a Child Protection Register, a parent may wish to challenge that decision and have the child removed. In *R v Kent County Council, ex parte B* [1996] Lexis Citation 1187, a father made an application for judicial review to have his elder son removed from the Child Protection Register. The child's name was placed on the register as the local authority had concerns regarding emotional abuse of the child. The local authority originally involved was Kent County Council, and it was their decisions and procedures, which the father sought to challenge. The father and his family moved to Yorkshire and the child was removed from the Kent 'at risk' register and placed on the register of the authorities in Yorkshire. Later, the child was removed from the 'at risk' register. The father felt aggrieved about what had happened and renewed his application notwithstanding that the relevant decisions had become academic. Hobhouse LJ in the Court of Appeal said:

> Questions of this kind give rise to strong passions, as has been recognised in the courts on a number of occasions. Parents, quite understandably, consider that they are being criticised or accused. They feel strongly about the implications of having one of their children placed on the at-risk register. Therefore, they understandably take an active part in the proceedings and assessments which lead up to the child being placed on an at-risk register and, in some cases, they thereafter pursue their own perception of the situation in the courts.

Recognising these sentiments the Court of Appeal in the case of *R v Harrow London Borough, ex parte D* [1990] 1 WLR 421 in the judgment of Butler-Sloss LJ to which Douglas Brown J in the case of *R v Kent County Council, ex parte B* [1996] [1996] Lexis Citation 1651, observes:

> In coming to its decision, the local authority is exercising a most important public function which can have serious consequences for the child and the alleged abuser (and) it would also seem that the recourse to judicial review is likely to be, and undoubtedly ought to be, rare. Local authorities have laid on them by Parliament the specific duty of protection of children in their area. The case conference has a duty to make an assessment as to abuse and the abuser if sufficient information is available. Of its nature, the mechanism of the case conference leading to the decision to place names on the register, and the decision-making process, is unstructured and informal [16–17].

Butler-Sloss LJ points out that it is not a judicial process, and in refusing the applications said:

> In proceedings in which the child is the subject, his or her welfare is paramount. In balancing adequate protection for the child and fairness to an adult, the interest of an adult may have to be placed second to the needs of the child. All concerned in this difficult and delicate area should be allowed to perform their task without looking over their shoulder all the time for the possible intervention of the court. The important power of the court to intervene should be kept very much in reserve, perhaps confined to the exceptional case which involves a point of principle which needs to be resolved, not only for the individual case but cases in general, so as to establish that they are not being conducted in an unsatisfactory manner. In a normal case where criticism is made of some individual aspect of procedure, which does not raise any point of principle, leave should be refused [17].

It is to be noted that the same reasoning informs the approach of the courts to interim care orders where in *D v Bury Metropolitan Borough Council; H v Bury Metropolitan Council* [2006] 1 WLR 917 it was held that a local authority investigating the possibility of child abuse did not owe a duty of care to the parents of the child, the only duty owed was to carry out its plans for child protection in a professional manner.

Child protection conference

Investigations of child abuse require professionals to work together and to convene a child protection conference (within 15 days of the last strategy discussion). The object of the child protection conference is to decide whether or not there is any foundation for the reasonable suspicion of significant harm, which resulted in the original referral. At the child protection conference, all relevant parties are required to be present. This includes doctors, social workers, teachers and other professionals involved with the child. Parents are also encouraged to be present. The participation of parents is important, as, prior to the CA 1989, parents were excluded and not properly informed, and their exclusion was one of the criticisms made in the Cleveland Inquiry.

However, parents may be reluctant to cooperate since it is they who are suspected of harming the child. Under such circumstances, where parents resist and challenge the investigation, and are obstructive, the presence of parents at such conferences may not be helpful. In some cases, the parents refuse to participate. Again, research is desperately needed at each stage of this process. The decision for the child protection conference is whether the child should be placed on, or removed from, the Child at Risk Register.

The test for convening a child protection conference is established in R (on the application of Redmond) and others v Health Service Commissioner [2005] EWCA Civ 1578 where Henriques J cites the evidence of a principal family support and child protection adviser, who said: 'The test for a child protection conference is "is the child at continuing risk of significant harm?" ' Where a child protection conference has indicated that s 47 court proceedings should be initiated, s 31(9) gives the local authority this power.

Care plans

There is a duty placed on the local authority to prepare a care plan in respect of a child to ensure that the future plans for the child are clearly considered, and communicated to all those involved, in order to achieve the objectives of the Protocol for Judicial Case Management in Public Law Children Act Cases, June 2003 (Hershman and McFarlane 2007). (See also *Practice Direction (Public Law Proceedings) (Guide to Case Management)* April 2010.)

The key objective of the Protocol is to avoid delay. Yet, as has been reported:

> *The average care case lasts for almost a year. This is a year in which the child is left uncertain as to his or her future, is often moved between several temporary care arrangements, and the family and public agencies are left engaged in protracted and complex legal wranglings. Though a fair and effective process must intervene before a child is taken from its parents, we believe it is essential that unnecessary delay is eliminated and that better outcomes for children are families are thereby achieved. This protocol sets a guideline of 40 weeks for the conclusion of care cases . . . It sets out a timetable for the several hearings and applications and directions involved in such cases. One of the obligations placed on local authority is to devise and present a care plan. The Social Services Assessment and Care Planning Aide-Memoire sets out a timetable, which a referral (above triggers) followed by a decision not to take any action or else to undertake an initial assessment.*
>
> (See 'Protocol for judicial case management in public
> law Children Act cases'.)

In *London Borough of Enfield v E (Unconscionable Delay)* [2024] EWFC 183, this case case took 131 weeks to come to court as against the time limit of 26 weeks.

Local authority – duty to investigate s 47

A reasonable suspicion of 'significant harm' is sufficient.

Section 47 provides:

(1) Where a local authority is informed that a child who lives, or is found, in its area: (i) is the subject of an emergency protection order; or (ii) is in police protection or has reasonable cause to suspect that a child who lives, or is found, in its area, is suffering, or is likely to suffer, significant harm.

Charles J, in *A v General Medical Council and another* [2004] EWHC 880 (Admin), said:

The . . . trigger for the duty imposed by s 47 namely 'reasonable cause to suspect' is lower than the trigger for other provisions (e.g. ss 31, 38, 44, 46). This reflects the purpose of the duty imposed by s 47. That duty is to make enquiries to enable properly informed decisions to be made.

In *Re S (Sexual Abuse Allegations: Local Authority Response)* [2001] 2 FLR 776 the court held that even where a suspected perpetrator had been acquitted in a criminal trial, the local authority was still entitled to make a finding of significant harm and take whatever protective measures they consider necessary. Approximately 65,000 children were the subject of s 47 investigations in England in the year to 31 March 2003 (DES figures). By 2021, this figure had risen to 198,790, and by 2023 to 225,400. (See 'Children in Need Reporting year statistics 2023'). This exponential rise must be seen in the context of cuts to local authority funding discussed in the concluding remarks at the end of this chapter.

Following this decision a core assessment will be conducted which must be completed within 45 days of the initial assessment.

TABLE 14.4 Number of Section 47 enquiries and initial child protection conferences and number of children on a child protection plan

	2013	2014	2015	2016	2017	2018	2019	2020	2021	2022	2023
s 47 investigations	127,190	142,710	160,490	172,510	185,680	198,090	201,170	201,000	198,790	217,800	225,400
Number of child protection conferences	60,080	65,190	71,410	73,050	76,930	79,470	77,440	77,470	72,580	73,790	74,380
Child protection plan	43,190	48,300	49,690	50,130	51,080	53,790	52,260	51,510	50,010	50,920	50,780

Source: Children in Need Reporting year 2023 – Explore education statistics https://explore-education-statistics.service.gov.uk/find-statistics/characteristics-of-children-in-need/2021 (accessed 12.05.2024)

Local authority failings

In *Mairs v Secretary of State for Education and Skills* [2005] EWHC 996 (Admin), the court found that there was a failure to hold a child protection conference in respect of Victoria Climbié. In September 2002, a disciplinary hearing was convened in relation to Ms Mairs, the social worker in the case, which she declined to attend. The hearing concluded by dismissing her for gross misconduct. That misconduct included, among other things, a conceded failure to provide management direction to social workers managed by her. An aspect of the gross misconduct found proved was that she failed to act upon knowledge in relation to Victoria Climbié that (it was concluded) that she had gained on 15 November 1999 at a supervision session with Lisa Arthurworrey. 'It was also found that she had misled the Part 8 Inquiry by denying this knowledge (which had resulted in that Inquiry accepting that she was "unaware of the allegations until after (Victoria's) death)".'

Child protection and public authority liability and human rights

Where a local authority fails to protect a child in its care, can the local authority be held liable for this failure? The relevance of Art 3 (inhuman and degrading treatment) of the ECHR has been recently tested in cases where violence is directed towards children, thereby establishing the liability of local authorities. In *Z v United Kingdom* [2001] 34 EHRR 97, the children were subject to neglect and brought an action against the local authority for failure to protect. The neglect included starvation, living in filthy conditions and sleeping on urine-soaked mattresses. The children scavenged in bins for food, soiled their pants, smeared excrement on the windows of their bedroom and their mattresses were sodden with urine. Despite several meetings with social services over a period and a case conference, no steps were taken to remove the children from their carers. Full care orders were eventually made in 1993; six years after the family were first reported to the social services. The four siblings all lodged a complaint with the European Court of Human Rights invoking Articles 3, 6, 8 and 13 of the ECHR, alleging, *inter alia*, that the local authority had failed to protect them from inhuman and degrading treatment (Article 3), that their respect for family life had been breached (Article 8), that they had been denied access to court (Article 6) and that they had not been afforded any effective remedy for the damage suffered (Art 13). The Official Solicitor, as next friend for the children, commenced proceedings against the local authority claiming damages for negligence and/or breach of statutory duty. The Court held that there was a contravention of Article 3 in that the local authority had failed to protect the applicants from serious long-term neglect and abuse (see also *E and others v United Kingdom* [2003] 36 EHRR 31).

Osman v United Kingdom [1999] 1 FLR 193 is relevant, and local authorities have a positive obligation to protect the lives of children known to them in accordance with Article 2, the right to life obligation and must take appropriate steps to safeguard life (*X v United Kingdom* (1979)). *Osman v United Kingdom* (earlier) qualified the duty by a requirement on the applicant to prove that the police authority, in the instant case, 'knew or ought to have known of a real and immediate risk to the life of the person from the criminal acts of another' (at [115–116]).

The *Osman* case has implications, for police and other public authorities (see *also R (Plymouth City Council) v HM Coroner for the County of Devon and Secretary of State for Education and Skills* [2005] EWHC 1014 (Admin); [2005] 2 FLR 1279). *D v East Berkshire Community Health NHS Trust and others MAK and another v Dewsbury Healthcare NHS Trust and another RK and another v Oldham NHS Trust and another* [2005] UKHL 23; [2005] AC 373. The House of Lords considered whether a duty of care was owed by healthcare professionals or social workers to parents. In the words of Lord Nicholls:

> *The law has moved on since the decision of your Lordships' House in X (Minors) v Bedfordshire County Council (1995). There the House held it was not just and equitable to impose a common law duty on local authorities in respect of their performance of their statutory duties to protect children. Later cases, mentioned by my noble and learned friend, Lord Bingham of Cornhill, have shown that this proposition is stated too broadly. Local authorities may owe common law duties to children in the exercise of their child protection duties.*

Orders during the preliminary stage

Following a s 47 investigation, the local authority may decide that there are no further concerns in respect of the child and thus no further investigation or intervention necessary. This being the case they must, in accordance with s 47(7) decide whether it would be appropriate to review the case at a later date, and if they so decide then to arrange a date for that review.

Where there is 'reasonable cause to suspect that a child is suffering or is likely to suffer significant harm' four orders may be applied for. The emergency protection order (EPO) s 44 (1) and exclusion order s 44A with the power to include an exclusion requirement, police protection order s 46 are by their very nature emergency orders and are likely applied for immediately a concern for child protection is made where the concern is of such seriousness that immediate action is required. The order for child assessment s 43(1) is likely made during the process of the inquiries.

Emergency orders

Emergency protection order

Anyone can apply for an emergency protection order (EPO). The grounds for an EPO are that the child is likely to suffer significant harm if not removed (s 44(1)(a)(i)) or if he or she does not remain in a place in which he or she is accommodated (s 44(1)(a)(ii)) or enquiries are being frustrated (s 44(1)(b)).

As Davis (2007) notes: 'Inevitably, EPO applications usually proceed on the evidence of the local authority alone; even if the parents are present, their chances of presenting an opposing case are severely limited (the Masson 2005 study found an active contest in only 7 out of 60 cases where parents were notified).' Such an order may be made immediately on a referral of harm or at any later stage. It is ex parte and involves immediate removal of the child until a later date. (See Halsbury's Grounds for Emergency Protection Order.)

In *Re M (Care Proceedings: Judicial Review)* [2003] EWHC 850 (Admin) Munby J said that an EPO required 'exceptional justification' and such an order is only appropriate: 'if immediate separation is essential to secure the child's safety; (and that) "imminent danger" must be "actually established" '. Munby J in *X Council v B (Emergency Protection Orders)* [2005] 1 FLR 341 said: 'an EPO summarily removing a child from his parents, is a terrible and drastic remedy' and an 'extremely harsh' measure, requiring 'exceptional justification' and 'extraordinarily compelling reasons'. He went on to review the law and practice relating to EPOs.

The Munby principles were applied in *Re X: Emergency Protection Orders* [2006] EWHC 510 (Fam), in which the mother drew attention to the child and to herself by inventing the child's illness (FII). There was no suggestion at the case conference that the child should be removed from the care of the parents, either immediately or at all. Yet, on a later date, the social worker and team manager decided that the child should be removed immediately and applied to the court for an EPO, by making misleading statements to the court. The court granted an EPO, and the child was removed from her mother's care by four uniformed police and social workers from the hospital. After one year in care the local authority abandoned its reliance on any allegation of sexual abuse or induced or fabricated illness, basing their application instead on emotional abuse. The court did not find the threshold met. McFarlane J reiterated the 14 principles and guidance laid down by Munby J. These principles remain in 2024 good and settled law.

In *A v East Sussex County Council* [2010] EWHC 2771 (Admin), the court said even in an emergency it was desirable, where possible, for a local authority to work in partnership with parents. (See *A Local Authority v EBY and others* [2023] EWHC 2494 (Fam); see also a case where procedure was not followed and there was no basis for it *Re Emma and Harry (children); A local authority v Mrs X (a mother) and others* [2023] EWFC 69.)

Whilst anyone can apply for an EPO, applicants are normally the NSPCC or the local authority. Importantly and uniquely, hearsay evidence, such as the evidence of a police officer to the effect that a child told him that she had been abused, even though normally excluded, is permissible (Civil Evidence Act 1968) although the use of hearsay is not admissible in all children cases. The child must normally be allowed to return home the moment that it appears to the applicant that it is safe to do so (s 44(10), (11)). The EPO confers on the applicant parental responsibility for the duration of the order. Contact with parents may be maintained, although this is subject to the court's power to give directions.

Under s 44(6) where the court orders an EPO, it may also give directions for other assessments to be made, including medical, psychological and social work reports.

The court may give directions for contact under s 44(6)(a) and medical and psychiatric assessment under s 44(6)(b).

Alternatively, the court may prohibit contact altogether. In *Re A (A Child) (Mental Health of Mother)* [2001] EWCA Civ 162, the mother arrived in the UK from Holland on the day that her baby was due to be born. Due to concerns about the mother's mental health, the mother and baby V were admitted to a residential unit for a psychiatric assessment of the mother and an assessment of the mother's parenting skills. The local authority applied for an EPO when the mother left the unit. She was certified as incapable of managing her affairs and her daughter was removed from her care and placed with foster parents whilst the authority brought care proceedings.

The decision is final and there is no right of appeal of an EPO. In *Re M (Care Proceedings: Judicial Review)* [2003] EWHC 850 (Admin) discussed earlier, Munby J held that judicial review was not appropriate to challenge a local authority's decision to make an application for an EPO. This remains the position.

Ex parte orders and human rights challenges

Because of the draconian effect of an EPO on parents, and potentially on the child, in that it removes a child from the parents' care without any advance warning, and in the absence of allowing them to be heard, litigation has centred on the human rights precepts with regard to the parental right to a fair hearing (Article 6 of the ECHR) and the need to balance the rights of the child and the family rights of parents (Article 8). In *X Council v B (Emergency Protection Orders)* (2005) cited earlier, Munby J outlined the interrelationship of parents' and children's rights in these orders:

> *Where the application for an EPO is made ex parte (without notice) the burden on the local authority is even heavier. In the first place, the local authority must make out a compelling case for applying without first giving the parents notice. As I have already observed, the Strasbourg court accepts that there may be situations justifying an ex parte application. Thus in* P, C and S v United Kingdom *(2002) 35 EHRR 31, (2002) 2 FLR 631 the court specifically held (at para [127]) that the local authority could not be criticized for using the ex parte procedure, and in* Covezzi and Morselli v Italy *(2003) 38 EHRR 28 the challenge failed, even though the application had been made without notification to the parents. But in* Venema v The Netherlands *(2003) 1 FLR 552 where the order was made without notification to the parents, and without there having been any discussion with the parents, this lack of involvement was held (see paras (98)–(99)) to have been a breach of Article 8, the parents having been presented with 'a fait accomplis without sufficient justification'. Likewise, in* Haase v Germany *(2004) 2 FLR 39 where there had been an ex parte application, the court held (see paras (96)–(105) that there had in all the circumstances been a breach of Article 8. In particular it held (at para [99]) that there had been no urgency so as to justify the making of an ex parte order.*

Contact with the child and emergency protection order

Section 44 (13) makes provision for contact with children who are subject to an emergency protection order in the following terms:

> Where an emergency protection order has been made with respect to a child, the applicant shall, subject to any direction given under subsection (6) allow the child reasonable contact with – (a) his parents; (b) any person who is not a parent of his but who has parental responsibility for him; (c) any person with whom he was living immediately before the making of the order; (d) any person named in child arrangements order as a person with whom the child is to spend time or otherwise have contact; (e) any person who is allowed to have contact with the child by virtue of an order under section 34; and (f) any person acting on behalf of any of those persons.

In *Kirklees Metropolitan District Council v S (Contact to Newborn Babies)* [2006] 1 FLR 333, the court had ordered daily contact where the mother, a drug addicted user, had her newly born baby removed from her care. Following an EPO, the mother was to have daily supervised contact when the EPO expired, and an ICO (interim care order) for eight days was put in place. Munby J said:

> *If a baby is to be removed from his mother, one would normally expect arrangements to be made by the local authority to facilitate contact on a regular and generous basis. It is a dreadful thing to take a baby away from his mother: dreadful for the mother, dreadful for the father and dreadful for the baby. If the state, in the guise of a local authority, seeks to intervene so drastically in a family's life – and at a time when ex hypothesi its case against the parents has not yet even been established – then the very least the state can do is to make generous arrangements for contact. And those arrangements must be driven by the needs of the family, not stunted by lack of resources. Typically, if this is what the parents want, one will be looking to contact most days of the week and for lengthy periods. And local authorities must be sensitive to the wishes of a mother who wants to breast-feed and must make suitable arrangements to enable her to do so – and when I say 'breast-feed', I mean just that, I do not mean merely bottle-feeding expressed breast milk. Nothing less will meet the imperative demands of the European Convention. Contact two or three times a week for a couple of hours a time is simply not enough if parents reasonably want more.*

The local authority appealed against the order for daily contact. Bodey J dismissed the appeal.

EPO's have been granted in cases allegedly involving radicalisation. See Ahdash (2023) in which she raises a concern with the radicalisation cases which have enabled, she says, the State to 'do' counterterrorism, covertly and dangerously through the family courts. *Re X (children) and Y (children) (emergency protection orders)* [2015] EWHC 2265 (Fam) involved four children: X1, a boy born in 2002; X2, a girl born in 2008; X3, a girl born in 2010; and X4 a boy born in 2012. The parents were MX (the mother) and FX (the father). In March 2015, the mother and the four children, together with the maternal uncle and maternal grandmother, were detained at an airport in the United Kingdom as they were about to board a flight to Turkey. The

TABLE 14.5 Number of children involved in public law applications for EPO and number of orders applied for and made

EPO*	2011	2015	2017	2018	2019	2020	2021	2022
Number of children involved in applications-public hearings3b	1918	1688	1600	1734	1414	1232	1160	1240
Number of orders applied for public hearings3a	1213	1024	940	982	874	750	700	719
Number of orders made 4a	775	635	668	724	691	650	543	n/a

Source: Family Court accessible tables July-Sept 2023. Table 3b and 3a and 4a respectively. Figures relate to proceedings in public law only. EPO also ordered in private law application especially with regard to authority to obtain information on missing children in 2021.*Excludes applications to extend, vary or discharge www.gov.uk/government/statistics/family-court-statistics-quarterly-july-to-september-2022 (accessed 5.05.2024)

three adults were arrested by the police and subsequently released. The local authority (A) was granted emergency protection orders in relation to all four children who were placed with foster carers. The local authority applied for care orders in relation to all four children and interim care orders were made.

Exclusion order provision

The CA 1989 made no provision for removing the suspect abuser from the family home and so the solution to child protection rested with the removal of children from their home. This practice was widely criticised. In 1992, the Law Commission considered the removal of the suspect abuser in their report, *Family Law, Domestic Violence and Occupation of the Family Home*, recommending a short-term ouster order with the power to attach a power of arrest.

> *There are obviously cases where a child needs immediate and guaranteed protection from risk of serious harm, which can only be given by removal from home. There are other cases where instant removal is not obviously the answer, but there are serious concerns, and it is difficult to know whether the trauma to the child of a hasty or unjustified removal will be greater than the hazards of leaving him at home pending further investigations. Sudden removal from home, whatever its deficiencies, always carries some risk to the child's welfare, varying with the age of the child and how the removal is done.*
>
> (paras [6.15–6.22])

The Family Law Act 1996, s 52, Sch 6, para 3, and Sch 6, para 1, introduced amendments to the CA 1989 which provided for the removal of an alleged abuser from the home under an exclusion order, where the courts had granted an EPO (CA 1989, s 44A) or an interim care order (s 38A). The provision also allows the court to accept undertakings from the suspect in respect of the exclusion requirement for EPOs (s 44B) and interim care orders (s 38B).

The new exclusion provision has been little used, perhaps because of real problems with its effectiveness. The duration of an exclusion order is limited to 15 days, after which the abuser will be allowed to return. (See Practice Direction PD12k: *Children Act 1989: Exclusion Requirement*) under which the court may attach a power of arrest to an exclusion order.) Furthermore, an exclusion order can only be made where

> *that another person living in the dwelling – house (whether the parent of the child or some other person) – (i) is able and willing to give to the child the care which it would be reasonable to expect a parent to give him, and (ii) consents to the inclusion of the exclusion requirement.*

This consent condition undermines the purpose of the order and puts the onus on the applicant. It is inconsistent with thinking on domestic abuse and violence in holding the other party to ransom by sacrificing the protection of children on their compromised consent which they may be afraid to give because of coercion control and fear of further violence. Moreover, no figures are collected on the number of such applications. Thus, the use of this provision cannot be monitored or evaluated, or the Government be held to account.

Consider the case of *W v Middlesbrough Borough Council (Exclusion Order Evidence)* [2000] 2 FLR 666, in which the court stated:

> *The object of serving a statement of the evidence relied upon by an applicant seeking to exclude a person from the family home was to ensure that the relevant party was made aware of the evidence upon which the exclusion requirement had been based. It was essential that the statement not only should set out the factual material clearly but also had to contain reference to the evidence supporting the relevant provisions of the CA 1989.*

Cazalet J in the Family Division, so held when allowing an appeal against the decision of Teesside Family Proceedings Court on 6 March 2000 whereby the appellant father, W, was committed to two months' imprisonment suspended for six months for breach of an exclusion order with power of arrest attached, which was attached to and formed part of an interim care order made by the same court on 4 February 2000 in respect of three children, on the grounds that it was manifestly excessive in the light of the change of circumstances since the order was made.

Police removal s 46

In ensuring the protection of children, a police officer may remove a child, under CA 1989, s 46(1) for 72 hours.

In protecting children, the use of police protection is common practice. One study found that in 39 out of 86 families where EPOs were made, the child had already been taken into police protection (Masson 2005). Police protection is a vital aspect of child protection as Masson observes: 'Court processes were insufficiently responsive to be relied on in "real emergencies" and largely unavailable out of office hours. This was tolerated because police protection powers could be used to solve the problem'

(2005: 96). In *A v East Sussex County Council and Chief Constable of Sussex Police* [2010] EWCA Civ 743, the mother sought damages under the Human Rights Act 1998, s 7, against the local authority and the police. The court held that the judge was entitled to conclude that the decision to remove the child was justified and that in the circumstances it was impractical to convene a family proceedings court. See *B (a child) (care proceedings: jurisdiction) Re* [2013] EWCA Civ 1434, and *Kiam v Crown Prosecution Service* [2014] EWHC 1606 (Admin) which detail the differences between an EPO under s 44 and the exercise of police powers under s 46 of the CA 1989. A s 46 removal may be the first step which later includes an application for an EPO (see *Langley v Liverpool City Council* [2005] EWCA Civ 1173).

Child assessment order s 43

Once an investigation has commenced, it will be necessary to gather all the evidence with regard to the concern that the child is at risk of suffering from significant harm, including medical, psychological, psychiatric and educational, and any other relevant information.

In cases where the child is of a young age, it is for the parent with parental responsibility to give consent to medical assessments being carried out on their child. Where those with parental responsibility refuse to consent and obstruct the investigation it may be necessary for an application to be made for a child assessment order (CAO) (s 43(1)).

The child may also refuse to consent (and is entitled to do so if he or she is Gillick competent *Gillick v West Norfolk and Wisbech Area Health Authority* [1986] AC 112 (see earlier, s 43(8) and 44(7) FPR, r 92A (see *The Children Act 1989 Guidance and Regulations* 1991 [4.8]). A CAO is an order of short duration (seven days) which allows for the necessary assessments of the child to be carried out. A local authority or the NSPCC may apply for this order. Unlike an EPO, this order cannot be made ex parte. The applicant must take such steps as are practicable to ensure that the child, the parents and anyone else with parental responsibility, are given notice. The court, in considering whether to grant such an order, must also consider whether it ought to make an EPO rather than a CAO (s 43(4)(b)).

In practice, such orders are rare; 104 applications for a CAO were made in 2022 (see 'Family court statistics quarterly accessible tables, 2022' Table 3b) possibly because, where the parents are refusing to cooperate, it is considered wiser and safer for the child concerned for the court to make an EPO which can also have a court directed assessment attached. Most assessments of children are undertaken with parental consent or, more accurately, without parental opposition. An EPO operates by removing the child from the home, although in the case of a CAO, removal from the home for an overnight stay is rare (s 43(9)). Very few orders are actually made for a CAO numbering some 22 in 2020. ('See Family Court statistics Quarterly Accessible Tables 2022' Table 4a for 2020.)

Court interim orders

Division of functions

The statutory scheme includes, *inter alia*, the following division of functions as between local authorities and the courts: (i) the decision to apply for a care or supervision order under Part IV of the 1989 Act is that of the local authority (or an authorised person) and not the court; (ii) decisions about the conduct of proceedings are exclusively those of the court; (iii) the decision whether to make an order and if so, what order is exclusively that of the court. Where the local authority is intent on making an application for a care or supervision order (CA 1989, s 37(2)(a)) an interim order under s 38(1) may be made.

Interim care orders

The House of Lords considered the procedure followed in the making of care orders in two cases and resolved that a care plan should have been set out and an interim care order should have been made in one of them (see *Re S (Minors) (Care Order: Implementation of Care Plan) In Re W (Minors) (Care Order: Adequacy of Care Plan)* [2002] UKHL 10).

Section 38 (1) provides:

(1) Where – (a) in any proceedings on an application for a care order or supervision order, the proceedings are adjourned . . . the court may make an interim care order or interim supervision order with respect to the child concerned. (2) A court shall not make an interim care order or interim supervision order under this section unless it is satisfied that there are reasonable grounds for believing that the circumstances with respect to the child are as mentioned in section 31(2).

The interim threshold

The court that must be satisfied as to the existence of reasonable grounds, however, there is relatively little direct authority on the application of s 38(2). It has been said that 'reasonable grounds for suspicion' adequately define it. In *Re GR (Care Order)* [2010] EWCA Civ 871, Lady Justice Black who set out the procedure said: 'It is trite law that the question must be approached in two stages.' That is to say, 'reasonable grounds to believe' and a 'necessity'.

Section 38(2) does not require the court to make findings of fact to the civil standard, nor to be satisfied that the main threshold document is proved. Instead, the section requires the court to be satisfied that 'there are reasonable grounds' for believing that the threshold in section 31 is made out. It follows that, at an interim hearing, rarely, if ever, will findings of fact be made that will have the effect of establishing the threshold at a final hearing.

In *G (children: fair hearing)* [2019] EWCA Civ 126, Peter Jackson LJ gave permission to appeal and directed the rehearing of an initial interim care order application because . . . ICO's have generated much discussion in recent years. McKenna (2019) observes: 'Practitioners need to be continually asking themselves: (1) Is shared parental responsibility really required? (2) Is there risk of immediate harm? (3) What/ where is the evidence for that risk? (4) Is an ICO inevitable or can a realistic challenge to it be mounted?' In *Re C (Permission to withdraw: Medical evidence: Interim Threshold not crossed)* [2018] EWFC B37 the court said:

> *where no agreement as to how bruises were sustained [30]. In all the circumstances and having regard to all the evidence I had seen and heard, I would not have been able to conclude that these marks were bruises, and I could not therefore have found that A had sustained an injury in her parents' care. Interim threshold has not been crossed.*

Interim supervision order

An interim supervision order (ISO) requires a child to be supervised by a social worker for the period up to the court final hearing usually with provision for the child to continue to reside with their parents rather than in local authority care (see *Re JW (children) (care order)* [2023] EWCA Civ 944).

Child protection requires truth – fact finding expert opinion and the truthful parent

In this the final section of this chapter the importance of truth is considered both from medical experts in arriving at causation and from parents in disclosing how the injury occurred. The court in arriving at a decision with regard to these provisional orders and also the final orders (discussed in Chapter 15) will gather all the information including evidence of medical experts and the statement of the parent carers.

What is truth? The medical expert

The medical expert (paediatrician, pathologist, psychiatrist, neuropathologist, etc) is central to this fact-finding exercise in determining whether the injury is accidental or non-accidental (NAI). Seagrim (2023) refers to Jackson LJ's guidance in *A County Council v DP, RS, BS (by the Children's Guardian)* [2005] EWHC 1953 (Fam) that: '[22](i) When considering the welfare of the child, the significance to the individual child of knowing the truth can be considered, as can the effect on the child's welfare of an allegation being investigated or not.'

In the investigation of a child's injury, the opinion of the medical expert (paediatrician, neurologist, etc) is pivotal in determining causation. The medical expert presents the clinical findings, forms an assessment and may also express an opinion on the issues in the case which may also include the ultimate issue. However, no fact finder is bound by such an opinion, and it is for the judge as fact finder to decide particular issues in his or her finding of fact. In many cases, evidence of causation may be undisputable and self-evident, as was apparent in the deaths of

Victoria Climbié, Arthur Labinjo-Hughes and Star Hobson. In other cases, there will be a likely contest between the expert called on behalf of the local authority and the expert called on behalf of the parents. Whilst the role of experts is pivotal in determining the outcome of local authority application, it is incumbent on practitioners and judges to be cautious when considering the findings and conclusions of experts and not to be blindly overwhelmed by expert knowledge of which they may have little or no understanding. Certainly, the legal profession as a whole must bear some responsibility for not properly challenging experts and their findings simply because they did not understand them. This complacency has resulted in experts presenting flawed conclusions from bowdlerised applications of probability theory with disastrous consequences for families whose children were removed from them, taken into care, and adopted, and in some cases the parent wrongfully prosecuted for child cruelty and in some cases manslaughter (see the *Webster* case, *Webster and another v Norfolk County Council* [2009] EWCA Civ 59, cited in Chapter 10).

In 1987, in Middlesbrough, Cleveland, an unprecedented number of young children were diagnosed by paediatricians as having suffered from child sexual (anal) abuse. In arriving at this finding, the anal dilation or dilatation test was used as a diagnostic indicator in determining whether child sexual abuse had occurred. Paediatrician Dr Marietta Higgs found anal rape in a large number of children relying largely, but not exclusively, on the anal dilatation test (which depended on reflex dilation of the anal sphincter when the buttocks near the anus were pressed). Children who had been admitted into hospital for a variety of conditions, not only ano genital problems were anally examined and this test (with no historicity or scientific evidence base) was used to make a finding of sexual abuse. As a result, a significant number of children were removed from their homes under EPOs (formerly place of safety orders). This particular test was later wholly discredited.

By 2000, injuries of subdural haematoma and retinal haemorrhaging were considered symptomatic of deliberately inflicted injury. As a result, many parents were convicted in the criminal courts of abuse including murder and manslaughter where children had died, and parallel care proceedings in the civil courts resulted in other children of the family being subject to care proceedings and placed for adoption. The cases of 'Shaken Baby Syndrome' (SBS) and 'Sudden Infant Death Syndrome' (SIDS) cases are illustrative. In the criminal trial of Sally Clark, a mother charged and convicted with the murder of her own babies, (convictions quashed on appeal) the experts were in conflict. In relation to the statistical evidence the defence relied on CONI figures (as opposed to the CESDI figures relied on by the prosecution) and Professor Berry's evidence that the risks were inherently greater in a family that had already had a SIDS death. In these SBS cases, some experts relied on a bowdlerised version of probability theory, and drew conclusions based more on intuitive heuristics than hard evidence, in advancing their claims and findings on causation. Put simply it was said that since the chances of two unexplained cot deaths occurring in a family were remote then the only explanation possible was that the injuries were deliberately inflicted. Sir Roy Meadow, the prosecution's medical expert, when giving evidence in the criminal trial of Sally Clark said: 'one cot death in a family is a tragedy, two is suspicious and three is murder'. In that case, he said that the chances of there being two innocent cot deaths in any one family were in excess of one in 73 million. (He reached this figure by multiplying the statistical chance of one cot death (one in 8,600) again by 8,600 to accommodate two cot deaths; a statistic he later accepted as flawed). Looking at Meadow's statistical hyperbole from another angle: if he concluded, as he did, that the chance of two cot deaths occurring was one in 73 million, given that the population of the UK is 67 million, that would mean that Sally Clark was the only mother who had two children who had died in this way. Yet, Sally Clark herself knew of 40 other families who shared the same experience.

The true number the murder trial jury should have heard is that once you have suffered one cot death, the chances of a second are 60–1. The statistic Meadow gave the court was untrue. (See Delgado 2021). But it was too late for many parents who had lost their other children in care and adoption proceedings.

By 2004–5 it was conceded that the medical opinion upon which the courts had relied in several of these earlier cases was flawed. Successful appeals in the criminal courts followed, including the appeal of Sally Clark although her conviction quashed in 2006, in 2007 she took her own life unable to cope with the trauma of losing her two sons and being unjustly accused and imprisoned and having lost the right to be a mother to her surviving son. By July 2005, the GMC struck Professor Meadow off the medical register after finding him guilty of serious professional misconduct. The council decided he gave 'erroneous' and 'misleading' evidence at Mrs Clark's trial (Utley 2005). A study published in December 2004, in *the Lancet* found that second cot deaths in the same family were far more likely to result from natural cases than abuse.

Be vigilant

In 2002 Dame Elizabeth Butler-Sloss expressed the need for caution in too readily accepting expert evidence.

In *Re A and D (Non-Accidental Injury: Subdural Haematomas)* [2002] 1 FLR 337, a baby was admitted to hospital, suffering from convulsions. Upon clinical examination, the child presented with two acute subdural haematomas, a fresh haemorrhage and bilateral retinal haemorrhages. The paediatrician concluded that the injury appeared to be non-accidental and was probably caused by shaking. The parents replied that the injury to the baby might be the result of rough play. Seven consultants submitted reports, and six gave oral evidence. Although the court found that the CA 1989, s 31 threshold conditions had been met, Dame Elizabeth Butler-Sloss said, 'the courts must be careful not to jump to conclusions, nor to accept too readily the diagnosis of non-accidental injury in "brain injury" cases'. And in *Re U (A Child); Re B (A Child) (Serious Injury: Standard of Proof)* [2004] EWCA Civ 567 she stressed the need for careful analysis of findings in SBS cases:

> The cause of an injury or an episode that could not be explained scientifically remained equivocal; recurrence was not in itself probative; particular caution was necessary in any case where the medical experts disagreed; the court always had to be on guard against the over-dogmatic expert; and the judge in care proceedings should never forget that today's medical certainty might be discarded by the next generation of experts.

Experts are placed under a duty to inform the solicitor of any conflicting findings which controvert their own:

> iv.If an expert has carried out experiments or tests which tend to disprove or cast doubt on the opinion he is expressing (or knows that such experiments or tests have been carried out in his laboratory) he is under a clear obligation to bring the records of such experiments and tests to the attention of the solicitor instructing him (so that it may be disclosed to the other party) or to the expert advising the other party directly (R v Ward [1993] 2 All ER 577 at 632).
>
> The CrimPR do not supplant or detract from the prosecution's general duty of disclosure in respect of scientific evidence, which exists irrespective of any defences request, extends to anything which may arguably assist the defence, and obliges the prosecution to make full and proper inquiries of forensic scientists in order to ascertain whether there is discoverable material. In Clark [2003] EWCA Crim 1020, D's convictions for the murder of her two infant sons were quashed where a forensic pathologist, in breach of normal practice, had omitted from his autopsy report and had failed to disclose the fact that, in the case of one of the infants, following microbiological examination of certain bodily fluids, a form of bacteria which in some parts of the body can prove lethal had been isolated.
>
> (Blackstone's Criminal Practice 2024 F11.47)

In *R v Cannings* [2004] EWCA Crim 1; [2004] 1 WLR 2607, the appellant was convicted of the murder of two of her four children who had died aged 7 weeks and 17 weeks. The Crown's case depended on expert evidence, which again relied heavily on a truncated version of probability theory. But it was not reliance on flawed probability theory alone which presented as the only error in the case. Where there are two deaths in the family, the defence make an application to sever the indictment, that is, to try each case separately. A decision to sever the indictment rests with the judge who, in exercising his discretion, will consider whether the facts in the two deaths are sufficiently similar and whether the probative value exceeds the prejudicial effect in refusing an application. (See Michael Mansfield KC who represented Cannings, Mansfield 2010: 53.) Meanwhile new medical findings on SBS were emerging establishing that sudden infant death may be the result of a range of other factors, including a gene, and that injuries observed in SBS cases may be occasioned by very little force ('a head rocking back and forth') and that such injuries may be the result of the birthing process itself (Foreman et al. 2015).

In *Devon County Council v EB and others* [2013] EWHC 968 (Fam), sub *nom Re EY (Fact-Finding Hearing)* [2023] EWCA Civ 1241, Baker LJ summarised the correct approach. 'Findings of fact must be based on evidence. Whilst the opinions of medical experts are important, they have to be considered in the context of all the evidence. The Court must be cautious as to scientific evidence expressed as certainty,' and where a cause cannot be established i.e. unknown aetiology this does not mean that non-accidental injury is proven. Baker LJ sets out the distinct roles of the court and the expert, it being for the court: 'to weigh up the expert evidence against its findings on the other evidence' (see *A County Council v K, D and L* [2005] EWHC 144 (Fam)) and reiterates the wider principle articulated by Butler-Sloss P in *Re T (Abuse: Standard Of Proof)* [2004] EWCA Civ 558 that: 'evidence cannot be evaluated and assessed in separate compartments . . . the judge has to have regard to the relevance of each piece of evidence to other evidence and exercise an overview of the totality'. The Court of Appeal found that the judge in EY was obliged to evaluate the expert opinion in the context of the totality of the evidence and had 'misunderstood' the scope of the instruction with the appeal allowed primarily on the way he carried out his evaluation and his reasons for rejecting the expert opinion (see further Bilson 2023).

Undoing earlier decisions and fresh medical evidence

In *Norfolk County Council v C* [2007] EWHC 1556 (Fam), in care proceedings it was found that that non-accidental injuries had been caused to a child. The child and two siblings were placed in care and were later adopted. A further child was born, and the local authority started care proceedings in respect of this fourth child. After the parents and the child underwent a successful residential assessment the local authority sought permission to withdraw the application in respect of the fourth child. Further medical evidence had been obtained in respect of the injured child: this would form the basis of an appeal to the Court of Appeal in respect of the earlier orders made in connection with the first three children.

However not all decisions can be undone. Many children were taken into care, adopted and parents convicted of criminal offences following the flawed evidence on Shaken Baby Syndrome (SBS) and Sudden Infant Death Syndrome (SIDS). Mansfield (2010: 53) writes with regard to the case of the Webster family whose child was adopted following a finding made by the local authority of abuse by them against their child.

> The court was unable to undo the formality of the adoption orders and observed that if there is a lesson to be learned from the case it is the need to obtain second opinions on injuries to children at the earliest opportunity, particularly in cases where, as here, the fault was unusual.

Protecting parents – the right not to self-incriminate

The second theme in this search for truth is the statements of the parents/carers.

With regard to their evidence Parliament decided that the public importance of child protection inquiries and the need to discover the truth about causation overrides the private right to claim privilege, such that in proceedings under Parts IV (care and supervision) and V (child protection) of the CA 1989, witnesses can be compelled to give self-incriminating evidence. CA 1989, s 98:

(1)   In any proceedings in which a court is hearing an application for an order under Part IV or V, no person shall be excused from –

(a)   giving evidence on any matter; or answering any question put to him in the course of his giving evidence, on the ground that doing so might incriminate him or his spouse of an offence.

And so, the privilege against self-incrimination is suspended and notwithstanding the provision of s 14 of the Civil Evidence Act 1968 which protects witnesses in civil proceedings from self-incrimination, parents can be compelled to give evidence at any stage of care proceedings. Hale LJ in *Re Y and K (Split Hearing: Evidence)* [2003] EWCA Civ 669 sets out the position which remains good law in 2024–5.

> *We are glad, therefore, to have the opportunity today of clarifying the situation. Parents can be compelled to give evidence in care proceedings; they have no right to refuse to do so; they cannot even refuse to answer questions, which might incriminate them. The position is no different in a split hearing from that in any other hearing in care proceedings. If the parents themselves do not wish to give evidence on their own behalf there is, of course, no property in a witness. They can nevertheless be called by another party if it is thought fit to do so, and the most appropriate person normally to do so would be the guardian acting on behalf of the child.*

Whilst s 98(2) limits the use to which evidence given under compulsion can be put (conditional secondary privilege) as the case law demonstrates and following the rulings authorising disclosure in *Re L (a minor) (Police Investigation: Privilege)* [1996] 1 FLR 731, HL, and *Re EC (Disclosure of Material), sub nom Re C* [1996] 2 FLR 725 CA the preservation of the principle of encouraging frankness through promising confidentiality is being compromised with the result that parents/carers are now less likely to assist in the discovery of causation.

Legal practitioners can no longer assure their clients that what they say will not be disclosed. When the police make applications for disclosure of such incriminating documents and/or transcripts, the civil court may grant the application, leaving it to the criminal courts to shut a stable door and ensure a fair trial may exclude such evidence. In *Re AB (A Child) (Care Proceedings: Disclosure of Medical Evidence to Police)* [2002] 1 FLR 579 Wall J said there was a particular duty laid on lawyers to explain s 98 clearly to their clients.

The Family Proceedings (Amendment No 4) Rules 2005 (SI 2005/1976) extended the parties permitted to have access to documents, information and findings at the welfare and threshold stages of care proceedings. The report *Disclosure of Information in Family Proceedings Cases Involving Children: Response to the Public Consultation* tried to achieve a balance between, 'allowing legitimate access to information to those who need it . . . against the need not to discourage those giving evidence or statements from full and frank disclosure'. Reed (2014) asks whether s 98 of the Children Act 1989 is bad or just misunderstood, and sets out the amendments all of which have diluted any protection of truthful parents, including amendments of both primary and secondary legislation, the implementation of s 119 of the Criminal Justice Act 2003 relating to the admissibility of previous inconsistent statements as evidence in criminal proceedings, the relaxation of the rules on disclosure begun by the amendment in 2005 of the (then) Family Proceedings Rules 1991, r 12.73 and PD 12G of the Family Procedure Rules 2010 (FPR 2010) (and there are mirror provisions in r 14.14/PD14E relating to adoption/placement proceedings) which permitted automatic disclosure of information to the police and Crown Prosecution Service ('CPS') for specified purposes only (namely the furtherance of criminal investigation or to allow the CPS to discharge its functions) (see Edwards 2007, 2009).

Reed (2014) reviews the cases of *A Local Authority v DG and Others, X and Y (Children: Disclosure of Judgment to Police)* [2014] EWHC 734 (Fam) *Y v Z (Publicity: Sch 1 Proceedings)* [2014] EWHC 650 (Fam) concluding that that any protection is illusory and sets out the need for judicial guidance. (See also *Re EC Disclosure, In Re O (children) (privilege against self-incrimination)* [2023] EWFC 14.)

In *Re P (Children) (Disclosure)* [2022] EWCA Civ 495 the court set it out starkly the father said he had a binary choice of silence and unfairness in a family court proceedings against disclosure where a criminal investigation was pending. The court said:

> [3] *His privilege against self-incrimination entitles him to refuse to answer questions when giving evidence in court that tends to incriminate him. The privilege extends to refusing to answer such questions from a Cafcass officer because his answers would be admissible in the family proceedings. He would also be entitled to avoid making incriminating statements in any written evidence he produced in the proceedings. The privilege does not entitle a witness or party to refuse to engage at all. In simple terms, a witness would not be entitled to say that he or she refuses to answer any and all questions.*

Concluding remarks – how well is the local authority doing in child protection?

As Munby LJ has said in his lecture 'Care Cases: The Looming Crisis' (2014), a significant aspect of that crisis concerns what he identified as 'local authority behaviour'. However, the cut to funding is significant in looking at the total context of child neglect and abuse. A joint report by Barnardo's, the Children's Society, Action for Children, the NSPCC and the National Children's Bureau, shows that funding for children's services has fallen by £2.2 billion from 2010/11–2018/19, a 23 per cent reduction, impacting on early intervention services, leading to spending on early help dropping by almost half (46 per cent) during this period (see Children's Services Funding Alliance Evidence CSFA). The CSFA suggests that cuts to children's services funding have affected areas with the highest levels of deprivation [P 5] and the report found that since 2010/11, the most deprived local authorities have experienced twice the size of cut to funding available as the least deprived areas affecting local authority and children's services budgets.

All of this impacts on local authorities' ability and preparedness to support families in need and to prevent neglect and abuse. As McFarlane LJ in the Bridget Lindley lecture (2017) acknowledged:

> Into this complicated mix, we must introduce the impact of resources, or the lack of them. In a neglect case, where permanent removal is a borderline decision, the question of what resources can be introduced into the home to support the parents may be determinative of the outcome. Resources have never been limitless and in the current times they are often scarce. Where, prior to court proceedings, the available support to a family is considered by social services to be insufficient, but a risk of significant harm to the child has been identified, then that risk cannot be left unaddressed.

The funding crisis is also a crisis of geography. The Barnardo's report also found a North–South divide in the scale of cuts in funding and reductions in local authority spending with the North East and London being worst affected. Safeguarding by geography and 'The English Indices of Deprivation 2019, IoD2019' show which areas are the most deprived.

> *Middlesbrough, is the most income-deprived local authority in England, with a 40% rise in children referred to social services in the last year.*
>
> *Rochdale, in Greater Manchester, ranked 15th on the government's index of multiple deprivation, received 420 referrals to children's social care in July this year, 35% more than in July 2019, when there were 310. The town also saw a 35% increase in families at its early help and safeguarding hub, with 1,310 contacts this July.*
>
> *In Hull, there has been a 19% increase in 'troubled families' needing extra support in the last year while the number of children in care has risen 9%. A shortage of foster carers meant 55 looked-after children in the city moved between seven or more placements between June 2020 and June 2021.*
>
> (See 'Independent review of children's social care')

The impact of deprivation surfaces in the family courts in care proceedings investigations.

Adding into this mix is 'over referrals' to local authority social services the majority of referrals when closely examined do not raise any concerns and these needless investigations drain resources from the more pressing and urgent cases. After all, local authority proceedings begin with a referral and it is at this input point that research also needs to be conducted. The 'Crisis' is reflected in the demise of legal aid where families are left to self-litigate.

Jo Delahunty concludes her 2019 lecture by saying that what needs to develop is the willingness of the Government to provide the essential funds for training, community and court services.

Self-test questions

1. Bembo Ndosi telephoned the local authority social services department because Omar, a child who lives next door, regularly rings on his doorbell asking for money to buy food. Omar says that his mother isn't in the house, and it is cold, and that he hasn't had breakfast or dinner and is hungry and that he hasn't seen his mother for three days and his mother left bread and margarine on the kitchen table and told him that she would be back at the end of the week. Bembo has also noticed a bruise on Omar's cheek. Bembo decides to telephone the local authority social services department because he is concerned about Omar.

   What is the role of the local authority with regard to Omar and what action should be taken?

2. To what extent is the parental right to a fair hearing (Article 6 of the ECHR) and the need to balance the rights of the child and the family rights of parents (Article 8) relevant considerations when making an emergency protection order (EPO)? And what guidance ensures that EPO's are granted only where absolutely necessary?

3. Edwards argued in 2005 that: 'The rich evidential jewel of "frankness" in civil courts in child protection proceedings is currently under siege.' Is this still the case in 2024?

   Discuss with reference to the self-incrimination privilege in care proceedings.

4. Jimmy tells his school teacher that Mummy and Daddy are always fighting and that he saw Daddy put his hands around mummy's neck and she couldn't breathe. Mummy told Jimmy not to tell anyone. What should the school do, if anything, and what course of action could be taken?

References

Ahdash, Fatima, 'Countering Terrorism in the Family Courts: A Dangerous Development' [2023] *Modern Law Review* 1197

Bainham, Andrew, 'Private and Public Children Law; an Under Explored Relationship' [2013] *Child and Family Law Quarterly* 138

Barnett, Adrienne, 'Greater Than the Mere Sum of Its Parts: Coercive Control and the Question of Proof' [2017] *Child and Family Law Quarterly* 379

Batty, David, 'Case Highlights Rural Councils' Funding Problems' *Guardian Report* (02.10.2001) Case highlights rural councils' funding problems | Children | The Guardian https://www.theguardian.com/society/2001/oct/02/childrensservices2

BBC video www.bbc.co.uk/news/uk-england-leeds-59599884) (accessed 05.05.2024)

Bilson, Andy and Charlotte Image-Flower, 'Bruising in Non-Mobile Infants: Challenging Assumptions and Reassessing the Evidence' [2023] *Family Law* 1194

Blackstone's Criminal Practice (Oxford University Press 2023) https://global.oup.com/booksites/content/9780192870278/

Brownmiller, Susan, *Waverley Place* (Grove 1990)

Butler-Sloss, E, 'Cleveland Inquiry' Report of the Inquiry into Child Abuse in Cleveland (Cm 412 1988)

Campbell, Duncan, Sam Jones and David Brindle, '50 Injuries, 60 Visits – Failures That Led to the Death of Baby P: Review Ordered After Mother and Two Men Convicted Over Death of Toddler Failures That Led to the Death of Baby P' *The Guardian* (11.11.2008) https://www.theguardian.com/society/2008/nov/12/baby-p-child-protection-haringey

Child Abuse Extent and Nature – Appendix Tables – Office for National Statistics www.ons.gov.uk/peoplepopulationandcommunity/crimeandjustice/datasets/childabuseextentandnatureappendixtables) (accessed 05.05.2024)

Child Abuse in England and Wales – Office for National Statistics www.ons.gov.uk/peoplepopulationandcommunity/crimeandjustice/bulletins/childabuseinenglandandwales/march2020 (accessed 05.05.2024)

Children in Need Reporting Year 2022 – Explore Education Statistics https://explore-education-statistics.service.gov.uk/find-statistics/characteristics-of-children-in-need/2022 (accessed 05.05.2024)

Children in Need Reporting Year 2023 – Explore Education Statistics https://explore-education-statistics.service.gov.uk/find-statistics/characteristics-of-children-in-need (accessed 05.05.2024)

Children's Services Funding Alliance (CSFA) Written evidence Submitted to Public Accounts Committee COVID-19: Local Government Finance https://committees.parliament.uk/writtenevidence/23632/pdf/ (accessed 05.05.2024)

Cretney, Stephen and Judith Masson, *Principles of Family Law* (Sweet and Maxwell 2003)

Davis, Lynn, 'Protecting Children in an Emergency – Getting the Balance Right' (2007) 37 *Family Law* 728

Delahunty, Jo, 'The 30th Anniversary of the Children Act Lecture Delivered at Gresham College' (2019) www.gresham.ac.uk/sites/default/files/2019-01-31_JoDelahunty_30thAnniversary OfTheChildrenAct89.pdf (accessed 05.05.2024)

Delgado, Kasia, 'The Woman Behind Sally Clark's Prison Release: "Any of Us Could Be Accused of Killing Our Babies"' *The Guardian* (inews.co.uk) (19.11.2021) https://inews.co.uk/ news/long-reads/sally-clark-prison-release-lawyer-accused-killing-babies-1308182

Department for Education and Skills, *Statistics of Education: Referrals,* Assessments and Children and Young People on Child Protection Registers: Year Ending 31 March 2003 (The Stationery Office 2004) (accessed 05.05.2024)

Department for Education and Skills, *Statistics of Education: Referrals,* Assessments and Children and Young People on Child Protection Registers: Year Ending 31 March 2004 (The Stationery Office 2005) (accessed 05.05.2024)

The Department of Health Publication, The Children Act 1989 Guidance and Regulations *Vol 1 Court Orders* (HMSO 1991) (accessed 05.05.2024)

Devine, Lauren and Stephen Parker, 'Rethinking Child Protection' (2023) https://suitable-education.uk/rethinking-child-protection-serious-reform-needed-research-by-devine-and-parker/ (accessed 05.05.2024)

Disclosure of Information in Family Proceedings Cases Involving Children Response to the Public Consultation CM 6623 (publishing.service.gov.uk) https://assets.publishing.service.gov. uk/media/5a7c47d2ed915d76e2ebc4d2/6623.pdf (accessed 12.05.2024)

Edwards, Susan, 'Disclosure: Sacrificing the Privilege of Self-Incrimination for the Greater Good of Child Protection?' [2007] *Family Law* 510

Edwards, Susan, *Female Sexuality and the Law* (Martin Robertson 1981)

Edwards, Susan, 'Sealing One's Own Fate: Disclosure of Documents in Care Proceedings – on the Trail to the Abrogation of a Fair Trial' [2005] *Child and Family Law Quarterly* 13

Edwards, Susan, 'The Self-Incrimination Privilege in Care Proceedings and the Criminal Trial and "Shall Not Be Admissible in Evidence"' [2009] *Journal of Criminal Law* 48

Edwards, Susan, *Sex and Gender in the Legal Process* (Blackstone Press 1996)

The English Indices of Deprivation 2019, IoD2019, English Indices of Deprivation 2019 – GOV. UK (www.gov.uk) www.gov.uk/government/statistics/english-indices-of-deprivation-2019; https://assets.publishing.service.gov.uk/government/uploads/system/uploads/attachment_ data/file/835115/IoD2019_Statistical_Release.pdf (accessed 12.05.2024)

Family Court Statistics Quarterly Accessible Tables www.gov.uk/government/statistics/family-court-statistics-quarterly-july-to-september-2022 (accessed 05.05.2024)

Ferenczi, Sandor, 'Confusion of Tongues Between Adults and Child' English Translation in International Journal of PsA. (1949), 30, 225 'Confusion of Tongues Between Adults and Child' in Martin Balint (ed) and E Mosbacher et al. (trans) *Final Contribution to the Problems and Methods of Psychoanalysis* (Karnac Books 1955)

Firestone, Shulamith, *The Dialectic of Sex* (Paladin 1972)

Foreman, David M, Nicky Best, Frank D Dunstan, Neil McIntosh and Deborah Ashby 'Improving Child Protection by Integrating Research Evidence and Clinical Experience' [2015] *International Journal of Law, Policy and the Family* 301

Fortin, Jane, *Children's Rights and the Developing Law* (Cambridge University Press 1998)

Gibbons, Jane, B Gallagher, C Bell and D Gordon, *Development After Physical Abuse in Early Childhood: A Follow-Up Study of Children on Protection Registers* (HMSO 1995)

Gilliatt, Jacqui, 'Relaunch of the Public Law Outline Part I' [2023] *Family Law* 721

Hale, Baroness, 'Family Rights Group 40th Anniversary Lecture' [2014] *Family Law* 1658

Halsbury's Grounds for Emergency Protection Order 666, *Halsbury's Laws of England* Children Vol 9 (2023) paras 1–722; Vol 10 (2023) paras 723–1311

Hershman, David and Andrew McFarlane, *Children Act Handbook* (Jordan 2007)

House of Commons Hansard Debates for 16.07.2003 (pt 30) (parliament.uk) https://publications.parliament.uk/pa/cm200203/cmhansrd/vo030716/debtext/30716-30.htm (accessed 05.05.2024)

Independent Review of Children's Social Care – Final Report (publishing.service.gov.uk) https://assets.publishing.service.gov.uk/government/uploads/system/uploads/attachment_data/file/1141532/Independent_review_of_children_s_social_care_-_Final_report.pdf (accessed 05.05.2024)

ITV News 'Nan of Murdered Boy Speaks Out Young Arthur Labinjo-Hughes "Must Have Had Sense of Impending Doom", Says Grandmother' (2021) https://www.youtube.com/watch?v=dKRFyTPrkW0 (accessed 05.05.2024)

Jackson, Peter, 'Is Family Law Law? The Nicholas Wall Memorial Lecture 2023' (2023) *Family Law*796www.judiciary.uk/the-nicholas-wall-memorial-lecture-given-by-lord-justice-peter-jackson-is-family-law-law/ (accessed 05.05.2024)

Labinjo-Hughes, Arthur, YouTube www.youtube.com/watch?v=dKRFyTPrkW0 (accessed 05.05.2024)

Law Commission, 'Family Law, Domestic Violence and Occupation of the Family Home' (1992) www.gov.uk/government/publications/family-law-domestic-violence-and-occupation-of-the-family-home (accessed 05.05.2024)

Lord Laming, The Victoria Climbié Inquiry Report (2003) www.gov.uk/government/publications/the-victoria-climbie-inquiry-report-of-an-inquiry-by-lord-laming (accessed 05.05.2024)

Lyon, Cathy, Cobley C Christina, S Petrie and C Reid, *Child Abuse* (3rd edn, Family Law 2003)

Mansfield, Michael, *Memoirs of a Radical Lawyer* (Bloomsbury 2010)

Masson, Judith, 'Emergency Intervention to Protect Children: Using and Avoiding Legal Controls' (2005) 17(1) *Child and Family Law Quarterly* 75

McFarlane, Andrew, 'Holding the Risk: The Balance Between Child Protection and the Right to Family Life' The Bridget Lindley OBE Memorial Lecture (2017) *Family Law* 610 www.judiciary.uk/wp-content/uploads/2022/07/lecture-by-lj-mcfarlane-20160309.pdf (accessed 12.05.2024)

McFarlane, Andrew, 'A View from the President's Chambers: July 2023' [2023] *Family Law* 1024

McKenna, Anna, ' Interim Care Orders – Are They Being Sought and Made on a Proper Basis or Is There a Real Prospect of a Successful Challenge at an Early Stage?' [2019] *Family Law* 533

Miller, Alice, *Thou Shalt Not Be Aware: Society's Betrayal of the Child* (Farrar Straus Giroux 1984)

Mistry, Pritti, 'Star Hobson: The Short Life and Death of a Beloved Toddler' *BBC News* (14.12.2021) https://www.bbc.co.uk/news/uk-england-leeds-59599884 (accessed 05.05.2024)

'Multi-Agency Safeguarding and Domestic Abuse Briefing paper' (2022) The Child Safeguarding PracticeReviewPanel'swww.gov.uk/government/publications/multi-agency-safeguarding-and-domestic-abuse-paper (accessed 05.05.2024)

Munby, Sir James, 'The Crisis in Private Law' (2020) https://transparencyproject.org.uk/the-crisis-in-private-law-by-sir-james-munby/(accessed 12.05.2024)

Munby, Sir James, 'A View from the President's Chambers, Care Cases: The Looming Crisis' (2014) www.judiciary.uk/wp-content/uploads/2014/08/pfd-view-15-care-cases-looming-crisis.pdf (accessed 12.05.2024)

'National Review into the Murders of Arthur Labinjo-Hughes and Star Hobson' www.gov.uk/government/publications/national-review-into-the-murders-of-arthur-labinjo-hughes-and-star-hobson; Child Protection in England https://assets.publishing.service.gov.uk/media/628e262d8fa8f556203eb4f8/ALH_SH_National_Review_26-5-22.pdf (accessed 05.05.2024)

Practice Direction (PD) 12J Child Arrangements & Contact Orders: Domestic Abuse and Harm (accessed 12.05.2024)

Practice Direction (Public Law Proceedings) (Guide to Case Management): April 2010 (accessed 12.05.2024)

Practice Direction 12k – Children Act 1989: Exclusion Requirement (Justice.Gov.Uk) www.justice.gov.uk/courts/procedure-rules/family/practice_directions/pd_part_12 (accessed 08.05.2024)

Protocol for Judicial Case Management in Public Law Children Act Cases (June 2003)

Protocol for Judicial Case Management in Public Law Children Act Cases www.i-law.com/ilaw/doc/view.htm?id=163927 (accessed 08.05.2024)

Proudman, Charlotte, 'Setting Parents Up to Fail: Punishing Hopeless Parents Is Integral to Care Proceedings' (2012) *Family Law* 987

Reed, Lucy, 'Section 98 of the Children Act 1989: Bad or Just Misunderstood?' (2014) *Family Law* 1003

Seagrim, William, 'To Fact-Find, or Not to Fact-Find, That Is The Question' [2023] *Family Law* 1214

The Statutory Guidance – Safeguarding and Promoting the Welfare of Children Affected by Parental Alcohol and Drug Use: A Guide for Local Authorities www.gov.uk/government/publications/safeguarding-children-affected-by-parental-alcohol-and-drug-use/safeguarding-and-promoting-the-welfare-of-children-affected-by-parental-alcohol-and-drug-use-a-guide-for-local-authorities (accessed 05.05.2024)

Tardieu, Auguste, 'A Medico-legal Study of Assaults on Decency' 1857 in Jeffrey Masson (ed) *The Assault on Truth* (Faber and Faber 1984)

Utley, Tom, 'How Could an Expert Like Roy Meadow Get It So Terribly Wrong?' *The Telegraph* (15.07.2005)https://www.telegraph.co.uk/comment/personal-view/3618377/How-could-an-expert-like-Roy-Meadow-get-it-so-terribly-wrong.html (accessed 30.08.2024)

Ward, Hannah, *Paul: Death Through Neglect* (Bridge Child Care Development Service, Islington Area Child Protection Committee 1991) (accessed 12.05.2024)

Wright, Lauren, Hansard Debate (16.10.2001) vol 372 col 222wh-225wh https://hansard.parliament.uk/Commons/2001-10-16/debates/9ce68945-66c6-49bc-9a74-d104da8cc788/ (accessed 05.05.2024)

Further reading

Child Protection in England (May 2022) (publishing.service.gov.uk) https://assets.publishing.service.gov.uk/government/uploads/system/uploads/attachment_data/file/1078488/ALH_SH_National_Review_26-5-22.pdf (accessed 13.05.2024)

Department of Health, Working Together (DOH 1991)

Edwards, Susan, 'Child Protection: Trapped in the Middle of the Edge' [2009] *Family Law* 220

Foreman, David M, 'Improving Child Protection by Integrating Research Evidence and Clinical Experience' [2015] *International Journal of Family Law* 301

Howe, David, Child Abuse *and Neglect: Attachment,* Development and Intervention (Palgrave Macmillan 2005)

Kennedy, Sue, *Seeing the Child in Child Protection Social Work* (Red Globe Press 2020)

Munro, Eileen, *Effective Child Protection* (3rd edn, Sage 2019)

Thompson, Liza, 'Impossible expectations? Abused mothers' experiences of the child protection and Family Court Systems' [2020] *Child and Family Law Quarterly* 31

15

'Significant harm'

Judicial interpretations and state politics

SUMMARY

This chapter title carries a bold and controversial statement. It is of course the case that it is judges who interpret the law and apply it in child protection proceedings. But judicial decision making in family law is not hermetically sealed from the fact specific nature of every single case that comes before the court and social policy, family policy and political opinion will influence a society's determination to protect children so far as funding will allow. Where society fails to adequately fund children's services and support families such cases will inevitably come before the family court as care proceedings for neglect as the data show. Lord Mackay of Clashfern, the Lord Chancellor, in opening the debate on the Children Bill in 1989 said:

> Public child care law is a subject of fundamental importance, with two main aspects: first, the responsibility which Parliament gives the executive, mainly the local authority, to intervene in private family life on behalf of the community in order to help the children; and secondly, the court processes for adjudication in respect of such intervention.
>
> *(Vol 502 col 488)*

This chapter explores the law and its application and also considers critically some of the main concerns that have arisen around practice which are interwoven throughout this discussion of the law and cases before the courts and judicial determination and interpretation of statute.

Key thematic issues raise concern over the disproportionate number of ethnic minority children in care and the disproportionate number of care proceedings brought by local authorities involving children from minority ethnic families. Research conducted by the Nuffield Family Justice Observatory on 'Ethnic inequalities' found that black ethnic minority children are more likely to be in care and in London 60 per cent of children in care proceedings were black, Asian or of mixed parentage.

DOI: 10.4324/9781003435020-15

The widening of the understanding and application of significant harm lowering the threshold, in certain circumstances, is also contentious and especially when resources are limited (See further Chapter 14).

Concerning the substantive law the impact of the Domestic Abuse Act (DAA) (2021) has made important and significant strides in understanding and identifying harm to adults (addressed in Chapter 5) and children including strangulation and the widening and reframing of domestic violence as domestic abuse including coercive and controlling conduct, which are all part of the dynamics of family violence, largely male, towards both women and children, are specifically recognised. Such understandings have impacted on local authority care applications and on the courts' s 31 threshold findings of significant harm.

Some of the key interpretive and procedural issues have concerned the standard of proof, uncertain perpetrators and the fact that children remain in the home under care orders. The civil standard of proof which is balance of probabilities may be considered so axiomatic as not to warrant any discussion. However, it has held a contested place in care proceedings cases specifically with regard to its interpretation in determining sexual abuse allegations (see House of Lords in *Re H and R* [1996] AC 563 at 586H, [1996] 1 All ER 1, [1996] 1 FCR 509 later in this chapter) where a higher threshold was required for such cases which arose because of postures of disbelief about the sexual abuse of children by parents held at that time and therefore cannot avoid some considerable discussion. If not only as a reminder and warning that judicial attitudes, presumptions and stereotypical prejudice impact on decisions and continue to do so (see *Re H-N and others (children) (domestic abuse: finding of fact hearings)* [2021] 2 FLR 1116 discussed further in Chapter 5) leading to criticism by fellow judges and from some practitioners, one at least who has spoken out of 'a boys club'. As for *Re H and R*, it was not until 2008 that this erroneous interpretative nuancing was given 'quietus' in the House of Lords judgment in *Re B (Children) (Sexual Abuse: Standard of Proof)* [2008] UKHL 35.

There also remains the unresolvable problem of identifying the perpetrator when likely perpetrators deny complicity in a child's suffering. Such denials present an ongoing problem for determining future risk to children of the family.

Lord Justice Munby (2016a) referred to the rising number of care proceedings and cuts to local authority funding as the 'looming crisis'. There is also the overriding concern that there are wide regional variations in family justice. One of the findings of the Public Law Working Group (PLWG) concerned the number of care orders that are made where children remain in the abusive home. Both these issues are addressed by McFarlane LJ in *Re JW (Child at Home Under care order)* [2023] EWCA Civ 944 [1][30].

The evolving interpretation of what conduct and behaviour amounts to a finding of significant harm for the purpose of s 31 of the Children Act (CA) has extended in responding to wider understandings of harm as society's and the legal perception of harm develops. Such changing understandings are reflected in court decision making. For example, the ubiquity and accessibility of online pornography would not have been contemplated as a possible harm when the CA became law in 1989 or indeed the potential harm to children of an unregulated www which is now understood and recognised in the Online Safety Act (2023) s 12, 'safety duties to protect children'. The digital era and the smartphone are recognised as harmful and damaging children's mental health, and Government guidance issued to schools, although not yet statutory, advises schools to ban the use of phones during the school day (see Press release 'Government launches crackdown on mobile phones in schools' 19 February 2024). This will be the next concern for local authorities when parents are unable to regulate their child's use of social media and where it is a contributory factor to the child's well-being.

The confluence of state security concerns in the criminal law arena has split over into family law and led to drawing into the 'significant harm' s 31 CA fold, a particular politico/ideological position within family life which is deemed to be harmful to children. In 1940s and 1950s America, the politico/ideological fear was communism. In 1938, the House Committee on Un-American Activities, or HUAC, a special committee in the US House of Representatives, was tasked with investigating individuals and organisations who were considered subversive. A key concern was infiltration of such ideas in the school system. In the UK state security has deemed what are considered to be extreme forms of political conduct, specifically support for particular Islamic terrorist activities at the end of a continuum as well as conduct which includes expressing views antithetical to UK foreign policy, UK sale of arms, to expressing outrage about the onslaught of Gaza, all of which come under the umbrella of the vague, lose and non-specific term 'radicalisation' considered harmful to children which may warrant removal of children from the family home.

In care proceedings cases, as Peter Jackson LJ in 'The Nicholas Wall Memorial Lecture 2023' [2023] said:

> A further aspect of family law is that it is usually more concerned with prediction than other branches of law. A criminal or civil court may centrally be deciding whether an assault occurred or whether a trader acted dishonestly; the family court may be asking whether a parent injured a child, but for it that is not the ultimate question. It has to go on and look to the future and ask itself what sort of a person this parent is. If they did it before, will they do it again? This involves an effort to understand what the person is really like and then to work out what the child really needs.

Prediction, as will become clear in this chapter especially, requires the court to consider the likelihood that a child will suffer harm in the future.

Ultimately, the application of the law in care proceedings brought by the local authority and the impact judicial decision making and judgments made in the appellate courts have an impact and cast a shadow on local authority decisions to initiate care proceedings and ultimately impact child protection. As Mnookin and Kornhauser (1979) in the context of divorce law negotiations wisely observed, it is the higher courts that cast a shadow on the law and on decisions to engage with the law. Here, in child protection this shadow cascades down and determines whether and what kind of future applications are made. Munby LJ in his '15th View from the President's Chambers, Care Cases: The Looming Crisis' (2016b) calls for research: into the extent to which local authority behaviour is in response to the actual or perceived effect of judicial rulings.

Social policy and the threshold

Determination of whether the commission or omission of parental conduct meets the threshold of significant harm necessitating a care or supervision order is a matter for judges and the several iterations of the statutory guidance 'Working together to safeguard children' together with the several Practice Directions that have shaped their decision making. However, the cases that are put up to the courts for determination is a matter for the local authority. Since 2013, Munby LJ has said that one of the reasons for the rise in applications is that the local authority threshold for care proceedings has been lowered (see Munby LJ 2016a; Devine and Parker 2023). Devine and Parker's examination of the available data for 2019/2020 found that of families referred to the local authority, 88 per cent did not meet the CA, s 47 threshold to trigger a local authority investigation. Section 47 provides:

> *(1) Where a local authority – (a) are informed that a child who lives, or is found, in their area – (i) is the subject of an emergency protection order; or (ii) is in police protection; (iii) have reasonable cause to suspect that a child who lives, or is found, in their area is suffering, or is likely to suffer, significant harm, the authority shall make, or cause to be made, such enquiries as they consider necessary to enable them to decide whether they should take any action to safeguard or promote the child's welfare.*

Since local authority children's services budgets are greatly reduced whilst at the same time, they are being expended on referrals some of which prove to have been unnecessarily investigated, there is less funding for the serious cases resulting in many children being inadequately protected. The *National Review into the Murders of Arthur Labinjo-Hughes and Star Hobson* concluded that there was insufficient multi-agency working and sense of urgency.

Drawing on the *Department for Education, Working Together to Safeguard Children*, data and statutory guidance, Devine and Parker (2023) found that whilst 600,000 families are affected each year, around 31 per cent of child protection assessments do not yield sufficient evidence of abuse to have merited a referral at all. Devine and Parker use the term 'assessment' in the context of a local authority social work process to decide whether a child is 'in need' under s 17 of the CA 1989 or 'at risk of or suffering significant harm' to initiate a s 47 CA 1989 investigation prior to commencing proceedings.

The legal framework

Section 31 – threshold finding of 'significant harm'

The court, having considered the case for the local authority including the response of parents, other interested parties, the children's guardian, and all the supporting and controverting rebuttal evidence, must make a finding of whether there is evidence of 'significant harm' having occurred ('is suffering') in the present or else ('likely to suffer') in the future. This involves a finding of causation in the past and of risk in the future, and is called the 'threshold finding', as cited by Peter Jackson LJ earlier.

The CA 1989, s 31(2)(a), states:

> the court must be satisfied on the civil standard of proof, that is, on the balance of probabilities, (i) that the child 'is suffering, or is likely to suffer, significant harm' and [that] the harm or likelihood of harm, is attributable to s 31(2)(b)(i) the care given to

> *the child, or likely to be given to him if the order were not made, not being what it would be reasonable to expect a parent to give him; or (ii) the child is beyond parental control.*

It is, as Lord Wilson said in *Re B* [2013] 3 All ER 929 a matter of discretion and judgment and is certainly the case as is discovered later in the analysis of *Re H and R* [1996] AC 563 at 586H, [1996] 1 All ER 1, [1996] 1 FCR 509.

If the court makes a finding of 'significant harm' it will then go on to consider whether to make a care or supervision order under s 31 of the CA (interim orders prior to this final hearing are discussed in Chapter 14) or whether, in applying the non-interventionist presumption, it is better for the welfare of the child not to make an order at all (CA 1989, s 1(5)). If, having decided to make an order, the court must then determine whether any additional orders, for example, an order for residence or contact with family members (CA 1989, s 8) should also be considered.

Split hearings

Some care proceedings applications proceed as split hearings (see *Re B (Split Hearing: Jurisdiction)* [2000] 1 FLR 334; *Re G (A Child) (Care Order: Threshold Criteria)* [2001] 1 FLR 872, UKHL 18; *Re B (children) (Non-accidental Injury)* [2002] EWCA Civ 902, [2003] UKHL 18, sub nom *Re O and another (Children) (Non-accidental Injury)* (2003); *Re Y and another (Children) Care Proceedings: Split Hearing)* [2003] EWCA Civ 669). Here, the court considers separately the factual matters, that is, the evidence from the local authority which supports their application and the evidence from the suspect abuser(s) which refutes or concedes the local authority case. Whilst split hearings are useful the delay which such a hearing occasions has to be proportionate to the benefit and continues to be a matter of current debate. For example, the fact-finding hearing in Nottinghamshire *County Council v Mother and others* [2024] EWHC 666 (Fam) was heard over five days.

It is generally agreed as Hale LJ in *Re G (A Child) (Care Order: Threshold Criteria)* [2001] 1 FLR 872, UKHL 18 said:

> *Split hearings like this can be very useful when there are early decisions which can be made about factual disputes, for example as to the causation of a child's injuries. But the early hearing has to be early, not many months into the case, and it has to be clearly focused.*

In *Re F-H (Dispensing with Fact-Finding Hearing)* [2008] EWCA Civ 1249 where there were allegations of sexual abuse by an adult half-sibling or sibling of four children the court considered in what circumstances it was appropriate for a judge, at the outset of a pre-arranged fact-finding hearing, to decline to conduct it. The Court of Appeal said: '[26] There is no doubt that in family proceedings the court has a discretion whether to hear evidence in relation to disputed matters of fact with a view to determining them.'

In *A County Council v DP and Others* [2005] EWHC 1593 (Fam) McFarlane J identified nine matters which the court should bear in mind before deciding whether to conduct a particular fact-finding exercise [24]. (See also *Practice Direction, Split Hearings* [2010] 2 FCR 271.) In *AA v NA (Appeal: Fact-Finding)* [2010] EWHC 1282 (Fam) the guiding principles with regard to a fact-finding hearing were restated and reiterated.

The delay point was dealt with in *Re S (Split Hearing)* [2014] 1 FLR 1421 where the child suffered two skull fractures with associated brain haemorrhage and swelling, the judge conducted a fact-finding hearing and concluded that whilst the child suffered significant harm while in the care of the parents and that the harm was caused by an injury, he was not satisfied that either of the parents had deliberately inflicted the injury. The LA authority appealed. The court reiterated the position and held:

> [3] A split hearing was only justifiable where the delay occasioned was in furtherance of the overriding objective in r 1 of the Family Procedure Rules 2010 (FPR 2010). . . . Even where it was asserted that delay would not be occasioned. The use of split hearings had to be confined to cases where there was a stark or discrete issue to be determined and an early conclusion on that issue would enable the substantive determination (i.e. whether a statutory order was necessary) to be made more expeditiously ([27] [31]).

However, even where a fact-finding hearing is dispensed with, as for example, in *L (A Child)* [2009] EWCA Civ 1008 where the parents accepted that the injuries to the child were non-accidental, the evidence to establish causation is still needed to be considered at some point.

The complexity of the case is also a determining factor in the need for a split hearing. In *Lancashire County Council v M and others* [2023] EWHC 3097 (Fam) the circumstances of this case involved sexual abuse allegations. Hayden J clearly indicated the need for a fact-finding hearing. Similarly, in *Re EY (Fact-Finding Hearing)* [2023] EWCA Civ 1241 the complexity of the case, its history and multifaceted concerns over a period of time necessitated a fact-finding hearing.

(See also *Re H-N and Others (Children) (Domestic Abuse: Finding of Hearings)* [2021] 2 FLR 1116; *Warwickshire County Council v A Mother and A Father and X and Z* [2023] EWHC 399 (Fam).)

Evidence – burden and standard

The burden of proof required to establish that a child 'is suffering or likely to suffer significant harm' s 31, is iterated by Wall LJ in *Re K (Care: Threshold Criteria)* [2005] EWCA Civ 1226, [2006] 2 FLR 868:

> The burden of establishing the threshold criteria lies of course on the local authority, and the reason for a split hearing is frequently that the facts on which the threshold criteria depend are disputed by the parents, and if resolved in the parents' favour would bring the proceedings to an end.

The standard of proof, which in civil cases is on the balance of probabilities has evoked, surprisingly, much dissension especially where there are allegations of a sexual nature (discussed later).

Veal J in *A Mother v A Father* [2024] EWFC 53 (B) iterates both the burden and standard:

> *[40] In resolving disputed issues of evidence in this court, where a person asserts a particular fact, it is that person who must prove it. Because the mother makes the allegations which I am to determine, she bears the burden of proving them. At no stage does the burden reverse. The father has to prove nothing. [41] The standard of proof is the balance of probabilities. In other words, if it is shown that any particular fact is more likely than not to be true, then it is treated as having happened; if it is not proved, then the fact is treated as not having happened. This is sometimes referred to as the binary effect. The court is entitled to take into account inherent probabilities and improbabilities in deciding whether a fact is proved, but must base its findings on evidence, including reasonable inferences, and not speculation: Re B [2008] UKHL 35.*

What conduct falls under 'significant harm' s 31(10)?

Under the CA 1989 s 31(2)(b), the harm, or likelihood of harm must be 'significant' (s 31(10)). In Chapter 14, the several forms of significant harm discussed included physical, sexual, emotional abuse and neglect, and by the Adoption and Children Act (ACA) 2002, s 120, new social policy concerns specifically included: 'In section 31 of the 1989 Act (care and supervision orders), at the end of the definition of "harm" in subsection (9) there is inserted "including, for example, impairment suffered from seeing or hearing the ill-treatment of another"'.

Other types of harm that have been defined and developed in the case law have included, amongst many others, 'parental alienation', fabricated illness (FII), forced marriage and female genital mutilation. In *Re M Minors (Children) (Repatriated Orphans)* [2002] EWHC 852 (Fam) Singer J said: 'both abduction and imposed marriage are child abuse'. In *Re B and G (children) (care proceedings)* [2015] EWFC 3 care proceedings commenced in relation to two children: B, a boy, and G, a girl, both of whom were under the age of 5 years. The family was of African origin and practicing Muslims. Concerns were raised over whether the girl had been subjected to some form of FGM after blood was discovered by staff at the nursery she attended. Both children were placed in foster care. The court held that any form of FGM constituted 'significant harm' within the meaning of ss 31 and 100 of the 1989 Act. Although in the instant case the court held that there was insufficient evidence of FGM now or risk in the future. The court also emphasised the need for greater understanding of what FGM amounted to and advised caution not to jump to the wrong conclusions.

Significant harm is also recognised, and not without considerable controversy, where parents who hold particular views have been alleged to 'radicalise' their children (see Ahdash 2018; Edwards 2023). The wording of the Act was not intended to be unduly restrictive as Sir Stephen Brown, in *Newham London Borough Council v AG* [1993] 1 FLR 28, emphasised. Cases brought before the courts have shown it not to be so.

It is perhaps worth reflecting here again on Devine and Parker's (2023) research and the disproportionate number of referrals to the local authority that resulted in no action being taken, strongly indicating a need for caution on the part of referrers especially with regard to suspicion of some kinds of harms. At the same time for caution, Baroness Hale in her lecture '30 Years of the Children Act' recognised, in cases like the death of Baby P:

> Numerous opportunities to realise that he was being ill-treated were missed by both health and children's services, children's services became more and more risk-averse and the number of care proceedings rocketed, putting a major strain on the family justice system, as well as on the resources available to children's services for preventive and rehabilitative work with families [17].

There is a fine balance, and again to reiterate, it is a matter of discretion and judgement.

Judicial interpretation

Sir James Munby's trenchant observations in his lecture 'The Crisis in Private Law' (2020) are also relevant to public law. As Munby LJ rightly recognises we do not know enough about how the courts deal with cases and with far too little research and lack of accessible data, adding:

> Our public law system is under considerable scrutiny and attack, but most of that is directed either to those parts of the legislation which, for example, permit a care order to be made where there is no more than a risk of future emotional harm or which enable the court to make an adoption order against parental opposition, or to the actions of local authorities and guardians; there is much less direct criticism of judges.

What degree of harm is recognised as significant?

The CA 1989 offers no guidance on the degree of harm likely to satisfy the 'significant' threshold. In *Humberside County Council v B* [1993] 1 FLR 257 Booth J accepted the local authority's submission that a dictionary definition should be used, where the definition of 'significant' turned upon (1) whether the harm was 'considerable, noteworthy or important' and (2) that the harm should also be considered in the context of the child's future. This leaves considerable discretion to the court in assessing harm and future risk.

In *L (a child) (care proceedings: responsibility for child's injury)* [2006] EWCA Civ 49 a finding of 'accidental injury' was not sufficient to satisfy the threshold criteria. In this case, the court held that the local authority must define precisely what facts it is inviting the court to find. The Court of Appeal held that the judge was wrong to have concluded that the threshold criteria were satisfied because either the mother or the father was responsible for the injuries. However, where accidental injuries amounted to a failure to protect a child such a finding would be relevant to the threshold criteria because it could be evidence of a failure on the part of the parents to provide adequate care for the child (s 31(2)(b)(ii)).

In *Re L Children* [2006] EWCA Civ 1282 the parents' learning difficulties were not in themselves considered sufficient justification for finding the threshold criteria to be satisfied.

> In *B Slough Children First applicant and Mother (1) F (2) SK (The Child) (3)* [2024] EWFC 31, sub nom *Slough Children First v Mother, Father, SK (The Child) (2024)* after a lengthy fact-finding hearing, involving a child with a tibia injury where the parents had actually contacted their GP who had reassured them and as a result they did not seek any subsequent hospital care, and where the court found that it was unknown whether the child's vitamin D deficiency resulted in increased bone fragility compared to children without this deficiency and the force required to fracture this child's leg remained 'unknown', the court said there was no finding that the parents' failure to seek medical attention in hospital for the child had been unreasonable.

Objective and subjective tests

In attempting to measure whether a standard of care is substandard or defective or whether the health and development of a child is substandard or defective, an objective and a subjective assessment of harm is made. The objective test relies on evidence of the nature and extent of harm. So, indecently touching a child or directing or enticing a child to indecently touch an adult (see *Lancashire County Council v M and others* [2023] EWFC 30) is, of its very nature, 'significant harm'.

Deliberately breaking a child's arm is, by its very seriousness, 'significant harm'. However, in *Re W (A Child) (Care Proceedings)* [2007] EWCA Civ 102 Wall LJ said:

> *[37] . . . in the overall context of the issues raised in this case, we do not think that, of itself a single blow by the father (or even more than one blow) would be sufficient to satisfy the threshold criteria under the first limb of CA 1989, section 31 (Referring to the 'is suffering or is likely to suffer' limb.)*

The subjective test, by contrast, relies on the impact of the harm on the individual child concerned. Thus, harm may be considered 'significant' if a child is deeply affected by what has happened, whereas another child may not be affected to such a degree. Impact awareness is also subject to changes over time. There was a time when children were supposed to simply 'get over it', or 'put up with it' or 'bury it'. Contemporary understanding of impact today focuses much more on the psychodynamic. In addition, abused children may live in denial in order to cope and survive and bury or minimise their experience and may also feel conflicted by feelings of loyalty to the abuser or to the non-abusive parent, and therefore any attempt to measure impact is affected very much by societal and individual construction. Children who were sexually abused in the Cleveland cases (Chapter 14) were reported as saying of the fathers who had sexually abused them: 'I loved him really.' Evidence to the Inquiry also reported that the child's face would light up when the father who had abused them entered the room. A conflicting sense of obligation and responsibility resulted in this child saying:

I thought any adult would not believe me – they would think I was making up a story. . . .
I didn't know what might happen. For my brother's sake I didn't want my family split
up. . . . I loved my father so much. I respected him as a father. But I was confused, didn't
understand. I wanted it to stop. I hated that part of it so much.

(Cleveland Inquiry 9)

How is the objective test of 'significant harm' measured?

The 'similar child' comparator test considers what can reasonably be expected with
regard to the health and development of a similar child and the standard of care that
can be expected of a reasonable parent. In assessing the harm to a child, the court will
consider evidence of the standard of care including physical and emotional that one
might expect a reasonable parent to provide for a child and will compare the child
with children of a similar background, age and gender and other relevant measures
and characteristics according to the health and development expected of an average
child. The guidance offered in the CA 1989, s 31(10) states: 'Where the question of
whether harm suffered by a child is significant turns on the child's health or
development, his health or development shall be compared with that which could
reasonably be expected of a similar child.' Expert evidence may be called upon to
address what would be expected and the range of normality. (The case of Re O (A
Minor) (Care Order: Education Procedure) [1992] 2 FLR 7 has been cited and used as an
example of the comparator test.)

The wording of s 31(10) is: 'which could reasonably be expected of a similar
child', and guidance from the DHSS *Review of Child Care Law* 1985 [5.15] indicates
that the deficit has to be 'substantial'. In *Re C (A Minor) (Care: Child's Wishes)* [1993]
1 FLR 832 Waite J upheld the findings of the justices, who concluded:

> we have considered whether the grounds under s 31 have been met. We find that the child
> has been suffering from significant harm and that her development has been impaired, and
> her health has suffered compared with a similar child of her age and similar background and
> this harm or likelihood of harm is attributable to the care given to the child in the past and
> likely to be given to her in the future if an order were not made.

Often there is no need for a comparator since the evidence of significant harm is
undisputable as were the injuries and their causation sustained by Victoria Climbié
(Laming Report [1.5]). (See also Chapter 14.)

Similar children: similar to whom and to what?

However, when assessing, for example, some types of emotional harm or neglect,
subjective evaluative judgments may be open to criticism especially where an
idealised standard of childhood from a dominant perspective is extolled as the
normative standard. It is to be remembered that Lord Templeman in *Re KD (A
Minor) (Ward: Termination of Access)* [1988] AC 806, at 812: said:

> *The best person to bring up a child is the natural parent. It matters not whether the parent*
> *is wise or foolish, rich, or poor, educated or illiterate, provided the child's moral and physical*
> *health are not endangered. Public authorities cannot improve on nature.*

This presumption has been echoed in other cases. In a case involving international adoption, Bracewell J said in *Re R (No 1) (Inter-Country Adoption)* [1999] 1 FLR 104: 'The case is not a contest between a middle-class lifestyle in Wales with all the comforts and advantages, and on the other hand poverty and deprivation in Bucharest.'

Debate – different but normal?

In some situations, it is difficult to draw a line and determine what is a normal standard of family life and at what point family life is harmful and what exactly is the tipping point or threshold. Sexual abuse may be easier to assess than physical, emotional abuse or neglect. Freeman (1993), critical of the normative expectation of family life, said at least for 1993 that it was located within the dominant white English Christian culture. Jivraj and Herman (2009) in critiquing judgments in private law asserted:

> we argue that, within these judicial texts, a way of thinking can be identified that is, at times, orientalist, racialised, and Christian. We use the words 'racialisation' and 'racialised', not as terms of art, but to signify a particular form of understanding and way-finding – usually through phenotypical signifiers or characteristics – when encountering persons perceived as alien to the 'home' environment.

(See Ahdash 2018)

The following two cases reflect the courts' earlier treatment of and attitudes to diverse parenting practices. In *Re H (Minors) (Wardship: Cultural Background)* [1987] 2 FLR 12, where the court acknowledged: '[15] This lady has had a refugee history of a very dramatic kind.' A referral to social services was made, which followed the discovery of injuries on P at school, and serious cuts and bruises on his face and head. A non-accidental injury conference resulted, and the names of all three children of the family were placed on the child abuse register. Injuries included the children being beaten with a stick and hit across the face with a flip flop sandal. Whilst the court took the view that the children should be placed with long term foster parents with a view to adoption, Callman J said: '[17] I must consider the case against the reasonable objective standards of the culture in which the children have hitherto been brought up, so long as these do not conflict with our minimal acceptable standards of child care in England' (discussed in detail in Chapter 9). In *R v Adesanya* (1974) *The Times*, 16 and 17 July, where a mother had made tribal markings on her son's face and was charged with assault Mrs Adesanya's main line of defence was that she had merely inflicted the markings in deference to preserving his cultural identity. King Hamilton J said: 'Nigerian custom (Mrs Adesanya was Yoruba) was no defence to the charge of assault occasioning bodily harm.' But given that the mark was not serious and given the mother's explanation he imposed a conditional discharge (see Poulter 1988). See more recently *Re A (A child: Wardship: Fact finding: Domestic Violence)* [2015] EWHC 1598 (Fam), where Pauffley J accepted that at times different cultural approaches to physical chastisement may be highlighted and whilst not excusing such behaviour as appropriate given UK laws and standards, at times a cultural allowance might be given.

> *[67] I do not believe there was punitively harsh treatment of A of the kind that would merit the term physical abuse. Proper allowance must be made for what is, almost certainly, a different cultural context. Within many communities newly arrived in this country, children are slapped and hit for misbehaviour in a way which at first excites the interest of child protection professionals.*

Scrutiny of judicial decision making and assumptions and reasoning and on what basis local authorities initiate care applications and on what ground referrals are made to local authorities is even more pertinent especially at a time when digital and social media create particular 'moral panics' which may heighten suspicions and generate an overzealousness by those who refer their concerns to the local authority. For example, the drawing in of so called 'radicalisation' with its lack of specificity, into the panoply of referrals and care applications does suggest that the labelling of certain beliefs and conduct as potentially meeting the threshold certainly in some cases goes beyond objective standards and reflects the impact of state ideological control.

Ethnic minority children in care

Throughout the care system at the referral, investigation and hearing stages judgements continue to be made on the basis of class, culture, race, ethnicity, gender and other factors. Cobley and Sanders (2003: 107) found that doctors were less likely to make referrals to social services of children of middle-class parents. Owen and Statham (2009) in their report, 'Disproportionality in Child Welfare, The Prevalence of Black and Minority Ethnic Children within the "Looked After" and "Children in Need" Populations and on Child Protection Registers in England' found:

> *Children of mixed ethnic background are over-represented in all three categories, . . . black children are over-represented among children in need in general and among children who are looked after as a specific group, . . . Once in care, Black Caribbean children are almost twice as likely to experience a placement in residential care compared with Bangladeshi children.*

These findings were replicated in the Nuffield Observatory report (see Roe 2021). Olivia Edwards (2021), for example, explores the findings of the Northern Circuit race panel report concerning the investigation into racial barriers to ethnic minorities into the Bar, the increase of ethnic minority children into the care system and increased migration. Anecdotal evidence gathered from ethnic minority barristers at 18 St John Street Chambers Manchester in June 2021 (cited in Edwards 2021 earlier) in relation to the challenges experienced for non–white families in the care system found that ethnic minority parents involved in public law care proceedings struggle to verbalise their case effectively. The potential for unconscious bias by all levels of the court system, judiciary and legal representatives was apparent. There was a lack of support services for ethnic minority parents to educate parents as to the standards and expectations of parenting in the UK and that many ethnic minority parents were economically disadvantaged not always being able to meet their children needs. Edwards (2021) also reports on Paul Bywaters' study which found that black Caribbean children are 20 times more likely than other children to be in the care system. (See also Roe and Rehill 2021.)

Poverty, deprivation and s 17

Poverty and deprivation appear to be the overriding factor especially in cases of neglect, and these variables intersect with class and ethnicity as Edwards 2021 above found. This has been an ongoing contributory factor (see Proudman 2012). Brophy and Cover (2012) offer some further observation on the intersectionality of class, race, ethnicity and disadvantage. Research over many years of care proceedings (Harwin and Alrouh 2017; Masson 2022; Alrouh et al. 2022; Delahunty 2019) demonstrates that the families involved in care proceedings are complex with multiple problems and needs.

> For the most part they are drawn from the poorest households in society, . . . parents have problems which are not properly assessed and diagnosed until they are subject to proceedings based on allegations of neglect/ill-treatment of their children; it is at that point that co-morbidity is clearly identified.
>
> (Brophy and Cover 2012)

Proudman's (2012) robust critique of the care system and lack of funding and support given to families in need and lack of adherence to s 17 of the CA also identifies the prevalence of the poverty and disadvantage dimension.

> Often families are from the most impoverished households where parents and children are at the bottom of the social and economic strata. Many parents live a destitute life. To compound this, many of their problems are not properly assessed, diagnosed, or treated until they are subject to care proceedings based on allegations of neglect and/or ill-treatment of their children.

Sir Andrew McFarlane's 2017 lecture 'Holding the Risk: The Balance between Child Protection and the Right to Family Life' also identifies the impact of poverty and disadvantage on neglect. (See also Mornington and Guyard-Nedelec 2009.)

Section 17 CA 1989 states that it is the general duty of every local authority to safeguard and promote the welfare of children within their area who are in need; to promote the upbringing of such children by their families and importantly provide a range and level of services appropriate to those children's needs.

Section 17 (10) sets out:

> For the purposes of this Part a child shall be taken to be in need if – (a) he is un-likely to achieve or maintain, or to have the opportunity of achieving or maintaining, a reasonable standard of health or development without the provision for him of services by a local authority under this Part; (b) his health or development is likely to be significantly impaired, or further impaired, without the provision for him of such services; or (c) he is disabled, and 'family', in relation to such a child, includes any person who has parental responsibility for the child and any other person with whom he has been living.

However, there is little evidence of this early support and intervention and rather more of crisis management through care orders and adoption. It is here that the much-needed children social care support is needed. The Independent Review of Children's Social Care 2023 reporting on child poverty said, 'An urban local authority in the Midlands has an overall population size of 300,000, 90,000 are children, making up 30% of the population. In certain parts of the local authority, it is estimated that 45% of children are living in poverty' (50).

Providing a reasonable standard of parental care

Children may also suffer significant harm because they are beyond parental control, or their parents themselves are ill, disabled or lacking in caring skills and unable to adequately parent necessitating s 20 CA orders for accommodation (discussed later). The parents in *J v C* [1970] AC 668 (see also Chapter 12) said the court, were unimpeachable but the mother was too ill to adequately care for the child. In *Re C (Child's Wishes)* [1993] 1 FLR 832,1 FCR 810, a single parent father was elderly and in poor health and also considered unable to provide adequate care. In *Re W (Minors: Sexual Abuse Standard of Proof)* [1994] 1 FLR 419, the mother was considered to be incapable of adequately caring for her children because she had the mental capacity of a 10-year-old child. In *Re C (A Minor)* [1995] 20 September CA, [1995] Lexis Citation 1364, the parents were unable to look after the child because of the mother's physical problems and the father's manic depression.

In such cases, 'children in need' and their families require local authority support (s 17 of the CA) to assist the family and enable children to be given the support they need to allow them to remain within their birth family. The State is unable or unwilling to adequately fund the support which is needed in these early stages (Proudman 2012). McFarlane LJ (2017) has rightly observed that it is low to medium level of persistent neglect that make up the majority of care and adoption cases.

Observing the child or the standard of parental care: s 38(6) residential assessments

During the course of care proceedings, in order to establish whether there is any prospect of the parents being able to adequately care for the child an application may be made for a s 38(6) residential assessment.

(6) Where the court makes an interim care order, or interim supervision order, it may give such directions (if any) as it considers appropriate with regard to the medical or psychiatric examination or other assessment of the child; but if the child is of sufficient understanding to make an informed decision he may refuse to submit to the examination or other assessment.

However, such assessments have been given very wide interpretation by the courts to include assessments of parenting capacity. Such assessments take place over a number of weeks, they are costly, and funding is controlled by the Legal Services Commission. The environment is artificial where families are monitored by a range of experts and observed by camera with regard to their interactions with their children. It provides parents with the opportunity to demonstrate their ability to parent and provides an opportunity for the local authority to determine whether parents can adequately care for their children. It is a matter for the judge in the course of care proceedings whether to grant an application for such an assessment if it is considered that there is any prospect at all of the ability to parent. Cases of neglect and lack of attachment are more likely than other categories of alleged harm to be considered. (See *Re C (Interim Care Order: Residential Assessment)* [1997] 1 FLR 1; and *Re G (Interim Care Order: Residential Assessment)* [2005] UKHL 68). Proudman (2012) is sceptical:

> assessments provided for under s 38(6) of the 1989 Act, conclude with the evidence, that parents cannot adequately meet their children's needs because parents are perceived as failures; this does little to help parents. Instead, such assessments merely legitimise the need for care proceedings.

Is there a right to a residential assessment?

In *TL v Hammersmith and Fulham London BC sub nom, Re T (a child) (residential parenting assessment)* [2011] EWCA Civ 812, [2011] 3 FCR 343, [2012] 2 FLR 308, the local authority initiated care proceedings. The mother applied for a s 38(6) assessment in respect of the third child. The judge refused the mother's application and considered that nothing could be achieved by a residential assessment, reiterating the principles in the leading cases (see *Re C (Interim Care Order: Residential Assessment)* [1997] 1 FLR 1, and *Re G (Interim Care Order: Residential Assessment)* [2005] UKHL 68 earlier). For successful appeals against refusal see *Re L and H (Residential Assessment)* 2007] EWCA Civ 213; where the judge had made an error of law see *Re B (Care Proceedings: Expert Witness)* [2007] EWCA Civ 556; where the factual circumstances had changed see *Re K (Care Order)* [2007] EWCA Civ 697. Thornton's (2024) assessment of the current situation in reviewing recent cases, returns the matter to the question of funding for such placements. This was a problem outlined by Baroness Hale in (*In Re G (A Minor) (Interim Care Order: Residential Assessment)* [2005] 3 WLR 1166 [70]). In 2024–5 funding is even more restricted.

Present significant harm: a temporal question

The s 31 threshold allows for a final order for care or supervision to be made where one of two conditions can be established – the child 'is suffering' or 'is likely to suffer' significant harm in the future.

'Is suffering'

'Is suffering' refers to the present. A previous issue for the courts had been at what point in time is the harm to have occurred from which protection is needed? It is settled law following *Re M (A Minor) (Care Order: Threshold Conditions)* [1994] 2 AC 424 that the relevant time is at the date when the local authority initiates the investigation and not the time at which the court hears the application. Lord Mackay Re M said: 'There is nothing in s 31(2) which, in my opinion, requires that the conditions to be satisfied are to be dissociated from the time of the making of the application by the local authority.'

Lord Templeman said:

> My Lords, this appeal is an illustration of the tyranny of language and the importance of ascertaining and giving effect to the intentions of Parliament by construing a statute in accordance with the spirit rather than the letter of the Act.

In assessing present harm, suspicion is not enough to find the s 31 threshold test met. Proven facts are required. Suspicion is only sufficient for the LA to commence protection proceedings under s 47 of the CA 1989.

Is suffering – physical abuse – the factual basis

In *Birmingham City Council v AG and others* [2009] EWHC 3720 (Fam), the threshold conditions were met where one child was starved to death and the remaining children were found in a state of malnourishment where the comparator the research evidence submitted was drawn from concentration camps, famine regions and knowledge of end stage anorexia.

Is suffering – sexual abuse – the factual basis

Where sexual abuse is alleged as having occurred a finding by the court that the child has suffered sexual abuse is extremely serious for the perpetrator especially where there are parallel criminal proceedings. Baroness Hale said in *Re B* [2008] UKHL 35 in a case involving allegations of a sexual nature where the judge said he could not decide one way or the other, that judges must not 'sit on the fence'. 'He is not allowed to sit on the fence. He has to find for one side or the other.'

The judicial reluctance to make a finding of sexual abuse has frequently resulted in the court making a threshold finding of emotional abuse or neglect in order to achieve the necessary outcome of taking a child at risk into care. However, where a judge makes a finding of significant harm on another factual basis thereby eschewing a finding of sexual harm any later work undertaken with the family will then focus on emotional rather than sexual abuse and thereby expose the child to future risk and also open the door to appeal. The difficulties in this alternative route into care are fraught and misconceived as the case that follows demonstrates.

In *Re W (A Child) (Care Proceedings)* [2007] EWCA Civ 102, cited earlier, W, who was 2 years of age, was taken into care. Experts concluded that she had been 'grossly anally abused'. The judge found, *inter alia*, that W had not suffered sexual abuse although found that there was a failure on the part of the mother to protect W (s 31(2)(b)(i)). A care order was made with a freeing order for adoption. The mother appealed against the care order on the basis that if the judge had failed to find that there was evidence of sexual abuse how could he go on to find that she had failed to protect. In this case the appeal was allowed and remitted for a rehearing.

General principles pre-emptive strike

CA 1989, s 31(2)(a)(b) provides protection against harm in the future. Such applications are made in order to protect other siblings in the family where a finding of 'is suffering' significant harm has already been made in respect of another sibling or, for example, where a sibling has died as a result of harm.

Prior to the CA 1989, before a care order was made, proof of present harm was required, and whilst the courts could consider future risk to a child, no order could be made solely on this basis (*Essex County Council v TLR and KBR (Minors)* [1978] Fam Law 15). The Children and Young Persons Act 1969, s 1(2) provided that a juvenile court could make a care order in respect of a child or young person (a person under 17 years) if it was satisfied that any of certain specified conditions are satisfied in respect of him including proper development. However, where future risk was suspected, little could be done to protect the child.

It was the catalogue of murders of children, and public and parliamentary concern, that pressed for a pre-emptive strike in cases where children needed protection from future harm. Maria Colwell, aged 7, was killed by her stepfather in 1973; she had internal injuries, bruising and had been starved. Jasmine Beckford, aged 4, died in 1984; she was starved and beaten by her stepfather. Tyra Henry, aged 21 months, died in 1984; her father and her mother beat her. Fifty bite marks were found on her body. Heidi Koseda, aged 5, died of thirst and hunger in 1985. Kimberly Carlisle died in 1986. She was 4 and was starved and was beaten to death by her father. These and other deaths might have been prevented (see Batty 2003 'Catalogue of Cruelty'). It was the deaths of these and other children in similar circumstances which led to the second limb of CA 1989, s 31 (2)(b) which authorises the removal of a child where it is considered that a child 'is likely to suffer, significant harm' in the future.

The case of Southwark *London Borough Council v B* [1998] 2 FLR 1095 raised again the temporal question, and the relevant time of 'likely to suffer'. Counsel for the mother contended that the relevant time for consideration was at the date of the hearing. If this was indeed the correct interpretation, since measures had already been taken by the LA to protect the child by the time of the hearing then few children would be deemed to be 'likely to suffer' and the statutory provision would be otiose. The court held that the House of Lords decision established in *Re M (a Minor) (Care Order: Threshold conditions)* [1994] 2 AC 424 'applied to both limbs of the threshold criteria, and the relevant date in respect of both actual harm and the likelihood of harm was the date upon which the local authority initiated protective arrangements for the relevant child'.

Retrospectivism and prospectivism

The principle that suffering in the past is a guide to the future was asserted in *Re B (A Minor) (Care Order: Criteria)* [1993] 1 FLR 815, as Douglas Brown J said: 'The court is not confined, in my judgment, to conditions obtaining at the date of the hearing in determining this question.' The court can also look into the future. In *Re H (A Minor) (Section 37 Direction)* [1993] 2 FLR 541, Scott Baker J emphasised that

> the likelihood of harm is not confined to present or near future but applies to the ability of a parent or carer to meet the emotional needs of a child in the years ahead. I am not limited . . . to looking at the past and immediate future. If a court concludes that a parent, or a carer, is likely to be unable to meet the emotional needs of a child in the future – even if years hence – my view is that the condition in s 31(2) would probably be met.

In *Newham London Borough Council v Attorney General* [1993] 1 FLR 28, Sir Stephen Brown P argued that 'likely' did not have to be strictly construed: quoting, with approval, Lord Reid in *Davies v Taylor* [1974] AC 207 who said:

> but you cannot prove that a future event will happen, and I do not think that the law is so foolish as to suppose that you can. All that you can do is to evaluate the chance. Sometimes it is virtually 100% sometimes virtually nil. But often it is somewhere in between.

The court in *Newham* above concluded that: 'in looking to the future the court has to assess the risk. Is this child likely to suffer significant harm?'

Evaluating the future risk of harm – facts not suspicion

However, the fact that an event has occurred in the past does not necessarily mean that it will happen again in the future. (See in *Re S-B (Children) (Non-Accidental Injury)* [2009] UKSC 17 a decision which has been the subject of much debate.)

Finding significant harm – but for which harm?

In evaluating the risk of future harm, the courts are reluctant to make a finding of sexual harm (as indicated earlier) and are more likely to make a finding of emotional harm or neglect. (See comparative categories of recorded harms in Chapter 14, Table 14.1 'Number of children who were the subject of a child protection plan on 31 March by category of abuse'.)

No finding of sexual abuse

Re G and R [1995] 2 FLR 867 concerned a number of children from various families where the local authority alleged that the families had been involved in a paedophile ring. In the G family, in respect of siblings D, K and L, the local authority made care applications. D, the court found, had been smacked, and this the court found was sufficient to grant a care order. The stepfather appealed. The court could find no fault with the finding of the court of first instance. K was neglected on ten occasions and admitted to the Accident and Emergency Department; there was evidence of inadequate parenting but no evidence of cruelty. The threshold conditions were satisfied for inadequate parenting and a care order was made on the basis of the possibility of further sexual abuse. With regard to L the court found that the child was not suffering harm but considered that the child was likely to suffer harm because of the evidence relating to K and made an order. The mother and stepfather appealed on the basis of the judge's finding of significant harm in the future. Physical or sexual abuse was not made out in L and K's case, and poor parenting (neglect) was finally the basis for the order.

The much contested case – *Re H and R* (1995) 'likely to suffer'

In *Re H and R* [1995] (CA) 1 FLR 643, a stepfather was acquitted in criminal proceedings (where the standard of proof is beyond all reasonable doubt and heard before a jury) of the rape of one of his stepchildren, D1. The local authority applied for a care order in respect of the remaining siblings D2, D3 and D4, as they were likely to suffer significant harm in the future. The Court of Appeal found that since it had not been proven that the stepfather had sexually abused the stepdaughter in the criminal proceedings with the higher standard of proof of 'beyond all reasonable doubt' or as expressed 'are you sure', there were no grounds upon which to find that the remaining children were likely to suffer significant harm in the future.

The Court of Appeal departed from the civil standard of 'on the balance of probabilities', and held that the standard of proof in sexual abuse cases for the purpose of care proceedings involved a two-stage test. Firstly, that the standard was beyond the mere balance of probabilities, and secondly, that there was a real possibility that the child would suffer significant harm and not the threshold of more likely than not (Sir Stephen Brown P and Millett LJ, Kennedy LJ dissenting). The ruling was appealed to the House of Lords, *H (minors) (sexual abuse: standard of proof), Re* [1996] AC 563. In the House of Lords judgment, Lord Goff of Chieveley, Lord Browne-Wilkinson, Lord Mustill, Lord Lloyd of Berwick and Lord Nicholls of Birkenhead (Lord Browne-Wilkinson and Lord Lloyd dissenting) concurred with the Court of Appeal in all its respects and went on to create much confusion. Lord Nicholls said:

> In s 31(2)(a) 'likely' is being used in the sense of a real possibility, a possibility that cannot sensibly be ignored having regard to the nature and gravity of the feared harm in the particular case. By parity of reasoning the expression 'likely to suffer significant harm' bears the same meaning elsewhere in the Act: for instance, in ss 43, 44 and 46. 'Likely' also bears a similar meaning, for a similar reason, in the requirement in s 31(2)(b) that the harm or likelihood of harm must be attributable to the care given to the child or 'likely' to be given him if the order were not made. Although the result is much the same, this does not mean that where a serious allegation is in issue the standard of proof required is higher. It means only that the inherent probability or improbability of an event is itself a matter to be taken into account when weighing the probabilities and deciding whether, on balance, the event occurred. The more improbable the event, the stronger must be the evidence that it did occur before, on the balance of probability, its occurrence will be established.

Lord Browne-Wilkinson in his dissenting judgment said that the facts necessary to establish that a child 'is suffering' significant harm are not the same facts as are necessary to establish that a child is 'likely to suffer' significant harm and his judgment is inclined towards suggesting that there are two different standards of proof.

> *Where I part company is in thinking that the facts relevant to an assessment of risk ('is likely to suffer . . . harm') are not the same as the facts relevant to a decision that harm is in fact being suffered. In order to be satisfied that an event has occurred or is occurring the evidence has to show on the balance of probabilities that such an event did occur or is occurring. But in order to be satisfied that there is a risk of such an occurrence, the ambit of the relevant facts is in my view wider. The combined effect of a number of factors which suggest that a state of affairs, though not proved to exist, may well exist is the normal basis for the assessment of future risk. To be satisfied of the existence of a risk does not require proof of the occurrence of past historical events but proof of facts, which are relevant to the making of a prognosis.*

Lord Browne-Wilkinson referred to the findings of the judge in the criminal trial who said:

> *I cannot be sure to the requisite high standard of proof [the criminal standard of beyond reasonable doubt] that [D1's] allegations are true. . . . This is far from saying that I am satisfied the child's complaints are untrue. I do not brush them aside as the jury seem to have done. I am, at least, more than a little suspicious that [Mr R] has abused her as she says. If it were relevant, I would be prepared to hold that there is a real possibility that her statement and her evidence are true. Nor has [Mr R] by his evidence and demeanour, not only throughout the hearing but the whole of this matter, done anything to dispel those suspicions.*

Lord Browne-Wilkinson in his dissenting judgment said:

> *that conclusion that there was a real possibility that the evidence of D1 was true was a finding of fact based on evidence and the micro facts that he had found. It was not a mere suspicion as to the risk that Mr R was an abuser: it was a finding of risk. My Lords, I am anxious that the decision of the House in this case may establish the law in an unworkable form to the detriment of many children at risk.*

It is worth here reflecting again on what Peter Jackson LJ said albeit later in 'The Nicholas Wall Memorial Lecture 2023' (2023):

> *A further aspect of family law is that it is usually more concerned with prediction than other branches of law. That being said prediction is not a science in this area and is so easily preyed upon by assumptions and disbelief.*

But put children at risk, Lord Nicholls' assertions in *Re H and R* certainly did.

Sexual abuse and probability theory

The problem with bowdlerised applications of probability theory is noted here. Lord Nicholls contends that the probability of child sexual abuse occurring in the general population is a factor to take into consideration when assessing whether child sexual abuse has occurred in any particular case. His view is informed by a posture of disbelief and scepticism and based on statistical prevalence which is irrelevant as to whether in a particular situation an event happened or not. For example, in a population of 65 million around 600 homicides occur each year. Some might say 'not many' or may say that homicide is 'not very prevalent', or 'not 'likely to occur', but the deaths are deaths none the less. No one would say that any particular death was unlikely to be murder by relying on statistical prevalence.

Lord Nicholls relies on three presumptions and because of the 'power' and weight attached to House of Lords judgments his ruling became elevated to a quasi 'rule of law' status impacting on other judicial decisions and on local authority application. Firstly, he said: 'the less likely it is that the event occurred . . . the more improbable the event, the stronger must be the evidence that it did occur' [17]. Secondly, he said: 'the probability standard can accommodate one's instinctive feeling that even in civil proceedings a court should be more sure before finding serious allegations proved than when deciding less serious or trivial matters' [17]. And thirdly, with his call for 'more sure' he inserts a standard of proof that is higher than the civil standard of balance of probabilities uttering: 'the more serious an allegation the more evidence is required to prove it'.

Re H and R's legacy has beleaguered the arena of child protection by reinforcing the long-established belief of the improbability of child sexual abuse by family members and child sexual abuse denial as detailed in Alice Miller's book *Thou Shalt Not Be Aware: Society's Betrayal of the Child* (1984). Lord Nicholls asserted: 'The inherent probability or improbability of an event is itself a matter to be taken into account when weighing the probabilities and deciding whether, on balance, the event occurred' [17]. This judgment in all its aspects created an uncertainty for local authorities who were from then onwards reluctant to commence applications for care orders where sexual abuse was suspected under s 31(2) of the Act because of likelihood of failure, thus leaving many children at risk, exactly as Lord Browne-Wilkinson's dissenting judgment had predicted.

Care proceedings applications of sexual abuse in the shadow of *Re H and R*

Re H and R [1996] AC 563 at 586H, [1996] 1 All ER 1, [1996] 1 FCR 509 cast a shadow on local authority applications for child protection and on subsequent court judgments as it did in *Re M and R (Minors) (Sexual Abuse: Expert Evidence)* [1996] 4 All ER 25 where one of six children alleged that he and several of the other children had been sexually abused by their mother and two men. The four younger children were placed with foster parents pending the outcome of the local authority's application for full care orders. The judge considered medical evidence, video-recorded interviews with the children and the expert evidence from two child psychiatrists. The judge concluded that, although the balance of the psychiatric evidence was unanimously to the effect that sexual abuse had probably occurred (note sufficient for the civil standard), he was not satisfied on the balance of probabilities that the allegations of sexual abuse were proved (applying the HL *Re H and R* standard). He was, however, satisfied that the threshold was met in respect of emotional abuse and made interim care orders, after having regard to the welfare principle in CA 1989, s 1. The local authority, supported by the guardian ad litem, appealed, contending principally that the judge, having found that there was a real possibility that sexual abuse had occurred, had erred in law in not taking into account the allegations of sexual abuse in his assessment of the welfare of the children.

The Court of Appeal held:

> When assessing under s 1(3)(e) of the 1989 Act whether a child was at risk of suffering harm, the court could have regard only to any harm that the child had suffered or was at risk of suffering if it was satisfied on the balance of probabilities that such harm or risk of harm (i.e. a real possibility of future harm) in fact existed,

and followed the spirit of Re H and R in the higher threshold expressed in the phrase 'real possibility'.

Subsequent cases struggled to make it clear that the balance of probabilities to be determined was nonetheless the civil standard and nothing else. (See Re T (Abuse: Standard of Proof) [2004] EWCA Civ 558.)

Setting the record nearly straight – Standard of proof – Re B (2008)

In Re B (Children) (Care Proceedings: Standard of Proof) (CAFCASS intervening) [2008] 3 WLR 1, the House of Lords laid much of this past to rest. Jo Delahunty and Alison Grief (2008) in an analysis of Re B discuss what they regard as: 'The judicial rebellion against Re H and R.'

> Sex abuse, thought to be difficult to prove, was often put to one side in child pro-tection registration or in court hearings and a lowest case denominator approach adopted for categorisation for threshold findings sought: for example, neglect rather than sexual abuse. This course potentially exposed a child to a risk that was not properly identified, proved, and managed whilst also allowing the stain of suspicion to linger in referral and case records tainting the assessment of parent and child alike.

In Re B (2008), the House of Lords (Lord Hoffmann, Lord Scott of Foscote, Lord Rodger of Earlsferry, Lord Walker of Gestingthorpe and Baroness Hale of Richmond) dismissed an appeal by two children, N, a girl aged 9, and A, a boy aged 6, through their guardian. The husband and wife lived in the family home with their children, N and A, and the wife's children of a previous marriage, S, a boy aged 17, and R, a girl aged 16. In 2006 the husband left and applied for residence orders in respect of N and A. The district judge made interim care orders in respect of R as well as N and A, on the basis of a plan to remove them from the wife and place them with the husband at his parents' home. R subsequently alleged that the husband had sexually abused her and had physically assaulted her and S. The husband denied the allegations. R was placed with foster carers and then returned to the wife and N and A were moved to foster carers. At a fact-finding hearing to ascertain whether the threshold criteria s 31(2) were satisfied, the judge could not find that it was 'more likely than not' that R was telling the truth, nor could he find that it was 'more likely than not' that the husband was telling the truth. The judge Charles J [2007] EWHC 2688 (Fam) also recused himself from the case. On the children's appeal by leapfrog procedure the case was considered by the House of Lords and the judge was subsequently criticised for 'sitting on the fence'. Lady Hale echoed the dissenting opinion of Lord Lloyd in *Re H and R* who said: 'Where it is claimed that the child has suffered or is suffering significant harm the standard of proof is the simple balance of probabilities, no matter how serious the underlying allegation' (at 13 [2]). Lord Hoffmann said in *Re B*: 'I think that the time has come to say, once and for all, that there is only one civil standard of proof and that is proof that the fact in issue more probably occurred than not [13]'.

Re B (2008) did more that reassert the civil standard of proof, it set aside the postures of what can be believed or disbelieved and the demolished any suggestion that 'instinct' has a role in evaluating evidence of the occurrence of sexual abuse. Lady Hale severs 'seriousness' from 'probability' and echoes Lord Lloyd's dissent in *Re H and R* when he said: 'the subsection (s 31) does not require a degree of probability commensurate with the seriousness of the allegation'. Lady Hale contends: '[72] As to the seriousness of the allegation, there is no logical or necessary connection between seriousness and probability.' Lord Hoffmann, in *Re B*, concurs with Lady Hale and says: '[5] Some confusion has however been caused by dicta which suggest that the standard of proof may vary with the gravity of the misconduct alleged or even the seriousness of the consequences for the person concerned.'

Lady Hale concludes offering this damning assessment.

> *[64] Lord Lloyd's prediction proved only too correct. Lord Nicholls's nuanced explanation left room for the nostrum: 'the more serious the allegation, the more cogent the evidence needed to prove it, to take hold and be repeated time and time again in fact-finding hearings in care proceedings. . . . It is time for us to loosen its grip and give it its quietus.*

However, all is not completely resolved or cast aside. Lord Hoffmann, in *Re B*, though embracing the rejection of the language of the instinctual presumption in *Re H and R*, says: 'If a child alleges sexual abuse by a parent, it is common sense to start with the assumption that most parents do not abuse their children', replacing the word instinct with common sense which after may amount to the same thing.

There is also a lingering survival of Lord Nicholls' concept of 'inherent probabilities'. Lady Hale in *Re B* said this: 'The inherent probabilities are simply something to be taken into account, where relevant, in deciding where the truth lies' ([70]). Leaving 'inherent probabilities' as a matter 'to be taken into account, where relevant' allows scepticism to creep in through the side door and infect and influence, and again passing off subjectivism for objectivism. Hayes agrees that *Re B* is not stripped entirely of all assumptions, as inherent probability is not totally disbanded, and the use of the term 'common sense' makes the application of 'instinct' more palatable. Should inherent probabilities be taken into account at all and what does it mean anyway?

As for the prognosis of this case the appeal was dismissed:

> *[82] I would therefore send the case back for the experts to be instructed and the judge to complete his hearing of the case in the light of the judgments in this House. As with so many family cases, it is likely that things have moved on since these proceedings were begun. The problems which loomed so large in the past may have receded while others have reared their heads. In family life, as in family proceedings, nothing stands completely still.*

Matters of proof and general allegations

A significant step forward in child protection in sexual abuse cases was made in *P (A Child)* [2010] EWCA Civ 672 in respect of two children, D six years of age and E three years of age, who were placed in foster care and then said 'worrying things' about the father prior to the placement with foster carers. Here, the court concluded that it is open to a judge conducting a fact-finding hearing to make a finding in general terms that it is probable a party has behaved towards and touched a child in an inappropriate sexual manner. This decision is important as it provides protection for children where it is not possible to make a finding on each particular or indeed any particular allegation but, on the case as a whole. In this case, the allegations and description of events made by the child to the foster carer were considered so alien to a child of such years that the only conclusion that could properly be drawn was that such events had in fact happened.

The Court of Appeal dismissed the appeal unanimously and referred to the finding of the judge in the hearing who said:

> [8] (31–32)] *Some of what [E] says may have an innocent explanation. Evidence of her apparently 'masturbating' would have no probative value on its own. Equally, evidence of her 'trying to wee like Daddy' should not be held against [the father]. I accept that [the father] would have several innocent reasons for touching [E] in the vaginal area. He has proffered explanations for some of what has been described. But why would [E] allege not only that her father had 'played' with her vagina but that he 'touched' her vagina 'with his bum' which in this context must surely mean his penis 'and it hurt' if that is quite untrue? Why would she say her father had 'licked' her vagina, and put his fingers in her vagina, if he had not? Even more worryingly, where has she got this concept of Daddy's 'bum' (I presume penis) 'coming out of his house to say hello [E] I love you'? The obvious adult interpretation is that this is her father with an erection. These are descriptions that would be alien to a child of this age who had not been exposed to inappropriate sexual activity. To ignore this evidence and say that it amounts to nothing probative would, in my judgment, be shutting one's eyes to the obvious.*

On appeal counsel for the father said it would be wrong to rely on this hearsay. Lord Justice Thorpe said, 'There is no foundation for the suggestion that this was a mere expression of judicial suspicion and dismissed the appeal.'

(See also Hayden J *Lancashire County Council v M and others* [2023] EWFC 30 and his assessment of the child's account and veracity [24].) Family law is indeed about making a judgment as Sir Peter Jackson said in the Nicolas Wall lecture (2023). Lord Wilson in *Re B* [2013] 3 All ER 929 said: 'It is a type of decision which is often described as involving the exercise of judgement [57].'

In *A London Borough Council v K and Others* [2009] EWHC 850 (Fam), the judge drew a rather different conclusion of the children's evidence and found the children's allegations untrue and considered that the children had been coached. Baker J said:

> *This is, at first, strong submissions and, on viewing the ABE interviews alone, one might find it hard to imagine how the children could possibly have acquired the knowledge about these matters without direct experience. But I am satisfied that much of what the children have said is untrue, including allegations about matters that one might have thought*

would be outside the experience of children, even in these days of sexual freedom and licence – for example, the descriptions of group sex and the account of fists being inserted into bottoms.

Truth – uncertain perpetrators and physical injury

The importance of truth and disclosure has already been raised in Chapter 14 in the context of protecting the child from future risk and harm. Here, truth is important in discovering which of a number of possible parents/carers inflicted the harm in order to protect children in second or third newly constituted families. In cases where child abuse is alleged the parent/carer invariably denies the allegations and in cases involving physical harm some blame each other.

As HHJ Masterman in his original judgment in *Re J (children) (non-accidental injury: past possible perpetrator in new family)* [2012] 2 FCR 1 (later at [4]) asserts: 'each maintains their innocence and protests the innocence of the other, only conceding the other's guilt when forced by logic in cross examination'.

Where it is not clear which of a number of possible people have perpetrated the abuse, the court in taking measures to protect the child and future children whom the parties under suspicion may parent either deem all the parties concerned a potential risk to children or none of them. Either way an injustice may be perpetrated. Such cases have come to be known as the 'uncertain perpetrator' cases. In the absence of any inculpatory statements and only denials from the possible perpetrator parties it has been impossible to establish with certainty who is responsible for the child's injuries, which is an insuperable and ongoing problem for the local authority and the court.

Early cases resolved the risk to the child by finding that care was inadequate in the absence of being able to name a perpetrator. In *Lancashire County Council v A* [2000] 2 AC 147:

The judge was unable to conclude that the harm was attributable to either of the parents and dismissed the application. The Court of Appeal held that the 'attributable' condition in s 31(2)(b)(i) was satisfied if the harm was attributable to an absence of proper care and reversed the judge's decision. A's parents appealed to the House of Lords, who dismissed the appeal.

The Domestic Violence, Crime and Victims Act (DVCVA) 2004, s 5 provided some remedy:

(1) A person ('D') is guilty of an offence if – (a) a child or vulnerable adult ('V') dies [F1or suffers serious physical harm] as a result of the unlawful act of a person who – (i) was a member of the same household as V, and (ii) had frequent contact with him.

Although this legislation could not solve the problems presenting in the family courts. Judges are agreed that even where it is unclear who the perpetrator is, a risk of future harm is still posed to any subsequent children in new relationships that the original possible perpetrator parties may form in the future.

See also *Re K (Care: Threshold Criteria)* [2005] EWCA Civ 1226, [2006] 2 FLR 868 where:

> *[4] The risk of significant harm in the present context was much wider than the purely physical and the court needed to consider the whole family dynamic, including the whole ambit of the elder child's relationship with his baby brother, in relation to the likelihood of significant harm. The judge was wrong to find that the elder child had not suffered or was not likely to suffer significant harm as a consequence of domestic violence and wrong not to find that there was a real possibility of harm if his poor school attendance were not rectified.*

The question posed in *Re S-B (children) (perpetrator: non-accidental injury) (2009), Re sub nom S-B (children) (care proceedings: standard of proof) SB* [2009], [2010] 1 All ER 705 was whether an order could be made where the perpetrator could not be identified. Baroness Hale ordered that the case be sent back for a complete rehearing before a different judge. The Supreme Court found that, in a case where non-accidental injuries had been caused to a child, but the perpetrator had not been identified, the test to be applied regarding identification of perpetrators was on the balance of probabilities. It further found that there was no obligation on a judge to decide who had caused the harm to the child, and it was not a necessary ingredient of the threshold criteria pursuant to s 31 as to whether there was significant harm.

Subsequent cases struggled with the dilemma of being unable to find for an unnamed perpetrator where there was silence and collusion between parties. In *Re K (Care Proceedings)* [2010] EWHC 3342 (Fam), a father had been acquitted of the murder or manslaughter of his 10-month-old daughter. The LA chose not to bring care proceedings with regard to the two surviving children of the family whom they considered would not be at risk since they were in the sole care of the father's former partner. The father then became involved with a new partner and they had two children together, and in addition the father took on a parenting role in respect of the mother's two elder children. The local authority issued care proceedings after one of the children suffered severe burns while in the mother's care, having been left alone in the bath. The mother pleaded guilty to neglect. The local authority then sought a fact-finding hearing in relation to the father's alleged involvement in his daughter's death. The mother and father argued that such an enquiry was neither necessary nor proportionate to the issues in the care proceedings. The court refused to hold a fact-finding hearing in respect of the father's alleged involvement in the death of his daughter. Hedley J said:

[17] The essence of the decision (so far as is material to this point) in Re B, O & N is to be found in para [31] of the speech of Lord Nicholls of Birkenhead where he says this: 'In "uncertain perpetrator" cases the correct approach must be that the judge conducting the disposal hearing will have regard, to whatever extent is appropriate, to the facts found by the judge at the preliminary hearing. Nowadays the same judge usually conducts both hearings, but this is not always so. When the facts found at the preliminary hearing leave open the possibility that a parent or other carer was a perpetrator of proved harm, it would not be right for that conclusion to be excluded from consideration at the disposal hearing as one of the matters to be taken into account. The importance to be attached to that possibility, as to every feature of the case, necessarily depends on the circumstances. But to exclude that possibility altogether from the matters the judge may consider would risk distorting the court's assessment of where, having regards to all the circumstances, the best interests of the child lie. . . . [18] That seems to me plainly to establish that where significant harm and attribution have been established, that the threshold criteria have been made out, then the 'uncertain perpetrator' may be the subject of a risk assessment in respect of other children with whom he may come into contact. Difficult as that task can sometimes be, it is one that is regularly undertaken in Children Act proceedings consequent on a fact-finding hearing. The tenor of Baroness Hale of Richmond's judgment in Re S-B does not appear to contain any suggestion of doubt as to the correctness of the views expressed in Re B, O & N'.

Re F (*A Child*) [2011] EWCA Civ 258, again a case with an unnamed perpetrator, Orrell J failed to make an order where the perpetrator was unknown. The Court of Appeal dismissed the appeal of the Local Authority. In Re J (*children*) (*non-accidental injury: past possible perpetrator in new family*) [2012] 2 FCR 1, the Court of Appeal said the case was similarly characterised by collusion.

On 29 March 2004, a three-week-old baby, T-L, was found dead in the bed of her parents in hostel accommodation where they were staying in South Wales. JJ was T-L's mother and SW her father. A post-mortem examination showed that T-L had sustained 17 fractures to her ribs a week or more prior to her death, together with bruising to her face, a shoulder and arm. The cause of death was asphyxia by obstruction of her airways. Following the birth of their second child, S, in August 2005, care proceedings were immediately instigated, and, in due course, a fact-finding hearing was conducted focusing on T-L's injuries and death. Each parent maintained their innocence and protested the innocence of the other. The judge held that they were colluding with one another to hide the truth; one parent was protecting the other or they were both protecting each other. He further found that they had deliberately kept T-L away from appointments with health professionals so that her bruises would not attract unwelcome attention. In consequence of those findings, a care order was made in relation to S and the local authority was authorised to place him for adoption.

McFarlane LJ said (per curiam):

The difficulties that have arisen in this case, in Re F (a Child) [2011] EWCA Civ 258, and no doubt elsewhere, originate from the Re B and W (threshold criteria) [1999] All ER (D) 880, case in the Court of Appeal and have been given additional focus and emphasis by Baroness Hale's words in paragraph 49 of Re S-B (children) (perpetrator: non-accidental injury) *[2010] 1 All ER 705. We were told, and I readily accept, that the situation is a cause for concern amongst child protection agencies. Given the importance of the point in terms of its impact on the ground for families and for those charged with protecting children, there is a pressing need for the issue to be determined by the Supreme Court so that a clear and full statement of the applicable law is achieved (see [130], [131] of the judgment).*

(See for further clarification Brian Sloan 'Uncertain Perpetrators' YouTube.)

Later, in *Re B children uncertain perpetrator* [2019] EWCA Civ 575 where three sisters aged between 5 and 10 years old were found to have been infected with gonorrhoea, Jackson LJ said:

> *a decision to place a person within the pool of perpetrators is not a finding of fact in the conventional sense. . . . The concept of the pool of perpetrators . . . does not alter the general rule on the burden of proof. Where there are a number of people who might have caused the harm, it is for the local authority to show that in relation to each of them there is a real possibility that they did it. No one can be placed into the pool unless that has been shown.*
>
> ([47–48])

(See also *Re A, B, & C fact finding gonorrhoea* [2023] EWCA Civ 437).

Re R (A Child: Possible Perpetrator) [2019] EWCA Civ 895 dealt with a case of non-accidental injury, in a fact-finding judgment. The judge, who knew the family dynamics well and had case managed throughout the care proceedings, concluded that the parents and/or the grandmother was responsible. The grandmother now challenged her inclusion in the pool of perpetrators but did not challenge findings that she had failed to protect the child from her parents by facilitating unauthorised contact, lying to professionals and the court, and putting protection of the parents ahead of protection of the child.

See also *Re A (Children) (Pool of Perpetrators)* [2022] EWCA Civ 1348, an appeal against orders made in care proceedings by HHJ Moradifar. Here the judge made a series of findings against the parents of a baby, 'A', who following an incident had sustained life-threatening injuries whist in the care of her parents. The court held, among other things, that the finding that the father was in the pool of potential perpetrators could not stand. The appeal was allowed on all grounds and remitted to a different judge for a rehearing only as to perpetration of the head injuries and fractures and the state of knowledge and actions of any non-perpetrator.

In exercising discretion and judgement Elizabeth Laing (dissenting) however took a different view and would have dismissed the father's appeal [60]. These cases are much contested. (See for further discussion Brown 2023.)

The expansion of emotional harms

Outside the sphere of physical, sexual harm or neglect is the arena of emotional harm which often encompasses multiple layers of harm and is particularly subject to changing conceptions of harm. Emotional harm, coercive and controlling conduct of children was indeed the mainstay of patriarchal control in the nineteenth century and twentieth century and conduct that was condoned, expected, excused and at times exonerated (see Gordon and Nair 2006).

Emotional abuse

Forms of emotional abuse that have come before the courts are extremely varied.

In *Local Authority v C (E and another intervening)* [2004] EWHC 2580 (Fam), the court took the view that the child was likely to suffer significant harm as both his parents believed, or said they believed, that he had been conceived as a result of a miracle birth and were determined in continuing in this delusion. The parents had been unable to have children. They had joined a religious group which embraced traditional African custom and Christian belief. One of this group's beliefs was in the power of divine intervention to facilitate miracle births. Whilst all medical tests confirmed that the mother was not pregnant, she continued to believe she was pregnant and went to Kenya, where she met a man whom she thought was a doctor. He told her she was 12 months' pregnant. During some procedure she was tricked into believing she had given birth to a child, G, who she brought to England. (See also *Re E (a child) (fact-finding hearing: assessment of biological parents)* [2011] EWHC 3453 (Fam), a case that concerned miracle birth and a suspected case of child trafficking of E whom the 'parents' declared as their own child.)

The radicalisation cases

More recently, children have been subject to care proceedings because of so-called radicalisation where the local authority has raised concerns about potential physical as well as emotional harm following referrals which given the outcome of some of the applications where the court found no evidence to justify a s 31 finding, raises interesting questions about moral panics and interpretation of the Government's 'Prevent guidance' under the Counter-Terrorism and Security Act 2015 (CTSA 2015), s 26 which requires specified authorities including nurseries and schools to '(1) A . . . in the exercise of its functions, have due regard to the need to prevent people from being drawn into terrorism'. (See Prevent Duty Guidance.)

It is to be noted too, although it would appear that this is a perspective set aside so far as some local authority applications suggest, that as Black LJ in the Court of Appeal *B (A Child)* [2012] EWCA Civ 1475 said:

> *[116] . . . society must be willing to tolerate very diverse standards of parenting, including the eccentric, the barely adequate and the inconsistent . . . it is not the provenance of the state to spare children all the consequences of defective parenting. . . . The threshold must be something unusual . . . more than commonplace human failure or inadequacy.*

What do these radicalisation cases so called actually involve? Well, a variety of conduct ranging from being exposed to violent videos, supporting Islamic state, travelling alone or with parents to Syria, to at the other end of the spectrum being critical of the Government's position regarding the war in Iraq or the invasion of Palestine, or collecting at school charitable monies to support the starvation of children in Gaza etc. The courts have been less persuaded by some of these applications. Woodward-Carlton (2019) points out that in LA applications for care proceedings brought on the basis of so-called radicalisation judges have rigorously applied the threshold criteria, refusing such applications as not meeting the threshold (see also Edwards 2023). Newton J, in *A Local Authority v M* [2016] EWHC 1599 (Fam), expresses scepticism when he asked the pointed question: 'whether, and in what circumstances, the religiously motivated views of a parent or parents are so harmful that the State should intervene to protect the child? [3]'.

In *London Borough of Tower Hamlets v B* [2015] EWHC 2491 (Fam), a girl who was 16 year of age was very unhappy having been placed outside her family for her protection since they had failed to prevent her from boarding a flight to Syria. In his judgment Hayden J recognised the sexual exploitation and sexual trafficking element when in considering several cases he said:

> [5] *In each of these cases however these young women have boundless opportunities, comfortable homes and carers who undoubtedly love them, but they have been captured, seduced, by a belief that travelling to Syria to become what is known as 'Jihadi brides' is somehow romantic and honourable both to them and to their families.*

Having already placed her in care outside her family which was not successful, Hayden J considered that her welfare could best be served by being allowed to return home under a care order to protect her psychological well-being where a 'crucial part of her humanity' had already been damaged. In *Re X (Children) (No 3)* [2015] EWHC 3651 (Fam), where children accompanied by their mother were intercepted prior to boarding a flight destined for Turkey, Sir James Munby discharged the care and wardship proceedings, since: 'The local authority, for its part, has not proved either that the materials found at her home have the significance which was suggested or, more generally, that she is a radical or extremist [111]'. In *Re C, D and E (Children) (Radicalisation: Fact-Finding)* [2016] EWHC 3087 (Fam), Cobb J was tasked to consider the true purpose of a family trip to Europe including Germany and whether the destination was Syria, Iraq or ISIS controlled State. He said:

> [115] *While . . . the conduct of the parents between January and July 2015 does indicate that they hold, or held beliefs of an extremist or radicalised nature, there is no evidence . . . that the parents have actually exposed, or taken any steps to promulgate to, their children these views, neither C nor D show any indicator of having been radicalised.*

In *Re K (Children)* [2016] EWHC 1606 (Fam), a case which involved children of 12, 14 and 15 years, the parents were loving and caring and held beliefs which the LA and court accepted was 'terrorism'. Hayden J, not without some contra consideration, supported the local authority's withdrawal of application for care [6]. He conceded that there must be some evidence of active radicalisation and a nexus between active promotion of such ideology and overt behaviours [22] [24].

MacDonald J was unable to find the threshold satisfied in *A Local Authority v HB and Others* [2017] EWHC 1437 (Fam). Here, the mother's care was exemplary. It was alleged that on one occasion she took the children to a town in Turkey close to the Syrian border, and on two occasions was stopped from leaving the UK with large sums of money which it was thought was for the purpose of providing funds to persons associated with the Islamic State. MacDonald J said: 'I am not satisfied that local authority has proved its case to the standard required by the law' [103].

There are some cases where the courts have found the threshold met. In *A Local Authority v M* [2016] EWHC 1599 (Fam) where the mother wanted to take her children to Syria and was herself involved in ISIL and was subsequently convicted of child abduction and sentenced to three years' imprisonment, Newton J queried: 'whether, the State should intervene to protect the child?' In *Leicester City Council v T* [2016] EWFC 20, the court ordered that the children should remain living with the maternal grandmother where the mother was stopped at the airport with her young children on her way to Syria. In *Re M (Children)* [2019] EWCA 1364, two British nationals travelled to Syria, formed a relationship, married and had two children and on their return to the United Kingdom were arrested under s 41 of the Terrorism Act 2000. The children of 3 and 2 years were taken into police protection and placed in foster care. An interim care order was made. In *A Local Authority v A Mother and others* [2020] EWHC 3496 (Fam), the mother and father went to ISIL in 2015. J was born later. The parents were arrested in 2017 on the Turkish border. The father was imprisoned there, and the mother and child allowed to return to the UK. The court concluded that the mother, although she had made progress, would radicalise J and remove J from the jurisdiction. Care proceedings concluded with the making of a special guardianship order (SGO) placing J in the care of CC, the paternal great uncle, coupled with a 12-month supervision order.

Of course, whilst the object in these rare cases is to use the family court system to protect the child where the local authority and other agencies have failed to protect, the child may be punished by other legal and so-called security measures (*Begum v Secretary of State for the Home Department* [2024] EWCA Civ 152; Edwards 2023).

The 2024 July – August riots by right wing racist extremists, were driven by deep-rooted Islamophobia, inciting men and women to burn mosques and attack hotels housing asylum seekers (Cordall 2024). This was contributed to by a long-standing political discourse which normalised anti - Muslim hatred (Edwards 2021). The criminal convictions of adults who are parents and the involvement of children pose questions for family law especially whether parents with such views and conduct are fit to parent. The remark made by the judge in *Re A (Application for Care and Placement Orders: Local Authority Failings)* [2015] EWFC 11, [2016] 1 FLR 1, that 'The father's membership probably only for a short time, of the EDL is neither here nor there' [71] would now be viewed very differently. It is important that organisations and the government rewrite their guidance on 'radicalisation' accordingly?.

'No order' presumption (CA 1989, s 1(5))

As in private proceedings, similarly here in public proceedings, the court must decide, once the threshold has been met, whether it is better to make an order for the child than not to make an order at all.

At the time of the introduction of CA 1989, s 1(5) at the Children Bill stage the Lord Chancellor, Lord Mackay of Clashfern, said:

> There is a prohibition in subsection 4 against courts making any order . . . unless that would be better for the child. There is a danger that a child may be put in LA care because of inadequate home circumstances but without evidence that this would improve the situation.
>
> (1988 vol 502 col 490)

This has turned out to be a prophetic warning when one sees the number of cases where children are removed because of inadequacy and without any local authority support (s 17) that might have averted this eventuality. (See *Re G (Children) (Residence Order: No Order Principle)* [2006] 1 FLR 771.) In *Northamptonshire County Council v S and others* [1993] Fam 136, Ewbank J's interpretation of s 1(5) described the correct procedure as:

> *The fact that the threshold test is met does not mean that the family proceedings court has to make a court order . . . the justices have the choice once the threshold conditions are met of making a care order, of making a supervision order, or of making any other order under the Children Act 1989.*

The burden is on the local authority who bring the application to explain to the court why an order for care or supervision is better than leaving things as they are. (See earlier in this chapter Veal J in *A Mother v A Father* [2024] EWFC 53.) In the early days, it would appear that judges (see *Kent County Council v C* [1993] 1 FLR 308) considered the 'no order' principle only where there was a contest. The importance of the two-stage process was enunciated in *Re CH (Care or Interim Care Order)* [1998] 1 FLR 402.

Parental cooperation

Parental cooperation with the local authority throughout the investigation has a significant impact on the outcome (disposal) of the case and in influencing the court in their decision whether to make a final order or no order at all. It has also been suggested that the conditions where 'no order' will be made are those where the prognosis for change is reasonable and parents show a willingness to cooperate with voluntary arrangements. However, it can never be right, for example that parental willingness to cooperate should prejudice risk assessment and child safety. (See Assessing Parental Capacity to Change 2014.)

In *Re M (A Minor) (Application No 2)* [1994] 1 FLR 59, there was evidence of both neglect and physical abuse; the child had a duodenal haematoma, was underweight, was emaciated, and there was evidence of multiple bruising to the shins, knees, buttocks, face, chest and back, which the mother and boyfriend denied causing. The local authority applied for a care order subject to the child residing with the maternal grandparents. The judge found that the child was likely to suffer significant harm although the judge was not prepared to find that the mother or boyfriend had beaten or starved the child. The judge refused the care order of the local authority and refused the residence order sought by the maternal grandparents and granted the mother's application for a residence order and made it subject to a condition that she continue to reside at the home of the boyfriend's parents. In considering s 1(5), he concluded that he would: 'give the parents a chance', and the child was returned to the mother. This was even though the child had told her foster mother: 'On Christmas Day I could not finish my dinner. Daddy started kicking me and punching – then Mummy.' The Court of Appeal could find no fault with the judge's handling of the case and the appeal was dismissed.

Whilst there are no statistics available on 'no order' orders in 2024, *Judicial Statistics* for 2005 recorded 250 'no order' orders for care and ten 'no order' orders for supervision in all tiers of the courts including family proceedings, county court and high courts.

Applications are also withdrawn where cases are unlikely to succeed. See *Re N (Leave to Withdraw: Care Proceedings)* [2000)] 1 FLR 134 where the court refused the application to withdraw. For cases where an application to withdraw was granted, see *London Borough of Southwark v B* [1993] 2 FLR 559; *R v Birmingham Juvenile Court, ex parte G and others (Minors)*, sub nom *R v Birmingham Juvenile Court, ex parte R (A Minor)* [1990] 2 QB 573. Withdrawals are costly and where a council commenced a care proceedings application which the court said had fallen below accepted standards, the council was ordered to pay £100,000 in court costs (see *Coventry City Council v X, Y and Z (Care Proceedings: Costs: Identification of Local Authority)* [2010] 1 FLR 977).

TABLE 15.1 Number of care and supervision orders made

	2011	2013	2015	2017	2019	2020	2021
Care Order made 4a	6,668	9,354	7,518	9,539	8,633	7,500	7,666
Number of children involved 4b	10,942	15,186	12,353	15,167	13,819	12,078	12,359
Number of children involved in applications 3b	20,188	19,307	21,590	25,545	23,030	23,034	20,228
Supervision orders made 4a	3,045	4,566	4,307	4,675	4,098	3,301	3,452
Number of children involved 4b	5,135	7,708	7,485	8,111	7,136	5,586	5,994
Children involved in applications 3b	1,236	1,170	1,519	2,597	2,525	2,553	2,900

Source: Taken from Family Court Statistics Quarterly Accessible Tables 2023
Table 4a – Orders made. Table 4b – Number of children involved in orders made. Table 3b – Number of children involved in applications.
www.gov.uk/government/statistics/family-court-statistics-quarterly-july-to-september-2023 (accessed 3.05.2024)

Voluntary agreement (CA 1989, s 20)

Many children who are the subject of child protection enquiries do not become involved in the legal proceedings detailed earlier. Many children who leave home for a period of time are accommodated by foster parents or other family members (Child Protection: Messages from Research 1995: 56). The CA 1989 has at its heart the principle of partnership. The Act introduced the provision of support services under Part III of the Act.

At the Bill stage Lord Mackay said: 'Parts VI and VII replace with amendments existing provisions of the Child Care Act 1980 on local authority community homes, the regulation of voluntary homes and responsibilities to children accommodated in those homes.'

Voluntary agreements under s 20 of the CA 1989 'Provision of accommodation for children: general.

(1) Every local authority shall provide accommodation for any child in need within their area who appears to them to require accommodation as a result of –
   (a) there being no person who has parental responsibility for him;
   (b) his being lost or having been abandoned; or
   (c) the person who has been caring for him being prevented (whether or not permanently, and for whatever reason) from providing him with suitable accommodation or care'
   (See the UK Supreme Court decision in *Williams v London Borough of Hackney* [2018] UKSC 37).

Children in voluntary care numbered in 2007 – 17,200; 2008 – 17,280; 2009 – 19,310; 2010 – 20,710; and 2011 – 20,430 (See Harker 2012). The Public Law Working Group PLWG 2021 considered how children and young people may safely be diverted from becoming the subject of public law proceedings. This was chaired by Keehan J who highlighted the egregious abuses of s 20 in *Herefordshire Council v AB* [2018] EWFC 10. It is to be noted that children accommodated pursuant to s 20 do not have the benefit of an independent children's guardian, parental responsibility does not pass to the authority, parental consent is required (and the child returned if and when it is withdrawn) and the court does not have the ability to control planning.

Supervision orders

Alternatively, the court may make a supervision order (CA 1989, s 31(1)(b)), which places a child under the supervision of a local authority supervisor. The duty of the supervisor is 'to advise, assist and befriend' the child. It is to be noted, however, that the order is to give the local authority the opportunity of monitoring the welfare of the child.

Whilst the order allows the local authority access to the child so that the relevant checks can be made, the order does not allow for conditions to be imposed upon them. This may seem strange, when after all the primary object of the order is to monitor the care parents or carers are giving the child.

Whilst conditions have been incorporated into the CA 1989, there are problems since parental responsibility does not lie with the local authority. With this order, as with the care order, again there are a number of placement options, although the child is placed usually at home or with those exercising parental responsibility. Thus, such orders may also be accompanied by a residence order to the person who is looking after the child.

In *Re B (Care or Supervision Order)* [1996] 2 FLR 693, Holman J laid down the principles to be applied when making this determination:

> On the choice between a care order or a supervision order there are now a number of authorities. It is now clear that it can be appropriate to make a full care order even though all parties, including the guardian ad litem and the court itself, agree that the child should not in fact be removed from the daily care of living with its parents; and the local authority only wish and propose that there should be a supervision order. However, it is also clear and obvious that a care order is a stronger and more serious order to make. A care order rather than a supervision order should only be made if the stronger order is necessary for the proper protection of the child. . . . There is a fundamental difference between these two orders. In the one case it is the local authority, which has to undertake the safeguarding of the child, in the other case it is the mother.
>
> ([698])

In *Re K (Supervision Orders)* [1999] 2 FLR 303, the mother's fourth child died when he was 1 month old. The local authority commenced proceedings in respect of the three surviving children. The local authority and the parents had reached a sensible agreement, which clearly protected the children. Once the threshold criteria were satisfied, in considering whether to make a supervision order or no order in accordance with CA 1989, s 1(5) there had to be something in the making or operation of a supervision order which made it better for the children for it to be made. It would be wrong to make a supervision order where the duties imposed on the local authority under Part III of the 1989 Act to provide services for children and their families would be sufficient to meet the children's needs, as the court should start with a preference for the less interventionist approach rather than the more interventionist approach.

The conclusion was that a supervision order was better for the children than no order at all.

In *Re B (Children)* [2006] EWCA 1186 (Fam), supervision orders were made in respect of three children following a finding with regard to one of them (J) of bilateral subdural haemorrhages. These injuries had been discovered following the child (J) being accidentally dropped at a wedding party on 6 November 2004, by a guest who had been holding the child. However, examination of the child following an MRI scan on 10 and 11 November disclosed injuries of more than two weeks' duration. In the Plymouth County Court on 24 June 2005, HHJ Tyzack QC found that:

> on a balance of probability, on a date unknown but two – three weeks before 10.11.04, either the mother or the father (but likely to be the mother) caused [J] to suffer bilateral

subdural haemorrhages probably by shaking her on one occasion. The retinal haemorrhages probably occurred at the same time.

The Court of Appeal, Longmore LJ (Laws LJ and Ward LJ concurring) asserted:

In these circumstances, while it is perfectly possible to acknowledge there may be suspicion, I cannot think it was right for the judge, with respect, to have found on the balance of probabilities that J was non-accidentally injured while in the control of her parents. The evidence does just not have that degree of cogency which is required to overcome the unlikelihood of the serious allegation that is being made, to adapt the words of Ungoed-Thomas J. approved by Lord Nicholls in Re H and R *[1996] AC 563 at 586H, [1996] 1 All ER 1, [1996] 1 FCR 509. As Lord Nicholls also said, a judicial suspicion is not a proper factual basis on which the court's jurisdiction can be exercised '. . . because that is no more than a judicial state of uncertainty about whether or not an event happened'.*

The length of the supervision order is normally one year and can be extended but not beyond three years. A care order lasts until the child is 18 years of age unless it is ended before. In 2023, the Public Law Working Group (PLWG) 2023 announced their *Supervision Order Report*, following findings reported by Harwin and Alrouh 2017.

In *JW (Child at Home under Care Order)* [2023] EWCA Civ 944, Sir Andrew McFarlane P, Lady Justice Macur and Lord Justice Coulson said:

[15–16] In contrast to a care order, a child under a supervision order is not being 'looked after' by the local authority and the authority neither has parental responsibility for the child, nor the power to direct how those who do have parental responsibility may exercise it. By CA 1989, Sch 3, para 2, a supervision order may require the child to comply with any directions given from time to time by the supervising officer. If the person responsible for the child's care (for example a parent) consents, the supervision order may include a requirement for the responsible person to comply with directions and other requirements [Sch 3, para 3]. There is no express requirement for the supervising officer to visit the child during the life of the order or to keep the plans for the child under review.

Supervision v care

The PLWG noted that supervision orders have the highest (20 per cent) risk of breakdown and return to court for further care proceedings within five years. They found that there are widespread professional concerns that supervision orders 'lack teeth' and made several recommendations noted in *JW* earlier.

Care orders at home

The PLWG recommended that: a care order should not be used solely as a vehicle to achieve the provision of support and services after the conclusion of proceedings.

They also noted that a care order on the basis that the child will be living at home should only be made when there are exceptional reasons for doing so. It should be rare in the extreme that the risks of significant harm to a child are judged to be sufficient to merit the making of a care order but, nevertheless, as risks that can be managed with the child remaining in the care of parents; that unless, in an exceptional case, a care order is necessary for the protection of the child, some other means of providing support and services must be used; that where a child is to be placed at home, the making of a supervision order to support reunification may be proportionate; and where a supervision order is being considered, the best practice guidance in the PLWG April 2023 report must be applied. The PLWG recommendations and guidance can be reduced to the following short points: '(a) a care order should not be used solely as a vehicle to achieve the provision of support and services after the conclusion of proceedings; (b) a care order on the basis that the child will be living at home should only be made when there are exceptional reasons for doing so. It should be rare in the extreme that the risks of significant harm to a child are judged to be sufficient to merit the making of a care order but, nevertheless, as risks that can be managed with the child remaining in the care of parents; (c) unless, in an exceptional case, a care order is necessary for the protection of the child, some other means of providing support and services must be used; (d) where a child is to be placed at home, the making of a supervision order to support reunification may be proportionate; (e) where a supervision order is being considered, the best practice guidance in the PLWG April 2023 report must be applied. In particular, the court should require the local authority to have a Supervision Support Plan in place.'

Regional disparities – care supervision North and West and South and East divide

In *JW (Child at Home under Care Order)* [2023] EWCA Civ 944, McFarlane LJ (cited earlier) expressed concern with what he recognised as family justice by geography, North and West and South and East:

> *[1] For some years it has been recognised that a difference exists in the approach taken by courts in different regions when determining whether a final care order, supervision order or no order should be made when care proceedings conclude with a plan for the subject child to be placed, or remain living, at home with their parent(s). Broadly speaking, if a line is drawn from Hull down to Bristol and beyond, courts in England and Wales that are North and West of that line will often make a care order in such cases, in contrast to courts South and East of the line where normally a supervision order or no public law order will be made. My experience is that the judges who sit on one side of the line or the other are confident that the approach taken in their area is the correct one.*

He went on to echo the fundings of the PLWG which in addition to noting the variations in care and supervision orders said:

[158–159] There is a risk that the making of a care order at home provides false assurances to partner agencies because the local authority is neither involved in, nor has a thorough oversight of, the child's day-to-day care. The making of a care order should not be used as a vehicle to achieve the provision of support and services after the conclusion of proceedings. Unless a final care order is necessary for the protection of the child, an alternative means/route should be made available to provide this support and these services without the need to make a care order.

Finale – how better can we protect children?

Proportionality question and the Human Rights Act (HRA)

The ultimate question is to hold the law to account in child protection whilst at the same time respecting the rights of families and children. Baroness Hale in her reflections on '30 Years of the Children Act' remarked: 'looking back, although we were aware of the European Convention on Human Rights, it played a remarkably small part in our thinking'. In *Re O (Supervision Order)* [2001] EWCA Civ 16; [2001] 1 FLR 923, Baroness Hale remarked on the need for proportionality. Certainly, this question of removing a child from home and placing a child in care has been seen to engage human rights issues of proportionality particularly in the recent case law. McFarlane LJ in *JW* (2023) stressed:

> *[28] viii) the protection of the child is the decisive factor, but proportionality is key when making the choice between a care and supervision order for a child who is placed at home; . . . [37] This can only be justified if it is necessary and proportionate to the risks of harm of the child . . . and the need to apply the s 1(5), CA 1989, the least interventionist approach [47].*

In contrast to the earlier case law dating following the implementation of CA 1989, it can be seen that the PLWG recommendations and best practice guidance places greater emphasis upon the need for proportionality in the face of significantly greater power afforded to a local authority under a care order. Drawing together some concluding thoughts and concerns regarding child protection, Sir Andrew McFarlane has raised the concern about the need for balance between child protection upholding the right to family life and the question of proportionality (discussed earlier in *JW*).

Concern has already been expressed widely amongst the judiciary that whilst delay is harmful to the child, at the same time, fast tracking children from care into adoption to satisfy the drive to avoid delay may be overriding the right to family life. Indeed, if there were adequate resources and support for families particularly where neglect is the problem such families may not lose their children. McFarlane LJ (2017) observes that in a borderline case of neglect the question of whether resources can be introduced into the home to support parents may be determinative of the outcomes the court is then faced with removal as the only option.

The case of *J v C* [1970] AC 668 (addressed in Chapter 9) clearly demonstrated the determination of the local authority to support a child and parents to live as a family where the mother was ill with a view to rehabilitating the child with the family, sadly even with continual foster carer support over several years that could not be achieved.

The support given to children in need under s 17 of the CA 1989 has suffered drastic cuts as has Government funding of family proceedings and the threshold has also affected many parties. For example, in *T (Children)* [2012] UKSC 36 the grandparents were joined as parties in allegations of sexual abuse against their grandchildren. The court of first instance made no findings against them. They did not qualify for legal aid and took out a loan to cover their representation. The Court of Appeal ruled that they should not be required to bear their own costs. The Supreme Court concluded that the general practice of not awarding costs in care proceedings against a party, including a local authority, in the absence of reprehensible behaviour or an unreasonable stance, is one that accords with the ends of justice, and which should not be subject to an exception in the case of split hearings. The Supreme Court heard the appeal on the basis that the grandparents in this case would be allowed to recover their costs whatever the outcome. Proudman (2012) writes providing compelling evidence for the need to put more money and resources into the child care system. Baroness Hale in 2014 '40th Anniversary of the Family Rights Group' berated the reduction in children's services.

Within the courtroom there are also concerns. The problem of 'uncertain perpetrators' and protecting children remains debated, uncertain and unsatisfactory. Baroness Hale's judgment in *Re S-B* remains the legal position. Elizabeth Laing J's dissent in *Re A (Children)* [2023] 1 WLR 1743 (earlier) is completely understood, and the unknown and unidentified threat remains for many children.

The question of crossing the threshold remains a matter of judgement. As Lord Wilson SCJ in *Re B (a child) (care order: proportionality: criterion for review)*, [2013] 3 All ER 929 put it:

> [57] The final step in relation to the s 31(2) threshold issue required the judge to address the question whether, on the primary facts he had found and assessments he had made, the threshold was crossed in this case. The decision on that question is certainly not one of law, but it is not one of primary fact either. It is a type of decision which is often described as involving the exercise of judgment, but it may fairly be said that this is not a very illuminating characterisation, because the determination of an issue of law or of an issue of fact also involves the exercise of judgment.

That exercise is not cast in stone.

Predicting that following *Re H-W (children) (No 2)* [2022] UKSC 17 the shadow of the law will be cast on local authority applications for care which may decline thereby resulting in more supervision orders, since they are less likely to be appealed, all of which have major implications for child protection. Judith Masson (2022) considers the consequences of the decision in *Re H-W (above)* and warns of the increase in appeal applications, increased pressure on the family court and on family judges, and longer waits for decisions for children and parents. Looking at the statistics she observes that following *Re B-S*, the number of family appeals to the Court of Appeal doubled from 40 in 2012 to 96 in 2013, reaching a peak of 132 in 2016 (RCJ Annual Statistics, table 3.9). Rehearings will add to the pressure on the family court (National Statistics Citation 2022).

The future is bleak despite the optimism of David Johnston MP speaking on behalf of the Government on 18 December 2023, on Children's Social Care in the Commons on the several recent measure to improve child protection. The delays in hearing public family law cases continue, as the latest data show that the 26-week target now stands at 46 weeks. The independent review 'A Failure of Implementation' (Children and Families Act 2014 Committee Report) 'called for the immediate investment of £2.6 billion to address the existing crisis in children's social care and a revolution in family help to prevent children entering care where possible'. Yet the Government pledge only additional £1 billion on children's social care over 10 years.

The Final Report of the independent review of children's social care (MacAlister 2023) calls for a move to 'reclaim the original intention of section 17 as a broad, flexible "Family Help" category'.

> We must reset the system and build a new Family Help approach, combining work currently done at targeted early help and work done under child in need. This will take us back to the original intentions of section 17 of the Children Act 1989, and genuinely fulfil its intention of safeguarding and promoting the welfare of children within their families.

> Whilst the overall duty defined in section 17 is the right one, the work can most plainly be described as "Family Help", emphasising both the whole family nature of the work and its focus on meeting need through support. Working Together should be amended throughout to reflect this and the principles set out in this chapter.
>
> (54)

As practitioners, academics and families and children are agreed we must do better.

Self-test questions

1. The Domestic Violence, Crime and Victims (Amendment) Act 2012, extends s 5 of the Domestic Violence, Crime and Victims (Amendment) Act 2004 to apply to the death or serious physical harm to a child or vulnerable adult. However, the situation in the family court is somewhat different and the stalemate reached in the family court with regard to uncertain perpetrators may need to be reconsidered.

   Discuss.

2. In applications for care proceedings made by local authorities on the basis of radicalisation evidence judges have rigorously applied the threshold criteria, insisting on the need for cogent evidence of actual or likely harm before sanctioning compulsory state intervention in private and family life.

   Assess this statement through an evaluation of the case law.

3. Can there ever be one normative standard of parenting below which it must be found that significant harm has occurred or is likely to occur, or must each case be looked at on its facts and by taking into account the social and cultural context?

4. One of the findings of the Public Law Working Group (PLWG) concerns the number of care orders that are made where children remain in the abusive home. This issue is addressed by McFarlane LJ in *Re JW (Child at Home Under care order)* [2023] EWCA Civ 944 [1][30]. To what extent might this undermine the protection of children, and what are the options open to the court?

References

Ahdash, Fatima, 'The Interaction Between Family Law and Counter-Terrorism: A Critical Examination of the Radicalisation Cases in the Family Courts' [2018] *Child and Family Law Quarterly* 389

Alrouh, Bachar, Claire Hargreaves, Linda Cusworth, Karen Broadhurst, Laura North, Lucy Griffiths, Steffi Doebler, Ashley Akbari, Ian Farr and Laura Cowley, What Do We Know About Ethnic Diversity in the Family Justice System in England? (2022) www.cfj-lancaster.org.uk/files/pdfs/nfjo_report_diversity_england.pdf (accessed 03.05.2024)

Assessing Parental Capacity to Change (2014) https://assets.publishing.service.gov.uk/government/uploads/system/uploads/attachment_data/file/330332/RR369_Assessing_parental_capacity_to_change_Final.pdf (accessed 03.05.2024)

Batty, David, 'Catalogue of Cruelty' *The Guardian* (27.01.2003) www.guardian.co.uk/society/2003/jan/27/childrensservices.childprotection (accessed 03.05.2024)

Brophy, Julia and Martha Cover, 'Children, the Recession, and Family Courts' [2012] *Family Law* 526

Brown, Nick, 'Threshold Findings and the Criminal Standard' [2023] *Family Law* 1451

Butler-Sloss, Dame Elizabeth, 'Cleveland Inquiry' Report of the Inquiry into Child Abuse in Cleveland (Cm 412 1988)

Children Bill [H.L] Debate (06.12.1988) vol 502 https://api.parliament.uk/historic-hansard/lords/1988/dec/06/children-bill-hl c488 (accessed 30.04.2024)

Children Bill [H.L] Debate (06.12.1988) vol 502 https://api.parliament.uk/historic-hansard/lords/1988/dec/06/children-bill-hl (accessed 03.05.2024)

'Children's Social Care' Hansard https://hansard.parliament.uk/commons/2023-12-18/debates/23121857000014/Children (accessed 03.05.2024)

Cobley, Cathy and Tom Sanders, 'Shaken Baby Syndrome Child Protection Issues When Children Sustain a Subdural Haemorrhage' (2003) 25 *Journal of Social Welfare and Family Law* 101

Cordall, Simon Speakman '"In Lancaster, the People Have Been Lovely": A UK City Resists Race Riots' (2024) https://www.aljazeera.com/news/2024/8/6/isolated-uk-cities-push-back-against-the-violence-of-the-far-right (accessed September 1 2024)

Delahunty, Jo, 'The 30th Anniversary of the Children Act 1989: Is It Still Fit for Purpose' (2019) www.gresham.ac.uk/sites/default/files/2019-01-31_JoDelahunty_30thAnniversaryOfThe ChildrenAct89.pdf (accessed 30.04.2024)

Delahunty, Jo and Alison Grief, 'The Judicial Rebellion Against Re H and R' [2008] *Family Law* 70

Department of Health, *Child Protection: Messages from Research* (HMSO 1995) (accessed 3.05.2024)

Department of Health and Social Security, *Review of Child Care Law* (DHSS 1985) https://archive.org/details/op1275285-1001 (accessed 30.04.2024)

Devine, Lauren and Stephen Parker, 'Rethinking Child Protection' (2023) https://suitable-education.uk/rethinking-child-protection-serious-reform-needed-research-by-devine-and-parker/ (accessed 30.04.2024)

Edwards, Olivia, 'Race and Culture in Family Law' [2021] *Family Law* 1174

Edwards, Susan, 'Radicalisation: Antithetical Jurisdictions of Protection and Punishment' [2023] *Family Law* 684

'A Failure of Implementation' (Children and Families Act 2014 Committee Report) House of Lords https://committees.parliament.uk/publications/31839/documents/179148/default/

Family Justice Review (March 2011) www.guardian.co.uk/society/2003/jan/27/childrensservices.childprotection

Freeman, Michael, 'Legislating for Child Abuse: The Children Act and Significant Harm' in Allan Levy (ed) *Refocus on Child Abuse* (Hawksmere 1993) 18

Gordon, Eleanor and Gwyneth Nair, 'Domestic Fathers and the Victorian Parental Role' [2006] *Women's History Review* 4

Hale, Baroness, '30 Years of the Children Act' www.supremecourt.uk/docs/speech-191113.pdf (accessed 30.04.2024)

Hale, Baroness, 'Family Rights Group 40th Anniversary Lecture' [2014] *Family Law* 1658

Harker, Racheal, 'Children in Care in England: Statistics Single Placements' Ministry of Justice Standard Note: SN/SG/4470 Social and General Statistics (2012)

Harwin, Judith and Dr Bachar Alrouh, 'Supervision Orders and Special Guardianship: How Risky Are They? Findings from a National Study of Supervision Orders and Special Guardianship' [2017] *Family Law* 513

Independent Review of Children's Social Care Research Report (May 2022) https://assets.publishing.service.gov.uk/media/640a17f28fa8f5560820da4b/Independent_review_of_children_s_social_care_-_Final_report.pdf (accessed 13.05.2024)

Jackson, Peter, 'The Nicholas Wall Memorial Lecture 2023, 'Is Family Law Law?' [2023] *Family Law* 796

Jivraj, Suhraiya and Didi Herman, '"It Is Difficult for a White Judge to Understand": Orientalisation, Racialisation and Christianity in English Child Welfare Cases' [2009] *Child and Family Law Quarterly* 28

Judicial Statistics 2005 Cm 6903 Table 5.2 p 66 www.gov.uk/government/statistics/judicial-statistics-revised-england-and-wales-for-the-year-2005 (accessed 03.05.2024)

Lord Laming, 'The Victoria Climbié Inquiry Report of Lord Laming' (2003) www.gov.uk/government/publications/the-victoria-climbie-inquiry-report-of-an-inquiry-by-lord-laming (accessed 13.05.2024)

MacAlister, Josh, 'Independent Review of Children's Social Care: Final Report' – GOV.UK (www.gov.uk) (2023) https://www.gov.uk/government/publications/independent-review-of-childrens-social-care-final-report (accessed 13.05.2024)

Masson, Judith, 'Judging Care Proceedings – It's Not What You Do It's the Way That You Do it' (2022) *Journal of Social Welfare and Family Law* 533

McFarlane, Andrew, 'Holding the Risk: The Balance Between Child Protection and the Right to Family Life' The Bridget Lindley OBE Memorial Lecture (2017) *Family Law* 610 www.judiciary.uk/wp-content/uploads/2022/07/lecture-by-lj-mcfarlane-20160309.pdf (accessed 12.05.2024)

Miller, Alice, *Thou Shalt Not Be Aware: Society's Betrayal of the Child* (Farrar Straus Giroux 1984)

Mnookin, Robert and Lewis Kornhauser, 'Bargaining in the Shadow of the Law: The Case of Divorce' [1979] *The Yale Law Journal* 950

Mornington, Alicia-Dorothy and Alexandrine Guyard-Nedelec, 'Is Poverty Eroding Parental Rights in Britain? The Case of Child Protection in the Early Twenty-First Century' in Nicolás Brando and Gottfried Schweiger (eds), *Philosophy and Child Poverty: Reflections on the Ethics and Politics of Poor Children and Their Families* (Springer 2019) 341–361

Munby, Sir James LJ, '14th View from the President's Chambers: Care Cases: Settlement Conferences and the "Tandem" Model' [2016a] *Family Law* 1102 https://transparencyproject.org.uk/the-crisis-in-private-law-by-sir-james-munby/

Munby, Sir James LJ, '15th View from the President's Chambers: Care Cases: The Looming Crisis' [2016b] *Family Law* 1227 www.judiciary.uk/wp-content/uploads/2014/08/pfd-view-15-care-cases-looming-crisis.pdf (accessed 13.05.2024)

Munro Review of Child Protection: Final Report – a Child-Centred System (2011) www.gov.uk/government/publications/munro-review-of-child-protection-final-report-a-child-centred-system (accessed 13.05.2024)

'National Review into the Murders of Arthur Labinjo-Hughes and Star Hobson' www.gov.uk/government/publications/national-review-into-the-murders-of-arthur-labinjo-hughes-and-star-hobson (accessed 05.05.2024)

Nuffield Family Observatory www.nuffieldfoundation.org/news/extreme-ethnic-inequalities-in-the-care-system#:~:text=There%20are%20extreme%20inequalities%20between%20ethnic%20groups%20in,%E2%80%98Black%20Caribbean%E2%80%99%20children%20are%2020%20times%20more%20likely (accessed 06.05.2024)

Owen, Charlie and June Statham, 'Disproportionality in Child Welfare the Prevalence of Black and Minority Ethnic Children within the "Looked After" and "Children in Need" Populations and on Child Protection Registers in England' (2009) Thoman Coram Research Institute Research Report DCSF-RR124 University of London (accessed 06.05.2024)

Poulter, Sebastian M, *Ethnicity, Law, and Human Rights: The English Experience* (Oxford Clarendon 1988).

Press Release, 'Government Launches Crackdown on Mobile Phones in Schools' (19.02.2024) www.gov.uk/government/news/government-launches-crackdown-on-mobile-phones-in-schools (accessed 06.05.2024)

Prevent Duty Guidance www.gov.uk/government/publications/prevent-duty-guidance (accessed 06.05.2024)

Proudman, Charlotte, 'Setting Parents Up to Fail Punishing Hopeless Parents Is Integral to Care Proceedings' [2012] *Family Law* 987

Public Law Working Group, Best Practice Guidance: Section 20 / Section 76 Accommodation (March 2021) www.judiciary.uk/wp-content/uploads/2021/03/S-20-s-76-BPG-report_clickable.pdf (accessed 03.05.2024)

Publication of the Public Law Working Group Supervision Order Report – and Webinar (24.04.2023) www.judiciary.uk/guidance-and-resources/publication-of-the-public-law-working-group-supervision-order-report-and-webinar-today-24-april-2023/ (accessed 3.05.2024)

Roe, Alice and Jordan Rehill, 'Unequal Chances? Ethnic Disproportionality in Child Welfare and Family Justice' [2021] *Family Law* 730

Sloan, Brian, 'Uncertain Perpetrators' www.youtube.com/watch?v=WYhaxBanCts (accessed 13.05.2024)

Thornton, Alice, 'The Limitations of Section 38(6) of the Children Act 1989' [2024] *Family Law* 70

Volume 832: Debated on Wednesday (06.09.2023) (Col 68gc) (accessed 03.05.2024)

Woodward-Carlton, Damian, 'Radicalisation and the Family Courts' [2019] *Family Law* 752

Working Together to Safeguard Children – Statutory Guidance https://assets.publishing.service.gov.uk/media/65cb4349a7ded0000c79e4e1/Working_together_to_safeguard_children_2023_-_statutory_guidance.pdf (accessed 30.04.2024)

Further reading

Bridge, Caroline, 'Case Reports: Family Proceedings' [2010] *Family Law* 236

Dalgarno, Elizabeth, Donna Bramwell, Arpana Verma, and Sonja Ayeb-Karlsson, 'Let's Excuse Abusive Men from Abusing and Enable Sexual Abuse: Child Sexual Abuse Investigations in England's Private Family Courts' [2024] *Journal of Social Welfare and Family Law* in press

Dalgarno, Elizabeth, Sonja Ayeb-Karlsson, Donna Bramwell, Adrienne Barnett and Arpana Verma, 'Health-Related Experiences of Family Court and Domestic Abuse in England: A Looming Public Health Crisis' [2024] *Journal of Family Trauma, Child Custody & Child Development* 1

Department of Health, The Children Act *1989:* Guidance and Regulations, *vol 1: Court Orders* (HMSO 1991)

Edwards, Susan, 'The Domestic Violence Crime and Victims Act 2004' [2006] *Denning Law Journal* 243

Edwards, Susan, *Sex and Gender in the Legal Process* (Blackstone Press 1996)

Eddon, George, 'Placing Children with Family Members' [2006] *Family Law* 949

Foreman, David M, 'Improving Child Protection by Integrating Research Evidence and Clinical Experience' [2015] *International Journal of Family Law* 301

Fortin, Jane, 'Significant Harm Revisited' [1998] *Journal of Child Law* 151

Griffith, Robert, *The Politics of Fear: Joseph R. McCarthy and the Senate* (2nd edn, University of Massachusetts Press 1987)

Hayes, Mary, '"Why Did the Courts Not Protect This Child"? Re SB and Re F' [2012] *Family Law* 169

Hayes, Mary and J Hayes, 'Shocking Abuse followed by a Staggering Ruling: Re MA (Care Threshold)' [2010] *Family Law* 166

HMSO, *Child Protection;* Messages from Research (HMSO 1995)

Mornington, Alicia-Dorothy and Alexandrine Guyard-Nedelec, 'Is Poverty Eroding Parental Rights in Britain? The Case of Child Protection in the Early Twenty-First Century' in Nicolás Brando and Gottfried Schweiger (eds) Philosophy *and Child Poverty Reflections on the Ethics and Politics of Poor Children and Their Families* (Springer 2019)

Welbourne, Penelope, 'Safeguarding Children on the Edge of Care: Policy for Keeping Children Safe After the Review of the Child Care Proceedings System, Care Matters and the Carter Review of Legal Aid' [2008] *Child and Family Law Quarterly* 335

16

Financial provision for children

SUMMARY

In this chapter we consider the ways in which the law organises financial support for the children of the family, including a civil partnership family. We examine the role of the courts and the role of the Child Maintenance Service (formerly the Child Maintenance and Enforcement Commission (C-MEC), and the Child Support Agency), in managing financial provision. The overarching principle with regard to child maintenance is the precept of parental responsibility whereby the legal parent is responsible for maintaining the children of the family. There has been a shift away from State-sponsored support for the child to enforcing parental responsibility even where the level of financial support a legal parent can make is only nominal. Where there is some income, both legal parents are required to make a financial contribution to the upbringing of their offspring. Where the level of income is inadequate, welfare benefits may supplement by 'top up' what is required to financially support a child. Parents may also negotiate their financial responsibility through the private arrangements made by the courts under the Matrimonial Causes Act – MCA 1973 and the Children Act 1989. The Child Support Agency, once responsible for calculating how much parents were to contribute financially towards supporting their children and also the enforcement of child payments, has been replaced firstly by the Child Maintenance and Enforcement Commission and subsequently by the Child Maintenance Service. Enforcement has always been problematic especially where the absent parent – usually the father – defaults and fails to make financial provision.

At the heart of the legislation is the welfare of the child (s 2 of the Child Support Act 1991). This is also found in the law regulating private arrangements for children MCA 1973).

In this chapter we consider how far the legislation has obviated the need for parents to go to court to recover child maintenance where the parent with care is reliant on a spouse's/non-resident parent's contribution to maintaining the child in their care, and whether the Child Support Act 1991 and subsequent Acts and its various agencies have improved the financial position and security of children. We also examine and review the role of the Child

DOI: 10.4324/9781003435020-16

Maintenance Service and the approach that it takes, in particular the move towards private ordering rather than State intervention.

We consider the workings of the law relating to private arrangements for child maintenance (Domestic Proceedings and Magistrates' Courts Act 1978, Matrimonial Causes Act 1973, Children Act 1989, s 15 and Sch 1). This pertains in the more wealthy parental arrangements where there is sufficient income to provide more than adequately for the child.

Background to child support

Child poverty

Child poverty has been identified as one of the main causes of many social problems besetting society at present. The figures for child poverty have consistently been rising according to figures from the Child Poverty Action Group.

- 350,000 more children were pulled into relative poverty (after housing costs) in 2021–22. That means 4.2 million children (29 per cent of all UK children) were in poverty – up from 3.6 million in 2010–11;
- 45 per cent of all children in poverty were in families with a youngest child aged under 5 (Wikeley 2008)

Child poverty has serious effects on the life chances of a child. According to research carried out by Dr Barnados, the Rowntree Trust and the Child Poverty Action Group, children from one-parent homes are calculated to be more likely to suffer long-term health conditions and are less likely to proceed to high education (see Barnados 2022).

The Royal College of Paediatrics and Child Health has identified a strong relationship between being from a low-income family and being a Special Education Needs and Disabilities (SEND) child. Over one quarter (27.2 per cent) of children who are categorised as having SEND are eligible for free school meals (FSM), suggesting that they are from a low-income household. In addition, children recognised as having SEND are more likely to achieve lower grades and experience poverty in the future, reducing their life chances as adults (RCPCH 2022).

Child support: theoretical background to the financial support of children

Theories behind child support usually focus on whom the burden of payment for a child should fall. Should it be the State or should the cost of support fall to the parents or should it be split between the two? A simplistic approach would be to say the responsibility of paying for the maintenance of a child should fall on the shoulders of the parents and a non-resident parent should continue to pay for the children. The parents created the child and so must bear responsibility of the costs of bringing up the child. Balanced against this and underpinning any discussion must be the welfare of the child and the need to ensure that children from single parent homes are not disadvantaged.

Theoretical basis of child support

Various theories have been propounded as to where the responsibility for financial support should lie.

1. **The causation theory.** This theory is based on the idea that if parents have conceived a child, then those parents have the moral duty to care and maintain that child and cover all the financial costs involved. Scott Altman in his wider ranging discussion of the theories of child support rejected causation as a theoretical basis of child support preferring the prevention of harm theory. This is not all it seems, as his argument is that in financially supporting a child a parent is demonstrating love which in turn will prevent the child from suffering from psychological harm. This is based on studies showing that a parent who financially supports a child is more likely to keep in touch with that child and to visit regularly (see Altman 2003). The problem with arguing that a parent should take financial responsibility for children is that it ignores the fact that many parents do not have the means to pay. Research carried out across the EU and across many countries into child maintenance showed that it is usually the parents earning below the minimum wage that are more likely to default on payments (see Takayesu and Eldred 2016).

2. **Children's rights:** The basis of this is the UNCRC which incorporates under Article 27 the right of every child to an adequate standard of living. The United Kingdom has ratified the Convention, and the Government is committed to consider the Convention whenever legislation is introduced.

   Article 27(4) of the UNCRC 1989 mandates child maintenance and support:

   > *States Parties shall take all appropriate measures to secure the recovery of maintenance for the child from the parents or other persons having financial responsibility for the child, both within the State Party and from abroad. In particular, where the person having financial responsibility for the child lives in a State different from that of the child, States Parties shall promote the accession to international agreements or the conclusion of such agreements, as well as the making of other appropriate arrangements.*

   Under the Convention a child has a right to financial support and the State is committed to recover unpaid maintenance. Applying this theory the responsibility for securing financial support of children from a parent lies with the State although the responsibility for payment should lie with the parents.

3. **The needs of children.** Some argue that the argument should focus more on the needs of children and the prevention of poverty amongst a vulnerable group in society. Sally Sheldon has put forward a powerful argument that the State

should carry the prime responsibility for supporting children financially. She argues that simply to leave all children subject to the vagaries of the economic means of their parents has resulted in widespread poverty. She counters the arguments of men's groups who say it is unfair to hold fathers financially liable for child support because it is women who control the decision to continue or terminate a pregnancy by arguing that a more effective way to support children would be to move towards a collective model where the State becomes responsible for the financial support of children (see Sheldon 2003).

Child support: history

Historically the burden of providing for child maintenance fell to the local parish who had power to recover the cost from the parents. The most punitive aspect of this was the burden placed on a single mother. When an illegitimate child was born it remained the mother's responsibility to financially provide for the child. A mother could of course take steps to pursue the biological father through the courts to try and recover child maintenance regardless of the legitimacy of the child. Women, throughout history, have been presented with the unenviable choice of pursuing fathers for child maintenance both for their legitimate and illegitimate children, or else face certain hardship or destitution and poverty. For some mothers, who became destitute, their only recourse, until the last century, was to place themselves at the mercy of the parish which meant that in order to survive they would be forced to go into an adult workhouse (essentially no more than a shelter) and be separated from their children, who would be cared for in a workhouse for children. In both, conditions of life were subsistence. From 1733, the **Bastardy Act** ordered that fathers of illegitimate children should be committed to jail unless they made arrangements to indemnify the parish (who were responsible for the so called workhouses) for the upkeep of their child. In 1871, the **Bastardy Laws (Amendment) Act** gave the mother of an illegitimate child the right to apply to a court for a maintenance order against the father of the child. A father of an illegitimate child was at risk of being sent to prison if he failed to make payments towards any child which was proved to be his. Proof often posed a problem in a time when paternity blood tests were not available. Nicholas Wikeley cites examples of unmarried mothers falsely claiming that a wealthy man living locally was the father of her children, claims which he would be unable to refute (Wikely 2006). Legislation was introduced in the Poor Law Amendment Act 1834 which required a higher level of proof of a claim that someone was the father of a child. This prevented many of the more bizarre and random claims made and placed the responsibility of maintenance of an illegitimate child onto the mother.

In *Ward v Byham* [1956] 1 WLR 496, the unmarried cohabiting biological parents of a child separated. Denning LJ reaffirmed the respective legal position of the biological parents, where the mother brought a claim for the sum of £1 a week in respect of the maintenance of her illegitimate child: 'By statute the mother of an illegitimate child was bound to maintain it, whereas the father is under no such obligation' (see National Assistance Act 1948, s 42).

When these various laws were abolished after the Second World War, enforcement of maintenance obligations against fathers fell to private law. There was no intervention by the State if a father persistently failed to provide financial support. Enforcement was always difficult if a father failed to make a payment and usually the only way to recover outstanding sums was through the courts. This was far from satisfactory. It was very expensive as often costs were far in excess of the payments involved and the courts had no power to trace an absent parent, usually the father. The decisions were often inconsistent and varied according to who heard the case. There was also a rise in single parent families but less than a quarter were receiving maintenance from the father as stated by the Lord Chancellor at the time Lord Mackay of Clashfern in a statement to the house on child maintenance:

> *Only 30 per cent. of lone mothers and 3 per cent. of lone fathers receive maintenance regularly. Over million lone parents and their children depend on income support. In 1989 only 23 per cent. of lone parents who were receiving income support received maintenance. Ten years ago the figure was 50 per cent. Income support represents 45 per cent. of the income of all lone parents. The cost in real terms to the taxpayer has risen from £1.4 billion in 1981–82 to £3.2 billion in 1988–89.*

> (Hansard 1990)

Against this background the Government sought to create an alternative central scheme which would bring consistency and predictability and would seek to place the responsibility for the maintenance of children with the parents and primarily the fathers.

The background to the Child Support Act 1991

The White Paper *Children Come First* (1990) (Cm 1264) which foreshadowed the CSA 1991 reported that many absent fathers made no provision for their families, and it was this failure that the Government sought to address. An equally important motivation for the legislation was that the cost to the public purse of child maintenance was a cost that the State was no longer prepared to shoulder. The Government's objective was to transfer, wherever possible, the responsibility of this financial burden onto the absent or non-resident parent by creating an effective enforcement mechanism.

The White Paper stated:

> *The present system of maintenance is unnecessarily fragmented, uncertain in its results, slow and ineffective. It is based largely on discretion. The system is operated through the High and county courts, the magistrates' courts, the Court of Session and the sheriff courts in Scotland and the offices of the Department of Social Security. The cumulative effect is uncertainty and inconsistent decisions about how much maintenance should be paid. In a great many instances, the maintenance awarded is not paid or the payments fall into arrears and take weeks to re-establish. Only 30 per cent of lone mothers and 3 per cent of lone fathers receive regular maintenance for their children. More than 750,000 lone parents depend on income support. Many lone mothers want to go to work but do not feel able to do so.*

The cost of child maintenance to the public purse had grown in the years preceding the CSA 1991 as a result of the increasing number of children dependent on State welfare following a rise in divorce and an increase in one-parent families. In 1968,

54,036 divorce petitions were filed and by 1978, there were 142,726 divorce decrees (absolute), compared with 152,139 in 1988. The Government under Margaret Thatcher strongly supported the policy that the financial responsibility for children fell to the parents rather than the State.

Recovery of maintenance prior to the Child Support Act 1991

Research conducted by Edwards and Halpern during the period immediately prior to the CSA 1991 which examined financial provision in the county courts, trends in ancillary relief and income related orders for children and for the spouse including interviews with solicitors discovered that child maintenance was infrequently awarded, and when awarded went unpaid, leaving many children reliant on state support. Even in those cases where a maintenance order was made by the courts in favour of a dependent child, the financial reality of those orders was that many were made for nominal sums of as little as £1 per year. The nominal order was put in place to ensure that whilst the absent parent had no resources to provide for the child at the time of making the order, it allowed for a reconsideration of the maintenance assessment at a later date should the absent parents circumstances change. They found that, 'only 26.5 per cent of dependent children under 16, and only 18 per cent of children under 18 and over 16 receive an order for maintenance' (1990: 75). They also found that 50 per cent of all orders made actually went unpaid. Significantly, 61 per cent of non-payers cleared their arrears once enforcement proceedings were commenced, whilst in the remaining 39 per cent of cases, orders could not be enforced because there were obvious financial difficulties or the ex-spouse was untraceable. Edwards and Halpern pioneered important research in this field exposing the ineffectiveness of the pre-1991 system of child maintenance (see Edwards and Halpern 1990, 1992).

Felicity Kaganas and Christine Piper note that Edwards and Halpern:

> with a 'cynical eye' saw [the government move as an] unsuccessful attempt to introduce equality between parents. They maintained that the Children Act 1989, along with the Child Support Act 1991 and the Criminal Justice Act 1991, included provisions designed as mechanisms to restructure thinking on parental responsibility so as to legitimate a reduction in state support for members of the family.
>
> (Kaganas and Piper 2002)

It was against this background that the CSA 1991 was enacted and the Child Support Agency (CS Agency) (the mechanism for collection and enforcement of child payment) was established. This body took over the responsibility for calculating child maintenance payments and securing enforcement of any payments. As Bird wrote:

> Before 1990, the idea that the courts were not the appropriate forum for decisions as in child maintenance when the parents could not agree would have seemed foreign to most lawyers . . . maintenance of children was regarded as a branch of family law which naturally fell within the jurisdiction of the courts, and there were few who thought that it should be removed into some free-standing system. Nevertheless, this is what the 1991 Act attempted to achieve.
>
> (Bird1996)

The Act and the creation of the Child Support Agency received considerable support at the time because it was perceived that it was far better to have a single agency vested with all powers connected with child support rather than the piecemeal approach which existed. The Act aimed to address multiple issues, and it soon ran into difficulties. Perhaps the worst aspect of the legislation was that instead of addressing the problem of enforcement of maintenance for children it focused more on the reduction of state benefits (see generally King and Crewe 2014).

The purpose of the Child Support Act 1991

Despite its shortcomings, for the first time, the CSA 1991 placed the responsibility to maintain the child on both biological parents regardless of marital status. In this regard, it strove to bring about equality between biological parents with regard to their duty to maintain the child regardless of marital status, whether married, or unmarried, in a civil partnership, separated, divorced, living together or living apart. This had not been the situation at common law.

In *Huxley v Child Support Officer* [2000] 1 FLR 898), Hale LJ, with the concurrence of Auld and Pill LJJ, characterised the regime established by the 1991 Act:

> *The child support system has elements of private and public law but fundamentally it is a nationalised system for assessing and enforcing an obligation which each parent owes primarily to the child. It replaces the powers of the courts, which can no longer make orders for periodical payments for children save in very limited circumstances. Unless she can secure a voluntary agreement at least as high as that which the CSA would assess, the PWC (parent with care) is expected to look to the Agency to assess her child support according to the formula, whether or not she is on benefit. The fact that it does her no direct good if she is on means-tested benefits, and that much CSA activity so far has been in relation to parents on benefit, does not alter the fundamental characteristics of the scheme.*

The Child Support Act 1991

With regard to domestic legislation the Child Support Act 1991, s 1(1) (CSA 1991) mandated financial maintenance for children by requiring the legal parent (biological/adoptive parents of a child and those legal parents under the HFEA 1990), both the parent with residence and the absent/non-resident parent, to meet their respective responsibilities. It established a State mechanism to assist in enforcing that obligation, and in addition it provided a system of penalties for those who failed to comply. This enforcement objective was furthered in the subsequent legislation.

Duty to maintain a qualifying child: Child Support Act 1991

The key features of the child support system are firstly that child support is calculated via a formula which applies to all cases and secondly the Government service now called the Child Maintenance Service has responsibility for both applying the formula and collecting the child support.

The CSA 1991, s 1(1) provides that 'each parent of a qualifying child is responsible for maintaining him'. Section 1(2) states:

> a non-resident parent shall be taken to have met his responsibility to maintain any qualifying child of his by making periodical payments of maintenance with respect to the child of such amount, and at such intervals, as may be determined in accordance with the provisions of this Act.

However, it is to be noted that the Act only applies to parents who are not living together. The law does not intervene where parties are living together. The law is unconcerned with how parents deal with family finances whilst a relationship is ongoing save for children who are at risk of suffering significant harm. Curiously, once the Child Maintenance Service becomes involved and the formula has been applied a parent may be required to pay far more than previously within the relationship.

A qualifying child

Maintenance is paid to the primary care of a 'qualifying child' who is defined as a child or young person:

Age of qualifying child

A 'qualifying child' for the purpose of the CSA 1991 is a child where one or both of his parents in relation to him are absent parents (s 3(1)). A child is a person under 16 years or else under 20 years if in full-time education or has registered for work based learning (CMOP 2008, s 42 amends s 55 of the CSA).

Note the age of the upper limit of a qualifying child has increased from 19 to 20 years; this further extends the upper age limit for parental responsibility diverting for as long as is possible State responsibility for the financial 'burden' of persons who elsewhere are adults (see Childs and Boden 1996 for an interesting discussion). Clearly we have a curious development and must ask, when is a child a child and for what purpose?

Maintaining other children

The non-resident parent may be maintaining several children in more than one household, where for example a man has several children by different mothers.

What of children of the civil partnership union?

Following the Civil Partnership Act 2004, a 'child of the family' is a child within a civil partnership family. As Bamforth writes:

> The meaning of 'family life' was addressed in Secretary of State for Work and Pensions v M, which concerned the basis on which child maintenance payments were calculated under the Child Support Act 1991 and accompanying secondary legislation.

> *The claimant argued that a parent who now lived with a same-sex partner was assessed less generously than a parent who lived with an opposite-sex partner, and that this difference fell foul of Article 14 coupled with the 'family life' limb of Article 8. Since the majority judgments placed considerable weight on the Strasbourg 'margin of appreciation' and four of the five judgments differed about how the Strasbourg Court would now interpret 'family life', the decision offers an ambiguous, but probably discouraging, message to those concerned to challenge the marriage/civil partnership distinction. Turning first to the ambit of 'family life', Lord Nicholls was confident that the Estevez exclusion of same-sex couples from this limb of Article 8 still applied, and asserted that since signatory States enjoyed a wide margin of appreciation in this area, '[f]or the time being the respect accorded' to same-sex relationships was a matter for them. Article 14 was thus not engaged. Lord Mance also invoked Estevez and the wide 'margin', but was far less categorical in that he linked the existence of the wide 'margin' to the time period 'very shortly before the period relevant to the present appeal'. While the claimant's same-sex relationship did not fall within the ambit of family life at that time, Lord Mance had 'little doubt' that were a similar question to arise based on contemporary circumstances, it 'could well be regarded, in both Strasbourg and the United Kingdom, as involving family life for the purposes of [A]rticle 8. at para [152].*

> (Bamforth 2007)

Wikeley criticises the primacy accorded to the genetic link between parent and child – 'qualifying child' – at the heart of the duty to maintain embodied in the CSA 1991. He argues that the CSA's insistence on genetic parentage reflects in an 'atavistic way' the concerns of the nineteenth-century Poor Laws and the Bastardy Laws. He contends that the genetic link between parent and child actually no longer fits into the reality of parenthood in the contemporary family. In furthering this argument he cites the way in which the genetic link argument is flawed in that it ignores scientific advances with regard to IVF, and that private law arrangements for financial provision of children under the Matrimonial Causes Act 1984, s 25 have already made provision for stepchildren and other children of the family to be maintained by a non-biologically related parent (Wikeley 2006).

Resident parent

A resident parent is the parent with care (the natural or adoptive parent or person who in accordance with the Human Fertilisation and Embryology Act 1990, s 30 becomes the parent, see ss 33 and 35 of the Human Fertilisation and Embryology Act 2008). The non-resident parent is the parent who does not have the day to day care of the child (CSA 1991, s 3(2)).

Person with care

The person with care is defined in s 3(3) as 'A person is a "person with care", in relation to any child, if he is a person – (a) with whom the child has a home, (b) who usually provides day to day care for the child (whether exclusively or in conjunction with any other person)'.

The terms non-resident parent and person with care have created some uncertainty. As we have seen there is a drift towards shared residence orders with regard to children even where one parent numerically has the care of the child over a greater number of days than the other parent. A shared residence order was also seen to have an advantage in relocation matters in *K v K* (Relocation: Shared Care Arrangement) [2011] EWCA Civ 793. The Child Support (Maintenance Calculations and Special Cases) Regulations 2000 SI 2001/155. reg 8 states that a person who provides day to day care is to be treated as a non-resident parent where the care provided is less that the other parent providing day to day care.

There is no statutory definition of 'day to day care'. The issue was considered recently in *DW v Secretary for State for Work and Pensions and Another* [2023] UKUT 19 (AAC). In this case the parents shared care and had equal overnight care of their child but the mother provided a greater degree of day to day care which meant the father could be considered the non-resident parent. In considering what is meant by day to day care it was held that it involves more than a mere counting of days and nights. It involves the exercise of judgment in respect of parenting tasks and responsibilities and the personal care provided for the child.

The Child Support Agency – Child Support Act 1991 and maintenance assessment

Where a child is born to a married or unmarried couple, or a couple in a civil partnership and the resident parent (usually the mother) is without independent means of support and is in need of income support both for herself and for the child, before the State could assist the resident parent, the resident parent is required to apply to the Child Support Agency (now the Child Maintenance Service) under the CSA 1991, s 4(1) for a maintenance assessment. The formula for any assessment is made under the Child Support Maintenance Calculation Regulations 2012. This assessment is based on the needs of the child and the respective incomes of the parties. The non-resident parent, or the parent with care, could apply. Usually, it is the mother who is in receipt of income support/family credit who applies for a maintenance assessment. The applicant for a maintenance assessment is required to provide all the necessary information to the Secretary of State including financial information as well as naming the father. Under s 6(10), this obligation to disclose the name and details of the non-resident parent could be waived by statutory instrument in certain prescribed circumstances and the furious debate that followed this resulted in repeal under the Child Maintenance and Other Payments Act 2008.

Failings of the CSA enforcement mechanism and subsequent reforms

Part of the overriding objective said the Government when it introduced the Child Support Act 1991 was to address the problem of child poverty. But did the CSA 1991 take children out of poverty? Ann Halpern, Susan Edwards, and Carole Gould (1990) wrote:

> *We believe that it makes little sense to make orders for financial support which are unlikely to be paid or which are paid with considerable difficulty . . . A clear social policy which seeks to address the poor economic position of women on divorce, guided by the recognition that it is the product of their position within the family and the social structure, would do more to alleviate the problems of divorced mothers and children than anything else. Social policy could now recognise that the best way to protect children of the divorced is not to force mothers to remain at home caring for children whilst reliant on a mixture of state support, maintenance and part time earnings, but to actively encourage mothers into employment.*
>
> ('The Continuing Saga of Maintaining the Family after Divorce' (1990) *Family Law* 31)

And did the CSA 1991 put children first as it claimed it would? Or was there evidence that it put the taxpayer first? In addition the Act and its Schedules have been criticised for not being intelligible. In *Re C* (1994) the court said:

> *The Child Support Act 1991 provides that, each parent of a qualifying child is responsible for maintaining him at a rate fixed by mathematically obtuse calculations in innumerable unintelligible Schedules.*

And was the enforcement mechanism effective as it claimed it would be? During 1993, 5,954 applications to register maintenance orders in magistrates' courts were granted, 24 per cent less than in 1992. In addition, 2,782 attachment of earnings orders were made compared with 2,553 in 1992. Roger Bird commented:

> *More significantly, a series of both official and independent reports began to highlight serious deficiencies in the performance of the Child Support Agency, and hardships, which resulted from the rigid interpretation of the formulae. A pattern emerged of critical Select Committee Reports every Autumn, followed by amended Regulations the following Spring. The Child Support Agency failed to meet its performance targets for 1993/94, the Select Committee Report published in November 1994 was highly critical; the Ombudsman Report revealed serious misadministration.*

In 2005, there were 640 applications made for attachments of earnings orders on maintenance orders and 623 orders made, compared with 156 in 2000, whilst 1,033 maintenance orders in the magistrates' courts were registered, compared with 1,070 so registered in 2000 suggesting little change or improvement in enforcement. According to the National Audit figures of 2005 there were an estimated £3.5 billion of outstanding arrears and of that over 60 per cent were now deemed to be uncollectable (Gov.UK 2006).

The CSPSSA 2000, s 17 amended the CSA 1991, in order to provide a wider arsenal of enforcement and s 39(a) provided for driving disqualification but this also proved of little value.

Wikeley writes that in the first five years after bringing into force the CSPSSA 2000, as few as 11 driving licences were removed and 63 suspended disqualification orders were made. Did the threat of the sanction act as a draconian sword of Damocles? In short the mechanism failed; it was cumbersome, incomprehensible and delayed in getting payments to children.

On 9 September 2005, Frank Field announced that the CS Agency was in 'meltdown'. Despite the avowed objective of the CSA 1991 of 'children come first', the new system did not deliver a service to children: there were substantial delays with forwarding money to single parents lengthening from an average 12 to 15 weeks in 2003 to an estimated 15 to 22 weeks in 2004; children remained in poverty: only 61,000 of the 478,000 parents who had applied for support since the introduction of the computer system in 2002 (supposedly to improve the efficiency of the CS Agency) had received any money at all 18 months later in 2004. In fact, it would seem that the CSA 1991 made matters worse for children.

In addition, resident and non-resident parents made a series of legal challenges against the agency which they considered had failed to recover payments from absent parents.

> See *R (on the application of Kehoe) v Secretary of State for Work and Pensions* [2005] UKHL 48 – in this case Mrs Kehoe was owed £17,000 in unrecovered maintenance. It was held in this case that a parent had no right to challenge how the Child Support Agency chooses to enforce or does not enforce a calculation. The parent with primary care could not take action to enforce. It therefore ties the hands of a parent who must rely on the Government agency to act on their behalf in the best way that it chooses.

In addition, the courts came to assess what finances/assets were available to be divided between the parties on the breakup of a marriage, in cases where the family might also depend on the State. Some judgments reflected the view that the court, in reaching a decision as to settlement, could take into account the State benefits that would be paid to the spouse on divorce/separation in assessing the income of each of the parties.

Reform and the Child Maintenance and Other Payments Act 2008

The White Paper *A New System of Child Maintenance* (2006) claimed to put forward a new and radical scheme to that which already existed and proposed a new formula for assessment, including departures from the formula, extensions to the existing system of enforcement and a new system for appeals. This was followed by the publication of the Child Maintenance and Other Payments Bill on 6 June 2007.

The Bill proposed to establish a new child maintenance delivery organisation – the Child Maintenance and Enforcement Commission – to simplify how child maintenance is calculated, and to introduce tougher enforcement powers to collect arrears. It was recognised that the Child Support Agency had been a failure. In addition, existing parents with care whose application for child maintenance was made under s 6 (and was therefore compulsory) would have a choice of withdrawing from the statutory scheme should they wish to do so. Following the Henshaw recommendations (Recovering Child Support (2006)) radical reform was introduced to deal with the failings of its predecessor especially by s 2(1) of the Act which relates to 'effective maintenance arrangements'.

The Child Maintenance and Other Payments Act 2008 created a series of free-standing provisions (Parts 1 and 2) and extensively amended the 1991 Act. So, for example, reform was made to enforcement matters and introduced to the calculation process, i.e. process of calculating how much was owed by the parent. Under this new Act parents would no longer be required to authorise the Secretary of State to collect child support maintenance through the C-MEC. However, voluntary arrangements were encouraged (s 2(2)(a)), and an 'effective . . . arrangement' could be voluntary or statutory (s 11 of the 1991 Act). Although where parents chose to register with the C-MEC, following the Child Maintenance and Other Payments Act 2008, the Child Maintenance Service would recover payment from aberrant absent parents. This new collection agency set out to provide a more robust enforcement mechanism than its predecessor. So aberrant parents would be fined if they were pursued on two or more occasions through the courts. Under the new system, parents would be contacted by the authorities within three days if they failed to make a single payment for their children.

The role of the new Commission was to facilitate child support, and encouraging the payment of maintenance and compliance is a central objective. Wikeley suggests that it is 'carrots and sticks':

> The main carrot is the increased maintenance disregard for PWC (parent with care) who are on means – tested benefits. The sticks are a whole new range of weapons which have been added to the Commission's collection and enforcement armoury. At the time of writing most of these latter measures have yet to be brought into force and are expected to come into operation between 2009 and 2011.
>
> (Wikeley 2008)

Who pays – Whose child is it anyway? Paternity

Under the CSA 1991, s 1(1) only the legal parents have a duty to maintain the child. Determining who is the natural or biological father often requires proof of paternity, as absent fathers may dispute paternity. The motivation to establish or disavow the genetic link with a child, for the purpose of the CSA 1991, s 26 at least, has been a financial one. For the resident parent in need of financial support from the non–resident parent, establishing paternity is crucial. Whilst for the person named as the father by the resident parent a blood test which disproves paternity is the only way in which financial responsibility can be avoided. Wikeley examined the centrality that paternity testing has had, not on parental responsibility, nor parenthood, but on the legal obligation to pay for the child. Wikeley showed that, for example, 200,000 cases each year involve a denial of paternity. Of those 20,000 are subject to testing and in 2,000 cases the denial of paternity is upheld (2001 figures) (Wikely 2006).

Under CSA 1991, s 27, an application can be made for declaration of paternity. 'Paternity suits' have become of enormous public interest, especially where celebrities are involved, where so often their denials of paternity are exposed as lies by the unassailable truth of DNA findings.

In *L v P (Paternity Test: Child's Objection)* [2010] EWCA Civ 1145, a child of 15 refused to take a blood test which would establish paternity, and the court held it had no power to order the test. The child was mature and rational and fully able to decide the issue. It meant the presumption of paternity could not be disproved.

The 'best interests' test displaces the 'welfare paramount' test because of the human rights issues around paternity, including the competing rights of parents and putative parents to know the genetic origins of the children for whom they are responsible or about whom they wish to know, and the right of the child to know his or her genetic heritage.

Presumption of paternity

Since the introduction of the Child Support, Pensions and Social Security Act 2000 (CSPSSA 2000), s 15, the CSA could automatically assume the non-resident parent to be the father of a child if,

> he was married to or the civil partner of the mother at some stage between conception and birth unless the child is adopted; he is registered as the father on the birth certificate; or a DNA test shows he or she is the parent or he refuses to take scientific (for example DNA) tests

Some of these conditions are contentious, and paternity cannot be presumed. First, being married to the mother between conception and birth no longer leads to a foregone conclusion that the husband is the father. Second, whilst registration on the birth certificate is probably the most reliable it is not a certainty of paternity. Third, a refusal to take a scientific test may in fact indicate that the person so refusing is not the biological father but there may also be reasons why a biological father might refuse. Where a non-biological father refuses to take a blood test, it may be that he wishes to continue acting in the capacity of father and in the belief that he is the father which may indeed be in the best interests of the child in his care and the family. If it is later proved through a DNA test that someone is not the parent the Child Maintenance Service may refund the payments you've made since the date you denied you were the parent or offset the amount you've paid in child maintenance against maintenance for another child you pay for and refund the cost of any DNA tests arranged through the service or ask the other parent to pay back any child maintenance to you.

Whose child is it? – non-paternity issues

In *T v B* [2010] EWHC 1444 (Fam), the respondent – a female – had lived with the female applicant but not in a legal civil partnership. The applicant became pregnant by artificial insemination after a joint application by the parties, and in 2000 a child was born. The question arose whether the respondent was a parent under Sch 1 of the Children Act 1989 so that the court had jurisdiction to make an order against her for financial relief. The court concluded that while the respondent was a parent of the child as identified in *Re G* [2006] 2 FLR 1092 (namely as a social and psychological parent) it was held that the word 'parent' in Sch 1 means legal parent and that it is for the legislature to determine who should be liable to financial claims for the benefit of children and the extent to which it includes those who are not the legal parents of children but are either to be treated as parents or are otherwise to be made liable.

Parental responsibility – financial responsibility and contact issues

Absent fathers (non-resident parents) who have been pursued for maintenance and have made maintenance payments for the upkeep of their children have regarded contact with the child as a right which should follow automatically. But making maintenance payments and fulfilling the statutory obligation to maintain does not grant the payer any automatic entitlement either to parental responsibility rights or where there is parental responsibility the right to contact with the child concerned. There has been a common misconception that payment of maintenance towards a child should be linked with contact with that child. The current law seeks to break the link between the two and ensure that every non-resident parent should pay towards the maintenance of that child.

In *R v Halifax Justices ex parte Woolverton* [1981] 2 FLR 369 the husband fell into arrears with maintenance payments; the husband sought to get the arrears remitted because obstacles were put in his way by the wife with regard to access. The court held that it was wrong to order remission of arrears of child maintenance as a penalty to the wife for failing to allow access.

In addition, there is a further issue with regard to the maintenance requirement where, for example, the child is staying with the non-resident parent and the non-resident parent is paying maintenance for the child with regard to the time spent and the deduction of the maintenance payment. The Court of Appeal, in *Re B (Contact: Child Support)* [2006] EWCA Civ 1574 decided this vexed and ongoing question.

The parents had one daughter aged 11 who lived with her mother after the relationship broke down. There was ongoing contact litigation between the parties with regard to exactly how much contact the father should have. The daughter expressed her wish to have less contact time with the father and in March 2006 the court reduced that to 93 nights per year. The father saw this reduced staying contact as an attempt to increase the father's child support liability and in effect the father received no discount on his child support liability for the staying contact of 93 days annually. If the father had been assessed under the new scheme he would have received some recognition for the staying contact. (See Gilmore 2007 where Stephen Gilmore argues that the Court of Appeal was mistaken in not taking into account the impact that any decision on contact may then have on a parent's liability to pay child support to the other under the Child Support Act 1991.)

How much is a child worth? The maintenance formula

The current child support formula for calculating the amount a non-resident parent must pay towards a child is set down in the Child Maintenance and Other Payments Act 2008 and the Child Support Maintenance Calculation Regulations 2012.

One of the main criticisms of the formula introduced in 1991 was that it was far too complicated. The formula was simplified under the CSPSSA 2000, but it was still based on a range of criteria.

Wikeley analysed the early years of the CS Agency, together with the need to make changes to the formula for assessment and modifications to the formula. These included: a reduction in the carer component of the maintenance requirement, adjustments to the protected income formulae, adjustments in the formula to accommodate the costs of high travel to work, a broad brush approach to take account of capital and property settlements, full allowance in exempt income for the housing costs of new partners and stepchildren, followed by departure directions (Wikeley 2006).

Maintenance calculations

It is beyond the scope of this chapter to consider in any great detail the system of maintenance and calculations, but this is a brief account as the system currently stands.

Today the focus is on encouraging a couple who separate to draw up their own arrangements with regard to maintenance for their children.

i.   'The Family-based arrangement'. Under this scheme parents agree maintenance but will often use the maintenance calculator or any other tools available the Child Maintenance Service website. The change in emphasis under the new rules is towards agreement between couples and away from the State acting as an enforcement agency with all the additional costs involved. It is assumed that arrangements drawn up between the parties are far less likely to be acrimonious and far more likely to be adhered to by the non-resident parent.

ii. Where the family-based arrangement breaks down or if the parties fail to agree on maintenance then either party can apply to the Child Maintenance Service (CMS). This body which has replaced the Child Support Agency and the Child Maintenance and Enforcement Commission offers a range of services. These include a Direct Pay service under which the CMS will calculate the amount of child maintenance to be paid and the non-resident parent will undertake to pay the primary carer direct. Where this system does not work then the CMS will firstly calculate the amount to be paid and then undertake to collect it directly from the non-resident parent. This system called the 'Collect and Pay' service involves a number of additional costs including a basic £20 charge and then an additional 20 per cent on top of the maintenance for administrative costs. There is also a deduction of 4 per cent from the maintenance due to the primary carer. Recent statistics from the Child Maintenance Service Statistics website show that during the quarter ending September 2023, £342.3 million child maintenance was due to be paid either via the Direct Pay service or the Collect and Pay service. Of this £263.2 million was arranged through the Direct Pay service and £79.1 million was arranged through the Collect and Pay service.

(Gov.UK 2023)

iii. Where family-based arrangements break down and Direct Pay and Collect and Pay are not working, then there are a number of other enforcement mechanisms available. These are usually court based and are regarded today as a last resort.

A flat fee of £20 is charged for all applications. This is waived only in extreme cases such as applicants under 19 or victims of domestic violence. The flat charge was waived in over 54 per cent of cases in 2023 (Gov.UK 2023).

The problem with the fees for enforcement is that the child is most likely to suffer as it reduces the amount received. This has been criticised by Gingerbread, the charity which supports single parent families. Victoria Benson, Chief Executive of Gingerbread, said in 2021:

> It is a child's legal right to be supported by both parents, and the Child Maintenance Service was established to help to enforce this right. Yet the very service designed to protect this right is not only failing them but charging them, too. While it's right that the government should collect maintenance on behalf of children where it is not willingly paid, it is incredibly unfair that fees are deducted from this money before it is passed on. (www. gingerbread.org.uk/our-work/news-and-views/dwp-unfair-child-maintenance-fees-408-million-owed)

Gillian Douglas points out that there are a number of barriers put in place to prevent the parent with care from recovering maintenance from the non-resident parent:

> This message is then reinforced through the barriers put in the way of parents trying to use the child support system.
> Firstly, the website that provides the basic information and first point of contact with the system strongly promotes the use of private agreements. Secondly, a parent must have a 'gateway conversation' with the Child Maintenance Service to discuss the options available before proceeding to use the system. Thirdly, there is a charge of £20 to make an application. Fourthly, there is a collection fee if the parent wishes the Service to collect the money on her behalf. The paying parent is required to pay 20% on top of the calculated amount, and 4% is deducted from the amount paid to the recipient.

She adds that it is possible that a non-resident parent can escape the system altogether: 'If a parent is sufficiently determined, deluded or desperate to overcome these hurdles, she will then find that, should the Service fail to collect the payments due, she has no standing to seek to recover the money herself' (Douglas 2016).

It seems as though the very people the system is designed to support are left powerless in many cases.

Calculating the formula for payment

The basic rate

The gross income of the paying parent is calculated looking at their income before tax and national insurance has been assessed but pension contributions can be deducted which can reduce liability. The general rule is that the non-resident parent who earns between £1 and £800 per week should pay 12 per cent for one child, 16 per cent for two children and 19 per cent for three or more children. Where income rises above £800 the percentages are reduced to 9 per cent for one child and 25 per cent for two children and 15 per cent for three or more children for any income earned over £800. The total income that can be included in the assessment is capped at £3000 per week. Any gross income in excess of £3000 is ignored for the purposes of the calculation.

Adjustments to the formula

Where the non-paying parent has other 'qualifying' children then the total gross income will be reduced before the formula is applied.

If the income of the non-resident parent falls below £200 per week then the parent will pay a reduced rate and if it falls below £100 then a flat rate of £7 is applied.

Adjustments are made to the formula where care is shared. This can be a contentious issue, and it is an area where disputes arise as to how many nights are spent in each household. As shown in *DW v Secretary of State for Work and Pensions and another* (2023) discussed earlier the courts tend to look at the question of care in a broader way than merely counting nights spent in a particular household.

The 2012 Regulations have included variations introduced in 2000; see Child Support (Variations) Regulations 2000 SI 2001/156. These variations may take into account special expenses. These include the cost of travelling to work. This may be significant where parents work a long way from their home. Also included are the travel costs of maintaining contact with a child. Again, this could be significant where parties live a distance away from each other. Also included are the costs incurred where the applicant or a dependent is ill or disabled.

Enforcement

Enforcement rests with the Secretary for State through the Child Maintenance Service. These derive from the 1991 Act and include the right to require the employer to deduct sums from the non-paying parent's earnings or deduct sums from benefits or amounts paid by way of pension. Money can also be taken directly from a bank or building society account. These can all be done without a court order. There are also court-based means of enforcement which would involve applying to the court for a liability order and once the order is made the service can instruct bailiffs to seise possessions of the non-paying party. As a last resort the service can apply for a committal order which could result in the non-paying party going to prison.

New powers were introduced in the Child Support (Enforcement) Act 2023 which would allow the Child Maintenance Service to make an administrative liability order against a person who has failed to pay child maintenance and is in arrears. The advantage of this is that it removes the need to take court action as it is a purely administrative process. There would be appeal rights for any parent who believes that the order has been wrongly made. The proposed introduction of these orders is currently going through a consultation process.

Domestic abuse cases

Over half the cases dealt with by the service in 2023 involved domestic abuse. Many would argue that those who have suffered domestic abuse are poorly dealt with under the scheme. The scheme leans in favour of informal arrangements between the parties but where domestic abuse is involved it is not only unfeasible in most cases it could also be simply dangerous as it may involve the applicant disclosing information which could put them at risk. The non-payment of maintenance for a child could also be seen as a form of economic abuse. Drawing on examples from the Australian Child Support program Kristin Natalier demonstrates that the withholding of child support particularly where a parent has the means to pay is a form of economic abuse, a continuing form of control (Natalier 2018). There has been no attempt to waive the 4 per cent reduction in maintenance for domestic abuse cases although the £20 application fee can be waived. The reforms of the system brought about since 1991 are significant, but many issues still need to be addressed.

Evaluation of the Child Maintenance Service

In an attempt to bring more stability to the system of child maintenance all calculations made after the changes introduced in 2012 are subject to annual review but cannot be reviewed before the annual review unless there is a real change of circumstances. This is most likely to be based on an increase or decrease in income. The trigger for a review will be a 25 per cent change in income (see Child Support Maintenance Calculations Regulations 2012). This has been welcomed as a way of bringing certainty and stability.

A major criticism of the new system lies in the charges that can be exacted. Firstly for use of the system wherein a flat fee of £20 is charged where the Child Maintenance system is used but an additional charge is exacted where a non-resident parent fails to makes payments. If the failure to pay is through financial difficulties the charges will only exacerbate the problems. A £20 to use the system is not negligible where the parties are already in poverty. Many parents on low incomes will not use the service for this reason.

Further as discussed earlier if a non-paying parent uses the system to evade payment then the enforcement system is problematic because it lies with the Government and the parent with care has no means to enforce herself.

There is also an argument that the system still fails those suffering domestic abuse. The pressure on parents to make their own arrangements for financial support is not feasible for a parent with care at risk of domestic abuse. Even the disclosure of financial information may put a parent at risk. Financial support of children can also become a weapon in the hands of an abuser as discussed earlier.

Residual role of the courts

The court still has a residual role in cases which are exceptions to the general rule set out in s 8(1) and 8(3) of the CSA 1991 'no court shall exercise any power which it would otherwise have to make, vary or revive any maintenance order'.

The general rule is that the court cannot make an order where there is jurisdiction to make an order under the child support scheme. There are a number of exceptions which allow the court jurisdiction. These include where one or more of the relevant parties is not habitually resident in the UK; a child support order cannot be made against a stepparent who has previously supported the child or the child involved is not a qualifying child for the purposes of the Child Support Act.

The private arena of child support

Neville Brown asserted in 1968 that 'the law of maintenance has become a treacherous quagmire' (Brown 1968). Some 50 years later these words still ring true. Part of the quagmire to which Brown referred was that there were two systems of maintenance, one in the divorce courts and the other in the magistrates' matrimonial jurisdiction. The failure of the system of private maintenance to recover monies from non-resident fathers for child support, and the divorce explosion in the 1960s, together with the rise in childbirth amongst unmarried and divorced women with their dependent children created an exponential rise of dependency on the State. With the advent of the CS Agency following the CSA 1991 it was envisaged that there would be a residual role for the courts in respect of those parents not in receipt of State benefit and therefore not mandated to go through the CS Agency with regard to an assessment of child maintenance. Indeed, in the early days after the CSA 1991, John Dewar argued in 1992 that with the introduction of the Act, it seemed unlikely that MCA 1973, ss 23–25 would survive for much longer.

However, the MCA 1973 has survived. And indeed since no one is mandated to apply to the Child Maintenance Service cases concerning financial provision for children still do proceed through the courts.

So what then is the role of the MCA 1973?

MATRIMONIAL CAUSES ACT 1973, SS 23–25

The Matrimonial and Family Proceedings Act 1984 (MFPA 1984) amended the MCA 1973 in two significant ways; first, in the event of divorce or nullity (dissolution of civil partnerships), the court should give first consideration to the welfare of a minor or any child of the family when making financial arrangements. Section 25 provides that 'it shall be the duty of the court' when deciding whether, and in what manner to exercise powers including those referred to earlier to have regard to 'all the circumstances of the case, first consideration being given to the welfare, while a minor, of any child of the family who has not attained the age of eighteen'.

Note that the legislation mentions first consideration must be given to a child of the family and secondly, the court should try to achieve a 'clean break' between the parties in respect of financial settlement. The MCA 1973, s 25 as amended provided for the following orders to be made: capital lump sum, matrimonial property, orders for weekly periodical payments for a wife (two types, fixed term/periodical payments), orders for weekly periodical payments for a child. Section 25(3) sets out the matters to which the court must have regard when making orders for children. These factors include: the financial needs of the child, financial resources of the child, physical or mental disability, the child's education.

Financial provision for spouse carers

Clean break and children

If the parents of a child were married or civil partners and are now going through a divorce or dissolution then the court has the power to make a range of financial orders in favour of any child who is a 'child of the family' (s 23 of the Matrimonial Causes Act 1973; s 72 of the Civil Partnership Act 2004). A 'child of the family' was defined in s 52 of the Matrimonial Causes Act as a child of both the parties or any other child who has been treated by both parties as a child of their family.

After 1984, following implementation of the clean break principle, there was a decline in periodical payments to wives and a move wherever possible to lump sum settlements.

In *S v S* [1986] Fam 189, the husband, Ringo Starr (the Beatles drummer), was extremely wealthy, and the court had to decide whether to grant the variation application by Starr (Starkey) in making a once and for all capital settlement. The court did so, ending the wife's periodical payments of £70,000 per annum, substituting a capital lump sum. The clean break was to be achieved by considering earning capacity and the steps each party should/could take to acquire this. This soon became a controversial issue, as often scant regard was paid to the reality of a wife who had not worked and instead had cared for a family, who was unable or less able to provide a prospective employer with skills, experience and qualifications, and therefore whose position in the labour market was not a strong one.

It became apparent that maintenance for children could not be considered in isolation from maintenance payments and/or other financial settlement on the resident parent. Indeed, financial provision for children in its various forms was enmeshed with financial provision for the carer. (It is to be noted that in those cases where the Child Maintenance Service has jurisdiction the courts have no power to order a maintenance order.)

The courts can however make periodical payments orders for the benefit of children of the family with the consent of both parties. In addition since the Child Maintenance Service maintenance calculation only covers gross income of up to £3,000 per week it cannot consider cases involving wealthy parents and so such cases come under the jurisdiction of the courts.

The Children Act 1989, schedule 1, paragraph 1 and paragraph 2 – who can make the application?

> Where the parents of a child are not married or in a civil partnership then neither the Matrimonial Causes Act nor the Civil Partnership Act will apply. An application under the Children Act can be made by a parent, guardian or special guardian or the person named in a child arrangements order as a person with whom the child is to live.

This could be a grandparent making the application on behalf of the child for payments from one or both parents. For the purposes of the Act parent is given a very wide definition to include married and unmarried parents, same-sex parents and any party to a marriage or civil partners in relation to whom the child is a child of the family. This provision can also be used where one parent is outside the jurisdiction which is significant since the Child Support provisions would not apply.

The Act also allows an adult child to make an application against his or her parents but only where the parents are living in separate households. The child must either be in full-time education or special circumstances apply for example the child has a disability.

The respondent to the application includes the parents or stepparents but not guardians or special guardians.

Financial orders under the Children Act 1989

A wide number of orders can be made including periodical payments and lump sum orders. The powers of the court differ as to whether the application is from an adult child or a minor with the powers reduced in the case of an adult child. The three main orders are;

a. **Periodical payments.** These are payments made on a regular basis to the applicant for the benefit of the child. They can be secured or unsecured. If the respondent fails to make the payment where the payment is secured it is possible to seek an order for sale of the asset. The power to make periodical payments is more limited since this is the jurisdiction of the Child Support Act and applies only in exceptional cases such as where a parent is outside the jurisdiction or the paying parent earns in excess of £3000 per week. If the case transfers to the Child Maintenance Service then the payments under the Children Act will cease.

b. **Transfer or settlement of property.** This is most likely in connection with the family home. No minor can own property under law, so this would have to be property held under a trust. In *A v A (Financial Provision for Child)* [1995] 1 FCR 309, Ward J made a property settlement for the child and held that it should be by way of trust rather than an outright transfer to the child. 'The terms of that trust . . . should be that the property be conveyed to trustees . . . to hold the same for A for a term which shall terminate six months after A has attained the age of 18, or six months after she has completed her full-time education, which will include her tertiary education, whoever is latest. . . . The mother's obligation is to look after A, and A's financial need is to provide a roof over the head of her caretaker.' There are wide powers under the Act and include the power to transfer a secured tenancy from one parent to the sole name of the other as shown in *K v K (Minors: Property Transfer)* [1992] 2 FLR 220.

c. **Lump sums.** The court has the power to order lump sum payments either in one sum or in separate instalments. The power can be used to order a lump sum to be used in a range of ways and not simply towards the care of the child. It was held in *CF v KM (Financial Provision for a Child: Costs of Legal Proceedings)* [2011] 1 FLR 208 that courts had jurisdiction under the Children Act 1989

Sch.1 para 1(2)(c) to order a lump sum payment to contribute to the costs of a claim under Sch.1 and to the costs of proceedings under s 8 during the course of the proceedings.

Under Schedule 1 Paragraph 4 when considering applications under the 1989 Act the court must consider all the circumstances including:

a.   The income, earning capacity, property and other financial resources which [the applicant, parents and the person in whose favour the order would be made] has or is likely to have in the foreseeable future;

b.   the financial needs, obligations and responsibilities which each person mentioned in sub-paragraph (4) has or is likely to have in the foreseeable future;

c.   the financial needs of the child;

d.   the income, earning capacity (if any), property and other financial resources of the child;

e.   any physical or mental disability of the child;

f.   the manner in which the child was being, or was expected to be, educated or trained.

'All the circumstances' of the case includes considering the standard of living enjoyed by the parents in relation to the child. So awards have been made which ensure that in circumstances where one parent is very wealthy the parent with care lives in circumstances which are such that a child feels comfortable living in the houses of both parents. In *J v C (Child Financial Provision)* [1999] 1 FLR 152, provision was made for a child of unmarried parents whose relationship broke down before the child was born. The father became a millionaire after winning the national lottery and the mother who was living on benefits in rented accommodation made an application under Schedule 1. Hale J discussed how the court should approach cases where one parent becomes wealthy after the breakdown of the relationship and held that the child is entitled to be brought up in circumstances which bear some sort of relationship with the non-resident parent's current resources and standard of living. The court ordered the father to buy the mother a four bedroomed house to be held on trust until the child was 21 or completed full-time education as well as enough money to furnish the property and also to buy her a car. In *Re P (A Child: Financial Provision)* [2003] EWCA Civ 837, an extremely wealthy businessman was ordered to pay substantially increased payments to the mother of a child born after a period of cohabitation. The judge at first instance had made provision for a house for the mother and costs of furnishing the house and provision for a car and periodical payments, but on appeal these were increased. The main principles from *J v C* were followed. Bodey J commented:

> it is in quantifying the mother's reasonable needs as carer of the child that a tension emerges in such cases as this where the father is very wealthy. This tension is between seeking to achieve that the child has a standard of living bearing some sort of relationship with the father's current resources and standard of living, yet that the mother is not in the process provided for just the same as if she and the father had undertaken the commitment of marriage.

The Court of Appeal raised the amount awarded for the purchase of a house from £450,000 to £1 million as well as £100,000 for the internal decoration of it (raised from £30,000) and periodical payments of £70,000 raised from £35,000. In *CA v DR* [2021] EWFC 21, a very wealthy father was ordered to make a lump sum payment allowing the mother to buy a large house with at least five bedrooms in Kent as well as an allowance of £110,000 every four years to purchase a new car. The court refused to make an additional order for pension contributions for her benefit, something the court determined was not permitted under Sch 1.

In *UD v DN* [2022] EWCA 1947 (Civ), the Court of Appeal reviewed an order made by the High Court in favour of adult children. He held that the court had such a power if the application had been made before the children reached their 18th birthdays and if there were exceptional circumstances. There was evidence that the very wealthy father had been abusive to the children in the past. This had been the first such order made in favour of adult children. The Court of Appeal overturned the decision but upheld the power of a court to make such an order. According to Lord Justice Moylan: 'it is, in my view, clear that such power as there is to order financial provision in favour of an adult child who is not in education or training is limited to "special" or "exceptional" circumstances'. He concluded that there were no such circumstances in this case. He said that:

> With all due respect to the Judge, seeking to protect children from financial pressure or 'manipulation' that a parent might seek to exert does not begin to come within the scope of a 'special' or 'exceptional' circumstance which would justify the outright capital award which the Judge made or, indeed, any award.

Human rights and child support under the 1991 Act: legal challenges

As discussed earlier the failures of the Child Support Agency resulted in an application, amongst others, by a mother testing whether the CSA 1991 was human rights compliant, since she was excluded from access to the court in her efforts over a long period to get the non–resident parent to pay what he owed, that is to effect the order made in favour of the child in her care.

In *R (Kehoe) v Secretary of State for Work and Pensions* [2005] UKHL 48, the mother sought a declaration that the provisions of the CSA 1991 were incompatible with Art 6 of the ECHR because they had the effect of denying a parent access to court in connection with disputes as to whether the non-resident parent had paid or ought to pay the sums due under a maintenance assessment, or as to the manner in which the maintenance assessment should be enforced. She sought a further declaration that delay on the part of the CS Agency constituted a breach of her Art 6 rights, and claimed damages under the Human Rights Act 1998, s 7. The Secretary of State appealed against the judge's finding that the mother's inability personally to enforce arrears of maintenance engaged her Art 6 rights. The mother cross-appealed against the judge's conclusion that the scheme under the CSA 1991 was compliant with Art 6 of the ECHR. The court allowed the Secretary of State's appeal, dismissing the mother's cross-appeal.

(See Wikeley 1995 and 2006 for a more detailed discussion of this decision.)

Wikeley concludes that children have a right to child support and that it is incumbent on the Government, as expressed in Treaty obligations, to develop a system that is effective. He argues, too, that higher child support liabilities have a beneficial effect not just on children's material well-being but on their 'post separation cognitive development' (p 473). Children's material and psychological well-being depends upon an adequate and effective system of financial provision.

In *R (Green) v Secretary of State for the Department for Work and Pensions* [2010] EWHC 1278 (Admin), the parents had agreed that their child was to be educated privately and they took out a policy to cover the expense. However, when the policy matured it was insufficient so the father paid the outstanding school fees. The mother applied to the Child Support Agency (CSA), acknowledging that the father paid the school fees but explaining that she received no child maintenance. The father told the CSA that he paid the school fees, and the CSA asked the mother if she was willing to have such payments offset against child maintenance, she said that she was not. The CSA assessed the child maintenance due from the father at £74.70 pw, making no allowance for the father's school fees payments. The school fees were £270 per term, and the father had made a lump sum payment of £6,000 to the school to secure the child's place until he was 16. His appeal was unsuccessful; he was told that payment of school fees was voluntary, and the CSA served the father with a notice of intention to apply for a liability order in respect of arrears of £10,203.14. The father commenced judicial review proceedings, arguing that the CSA had failed to exercise its discretion as to whether to offset the school fees. The court granted judicial review and quashed the decision not to offset the school fees.

See also *Bird v Secretary of State for Work and Pensions* [2008] EWHC 3159 where it was held that the payment of mortgage instalments could be offset against maintenance payments.

In *Child Maintenance and Enforcement Commission v Beesley and Whyman* [2010] EWCA 1344 (Civ), the non-resident father was liable to pay child support, and his arrears amounted to £25,610.90. An individual voluntary arrangement (IVA) was agreed by the father's creditors. The father's case was that the C-MEC was bound by the terms of the IVA. The C-MEC submitted that it was not. The judge held that the C-MEC was a creditor capable of being bound by an IVA, but set aside the IVA on the ground that it unfairly prejudiced the Commission. The Commission appealed; the father cross-appealed. The court allowed the appeal, dismissing the cross-appeal.

Financial support for children: the future

In a matter of just over 30 years three separate Government bodies have been responsible for overseeing the financial support given to children. It was assumed that the role of the courts would be merely residual, but cases continue to be heard in both the High Court and the magistrates' courts.

The introduction of a system which encourages parents by a number of means, 'carrots and sticks' as described by Nicholas Wikeley, to draw up their own arrangements is a system to be applauded but whether this is addressing all the faults of the ill-fated Child Support Agency is doubtful. Arrears still accrue, but the new system has limited scope for appealing assessments which may be incorrect and may be the very reason for arrears building up. An inherent problem remains in the new system that parents with care are penalised financially for the failure of a non-paying parent which appears as a double penalty. Finally the failure to pay by so many non-resident parents remains a difficult issue which repeated attempts to address have rarely been successful.

Self-test questions

1. John Dewar argued that with the introduction of the CSA 1991, it seemed unlikely that the MCA 1973, ss 23–25 could survive for much longer without a root and branch reappraisal. To what extent is this argument true today? Has the MCA 1973 a continuing role to play in assessing financial maintenance for a child?

2. What are the problems for mothers who have experienced domestic violence in the requirement that naming the non-resident father is a precondition of receiving benefit? Consider changes made to the current legislation which addresses this. To what extent do these changes protect mothers who have experienced domestic abuse?

3. What is the logic behind the thinking that places the resident parent as central in disclosing details of the non-resident parent for the purpose of child support but, as *Kehoe* demonstrates, denies the resident party the right to participate in the proceedings for enforcement? Has that logic now been set aside?

4. Kai and Jan have lived together for six years. Kai is the chief executive of a large company and travels regularly; Jan works in finance but since having twins four years ago she has only worked part time. They have a large house near the sea in Sussex and a flat in London which is sufficiently large for a live-in nanny to have a separate flat. They split up last year. Jan moved out and is currently living in a modest flat in London without room for a nanny, making it very difficult for her to work. Kai is paying towards the care of the children, but his payments are irregular and Jan is struggling to cope. The children stay with him once a month for a weekend at the London flat.

    Advise Jan on what steps she should take to ensure that Kai pays regularly towards the children. What difference would it make to your advice if Kai had a less well paid job?

References

Altman, Scott, 'A Theory of Child Support' (2003) 17 *International Journal of Law, Policy and the Family* 173

https://api.parliament.uk/historic-hansard/lords/1990/oct/29/child-maintenance

Barnados 'At What Cost?' (October 2022) www.barnados.org.uk/sites/default/files/2022 (accessed 10.09.2024)

Bamforth, Nicholas, 'The Benefits of Marriage in All But Name? Same-Sex Couples and the Civil Partnership Act 2004' [2007] *Child and Family Law Quarterly* 133

Bird, Roger, *Child Maintenance* (3rd edn, Family Law 1996)

Brown, L Neville, 'Maintenance and Esoterism' (1968) 31 *Modern Law Review* 121

Childs, Mary and Rebecca Boden, 'Paying for Procreation: Child Support Arrangements in the UK' (1996) 4(2) *Feminist Legal Studies* 131

DHSS White Paper, Children Come First (Cmd 1264, 1990)

Douglas, Gillian, 'Towards an Understanding of the Basis of Obligation and Commitment in Family Law' (2016) 36 *Legal Studies – Society of Public Teachers of Law*

Edwards, Susan and Ann Halpern, 'Regional "Injustice" Financial Provision on Divorce' [1990] *Journal of Social Welfare Law* 71

Edwards, Susan and Ann Halpern, 'Parental Responsibility: An Instrument of Social Policy' [1992] *Family Law* 113

Edwards, Susan, Ann Halpern and Carole Gould, 'The Continuing Saga of Maintaining the Family after Divorce' [1990] *Family Law* 31–35

Gingerbread, 'Gingerbread Calls on the Government to Scrap Unfair Child Maintenance Fees' (2021)www.gingerbread.org.uk/our-work/news-and-views/dwp-unfair-child-maintenance-fees-408-million-owed[0]

Gov.UK, 'Child Support Agency Annual Report and Accounts 2005/2006' (2006) https://assets.publishing.service.gov.uk-child-support-agency-annual-accounts-2005/06

Gov.UK, 'Child Maintenance Service Statistics Data to September 2023' (2023) www.gov.uk/government/statistics/child-maintenance-service-statistics-data-to-september-2023[0]

Hansard, 'Child Maintanence' HL Deb vol 522 cc1695-708 (29.10.1990) https://api.parliament.uk/historic-hansard/lords/1990/oct/29/child-maintenance[0] [0](accessed 10.09.2024)

Kaganas, Felicity and Christine Piper, 'Shared Parenting – a 70% Solution?' [2002] *Child and Family Law Quarterly* 365

King, Anthony and Ivor Crewe, *Chapter 6: Blunders of Our Governments* (Oneworld 2014)

Natalier, Kristin, 'State Facilitated Economic Abuse: A Structural Analysis of Men Deliberately Withholding Child Support' (2018) 26 *Feminist Legal Studies* 121

RCPCH, 'Child Health Unequalities Driven by Child Poverty in the UK – Position Statement' (2022) www.rcpch.ac.uk/resources/child -health-inequalties-position-statement (accessed 10.09.2024)

Sheldon, Sally, 'Unwilling Fathers and Abortion: Terminating Men's Child Support Obligations' (2003) 66 *Modern Law Review* 175

Takayesu, Mark and Steven Eldred, 'Setting Appropriate Child Support Orders and Addressing Barriers: Research and Policy Implications to Improve Payments and Compliance' in Paul Beaumont et al. (eds) *The Recovery of Maintenance in the EU and Worldwide* (Hart 2016)

Wikeley, Nicholas, 'Child Support: Carrots and Sticks' [2008] *Family Law* 1102 https://cpag.org.uk/news/official-child-poverty-statistics-

Wikeley, Nicholas, *Child Support Law and Policy* (Hart Publishing 2006)

Wikeley, Nicholas, 'A Duty but Not a Right: Child Support After R (Kehoe) v Secretary of State for Work and Pensions' [2006] *Child and Family Law Quarterly* 287

Wikeley, Nicholas, 'Kehoe v Secretary of State for Work and Pensions: No Redress When the Child Support Agency Fails to Deliver' (1995) 17(1) *Child and Family Law Quarterly* 113

Further reading

Eekelaar, John, 'Are Parents Morally Obliged to Care for Their Children?' (1991) 11 *Oxford Journal of Legal Studies* 340

Ellman, Ira, Stephen McKay, Joanna Miles and Caroline Bryson, 'Child Support Judgments: Comparing Public Policy to the Public's Policy' (2014) 28 International Journal of Law, Policy and the Family 274

Gilmore, Stephen, 'Re B (Contact: Child Support) – Horses and Carts: Contact and Child Support' [2007] Child and Family Law Quarterly 357

Henshaw Recommendations (Recovering Child Support (2006) Cm 6894)

Mahmoud, Sharon and Catherine Hallam, 'Schedule 1 and the CSA: Getting into the Top Up Zone' [2011] Family Law 266

Married or Not in Britain Today, Key Facts, Key Trends www.oneplusone.org.uk

Millar, Jane, 'Family Obligations and Social Policy: The Case of Child Support' (1996) 17 Policy Studies 181

Pirrie, James, 'Child Support Update, Part 1' [2002] Family Law 195

The Rt Hon Lord Justice Thorpe, 'London – the Divorce Capital of the World' [2009] Family Law 21

Index

Note: page numbers in **bold** indicate a table on the corresponding page.

abduction 262–3, 414–16, 419–20;
prohibited steps and different
domiciles 414–16; relocation
residence and contact 414–15; and
wardship 415–16, 459–63
abortion 450
abuse 7; 1970s reform measures 117;
assault and coercive control 121–3;
child abuse 468–79, **479**; and child
support 572; civil remedies for
domestic violence and abuse 123–4;
contact with abusive parents 406–10;
contemporary definitions and very
public cases 110–15; court's discretion
133; domestic abuse is also a pattern of
abuse 114–15; domestic abuse
incidence and the criminal law
119–23; domestic abuse may also
include sexual abuse 113–14; domestic
violence/abuse protection orders/
notices 141; dowry abuse 140; of the
elderly 232–3; emotional 538;
enforcement 133, **134**; entitled
persons 124–8; ex parte orders
(without notice) occupation and
non-molestation 134–6; explanations
of domestic abusee 117–18; female
genital mutilation protection orders
140, **141**; feminist jurisprudential
challenges 119; forced marriage
136–9, **139**; history 115–19; legal
landmarks 116–17; and the media

446–7; more protection needed
141–5; non-entitled persons 128–30;
non-molestation orders 131–4;
number of occupation and
non-molestation order applications
and orders granted 130–1, **131**;
occupation rights 124–31; other forms
of abuse and legal protections 136–41;
pattern of 114–15; return hearings
135–6; risk domestic abuse (child)
424–5; sexual 113–14; summary
109–10; undertakings 134; what
constitutes non-molestation 131–2;
who may apply 132–3; *see also* child
abuse; child protection; significant
harm
academic community 358
accountability 12
activism, judicial 373–6
adolescent autonomy: adolescent
participation in legal proceedings
367–73; changing attitudes 371–2;
chronological age 354; competent/
incompetent putative transgender
adolescent 365–7; end game 376–7;
family proceedings 372–3; from
consequences to competence 358–9;
general principles and sources of law
343–9; how can an adolescent acquire
competence 353–5; judicial activism
or judicial paternalism 373–6; maturity
to understand 354–5; medication/

sedation 362–3; not old enough or not of sufficient understanding 368–9; only a right to refuse consent 355–9; organ transplant 361–2; reaction of academic community 358; refusal 359–63; sexual intercourse and the dissenters 352–3; simply inappropriate 370–1; summary 342–3; test of competency 367–8; three ages and stages of child rights 346–9; under 16-year-olds and the Gillick competence precept 350–3; voice of the child 345–6; wardship 363–7

adoption: adoption order 321–2; adoption or special guardianship order 322–9, **323**; adoptive parents 294; appealing adoption order and refusal 326; appealing/revoking placement order 320; appealing a special guardianship order 324–5; birth fathers following adoption 290–1; blood tie 336–7; child's presence 322; contact with parents 329–30; court orders 313–19; current legal framework 307–12; discharging a special guardianship order 325–6, **325**; dismissing appeals 326; dispensing with consent 315–18; grandparents 331; history of UK adoption 303–4; international adoption 331–4; legislation 304; 'nothing else will do' 334–7; opposing making of an adoption order 326–7; other orders 329–31; overarching principles, judicial decision making and consent 313–15; placement order 319–21; post adoption contact 335–6; racial and cultural origin 310–11; by relatives/foster parents 307; religious preferences 311–12; residence orders rather than adoption 329; setting aside adoption order 327–9; siblings 330–1; by stepparents 306; suitability and matching 307–8; summary 301–2; upholding placement order 321; waiting time 318–19; welfare v best interests 332–4; when adoption is cheap 334–5; who can be adopted and who can adopt 304–7

adult children: care for elders 231–2; financial maintenance 248–50

adultery 153–6, 165–6

advance decisions 229

age: and child custody 392–3, 394–5; civil partnership 40–1; financial consequences 203–4; marriage 24; not old enough or not of sufficient understanding 368–9

agreements, judicial approaches to 209–22; agreements made in relationship breakdown 209–11; cohabitants 218–22; pre-nuptial or pre-civil partnership agreements 211–18

agreements, relationship/pre-nuptial 208–9, 211–18

agreements to enter into a civil partnership 20

agreements to share the property 84–96; detrimental reliance 87; familial approach to agreements 86–7; financial detriment 87–8; move to pragmatism 89–96; quantification of the beneficial interest 89, 91–6

alternative divorce models 165–7

Anglican Church, marriage in 31–2

anticipatory declarations: wardship 444–5

assault 121–3

assumption of responsibility: and death 244–5

asylum-seeking children, unaccompanied: and wardship 462

attachment (parent/child relationship) 277–81

attachment orders 188

autonomy *see* adolescent autonomy

bankruptcy: trusts of land 104–5

bars to relief: where civil partnership is voidable 70; where marriage is voidable 68

behaviour 156–8

beneficiaries: trusts of land 104

best interests v welfare 332–4

bilateral agreements: and child custody 419–20

biological heterosexual family 265–7

biological parentage/origins 562; and contact 336–7; court orders parental responsibility 287–9; father's rights are 'sacred' 258–9; and the natural parent presumption 265–8

birth fathers following adoption 290–1

blood transfusions/blood products 359–63

bona vacantia 240

breakdown of marriage 161–2; by both parties 166; by one party 166; procedure for divorce 162

burden of care: elders 231–2

buying a house 79–82; equitable title 80–2; legal ownership 79–80

CAFCASS *see* Children and Family Court Advisory and Support Service (CAFCASS)

CAO *see* child arrangement order (CAO); child assessment order (CAO)

capacity to marry 23–4

capacity to register a civil partnership 38–9

care for the child, responsibility to 282

care of elders 231–2

care plans: child protection 487

care orders: at home 545–6; and sexual abuse 530–4

carers: adoptive parents 294; attachment 277–81; biological father's rights are 'sacred' 258–9; biological heterosexual family 265–7; biological parents and the natural parent presumption 265–8; court denial of parental responsibility applications 291; court orders parental responsibility 286–94; deciding in favor of non-biological over natural parents 261; de facto fathers' right to truth 291; demise of paternal authority and rise of parental responsibility 259–63; the exclusive father 257–9; family rights 295–6; fathers 261–2, 285; financial provision for spouse carers of children 574; foster parents 295; gestational parentage 268–77; international arrangements (surrogacy) 276–7; 'in the custody of the parent' 260–1; kidnapping and child abduction 262–3; legal parents and parental responsibility 281–4; the limits of language 279–80; mothers 285; mothers over fathers 261–2; mothers refusing to consent to blood tests 287–9; other parents 294–5; parental responsibility order 286–7, **287**; parental responsibility when not the parent 294; parenting histories 257–9; putting biological parentage to proof 287; reproductive technology and the legal parent 268–71; reproductive technology reform 273–4; responsibility to act for the child in legal proceedings 284; responsibility to care for the child 282; responsibility for the child's religion 283; responsibility to consent to medical treatment of the child 284; responsibility to ensure the child's education 282–3; responsibility involves administering child's property and enter into contracts 284; responsibility to protect the child and not to inflict punishment or physical discipline 283–4; responsibility to withhold consent or consent to marriage overridden by statute 284; right of child to know 289–91; sexual orientation and gender reassignment 278–9; social and psychological parentage 277–81; special guardians/guardians 295; statutory exceptions to the natural parent presumption 267–8; summary 255–6; surrogacy 274–7; terminating parental responsibility 291–4; three parents 273; transgender father 280–1; transgender parentage and IVF 271–2; the unfit parent 263–5; unmarried fathers 285–6; who is entitled 285–6; who is a parent in fact 263–5

care v supervision 545–7

Catholic marriage 32

causation theory 556

chameleon concept of unreasonableness 315–18

change in circumstances, likely effect on the child 394

Child AB 398–9

child abuse: changing perceptions of abuse 469–70; from discrete incidents to totality context 472–8; emotional abuse 475–8; epidemic 478–9, **479**; historical denial 468–72; neglect 478; physical abuse 473–4; sexual abuse 474–5; slow death in full view of protective agencies 470–72; totality context approach 473–8; *see also* child protection

child arrangement order (CAO): for contact 403–6; for residence 401–3, **401**

child assessment order (CAO) 496

child custody: abusive partners and contact strategies 406–10; child arrangement order (CAO) for contact 403–6; child arrangement order (CAO) for residence 401–3, **401**; child does not want contact 404–6; child objections 421–2; child voice in international relocation 420–1; child welfare paramount 389–90; conciliation and mediation 387–8; different domiciles 414–16; disagreements, education, name change, health care 411; enforcing contact 410; grandparents 409–10; history 383–5; 'implacable hostility' 407–9; international law 416–25; international relocation and abduction 414–25; legal framework 388–9; legitimacy crisis in private law 425–6; no presumption in favour of applicant parent 422–5; 'pro contact' even where domestic violence 406–7; prohibited steps order 412–16; regional variations in orders 413–14, **414**; removal and return, deciding the case, habitual residence 418–20; right to contact 403–4; shared residence 402–3; specific issue order 410; summary 381–3; welfare checklist 391–401; when parents fall out today 385–6

Child Maintenance system: evaluation of 572

child protection 8; changing perceptions of abuse 469–70; child protection conference 487; child protection plan 485–6; child protection register 485; court interim orders 497–8; court ordered investigations 484–9, **488**; division of functions 497; emergency orders 490–4, **494**; emotional abuse 475–8; epidemic of abuse 478–9, **479**; exclusion order provision 494–6; high profile cases 468; historical denial of abuse 468–72; how well is local authority doing in child protection 504–5; interim care orders 497–8; interim supervision order 498;

investigative process 481; legal and procedural framework of safeguarding 479–90; medical expert 498–502; neglect 478; orders during the preliminary stage 490–6; partnership principle 480–1; physical abuse 473–4; and public authority liability and human rights 489–90; referral process 482–3, **482–3**; requires truth 498–504; right not to self-incriminate 502–4; sexual abuse 474–5; significant harm 481; slow death in full view of protective agencies 470–2; summary 467–8; totality context approach to abuse 472–8

children 7–8; abduction 262–3; child poverty 555; children of children who have killed 445–6; ethnic minority children in care 521; intolerable life 454–7; and the media 445–7; observing the child 523–4; qualifying child 560–1; responsibility to act in legal proceedings 284; responsibility to care for 282; responsibility to consent to medical treatment of 284; responsibility to ensure education of 282–3; responsibility involving property and contracts 284; responsibility to protect 283–4; responsibility for religion of 283; responsibility to withhold consent or consent to marriage 284; rights of (general principles and sources of law) 343–9; sexual exploitation 448–9; similar children 519–20; three ages and stages of 346–9; voice of 345–6; *see also* adolescent autonomy; adoption; adult children; child abuse; child custody; child protection; child support; parents/parenting; significant harm; wardship

child protection: changing perceptions of abuse 469–70; child protection and public authority liability and human rights 489–90; child protection requires truth 498–504; court interim orders 497–8; court ordered investigations 484–9, **488**; division of functions 497; emergency orders 490–4, **494**; emotional abuse 475–8; epidemic of abuse 478–9, **479**; exclusion order provision 494–6; high

profile cases 468; historical denial of
abuse 468–72; how well is local
authority doing in child protection
504–5; interim care orders 497–8;
interim supervision order 498;
investigative process 481; legal and
procedural framework of safeguarding
479–90; medical expert 498–502;
neglect 478; orders during the
preliminary stage 490–6; partnership
principle 480–1; physical abuse
473–4; referral process 482–3, **482–3**;
right not to self-incriminate 502–4;
sexual abuse 474–5; significant harm
481; slow death in full view of
protective agencies 470–2; summary
467–8; totality context approach to
abuse 472–8
Children and Family Court Advisory and
Support Service (CAFCASS) 313,
410, 415, 422, 453, 504, 531
children and family life: adoptive parents
294; attachment 277–81; biological
father's rights are 'sacred' 258–9;
biological parents and the natural
parent presumption 265–8; court
denial of parental responsibility
applications 291; court orders parental
responsibility 286–94; deciding in
favour of non-biological over natural
parents 261; de facto fathers' right to
truth 291; demise of paternal authority
and rise of parental responsibility
259–63; the exclusive father 257–9;
fathers 261–2, 285; foster parents 295;
gestational parentage 268–77;
international arrangements (surrogacy)
276–7; 'in the custody of the parent'
260–1; kidnapping and child
abduction 262–3; legal parents and
parental responsibility 281–4; the
limits of language 279–80; mothers
285; mothers over fathers 261–2;
mothers refusing to consent to blood
tests 287–9; other parents 294–5;
parental responsibility order 286–7,
287; parental responsibility when not
the parent 294; parenting histories
257–9; putting biological parentage to
proof 287; reproductive technology
and the legal parent 268–71;
reproductive technology reform

273–4; responsibility to act for the
child in legal proceedings 284;
responsibility to care for the child 282;
responsibility for the child's religion
283; responsibility to consent to
medical treatment of the child 284;
responsibility to ensure the child's
education 282–3; responsibility
involves administering child's property
and enter into contracts 284;
responsibility to protect the child and
not to inflict punishment or physical
discipline 283–4; responsibility to
withhold consent or consent to
marriage overridden by statute 284;
right of child to know 289–91; sexual
orientation and gender reassignment
278–9; social and psychological
parentage 277–81; special guardians/
guardians 295; statutory exceptions to
the natural parent presumption 267–8;
surrogacy 274–7; terminating parental
responsibility 291–4; three parents
273; transgender father 280–1;
transgender parentage and IVF 271–2;
unfit parent 263–5; unmarried fathers
285–6; who is entitled 285–6; who is
a parent in fact 263–5
child support: background 555–7, 558–9;
calculating the formula for payment
570–3; child poverty 555; Child
Support Agency (CSA) 563–5;
financial provision for spouse carers
574; history 557–8; and human rights
577–9; parental responsibility 568–70;
private arena of 573; purpose 560–3;
recovery of maintenance 559–60;
reform 565–8; theoretical background
555–6; theoretical basis 556–7; who
can make the application 574–7
Child Support Agency (CSA) 563;
failings of enforcement mechanism
and subsequent reforms 563–5
child welfare: abusive partners and contact
strategies 406–10; child arrangement
order (CAO) for contact 403–6; child
arrangement order (CAO) for
residence 401–3, **401**; child does not
want contact 404–6; child objections
421–2; child voice in international
relocation 420–1; child welfare
paramount 389–90; conciliation and

mediation 387–8; different domiciles 414–16; disagreements, education, name change, health care 411; enforcing contact 410; grandparents 409–10; history 383–5; 'implacable hostility' 407–9; international law 416–25; international relocation and abduction 414–25; legal framework 388–9; legitimacy crisis in private law 425–6; no presumption in favour of applicant parent 422–5; 'pro contact' even where domestic violence 406–7; prohibited steps order 412–16; regional variations in orders 413–14, **414**; removal and return, deciding the case, habitual residence 418–20; right to contact 403–4; shared residence 402–3; specific issue order 410; summary 381–3; welfare checklist 391–401; when parents fall out today 385–6

circumcision: and custody 397–8

civil ceremonies 29–32; marriage ceremony 30–1; preliminary requirements 29; Quaker and Jewish marriages 32; religious ceremonies 31–2

civil partnerships 15–16, 38; age 40–1; agreements to enter into 20; already in a registered civil partnership 26–9, 41; bars to relief 70; capacity to register 38–9; and child support 561–2; consequences of nullity 70–2; death 242–5; delay 70; dissolution 168–9; domestic abuse 129; formalities of 41–2; mental capacity 41; prospective civil partners 222–3; statutory right of occupation for civil partners 103; voidable 69–70

'clean break' principle 196–7; and child support 574

coercive control 121–3

cohabitation: continuing cohabitation 158; domestic abuse 130; and the family home 78; financial consequences 218–22; heterosexual and same-sex 5–6, 42–5; marriage by cohabitation and repute 56; non-sexual 5–6, 17–19; presumption of marriage by 33–7; resumption of cohabitation 159–60; succession 242–5

common law marriage 33

compensation: proprietary estoppel 101

competence: in family proceedings 372–3; test of competency 367–8; see also Gillick competence

conciliation: custody battles 387–8

conduct: post-separation assets 205–7; rights of maintenance 178

consent: adolescent autonomy 355–63; adoption 313–18

constructive trusts 83–96; detrimental reliance 87; familial approach to agreements 86–7; financial detriment 87–8; move to pragmatism 89–96; quantification of the beneficial interest 89, 91–6

contact: and abusive partners 406–10; and child support 568–70; contact orders 403–6; and emergency protection order 493–4, **494**; and relocation residence 414–15; and wardship 461–3

continuing cohabitation 158

contracts for maintenance 176

contracts with children 284

conventions see international conventions

court, residual role of (child support) 572–3

court interim orders (child protection) 497–8; division of functions 497; interim care orders 497–8; interim supervision order 498

Court of Protection 230, 244, 436

court ordered investigation (child protection) 484–9, **488**; care plans 487; child protection conference 487; child protection plan 485–6; child protection register 485; duty to investigate 488–9

court orders (adoption) 313–19

court orders (parental responsibility) 286–7, **287**; and biological parentage 287–9; court denial of applications 291; de facto fathers' right to truth 291; right of child to know 289–91; termination 291–4; when not the parent 294

court proceedings, adolescent participation in 367–73; see also right to decide and to participate in court proceedings

court's discretion: domestic abuse 126–8, 129–30, 133; rights to maintenance 177

creditors: trusts of land 104–5

criminal law: and domestic abuse 119–23

culture: and adoption 310–11; and child custody 395–7

custody, child: abusive partners and contact strategies 406–10; child arrangement order (CAO) for contact 403–6; child arrangement order (CAO) for residence 401–3, **401**; child does not want contact 404–6; child objections 421–2; child voice in international relocation 420–1; child welfare paramount 389–90; conciliation and mediation 387–8; different domiciles 414–16; disagreements, education, name change, health care 411; enforcing contact 410; grandparents 409–10; history 383–5; 'implacable hostility' 407–9; international law 416–25; international relocation and abduction 414–25; legal framework 388–9; legitimacy crisis in private law 425–6; no presumption in favour of applicant parent 422–5; 'pro contact' even where domestic violence 406–7; prohibited steps order 412–16; regional variations in orders 413–14, **414**; removal and return, deciding the case, habitual residence 418–20; right to contact 403–4; shared residence 402–3; specific issue order 410; summary 381–3; welfare checklist 391–401; when parents fall out today 385–6

death: applications for financial maintenance 240–50; and child abuse 470–2; common law 234; family life after 250–3; funeral arrangements 235–7; impact on family life 233–4; intestate succession 238–40; life ending decisions (wardship) 451–9; presumption of 234–5; testate succession 237–8

decision, substitute: elders 228–31

declaration of parentage and identity 289–90

definitions/overviews: adultery 156; already married or in a registered civil partnership 26–9; civil ceremonies 29–32; civil partnership 20, 38–42; cohabitation 42–5; domestic abuse 110–15; engagement 19–20; family 4–5; family home 75–7; family law 1–3; informal marriage 33–8; marriage 20–6, 29–32; nullity 48–9; parent 263–6; rights of the child and adolescent 343–9

degrees of relationship, prohibited 25–6

delay: civil partnership 70; marriage 68–9

deportation, resisting 463

deprivation 522–3

deputies 230

desertion 158–9

detriment: proprietary estoppel 98–100

detrimental reliance: constructive trusts 87

different domiciles 414–16

disability 204–5

disagreements: and child custody 411

disasters, child victims of: and media interest 447

division of functions 497

divorce 6–7, 152–3, 155–6; adultery 156; alternative models 165–7; background to 154–5; behaviour 156–8; consequences 169; desertion 158–9; grave hardship 160–1; grounds for the decree 167–8; intolerability 156; irretrievable breakdown of marriage 161–2; judicial separation 167; new procedure 161–8; religious courts 168–9; resumption of cohabitation 159–60; statistical evidence of 153–4

domestic violence and abuse 7; 1970s reform measures 117; assault and coercive control 121–3; and child support 572; civil remedies for domestic violence and abuse 123–4; and contact 406–7; contemporary definitions and very public cases 110–15; court's discretion 133; domestic abuse is also a pattern of abuse 114–15; domestic abuse incidence and the criminal law 119–23; domestic abuse may also include sexual abuse 113–14; domestic violence/abuse protection orders/ notices 141; dowry abuse 140; enforcement 133, **134**; entitled

persons 124–8; ex parte orders (without notice) occupation and non-molestation 134–6; explanations of domestic abusee 117–18; female genital mutilation protection orders 140, **141**; feminist jurisprudential challenges 119; forced marriage 136–9, **139**; history 115–19; legal landmarks 116–17; more protection needed 141–5; non-entitled persons 128–30; non-molestation orders 131–4; number of occupation and non-molestation order applications and orders granted 130–1, **131**; occupation rights 124–31; other forms of abuse and legal protections 136–41; return hearings 135–6; risk domestic abuse 424–5; summary 109–10; undertakings 134; what constitutes non-molestation 131–2; who may apply 132–3; *see also* abuse
Domestic Proceedings and Magistrates' Court Act (DPMCA) 177–8
dowry abuse 140
DPMCA *see* Domestic Proceedings and Magistrates' Court Act (DPMCA)
dual approach 15–17
duress 59–60
duties: to deal with the deceased's body 235–7; to maintain a qualifying child 560–1

ECtHR *see* European Court of Human Rights (ECtHR)
education of children: and custody 393–4, 411; responsibility to ensure child's education 282–3
elderly, the: abuse of 232–4; adult children 231–2; applications for financial maintenance 240–50; burden of care 231–2; common law 234; death 234–52; family life after death 250–3; funeral arrangements 235–7; impact of death on family life 233–4; intestate succession 238–40; mental capacity 227–31; presumption of death 234–5; social care 231; substitute decisions 228–31; summary 227; testate succession 237–8
emergency orders 490–4; contact with the child and 493–4, **494**; emergency protection order (EPO) 490–2; ex parte orders and human rights challenges 492
emotional abuse 475–8, 538
emotional harms 537–40; emotional abuse 538; radicalisation cases 538–40
emotional needs of the child: and custody 393–4
ending relationships: alternative divorce models 165–7; civil partnerships 168; consequences of divorce 169; critique of the law 163; defence of grave hardship 160–1; divorce (background) 152–9; the five facts 156–9; government's response 164–5; grounds for the decree 167–8; irretrievable breakdown of marriage 161–2; judicial separation 167; new procedure 161–8; religious courts 168–9; resumption of cohabitation 159–60; road to reform 163–4; summary 152; *see also* financial consequences of relationships
enforcement: child support 563–5, 571; contact 410; non-molestation orders 133
engagement to marry 17, 19–20
EPO *see under* emergency orders
equitable title: buying a house 80–2
estoppel license 101; *see also* proprietary estoppel
ethnicity: and adoption 312; ethnic minority children in care 521
European Court of Human Rights (ECtHR) 9, 18–19, 24–6, 42, 142, 237, 270, 280–1, 289, 321, 337, 470, 489
evidence: burden and standard 515–16; undoing earlier decisions and fresh medical evidence 502
exceptional circumstances: family home 105–6
excluded/exempt relationships 5–6, 17–19
exclusion order provision 494–6; child assessment order 496; police removal 495–6
ex parte orders (without notice): and human rights challenges 492; occupation and non-molestation 134–6
expert opinion (child protection) 498–504; be vigilant 500–502;

medical expert 498–502; protecting parents 502–4; undoing earlier decisions and fresh medical evidence 502

explicit representations 97–8

express trusts 175

fact finding (child protection) 498–504; be vigilant 500–502; medical expert 498–502; protecting parents 502–4; undoing earlier decisions and fresh medical evidence 502

faith: and child custody 395–7

family: evolving definitions of 4–5; international 8–9

family home: beneficiaries 104; civil partnership 102–3; cohabitants and the family home 78; compensation 101; constructive trusts 83–4; creditors and bankruptcy 104–5; detriment 98–9; effect of statutory right on third parties 104; equitable title 80–2; estoppel license 101; exceptional circumstances 105–6; fee simple 100–101; home sharing 78–9; legal ownership 79–80; nature of the representation 97–8; problems of home ownership 77; property in joint names 91–6; property is in sole name 84–91; proprietary estoppel 96–102; reliance 99–100; resulting trusts 82–3; statutory right of occupation for spouses and civil partners 103; summary 75; wide range of remedies 100–101

family law (introduction): accountability 12; challenges to 6–8, 10; child protection 8; children 7–8; definition 1–3; divorce 6–7; domestic abuse 7; evolving definitions of family 4–5; excluded relationships 5–6; financial matters 7; human rights 9; international conventions 9–10; international family 8; judges 10–12; rights and obligations 3

family life: abuse of the elderly 232–4; adult children 231–2; applications for financial maintenance 240–50; biological heterosexual family 265–7; burden of care 231–2; common law 234; after death 250–52; family rights 295–6; funeral arrangements 235–7;

interstate succession 238–40; mental capacity amongst older people 227–31; presumption of death 234–5; social care 231; substitute decisions 228–31; summary 227, 255–6; testate succession 237–8; see also children and family life

fathers: birth fathers following adoption 290–1; and child support 566–7; de facto fathers' right to truth 291; mothers over 261–2; parental responsibility 285–6; parenting histories 257–9; putative fathers' right to know 290; stepfathers 294–5; transgender 280–1; unmarried fathers 285–6; see also parents/parenting

fault-based divorce 166

fee simple: proprietary estoppel 100–101

female genital mutilation (FGM): protection orders 140, **141**; significant harm 516

feminist jurisprudence: and domestic abuse 119

fiancées 222–3

financial awards 181–2

financial consequences of relationships: agreements made on relationship breakdown 209–111; cohabitants 218–22; fiancées and prospective civil partners 222–3; general overview 178–80; guidance from case law 189–93; judicial approaches to agreements 209–22; judicial intervention 189; lack of overall guiding objective 189; looking afresh 186–8; 'non-relationship assets' 198–200; orders available to the court 181–6; personal property 173–4; post-separation assets 200–207; potential reform for the award of financial remedies 207–8; reaching financial settlement 180–1; reform of the guidelines 207; relationship or pre-nuptial agreements 208–9, 211–18; return to statutory guidelines 193–8; rights to maintenance during the relationship 176; statutory rights to maintenance 176–8; summary 172–3; trusts 174–6

financial detriment: constructive trusts 87

financial maintenance/provision: abolition of a wife's right 176;

cohabitation 221–2; contracts for
maintenance 176; and death 240–50;
for spouse carers of children 574; *see
also* financial provision for children
financial matters 7
financial needs 209
financial orders 71–2; child support
575–7
financial provision for children:
background 555–7, 558–9; calculating
the formula for payment 570–3; child
poverty 555; Child Support Agency
(CSA) 563–5; financial provision for
spouse carers 574; history 557–8; and
human rights 577–9; parental
responsibility 568–70; private arena of
573; purpose 560–3; recovery of
maintenance 559–60; reform 565–8;
theoretical background 555–6;
theoretical basis 556–7; who can make
the application 574–7
financial responsibility: child support
568–70
financial settlement 180–1
finding significant harm 527
forced marriages 60–3, 136–9, **139**, 437
formalistic approach of the State 15–19
formalities: civil partnership 41–2;
marriage 29
formation of relationships: already
married or in a registered civil
partnership 26–9; civil ceremonies
29–32; civil partnership 20, 38–42;
cohabitation 42–5; engagement
19–20; family 4–5; family law 1–3;
informal marriage 33–8; marriage
20–6, 29–32
foster parents 295; adoption by 307
functional approach of the State 15–19
funeral arrangements 235–7
future risk of harm 527

gender reassignment: and parentage
278–9
genetic parentage 265–8, 562; *see also*
biological parentage/origins
gestational parentage 268–77
gifts: resulting trusts 83
Gillick competence 350–9, 364–7
grandparents: and adoption 331; contact
with 409–10
grave hardship 160–1

guardians 295
guidelines (financial consequences)
193–6; lack of 189–93; and the
principle of fairness 196–9; reform
of 207

habitual residence 459–63; and child
custody 418–20; not habitually
resident 460–1
harm: and custody 399–400; and
domestic abuse 126–8; emotional
537–40; *see also* significant harm
health care: and child custody 411
heterosexual family 265–7
Hindu marriage 32
home *see* family home
home sharing 78–9
housebound, the: marriages of 32
household: living together as if spouse or
civil partner 242–5
human rights 9; and child protection
489–90; and child support 577–9; and
ex parte orders 492

ICSI *see* Intra-cytoplasmic Sperm
Injection (ICSI)
identity, declaration of 289–90
'implacable hostility' 407–9
implied representations 98
implied trusts *see* informal trusts/implied
trusts
indirect letter contact 405–6
infants, rights of 347–9
informal marriage 33–8
informal trusts/implied trusts 82, 176;
constructive trusts 83–4; resulting
trusts 82–3
inherent jurisdiction 436–8; confluence
of wardship and 438; forced
marriage 437
injury *see* physical injury
injustice to the respondent: civil
partnership 70; marriage 68–9
interim care orders 497–8; interim care
threshold 497–8
interim supervision order 498
international adoption 331–2; welfare v
best interests 332–4; *see also* adoption
international conventions 9–10
international family 8
international law 416–25; child's
objections 421–2; child's voice in

international relocation 420–1; no presumption in favour of applicant parent 422–5; removal and return, deciding the case, habitual residence 418–20

international relocation 414–16; child's voice in 420–1; prohibited steps and different domiciles 414–16; relocation residence and contact 414–15; wardship and specific issue orders 415–16

interstate succession 238–40

'in the custody of the parent' 260–1

intolerability 156

Intra-cytoplasmic Sperm Injection (ICSI): and the legal parent 268–71; reform 273–4; three parents 273; and transgender parentage 271–2

investigative process: safeguarding 481

in vitro fertilisation (IVF): and the legal parent 268–71; reform 273–4; three parents 273; and transgender parentage 271–2

irretrievable breakdown of marriage 161–2; by both parties 166; by one party 166; procedure for divorce 162

'is suffering' 524–5; physical abuse 525; sexual abuse 525

IVF *see* in vitro fertilisation (IVF)

Jewish marriage 32

joint names, property purchased in 91–6

joint tenancy 80–1

judges 10–12

judicial activism 373–6

judicial interpretation: significant harm 517–20

judicial paternalism 373–6

judicial separation 167; effect of 168; grounds for the decree 167–8

jurisdiction: abduction and habitual residence 459–63; from ancient to modern jurisdiction of wardship 434–6; applications without notice 442; child's perspective 454–7; child sexual exploitation 448–9; confluence of inherent jurisdiction and wardship 438; contact 461–3; contemporary high profile wardship cases 434; ease suffering or prolong life 453–4; forced marriage 437; inherent jurisdiction 436–8; legal framework of wardship 438–40; life ending decisions 451–3; limitless jurisdiction 445–7; minors and inherent jurisdiction 443–4; not habitually resident 460–1; no wardship before birth 444–5; Official Solicitor 439; orders to prevent undesirable association 448–50; orders relating to medical treatment 450–9; orders to restrain publicity 445–7; Practice Direction 438–9, 445–63; procedure and principles 439–40; radicalisation 449–50; recent disagreements 457–9; reform of wardship 463; restricting wardship 442–3, 444–5; seek and find orders 450; strictly wardship 440–5; summary 433; surrogacy 451; termination and sterilisation 450–1; who can make application in wardship 441–2

kidnapping 262–3

knowledge of the petitioner/applicant: civil partnership 70; marriage 68–9

language, limits of 279–80

lasting power of attorney (LPA) 229–32

leave to appeal 185–6

legal frameworks: adoption 307–12; child custody 388–9; significant harm 513–15; wardship 438–40

legal parents: and parental responsibility 281–5; and reproductive technology 268–71

legal proceedings *see* court proceedings

legitimacy crisis in private law 425–6

'let die' 453

liability, public authority: and child protection 489–90

life ending decisions: child's perspective 454–7; easing pain and suffering 451–3; ease suffering or prolong life 453–4; recent disagreements 457–9

'likely to suffer' 528–30; probability theory 529–30

limitless jurisdiction 445–7; children of children who have killed 445–6; and the media 446–7; Practice Direction 445–7; publicity privacy and children's rights 445

living wills 229

loans: resulting trusts 83

local authority: changing perceptions of abuse 469–70; child protection and public authority liability and human rights 489–90; child protection requires truth 498–504; court interim orders 497–8; court ordered investigations 484–9, **488**; division of functions 497; emergency orders 490–4, **494**; emotional abuse 475–8; epidemic of abuse 478–9, **479**; exclusion order provision 494–6; high profile cases 468; historical denial of abuse 468–72; how well is local authority doing in child protection 504–5; interim care orders 497–8; interim supervision order 498; investigative process 481; legal and procedural framework of safeguarding 479–90; medical expert 498–502; neglect 478; orders during the preliminary stage 490–6; partnership principle 480–1; physical abuse 473–4; and proof of parentage 289; referral process 482–3, **482–3**; right not to self-incriminate 502–4; sexual abuse 474–5; significant harm 481; slow death in full view of protective agencies 470–2; summary 467–8; totality context approach to abuse 472–8

looking afresh 186–8
lump sum orders 183–4, 575–7

maintenance *see* financial maintenance/ provision
manipulation: and home right 104
marriage: age 24; already married 26–9; bars to relief 68; capacity to marry 23–4; civil ceremonies 29–32; consequences of nullity 70–2; death 242–5; domestic abuse 129; duress 59–60; forced marriages 60–3, 136–9, **139**, 437; formalities of 29; history and background 20–2; informal 33–8; knowledge of the petitioner and injustice to the respondent 68–9; marriage by cohabitation and repute 56; mistake 63; or otherwise 66–8; overseas marriages 54–5; prohibited degrees of relationship 25–6; right to marry 22–3; sham marriages 63–5; of the sick, the housebound or prisoners

32; statutory right of occupation for spouses 103; unsound mind 65–6; void 37–8, 49–56; voidable 49–50, 57–68; of young children 284; *see also* divorce; engagement to marry; same-sex marriage
Martin orders 185
matching: adoption 307–9
matrimonial property agreements 209
maturity to understand 354–5
media, the: and child custody 398–9
mediation: child victims of disasters 447; custody battles 387–8; and limitless jurisdiction 446–7; victims of child abuse 446–7
medical expert 498–502; be vigilant 500–502; undoing earlier decisions and fresh medical evidence 502
medical treatment/medication: refusing medication 362–3; responsibility to consent to medical treatment of the child 284; and wardship 450–59
mental capacity: civil partnership 41; elders 227–31
mental disability 204–5
Mesher orders 184–5
minors: and the inherent jurisdiction 443–4; restricting wardship suborned to Secretary of State power 443–4; *see also* children
mistake, marriages based on 63
monies attributable to some other motive: resulting trusts 83
moral panics 482–3
mothers: court orders parental responsibility 287–9; over fathers 261–2; parental responsibility 285; stepmothers 294–5; *see also* parents/ parenting
Muslim marriage 32

name change: and child custody 411
natural parent presumption 265–7; statutory exceptions to 267–8
nature of the representation 97–8
needs of the child: and child support 556–7; and custody 393–4, 400
neglect 478
non-accidental injury 473–4
Non-Conformist Christian marriage 32
non-financial detriment: constructive trusts 88

non-marriages *see* non-qualifying
marriages/non-marriages
non-molestation orders 130–4, **131**, **134**;
ex parte 134–6
non-paternity issues 567–8
non-qualifying marriages/non-marriages
37–8
non-relationship assets 198–200
'no order' principle: child custody
400–401; significant harm 540–1
no presumption in favour of applicant
parent 422–5; child at risk 422–4; risk
domestic abuse 424–5
'nothing else will do' (adoption) 321–2,
334–7
not old enough or not of sufficient
understanding 368–9
nullity: bars to relief where a marriage is
voidable 68; concept 48–9;
consequences for married couples and
civil partners 70–2; duress 59–60;
forced marriages 60–3; grounds on
which a civil partnership will be
voidable 69–70; knowledge of the
petitioner and injustice to the
respondent 68–9; marriage by
cohabitation and repute 56; mistake
63; or otherwise 66–8; overseas
marriages 54–5; religious decrees of
72; sham marriages 63–5; summary
48; unsound mind 65–6; void or
voidable relationships 49–68

objections of the child: custody 421–2;
see also voice of the child
objective tests: significant harm 518–19
obligations 3
observing the child 523–4
occupation orders 130, **131**; ex parte
134–6
occupation rights: and domestic abuse
124–31; entitled persons 124–8;
non-entitled persons 128–30;
non-molestation order applications
and orders granted 130–1, **131**
Official Solicitor 439
'on demand' divorce 166
orders during the preliminary stage (child
protection) 490–6; child assessment
order 496; contact with the child and
emergency protection order 493–4,
494; emergency orders 490–4, **494**;

emergency protection order 490–2;
exclusion order provision 494–6; ex
parte orders and human rights
challenges 492; police removal 495–6
orders relating to medical treatment
450–59; child's perspective 454–7;
ease suffering or prolong life 453–4;
life ending decisions 451–3; recent
disagreements 457–9; surrogacy 451;
termination and sterilisation 450–1
orders to prevent undesirable association
448–50; child sexual exploitation
448–9; radicalisation 449–50; seek and
find orders 450
orders to restrain publicity 445–7;
children of children who have killed
445–6; media intrusion/interest
446–7; publicity privacy and
children's rights 445
organ transplant 359–63
orientalism: and child custody 398–9
or otherwise 66–9
overseas marriages 54–5
ownership of family home: buying a
house 79–80; problems of 77; *see also*
family home

pain and suffering: life ending decisions
451–4
'parental alienation' 407–9
parents/parenting: adoptive parents 294;
attachment 277–81; biological father's
rights are 'sacred' 258–9; biological
heterosexual family 265–7; biological
parents and the natural parent
presumption 265–8; child support
568–70; contact with (adoption)
329–30; cooperation (significant harm)
541–3; court denial of parental
responsibility applications 291; court
orders parental responsibility 286–94;
deciding in favor of non-biological
over natural parents 261; de facto
fathers' right to truth 291; demise of
paternal authority and rise of parental
responsibility 259–63; the exclusive
father 257–9; family rights 295–6;
fathers 261–2, 285; foster parents 295;
gestational parentage 268–77;
international arrangements (surrogacy)
276–7; 'in the custody of the parent'
260–1; kidnapping and child

abduction 262–3; legal parents and parental responsibility 281–4; the limits of language 279–80; mothers 285; mothers over fathers 261–2; mothers refusing to consent to blood tests 287–9; other parents 294–5; parental responsibility order 286–7, **287**; parental responsibility when not the parent 294; parenting histories 257–9; putting biological parentage to proof 287; reasonable standard of parental care 523–4; reproductive technology and the legal parent 268–71; reproductive technology reform 273–4; resident parent 562; responsibility to act for the child in legal proceedings 284; responsibility to care for the child 282; responsibility for the child's religion 283; responsibility to consent to medical treatment of the child 284; responsibility to ensure the child's education 282–3; responsibility involves administering child's property and enter into contracts 284; responsibility to protect the child and not to inflict punishment or physical discipline 283–4; responsibility to withhold consent or consent to marriage overridden by statute 284; right of child to know 289–91; right not to self-incriminate 502–4; sexual orientation and gender reassignment 278–9; social and psychological parentage 277–81; special guardians/ guardians 295; statutory exceptions to the natural parent presumption 267–8; summary 255–6; surrogacy 274–7; terminating parental responsibility 291–4; three parents 273; transgender father 280–1; transgender parentage and IVF 271–2; the unfit parent 263–5; unmarried fathers 285–6; who is entitled 285–6; who is a parent in fact 263–5; *see also* custody, child; private disputes; responsibility, parental
partnership: and custody battles 387–8
partnership principle 480–1
paternal authority *see* fathers
paternalism, judicial 373–6
paternity: and child support 566–7; presumption of 567

pension sharing orders 188
periodical payments 183–4, 575
perpetrators, uncertain 534–43; expansion of emotional harms 537–40; 'no order' presumption 540–1; parental cooperation 541–2, **542**; voluntary agreement 543
personal property 173–4
personal relationships, State intervention in: agreements to enter into civil partnership 20; already married or in a registered civil partnership 26–9; civil ceremonies 29–32; civil partners 38–41; cohabitation 42–5; definitions and formation of relationships 19–45; engagement 19–20; form v function 15–19; formalities of civil partnership 41–2; formalities of marriage 29; informal marriage 33–8; marriage 20–6; marriages of the sick, the housebound or prisoners 32; mental capacity 41; relationships exempt from legal intervention 17–19; summary 14; which relationships should be recognised 15–17
person with care 562–3
physical abuse (non-accidental injury) 473–4; 'is suffering' 525
physical disability 204–5
physical discipline, responsibility not to inflict 283–4
physical injury 534–43; expansion of emotional harms 537–40; 'no order' presumption 540–1; parental cooperation 541–2, **542**; voluntary agreement 543
physical needs of the child: and custody 393–4
placement order: adoption 319–21
police removal 495–6
politics *see* state politics
post-separation assets 200–207; increase in earning capacity 201–7
poverty 522–3; child poverty 555
Practice Directions 438–9; orders to prevent undesirable association 448–50; orders relating to medical treatment 450–59; orders to restrain publicity 445–7; wardship, abduction and habitual residence 459–63
pragmatism: constructive trusts 89–96
pre-civil partnership agreements 211–18

pre-emptive strike: evaluating future risk of harm 527; finding significant harm 527; no finding of sexual abuse 527–8; retrospectivism and prospectivism 526–7; significant harm 526–8
pre-nuptial agreements 208–9, 211–18
presumption of advancement: resulting trusts 83
presumption of marriage by cohabitation and repute 33–7, 56
prisoners: marriages of 32
private arena of child support 573
private disputes: abusive partners and contact strategies 406–10; child arrangement order (CAO) for contact 403–6; child arrangement order (CAO) for residence 401–3, **401**; child does not want contact 404–6; child objections 421–2; child voice in international relocation 420–1; child welfare paramount 389–90; conciliation and mediation 387–8; different domiciles 414–16; disagreements, education, name change, health care 411; enforcing contact 410; grandparents 409–10; history 383–5; 'implacable hostility' 407–9; international law 416–25; international relocation and abduction 414–25; legal framework 388–9; legitimacy crisis in private law 425–6; no presumption in favour of applicant parent 422–5; 'pro contact' even where domestic violence 406–7; prohibited steps order 412–16; regional variations in orders 413–14, **414**; removal and return, deciding the case, habitual residence 418–20; right to contact 403–4; shared residence 402–3; specific issue order 410; summary 381–3; welfare checklist 391–401; when parents fall out today 385–6
probability theory 529–30
'pro contact' even where domestic violence 406–7
prohibited degrees of relationship: marriage 25–6
prohibited steps 414–16
prohibited steps order 412–14; regional variations in orders 413–14, **413**
proof, matters of: significant harm 533–4

proof, standard of: significant harm 530–4
property: of children 284; and rights to maintenance during a relationship 173–8; transfer of 184–5, 575
property adjustment orders 184
proportionality question 547–9
proprietary estoppel 96–102; compensation 101; detriment 98–9; fee simple 100–101; license 101; nature of the representation 97–8; problematic remedy 102; reliance 99–100
prospective civil partners 222–3
prospectivism 526–7
protection, child: changing perceptions of abuse 469–70; child protection and public authority liability and human rights 489–90; child protection requires truth 498–504; court interim orders 497–8; court ordered investigations 484–9, **488**; division of functions 497; emergency orders 490–4, **494**; emotional abuse 475–8; epidemic of abuse 478–9, **479**; exclusion order provision 494–6; high profile cases 468; historical denial of abuse 468–72; how well is local authority doing in child protection 504–5; interim care orders 497–8; interim supervision order 498; investigative process 481; legal and procedural framework of safeguarding 479–90; medical expert 498–502; neglect 478; orders during the preliminary stage 490–6; partnership principle 480–1; physical abuse 473–4; referral process 482–3, **482–3**; right not to self-incriminate 502–4; sexual abuse 474–5; significant harm 481; slow death in full view of protective agencies 470–2; summary 467–8; totality context approach to abuse 472–8
protection notices: domestic violence/abuse 123, 141
protection of rights in the family home: beneficiaries 104; civil partnership 102–3; cohabitants and the family home 78; compensation 101; constructive trusts 83–4; creditors and bankruptcy 104–5; detriment 98–9; effect of statutory right on third parties

104; equitable title 80–2; estoppel license 101; exceptional circumstances 105–6; fee simple 100–101; home sharing 78–9; legal ownership 79–80; nature of the representation 97–8; problems of home ownership 77; property in joint names 91–6; property is in sole name 84–91; proprietary estoppel 96–102; reliance 99–100; resulting trusts 82–3; statutory right of occupation for spouses and civil partners 103; summary 75; wide range of remedies 100–101

protection orders: domestic violence/abuse 141; female genital mutilation 140, **141**; forced marriage 138–9, **139**

psychological parentage 277–81

public authority liability: child protection 489–90

publicity privacy 445

public law procedure: changing perceptions of abuse 469–70; child protection and public authority liability and human rights 489–90; child protection requires truth 498–504; court interim orders 497–8; court ordered investigations 484–9, **488**; division of functions 497; emergency orders 490–4, **494**; emotional abuse 475–8; epidemic of abuse 478–9, **479**; exclusion order provision 494–6; high profile cases 468; historical denial of abuse 468–72; how well is local authority doing in child protection 504–5; interim care orders 497–8; interim supervision order 498; investigative process 481; legal and procedural framework of safeguarding 479–90; medical expert 498–502; neglect 478; orders during the preliminary stage 490–6; partnership principle 480–1; physical abuse 473–4; referral process 482–3, **482–3**; right not to self-incriminate 502–4; sexual abuse 474–5; significant harm 481; slow death in full view of protective agencies 470–2; summary 467–8; totality context approach to abuse 472–8

punishment, responsibility not to inflict 283–4

putative fathers: right to know 290

putative transgender adolescents 365–7

Quaker marriage 32

qualifying child 561; age of 561; duty to maintain 560–1

quantification of beneficial interest: constructive trusts 89

race: and adoption 310–11, 312

radicalisation 449–50, 538–40

reasonable financial provision 245–8

reasonable standard of parental care 523–4; residential assessments 523–4

referral process: safeguarding 482–3, **482–3**

refusal to consent 355–63

relationship agreements 208–9

relationship status 70–1

relatives, adoption by 307

reliance: proprietary estoppel 99–100

religion: and adoption 311–12; and custody 397–8; religious ceremonies 31–2; religious decrees of nullity 72; responsibility for child's religion 283

relocation residence 414–15

removal and return: and child custody 418–20

reporting suspicions 482–3, **482–3**

representation, nature of 97–8

reproductive technology: and the legal parent 268–71; reform 273–4; three parents 273; and transgender parentage 271–2

repute *see* presumption of marriage by cohabitation and repute

residence orders 329

residential assessments 523–4; right to 524

resident parent: and child support 562

residual role of the courts: child support 572–3

resisting deportation 463

responsibility, assumption of: and the deceased 244–5

responsibility, parental 281–2; to act for the child in legal proceedings 284; to care for the child 282; for the child's religion 283; and child support 568–70; to consent to medical treatment of the child 284; court orders 286–94, **287**; to ensure the child's education 282–3; involves administering child's property and enter into contracts 284; other parents 294–5; to protect the child and not to inflict punishment or physical discipline 283–4; and its responsibilities 282–4; to withhold consent or consent to marriage overridden by statute 284; who is entitled 285–6

resulting trusts 82–3

resumption of cohabitation 159–60

resuscitation 454–5

retrospectivism 526–7

return hearings: ex parte orders 135–6

revocation of wills 71

rights 3; applications for financial maintenance 240–50; to deal with the deceased's body 235–7; de facto fathers' right to truth 291; interstate succession 238–40; occupation rights 124–31; and publicity privacy 445; putative fathers' right to know 290; right of child to know 289–90; rights to deal with deceased's body 235–7; rights to maintenance 176–8; right to marry 22–3; right to residential assessment 524; right not to self-incriminate 502–4; right to refuse consent 355–63; statutory right of occupation for spouses 103–4; testate succession 237–8; theoretical basis of child support 556; trusts of land 104–5; see also rights in the family home; right to decide and to participate in court proceedings

rights in the family home: beneficiaries 104; civil partnership 102–3; cohabitants and the family home 78; compensation 101; constructive trusts 83–4; creditors and bankruptcy 104–5; detriment 98–9; effect of statutory right on third parties 104; equitable title 80–2; estoppel license 101; exceptional circumstances 105–6; fee simple 100–101; home sharing 78–9; legal ownership 79–80; nature of the representation 97–8; problems of home ownership 77; property in joint names 91–6; property is in sole name 84–91; proprietary estoppel 96–102; reliance 99–100; resulting

trusts 82–3; statutory right of occupation for spouses and civil partners 103; summary 75; wide range of remedies 100–101

right to decide and to participate in court proceedings: adolescent participation in legal proceedings 367–73; changing attitudes 371–2; chronological age 354; competent/incompetent putative transgender adolescent 365–7; end game 376–7; family proceedings 372–3; from consequences to competence 358–9; general principles and sources of law 343–9; how can an adolescent acquire competence 353–5; judicial activism or judicial paternalism 373–6; maturity to understand 354–5; medication/sedation 362–3; not old enough or not of sufficient understanding 368–9; only a right to refuse consent 355–9; organ transplant 361–2; reaction of academic community 358; refusal 359–63; sexual intercourse and the dissenters 352–3; simply inappropriate 370–1; summary 342–3; test of competency 367–8; three ages and stages of child rights 346–9; under 16-year-olds and the Gillick competence precept 350–3; voice of the child 345–6; wardship 363–7

risk: child at risk 422–4; risk domestic abuse 424–5

safeguarding: court ordered investigation 484–9, **488**; investigative process 481; legal and procedural framework 479–90; partnership principle 480–1; public authority liability and human rights 489–90; referral process 482–3, **482–3**; significant harm 481

same-sex marriage 15–16

Secretary of State powers: and wardship 443–4

sedation, refusing 362–3

seek and find orders 450

self-incrimination: protecting parents 502–4

settlement of property 575

sex of the child: and custody 394–5

sexual abuse 113–14, 474–5; care proceedings application of 530–4; 'is suffering' 525; no finding of 527–8; and probability theory 529–30

sexual exploitation, child 448–9

sexual intercourse 352–3

sexual orientation: and parentage 278–9

sham marriages 63–5

shared residence order 402–3

siblings: and adoption 330–1

sick, the: marriages of 32

significant harm 481; care proceedings applications of sexual abuse 530–4; different but normal 520–1; duty to investigate 488; ethnic minority children in care 521; evaluating the future risk of harm 527; evidence 515–16; expansion of emotional harms 537–40; finding significant harm 527; general principles pre-emptive strike 526–8; how better can we protect children 547–9; 'is suffering' 524–5; judicial interpretation 517–20; legal framework 513–15; 'likely to suffer' 528–30; matters of proof and general allegations 533–4; no finding of sexual abuse 527–8; 'no order' presumption 540–1; parental cooperation 541–2, **542**; poverty and deprivation 522–3; proportionality question 547–9; providing a reasonable standard of parental care 523–4; social policy and the threshold 512–13; standard of proof 531–2; summary 510–12; supervision v care 545–7; supervision orders 543–7; temporal question 524–5; threshold finding of 'significant harm' 513–15; truth 534–43; voluntary agreement 543; what conduct falls under 'significant harm' 516–24

Sikh marriage 32

social care: elders 231

social parentage 277–81

social policy: significant harm 512–13

special guardianship orders (SGOs) 295, 322–6, **325**

specific issue order 410; and wardship 415–16

split hearings 514–15

standard of living 202–3

standard of parental care, reasonable 523–4; residential assessments 523–4

standard of proof: significant harm 530–4

State intervention in personal relationships: agreements to enter into civil partnership 20; already married or in a registered civil partnership 26–9; civil ceremonies 29–32; civil partners 38–41; cohabitation 42–5; definitions and formation of relationships 19–45; engagement 19–20; form v function 15–19; formalities of civil partnership 41–2; formalities of marriage 29; informal marriage 33–8; marriage 20–6; marriages of the sick, the housebound or prisoners 32; mental capacity 41; relationships exempt from legal intervention 17–19; summary 14; which relationships should be recognised 15–17

state of affairs 166

state politics: care proceedings applications of sexual abuse 530–4; different but normal 520–1; ethnic minority children in care 521; evaluating the future risk of harm 527; evidence 515–16; expansion of emotional harms 537–40; finding significant harm 527; general principles pre-emptive strike 526–8; how better can we protect children 547–9; 'is suffering' 524–5; judicial interpretation 517–20; legal framework 513–15; 'likely to suffer' 528–30; matters of proof and general allegations 533–4; no finding of sexual abuse 527–8; 'no order' presumption 540–1; parental cooperation 541–2, **542**; poverty and deprivation 522–3; proportionality question 547–9; providing a reasonable standard of parental care 523–4; social policy and the threshold 512–13; standard of proof 531–2; summary 510–12; supervision v care 545–7; supervision orders 543–7; temporal question 524–5; threshold finding of 'significant harm' 513–15; truth 534–43; voluntary agreement 543; what conduct falls under 'significant harm' 516–24

status quo principle: child custody 394

stepparents: adoption by 306; parental responsibility 294–5

sterilisation 450–1
subjective tests: significant harm 518–19
substitute decision: elders 228–31
suitability: adoption 307–9
supervision orders 543–7; supervision v
   care 545–7
surrogacy 274–6; international
   arrangements 276–7; and
   wardship 451
suspicions, reporting: safeguarding 482–3,
   482–3

tenancy: joint tenancy 80–1; tenants in
   common 81–2
terminating parental responsibility 291–4
testate succession 237–8
test of competency 367–8
theoretical basis of child support 556–7;
   causation theory 556; children's rights
   556; needs of children 556–7
third parties: effect of home right on 104
three parents 273
thresholds: significant harm 512–13
time bar: and death 241
totality context approach 472–8;
   emotional abuse 475–8; neglect 478;
   physical abuse 473–4; sexual abuse
   474–5
transfer of property 184–5, 575
transgender adolescents 365–7
transgender parentage 271–3; transgender
   father 280–1
transplant decisions 455–7
'treat to ease pain and suffering' 453–4
trusts 174–5; express trusts 175; informal
   trusts 176; trusts of land 104–5; *see also*
   informal trusts/implied trusts
truth (child protection) 498–504; be
   vigilant 500–502; medical expert
   498–502; protecting parents 502–4;
   undoing earlier decisions and fresh
   medical evidence 502
truth (significant harm) 534–43;
   expansion of emotional harms
   537–40; 'no order' presumption
   540–1; parental cooperation 541–2,
   542; voluntary agreement 543
turning the other way 482

unaccompanied asylum-seeking children:
   and wardship 462
unborn, the: rights of 346–7

uncertain perpetrators 534–43; expansion
   of emotional harms 537–40; 'no
   order' presumption 540–1; parental
   cooperation 541–2, **542**; voluntary
   agreement 543
UNCRC *see* United Nations
   Convention on the Rights of the
   Child 1989 (UNCRC)
undertakings: non-molestation
   orders 134
understanding of the child 368–9; and
   child custody 392–3
undesirable association, orders to prevent
   448–50; child sexual exploitation
   448–9; radicalisation 449–50; seek and
   find orders 450
unfit parent 263–5
United Nations Convention on the
   Rights of the Child 1989 (UNCRC)
   283, 337, 344–5, 389, 392, 403, 417,
   421, 479, 556
unmarried fathers: parental responsibility
   285–6
unreasonableness: and adoption 315–18
unsound mind 65–6

variation of periodical payments 183–4
vexatious litigation: custody battles 390
voidable relationships: bars to relief 68;
   civil partnership 69–70; duress 59–60;
   forced marriages 60–3; marriages
   49–68; mistake 63; or otherwise 66–8;
   sham marriages 63–5; unsound mind
   65–6
void relationships 37–8, 49–56;
   consequences of nullity 70–2;
   marriage by cohabitation and repute
   56; overseas marriages 54–5
voice of the child 345–5; in international
   relocation 420–1
voluntary agreement 543

waiting time: adoption 318–19
wardship 363–7: abduction and habitual
   residence 459–63; from ancient to
   modern jurisdiction of 434–6;
   applications without notice 442;
   child's perspective 454–7; child sexual
   exploitation 448–9; confluence of
   inherent jurisdiction and 438; contact
   461–3; contemporary high profile
   cases 434; ease suffering or prolong life

453–4; forced marriage 437; inherent jurisdiction 436–8; legal framework of 438–40; life ending decisions 451–3; limitless jurisdiction 445–7; minors and inherent jurisdiction 443–4; not habitually resident 460–1; no wardship before birth 444–5; Official Solicitor 439; orders to prevent undesirable association 448–50; orders relating to medical treatment 450–9; orders to restrain publicity 445–7; Practice Direction 438–9, 445–63; procedure and principles 439–40; radicalisation 449–50; recent disagreements 457–9; reform of 463; restricting 442–3, 444–5; seek and find orders 450; and specific issue orders 415–16; strictly wardship 440–5; summary 433; surrogacy 451; termination and sterilisation 450–1; who can make application 441–2

welfare of the child: abusive partners and contact strategies 406–10; and adoption 302, 304–6, 308–9, 313–15, 318, 320; child arrangement order (CAO) for contact 403–6; child arrangement order (CAO) for residence 401–3, **401**; child does not want contact 404–6; child objections 421–2; child voice in international relocation 420–1; child welfare paramount 389–90; conciliation and mediation 387–8; different domiciles 414–16; disagreements, education, name change, health care 411; enforcing contact 410; and family life 261, 263, 265; grandparents 409–10; history 383–5; 'implacable hostility' 407–9; international law 416–25; international relocation and abduction 414–25; legal framework 388–9; legitimacy crisis in private law 425–6; no presumption in favour of applicant parent 422–5; 'pro contact' even where domestic violence 406–7; prohibited steps order 412–16; regional variations in orders 413–14, **414**; removal and return, deciding the case, habitual residence 418–20; right to contact 403–4; shared residence 402–3; specific issue order 410; summary 381–3; welfare checklist 391–401; when parents fall out today 385–6

welfare v best interests 332–4

wills, revocation of 71